EVANGELIZOLOGY

A Biblical, Historical, Theological
Study of Evangelizing

Volume Two:
Commission, Practice,
and Follow-Up

By Thomas P. Johnston

Forewords by Darrell W. Robinson
and Robert E. Coleman

Evangelism Unlimited, Inc.
P.O. Box 1152, Liberty, MO 64069-1152, U.S.A.
Webpage: www.evangelizology.org;
Email: tom@evangelismunlimited.org

2014 Edition

ISBN: 978-0-9831526-5-1

Published by Evangelism Unlimited, Inc.
Liberty, Missouri

Dewey Decimal Classification: 269.2
Subject Heading: EVANGELISTIC WORK \ WITNESSING

Unless otherwise noted, Scripture is quoted from the New American Standard Bible or the New American Standard Updated edition, © Copyright the Lockman Foundation 1960,1962, 1963, 1968, 1971, 1972, 1973, 1975, 1977, 1988, 1995. Used by permission. Most other Scripture cited are taken from BibleWorks 7, 8, or 9 (BibleWorks, P.O. Box 6158, Norfolk, VA 23508, service@bibleworks.com), with the exception of some 14th-17th Century French and English versions; the Contemporary English Version, © American Bible Society 1991, imprimatur 22 Mar 1991; and the Good News Translation or Today's English Version, second edition, © American Bible Society 1978, 1992, imprimatur 10 Mar 1993.

Greek text is from the Nestle-Aland 27th edition (from BibleWorks 7, 8, or 9), unless otherwise noted. Hebrew citations from the Biblia Hebraica Stuttgartensia, unless otherwise noted. Likewise citations from Barclay-Newman (Barclay M. Newman, Jr., *A Concise Greek-English Dictionary of the New Testament* [1971, 1993),Friberg Lexicon (Timothy and Barbara Friberg, *Analytical Lexicon to the Greek New Testament* [1994, 2000]); Gingrich Lexicon (*Greek-English Lexicon of the New Testament and Other Early Christian Literature*, 3rd ed [2000]); Liddell-Scott Lexicon (*The Abridged Liddell-Scott Greek-English Lexicon*); Louw-Nida (*Louw-Nida Greek-English Lexicon of the New Testament Based on Semantic Domains* [1988]); Lust-Eynikel-Hauspie (*A Greek-English Lexicon of the Septuagint* [1992, 1996]); Thayer's (C. L. W. Wilke, C. G. Grimm and Joseph Henry Thayer, *A Greek-English Lexicon of the New Testament* (1851, 1861-1868,1879, 1889]); and Tischendorf (*The Constantinus Tischendorf Apparatus* [1869, 1872, 1984, 2003]).

Cover design by Cory Thomason. Some inside artwork by Mike Longinow (The Spiritual Battle, 105; Its in the Word, 230; Electric Bible, 482; Handshake, 807).

Dedication

I dedicate this work to my beloved wife of almost 29 years, Raschelle. I began these notes during the first year of our marriage, and have continued to work on them ever since. Without Raschelle's love, understanding, commitment, and sacrifice, this study would never have been possible.

Abbreviations

The following abbreviations are used (almost all versions of the Bible):

BBE=Bible in Basic English (Cambridge, 1949/1964);*

BYZ=Byzantine Textform (Chilton, 2005; Bibleworks);*

CEV=Contemporary English Version (1991);*

CJB=Complete Jewish Bible (1998);*

CSB=Holman Christian Standard (Nashville: Lifeway, 1999, 2000, 2002, 2003, 2009);*

CSBO=CSB versions prior to the 2009 edition;*

DRA=Douais-Rheims (1899);*

DS=Denzinger, Heinrich, et al. *Symbols et Definitions de la Foi Catholique: Enchiridion Symbolorum* (Paris: Cerf, 2005).

ESV=English Standard Version (2001, 2007, 2011);*

FGN [or GEN]=French Geneva (1560; http://biblegeneve.com/nt1669, 1669);

FJB [or FBJ]=French Jerusalem Bible (1973);*

GNV [or EGN]=English Geneva Bible (1560; Hendricksen, 2007; Bibleworks, 1599);*

GOT=Greek Orthodox Text (Athenian Bible Society, 1928, 2004; also Bibleworks)*

FLF=French Lefevre Bible NT (bibliotheque national de France [online], 1530);

FLV=French Louvain Bible (bibliotheque nationale de France [online], 1550);

GNT=Good News Translation (American Bible Society, 1993);

GWN=God's Word to the Nations (1995);*

KJV=King James Version (1611/1769);*

LXE=Brenton' English Translation of the Septuagint (1844; 1851);

MIT=MacDonald Idiomatic Translation of the NT (2006);*

MRT=French Martin (http://www.biblemartin.com/bible/bible_frm.htm, 1744);

NA27=Nestle-Aland 27th (1993);*

NAB=New American Bible (1900, 1970, 1986, 1991);*

NAS [or NASB]=New American Standard (1976);*

NAU=New American Standard Updated (1995);*

NIV=New International Version (1984, 2011);*

NJB=[English] New Jerusalem Bible (1985);*

NKJ [or NKJV]=New King James (1982);*

NLT=New Living Translation (2004);*

RSV=Revised Standard Version (1952);*

SEM=French Le Semeur (International Bible Society, 1992, 1999);

TOB=French Traduction Oecumenique de la Bible (1988);*

VUL=Latin Vulgate (435, 1969, 1975, 1983).*

Other Bible versions cited include: French Darby (1859/1884);* English Darby (1884/1890);* James Murdock NT (1851);* French Ostervald (http://lirelabible.com/bibles-php/index.php?version=ostervald-NT, 1744); French Segond (1910);* Wycliffe 1st ed (1384; Oxford, 1850); Wycliffe 2nd ed (1388);* Young's Literal (1862/1898);* as well as five German, three Italian, five Portuguese, and one Spanish translation.*

*Versions used from Bibleworks 8.0, Bibleworks 9.0, and/or add-ons.

Forewords

What a TREASURE our Sovereign God has given to His church through Dr. Tom Johnston's *Understanding Evangelizology*. This book provides a wealth of comprehensive Biblical, historical, and statistical resource material on Evangelism.

Every theology professor, Bible teacher, student of theology, pastor, and leader will greatly profit by having Dr. Johnston's book of research on Evangelism in their basic "tool kit" for balanced Biblical studies. He provides an extensive bibliography on Personal Evangelism dated from the 1700's to 2005. The Biblical terms used in both the Old and New Testaments that form a foundation for Evangelism are set forth along with all the Greek words and Scripture references to Evangelism.

Dr. Johnston's book covers every conceivable subject that I could imagine on Evangelism. He gives excellent charts and illustrations as he outlines such subjects as the Biblical Theology of Evangelism; the Practical Theology of Evangelism; A Biblical Theology of Follow-up; and the Local Church Evangelism Strategy.

Dr. Tom Johnston is truly "scholarship on fire!" He is an outstanding theologian, professor, pastor, preacher, and he practices what he writes, teaches and preaches in his life of personal witness for Christ to those who need to know Him.

My only regret is that I did not have this book from the beginning of the pastoral and evangelistic ministry to which God called me.

Dr. Darrell W. Robinson
The Woodlands, Texas, 2006.

Evangelism begins before the foundation of the world when the Lamb is slain in the heart of God. That amazing act of redemptive love which came into focus at Calvary brings creatures of time to measure life now by the values of eternity. In so doing, we are made to face the cross on which the Prince of Glory died, and broken and contrite in spirit, offer ourselves to Him who poured out His blood for us.

That commitment to Christ, through the power of His Spirit, transforms us into an emissary of the Gospel as the love of God is shed abroad in our heart. The priorities of our Lord reorder our agenda of concern, and we begin to think in terms of His kingdom, which might be called a "mindset of eternity."

That is why these notes compiled by Tom Johnston are so helpful. They lift up evangelism from the biblical perspective, coming to groups with both theory and practical ministry of the Word.

What gives this kind of study authenticity is the author's own personal life-style. I have known Tom for a number of years, and can say that he sincerely seeks to practice what he teaches. He is a fearless witness, yet always compassionate, and ever seeking more understanding. I appreciate such a man, and it is a pleasure to commend his thoughts to you.

Dr. Robert E. Coleman
Deerfield, Illinois, 1992

Contents

VOLUME ONE

"Boldly, As I Ought to Speak" (Eph 6:20)

"I Must Evangelize Other Cities Also" (Luke 4:43)

"Teaching Them to Observe" (Matt 28:20)

"I Will Build My Church" (Matt 16:18)

Preface

Walter Rauschenbusch began his *A Theology for the Social Gospel* with the following two sentences: "We have a Social Gospel. We need a systematic theology large enough to match it and vital enough to back it." I would like to change his logical progression a bit, and say: "We have a Great Commission. We need a theology of evangelism large enough to match it and vital enough to back it."

While God's Word was, is, and will always be very much sufficient to back up the Great Commission, these notes seek to look at evangelism from the Bible first, from the history of the churches and systematic theology second, and lastly from culture. This order is usually reversed in most works on evangelism. Even critical hermeneutics cannot look at the words of the Bible without first analyzing the recent historical approaches to words, phrases, arguments, and genres. In this process the priority of the message of the Bible can sometimes be lost due to linguistic arguments of some type or other.

I recently read in the preface of the 2nd volume of Matthew Henry's Bible Commentary the following, "*Brevis esse laboro, obscurus fio*—labouring to be concise I become obscure." It occurred to me that these words may relate to this present volume. Several years ago I determined that, due to the apparent lack of a comprehensive biblical overview of evangelism, brevity would not befit the subject at hand.

My late father, Arthur P. Johnston, conceived of a theology of missions and evangelism as an iceberg. 90% of the iceberg is under the waterline. Likewise, he taught that the 10% of missions and evangelism above the waterline corresponds to the principles and practice of the same. Meanwhile, the 90% below the waterline represent the theological foundations that buttress missions and evangelism. It would be foolish and self-defeating to teach the principles and practice of New Testament evangelism, without at the same time devoting some space to the 90% of biblical-historical-theological material that undergirds the same.

Therefore, my goal in making these class notes available is not to render obscure the work of the Gospel, nor to make evangelizing overly complex, but rather to highlight the teachings of the Bible, and to simultaneously examine avenues by which deviations from the Bible's teaching are constantly being made. Each chapter has biblical meat which drives an urgent evangelism, and likewise includes various theological or practical points which may undermine the very subject at hand. My desire is to show the breadth of issues related to the study of evangelism, hence evangelizology. Indeed, the Christian faith is like a well ordered row of dominos. When one domino moves, the remaining dominos likewise move. Hence, "A little leaven leavens the whole lump." Methodology of evangelism is often one of the first dominos moved, which ends up altering all of Christian doctrine itself. Therefore, while not discussing every point in any class, nor looking up every verse with my students, main points are highlighted during class, with the remaining material as a type of encyclopedic resource for further study and inquiry into evangelizology.

As far as evangelizology as a "Classical Theological" discipline. Since the writings of Augustine, particularly those compiled as *Contra Donatisten* (Against the Donatists), and since the so-called Soteriological Controversy which led to the Second Council of Orange (529 A.D.), Sacramental writings have framed the question of "Classical Theology." The Medieval authors, such as Master Peter "the Lombard" and Thomas Aquinas, only furthered the Sacramental cause. Schleiermacher and Schaff, in their writings on the "Study of Theology" did not very much alter the course set before them. The Evangelical Gospel and its corresponding evangelizing have had a tough go of it in historical writings. B. H. Carroll, fouding president of Southwestern Baptist Theological Seminary was correct in his assessment of this struggle. He spoke in 1906 to the Southern Baptist Convention on the creation of a "Department of Evangelism":

"Let us give the report a rousing, unanimous endorsement.
"The bedrock of Scripture underlies it. Experience demonstrates its wisdom and feasibility. If the Home Board may employ any man, it may employ evangelists. Altogether, then, with a ring, let us support this measure. If I were the secretary of this board I would come before this body in humility and tears and say: 'Brethren, give me evangelists. Deny not fins to things that must swim against the tide, nor wings to things that must fly against the wind.'" (Charles S. Kelley, *How Did They Do It?* [Insight, 1993], 14).

Alas, there will always be a battle involved for both the work of the evangelist and for New Testament evangelism! But we must not lose heart.

The question for contemporary Baptist and Conservative Evangelical academia comes by way of a plea off the pen of the Apostle Paul: "Therefore do not be ashamed of the testimony of our Lord, or of me His prisoner; but join with *me* in suffering for the gospel according to the power of God" (2 Tim 1:8). There is a shame involved in participation in Pauline or New Testament evangelism. Later Paul wrote, "At my first defense no one supported me, but all deserted me; may it not be counted against them" (2 Tim 4:16). Could the Apotles of the Lord in Jerusalem be counted among these "all"? Or is Paul speaking of his missionary team? Either interpretation is sorrowful. My request to the reader is to consider Paul's plea in 2 Timothy 1:8, while reading these note that are doubtless flawed and feeble. Please consider that any areas of disagreement or any errors you may find originate in a sincere desire to plumb the depths of Scripture in the area of biblical evangelizology.

As the Book of Proverbs says, "He who has knowledge spares his words, *And* a man of understanding is of a calm spirit. Even a fool is counted wise when he holds his peace; *When* he shuts his lips, *he is considered* perceptive" (Prov 17:27-28). Then two verses later we read, "A fool has no delight in understanding, But in expressing his own heart" (Prov 18:2). In this light, perhaps no one ought ever to write a book. And if someone did write down his thoughts, he ought to follow Proverbs 18:1, "A man who isolates himself seeks his own desire; He rages against all wise judgment." There is always a danger of isolating oneself by finding fault with everyone else. Knowledge can always be dangerous and lead to pride (1 Cor 8:1). May the reader be assured that this author recognizes that he also is in the midst of a journey to understand the depths of the teachings of the Word of God.

It is my prayer that these efforts will encourage new avenues of study into biblical evangelizing, allowing the very words of God's Word to motivate His children to evangelize in concert with what He has revealed in His Scriptures. This work is therefore offered to that end, that, according to God's will, He would usher in a needed awakening of New Testament evangelism among His people.

Thomas P. Johnston
Liberty, Missouri, U.S.A.
December, 2013.

Executive Brief for *Evangelizology*

Introduction:

This Executive Brief will break down the important points in each chapter of *Evangelizology*. Hopefully this brief will accomplish two things: (1) Provide readers an understanding as to why the chapter is included as part of the notes; and (2) Allow readers to gain an understanding of the prioritative elements in each chapter. This Executive Brief is like a "Cliff Notes" version providing the thoughts behind the inclusion of each chapter in these volumes.

Regarding the Appendixes:

Please notice in the Table of Contents that some of the chapters include appendixes and some do not. The appendixes are generally material related to the content of the chapter, but not included as part of the chapter or the lecture notes. As these notes are somewhat exhaustive from a biblical-historical-theological point of view, a number of items have come up that are directly or indirectly related to how evangelism was/is practiced and taught in the classroom. These items are included as appendixes.

Chapter One:

The purposes for Chapter One are two-fold. First, it was my goal to give a quick introduction to the rudimentary aspects of evangelism through the discussion of the tools for the evangelist: tracts, questionnaire forms, etc. Second, it was my goal to provide an overview of the massive bibliography available in the area of evangelism. This second point shows the scope of a discussion of evangelism in several ways: amount of material, variation in viewpoints and emphases, and changes in emphases over time. Right from my very first class, students are required to begin sharing the Gospel. So for this reason I have included an early discussion of Gospel tracts and Gospel presentations. My father once asked me, "Tommy, how do you know that your students are saved?" This question rang in my heart for quite a number of years. It was because of that comment that I added the material on the first page of my notes.

Chapter Two

Chapter Two begins the material related to the Christian's calling to evangelize. Because the Christian's practice of evangelizing is directly related to Christ's command and God's prompting in that direction, I begin to introduce the Christian's call to evangelism in Chapter Two. In this case, Chapter Ten on the Great Commission is a parallel portion, looking at the same topic through the lens of Christ's Great Commission. The two main sections of Chapter Two are a section on 1 Peter 2:9-10 and metaphors for evangelism as related to the Christian. Both of these begin to build a base upon which students will begin to lay a foundation of the biblical material on the subject of evangelism.

Chapter Three

Chapter Three begins to deal with the heartbeat of evangelism: the spiritual passion and the spiritual battle. The chapter begins to provide a historical introduction of what some people said about soul-winning. It then goes into the "Spiritual Passions" chart. The goal of the "Spiritual Passion" chart is to show that as a result of our response of faith in the Gospel, God will grow our spiritual passions, including a passion for Him, His Word, prayer, and obedience. This will lead to changes in how we live and communicate, with God, God's people in the church, and lost folks outside the church. The spiritual battle cannot be ignored as we develop a heart for the lost. It is in the beginning of the budding of spiritual concern for others that Satan comes in to steal, kill, and destroy. In fact, one of the primary instances of spiritual battle takes place at the point of sharing the Gospel with lost souls. This is when Satan becomes very active to keep us quiet (cf. Acts 18:9-10). These notes overview the plots and wiles of the Devil as he opposes the proclamation of the Gospel.

Chapter Four

Chapter Four develops two ideas that were born in my mind and heart through my early involvement in evangelism: Tremendous Truths and Unchangeable Realities. In my opinion Christians who understand these truths early as they develop in the practice of evangelism, will be protected from discouragement when the wiles of the Devil, as described in the previous chapter, come upon them (cf. Acts 22:18-22). Unchangeable Realities are four realities in evangelism, which it seems to this author are impossible to avoid: fear, difficulties, antagonism, and persecution. Tremendous Truths are biblical points which God has provided in His Word to encourage the Christian to press on in evangelism regardless of the Unchangeable Realities.

Chapter Five

Chapter Five highlights some motivations for evangelism. While there are numerous motivations in the Bible, these notes highlight some of the main ones communicated by Jesus or Paul. Then the chapter spends more time focusing on the urgency of evangelism. These urgencies are biblical and theological truths that convert the priority of evangelism from one among many to the pan-ultimate priority of life. Should Christians and students meditate on these urgencies, perhaps putting them in their daily prayer list, it may radically transform their lives!

Chapter Six

Chapter Six speaks of the Bible and evangelism. Because the Bible is the only document that will constantly bring our focus heavenward and lead us to unite with God, Christ, and the Gospel in bringing salvation to lost souls, it is vital and essential that all of evangelism be built upon a solid understanding of the nature and purpose of the Bible. When this foundation has been developed, at the very end of the chapter, I have included a section on the use of the Bible in witness for Christ.

Chapter Seven

The largest and most comprehensive chapter in *Evangelizology* is Chapter Seven on "Defining Evangelizing." I began these notes by taking the notes that my father used at Trinity Evangelical Divinity School for his "Theology of Missions and Evangelism" class in the 1980s. He highlighted historic definitions of evangelism to help students understand some of the issues in defining evangelism. While this approach was informative and helpful, I felt after sitting in that class and actually teaching through the notes several times, that they lacked the biblical power and guidance. It appeared to me rather to be men in history quarreling over details in a definition of evangelizing. It was not until some years later that I began to compile actual verbs which described evangelizing, and found many-many verbs on this subject.

Three pages into Chapter Seven, I provide a "Chapter Breakdown" which explains the content of the chapter. The reader will note that the chapter begins with some historic definitions of evangelism (as I mentioned in the paragraph above), and goes from there. The two most important aspects of this chapter include (1) the work that I have done uncovering the translation of the verb "evangelize" and (2) my notes "Five Categories of New Testament Terms for Evangelism." Please see the chart right before this last section, in which I graphically portray the five categories. The massive category involves the development of the 120 or so verbs and the 15 or so nouns used in the Greek text of the NT for the act of evangelizing. The student may be pleased to hear that I have begun a similar study of verbs for follow-up and discipleship in Chapter 26.

Chapter Eight

Because conversion is such a central part of reason for evangelism (to "make disciples," Matt 28:19), and because philosophical theology has sequestered and squelched some of the important aspects of conversion, it was deemed necessary to include a chapter on this subject. When the teaching of the Bible is considered at face value, many of the current debates in the area of conversion dissipate. However, when philosophical theology, with its "classical" approach to theological categories, is front and center, then an evangelistic theology of conversion becomes confused and even turns anti-evangelistic. It is all about the framing of the question. Therefore the topics presented in this chapter seek to re-center the question on the Great Commission and evangelism, while pointing out some unhelpful views of certain theologians and churches.

Chapter Nine

Chapter Nine is a chapter on the evangelist. The existence and development of this chapter was in two phases. During the first phase, I felt that there was a gift of evangelism, as well as a gift of the evangelist. So this chapter explains the spiritual gifts, and the role of the evangelist in the local church. In the second phase I began noticing the exclusion of the mention of the evangelist in almost all of my seminary textbooks. This disconcerting thought began to captivate my thoughts, especially in light of the historical notes that I have compiled in Chapter Seven and some of the notes on the translation of Matthew 28 that I have compiled in Chapter Twenty-Six. These three strands coming together led me to consider the unfortunate historiography of Church History in which I had been operating.

Meanwhile I had the privilege of purchasing a 1964 reprint of the 1570 French Martyrology of Jean Crespin, a Geneva publisher who had published 53 of John Calvin's books, as well as an edition of the English Geneva Bible. This Martyrology, which listed Protestant martyrs from 1410-1570, opened my eyes to evangelists in Church History prior to the First Great Awakening in England and the United States. Please consider from this chapter the importance of the evangelist for the NT church. Whereas the word "Pastor" (for shepherd) is used once in the NT, the word "evangelist" is used three times. This chapter may provide for a complete rethinking and reconfiguration of our classes in pastoral ministry and macro-ecclesiology

Chapter Ten

Chapter Ten focuses on the Great Commission. If the Great Commission is truly the single most important mandate given by Christ to His church, then it follows that it would be helpful to know what it is and what it means. The goal of this rather extensive chapter seeks to flesh out the biblical mandate of Christ's Great Commission mandate. I have gone about seeking to understand the Great Commission in several ways in this chapter. After some preliminary points, I seek to flesh out each of the five Great Commission passages. I discuss and have charts and graphs discussing the interrelationship of the Great Commission passages. I look at other commands to evangelize in the Bible, of which there are quite a few. Then we look at OT sequels to the Great Commission passages. Toward the end of the chapter, I discuss distractions or other commands that appear to compete with the Great Commission for preeminence in the local church. It is my wish that this chapter will help keep the Christian, pastor, and church on focus in fulfilling the Great Commission.

With this in mind, I began to evaluate the strengths and weaknesses of four categories of evangelism programs: initiative evangelism methodologies, relational or lifestyle evangelism methodologies, servant evangelism methodologies, and special event methodologies. Whereas there can be huge methodological arguments and significant discussions and disagreements on these methodologies, a discussion of strengths and weaknesses ought not be ignored. It is for this reason that I have kept this chapter for the very end of the book. Without the conceptual framework of the earlier portions of the book, a discussion of methodologies is so animated so as to be almost fruitless.

Chapter Eleven

Chapter Eleven and Twelve provide an introduction to the spiritual basis for evangelism: God's involvement with the evangelist and man's lost spiritual state related to evangelism. Both of these topics are pretty well attested to in Scripture, but do not seem to be covered in systematic theology class, because they do not coincide with the way that sacramental theologians have framed the issues dealt within their so-called "classical" categories of systematic theology. This is where *evangelizology* fits in this picture. *Evangelizology* does not frame the question of issues based on Augustine, Peter the Lombard, Thomas Aquinas, Friedrich Schleiermacher, or Philip Schaff. *Evangelizology* seeks to approach evangelism (and theology) from the priority of the Bible, being considered first and foremost from the standpoint of the Great Commission and evangelism on the highways and byways, rather than from the tenets of scholastic philosophical theology.

So with this context in mind, Chapter Eleven considers how man can and does partner with God in evangelizing, which actually leads to an eternal salvation for the elect. It is clear, by the way, why the sacramental theologians, including Augustine, did not speak of this in their deliberations. For them, the "signs and symbols" of the sacraments communicated "grace" to the recipient. For Evangelicals, the Holy Spirit works in, with, and by the Word of God proclaimed to bring forth eternal fruit in the life of the person who has a hearing of faith. This chapter cuts new ground for theological deliberation, as it is completely intertwined with the necessity for the evangelizing mandate.

Chapter Twelve

Chapter Twelve is a very short chapter, which considers why people have not yet come to Christ, the profile of an open heart, biblical presuppositions, times of openness, and spiritual steps. These are imminently practical aspects that we need to keep in mind as we evangelize.

Chapter Thirteen

Chapters Thirteen through Fifteen provide an overview of some practical pointers prior to and to initiate personal evangelism conversations. Chapter Thirteen highlights pointers that may sometimes be used in preparing groups for evangelism ministry.

Chapter Fourteen

Chapter Fourteen considers beginning a spiritual conversation with someone. It actually plumbs some of the 52 personal evangelism conversations in the Gospels and the Book of Acts, as well as some Old Testament precedents. After looking at some personal evangelism conversation starters in the Bible, it then includes some pointers and principles for starting evangelism conversations today.

Chapter Fifteen

Chapter Fifteen takes the spiritual conversation, once it has begun as described in Chapter Fourteen, to the level of spiritual challenge. I have called it, "Getting into Spiritual Things." Moving a conversation from a surface discussion to the level of "warning" someone (as described in Ezekiel 3:17-19) takes love, tact, determination, and boldness. This chapter delineates the challenges to making this transition, and provides pointers, examples, and encouragement.

Chapter Sixteen

Storying became a faddish interest in the mid-1990s. Whereas the personal testimony is important, in some cases it has spun out into undermining the proclamation of the Gospel. Chapter Sixteen seeks to walk the fine line between a positive approach to personal testimony and a cautious approach to some aspects of storying.

I am reminded of some words of my father, who was a World War II veteran, missionary in France, seminary professor, and founding president of Tyndale Theological Seminary, when I told him that I was teaching my evangelism class how to prepare a personal testimony. He said, "Why are you doing that?" I was struck that not everyone felt that using a personal testimony was an essential need for personal evangelism.

Chapter Seventeen

Chapter Seventeen is another massive chapter in *Evangelizology*. It did not begin that way. In my early years of teaching, I would have gone through the "Simple Gospel" with my class, an explained the rudiments of what we need to share so that we can lead someone to Christ. However, as time went on, I noticed that little foxes, often brought up in theology classes or church history classes, can completely pull the rug out from under the simple Gospel, leaving the student with no Gospel at all. Furthermore, as explained briefly in my introductory notes to Chapter Eleven, as sacramental and formal theologians get a hold of the Gospel, over the many centuries of Church History, those things that are discussed about the Gospel have drifted into philosophical theology, sometimes appearing completely unrelated to the message that ought to be shared to lead someone to Christ.

Thus, over the years (since 1985), Chapter Seventeen has grown and grown. It has grown in two ways. First, I have included clear points that often undermine the Simple Gospel, such as a gradual conversionism. Second, I have sought to elucidate those items that affirm and confirm the Simple Gospel message, such as individualism. Again, this chapter began through taking my father's notes and expanding them from about 6-7 pages. The professor and student will find the material on the simple Gospel at the very end of this chapter.

Chapter Eighteen

Once a conversation has begun, once the Gospel has been shared, then the spiritual battle becomes clear and the conversation proceeds into what I call, "Levels of Openness." Chapter Eighteen considers this process, in the middle of or at the conclusion of a Gospel presentation, where again, people fall into some pretty consistent categories (perhaps much like the Parable of the Sower in Chapter 25). These categories are helpful to keep in mind, as the personal evangelist seeks to know how to proceed with the individual.

The levels are pretty cut and dried: the open person, the close person, the non-committal person, and the spiritually stagnant. To these four I also added "the Messenger of Satan," which appears to be a unique category of people that the personal evangelist will encounter who will seek to discredit or discourage the personal evangelist. This last group provides the greatest challenge in the ministry of personal evangelism, and must be seen in a proper biblical and spiritual sense, lest the personal evangelist be discouraged and cease evangelizing altogether.

Chapter Nineteen

Chapter Nineteen provides an overview of smokescreens and objections to the Gospel, as well as a little taste of street apologetics. Whereas much of what is taught as "classical" apologetics may have very little relation to the issues which real people are facing on the highways and byways, street apologetics is born out of encounters with real people on the street. In that way, it may be helpful for the student to consider. Issues will vary from people to people and from culture to culture. The evangelist needs to arm himself to know how to give an answer to lead people to salvation in Jesus Christ. I am also convinced, especially in this area, that the Holy Spirit provides specific answers during specific conversations to answer difficult people who are encountered (consider Ezek 3:8-9; Matt 10:19-20; Acts 13:9-11).

Chapter Twenty

Chapter Twenty is called "Results, Reactions, and Responses." This chapter reinforces the interrelationship between proclaimer, Christ, and God, also confirming the interrelationship in the reactions of people to each. These interrelationships include reactions and verbal responses to the Gospel message. Again, this clearly biblical interrelationship encourages the faithful personal evangelist in his ministry and resolve. Is this interrelationship as described in Chapter Twenty not another area that is quite ignored in "classical" theological studies?

Chapter Twenty-One

The need for a verbal commitment to Jesus Christ through prayer is confirmed throughout the Bible, but especially in the words of Jesus in John 4:10, "…you would have asked Him, and He would have given you living water." The necessity for verbally "asking" for salvation is the topic of Chapter Twenty-One, titled, "Commitment and Prayer." Rather than the prayer prayed over an infant whose eyes are not yet opened, while some water is being poured, sprinkled, or rubbed into their hair, the prayer of repentance of the sinner in response to the Gospel presentation is clearly in keeping with the examples and teaching of the Word of God. It is in effect a type of "Sinner's Prayer." Corporate reciting of a creed, corporate singing of "I Love You, Lord," nor any sacrament can replace the sinner broken by his sin, and humbly confessing his need for the cleansing blood of Jesus to be poured over his soul.

Chapter Twenty-Two

Chapter Twenty-Two follows up on the decision by discussing the invitation to receive Christ as Savior and Lord. Again, the many examples of the Bible and the teaching of the Bible are brought to bear on this—another divisive subject. It goes without saying that the 85% of people who call themselves Christian, who do not believe in conversion as a divine appointment following the verbally proclaimed Gospel from the lips of an evangelist, also balk at an invitation. To them, conversion is not transacted in such a "simplistic" way. To them, conversion is transacted by the water on the unknowing infant's head or even perhaps by some divine decision prior to the creation of the world. Thus, these "Christians" are insulted at the idea of an invitation to receive Christ, and especially at the prospect of "assurance of salvation" from God, confirmed at the heels of such a decision for Christ. Yes, while there are many controversial issues in these notes, the invitation is another one. This author attempts to bring the Bible, theology, and church history to bear on this subject for the enlightenment of the reader.

Chapter Twenty-Three

Chapter Twenty-Three is another very short but very important chapter. It relates to immediate follow-up after the evangelistic conversation, focusing primarily on those who did make a positive response to the Gospel. There is also included a suggested protocol for evaluating a Gospel conversation. This evangelist has been beat down many times after a conversation by the Accusers words, "You didn't say the right thing!" "Why didn't you say this?" "Why didn't you say that?" Sometimes introspection is helpful. But usually it can be destructive. Proper evaluation can help.

Chapter Twenty-Four

Chapter Twenty-Four addresses the need for and the link between the evangelistic conversation, conversion, and Water Baptism within the local church. This chapter also addresses some confusing and unexpected consequences of infant baptism upon the evangelism enterprise of the church.

Chapter Twenty-Five

While a short chapter, Chapter Twenty-Five may be one of the more important chapters in the entire book. In the estimation of this author, Christ provides His disciples with a theological rubric within this parable. There are the saved; there are the lost; and then there are two groups that can make us feel uncomfortable, the shallow soil and the weed-infested soil. Whereas "classical theologians" can describe the saved and the lost, according to their categories of logic, they have more difficulty with the two middle soils. However, pastoral ministry and evangelism ministry make it abundantly clear that the middle soils do exist, and that they do infect the church and discourage the evangelist. It is my feeling that Christ gave this parable as an encouragement to His disciples to press on, even though some (or much) seed does fall on shallow soil and some (or much) seed does fall on weed-infested soil.

Chapter Twenty-Six

In Chapter Twenty-Six, I seek to provide a link between evangelism, follow-up, and discipleship. I delve into the pages of history to pull the reader out of the contemporary battles in this area. Then deal with some definitional issues. Perhaps the discussion of Matt 28 and its translation may be a benefit to the reader, as well as the sequel of verbs describing the follow-up activity of the apostles in the Book of Acts. Do not these verbs describe what the local church is all about, and what it should be doing?

After laying out the verbs, I discuss the importance of follow-up, from the standpoint of my early years in the ministry wherein I was strongly influenced by the discipleship movement. While very grateful for those years of training and thought, I must confess that I had to scour the pages of the Bible to find strong admonitions and examples of discipleship and mentoring. When I used similar efforts in seeking information on evangelizing, it resulted in the content of Chapter Seven.

The appendixes to Chapter Twenty-Six provide an evaluation of some polemical hot-points in the local church and its view of evangelism and discipleship.

Chapter Twenty-Seven

Just as *Evangelizology* includes a chapter on the Bible and another chapter on God's role in evangelism, so in the follow-up section of the book, I have included a section on God and the Bible in follow-up. Again, because of our Pelagian tendency to place all the weight of responsibility for follow-up upon the shoulders of the evangelist, Chapter Twenty-Seven provides a counter-balance as to God's self-disclosed responsibility in follow-up, as well as the power of the Word of God in follow-up.

Chapter Twenty-Eight

Finally, Chapter Twenty-Eight gives some graphically-portrayed schemes for follow-up and spiritual growth. Perhaps these can guide the evangelist as he assists those that he has led to Christ in their walk with the Lord.

Chapter Twenty-Nine

Chapter Twenty-Nine provides practical notes for developing and maintaining a regular visitation program in a local church. Visitation Initiative gives the skeleton or framework through which any local church can custom-design its own evangelism and visitation ministry. This chapter was developed when I was a part-time pastor of visitation at a local church, and was frankly overwhelmed by the task. Hopefully this will provide a bite-sized and workable solution to this often neglected area of local church life.

Chapter Thirty

Chapter Thirty came to my attention as I began to notice that many of the evangelism programs developed for small groups or for the local church fell into some pretty well-defined categories. Because of this commonality, rather than evaluating them individually, I wondered about evaluating the various methodologies as groupings or categories.

Chapter Thirty-One

Chapter Thirty-One provides the next logical step for these notes. If all that has been noted is true and is biblical, then how do these truths correspond to theological categories as they are noted today? Further, can deviancies from the personal gospel be noted and analyzed? While the chapter on the gospel message considered issues related to the gospel, Chapter Thirty-One concerns issues that correspond to a theology of evangelism.

Recommendations for the Use of These Notes for Teaching

These notes comprise a many of my findings in the biblical, historical, and theological research of evangelism. They have been compiled to provide an introduction to evangelizology all in one place, roughly similarly to how an *Introduction to Christian Theology* provides notes for several classes in theology under one cover. The following comments are meant to assist anyone who would like to teach from these notes.

There are three questions which need to be answered prior to proceeding with the use of these notes: What level is the class? General church members, college-level, masters level, or doctoral level. What is the length of the class? Several hours long, four to six hours, a 2 credit hour semester class, or above. What is the purpose of the class? To teach people to share their faith, to give a foundation for evangelizing, to teach about the Great Commission, word studies on proclamational words, translation studies on gospel or evangelistic passages, evaluating evangelism methodologies, etc.

Once these questions have been answered, it is recommended that only those chapters pertaining to the subject be considered. The Table of Contents should give a clear understanding on what the content of each chapter entails. Likewise, following each chapter, there may be a number of appendixes which either directly or indirectly relate to the chapter. These also may be found to be of interest for study and reflection.

For example, if teaching a seminar on evangelizing in the local church setting, the following is suggested: (1) From Chapter 5, speak about the urgency of evangelism, using one verse for each urgency (30 minutes); (2) From Chapter 4, address "Steadfast Truths in Evangelism," again using one verse for each truth (30 minutes); and (3) From Chapter 1, walk through one Gospel presentation listed in the chapter (30 minutes).

Chapters 10-24 (in Vol 2) are designed to a 3-hour undergraduate course in evangelism, whereas Volumes 1-2 are designed to provide a thorough 3-hour master's level introduction to evangelism (not including the additional appendixes at the end of each chapter). On the masters-level, I divide Chapter 5 into two 1.5 hour sessions, and likewise Chapter 7. Chapters 13-14 and Chapters 15-16 are each combined into one 1.5 hour session.

Most chapters are organized with core teaching. The core teaching is preceded by issues that are meant to be a "Hook" into the subject. These introductory comments may be perused by the teacher for use as a hook, or he may want to enter the core subject of the chapter directly. I have found that when I have a short time to cover a chapter, I begin with the conclusion of the longer chapters chapter (such as Chapters 7, 8 or 17), and then work my way back toward the beginning of the chapter. Remember that the Table of Contents contains a listing of appendixes after certain chapters—these appendixes are not meant to be lecture material, but to provide further reflection on the subject of the chapter.

Most chapters were originally designed for a class of 1.5 hours in length. However, due to my biblical and historical research in these past 25 years, some chapters have grown in size due to the amount of material included in them. (This author has been overwhelmed at the amount of biblical material on the concept of evangelizing!) Each chapter still has a core amount of material which could be covered in about 1.5 hours.

It is my prayer that the reader will find encouragement in these words as he considers the best use of this volume in teaching New Testament evangelizing.

Respectfully submitted,

Thomas P. Johnston, Ph.D.

CHAPTER 10
The Great Commission

Why Study the Great Commission?

> "This evangelistic work of declaring the Gospel is the primary ministry that the church has toward the world."[759]

Can this statement of Wayne Grudem be real? Is it not just hyperbole? In fact, were not the final words of Jesus to His disciples a figure of speech, an overstatement to make a point?

Grudem's generous and yet fully biblical viewpoint of the primacy of "declaring the Gospel" comes under continual fire from many directions. One of these directions is in the battle over the definition of the Great Commission. The ultimate or primary mission of the church is hotly debated and discussed.[760]

Perhaps the words of Peter Drucker may prove insightful here:

> "A striking social phenomenon of the last 30 years in the United States, the explosive growth of the new 'mega-churches' (now beginning to be emulated in Europe), rests on these institutions' dedication to a single purpose: the spiritual development of the parishioners. Just as the decline of their predecessors, the liberal Protestant churches of the early years of the 20th century, can largely be traced to their trying to accomplish too many things at the same time, above all, to their trying to be organs of social reform as well as spiritual leaders.
> "The strength of the modern pluralist organization is that it is a single-purpose institution."[761]

What is the churches single mission? How about Christ's Great Commission? Is it too narrow-minded to take the advice of Peter Drucker and consider the mission that Christ gave His Church?

Note also the helpful clarification of Mark Dever, as related to the definition of evangelism and the Great Commission:

> "Evangelism is not declaring God's political plan for the nations nor recruiting for the church—it is the declaration of the gospel to individual men and women. …
> "By far the greatest danger in apologetics is being distracted from the main message. Evangelism is not defending the virgin birth or defending the historicity of the resurrection. …
> "Evangelism is not the imposition of our ideas upon others. It is not merely personal testimony. It is not merely social action. It may not involve apologetics, and it is not the same thing as the results of evangelism. Evangelism is telling people the wonderful truth about God, the great news about Jesus Christ. When we understand this, then obedience to the call to evangelize can become certain and joyful. Understanding this increases evangelism as it moves from being a guilt-driven burden to a joyful privilege."[762]

Introduction: What's so Great about the Great Commission?
Or—Reasons the Great Commission Passages Communicate Christ's Ultimate Purpose for His Church!

1. Of the place of the Great Commission in the ministry of Christ:
   a. A commissioning is repeated in each Gospel and in Acts, after Christ's resurrection and before His ascension
   b. These Commissionings involve the *very last words of Christ* in the Gospels of Matthew, Mark, Luke, and in Acts

---

[759]Wayne Grudem, *Systematic Theology* (Grand Rapids: Zondervan, 1994), 868.

[760]David Bosch wrote, "The harsh realities of today compel us to re-conceive and reformulate the church's mission, to do this boldly and imaginatively, yet also in continuity with the best of what mission has been in the past decades and centuries" (Bosch, *Transforming Mission*, 8). He then spent 562 pages seeking to elucidate this subject, although he made no mention of the Medieval terms used to describe mission, as found in later in the introduction to Chapter 26. The subject is quite complex and far reaching.

[761]Peter Drucker, "The New Pluralism," *Leader to Leader* (Fall 1999): 22.

[762]Mark Dever, *The Gospel and Personal Evangelism* (Wheaton, IL: Crossway, 2007).

    c.   These Commissionings involved "Christ's resurrection proclamation"[763]

2.   The main verbs in Matthew, "win disciples" (Matt 28:19, μαθητεύσατε),[764] and Mark, "preach" (Mark 16:15, κηρύξατε) are in the imperative [aorist], as is Luke's "stay" (Luke 24:49, καθίσατε). John's "I am sending you" (John 20:21, κἀγὼ πέμπω ὑμᾶς) is in the present indicative active. Luke is in the aorist infinitive, literally, "to preach," or, "shall be preached" (Luke 24:47, κηρυχθῆναι), and Acts is in the indicative future middle voice, "Ye shall be" (Acts 1:8, ἔσεσθέ). All have the weight of a command of Christ.

3.   The Great Commission in Luke provides:
    a.   The climax or culmination of the Luke's development and communication of the Evangel[765]
    b.   The interpretation of the death and resurrection of Christ by Jesus Himself after it took place, Luke 24:46-47
    c.   The addition of the Gospel (death and resurrection of Jesus) to the preaching of "repentance for the forgiveness of sins" which had hithertofore been the primary focus, Matt 3:2; 4:17; Mark 6:12; Luke 3:3; 15:3, 5:
       1)   Rather than being the entry point of the decision to follow Christ, "repent and believe," repentance moved to being the desired response after the Gospel preaching, Luke 24:47; Acts 2:38.

4.   The Great Commission in Acts (Acts 1:8) is the organizational theme for and focus of the book of Acts, making it the central interpretive motif (CIM) for the nascent church, as well as for the church in the history of the churches.

5.   The Great Commission provides for a continuation of Jesus' evangelism ministry in Luke: cf. Luke 4:43; 8:1; 9:6 (note context, 9:18-22); 10:1ff.; 20:1 (compare with verbs in Acts 5:42)

6.   The Great Commission is also contained in summary statements discussing Jesus' ministry in Acts: Acts 1:1-4; 9:15-16; 10:42; 13:31-32 (cf. Matt 10:27)

7.   Centrality of the Great Commission in the Organization of Luke-Acts: Acts 1:1-8 (English ASV):

    v 1 Τὸν μὲν πρῶτον λόγον ἐποιησάμην περὶ πάντων, ὦ Θεόφιλε, ὧν ἤρξατο ὁ Ἰησοῦς ποιεῖν τε καὶ διδάσκειν,
        In the former treatise I made [concerning all], O Theophilus, [] that Jesus began both to do and to teach,

    v 2 ἄχρι ἧς ἡμέρας **ἐντειλάμενος** τοῖς ἀποστόλοις διὰ πνεύματος ἁγίου οὓς ἐξελέξατο ἀνελήμφθη.
        until [after] the day in which [] **he had given commandment** through the Holy Spirit unto the apostles whom he had chosen, [he was received up]:

        ἐντειλάμενος (vpamnms) is a unique form of the verb ἐντέλλομαι (cf. Acts 13:47). Note that Acts 15:24, διεστειλάμεθα (viam1pp) "to whom we gave no command" or "instruction," uses a different prepositional prefix, δια (most versions translate this verb in the singular). Acts 18:2; 20:13; 23:31 use διατάσσω [Byz of 18:2, τάσσω], meaning command, order, give instructions, arrange.

        The same term for giving commandment is used in the OT Septuagint for:
       1)   God giving commandment to Moses as to when to speak and what to say to the people of Israel, Deut 1:3

---

[763]H. N. Ridderbos, *Matthew* (Grand Rapids: Zondervan, 1987), 553; quoted in Danny Vance, "A Crucial Missing Link in Local Church Evangelism in the Twenty-First Century"; D.Min. dissertation, Midwestern Baptist Theological Seminary (2007), 26.

[764]I must give credit to Samuel Zwemer for preceding me in coining the term "win disciples," which I gleaned from the following quote: "It is time that protest be made against the misuse of the word evangelism. It has only one etymological, New Testament, historical and theological connotation, namely, to tell the good news of One who came to earth to die on the cross for us: who rose again and who ever lives to intercede for those who repent and believe the Gospel. To evangelize is to win disciples, to become fishers of men, to carry the Gospel message directly to all nations" (Samuel Zwemer, *Evangelism Today: Message not Method,* 4th ed. [New York: Revell, 1944], 17). It must also be noted that "won ... disciples" is found as the translation of μαθητεύω in the NIV's translation of Acts 14:21, "They preached the good news in that city and **won** a large number of **disciples**."

[765]Thomas P. Johnston, "A Summary Study of the Progressive Communication of the Gospel in Luke"; unpublished notes, n.d.

2) Moses gave commandment to the judges, Deut 1:16
3) Moses gave commandment to the people concerning all that they were to do, Deut 1:18
4) God gave commandment as to where to go Deut 1:19; 2:4; which Moses obeyed, Deut 1:19; and which the people obeyed, Deut 2:37
5) The people of Israel disobeyed the clear command of God, Deut 1:41
6) Moses commanded the people to take the land which the Lord God was giving them, Deut 3:18
7) Moses gave commandment to Joshua, Deut 3:21

The Greek word ἐντέλλομαι is used 86 times in Deuteronomy, 375 times in the OT LXX, 15 times in the NT, for a total of 390 times in Holy Writ.

Comparing Translations of ἐντέλλομαι

Verses	KJV (1611, 1769)	NASB (1977)	NIV (1984)	NJB* (1985)	ABS' CEV* (1991)
Deut 3:18	And I commanded you at that time	Then I commanded you at that time	I commanded you at that time	I then gave you this order	At that time I told the men of Reuben, Gad, and East Mannaseh
Deut 3:21	And I commanded Joshua at that time, saying	And I commanded Joshua at that time, saying	At that time I commanded Joshua	I then gave Joshua this order	Then I told Joshua
Deut 3:28	But charge Joshua	But charge Joshua	But commission Joshua	Give Joshua your instructions	...and tell him what he must do
Acts 1:2	Until the day in which he was taken up, after that he through the Holy Ghost had given commandments unto the apostles whom he had chosen	until the day when He was taken up, after He had by the Holy Spirit given orders to the apostles whom He had chosen	until the day he was taken up to heaven, after giving instructions through the Holy Spirit to the apostles he had chosen	until the day he gave his instructions to the apostles he had chosen through the Holy Spirit, and was taken up to heaven	until he was taken up to heaven. But before he was taken up, he gave orders to the apostles he had chosen with the help of the Holy Spirit
Acts 13:47	For so hath the Lord commanded us	For thus the Lord has commanded us	For this is what the Lord has commanded us	For this is what the Lord commanded us to do when he said	The Lord has given us this command

Regardless of the order of the phrases in Acts 1:2, Christ gave His church one clear command (commission) before He ascended into heaven, that is the "Great Commission"!

v 3 οἷς καὶ παρέστησεν ἑαυτὸν ζῶντα μετὰ τὸ παθεῖν αὐτὸν ἐν πολλοῖς τεκμηρίοις, δι᾽ ἡμερῶν τεσσεράκοντα ὀπτανόμενος αὐτοῖς καὶ λέγων τὰ περὶ τῆς βασιλείας τοῦ θεοῦ·
To whom he also showed himself alive after his passion by many proofs, appearing unto them by the space of forty days, and speaking the things concerning the kingdom of God:

v 4 καὶ συναλιζόμενος παρήγγειλεν αὐτοῖς ἀπὸ Ἱεροσολύμων μὴ χωρίζεσθαι ἀλλὰ περιμένειν τὴν ἐπαγγελίαν τοῦ πατρὸς ἣν ἠκούσατέ μου,
and, being assembled together with them, he charged them not to depart from Jerusalem, but to wait for the promise of the Father, which, said he, ye heard from me:

v 5 ὅτι Ἰωάννης μὲν ἐβάπτισεν ὕδατι, ὑμεῖς δὲ ἐν πνεύματι βαπτισθήσεσθε ἁγίῳ οὐ μετὰ πολλὰς ταύτας ἡμέρας.
For John indeed baptized with water; but ye shall be baptized in the Holy Spirit not many days hence.

v 6 Οἱ μὲν οὖν συνελθόντες ἠρώτων αὐτὸν λέγοντες· κύριε, εἰ ἐν τῷ χρόνῳ τούτῳ ἀποκαθιστάνεις τὴν βασιλείαν τῷ Ἰσραήλ;
They therefore, when they were come together, asked him, saying, Lord, dost thou at this time restore the kingdom to Israel?

v 7 εἶπεν δὲ πρὸς αὐτούς· οὐχ ὑμῶν ἐστιν γνῶναι χρόνους ἢ καιροὺς οὓς ὁ πατὴρ ἔθετο ἐν τῇ ἰδίᾳ ἐξουσίᾳ,
And he said unto them, It is not for you to know times or seasons, which the Father hath set within His own authority.

v 8 ἀλλὰ λήμψεσθε δύναμιν ἐπελθόντος τοῦ ἁγίου πνεύματος ἐφ᾽ ὑμᾶς καὶ ἔσεσθέ μου μάρτυρες ἔν τε
Ἰερουσαλὴμ καὶ [ἐν] πάσῃ τῇ Ἰουδαίᾳ καὶ Σαμαρείᾳ καὶ ἕως ἐσχάτου τῆς γῆς.
But ye shall receive power, when the Holy Spirit is come upon you: and ye shall be my witnesses both in
Jerusalem, and in all Judaea and Samaria, and unto the uttermost part of the earth.

7. Conclusion: So what's so great about the Great Commission?

   a. Because of its potential weight as the CIM of the New Testament church, the Great Commission
       forms the hermeneutical grid by which all other biblical passages ought to be interpreted (!)

   b. For example, consider the statements:

      1) What is more important for the Great Commission, evangelism or discipleship?
         a) Does a certain reading of Matthew 28's Great Commission really overturn the weight of
             the Commissioning in Mark, Luke, and Acts?
         b) Does the reading of Matthew 28 as "m-m-m-make disciples" really overturn the entire
             example of the ministry of the church as found in the Book of Acts?
         c) In other words, do 2 of the 4 uses in the New Testament of μαθητεύω (for make or win
             disciples) eclipse the weight of its other two uses, as well as that of the 55 uses of the
             verb εὐαγγελίζω (meaning evangelize)?

      2) Should not the main focus of the church's mission be to "seek and to save them that are
          lost"?

      3) Or should rather the main focus of the church be "teaching them to obey"?

      4) And is "teaching to obey" not merely leading people to practice the spiritual disciplines, of
          which some attest that evangelism is merely one of several?

      5) Is it not, however, human-centered to think that we ought to "reproduce ourselves in other
          people's lives"?
         a) What about "Christ in you the hope of glory" (Col 1:27)?
         b) What about "that they may know you,… and Jesus Christ whom You have sent" (John
             17:3)?

      6) Is it right to be seeking to pour ourselves into the lives of others?
         a) Does not the Word of God transform lives (John 17:8), and does not the Word of God
             penetrate much more deeply than my life ever can or ever will (Heb 4:12-13)?

   c. Yes, because the Great Commission becomes a hermeneutical grid, not only for the
       interpretation of the Bible and theology, but also for the formulation of local church ministry and
       practice, it is essential that it be understood biblically!
      1) A discussion of the Great Commission is not a secondary issue;
      2) It is the life-blood of a Great Commission church, a New Testament church;
      3) Whether we realize it or not, everything else flows from our understanding of Christ's Great
          Commission given to His Church!

Preliminary Issues in a Study of the Great Commission:

1. **Lifestyle or initiative—Passive or Active?**

   a. Does "Go" in the Great Commission really mean "Go"?

      1) Is not "Go" (in Matthew 28:19) a participle, which really means "Going"

      2) Cannot "Going" also be translated "As you go" or "while you go"? Or…

      3) "As you go [on your way]" or similarly,

      4) "While you go [your own way]", or in other words,

      5) "[No need to] go out of [your own way]", therefore,

      6) "[No need to] go" or

7) "[Why don't you just] stay [where you are and live for the Lord]"?

   a) In other words, no need to "Go" or change anything, just do what you are already doing; and/or

   b) No need to "Go," just do what you are already doing, but now do it "to the glory of God";

8) In fact, could it not be that for most disciples, Jesus did not really mean "Go" when He said "Go" in Matthew 28, He really meant "Stay!":

9) In fact, is not teaching that "Go" means "Go" really misrepresenting the meaning of what Jesus was teaching?

   a) Is not emphasizing "Go," therefore, unnecessarily putting guilt trips on unsuspecting Christians, to whom Jesus never meant to say "Go!"?

   b) In fact, did not Jesus specifically state that the disciples were to remain "in the world"?

      (1) John 17:11, "And I am no more in the world; and *yet* they themselves are in the world"

      (2) John 17:15, "I do not ask Thee to take them out of the world"

      [By the way: these are purposeful partial quotes of verses, which omit the evangelistic context, to show how some make this point!]

10) In fact, proceeds this argumentation, we ascertain [from conjecture] from the Beatitudes of Jesus, the Golden Rule, and the Greatest Commandment, that Jesus never mean "Go" when He said "Go!" in the Great Commission!

11) Those who continue to teach "Go!" are unnecessarily literalistic, emphasizing the need for mission trips, and the initiating of evangelistic conversations, rather than interpreting the Bible through:

   a) Modern psychological and sociological categories

   b) The categories of ancient philosophy or Greek Stoicism, or

   c) The contemporary teachings of Madison Avenue and the *Harvard Business Review*!

12) Notice that just described is a [not so] sneaky walk around logic's "Square of Opposition":

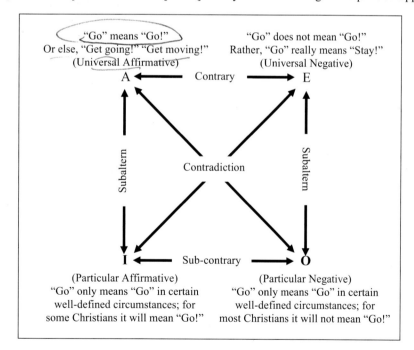

13) Note also that this progression shows a fairly common "logical" way in which the concept "Go" can be completely reversed and made to mean "Stay"!

   a) However, the "sending passages" of Matt 10, Mark 6, and Luke 9 and 10 cannot be equated with an "as you go" type of interpretation

   b) Thereby, those same sending passages are rarely even considered as foundational for evangelism training today!

b. What of the example of Abraham?

   Heb 11:8, "By faith Abraham, when he was called, obeyed by going out to a place which he was to receive for an inheritance; and he went out, not knowing where he was going."

   1) Interestingly, the 1910 French Louis Segond translated the word "when he was called" as "at his vocation" (a borrowed term from the Latin Vulgate's "qui vocatur"), strongly suggesting that the Vulgate framed the concept of "go" in this verse as directed only for priests and monks, not for laity!
      a) Which, by the way, conforms with Rome's theology of the Sacrament of Holy Orders
      b) Which is an example of view of the Great Commission forcing a translation or interpretation!

   2) Cambridge's Bible in Basic English (1949/1962) set a similar clerical-only precedent in the translation of this word, using the word "ordered":

      Heb 11:8, "By faith Abraham did as God said when he was ordered to go out into a place which was to be given to him as a heritage, and went out without knowledge of where he was going"

   3) However, almost all translations translate καλέω in this verse as "called" which does not limit the interpretation of the verse to clergy only

c. "Onward, Christian Soldiers!"
   1) Does not the term "Onward" express the same thought as "Go"?
   2) "Go" seems to emphasize geographic displacement, whereas "Onward" seems to emphasize "get moving!"
      a) By the way, the Great Commissions in Matthew and Mark use the Greek verb πορεύομαι, which implies geographic displacement (e.g. proceed); it is also used in Matt 10:6, 7
      b) The Greek verb ὑπάγω, meaning in a more direct and almost harsh sense "Go!", is used in Luke 10:3
   3) The geographic aspect of the Great Commission command is obvious, and for those who are not crossing oceans and seas, they cannot be static, but must move onward to fulfill Christ's Great Commission!

d. As noted above, has not some recent lifestyle literature in evangelism resulted in a serious downgrade of the biblical concept of "Go"?

2. **Itinerating or not?**

a. Can New Testament evangelism be accomplished within the four walls of the church alone? [A local church ministering as if it is on house arrest]

b. What of the examples in the ministry of Jesus of:
   1) His itinerant ministry?
   2) His lack of willingness to stay in one location, even when asked?
   3) His sending His disciples to go from "city to city"?

c. What does "going" mean in the context of 21st century Christianity?

d. Are we guilty of ignoring a clear element of New Testament evangelism, that is found both in the Gospels, as well as in the Book of Acts, because it is inconvenient, or does not follow our current way of thinking? Note the words of Barrett on the term *evangelize*:

   "To evangelize either individual or substantial population is not necessarily gradual, indefinite, lengthy, protracted, or interminable process: it is usually or normally a short definite accomplishment, completed over a relatively short, definite period of time."[766]

e. Ought we not to regularly gauge our lives and ministries by the Bible, and reorient them as necessary?

---

[766]David B. Barrett, *Evangelize! A Historical Survey of the Concept* (Birmingham, AL: New Hope, 1987), 13.

f. What does the clear itinerating element in NT evangelism mean for what Joe Aldrich called "ambushes and forays"?[767]

g. What of our tendency to send people on non-evangelistic mission trips to repair churches and orphanages? Is this tendency in line with the NT mission trips in Matt 9, Mark 6, Luke 9, and Luke 10, or the examples in the Book of Acts?

3. **Mission or Missions**?

a. An undercurrent in this discussion is the question of the validity of use of the term "missions" (plural), rather than "mission" (singular)

b. "Missions" (plural) has a tendency to view evangelism as a temporal task, much like when Jesus sent out his disciples in Matt 10, Mark 6, and Luke 9, 10; e.g. you go, preach, and come back.

c. "Mission," however, is much more broad that mere missionary trips, it implies lifestyle, a wholistic view of discipleship or social ministry, and the life of the "evangelist," those he is seeking to reach, and the totality of church life

d. Again one's use of these words has an important impact on one's view and application of the Great Commission, to which this chapter is devoted!

4. **Do not some verses state specifically not to evangelize [as rightly or wrongly interpreted]?**

a. By way of principle:

(1) Matt 6:1, "Beware of practicing your righteousness before men"
   (a) Does this relate to evangelism? No.
   (b) Unless we are peddling the word, 2 Cor 2:17
   (c) Or unless we are preaching ourselves, 2 Cor 4:5

(2) Matt 7:6, "Do not throw pearls to swine"
   (a) Does this not relate to evangelism without shaking the dust off of our feet when the Word is rejected?
   (b) Once the message has been rejected, via blasphemy and contradiction, then the admonition is to "move on" to someone else

(3) Matt 13:30, "Allow both to grow together"
   (a) An African once used this verse of Muslims: "Let them be! Don't even try to evangelize them, God will divide the wheat and the tares at the time of harvest"
   (b) His interpretation, however, seems unrelated to the text, as it would seem from the passage that Jesus was speaking not of Muslims, who do not call Jesus, "Lord," but of false Christians (the tares among the wheat), similar to those who say "Lord, Lord" in Matt 7:21-23

(4) Luke 15:8, "Sweep the house and search carefully until she finds it"
   (a) A pastor in Missouri once spoke this to his congregation that their responsibility was not to evangelize the world, but only to seek out those from "within the house" (former members of the church) who had drifted from the fellowship of the church.
   (b) While not a bad approach for a new pastor to a church, using only this approach appears to ignore the geographic extent of the Great Commission (the whole world), as well as its sociological extent (all its people), Mark 16:15; Matt 28:19

(5) 1 Thess 4:10b-12, "But we urge you, brethren, to excel still more, and to make it your ambition to lead a quiet life and attend to your own business and work with your hands, just as we commanded you; so that you may behave properly toward outsiders and not be in any need"
   (a) These verses were used by the French and German Reformers against the door-to-door begging of some of the monastic orders
   (b) Likewise, these verses became important to Mennonite, Hutterite, and Amish groups, who value hard work, and sometimes [contemporaneously] seem to devalue evangelism

---

[767]Joseph Aldrich, *Life-Style Evangelism* (Portland, OR: Multnomah Press, 1981), 79.

(c) Paul combined the two ideas (evangelism and working with his hands) in Acts 20, speaking of working with his own hands (20:23-25), as well as his ministering the gospel (20:18-27)—"night and day," 20:31!

(d) Because of verse like these, some Swiss Brethren churches will not pay a pastor, but rather will be led by a teaching elder, who earns an income in some other way

(6) Heb 8:11, "And they shall not teach everyone his fellow citizen, And everyone his brother, saying, 'Know the LORD,' For all shall know Me, From the least to the greatest of them"

(a) The eschatological context of this quote from Jeremiah 31:34, while clearly referring to the new covenant, does not make evangelism unnecessary in the new covenant

(b) The key words are "everyone his brother," which seems to imply that within the family of God, He will make Himself known

(7) James 3:1, "Let not many *of you* become teachers, my brethren, knowing that as such we shall incur a stricter judgment"

(a) Again, this passage seems unrelated to evangelism; it is a warning for the fulfillment of a command (or obedience in the use of the gift of teaching)

(b) Obedience to the command to evangelize must be obeyed, while remembering that we will be responsible for what we do teach

(8) 1 Pet 3:1, "That they may be won without a word"

(a) Again, using this passage to say that evangelism is non-verbal is misinterpreting the verse (isogesis), while using it to negate a clear command

(b) The command is for the verbal proclamation of the Gospel, and is unrelated to what God may use in the life of any person to draw them to Christ

(c) The text of 1 Peter 3 implies that the unsaved husband has already heard the Gospel, the seed has already been planted, now God will use the silent witness and submission of the believing wife to draw her husband to Him, according to His will (1 Cor 7:16)

b. Specific contexts in which some are commanded not to evangelize or to wait:

(1) Matt 10:5, "These twelve Jesus sent out after instructing them, saying, 'Do not go in *the* way of *the* Gentiles, and do not enter *any* city of the Samaritans'"

(2) Luke 24:49, "And behold, I am sending forth the promise of My Father upon you; but you are to stay in the city until you are clothed with power from on high."

(3) Acts 16:6-7, "And they passed through the Phrygian and Galatian region, having been forbidden by the Holy Spirit to speak the word in Asia; and when they had come to Mysia, they were trying to go into Bithynia, and the Spirit of Jesus did not permit them."

c. In this light, Chart 7, "Alternatives to Mere Proclamation," in my *Charts for a Theology of Evangelism* (Nashville: Broadman, 2007), lists 57 [possible] arguments against mere proclamation into the following categories:

1) Biblically-derived (10 cited reasons)
2) Non-biblical (7 reasons)
3) Ecclesiological (9 reasons)
4) Sacramental (4 reasons)
5) Good works (9 reasons)
6) Miracles (5 reasons)
7) Attitude (3 reasons)
8) Spiritual maturity (10 reasons)

None of which (I believe) displace the priority of the Great Commission as the command to evangelize.

Some questions:

1) How are we to understand these verses in light of the Great Commission passages and emphases in the Bible?

2) Do they provide parameters for the accomplishment of the Great Commission, or do they completely negate the weight and thrust of the Great Commission passages?

3) Can both sets of commands or teachings be understood simultaneously (the unity of Scriptures as one voice of the Holy Spirit)?

5. **Punctiliar or Linear Action?**

    a.   How much linear action can be attributed to μαθητεύω [make/win disciples] in Matt 28 (which verb is in the aorist tense, by the way) to counter the punctiliar action of κηρύσσω [preach] in Mark 16 and Luke 24 or μαρτυρέω [bear witness] in Luke 24 or Acts 1?

    b.   How does the Acts 1:2 translation of the participle ἐντέλλομαι (aor-mid-nom-masc-sing) into a plural form impact this question?

        1) Plural in the English (as an equivocating colloquialism):

            a) KJV, "after that he ... had given commandments"

            b) Bible in·Basic English (1949/1964), "after he had given his orders"

            c) NAS, "after he had ... given orders"

            d) NKJ, "after He ... had given commandments"

            e) NIV, "after giving instructions"

            f) ESV, "after he had given commands"

            g) NLT, "after giving his chosen apostles further instructions"

            h) CSB, "after giving instructions"

            i) NET, "after he had given orders"

        2) Singular in the English:

            a) Darby (1884/1890), "having ... charged [the apostles]"

            b) ASV, "had given commandment"

            c) RSV, "after he had given commandment"

         3) As an active verb:

            a) James Murdock (1852), "after he had instructed those legates"

        4) Some thoughts:

            a) Issue regards how many commandments Christ gave His disciples: was it one (hence the Great Commission), or many?

            b) If "giving instructions" in Acts 1:2 parallels Acts 10, is the emphasis of the Great Commission sowing or reaping? …

    c.   If the emphasis of the Great Commission is punctiliar, is that emphasis on sowing, reaping, or growing?

Is the Emphasis of the Great Commission Sowing, Reaping, or Growing?

[John 4:37, "For in this *case* the saying is true, 'One sows, and another reaps.'"]

Passage	Matt 28:19-20	Mark 16	Luke 24:47	John 20:21	Acts 1:8
Active Verb	"Win disciples" or "Make disciples"	"Preach the gospel"	"Repentance for forgiveness of sins should be proclaimed"	"As the Father has sent Me, I also send you"	"You shall be testifiers of Me"
Emphasis	"Win"—Reaping or "Make"—Reaping or Growing	Sowing	Sowing	Sowing, reaping, and growing	Sowing

6. **Exclusively Spiritual or Not?**

   a. What of the "as" (Gk. καθὼς) in John 20:21? What is its significance? There seems to be considerable leeway taken in using the "as" to apply to multiple aspects of the Christian life: For example: the following exemplifies how John 20:21 was applied to the Trinitarian theology of mission of the Orthodox Bishop Anastasios (Yannoulatos) of Androussa, Greece:

> "The conjunction 'as' which is found in John 20:21, remains very decisive for Orthodox mission. It is I who always remain your model, Christ stresses. You must walk in my footsteps and follow my example. Christological dogma defines the way of the mission of the Trinitarian God, which the faithful continue. The most crucial point of mission is not what one announces, but what one lives, what one *is*."[768]

      a) Notice that the "as" in John 20:21 is used to state that "the crucial point of mission is not what one announces"! What of Luke's Great Commission, Luke 24:46-47?

      b) Rather, as Anastasios posited, the "as" in John 20:21 shows that our lifestyle is the crucial point in mission. Does this match with a plenary view of the Great Commission?

So then, does the "as" in John 20:21 carry such hermeneutical weight that it can completely overturn:

1) The clear proclamational/conversionist emphasis of all the other Great Commission passages?
2) The plenary example of the book of Acts?
3) The theological weight of justification by faith in Romans?
4) And provide for non-spiritual elements in the Great Commission, such as:
   a) The founding of educational institutions,
   b) Encouraging political agendas,
   c) Commanding Christians to feed the hungry,
   d) Emphasizing lifestyle, such as the ancient monastic vows of poverty (Jesus was poor), chastity (Jesus never was married), and obedience (Jesus was absolutely obedient to the Father)?
5) Thereby inserting multitudinous non-Evangelical elements into the theology of the "true" mission of the church?

   b. How flexible is "win disciples" (μαθητεύω) in Matt 28:19 as regards non-spiritual elements of the Gospel, such as...
1) Founding Christian day cares for children?
2) Founding educational institutions?
3) Providing for pastoral counseling, etc.?
[Granted this emphasis for those who are already disciples is included in the "teaching them to obey" of Matt 28:20]

7. **Dispensational/Hermeneutical Questions:**

   a. Does the OT teach "come" (centripetal) and the NT teach "go" (centrifugal)?

   b. Does the OT teach lifestyle (Lev 18:5) and the NT teach proclamation (Mark 16:15)?

   c. Does the OT teach works (lifestyle) and the NT teach faith alone (as a response to proclamation)?

   d. While there is a major section below on the OT precedents for the Great Commission, by way of preliminary consideration:
1) From learn to win disciples!
   a) From μανθάνω ("learning," Deut 5:1) to μαθητεύω ("winning disciples," Matt 28:19)!
   b) From learning φυλάξεσθε ποιεῖν αὐτά ("keeping to do them," Deu 5:1 BGT) to ποιήσω ὑμᾶς γενέσθαι ἁλιεῖς ἀνθρώπων ("I will make you become fishers of men," Mark 1:17)

---

[768]Anastasios (Yannoulatos) of Androussa, "Orthodox Mission—Past, Present, Future," in *Your Will Be Done: Orthodoxy in Mission*," edited by George Lemopoulos (Geneva: WCC, 1988), 79-81; quoted in Norman E. Thomas, ed., *Classic Texts in Mission and World Christianity* (Maryknoll, NY: Orbis, 1995), 120.

      c) From learning God's δικαιώματα ("judgments," Deut 5:1) to evangelizing God's δικαιοσύνη ("righteousness," Rom 1:17)

    2) From scattering being a curse to going into all the world as a command!

      a) The scattering into all the world, commanded in the Great Commission, is mentioned as a curse in the OT (Lev 26:33; Deut 4:27; 28:64; 30:3-5), and so is being driven to all the nations and the peoples (Deut 4:27; 28:37; cf. Jer 8:3), even to the ends of the earth (Deut 30:4).

      b) And the gathering together into the land, and possessing it (remaining stationary for a long time), is repeatedly mentioned as a blessing, Deut 17:20; 30:1-5; cf. Psa 106:47

      c) And yet Christ commanded this geographic scattering as part of His Great Commission!

8. **Particularity versus Universiality:**

    a. To whom is the Great Commission addressed and under what circumstances (e.g. the Apostles, pastors, missionaries, or all Christians)?

    b. Is the Great Commission confined to unreached areas only (prior to an established church, as Gustav Warneck)?

    c. Was the Great Commission only meant for Apostolic Christianity or the Apostolic era (as Calvin believed of the gift of the evangelist)?

    d. Are the lost to "be discipled," or is this a term that can only be applied to the saved?

9. **The Importance of Matthew 10 in Evangelism:**

    a. On support in missions:

> "Do not acquire gold, or silver, or copper for your money belts, or a bag for *your* journey, or even two tunics, or sandals, or a staff; for the worker is worthy of his support" (Matt 10:9-10).

Introduction: Was this not evangelism from the posture of inferiority?
Not knowing the particulars of language, customs, or culture
Not having established relationships or a longstanding reputation in the community
Not having the financial means to survive, even in the basics, such as eating, clothing, and sleeping accommodations (e.g. Heb 11:37)
Consider…

    1) He sent them as traveling evangelists; they were always strangers wherever they went:

      a) Meaning that they may not know the local dialect, likely spoke with an accent, and may not even have known the language at all (e.g. Acts 14:11):

        (1) Granted in Matthew 10 they were sent to the "lost sheep of the house of Israel" (Matt 10:6)

        (2) But was this limitation not lifted in Matthew 28:19-20?

      b) As far as evangelism methodology, the traveling evangelism meant:

        (1) No **"presence evangelism"**—wherever they went they had no reputation, no connections, no political clout, no building, no house, no property (Deut 28:37)

        (2) No **"lifestyle evangelism"**—taking the time by a long lifestyle to win a hearing for the Gospel

          (a) Although the opposite is true, "I went by the field of a lazy man…" (Prov 24:30-34)

        (3) No **"relationship evangelism"**—they were strangers, without an opportunity for long term relationships:

          (a) Although most evangelists can "build relationships" very quickly, like Jesus and the Woman at the Well in John 4

    2) He sent them with no money or moneybelt:

      a) Does not Prov 14:20 state: "The poor is hated even by his neighbor, But those who love the rich are many"?

        (1) Jesus sent them out without enough money for a single meal, a hotel room, or a change of clothes!

    b) As far as evangelism, no money meant:

        (1) No "**service evangelism**" or "**servant evangelism**"; they could not provide service to the poor or needy, because they themselves were needy!

        (2) No "**socio-political transformation**"; they did not have social or political clout nor the stature of their wealth; they came on the basis of their message alone

    c) No money also meant:

        (1) No budgets or fund raising

        (2) No red tape or budget requests

        (3) No control from a funding source

    d) No money meant that Christ was going to keep His servants "lean and mean"—relying only on Him by faith, Heb 11:8-10

3) He sent them with no change of clothes:

    a) Meaning that they needed to be served by those whom they reached out to, even more than housing, but also in the washing of clothes

    b) Meaning that they dressed as the Lord would provide through those whom He foreordained to provide clothing for them

        (1) Meaning that they dressed like the people to whom they went fairly quickly as their original clothing wore out

    c) Meaning no clerical collar, no monastic robes, and no special haircut (a tonsure)!

    d) Meaning also that sometimes they had no place to lay their heads, just as Jesus (Matt 8:20; Luke 9:58)

4) Without even food:

    a) Meaning that multiple times during the day they were needy for food, or else they went without food (Deut 28:47-48; 1 Cor 4:11; 2 Cor 11:27)

    b) Meaning that they were completely dependent on God for food, even as Elijah (1 Kings 17:8-16; 19:5-8) and Jesus (during His temptation, as a temptation!)

    c) Meaning that they went without food, even though they were grateful to the Lord (Deut 28:47-48; Phil 4:4, 11-12)

b. However, it seems like Jesus was giving a perfect recipe for truly indigenous evangelism ministry!

  1) Notice how the ministry would become almost immediately indigenous:

    a) Eat their food

    b) Sleep in their homes

    c) Wear their clothes (after their own clothing wore out)

  2) It sounds like effective methods of evangelism in the history of the churches:

    a) 12th and 13th Century "Poor Men of Lyons," the Medieval Hermits, the *Beghards*, the Albigensian and Waldensian preachers

    b) 14th and 15th Century Wycliffe's Lollards

    c) 17th Century French desert church evangelist and preacher Claude Brousson

    d) 18th and 19th Century Baptist Preachers and Methodist Circuit Riders

    e) 19th Century Evangelical missionaries (e.g. J. Hudson Taylor)

  3) Does this not also sound very much like Book of Acts evangelism?

c. Notice also some other considerations as to obedience in the Matt 10:9-10 commands:

  1) There is no financial overhead and very little if any administrative time or cost (buildings, salaries, budgets, organization, etc.) in this type of evangelism ministry

  2) Everyone is involved in front-line ministry:

    a) Likewise, there is very little hierarchy in such a ministry, even leaders are involved in the same ministry as all the others

    b) Notice that Jesus sent out His disciples to do what He himself had been doing (Matt 9:35), and what He Himself continued to do (Matt 11:1); in other words, He did not graduate from a ministry of itinerant evangelism to a desk job!

        (1) And was not "everyone in front line ministry"[769] exemplified by Jesus (both before and after his teaching and sending)?

              Matt 9:35, "And Jesus was going about all the cities and the villages, teaching in their synagogues, and proclaiming the gospel of the kingdom, and healing every kind of disease and every kind of sickness"

              Matt 11:1, "And it came about that when Jesus had finished giving instructions to His twelve disciples, He departed from there to teach and preach in their cities"

        (2) As was also prophecied of Jesus?

              Isa 61:1-2, "The Spirit of the Lord God is upon me, Because the LORD has anointed me To bring good news to the afflicted; He has sent me to bind up the brokenhearted, To proclaim liberty to captives, And freedom to prisoners; To proclaim the favorable year of the LORD, And the day of vengeance of our God; To comfort all who mourn"

              Matt 11:2-6, "Now when John in prison heard of the works of Christ, he sent *word* by his disciples, and said to Him, "Are You the Expected One, or shall we look for someone else?" And Jesus answered and said to them, "Go and report to John what you hear and see: *the* blind receive sight and *the* lame walk, *the* lepers are cleansed and *the* deaf hear, and *the* dead are raised up, and *the* poor have the gospel preached to them. "And blessed is he who keeps from stumbling over Me"

        (3) In fact, it even appears that the very ministry methods of Jesus caused John the Baptist consternation!

  3) Perhaps these factors are why true Matthew 10 evangelism is so easy to whitewash from the pages of history, with very little physical trace of its existence:

    a) Whereas the massive territorial churches, with their buildings, budgets, affluence, political and economic influence, and hierarchy, want to be and are remembered in the annals of history (thereby showing their mission and priorities)

    b) Those obedient to Christ's commissioning would barely be noticed or known, much like the ministries of Isabeau and Pintarde mentioned at the end of Chapter 2

    c) By the way, is this not also true of many of today's house church movements and other movements?[770]

  4) Why would Jesus have wanted it so? Are there lessons to be taken away from such a commissioning?

---

[769]Sounds like Wesley's "All at it, Always at it!": "Every true convert to Christ is a commissioned evangelist.... The method of the Wesleyans was in perfect accord with the prescription of the Word; and was equally adapted to the eighteenth, nineteenth, or twentieth century—'All at it: always at it'—every convert to Christ a commissioned Evangelist" (W. B. Riley, *The Crisis of the Church* [New York: Cook, 1914], 80).

[770]For example, the only mention of Billy Graham in the 1,016 page biography of Pope John Paul II by George Weigel relates to John Paul II's being in Poland one more day (3 Oct 1978) than what he told Billy Graham:

    "Cardinal Wojtyla went to Warsaw October 2 for a meeting of the Main Council of the Polish Episcopate, thus missing the American evangelist Billy Graham, whom he had given permission to St. Anne's Church. In Warsaw he stayed at the Ursuline convent, where the sisters remembered him as looking very serious. Wojtyla left for Rome at 7:30 a.m. the next morning, along with Cardinal Wyszyński. By 11 a.m. on October 3, the Primate of Poland and the Archbishop of Kraków were in St. Peter's Basilica praying at the bier of John Paul I" (*Witness to Hope: The Biography of John Paul II* [New York: HarperCollins, 1999, 2001], 248).

Thus he may have misled the gracious Billy Graham that he was actually leaving Poland that same day (2 Oct 1978; see William Martin, *A Prophet with Honor: The Billy Graham Story* [New York: Morrow, 1991], 490). For those who can read ecclesiastical sign, could this misleading be a token that John Paul II did not honor his word to a heretic, following in the footsteps of many of his predecessors (e.g. John XXIII's word of safe passage to the Council of Constance to John Hus which was then rescinded)?

    d. Of the enemies of the Gospel:

       Introduction: Matthew 10, with its strong emphasis on persecution and hardship, makes it very clear that the Gospel of Jesus Christ has enemies…

      1) Listen to some of these incredible passages:

         a) Some will not receive the messenger of the Gospel, nor heed the words of the Gospel:
Matt 10:14, "And whoever does not receive you, nor heed your words, as you go out of that house or that city, shake off the dust of your feet"

         b) The world at large is not typified as being neutral to the Gospel, but rather of being wolves against the Gospel:
Matt 10:16, "Behold, I send you out as sheep in the midst of wolves; therefore be shrewd as serpents, and innocent as doves"

         c) The world at large demands that the evangelist be "shrewd as a serpent"!
Matt 10:16, "Behold, I send you out as sheep in the midst of wolves; therefore be shrewd as serpents, and innocent as doves"

         d) Christ commands his disciples to "beware of men":
Matt 10:17, "But beware of men; for they will deliver you up to *the* courts, and scourge you in their synagogues"

         e) Christ prophecies what will happen to Christians that are arrested for the Gospel:[771]
Matt 10:17-18, "But beware of men; for they will deliver you up to *the* courts, and scourge you in their synagogues; and you shall even be brought before governors and kings for My sake, as a testimony to them and to the Gentiles"

         f) This persecution is not "if" but "when":
Matt 10:19, "But when they deliver you up, do not become anxious about how or what you will speak; for it shall be given you in that hour what you are to speak"

         g) Persecution will enter and divide even to the point of the nuclear family:
Matt 10:21, "And brother will deliver up brother to death, and a father *his* child; and children will rise up against parents, and cause them to be put to death"

         h) The prophecied level of persecution will be raised even to the point of the death penalty (e.g. Acts 8:1; 12:2; 21:31; 22:22); note the parallelism in Jesus twice mentioning the death penalty:
Matt 10:21, "And brother will deliver up brother to death, and a father *his* child; and children will rise up against parents, and cause them to be put to death"

         i) Jesus used the word "all" to describe the level of antagonism of the world of men against the Gospel:
Matt 10:22, "And you will be hated by all on account of My name, but it is the one who has endured to the end who will be saved"

           In my minds eye, I see a Christian in a Muslim country with a Bible, huddled in a corner reading the Bible by candlelight, fearful of being caught by anyone finding him reading this forbidden book.

         j) The promise of salvation is directly linked to endurance through persecution for the Gospel:
Matt 10:22, "And you will be hated by all on account of My name, but it is the one who has endured to the end who will be saved"

         k) The Christian is not to capitulate to persecution, but rather to flee to the next city:
Matt 10:23, "But whenever they persecute you in this city, flee to the next; for truly I say to you, you shall not finish *going through* the cities of Israel, until the Son of Man comes"

---

[771]And, lo and behold, this is exactly what has been noted in 16th, 17th and 19th Century Protestant Church Histories that are labeled "Martyrologies" and then, it appears, virtually ignored by contemporary English church historians.

l) Another amazing promise is linked to the necessity of fleeing persecution, that of the timing of the return of Christ:

Matt 10:23, "But whenever they persecute you in this city, flee to the next; for truly I say to you, you shall not finish *going through* the cities of Israel, until the Son of Man comes"

m) Persecution is directly related to the Christians relationship with Christ:

Matt 10:24-25, "A disciple is not above his teacher, nor a slave above his master. It is enough for the disciple that he become as his teacher, and the slave as his master. If they have called the head of the house Beelzebul, how much more the members of his household!"

Persecution is not for personal or relational reasons, rather as in Matt 10:14, it is because of an antagonism to the words of Christ (cf. Mark 8:38).

Note the level of antagonism, along with the confusion that it causes to those who do not know or understand, to label the true Christian as related to Beelzebub.

Herein perhaps lies the key for not seeking to be amenable to "all other Christians" by seeking to show the longstanding orthodoxy of Evangelical beliefs according to the grid developed through what remains of Early Church theology.[772]

o) Christ twice commands his disciples not to live in fear, contrary to what may be the natural response to such bad news, because of sure just retribution at the end of time:

Matt 10:26, "Therefore do not fear them, for there is nothing covered that will not be revealed, and hidden that will not be known"

Matt 10:31, "Therefore do not fear; you are of more value than many sparrows"

Which retribution matches the level of persecution promised in Matt 10:21
Which level of retribution is expanded in Matt 10:27

p) Further excellent teaching is found in Matt 10:32-42, which is beyond the scope of this study at this time ☺

2) Lessons on enemies of the Gospel:

a) It is abundantly clear, just in looking at Matt 10, that Christ prepared His disciples for the persecution of which we read in the Book of Acts

b) It is very naïve to assume that we have no enemies if we are working for Christ, cf. Acts 22:19-20

---

[772]Consider the title of this article: Yves Krumenacker, "La généalogie imaginaire de la Réforme protestante" [The imaginary genealogy of the Protestant Reformation], *Revue Historique*, 638 (2006/2):259-89. Consider its English abstract: "The advent of Protestantism appeared to the Christians who were faithful in Rome like an innovation and thus an error. This is why the Reformers wanted to show that they had predecessors. Luther was interested in Hus. Flacius Illyricus, then Crespin and Goulard drew up lists of 'witnesses of the truth' persecuted by Rome. One then imagined a continuity of the true Christian tradition, by giving a significant place to Cathares and Waldensians: one can find that in the French Protestant histories of the Church at the XVIIth century. This type of history is declining with XVIIIth, except at Basnage, because of the progress of historical knowledge. But it reappears at the next century, in a nationalist context: if Waldensians are Protestants, it is possible to give a French origin to the Reformation. This history takes also a regionalistic color, when one starts to bind the 'southern spirit' to the defense of freedom, specially religious freedom. This is why it could be maintained until nowadays" (ibid., 289).

e. Considering Paul's possible use of Matt 10 in 2 Tim 2:11-13:

Immediately prior context: persevering in evangelism through suffering, following the example of Christ, 2 Tim 2:8-10 (cf. 1 Pet 4:16)…

Paul's Possible Use of the Antecedent of Matt 10 in 2 Tim 2:11-13

2 Tim 2:11-13	Some Parallels from the Gospels	Comments
Πιστὸς ὁ λόγος· *This is* a faithful saying:		Used in 1 and 2 Timothy
εἰ γὰρ συναπεθάνομεν, καὶ συζήσομεν For if we died with *Him*, We shall also live with *Him*	Matt 10:39, "and he who loses his life for My sake will find it" (cf. Matt 16:25)	
εἰ ὑπομένομεν, καὶ συμβασιλεύσομεν· If we endure, We shall also reign with *Him*	Matt 10:22, "And you will be hated by all for My name's sake. But he who endures to the end will be saved" (cf. Matt 24:13; Mark 13:13) Luke 21:19, "By your endurance you will gain your lives [souls; τὰς ψυχὰς ὑμῶν]" Luke 22:28-30, "But you are those who have continued with Me in My trials. 29 And I bestow upon you a kingdom, just as My Father bestowed *one* upon Me, 30 that you may eat and drink at My table in My kingdom, and sit on thrones judging the twelve tribes of Israel" (cf. Matt 19:28)	Rev 20:6, "Blessed and holy *is* he who has part in the first resurrection. Over such the second death has no power, but they shall be priests of God and of Christ, and shall reign with Him a thousand years" Cf. "kingdom of priests" 1 Pet 2:9; etc.
εἰ ἀρνούμεθα, κἀκεῖνος ἀρνήσεται ἡμᾶς· If we deny *Him*, He also will deny us.	Matt 10:33, "But whoever denies Me before men, him I will also deny before My Father who is in heaven" (cf. Luke 12:9)	Parallel passages also use the concept of "be ashamed of" (Mark 8:38; Luke 9:26); a concept which is well developed by Paul, Rom 1:16, and especially in 2 Tim 1:8, 12, 16; 2:15

εἰ ἀπιστοῦμεν, ἐκεῖνος πιστὸς μένει·
 If we are faithless, He remains faithful;
	Related to Peter's triple denial of Christ?
	
	 Luke 22:31-34, "And the Lord said, 'Simon, Simon! Indeed, Satan has asked for you, that he may sift *you* as wheat. 32 But I have prayed for you, that your faith should not fail; and when you have returned to *Me*, strengthen your brethren.' 33 But he said to Him, 'Lord, I am ready to go with You, both to prison and to death.' 34 Then He said, 'I tell you, Peter, the rooster shall not crow this day before you will deny three times that you know Me'"
		ἀπιστέω (7 NT uses), meaning:
		  Friberg: 1) *not believe, refuse to believe, be distrustful* (LU 24.11); (2) as acting disloyally *be unfaithful, prove false*
		  Gingrich: disbelieve, refuse to belief; be unfaithful, Mark 16:11, 16; Luke 24:11, 41; Acts 28:24; Rom 3:3; 2 Tim 2:13 [NA27 adds 1 Pet 2:7]
		  Louw-Nida: to believe that something is not true - 'to not believe, to disbelieve, to not think to be true.' ἀκούσαντες ὅτι ζῇ καὶ ἐθεάθη ὑπ᾽ αὐτῆς ἠπίστησαν 'when they heard her say that he was alive and that she had seen him, they did not believe her' Mk 16.11
		  UBS Lexicon: fail or refuse to believe; prove or be unfaithful
		 God is faithful, 1 John 1:9, etc.

ἀρνήσασθαι ἑαυτὸν οὐ δύναται. He cannot deny Himself.	Related to Jesus telling His followers, "Let him deny himself, and take up his cross, and follow Me" (Matt 16:24; Mark 8:34; Luke 9:23)	

f. Finally, remembering also the Lucan disclaimer of some of the content of the Matt 10 commands:

Luke 22:36-40, "Then He said to them, 'But now, he who has a money bag, let him take *it*, and likewise a knapsack; and he who has no sword, let him sell his garment and buy one. For I say to you that this which is written must still be accomplished in Me: "And He was numbered with the transgressors." For the things concerning Me have an end.' So they said, 'Lord, look, here *are* two swords.' And He said to them, 'It is enough.' Coming out, He went to the Mount of Olives, as He was accustomed, and His disciples also followed Him. When He came to the place, He said to them, 'Pray that you may not enter into temptation.'"

10. **What of Insubordination in Fulfilling the Great Commission**?

So what of those who are "not under orders" (ἀνυπότακτοι [Tit 1:10]), those independent of, or not subject to the head (ἀνυπότακτοι [Heb 2:8]), which is Christ?

Titus 1:10 (CSB), "For there are also many rebellious people, idle talkers and deceivers, especially those from Judaism" (Tit 1:10)

Translations of ἀνυπότακτοι in Titus 1:10
[Disobedient to the Bible (or to Christ) or rebellious against human or ecclesial authority?]

Tyndale (1388); Geneva; DRA⊕	KJV; Bishops; ERV; ASV	Webster's (1833); Darby	Etheridge (1849) (from Syriac)	Murdock (1851) (from Syriac)	Young's (1862); RSV; NKJ; ESV	Bible in Basic English (1949)	NJB⊕ (1985)	NAS (1977)	NIV (1984); NLT; CSB; NET	NAB⊕ (1991)	God's Word to the Nations (1995)
Disobedient	Unruly	Disorderly	Not in subjection	Unsubmissive	Insubordinate	Who are not ruled by law	People who are insubordinate	Rebellious Men	Rebellious people	Rebels	Believers … who are rebellious
For ther are many disobedient and talkers of vanite and disceavers of myndes namely they of the circumcision	For there are many unruly and vain talkers and deceivers, specially they of the circumcision	For there are many disorderly and vain talkers and deceivers, specially they of the circumcision	For there are many who are not in subjection, and whose words are vain, and make the minds of men to err, especially those of the circumcision	For many are unsubmissive, and their discourses vain; and they mislead the minds of people, especially such as are of the circumcision	for there are many both insubordinate, vain-talkers, and mind-deceivers – especially they of the circumcision –	For there are men who are not ruled by law; foolish talkers, false teachers, specially those of the circumcision	And in fact there are many people who are insubordinate, who talk nonsense and try to make others believe it, particularly among those of the circumcision	For there are many rebellious men, empty talkers and deceivers, especially those of the circumcision	For there are many rebellious people, mere talkers and deceivers, especially those of the circumcision group	For there are also many rebels, idle talkers and deceivers, especially the Jewish Christians	There are many believers, especially converts from Judaism, who are rebellious. They speak nonsense and deceive people

Friberg stated that the word ἀνυπότακτοι literally means "not under orders." The same word is used of being subject to Christ in Heb 2:8.

What of those who claim to be in subjection to Christ, but are not in subjection to the Great Commission? But then, it depends what is meant by "being in subjection to the Great Commission," or again, it depends what is meant by Great Commission?

What of Matt 10:32-33 and the link with salvation in this regard?

Matt 10:32-33, "Everyone therefore who shall confess Me before men, I will also confess him before My Father who is in heaven. But whoever shall deny Me before men, I will also deny him before My Father who is in heaven."

So these notes on the Great Commission find themselves as prioritative as regards obedience of the Great Commission: what is the New Testament Christian to obey as regards the Great Commisison? Let's look into this topic…

11. Also note my *Charts for a Theology of Evangelism*:[773]

a. Competition for the Main Idea

b. Verbs for Great Commission Methodology

---

[773]Johnston, *Charts for a Theology of Evangelism* (Nashville: Broadman, 2007).

    c.   Twelve approaches to the Great Commission, the Christian Life, and Holy Living

    d.   What is commanded in the Great Commission?

In the Great Commission, the Christian Is Commanded to Evangelize![774]

    1. The Great Commission:

        a.   The five passages:
            1)   "Win disciples," Matt 28:18-20: going; [winning]; baptizing; teaching.
            2)   "Go... and preach the Gospel," Mark 16:15 ff.
            3)   "Repentance for the forgiveness of sins would be proclaimed in His name," Luke 24:46-49
            4)   "As the Father has sent Me, so send I you," John 20:21[775]
            5)   "And you will be My testifiers," Acts 1:8

        b.   To whom are the Great Commission passages addressed?

            1)   The audience in context, the 12 disciples, 120 (Acts 1:15), or the 500 (1 Cor 15:6)

            2)   This is a command to all followers of Jesus:
                a)   Following the use of the word disciple, Matt 28:19-20 >> Mark 1:17, 15:16, for disciple speaks of all followers of Jesus Christ.
                b)   This is a command of Christ, and obedience to Christ's commands is not an option for the believer, John 14:21, 15:14, 1 John 2:3-6 (or "keeping His word," John 17:6).

            3)   The Great Commission is binding as a command on **all** Christians[776]
                a)   Herein Evangelicals stand in sharp contrast to the Church of England, whose "39 Articles" forbid public preaching [evangelizing] by anyone who has not been given "public authority" to do such (i.e. been ordained by the Church of England)[777]
                b)   Likewise, Evangelicals stand in sharp contrast to the Church of Rome, which requires that they discover, train, approve, appoint, and oversee all those who preach the Gospel,

---

[774]Mark Liederbach appears to downgrade this motivation, by categorizing it as "deontological": "The second type of motivation that I will evaluate is the idea that all Christians should do evangelism because we are commanded to do it. … This form of motivation is what an ethicist would call deontological. The emphasis here is on duty, obedience to command, or rule keeping. Deontology maintains that proper moral behavior is determined by focusing on the nature of the act itself. The value of the activity, then, has little to do with motive, results, even the character of the one performing the action. Rather, the value of the activity in question is determined solely by the inherent 'rightness' or 'wrongness' of the thing done or left undone. … From the deontological point of view, evangelism is right because God commanded it. Thus, because we are commanded by Christ to go to the world, we should go and evangelize. … Only when the command to evangelize is tied to the person and worship of God [where is Christ?] will knowledge of what we ought to be [be] transformed into a part of the 'art of living well' that Bavinck refers to and which we long for it to be" (Mark D. Liederbach, "Ethical Evaluation of Modern Motivations for Evangelism," 5, 7).

[775]Other passages in John are sometimes cited as Great Commision passages, such as John 15:26-27, "When the Helper comes, whom I will send to you from the Father, *that is* the Spirit of truth, who proceeds from the Father, He will bear witness of Me, and you *will* bear witness also, because you have been with Me from the beginning." While this passage is remarkably similar to Acts 1:8, it was not given during a post-resurrection appearance of Jesus.

[776]Clearly the Great Commission passages are meant for all Christians, not solely for those who may have "the gift of evangelism." In fact, all of the general commands, analogies, and metaphors of Scripture regarding evangelism are inclusive of all Christians. Donald A. Carson speaking of Matthew 28:19-20 concluded that, "Either way it is binding on *all* Jesus' disciples to make others what they themselves are—disciples of Christ." [italics his] Donald A. Carson, "Matthew", *Expositor's Bible Commentary*, Frank E., Gaebelien ed. Grand Rapids: Zondervan, 1984, Vol. 8, 596; see also Roland Q. Leavell, *Evangelism: Christ's Imperative Commission*, rev ed. (Nashville: Broadman, 1979) and John Ed Mathison, "How Does a Church Develop a Heart and a Vision for Evangelism?" *Decision Magazine* (April 1989), 29, 38.

[777]"Article 23: Of Ministering in the Congregation: It is not lawful for any man to take vpon hym the office of publique preachyng, or ministring the Sacramentes in the congregation, before he be lawfully called and sent to execute the same. And those we ought to iudge lawfully called and sent, whiche be chosen and called to this worke by men who haue publique aucthoritie geuen vnto them in the congregation, to call and sende ministers into the Lordes vineyarde" (39 Articles of the Church of England [1572]; available from: http://www.episcopalian.org/efac/1553-1572.htm; accessed: 21 Oct 2004; Internet).

giving this unique and particular privilege the title of "Sacrament of Holy Orders"[778]
Several things emanate from this "Sacrament" (which apparently goes back to Pope Gregory I [A.D. 590-604]):

(1) One who dares to preach the Gospel without having received this "means of grace" is going against the heart of salvation for the Church of Rome (one of the Seven Sacraments)

(2) By the 12th Century, receiving the Sacrament of Holy Orders also meant living a celebate life in a commune without the private ownership of anything (cf. the three Benedictine Vows)

(3) Those not receiving the grace of the "Sacrament of Holy Orders" where to receive the "Sacrament of Holy Matrimony," get married, have children, and not speak about the Gospel of salvation in the privacy of their own homes nor out in public

It is difficult to calculate the negative impact of these two "sacraments" which eliminate the possibility of forming Gospel-oriented families and deny Christians the opportunity to obey the Great Commission

2. UNPACKING THE GREAT COMMISSION PASSAGES:

a. An evaluation of the emphases in each Great Commission Passage...

---

[778]"875 'How are they to believe in him of whom they have never heard? And how are they to hear without a preacher? And how can men preach unless they are sent?' No one—no individual and no community—can proclaim the Gospel to himself: 'Faith comes from what is heard.' No one can give himself the mandate and the mission to proclaim the Gospel. The one sent by the Lord [e.g. Christ or his supposed 'Vicar' the Pope] does not speak and act on his own authority; not as the member of the community, but speaking to it in the name of Christ. No one can bestow grace on himself; it must be given and offered. This fact presupposes ministers of grace [ministers of the sacraments], authorized and empowered by Christ [and his 'Vicar' on earth]. From him, they receive the mission and faculty ('the sacred power') to act *in persona Christi Capitis* ['in the person of headship Christ'?]. The ministry which Christ's emissaries do and give by God's grace what they cannot do and give by their own powers, is called a 'sacrament' by the Church's tradition. Indeed, the ministry of the Church is conferred by special sacrament" (*Catechism of the Catholic Church*, ed. by Joseph Cardinal Ratzinger [Rome: Libreria Editrice Vaticana, 1994; London: Geoffrey Chapman, 1994], §875).

MATTHEW'S GREAT COMMISSION

1) **Matthew** emphasizes winning and teaching disciples with the use of μαθητεύω as the main verb, and three participles modifying the command to "win/make disciples": by (1) going [and preaching], (2) baptizing/immersing, and (3) teaching to obey:

a) "Of all nations" in Matt 28:19:

Introduction: Matthew 28's "pan ta ethne" became a mantra for Donald McGavran, as he sought to find the concept of "People Movements" in the Great Commission of Jesus. It appears that he missed the fact that the "them" in Matt 28:19 was masculine, while the word "nations" was neuter—exegetically, they cannot correspond to one another!

Further, a romanticized conception of God's dealing with "the nations" in the Old Testament is brought to reality in Deut 19:1:

Deut 19:1 (HSCB), "When the LORD your God annihilates the nations whose land He is giving you, so that you drive them out and live in their cities and houses"

Neither did Jesus ask His disciples to evangelize among the nations in Matt 10:5-6:

Matt 10:5-6, "These twelve Jesus sent out after instructing them, saying, 'Do not go in *the* way of *the* Gentiles, and do not enter *any* city of the Samaritans; but rather go to the lost sheep of the house of Israel'"

Yet in Matthew 28:19, Jesus removed this ethnic restriction in the presentation of the Gospel! So what are some lessons from the "all nations" in Matt 28:19?

(1) The implication of a plain reading of the text may be that "all nations" can be or will be "discipled" or "taught" in a universalist or triumphalist sense:

(a) However, other Scriptures, such as Matt 7:13-14 and 1 Cor 9:22, show us that the implication of Jesus was not a universal salvation (aka. universalism), nor even that everyone should or would respond to the Gospel if it is properly presented to them!

(2) Perhaps a better interpretation of the accusative (πάντα) may be: "from among all nations," or "out of all nations," clearly showing that individuals are being snatched out from among all nations (as in [ἐκ πάσης] in Rev 5:9, "from every tribe and tongue and people and nation"):

"And they sang a new song, saying, 'Worthy art Thou to take the book, and to break its seals; for Thou wast slain, and didst purchase for God with Thy blood *men* from every tribe and tongue and people and nation. And Thou hast made them *to be* a kingdom and priests to our God; and they will reign upon the earth.'"

(a) The *Complete Jewish Bible* (1998) translated Matt 28:19 with this particularist emphasis:

"Therefore, go and make people from all nations into *talmidim*, immersing them into the reality of the Father, the Son and the *Ruach HaKodesh*, and teaching them to obey everything that I have commanded you. And remember! I will be with you always, yes, even until the end of the age."

Note the impact of the "from" instead of the "of" as in most other English translations.

(b) Consider the clause in Deut 4:34 that parallels or prefigures the result of the Great Commission in a particularist sense:

NKJ: "Or did God *ever* try to go *and* take for Himself a nation from the midst of *another* nation…?"
Darby: "Or hath God essayed to come to take him a nation from the midst of a nation…?"
LXX: εἰ ἐπείρασεν ὁ θεὸς εἰσελθὼν λαβεῖν ἑαυτῷ ἔθνος ἐκ μέσου ἔθνους

Does not God seeking and snatching a "nation from the midst of a nation" describe the Great Commission?

(c) Consider also God's work of gathering in from among the nations in Deut 30:3:

Deut 30:3, "then the LORD your God will restore you from captivity, and have compassion on you, and will gather you again **from all the peoples** [ἐκ πάντων τῶν ἐθνῶν] where the LORD your God has scattered you"

Again we find a gathering "out from among" emphasis, which seems to parallel both Matt 28:19 and Rev 5:9

(d) Therefore a more exacting translation of Matthew 28:19 may preferably translate the accusative of πάντα as follows, "Go, [make/win] disciples from all nations…"

b) "Them" in Matthew 28:19, "baptizing/immersing them," shows:

(1) As mentioned above, the masculine plural "them" [αὐτοὺς] does not necessarily match with the neuter plural "all nations" [τὰ ἔθνη], especially if the point above is a correct interpretation:

(a) Rather, it seems to be referring to those "out of" the nations that are won as or become "disciples", thereby referring to the particular group of those who are won as disciples

(b) This application of the baptized referring to a particular group also applies to the masculine plural of the "them" [αὐτοὺς] in "teaching them to keep" in v. 20

(c) This **particularist interpretation**, it must be remembered, may fly in the face of various churches, and therefore be telegraphed to their writings an interpretations of this Great Commission, as well as in their lexicons and other Bible helps, for example:
[1] **Territorial churches** (Catholic, Orthodox, Anglican, Lutheran),
[2] **Non-conversionistic churches** (i.e. Liberal Protestant and Liberal Baptist, etc.), and/or
[3] Churches, theologians, and practitioners who believe in or practice a form of **Universalism** (most authors in Christendom)

(2) If "them" speaks only of disciples that are won, then it follows (from plenary inspiration and context) that they must have first heard the preaching of the Gospel:

(a) Is this omission of "preaching" not an example of an ellipsis as a figure of speech,[779] wherein "Go and preach" is reduced to "Go", perhaps for greater emphasis on the omission or to reduce unnecessary redundancy?
[1] To begin with:
[a] Matt 28:19 uses the Greek word πορεύομαι, which means "Go"
[2] Likewise, this exact same word is used in combination with preaching in Matthew:
[a] "Go and preach, saying, 'The kingdom of heaven is at hand,'" Matt 10:7 (translation mine)
[b] "Go and report to John what you hear and see," Matt 11:4
[3] Also there are other uses of "Go" (πορεύομαι) in Matthew which also parallel Matthew's Great Commission:
[a] "Go to the lost sheep of the house of Israel," Matt 10:6
[b] "Go and search for the one that is straying, Matt 18:12
[c] "Go therefore to the main highways, and as many as you find *there*, invite to the wedding feast," Matt 22:9
[d] "Go quickly and tell His disciples that He has risen from the dead," Matt 28:7

---

[779]"The omission of one or more words that are obviously understood but that must be supplied to make a construction grammatically complete" (*Webster's New Collegiate Dictionary* [Springfield, MA: Merriam, 1977]).

[4] Notice also the parallel missional texts in Matthew, with both movement and mission:

[a] "John the Baptist came, preaching in the wilderness of Judea, saying, 'Repent, for the kingdom of heaven is at hand,'" Matt 3:1-2

[b] "From that time Jesus began to preach and say, 'Repent, for the kingdom of heaven is at hand,'" Matt 4:17

[c] "Follow Me, and I will make you fishers of men," Matt 4:19

[d] "And Jesus was going about [περιάγω] all the cities and the villages, teaching in their synagogues, and proclaiming the gospel of the kingdom, and healing every kind of disease and every kind of sickness," Matt 9:35

[e] "Therefore beseech the Lord of the harvest to send out [ἐκβάλλω] workers into His harvest," Matt 9:38

[f] "Behold, I send you out [ἀποστέλλω]…" Matt 10:16

[g] "…He departed [μεταβαίνω] from there to teach and preach in their cities, Matt 11:1

[h] "Behold, the sower went out [ἐξέρχομαι] to sow," Matt 13:3

(b) Like all the examples, because there can be no faith without hearing (Acts 15:7-11; Rom 10:17), it is clear that the necessary preaching was an unrepeated part of Jesus' command to "Go"—as is clearly mentioned in other Great Commission passages:

[1] Mark 16:15, "Go … and preach"

[2] Luke 24:47-48, "Repentance … shall be preached … You are testifiers of these things"

[3] Acts 1:8, "You shall be My testifiers"

(c) Were "Go" to include an ellipsis, as conjectured and ascertained, then the construction would flow in the following order:

Go!—[Preach!]—Win disciples!—Baptize!—Teach to obey![780]

(3) If "them" speaks only of disciples that are won, then it follows that only those disciples that are won [μαθητεύω] should be baptized/immersed:

(a) That the winning of the disciple is a completed action prior to the baptism/immersion, thereby nullifying both infant and generalistic baptism as being taught in this verse:

[1] This **baptistic interpretation** flies in the face of all denominations and churches that baptize infants: the Eastern Orthodox, Church of Rome, Lutheran, Anglican/Episcopalian, Reformed, Presbyterian, Methodist, etc.; remembering that their view of infant baptism will be transported into their writings, lexicons, and Bible helps:

[2] For example, notice the "born again" language as applied to baptism:

[a] In the 39 Articles of the Church of England (used by Anglicans and Episcopalians)[781]

---

[780]Notice the snide words of Calvin against the [ana]Baptists' use of Matthew 28 for believer's baptism: "To prove this, they allege the passage of Saint Matthew (28:19), where Jesus Christ tells to his Apostles: Go, and teach all people, baptizing them, in the name of the Father, and of the Son, and of the Holy Spirit: to which they add this sentence from Mark (v. 16): Who believes, and is baptized, will be saved. Behold, this seems to them an invincible foundation" (Jehan Calvin, "Brieve Instruction pour Armer tous Bons Fideles contre les Erreurs de la Secte Commune des Anabaptistes"; or: "Brief Instruction to Arm All Good Faithful [Ones] against the Errors of the Common Sect of the Anabaptists" [Geneva: Jehan Girard, 1544]; in *Corpus Reformatorum*, vol 35; Ioannis Calvini, *Opera Quae Supersunt Omnia*, vol. 7 [Brunsvigae: Schwetschke, 1868], 45-142). Translation mine.

[781]"XXVII. Of Baptisme. Baptisme is not only a signe of profession, and marke of difference, whereby Christian men are discerned from other that be not christened: but is also a signe of regeneration or newe byrth, whereby as by an instrument, they that receaue baptisme rightly, are grafted into the Church: the promises of the forgeuenesse of sinne, and of our adoption to be the sonnes of God, by the holy ghost, are visibly signed and sealed: fayth is confirmed: and grace increased by vertue of prayer vnto God. The baptisme of young children, is in any wyse to be retayned in the

        [b] In the Methodist Discipline[782]

        [c] In the *Catechism of the Catholic Church*[783]

  (b) The issue of baptism by immersion also comes into this verse:

    [1] Immersion is the only form of baptism exemplified in the Bible:

        [a] John the Baptist baptized in the Jordan river, Matt 3:6; Mark 1:5, 9;

        [b] "After being baptized, Jesus went up immediately from the water," Matt 3:16

        [c] "I came baptizing in water," John 1:31, "in water"

        [d] The need for "much water," John 3:23

        [e] "They both went down into the water," Acts 8:38

    [2] Also, immersion is the only form of baptism which parallels the imagery in the NT:

        [a] "Buried with him in baptism," Rom 6:4; Col 2:12

        [b] "Passing through the sea," 1 Cor 11:1-2

        [c] "Clothed with Christ," Gal 3:27

    [3] On top of that, the Greek word βαπτίζω actually means "to immerse":

        [a] Friberg lexicon: "strictly *dip, immerse* in water"

        [b] Lidell-Scott-Jones: "*to dip in* or *under water*"

        [c] Thayer's: Meaning #1: "**1.** properly, *to dip repeatedly, to immerge, submerge*"

        [d] Gingrich lexicon: "*dip, immerse*"

    [4] Therefore, it seems clear that the word "baptize" (which is a transliteration) could or should be translated "immerse"

  (4) If "them" in verse 19 speaks of disciples that are won, then it follows that the "them" in verse 20 refers to disciples that have been won and baptized (after believing as in Mark 16:16):

    (a) That the winning of the disciple is a completed action prior to the immersion, thereby separates the action of "win disciples" from the "teaching them to obey" in verse 20:

        [1] Which implication is that the local church is primarily and predominantly for saved people to be taught to obey

---

Churche, as most agreable with the institution of Christe" ("39 Articles of Religion" [1572]; available at: http://www.episcopalian.org/efac/1553-1572.htm; accessed: 21 Oct 2004; Internet).

[782]"XVII—Of Baptism: Baptism is not only a sign of profession and mark of difference whereby Christians are distinguished from others that are not baptized; but it is also a sign of regeneration or the new birth. The Baptism of young children is to be retained in the Church" (*Methodist Book of Discipline* [1784, 1808]; available at: http://archives.umc.org/interior.asp?ptid=1&mid=1817; accessed: 22 Feb 2007; Internet).

[783]"1262. The different effects of Baptism are signified by the perceptible elements of the sacramental rite. Immersion in water symbolizes not only death and purification, but also regeneration and renewal. Thus the two principal effects are purification from sins and the new birth in the Holy Spirit [*Council of Florence* (1439)].

"1265. Baptism not only purifies from all sins, but also makes the neophyte 'a new creature', an adopted son of God, who has become a 'partaker of the divine nature', member of Christ and co-heir with him, and a temple of the Holy Spirit.

"1266. The Most Holy Trinity gives the baptized *sanctifying grace*, the grace of *justification*:

- enabling them to believe in God, to hoppe in him and to love him through the *theological virtues*;

- giving them the power to live and act under the promptings of the Holy Spirit through the *gifts of the Holy Spirit*;

- allowing them to grow in goodness through the *moral virtues*.

Thus the whole organism of the Christian's supernatural life has its roots in Baptism.

"1274. The Holy Spirit has marked us with the '*seal of the Lord*' (*Dominicus character*) 'for the day of redemption'. 'Baptism indeed is the seal of eternal life.' The faithful Christian who has 'kept the seal' until the end, remaining faithful to the demands of his Baptism, will be able to depart this life 'marked with the sign of faith', with his baptismal faith, in expectation of the blessed vision of God – the consummation of faith – and in the hope of resurrection" (*Catechism of the Catholic Church* [Rome: Vatican, 1994; London: Geoffrey Chapman, 1994], §1262, 1265, 1266, 1274).

[2] Which **particularistic interpretation** flies in the face of:

[a] **Seeker sensitive churches** who seek by their church services and their worship to woo non-believers into the kingdom of God, and may likewise not ground disciples in the faith as they ought to do

[b] **Territorial churches** who wrongly take it upon themselves to teach all people [whom they have baptized as infants] in the same way, as if the converted and unconverted are able to discern the same spiritual truths.

Again, this generalistic interpretation will be presumed and assumed in all their writings and in all the Bible helps that they publish.

(b) This clear distinction between the two actions of "win disciples" and "teaching to obey" is taught throughout the book of Acts by different sets of verbs (compare the lists of verbs on evangelism in Chapters 7 and life in the church in Chapter 26)

(c) This distinction leads to a number of interesting conclusions:

[1] Winning a disciple is the result of evangelizing:
  [a] "Disciples" were the immediate result of evangelistic activity, Acts 6:1, 7; 14:21
  [b] For the first time, the disciples (the fruit of Paul and Barnabas' evangelistic ministry) were called "Christians" in Antioch, Acts 11:26
  [c] In Paul's ministry in Ephesus, he evangelized in the synagogue (Acts 19:8), and later because of antagonism, "withdrew the disciples"—the fruit of his evangelistic ministry, to the school of Tyrannus (Acts 19:9)

[2] Winning a disciple speaks of conversion or the beginning of the Christian life:
  [a] For Joseph of Arimathea (Matt 27:57), the word μαθητεύω could not have meant "spend two years walking with and being mentored by Jesus"
  [b] Nor could it have meant a prolonged time for Paul's ministry in Acts 14:21

[3] That the disciple is won as a disciple prior to his being baptized is also taught in this verse:
  [a] Rather persons in church history have turned the winning of a disciple into a human work that necessitates a prolonged period of time, seeking to disciple all people generally who were baptized as infants
  [b] This verse teaches, as we will note below, that the person must be a disciple prior to being baptized!

[4] Winning disciples shows that God does not want His people to evangelize without aim or purpose (cf. 1 Cor 9:26):
  [a] Their aim is to win disciples (1 Cor 9:19-22)
  [b] They are to tirelessly give themselves to this one task (2 Cor 12:15)

[5] The need to win disciples prior to teaching them shows that the New Testament church is always a first generation Christian church:
  [a] No one gains membership into the church through natural descent of human blood line (cf. John 1:12-13)
  [b] Being won as a disciple relates to being born again, and does not follow a class on theology (catechism)

     [6] There is a separation between winning and teaching:

        [a] One ought not spend time trying to teaching a lost person "to do all that" Jesus commanded—in order that they then may become saved![784]

        [b] Mixing up the order of these commands led Augustinian Catholics (with their sacraments), and similarly the Monastic movement (Monks) down the wrong path of salvation apart from grace through faith in response to the Gospel message!

  (d) Non-conversionistic churches will cringe at translating Matthew's Commission with a conversionist bent—again reducing the likelihood that a broadly-received Bible will ever translate μαθητεύω as "win disciples"!

c) Similarly, regarding Acts 14:21's use of μαθητεύω:

"After they had evangelized [εὐαγγελίζω, vpamnmp] that city and won many disciples [μαθητεύω, vpaanmp] they returned to Lystra and to Iconium and to Antioch,"

Where the verbs "evangelize" and "winning disciples" were used together as:

(1) Related actions, quite likely both referring to the beginning of salvation:

    (a) Some scholars place the context of Paul's second missionary journey in A.D. 45-47,[785] others 47-48,[786] making the entire missionary journey one of two years, which does not allow for a prolonged [2-3 year] discipleship program to be implemented in each town listed in the text (the phases and indented towns below come from Schnabel's chronology, where he posited a trip from 45-47 A.D., adding the logical towns assuming the travel from one city to the next):

    [1] Phase One:

      [a] Sailed to the Island of Cyprus, Acts 13:4

      [b] City of Salamis, 13:5

        {1} Kition

        {2} Amathos

        {3} Neapolis

        {4} Kourion

      [c] Ministry in the city of Paphos, 13:6

    [2] Phase Two:

      [a] Sailed to Perga in Pamphylia, 13:13

        {1} Ariassos?

        {2} Komama?

        {3} Lysinia? (Pisidia)

        {4} Ilyas

        {5} Eudoxiopolis?

        {6} Apollonia?

        {7} Tymandos?

      [b] Antioch in Pisidia, 13:14

        {1} Neapolis

        {2} Pappa

      [c] Iconium, 14:1

---

[784]"The work of conversion, of repentance from dead works, and faith in Christ, must be taught first and in a frequent and thorough manner. The stewards of God's household must give to each their portion in their season. We must never go beyond the capacities of our people, nor should we teach Christian maturity to those who have not yet learned the first lesson" (Richard Baxter, *The Reformed Pastor* [Portland, OR: Multnomah, 1982; based on William Orme's edition of 1920, first edition, 1656], 15). "The work of conversion is the first and most vital part of our ministry. For there are those who are Christian only in name, who have need to be truly 'born again.' ... The next part of the ministry is the upbuilding of those that are truly converted'" (ibid., 73).

[785]Eckhard J. Schnabel, *Early Christian Mission,* vol 2, *Paul and the Early Church* (German edition, 2002; Downers Grove, IL: InterVarsity, 2004),

[786]"Chronological Table" in F. F. Bruce, *The Acts of the Apostles,* 2nd ed. (Grand Rapids: Eerdmans, 1952), 55.

> [d] Lystra
> > {1} Dalisandos
> > {2} Kodylessos
> > {3} Posala
> > {4} Ilistra
> > {5} Laranda
> [e] Derbe in Lycanoia, 14:6
> [3] Phase Three:
> > [a] Derbe, 14:20
> > [b] Lystra, 14:21
> > [c] Iconium, 14:21
> > [d] Antioch, 14:21
> [4] Phase Four:
> > [Passed through the regions of Pisidia and Pamphylia, 14:24]
> > [a] Perge, 14:24
> > [b] Attalia, 14:25
> > [c] Antioch, 14:26

(2) In Acts 14:21, both evangelism and winning disciples were completed actions (aorist tense)

(3) Therefore, "evangelism" and "winning disciples" [or making disciples or discipleship] may not really be as different as some have made them out to be:

(a) Notice, however, how Howard Hendricks counter-positioned evangelism and discipleship:

> "'Make disciples' is the mandate of the Master (Matthew 28:19-20). We may ignore it, but we cannot evade it.
> "Our risen Christ left this legacy—the magna charta of the church. He provided both the model and the method. His life—and death—recast the lives of men. He demonstrated that you have not done anything until you have changed the lives of men.
> "'Follow Me,' He urged His men. And then that staggering assurance: 'Lo, I am with you *always*...' Somehow we have forgotten that this promise is linked to a process. We cannot embrace the *promise* and ignore the *process*."[787]

(b) Notice Hendricks':

[1] Strong emphasis on "process," with a correlating disemphasis on the point or time and place of conversion.

[2] Note also the partial quote of Matt 4:19, with the removal of "and I will make you fishers of men." Perhaps it was ignored or overlooked because fishing does not emphasize process, but rather the punctiliar act of catching the fish. A phrase that would not buttress the point he was seeking to make.

[3] Notice the onus of the responsibility is placed on the shoulders of the [unworthy] "discipler":
  [a] "**You** haven't done anything until **you** have changed the lives of men"; which emphasis is actually not completely biblical as regards the Holy Spirit's role in conversion (cf. Gal 3:1-5)!
  [b] One wonders if a Christian being "born of the Holy Spirit" has any lasting impact in the life of the new believer? It appears not, from Hendricks' point-of-view, much against what most Evangelical Systematic Theologies would affirm about conversion and salvation!
  [c] Likewise, I have heard repeated, "You must reproduce yourself in your disciple!" What? I have too much evil within me. I want Jesus to be formed in those with whom I work, not Tom Johnston!

---

[787]Howard Hendricks, "Foreword," in Walter A. Hendrichsen, *Disciples Are Made—Not Born: Making Disciples Out of Christians* (Wheaton, IL: Victor, 1974; 23rd printing, 1985), 5. Italics from original.

(c) In this case, Hendricks exemplifies a missional turn which took place in the middle 1970s:

[1] From evangelism as being the primary thrust of the Evangelical church

[2] To discipleship as a process-oriented task being the primary thrust of the church, of which evangelism is considered a silent assumption (at least in their reading of Matt 28)

[3] See Chart 5 in my *Book of Charts for a Theology of Evangelism* titled, "Twelve Approaches to the Great Commission and the Christian Life."

(d) Notice, however, that Hendrick's view is not new, it not only mirrors the monastic views of the Dark Ages, but it also mirrors the contemporary Roman Catholic view of "make disciples":

"We should take careful note of the fact that Christ did not send His disciples to convert the whole world to the Church but rather to send them out to teach or make disciples of all nations."[788]

"In the past we wrongly conceived the mission task in terms of converting as many as possible, overlooking the fact that Christ commanded the apostles to teach or make disciples of all nations, not to convert them."[789]

[1] Notice that this Roman Catholic gentleman's views seem to appreciate the process orientation of the discipleship movement

[2] Notice also his uncomfortable use of "we," referring to Catholics and Evangelicals in the second person plural. To find true spiritual conversion in official Roman documents, one has to reach back prior to the sacramentalism of Ambrose and Augustine!

[3] Notice his use of "converting as many as possible" as a past view, and Christ's use of "making disciples" as "not to convert them"!

For an "infallible" view of what Rome teaches on evangelism and conversion as a process, beginning with [Holy] Baptist, and constantly nurtured through the [Holy] Eucharist, and the Church of Rome's place in evangelism, see [Pope] Paul VI's encyclical, *Evangelii Nuntiandi*: On Evangelization in the Modern World (8 Dec 1975)[790]

[4] Rather, Rome's Great Commission for its priests and hierarchy is found in Hebrews, that being continually offering sacrifices (especially "The [perpetual sacrifice of the] Mass"):

Heb 9:6 (DRA), "Now these things being thus ordered, into the first tabernacle the priests indeed always entered, accomplishing the offices of sacrifices" (cf. Heb 5:1-3)

Heb 9:9 (DRA), "Which is a parable of the time present: according to which gifts and sacrifices are offered, which can not, as to the conscience, make him perfect that serveth, only in meats and in drinks"

The observant reader may want to consider how these verses have been translated in order to accommodate such an interpretation...

---

[788]Ronan Hoffman, [in response to: 1967: Are Conversion Missions Outmoded?] "Yes! Conversion and the Mission of the Church," in Donald McGavran, ed., *Eye of the Storm: The Great Debate in Mission* (Waco, TX: Word, 1972), 71.

[789]Ibid., 77.

[790]John Paul II, *Evangelii Nuntiandi: On Evangelization in the Modern World* (Rome: 8 Dec 1975) (online): available at: http://listserv.american.edu/catholic/church/papal/paul.vi/p6evang.txt; accessed: 8 Sept 2004; Internet.

Translations of Hebrews 9:6

Byzantine Textform	NKJ	NAS	NJB*	NAB*	GNT*
Τούτων δὲ οὕτως κατεσκευασμένων, εἰς μὲν τὴν πρώτην σκηνὴν διὰ παντὸς εἰσίασιν οἱ ἱερεῖς, τὰς λατρείας ἐπιτελοῦντες·	Now when these things had been thus prepared, the priests always went into the first part of the tabernacle, performing the services.	Now when these things have been thus prepared, the priests are continually entering the outer tabernacle, performing the divine worship,	Under these provisions, priests go regularly into the outer tent to carry out their acts of worship,	With these arrangements for worship, the priests, in performing their service, go into the outer tabernacle repeatedly,	This is how things have been arranged. The priests go into the outer tent to perform their duties,

(e) Likewise, following the pattern of the Medieval church interpretation of Matthew's Great Commission, the King James use of "teach" in Matt 28:19 for the Greek verb μαθητεύω, and its use of the verb "teach" for the Greek verb διδάσκω in Matt 28:20 further communicated soteriological nuance:

[1] The KJV merely followed the precedent set by Jerome's Vulgate, as he used the verb *docete* (Latin for teach) in both places

[a] A precedent which allowed the Vulgate to be a monastic-friendly and sacramental-friendly translation

[2] Using the same verb (teach) to describe the ministry toward the lost of "winning disciples" and ministry toward those who are baptized disciples confused the fast difference between evangelism and teaching to obey within the church

[3] Likewise the KJV's translation confused justification with sanctification[791] (a distinction which territorial or sacramental churches are wont to ignore)

d) "Make [to become] disciples" or "Win disciples" in Matt 28:19:

(1) That "make disciples" speaks of the beginning of faith, rather than a prolonged period in the Christian life which continues indefinitely after conversion, is made evident by the use of the verb μαθητεύω in Matt 27:57; the following are four contemporary translations of the verse:

NAS (1977): "And when it was evening, there came a rich man from Arimathea, named Joseph, who himself **had also become a disciple** of Jesus."

NKJ (1982): "Now when evening had come, there came a rich man from Arimathea, named Joseph, who himself **had also become a disciple** of Jesus."

NIV (1984): "As evening approached, there came a rich man from Arimathea, named Joseph, who **had himself become a disciple** of Jesus."

HSCB (2005): "When it was evening, a rich man from Arimathea named Joseph came, who himself **had also become a disciple** of Jesus."

Nestle-Aland 27th Edition: Ὀψίας δὲ γενομένης ἦλθεν ἄνθρωπος πλούσιος ἀπὸ Ἀριμαθαίας, τοὔνομα Ἰωσήφ, ὃς καὶ αὐτὸς **ἐμαθητεύθη** τῷ Ἰησοῦ·

(2) Some thoughts about the translation of μαθητεύω as "had become a disciple" in Matt 27:57:

(a) The name of Joseph of Arimathea shows up uniquely at the end of each of the four Gospels (Matt 27:57; Mark 15:43; Luke 23:50-51; John 19:38):

[1] Mark 15:43 he described Joseph as, "who himself was waiting for the kingdom of God"

[2] Luke 23:50-51 stated of Joseph:

[a] "Who was a member of the council"

[b] "A good and righteous man"

---

[791]"17. Of the Righteous and the Wicked: We believe that there is a radical difference and essential difference between the righteous and the wicked; that such as through faith are justified in the name of the Lord Jesus and sanctified by the Spirit of our God, are truly righteous in his esteem; while such as continue in impenitence and unbelief are in his sight wicked, and under the curse; and this distinction holds among men both in and after death" ("New Hampshire [Baptist] Confession [1833]," in Lumpkin, William L. *Baptist Confessions of Faith,* rev. ed. [Valley Forge: Judson, 1959, 1969]).

[c] "He had not consented to their plan of action" (cf. Nicodemus, John 7:50-52; Gamaliel, Acts 5:33ff., who taught Paul, Acts 22:3)

[d] "A man from Arimathea, a city of the Jews

[e] "Who was waiting for the kingdom of God"

[3] John elaborated:

[a] "Being a disciple of Jesus"

[b] "But a secret one, for fear of the Jews" (cf. John 3:1-2; 12:42-43)

Various Translations of "secretly" John 19:38

Was Joseph a secret disciple of Jesus, or did he secretly ask for the body of Jesus, or both?

Byzantine	Wycliffe (1388)	Tyndale (1534); cf. Geneva; Webster's; Young's; NET; CSB	New American Bible* (1901, 1991); cf. NLT	NAS (1977); cf. NJB*	NIV (1984)	KJV (1611, 1769); cf. Darby; English Revised; ASV; RSV; ESV	NKJ (1982)
Μετὰ ταῦτα ἠρώτησεν τὸν Πιλᾶτον Ἰωσὴφ ὁ ἀπὸ Ἀριμαθαίας, ὢν μαθητὴς τοῦ Ἰησοῦ, κεκρυμμένος δὲ διὰ τὸν φόβον τῶν Ἰουδαίων, ἵνα ἄρῃ τὸ σῶμα τοῦ Ἰησοῦ· καὶ ἐπέτρεψεν ὁ Πιλάτος. Ἦλθεν οὖν καὶ ἦρεν τὸ σῶμα τοῦ Ἰησοῦ.	But after these thingis Joseph of Armathi preyede Pilat, that he schulde take awei the bodi of Jhesu, for that he was a disciple of Jhesu, but priui for drede of the Jewis. And Pilat suffride. And so he cam, and took awei the bodi of Jhesu.	After that Ioseph of Aramathia (which was a disciple of Iesus: but secretly for feare of the Iewes) besought Pylate that he myght take doune the body of Iesus. And Pylate gave him licence.	After this, Joseph of Arimathea, secretly a disciple of Jesus for fear of the Jews, asked Pilate if he could remove the body of Jesus. And Pilate permitted it. So he came and took his body.	And after these things Joseph of Arimathea, being a disciple of Jesus, but a secret *one*, for fear of the Jews, asked Pilate that he might take away the body of Jesus; and Pilate granted permission. He came therefore, and took away His body.	Later, Joseph of Arimathea asked Pilate for the body of Jesus. Now Joseph was a disciple of Jesus, but secretly because he feared the Jews. With Pilate's permission, he came and took the body away.	And after this Joseph of Arimathaea, being a disciple of Jesus, but secretly for fear of the Jews, besought Pilate that he might take away the body of Jesus: and Pilate gave *him* leave. He came therefore, and took the body of Jesus.	After this, Joseph of Arimathea, being a disciple of Jesus, but secretly, for fear of the Jews, asked Pilate that he might take away the body of Jesus; and Pilate gave *him* permission. So he came and took the body of Jesus.
Notice the comma added prior to the word "secretly" adding some ambiguity	The "privi" is associated with his being a disciple; the period breaks the two ideas	The parentheses make it clear that Joseph was a secret disciple	Moved the word secret prior to the phrase about being a disciple	Add interpretive word "one" to emphasize that it relates to his being a secret disciple	Use punctuation to separate the clauses, as in the 1388 Wycliffe	Slightly open to interpretation	Through punctuation, make "secretly" an adverb of asking for the body of Jesus

[c] John is also unique to include Nicodemus in the burial narrative of Jesus, 19:39

[4] Matthew simply used the verb μαθητεύω that Joseph "had become a disciple of Jesus [τῷ Ἰησοῦ]"!

(b) It is clear that:

[1] Nothing else is said of Joseph of Arimathea except for in the passion narratives of Jesus:

[a] Therefore, Joseph could not have been "discipled" (or mentored) by Jesus for two or three years

[b] At best Joseph would have been in the crowds following Jesus and hearing Him speak (i.e. large group cognitive communication, as decried by some of our education specialists), although even this is somewhat unlikely in light of John 12:42-43, other than the fact that scribes and pharisees were sent to spy out what Jesus was saying to find fault with Him and ask Him difficult questions

[2] Nor was Joseph of Arimathea ever listed as one of the twelve apostles:

[a] He is not listed among the disciples in any list, and it is unlikely that he was one of the 70 others in Luke 10, as he was a "secret disciple"

[b] Therefore his "having become a disciple" (Matt 27:57) or his being called a "disciple of Jesus" (John 19:38) could not have been from a prolonged intentional relationship with Jesus (which while being important, is the view of "make disciples" in the interpretation of Matt 28:19 portrayed by most experts)

[3] Therefore, Joseph of Arimathea could not have gone through the three year *The Training of the Twelve* as in A. B. Bruce's book by that title, that has helped shape the discipleship movement.[792]

[a] The only way to make a long term relationship possible between Jesus and Joseph of Arimathea would be to adhere to an argument from silence

[b] However, it would not have been possible for Joseph to be an overt disciple, as he was said to be a secret follower, John 19:38—even after the death of Christ!

[4] Yet Joseph of Arimathea was made a "disciple of Jesus":

[a] Matthew stated that Jesus "had become a disciple of Jesus [ὃς καὶ αὐτὸς ἐμαθητεύθη τῷ Ἰησοῦ]"

[b] John called Joseph of Arimathea a disciple of Jesus [ὢν μαθητὴς τοῦ Ἰησοῦ], using the noun μαθητής (nominative masculine singular), the special word that is [naively] thought to distinguish between a "convert" and a "disciple"

[c] Whereas Matt 28:19 does not include the predicate "of Jesus" (i.e. "win disciples to Jesus"), this can be gleaned from Matt 27:57 and John 19:38, leading one to consider that Matt 28:19 could be interpreted, "Go win disciples [unto Jesus] from all nations…"

{1} The implication being that a person is instantaneously made into a disciple of Christ, and not a disciple of a particular person or movement

{2} Historically, this implication differentiates Protestantism from the Church of Rome's monastic movement, whose monks became disciples of particular people who wrote out specific "Rules" that their devotees were to follow (Benedictine, Fransiscan, Dominican, etc.), and unto whom they even made a vow of obedience!

{3} Some current discipleship programs and guidelines for spiritual disciplines come dangerously close to Rome's works-oriented monastic practices

(c) Clearly:

[1] The use of μαθητεύω in Matthew 27:57 cannot refer to a long-term process of discipleship, which definition is usually associated with the verb in Matthew 28:19

[2] The view that term "disciple" refers to something different than a convert, believer, or "Christian" (Acts 11:26), as noted above, is also suspect from this and related passages

[3] Also the commonly used designation, "He is my disciple" or "I am his discipler," is not warranted from this passage, as Christians are to be disciples "of Jesus"!

---

[792]"Probably the most careful study to date in the Master's larger plan of evangelism has been done in reference to the training of the disciples, of which A. B. Bruce's *The Training of the Twelve* is the best" (Robert Coleman in *The Master Plan of Evangelism* [Old Tappan, NJ: Revell, 1964], 14; referencing A. B. Bruce *The Training of the Twelve* [1st edition, 1872; 2nd edition, 1899; 3rd edition New York: Richard B. Smith, 1930]).

(3) More about no specific use of the English verb "make" in translating Matthew 28:19:

    (a) Had Jesus wanted to use the verb "make" in Matt 28:19, He had already used "make" [ποιέω] twice in Matthew in parallel contexts:

        [Wherein ποιέω (from which is translated the word "make") is said to mean: "do, make" or "do, cause, accomplish, also keep, carry out, practice, etc."][793]

        [1] Matt 4:19, "And He said to them, 'Follow Me, and I will **make** [ποιήσω] you fishers of men.'"

        [2] Matt 23:15, "Woe to you, scribes and Pharisees, hypocrites, because you travel about on sea and land to **make** [ποιῆσαι] one proselyte; and when he becomes one, you make him twice as much a son of hell as yourselves"

    (b) He was even more emphatic in Mark 1:17, using two verbs, "make" as well as "become": "And Jesus said to them, 'Follow Me, and I will **make you become** [ποιήσω ὑμᾶς γενέσθαι] fishers of men.'"

        [1] γίνομαι ["become"] is said to mean: "capable of many translations in various contexts, of which these are typical; 1. be born or produced 2. be made or created, be done; be established 3. happen, take place 4. become 5. be largely"[794]

    (c) Likewise, John 4:1 is even more pointed, in that Jesus "made disciples" (μαθητὰς ποιεῖ), literally, "he was making disciples":

        [1] Byzantine: ὅτι Ἰησοῦς πλείονας μαθητὰς ποιεῖ καὶ βαπτίζει ἢ Ἰωάννης-

        [2] NKJ: "that Jesus made and baptized more disciples than John"

    (d) Although these other verbs were clearly available in the contemporary Greek, available in the vocabulary of Jesus, and even in the Book of Matthew (in the case of Matt 4:17; 23:15), Jesus did not use them in His Great Commission in Matthew 28:19; He merely used the verb μαθητεύω.

(4) The aorist tense used in all four uses of the verb μαθητεύω also points to the punctiliar action of this verb, as related to a person beginning his/her relationship with Jesus Christ (Matt 13:52; 27:57; 28:19; Acts 14:21):

    (a) Had Jesus wanted to emphasize the linear, He could have or should have used either the present or imperfect tenses[795]

    (b) Since Jesus chose the aorist to communicate His commissioning, then it seems likely that μαθητεύω in Matt 28:19 refers primarily to the beginning of faith:

        [1] If this is true, that μαθητεύω refers primarily to the beginning of faith, or conversion, then it does not refer to the process of catachetics, spiritual development, or mentoring normally associated with this verse; rather, catechetics is found in verse 20, "teaching them to keep..."

        [2] If this is true, then the constant and unavoidable bickering and positioning between the "evangelism" and "discipleship" sectors in the Evangelical church based on Matt 28:19 is unnecessary:

            [a] Yes, "teaching to observe" is found in the Matt 28:20

            [b] But it is subservient to the main verb, that of "winning disciples" in Matt 28:19.

---

[793]"Shorter Lexicon of the Greek NT (Gingrich, Danker)," BibleWorks 7.0.

[794]Ibid.

[795]"As we saw in Lesson 3, the Greek Present tense corresponds most closely to the English Present Continuous tense, usually referring to continuous or repeated action in the present" (J. W. Wenham, *The Elements of New Testament Greek* [Cambridge: University Press, 1965], 54).

(c) If μαθητεύω in Matt 28:19 refers primarily to the beginning of faith, then Matt 28's commissioning is not divorced from Jesus' sending of the 12 in Matthew 10:

[1] Therefore, Matthew 10 provides an expansive explanation of the commissioning in Matthew 28 (reflexive property of the two passages ☺)

[2] Matthew 10 emphasizes:

[a] Authority: power over unclean spirits (10:1, 8), to heal (10:1, 8)

[b] Physical displacement: going (10:7, 23), entering villages (10:11, 14-15, 23), entering homes (10:12-13, 14), being received (Matt 10:14, 40-42), being sent (10:16)

[c] Saying something: preaching (10:7, 27), speaking certain words (10:7, 14, 19-20, 27), confessing Christ before men (10:32-33)

[d] Persecution: not listening (10:14), lambs in the midst of wolves (10:16), delivered up (10:17, 19, 21), whipped (10:17), put to death (10:21, 28), hated by all (10:22), persecution (10:23), called Beelzebub (10:25), division (10:34-36)

[e] Commitment: persevere (10:22), not fear man (10:26, 28, 33), love Christ more than parents (10:37), take up one's cross (10:38), lose one's life (10:39)

[3] Wasn't the Book of Acts a picture of Matthew 10 evangelism?

(d) If Matt 28:19 emphasizes the beginning of salvation for the listener, then the chasm between the 54/55 NT uses of εὐαγγελίζω ("evangelize") is not that far from the 4 NT uses of μαθητεύω ("win disciples"); the dichotomy that we have created between evangelism and discipleship is not God's, it is man's!

(e) If this is true, then it strongly impacts our view of the mission of the church, and reorients the "Evangelical" church to reemphasize evangelizing—how refreshing!

(5) Thoughts on use of the word "win":

(a) Use of the word "win" correlates with Paul's five uses of κερδαίνω in 1 Corinthians 9:19-22:

[1] 1 Cor 9:19-22, "For though I am free from all *men*, I have made myself a slave to all, that **I might win** the more. [20] And to the Jews I became as a Jew, that **I might win** Jews; to those who are under the Law, as under the Law, though not being myself under the Law, that **I might win** those who are under the Law; [21] to those who are without law, as without law, though not being without the law of God but under the law of Christ, that **I might win** those who are without law. [22] To the weak I became weak, that **I might win** the weak; I have become all things to all men, that I may by all means save some."

[2] In fact, so closely is the term "win" associated with salvation, that in his summary at the end of verse 22, Paul changed his pattern and used the word "save" [σώζω]; cf. 1 Cor 10:33; Jude 23

(b) This corresponds with other verses in which God's word highlights the role of the proclaimer:

[1] Notice for example, 1 Cor 3:5, "What then is Apollos? And what is Paul? Servants **through whom you believed**, even as the Lord gave *opportunity* to each one."

[2] Acts 19:26, "This Paul has **persuaded** and turned away a considerable number of people"; cf. Acts 28:23-24

[3] Acts 11:21, "And the hand of the Lord was with them, and a large number who believed **turned** to the Lord"

(c) The translators of the NIV used the word "win" ["won"], rather than "make" ["made"] as most other translations do, in their translation of μαθητεύω in Acts 14:21: "They preached the good news in that city and won a large number of disciples. Then they returned to Lystra, Iconium and Antioch"

   [1] Indicating that the translators determined that the verb μαθητεύω was referring to the result of immediate salvation, rather than its long-term continuation

(d) Historically speaking:

   [1] It is interesting to note, the *Oxford Latin Dictionary* (1968-1973) gives the meaning of *evangelizo* in Classical Latin (First Two Centuries) as: "(1) to preach, declare, proclaim, bring good tidings, and (2) to evangelize, preach to, win to the Gospel by preaching."[796]

   [2] The meaning for Thomas Aquinas is given as: "to preach, declare, proclaim, always with the notion of bringing clad tidings, proclaiming the Gospel; to evangelize, to win to the Gospel by preaching."[797]

(e) Therefore, use of the English word "win" in Matthew 28:19 is not without biblical or historical precedent.

(6) Some thoughts on "discipleship" as a movement:

(a) The grammatical provenance of the term "discipleship":

   [1] If Matt 27:57 referred to the beginning of Joseph of Arimathea's faith,

   [2] And if a lost person ought not be baptized, unless he is first won as a disciple,

   [3] And if a lost person cannot be taught to obey all that Christ has commanded, unless he is first won as a disciple,

   [3] Then it follows that Matthew 28:19 must refer solely to the initiation of faith, and not the continuation thereof;

   [4] Then, properly speaking, the concept of "discipleship" does not properly come from Matt 28:19, but rather from Matt 28:20, "teaching to obey"

   [5] Therefore the "discipleship movement" *per se* is derived from a misreading of Matthew 28:19 as speaking more of the continuation of faith than uniquely of the act of initiation in faith (as a response to hearing the Gospel)

(b) Likewise, historically speaking:

   [1] Roman Catholic monasticism has its roots in a combination of Greek ascetism (Stoicism), and Greek philosophical pedagogy

   [2] Early Protestants shunned this notion of spiritual growth through lifestyle discipleship (see Francois Lambert d'Avignon's testimony appended to Chapter 26)

   [3] As is noted in Chapter 26, both graphically and in the text, John Darby was the first to translate Matt 28:19 in English "make disciples" in 1884

   [4] Once this soon-to-become equivocal translation came into common usage in English (through most subsequent English translations), then the concept of discipleship began to gain traction among Evangelicals in the English-speaking world, to the detriment of a primary focus on evangelism (in many cases)

(7) Remembering that:

(a) The mainline and territorial church authors will virtually never agree with using "win disciples" because they view of conversion as a process, they often have a generalistic view of baptism, as well as tend toward a universalistic view of salvation

---

[796]David B. Barrett, *Evangelize! A Historical Survey of the Concept* (Birmingham, AL: New Hope, 1987), 21.
[797]Ibid., 22.

(b) Some contemporary authors display significant antipathy to the concept of "winning" persons to Christ[798]

(c) There are Not-for-Profit ministries (that need to protect their funding base) and academic disciplines (that need to protect their degrees and programs) whose existence or priority is predicated on the fact that "make disciples" in Matthew 28:19 speaks of a prolonged process (of mentoring in the spiritual disciplines); therefore, one can expect resistance from these people to the interpretation that μαθητεύω deals primarily or only with the conversion of an individual or the act of placing his/her faith in Christ;

(d) Likewise, there are some semi-conservative professors, pastors, and authors who harbor antagonism to initiative evangelism; one can also expect resistance and antagonism from these people to translating μαθητεύω as "winning disciples"

(e) Therefore, consider the end result of various conceptions of the verbs in Matthew's Great Commission, as it relates to the *ordo salutis*, or the "Order of Salvation"

Various Orders of Salvation Based on Verbs in Matthew 28:19-20

Orders of Salvation	First Stage	Second Stage	Third Stage	Fourth Stage
Canonical order	1. Go [Πορευθέντες]	2. Win as a disciple [μαθητεύσατε]	3. Baptize/immerse [βαπτίζοντες]	4. Teach to obey [διδάσκοντες αὐτοὺς τηρεῖν]
Anabaptist, Baptist, or Baptistic; Conversion-focused	1. Go, evangelize	2. Win other persons as disciples of Jesus	3. Baptize/immerse only those that are won as disciples of Jesus	4. Teach those that are won and are baptized to follow all the commands of Christ
Discipleship or Relationship-focused; Mentoring or Leadership Development-oriented; or Seeker-Sensitive	4. Teaching them to obey, through (a) building relationships, (b) mentoring within and outside of the local church, and (c) teaching to worship God	2. Gradually making them into a disciple; gradually winning them as a disciple which will usually take time; watch out for over-emphasizing the point of conversion	3. Time or manner of baptism doesn't matter, it is a secondary issue	1. Need to go is secondary to the Great Commission; stay where you are and be faithful; be "salt and light" in your context
Protestant Sacramental	3. Baptize all infants of members in good standing	4. Teach those that are baptized to obey through catechism and the teachings of the church	2. Those baptized/ sprinkled and taught will gradually develop as disciples; "evangelism" (whatever that may mean) is only for those outside the fold	1. All faithful should do good deeds; otherwise, no need not go, except for approved clergy and missionaries
Roman Catholic Sacramental	3. Baptize all infants of members in good standing or not; the lifestyle or credentials of the baptizer do not negate the effect of the sacrament *ex opere operato*	4. Teach those that are baptized to obey through Catechism, the Sacraments, and other approved teachings of the church	2. Those baptized [or sprinkled] and taught will gradually develop as disciples; need to use apologetics to reach those outside the fold of the Church	1. All faithful should do good deeds; otherwise, faithful prohibited from going and preaching, except for ordained clergy and missionaries

*Making an issue of believers' baptism would eliminate Evangelical pedobaptist churches from most cooperative evangelism efforts (e.g. some Presbyterians and Methodists). Therefore, in an effort to be ecumenically-minded, and perhaps to show the unity and size of the combined Evangelical churches, some mainstream evangelists tend to downplay issues like believer's baptism. Therefore, in practice, those doing the evangelism are not very clear on the Matthew 28 pattern of ministry, nor on their convictions concerning believers' baptism.

---

[798]E.g. Brian McLaren, *More Ready than You Realize: Evangelism as Dance in the Postmodern Matrix* (Zondervan, 2002).

e) There may be a further lesson in the words "of/from all nations" (πάντα τὰ ἔθνη) in Matthew 28:19:

    (1) As part of the curse of God in the book of Deuteronomy, God's disobedient people were to be scattered:

        (a) Deut 4:27, "And the LORD will scatter you among the peoples" (Gk. καὶ διασπερεῖ κύριος ὑμᾶς ἐν πᾶσιν τοῖς ἔθνεσιν)

        (b) Deut 28:64, "Among all people" (Heb 'am; Gk εἰς πάντα τὰ ἔθνη)

        (c) Deut 28:65, "Among the nations" (Heb gowi; Gk ἐν τοῖς ἔθνεσιν)

        (d) Deut 30:3, to "all the peoples" (Heb 'am; Gk ἐκ πάντων τῶν ἐθνῶν)

    (2) This same implication was also affirmed by other verses:

        (a) Psa 106:47, "Save us, O LORD our God, And gather us from among the Gentiles (καὶ ἐπισυνάγαγε ἡμᾶς ἐκ τῶν ἐθνῶν)"

    (3) What is the implication of being called unto a curse in the geographic expansion mandated by Christ's Great Commission?

        (a) God knew that scattering His people was difficult, that is why He made it a curse upon them in Deut 28

        (b) The geographic movement mandated by the Great Commission brings stress, pain, and discomfort at every level—as exemplified in the ministry of Paul

        (c) The common tendency may be to turn the difficulties of fulfilling the Great Commission into a bed of ease, or to ignore this clear part of the mandate by turning it into "as you go" (as noted above)—thereby removing the curse inherent with the command, "Go"!

        (d) Herein may be part of the need to fulfill the Great Commission, not trusting in our own understanding, but rather trusting Him, Prov 3:5-6; for example:

            [1] Deut 28:29, "and you shall grope at noon, as the blind man gropes in darkness, and you shall not prosper in your ways; but you shall only be oppressed and robbed [διαρπάζω] continually, with none to save you"

            [2] Matt 12:29, "Or how can anyone enter the strong man's house and carry off his property, unless he first binds the strong *man*? And then he will plunder [διαρπάζω] his house"

            [3] Heb 10:34, "For you showed sympathy to the prisoners, and accepted joyfully the seizure [ἁρπαγή] of your property, knowing that you have for yourselves a better possession and an abiding one"

        (e) More on these parallels with the blessings and curses of Deuteronomy below in the section title "The Search for OT Sequels to the NT Great Commission Passages"

f) A possible translation of Matthew 28:19-20, following some of the considerations above is may be:

"Go! Win disciples from all nations! Baptize them in the name of the Father and the Son and the Holy Spirit! Teach them to observe all that I commanded you! And lo, I am with you always, even to the end of the age" (Matt 28:19-20)

Or even:

"Onward! Win disciples from all nations! Immerse them in the name of the Father and the Son and the Holy Spirit! Teach them to observe all that I commanded you! And lo, I AM with you all the days, even unto the consummation of the age" (Matt 28:19-20)

g) Lastly on Matthew 28, it seems that some Christians may consider Matthew 28 as:

   (1) The only complete Great Commission passage:

   (a) For example, note the words of Joe M. Kapolyo, Principal of All Nations Christian College:

   > For the majority of Christians mission starts and ends with Matt 28:18-20. This text occupies a significant place in our understanding of mission, but is just the apex of everything the Bible has to say about God and mission.[799]

   (2) And likewise that the Great Commission refers primarily to Christian spiritual development and growth, and only peripherally to evangelism (if at all)

   (3) **However, there exist four other Great Commission passages that ought not be ignored**; these complement (rather than contradict) and illuminate the breadth of what Jesus had in mind in what He commanded His disciples after the resurrection...[800]

   (a) By the way, translating μαθητεύω as "win disciples" corresponds with the teaching in the other Great Commission passages, removes the ambiguity that has become associated with "make disciples", and eliminates the methodological battles that exist between uses of the Great Commission passages (I am of Matthew, I am of Mark, I am of John, etc... (1 Cor 1:12])

   (b) Therefore, μαθητεύω highlights the result to some (they are won as disciples of Jesus), whereas Mark and Luke highlight the proclamation necessary to produce that result in some.

---

[799]Joe M. Kapolyo, "The Easneye Lectures," in Richard Bauckham, *Bible and Mission: Christian Witness in a Postmodern World* (Grand Rapids: Baker, 2003), viii.

[800]See chart below, "Semantic Range of the Great Commission Passages."

MARK

2) **Mark** emphasized proclamation (κηρύσσω) of the Gospel and the geographic and sociological extent of this task by repetition of the idea of "all the world" and "all creation."

a) Mark 16:15-16 makes it clear that the Commission includes:

(1) Two actions prior to the person believing or not believing:

(a) Go (Πορευθέντες);

(b) Preach (κηρύξατε):

Unfortunately for primacy of preaching in Mark's Great Commission, Gustav Warneck, The "father of Protestant missiology," stated that "mere evangelism does not suffice."[801] Therefore, in fact, he negated Mark's Great Commission as being a sufficient revelation of Christ's Great Commission.

Added to this antagonism to Mark's Great Commission, is the textual question of the end of Mark. Some ancient manuscripts, such as Sinaiticus and Vaticanus, appear to omit Mark's Great Commission altogether, leading some NT scholars to call into question its reliability. Some preliminary comments are found below.

(2) One message: the Gospel (τὸ εὐαγγέλιον).

(3) Two ways of describing the targets of the preaching:

(a) Into all the world (εἰς τὸν κόσμον ἅπαντα);

(b) To all creation (πάσῃ τῇ κτίσει).

(4) Individual people who respond in two different ways:

(a) Those who believe ('Ο πιστεύσας);

(b) He who does not believe (ὁ δὲ ἀπιστήσας), or "he who is unbelieving":

The individualism here is dramatic and telling, "he who believes", and "he who does not believe," is accentuated by Jesus' use of the singular. Jesus is not shy about His desired and intended response, to believe.

As far as repentance, which is found in Luke's Great Commission, Mark's omission may easily be construed an ellipsis, as repentance and belief are used in parallel in Mark 1:14-15.

(5) A first response for those who do believe:

(a) "And is baptized (καὶ βαπτισθεὶς):

The chronological order of the verbs, conjoined by the conjunction "and" leads to two opposing, and yet similar approaches to baptismal regeneration: (1) Some teach that a person is not saved after believing until they are baptized (e.g. Disciples of Christ), and (2) Others teach that baptism can be applied to an infant, before they believe, and that they are saved by baptism, preparing them for the confirming of that baptism later; these also believe in baptismal regeneration (see the Appendix following Chapter 24).

Baptists, since the 1527 *Schleitheim Confession* take these two verbs to be chronological.[802] Thus emphasizing the proper order: active faith first, baptism by immersion second.

---

[801]"This last task is the task of missions [the solid founding of the Christian church]; the limitation of this task to mere evangelisation confounds means and goal. Mere preaching does not suffice; it is to be the means of laying the foundation of the Church. ...mere* announcement of the Gospel is not sufficient for this" (Gustav Warneck, *Outline of the History of Protestant Missions*, 3rd English ed. [from 8th German ed. of 1904] (New York: Revell, 1906), 407.

[802]"First. Observe concerning Baptism: Baptism shall be given to all those who have learned repentance and amendment of life, and who believe truly that their sins are taken away by Christ, and to all those who walk in the resurrection of Jesus Christ, and wish to be buried with Him in death, so that they may be resurrected with Him, and to all those who with this significance request it [baptism] of us and demand it for themselves" ("Schleitheim Confession [1527]," in *Baptist Confessions of Faith*, ed. by William L. Lumpkin [Valley Forge: Judson, 1959, 1969], 25).

(5) The two individual responses result in two very different outcomes:
(a) "Will be saved" (σωθήσεται);
(b) "Will be condemned" (κατακριθήσεται).

b) κηρύσσω in Mark 16:15 is a natural flow of the preaching of John the Baptist in Mark (1:4) and Jesus (1:14-15), the call of the apostles (3:14-15) and their preaching (6:12-13), as well as the sending forth of the former demoniac (5:19-20)

(1) In this case, κηρύσσω [preach] is a parallel rendering to εὐαγγελίζω [evangelize]:

(a) Compare the parallel passages of Mark 6:12-13 and Luke 9:6
Mark 6:12-13, "And they went out and preached [κηρύσσω] that *men* should repent. And they were casting out many demons and were anointing with oil many sick people and healing them"
Luke 9:6 And departing, they *began* going about among the villages, preaching the gospel [εὐαγγελίζω], and healing everywhere

(b) See also Acts 8:4-5:
Acts 8:4-5 "Therefore, those who had been scattered went about preaching [εὐαγγελίζω] the word. And Philip went down to the city of Samaria and *began* proclaiming [κηρύσσω] Christ to them"

(2) κηρύσσω in Mark 16:15 is the only **method** of communication:

(a) Mark therefore emphasizes the heralding forth of the message of the Gospel, much like the heralds of the king would announce an official proclamation of the king!

(b) In this sense, κηρύσσω in Mark 16:15 parallels 1 Peter 2:9's use of ἐξαγγέλλω, "that you may proclaim" as the main verb in this important Peter's first epistle

(c) Whereas Matthew emphasized through use of μαθητεύω the **result** in those who were foreordained unto salvation as they heard the life-saving message and were won as disciples.

c) The textual critical question regarding the authenticity of this text [as not being found in the earliest originals] does not minimize the breadth or emphasis of evangelism in other parts of the New Testament:

(1) It is clearly an argument from silence in both directions

(2) The Byzantine tradition and Majority Text affirm its authenticity

(3) In fact, may the science of "Textual Criticism" be tainted as regards the two oldest manuscripts of the New Testament?[803]

(a) Could Sinaiticus have been planted for Tischendorf to find?[804]
[1] Was it not supposedly a rejected or faulty manuscript? Was it in fact authentic? Did its originators have a theological or methodological agenda?
[2] Does the existence of one manuscript lacking the end of Mark 16 mean anything? Is it not true that there was Great Commission battles going back

---

[803]See my comments at the end of Chapter 6, "Some Thoughts about Bible Translation."

[804]"On the afternoon of this day I was taking a walk with the steward of the convent in the neighbourhood, and as we returned, towards sunset, he begged me to take some refreshment with him in his cell. Scarcely had he entered the room, when, resuming our former subject of conversation, he said: 'And I, too, have read a Septuagint'— i.e. a copy of the Greek translation made by the Seventy. And so saying, he took down from the corner of the room a bulky kind of volume, wrapped up in a red cloth, and laid it before me. I unrolled the cover, and discovered, to my great surprise, not only those very fragments which, fifteen years before, I had taken out of the basket, but also other parts of the Old Testament, the New Testament complete, and, in addition, the Epistle of Barnabas and a part of the Shepherd of Hermas" (source: wikipedia; Constantin von Tischendorf, *When Were Our Gospels Written? An Argument by Constantine Tischendorf. With a Narrative of the Discovery of the Sinaitic Manuscript* [New York: American Tract Society, 1866]).

into the first century (cf. Book of Galatians), not to mention the fourth and fifth centuries (Augustine, *Contra Donatisten* [approx A.D. 402-412])?

(b) Could Vaticanus have been tampered with, as some allege? Why was the Catholic Church so secretive of its being found? What of the 795 "umlauts" in the margin seemingly indicating textual uncertainty?

d) Whatever the case, that Mark's Great Commission focuses on the proclamational event, and the corresponding response to this event, is clear.

LUKE

3) **Luke** stated the Great Commission in a prophetic sense, emphasizing the proclamation of repentance for the forgiveness of sin in the name of Jesus, the witness [μάρτυρος] of the disciples, and the necessary power of the Spirit:

   a) **Luke** combined, Luke 24:46-47:

      (1) Meat of the message: "Thus it is written," Luke 24:46

      (2) Message: "that the Christ would suffer and rise again from the dead the third day"
         (a) The Evangel as the center of Gospel proclamation (though it may be foolishness to some, 1 Cor 1:18-25)
         (b) This commissioning comprises Christ's divine interpretation of His own death and resurrection to the disciples who did not yet understand its meaning, purpose, or place in salvation, Luke 24:25-27
         (c) The preaching of this Gospel (or the cross, 1 Cor 2:2), should necessarily be followed by a call for repentance

      (3) Method: "would be proclaimed," v 46

      (4) Applications of the phrase: "Repentance for the forgiveness of sin"
         (a) As the thrust or culmination of "the preaching" anticipated as a response to the Gospel message of v 46 (i.e. the cross, 1 Cor 2:2)
         (b) As the response necessarily desired by the messenger of the cross
         (d) As the only appropriate response by someone wishing to find forgiveness of sin in the cross of Christ

      (5) Fulfillment of the commission: "would be proclaimed in his name to all nations"

   b) Further elements in Luke, Luke 24:48-49:

      (1) Geographic element—expanded in the Book of Acts 1:8

      (2) Testimonial element, "You are witnesses of these things"
         A parallel concept to that mentioned in Deut 4:35:
            NAS: "To you it was shown that you might know that the LORD, He is God; there is no other besides Him"
            French Segond Revisee Geneve: "Tu as été rendu témoin de ces choses [you were made witnesses of these things], afin que tu reconnaisses que l'Éternel est Dieu, qu'il n'y en a point d'autre"
            From the Hophal of *ra'ah*: to be shown, to be made to see, *even* [chosen] to see; *hence* to be made witnesses of
            By the way, this phrase was missing from Migne's Latin Vulgate, and was reinserted into the post-Vatican II "Nova Vulgata" (25 April 1979)

      (3) The promise of the Holy Spirit

      (4) The power of the Holy Spirit

   c) Some implications of Luke:
      (1) As the most complete and contextual theological Great Commission passage
      (2) As the interpretive grid for all Gospel preaching in the Book of Acts

JOHN

4) **John** 20:21 emphasized the exemplary role of Christ in the accomplishment of the Great Commission. The personal evangelism of Jesus is much attested in this Gospel.[805]

   a) Note the comment of the Apostle Paul in 1 Cor 11:1, "Be imitators of me, just as I also am of Christ" (cf. 1 Cor 10:32-33).
      (1) In the case of 1 Cor 11:1, Paul was the biblically-ordained example of following the exemplary role of Christ;
      (2) Notice the words of Solomon Stoddard: "Christ knew how to deal with Souls, and Paul followed His Example."[806]

   b) As noted above, the "as" in John 20:21 is often used as a prooftext to allow for the necessity or priority of non-spiritual elements in the communication of the Gospel (e.g. feeding the hungry). See in Chart 65, "Guide to Evangelical Drift Portrayed in Charts 66-75" my *Charts for a Theology of Evangelism.*
      (1) Some will say, "it's not an either/or, it's a both/and"
      (2) True, but what was the one Great Commission that Christ gave? "Go into all the world and feed all the hungry people?"
      (3) Adding the physical to the spiritual muddies the power and eventually nullifies the spiritual emphasis of the Great Commission

---

[805]Merrill C. Tenney, *The Gospel of John* (Grand Rapids: Eerdmans, 1948), 313-16, calls of the twenty-seven spiritual conversations of Jesus "interviews." These give cohesive flow to the Gospel of John.

[806]Richard L. Bushman, ed. *The Great Awakening: Documents on the Revival of Religion, 1740-1745* (Chapel Hill, NC: University Press, 1969), 13.

5) **Luke in Acts** 1:8 reemphasized in a prophetic sense the testifiers (μάρτυρος) and the power (δύναμις) of the Holy Spirit, as found in the Lucan Great Commission; however some new material is emphasized:

a) A distinction from Luke in the person of the witness or testifier:
  (1) Whereas the Gospel of Luke emphasizes the testimonial element, "witnesses of these things"
  (2) Jesus in Acts emphasizes His ownership of the testifiers, "You shall be My witnesses"
  (3) Perhaps this ownership is related to the fact that Jesus had and has the right to command [ἐντέλλομαι] His disciples, Acts 1:2
  (4) Likewise Christ continues to own them in trials, hardships, and persecutions (cf. Rom 8:35-37)

b) Jesus repeated the geographic extent of Great Commission with the same language as the curse of being scattered in Deuteronomy (as was noticed above with Matthew's Great Commission):
  (1) Deut 28:64a, "Moreover, the LORD will scatter you among all peoples, from one end of the earth to the other end of the earth"
  (2) Deut 30:4a, "If your outcasts are at the ends of the earth, from there the LORD your God will gather you"

c) This curse parallels Paul's mention of being "offscouring" and "refuse" in 1 Cor 4:13, as Deut 30:4 calls the people of God in the many lands of the earth, "outcasts"

d) Some thoughts about the geography of the Great Commission:

  (1) Where were the disciples when they received the Great Commission?
    (a) Matthew 28:16, Mark 6:7, and John seem to indicate that the disciples were in Galilee
    (b) Mark 16:7 appears to say to the women to hurry, because Peter was going to Galilee; then Mark 16:14 gives another scene much like the upper room in Jerusalem
    (c) In Luke 24:33, the disciples appear to have been gathered in Jerusalem in an upper room when they received the Great Commission
    (d) In John 20:21, the disciples were still in Jerusalem; eight days later, they still appear to be in Jerusalem, John 20:26; then in John 21 the epilogue is written from the area of the "Sea of Tiberias" or the Sea of Galilee
    (e) In Acts 1:12, following the reception of the Great Commission, we have the disciples returning to Jerusalem to receive the Holy Spirit
    (f) Some conclusions:
      [1] There is clearly room for several different commissioning being stated over the 40 days in which Jesus appeared to them
      [2] However, it seems clear that there are three phases: Jerusalem, Galilee, and back in Jerusalem
      [3] The addition of a geographic element adds not only credibility to each of the accounts, but also interpretive depth

  (2) Some thoughts about the geographic element in the Great Commission:

    (a) The disciples were told to make Jerusalem the starting point of their mission, while they were in Galilee:
      [1] Jerusalem was not where they were located at the time; so it require geographic displacement just for them to go to Jerusalem, returning to Jerusalem was the starting point of their obedience
      [2] The disciples did return to Jerusalem, even though they feared the Jews, John 20:19

[3] Apparently, Jerusalem, with the Temple, was the place from which God had promised that He would bless the world:
[a] It was the place God had chosen for the people, Deut 12:5, 11, 18; 31:11
[b] Jerusalem is also a type of Christ's church, Psa 51:18; 122:1-9
[4] Jerusalem was the starting point of the ministry of Paul, Rom 15:19

(b) Jerusalem was also the place of persecution:

[1] Note the ode of Jesus: "O Jerusalem, Jerusalem, who kills the prophets and stones those who are sent to her! How often I wanted to gather your children together, the way a hen gathers her chicks under her wings, and you were unwilling," Matt 23:37

[2] Note the historical reality of Jerusalem: "Therefore, behold, I am sending you prophets and wise men and scribes; some of them you will kill and crucify, and some of them you will scourge in your synagogues, and persecute from city to city, that upon you may fall *the guilt of* all the righteous blood shed on earth, from the blood of righteous Abel to the blood of Zechariah, the son of Berechiah, whom you murdered between the temple and the altar. Truly I say to you, all these things shall come upon this generation," Matt 23:34-36

[3] Jerusalem was the place where Christ was crucified, Luke 9:51; 23:7, 28; 24:18

[4] Jerusalem was the central location for Saul's persecution of believers, Acts 8:2, "he might bring them bound to Jerusalem" (cf. Acts 9:13, 21)

[5] Jerusalem was the place that would violently reject the evangelizing of the Apostle Paul:
[a] Paul's early evangelizing in Jerusalem, Acts 9:28
[b] Their rejection of Paul, Acts 21:27-32; 22:18, 22

[6] Jerusalem was the place where Paul would be arrested and held illegally by the Romans (Acts 23:26-30; 24:26; 26:32), as well as plotted against by the Jews (Acts 23:12-22)

(c) What then may be some implications of "beginning from Jerusalem" (Luke 24:47; Acts 1:8)?

[1] God fulfilled His promise to bless the world from Jerusalem

[2] God's people (both Israel and in the church) are:
[a] Often in rebellion against God, and therefore
[b] The starting point of fulfilling the Great Commission, and therefore
[c] Revival ministry is a necessity!

[3] Christ sent His disciples back to preach where the ministry was very difficult
[a] Ease of ministry or "abundant harvest" does not necessarily imply the will of God, 1 Cor 16:8-9

(d) What of "in all Judea and Samaria" (Acts 1:8)?
[1] The apostolic church became a regional church by Acts 5:16, "And also the people from the cities in the vicinity of Jerusalem were coming together, bringing people who were sick or afflicted with unclean spirits; and they were all being healed."
[2] It seems that it took persecution for the disciples to venture beyond a "come and see" regional-type church, Acts 8:1-4
[3] A saved Hellenistic Jew, Philip, seems to be the first to venture into Samaria, with much success, Acts 8:5-12

(e) Somehow, although others were being persecuted for their evangelism, the apostles stayed back in Jerusalem, Acts 8:25; 15:2
[1] Is this a signal that the apostles had ceased to be evangelistic?

[2] Or was this a sign that the apostles knew that the Great Commission must originate from Jerusalem, as they also were persecuted in Jerusalem, Acts 12:1-4?

[3] Therefore, Paul and Barnabas came to Jerusalem to find answers to the Judaizer problem, Acts 15

[4] Yet those who were of reputation contributed nothing to Paul, Gal 2:6

[5] And the apostles did not host Paul when he came to Jerusalem, Acts 21:16

(f) God seems to have allowed Jerusalem to include some variance as to application and interpretation

b. **Some Distractions or Alternatives** to the Great Commission:[807]

1) Matt 7:12 or Luke 6:31 (the "Golden Rule") as the Great Commission for the unregenerate

2) The Matthean Beatitudes (Matt 5:3-12) as the "Great Commission" of liberalized Protestants or Stoicized Christians ("act in this way, and you will be acting Christianly")

3) Rom 12:1 as the Great Commission for the Gospel lifestyle

4) 2 Tim 2:2 as the Great Commission for the discipleship movement

5) Phil 3:17 (imitating a pattern of life) as the Great Commission for the monastic movement, as well as possibly for the contemporary Spiritual Disciplines movement

6) 2 Thess 2:15; 3:6 (the passing on of oral traditions) as the Great Commission for Roman Catholics?

7) While many of the commands are important, they do not carry the practical or missional weight of the post-resurrection Great Commission passages

8) Notice for example various divergent views of mission and their result...

Considering Divergent Views of Mission

Preach the Gospel	Mentor Leaders	Correctly Parse Culture	Adroitly Rule over Creation	Perpetually Offer Sacrifices
"And He said to them, 'Go into all the world and preach the gospel to all creation,'" Mark 16:15	"And the things which you have heard from me in the presence of many witnesses, these entrust to faithful men, who will be able to teach others also," 2 Tim 2:2	"And of the sons of Issachar, men who understood the times, with knowledge of what Israel should do, their chiefs were two hundred; and all their kinsmen were at their command, "1 Chron 12:32	"And God blessed them; and God said to them, 'Be fruitful and multiply, and fill the earth, and subdue it; and rule over the fish of the sea and over the birds of the sky, and over every living thing that moves on the earth,'" Gen 1:28	"Now when these things have been thus prepared, the priests are continually entering the outer tabernacle, performing the divine worship," Heb 9:6
Evangelize as the priority	Mentor as a priority	Be culturally-relevant as a priority	Emphasize the preservation of the earth	Emphasize priests regularly saying and giving Mass

---

[807]Chart 7, "Alternatives to Mere Proclamation" includes 57 alternatives to "mere" proclamation as the main mission of the church (Johnston, *Charts for a Theology of Evangelism*, 20-23).

c. **Finding Unity in The Great Commission Passages**:

1) For example, a linear approach to the Great Commission Passages:

What Is Commanded in the Great Commission?
A Linear View of the Five Great Commission Passages[808]

The Missionary Call	Geographic Extent			Missionary Method		Missionary Message		Necessary Nurture	Missionary Example	Necessary Power	A Sure Fulfillment
Going; Go	"All the world ... to all creation"	"To all nations, beginning from Jerusalem"	(1) Jerusalem, (2) Judea, (3) Samaria, (4) uttermost parts of the earth	Preach; proclaim; bear witness	With the result of: Winning disciples	The Gospel: "the Christ should suffer and rise again from the dead the third day"	The Message: "repentance for the forgiveness of sins ... in His name"	(1) baptizing (2) teaching to obey	Christ	Holy Spirit	Prophetically Stated
Matt 28:19; Mark 16:15	Mark 16:15	Luke 24:47	Acts 1:8	Mark 16:15; Luke 24:47-48; Acts 1:8	Matt 28:19	Mark 16:15; Luke 24:46	Luke 24:47	Matt 28:19-20	John 20:21	Acts 24:49	Luke 24:47; Acts 1:8

2) Christ is not divided (cf. 1 Cor 1:13), nor does the Holy Spirit speak in contradictory terms: Introduction: Coherence or unity of God's revelation of Himself in the Scripture[809]
   a) The Great Commission passages do not teach contradictory truths, but rather complimentary truths
   b) Therefore the semantic range of the Great Commission passages must overlap, for example…

---

[808]Expanded in Chart 3, "A Linear View of the Five Great Commission Passages" (Johnston, *Charts for a Theology of Evangelism*, 14-15).

[809]"Further, since the Bible does have an objective meaning which we come to understand through the process of illumination, illumination must have some permanent effect" (Millard J. Erickson, *Christian Theology* [Grand Rapids: Baker, 1983], 1:253).

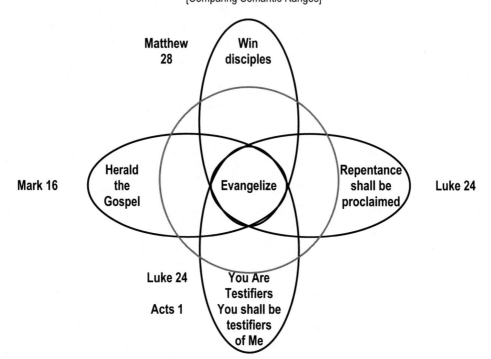

Semantic Range of the Great Commission Passages[810]
[Comparing Semantic Ranges]

Matthew 28 — Win disciples

Mark 16 — Herald the Gospel

Evangelize

Luke 24 — Repentance shall be proclaimed

Luke 24
Acts 1 — You Are Testifiers / You shall be testifiers of Me

3)   Or consider also…

A Paradigm for the Interworking of the Great Commission Passages

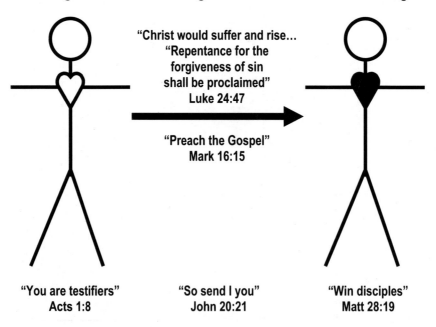

"Christ would suffer and rise…
"Repentance for the
forgiveness of sin
shall be proclaimed"
Luke 24:47

"Preach the Gospel"
Mark 16:15

"You are testifiers"
Acts 1:8

"So send I you"
John 20:21

"Win disciples"
Matt 28:19

4) An expansion of the NT revealed missionary method:
  a) Using the Matthean Great Commission and expanding its methodology with terminology from the Gospels and the book of Acts;
  b) Passages in the following chart were chosen because they provided several verbs to describe some aspect of the method in the context…

EXAMPLES AND EXPANSIONS OF GREAT COMMISSION'S METHODOLOGY[811]

Rubric: Matt 28:19-20	Going (πορεύομαι)	Win Disciples (μαθητεύω)	Baptizing (βαπτίζω)	Teaching to Observe (διδάσκω + τηρέω)
Matt 3:1-2	Came (παραγίνομαι)	Preaching (κηρύσσετε) Saying (λέγω)		
Matt 4:17	[v. 13 "came and settled"]	Preach (κηρύσσω) Say (λέγω)		
Matt 4:23	Went about (περιάγω)	Teaching (διδάσκω) Proclaiming (κηρύσσω) Healing (θεράπεύω)		
Matt 9:35	Went about (περιάγω)	Teaching (διδάσκω), Preaching (κηρύσσω), Healing (κηρύσσω)		
Matt 10:7	As you go (πορευόμενοι)	Preach (κηρύσσω) Saying (λέγω)		
Matt 11:1	Departed (μεταβαίνω)	Teaching (διδάσκω), Preaching (κηρύσσω)		
Matt 13:1-3	Went (ἔρχομαι) Sitting (κάθημαι)	Spoke (λαλέω) [in parables]		[to hide the meaning from the multitudes, 13:10-17]
Mark 1:14	Came into (ἔρχομαι)	Preaching (κηρύσσω)		
Mark 1:38	Let us go (ἄγω)	That I may preach (κηρύσσω)		
Mark 1:39	Went (ἔρχομαι)	Preaching (κηρύσσω) Casting out (ἐκβάλλω)		
Mark 1:45	Went out (ἐξέρχομαι)	Proclaim (κηρύσσω) Spread the news (διαφημίζω)		
Mark 2:13	Went out (ἐξέρχομαι)	Again (πάλιν) Was teaching (διδάσκω)		
Mark 3:14-15	[and that might He] send [them] out (ἀποστέλλω)	To preach (κηρύσσω) To have authority (ἔχω + ἐξουσία) + to cast out (ἐκβάλλω)		[so that they would be with Him]
Mark 5:19-20	Go (ὑπάγω), Went away (ἀπέρχομαι)	Report (ἀπαγγελλω), Began to proclaim (ἄρχω + κηρύσσω)		
Mark 6:12-13	Went out (ἐξέρχομαι)	Preached (κηρύσσω + μετανοέω), Casting out (ἐκβάλλω), Anointing (ἀλειφω), Healing (θεράπεύω)		
Mark 10:1	Arose (ἀνίστημι) + went forth (ἔρχομαι)	According to his custom (ὡς εἰώθει) + again (πάλιν) Began to teach (διδάσκω)		
Mark 16:15	Go (πορεύομαι)	Preach (κηρύσσω)		
Mark 16:20	Went forth (ἐξέρχομαι)	Preached (κηρύσσω)		
Luke 3:3	Came (ἔρχομαι)	Preaching (κηρύσσω)	a baptism of repentance for the forgiveness of sins	
Luke 4:14-15	Returned (ὑποστρέφω)	Teaching (διδάσκω)		
Luke 4:44		Was preaching (εἰμί + κηρύσσω)		
Luke 8:1	Traveled about (διοδεύω)	Preaching (κηρύσσω), Evangelizing (εὐαγγελίζω)		
Luke 9:2	Sent [them] (ἀποστέλλω)	To preach (κηρύσσω)		

[811]Ibid., Chart 4, "Verbs for Great Commission Methodology," 16-17.

Rubric	Going (πορεύομαι)	Win Disciples (μαθητεύω)	Baptizing (βαπτίζω)	Teaching to Observe (διδάσκω + τηρέω)
Luke 9:6	Departed (ἐξέρχομαι), Went (διέρχομαι)	Evangelizing (εὐαγγελίζω), Healing (θεράπεύω)		
John 4:1		Jesus was making … more disciples ('Ιησοῦς πλείονας μαθητὰς ποιεῖ)	Baptizing (βαπτίζει)	
John 4:2			Jesus Himself was not baptizing, but His disciples were ('Ιησοῦς αὐτὸς οὐκ ἐβάπτιζεν, ἀλλ' οἱ μαθηταὶ αὐτου)	
Acts 5:20-21	Go (πορεύομαι), Went in (εἰσέρχομαι)	Speak (λαλέω), Teach (διδάσκω)		
Acts 5:42	Not cease (οὐκ παύω)	Teach (διδάσκω), Evangelizing (εὐαγγελίζω)		
Acts 8:4	Scattered (διασπείπω), Went about (διέρχομαι)	Evangelizing (εὐαγγελίζω)		
Acts 8:5	Went down (κατέρχομαι)	Preached (κηρύσσω)		
Acts 8:12		Evangelized (εὐαγγελίζω)	Baptized (βαπτίζω)	
Acts 8:25	Started back (ὑποστρέφω)	Evangelizing (εὐαγγελίζω)		Solemnly testified (διαμαρτύρομαι), Spoken (λαλέω)
Acts 8:26-39	Get up (ἀνίστημι), Go (πορεύομαι), Got up (ἀνίστημι), Went (πορεύομαι), Go up (προσέρχομαι), Join (κολλάομαι), Ran up (προστρέχω)	Evangelized (εὐαγγελίζω)	Baptized (βαπτίζω), Baptized (βαπτίζω)	No longer saw [him] (ouk oraō)
Acts 8:40	Was found (εὑρίσκω), Passed through (διέρχομαι)	Kept evangelizing (εὐαγγελίζω)		
Acts 10:37		Proclaimed (κηρύσσω)	Baptism [noun] (βάπτισμα)	
Acts 10:42		To preach (κηρύσσω) Solemnly to testify (διαμαρτύρομαι)		
Acts 14:6-7	Fled (καταφεύγω)	Evangelized (εὐαγγελίζω)		
Acts 14:20-22	Departed (ἐξέρχομαι)	Evangelized (εὐαγγελίζω), Won Disciples (μαθητεύω)		
	Returned (ὑποστρέφω),			Strengthening (ἐπιστηρίζω), Encouraging (παρακαλέω)
Acts 16:9-10	Come over (διαβαίνω) Sought to go (εὐθέως ἐζητήσαμεν ἐξελθεῖν)	Help us (βοηθέω) Evangelize (εὐαγγελίζω)		
Acts 17:2-3	Went in (εἰσέρχομαι)	Reasoned (διελέγομαι), Opening (διανοίγω), Setting forth (παρατίθημι), Protesting (καταγγέλλω)		Reasoned (διελέγομαι)
Acts 18:9	Do not fear (μη φοβέομαι)	Speak (λαλέω), Do not be silent (μη σιωπάω)		
Acts 19:8-9	Entered (εἰσέρχομαι)	Bold speech (παρρησιάζομαι), Reasoning (διαλέγομαι), Persuading (πείθω)		
Acts 19:13		Preaches (κηρύσσω)		

Rubric	Going (πορεύομαι)	Win Disciples (μαθητεύω)	Baptizing (βαπτίζω)	Teaching to Observe (διδάσκω + τηρέω)
Acts 20:18, 20, 25, 31	Set foot (παραγίνομαι)	Not shrink + declaring (ouden upostellō + anaggellō), Teaching (διδάσκω) Preaching (κηρύσσω)		Not cease + admonish (ouk pauō + noutheteō)
Acts 28:30-31	Welcoming (ἀποδέχομαι) + [All who] came in (εἰσπορεύομαι)	Preaching (κηρύσσω), Teaching (διδάσκω)		
Rom 10:15	How beautiful are the feet (ὡς ὡραῖοι οἱ πόδες)	Of those who evangelize peace (τῶν εὐαγγελιζομένων εἰρήνην) Who evangelize good (τῶν εὐαγγελιζομένων τὰ ἀγαθά)		
Rom 15:20		Make it my ambition (φιλοτιμέομαι) + to evangelize (εὐαγγελίζω)		
1 Cor 1:17	Send (ἀποστέλλω)	To evangelize (εὐαγγελίζω)	Not to baptize (βαπτίζω)	
1 Cor 9:6		To evangelize (εὐαγγελίζω) [Do not] evangelize (εὐαγγελίζω)		
1 Cor 15:1-2		Evangelized (εὐαγγελίζω) Evangelized (εὐαγγελίζω)		Make known (γνωρίζω) Received (παραλαμβάνω) Stand (ἵστημι) Saved (σῴζω) Hold fast (κατέχω)
2 Cor 2:12	Came (ἔρχομαι)	[No verb] unto the Gospel of Christ (εἰς τὸ εὐαγγέλιον τοῦ χριστοῦ)		
1 Thess 2:1-2	Our entrance (εἴσοδος) to you	Boldness to speak (παρρησιάζομαι) Speak (λαλέω)		
2 Thess 3:1	That the word of the Lord may spread rapidly [run] (ἵνα ὁ λόγος τοῦ κυρίου τρέχῃ)			just as it did also with you (καθὼς καὶ πρὸς ὑμᾶς)

d. The Great Commission commands all Christians to evangelize, which is the **verbal** proclamation of the Gospel of Jesus Christ. Note the words of the *Baptist Faith and Message 2000*:

"It is the *duty and privilege of every follower of Christ and of every church* of the Lord Jesus Christ to endeavor to make disciples of all nations. The new birth of man's spirit by God's Holy Spirit means the birth of love for others. Missionary effort on the part of all rests thus upon a spiritual necessity of the regenerate life, and is expressly and repeatedly commanded in the teachings of Christ. The Lord Jesus Christ has commanded the preaching of the gospel to all nations. It is the duty of every child of God to seek constantly to win the lost to Christ by *verbal witness* undergirded by a Christian lifestyle, and by other methods in harmony with the gospel of Christ. Genesis 12:1-3; Exodus 19:5-6; Isaiah 6:1-8; Matthew 9:37-38; 10:5-15; 13:18-30, 37-43; 16:19; 22:9-10; 24:14; 28:18-20; Luke 10:1-18; 24:46-53; John 14:11-12; 15:7-8,16; 17:15; 20:21; Acts 1:8; 2; 8:26-40; 10:42-48; 13:2-3; Romans 10:13-15; Ephesians 3:1-11; 1 Thessalonians 1:8; 2 Timothy 4:5; Hebrews 2:1-3; 11:39-12:2; 1 Peter 2:4-10; Revelation 22:17."[812]

e. For further clarity on the role of proclamation, please note the addendum at the end of this chapter entitled, "Evangelism as the Means to an End or as an End in Itself." This addendum also includes a chart titled, "Evangelizing and the Great Commission's Fulfillment"

---

[812]"XI. Evangelism and Missions," in *The Baptist Faith and Message* (2000); accessed 14 August 2002; available from: http://www.sbc.net/bfm/default.asp; Internet. Emphasis mine.

3. The extent of the Great Commission is all inclusive:[813]

   a. **Geographical extent** (cf. Isa 24:14-16)
     1) "Everywhere," Luke 9:60
     2) "Jerusalem, all Judea, Samaria, and unto the remotest part of the earth," Acts 1:8 (cf. Isa 41:9)
     3) "Go into all the world... to all creation," Mark 16:15
     4) "The whole world," Matt 24:14
     5) "Throughout the whole earth," Rom 9:17 (cf. Psa. 66:1)
     6) "Give ear, O heavens, and let me speak; And let the earth hear the words of my mouth," Deut 32:1
     7) "So as to preach the gospel even to the regions beyond you, *and* not to boast in what has been accomplished in the sphere of another," 2 Cor 10:16

   b. **Sociological extent** (cf. Psa 148:11-13, Rev 5:9)
     1) "All nations," Matt 24:14, 28:19, Mark 13:10, Luke 24:47
     2) "All the peoples," Isa 56:7; "O peoples," Psa 66:8; "to the people," Acts 13:31
     3) "All the families of the earth," Gen 12:3
     4) "All men," 1 Cor 9:22 (cf. Col 1:28)
     5) "Gentiles" [the nations], Is 42:6; 49:6; Acts 13:46-48; 15:7-11
     6) "The foreigner," 1 Kg 8:41-43
     7) "The foreigner ... all the peoples of the earth," 2 Chron 6:32-33
     8) "The poor," Gal 2:10 (cf. Jms 2:5-9)
     9) "The cities of Judah," Matt 10:23
     10) "Kings," Acts 9:15 (cf. Psa 119:46)

   c. **Spiritual extent**:
     1) "And thus I aspired to preach the gospel, not where Christ was *already* named, that I might not build upon another man's foundation," Rom 15:18-21 (cf. Rom 10:14-15)
     2) Those not reconciled to God, 2 Cor 5:20
     3) Those "appointed to eternal life," Acts 13:48

4. **Prophecies on the fulfillment of the Great Commission**:
   a) As the fulfillment of Old Testament prophecy, Luke 24:46-47
   b) Of the propagation of the God's Word, Psa 147:15 (cf. 2 Thess 3:1)
   c) Of righteousness and salvation going forth to the nations from Zion, Isa 62:1-2
   d) Of those who obey the Great Commission, Psa 68:11, Isa 43:21, John 15:26-27, Acts 1:8
   e) Of those who receive the Gospel, Isa 24:13-16
   f) Of the earth being full of the knowledge of the glory of God, Hab. 2:14
   g) As necessary before the return of Christ, Matt 24:14, Mark 13:10
   h) Of those before the throne of God, Rev 5:9

5. Conclusions:

Note the words of Paul in the closing doxology in Romans [16:25-27]:

    Byzantine: Τῷ δὲ δυναμένῳ ὑμᾶς στηρίξαι κατὰ τὸ εὐαγγέλιόν μου καὶ τὸ κήρυγμα Ἰησοῦ χριστοῦ, κατὰ ἀποκάλυψιν μυστηρίου χρόνοις αἰωνίοις σεσιγημένου, φανερωθέντος δὲ νῦν, διά τε γραφῶν προφητικῶν, κατ' ἐπιταγὴν τοῦ αἰωνίου θεοῦ, εἰς ὑπακοὴν πίστεως εἰς πάντα τὰ ἔθνη γνωρισθέντος, μόνῳ σοφῷ θεῷ, διὰ Ἰησοῦ χριστοῦ, ᾧ ἡ δόξα εἰς τοὺς αἰῶνας. Ἀμήν.

    NAS: "Now to Him who is able to establish you according to my gospel and the preaching of Jesus Christ, according to the revelation of the mystery which has been kept secret for long ages past, but now is manifested, and by the Scriptures of the prophets, according to the commandment of the eternal God, has been made known to all the nations, *leading* to obedience of faith; to the only wise God, through Jesus Christ, be the glory forever. Amen."

    My tweak: "Now to Him who is able to establish you according to my gospel and the preaching of Jesus Christ, according to the revelation of the mystery which has been kept secret for long ages past, through the Scriptures of the prophets, according to the commandment of the eternal God, being made known unto the obedience of faith among all the nations; to the only wise God, through Jesus Christ, be the glory forever. Amen."

---

[813]T. Johnston, *Mindset*, Chap 6, VI.E, develops this theme from an Old Testament vantage point beginning with the Psalms. There is found a wide breadth of material and the conclusions are virtually identical.

J.E. Conant wrote, "The Commission according to Mark, therefore, in one phrase from Matthew, tells us that witnessing is the main work of the whole church in the whole world throughout the whole age."[814]

C. Other Commissionings in the Bible:

1. A selection of the OT commands:[815]

   Introduction:

   Most OT examples are not in command form, at least in the way they are commonly translated into English; e.g. Psa 35:8; 51:13; 118:17; cf. Isa 42:12; 43:21;

   Some OT relate to sinners turning or converting, Psa 51:13; Mal 2:6; cf. Ezek 18:30-32; 33:11

   Other commands relate to the action of going to gather, Psa 50:5

   a) In the Psalms:

      1) Psa 9:11, "Sing praises to the Lord, who dwells in Zion; **Declare** (Heb *saphar;* LXX διηγέομαι) among the peoples His deeds."

      2) Psa 22:31, "They will come [go (Heb *bo*; LXX ἔρχομαι) and will declare [Heb *nagad*; LXX, ἀναγγέλλω] His righteousness To a people who will be born, that He has performed *it.*

      3) Psa 35:28, "And my tongue shall declare Thy righteousness *And* Thy praise all day long"

      4) Psa 64:9, "Then all men will fear, And will declare the work of God, And will consider what He has done"

      5) Psa 66:8, "Bless the Lord, O peoples, And **sound His praise abroad**" (Fr. NEG, "Peuples, bénissez notre Dieu, Faites retentir sa louange !")

      6) Psa 71:15, "My mouth shall **tell** of Your righteousness *And* of Your salvation all day long"

      7) Psa 75:1, "Men declare (*saphar*) Thy wondrous works"

      8) Psa 79:13, "So we Your people and the sheep of Your pasture Will give thanks to You forever; To all generations we will **tell** of Your praise"

      9) Psa 92:1-2, "It is good to give thanks to the LORD, And to sing praises to Thy name, O Most High; To declare Thy lovingkindness in the morning, And Thy faithfulness by night"

      10) Psa 96:2-3, "Sing to the Lord, bless His name; **Proclaim good tidings of His salvation from day to day. Tell of His glory among the nations**, His wonderful deeds among all the peoples."
      Greek (second line in v. 2), εὐαγγελίζεσθε ἡμέραν ἐξ ἡμέρας τὸ σωτήριον αὐτοῦ
      My English: "Evangelize from day to day of His salvation"

      11) Psa 105:1-2, "Oh give thanks to the lord, call upon His name; **Make known His deeds among the peoples**. Sing to Him, sing praises to Him; **Speak of all His wonders**."

      12) Psa 145:4, 11-12, "One generation shall praise Your works to another, And shall declare Your mighty acts. … They shall speak of the glory of Your kingdom And talk of Your power; To make known to the sons of men Your mighty acts And the glory of the majesty of Your kingdom"

   b) Some General OT Commissionings in the Prophets:

      1) **Isa 40:9**, "Get yourself up on a high mountain, O Zion, bearer of good news, Lift up your voice mightily, O Jerusalem, bearer of good news; Lift *it* up, do not fear. Say to the cities of Judah, 'Here is your God!'"
      Greek: ἐπ' ὄρος ὑψηλὸν ἀνάβηθι ὁ εὐαγγελιζόμενος Σιων ὕψωσον τῇ ἰσχύι τὴν φωνήν σου ὁ εὐαγγελιζόμενος Ιερουσαλημ ὑψώσατε μὴ φοβεῖσθε εἰπὸν ταῖς πόλεσιν Ιουδα ἰδοὺ ὁ θεὸς ὑμῶν
      My English [note the need for taking a stand, and raising one's voice]:
      "Get up on a high mountain [high place], O evangelizer of Zion;
      "With strength raise your voice, O evangelizer of Jerusalem;
      "Lift *it* up, be not afraid;
      "Say to the cities of Judah, 'Behold your God!'"

---

[814]J. E. Conant, *Every Member Evangelism* (New York: Harper, 1922), 7.

[815]These are just a few examples of the wealth of material on this subject in the Psalms. For greater detail see T. Johnston, *Mindset*, Chap 6, V., "An Expanded Study of Testifying in the Psalms." For our use here, I have only listed several direct commands. There are many testimonials concerning testifying throughout the Psalms—in fact, the latter is by far in the majority (e.g. Psa 40:10; 71:15-16).

2) **Isa 49:6**, "He says, 'It is too small a thing that You should be My Servant To raise up the tribes of Jacob, and to restore the preserved ones of Israel; I will also make You a light of the nations So that My salvation may reach to the end of the earth'" (cf. Isaiah 42:6)

   Paul applied this verse as a commissioning for his own ministry of evangelism, even unto Gentiles, Acts 13:47 ("for so the Lord commanded [ἐντέλλομαι] us")

   The French Segond Revise Genève translated the last phrase in Isaiah 49:6, "Pour porter mon salut jusqu'aux extrémités de la terre" (my trans. "to carry my salvation unto the ends of the earth")

3) **Isa 52:7**, "How lovely on the mountains Are the feet of him who brings good news, Who announces peace And brings good news of happiness, Who announces salvation, *And* says to Zion, "Your God reigns!""

   Greek: ὡς ὥρα ἐπὶ τῶν ὀρέων ὡς πόδες εὐαγγελιζομένου ἀκοὴν εἰρήνης ὡς εὐαγγελιζόμενος ἀγαθά ὅτι ἀκουστὴν ποιήσω τὴν σωτηρίαν σου λέγων Σιων βασιλεύσει σου ὁ θεός

   My English [notice the five proclamational verbs in the Hebrew!]:
   "How beautiful upon the hills
   "Are the feet of **those evangelizing**,
   "**Announcing** peace;
   "**Those evangelizing** good,
   "**Announcing** salvation, [LXX, "that announce salvation"]
   "**Saying** unto Zion, "Your God reigns!"
        [i.e. NT "kingdom of God"]

4) Jer 4:16 (KJV), "For a voice declareth from Dan, and publisheth affliction from mount Ephraim. Make ye mention to the nations; behold, publish against Jerusalem, *that* watchers come from a far country, and give out their voice against the cities of Judah"

c) Some Specific OT Commissionings:

1) Isa 6:8-9, "Go and tell this people"

2) To Jeremiah:

   Jer 1:7, "Do not say, 'I am a youth,' Because everywhere I send you, you shall go, And all I command you you shall speak"

   Jer 1:17, "Now, gird up your loins, and arise, and speak to them all which I command you. Do not be dismayed before them, lest I dismay you before them"

   Jer 3:12, "Go, and proclaim these words toward the north and say, 'Return, faithless Israel,' declares the LORD; 'I will not look upon you in anger. For I am gracious,' declares the LORD; 'I will not be angry forever'"

   Jer 5:19, "And it shall come about when they say, 'Why has the LORD our God done all these things to us?' then you shall say to them, 'As you have forsaken Me and served foreign gods in your land, so you shall serve strangers in a land that is not yours'"

   Jer 7:2, "Stand in the gate of the LORD's house and proclaim there this word, and say, 'Hear the word of the LORD, all you of Judah, who enter by these gates to worship the LORD!'"

   Jer 7:25, "And you shall speak all these words to them, but they will not listen to you; and you shall call to them, but they will not answer you"

   Jer 7:27-28, "And you shall speak all these words to them, but they will not listen to you; and you shall call to them, but they will not answer you. And you shall say to them, 'This is the nation that did not obey the voice of the LORD their God or accept correction; truth has perished and has been cut off from their mouth'"

   Jer 8:4, "And you shall say to them, 'Thus says the LORD, "Do *men* fall and not get up again? Does one turn away and not repent?"'"

   Jer 10:11, "Thus you shall say to them, 'The gods that did not make the heavens and the earth shall perish from the earth and from under the heavens'"

   Jer 11:2-3, "Hear the words of this covenant, and speak to the men of Judah and to the inhabitants of Jerusalem; and say to them, 'Thus says the LORD, the God of Israel, "Cursed is the man who does not heed the words of this covenant"'"

   Jer 13:12-14, "Therefore you are to speak this word to them, 'Thus says the LORD, the God of Israel, "Every jug is to be filled with wine."' And when they say to you, 'Do we not very well know that every jug is to be filled with wine?' then say to them, 'Thus says the LORD, "Behold I am about to fill all the inhabitants of this land—the kings that sit for David on his throne, the priests, the prophets and all the inhabitants of Jerusalem—with drunkenness! And I will dash them against each other, both the fathers and the sons together," declares the LORD. "I will not show pity nor be sorry nor have compassion that I should not destroy them"'"

   Jer 13:18, "Say to the king and the queen mother, 'Take a lowly seat, For your beautiful crown Has come down from your head'"

Jer 14:17, "And you will say this word to them, 'Let my eyes flow down with tears night and day, And let them not cease; For the virgin daughter of my people has been crushed with a mighty blow, With a sorely infected wound'"

Jer 15:2, "And it shall be that when they say to you, 'Where should we go?' then you are to tell them, 'Thus says the LORD: "Those *destined* for death, to death; And those *destined* for the sword, to the sword; And those *destined* for famine, to famine; And those *destined* for captivity, to captivity"'"

Jer 16:11-12, "Then you are to say to them, '*It is* because your forefathers have forsaken Me,' declares the LORD, 'and have followed other gods and served them and bowed down to them; but Me they have forsaken and have not kept My law. You too have done evil, *even* more than your forefathers; for behold, you are each one walking according to the stubbornness of his own evil heart, without listening to Me'"

Jer 17:19-20, "Thus the LORD said to me, 'Go and stand in the public gate, through which the kings of Judah come in and go out, as well as in all the gates of Jerusalem; and say to them, "Listen to the word of the LORD, kings of Judah, and all Judah, and all inhabitants of Jerusalem, who come in through these gates…"'"

Jer 18:10, "So now then, speak to the men of Judah and against the inhabitants of Jerusalem saying, 'Thus says the LORD, "Behold, I am fashioning calamity against you and devising a plan against you. Oh turn back, each of you from his evil way, and reform your ways and your deeds"'"

Jer 19:2-3, "Then go out to the valley of Ben-hinnom, which is by the entrance of the potsherd gate; and proclaim there the words that I shall tell you, and say, 'Hear the word of the LORD, O kings of Judah and inhabitants of Jerusalem: thus says the LORD of hosts, the God of Israel, "Behold I am about to bring a calamity upon this place, at which the ears of everyone that hears of it will tingle"'"

Jer 19:10-11, "Then you are to break the jar in the sight of the men who accompany you and say to them, 'Thus says the LORD of hosts, "Just so shall I break this people and this city, even as one breaks a potter's vessel, which cannot again be repaired; and they will bury in Topheth because there is no *other* place for burial"'"

Jer 22:1, "Thus says the LORD, 'Go down to the house of the king of Judah, and there speak this word'"

Jer 21:8, "You shall also say to this people, 'Thus says the LORD, "Behold, I set before you the way of life and the way of death"'"

Jer 21:11, "Then *say* to the household of the king of Judah, 'Hear the word of the LORD…'"
[These Jer 21 examples are Jeremiah commissioning messengers to the King of Israel]

Jer 22:1-3, "Thus says the LORD, 'Go down to the house of the king of Judah, and there speak this word, and say, "Hear the word of the LORD, O king of Judah, who sits on David's throne, you and your servants and your people who enter these gates. Thus says the LORD, 'Do justice and righteousness, and deliver the one who has been robbed from the power of *his* oppressor. Also do not mistreat *or* do violence to the stranger, the orphan, or the widow; and do not shed innocent blood in this place'"'"

Jer 23:33, "Now when this people or the prophet or a priest asks you saying, 'What is the oracle of the LORD?' then you shall say to them, 'What oracle?' The LORD declares, 'I shall abandon you'"

Jer 25:30, "Therefore you shall prophesy against them all these words, and you shall say to them, 'The LORD will roar from on high, And utter His voice from His holy habitation; He will roar mightily against His fold. He will shout like those who tread *the grapes*, Against all the inhabitants of the earth'"

Jer 26:2-4, "Thus says the LORD, 'Stand in the court of the LORD's house, and speak to all the cities of Judah, who have come to worship *in* the LORD's house, all the words that I have commanded you to speak to them. Do not omit a word! Perhaps they will listen and everyone will turn from his evil way, that I may repent of the calamity which I am planning to do to them because of the evil of their deeds. And you will say to them, "Thus says the LORD, 'If you will not listen to Me, to walk in My law, which I have set before you…'"'"

Jer 28:13, "Go and speak to Hananiah, saying, 'Thus says the LORD, "You have broken the yokes of wood, but you have made instead of them yokes of iron"'"

Jer 29:24, "And to Shemaiah the Nehelamite you shall speak, saying"

Jer 34:2, "Thus says the LORD God of Israel, 'Go and speak to Zedekiah king of Judah and say to him: "Thus says the LORD, 'Behold, I am giving this city into the hand of the king of Babylon, and he will burn it with fire'"'"

Jer 35:2, "Go to the house of the Rechabites, and speak to them, and bring them into the house of the LORD, into one of the chambers, and give them wine to drink"

Jer 35:12-13, "Then the word of the LORD came to Jeremiah, saying, 'Thus says the LORD of hosts, the God of Israel, "Go and say to the men of Judah and the inhabitants of Jerusalem, 'Will you not receive instruction by listening to My words?' declares the LORD""""

Jer 37:6-7, "Then the word of the LORD came to Jeremiah the prophet, saying, 'Thus says the LORD God of Israel, "Thus you are to say to the king of Judah, who sent you to Me to inquire of Me: 'Behold, Pharaoh's army which has come out for your assistance is going to return to its own land of Egypt""""

Jer 39:16, "Go and speak to Ebed-melech the Ethiopian, saying, 'Thus says the LORD of hosts, the God of Israel, "Behold, I am about to bring My words on this city for disaster and not for prosperity; and they will take place before you on that day""""

[By the way, seeing all these examples gives greater clarity to the words of Jesus, when He said, "Blessed are you when *men* cast insults at you, and persecute you, and say all kinds of evil against you falsely, on account of Me. Rejoice, and be glad, for your reward in heaven is great, for so they persecuted the prophets who were before you" (Matt 5:11-12)

3) To Ezekiel:

Ezek 2:4, "And I am sending you to them who are stubborn and obstinate children; and you shall say to them, 'Thus says the Lord God.'"

Ezek 2:7, "But you shall speak My words to them whether they listen or not, for they are rebellious"

Ezek 3:1, "Then He said to me, 'Son of man, eat what you find; eat this scroll, and go, speak to the house of Israel'"

Ezek 3:4, "Then He said to me, 'Son of man, go to the house of Israel and speak with My words to them'"

Ezek 3:11, "And go to the exiles, to the sons of your people, and speak to them and tell them, whether they listen or not, 'Thus says the Lord God.'"

Ezek 3:17, "Son of man, I have appointed you a watchman to the house of Israel; whenever you hear a word from My mouth, warn them from Me" (cf. Ezek 33:7ff.)

Ezek 3:27, "But when I speak to you, I will open your mouth, and you will say to them, 'Thus says the Lord God.' He who hears, let him hear; and he who refuses, let him refuse; for they are a rebellious house"

Ezek 6:1-3, "And the word of the LORD came to me saying, 'Son of man, set your face toward the mountains of Israel, and prophesy against them, and say, "Mountains of Israel, listen to the word of the Lord God! Thus says the Lord God to the mountains, the hills, the ravines and the valleys: 'Behold, I Myself am going to bring a sword on you, and I will destroy your high places""""

Ezek 11:5, "Then the Spirit of the LORD fell upon me, and He said to me, 'Say, "Thus says the LORD, 'So you think, house of Israel, for I know your thoughts""""

Ezek 11:15-17, "Son of man, your brothers, your relatives, your fellow exiles, and the whole house of Israel, all of them, *are those* to whom the inhabitants of Jerusalem have said, 'Go far from the LORD; this land has been given us as a possession.' Therefore say, 'Thus says the Lord God, "Though I had removed them far away among the nations, and though I had scattered them among the countries, yet I was a sanctuary for them a little while in the countries where they had gone."' Therefore say, 'Thus says the Lord God, "I shall gather you from the peoples and assemble you out of the countries among which you have been scattered, and I shall give you the land of Israel.""'"

Ezek 12:23, "Therefore say to them, 'Thus says the Lord God, "I will make this proverb cease so that they will no longer use it as a proverb in Israel." But tell them, "The days draw near as well as the fulfillment of every vision""""

Ezek 12:25, "'For I the LORD shall speak, and whatever word I speak will be performed. It will no longer be delayed, for in your days, O rebellious house, I shall speak the word and perform it,' declares the Lord God"

Ezek 12:26-28, "Furthermore, the word of the LORD came to me saying, 'Son of man, behold, the house of Israel is saying, "The vision that he sees is for many years *from now*, and he prophesies of times far off." Therefore say to them, "Thus says the Lord God, 'None of My words will be delayed any longer. Whatever word I speak will be performed,' declares the Lord God""""

Ezek 13:2, "Son of man, prophesy against the prophets of Israel who prophesy, and say to those who prophesy from their own inspiration, 'Listen to the word of the LORD'"

Ezek 13:17-18, "Now you, son of man, set your face against the daughters of your people who are prophesying from their own inspiration. Prophesy against them, and say, 'Thus says the Lord God, "Woe to the women who sew *magic* bands on all wrists, and make veils for the heads of *persons* of every stature to hunt down lives! Will you hunt down the lives of My people, but preserve the lives *of others* for yourselves?""""

Ezek 14:4, "Therefore speak to them and tell them, 'Thus says the Lord God...'"

Ezek 14:6, "Therefore say to the house of Israel, 'Thus says the Lord God, "Repent and turn away from your idols, and turn your faces away from all your abominations"'"

Ezek 16:2-3, "Son of man, make known to Jerusalem her abominations, and say…"

Ezek 20:3-5, "Son of man, speak to the elders of Israel, and say to them, 'Thus says the Lord God, "Do you come to inquire of Me? As I live," declares the Lord God, "I will not be inquired of by you"' Will you judge them, will you judge them, son of man? Make them know the abominations of their fathers; and say to them, 'Thus says the Lord God, "On the day when I chose Israel and swore to the descendants of the house of Jacob and made Myself known to them in the land of Egypt, when I swore to them, saying, I am the LORD your God"'"

Ezek 20:27, "Therefore, son of man, speak to the house of Israel, and say to them, 'Thus says the Lord God, "Yet in this your fathers have blasphemed Me by acting treacherously against Me"'"

Ezek 20:30, "Therefore, say to the house of Israel, 'Thus says the Lord God, "Will you defile yourselves after the manner of your fathers and play the harlot after their detestable things?"'"

Ezek 20:45-47, "Now the word of the LORD came to me saying, 'Son of man, set your face toward Teman, and speak out against the south, and prophesy against the forest land of the Negev, and say to the forest of the Negev, "Hear the word of the LORD: thus says the Lord God, 'Behold, I am about to kindle a fire in you, and it shall consume every green tree in you, as well as every dry tree; the blazing flame will not be quenched, and the whole surface from south to north will be burned by it'"'"

[And there are many more… in Ezekiel and in the other prophets; I quoted these to provide a taste of the antecedent Scripture to both the sending passages in Matt 10 and Luke 9-10, as well as Great Commission passages]

    4) To Jonah:

        (a) Jonah 1:2, "Arise, go to Nineveh the great city and cry (Heb *qara'*; LXX κήρυξον) against it, for their wickedness has come up before Me."

            ἀνάστηθι καὶ πορεύθητι εἰς Νινευη τὴν πόλιν τὴν μεγάλην καὶ κήρυξον ἐν αὐτῇ ὅτι ἀνέβη ἡ κραυγὴ τῆς κακίας αὐτῆς πρός με

        (b) Jonah 3:2, "Arise, go to Nineveh the great city and proclaim to it the proclamation which I am going to tell you."

            ἀνάστηθι καὶ πορεύθητι εἰς Νινευη τὴν πόλιν τὴν μεγάλην καὶ κήρυξον ἐν αὐτῇ κατὰ τὸ κήρυγμα τὸ ἔμπροσθεν ὃ ἐγὼ ἐλάλησα πρός σέ

Some Interesting OT combinations:

    Psa 40:5, declare and speak (*nagad* and *dabar*)

    Psa 106:2, speak and show forth (*malal* and *shama*)

    Isa 40:9, get up and evangelize; get up and evangelize, do not fear, say

    Isa 52:7, evangelize, announce, evangelize, announce, say

2. Other NT Commissionings:

  a. Jesus to those He healed:

    1) "Go home to your people and report to them what great things the Lord has done for you," Mark 5:19; Luke 8:39

    2) "Go and show yourself to the priest for a testimony to them," Mark 1:44; Luke 5:14 (cf. Luke 17:14)

  b. Christ to his disciples:

  Introduction: The call of Jesus to His disciples was:

    "Follow Me and I will make you fishers of men," Matt 4:19

    "Follow Me and I will make you become fishers of men," Mark 1:17

    "Do not fear, from now on you will be taking men alive," Luke 5:10

    1) "And as for you go, preach, saying, 'The kingdom of heaven is at hand,'" Matt 10:7 (cf. Matt 3:2; 4:17)

    2) "What I tell you in the darkness, speak in the light; and what you hear *whispered* in *your* ear, proclaim upon the housetops," Matt 10:27

    3) "And He summoned the twelve and began to send them out in pairs; and He was giving them authority over the unclean spirits," Mark 6:7

    4) "But as for you, go and proclaim everywhere the kingdom of God," Luke 9:60 (cf. Luke 9:2)

    5) "And you will bear witness also, because you have been with Me from the beginning," John 15:27

    6) "And He ordered us to preach to the people, and solemnly to testify that this is the One who has been appointed by God as Judge of the living and the dead," Acts 10:42

  c. In the parables of Christ (cf. Matt 13:3, 19, 44-46):

     1) "Go therefore to the main highways, and as many as you find there, invite to the wedding feast," Matt 22:9

     2) "Go out at once into the streets and lanes of the city and bring in here the poor and crippled and lame," Luke 14:21

     3) "Go into the highways and along the hedges, and compel them to come in, that my house may be filled," Luke 14:23

  d. To the Apostle Paul (notice how Paul fulfilled Christ's Acts 1:8 commission both of being a testifier [μάρτυς] and of testifying [μαρτυρέω]):

     1) "Go, for he is a chosen instrument of Mine, to bear My name before the Gentiles and kings and the sons of Israel; for I will show him how much he must suffer for My name's sake," Acts 9:15-16

     2) "Set apart for Me Barnabas and Saul for the work to which I have called them," Acts 13:2

     3) "For thus the Lord has commanded us, 'I have placed You as a light for the Gentiles, That You should bring salvation to the end of the earth,'" Acts 13:47

     4) "'Come over to Macedonia and help us.' When he had seen the vision, immediately we sought to go into Macedonia, concluding that God had called us to preach the gospel [to evangelize] them" Acts 16:9-10

     5) "And the Lord said to Paul in the night by a vision, 'Do not be afraid *any longer*, but go on speaking and do not be silent; for I am with you, and no man will attack you in order to harm you, for I have many people in this city.'" Acts 18:9-10

     6) "For you will be a witness [μάρτυς] for Him to all men of what you have seen and heard." Acts 22:15

     7) A two-part calling:

       a) "and I saw Him saying to me, 'Make haste, and get out of Jerusalem quickly, because they will not accept your testimony about Me,'" Acts 22:18

       b) "And He said to me, 'Go! For I will send you far away to the Gentiles.'" Acts 22:21

     8) "Take courage; for as you have solemnly witnessed [διαμαρτύρομαι] to My cause at Jerusalem, so you must witness [μαρτυρέω] at Rome also," Acts 23:11

     9) "And I said, 'Who are You, Lord?' And the Lord said, 'I am Jesus whom you are persecuting. But get up and stand on your feet; for this purpose I have appeared to you, to appoint you a minister [ὑπηρέτης] and a witness [μάρτυς] not only to the things which you have seen, but also to the things in which I will appear to you; rescuing you from the *Jewish* people and from the Gentiles, to whom I am sending you, to open their eyes so that they may turn from darkness to light and from the dominion of Satan to God, that they may receive forgiveness of sins and an inheritance among those who have been sanctified by faith in Me.' So, King Agrippa, I did not prove disobedient to the heavenly vision, but *kept* declaring [ἀπαγγέλλω] both to those of Damascus first, and *also* at Jerusalem and *then* throughout all the region of Judea, and *even* to the Gentiles, that they should repent and turn to God, performing deeds appropriate to repentance," Acts 26:15-18

  e. To other NT people:

     4) To the Apostles: "Go your way, stand and speak to the people in the temple the whole message of this Life," Acts 5:20

     5) To Philip: "But an angel of the Lord spoke to Philip saying, 'Arise and go south' ... 'Go up and join this chariot,'" Acts 8:26, 29

     6) To Ananias: "But the Lord said to Him, 'Go!'" Acts 9:15

     7) To Peter: "And the Spirit told me to go without misgivings," Acts 11:12

     8) To Timothy: "Preach the word; be ready in season and out of season," 2 Tim 4:2

     9) To Timothy: "Do the work of an evangelist," 2 Tim 4:5

     10) To Titus: "These things speak and exhort and reprove with all authority. Let no one disregard you," Tit 2:15

  g. Further general OT and NT commands:

     1) Prov 24:11-12

     2) Isa 43:10-11

     3) 1 Pet 3:15

D. The Search for OT Sequels to the NT Great Commission Passages (taking our lead from words of Jesus, Who said, "Thus it is written" (Luke 24:46):

This topic is fraught with theological and missiological disagreement (due to literal versus figurative views of the atonement and the Great Commission, Covenant versus Dispensational theologies, Evangelical versus Sacramental interpretations, etc.). That being said, it is instructive to consider and understand the issues in delineating an OT parallels or antecedent Scriptures, as these impact the practice or method of fulfilling the Great Commission.

1. **NT Great Commission and Deuteronomy's "Conquest Tread:"**[816]

Introduction:

The Promise: "Every place on which the sole of your foot treads shall be yours" (Deut 11:24 [NKJ])

1) Deuteronomy, written as an executive brief (chapter 1) for the Israelite King (Deut 17:18-20), then becoming an in-depth class from God, urged the conquest tread of the kings of Israel and/or Judah:

a) Notice God's repetition of the exact borders and boundaries (giving the young King of Israel a spiritual vision), Deut 1:6-7; 2:24, 36-37; 3:8-9, 12-17; 4:44-49; 7:1-2; ... 34:1-3

Deut 11:24 "Every place on which the sole of your foot treads shall be yours: from the wilderness and Lebanon, from the river, the River Euphrates, even to the Western Sea, shall be your territory"

(1) Notice that in a plural context, God emphatically tells the king that these will be his borders (singular), Deut 11:24, "...shall be yours (plural); ... shall be your (singular) territory [border]"

(2) By the way, it appears that these borders were never reached by any king of Israel or of Judah!

b) Notice God's repetition of the fact that He swore to give and gave this specific land to the people of Israel, and that they should possess it, Deut 1:8; 2:24, 29-31, 33; 3:2, 18, 20, 26-28; 4:1, 5, 26; 5:31, 33; 6:3, 10-11, 18, 23; 7:1, 18, 22-24; 8:1, 7-9; 9:1-6; 10:11; 11:8-12; ... 34:4

(1) As well as the land that He did not give to them, Deut 2:5, 9, 19, 37

c) And yet they did not automatically get the land, they had to fight for it; there were enemies in the land; God had predestined the need for battles and warfare!

2) In an analogous way, the same commissionings apply to the NT Christian with some NT distinctions:

a) By faith, take the land for the Gospel

b) Do not fear for Christ said, "I am with you!"

3) First let's notice the Deuteronomic commissioning, then consider the comparisons with the NT Great Commission passages and related passages.

a. Various commissionings in Deuteronomy (not exhaustive):

1) Deut 1:21, "See ... go up, take possession" (please note that the verbs in this verse are all in the singular)

a) Some positives:

1:21, "See" (John 4:35 has three verbs for seeing)

1:21, "Go up" (Heb 'alah': rise up, get up, climb, ascend; parallel to Isa 40:9, "Get thee up [on a high place]")

1:21, "take possession" (Heb yarash; [imperative]: possess the land:

NT parallel to evangelizing leading to the "kingdom of heaven" being at hand (cf. Matt 3:2; 4:17; 10:7; Luke 10:9, 11)

---

[816]"It is not wise to say that *soul winning* is the main thing or that *soul building* is the main thing. They are Siamese twins of God's gospel, going hand in hand, and they ought to keep up with each other.... And this leads me to say that the main thing in the Kingdom of God is the evangelistic spirit, the martial note and conquest tread" (L. R. Scarborough, *Recruits for World Conquest* [New York: Revell, 1914], 58).

NT parallel to evangelizing leading to the rule of Christ in the hearts of those who respond favorably

A morphological search on the Hebrew verb yarash yields 71 hits in Deuteronomy; likewise, there are 52 uses of the English verb "possess" in Deuteronomy; almost all of these are related to God's gift of "the land"

b) Some negatives:

1:21, "Do not fear"

1:21, "Do not be dismayed [or discouraged]"

1:29, "Do not be shocked, nor fear them"

[after their disobedient response to their sociological survey]

1:42, "Do not go up nor fight, for I am not among you"

2) Deut 2:24, "Arise, set out … Look! I have given…"

2:25, "This day I will begin to put the dread and fear of you upon the peoples everywhere"

2:31, "See, I have begun to deliver … that you may possess his land"

3) Deut 3:2, "Do not fear him, for I have delivered him…"

4) Deut 3:18, "The LORD your God has given you this land to possess it"

3:21, "Your eyes have seen"

3:22, "Do not fear them, for the LORD your God is the one fighting for you."

5) Deut 3:27, "Go up to the top of Pisgah"

3:28, "But charge Joshua and encourage him and strengthen him, for he shall go across at the head of this people, and he will give them as an inheritance the land which you see"

[an interesting analogy is being made between Joshua and Jesus; Joshua meaning "The LORD saves," and Jesus meaning "the LORD saves"]

6) Deut 7:17, "If you should say in your heart, 'These nations are greater than I; how can I dispossess them?'"

7:18, "You shall not be afraid of them

7:21, "You shall not dread them

7:22, "The Lord your God will clear away…"

7:24, "He will deliver…"

7) Deut 9:23, "And when the LORD sent you from Kadesh-barnea, saying, 'Go up and possess the land which I have given you,' then you rebelled against the command of the LORD your God; you neither believed Him nor listened to His voice"

8) Deut 10:11, "Arise, proceed on your journey ahead of the people"

10:11, "That they may go in and possess the land"

i) Deut 11:8, "so that you may be strong and go in and possess the land…"

j) Deut 31:23, "Then He commissioned Joshua the son of Nun, and said, 'Be strong and courageous, for you shall bring the sons of Israel into the land which I swore to them, and I will be with you.'"

Comparing Deuteronomy's "Conquest Tread" with the NT Great Commission

Aspects		Deuteronomy	New Testament
God's Vision	Similarity	See, Deut 1:21 (2nd person sing); 2:31 Look, Deut 2:24 Your eyes have seen, Deut 3:21 Lift up your eyes and see, Deut 3:27	Behold, Lift up your eyes, and see, John 4:35 "Come over to Macedonia and help us," Acts 16:9
God's Calling	Similarity	Go up, Deut 1:21 (2nd person sing) Arise, set out, Deut 2:24 Go up, Deut 9:23 (2nd person pl) Arise, proceed, Deut 10:11 That they may go in, Deut 10:11	Go, Matt 28:19; Mark 16:15 So send I you, John 20:21 To all nations, Luke 24:48
Purpose	Dissimilarity	People don't matter (they must be annihilated, Deut 7:24) What matters is taking the land! The people must be dispossessed (Deut 7:17-26)	The land doesn't matter (other than peace to tell the people, 1 Tim 2:1-4) What matters are the people, Mark 15:16! Let them possess their own land, Rom 13:1ff.
		To take the land, Deut 1:21 (2nd person sing); 9:23 (2nd person pl); 31:23 (to Joshua) [Was it not this type of teaching that drove the Medieval Church of Rome's military crusades and Holy Inquisitions? "Annihilate the infidels; take the 'Holy Land', take Constantinople, take Southern France, take Bohemia, whatever the cost; kill all the inhabitants, drive them out of the land"] [For Rome's inquisition methodology against the Albigenses from Southern France and the Hussites of Bohemia, see Deut 13:12-18; 17:1-7, whereas "other gods" is interpreted as "other churches", likewise "other nation," 7:22, is "other church"; I often heard as a youth in France, "j'ai déjà ma religion!" (meaning: I already have my [own] religion)]	The kingdom of heaven is at hand, Matt 3:2; 4:17; 10:7 Possess the land spiritually, Luke 17:20-21; John 18:36 Clearly the Great Commissions have a geographic element to them: "All nations," Matt 28; "All the world ... all creation," Mark 16; "Unto the uttermost parts of the earth," Acts 1:8
The nations	Disimilarity	"And you shall consume all the peoples [τῶν ἐθνῶν] whom the LORD your God will deliver to you; your eye shall not pity them, neither shall you serve their gods, for that *would be* a snare to you," Deut 7:16	"Go therefore and make disciples of all the nations [τὰ ἔθνη], baptizing them in the name of the Father and the Son and the Holy Spirit, 20 teaching them to observe all that I commanded you; and lo, I am with you always, even to the end of the age," Matt 28:19-20
Weapon	Dis-similarity	A carnal weapon: physical sword	A spiritual weapon: the sword of the Spirit (Eph 6:17) and the power of the Gospel of Christ (Rom 1:16) The weapons of our warfare are not carnal, but spiritual..., 2 Cor 10:3-5
Method	Similarity	The need for walking: "set your foot," Deut 11:24	The need for walking: "Go!" Matt 10:5-6, 14
Method	Dis-similarity	Military battle, with the Lord fighting for them	Method: "Preach the Gospel," Mark 16:15; Luke 24:46-47 Method: Testify of Christ, Acts 1:8 Method: Win disciples, Matt 28:19-20
God's promised presence	Similarity	The LORD your God is fighting for you, Deut 1:30; 3:22; 31:3-5	Lo, I am with you, Matt 28:20; Acts 18:10

Aspects		Deuteronomic	New Testament
God's needed presence	Similarity	When God was present—victory, Deut 2:31; 3:2-7 When God was not present—defeat, Deut 1:34-46	God's presence gives power (shown by the infilling of the Spirit), Acts 2:14; 6:15; 13:9; and boldness in speech, Acts 4:31
God's direct involvement	Similarity	"The LORD your God who goes before you will fight on your behalf," Deut 1:30 "But the LORD thy God shall deliver them unto thee, and shall destroy them with a mighty destruction, until they be destroyed," Deut 7:23 (KJV)	The Holy Spirit will convict the world of sin and righteousness and judgment, John 16:8 The Word of God is quick and lively, sharper, piercing, able to judge, no creature hidden before him, Heb 4:12-13 The Word of the Lord was growing mightily and prevailing, Acts 19:20
Identified Foes	Dissimilarity	Enemies are all the nations around Conquer and subdue your enemies False teachers and false prophets as enemies	All the nations around are intented recipients for the gospel Love your enemies Satan as our arch-enemy, so also the antichrist, shun false teachers and false prophets
Being over-whelmed with the task	Similarity	"If you should say in your heart, 'These nations are greater than I; how can I dispossess them?'" Deut 7:17	"But Ananias answered, 'Lord, I have heard from many about this man, how much harm he did to Thy saints at Jerusalem; and here he has authority from the chief priests to bind all who call upon Thy name.' But the Lord said to him, 'Go...'" Acts 9:13-15; cf. Acts 18:9-10
Need strong and coura-geous people and leaders	Similarity	To people: "Be strong and courageous," Deut 31:6 To Joshua: "Be strong and courageous," Deut 31:7	To all Christians: "Be strong in the Lord and in the strength of his might," Eph 6:10; "Be steadfast, immovable," 1 Cor 15:58; "Be on the alert, ... act like men, be strong," 1 Cor 16:13
Names of leaders in warfare	Dissimilarity	The priest: "So it shall be, when you are on the verge of battle, that the priest shall approach and speak to the people," Deut 20:2 Officers: "Then the officers shall speak to the people, saying: 'What man *is there* who has built a new house and has not dedicated it? Let him go and return to his house, lest he die in the battle and another man dedicate it'" Deut 20:5	Jesus -> Disciples = Apostles, Matt 10:1-5; Mark 6:7; Luke 9:1-2 Jesus -> Seventy others, Luke 10:1 Jesus -> Eleven + 2 from road to Emmaus + others with them, Luke 24:33-36 Apostles + 120, Acts 1:15 Seven deacons, Acts 6:5-6; 8:5ff. All the disciples, except Apostles, Acts 8:1, 4 Saul = Paul, Acts 9:15-16 Paul, Barnabas + their many companions, Acts 13:2-3 Evangelist, Acts 21:8 Prophet, Acts 21:10 Preacher, apostle, teacher, 1 Tim 2:7; 2 Tim 1:11 Eph 4:11: Apostles; Prophets; Evangelists; Pastors; Teachers.
Need fearless people and leaders	Similarity	To people: "Do not be afraid or tremble," Deut 31:6 (cf. Isa 40:9) To Joshua: "Do not fear or be dismayed," Deut 31:8	As evangelism training: "Do not fear them," Matt 10:26, 28, 31 To Paul: "Do not be afraid *any longer*, but go on speaking and do not be silent; for I am with you," Acts 18:9-10

Aspects		Deuteronomic	New Testament
Promised blessing or persecution	Dissimilarity	**For obedience**: "And all these blessings shall come upon you and overtake you, because you obey the voice of the LORD your God: ... The LORD will cause your enemies who rise against you to be defeated before your face; they shall come out against you one way and flee before you seven ways. ... Then all peoples of the earth shall see that you are called by the name of the LORD, and they shall be afraid of you," Deut 28:2, 7, 10 **For disobedience**: "But it shall come to pass, if you do not obey the voice of the LORD your God, to observe carefully all His commandments and His statutes which I command you today, that all these curses will come upon you and overtake you: ... The LORD will cause you to be defeated before your enemies; you shall go out one way against them and flee seven ways before them; and you shall become troublesome to all the kingdoms of the earth, Because you did not serve the LORD your God with joy and gladness of heart, for the abundance of everything, therefore you shall serve your enemies, whom the LORD will send against you, in hunger, in thirst, in nakedness, and in need of everything; and He will put a yoke of iron on your neck until He has destroyed you," Deut 28:15, 25, 47-48 Yet notice some of the Psalms on persecution: Psa 80:5-6; 83:1-4; 94:4-5; etc.	**For obedience**: "But beware of men, for they will deliver you up to councils and scourge you in their synagogues. You will be brought before governors and kings for My sake, as a testimony to them and to the Gentiles. But when they deliver you up, do not worry about how or what you should speak. For it will be given to you in that hour what you should speak; for it is not you who speak, but the Spirit of your Father who speaks in you. Now brother will deliver up brother to death, and a father *his* child; and children will rise up against parents and cause them to be put to death. And you will be hated by all for My name's sake. But he who endures to the end will be saved," Matt 10:17-22 **For obedience**: "Yet if *anyone suffers* as a Christian, let him not be ashamed, but let him glorify God in this matter. For the time *has come* for judgment to begin at the house of God; and if *it begins* with us first, what will *be* the end of those who do not obey the gospel of God? Now 'If the righteous one is scarcely saved, Where will the ungodly and the sinner appear?' Therefore let those who suffer according to the will of God commit their souls *to Him* in doing good, as to a faithful Creator," 1 Pet 4:16-19
Result	Dis-similarity	Conquer land and possess it; Possess the Lord's promised land [or in the crusades: the "Holy Land"]	Conquer souls: Fish for men, Matt 4:19; Mark 1:17 Win disciples, Matt 28:19-20 Take men alive, Luke 5:10 Snatch souls from the fire, Jude 22-23

b.   The "Conquest Tread" also coincides with Paul's repeated use of military imagery to describe the spiritual battle (2 Cor 10:3-5; Eph 6:10-20; etc.; cf. Jer 1:9-10)

c.   The "Conquest Tread" also coincides with prior proto-Evangelical and Evangelical military imagery:

   1)   In 1326-1327, a so-called "heretical" sect appeared in Portugal called "Gendarmes de Jesus" [lit. "Police (armed-people) of Jesus"]; this movement spread throughout Tuscany and Senes.[817]

   Armed with "the sword of the Spirit, which is the Word of God," Eph 6:17

   2)   William Booth's "Salvation Army"

   3)   L.R. Scarborough speaking of the Great Commission as "the Martial Note and Conquest Tread"[818]

   4)   The post-World War II missions and evangelism agencies called Far Eastern Gospel Crusade, Campus Crusade for Christ, Operation Mobilization, etc.

   5)   Billy Graham calling his revival meetings "crusades"

   In this regard, there is an interesting photo of Billy Graham, Chuck Templeton, and Youth for Christ founder, Torrey Johnson, looking at a map as they planned their 1946 post-WWII offensive of the Gospel in Europe.[819]

---

[817]Jean Crespin, *Histoire des vrays Tesmoins de la verite de l'evangile, qui de leur sang l'ont signée, depuis Jean Hus iusques autemps present* (Geneva, 1570; reproduction, Liège, 1964).

[818]"It is not wise to say that *soul winning* is the main thing or that *soul building* is the main thing. They are Siamese twins of God's gospel, going hand in hand, and they ought to keep up with each other.... And this leads me to say that the main thing in the Kingdom of God is the evangelistic spirit, the martial note and conquest tread" (L. R. Scarborough, *Recruits for World Conquest* [New York: Revell, 1914], 58).

[819]Billy Graham, *Just as I Am* (San Francisco: HarperCollins, 1997), photo facing page 105.

I included a section in my *Examining Billy Graham's Theology of Evangelism* titled "Graham's World Conquest Methodology."[820]

6) I myself led an evangelism team, the "Trinity Evangelistic Team" or "TET" for short, which we called the "TET Offensive," based on the Vietnam War

7) It is amazing how military imagery seems to naturally parallel aggressive evangelism!

2. **Matthew 28:19-20**—locating OT parallels for Matthew's Great Commission emphasis depends on how it is translated[821] (notice how the translation colors the parallels):

a. The Latin tradition translated Matthew 28:19's μαθητεύω as *docete* or "teach":

1) This translation parallels Deuteronomy's use of *doceo* in Deut 4:1, in which Moses was a spokesperson of God to teach commands and statutes to the people of Israel

2) Likewise, it is understandable that Jerome looked at Jesus as a second Lawgiver, merely giving a new Law to the Church

3) This author wonders how the various Donatist translations dealt with this important verb in Matthew 28:19; furthermore, how much did Jerome's sacramental theology influence his compiling of the Latin Vulgate for the Bishop of Rome, Damasus?[822]

4) If such was the case, that Jerome's theology influenced his translation of this important word, then his influence on the Western Church lasted more than a millennia!

b. Calvin's 1560 French Geneva Bible translated μαθητεύω as "indoctrinate":

1) English Bibles from Wycliffe's 2nd edition to the King James Version also used "teach" in Matthew 28, as that followed "docete" in the Latin Vulgate

2) This translation parallels Deut 6:7 addressed to all fathers, "You shall teach them [*shanan*] diligently to your sons and shall talk of them…"

3) The message to be taught are "these words which I am commanding you" (Deut 6:6)

4) It must be noted that the emphasis of Deut 6:7 is within the family unit, whereas the emphasis of Matt 28 is "all nations"—quite a difference in scope

c. The King James Version translated μαθητεύω as "teach":

1) This translation parallels Deut 4:14, where Moses was commanded by God to teach the people, "And the LORD commanded me at that time to teach [*lamad*] you statutes and judgments, that ye might do them in the land whither ye go over to possess it"

2) Whereas in the Old Covenant, commissionings were generally to specific people (in this case Moses), under the Great Commission of Jesus, all of Christ's followers are commanded to teach all nations

3) Similarly, in this specific verse, the command is directed for Moses to teach the sons of Israel. However, the impact would be felt by the nations around (Deut 4:6), similarly to the prayer of Solomon at the dedication of the Temple (2 Chron 6:32-33)

d. Webster's Bible of 1833 translated μαθητεύω as "disciple":

1) Webster broke from Jerome's precedent, as lodged in the KJV

---

[820]Thomas P. Johnston, *Examining Billy Graham's Theology of Evangelism* (Eugene, OR: Wipf & Stock, 2003), 19-24.

[821]For example, see Chapter 26 on the history of translations of Matt 28:19.

[822]If Migne's Vulgate is accurate, it appears that a sacramentalism crept into the translations of Deuteronomy, for example in Deut 4:8 and 11:32, in translating "statutes" (Heb. *choq*) as "ceremonies": cf. the 1899 Douai-Rheims translation of Deut 4:8, "For what other nation is there so renowned that hath ceremonies, and just judgments, and all the law, which I will set forth this day before your eyes?" and of Deut 11:32, "See therefore that you fulfill the ceremonies and judgments, which I shall set this day before you." The *Nova Vulgata*, approved by Pope John Paul II (1982), a methodical revision of the Migne edition Vulgate, changed this word in 4:8 from "caeremonias" to "praecepta" and in 11:32 from "caeremonias" to "omnia praecepta" (surprisingly listen to this anathema from the Fourth Session of the Council of Trent [1546], "If anyone does not accept as sacred and canonical the aforesaid books in their entirety and with all their parts, as they have been accustomed to be read in the Catholic Church and as they are contained in the old Latin Vulgate Edition, and knowingly and deliberately rejects the aforesaid traditions, let him be anathema" [19th Ecumenical Council, the Council of Trent; available from: http://www.forerunner.com/chalcedon/ X0020_15._Council_of_Trent.html (online); accessed 8 Jan 2005; Internet]).

2) While quite similar to the word "teach", visions of Greek peripatetic learning can be gleaned from this term, along with parallels in the OT, such as Moses and Joshua, Elijah and Elisha, the sons of the prophets, etc.

3) Psa 105:1, "Make known His deeds among the peoples"

   a) Make known comes from the Hebrew *yada'* (hiphil imperative masculine plural), meaning (*Abridged Brown-Driver-Briggs*) make known, declare, teach, make one known, teach the difference between, discriminate between

   b) Slightly more receptor-oriented than straight teaching

e. Darby's French NT translation of 1859 translated μαθητεύω "make disciples," which came into English Bibles through Darby's 1884 English translation, and continues to be the prominent use as a translation of μαθητεύω today:

   1) The emphasis moved from teaching the word of God, to seeking and/or developing a human methodology of "teaching to obey"

   2) Hence, the first edition of A.B. Bruce's *The Training of the Twelve* appeared in 1872, analyzing the reproducible [human] methods of Jesus to "make disciples"

   3) However, "make disciples" may be considered a synonym of "win disciples" (following NIV's translation of Acts 14:21), in which case instantaneous conversion is emphasized—it would seem that the Greek aorist tense and the French word "faites" (from which Darby introduced the English term "make") have more of a punctiliar emphasis, rather than the strong linear emphasis generally associated with "make disciples" (See much more detail here in Chapter 26)

f. The "go" and the "all nations" have their earliest antecedent Scripture in God's call of Abraham (Gen 12:1-3):

   1) "All authority has been given to Me in heaven and on earth:
      2 Chron 17:7, officials are commissioned by King Jehoshaphat in the third year of his reign to teach the Law of the Lord
      2 Chron 30:6, couriers are commissioned and commanded by King Hezekiah with a proclamation to repent and return to God

   2) "Go"
      Gen 12:1, "Go forth from your country"
      Deut 1:8, "Go in and possess…", 21, "Go up, take possession…":
      (1) Deut 4:1, "that you may live and go in and take possession"; 6:18, "that you may go in and possess the good land"; 8:1; 9:1, 23; 10:11; 11:8, 31
      (2) Deut 21:10, "When you go out to battle against your enemies"; 23:9, "When you go out as an army against your enemies"
      2 Chron 17:7, King Jehoshaphat sent officials
      2 Chron 30:6, King Hezekiah sent couriers
      Isaiah 40:9, "Get yourself up"
      Jonah 1:2, "Arise, go"
      Jonah 3:2, "Arise, go"

   3) "teach-win disciples"

      a) 2 Chron 17:7-9, King Jehoshaphat sent revival teams throughout the land of Judah and Israel to teach the people:
         (1) Note the emphasis on "teach" in verse 9, "And they taught in Judah, *having* the book of the law of the LORD with them; and they went throughout all the cities of Judah and taught among the people"

      b) 2 Chron 30:6, King Hezekiah, of Judah, sent couriers to call the Israelites to repent, return to the Lord, and come to the Passover celebration, "Come to the feast" (cf. Luke 14:16-24)

   4) "all the nations"
      a) Gen 12:3, "And in you all the families of the earth will be blessed."
      b) Deut 28:65, "Among those nations [to whom the Lord would scatter His people as a cure]"

    c) 2 Chron 6:32-33, "Also concerning the foreigner who is not from Thy people Israel, when he comes from a far country for Thy great name's sake and Thy mighty hand and Thine outstretched arm, when they come and pray toward this house, [33] then hear Thou from heaven, from Thy dwelling place, and do according to all for which the foreigner calls to Thee, in order that all the peoples of the earth may know Thy name, and fear Thee, as *do* Thy people Israel, and that they may know that this house which I have built is called by Thy name"

    d) Psa 96:3, "Tell of His glory among the nations, His wonderful deeds among all the peoples"

    e) Psa 105:1, "Make known His deeds among the peoples"

    f) Isa 42:4, "καὶ ἐπὶ τῷ ὀνόματι αὐτοῦ ἔθνη ἐλπιοῦσιν"—and in his name the nations will hope

g. On Accommodation and Syncretism: Deut 18:9 as an antithetical parallel to Matt 28:19-20: Introduction: Notice the duality of verbs and the antithetical content of the instruction:

Comparing Matt 28, Mark 16 with Deut 18:9

	Matthew 28	Mark 16	Deut 18:9
Command to go: —Context: when they enter the land	"Go therefore and make disciples of all the nations"	"Go into all the world and preach the gospel to every creature"	"When you come into the land which the LORD your God is giving you"
What to do: —No Deuteronomic parallel	(2) "Win disciples" (3) "Baptizing them in the name of the Father and of the Son and of the Holy Spirit"	(1) "Preach the Gospel" (2) "He who believes" (3) "And is baptized will be saved" (4) "He who does not believe will be condemned"	
Follow-up verbs: —Cautionary command	"Teaching them to observe" BYZ: διδάσκοντες αὐτοὺς τηρεῖν		"You shall not learn to follow" LXX: οὐ μαθήσῃ ποιεῖν
Follow-up content: —Cautionary content	"All things that I have commanded you" BYZ: πάντα ὅσα ἐνετειλάμην ὑμῖν		"The abominations of those nations" LXX: κατὰ τὰ βδελύγματα τῶν ἐθνῶν ἐκείνων
Promise: —No Deuteronomic parallel	"And lo, I am with you always, *even* to the end of the age." Amen"		

Considering applications related to syncretism and accommodation from Deut 18:9:

    a) For evangelism: It appears that when one goes out and seeks to share the Gospel and engage another culture, there is the tension between the reproach of the Gospel and acceptance of "neutral" cultural norms that are tangential to the Gospel, and may even be used as bridges for the Gospel. Deut 18:9 provides a warning of going too far

    b) In missions: The same problem of accommodation or syncretism exists in seeking to engage culture, as noted above under evangelism. In this case it is often in reference with the predominant religious belief-system of a given culture. Again, Deut 18:9 provides an appropriate cautionary warning

    c) In apologetics: Often, as apologetics is viewed primarily as a means of evangelism, rather than as a means of edification, those who practice apologetics often gravitate toward a type of syncretism or accommodation of ideas. The very real danger is in allowing the pagan beliefs to frame the question, rather than Scripture

3. **Mark 16:15**:

    a. May glean from Jonah 3:2, "Arise, go to Nineveh the great city and proclaim to it the proclamation which I am going to tell you"

        1) Arise and go = "go"

        2) Specific—to Nineveh (virtually uttermost parts of the earth at the time) = "into all the world"

        3) Proclaim (κηρύσσω) the proclamation (κήρυγμα) = "preach [κηρύσσω] the Gospel"

  b. May glean from the proclamational verses in the Psalms and Isaiah as noted above, especially perhaps Psa 96:2-3:
    1) "Preach the Gospel"—"Evangelize of His salvation from day to day"
    2) "Into all the world"—"Tell of His glory among the nations"
    3) "To all creation"—"His wonderful deeds among all the peoples."

  c. As far as the recipient of the message, the following may be parallels:
  [See especially "Sociological extent of the Great Commission"]
    1) "In the sight of the peoples who will hear all these statutes," Deut 4:6

4. **Luke 24:46-48**:

  a. May glean from 2 Chron 30:1-12, esp. v 6:

    1) The king (Hezekiah) commissioned and commanded couriers

      a) Verse 6 reads (in English Geneva Bible), "So the postes went with letters by the commission of the King, and his princes, throughout all Israel and Iudah, and with the commandement of the King, saying, Ye children of Israel, turne againe vnto the Lord God of Abraham, Izhak, and Israel, and he will returne to the remnant that are escaped of you, out of ye hands of the Kings of Asshur"

      b) Notice:
        1) The messengers (of the King's proclamation) are likened to swift-footed couriers
        2) They are both commissioned and commanded
        3) Their message was the proclamation of the King

    2) To go from city-to-city, not only in Judah, but also in Samaria (vv 10-11, "Through the country of Ephraim and Manasseh, and as far as Zebulun")

    3) With a proclamation (*kerygma*) to repent (turn) and obey the Lord (in observing Passover in Jerusalem)

  b. The following verses in Luke's Great Commission may also glean from numerous other verses:

    1) Luke 24:46, "Thus it is written, that the Christ would suffer and rise again from the dead the third day," Isa 52:13-53:12

    2) Luke 24:47:

      a) "And that repentance for forgiveness of sins"
        (1) Note the condition of repentance for forgiveness:
          2 Chron 7:14, "and My people who are called by My name humble themselves and pray and seek My face and turn from their wicked ways, then I will hear from heaven, will forgive their sin and will heal their land"
          Isa 59:20, "'And a Redeemer will come to Zion, And to those who turn from transgression [ἀποστρέψει ἀσεβείας] in Jacob,' declares the LORD"
          Jer 36:3, "Perhaps the house of Judah will hear all the calamity which I plan to bring on them, in order that every man will turn from his evil way; then I will forgive their iniquity and their sin"
        (2) Jer 31:34, "for I will forgive their iniquity, and their sin I will remember no more"

      b) "would be proclaimed in His name to all the nations," Isa 42:9-12
        (1) See all the OT proclamational verses listed for Matthew above, and in Chapters 2, 7, and earlier in this chapter

      c) "beginning from Jerusalem," Psa 20:2; 128:5; 134:3; 135:21; Isa 59:20
        (1) Micah 4:2, "For from Zion will go forth the law, Even the word of the LORD from Jerusalem"

    3) Luke 24:48, "You are witnesses of these things" (cf. Deut 4:35)
      a) Isa 43:10, "'You are My witnesses,' declares the LORD, 'And My servant whom I have chosen, In order that you may know and believe Me, And understand that I am He'"
      b) Isa 43:12, "'It is I who have declared and saved and proclaimed, And there was no strange *god* among you; So you are My witnesses,' declares the LORD, 'And I am God'"

c) Isa 44:8,. "Do not tremble and do not be afraid; Have I not long since announced it to you and declared it? And you are My witnesses. Is there any God besides Me, Or is there any *other* Rock? I know of none"

d) Luke 24:49, "And behold, I am sending forth the promise of My Father upon you," Joel 2:28-29

5. **John 20:21**, "Peace *be* with you; as the Father has sent Me, I also send you"

Deut 18:18-19, "I will raise up a prophet from among their countrymen like you, and I will put My words in his mouth, and he shall speak to them all that I command him. It shall come about that whoever will not listen to My words which he shall speak in My name, I Myself will require *it* of him."

Isa 40:11, "Like a shepherd He will tend His flock, In His arm He will gather the lambs And carry *them* in His bosom; He will gently lead the nursing *ewes*"

Jer 23:3-6 "'Then I Myself shall gather the remnant of My flock out of all the countries where I have driven them and shall bring them back to their pasture; and they will be fruitful and multiply. I shall also raise up shepherds over them and they will tend them; and they will not be afraid any longer, nor be terrified, nor will any be missing,' declares the LORD. 'Behold, *the* days are coming,' declares the LORD, 'When I shall raise up for David a righteous Branch; And He will reign as king and act wisely And do justice and righteousness in the land. In His days Judah will be saved, And Israel will dwell securely; And this is His name by which He will be called, "The LORD our righteousness."'"

Ezek 34:11-16, "For thus says the Lord God, 'Behold, I Myself will search for My sheep and seek them out. As a shepherd cares for his herd in the day when he is among his scattered sheep, so I will care for My sheep and will deliver them from all the places to which they were scattered on a cloudy and gloomy day. And I will bring them out from the peoples and gather them from the countries and bring them to their own land; and I will feed them on the mountains of Israel, by the streams, and in all the inhabited places of the land. I will feed them in a good pasture, and their grazing ground will be on the mountain heights of Israel. There they will lie down in good grazing ground, and they will feed in rich pasture on the mountains of Israel. I will feed My flock and I will lead them to rest,' declares the Lord God. 'I will seek the lost, bring back the scattered, bind up the broken, and strengthen the sick; but the fat and the strong I will destroy. I will feed them with judgment.'"

6. **Acts 1:8** (see Mark and Luke above)

a. Further thoughts about "the ends of the earth" in Acts 1:8:
1) The message of the Bible is addressed to the "earth," Deut 32:1; Isa 1:2
2) It is through this message that Abraham's blessing reaches "all the families of the earth," Gen 12:3
3) This message of the Bible, when proclaimed in all the earth, actually feeds and nurtures the earth, Deut 32:1-2; Isa 55:10-11

7. Furthermore, fulfilling the Great Commission and the Curses of Deuteronomy 28:

a. Mentioned above (in the section describing Matthew 28) is the concern that the geographic expansion mentioned in the curses of Deuteronomy 28 was included in Matthew's Great Commission, through the words "of/from all nations" (πάντα τὰ ἔθνη) in Matthew 28:19:

1) As part of the curse in the book of Deuteronomy, God's disobedient people were to be scattered:
a) Deut 28:64, "Among all people" (Heb 'am; Gk εἰς πάντα τὰ ἔθνη)
b) Deut 28:65, "Among the nations" (Heb gowi; Gk ἐν τοῖς ἔθνεσιν)
c) Deut 30:3, to "all the peoples" (Heb 'am; Gk ἐκ πάντων τῶν ἐθνῶν)

2) Therefore, as it were, Jesus was calling the results of the Deuteronomic curse upon His disciples when He sent them out:
a) Perhaps this was why the Jerusalem Jews reacted so negatively to Paul when he repeated the words of God, "Go! For I will send you far away to the Gentiles," Acts 22:21
b) The Jews wanted capital punishment for Paul
c) Notice the exact words in the Greek: "Πορεύου, ὅτι ἐγὼ εἰς ἔθνη μακρὰν ἐξαποστελῶ σε," Acts 22:21

        d) Notice Deuteronomy 28:37, "among all the people where the LORD will drive [Darby: 'lead'] you" [ἐν πᾶσιν τοῖς ἔθνεσιν εἰς οὓς ἂν ἀπαγάγῃ σε κύριος ἐκεῖ]

  b. How about the three curses: Hunger—Thirst—Nakedness?

     1) As the curse of God, Deut 28:47-48

     2) The promise of Christ:
        a) Matt 6:31-33
        b) cf. John 6:35

     3) The result in Paul's life of the fulfilling the Great Commission:
        a) 1 Cor 4:11
        b) 2 Cor 11:27

     4) Care for others in the life of the true believer:
        a) Care for the traveling evangelists, Matt 10:40-42
        b) Care for others, Matt 25:35-38, 41-44

  c. There is more material to be uncovered as to the relationship of the Great Commission, evangelizing, and NT persecution for evangelizing (e.g. Rom 8:36)

D. Other Commands to "Go" in the Bible:[823]

"Go" implies not only a change in geography, but the making a concerted effort!

Stephen F. Olford in *The Secret of Soul-Winning* discusses "The Soul-Winner's Travail." His comments are based on 1 Thess 2:9:

> The expression "travail" here denoted the toil, labor, and weariness which were involved in bringing those men and women at Thessalonica to a personal knowledge of Christ. Souls are not easily won, although they may appear to be when we observe the glamorized mass evangelism of a modern age. Men can never be born into the kingdom of God without tears and travail. Even if the evangelist does not pay the price, God has His own who are prepared to suffer with Christ in order to bring to birth His redemptive purposes in the world.[824]

1. Jesus commands the Christian to "Go!" Matt 28:19-20, Mark 16:15
    Please note the unfortunate downgrade of the term "Go" which is sometimes found in lifestyle literature, above in this chapter: "Some Issues in the Study of the Great Commission," "1. Lifestyle or Initiative?"

2. The lost need someone to make an effort to reach them:

  a. The principle:
     1) "The harvest is plentiful but the laborers are few," Matt 9:36-38, Luke 10:2
     2) "I sent you to reap that for which you have not labored; others have labored, and you have entered into their labor," John 4:38
     3) "And how shall they preach unless they are sent?" Rom 10:14-15
     4) "But by the grace of God I am what I am, and His grace toward me did not prove vain; but I labored even more than all of them, yet not I, but the grace of God with me," 1 Cor 15:10
     5) "Having shod your feet with the preparation of the Gospel of peace," Eph 6:15
     6) "Always being ready to make a defense to every one who asks," 1 Pet 3:15

  b. The spheres:
     1) Going to one's family, Mark 5:19
     2) Going to the next town, Luke 4:43-44
     3) Going to another region, 2 Cor 10:15-16
     4) Going to the uttermost parts of the earth, Matt 28:19-20, Mark 16:15, Acts 1:8

---

[823]A study of the word "Go" in the Bible proves very enlightening, as this section is only a mere sampling.

[824]Stephen F. Olford, *The Secret of Soul-Winning* (Chicago: Moody, 1963), 79. Olford's comments do not discount the effectiveness of mass evangelism as seen in the Bible and throughout the history of the church. However, for those who preach the Gospel to their neighbor or to many in an auditorium, there is travail of soul.

    c. The reality:
        1) Being driven to all nations in Deut 28 is listed as one of the curses of God:
            a) "And you shall become a horror, a proverb, and a taunt among all the people where the LORD will drive you" Deut 28:37
            b) "Moreover, the LORD will scatter you among all peoples, from one end of the earth to the other end of the earth; and there you shall serve other gods, wood and stone, which you or your fathers have not known. And among those nations you shall find no rest" Deut 28:64-65a
        2) Therefore, it cannot be expected to be an easy thing to "go to all nations"—yet it is commanded!

3. Biblical examples of making an effort:
    a. In the ministry of Jesus, Mark 1:38; Luke 4:42-44
    b. In the evangelism of the Apostle Paul, 1 Cor 9:16, 22; 10:33; 2 Cor 5:9, "nous nous efforçons [we force ourselves],"[825] Col 1:29, "And for this purpose also I labor," 1 Thess 2:9-10 (cf. Acts 18:9-11)

4. Some biblical examples of going:

    a. In the OT: Isa 6:8-9; 52:7; 55:12; Jer 1:7; Ezek 2:3; 3:3; 33:2, Jonah 1:2; 3:2

    b. In the NT: Jesus, the disciples (Matt 10; Mark 6; Luke 9, 10), the apostles after Pentecost, Stephen, Philip, Barnabas, Paul (see below)

    c. Several people took the initiative for salvation or eternal life:
        1) The Rich Young Ruler, Mark 10:17-22, Luke 18:18-23
        2) Luke 10:57-62, Several people come to Jesus after He says "Follow-Me" (v. 59).
        3) Nicodemus, John 3:1-21
        4) The jailer came to Paul and Barnabas for salvation, Acts 16:30

Evaluation: There is an effort to be made in reaching out to the lost. In a few cases, some came to Jesus for salvation or eternal life. In the same way, sometimes people come to those who are aggressively seeking the lost for salvation (1 Pet 3:15).[826] These opportunities are the exception and not the rule, nor the command:

> Johan Lukasse applied this principle of "going" to the local church:
>
> > Often we have reversed the command of Jesus Christ, "Go into all the world and preach the good news to all creation" (Mk. 16:15), by turning this 'go' evangelism into 'come' evangelism. We invite people to attend a Sunday service, to come to hear the preacher, to come to join this or that, but Jesus said, "Go." We need to visit people and build up relationships and introduce them to Christ.[827]

E. Examples of obedience to the Great Commission:

1. Two remarkable examples:
    a. Paul at the marketplace every day, Acts 17:16-17
    b. Paul going house-to-house, Acts 20:20-21 (cf. Acts 5:42)

2. Select summary statements of ministry in Luke-Acts:
    Luke 4:15, "And He *began* **teaching** in their synagogues and was praised by all"
    Luke 4:40, "So He kept on **preaching** in the synagogues of Judea"
    Luke 8:1, "Soon afterwards, He *began* going around from one city and village to another, **proclaiming and preaching [evangelizing] the kingdom of God**. The twelve were with Him"
    Luke 9:2, "And He sent them out to proclaim the kingdom of God and to perform healing"
    Luke 9:6, "Departing, they *began* going throughout the villages, preaching the gospel and healing everywhere"

---

[825]From *Nouvelle Edition the Genève* (Société Biblique de Genève, 1979). The French John Darby (1800-1882) translation is even more emphatic here, "nous nous appliquons avec ardeur [we apply ourselves with zeal]." The Greek φιλοτιμούμεθα indicates the idea of aspiration, which is emphasized in the French translation tradition.

[826]Billy Graham is such an example. In his book, *How To Be Born Again* (Waco, TX: Word, 1977), 19-20, Dr. Graham spoke of a famous scientist from an eastern university who asked to see him one day. He had seen Billy Graham on television and felt that the evangelist knew the meaning of life. Those who are sowing the seed, will reap with joy.

[827]John Lukasse, *Churches with Roots* (Bromley, Kent, England: MARC, 1990), 108-09.

Luke 10, 1, "Now after this the Lord appointed seventy others, and sent them in pairs ahead of Him to every city and place where He Himself was going to come"

Luke 13:10, "And He was teaching in one of the synagogues on the Sabbath"

Luke 13:22, "And He was passing through from one city and village to another, teaching, and proceeding on His way to Jerusalem"

Luke 20:1, "On one of the days while He was teaching the people in the temple and preaching the gospel, the chief priests and the scribes with the elders confronted *Him*"

Acts 4:31, "And when they had prayed, the place where they had gathered together was shaken, and they were all filled with the Holy Spirit and *began* to **speak the word of God** with boldness"

Acts 5:42, "And every day, in the temple and from house to house, they kept right on **teaching and preaching [evangelizing] Jesus *as* the Christ**"

Acts 8:4-5, "Therefore, those who had been scattered went about **preaching [evangelizing] the word**. Philip went down to the city of Samaria and *began* **proclaiming Christ** to them"

Acts 8:25, "So, when they had **solemnly testified and spoken the word of the Lord**, they started back to Jerusalem, and were **preaching the gospel [evangelizing]** to many villages of the Samaritans"

Acts 8:40, "But Philip found himself at Azotus, and as he passed through he kept **preaching the gospel [evangelizing]** to all the cities until he came to Caesarea"

Acts 9:27, "But Barnabas took hold of him and brought him to the apostles and described to them how he had seen the Lord on the road, and that He had talked to him, and how at Damascus he had **spoken out boldly in the name of Jesus**"

Acts 9:28, "And he was with them, moving about freely in Jerusalem, **speaking out boldly in the name of the Lord**"

Acts 11:20, "But there were some of them, men of Cyprus and Cyrene, who came to Antioch and *began* **speaking** to the Greeks also, **preaching the Lord Jesus**"

Acts 13:5, "When they reached Salamis, they *began* to **proclaim [*kataggello*] the word of God** in the synagogues of the Jews"

Acts 14:7, "and there they continued to **preach the gospel [evangelize]**"

Acts 14:21 (NIV), "They **preached the good news** in [**evangelized**] that city and **won** a large number of **disciples**. Then they returned to Lystra, Iconium and Antioch"

Acts 14:25, "When they had **spoken the word** in Perga, they went down to Attalia"

Acts 15:35, "But Paul and Barnabas stayed in Antioch, **teaching** and **preaching [evangelizing]** with many others also, the word of the Lord."

Acts 15:36, "Let us return and visit the brethren in every city in which we **proclaimed [*kataggello*] the word of the Lord**, *and see* how they are."

Acts 16:6, "They passed through the Phrygian and Galatian region, having been forbidden by the Holy Spirit to **speak the word** in Asia"

Acts 16:10, "When he had seen the vision, immediately we sought to go into Macedonia, concluding that God had called us to **preach the gospel [evangelize]** to them"

Acts 17:13, "But when the Jews of Thessalonica found out that **the word of God had been proclaimed [*kataggello*]** by Paul in Berea also, they came there as well, agitating and stirring up the crowds"

Acts 18:11, "And he settled *there* a year and six months, **teaching the word of God** among them" (note that his purpose for teaching was evangelistic, Acts 18:10, "for I have many people in this city")

Acts 19:8, "And he entered the synagogue and continued speaking out boldly for three months, **reasoning and persuading *them* about the kingdom of God**"

Acts 20:20-21, "How I did not shrink from **declaring to you anything that was profitable**, and **teaching** you publicly and from house to house, **solemnly testifying** to both Jews and Greeks of repentance toward God and faith in our Lord Jesus Christ"

Acts 20:27, "For I did not shrink from **declaring to you the whole purpose of God**"

Acts 24:24, "But some days later, Felix arrived with Drusilla, his wife who was a Jewess, and sent for Paul, and **heard him *speak* about faith in Christ Jesus**"

Acts 26:20, "but *kept* **declaring** both to those of Damascus first, and *also* at Jerusalem and *then* throughout all the region of Judea, and *even* to the Gentiles, that **they should repent and turn to God**, performing deeds appropriate to repentance"

Acts 28:31, "**preaching the kingdom of God and teaching concerning the Lord Jesus Christ** with all openness, unhindered"

Summation of the 24 summary statements in Acts:

Method: evangelize (8 times); speak (5 times); teaching (4 times); proclaim [*kataggello*] (thrice); declare (thrice); bold speech (twice); solemnly testify (twice); preaching (once); reason and persuade (once); listen [hear] (once)

Message: word of God (4 times); word of the Lord (3 times); word (3 times); Lord Jesus (once); Lord Jesus Christ (once); Christ (once); Jesus as the Christ (once); name of Jesus (once); name of the Lord (once); faith in Christ Jesus (once); kingdom of God (twice); repent and turn to God (once); repentance toward God and faith in our Lord Jesus Christ (once); the whole purpose of God (once)

3. Other examples of obedience:
    a.   Mark 5:20; Luke 8:39
    b.   Mark 16:10, 20
    c.   1 Cor 16:9-10
    d.   Gal 4:13
    e.   1 Thess 2:1-2

4. Examples of disobeying the command (or opportunity) to preach:
    1)   Jonah, Jonah 1:2-3
    2)   The case of the fearful "rulers" who would not confess Christ openly for fear of the Jews, John 12:42-43 (cf. John 7:13; 19:38):

    "Nevertheless many even of the rulers believed in Him, but because of the Pharisees they were not confessing *Him*, lest they should be put out of the synagogue; for they loved the approval of men rather than the approval of God."

    3)   The case of Peter denying Christ, Matt 26:69-75 and parallels
    4)   The case of John Mark withdrawing from the missionary journey, Acts 13:13; 15:38
    5)   The case of Paul's fear and silence, Acts 18:9-10

F.   Results of obedience:[828]

1. Souls are saved (cf. Psa 51:13; Mal 2:6):
    Acts 2:41, So then, those who had received his word were baptized; and that day there were added about three thousand souls"
    Acts 11:21, "And the hand of the Lord was with them, and a large number who believed turned to the Lord"

2. Rejoicing:
    Acts 8:8, "So there was much rejoicing in that city"
    Acts 8:40, "and the eunuch no longer saw him [Philip], but went on his way rejoicing"
    Acts 13:52, "And the disciples were continually filled with joy and with the Holy Spirit"

3. Churches are planted:
    Acts 16:40, "They went out of the prison and entered *the house of* Lydia, and when they saw the brethren, they encouraged them and departed"
    Acts 18:7-8, "Then he left there and went to the house of a man named Titius Justus, a worshiper of God, whose house was next to the synagogue. Crispus, the leader of the synagogue, believed in the Lord with all his household, and many of the Corinthians when they heard were believing and being baptized"

4. Churches grow:
    Acts 2:47, "So then, those who had received his word were baptized; and that day there were added about three thousand souls"
    Acts 5:14, "And all the more believers in the Lord, multitudes of men and women, were constantly added to *their number*"

G.   Obedience to the Great Commission relates to other aspects of following Christ:

Introduction:

a.   Obedience to the Great Commission does not compete with or contradict other commands

b.   Obedience to the Great Commission does not conflict with or alter the other commands of Scripture
    1)   By the way, false dichotomies and segmentations abound with virtually every other command in Scripture, from theological to practical

---

[828]The results of disobedience in fulfilling this command are very sad. See Chapter 20, "Results, Reactions, and Responses," D. 5, "The Results of No Verbal Witness of God's Word."

    c. Obedience to the Great Commission, in fact, compliments all the other commands of Scripture and motivates the Christian to obey them

1. Verbal proclamation follows the purpose of Jesus on earth:
    a. His **revelatory** purpose, Matt 17:5, Mark 1:11, John 12:45; 14:9
    b. His **redemptive** purpose, Mark 10:45, John. 1:29
    c. His **prophetic** purpose, Luke 24:44 (cf. John 19:28, 1 Cor 15:3-4)
    d. His **evangelistic** purpose, Luke 4:43-44 (cf. Matt 4:17, 9:35, Mark 1:14-15)
    e. His **exemplary** purpose, John 13:14-15 (cf. Mark 10:45, John 20:21, 1 Cor 11:1)

2. Verbal proclamation follows the example of Jesus on earth (cannot have *imitatio Christi*—the imitation of Christ without aggressive proclamational evangelism):

    a. Following Jesus' example in evangelism, Mark 10:45, Luke 4:43-44; John 20:21

    b. Following Jesus' example in obedience:
       1) Jesus' submission to God the Father's will, Matt 26:42, John 17:4, Phil 2:7
       2) Jesus learned obedience, Heb 5:8
       3) The importance of obedience for the Christian, John 3:36, 13:17, 14:21, 23-24, James. 1:22, 1 John 2:3-6, 5:3, 3 John 6, Rev 14:12

    c. Following Jesus' example of service:
       1) Jesus came to serve, Mark 10:45
       2) Evangelism is serving others, I Pet. 1:12
       3) Evangelism allows Christ to work through us, Rom 15:18

3. Verbal proclamation glorifies God:
    a. The Christian is commanded to glorify God, 1 Cor 10:31, Col 3:17, 1 Pet 4:11
    b. Evangelism glorifies God, John 15:8 (cf. John 4:36, "fruit for life eternal")

Conclusion: Millard J. Erickson wrote, "This was the final point Jesus made to His disciples. It appears that He regarded evangelism as the very reason for their being."[829]

Note the Great Commission and Logic's Square of Opposition…

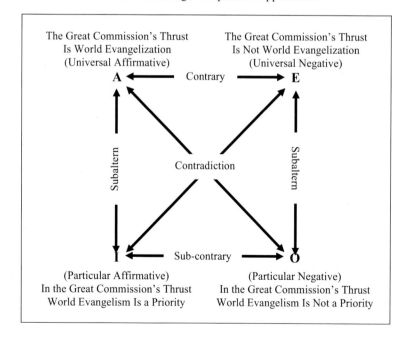

The Great Commission's Thrust Is World Evangelization (Universal Affirmative) **A** — Contrary → **E** The Great Commission's Thrust Is Not World Evangelization (Universal Negative)

Subaltern — Contradiction — Subaltern

I ← Sub-contrary → **O**

(Particular Affirmative) In the Great Commission's Thrust World Evangelism Is a Priority

(Particular Negative) In the Great Commission's Thrust World Evangelism Is Not a Priority

---

[829]Millard J. Erickson, *Christian Theology* (Grand Rapids: Baker, 1985), 1052.

H. Additions to the Great Commission and/or "Preach the Gospel and …":

The existence of other commands compliments and does not contradict, negate or alter the thrust of the Great Commission passages:

> "If Christians don't become comfortable with outreach, Bible study is academic, prayer is boring, and fellowship is superficial.[830]

> "Without outreach, the [small] group will die a natural death and produce lopsided Christians. Christians who know the Bible, love to fellowship with other Christians, and pray on a regular basis, but don't do outreach *militate against the cause of Christ*."[831]

Question on Galatians 2:6—
Additions to Proclamation or to Message?
Or, Is Galatians 1:8-9 about Method or Message?

Original	Left Ambiguous [allowing for methodology]				Imply "Message"		Add the Word "Message" to the Text				
Byzantine Textform	English Geneva (1560)	New King James (1982)	King James Version (1611, 1769)	New American Standard (1977)	Bible in Basic English (1949, 1964)	New American Bible⁺ (1970)	New Jerusalem Bible⁺ (1985)	NIV (1984)	God's Words for the Nations (1995)	ABS's CEV⁺ (1995)	NET Bible (2004, 2005)
Ἀπὸ δὲ τῶν δοκούντων εἶναί τι ὁποῖοί ποτε ἦσαν οὐδέν μοι διαφέρει· πρόσωπον θεὸς ἀνθρώπου οὐ λαμβάνει ἐμοὶ γὰρ οἱ δοκοῦντες οὐδὲν προσανέ-θεντο·	But of them which semed to be great, I was *not taught* (what they were in time passed, it maketh no matter to me: God accepteth no mans persone) neverthe-less, they that are the chiefe, did communi-cate nothing with me.	But from those who seemed to be somethin—what-ever they were, it makes no difference to me; God shows personal favoritism to no man—for those who seemed to be something added nothing to me.	But of these who seemed to be somewhat, (whatsoever they were, it maketh no matter to me: God accepteth no man's person:) for they who seemed to be something in conference added nothing to me:	But from those who were of high reputation (what they were makes no difference to me; God shows no partiality)— well, those who were of reputation contributed nothing to me.	But from those who seemed to be important (whatever they were has no weight with me: God does not take man's person into account): those who seemed to be important gave nothing new to me	But from those who were reputed to be important (what they once were makes no difference to me; God shows no partiality) — those of repute made me add nothing.	but those who were recognised as important people— whether they actually were important or not: There is no favouritism with God— those recognised leaders, I am saying, had nothing to add to my message.	As for those who seemed to be important —whatever they were makes no difference to me; God does not judge by external appearance —those men added nothing to my message.	Those who were recognized as important people didn't add a single thing to my message. (What sort of people they were makes no difference to me, since God doesn't play favorites.)	Some of them were supposed to be important leaders, but I didn't care who they were. God doesn't have any favorites! None of these so-called special leaders added anything to my message.	But from those who were influential (whatever they were makes no difference to me; God shows no favoritism between people)– those influential leaders added nothing to my message.

The Greek verb προσανατίθημι is found twice in the NT, and only in Galatians: 1:16; 2:6.

The French *Le Semeur* (1992, 1999) for the last phrase is even more dynamic reading, "Oh well, these very influencial people imposed no other directives upon me" (notice that these others are characterized as "very influential people who impose directives"—in sync with the Roman Catholic hierarchy and the encyclicals of the Bishop of Rome).

Notice some issues in the translation of this verse…

a. Is the main thrust of the Book of Galatians the message or the method?

    1) This issue parallels the issue in translating 1:8-9

b. At issue is also the translation of the verb προσανατίθημι, which is unique to Galatians, and forms one of the main elements in the message of Galatians:

    1) Paul did not communicate with, confer with, or consult flesh and blood

    2) The great or those of high reputation added or contributed nothing to Paul

---

[830]Bill Hull, *The Disciple Making Pastor* (Old Tappan, NJ; Revell, 1988), 176.

[831]*Ibid.,* 179 (italics mine).

c. At issue is the evangelism methodology of Paul, which is not unrelated to the message that he preached:

1) Did he need to do more than just proclaim or evangelize?

2) The only advice given here is in 2:10, "only remember the poor"—again advice dealing with methodology:

   a) Could it be that the apostles were more comfortable with servant evangelism?

   b) Could it be that this was the "I am of Christ" contingent in the church of Corinth?

   c) Was the church in Jerusalem so interested in lifestyle issues that they had lost the preach in the Great Commission?

   d) When those of James came to Antioch, Peter began to stand aloof from the Gentiles (2:11-12)—that was not very evangelistic, it was lifestyle!

d. The changing of the dative ἐμοὶ to a genitive, and then the addition of the word "message" in both the New International Version and in the Catholic New Jerusalem Bible brings consternation

1. **Understanding the Great Commission in light of other biblical commands**:[832]

a. **Love:**

1) Aspects of Love in the Bible

   a) Deut 6:5, "And you shall love the Lord your God with all your heart and with all your soul and with all your might." (cf. Matt 22:36-40, Mark 12:28-31)

   b) Lev 19:18, "But you shall love your neighbor as yourself; I am the Lord." (cf. Matt 22:36-40, Mark 12:28-31):

     (1) Love for God is needed first before we can love our fellow man or even our brother in Christ, 1 John 5:2

     (2) If a knowledge and acceptance of the forgiveness of the Lord Jesus is the most important thing for the Christian, it must be the most important thing for his neighbor also![833] The command for evangelism is clearly implied in this command.

     (3) Eli the priest honored his sons above God, therefore, displacing the order of these commands, I Sam 2:29. It is possible to let our priorities become incorrect even though we seem to be doing good.

   c) John 13:35, "By this all men will know that you are My disciples, if you have love for one another."

   d) Romans 13:8-10, "Owe nothing to anyone except to love one another; for he who loves his neighbor has fulfilled *the* law. For this, 'You shall not commit adultery, You shall not murder, You shall not steal, You shall not covet,' and if there is any other commandment, it is summed up in this saying, 'You shall love your neighbor as yourself.' Love does no wrong to a neighbor; love therefore is the fulfillment of *the* law"

   5) 1 John 2:15, "Do not love the world, nor the things in the world. If any one loves the world, the love of the Father is not in Him."

2) Sample approaches to love as the priority:

   a) Charles Arn:

     "The great commission—to make disciples—and the great commandment—to love—are inseparably linked. The *mission* Christ gave us is to make disciples. The *model* He gave us is love

---

[832]Resulting from this study, I have noted a total of 57 additions or alterations of the Great Commission in Chart 7, "Alternatives to Mere Proclamation," in my *Charts for a Theology of Evangelism* (Nashville: Broadman, 2007), 22-25.

[833]Contra John R. W. Stott, *Christian Mission in the Modern World* (Downers Grove, IL; InterVarsity, 1975), 29.

... the *method* He gave us is love ... the *motive* He gave us is love ... the *message* He gave us is love."[834]

b)   John Shore (as an example of the logic involved and impact):

(1)   Shore began his argument with equating the Great Commission and the Great Commandment as twin commands:

"And what I'm suggesting we concentrate *upon* is this book's Core Idea, which is that here in America we (lovely, lovely) Christians have for so long now been so energetically endeavoring to fulfill the Great Commission that it's reasonable to wonder whether or not at this point we are, by continuing to press upon people a belief system they already know about and have already rejected, working to the detriment of the Great Commission, but also against that *other* humongous To Do item Jesus gave us—the Great Commandment.

I mean, I'm totally just an Average Layperson, for sure—but I'm pretty sure that's all anyone needs to be in order to at least know that Christ gave his followers two Colossal Directives: the Great Commission and the Great Commandment, right? The former, of course, tells us (in so may words) to do our best to try to convert nonbelievers into Christians ('Therefore go an make disciples of all nations ... teaching them to obey everything I have commanded you.'); the latter (after the 'Love the Lord Your God with all your heart') enjoins us to 'Love your neighbor as yourself."[835]

(2)   Shore restated the argument (above) that most if not all Americans have heard the Gospel, or that the Great Commission has been fulfilled in the U.S.:

"Yay! Pretty much every last, single person in America has heard the word of God! The Great Commission has gone a very long way toward being fulfilled right here in our own backyard!

"Whoo-hoo!

"We rock!

"Well done, good and faithful servants"

"Glory be to God!

"So. Now what?"

"Well, the contention of this book is that now that it's safe to assume that all of our neighbors already know the story of Christ and the Bible and so on, it might be a good time to take some of that enormous energy we currently spend on converting those same people, and to focus it instead on 'just' loving them as much as we love ourselves."[836]

(3)   Shore then related his logic to the Great Commission in the very next paragraph:

"In other words, I think that here in the great, gospel-saturated U.S. of A., it's time to shift our concentration from fulfilling the Great Commission to fulfilling the Great Commandment."[837]

(4)   After denigrating initiative evangelism, Shore continued, giving the context for the title of his book:

"It's not good for the Great Commission because it simply doesn't work: A person on the receiving end of the message that in order to become a better (or at least 'okay') person they need to undergo a radical transformation is generally inspired to do nothing so much as hightail it away from the messenger. And it's not good for the Great Commandment, either, since once an evangelizer and his or her would-by Christian have split up, their relationship is finished—and unless the Hallmark company has come up with some truly amazing new card I haven't yet heard about, it's not possible to love someone with whom you have no relationship at all.

"The bottom line is that no matter how artfully we put it, or how passionately or sincerely we mean them well, when we convey to an unbeliever the message that they really

---

[834]Charles Arn, "A Response to Dr. Rainer: What Is the Key to Effective Evangelism?" *Journal of the American Society for Church Growth* 6 (1995): 77-78.

[835]John Shore, *I'm OK—You're Not: The Message We're Sending to Unbelievers and Why We Should Stop* (Colorado Springs: NavPress, 2007), 11-12.

[836]Ibid., 14.

[837]Ibid.

need to become a Christian, the only thing they can possibly understand us to be saying—the only thing *we'd* hear if we were in their shoes[838]—is that we're okay, and that they definitely are not.

"We're great; they're on their way to perdition.

"A message not exactly cockle-warming to hear. Which is why unbelievers, as we all know, never listen to it for long at all."[839]

(5) Finally, Shore placed the Great Commandment as a priority above the Great Commission (an amazing admission):

"Besides, doesn't as Great Commandment totally trump a Great Commission? Isn't it a much bigger deal to be *commanded* to do something than it is to be *commissioned* to do it?...

"The point it: Just on the *face* of it, shouldn't we pay a lot more attention to fulfilling the Great Commandment than we do to fulfilling the Great Commission? (Yes. I'm submitting that the answer is 'Yes.')

"And let us, by the by [sic.], not forget that Jesus himself never referred to what he said in Matthew 28 as the 'Great Commission'—that those words are *our words*, not his."[840]

c) Further recent books in this area:

(1) Apparently, in 2007, NavPress seems to have decided to create a new marketing wave [possibly to parallel or compete with Zondervan's *EmergentYS* line?] by focusing on love as the overriding commandment over the Great Commission, and, along with John Shore's *I'm OK—You're Not: The Message We're Sending to Unbelievers and Why We Should Stop*, they published three companion volumes:
  (a) Paul Borthwick, *Stop Witnessing ... and Start Loving*.
  (b) Paul Miller, *Love Walked Among Us*.
  (c) Scott Morton, *Down-toEarth Discipling*.

(2) Moody Press also published on this topic: Timothy George and John Woodbridge, *The Mark of Jesus: Loving in a Way the World Can See* (Chicago: Moody, 2005).

(3) A quick perusal of the chronological bibliography at the end of Chapter One in this text should show how many books are published in this vein on a regular basis. Consider also, for example, the "Friendship/Lifestyle Evangelism" wave from 1974-1981.

3) Analysis:

a) If anything, the commands to love in the Bible encourage obedience to the Great Commission:
  (1) God's love actively brought salvation to us, John 3:16, Rom 5:8, 1 John 4:10
  (2) Our love for others, if it is from God, will lead us to actively pursue bringing salvation to others (cf. 2 Cor 5:14; e.g. J. I. Packer quote above).

b) Also, are not the quotes of Jesus in Matt 22:37-39 (and parallels) merely a summary or restatement of the Law of Moses, which was therefore fulfilled by Jesus, and not part of the "law of Christ" (1 Cor 9:21)?
  (1) As such, they are not salvific, lest we make Jesus into a Moses, as was noted by Luther,[841] and as was confirmed by [Pope] Leo XIII[842]

---

[838]Reminiscent of the book: John Kramp, *Out of Their Faces and Into Their Shoes: How to Understand Spiritually Lost People and Give Them Directions to Find God* (Nashville: Broadman and Holman, 1995).

[839]John Shore, I'm OK—You're Not, 16.

[840]Ibid., 16, 17.

[841]"Therefore, beware lest you make Christ into a Moses, and the gospel into a book of law or doctrine, as has been done before now, including some of Jerome's prefaces" (Martin Luther, "Preface [to New Testament]," in *Martin Luther,* John Dillenberger, ed. [Garden City, NY: Anchor, 1961], 17).

[842]"If Sacrifices are abolished, Religion can neither exist nor be conceived. The Evangelical Law is not inferior, but superior, to the Old Law. It brings to perfection what the Old Law had merely begun." (Leo XIII, *Caritatis Studium* [25 July 1898]; available at: http://www.ewtn.com/library/ENCYC/L13CARIT.HTM; accessed: 8 Sept 2004; Internet).

(2) Nor is the "Great Commandment" ever said to summarize the New Covenant

(3) The "Great Commandment," the second commandment, and their corollary, the "Golden Rule" (Rom 13:19) summarize the Old Covenant

(4) Under the New Covenant, Jesus gave a "New Commandment," in which He limited the command to mean love toward believers, "love one another"

(5) True, non-conservative theologians (falsely) try to insert (at this point) the collectivist idea of the "Brotherhood of Men" and the "Fatherhood of God"

(6) However, "One another" from the mouth of Jesus to His disciples in the upper room, and from the Apostle John in his epistles, is clearly communicated within the context of the household of faith, and parallels Paul admonition in Gal 6:10:

> "So then, while we have opportunity, let us do good to all men, and especially to those who are of the household of the faith"

(7) My experience in local church ministry has shown me that those churches who do not obey the differentiation of Paul in Galatians 6:10, because unending need exists, and because they help all people (proudly) without regard to their being converted Christians or not, ultimately neglect even the believers within their own churches! A very sad state of affairs for any local church. How quickly non-conversionistic pastors, churches, and schools become anti-conversionistic!

4) A special analysis of 1 Corinthians 13:4-8:

> "Love is patient, it is kind; love is not jealous; love is not boastful, it is not arrogant, it is not disgraceful, it does not seeks its own, it is not irritable, it does not devise evil, it does not rejoice in unrighteousness, but celebrates in truthfulness; it bears all things, it believes all things, it hopes all things, it endures all things. Love is never destroyed. But for prophecies, they will be nullified; as for tongues, they will cease; as for knowledge, it will be nullified" (trans. mine).

a) Is this definition of love a list of virtues by which a person is saved?
   (1) No! Not only is God the initiator of love (1 John 4:19), "We love, because He first loved us."
   (2) But He is the initiator of our salvation, (1 John 4:10), "In this is love, not that we loved God, but that He loved us and sent His Son *to be* the propitiation for our sins."
   (3) God gives us His love, we cannot work it up (Rom 5:5), "and hope does not disappoint, because the love of God has been poured out within our hearts through the Holy Spirit who was given to us."

b) If love "bears all things," does God not show love if He holds mankind accountable for sin? No! Note the uses of "those who practice such things shall not inherit the kingdom fo heaven" (Rom 1:32; 2:2; Gal 5:21; cf. 1 Cor 6:9-10)

c) If love never fails, and prophecies will be nullified, then is love (lifestyle, friendship, and service), more important than prophesying (evangelizing and preaching) in evangelism, especially in light of 1 Cor 8:1, "Knowledge makes arrogant, but love edifies"? Again, no!
   (1) This reversal exemplifies the nullifying of a direct command, by the misapplication of a tangential principle; likewise, the Jews nullified the command of God to care for their parents by their sophistry, Matt 15:3-9

d) If knowledge will "pass away," is love therefore more important than knowledge? And is love therefore more important than doctrine or doctrinal statements, such as the BF&M?

No! It's not a matter of either-or, it's a matter of both/and:

> And the Word became flesh, and dwelt among us, and we saw His glory, glory as of the only begotten from the Father, full of grace and truth. John testified about Him and cried out, saying, "This was He of whom I said, 'He who comes after me has a higher rank than I, for He existed before me.'" For of His fullness we have all received, and grace upon grace. For the Law was given through Moses; grace and truth were realized through Jesus Christ. (John 1:14-17)

5) The antagonism to Jesus in John 10:31-39:
    a) v. 31, the Jews were planning to stone Jesus, v. 31
    b) v. 32, so Jesus appealed to His many good works as authenticating His message: "I showed you many good works from the Father; for which of them are you stoning Me?"
    c) v. 33, the Jews retorted that the good works of Jesus were basically meaningless, they were scandalized by His message: "For a good work we do not stone You, but for blasphemy; and because You, being a man, make Yourself out *to be* God"
    d) Some thoughts:
        (1) Clearly, the good works of Jesus were neutral as regards the message, it was His words that caused them to want to kill Him (capital punishment for His words—do we not seen this in Acts 22:22?)
        (2) Just as a miracle can be misinterpreted (Acts 14:11-12), so good works and love can be misunderstood and misapplied
        (3) The words, however, are direct and powerful (Rom 1:16), and they draw the foreordained result that God desires (Rom 10:16-17; John 6:68)

6) A though from J. I. Packer:

"My neighbor's deepest need is to know the love of God in Jesus Christ, and my claim to love him or her is hollow if I make no attempt to meet that need as best I can."[843]

b. Ministry/Service:
1) Jesus came to serve, Mark 10:45
2) The Christian is called to serve God, Psa 100:2
3) Evangelism is clearly serving the Creator rather than the creature (cf. Rom 1:25):

For am I now seeking the favor of men, or of God? Or am I striving to please men? If I were trying to please men, I would not be a bond-servant of Christ. Gal 1:10 (cf. Gal 1:6-12; 5:11)

4) Jesus' service evangelism of feeding 5,000 in John 6 accounted for no advance in followers. He started the chapter with 12 disciples and ended the chapter with 12 disciples, even though he had healed many, fed 5,000, and even walked on water!
    a) An interesting side note on this chapter:
        (1) Jesus may have even "lost" Judas due to the events in this chapter, 6:70-71
        (2) Notice that Judas seemed to have a fascination with acts of servanthood, John 12:4-6, as well as with personal financial gain
        (3) When did the Devil put into the heart of Judas to betray Jesus, was it John 6 or John 12? Interesting!
    b) How easy it is for God's people to have man's interests on their minds and not God's:
        (1) Notice what Jesus said of Peter:

"From that time Jesus Christ began to show His disciples that He must go to Jerusalem, and suffer many things from the elders and chief priests and scribes, and be killed, and be raised up on the third day. And Peter took Him aside and began to rebuke Him, saying, 'God forbid *it*, Lord! This shall never happen to You.' But He turned and said to Peter, 'Get behind Me, Satan! You are a stumbling block to Me; for you are not setting your mind on God's interests, but man's'" (Matt 16:21-23)

        (2) Remember that this weakness of Peter showed up again:

"Simon Peter therefore having a sword, drew it, and struck the high priest's slave, and cut off his right ear; and the slave's name was Malchus. Jesus therefore said to Peter, 'Put the sword into the sheath; the cup which the Father has given Me, shall I not drink it?'" (John 18:10-11; cf. Matt 26:51; Mark 14:47; Luke 22:49-51)

        (3) Jesus said to Pilate:

"Jesus answered, 'My kingdom is not of this world. If My kingdom were of this world, then My servants would be fighting, that I might not be delivered up to the Jews; but as it is, My kingdom is not of this realm'" (John 18:36)

---

[843]J.I. Packer, "Foreword" in Lewis A. Drummond, *The Word of the Cross* (Nashville: Broadman, 1992), 7.

(4) Jesus also said of His kingdom:

> "Now having been questioned by the Pharisees as to when the kingdom of God was coming, He answered them and said, 'The kingdom of God is not coming with signs to be observed; [21] nor will they say, "Look, here *it is*!" or, "There *it is*!" For behold, the kingdom of God is in your midst.'" (Luke 17:20-21)

(5) Was not this view of a future reward why the men of old were commended in Hebrews 11?

5) The divine miracles of Jesus, as supernatural acts of service, did not open the hearts of those that beheld them or received them:

  a) Notice this question of Jesus, "I showed you many good works from the Father; for which of them are you stoning Me?" (John 10:32)
    (1) Is not the response of the Jews telling? "For a good work we do not stone You, but for blasphemy; and because You, being a man, make Yourself out *to be* God (Joh 10:33 NAS)" (John 10:33)
    (2) Apparently, they didn't seem to mind the good works, but they did stumbled at His message, to the point of wanted to kill Him!

  b) Notice also this interesting narrative portion from John:

    > John 12:37-40, "But though He had performed so many signs before them, *yet* they were not believing in Him; that the word of Isaiah the prophet might be fulfilled, which he spoke, 'LORD, who has believed our report? And to whom has the arm of the Lord been revealed?' For this cause they could not believe, for Isaiah said again, 'He has blinded their eyes, and He hardened their heart; lest they see with their eyes, and perceive with their heart, and be converted, and I heal them.'"

6) Notice also that one of Paul's issue with the "James, Cephas, and John"—was this an issue brought up by the Judaizers against Paul's methodology of evangelism?

  > "And recognizing the grace that had been given to me, James and Cephas and John, who were reputed to be pillars, gave to me and Barnabas the right hand of fellowship, that we *might go* to the Gentiles, and they to the circumcised. *They* only *asked* us to remember the poor—the very thing I also was eager to do" (Gal 2:9-10)

  [also see my discussion of Galatians 6:10 above, which also fits with so-called servant evangelism]

c. **Worship:**

  Introduction: Over-emphasizing the worship of God, as may do the Westminster Confession,[844] is perhaps a common theologically-based approach to de-emphasize an urgent evangelism.[845]

  1) "I will be exalted among the nations, I will be exalted in the earth," Psa 46:10
  2) Consider the words of the Apostle Paul:

    > How shall they call upon Him in whom they have not believed?
    > And how shall they believe in Him whom they have not heard?
    > And how shall they hear without a preacher? (Rom 10:14)

---

[844]"1) What is the chief end of man? A. Man's chief end is to glorify God and to enjoy him forever" (Westminster Shorter Catechism," accessed 1 Dec 2005; from http://www.shortercatechism.com/resources/wscformats/BPC_wsc.doc; Internet).

[845]I have included significant quotes from a paper by Mark D. Liederbach, Associate Professor of Christian Ethics at Southeaster Baptist Theological Seminary, in his "Ethical Evaluation of Modern Motivations for Evangelism" (Mark D. Liederbach, "Ethical Evaluation of Modern Motivations for Evangelism" in which he followed this same line of reasoning, citing Dietrich Bonhoeffer's emphasis on the "who" (knowing Christ) before the "how" (preaching the Gospel). Liederbach made the glory of God his central interpretive motif to the detriment of the urgency of the evangelism mandate and examples (see footnote above under "The Urgencies of Evangelism," "2 The Lost Are Really Lost").

It is clear that without conversion to Christ (the new birth), no man can worship God in Spirit and in truth (cf. John 4:23-24). In fact they do not know whom nor why they are to worship. Evangelism is the only means of acquainting people to Jesus that they may worship Him. Thus evangelism is not only a chronological priority to worship, but it is also the priority of the Great Commission passages and the methodology in the Book of Acts. Note that there are few if any worship services in Acts (other than a non-voluntary audience in prison in Acts 16), while the Book of Acts is replete with examples of evangelism!

d. The Great Commission and/or Political Involvement?

1) The foreword to Charles Colson's *How Now Shall We Live?* explained his view of the mission of the church. Colson wrote:

"Don't get me wrong. We need prayer, Bible study, worship, fellowship, and witnessing. But if we focus exclusively on these disciplines—and if in the process we ignore our responsibility to redeem the surrounding culture—our Christianity will remain privatized and marginalized."[846]

2) Colson seemed to switch belief in the gospel for belief in a Christian worldview [aka. A Christianized moral philosophy]. He continued later:

"It is our contention in this book that the Lord's cultural commission is inseparable from the great commission. That may be a jarring statement for many conservative Christians, who, who through much of the twentieth century have shunned the notion of reforming culture, associating that concept with the liberal social gospel. The only task of the church, many fundamentalists and evangelicals believed, is to save as many lost souls as possible from a world literally going to hell. But this explicit denial of a Christian worldview is unbiblical and is the reason we have lost so much of our influence in the world. *Salvation does not consist simply of freedom from sin; salvation also means being restored to the task we were given in the beginning—the job of creating culture.*"[847]

[See the notes on historical tautology at the end of this Chapter in response to Colson's reinterpretation of the Nineteenth Century evangelicalism]

3) Colson continued:

"When we turn to the New Testament, admittedly we do not find verses specifically commanding believers to be engaged in politics or the law or education or the arts. But we don't need to, because the cultural mandate given to Adam still applies [Gen 1:28]."[848]

4) He buttressed his views with knowledge from special revelation and general revelation,[849] and through affirming, "all truth is God's truth."[850] Thus, due to the cultural mandate superseding theological distinctives, Colson continued:

"But if we are to have an impact on culture, the beginning point must be to take our stand united in Christ, making a conscious effort among all true believers to come together across racial, ethnic, and confessional lines.... This is difficult for many evangelicals (as well as Catholics and Orthodox) to accept, and understandably so.... Conservative believers are distrustful of ecumenism because of the danger of glossing over those differences. Focusing on worldview, however, can help build bridges."[851]

---

[846]Charles Colson and Nancy Pearcey, *How Now Shall We Live?* x.
[847]*Ibid.,* 295-96; emphasis mine.
[848]*Ibid.,* 296.
[849]*Ibid.,* 296-297.
[850]*Ibid.,* 189-199.
[851]*Ibid.,* 303-04.

5) Thus, it seems that Colson may have advised unity based on a Christian worldview [or moral philosophy], rather than based on the gospel and evangelism (or a cooperative document, such as the Baptist Faith and Message)!

e. The Glory of God?

Introduction: For some high Calvinists the "glory of God" (with its corollary "worship") is the Central Interpretive Motif (CIM) of the Bible and for all time. For example, John Piper began his explanation of this view in this way:

> Missions is not the ultimate goal of the church. Worship is. Mission exists because worship doesn't. Worship is ultimate, not missions, because God is ultimate, not man. When this age is over, and the countless millions of the redeemed fall on their faces before the throne of God, missions will be no more. It is a temporary necessity. But worship abides forever.
> Worship, therefore, is the fuel and goal of missions....
> Worship is also the fuel of missions....
> If the pursuit of God's glory is not ordered above the pursuit of man's good in the affections of the heart and the priorities of the church, man will not be well served and God will not be duly honored.[852]

Notice how this view changed Piper's approach to the message of salvation:

> The gospel demand that flows from God to the nations is an eminently shareable, doable demand, namely to rejoice and be glad in God.... What message would missionaries rather take than the message: Be glad in God! Rejoice in God! Sing for joy in God![853]

There seems to be a real lack of the gospel according to Luke 24:46-47 or 1 Corinthians 15:1-8 as the primary message. Piper seems not to ascribe to "I have determined to know nothing among you except Jesus Christ, and Him crucified" (1 Cor 2:2). Rather, Piper posited a "more profound message," the glory of God! What of the reproach of the Christ (Heb 11:26) or the shame of the cross (Heb 12:2)?

There was similarly a lack of clarity as regards "repentance for the forgiveness of sins" (Luke 24:47):

> His first and great requirement of all men everywhere is that they repent from seeking their joy in other things and begin seeking it only in him.[854]

This statement seems to be nothing more than a restatement of [St] Augustine's own spiritual journey, which in actuality had more to do with philosophical theology and less to do with the Gospel of Christ.[855]

Piper ended by restating the Great Commission(s) of Jesus Christ in his own terms:

> Missions is not the ultimate goal of the church. Worship is. Missions exists because worship doesn't. The Great Commission is first to delight yourself in the Lord (Ps 37:4). And then to declare, "Let the nations be glad and sing for joy" (Ps 67:4). In this way God will be glorified from beginning to end and worship will empower the missionary enterprise till the coming of the Lord.[856]

However, making the choice to use the "glory of God" as the unique or prior CIM to all others is not as clear from Scripture...

a) Paul argued that **the Jews made their boast in God** (Rom 2:17), *without* however submitting to or believing in Christ (as do also Muslims)!

---

[852]John Piper, "Let the Nations Be Glad!" in *Perspectives on the World Christian Movement: A Reader,* 3rd Ed., Ralph D. Winter and Steven C. Hawthorne, eds. (Pasadena: William Carey, 1981, 1992, 1999), 49. Piper provides a greater expansion of his view in *Let the Nations Be Glad: The Supremacy of God in Missions* (Grand Rapids: Baker, 1993).

[853]Piper, "Let the Nations Be Glad!" in *Perspectives,* 51.

[854]*Ibid.*

[855]See my notes in *UE,* Chapter 7, B. Some Historic Looks…, 2. On the Demise of Evangelism and Conversion Theology…, b. Augustine.

[856]*Piper, "Let the Nations Be Glad!" in Perspectives,* 52.

b)   Can not the necessity for and the practice of verbal evangelism be lost by philosophically-minded Calvinists (e.g. Joseph Hussey[857]), or at least be lowered from being the highest object of the church (e.g. John Gill[858])?

c)   It would seem preferable to use the hermeneutic of Jesus on the road to Emmaus and elsewhere, that the CIM of the Bible *is* the person and work of Christ (Luke 18:31-33; 24:25-27, 44-45). Christ and His death as the CIM is confirmed in the preaching of the Apostle Paul, "For I determined to know nothing among you except Jesus Christ, and Him crucified" (1 Cor 2:2; cf. 1 Cor 15:1-8).

d)   On the other hand, Charles Kelley explained that the "Great Commission Hermeneutic" propelled Southern Baptists in New Testament evangelism.[859]

e)   Furthermore, the responses demanded by these two CIMs are also quite different:

(1)   The response corresponding to the glory of God is worship… Yet unfortunately there are many cases of churches who have a doxology [of sorts] without proper soteriology!

(a)   Note the philosophical approach of father of Medieval scholasticism, Peter the Lombard (d. 1164) in his *Sentences*[860]

(b)   Another philosophical parallel is Blaise Pascal's "On the Conversion of the Sinner"[861]

---

[857]Joseph Hussey [1659-1726], *God's Operations of Grace: but No Offers of His Grace* (London: D. Bridge, 1707).

[858]John Gill, *Body of Divinity* (1769, 1770, 1839).

[859]Charles Kelley, *How Did They Do It? The Story of Southern Baptist Evangelism* (New Orleans: Insight, 1993), 119-131.

[860]"Among things, therefore, it must be considered, that as (St.) Augustine says in the same (book) [*On Christian Doctrine*, bk 1, ch 3, n 1], 'there are some things, which one is to enjoy, others, which one is to use, others, which enjoy and use. Those, which one is to enjoy, make us blessed; by those others, which one is to use, as ones tending towards beatitude we are helped and, as it were [*quasi*], propped up, so that we can arrive at those things, which make us blessed, and cleave to them. But between both things, which are enjoyed and used, we have been constituted, as it were,' as both Angels and Saints [*Angeli sancti*]. 'Moreover *to enjoy* is to cleave to any thing by love on account of its very self; but *to use* (is) to refer that which has come to be used to obtain that, which one is to enjoy; otherwise it is abusing, not using. For an illicit use ought to be named abuse [*abusum*] and/or an abuse [*abusio*]' [*ibid.*, ch 4 and 5]. 'The things, therefore, which one is to enjoy, are the Father and the Son and the Holy Spirit'" (Peter the Lombard, *Sentences*, bk 1, ch 1; accessed 16 May 2006; available from: http://www.franciscan-archive.org/lombardus/opera/ls1-01.html; Internet.

[861]"The first thing that God inspires in the soul that he deigns to truly touch, is a knowledge of and an extraordinary insight by which the soul considers things [material] and itself in a completely new way.

"This new light gives her [the soul] fear and brings her a troubled [spirit] that pierces the tranquility she found in the things that gave her pleasure.

"She can no longer taste with ease the things that charmed her. A continuous unscrupulous battle in the midst of pleasure, and an internal view keeps her from finding the usual tenderness associated with [material] things or else they are abandoned with illusiveness of heart.

"But she finds even greater bitterness with the exercises of piety and the vanity of the world. On one hand, the presence of visible objects touches it with more hope than the invisible, and on the other the solidity of the invisible touches it in a greater way than the vanity of the visible. And in this way the presence of the one and the solidity of the other argue against her affection; and the vanity of the one and the absence of the other excites her horror; in this way there is born in her a disorder and confusion that….

"This uplift is so imminent and transcendental, that it does not stop in the heavens: there is not enough to satisfy above the heavens, nor with the angels, nor with other more perfect beings. She traverses all the creatures, and cannot stop her heart until she arrives at the throne of God, in which she begins to find her rest and the goodness that is such that there is nothing more lovable, and that can be taken from her without her own consent.

"For even if she does not feel the charms by which God rewards pious habits, she understands nevertheless that the creature cannot be more lovable than the Creator, and her reason assisted with the light of grace shows her that there is nothing more lovable than God and that he can be taken only from those who reject him, because to desire him is to possess him, and to refuse him is to lose him.

"Hence she herself rejoices that she has found goodness that cannot be ravished from her as long as she longs for it, and of which there is none higher.

(c) One must remember that this philosophical approach to conversion was developed and taught as the Roman church was persecuting and executing the [so-called] Albigenses, as well as the Waldenses, Lollards, and the Hussites.

(2) However, the response corresponding to the New Testament Gospel is to repent and believe (cf. Mark 1:14-15; Luke 24:46-47)!

f) Please also see my notes following Chapter 5, "The Gospel of Christ or the Glory of God as Central Interpretive Motif?"

Evaluation:

1) Two common denominators in most concepts competing for priority over the Great Commission are:
   a) They are biblical
   b) They are important

2) However, they move aside the priority of the Gospel and the Great Commission in a subtle way—they redefine the issues and reframe the question:
   a) In that light, they do not represent "the whole counsel of God (Acts 20:27)
   b) Rather, an overemphasis on some aspect of biblical revelation, representing a partial understanding of God's revelation, often acquiescing to a non-initiative spirit and methodology of evangelism

3) They fall short of dealing adequately with the teaching of the New Testament, and in the long run can move local churches away from their evangelistic mandate.

I.   More Competing Priorities to the Great Commission:

1.   Go and Engage the Culture:

Introduction: Common among proponents of Apologetic Evangelism, is the concept of engaging the culture, using its arguments and its methods. While commendable on the surface, several dangers lie beneath the surface:

1. Engaging the culture using its arguments and issues may and *usually* does reframe the question away from the Gospel, biblical concepts, and biblical terminology.

2. Engaging the culture using its methods *quite often* removes the urgency from evangelism and changes the method to a non New Testament method.

2.   Social Transformation:

Social Transformation combines the service element mentioned above with a social zeal and political emphasis which transforms the Great Commission into a socio-economic enterprise. Every time period includes people, churches, and movements which morph in this direction. One example from the 19th Century may be the Salvation Army. World Vision was an "Evangelical" organization founded in 1950 by Bob Pierce, who preached two sermons at Billy Graham's famous 1949 Los Angeles crusade. A look at World Vision's six stated purposes can be compared to how Christ communicated the Great Commission in the Bible.[862]

"And in these new consternations she enters with new insight into the greatness of her Creator, and this with deep humiliations and adorations. She annihilates herself in his presence not being able to consider an idea of herself that is lowly enough, nor able to be able to conceive of a great enough revelation of this true sovereign, she makes new efforts to subjugate herself to the lowest abyss of nothingness, in considering God in his immensities which she multiplies; finally in his revelation, that saps all of her strength, she adores in silence, and she considers herself a vile and useless creature, and by these considerations reaffirmed, she adores him and blesses him, and would want to forever bless and adore him…" (Blaise Pascal, "Sur la Conversion du Pécheur," in *Pascal: Œuvres Complètes,* Louis Lafuma, ed. [New York: Macmillan, 1963]), 290-91. Translation by Thomas P. Johnston.

[862]The following are the six stated purposes of World Vision, International, from its webpage titled, "What We Do":

[1] "Transformational Development: Children are the hope for the world's future, yet they are its most vulnerable victims of conflict, disaster and poverty. Changing a child's life for the better is at the heart of the process of

3. Promote the Church of Rome and Its Priorities:

The primary mission for Rome seems to be the promotion of its existence and universal role.

    a. Rome succinctly stated its view of mission in the 1994 *Catechism of the Catholic Church*, after first restating that "outside the Church [of Rome] there is no salvation":

> "848 Although in ways known to himself God can lead those who, through no fault of their own, are ignorant of the Gospel, to that faith without which it is impossible to please him, the Church still has the obligation and also the sacred right to evangelize all men."[863]

---

transformational development. This process first helps people and their communities recognise the resources that lie within themselves to make change possible. As a result, health care, agriculture production, water projects, education, micro-enterprise development, advocacy and other programmes are carried out by the community with the support of World Vision.

    [2] "Emergency Relief: People whose lives are endangered by disasters or conflict need immediate, skilled assistance. World Vision is committed to respond to any major emergency around the world, through our own programs or in co-operation with partner agencies. For example, World Vision has responded to famine in Ethiopia and North Korea, hurricanes in Central America, earthquakes in El Salvador and India Taiwan and Turkey, and war refugees in Kosovo, Chechnya, Sierra Leone, Angola, and East Timor.

    "World Vision's focus on development is steadfast, even in emergency response situations. To do this World Vision:

- Encourages maximum participation from those being assisted
- Operates with sensitivity to the local culture and relationships
- Works whenever possible through national partners
- Gives immediate attention to economic recover
- Encourages peace building through reconciliation and enhancement of civil society
- Provides local preparedness training in disaster-prone areas

    [3] "Promotion of Justice: It is not enough to work with people to address the symptoms of their poverty. World Vision also addresses the complex, systematic factors that perpetuate poverty. World Vision supports community awareness of the collective ability to address unjust practices and begin working for change. World Vision speaks out on issues such as child labour, debt relief for poor nations, and the use of children as combatants in armed conflict.

    "World Vision International has endorsed the Universal Declaration of Human Rights and the United Nations Convention on the Rights of the Child as fundamental expressions of the freedoms and responsibilities that should exist in every country. Whenever possible, World Vision seeks opportunities to help reduce the level of conflict and to contribute to peaceful resolution and reconciliation.

    [4] "Strategic initiatives: As a Christian organisation, World Vision shares a special relationship with local churches of all Christian traditions. World Vision, in partnership with the church, works toward reducing poverty and advocating for justice through our development, relief and advocacy efforts.

    "World Vision invites Christian leaders to participate in conferences, consultations, training programmes and various educational opportunities. These diverse activities, which are typically the outcome of local initiatives, involve both clergy and lay people. World Vision welcomes opportunities to contribute to the life and work of the church in general.

    [5] "Public Awareness: World Vision encourages people to care about the needs of others, to understand the causes of poverty, and to offer a compassionate response. These efforts include collaboration with media and community participation in fundraising. In all its communications, World Vision upholds the dignity of suffering children and families in presenting explanations of the causes and consequences of poverty, war, neglect, and abuse. Its ministry seeks to touch the hearts and minds of both the poor and those with means.

    [6] "Witness to Jesus Christ: World Vision believes that God, in the person of Jesus Christ, offers hope of renewal, restoration, and reconciliation. It is this message that World Vision seeks to make known by life, deed, word, and sign.

    "World Vision's work of human transformation is holistic and ecumenical. It is holistic by valuing the spiritual as well as the physical and the personal as well as the social. It is ecumenical in its willingness to partner with all Christian churches in fulfilling the mission of Christ.

    "At the same time, World Vision is respectful of other faiths. It does not engage in proselytism or religious coercion of any kind. World Vision's programmes and services are available to people in need regardless of race, ethnic background, gender, or religion" (available from: http://www.wvi.org/wvi/about_us/what_we_do.htm; accessed 15 Dec 2005).

[863]1994 *Catechism of the Catholic Church*, §848.

[a] "Through no fault of their own": this universalistic statement undermines total depravity outside of God's saving work in the heart through the power of the Gospel proclaimed and received by faith

[b] "Known to God himself": describing God as having some secret way of saving people outside of that which He has made known in His Word, e.g. Thomistic Naturalism combined with pure Pelagianism

[c] "That faith without which it is impossible to please him" = for Rome, its Seven Sacraments, et al.

[d] "Evangelize all men" is described in §851 as bringing people to a knowledge of the truth, then stating, "But the Church, to whom this truth has been entrusted, must go out to meet their desire [Pelagianism], so as to bring them the truth [=Rome and all its Traditions]."[864]

b. Then, in stark contrast to Christ's Great Commission as understood by Evangelicals, the 1994 *Catechism of the Catholic Church* commissions its people, "The vocation of lay people," in a very unusual way:

> "899 The initiative of lay Christians is necessary especially when the matter involves discovering and inventing the means for permeating social, political and economic realities with the demands of Christian doctrine and life. This initiative is a normal element of the life of the Church:
>
> > "Lay believers are in the front line of Church life; for them the Church is the animating principle of human society. Therefore, they in particular ought to have an ever-clearer consciousness not only of belonging to the Church, but of being that Church, that is to say, the community of the faithful on earth under the leadership of the Pope, the Common Head, and of the bishops in communion with him. They are the Church [quoting from Pius XII, Discourse, 20 Feb 1946: AAS 38 (1946), 149; quoted by John Paul II, *Christifideles laici* (30 Dec 1988): 9]."[865]

c. Perhaps this methodology of "permeating social, political and economic realities" can coincide to some degree with the liberal Protestant social Gospel, however, in the case of mainstream Protestant churches, "social gospel" does not include making their specific churches or denominations the entire and only center of salvific reality for all of human life and activity.

d. Consider also the role of Mixed Marriages in fulfilling the Great Commission for Rome:

> "If after one admonition ... to the end of turning the catholic party from a mixed marriage, this one nevertheless persists in the desire to enter into this contract, and if it is noted that the marriage will continue notwithstanding, the Catholic clergy may accord his physical presence, but must observe the following precautions:
>
> "Firstly, that he not assist in such a marriage in a holy place, and that he not wear vestments giving the notion that it is a sacred rite, that he not pronounce ecclesiastical prayers on the contractants, and that he not bless them in any way.
>
> "Secondly, that he require on the part of the heretical party a written declaration by which, in the form of a vow, and in the presence of two witnessed who must also be signatories, he/she is obliged to permit their partner the free exercize of the catholic religion and to educate in this same religion all the children that will be born, without differentiation of sex. ...
>
> "Thirdly, that the catholic party itself also make a written declaration, sign by he/she and by two witnesses, in which he/she promises that not only will he/she never apostacize from the catholic religion,[866] but that she will educate it the same all children that will be born, and that he/she will tender with effectiveness unto the conversion of the other party, acatholic."[867]

---

[864]1994 *Catechism of the Catholic Church*, §851.

[865]1994 *Catechism of the Catholic Church*, §899.

[866]By the way, notice that from the perspective of Rome, Protestants and/or Evangelicals are members of another religion, foreign and quite different than their own. This same teaching is found over and over in their writings and "infallible" Traditions. Any attempt at cooperation is merely following the dictates of Aquinas, when Catholics are in a minority (see point "4) d)" below).

[867]Pius VI, *Exsequendo nunc* (13 July 1782), in Heinrich Denzinger, Peter Hünermann, and Joseph Hoffmann, *Symboles et définitions de la foi catholique* (*Enchiridion Symbolorum*), 38th ed. (Paris: Cerf, 1996), §2590.

e.   In conjunction with other statements of the Church of Rome, the following teaching may prove insightful:

1)   Thomas Aquinas (1275) on Catholics should act when in the minority:

> "On the other hand, the rites of other unbelievers, which are neither truthful nor profitable are by no means to be tolerated, except perchance in order to avoid an evil, e.g. the scandal or disturbance that might ensue, or some hindrance to the salvation of those who if they were unmolested might gradually be converted to the faith. For this reason the Church, at times, has tolerated the rites even of heretics and pagans, when unbelievers were very numerous."[868]

2)   Thomas Aquinas (1275) on Catholics laying ambushes for their enemies:[869]

> "I answer that, The object of laying ambushes is in order to deceive the enemy. Now a man may be deceived by another's word or deed in two ways. First, through being told something false, or through the breaking of a promise, and this is always unlawful. No one ought to deceive the enemy in this way, for there are certain 'rights of war and covenants, which ought to be observed even among enemies,' as Ambrose states (De Officiis i).
>
> "Secondly, a man may be deceived by what we say or do, because we do not declare our purpose or meaning to him. Now we are not always bound to do this, since even in the Sacred Doctrine many things have to be concealed, especially from unbelievers, lest they deride it, according to Mat. 7:6: 'Give not that which is holy, to dogs.' Wherefore much more ought the plan of campaign to be hidden from the enemy. For this reason among other things that a soldier has to learn is the art of concealing his purpose lest it come to the enemy's knowledge, as stated in the Book on Strategy [*Stratagematum i, 1] by Frontinus. Such like concealment is what is meant by an ambush which may be lawfully employed in a just war.
>
> "Nor can these ambushes be properly called deceptions, nor are they contrary to justice or to a well-ordered will. For a man would have an inordinate will if he were unwilling that others should hide anything from him."[870]

3)   Pius VI on the democratic form of government and the corresponding need to control education (1775):

> "4. … Since this cannot occur without careful education, it has been decreed accordingly that each diocese should establish a college for clerics in accordance with its means; if such a college already exists, it should be carefully preserved. …
>
> "Such colleges have been established and carefully equipped with suitable regulations and even greatly expanded in individual dioceses as Benedict XIV recommended to each of you as an indispensable part of your office.[6] So just as We must praise the outstanding labor and concern shown in founding and expanding these colleges, We must also urge on strongly those in whose diocese a college has not been established or completed.
>
> "7. When they have spread this darkness abroad and torn religion out of men's hearts, these accursed philosophers proceed to destroy the bonds of union among men, both those which unite them to their rulers, and those which urge them to their duty. They keep proclaiming that man is born free and subject to no one, that society accordingly is a crowd of foolish men who stupidly yield to priests who deceive them and to kings who oppress them, so that the harmony of priest and ruler is only a monstrous conspiracy against the innate liberty of man. …
>
> "… The holy Pope Leo used to say, 'We can rule those entrusted to us only by pursuing with zeal for the Lord's faith those who destroy and those who are destroyed and by cutting them off from sound minds with the utmost severity to prevent the plague spreading'[footnote 13: 'Epistles 7-8, chap. 2, to the bishops throughout Italy']."[871]

---

[868]Thomas Aquinas, *Summa Theologica*, SS, Q[10], A[11], "Whether the rites of unbelievers ought to be tolerated?" (online); available at: http://www.ccel.org/ccel/ aquinas/summa.html; accessed: 10 June 2008; Internet.

[869]Remembering that the Dominicans considered the Albigenses there "enemies": "Bishop Diego, borrowing from the enemy, recommended to the legates a new type of apostolate" (William A. Hinnebusch, O.P., *The History of the Dominican Order: Origins and Growth to 1500* [Staten Island, NY: Alba House, 1965], 1:23).

[870]Thomas Aquinas, *Summa Theologica*, SS, Q[40], A[3], "Whether it is right to lay ambushes in war?" (online); available at: http://www.ccel.org/ccel/ aquinas/summa.html; accessed: 10 June 2008; Internet.

[871]Pius VI, *Inscrutabile* (25 Dec 1775); available at: www.ewtn.com; accessed 8 Sept 2004; Internet.

4) Concluding comments:

    a) May these several quotes give an idea of similar quotations in the history of the Church of Rome, particularly prior to Napoleon's rule in Western Europe.

    b) May these quotes also provide insight to the observant reader as to how Rome has been taught to operate when it is in the minority.

J. In conclusion to notes on the Great Commission:

1. The often repeated quote of Wesley speaks to the centrality of the Great Commission:

    "You have nothing to do but to save souls. Therefore spend and be spent in this work. And go always, not only to those that want you, but to those that want you most. Observe: It is not your business to preach so many times, and to take care of this or that society; but to save as many souls as you can; to bring as many sinners as you possibly can to repentance, and with all your power to build them up in that holiness without which they cannot see the Lord."[872]

2. Now we can understand the urgency of Bailey E. Smith as he wrote:

    "Let me repeat a too-often forgotten truth. Witnessing is every Christian's responsibility. Escape cannot be found in some other achievement in Christian service. Oh, dear Christian, get hot on the trail for the souls of men."[873]

3. Or else we can see that George Truett was biblical (and not just expressing the views of his time, nor some pius platitudes) when he stated:

    "What great arguments shall I marshal to get us to do that right now? Shall I talk about duty? Then this is our first duty. And what great word that word duty is! Robert E. Lee was right, that matchless man of the South, when he wrote to his son saying: 'Son, the great word is duty.' Shall I talk about duty? My fellow Christians, your duty and mine, primal, fundamental, preeminent, supreme, tremendously urgent, is that we shall tell these around us that we want them saved."[874]

4. And W. A. Criswell was not exaggerating when he wrote:

    "If the pastor is under authority to do the work of an evangelist, then he must do the same thing; namely, he must use his church organization to win the lost. To what better use could they be dedicated. And what a powerful instrument for witnessing the pastor has in the marching members of his many-faceted ministry through the church. The way the church is put together is inherently, intrinsically made for soul winning, for reaching lost people. It is the thing that comes naturally."[875]

---

[872]John Wesley, "Charge to His Preachers," in Robert E. Coleman, *"Nothing to Do but to Save Souls"* (Grand Rapids: Zondervan, 1990), 1.

[873]Bailey E. Smith, *Real Evangelism* (Nashville: Broadman, 1978), 162.

[874]George W. Truett, *Quest for Souls* (New York: Doran, 1917), 72.

[875]W. A. Criswell, *Criswell's Guidebook for Pastors* (Nashville: Broadman, 1980), 233.

Chapter 10 Appendixes

Moving the Great Commission Off Center

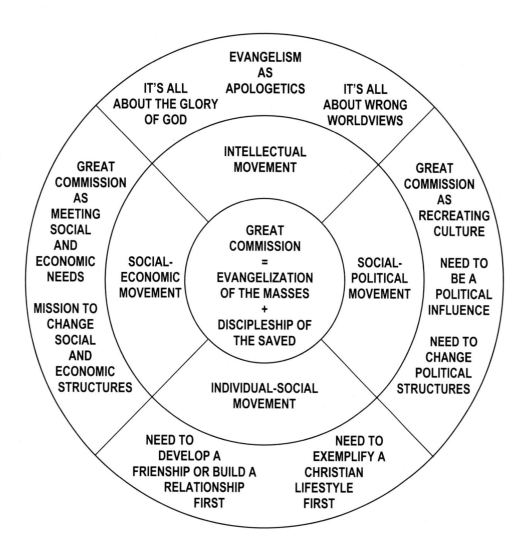

Challenge is to keep the main thing the main thing!

Evangelism as the Means to an End
Or as an End in Itself?

Introduction: This addendum will consider whether evangelism is an end in itself, or whether it is the means to an end to achieve a higher good. My Chart on "Alternatives to Mere Proclamation" provides 56 examples of aspects which are used either to replace evangelism or add to it.[876] My Chart on "Twelve Approaches to the Great Commission and the Christian Life"[877] also shows various emphases as to means and ends. However, the subject of this portion relates to this concern: "If I have shared the Gospel (evangelized), have I fulfill the Great Commission?"

Arguments for Evangelism as the Means to another End:

- Evangelism as a means to discipleship: Matthew 28:19 uses the verb μαθητεύω which since 1884 has been translated "make disciples" in English (beginning with John Darby's translation, see Chapter 26)
- Evangelism as a means to church planting: Matthew 16:18 emphasizes Jesus' purpose of building His church
- Evangelism as a means to glorify God: Arguing that God's ultimate purpose is to glorify Himself (Eph 1:6, 12), it is argued that evangelism is merely a means to that end.

Arguments for Evangelism as an End in Itself:

- Three Great Commission passages emphasize only proclamation (Mark, Luke, and Acts), whereas the other two are more open to interpretation (Matt, John)
- When Jesus sent out His disciples in Matthew 10, Mark 6, and Luke 9 and 10, it was to proclaim the Gospel and heal; nothing was said of follow-up or the development of converts into spiritual groups (same with Mark 5:19-20)
- When a city did not respond to their preaching, the disciples were to shake the dust off of their feet (Matt 10:14; Mark 6:11; Luke 9:5) and say, "Even the dust of your city which clings to our feet, we wipe off *in protest* against you; yet be sure of this, that the kingdom of God has come near," Luke 10:11; i.e. they had completed their mission in regard to that city!
- Luke 4:42-43 emphasizes that one purpose for Christ being sent was to "evangelize," which corresponds to several other purpose statements: He came to seek and to save the lost, Luke 19:10 (Matt 18:11); He came to call sinners to repentance, Matt 9:13; Mark 2:17; Luke 5:32; some of His early preaching only included the need to repent, Matt 4:17; 11:20 (cf. Mark 6:12; Luke 24:47; Acts 2:38; 5:31; 11:18)
- Paul was send, not to perform an ordinance of the church, baptism, but to evangelize, 1 Cor 1:17
- Paul's example in Acts is virtually silent as regards any type of discipleship program
- Evangelism as an end in itself is consistent with the teaching about the impact of the Word of God in Isaiah 55:10-11
- Rom 9:17 speaks of God's election ultimately resulting in His name being proclaimed (διαγγέλλω) in all the earth

Conclusions:

Coming back to the question in the introduction, "If I have evangelized, have I completely fulfilled the Great Commission?" The answer is "Yes."

The Great Commission is fulfilled by proper evangelizing. As the majority of people are on the wide road to perdition (Matt 7:13-14; 13:19), when they do not respond positively to the Gospel message, this is where the Great Commission stops for them (until the Holy Spirit provides another opportunity for witness).

Yet the answer seems to be "No," for those who listen to the Gospel (Acts 16:14). At this point, three soil types will respond positively to the Gospel (Matt 13:20-23 et al), and the true soil of their heart will

---

[876]Johnston, *Charts for a Theology of Evangelism*, Chart 7, "Alternatives to Mere Proclamation," 22-25.

[877]Ibid., Chart 5, "Twelve Approaches to the Great Commission and the Christian Life," 18-19.

become evident over time. In the case of those that respond positively, the evangelist is to seek to gather them into the fellowship of a local church.

Then as regards the title of this piece, evangelism is an end in itself, as regards the unregenerate. It only becomes a means to another end (discipleship and church planting) when there is a positive response to the Gospel.

EVANGELIZING AND THE
GREAT COMMISSION'S FULFILLMENT

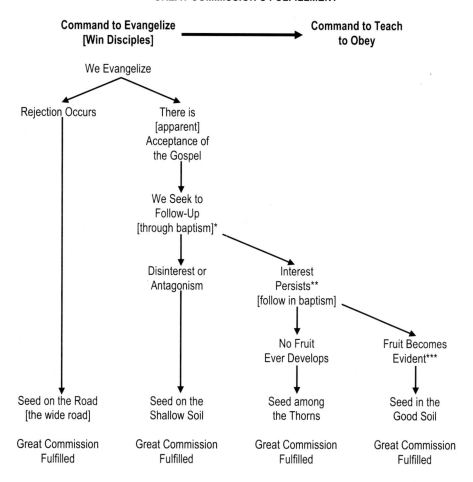

*These will likely never be baptized, as they will often stumble over the Gospel prior to that point.

** These likely will be baptized, join the church in fellowship, and perhaps join Sunday School—could these be the tares mentioned in the next parable, Matt 13:24-30?

*** These are baptized, join the church in fellowship, and soon get involved in evangelism, and may see some of their friends come to Christ.

Frequency and Duration in Witness

Introduction: This study was developed from a study of testifying in the Psalms (See also after Chapter 19, "Length of Time Evangelizing").

1. **The Duration in Terms of Speed:**
   a. "He sends forth His command to the earth; His word **runs very swiftly**," Psa 147:15
   b. "Finally, brethren, pray for us that the word of the Lord **may spread rapidly** and be glorified, just as *it did* also with you," 2 Thess 3:1
   c. "And believers were increasingly added to the Lord, multitudes of both men and women," Acts 5:14

2. **The Duration in Terms of Days:**
   a. From day to day: 1 Chr 16:23; Psa 96:2:
      1) Acts 2:47, "day by day"
      2) Acts 17:17, "every day"
   b. All day long: Psa 35:28; 71:8, 15, 24
   c. In the morning and at night: Psa 92:1-2
   d. Morning or evening: Eccl 11:6
   e. When you sit in your house and when you walk by the way and when you lie down and when you rise up, Deut 6:6

3. **The Duration in Terms of Time:**
   a. Continually: Psa 40:16, 70:4 (cf. Psa 34:1, Heb 13:15)
   b. Forever: Psa 75:10

4. **The duration in Terms of Life:**
   a. While alive: Psa 118:17
   b. Concerning youth: Psa 71:17
   c. Into old age: Psa 71:18; 92:1214-15
   d. From one generation to another: Psa 78:6; 145:4

5. **Conclusions**: The Gospel message needs to be proclaimed all the time if all peoples are going to be reached and if His word is obeyed:
   a. The urgency of the message is indicated by the swift nature of the propagation of the Gospel message
   b. The testifier should share at any time of the day, week, month or year that the opportunity is taken to share.
   c. The testifier should declare from his youth, into his old age and as long as he has breathe to tell of Jesus.
   d. This is the teaching of the apostle Paul to Timothy: 2 Tim. 4:2, "Preach the word; *be insistent* in season and out of season" [translation mine]. There seems to be no time when it is not right to speak for Jesus. It is always important (cf. Prov 3:27; Eccl 11:6; 2 Cor 3:12).

Various Translations of ἐπίστηθι (from ἐφίστημι) in 2 Tim 4:2

Insiste (insist)	Insist on it	Be urgent	Be instant	Persist in it	Be persistent	Persevere (persevere)	Fay diligéce (be diligent)	Be ready	Be prepared
Fr. Geneva; Fr. Martin; Fr. Darby; Fr. Segond; French Jerusalem	English Jerusalem Bible	English Darby; Revised Standard Version	English Geneva; King James Version	Holman Christian Standard	New Living Translation	French Lefèvre (1530)	French Louvain (1550)	New American Standard; English Standard Version	New International Version

Mordecai Ham on Preaching the Gospel and Prohibition (i.e. Socio-Political Involvement)

From: Edward E. Ham, *Fifty Years on the Battle Front with Christ: A Biography of Mordecai Ham* (Shelbyville, KY: Bible and Literature Missionary Foundation, 1950; St. John, IN: Larry Johnson, 2005), 103-04.

In January, 1916, Mr. Ham went to a meeting in Corpus Christi, Texas. Persistent rumors were circulated by the saloon crowd to the effect that Ham was a hired agent of the Anti-Saloon League, sent to clinch a victory for the Dries. The evangelist's own statement, concerning this matter, is interesting because it not only refutes the lie, but shows that he had never diverted from the main issue of his work, the preaching of Christ Jesus for the salvation of sinners.

"On reaching Corpus Christi from my home in Kentucky, I was informed that certain parties were industriously circulating the statement that the Ham-Ramsay revival meeting is to be merely a tail to a prohibition kite said to be nearly ready to fly…

"In answer to these rumors and surmises, I wish to make the statement below and to challenge any proof from any source to the contrary.

"…I have never delivered one address under the auspices of the Anti-Saloon League. I have never received one dollar from the Anti-Saloon League. I have never been sent anywhere by the Anti-Saloon League or any other organization. I have never gone anywhere to hold a meeting except on the invitation of the people of that place. The first invitation from the Corpus Christi Pastors' Association to hold a meeting here reached me several months ago; and neither in that invitation, nor in the more formal invitations subsequently sent me, in which the pastors were joined by their several official boards, nor in my acceptance of the same, nor in any correspondence relating thereto was any mention made of a prohibition campaign.

"I am an evangelist, called of God to preach salvation from sin through Jesus Christ, freely given to all who accept Him as their Saviour by repentance and faith. The experience of several years in this work has demonstrated to me that thousands of men reject Christ because they are not willing to give up drink; and that other thousands, who would be glad to be freed from the appetite for drink, nevertheless reject Christ because they do not believe that they have the strength to give it up. Being ignorant of things spiritual, they do not know that Christ will give them the necessary strength when they accept Him in good faith. Hence, I am persuaded that drink is the greatest hindrance to the salvation of men. For that reason I preach against it as faithfully as against any other sin. I could not do otherwise and remain true to my Divine call and commission.…"

Historical Fallacies and the Great Commission

Introduction:

Fallacies are found in every field of inquiry. However, it would seem that because evangelizing and the Great Commission illicit especially strong emotional feelings, this topic is prone to significant fallacious logic.

A. Tautology, the Great Commission and Social Responsibility:

1. The following paragraph written by the "Evangelical" Church historian George Marsden exemplifies a reason why very little is written about evangelism in many church histories. It comes from a discussion of 1947 evangelicalism during the first year of Fuller Theological Seminary:

> "Ockenga and his cohorts had no doubts that the responsibility for the reconstruction of the West lay primarily with America. In 1947 it would have been difficult to think otherwise. American evangelicals themselves had a heritage, going back to the Puritans, of believing that the nation had a special cultural mission as part of the history of redemption. The only hope to refurbish this dream, so deeply engrained in the American evangelical psyche, was to refurbish American evangelicalism itself. Evangelical Christianity then was truly the last hope for the world since it was the only hope for America.
>
> "Harold Ockenga took this thought a step further. When he spoke of 'Christian culture in the West,' he said in his Fuller convocation, he was using *west* in two senses. He was referring not only to Western civilization but also to the west coast, about which he proclaimed, 'The hour for the west to enter its maturity theologically is come.' Such language was bound to rankle mainline Protestants that had long had seminaries in California; but it made perfect sense given the premise of the address—that *evangelical* theology was the only adequate theology and therefore the only remaining hope for Western (and western) culture. The mission of the theological seminary involved much more than just training pastors and missionaries. It also involved a *cultural* task, the task of saving Western civilization."[878]

2. A tautology explained:[879]

    a. The tautology begins with the conclusion that the Bible is pluralistic, and does not give one clear mandate other than what is derived from the cultural context of the specific adherents.

    b. The tautology reinterprets the Great Commission from a psycho-social point of view:
        1) At this stage, evangelism and the power of the Gospel to change individual lives is either minimalized or ignored.
        2) Yet it is clear, even from Marsden's own writing, that soul-winning was *the* major focus of the early Fuller movement, and not the social reconstruction of American society.

        > "The idea [of Fuller] is to train young men to preach, to emphasize the great verities of the Word of God, and to lead people to Christ"[880]

        > "Such agencies became virtual subsects within the denominations, usually developing their own strict creeds to insulate themselves from any contamination of modernism. At the same time, because of their immense zeal for effective evangelistic outreach, they cultivated coalitions with other like-minded fundamentalists across denominational lines"[881]

        > "Missions was the paramount concern for all evangelicals"[882]

        And describing Ockenga's first inaugural address:

        > "Along with accepting the task of training men to save souls…"[883]

---

[878]George Marsden, *Reforming Fundamentalism: Fuller Seminary and the New Evangelicalism* (Grand Rapids: Eerdmans, 1987), 62.

[879]"The fallacy of tautological questions is the framing of a question in such a way that they are true by definition and cannot be empirically contradicted without self-contradiction. A tautological question is not really a question at all, but a declaration" (David H. Fischer, *Historians Fallacies: Toward a Logic of Historical Thought* (New York: Harper, 1970), 40-63.).

[880]George Marsden, *Reforming Fundamentalism*, 35, n. 5).

[881]Ibid., 38.

[882]Ibid., 41.

    c. Once the Great Commission is reinterpreted as seeking to effect social change, its worldwide focus, "Go into all the world," must be reinterpreted as a mere sense of cultural superiority with a "triumphalist" attitude, emphasizing the transplantation of [20th Century American] culture, as exemplified in the paragraphs above.

    d. Likewise, the placing of America in the "history of redemption," another misconception of the Great Commission, seems to be imported from a Modernist anti-Puritan rhetoric and betrays the Modernist downgrade of the spiritual nature of the Great Commission, were it to be taken seriously by anyone from any tongue, tribe, or nation.

    e. Thus the tautology is as follows:
      1) American evangelicals see their mission as the literal redemption of the world culture, because
      2) American evangelicals see their mission as the literal redemption of the world culture.

3. Related fallacies to tautology as regards the Great Commission and social responsibility are:

    a. A fallacy of factual verification: circular proof:

> "The *fallacy of circular proof* is a species of a question-begging, which consists in assuming what is to be proved."[884]

    b. A fallacy of causation: cum hoc, propter hoc:

> "The *fallacy of cum hoc, propter hoc* mistakes the correlation for cause. … Correlation itself can never establish cause. It can disestablish one—for there can never be a *regularistic* causal relationship without correlation. But there can often be a regular correlation without a cause."[885]

    c. A fallacy of semantical distortion: misplaced accent

> "The *fallacy of accent* occurs in an argument when meaning is distorted by emphasis…. Inuendo is a form of the fallacy of accent. … The fallacy of accent consists not in the use of emphasis, but in its unfair and inaccurate use."[886]

4. Further Analysis of Marsden's tautology:

    a. Marsden found what he presupposed in his preface, the desire for social transformation:

> "Like the New School evangelicals of the nineteenth century (and unlike both the strict Old School and the dispensationalists) these fundamentalists saw Christians as having the duty to transform culture in addition to their primary duty to evangelize."[887]

The insightful reader will note the comments of Robert Speer that contradict Marsden on this very issue his speech at the 1900 New York Ecumenical Missionary Conference, "The Supreme and Determining Aim" (see UE, Chapter 2, in the portion titled, "The Christian as Salt").

Likewise, the insightful reader will find the words of Evangelist Mordecai Ham's on "Preaching the Gospel and Prohibition" later in this chapter to be insightful as to Ham's approach to social issues. His words show the fallacy of Marsden's circular reasoning in this area.

    b. Marsden's fallacy of tautology was based on several [Modernist] presuppositions:
      1) Disbelief in the unified voice of the Holy Spirit…
      2) Who speaks through the Bible with one voice to all Christians, regardless of language, time, or culture…
      3) And who shapes their understanding of the Great Commission as the evangelization of the world.

---

[883]Ibid., 61.
[884]Fischer, *Historians Fallacies*, 49.
[885]Ibid., 167, 168.
[886]Ibid., 271, 273, 274.
[887]Marsden, *Reforming Fundamentalism*, 7.

    c. Tautology and its related fallacies:

        1) Were used by Adolph Harnack[888] when he described the social emphasis in the growth of the Early Church:

            a) Which seems to be picked up by Rodney Stark as he described the sociological reasons for the rapid expansion of the church, on the basis of why "people convert to new religions"[889]

            b) One will need to look long and hard in these books to find a discussion of the Great Commission or New Testament evangelization as being the primary reason for the growth of the Church, which makes sense because of their sociological *a priori*

        2) Similarly tautology is used in describing the social impact of D. L. Moody's ministry in Great Britain

        3) Likewise, the 19th Century hero for those who adhere to this tautology is often William Wilberforce, with his impact on the abolition of slavery in England (the so-called "great social sin" of Puritan America until the Civil War).

B. Fallacy ad Temperantiam and Evangelistic Focus:

    1. Fallacy ad temperantiam explained:

> "The *fallacy ad temperantiam* is an appeal to moderation, on the apparent assumption that truth, in Burke's phrase, is always a 'sort of middle.'"[890]

    Fischer continued:

> "A second form of the fallacy of argument *ad temperantiam* consists in substantive moderation. '*N'ayez pas de zèle,*' said Talleyrand. Many historians have made this *mot* into a motto. Ranke was one of them. Beard sneered that 'he could write of popes in a manner pleasing to both Catholics and Protestants of the upper classes.' That fact was owing not merely to an elitist common denominator but to an excess of substantive moderation. Ranke, I think, sometimes imagined that he had unlocked the inner secret of objectivity, when he had merely found a middling subjectivism."
>
> "Another example was MacAulay, who condemned historians who believed that to be impartial was 'to intersperse in due proportion epithets of praise or abhorrence.' MacAulay himself operated under a different assumption. To be impartial was, for him, to intersperse, in due proportion, epithets of abhorrence for all extremes. A recent work had analyzed the importance of 'middlingness' in his thought."[891]

    2. Fallacy ad temperantiam exemplified:

> "The book is scrupulously balanced and based on a wide range of sources, as one could expect from conscientious scholars. ...
>
> "The authors rescue Brousson from Protestant biographers by presenting a nuanced and believable picture of this martyr. Declining to give their readers 'a saintly prude ... without ordinary feelings or failings,' they argue that Brousson was 'far more complex' than his admirers have recognized. They

---

[888]Adolf von Harnack, *The Mission and Expansion of the Church in the First Three Centuries*, 2nd ed. (London: Williams and Norgate, 1908; New York: G. P. Putnam's, 1908). Michael Green provided a refreshing alternative in his *Evangelism in the Early Church* (Grand Rapids: Eerdmans, 1970).

[889]"Did Christianity grow so rapidly that mass conversions must have taken place—as Acts attests and every historian from Eusebius to Ramsay MacMullen has believed? Having established a plausible growth curve for the rise of Christianity, I will review sociological knowledge of the process by which people convert to new religions in order to infer certain requirements concerning social relations between Christians and the surrounding Greco-Roman world. The chapter concludes with a discussion of the legitimate uses of social scientific theories to reconstruct history in the absence of adequate information on what actually occurred.

"Since this book is a work of both history and social science, I have written it for a nonprofessional audience. In this way I can make sure that the social science is fully accessible to historians of the early church, meanwhile preventing social scientists from becoming lost amidst obscure historical and textual references" (Rodney Stark, *The Rise of Christianity: How the Obscure, Marginal, Jesus Movement Became the Dominant Religious Force in the Western World in a Few Centuries* [Princeton: University Press, 1996; San Francisco: HarperCollins, 1997], 3.).

[890]Fischer, *Historians Fallacies*, 296.

[891]Ibid., 297.

demonstrate, beyond question, that he was in fact guilty (as charged) of conspiring with the foreign enemies of France in a desperate attempt to halt the persecution of the Huguenots."[892]

a. The original author of this book on Claude Brousson was Walter Utt, who does not seem to have been "nuanced" enough. His 900 pages, described as representing "the life's work of Professor Utt," needed editing and pruning in order to be palatable to an Catholic-neutral English audience. Unfortunately for those interested in true history, it would seem that Strayer may have strayed to the middle t oprovide a more "nuanced" view of Brousson (for an example of Brousson's invitation in UE, see Chapter 22, "Is an Invitation Necessary for Effective Evangelistic Preaching?").

b. As a French-speaking and reading professor of "church history" myself, I am often dismayed by that which is published for English audiences as it relates to the history of the churches that took place in France. This is especially the case as it relates to Medieval France, as will be noted in the "Fallacy of Prevalent Proof" below.

4. Fallacy ad temperantiam discussed:

   a. The ever-changing and ever-readjusting "middle view," while it appeals to Hegelian dialectic, provides no foundation for the biblically-oriented Christian:
      1) The elusive middle-view often has ever-changing extremes
      2) The elusive middle-view allows for no sure foundation, such as an inerrant Bible

   b. The fallacy ad temperantiam distorts the telling of history:
      1) It denies the law of non-contradiction by forcing two opposing sides to be equally valid simultaneously
      2) It usually distorts both extreme views, because when one supposed "extreme" is invalidated (e.g. the desire to reach lost souls), the opposing view is also invalidated (the persecution of preachers of the simple Gospel)
      3) Likewise, when the true *sitz im leben* is distorted, then history is distorted.

C. Fallacy of Prevalent Proof in Historiography:

1. Fallacy of prevalent proof explained:

   "The *fallacy of prevalent proof* makes mass opinion into a method of verification."[893]

   When added to the *fallacy of argument ad temperantiam* the *fallacy of prevalent proof* can completely neuter historical facts.

2. Fallacy of prevalent proof exemplified:

   a. Prevalent proof and Patristics:

      1) Arguments from silence: These arguments abound in history, as for much of Western Church History there is only one view that has survived[894]

---

[892]Eric D. Anderson, "Preface," in Walter C. Utt and Brian E. Strayer, *The Bellicose Dove: Claude Brousson and the Protestant Resistance to Louis XIV, 1647-1698* (Brighton, Great Britain: Sussex, 2003; Portland, OR: Sussex, 2003), vii, viii.

[893]Fischer, *Historians Fallacies*, 51

[894]"Founding themselves upon this one-sided Medieval documentation, the modern theologians (from Döllinger to Father Dondaine, O.P.), the historians of religion (from Söderberg to Runciman), and the historians (from Arno Post to Christine Thouzellier) who studied and wrote on the subject up to the middle of the 20th Century, ended quite naturally to one consensual opinion, leaving the phenomena of the Cathars as a well-ordered question: catharism was a foreign body in Western Christianity and, as such, it was given over to failure. Heirs of Persian Manichaeanism and of the intervening *Mazdéism* of the Paulicians and Bogomils, it was characterized by a dualist doctrine of Oriental origin which it taught. Unrealistic, pessimistic, fundamentally anti-social, it had no chance of surviving in Western Christianity and very understandable repression of which it was the object—crusade and Inquisition—had only but accelerated the process of internal degeneration which would have without a doubt led to its disappearing.

"Paradoxically, it was in the publication and study of the inquisition archives that opened the first flaw of this wall of certainty" (Anne Brenon, *Les Archipels Cathares* [Cahors, France: Dire, 2000], 13. Translation mine).

2) Arguments from remaining manuscripts:

   a) Catholic monks, who were especially focused on propagating a sacramental (or sacerdotal) approach to salvation cleansed the records of the early church in their hands from any documents that would not promote their view

   b) The only caviat to this problem which lent to the Middle Ages the title "Dark Ages" is information from other churches, such as the Orthodox churches; the Orthodox record provides a different sacramental viewpoint to some of the issues in the Early Church

3) Arguments from the content and message of the Bible:

   a) The Bible read by Augustine, Ambrose, and Jerome, was the same Bible available to us

   b) The fact of their various interpretations do not always conform to contemporary biblical interpretation, often stems from their Ecclesiastical situation and the problems that they engaged, as well as the fact that they were very capable spokepersons for Rome's point of view, and therefore were deemed worthy for their writings to be copied and passed on to future generations

   c) A healthy skepticism as to the lack of balance in the material available is the only explanation for some of the skewed theological views that are often derived from Patristics

b. Medieval Historiography: some examples of issues:

   1) Regarding the scholarship of Jean Gonnet's and Amedeo Molnar's *Les vaudois au moyen age* (Torino: Claudiana, 1974) as regards the orthodoxy of the Waldenses; or likewise the scholarship of Michel Rubellin in his *Église et société d'Agobard à Valdèz* (Lyon, France: Presses Universitaires, 2003)

   2) Regarding the scholarship of Robert Ian Moore's *The Formation of a Persecuting Society* (Oxford: Blackwell, 1987, 1990, 1992, 1993, 1994, 1996, 1997, 1998, 1999, 2000).

   3) Regarding the scholarship of the professors in Monique Zerner, ed., *Inventer l'hérésie?Discours polémiques et pouvoirs avant l'inquisition*, Collection du centre d'études médiévales de Nice, vol. 2 (Paris: C.I.D., 1998).

   4) Regarding the words of Jean-Louis Biget, Jean Duvernoy, and Jacques Dalarun in *Évangile et évangélisme (XIIe-XIIIe siècle)*, Cahiers de Fanjeaux 34 (Toulouse, France: Éditions Privat, 1999).

c. Baptist origins:

   1) See Leon McBeth, *The Baptist Heritage*, 49ff.

D. Fallacy of Insidious Analogy:

1. Explained: A. J. P. Taylor in his introduction to *The Communist Manifesto*. Taylor quoted a couplet of Hilaire Belloc which explained why Europeans controlled huge properties on the continent of Africa:

   "We have the maxim gun,
   "And they do not"[895]

   Marx and Engels used the "maxim gun" to mislabel the bourgeoisie as the oppressing land-owners, and proletariat as oppressed working class, leading to the Russian Revolution.

2. The fallacy of labeling in the History of the Churches:

   a. "Church History" rather than "History of the Churches." It is fallacious to attempt to show that their has been one organization called the church throughout the history of the church. The Church of Rome likes to think thusly. Meanwhile it has systematically crushed and absorbed numerous revival movements in the Western church since the 3rd and 4th Centuries. However, the New Testament contains 35 uses of the plural "churches" (e.g. Acts 15:41; 16:5; Rom 16:4, 16; 1

---

[895]A. J. P. Taylor, Introduction, in Karl Marx and Friedrich Engels, *The Communist Manifesto* (Harmondsworth, Middlesex, England: Penguin books, 1967), 16.

Cor 16:1, 19; Gal 1:2, 22; Rev 1:4; etc.), thereby proving that God's New Testament ideal was not one centralized ecclesio-political organization, but rather a decentralized group of autonomous churches, led by local leaders.

b. The "Iconoclastic Controversy" in the 8th-9th Centuries were attempts by some elements in various church groupings to remain faithful to the Second Commandment, "You shall not make for yourself an idol" (Exod 20:4). Thus, rather than destroying the idols, it was the making of them that was the problem. Therefore this controversy should more clearly be called "Idol Worship Controversy."

c. The "Investiture Controversy" is another controversy with a confusing name. The title should more appropriately be called, "Debate Against the Three-Self Church," that being self-propagating, self-supporting, and self-governing. Rome was able to extirpate and eradicate self-governing churches, like those of the Cathars in Southern France, with barely a mention in any so-called "Church Histories."

d. The "Peasant Revolts," being peasants not desiring to worship according to the Church of Rome, but according to the dictates of their own conscience, leading Rome to send its forces against them. In this case these so-called "Revolts" were more appropriately "Rome's Crusades to Crush Freedom of Conscience."

e. The "Orange Riots" of New York (1870-1871). Again, another fallacious labeling. It was the Irish Catholics, the "Greens" who attacked the "Orangemen," putting an end to their parade. The Irish Catholics felt that it was a disgrace to their church that some Americans would celebrate the victory of the Protestant William of Orange over the Catholic King James II in the battle of Boyne on July 12, 1690.[896]

3. Other examples of fallacious labelling:

a. John Calvin being a "trained lawyer" as the reason behind his belief in the penal substitutionary atonement, whereas it is supposed that Thomas Anselm taught this doctrine because of his Medieval-feudal context

1) Likewise, on believers in the substitutionary atonement and their Medieval or judicial fetish

b. On the veracity and role of Protestant Martyrologies:

1) Greengrass and Jean Crespin's Martyrology[897]

2) Protestant Martyrologies and the label of sectarian bias

c. On New Testament evangelism as constantly considered "old fashioned" and out-of-date, etc.

E. The Fallacy of False Analogy:

1. The Fallacy of False Analogy Explained: "The *fallacy of false analogy* is a structural form of error which occurs when the analogical terms are shifted fron one analog to another. … This form of error is often exceedingly difficult to recognize, because it is often hidden in semantical ambiguity, or buried in some of the things which the author doesn't tell us."[898]

2. Some examples of false analogies in the History of the Churches:

a. Comparing those who believe in biblical inerrancy with those who are Docetists, believing that Jesus was not fully man:

"The foundational problem with this fundamental reading is that, refusing to keep in mind the historical character of divine revelation, she finds herself incapable of fully accepting the truth of the

---

[896]Michael A. Gordon, *The Orange Riots: Irish Political Violence in New York City, 1870 and 1871*. Ithica, NY: Cornell University, 1993.

[897]Mark Greengrass and Thomas S. Freeman, "The Acts and Monuments and the Protestant Continental Martyrologies" (copyright 2004, The John Foxe Project), from http://www.hrionline.ac.uk/johnfoxe/apparatus/greengrassessay.html; accessed 11 Oct 2007; Internet.

[898]Fischer, *Historians' Fallacies*, 251.

Incarnation itself. Fundamentalism flees the narrow relationship between the divine and the human as regards relations with God. He refuses to admit that the inspired Word of God was expressed in human language and that it was transmitted, under divine inspiration, by human authors with limited capacities and resources. For this reason, he tends to treat the biblical text as if it were dictated word for word by the Spirit and is not able to recognize that the Word of God was formulated in the language and the phraseology conditioned by this or that period."[899]

1) This accusation from the man who is currently Pope is astonishing, to say the least!

2) Was he, and other representatives on the Pontifical Commisison of which Ratzinger was President, not saying that those who believe in the inerrancy of Scripture are showing signs of Christological deviancy, by "refusing" to admit to the limitations of the human nature of the biblical revelation?

3) Ought the inerrantist rather, then, to believe that Jesus was merely half God and half man; and if that is the case, would that not also be a Christological heresy?

4) It is also interesting to note that the dictation theory is clearly taught in the Council of Trent and in Leo XIII's *Providentissimus Deus* (1893).

b. Comparing the Call for Sinners to Repent with Semi-Pelagianism[900]

1) This argument has led many a Evangelical and Protestant to part ways, and therefore:
a) Lose focus on the main thing: the Great Commission
b) In so doing, let their guard down to their true foe[901]

3. The fallacy of false analogy abounds in the History of the Churches, and unfortunately, as Fischer stated, it is often very difficult to catch!

F. Fallacy of Cum Hoc, Propter Hoc:

1. Fallacy explained:

"The *fallacy of cum hoc, propter hoc* mistakes correlation for cause."[902]

2. Fallacy exemplified:

a. Turning the Puritan application of Scripture to their arrival in the U.S. into some kind of Zionism:

1) Beginning with the fact that the Puritans were appreciative of their arrival in "New England"

2) Then showing that the Puritans and Pilgrims sought to apply Scriptures to their government and life in the U.S. (for example the quote of Acts 16:10 on the 1629 Massachusetts Bay Colony seal)

3) The fallacy comes true for these sociologically-biased historians when, due to the Puritan application of principles from the Scriptures:
a) Because the historians are working from a secular or sociological *a priori*, they fallaciously assume that the Puritans were working from their same *a* priori
b) Therefore they consider any attempt to convert the heathen Indians as an attempt at socialization, also considering any attempt at using the Bible to find governmental principles as the establishing of "theocracy"

---

[899]Joseph Cardinal Ratzinger, Pres., Commission biblique pontificale, *L'interprétation de la Bible dans l'Église* (Quebec: Fides, 1994; Paris: Cerf, 1994], 49; translation mine.

[900]See my notes on the Second Council of Orange (A.D. 529), following this chapter.

[901]Notice the Hussites who were weakened by division, and whose lands were invaded by Rome's armies in 1434: "A war broke out between the Taborites and the Ultraquists, allowing the Polish Hussites to gain the upper hand in Bohemia; Wladyslaw III of Varna definitively defeated the Hussites in the Battle of Grotniki, ending the Hussite wars" (Thomas P. Johnston, *Inquisition and Martyrdom (1002-1572): Being a Historical Study of Evangelism and Its Repression* [Liberty, MO: Evangelism Unlimited, 2009], 49-50).

[902]Fischer, *Historians' Fallacies*, 167.

c) Therefore, these historians fallaciously believed that the Puritans believed that the U.S. was a new Holy Land

d) This fallacious arguments are easily dismantled:

(1) By noting that the U.S. was the first Western pre-Napoleonic European power to include freedom of conscience as the First Amendment of its constitution, quite different than the Roman totalitarianism of most of Europe, and

(2) By understanding the conversionistic views of the early Puritans

4) Some historians go so far as to mock Solomon Stoddard's "Half-Way Covenant," which in their minds shows that "The Puritan experiment did not work!"

b. Other examples in American history related to the "Prohibition Era":

1) Because Evangelist Mordecai Ham preached on the evils of liquor, he was therefore paid by the prohibition crowd (an accusation that he denied, see below).

2) Because "organized crime" seemed to make money during the prohibition era, therefore:

a) Prohibition was the cause for the wealth of organized crime in America (via "Speakeasies"), rather than poor enforcement of the law, and

b) Prohibition, or the laws against the sale of alcohol, was responsible for the rise of organized crime in America; this exemplifies a *non sequetor* similar to, for example, a law against gun sales being responsible for the rise in illegal gun dealers

Conclusion:

For reasons of these fallacies, let the reader not be discouraged if he does not find ample evidence of evangelism in his readings in the history of the churches. Often those books that do emphasize evangelical faith are castigated and discredited by broad-minded historians (such as are the Protestant Martyrologies). Whereas the history of the churches is often rewritten with the omission of the sectarian tendency of evangelism.

Is It Possible to Study the Great Commission Hermeneutic in the Patristics Era?

Argument from Historical Distance:

The greater the historical distance, the greater the possibility of historical dissonance

We can establish that evangelists and evangelizing have been all but framed out of the Reformation era up to the First Great Awakening, is not the likelihood of the same even greater through the lens of the Medieval period and into the Patristic Era?

Argument from Question Framing, Selective Copying, or Intentional Deletion:

Is it not likely that copyists and historians have only dealt with material which is either beneficial to their cause or tangential to their cause

In other words, when there is *nihil obstat* (no obstacle), it can be copied, but if there is an obstacle to the copyist or historian, it ceases to be copied, or is burned (as was the command for the writings of Wycliffe)

Possible Repercussions of a Select Segmentation of Patristic Material:

Issues are framed in a view either positive or non-negative hermeneutic to the copyist or historian:

Such seems to be the case with the almost unique emphasis on Trinitarian theology and Christology, to the detriment of an Evangelical soteriology

Both Peter the Lombard's *Sentences* and Thomas Aquinas' *Summa* seem especially guilty of this question-framing

What remains of Augustine's writings seem especially potent in the area of question-framing, hence he is still used as a champion of scholars on both sides of the Sacramental divide

Issues that may bring distain to the ruling church are destroyed

Thus results the likelihood that material and issues are partially or seriously skewed away from the non-ruling church

Thus arguments are made using materials that lead to a predisposed hermeneutic, framing the question toward that hermeneutic

Hence, discussions of evangelizing or justification by faith are virtually impossible to find

The only hope lies in the fact that Patristic material is available in the many languages of the Mediterranean, which allows that question-framing has been less autocratic in that era

The Inverse Importance of the Study of "Church History I (0-1500 A.D.)":

Again, the issue of what constituted the real issues of the Patristic era must be viewed as clouded in historical obscurity

Also, the obscurity of the meaning of the "Classical Disciplines of Theology" remains as courses in theology and textbooks on the subject are constantly being taught or published with very few questioning the impact of the presentation of the topics, especially from a Great Commission hermeneutic

Could it therefore not be said that Church History I is the most important course in the seminary curriculum?

The Second Council of Orange (A.D. 529), Evangelism, and the Great Commission

As we will notice below, in an interesting and effective "turn of the tables", it appears that Pelagians and semi-Pelagians include those who think that unbaptized persons can respond to the Gospel message prior to their being baptized!

Introduction 1 (from http://www.fordham.edu/halsall/ basis/orange.txt (online); accessed: 5 June 2009; Internet):

> "The Council of Orange was an outgrowth of the controversy between Augustine and Pelagius. This controversy had to do with degree to which a human being is responsible for his or her own salvation, and the role of the grace of God in bringing about salvation. The Pelagians held that human beings are born in a state of innocence, i.e., that there is no such thing as a sinful nature or original sin.
>
> "As a result of this view, they held that a state of sinless perfection was achievable in this life. The Council of Orange dealt with the Semi-Pelagian doctrine that the human race, though fallen and possessed of a sinful nature, is still "good" enough to able to lay hold of the grace of God through an act of unredeemed human will."

Introduction 2 (from http://www.reformed.org/documents/canons_of_orange.html (online); accessed: 5 June 2009; Internet)—compare with the introduction above:

> "The Council of Orange was an outgrowth of the controversy between Augustine and Pelagius. This controversy had to do with degree to which a human being is responsible for his or her own salvation, and the role of the grace of God in bringing about salvation. The Pelagians held that human beings are born in a state of innocence, i.e., that there is no such thing as a sinful nature or original sin.
>
> "As a result of this view, they held that a state of sinless perfection was achievable in this life. The Council of Orange dealt with the Semi-Pelagian doctrine that the human race, though fallen and possessed of a sinful nature, is still "good" enough to able to lay hold of the grace of God through an act of unredeemed human will. The Council held to Augustine's view and repudiated Pelagius. The following canons greatly influenced the Reformed doctrine of Total Depravity."

Johnston's Preliminary Analysis: How do the Canons of the Council of Orange impact New Testament evangelism?

The importance of the teaching of the Second Council of Orange as far as the theological struggles related to evangelism in the English-speaking churches can scarcely be overstated. This council pits the currently-called Calvinists against the currently-called Arminians. And, yes, the issue relates to evangelism.

> Jesus rightly stated, "Every city or house divided against itself will not stand," Matt 12:25

> This issue provides the perfect knife to divide Bible-believing and conversion-believing Christians into opposing camps!

For example, notice this paragraph from the 1553 Forty-Two Articles of the Church of England:

> "VIII. *Of originall or birthe sinne.* Originall sinne standeth not in the folowing of Adam, as the Pellagianes doe vainelie talke, whiche also the Anabaptistes doe now a daies renue, but it is the fault, and corruption of the nature of euery manne, that naturallie is engendred of the ofspring of Adam, whereby manne is very farre gone from his former righteousnesse, whiche he had at his creation and is of his owne nature geuen to euill, so that the fleshe desireth alwaies contrarie to the spirit, and therefore in euery persone borne into this woride, it deserueth Goddes wrath and damnation And this infection of nature doeth remaine, yea in theim that are baptized, wherby the lust of the fleshe called in Greke φρονερα σαρκος, (whiche some do expoune, the wisedome, some sensualitie, some the desyre of the fleshe, is not subject to the lawe of GOD. And although there is no condemnation for theim that beleue, and are baptized, yet the Apostle doeth confesse, that concupiscence, and lust hath of it self the nature of sinne."[903]

---

[903]" Anglican Articles of Religion of 1553 and 1572," available at: http://www.episcopalian.org/ efac/1553-1572.htm; accessed 21 Oct 2004; Internet.

1. In order to properly understand this Council in its context, prior to reading the Canons, the reader should first read the Conclusion (at the second table [sections 26-27] below). In this way it will be clear to him what the "catholic" church taught at that time about the necessity of baptism as the original reception of, and in order to respond to future nurture in the grace of God:

    a. The will of man being so impaired that "no one can … believe in God":
        1) Thus when an evangelist tells an unbaptized person to believe in God, the unbaptized person cannot believe in God (i.e. Christ or the Gospel), because of an impaired nature, which can only be cleansed by the waters of Baptism, rightfully bestowed
        2) Or worse yet, if an evangelist says (with audacity and temerity) that infant baptism does not bestow any special grace or saving faith, but rather that a person must first repent and believe—then come the Canons of the Council of Orange to the rescue
        3) Lastly, if a person has already been baptized, they have no need to heed the call to repent and believe, since they have already done so by proxy through infant baptism, furthermore, deeds of penance and growth in faith are a constant part of the Christian life, their beginning point is the sacrament of "Holy Baptism" and their ending point [be it so] is the sacrament of "Holy Unction" prior to death

    b. No one can believe in God "unless the grace of divine mercy has preceded him"—and this [prevenient] grace of God comes uniquely and only through the sacrament of "Holy" Baptism,[904] and that baptism may even be conferred by "heretics" and "schismatics," given the proper formula is used:[905]

        1) Therefore a lost or unsaved person can only respond to the Gospel if they have first been baptized

        2) But, [infant] baptism *is* the new birth, therefore the [infant] baptized person needs no conversion to the Lord!

        3) Therefore, asking a baptized person to be converted is:
            a) Highly arrogant and opinionated on the part of the evangelist,
            b) A complete misreading the Bible, and a complete misunderstanding of [true] conversion and salvation (and especially the role of Baptism and the other "Sacraments" [means of grace] and Rome's hierarchy in this process), and
            c) Going against all the teachings of the "Church" on the subject

        4) Some further implications of this false teaching on baptism:
            a) Teaching that infant baptism removes original sin, in effect, makes any future sin for the baptized infant a matter of environmentalism—or: the "outside locus of sin" (i.e. "behavior is social")
            b) Just as sin does not reside within the baptized person (by his very nature), so neither does the Holy Spirit reside within the saved person (which theologians would consider Manicheanism), even though there is ample biblical evidence to the contrary, e.g. 1 Cor 6:19; 2 Tim 1:14
            c) The result is that the Holy Spirit must be received from the outside, i.e. through a sacrament—a sign or symbol made holy by the prayer of the priest (holy host, holy water, holy oil, etc.)
            d) So the implications of Infant Baptism and the entire Sacramental system of conversion is drastically different from a biblical theology and quite foreign to Evangelical theology!

    c. The Second Council of Orange then follows with a litany of verses often used by Evangelicals to describe conversion, but in this case wrongly used to describe the incomparable gift of Holy

---

[904]"It [Baptism] is called a *gift* because it is conferred on those who bring nothing of their own [not even the will to say a 'Sinner's Prayer']; *grace* since it is given even to the guilty" (*Catechism of the Catholic Church*, ed. by Joseph Cardinal Ratzinger [Rome: Libreria Editrice Vaticana, 1994; London: Geoffrey Chapman, 1994], §1216).

[905]*Catechism*, §838; referencing the Vatican II decree, *Unitatis Reintegratio*, §3; the acceptance of "heretical" baptism goes back to Gregory 1 (590-604), who accepted the baptism of the Arian Visigoths when they were [re]absorbed or reintegrated (using the verb in the Vatican II decree) into the fold of Rome.

Baptism, which is usually given to young infants, who are unable to speak or respond to the message of the Gospel in any way[906]

d. The Council of Orange provides the touchstone separating churches and denominations that practice infant baptism and those that do not:

1) At stake is the entire evangelism and conversion impetus of the church in question, that is, its Great Commission emphasis

2) It is no wonder that infant baptism has a strong tendency to diminish the evangelistic thrust of any church, particularly a state church, wherein it is assumed that every citizen of the state has been baptized

3) Remembering also that Calvin placed the entire argument for infant baptism, and therefore for the major salvific enterprise of the church on one phrase in 1 Cor 7:14 [Gk. νῦν δὲ ἅγιά ἐστιν; "but now they are holy"], for this verse provides his only non-deduced NT justification for the practice:[907]

1 Cor 7:14, "For the unbelieving husband is sanctified through his wife, and the unbelieving wife is sanctified through her believing husband; for otherwise your children are unclean, but now they are holy"

4) Therefore, based primarily on deduction from the OT, with not one example from the NT, through infant baptism, the "martial note and conquesat tread of the Gospel" is changed, and the entire salvific enterprise of the church suffers:

a) Changing the focus of salvation to seeking to persuade parents that they must bring their newborn babies for infant "baptism" as a NT rite of passage:

(1) Based on the deduction that the phrase "but now they are holy" in 1 Cor 7:14 relates specifically and primarily to salvation:
(a) Thereby undermining the entire weight of Scriptures alone, grace alone, and faith alone of NT salvation

---

[906]Recalling the five points of the Monk Henry [of Lausanne], against which wrote Peter [the Venerable of Cluny] in his *Contra Petrobrusianos* (1135-1140):

"1. Refusal to baptize infants, under the pretext that it is faith that saves and that a young infant could not have sufficient conscience to believe.

"2. Rejection of holy places; the Church of God does not consist of an assemblage of stones but of a spiritual reality, the communion of the faithful.

"3. The cross is not an object of adoration; it is on the contrary a detestable object, as the instrument of the torture and suffering of Christ.

"4. Priests and bishops dispense a lying teaching as to the matter of the Eucharist. The body of Christ was consumed only one time and only by the disciples, during the communion that preceded the Passion. All other later consumption is only vain fiction.

"5. The funeral liturgy in its whole (offerings, prayers, Masses, and alms) is useless; the dead can hope in nothing more than what they received when they were alive" (Dominique Iogna-Prat, "L'argumentation défensive: de la Polémique grégorienne au 'Contra Petrobrusianos' de Pierre le Vénérable," in *Inventer l'hérésie: Discours polémiques et pouvoirs avant l'inquisition*, Monique Zerner, ed., Collection du centre d'études médiévales de Nice, vol. 2 [Paris: C.I.D., 1998], 88; translation mine.).

[907]"It is true that when the children of the faithful arrived at the age of discretion, they may alienate themselves from God, and render void [Fr. et anneantir] the truth of Baptism ["The translator (into Latin) added: *quantum in ipsis est*"]. But this is not to say, that our Lord has not elect and separated them from others, in order to present to them His salvation. Otherwise, it would be in vain that Saint Paul said that the child having a faithful father or mother is sanctified, who would be base, if he was engendered from and a descendant of unbelievers (1 Cor 7:14). Because the Holy Spirit, author and source of all sanctification, testifies that the children of Christians are holy, is it for us to exclude them of such a good? Or if the truth of Baptism is in them, how do we dare deprive them of the sign, which is lesser and inferior?" ("John Calvin's Brief Instruction against the errors of the [ana]Baptists" (1544): Preface and Part One, on the Baptism of Little Children"; from Jehan Calvin, "Brieve Instruction pour Armer tous Bons Fideles contre les Erreurs de la Secte Commune des Anabaptistes" (Geneva: Jehan Girard, 1544); in *Corpus Reformatorum*, vol 35; Ioannis Calvini, *Opera Quae Supersunt Omnia*, vol. 7 (Brunsvigae: Schwetschke, 1868), 45-142; translated by Thomas P. Johnston).

        (b) Which conjecture also biblical revelation shows not to be the case, in the apostacy of the children of Israel in the OT (who were submitted to circumcision at infancy), e.g. Deut 31:26-27; the main theme of the Book of Judges

        (c) Which conjecture, furthermore, the NT shows not to be the case, 2 Tim 4:3-4

        (d) And which conjecture experience shows not to be the case, as children and/or grandchildren of godly born again Christians are constantly drifting from the Gospel they grew up with

    (2) Thereby the unknowing child receives assurance of salvation by virtue of:

        (a) His parents bringing him/her

        (b) To be baptized by an approved third party (human intermediary)

        (c) To whom the parents (and perhaps godparents) make certain vows

        (d) The third party speaks the proper formula of words prior to or during the sprinkling or pouring of water over its head

           [1] The water being considered an effective physical sign and symbol unto salvation

           [2] The baptismal formula, from Matt 28:19, also considered to have a supernatural salvific impact on the baby

        (e) And the third party then prays a type of Sinners Prayer on behalf of the child

           [1] This prayer being another confirmation that the rite must be valid, by virtue of its words and passion ("whatever you bind on earth will be bound in heaven," Matt 18:18)

    (3) In this system, it is clear that:

        (a) The way in which the approved third party is ordained may differ, as may be the vows or conditions that he or she are made to follow

        (b) The vows made or the words spoken by the parents may differ

        (c) The exact method of and location for the application of the water may differ (pouring on the forehead, sprinkling on the temple, a wet hand placed on the head, etc.)

        (d) The calling of the three persons of the Trinity, from Matt 28:19, is pretty much a standard

        (e) The exact words of the priest, pastor, or preacher prayed during or following the baptism (a Sinner's Prayer) may also differ

    (4) Nevertheless, this action done to a child when he/she is an infant, is said to apply all the benefits of salvation to the child, needing only to be "Confirmed" as a young adolescent:

        (a) Meanwhile, many who teach and practice infant baptism, loudly decry an adult crying out to God for salvation through use of some type of Sinner's Prayer

        (b) Quite a paradox!

b) Rather, the NT focus of salvation to involve seeking to convince persons who have arrived at a reasonable age to understand their sinful state, and of their need for repentance and the new birth:

    (1) That is, actually fulfilling the words of the Great Commission to "go and preach," "be testifiers," and "win disciples"

    (2) Thereby placing the assurance of salvation, not on some water sprinkled on the baby at infancy, but in the cognitive decision of that same person to:

        (a) Repent of sin and sinfulness;

        (b) Confess that sin to Christ as wrong;

        (c) Look only to Christ as the possibility for forgiveness of that sin;

        (d) Verbally cry out to Jesus for that forgiveness (in some way, hence a sinner's cry for mercy, or a Sinner's Prayer); and

        (e) Place one's life under the rulership of Christ and His Word, the Bible

(3) The only third party (or intermediary) is the Holy Spirit speaking to the heart of man through the powerful Word of God, using the words of the obedient herald of the Gospel to convict of sin, righteousness, and judgment.

e. Consider how the "Council of Orange" frames the question…

Charting the Second Council of Orange's Framing of the Question

	Infant Baptizers	Believer's Baptizers
Prior to Persons Receiving Baptism (regardless of the age)	Outside the water of Baptism persons cannot understand the Gospel; Outside the water of Baptism persons cannot respond positively to the Gospel call	Simply preaching the Gospel to lost persons is illegitimate, since only through the waters of Baptism can be cleansed of original sin (allowing their minds to discern spiritual truth), and receive salvation. Those who preach the Gospel expecting lost people to believe merely from hearing the Gospel: • Must not understand that the Holy Spirit must be dispensed with the sign of water • Must not understand that man in his own rational being cannot comprehend the things of God. Therefore, anyone who evangelizes indiscriminately must not believe in man's depraved nature, making them "semi-Pelagian"
What Baptism Does?	E.g. "39 Articles of the Church of England" [By Thomas Cramner (1553) and Matthew Parker (1572)] XXVII. *Of Baptisme* "Baptisme is not only a signe of profession, and marke of difference, whereby Christian men are discerned from other that be not christened: but is also a signe of regeneration or newe byrth, whereby as by an instrument, they that receaue baptisme rightly, are grafted into the Church: the promises of the forgeuenesse of sinne, and of our adoption to be the sonnes of God, by the holy ghost, are visibly signed and sealed: fayth is confyrmed: and grace increased by vertue of prayer vnto God. "The baptisme of young children, is in any wyse to be retayned in the Churche, as most agreable with the institution of Christe."	E.g. Balthasar Hubmaier "Summary of the Entire Christian Life" (1525) "From all this it follows that the outward baptism unto Christ is nothing else than a public profession of the inward obligation. By it, man confesses publicly that he is a sinner, and admits his guilt. Yet he believes that Christ, through His death, has atoned for his sins, and by His resurrection has made him righteous in the sight of God, our heavenly Father. Therefore he has determined to confess openly and publicly the faith and name of Jesus Christ."
After Receiving Baptism (regardless of age)	They will not refuse the grace of God, although they will need to add works to the graces that they receive by the Holy Sacraments of the Holy Roman Church Likewise they need not hear the Gospel again They have already responded to the Gospel (through baptism)	[Since Orange placed the focus on the waters of Baptism, everything is fine once persons have submitted to water Baptism] [Makes one wonder if this was why the so-called "Albigenses" or "Cathars" seemed to emphasize waterless Spirit-Baptism]
The Impasse	Someone who tries to evangelize a baptized person disagrees with the ancient teachings of the Roman Catholic Church, and is therefore a heretic Someone who tells an infant baptized person that he is not converted is a heretic	A Christian who refuses to confess Christ before men, will be denied by the Lord Jesus Christ, Mark 8:38 A Christian who disobeys the Great Commission is disobeying a clear command of Christ, which must be obeyed, Matt 28:19-20

f. Then the prior admission being made (Baptism is first necessary to understand the Gospel), the interpretation and application of the Council of Orange is completely changed thereby:

1) Quote: "According to the catholic faith we also believe that after grace has been received through baptism"
   a) The entire weight of all the argumentation of this council is poised on the sacrament of Holy Baptism, or infant baptism
   b) Pitting the supposed human agency of believing and the corresponding divine agency of regeneration, is an exercise to confuse Evangelicals, and divide them into two arbitrary camps, neither of which likely believes in baptismal regeneration.

    c) This struggle with baptism brings alive the issues that were discussed between Zwingli and Hubmaier on the issue of [re]baptism.

  2) Quote: "all baptized persons have the ability and responsibility, if they desire to labor faithfully, to perform with the aid and cooperation of Christ what is of essential importance in regard to the salvation of their soul"

    a) It is therefore not necessary for "baptized persons" to "repent and believe the Good News"!

      (1) "So long, evangelist, go elsewhere to preach your Gospel"

      (2) "You false teacher, go speak to someone else [the unbaptized]"[908]

      (3) [Hence, as the plowman precedes the planter of seeds, so the Evangelical missionaries plow the fields of world religions, while Rome comes in later to plant their seed in the plowed soil!]

    b) Even though (according to Rome) only the baptized, and they alone, can positively respond to the proclamation of the Word of God, because they have received the grace of Baptism!

      (1) Therefore, the only ones, who according to Roman theology can and will actually respond to the Gospel message, according to their theology, never hear it from a priest of the Church of Rome, but rather receive it through the signs and symbols of the Church instead—as the power is not in the Gospel proclaimed, it is in the signs and symbols of the Church!

      (2) A thereby a knot is tightened over the preaching of the Gospel to the unbaptized, while the baptized never hear it either; it is a Lose-Lose for evangelism and true conversion either way!

g. This complete turning of the tables is almost incomprehensible to the Evangelical mind, who may think that the Council of Orange is merely a Calvinism versus Arminianism debate:

  1) It is not: this debate very wisely and very poisonously, frames Evangelicalism into two camps, along with quotes of Scripture that they frequently use, to:

    a) Created, accentuated, or capitalized upon the Calvinist-Arminian type of debate driving an effective wedge into Evangelicalism (much like the Hussites were divided into two camps to be defeated in the 1400s); the motto being, "divide and conquer!"

    b) Forcing an artificial dichotomy that is not in the Bible (cf. Psa 119:9, etc.), to place the two groups at war against each other (which unfortunately we have willingly fulfilled)

    c) And then threw in the Sacrament of Holy Baptism, as if an afterthought, which blows away the confused minds of the Evangelicals, who have been trying to make sense of the arguments of this Council without reading the context provided by the Conclusion:

      (1) As Orange ignored the divine element (the power of the Word of God, the Gospel of Christ, the blood of Christ, and the grace of God)

      (2) Then they turned both the proclamation of the Gospel and its reception through repentance and faith into a human work of receiving some water on the outer man

      (3) While [guardedly] framing the issue of conversion and salvation via Augustine's theology of "signs and symbols"

      (4) As such, it appears that the Council of Orange is full of half truths and partial truths (equivocations)

  2) For example, there is no mention of the inherent power of the Word of God and/or the Gospel proclaimed to transform the hardest heathen heart; [909] in fact, the Holy Spirit

---

[908]Herein is where Evangelicals are useful to Rome, to bring in people of other faiths into "Christianity." Once brought into "Christianity," Rome can send its people to convert them to its version of the "Christian" faith.

[909]Notice J. Hudson Taylor on this concept: "The gospel itself is the power of God unto salvation to everyone that believeth. Now, there are different ways of preaching the gospel. There is the plan of preaching the gospel and looking forward to the gradual enlightenment of the people, to their being saved as it were by a process of gradual instruction and preaching. And there is another method of preaching the gospel; *believing it to be the power of God unto*

working in, with, and by the Word of God seems purposefully left out of the discussion, whereas the Holy Spirit working salvifically through the Sacrament of Baptism is promoted at the end!

h. In essence, the Council of Orange leveraged God's sovereignty and eliminated individual choice, not for the purpose of emphasizing the work of God through His Word to convict of sin and draw sinners to Christ, but for the purpose of promoting infant baptism:

1) The Second Council of Orange, and its acceptance as part of the "infallible" Tradition of the the Church of Rome, marks a clear departure of that church from New Testament evangelism

2) If infant baptism was the first soteriological watershed, several other points can be added to this sacrament:
   a) The primacy of the bishop of Rome and of his rulings came before, with Augustine's *Contra Donatisten* (A.D. 402-412; while it seems very likely that his *Contra Manichean* was also aimed at Evangelicals in his day)
   b) The sacrament of Penance and absolution of sins were already clearly taught by Jerome (~A.D. 435)
   c) The sacrament of the Eucharistic sacrifice was well developed by the time of Paschasius Radbertus (~A.D. 851)
   d) Confession to a priest as part of Penance and Absolution, and as required [annually] of all the citizens of a country with a Catholic sovereign, taught by 1215 (not so doing meant coming under Inquisition)

2. The following appear to be five foundations (among others) for New Testament Evangelism:

a. Assurance of salvation:
   = The person sharing is sure of his salvation
   + The person sharing is sure that he can guide the person listening on how to be saved

b. By the blood of Christ alone:
   = Faith alone in the finished substitutionary work of Christ on the cross as the only source of forgiveness of sins, salvation, and eternal life

c. Through the power of God's Word alone:
   = The person sharing believes that the Word of God and/or the Gospel, is the sword of the Spirit (Eph 6:17), and has inherent power (Heb 4:12-13; Rom 1:16-17; 1 Thess 2:13),
   + That it will bring about conviction of sin, righteousness, and judgment (John 16:8)
   ... Leading to a "hearing of faith" (Gal 3:1-5; Heb 4:2) in some who hear,
   ... Allowing for their instantaneous conversion, if they repent and believe in the Gospel (John 5:24; 1 John 5:13; e.g. Acts 16:14; 16:30-31)

d. Instantaneous conversion:
   = The person sharing believes from the words of Scripture that he can guide the contact to immediate repentance and salvation
   + Following a hearing of faith,
   + Even through saying a prayer of faith (Rom 10:9-10)
   ... Leading to immediate justification by faith (Rom 1:16-17)

e. The role of a sinner's prayer:
   = The sinner's prayer provides a guide to lead a person into verbal repentance of sin and verbal confession of Christ (Rom 10:9-10)

---

salvation; preaching it in the *expectation* that He who first brought light out of darkness can and will at once and instantaneously take the darkest heathen heart and create light within. That is the method that is successful. It has been my privilege to know many Christians – I am speaking within bounds when I say a hundred – who have accepted Jesus Christ as their Saviour the first time they ever heard of Him. The gospel itself is the power of God unto salvation" (J. Hudson Taylor, "The Source of Power," *Ecumenical Missionary Conference, New York, 1900* [New York, American Tract Society, 1900]: 1:91. emphasis mine).

… That being the only rightful "manner" of salvation (Acts 15:7-11; Rom 10:9-10, 13-15, 17); cf. the Medieval Cathar "*consolamentum*"

3. The fact that a person upon hearing the Gospel, must be given the opportunity to believe (following the biblical examples), and thus it appears that the person hearing must have freedom to receive Christ (the Holy Spirit's work in the heart not being fully discernible to the evangelist, but only to God):

   a. This entire Council was attacking the fact that a lost person can turn to Christ outside of the preceding sacrament of "Holy" Baptism:
      1) A lost person was redefined as someone not having been baptized
      2) A saved person was redefined as someone who has been baptized

   b. This Council attacked Evangelicalism at its heart, decisional preaching, the proclamation of the Gospel to the lost with a view to instantaneous conversion!
      1) Calling an unbaptized person to Christ was rendered illegitimate, being labeled "Semi-Pelagianism," a decision they could not make
      2) Calling a baptized person to Christ was also considered illegitimate, going against Rome's teaching on baptismal regeneration
      3) However, there did remain a misplaced decisional preaching in Rome's approach, of which examples are:
         a) [Pope] Urban II (1088-1099) called young men to take up arms to regain the "Holy" Land back for the Church of Rome[910]
         b) The decisional proclamation of the reconverted Waldensian Durand d'Osca (1208), which proclaimed the authority of the Roman Pontiff and of all the particular doctrines of Rome at that time[911]
         c) Bernard of Clairveaux calling his hearers in Southern France to take up the fight against the so-called heretical Cathars,[912] who were given the name "Albigensian [Fr. *Albigeois*]" by another "crusade preacher," Jacques de Vitry[913]

   c. This Council leveraged a tangential "theological problem" in its age to hereticize any evangelist who would call his audience to make a decision for Christ!

4. Final preliminary conjecture: These canons seem to be the result of taking an existing Evangelical-type doctrinal statement (perhaps of Donatist origin), set against a sacramental (aka. sacerdotal) view of conversion itself; and using as much as possible of its original points and Scriptures, the Council of Orange theologians put just enough nuance in necessary points to turn it into a sacramental statement!

   a. They turned the original arguments regarding conversion into a semantical game (playing with words, playing with the salvation of millions upon millions of lost souls)
   b. Truly, "A little leaven leavens the whole lump of dough" (Gal 5:9)!

---

[910]Jonathan Riley-Smith, *What Were the Crusades?* 3rd ed (San Francisco: Ignatius, 1977, 1992, 2002), 37-43.

911 Heinrich Denzinger, Peter Hünermann, and Joseph Hoffmann, *Symboles et définitions de la foi catholique* (*Enchiridion Symbolorum*), 38th ed. (Paris: Cerf, 1996), §790-797.

[912]Jean Duvernoy, *Le Catharisme: Histoire des Cathares* (Toulouse, France: Privat, 1979), 205.

[913]Jean Duvernoy, *Le Catharisme: La Religion des Cathares* (Toulouse, France: Privat, 1976), 227-33.

THE CANONS OF THE COUNCIL OF ORANGE (529 AD)[914] [WITH ANALYSIS]

CANON	ANALYSIS
CANON 1. If anyone denies that it is the whole man, that is, both body and soul, that was "changed for the worse" through the offense of Adam's sin, but believes that the freedom of the soul remains unimpaired and that only the body is subject to corruption, he is deceived by the error of Pelagius and contradicts the scripture which says, "The soul that sins shall die" (Ezek. 18:20); and, "Do you not know that if you yield yourselves to anyone as obedient slaves, you are the slaves of the one whom you obey?" (Rom. 6:16); and, "For whatever overcomes a man, to that he is enslaved" (2 Pet. 2:19).	1.1 As far as NT evangelism goes, the "error of Pelagius" here relates to the fact that an evangelist has the obligation to give the unsaved person the opportunity to repent and believe the Gospel, immediately upon the hearing of the Gospel, and to decide for or against Christ ("Choose you this day whom you shall serve," Josh 24:15; "Today if you hear His voice do not harden your heart," Psa 95:7; Heb 3:7, 15; 4:7; "now is the acceptable time, now is the day of salvation" 2 Cor 6:2); as this Canon is framed, it seems that for this type of decision to be possible, the evangelist has to have a "semi-Pelagian" view of the sin nature, wherein the lost person has some opportunity to believe within himself, his "will" therefore being "unimpaired"—with never a mention of the power of God's Word in this process (Heb 4:12-13; e.g. Acts 16:14): 1.1.1. This attacks evangelism at its heart: the point of decision, the invitation to repent and believe 1.1.2. Notice that this point removes and denigrates the individual obligation to decide for Christ, a position in which liberal Protestants would agree with Rome, in that they [liberal Protestants] would call an emphasis on personal conversion, an individualistic or personalistic tendency [rather than its inverse, their communitistic or socialistic tendency]) 1.2. The "error of Pelagius" here is that the entire body is "subject to corruption," a point for which Evangelicals are also considered as having "Manichean tendencies," whereas it is true that the entire body is subject to corruption (see my notes "Jesus on Total Depravity"); the deeper issue is twofold: 1.2.1. Whether relics, holy objects, sacred statues, or the Host in the Eucharist are really a part of the "new creation" and are truly "holy" as affirmed by the Church of Rome? 1.2.2. Whether humans, prior to conversion, are totally depraved in body, mind, soul, and spirit, and can do absolutely no good in the eyes of God, outside of first being converted? It seems that this truth is equivocated in this doctrine through the skillful application of their doctrine of Infant baptism, wherein the infant is cleansed of his "Original Sin" 1.2.3 It must be noted that from an Evangelical point of view, the sacraments (incl. "Holy" Baptism) do not, cannot, and will not confer any type of grace whatsoever, but are merely human actions (John 1:13), two of which are done in obedience to commands of Christ (Matt 28:19-20; Luke 22:19); in fact, not only do the other Five Sacraments add to the Scriptures (which is strictly forbidden, Deut 4:2; 12:32; Prov 30:6; Rev 22:18), but they rob God and the Holy Spirit of their part in salvation, making every aspect of salvation into the human work conferred by an earthly and physical action by a priest of Rome, John 6:28-29 1.2.4. Notice also how the Council of Orange skirts around the real issues of salvation by grace alone through faith alone upon the hearing of the Word of God proclaimed (Acts 15:7-11; Rom 10:17), the same being mimicked in the 1999 Lutheran-Catholic Declaration on Justification, in which salvation is by an equivocal "grace alone," but never by "faith alone"! 1.3. It would seem, therefore, from this Canon 1 of the Council of Orange, that anyone who feels that a person can and should make a decision for Christ upon hearing the Gospel can rightfully be accused of Pelagianism: 1.3.1. Isn't this the accusation of the high Calvinists against contemporary evangelists and evangelism? They deny NT evangelism on the basis of Augustinian anti-believer's baptism philosophical theology—perhaps without even realizing it! 1.3.2. Notice also that this same condemnation of decisional preaching by Rome led them to falsely accuse the Reformers of being "Humanists", and similarly the preachers of the Second Great Awakening in the U.S. are accused of preaching to move the "human will"[915] 1.4. Notice also that the entire logic of the Council of Orange stems from the writings of Augustine; this would be his third strike against Evangelicals: 1.4.1. *Contra Donatisten* prohibited local congregational or any other local form of church government, while denying local congregations their obligation to use 1 Timothy 3 as a measuring stick for their leaders, leading to a host of problems related to leadership, accountability, and immorality in the history of the Church of Rome 1.4.2. *Contra Manichean* discounted the concept of being "born again" (a new creation, 2 Cor 5:17) by the Holy Spirit by faith alone outside of the signs and symbols of the sacraments of the Church; this was an especially effective use of the fallacy of false composition by Augustine (see below) 1.4.3. Now the Council of Orange, based on Augustinian writings, attacks New Testament evangelism in a number of

---

[914]"The Second Council of Orange" (online); available at: From: http://www.fordham.edu/halsall/basis/orange.txt; accessed:

[915]"Protestant Evangelicalism of the 1820s and 1830s contributed a spiritual component to republican capitalism by preaching that human will, not divine power, could create order and virtue" (Michael A. Gordon, *The Orange Riots: Irish Political Violence in New York City, 1870 and 1871* [Ithica, NY: Cornell University Press, 1993], 11). Notice that Rome's antithesis of preaching human will is focused on the so-called divine reception of grace received only when a priest pours water over the head of an infant.

ways, as noted herein, calling those who practice New Testament evangelism "deceived by the error of Pelagius"

1.5. One cannot ignore the subtleties of the methods of argumentation used by Augustine, in which groupings were made in order to group Evangelical thought with false teachers who exhibited certain related tendencies, then accusing the Evangelicals of all the falsehoods related to those false teachers:

1.5.1. False grouping of groups of thought or beliefs, as in this case, is called the "fallacy of composition" in David Fischer's *Historians' Fallacies*[916]

1.5.2. The methodology used by Augustine as relates to the "fallacy of false composition" seems to be as follows:

1.5.2.1. The false teacher to be used for the fallacy of false composition has to be chosen very carefully; for he needs to exhibit at least one link of a distasteful teaching, which can then be used in labeling the target group, and yet he has to be a clear false teacher in some way (e.g. Manis for the Manicheans)

1.5.2.2. The false teacher, once found and chosen, is described in every detail to show his theological inadequacies

1.5.2.2.1. There seems to be an obsession, among Catholic apologists, to target any teaching that does not derive from their Traditions as the innovation of an individual

1.5.2.2.2. This obsession becomes a double-edged sword for them:

1.5.2.2.2.1. On one hand, to them, it proves that a teaching is not derived from a proper interpretation of Scripture, as it is not their interpretation of Scripture; the individual is therefore easy to anathematize and his memory and followers must then be extirpated

1.5.2.2.2.2. On the other hand, when individual after individual exhibit the same supposed "misinterpretation" of Scripture, for example by disbelieving in infant baptism (and so forth), it becomes more difficult for Catholic apologists to prove that it is truly a brand new innovation; so they must redouble their efforts to find other areas of theological distinction, even going to extremes to find them!

1.5.2.2.2.3. For example, in 1334, [Pope] John XXII wrote of the Fraticelli, "in this they follow the error of the Donatists" (of the 4th Century) and also, "Their third error conspires with the error of the Waldenses" and again, "The fourth blasphemy of these wicked [ones], bubbling forth from the poisonous source of the aforementioned Waldenses" (a 12th-13th Century group)[917]

1.5.2.2.2.3.1. It is difficult to find a teaching to be the particular innovation of an individual if it is admittedly held by others in the history of the churches, and yea, throughout the history of the churches!

1.5.2.2.2.4. Also, the Parliament of France (1527) accused the Protestant (called Lutheran at that time) distribution of vernacular Bibles as repeating the error of the Waldensians, Albigensians and Turlupins, the first two groups being 12th and 13th Century so-called heresies[918]

1.5.2.3. The one area of commonality, to be used to later force the fallacious grouping, is then described in great detail

1.5.2.4. The target group, which will be labeled as "heretical" via the false grouping is introduced as having the area of commonality described in 1.5.2.3., much to the glee of church administrators who do not

---

[916]"The *fallacy of composition* consists in reasoning improperly from a property of a member of group to a property of the group itself. This form of error is not restricted to groups of human beings but extends to all classes of things. And as such, it occurs in two varieties: First, it falsely extrapolates a quality of one group member to all group members. … Second, it is possible to transfer the quality of a member of the group to the group itself" (David H. Fischer, *Historians Fallacies: Toward a Logic of Historical Thought* [New York: Harper, 1970], 219); the *converse fallacy of difference* applies here also (Fischer, 223-24).

[917]Heinrich Denzinger, §912-914. Translation mine.

[918]"Although the sacred books might be translated into languages, in that they are in their nature holy and good: yet the great danger of permitting the promiscuous reading of them, when translated without any explanation, is sufficiently shewn by the Waldensians, Albigensians and Turlupins, who have spread abroad many errors through this cause" (Margaret Deanesly, *The Lollard Bible and Other Medieval Biblical Versions* [Cambridge University Press, 1920; Eugene, OR: Wipf and Stock, 2002], 387-88).

		appreciate the ecclesiastical competition of target group either
	1.5.2.5.	The one area of commonality is then expounded in great detail (using the fallacious semantical distortion of accent),[919] sometimes choosing only those people or practitioners from within the target group, who make sure targets to make the point, in order to set the stage for the next point
	1.5.2.6.	Once the false grouping is clearly established by the proponent as having the one area of commonality, then coming in for the kill, the target group is now accused, by the fallacy of the perfect analogy,[920] of every other area of falsehood already established in 1.5.2.2.

- 1.5.2.6.1. Examples of this fallacious grouping is very common in Early Church historiography and theology; it takes place regularly using the following categories:
  - 1.5.2.6.1.1. Gnosticism (believing that they have a "special" knowledge), for those who believe that when a person is "born again" through prayer that they receive special or new insight into the Bible (1 Cor 2:14) and God's work in the world (Eph 1:9)
  - 1.5.2.6.1.2. Docetic (believing that Christ was not human, but merely appeared human), for any who believe that the new birth (being "born again") is all and only wrought inwardly by the Holy Spirit, outside of any outward physical or human sign (water) or outside of seeking to transform society (as in liberation theology)[921]
  - 1.5.2.6.1.3. Marcionite (posited a "God" of the Old Testament as different than the "God" of the New), for those who believe in a New Testament church and New Testament evangelism, rather than a church with vestments, priests, and sacrifices (sacraments) which simultaneously deemphasizes man's depravity and the need for evangelism and conversion
  - 1.5.2.6.1.4. Manichean (dividing up the universe as a constant struggle between good and evil), for any who believe that there is such a category as "saved and lost" (Col 2:13), or who believe that Christians are in a spiritual battle with the forces of wickedness (2 Cor 4:3-4; 10:3-4)![922]
  - 1.5.2.6.1.5. Donatist (a separatist church movement in North Africa), for any who believe in a locally-ruled church or that the church is for believers only
  - 1.5.2.6.1.6. Pelagian (believing that man somehow has the ability to save himself), for any who believe that God can speak to the unbaptized soul to lead the person to repentance and faith, uniquely by the preaching of the gospel, outside of the use of an outward sign, symbol, or sacrament of the Roman church
  - 1.5.2.6.1.7. All these categories, and more, are constantly volleyed about in "academic" circles, and are regularly used as "maxim guns"[923] against authors, church leaders, and churches who happen to believe in New

---

[919] "The *fallacy of accent* occurs in an argument when meaning is distorted by emphasis" (Fischer, 271).

[920] "The *fallacy of the perfect analogy* consists in reasoning from a partial resemblance between two entities to an entire and exact correspondence" (Fischer, 247).

[921] "Even though fundamentalism is correct in insisting upon the divine inspiration of the Bible, the inerrancy of the Word of God and the other biblical truths included in the five fundamental points, its method of presenting these truths is embroiled in an ideology that is not biblical, though its representatives say they are. For they require an acceptance without compromise to rigid and imposing doctrinal attitudes, as the only source of teaching on the subject of the Christian life and salvation, a reading of the Bible that refuses all questioning and all critical research. ...

"The foundational problem with this fundamental reading is that, refusing to keep in mind the historical character of divine revelation, she finds herself incapable of fully accepting the truth of the Incarnation itself. Fundamentalism flees the narrow relationship between the divine and the human as regards relations with God. He refuses to admit that the inspired Word of God was expressed in human language and that it was transmitted, under divine inspiration, by human authors with limited capacities and resources. ...

"The fundamentalistic approach is dangerous, for she is attractive to persons who are looking for biblical answers to their life problems. She can trick them by offering them pious but illusory interpretations, rather than telling them that the Bible does not necessarily contain an immediate response to each of these problems. Fundamentalism invites, without saying it, a form of intellectual suicide. It places false sense of security to life, for it unconsciously confuses the human limitations of the biblical message with the substance of the divine message" (Commission biblique pontificale, *L'interprétation de la Bible dans l'Église*, 48-49, 50; translation mine).

[922] For example, see George Marsden, *Fundamentalism and American Culture: The Shaping of Twentieth-Century Evangelicalism, 1870-1925* [Oxford: University Press, 1980], 210-211; Mark Noll, *The Scandal of the Evangelical Mind* [Grand Rapids: Eerdmans, 1994], 245 (both texts are cited in Chapter 7).

[923] Hilaire Beloc, "Whatever happens, we have got / The Maxim gun, and have not" (*The Modern Traveller* [1898]).

Testament evangelism or biblical conversion!

1.5.2.6.2. One particularly insidious example of this methodology is found in the 1484 *Hexenhammer* or *Malleus Maleficarum* of the Dominican Inquisitors Heinrich Kramer and Jacob Sprenger, in which they asserted that witches and atheists do not allow their infants to be baptized by the churches of Rome, thus Anabaptists who do not allow their infants to be baptized must also be witches or atheists!

1.5.2.7. Because the false teacher has been well chosen for this task, it is impossible to deny that he is truly theologically erroneous:

1.5.2.7.1. Likewise, the target group is in a lose-lose, as they left seeking to argue tangential points on behalf of someone with whom they do not agree

1.5.2.7.2. Likewise, the target group is made to argue something that they have been framed to believe, thereby framing them in with a tangential question

1.5.2.7.3. Furthermore, historical distance makes it almost impossible to accurately prove what some of these people actually did believe in the first place, as most of the material comes from their antagonists ("The first to plead his case *seems* just, *Until* another comes and examines him," Prov 18:17)

1.5.2.8. Once the proper links have been made, the target group has now been labeled and destroyed theologically; furthermore, ammunition is given to all future generations that they can use the same fallacy of perfect analogy to attack other opponents who hold similar views:

1.5.2.8.1. There is a balance here (as noted above): for while admitting that others may have had or may have similar views in the future, it is important to Rome to name each group by a unique name, to show the initiator of the movement to be a theological innovator, with a completely foreign interpretation of the Scriptures that no one else has ever had (Hence, Manichean, Donatist, Petrobusian, Henrician, Cathar, Waldensian, Albigensian, Fraticelli, Wycliffite, Lollard, Hussite, Anabaptist, Lutheran, Huguenot, etc.)

1.5.2.8.2. Once the new name has been coined, then every attempt is made to point out the divergences between all the various groups, while likewise maintaining that Rome has always held the same view in all things; as noted in a particularly vehement anti-Protestant writing coming off the pen of Jacques-Benigne Bossuet in 17th Century France, titled, *History of the Variations of Protestant Churches*;[924] nevertheless, this writing had a long historical precedent of similar argumentation (e.g. Reinerius Saccho in A.D. 1250)

1.5.2.8.3. Rome's need to show that each group was an isolated individual having a completely novel theology and interpretation of Scripture has further bled over into denying any ties between:

1.5.2.8.3.1. Paulicians, Henricians, Petrobusians, and Waldenses

1.5.2.8.3.2. Bohemian Hussites and Alpine Waldenses

1.5.2.8.3.3. Alpine Waldenses and the Geneva Reformation

1.5.2.8.3. Meanwhile Rome has allowed for ties between:

1.5.2.8.3.1. The Bulgarian "Bogomiles" and the Cathars of Southern France (possibly due to the visit of the Bulgarian Orthodox Bishop Nicetas to Southern France in 1167)

1.5.2.8.3.2. The Fraticelli and the Donatists and the Waldensians (as noted above)

1.5.2.8.3.3. Wycliffe and Huss (in the Council of Constance, to condemn Hus to be burned at the stake)

1.5.2.8.3.4. Wycliffe and Luther (labeling Luther a Wycliffite, for a similar condemnation as that of Hus):

1.5.2.8.3.4.1. Luther, however, was not ignorant of what happened to Hus (100 years before his time), and the resulting crusade against the land of the Hussites[925]

---

[924]Jacques-Benigne Bossuet, *Histoire des variations des églises Protestantes* (Paris, 1688, 1740, 1760, 1821).

[925]"24. It is high time that we seriously and honestly consider the case of the Bohemians,[49] and come into union with them so that the terrible slander, hatred and envy on both sides may cease. As befits my folly, I shall be the first to submit an opinion on this subject, with due deference to every one who may understand the case better than I.

"First, We must honestly confess the truth, stop justifying ourselves, and grant the Bohemians that John Hus and Jerome of Prague were burned at Constance in violation of the papal, Christian, imperial safe-conduct and oath; whereby God's commandment was sinned against and the Bohemians were given ample cause for bitterness; and although they ought to have been perfect and to have patiently endured this great injustice and disobedience of God on our part, nevertheless they were not bound to approve of it and to acknowledge that it was well done. Nay, even to-day they should give up life and limb rather than confess that it is right to violate an imperial, papal Christian safe-conduct, and faithlessly to act contrary to it. So then, although it is the impatience

1.5.2.9. Once the target group is destroyed theologically, the next step is to work through political officials to have them outlawed and/or banished from their lands:

    1.5.2.9.1. This seemed to be a purpose of most of the Medieval Councils: 1st (1123), 2nd (1139), 3rd (1179), and 4th (1215) Lateran, 1st (1245) and 2nd (1274) of Lyons, Constance (1414), 5th Lateran (1512), Trent (1545-1564); not to mention the dozens of local councils not listed as "ecumenical councils"

    1.5.2.9.2. The decrees of the Councils and the Popes then being enforced by the local Bishops and/or traveling Papal Legates

1.5.2.10. There remains one important step, that is the step of (1) not copying and/or (2) destroying any documents that are or may be construed as being positive or beneficial to the viewpoint of the identified "heretic" and the entire target group (cf. Deut 7:24; 9:14; 12:3; 29:20; Psa 9:5; 16:4; 109:13; Zeph 1:4; e.g. of the Amalekites, Exod 17:14; Deut 25:19; of the Baals, Hos 2:17), so that future generations cannot assess for themselves the fallacy of false grouping, leaving the counter-argument an argument from silence (Notice the intentional silence about the errors of the Knights Templar in their dissolution by the 1311 Council of Vienna: "We are silent here as to detail because the memory is so sad and unclean"):

    1.5.2.10.1. Hence, all of the writings of the "pseudo Christian" [acc. to Constance] Wycliffe were condemned to be burned in 1410, following the 1408 Council of Oxford; the required burning of Wycliffe's books was again decreed in the 1415 Council of Constance ("for the condemnation of the said Wyclif and his memory");[926] the fact that we have so many of his documents extant is a miracle, given the power and authority of the Church of Rome, also being an attestation of the power of movable type invented in Guttenberg in 1455.

    1.5.2.10.2. The 1415 Council of Constance also decreed the burning of all of the books and works of John Hus, after burning him at the stake; the reason any of those remains is due to the strength of the Hussite movement in Bohemia, a movement which maintained political power until 1434, and which maintained ties to the Waldensian movement of the Italy's Piedmont area (See Gonnet and Molnar, *Les Vaudois au Moyen Age*)

    1.5.2.10.3. A side note is in order here:

        1.5.2.10.3.1. Most Protestants and Evangelicals (along with Luther) agree that 14th Century Wycliffe and 15th Century Hus taught Reformation-type doctrines; these facts are verifiable because of their manuscripts which still exist;

        1.5.2.10.3.2. If one goes back to the 12th-13th Century Waldenses, there is less clarity, as historical distance has lost virtually all of their records;

        1.5.2.10.3.3. If one goes back to the 11th-12th Century so-called Paulicians, Henricians (aka. Cathars or Albigenses), and Petrobusians it is even more difficult, the lens of historical distance being unclear as their names and writings are primarily known to us only through the antithetic writings of Rome

---

of the Bohemians which is at fault, yet the pope and his followers are still more to blame for all the trouble, error and loss of souls that have followed upon that council.

"I have no desire to pass judgment at this time upon John Hus's articles or to defend his errors, though I have not yet found any errors in his writings, and I am quite prepared to believe that it was neither fair judgment nor honest condemnation which was passed by those who, in their faithless dealing, violated a Christian safe-conduct and a commandment of God" (Luther, "An Open Letter to Christian Nobility"; available at: http://www.iclnet.org/pub/resources/text/wittenberg/luther/web/nblty-06.html; accessed: 11 Oct 2005; Internet).

[926]"After these things had again been brought to the notice of the apostolic see and a general council, the Roman pontiff condemned the said books, treatises and pamphlets at the lately held council of Rome [In 1412 (Msi, 27, 505-508)], ordering them to be publicly burnt and strictly forbidding anyone called a Christian to dare to read, expound, hold or make any use of any one or more of the said books, volumes, treatises and pamphlets, or even to cite them publicly or privately, except in order to refute them. In order that this dangerous and most foul doctrine might be eliminated from the church's midst, he ordered, by his apostolic authority and under pain of ecclesiastical censure, that all such books, treatises, volumes and pamphlets should be diligently sought out by the local ordinaries and should then be publicly burnt; and he added that if necessary those who do not obey should be proceeded against as if they were promoters of heresy. ...

"This holy synod, therefore, at the instance of the procurator-fiscal and since a decree was issued to the effect that sentence should be heard on this day, declares, defines and decrees that the said John Wyclif was a notorious and obstinate heretic who died in heresy, and it anathematises him and condemns his memory. It decrees and orders that his body and bones are to be exhumed, if they can be identified among the corpses of the faithful, and to be scattered far from a burial place of the church, in accordance with canonical and lawful sanctions" ("Council of Constance [1415]"; available at: http://www.dailycatholic.org/history/16ecume2.htm; accessed: 23 Sept 2004).

1.5.2.10.3.4. Knowledge of the non-Roman Western Church in the 5th through 11th Centuries is a virtual black hole, rightly called the "Dark Ages", with the Early Church only slightly more illuminated due to manuscripts available from the Eastern Orthodox Churches and other non-Latin sources

1.5.2.10.4. The lack of information in early church evangelism, or perhaps a misemphasis in the reporting of early church evangelism, led Adolph Harnack to a self-fulfilled prophetic approach to finding social activity as the method and power of Early Church evangelism:

1.5.2.10.4.1. Harnack's emphasis seems to have been recently picked up by Rodney Stark in his book on the growth of the early church

1.5.2.10.5. The result of a lack of information on the non-sacramental churches of the early church period and the early Middle Ages forces a study of such to be little more than a study of:

1.5.2.10.5.1. The legitimizing of Rome and its role

1.5.2.10.5.2. The development of the sacramental system and the benefits of such

1.5.2.10.6. Another comment may be appropriate here, Rome is not the only one guilty of using false grouping, this fallacy is also used with unfortunate effectiveness in contemporary times:

1.5.2.10.6.1. For example the label "Landmarkist" has been an effective verbal sledgehammer to discourage historical inquiry into the true church of the "Middle Ages"

1.5.2.11. Use "fallacy of false composition" on all competing church groups that have a similar area of commonality

1.5.2.12. Repeat as necessary.

1.5.3. Rome has made good use this sequence, based on the writings of Augustine, for many groupings which they deemed competitors to their church monopoly; the list is long, and many names are lost in the sands of time: the Paulicians, the Henricians, the Petrobusians, the Cathars, the Publicani, the Albigenses, the Waldenses, the Wycliffites, the Lollards, the Hussites, the Lutherans, the Calvinists, the Zwinglians, etc…

1.5.3.1. Then another game is played, as follows:

1.5.3.1.1. The historical dissonance argument, whereby, through returning to the original perpetrator or false teacher above, they can deny the application of the Second Council of Orange for contemporary issues, while using the findings of the Council to apply it to contemporary issues

1.5.3.1.2. The target group is made to focus so strongly on the contemporary issue of the historical perpetrator, so that they begin to teach the findings of the Council (such as the Second Council of Orange) as orthodoxy, not realizing that in so doing they are driving a double-edged sword through their own theology and practice

1.5.3.2. This game (1) clouds the real issues in the early church, (2) leads researchers down theological dead ends in research, by which they "learn but never come to a knowledge of the truth" (2 Tim 3:7), (3) causes Evangelical researchers either to agree with Rome's condemnations (due to partial information) or to defend those who have been chosen as straw men to falsely typify the teaching of an entire group or even a civilization, and (4) therefore Evangelical researchers may undermine their own theology by using Rome's partial data, often without even knowing it, because of a false historical analogy

1.5.3.2.1. Once Rome has found an Evangelical theologian who agrees with their condemnations, they promote the teachings of that Evangelical theologian, pitting Evangelical versus Evangelical (and thereby maintaining an innocent third-party position), a methodology which they have used since at least the 12th Century against the Albigenses, and then in the 15th Century against the Hussites

1.5.3.2.2. Then, using the fallacy of prevalent proof, a new Evangelical teaching emerges over time, following the question-framing received from the extant writings from Rome

1.5.3.2.3. It would seem like this game was played with the Landmark Controversies of the late 19th and early 20th Centuries among Southern Baptists (i.e. the Whitsitt Controversy), thereby cutting them from their pre-Reformation roots, cutting them from the immense bloodshed from the 12th-16th Centuries, leading to compromise in cooperation with the Church of Rome by the end of the 20th Century, as typified in the "Evangelicals and Catholics Together Statement" of 1994 (originally signed by two Southern Baptists, and then recinded on a vote of the SBC)

1.5.3.3. The most common use of this game is in Christology, whereas, the various "heretical" views of the interaction of the divine and human natures of Christ are used to described (see more detail above):

1.5.3.3.1. The doctrine of salvation (by which the "born again" emphasis of Evangelicals tends to be Docetic):

1.5.3.3.1.1. Docetism is the view that Christ merely appeared to come in the flesh, but He was only a ghost

1.5.3.3.1.2. Therefore those who believe that salvation is by faith alone, without water being sprinkled on the head, nor any other physical attribute of the sign or symbol of a sacrament, are considered docetic

1.5.3.3.1.3. Likewise, those who emphasize that salvation consists only of forgiveness of sins, entrance into spiritual sonship, and the granting of eternal life, while not emphasizing the God's rulership over all of the created order and participation in the redemption of life here-and-now, are merely betraying docetic tendencies, as have, in this view, conservative U.S. Evangelicals

1.5.3.3.1.4. Moreover, every attempt possible is being made to move Evangelicals from this position, including the revising of historical studies, etc.

1.5.3.3.2. The inspiration of Scripture (in which the inclusion of the human weaknesses and errors is merely consistent with the human part of Jesus in Chalcedon [see the 1994 *Pontifical Commission on Biblical Interpretation*, "Fundamentalist Interpretation"])

1.5.3.3.2.1. Consider the 1994 *Pontifical Commission*, headed by Joseph Cardinal Ratzinger, now [Pope] Benedict XVI[927]

1.5.3.3.3. The doctrine of the Eucharist (by which Rome views their belief in transubstantiation as being consistent with the orthodox view of the Trinity):

1.5.3.3.3.1. Again, the Zwinglian view that the elements of the Eucharist are in memorial only, is seen as ignoring the dual nature of the God-man in Christology

1.5.3.3.4. Virtually every doctrinal differentiation between Rome and Evangelicalism can be cited by Rome as being the result of a Christological misunderstanding.

1.5.4. Consider, for example, the possibility of using the "fallacy of false composition" to make all Baptists in the U.S.A. believe like the Baptist pastor from Topeka, Kansas, Fred Phelps, who has emphasized, "God Hates Gays":

1.5.4.1. There is ample evidence (newspaper, television, etc.) of what Fred Phelps taught, that he was a pastor, and that he called himself a Baptist

1.5.5.2. All that is needed is to make the link between Fred Phelps and every other Baptist in America (a fallacious argument, but not a very hard sell), and to ignore what all other Baptists teach

1.5.4.3. There we have it, all Baptists in America think, preach, and teach like Fred Phelps

1.5.4.3.1. This kind of argument could be used very effectively in France, much to the detriment and consternation of French Baptists who are forced to defend themselves from a view that they have never held, and who gain a jaded view of all American Baptists because of the false grouping

1.5.4.4. Now, as Rome's Bishop of the St. Joseph diocese (St. Joseph, Missouri), would you not want to encourage Fred Phelps, to send him support by secondary means, to purchase his books, to encourage those who are counseling him to go even farther? Why, yes you would! Fred Phelps is a perfect pawn for future use for the "fallacy of false composition," a fallacious method of argumentation used by Rome since Augustine (354-430 A.D.)

1.5.5. Imagine by the same methodology by making all Evangelicals in the U.S. into snake handlers, Mormons, or Jehovah's Witnesses (none of these false groupings are hard to "prove" for someone unfamiliar with the differences), or by making all TV evangelists into Jim Baker's or Jimmy Swaggart's (I have experienced this last false grouping in a Quebec newspaper, and the former in French writings on religions and cults):

1.5.5.1. It sets up a "guilty until proven innocent" scenario

1.5.5.2. It also sets up a "damned if I do, damned if I don't" scenario

1.5.5.3. The only way to avoid this fallacious grouping is to give in and join the Church of Rome, making one in a long series of compromises to the teachings of the Bible

---

[927]"The foundational problem with this fundamental reading is that, refusing to keep in mind the historical character of divine revelation, she finds herself incapable of fully accepting the truth of the Incarnation itself. Fundamentalism flees the narrow relationship between the divine and the human as regards relations with God. He refuses to admit that the inspired Word of God was expressed in human language and that it was transmitted, under divine inspiration, by human authors with limited capacities and resources. For this reason, he tends to treat the biblical text as if it were dictated word for word by the Spirit and is not able to recognize that the Word of God was formulated in the language and the phraseology conditioned by this or that period. He accords no attention to literary forms and to the human ways of thinking which are present in the biblical text, of which many are the fruit of an elaboration that stretched over long periods of time and wear the marks of strongly different historical situations" (Commission biblique pontificale, *L'interprétation de la Bible dans l'Église* [Quebec: Fides, 1994; Paris: Cerf, 1994], 49; trans. mine).

<table>
<tr>
<td></td>
<td>

1.5.6. By the way, what led me to consider this use of Augustine was three things:

    1.5.6.1. Rome finding "Manicheans" in every age, including U.S. Evangelicals being labeled as having "essentially Manichean" by George Marsden in his *Fundamentalism and American Culture*,[928] and having "Manichean tendencies" by Mark Noll in his *Scandal of the Evangelical Mind*.[929]

    1.5.6.2. The use of Augustine by Peter the Lombard, Bishop of Paris, in arguing for the "signs and the symbols" as the Central Interpretive Motif of a theology of salvation (hence, sacramentalism)[930]

    1.5.6.3. Thomas Aquinas' ample use of Augustine to promote the inquisitorial practices of the early Dominicans in his *Summa Theologica*.

1.5.7. Likewise confusing is the Reformed or high Calvinist use of Augustine to buttress select points of theology, such as predestination, which Augustine seemed to teach from a purely sacramental point of view, as we shall see below…

</td>
</tr>
<tr>
<td>

CANON 2. If anyone asserts that Adam's sin affected him alone and not his descendants also, or at least if he declares that it is only the death of the body which is the punishment for sin, and not also that sin, which is the death of the soul, passed through one man to the whole human race, he does injustice to God and contradicts the Apostle, who says, "Therefore as sin came into the world through one man and death through sin, and so death spread to all men because all men sinned" (Rom. 5:12).

</td>
<td>

2.1. True, but framing the question to confuse NT evangelists, and setting up the next points with some truth:

    2.1.1. Many of these points seem like they are taken from the selections of an unknown evangelistic and non-sacramental document, and then reframed to be used against them

2.2. Here is the framing of the question: if, from Canon 1, anyone thinks that people can decide for themselves about salvation after they have heard a clear Gospel presentation, likewise they are also affirming that Adam was not the Federal Head of sin, with which most conservative and even mildly Calvinistic Evangelicals heartily agree:

    2.2.1. Evangelistic persons are placed in a "no-win" situation:

        2.2.1.1. Do call people to decision (as Scripture affirms and exemplifies), and then do not believe that Adam's sin nature was passed on to all humanity (as the Scripture clearly teaches)

        2.2.1.2. Do not call people to decision (against the teaching and examples of Scripture), but do believe that Adam's sin nature was passed on to all humanity (as the Scripture clearly teaches)

    2.2.1. Canon 2 counterpoises two beliefs with a causal fallacy, by taking a practice and making it appear contradictory to an unrelated theological question, thereby making two biblical teachings appear contradictory

        2.2.1.1. The causal fallacy is called "the fallacy of *cum hoc, propter hoc*," which Fischer explained, "mistakes correlation for cause."[931] In this case, I am using this fallacy to describe, "you do this, therefore you must believe this"; whereas, it could also be described as a "false analogy" (see above)

2.3. Furthermore, the Council of Orange Divines applied equivocal language here, as causing even further theological confusion, since Canon 2 does not affirm Federal Headship (necessary for the concept of Substitutionary Atonement), rather it affirms either:

    2.3.1. A limited Federal Headship of Adam, or

    2.3.2. The Natural Headship of Adam, with its affirmation "not also that sin"

2.4. Canon 2 affirms that "sin, which is the death of the soul, passed through"; hence, sin, not depravity, pass through; does this mean in a Federal way, that the depraved nature was passed on prior to committing sin, or that sin's punishment, once a person necessarily sins was passed on? It is likely the second, as there is intentional equivocal language built into this Canon.

</td>
</tr>
<tr>
<td>

CANON 3. If anyone says that the grace of God can be conferred as a result of human prayer, but that it is not grace itself which makes

</td>
<td>

3.1. Is not this a Canon against a "Sinner's Prayer"? How amazing! And that in the 6th Century after Christ?

3.2. The second part of this Canon adds the concept of "grace", which has no direct relationship to a "Sinner's Prayer":

    3.2.1. From the Augustinian Sacramental perspective, the infusion of the grace of God cannot be bestowed by God outside of (1) the sacraments of the Roman Church and (2) the "signs and symbols" that correspond to the grace bestowed (new birth=holy water, Lord's Supper [Holy Eucharist]=holy wafer [Host], holy unction=holy oil, etc.); for Rome, the conferring of grace must always include a physical sign and/or symbol

    3.2.2. The "Sinner's Prayer" fails the sacramental test in several ways:

</td>
</tr>
</table>

---

[928]George Marsden, *Fundamentalism and American Culture: The Shaping of Twentieth-Century Evangelicalism, 1870-1925* (Oxford: University Press, 1980), 210-211.

[929]Mark Noll, *The Scandal of the Evangelical Mind* (Grand Rapids: Eerdmans, 1994), 245.

[930]Peter the Lombard, *Sentences,* Book 1, Distinction 1, Chap 1, "Every doctrine concerns things and/or signs"; available from: http://www.franciscan-archive.org/lombardus/opera/ls1-01.html; accessed: 16 May 2006; Internet.

[931]Fischer, 167-69.

<table>
<tr><td>

us pray to God, he contradicts the prophet Isaiah, or the Apostle who says the same thing, "I have been found by those who did not seek me; I have shown myself to those who did not ask for me" (Rom 10:20, quoting Isa. 65:1).

</td><td>

3.2.2.1. It is verbal only, so it does not include a physical "sign and symbol" associated with it

3.2.2.2. It is not conferred by the approved clergy of the Church of Rome, thus no grace of God can be conferred through a "Sinner's Prayer"

3.2.2.3. Furthermore, and even more problematic, the heretics [and less-likely schismatics] who do share the Gospel using a sinner's prayer in their call to commitment (called by the inquisitors of the Cathars "consolementum" and "worshipping the perfects" [as Rome did not believe that they were preaching Christ, so the heretics must have been preaching "themselves" 2 Cor 4:5]) are going against the teaching of Rome against the laity preaching the Gospel (which became a capital crime after 1184, 1215)

3.2.3. Therefore, from an Augustinian Sacramental position, a "Sinner's Prayer" does not, cannot, and can never suffice, for the eternal salvation of the soul (even though this is clearly taught in John 5:24; Acts 16:30-31; Rom 10:9-10, 13), whereas the prayer whispered over the Holy Water prior to Holy Baptism of infants does suffice![932]

3.2.4. Herein is the non-sequetor:

3.2.4.1. Prayer is valid, but just not the "Sinner's Prayer"

3.2.4.2. Yet the prayer of the priest over the Holy Water in preparation for the Sacrament of Holy Baptism is deemed efficacious

3.2.4.3. But the prayer of the sinner who repents is not deemed efficacious; and this quite against the examples and teachings of Scripture, for example:

3.2.4.3.1. King David who verbally repented, 2 Sam 12:13

3.2.4.3.2. King David after asking for a census to be taken, 1 Chron 21:8, "So David said to God, 'I have sinned greatly, because I have done this thing; but now, I pray, take away the iniquity of Your servant, for I have done very foolishly'"

3.2.4.3.3. The words of the Prodigal Son, Luke 15:18, 21

3.2.4.3.4. The repentant sinner, Luke 18:13, "God, be merciful to me a sinner!"
Etc.

3.2.4.4. Both are a matter of prayer—it is only the context that is different:

3.2.4.4.1. Initiation: parents (or other third party) versus the guilty individual

3.2.4.4.2. Timing: unconsciously (as an infant) versus consciously

3.2.4.4.3. Person involved: approved priest versus the person in need of grace

3.2.4.4.4. Efficacy (power): hierarchical ties to Bishop of Rome versus the Holy Spirit working directly on the individual heart

3.2.4.4.5. Intermediary: a priest versus no one!

3.2.4.5. The differences involved are stunning and unresolvable

3.3. Furthermore the question-framing in the second highlighted phrase is laughable: Does any Evangelical actually believe that it is possible for a lost person to, (1) hear the Gospel, (2) have a hearing of faith, (3) be challenged to pray a sinner's prayer, and (4) pray to repent and believe, outside of God's grace first working in, with, and by the Word of God, and God's Holy Spirit giving a hearing of faith by the grace of God, God's grace breaking the person's stubborn will and providing that the person have the will to repent and believe? Rather God's grace and Holy Spirit must superintend the entire process, as He is the giver of saving faith (Gal 3:22)!

3.3.1. Since the Council of Orange has purposefully omitted the power of the Word of God and the Gospel of Christ, and because they have limited the giving of grace to the signs and symbols of the sacraments of their church, they are left with denying that the grace of God operates through the Word proclaimed—a doctrine Rome has ignored for over a millenia and a half!

3.3.1.1. Pray tell, what then do they preach? The church, the saints, and the sacraments?

3.3.1.2. Where do they feel that their power lies? The keys given to Peter and his succesors (Matt 16:17-19)?

3.3.1.3. Does it not appear that the existence and growth of the Evangelical church a threat to their soteriological and ecclesiological monopoly? Absolutely!

3.4. Thus, as has been noted, this Canon contains a non sequetor, is it possible for a person to pray a true "Sinner's Prayer" from a contrite heart (Luke 18:13-14), outside the grace of God? And furthermore, if one does pray a "Sinner's Prayer" (whatever the particular wording, Rom 10:13) from a truly contrite heart (Psa 51:17), does not God hear, and hearing does He not forgive (1 John 1:9-2:2; 5:13-15)? Absolutely He does! He honors His Word, not the words of men from some particular church, no matter how old or how large it may be!

</td></tr>
</table>

---

[932]"¶1257The Lord himself affirms that Baptism is necessary for salvation. ... The Church does not know any means other than Baptism that assures entry into eternal Beatitude [for sure not a 'Sinner's Prayer,' as we note in the Council of Orange]; this is why she takes care not to neglect the mission that she has received from the Lord to see that all who can be baptized are 'reborn of the water and the Spirit.' *God has bound salvation to the sacrament of Baptism, but he himself is not bound by his sacraments*" (*Catechism of the Catholic Church*, §1257).

CANON 4. If anyone maintains that God awaits our will to be cleansed from sin, but does not confess that even our will to be cleansed comes to us through the infusion and working of the Holy Spirit, he resists the Holy Spirit himself who says through Solomon, "The will is prepared by the Lord" (Prov. 8:35, LXX), and the salutary word of the Apostle, "For God is at work in you, both to will and to work for his good pleasure" (Phil. 2:13).	4.1. Here the cleansing of the will allowing man to call out for the mercy of God is confused with the need for "Sacrament of Baptism" (of which Peter's successor in Rome alone holds the "keys") by which the will is first prepared to receive grace—again the sacramental view of salvation skews what is really being said; these are half truths.
	
	4.2. The irony is that the Church of Rome assumes that through the outward symbol of their "Holy Baptism" (given to an infant involuntarily and without their knowledge) the sinful nature is cleansed (this is their very long belief, as described by contemporary Rome in the *Catechism of the Catholic Church*)[933] therefore preparing the recipient of baptism to further receive the unending and always necessary emanations of grace for salvation for the rest of their life[934]—without any possibility of assurance of salvation, which is the No. 1 Cardinal Sin, "Pride" (by the way, Augustine decried the pride of the Manicheans, and Aquinas in his *Summa Theologica*, SS, has a section on the vainglory of the heretics)!
	
	4.3. True pride is believing that a priest pouring water into a infant's ear or forehead (1) confers grace, (2) removes the stain of original sin, (3) changes the infant's will, and (4) has anything to do with salvation (more about baptismal regeneration below)
	
	4.4. Notice how the effectuality of the Word of God is left out of Canon 4; again, the Council of Orange appears so bent on removing from man the responsibility of individually responding to God, that it frames the question in such a way that in calling for a decision for Christ the evangelist is seeking man's will to be the trigger for cleansing from sin; this question framing is hardly excusable:
	
	  4.4.1. Again we have the same problem that we discussed under Canon 1, so much of God's working through His Word and the Gospel of Christ is left out of the equation, that it posits a false premise
	
	  4.4.2. Again, from the human side of conversion, after hearing the Gospel, man's will must turn or change (in New Testament evangelism), as part of his conversion, and prior to God enacting regeneration and justification on his behalf; again the issues are looking at conversion from the standpoint of the evangelist (man), or from the standpoint of God; Scripture contains both simultaneously (in an fully God-fully man [hence, incarnational] way, to use Christological terms)
	
	  4.4.3. Canon 4 is framing the question as strongly and antithetically to New Testament evangelism as possible, by framing those who believe that man must decide for or against Christ, as believing that unsaved man has an untainted will allowing him to change, and likewise by that that change of man's will is the trigger for cleansing from sin:
	
	    4.4.3.1. Understandably, this is when high Calvinists become wary when they hear an evangelist asking people to say a sinner's prayer, and after this verbalized prayer, telling those who prayed that they are children of God, have eternal life, are born again, etc.
	
	    4.4.3.2. Again, however, from the standpoint of the evangelist, he is merely repeating concepts of "justification by faith" and assurance of salvation as found in the Bible (Isa 1:18; 53:4-6; 55:6-7; John 1:11-13; 3:16; 5:24; 2 Cor 5:17, 21; 1 Peter 2:24; 3:18; 1 John 5:11-15; etc.)
	
	    4.4.3.1. True, great care must be taken here not to go beyond Scripture by either subtracting from it or adding to it
	
	  4.4.4. Remember that Rome, through its Sacrament of Penance,[935] already well defined by the time of Jerome,[936] had the only authority to declare absolution from sin,[937] so Canon 4's issue is not, whether a man must

---

[933]"¶1263 By Baptism, *all sins* are forgiven, original sin and all personal sins, as well as the punishment for sin. In those who have been reborn nothing remains that would impede their entry into the Kingdom of God, neither Adam's sin, nor personal sin, nor the consequences of sin, the gravest of which is separation from God [and the representative of His Son on earth, the Vicar of Christ!]" (Ibid., §1263).

[934]"¶1426 *Conversion* to Christ, the new birth of Baptism, the gift of the Holy Spirit and the Body and Blood of Christ received as food have made us 'holy and without blemish', just as the Church herself, the Bride of Christ, is 'holy and without blemish'. Nevertheless the new life received in Christian initiation has not abolished the frailty and weakness of human nature, nor the inclination to sin that tradition calls *concupiscence*, which remains in the baptized such that with the help of the grace of Christ [i.e. these same sacraments] they may prove themselves in the struggle of the Christian life. This is the struggle of *conversion* directed toward holiness and eternal life to which the Lord nevere ceases to call us" (Ibid., §1426).

[935]"¶1422 Those who approach the sacrament of Penance obtain pardon from God's mercy for the offence committed against him, and are, at the same time, reconciled with the Church which they have wounded by their sins and which by charity, by example and by prayers labours for their conversion.

"1423 It is called the *sacrament of conversion* because it makes sacramentally present Jesus' call to conversion, the first step in returning to the Father from whom one has strayed into sin.

"It is called the *sacrament of Penance*, since it consecrates the Christian sinner's personal and ecclesial steps of conversion, penance and satisfaction.

	change his will prior to justification, Canon 4's issue appears to be the removal of the human mediation of a priest out of the equation 4.4.4.1. The framers of Canon 4 skillfully pitted the high Calvinists against the low Calvinists, while giving themselves enough wiggle room for their sacramental notions—an ingeniously evil argumentation, which they have propagated to divide Bible believing Christians since the time it was first put in print! 4.5. The Council of Orange may well show how some theologians can be and are encouraged to convert from high Calvinism straight into the Church of Rome, a strange change of allegiances, via the false premises and insidious analogies of these Canons.

CANON 5. If anyone says that not only the increase of faith but also its beginning and the very desire for faith, by which we believe in Him who justifies the ungodly and comes to the regeneration of holy baptism -- if anyone says that this belongs to us by nature and not by a gift of grace, that is, by the inspiration of the	5.1. Again we have a wrestling match between man being able of his own accord to call upon the name of the Lord to be saved, and the sheepish insertion of the concept of "holy" baptism (which is actually the center point of Rome's theology of salvation, see footnote below), and the idea of denying the very grace of God (by which Rome accuses all detractors who do not agree with their Seven Sacraments and all their other Holy Traditions, included in their list of detractors were/are all the Protestant Reformers).
	
	5.2. Again, in the mind of Rome, "Holy" Baptism = being born in the Spirit, born from above, etc.,[938] in Baptist theology baptism follows being born of the Spirit;[939] it's a question of which comes first, Baptism (which in Rome's case savingly amends the will), or conversion (which must then be followed by believer's baptism).
	
	5.3. Herein, Evangelicals who believe in infant baptism have a confusing dilemma (quite a few false premises in this Canon), trying to reconcile two opposing views of baptism's role in conversion (which was also an issue for the Reformers); no wonder Presbyterians, who adhere to infant baptism, ascribe that some grace is conferred thereby.
	
	5.4. A false premise involved in Canon 5:
	    5.4.1. Man's will [to chose to be saved] is posited *against* the grace of God itself; as if they are in opposition!
	        5.4.1.1. This is not the Bible's problem (for example note the verbs in Jer 35:15), but it is philosophical theology's problem (man's limited reason)
	        5.4.1.2. Even by positing this problem, the Council of Orange set in motion an artificial debate among born-again Christians, which comes first "the chicken or the egg?"
	        5.5.1.3. While many second generation Evangelical Christians may subtly and Roman Catholics not so subtly undermine God's role,[940] either through thinking that man is good enough to save himself

"1424 It is called the *sacrament of confession*, since the disclosure or confession of sins to a priest is an essential element of this sacrament. In a profound sense it is also a 'confession'—acknowledgement and praise—of the holiness of God and his mercy towards sinful man.

"It is called the *sacrament of forgiveness*, since by the priest's sacramental absolution God grants the penitent 'pardon and peace'

"It is called the *sacrament of Reconciliation*, because it imparts to the sinner the love of God who reconciles: 'Be reconciled to God.' He who lives by God's merciful love is ready to respond to the Lord's call: 'Go, first be reconciled to your brother' (Ibid., §1422-24).

[936]"*It may be that God will forgive thy sins.*' In view of the fact that the blessed Daniel, foreknowing the future as he did, had doubts concerning God's decision, it is very rash on the part of those who boldly promise pardon to sinners. And yet it should be recognized that indulgence was promised to Nebuchadnezzar in return, as long as he wrought good works" (*Jerome's Commentary on Daniel,* trans. by Gleason L. Archer, Jr. [Grand Rapids: Baker, 1958], 52).

[937]"Today the word 'ordination' is reserved for the sacramental act which integrates a man into the order of bishops, presbyters or deacons, and goes beyond a simple *election, designation, delegation* or *institution* by the community, it confers a gift of the Holy Spirit that permits the exercise of a 'sacred power' (*sacra potestas*) which can come only from Christ himself through his Church" (*Catechism of the Catholic Church,* §1538).

[938]"¶1213 Holy Baptism is the basis of the whole Christian life, the gateway to life in the Spirit (*vitae spiritualis iannua*), and the door which gives access to the other sacraments. Through Baptism we are freed from sin and reborn as sons of God; we become members of Christ, are *incorporated into the Church and made sharers in her mission: 'Baptism is the sacrament of regeneration through water and the word"* (Ibid., §1213).

[939]Note the eloquent words of Balthasar Hubmaier on the role of baptism in salvation: "From all this follows that this outward baptism unto Christ is nothing else than a public profession of the inward obligation. By it, man confesses publicly that he is a sinner, and admits his guilt. Yet he believes that Christ, through His death, has atoned for his sins, and that by the resurrection has made him righteous in the sight of God, our heavenly Father. Therefore he has determined to confess openly and publicly the faith and the name of Jesus Christ. Also he has promised to live henceforth according to the Word of Christ, but not in human strength, lest the same thing befall him as befell Peter" (Balthasar Hubmaier, "A Summary of the Entire Christian Life," W. O. Lewis, ed., trans. by G. D. Davidson [Liberty, MO: Archives, William Jewell College Library], 1:59-63).

| Holy Spirit amending our will and turning it from unbelief to faith and from godlessness to godliness, it is proof that he is opposed to the teaching of the Apostles, for blessed Paul says, "And I am sure that he who began a good work in you will bring it to completion at the day of Jesus Christ" (Phil. 1:6). And again, "For by grace you have been saved through faith; and this is not your own doing, it is the gift of God" (Eph. 2:8). For those who state that the faith by which we believe in God is natural make all who are separated from the Church of Christ by definition in some measure believers. | (through some form of universalism), or giving certain men (priests) the role of saving or denying salvation by their sacraments and anathemas (cf. the keys given to Peter), it is only Evangelical Christians that hold them both in check! |

5.5.1.4. This false dilemma communicated in the Council of Orange is really a false dichotomy, comparing apples and oranges , and making an issue of it; and lo and behold, has Calvinism and Arminianism become an issue, but not among liberal Protestants and Roman Catholics, rather, only for those who actually believe in the new birth and the absolute truthfulness of Scripture!

5.4.2. Baptism, "Holy" Baptism, is insidiously thrown in as an afterthought, when it is actually the centerpiece of Rome's theology of salvation (see below), again because this council was and is used to pit two Evangelical points against each other

5.4.3. Therefore, anyone who posits that man "must change his ways" (repent, e.g. Jer 35:15), or "must chose" (as is actually stated *maint* times in Scripture) following the proclamation of the Gospel, is actually, according to Canon 5, undermining the grace of God and/or going against the Reformed "Doctrines of Grace" so to speak, whereas the verses that these sacramentalists use as prooftexts are verses that they themselves neither believe, practice, nor honor!

5.5. Canon 5 confuses salvation, "unbelief to faith," with spiritual growth, "godlessness to godliness"

5.5.1. This confusion of justification and sanctification permeates the sacramental system, with its corresponding lack of "Assurance of salvation."

5.5.2. Furthermore, Infant Baptism mitigates against personal holiness, as it undermines the personal accountability of discipleship right at its start, personal obedience to the profession of Christ through believer's baptism

5.6. Their final argument, in their final sentence, further displays their confusion:

5.6.1. Preaching with the expectation that God can and will instantaneously convert the hearer of the Gospel, apart from the "Sacrament of Baptism," in a generalistic sense, is not making "all who are separated from the Church of Christ" into believers, but rather trusting and expecting that God will work in, with, and by His Holy Word to bring conviction of sin and the desire for repentance and faith!

5.6.2. It is clear from this document, that the Council of Orange sees Baptism and only Baptism as a supernatural work of God by which lost sinners are brought into the family of God

5.6.2.1. Thus according to this document, Baptism or Infant Baptism is the particularizing act by which God calls His elect!

5.6.2.2. Notice how far afield this position lies from "hearing and believing," John 5:24; 6:29

| CANON 6. If anyone says that God has mercy upon us when, apart from his grace [e.g. Baptism], we believe, will, desire, strive, labor, pray, watch, study, seek, ask, or knock, but does not confess that it is by the infusion and inspiration of the Holy Spirit within us that we have the faith, the will, or the strength to do all these | 6.1. Some theological landmines in Canon 6 seem to be: |

6.1.1. "Apart from his grace" = necessity for the prior reception of the sacrament of "Holy" Baptism, usually as an infant

6.1.2. "by the infusion and inspiration of the Holy Spirit within us" = this is what the sacrament of "Holy" Baptism does in Rome's mind; "Holy" baptism is being born again, being born of the spirit, being born of water, and receiving the washing of regeneration

6.1.3. "['Apart from his grace'] we have the faith" attacksProtestant/Evangelical belief in Scriptures alone, faith alone, grace alone (Acts 15:7-11)

6.1.3.1. From an Evangelical point-of-view, no faith is possible without first the preaching of the Word of God, the Holy Spirit in, with, and by that Word proclaimed, forming faith within the hearer, and causing him to respond by faith

6.1.3.2. From the point of view of an Evangelical, the Word of God proclaimed cannot understood, nor received, nor even believed by the infant who is being baptized, therefore nullifying it as an act of obedience

6.1.3.3. From the point of views of Rome, "Holy" Baptism, whenever applied by the priest (or with the proper words by a heretic), in a persons infancy or adulthood, is THE "key" to every other grace of God

6.1.3.4. Again from Rome's point-of-view, a lost person cannot understand the Gospel without first being baptized—which makes no sense to the Evangelical mind—and which completely undermines the urgency of the Great Commission, where Christ has never been preached (Rom 15:20)

6.1.4. "['Apart from his grace'] we have … the will" can be used as another jab at decisional preaching or the

---

[940] For example, read this philosophical double-speak: "848 Although in ways known to himself God can lead those who, through no fault of their own, are ignorant of the Gospel, to that faith without which it is impossible to please him, the Church still has the obligation and also the sacred right to evangelize all men" (1994 *Catechism of the Catholic Church*, §848).

things as we ought; or if anyone makes the assistance of grace depend on the humility or obedience of man and does not agree that it is a gift of grace itself that we are obedient and humble, he contradicts the Apostle who says, "What have you that you did not receive?" (1 Cor. 4:7), and, "But by the grace of God I am what I am" (1 Cor. 15:10).	6.1.5. "['Apart from his grace'] we have … the strength to do all these things as we ought" = in a typical sacramental sense, the Council of Orange cannot get out of its mind salvation through a life-long series of works, for which the needed spiritual strength is conferred through Baptism, et al. (contra the "faith alone" answer of Jesus in John 6:28-29)

6.1.6. "The assistance of grace … is a gift of grace itself": it is important to note, that for the Council of Orange, receiving "Holy" Baptism = receiving grace (infant or adult), pure and simple

6.1.7. "Depend on the humility alone" is downplaying the fact that prior to repentance, the unsaved must be broken by the Law of God, whereby every man (even the infant baptized) becomes accountable to God, Rom 3:10-20:

6.1.7.1. Remember, they are talking about babies receiving the infusion of grace, as found above

6.1.7.2. Remember also the teaching of Henry the Monk, as reported by Peter the Venerable, "Refusal to baptize infants, under the pretext that it is faith that saves and that a young infant could not have sufficient conscience to believe"; remember, at that time (1134 A.D.), as now, this teaching:

6.1.7.2.1. Henry's teaching countered that of the Council of Orange (from ~605 years before his time),

6.1.7.2.2. Henry's teaching made him a heretic in the eyes of Rome, and

6.1.7.2.3. Those who agree with Henry's teaching are guilty of points 1 and 2 above

6.1.7.3. It was the Law, not the sacraments, that Paul described as the schoolmaster to bring us to Christ "that we might be justified by faith" (Gal 3:24)

6.1.7.4. Perhaps this point is why Roman Catholics cringe and grow antagonistic to the Pauline Gospel, wherein it is taught that all men are sinners (regardless of the supposed reception of infant baptism)

6.2. The real issue of this Canon concerns the giving and reception of grace: the sacrament of "Holy" Baptism or a supernatural flooding of our soul by the Holy Spirit upon the hearing of the Gospel:

6.2.1. Jesus spoke to this issue when He said, "Let him who has ears hear"

6.2.2. Jesus also spoke to this issue when He used the illustration of wind with Nicodemus, "The wind blows where it wishes and you hear the sound of it, but do not know where it comes from and where it is going; so is everyone who is born of the Spirit" (John 3:8)

6.2.3. Much to the dismay of territorial church theologians, the new birth is not assured of everyone, rather it is a particular operation of the Spirit of God in the few, the elect (Matt 7:13-14; 1 Cor 9:22)

CANON 7. If anyone affirms that we can form any right opinion or make any right choice which relates to the salvation of eternal life, as is expedient for us, or that we can be saved, that is, assent to the preaching of the gospel through our natural powers without the illumination and inspiration of the Holy Spirit, who makes all men gladly assent to and believe in the truth, he is led astray by a heretical spirit, and does not understand the voice of God who says in the Gospel,	7.1. The Council of Orange "Divines" just laid down the anvil, clearly manifesting their antagonism to Evangelical Gospel preaching—it is no longer hidden and couched in mystery and double-speak!

7.2. The important phrase for the understanding of the whole Canon is "without the illumination and inspiration of the Holy Spirit":

7.2.1. Herein, Orange believes that this "illumination and inspiration" comes only one way, and that is not through Gospel preaching, but through the sacrament of "Holy" Baptism

7.2.2. Likewise, to them, according to this point, "Holy" Baptism of infants or whomever, "makes all men gladly assent to and believe in the truth":

7.2.2.1. Not only are they contradicting that the road is narrow, as noted above

7.2.2.2. But they are further making Baptism **the sure preparation** for the reception of the Gospel

7.2.2.3. Therefore they teach that a human work, enacted upon an unthinking child, not only ensures that the Holy Spirit will work savingly in their heart, but that through that human sign or symbol the Holy Spirit has already worked savingly in their heart

7.2.2.3.1. Thus their assurance of salvation (or lack of it) ought to be based on the power and efficacy of the water of Baptism bestowed by the proper prayer of the priest (whether he is godly or a sinner)

7.2.2.3.2. Whereas, assurance of salvation, for the Evangelical, lies in the power of the Holy Spirit to convict of sin, righteousness, and judgment, and to lead the person to cry out unto the Lord for salvation

7.2.3. "Believe in truth"—what truth?

7.2.2.1. The truth that only Rome's water Baptism saves?

7.2.2.2. The truth that Rome is the only true church?

7.2.2.3. The truth that all of Rome's teachings are infallible?

7.2.2.4. The truth that Rome alone and its hierarchy alone can interpret Scripture?

7.2.2.5. The truth that Rome's Eucharist by the words of the priest, and though it still looks like, feels like, and tastes like a wafer, is the actual "Body of Christ," worthy of veneration on the spot?

7.2.2.6. The truth that Rome's Pope is above all kings and peoples of the world, as he has told of himself that he wields the "Two Swords"?

7.2.2.7. The truth that anyone who contradicts Rome is a heretic, being led by a "heretical [demonic] spirit"

"For apart from me you can do nothing" (John 15:5), and the word of the Apostle, "Not that we are competent of ourselves to claim anything as coming from us; our competence is from God" (2 Cor. 3:5).	(therefore using the "H-Bomb")?
	
	7.2.2.6.1. Why doesn't Rome charge itself with a demonic spirit, as their ecclesiastical laws go directly against 1 Tim 4:1-4, which makes them guided by "doctrines of demons"?
	
	7.2.2.6.2. By the way, the word "heresies" is found in the list of sins (KJV, NKJ) in Gal 5:20, a transliteration of the Greek αἵρεσις; the same word is translated "factions" (NAS) and "sects" (Tyndale, Coverdale, Bishop's), coming from the Latin Vulgate's *sectae*
	
	7.2.2.6.3. The word "heresies" is also found in 2 Pet 2:1 (NAS, NKJ)
	
	7.3. In this first use of the words "heretical spirit" by the Orange Divines results in several points:
	
	    7.3.1. This Council of Orange draws the lines of demarcation for evangelism and cooperation:
	        7.3.1.1. New Testament evangelism is declared heretical by Rome!
	
	    7.3.2. This Council of Orange leaves no doubt as to what Rome believes about New Testament evangelism:
	        7.3.2.1. For the record, the Council of Orange is still part of the official symbols of Rome, being found in sections 370-397 of the 1997 Denzinger[941]
	        7.3.2.2. Futhermore, it is cited in the 1994 *Catechism of the Catholic Church* at least 3 times,[942] dealing with such topics as:
	            7.3.2.2.1. Original sin[943]
	            7.3.2.2.2. Prevenient grace, from Canon 7 (with its use of heresy with respect to "faith alone") is cited as a reference to a citation of Vatican II's *Dei Verbum* (§5)[944] which affirms the need for the reception of grace[945], to this citation is also appended a paragraph from Vatican I, further clarifying the need for Baptism prior to being able to respond in faith to the Gospel[946]
	            7.3.2.2.1. "Christ predestines no one to go to hell"[947]—the *reductio ad absurdum* argument used by Rome against the entire system of salvation "by Scriptures alone, by grace alone, through faith alone," upheld by Evangelicals, that only those who respond positively to the Gospel are saved, and therefore only those that respond positively are predestined or among the elect
	        7.3.2.3. Here is what Rome teaches about the role of "Holy" Baptism in responding to the preaching of the Gospel:
	            7.3.2.3.1. The un-Baptized are still in their original sin, have not received the gift of grace from the Holy Spirit, and therefore do not have the ability to respond savingly to the call of the Gospel—expecting that they can respond to the Gospel being considered "being led by a heretical spirit"
	            7.3.2.3.2. The Baptized have been cleansed of their original sin, have received the gift of grace from the Holy Spirit, and therefore will necessarily respond savingly to the call of the Gospel
	                7.3.2.3.2.1. Hence telling a baptized Catholic that he is in sin—is the sin of heresy
	                7.3.2.3.2.2. Hence telling a baptized Catholic that he is not saved is heresy
	                7.3.2.3.2.3. Hence telling a baptized Catholic that he must respond to the Gospel by faith to be saved is also heresy

---

[941]Heinrich Denzinger, et al., *Symboles et définitions de la foi catholique*, 38th ed. (Paris: Cerf, 1996).

[942]*Catechism of the Catholic Church*, 634.

[943]"The Church pronounced on the meaning of the data of Revelation on original sin especially at the second Council of Orange (529)" (ibid., §406).

[944]"To make this act of faith, the grace of God and the interior help of the Holy Spirit must precede and assist, moving the heart and turning it to God, opening the eyes of the mind and giving 'joy and ease to everyone in assenting to the truth and believing it' [citation: 'Second Council of Orange, Canon 7: Denzinger 180 (377); First Vatican Council, loc. cit.: Denzinger 1791 (3010)']" (Vatican II, "Divine Constitution on Divine Revelation" [18 Nov 1965]; available online at: listserv.american.edu/catholic/church/vaticanii/dei-verbum.html; accessed 19 April 2001; Internet).

[945]*Catechism of the Catholic Church*, §153.

[946]"Even though the consent [Lat. *assensus*] of faith is not-at-all a blind movement of the spirit, no one can yet give his support to the proclamation of the Gospel [Lat. *evangelicae praedicationi consentire*] in a way required to obtain salvation 'without the illumination and inspiration of the Holy Spirit who gives to all his unction once they support and believe the truth (2nd Council of Orange, DS 377). This is why faith in itself, even if it does not operate in charity, is a gift of God; and the act of faith is a salvific work, by which man offers to God himself his free obedience by acquiescing and cooperating with the grace toward which he may have resisted (see DS 1525 [Council of Trent's 'Decree on Justification,' Chapter 5, being 'On the necessity in adults for a preparation unto justification. Its origin.' (in which is taught the need for the prevenient grace [of Holy Baptism])]" (*Denzinger*, §3010).

[947]*Catechism of the Catholic Church*, §1037.

CANON 8. If anyone maintains that some are able to come to the grace of baptism by mercy but others through free will, which has manifestly been corrupted in all those who have been born after the transgression of the first man, it is proof that he has no place in the true faith. For he denies that the free will of all men has been weakened through the sin of the first man, or at least holds that it has been affected in such a way that they have still the ability to seek the mystery of eternal salvation by themselves without the revelation of God. The Lord himself shows how contradictory this is by declaring that no one is able to come to him "unless the Father who sent me draws him" (John 6:44), as he also says to Peter, "Blessed are you, Simon Bar-Jona! For flesh and blood has not revealed this to you, but my Father who is in heaven" (Matt. 16:17), and as the Apostle says, "No one can say 'Jesus is Lord' except by the Holy Spirit" (1 Cor. 12:3).	8.1. Orange is not allowing for middle ground—it is either all or nothing:
	    8.1.1. One cannot hold to Baptismal regeneration, as taught by Orange, and also believe in regeneration through the power of the Word of God proclaimed
	    8.1.2. Orange is clearly defining the parameters of the argument as an all or nothing—there is no room for NT evangelism here
	 8.2. Contra "grace alone" and "faith alone" bringing in the prior issue of man's weakened freewill [prior to receiving supposed divine work of baptism]
	 8.3. Someone preaching Isaiah 55:1 or Jeremiah 35:15 to a group of unbaptized people, therefore, according to the Council of Orange, "has no place in the true faith"
	    8.3.1. This explains Rome's antagonism to New Testament evangelism
	 8.4. The power of the Gospel proclaimed is left out, the argument of a "weakened" free will is brought to bear, as well as the inability to respond to the Gospel [outside of infant or adult baptism as mentioned in the conclusion]
	    8.4.1. God's divine revelation (Matt 16:17) is not attributed to the Word preached, but to the water poured over the head in baptism!

CANON 9. Concerning the succor of God. It is a mark of divine favor when we are of a right purpose and keep our feet from hypocrisy and unrighteousness; for as often as we do good, God is at work in us and with us, in order that we may do so.	9.1. Succor = aid
	    9.1.1. Hereby is affirmed a works salvation, especially of those who have been baptized and not converted, who may feel that because they are doing self-perceived good works, these must be must be proof of God working in them (cf. John 3:20-21)
	    9.1.2. Good works must follow conversion, but we are not saved by good works (Eph 2:8-10; James 2:17-18)
	 9.2. Contra mercy alone, outside of any prevenient meritorious works unto salvation, either before or after conversion (Luke 17:10)!
	 9.3. Meanwhile, taking a jab at evangelists or proclaimers of the Gospel that:
	    9.3.1. They are not "of a right purpose"—the accusation of illicit motivation being rife in ancient and contemporary history, including the accusation of Simony, or being in it for the money
	    9.3.2. They do not "keep their feet from hypocrisy"—a jab at the traveling or itinerating evangelist, as it taught in Matt 10 and is exemplified in Luke and Acts, and as is exemplified throughout the history of the churches
	    9.3.3. "Feet from … unrighteousness"—placing a moral stigma on those who do not agree with Orange's focus on salvation through infant baptism
	    9.3.4. The divines of Orange, however, "do good"—a sign that the church by this time had absorbed a social gospel, by doing good to fellow man
	    9.3.1. Even while they exalt themselves that they do good (contra Mark 10:18), they also affirm that it is due to the special work of God in their lives—affirming the divine origin of the goodness of their flesh; which seems O.K. until it is noted that their Evangelical antagonists place the work of God "in, with, and by" the Word of God

CANON 10. Concerning the succor of God. The succor of God is to be ever sought by the regenerate and converted also, so that they may be able to come to a successful end or persevere in good works.	10.1. Salvation is always a matter of unmerited favor!
	    10.1.1. Implying or setting up that God cannot be sought of the unregenerate
	    10.1.2. Undermining the assurance of salvation outside of personal effort to "seek" to persevere, but based solely on the grace of God alone, who will cause to persevere (Phil 1:6)

CANON 11. Concerning the duty to pray. None would make any true prayer to the Lord had he not received from him the object of his prayer, as it is written, "Of thy own have we given thee" (1 Chron. 29:14).	11.1. Back to the "Sinner's Prayer" originating in God—as any true prayer must! 11.2. Perhaps this is why memorized prayers, being "received from him," such as the Lord's Prayer or perhaps the Rosary, are so common within the Church of Rome?

CANON 12. Of what sort we are whom God loves. God loves us for what we shall be by his gift, and not by our own deserving.	12.1. No! God has loved and does love never deserving individuals, even while they are not deserving: 12.1.1. Prior to salvation, "while we were yet sinners" (Rom 5:7-9, Eph 2:4-7) 12.1.2. And even after salvation, we are not deserving Rom 7:24 (cf. Luke 17:10) 12.1.3. Yes, God even loves the world, John 3:16
CANON 13. Concerning the restoration of free will. The freedom of will that was destroyed in the first man can be restored only by the grace of baptism, for what is lost can be returned only by the one who was able to give it. Hence the Truth itself declares: "So if the Son makes you free, you will be free indeed" (John 8:36).	13.1. Man's supposed "loss of freewill" to respond savingly to the Gospel proclaimed makes Jesus' preaching in Luke 13:3, 5 sound ridiculous, and likewise for His preaching in Luke 11:29-32, with its use the example of Nineveh's repentance at the preaching of Jonah 13.1.1. Notice how "freewill" is described, such that, according to this Couincl, even the Holy Spirit working through the Word of God cannot penetrate man's fallen mind (outside of the infusion of grace through infant baptism) 13.2. Where in the Bible is it taught that "Holy" Baptism cleanses the infant who receives it from the stain of original sin, or that by that Baptism the infant receives back his free will unstained by sin—this is going far beyond the Scriptures, i.e. adding to Scripture 13.2.1. Augustine, in his desire to counter the conversionism of the so-called "Manicheans" and to safeguard [the sacrament of] baptism from the so-called Donatists, went far beyond Scripture in his argumentation
CANON 14. No mean wretch is freed from his sorrowful state, however great it may be, save the one who is anticipated by the mercy of God, as the Psalmist says, "Let thy compassion come speedily to meet us" (Ps. 79:8), and again, "My God in his steadfast love will meet me" (Ps. 59:10).	14.1. Going back to baptism, again 14.2. "Anticipated by the mercy of God," in other words, this Canon teaches foreknowledge, rather than election! 14.2.1. This foreknowledge is based on receiving the waters of baptism as an infant, rather than responding to the Gospel of Jesus Christ as a thinking adult (which is framed as Pelagianism) 14.3. Undermines the sorrowful state that is brought about when the Law of God crushes the heart (Gal 3:22-24), and when the Gospel preached and believed lifts that same burden! 14.4. In this Canon is an example of the complete misuse of Scripture, taking the coming of the compassion and mercy of God … to be found in the poured waters during infant baptism—whereas the infant cannot cry out for the mercy and love of God as is found in these verses!
CANON 15. Adam was changed, but for the worse, through his own iniquity from what God made him. Through the grace of God the believer is changed, but for the better, from what his iniquity has done for him. The one, therefore, was the change brought about by the first sinner; the other, according to the Psalmist, is the change of the right hand of the Most High (Ps. 77:10).	15.1. "Through the grace of God" = infant "Holy" Baptism again! 15.1.1. This Canon completely undermines the need for individual repentance and faith, subtly placing these prominent twin commands of New Testament evangelism with the sacramental rite, sign, and symbol of the poured [holy] waters Baptism 1.5.1.1.1. How long did it take for a special formula to be required for the "making" of so-called "holy water"—with a pinch of salt and a bit of spittle—which sounds more akin to Medieval Druidism? 1.5.1.1.2. Gregory I [the Great] (590-604) called for Augustine of Canterbury to use "holy water" to cleanse the well built temples of the English druids, in his letter to the Abbott Mellitus 1.5.1.1.3. Lorraine Boettner found that "holy water" was made with a pinch of salt and the blessing of a priest by A.D. 850 15.1.2. The "believer" in the case of Infant Baptism is the parent or godparent, believing in the Church and its sacraments on behalf of the incomprehending child 15.1.3. Notice how "the change of the right hand of the most high" is ascribed to a priest pouring this special water from an urn onto the head of a

	newly born infant
	15.2. "Shall we sin that grace may abound? May it never be!" Rom 6:1
CANON 16. No man shall be honored by his seeming attainment, as though it were not a gift, or suppose that he has received it because a missive from without stated it in writing or in speech. For the Apostle speaks thus, "For if justification were through the law, then Christ died to no purpose" (Gal. 2:21); and "When he ascended on high he led a host of captives, and he gave gifts to men" (Eph. 4:8, quoting Ps. 68:18). It is from this source that any man has what he does; but whoever denies that he has it from this source either does not truly have it, or else "even what he has will be taken away" (Matt. 25:29).	16.1. This Canon seems to be deprecating a person who has received Christ by faith prior to baptism, as though he has attained it with his own power: 　16.1.1. This may be foundational for what Aquinas called the "vainglory of the heretics" 16.2. "Supposed that he has received it … from without … in speech" 　16.2.1. Are these lines not against the "outward word" of the Gospel preached? 　16.2.2. Is not a response of faith in the "outward word" the heart of the proclamation of the Gospel, and the heart of Evangelicalism? 16.3. Missive from without = written communication or letter: 　16.3.1. This point seems to be directed against the direct action of God in the heart of man through His Word without any human intermediary or sacrament, contra 1 Thess 2:13; 2 Tim 3:14-17; He 4:12-13 　16.3.2. It also undermines the sufficiency of the Word, 2 Tim 3:16-17 　16.3.3. Is not Rome's water of baptism "from without" rather than "from within" in several ways? 　　16.2.3.1. It is physical ["holy"] water on the skin (cf. Heb 9:13-14; 1 Pet 3:21, "not the removal of dirt from the flesh, but an appeal to God for a good conscience") 　　　16.2.3.1.1. The Church of Rome will appeal to Platonic logic to prove that: 　　　　16.2.3.1.1.1. Because Peter holds the keys, 　　　　16.2.3.1.1.2. The bishop of Rome holds the keys, 　　　　16.2.3.1.1.3. And because the keys they hold are directly related to the sacraments, 　　　　16.2.3.1.1.4. Then the very moment that water is poured over the head of the infant child, 　　　　16.2.3.1.1.5. Grace is immediately conferred in the heart (*ex opere operato*), and 　　　　16.2.3.1.1.6. Original sin, or the guilty conscience of the child, is cleansed at that very moment (and aren't their mothers' relieved)! 　　16.3.3.2. Applied by man, a priest, regardless of his spiritual state (cf. *Contra Donatisten*) 16.4. "Form this source" = the hierarchy of Rome and its sacraments: 　16.4.1. This point seems to be against the imputation of a foreign righteousness, that is the righteousness of God, as is taught in 2 Cor 5:21; 1 Pet 2:24, by faith alone without a corresponding "sign or symbol" 　16.4.2. It almost seems that this point is against the reading of the pronouncements from the Bible on imputed righteousness (or even assurance of salvation) 16.5. Those with imputed righteousness by faith alone, according to this Council: 　16.5.1. Do not have imputed righteousness 　16.5.2. Or will somehow have their imputed righteousness somehow "taken away" from them? (Rom 8:35-39) 　　16.5.2.1. We have here a for-sure precedent to Rome anathematizing (removing grace), and later excommunicating (putting to death, normally by burning at the stake)
CANON 17. Concerning Christian courage. The courage of the Gentiles is produced by simple greed, but the courage of Christians by the love of God which "has been poured into our hearts" not by freedom of will from our own side but "through the Holy Spirit which	17.1. "Courage of the Gentiles" = courage of those who call themselves Christians outside of Rome and its sacraments 　17.1.1. Their courage in preaching the Gospel against all obstacles, by seemingly exerting their own freedom of will to preach the Gospel, much like Paul who was under compulsion to evangelize (1 Cor 9:16-

has been given to us" (Rom. 5:5).	17)? 17.1.2. Their steadfastness in maintaining their views until death? 17.1.3. Was this courage the assurance of salvation of true believers, later called vainglory by Aquinas? 17.2. What of the dropping in of the word "greed"? 17.2.1. Is this not another not so veiled attempt at making non-Roman Christian leaders into followers of Simon the Sorcerer (Acts 8:18-19)? 17.2.2. Is this not the same allegation that the 1994 Pontifical Commission on Biblical Interpretation alleges of Fundamentalists (defined by the Five Fundamentals of the 1895 Niagara Bible Conference), calling it tricking the unlearned "by offering them pious but illusory interpretations"?[948] 17.3. Rome was emphasizing a courage "to love" all men, a serious downgrade of the Great Commission to evangelize all men! 17.4. "Not by freedom of the will from our own side"—undermining "whosoever will come" (Mark 8:34; cf. Isa 55:1-3; John 3:16; Rom 10:13; Rev 21:6; 22:17)
CANON 18. That grace is not preceded by merit. Recompense is due to good works if they are performed; but grace, to which we have no claim, precedes them, to enable them to be done.	18.1. Must read this point knowing that the reception of grace = the "Holy" Baptism of an incomprehending infant 18.2. Even in an Augustinian document, Rome shows that it cannot get away from its frame of reference based on a works salvation: 18.2.1. We are not saved by works, Eph 2:8-9; Rom 4:2-5; 10:2-4; Gal 2:16 18.2.2. There is nothing that we can do for which we can receive any merit, even our good works are not our own, but Christ's worked through us, Eph 2:10; John 3:20-21
CANON 19. That a man can be saved only when God shows mercy. Human nature, even though it remained in that sound state in which it was created, could be [sic] no means save itself, without the assistance of the Creator; hence since man cannot safe-guard his salvation without the grace of God, which is a gift, how will he be able to restore what he has lost without the grace of God?	19.1. In what way does God savingly assist man to reveal His salvation? In the Word of God. Here is where the power of the Word should be emphasized, but it is not! 19.2. "Without the grace of God" = without "Holy" Baptism, a complete turn of the tables on the way God's grace is communicated to man, through the Scriptures alone and by faith alone
CANON 20. That a man can do no good without God. God does much that is good in a man that the man does not do; but a man does nothing good for which God is not responsible, so as to let him do it.	20.1. This Canon sets up Baptism as: 20.1.1. The work of God; in other words, a priest pouring water into the ear of an infant = the work of Almighty God to pout His Spirit and His grace, and to bring salvation to that infant; how presumptuous! 20.1.2. Therefore, without this prevenient work of the Spirit of God, man can do nothing, not even respond to the Gospel by faith! 20.2. One thinks that one is reading from an Evangelical playbook on this point, which leads me to surmise that the original canons were of an Evangelical nature, and were then twisted just enough to be useful as a tool for the sacramental arguments of Rome's theologians
CANON 21. Concerning nature and grace. As the Apostle most truly says to those who would be justified by the law and have fallen from grace, "If justification were through the law, then Christ died to no purpose" (Gal. 2:21), so it is most truly declared to those who imagine that grace, which faith in Christ advocates and lays hold of, is nature: "If justification were through nature, then Christ died to no purpose." Now there was	21.1. If nature = [natural] ability to respond to the Gospel proclaimed (as in the first several Canons), then they have just turned the tables on the New Covenant, turning it into the Old; meanwhile setting the stage for their Sacramental Covenant! 21.1.1. A very coy turn of the tables, through swapping words! 21.1.2. It looks like Matt 5:17 becomes the prooftext for Christ setting up a new Law, the Law of Grace, as it were, which requires Baptism as the first sacrament

[948]Commission biblique pontificale, *L'interprétation de la Bible dans l'Église* (Quebec: Éditions Fides, 1994; Paris: Les Éditions du Cerf, 1994), 50.

indeed the law, but it did not justify, and there was indeed nature, but it did not justify. Not in vain did Christ therefore die, so that the law might be fulfilled by him who said, "I have come not to abolish them <the law and prophets> but to fulfil them" (Matt. 5:17), and that the nature which had been destroyed by Adam might be restored by him who said that he had come "to seek and to save the lost" (Luke 19:10).	21.1.3. Somehow, in Rome's logic, once an infant has had the water poured in his ear, then his response to the means of salvation provided by Rome is no longer natural, but supernatural; in fact, as noted above, he has no need to respond to the Gospel, although he alone could do it from a supernatural state, for he already has responded to the gospel through the sacrament of [infant] baptism 21.2. Here all the verses noted above on justification by faith alone are completely ignored (Rom 1:16-17; 4:2-5; 10:2-4; Gal 2:16; Eph 2:8-9) 21.2.1. The giving of that faith itself being a gift, Gal 3:22
CANON 22. Concerning those things that belong to man. No man has anything of his own but untruth and sin. But if a man has any truth or righteousness, it is from that fountain for which we must thirst in this desert, so that we may be refreshed from it as by drops of water and not faint on the way.	22.1. Could this be responding to: "God has His part, man has his part, wherefore he must respond to God's Word"? 22.2. The "if" is a mute point, seems like the addition of Roman scholars who could not and cannot accept total depravity 22.2.1. Does this not correspond with Rome's attack on the Manichean Cathars of Southern France, that they were so negative that their civilization could not have lasted, and therefore needed to be wiped out (via the Albigensian Crusade which began in earnest from 1215-1255, followed by centuries of inquisition)?[949] 22.3. In this Canon, it is clear that that for which a lost person must faint, is not the righteousness of God, but is the fount of "Holy" Baptism

CANON 23. Concerning the will of God and of man. Men do their own will and not the will of God when they do what displeases him; but when they follow their own will and comply with the will of God, however willingly they do so, yet it is his will by which what they will is both prepared and instructed.	23.1. Another attack on the will of man to savingly respond to the Gospel proclaimed
	    23.1.1. Responding to God's call through His Word by the Gospel proclaimed is actually displeasing to God according to this Canon, as anyone who does so is following their own will and not complying with the will of God (as savingly and infallibly communicated to His Church, the Church of Rome, through its Holy Traditions, as found in this and other Councils of the said Church)
	    23.1.2. "However willingly they do so," no matter how willingly one submits his own will to that of the Holy Scriptures, it is not enough, until that will has been prepared and instructed by the will of God as communicated through Rome
	
	23.2. Again, the "but" statement seems like the addition of nuance to an original document

CANON 24. Concerning the branches of the vine. The branches on the vine do not give life to the vine, but receive life from it; thus the vine is related to its branches in such a way that it supplies them with what they need to live, and does not take this from them. Thus it is to the advantage of the disciples, not Christ, both to have Christ abiding in them and to abide in Christ. For if the vine is cut down another can shoot up from the live root; but one who is cut off from the vine cannot live without the root (John 15:5ff).	24.1. Rome = the true vine and Christ Himself
	    24.1.1. This is why the Pope taking on the various titles have massive theological significance for Rome
	    24.1.1. Remembering that it was not long before the Pope took the title "Vicar of Christ", meaning in the place of Christ; not following in allegiance to the Pope in their minds means not following Christ!
	
	24.2. The teaching, that latter became a threat, Rome is the only true vine, there is no life outside of the vine of Rome, and all her teachings, and all of her sacraments, and all of her hierarchy

---

[949]"Founding themselves upon this one-sided Medieval documentation, the modern theologians (from Döllinger to Father Dondaine, O.P.), the historians of religion (from Söderberg to Runciman), and the historians (from Arno Post to Christine Thouzellier) who studied and wrote on the subject up to the middle of the 20th Century, ended quite naturally to one consensual opinion, leaving the phenomena of the Cathars as a well-ordered question: catharism was a foreign body in Western Christianity and, as such, it was given over to failure. Heirs of Persian Manichaeanism and of the intervening *Mazdéism* of the Paulicians and Bogomils, it was characterized by a dualist doctrine of Oriental origin which it taught. Unrealistic, pessimistic, fundamentally anti-social, it had no chance of surviving in Western Christianity and very understandable repression of which it was the object—crusade and Inquisition— had only but accelerated the process of internal degeneration which would have without a doubt led to its disappearing.

"Paradoxically, it was in the publication and study of the inquisition archives that opened the first flaw of this wall of certainty" (Anne Brenon, *Les Archipels Cathares* [Cahors, France: Dire, 2000], 13; Translation mine).

CANON 25. Concerning the love with which we love God. It is wholly a gift of God to love God. He who loves, even though he is not loved, allowed himself to be loved. We are loved, even when we displease him, so that we might have means to please him. For the Spirit, whom we love with the Father and the Son, has poured into our hearts the love of the Father and the Son (Rom. 5:5).	25.1. Enter a theology of love (charity, love in action):
	    25.1.1. Remembering that the translation of one of the words for which Tyndale was burned was translating agape as "love" and not "charity"—"charity" being a work, "love" being an affection
	    25.1.2. Therefore, it is highly likely that the original Latin in the Canon is equivocal: not "love" only with all of its affectionate implications, but also "charity" with all of its corresponding actions
	
	25.2. Two further thoughts about love or charity:
	    25.2.1. Non-Roman partisans were accused of not loving Christ or His Church, because they were not speaking for Rome or the Pope
	    25.2.2. In fact they were accused of sowing discord and schism, which is sin against the charity to which Christ calls His Church:
	        25.2.2.1. For Aquinas, sowing discord and schism were worse than any other crimes (murder and theft), because they were crimes against the taproot of his theology, Rome and its Church
	        25.2.2.2. Herein enters the first Cardinal Sin, the sin of pride, thinking that you, as an individual know better than the Roman Church with all of her long history, Holy Traditions, and her divinely inspired and infallible interpretations of the Holy Scriptures!
	        25.2.2.3. She (the Church of Rome) is without spot, wrinkle or blemish (Eph 5:27); she has done no wrong and she can do no wrong; she is infallible!
	    25.2.3. Somehow, a love for charity led Rome to be most uncharitable to those who did not hold there sacramental view of salvation, and who, worse yet, sought to share the Gospel with others! The were interred in a wall, burned alive, had their head cut off, drowned, had wars called against them, whole cities and populations were decimated—all in the name of charity! What a paradox!

Concluding paragraphs of the 2nd Council of Orange (529)[950]

TEXT OF THE CONCLUDING PARAGRAPHS	ANALYSIS

"CONCLUSION. And thus according to the passages of holy scripture quoted above or the interpretations of the ancient Fathers we must, under the blessing of God, preach and believe as follows. The sin of the first man has so impaired and weakened free will that no one thereafter can either love God as he ought or believe in God or do good for God's sake, unless the grace of divine mercy has preceded him. We therefore believe that the glorious faith which was given to Abel the righteous, and Noah, and Abraham, and Isaac, and Jacob, and to all the saints of old, and which the Apostle Paul <sic> commends in extolling them (Heb. 11), was not given through natural goodness as it was	26.1. This regional council gave itself the weight of a creed (much like the so-called 8th Century "Creed of Athanasius"[951]):
	    26.1.1. Stating that it was correctly interpreting the Bible passages above, though it purposefully misquoted and distorted them, mainly framing out of the question (not dealing with) Scripture that would oppose its propositions
	    26.1.2. Stating that it is following the "interpretations of the ancient fathers"—further proof that the interpretations of the "ancient fathers" passed down to us off the pen of over a Millenium of monks are suspect at best
	    26.1.3. Using phrases (in this paragraph) as:
	        26.1.3.1. "We must, under the blessing of God, preach and believe as follows"
	        26.1.3.2. "We therefore believe"
	        26.1.3.3. "And we know and also believe"
	    26.1.4. Using phrases (in the next paragraph [#27]) as:
	        26.1.4.1. "According to the catholic faith we also believe"
	        26.1.4.2. "We not only do not believe"
	        26.1.4.3. "We also believe and confess to our benefit"
	        26.1.4.4. "We must therefore most evidently believe"
	
	26.2. Appeal is made to an "impaired and weakened free will" making it impossible for a person to believe in God:

---

[950]Denzinger added that these conclusions are from Cesar d'Arles (DS 396-397).

[951]"Whosoever will be saved, before all things it is necessary that he hold the Catholic faith, Which Faith except every one do keep whole and undefiled, without doubt he shall perish everlastingly. And the Catholic faith is this: that we worship one God in Trinity, and Trinity in Unity…" ("Creed of Athanasius," available at: http://www.rca.org/aboutus/beliefs/athanasian.php; accessed 28 Sept 2004; Internet).

before to Adam, but was bestowed by the grace of God. And we know and also believe that even after the coming of our Lord this grace is not to be found in the free will of all who desire to be baptized, but is bestowed by the kindness of Christ, as has already been frequently stated and as the Apostle Paul declares, "For it has been granted to you that for the sake of Christ you should not only believe in him but also suffer for his sake" (Phil. 1:29). And again, "He who began a good work in you will bring it to completion at the day of Jesus Christ" (Phil. 1:6). And again, "For by grace you have been saved through faith; and it is not your own doing, it is the gift of God" (Eph. 2:8). And as the Apostle says of himself, "I have obtained mercy to be faithful" (1 Cor. 7:25, cf. 1 Tim. 1:13). He did not say, "because I was faithful," but "to be faithful." And again, "What have you that you did not receive?" (1 Cor. 4:7). And again, "Every good endowment and every perfect gift is from above, coming down from the Father of lights" (Jas. 1:17). And again, "No one can receive anything except what is given him from heaven" (John 3:27). There are innumerable passages of holy scripture which can be quoted to prove the case for grace, but they have been omitted for the sake of brevity, because further examples will not really be of use where few are deemed sufficient.	26.2.1. Therefore being unable to respond to the Gospel, even though New Testament evangelism does not approach lost man in this way!
	
	 26.2.2. In New Testament evangelism (i.e. the Book of Acts), no mention is made of baptism as being a prerequisite to a response of faith; in fact quite the opposite (e.g. Acts 10:47; 15:7-11; 16:14, 30-31)
	
	 26.2.3. Two prooftexts, taken out of context, are falsely applied to the order of salvation (Mark 16:16; 1 Pet 3:20-21), requiring a "desire to be baptized" prior to a hearing of faith
	
	 26.2.4. Or to reduce this argument to its lowest common denominator, the message to be preached only by the approved "evangelists" credentialed by Rome is as follows—a baptism of penance for the forgiveness of [original] sins! Sounds like Jerome's Vulgate (quoting the 1899 Douais-Rheims Bible):
	
	   26.2.4.1. "John was in the desert baptizing, and preaching the baptism of penance, unto remission of sins," Mark 4:1
	
	   26.2.4.2. "And he came into all the country about the Jordan, preaching the baptism of penance for the remission of sins," Luke 3:3
	
	   26.2.4.3. "And that penance and remission of sins should be preached in his name, unto all nations, beginning at Jerusalem," Luke 24:47
	
	   26.2.4.4. "But Peter said to them: Do penance, and be baptized every one of you in the name of Jesus Christ, for the remission of your sins: and you shall receive the gift of the Holy Ghost," Acts 2:38
	
	 26.2.5. By the way, word "penance" is found 67 times in the Douais-Rheims Bible (a very literal [at times] translation of the Latin Vulgate into English in 1899), and the phrase "do penance" is found 29 times, "did penance" is found 5 times, and "done penance" is found 3 times
	
	 26.2.6. Jerome's translation of Rom 3:23 reads, "For all have sinned and do need the glory of God" (1899 Douais-Rheims), a further Augustinian gloss in his translation
	
	 26.2.7. True total depravity is much more strongly stated than the Augustinian "impaired and weakened free will"[952]
	
	 26.3. Again, the Council frames the question such that man's free will causes the coming of the grace of God, again making a mockery of the examples in the Book of Acts (as noted above)
	
	 26.4. Then the Council has the audacity of affirming that its approach, which will inject below water baptism by sprinkling as the reception of grace, proves the case for salvation by "grace"!

"According to the catholic faith we also believe that after grace has been	27.1. Finally, after spinning this long string of framed arguments to slice the Evangelical movement down the middle, the Council affirms that "grace is received through baptism"—which view

---

[952]"Chapter II: Concerning Man. Man is wicked, able to do nothing, foolish and reckless, full of falsehood and hypocrisy, fickle, variable, thinking only of evil and sin (Ps. 55; Rom. 3:9-12), into which he is conceived and born (Ps. 51:7), seeking for himself in everything and by everything. Esteeming only what benefits him, always wishing to magnify his works, powers, and virtues, full of ingratitude and disobedience: and hoping and dreaming of guarding his own inventions, laws, and ordinances more than those of God (Gen 3:1-6). He cannot bear to be humiliated, dishonored, and scorned; but wishes to exalt himself above God, above His holy Word, law, and commandment. And he is so full of all iniquity that he has lost all appearance of righteousness and sanctity. And still he is cursed, unhappy, and mendacious; as a rotten root of an evil tree can bring forth only evil fruit (Matt 7:17-18); for all is corrupted in him. Still, that death for the disobedience of the first man could bear fruit only in death and damnation, having all evil thoughts, because every product of the thoughts of his heart is only evil all the time: for he is flesh, and both that which comes from his heart and every affection of the flesh is evil (Gen 6:12; 8:21). …

"Chapter VI: Concerning Sin. Sin is nature corrupted and depraved, living for itself, loving itself, repugnant to the law of God (Rom 7:22-23), and hating it, loving carnal things, contemptuous of spiritual things (1 Cor 2:14), understanding nothing from God, full of all ignorance, bearing fruit in death. For sin is so cursed and wicked a source, that it can be only evil.

"And the more the right and good path is clearly revealed to it, the more it rejects and reviles it (Matt. 7:13-14). And if it does not die and is not destroyed by the death of Jesus, it will say the good is bad, and the bad is good, and the darkenss light, blaspheming the Holy Spirit, attributing injustice to God and to His innocence, and rising up against god and His Spirit, condemning Him for His Rule, because it wants renown and honor" ("William Farel's Summary (1529)," from James T. Dennison, Jr., *Reformed Confessions of the 16th and 17th Centuries in English Translation: Volume 1, 1523-1552* [Grand Rapids: Reformation Heritage, 2008], 55-56, 58-59).

received through baptism, all baptized persons have the ability and responsibility, if they desire to labor faithfully, to perform with the aid and cooperation of Christ what is of essential importance in regard to the salvation of their soul. We not only do not believe that any are foreordained to evil by the power of God, but even state with utter abhorrence that if there are those who want to believe so evil a thing, they are anathema. We also believe and confess to our benefit that in every good work it is not we who take the initiative and are then assisted through the mercy of God, but God himself first inspires in us both faith in him and love for him without any previous good works of our own that deserve reward, so that we may both faithfully seek the sacrament of baptism, and after baptism be able by his help to do what is pleasing to him. We must therefore most evidently believe that the praiseworthy faith of the thief whom the Lord called to his home in paradise, and of Cornelius the centurion, to whom the angel of the Lord was sent, and of Zacchaeus, who was worthy to receive the Lord himself, was not a natural endowment but a gift of God's kindness."

completely undermines evangelical theology of salvation by grace alone without any intermediary (cf. Warfield's *The Plan of Salvation* [1918])

27.1.1.   "…God himself first inspires in us … so that we may both faithfully seek the sacrament of baptism…"

27.1.2.   Herein it is clear from this text of the Council of Orange that Baptism is the first step in the order of salvation

27.1.3.   Therefore the message of Rome's approved evangelist should be for his hearers to "faithfully seek the sacrament of baptism" for themselves and their children—thereby placing a work of man in the place of faith

27.1.4.   Herein is perhaps why Paul's use of circumcision in Romans and Galatians is especially poignant as an argument against infant baptism:

27.1.4.1.   Infant baptism takes place prior to the age of accountability of a child, and is therefore conferred upon the child at the wishes of his parents or guardians, without his knowledge or approval, and without prior:

27.1.4.1.1.   Having been won as a disciple or Jesus (Matt 28:19), as was Joseph of Arimathea (Matt 27:57)

27.1.4.1.2.   Having believed (Mark 16:16; Acts 8:12, 13, 37; 18:8)

27.1.4.1.3.   Repentance for the forgiveness of sins (Acts 2:38)

27.1.4.1.4.   Receiving the word (Acts 2:41)

27.1.4.1.5.   Having personally requested baptism, (Acts 8:36)

27.1.4.1.6.   The removal of the veil of blindness (Acts 9:18)

27.1.4.1.7.   Having already received the Holy Spirit (Acts 10:47-48; 11:15-16)

27.1.4.1.8.   First the Lord opened Lydia's heart to respond to the words spoken by Paul (Acts 16:14-15)

27.1.4.1.8.1.   To believe that the message spoken by Paul was to be baptized prior to faith is (1) a misreading of all of Pauline theology, and (2) an argument from silence in Acts

27.1.4.1.9.   When the Philippian jailer asked what to "do" to be saved, Paul replied "believe" not in water baptism, but in the name of the Lord to be saved

27.1.4.1.9.1.   This "faith alone" corresponds with the words of Jesus to the incredulous crowds in John 6:28-29

27.1.4.1.9.2.   This "faith alone" corresponds to Rom 10:9-10, 13, 14-15

27.1.4.2.   Remembering that circumcision was a rite that went back to Abraham (Gen 17:10), prior to the giving of the Law to Moses

27.1.4.2.1.   Also remembering that Jerome in his introductions made Christ into a second lawgiver, thereby affirming Jerome's sacramental view of salvation

27.1.4.3.   Also remembering Paul's argument in Romans 4 that Abraham believed and received imputed righteousness prior to the giving of the rite of circumcision (Gen 15:6)

27.1.4.4.   Thus, Paul disproved any rite whatsoever prior to or alongside of faith in the following verses:

27.1.4.4.1.   Rom 1:16, "for everyone who believes"

27.1.4.4.2.   Rom 1:17, "from faith to faith"

27.1.4.4.3.   Rom 4:5, "But to the one who does not work, but believes in Him who justifies the ungodly, his faith is reckoned as righteousness"

27.1.4.4.4.   Gal 2:16, "nevertheless knowing that a man is not justified by the works of the Law but through faith in Christ Jesus, even we have believed in Christ Jesus, that we may be justified by faith in Christ, and not by the works of the Law; since by the works of the Law shall no flesh be justified"

27.1.4.4.5.   Gal 5:6, "For in Christ Jesus neither circumcision nor uncircumcision means anything, but faith working through love"; replacing "infant baptism" for "circumcision" reads as follows:

	27.1.4.4.5.1. "For in Christ Jesus neither infant baptism nor lack of infant baptism means anything, but faith working through love"
	27.1.4.4.5.2. Notice how this verse can be used as a backdoor for a non-negative view of infant baptism (à la "Normative Principle," allowing anything in the worship of the church not directly prohibited in Scripture [in contradistinction to Calvin's "Regulative Principle"])
	27.1.4.4.6. Gal 6:15, "For neither is circumcision anything, nor uncircumcision, but a new creation" (cf. 2 Cor 5:17)
	27.1.4.5. In fact, Paul emphasized God's work of salvation as a circumcision done without human hands, by God Himself through faith, Col 2:11-12 (cf. Rom 2:29)
	27.1.5. Concerning passages linking baptism with washing away sin:
	27.1.5.1. Acts 2:38 emphasized repentance prior to baptism
	27.1.5.1. Acts 22:16 emphasized that after faith and obedience of faith, Paul was to be baptized, symbolizing the washing away of his sins, as is taught in Rom 6:1-4; Col 2:11-12 (cf. Gal 3:27)
	27.2 "Have the ability" flies in the face of NT conversion and justification:
	27.2.1. Before conversion, man is "without strength" and incapable of following Christ and His commands, Rom 5:6
	27.2.2. About the sinner actually knowing the day and time of his salvation, not only is this the teaching of the Bible, it is the example of the Bible
	27.2.2.1. Asking to be saved, Acts 16:30
	27.2.2.2 Volitionally believeing in him "with all the heart," Acts 16:37
	27.2.2.3 Confessing Christ in the lips, Acts 16:37
	27.2.2.4. Those who knew the exact day and time of their conversion: Paul, the Woman at the Well, the Demoniac from Gerasenes, the Philippian Jailer, the Ethiopian Eunuch, Lydia from Thyatira, etc.
	27.2. The disclaimer, "if they desire to labor faithfully," accomplishes three things for the Orange divines:
	27.2.1. The disclaimer protects them [Rome] from the blame resulting from inevitable apostate members who they baptize, but who then live lives of debauchery (as an extreme example, Adolf Hitler)
	27.2.2. The disclaimer causes members of the Church of Rome to be ever beholden to Rome for the proper dispensation of further graces—i.e. it gives the Roman curia the upper hand over all Catholics:
	27.2.2.1. Consider in this light the title for [St.] Mary, "Mediatrix of all the graces of God"
	27.2.2.2. Consider also in this light Rome's 1993 *Catechism of the Catholic Church*, "Who Belongs to the Catholic Church" (§836-838); according to this section the only people who can be sure not to be saved are apostate Catholics:
	27.2.2.2.1. "Even though incorporated into the Church, one who does not however persevere in charity is not saved" (ibid., §837)
	27.2.3. The disclaimer removes any possibility of assurance of salvation, as it is always worked out by the unending and unsatisfying efforts of the adherent of Rome's theology
	27.2.3.1. Luther struggled with his soul due to the need for unending confessions, which is part of the "Sacrament of Penance"
	27.2.3.2. Likewise, Heb 10:4, "For it is impossible for the blood of bulls and goats to take away sins"
	27.3. The authors of the Council of Orange were not theological novices, but ever wise of Holy Scriptures, even as Satan used Scriptures when he tempted Jesus; they dealt with three examples of individuals who were not baptized (perhaps as types of all of them):
	27.3.1. Who were not baptized at all: Thief on the cross and Zacchaeus
	27.3.2. One who believed prior to baptism: Cornelius

27.3.3. How about Nicodemus or the Woman at the Well of whom it is never stated that they are baptized?

27.3.4. And how about the Ethiopian Eunuch, Lydia, and the Philippian jailer who were all baptized after faith (following the order of Mark 16:16; etc.), as were the visitors in the house of Cornelius?

27.3.5. How about the "disciples of John the Baptist" who received the water of John the Baptist and were not cleansed by the Holy Spirit (Acts 19:2)? And then when they were baptized, Paul did not use the Matt 28:19 Trinitarian formula?

27.3.6. The Orangians argument seems to be that for these people, they received a special endument of the gift of God's kindness (notice that they did not use the word "grace"), but that this gift of kindness was unique or restricted, but not exemplary of God's working, against all of the examples in the New Testament noted above!

27.4. The true "plan of salvation" of Orange is not clarified until it has spun a goodly web around New Testament evangelism (and likewise obedience to the Great Commission), reducing its necessity to nothing:

27.4.1. With [infant] baptism, a response to the Gospel is unnecessary, since it has already occurred by proxy, when a person was baptized as an infant

27.4.2. Without baptism, a response to the Gospel is impossible (unless a semi-Pelagian), since the only response possible is to faithfully seek out baptism from a duly appointed priest of Rome

27.4.3. Therefore, the proclamation of the Gospel in obedience to the Great Commission is not only unnecessary, it is twice anathemized by this Council

27.4.4. Perhaps this is why the Lutheran Gustav Warneck in his *History of Protestant Missions* (6th German ed., 1903; 3rd English ed., 1905) taught that NT evangelism was unnecessary after a church had been established in a country, since once a church was established, there was a vehicle for conferring the "ever-effective" waters of baptism in a country!

27.4.5. Was this same discussion the core of disagreement between Zwingli and Hubmaier in 1523-1525?

27.5. A last jab is struck via the silent argument of some receiving a "hearing of faith" which presupposes others not receiving it:

27.5.1. The accusation and anathema of anyone who believes in "double-predestination" (of those not receiving a "hearing of faith")

27.5.2. Jesus, however, "upped the ante" by stating that "Many will say to Me in that day. 'Lord, Lord,'" to which He will respond, "I never knew you" (Matt 7:21-23)

27.5.3. Likewise, some seed sown on the shallow soil is received immediately with joy, and then scandalizes [falls away], Matt 13:20-21 and parallels

Further Concluding Comments from Johnston:

1. Clearly the contribution of the Second Council of Orange relates not to freewill or predestination, but rather to the role of Baptism in conversion and salvation, highlighting Rome's right to bestow their "Holy" Baptism, by which the recipient, no matter how young he may be, is born again, born from above, receives the washing of regeneration, the washing of original sin, etc.

2. Most non-Roman Christians, Methodists, Presbyterians, Anglicans, Lutherans, and Eastern Orthodox, practice some form of infant baptism, thereby professing by their actions that there is some kind of hidden grace communicated through baptism, which makes them less volatile against Rome's theology on this point:

   a. Was believer's baptism a battle that Zwingli decided against fighting when he made a change on believer's baptism in 1523-1524, later arresting the "Anabaptist" doctor of theology, Balthasar Hubmaier, who himself was [re]baptized in 1525 by the "Anabaptist" Wilhelm Reublin in Waldshut

   b. There seems to be three levels of intensity of debate in the issue of believer's baptism:

      1) Agree with believer's baptism, but not to the point of [re]baptizing someone who has already been baptized as an infant (Hubmaier, 1523-1524)

      2) Agree with believer's baptism, to the point of [re]baptizing one who had been illegitimately baptized before (Hubmaier, 1525-1528, until his martyrdom in Vienna)

     3) Agree with believer's baptism, to the point of not allowing one's children to be baptized (the view which labelled Anabaptists as witches according to the widely printed 1484 guidelines of Rome's Grand Inquisitor in the region of Germany, Conrad of Marburg's *Hexenhammer,* or in Latin, *Malleus Maleficarum*)

    c. The aforementioned Protestant denominations seem to have decided that believer's baptism (and what it means for salvation) is not a position worth dying for!

3. Baptists, however, are especially egregious to Rome's theology in the 2nd Council of Orange, in that they do not allow for some form of grace being communicated through Baptism if administered prior to conversion; in fact, Baptists regularly have the audacity of rebaptizing those who have been baptized by Rome's hierarchy, therefore by their actions denigrating Rome's baptism,[953] and validating their own; in this way they are equal to or worse than the Donatists, against whom Augustine wrote, who had the audacity to rebaptize Roman believers!

4. This is perhaps why Baptists faced terrible persecution throughout the history of the Church, but especially during and after the Dark Ages

5. By the way, according to Rome, anyone baptized by the proper formula, baptized by a Roman priest or not, is baptized into the Church of Rome, and therefore comes under their rightful church discipline!

---

[953]Rome does not take this slight against their baptism very lightly. Listen to what the *Catechism* stated regarding one who has left their fold to find greener spiritual pastures in someother church [be it a "schismatic" church (defined as sacramental doctrine but not under Rome's hierarchy) or a "heretical" ecclesial community (not accepting a sacramental salvation [i.e. all Evangelicals])]: "837. 'Fully incorporated into the society of the Church are those who, possessing the Spirit of Christ [bestowed at infant baptism or at baptism some at some other time], accept all the means of salvation given to the Church together with her entire organization, and who—by the bonds constituted by the professions of faith, the sacraments, ecclesiastical government, and communion—are joined to the visible structure of the Church of Christ, who rules her through the Supreme Pontiff and the bishops. Even though incorporated into the Church, one who does not however persevere in charity is not saved. He remains indeed in the bosom of the Church, 'in body' not 'in heart'" (*Catechism of the Catholic Church* [London: Geoffrey Chapman, 1994], 194).

CHAPTER 11
God, Prayer, and Fasting in Evangelism
❖ ❖ ❖
God and Man in Evangelism

Introduction (an expansion of Hudson Taylor's watchword):

We have a living God (Psa 42:2), who has given us a living Word (Heb 4:12) and who is at work in the world today (2 Pet 3:9). When we are involved in evangelism, God works through His word, through His Spirit, through the blood of Christ, and through his servants in the present world!

Examples of God's divine *preparatio*
Sidonian widow prepared by God to assist Elijah, 1 Kg 17:9
Those appointed to eternal life, Acts 13:48
The Lord opened her heart to respond to the things spoken by Paul, Acts 16:14

However, due to the sometimes heated debate between God's and man's part in evangelism, I have included this discussion as food for thought.

Perhaps this was what Jesus was getting at when He asked the following question:

"And they came again to Jerusalem. And as He was walking in the temple, the chief priests, and scribes, and elders came to Him, and *began* saying to Him, 'By what authority are You doing these things, or who gave You this authority to do these things?' And Jesus said to them, 'I will ask you one question, and you answer Me, and *then* I will tell you by what authority I do these things. Was the baptism of John from heaven, or from men? Answer Me.'" (Mark 11:27-30)

Notice that Jesus was asking them a question that related to the God and man interaction in a divinely ordained religious rite, baptism! The chief priests, scribes and elders, however, did not want to answer the question…

"And they *began* reasoning among themselves, saying, 'If we say, "From heaven," He will say, "Then why did you not believe him?" But shall we say, "From men"?'—they were afraid of the multitude, for all considered John to have been a prophet indeed. And answering Jesus, they said, 'We do not know.' And Jesus said to them, 'Neither will I tell you by what authority I do these things'" (Mark 11:31-33)

Yes, just as in the case of the baptism of John the Baptist, there seems to be a "hypostatic union" when it comes to the ministry of evangelism!

Building from this question—Who Evangelizes?
Acts 17:
Paul evangelizes:
v. 18, "because he was preaching Jesus and the resurrection"
v. 22, "And Paul stood in the midst of the Areopagus and said…"
God evangelizes:
v. 30, "God is now declaring to men that all everywhere should repent"
Eph 2-3:
Jesus evangelizes:
2:17, "And He came and preached [εὐαγγελίζω] peace [Isa 52:7] to you who were far away, and peace to those who were near"
Paul evangelizes:
3:7, "To me, the very least of all saints, this grace was given, to preach [εὐαγγελίζω] to the Gentiles the unfathomable riches of Christ"

Many other passages delineate aspects of this hypostatic union in the Christian life and in the ministry of the Gospel…

A. Several Passages Exemplifying in the Relationship of God and Man:

Deut 11:29 (ESV)

GOD'S PART	MAN'S PART
And when the LORD your God brings you into the land	that you are entering to take possession of it, you shall set the blessing on Mount Gerizim and the curse on Mount Ebal.

Psalm 119:25-32

GOD'S PART	MAN'S PART
	25 My soul cleaves to the dust;
Revive me according to Your word.	26 I have told of my ways,
And You have answered me; Teach me Your statutes.	
27 Make me understand the way of Your precepts,	So I will meditate on Your wonders.
	28 My soul weeps because of grief;
Strengthen me according to Your word.	
29 Remove the false way from me,	
And graciously grant me Your law.	30 I have chosen the faithful way;
	I have placed Your ordinances *before me*.
	31 I cling to Your testimonies;
O LORD, do not put me to shame!	32 I shall run the way of Your commandments,
For You will enlarge my heart.	

John 6:35-40

GOD'S PART	MAN'S PART
35 Jesus said to them, "I am the bread of life;	he who comes to Me will not hunger, and he who believes in Me will never thirst.
	36 "But I said to you that you have seen Me, and yet do not believe.
37 "All that the Father gives Me [] I will certainly not cast out.	[will come to Me, and the one who comes to Me]
38 "For I have come down from heaven, not to do My own will, but the will of Him who sent Me.	
39 "This is the will of Him who sent Me, that of all that He has given Me I lose nothing, but raise it up on the last day.	
40 "For this is the will of My Father, [] will have eternal life, and I Myself will raise him up on the last day."	[that everyone who beholds the Son and believes in Him]

Acts 14:21-28

GOD	EVANGELIST
	21 After they had preached the gospel to that city and had made many disciples, they returned to Lystra and to Iconium and to Antioch, 22 strengthening the souls of the disciples, encouraging them to continue in the faith, and *saying*, "Through many tribulations we must enter the kingdom of God."
[they commended them to the Lord]	23 When they had appointed elders for them in every church, having prayed with fasting, [] in whom they had believed.
	24 They passed through Pisidia and came into Pamphylia. 25 When they had spoken the word in Perga, they went down to Attalia.
[from which they had been commended to the grace of God]	26 From there they sailed to Antioch, [] for the work that they had accomplished (εἰς τὸ ἔργον ὃ ἐπλήρωσαν).
[all things that God had done with* them and how He had opened a door of faith to the Gentiles.]	27 When they had arrived and gathered the church together, they *began* to report []
	28 And they spent a long time with the disciples.

*(note the word "with" in v 27 [not NIV's "through"] implies colaboring, cf. 2 Cor 6:1, συνεργέω)

Acts 13:2-12

GOD	EVANGELIST	CONTACT	ANTAGONIST
	2 While they were ministering to the Lord and fasting,		
the Holy Spirit said, "Set apart for Me Barnabas and Saul for the work to which I have called them."			
	3 Then, when they had fasted and prayed and laid their hands on them, they sent them away (ἀπολύω).		
4 So, being sent out (ἐκπέμπω) by the Holy Spirit,			
	They went down to Seleucia and from there they sailed to Cyprus. 5 When they reached Salamis, they *began* to proclaim the word of God in the synagogues of the Jews; and they also had John as their helper. 6 When they had gone through the whole island as far as Paphos, they found a magician,		
			a Jewish false prophet whose name was Bar-Jesus, 7 who was with the proconsul, Sergius Paulus, a man of intelligence.
		This man summoned Barnabas and Saul and sought to hear the word of God.	
			8 But Elymas the magician (for so his name is translated) was opposing them, seeking to turn the proconsul away from the faith.
[filled with the Holy Spirit,]	9 But Saul, who was also *known as* Paul, [] fixed his gaze on him, 10 and said, ...		
[the teaching of the Lord.]		12 Then the proconsul believed when he saw what had happened, being amazed at []	

Acts 15:7-11, Peter's testimony before the Jerusalem Council

GOD	EVANGELIST/JEWS	GENTILES
7 ... Brethren, you know that in the early days God made a choice among you,	That by my mouth	the Gentiles would hear the word of the gospel and believe.
8 And God, who knows the heart, []	Just as He also did to us;	[testified to them giving them the Holy Spirit,]
9 and He made no distinction	Between us and them,	cleansing their hearts by faith.
	10 Now therefore why do you put God to the test [] a yoke which neither our fathers nor we have been able to bear?	[by placing upon the neck of the disciples]
[through the grace of the Lord Jesus]	11 But we believe that we are saved []	in the same way as they also are

New Testament Uses of "Open" (διανοίγω)

GOD OPENING THE HEART [through things spoken]	PAUL OPENING THE GOSPEL
Acts 16:14 A woman named Lydia, from the city of Thyatira, a seller of purple fabrics, a worshiper of God, was listening; and the Lord opened her heart (ὁ κύριος διήνοιξεν τὴν καρδίαν) to respond to the things spoken by Paul	Acts 17:2-3 And according to Paul's custom, he went to them, and for three Sabbaths reasoned with them from the Scriptures, explaining (διανοίγων) and giving evidence that the Christ had to suffer and rise again from the dead, and *saying*, "This Jesus whom I am proclaiming to you is the Christ."

A closer look at Acts 16:13-14

GOD	EVANGELIST	CONTACT
	13 And on the Sabbath day we went outside the gate to a riverside, where we were supposing that there would be a place of prayer; and we sat down and began speaking	To the women who had assembled.
		14 A woman named Lydia, from the city of Thyatira, a seller of purple fabrics,
a worshiper of God,	[Paul's speaking implied from listening and from verse 13]	was listening;
and the Lord opened []	to the things spoken by Paul	[her heart to respond]

Acts 28:17-29

GOD	EVANGELIST	CONTACT	ANTAGONIST
	17 After three days Paul called together those who were the leading men of the Jews, and when they came together, he *began* saying to them…		
		21 They said to him, "We have neither received letters from Judea concerning you, nor have any of the brethren come here and reported or spoken anything bad about you	
		22 "But we desire to hear from you what your views are; for concerning this sect, it is known to us that it is spoken against everywhere."	[discuss antagonism]
		23 When they had set a day for Paul, they came to him at his lodging in large numbers	
[Holy Spirit at work through the Word!]	And he was explaining to them by solemnly testifying about the kingdom of God and trying to persuade them concerning Jesus, from both the Law of Moses and from the Prophets, from morning until evening		
[Holy Spirit at work through the Word!]	[by the things spoken (by Paul or by the Holy Spirit?)]	24 Some were being persuaded by the things spoken, but others would not believe	
		25 And when they did not agree with one another, they *began* leaving	
	after Paul had spoken one *parting* word, "The Holy Spirit rightly spoke through Isaiah the prophet to your fathers…		
		29 And when he had said these words, the Jews departed and had a great dispute among themselves	

A closer look at Acts 28:25-27 (quoting Isa 6:9-10)

GOD	EVANGELIST	CONTACT	RESULT
25 And when they did not agree with one another, they *began* leaving after Paul had spoken one *parting* word, "The Holy Spirit rightly spoke through Isaiah the prophet to your fathers,			
26 saying,	'Go to this people and say,	"You will keep on hearing, And you will keep on seeing,	but will not understand; but will not perceive;
		27 For the heart of this people has become dull, And with their ears they scarcely hear, And they have closed their eyes;	Lest they should see with their eyes, And hear with their ears, And understand with their heart and return, And I should heal them.'"

Rom 15:18-21

CHRIST	OT PROPHECY	EVANGELIST	GENTILES
[except what Christ has accomplished through me]		18 For I will not presume to speak of anything [], {}	{resulting in the obedience of the Gentiles by word and deed,}
19 in the power of signs and wonders, in the power of the Spirit;		so that from Jerusalem and round about as far as Illyricum I have fully *preached* the gospel of Christ.	
		20 And thus I aspired to evangelize, [] that I might not build upon another man's foundation;	[not where Christ was *already* named,]
	21 but as it is written, "They who had no news of Him shall see, And they who have not heard shall understand."		[regarding Gentiles]

1 Cor 15:10, Paul speaking of God's grace and his own labor

GOD	EVANGELIST
But by the grace of God I am what I am, and His grace toward me did not prove vain; [] yet not I, but the grace of God with me	[but I labored even more than all of them,]

Eph 2:8-10

GOD'S PART	MAN'S PART
8 For by grace you have been saved	through faith, and that not of yourselves;
it is the gift of God,	
	9 not of works, lest anyone should boast.
10 For we are His workmanship, created in Christ Jesus	
	for good works,
which God prepared beforehand	
	that we should walk in them.

Phil 2:12-13, God's work and man's work

GOD	CHRISTIAN
	So then, my beloved, just as you have always obeyed, not as in my presence only, but now much more in my absence, work out your salvation with fear and trembling;
13 for it is God who is at work in you, both to will and to work for *His* good pleasure	

Col 1:28-29

GOD	EVANGELIST
[Him] {Christ}	We proclaim [], admonishing every man and teaching every man with all wisdom, so that we may present every man complete in {}.
[according to His power, which mightily works]	For this purpose also I labor, striving [] within me

2 Thess 2:9-14

GOD TOWARD SAVED	GOD TOWARD LOST	SATAN TOWARD LOST	EVANGELIST	SAVED MAN	LOST MAN
		9 The coming of the *lawless one* is according to the working of Satan, with all power, signs, and lying wonders, 10 and with all unrighteous deception among those who perish,			because they did not receive the love of the truth, that they might be saved
	11 And for this reason God will send them strong delusion, that they should believe the lie, 12 that they all may be condemned				who did not believe the truth but had pleasure in unrighteousness.
because God from the beginning chose you for salvation through sanctification by the Spirit			13 But we are bound to give thanks to God always for you,	brethren beloved by the Lord, … and belief in the truth,	
14 to which He called you			by our gospel,	for the obtaining of the glory of our Lord Jesus Christ.	

In conclusion, there seems to be a "hypostatic union" when it comes to the ministry of evangelism!

Ours is to tell the Gospel message

God's is to do the supernatural work of opening the heart

God has a part and man has a part (cf. a type of hypostatic union, i.e. 100%-100%).

Evangelism, conversion, and spiritual growth are *not* a matter of sovereignty *versus* freewill. They are a matter of obedience to God's commands. To frame the question as sovereignty *versus* freewill is to depart from how the Bible frames the question. It is rather fully sovereignty *and* even seemingly fully freewill!

It may be that the best example to explain this cooperative working is the church as the bride of Christ, Eph 5:32:

Eph 5:32, "This mystery is great; but I am speaking with reference to Christ and the church."

1. If Christ is a typology of God's part in salvation, and if the church is a typology for man's part in salvation;
2. Then the complexity of the inner workings of God and man are best understood in this life in the complexity of the leadership of the husband over his wife:
   a. As man is the head of the wife, so Christ is the head of the church;
   b. As the wife ought to respect (Eph 5:33) and even obey her husband (1 Pet 3:6), so Christ loves the church, and gave Himself for it
3. So it is all about God in Christ—gloriam Christi soleus, and it is also all about man:
   a. Is not this issue (so called Calvinism vs. Arminianism) one of the greatest mysteries in the Christian life?
   b. And is not the husband-wife relationship an awesome metaphor for God to use in His Word to describe this interrelationship?
   c. Yes, indeed, "the mystery is great!"[954]

BIG IDEA #1: GOD IS INTIMATELY INVOLVED IN EVERY ASPECT OF EVANGELISM!

B. God's Desire Is the Salvation of Every Person:

1. God's perfect will, 1 Tim 2:4, 2 Pet 3:8-9 (cf. Ezek 18:23, 32, 33:11; Matt 18:14):
   1 Tim 4:10, "For it is for this we labor and strive, because we have fixed our eyes on the living God, who is the Savior of all men [cf. 1 John 2:1-2], especially the believers."

2. God's permissive will, 1 Cor 7:16 (cf. 1 Cor 9:22, "all" -> "some"):
   a. Man is to individually respond to God, Isa 55:6-7, Ezek 18:31, Rom 10:13
   b. Those who are saved:
      1) Few will find salvation, Matt 7:13-14; 22:14, Luke 13:23-30
      2) Jesus Christ is the first among **many** brethren, Rom 8:29, Heb 2:10
      3) God will save people from all nations, Psa 86:9, Rev 5:9
   c. Those who are lost:
      1) Many are those who are lost, Matt 7:13, Rev 20:8
      2) God takes no pleasure in the death of the wicked, Ezek 18:23, 32, 33:11
      3) All men will be forced to bow the knee to Christ, Phil 2:10-11 (see parallel with Joseph, Gen 37:5-11)

C. God Made Provision for Salvation:

1. Because of His Great Love, John 3:16; Rom 5:8; Eph 2:4 (cf. Eph 3:18-19)
2. God took the initiative to save man in sending Jesus Christ to die on the cross for sin, John 3:15-16; Rom 5:8; 1 Pet 3:18; 1 John 2:1-2
3. Therefore, God is often called the Savior, Psa 68:19; Isa 43:3, 14; Hos 13:4; Luke 1:47; 1 Tim 1:1; 4:10; Titus 1:3; Jude 24
4. God also has declared His salvation, Isa 43:12; 51:4.

D. The Trinity's Involvement in Particular Evangelism Situations:

1. Jesus commanded all of His disciples to evangelize, Mark 16:15 (e.g. Mark 1:16-18; cf. Matt 28:19-20; Luke 24:46-49; John 20:21; Acts 1:8)

2. God has given His Word as the message for the evangelist, 2 Tim 4:2 (cf. 1 John 2:21)

3. God stirs in His servants the urge to evangelize, Acts 17:16, 1 Cor 9:16

4. God trains His people, Psa 144:1

---

[954]And, by the way, the mystery here is not the infusion of the Holy Spirit within the sacraments in a Christological sense, as the Orthodox and Catholic Churches would have us think.

5. God leads His people:
   a. God opens doors for the preaching of the Gospel, Acts 14:27, 2 Cor 2:12 (cf. 1 Cor 16:9, Col 4:3, e.g. Acts 16:6-10).
   b. Sometimes doors for the Gospel are closed, 1 Thess 2:17-18.
   c. God can even lead through illness, Gal 4:13.

6. By God's Word the Holy Spirit gives specific leading to the evangelist in his conscience, e.g. Acts 8:29 (cf. Job 33:14-18; Prov 6:22; Acts 16:9, 18:9-10; Rom 2:15)

7. God opens the mouth of the evangelist (cf. Acts 4:29; Eph 6:19-20):
   Psa 51:15, "O Lord, open my lips, That my mouth may declare Your praise"
   Ezek 3:27, "But when I speak to you, I will open your mouth and you will say to them, 'Thus says the Lord GOD.' He who hears, let him hear; and he who refuses, let him refuse; for they are a rebellious house"

8. It is therefore God…
   a. Who is declaring the Gospel through the evangelist, Acts 17:30
   b. As well as His Holy Spirit, 1 Pet 1:12; Luke 12:12
   c. Yes, even "the Spirit of Your Father who speaks in you," Matt 10:20

   Consider also Heb 12:25 in this regard:

   > Heb 12:25, "See that you do not refuse Him who speaks. For if they did not escape who refused Him who spoke on earth, much more *shall we not escape* if we turn away from Him who *speaks* from heaven"

   If it is truly the Holy Spirit, or God Himself, speaking through His servant, the evangelist, and that particularly in times of persecution, then is it not God warning from heaven through His servants? In which case, it is clear why Jesus said:

   > Luke 10:16, "He who hears you hears Me, he who rejects you rejects Me, and he who rejects Me rejects Him who sent Me"; Matt 10:40; John 15:20

9. The evangelist should pray for God to grant boldness in evangelism:
   Acts 4:29, "And now, Lord, take note of their threats, and grant that Thy bond-servants may speak Thy word with all confidence…"

10. It is therefore God who…
    a. Through His Holy Spirit fills the evangelist to give him boldness in evangelism, Acts 4:31
    b. And likewise the hand of the Lord that accompanies the evangelist, Acts 11:21

11. Meanwhile, the Holy Spirit…
    a. Gives specific words to the evangelist, Matt 10:19-20, Mark 13:11, Luke 12:11-12, 21:14-15 (cf. Eph 6:19).
    b. Works in, with, and by His Word, Eph 6:17
    c. Speaks to man's spirit through His Word, Rom 8:16
    d. Preaches the Gospel, 1 Pet 1:12
    e. Prepares the heart of those who will be saved, John 3:8 (e.g. Acts 16:25-30)

12. God simultaneously prepares the heart of the person to hear the Gospel, Acts 8:30-31:
    a. For openness, Acts 8:30-31 (e.g. Acts 10:1-8)
    b. And even for hardness of heart, Isa 6:9-10, Ezek 2-3

13. The Holy Spirit often allows the spiritual condition of the heart to be evident, Acts 13:9-11, 14:9 (cf. Matt 6:22-23)[955]

14. God gives strength to meet the challenges of difficult people, Ezek 3:7-9

---

[955]"Fixing their/his gaze" (ἀτενίζω, Acts 6:15, 13:9) seems to imply some type of spiritual assessment. Jesus was noted to have the ability for this assessment throughout his ministry (e.g. Matt 9:4, 12:25). One clear example of this is the presence of the Holy Spirit was present in the face of Stephen as recorded in Acts 6:15 (F.F. Bruce). Whether it was a miracle of transformation evident to all or a miracle of vision for a particular person or group of people is uncertain, although the former is more likely. However, the fact is that the spiritual life of Stephen was made evident to onlookers, as it seems to be the case in the Peter's assessment of the lame man in Acts 3:4, or Paul's assessment of Elymas the magician in Acts 13:9 and of the lame man in Acts 14:9.

Comparing Translations of Ezek 3:8[956]

LXX	Wycliffe 2nd ed (1388)	King James Version (1611/1769)	New American Standard (1977)	New International Version (1984)	New Jerusalem Bible⁑ (1985)	French Le Semeur (1992, 1999; my trans)	God's Word for the Nations (1995)
καὶ ἰδοὺ δέδωκα τὸ πρόσωπόν σου δυνατὸν κατέναντι τῶν προσώπων αὐτῶν καὶ τὸ νεῖκός σου κατισχύσω κατέναντι τοῦ νείκους αὐτῶν	Lo! Y yaf thi face strongere than the faces of hem, and thi forheed hardere than the forheedis of hem	Behold, I have made thy face strong against their faces, and thy forehead strong against their foreheads	Behold, I have made your face as hard as their faces, and your forehead as hard as their foreheads	But now, I am making you as defiant as they are, and as obstinate as they are	But now, I am making you as defiant as they are, and as obstinate as they are	Oh well, I will give you a face as obstinant as theirs and a forehead as resolute as theirs	Yet, I will make you as stubborn and as hardheaded as they are

Notice that the more literal translations seem to have greater power.

Also note that the more dynamic translation of the New Jerusalem Bible is identical to that of the New International Version in this verse.

14. God gave Stephen the supernatural wisdom to deal with difficult people, Acts 6:10 (Luke 12:11-12)

15. God opens the heart of the person who He has made ready to listen and respond to the Gospel message, Acts 16:14 (see more on God bringing salvation below):
    a. Is this not when the grace of God "shines forth" [ἐπιφαίνω] for the individual (cf. Tit 2:11; 3:4)?
    b. Was this not the experience of the Apostle Paul (cf. Acts 9:3)?

16. The Holy Spirit shines in the heart (and sometimes on the face) of the evangelist, Acts 6:15, 2 Cor 3:18, 4:3-6 (cf. Exod 34:30-35)

17. God assures that His Word accomplishes His will, Isa 55:10-11

18. God performs the purpose of His messengers, Isa 44:26

E. God through the Holy Spirit Convicts Man:[957]
1. He convicts man as and when He wills it, John 3:8
2. He convicts man of sin, righteousness and judgment, John 16:8-11; e.g. Acts 24:25
3. Therefore, it is actually the Holy Spirit proclaiming through us, 1 Pet 1:12
4. God even allows difficulties to come into the lives of unbelievers in order to prepare them to seek Him for salvation, Job 33:17-28, 36:15

F. God Brings Salvation to the Open Heart:

Introduction: Note the main actor in salvation in Jer 31:31-34

1. God prepares the heart for the Gospel (*gracis preparatur*), Isa 25:9, 42:4, 45:24, 51:5, 60:9
    Luke 2:38 (NKJ), "And coming in that instant she gave thanks to the Lord, and spoke of Him to all those who looked for redemption in Jerusalem"
        Note on this verse (see charts below): The Latin Vulgate and most contemporary translations follow the Critical Edition Greek Text which drops the preposition "in," changing its translation to "of." This

---

[956]Likewise, consider the accusations against the Huguenot martyrs as being "opinionated," "stubborn," "obstinant," and "impertinent," before the Catholic clergy turned them over to be burned alive, because they would not recant: Of Thomas de Sainct-Paul, that he had "pertinacite et opiniastrete" (Jean Crespin, *Histoire des vrais tesmoins de la verite de l'evangile, qui de leur sang l'ont signée, depuis Jean Hus iusques autemps present* [Geneva, 1570; Liège, 1964], 185); of Jean Bertrand, that he was a "pernicieux Lutherien" (ibid., 433) and "opiniastrete" (ibid., 434); of Pierre Chevet, "heretique et schismatique" (ibid., 517); of Philbert Hamelin, "pertinax et obstine" (bid., 540v).

[957]Philipp Jacob Spener (1635-1705), sometimes called the Father of Pietism, summarizes the work of the Holy Spirit with regard to God's Word in his work *Theologische Bedencken*. Spener wrote, "The Holy Spirit works with, by, and in the Word (Der Heil. Geist ist allezeit mit/beh und in dem wort) of God to bring men to illumination, conversion, and the new birth." Philipp Jakob Spener, *Theologische Bedencken* (Halle, Germany: Erster Theil. Mit Chur-Furstl., 1700), 159; translation and citation by Arthur P. Johnston, *World Evangelism and the Word of God* (Minneapolis: Bethany Fellowship, 1974), 30.

change softens the stark evangelistic ministry of Anna unto prepared people "in Jerusalem" to communication to a theological worldview class of people who awaited the "redemption of Jerusalem." It is interesting to note that the Clementine Vulgate of 1598 has for this portion "redemption of Israel," showing that this has been an argued passage for quite some time—as has been the case for most evangelistically-oriented passages!

Original Language and Early Translations of the last phrase in Luke 2:38

Greek Orthodox NT	Stephanus (1550)	Scrivener's *Textus Receptus* [from Beza, 1598]	Vulgatam Clementinam (1598; Migne ed, 1880)	Tischendorf (1869-1872)	Wescott-Hort (1881)	Biblia Sacra Iuxta Vulgatam (1969, 1975, 1983)	Nova Vulgata (1979)	Nestle-Aland, 27th ed. (1993)	Byzantine (2005)
καὶ ἐλάλει περὶ αὐτοῦ πᾶσιν τοῖς προσδεχο-μένοις λύτρωσιν ἐν Ἰερουσαλήμ	καὶ ἐλάλει περὶ αὐτοῦ πᾶσιν τοῖς προσδεχο-μένοις λύτρωσιν ἐν Ἰερουσαλήμ	καὶ ἐλάλει περὶ αὐτοῦ πᾶσι τοῖς προσδεχο-μένοις λύτρωσιν ἐν Ἰερουσαλήμ	et loquebatur de illo omnibus, qui exspectabant redemp-tionem Israël.	καὶ ἐλάλει περὶ αὐτοῦ πᾶσιν τοῖς προσδεχο-μένοις λύτρωσιν Ἰερουσαλήμ.	καὶ ἐλάλει περὶ αὐτοῦ πᾶσιν τοῖς προσδεχο-μένοις λύτρωσιν Ἰερουσαλήμ	et loquebatur de illo omnibus qui expectabant redemp-tionem Hierusalem	et loquebatur de illo omnibus, qui exspectabant redemp-tionem Ierusalem.	καὶ ἐλάλει περὶ αὐτοῦ πᾶσιν τοῖς προσδεχο-μένοις λύτρωσιν Ἰερουσαλήμ.	καὶ ἐλάλει περὶ αὐτοῦ πᾶσιν τοῖς προσδεχο-μένοις λύτρωσιν ἐν Ἰερουσαλήμ

Bruce M. Metzger, *A Textual Commentary on the New Testament Greek* (UBS, 1993), offered the following comment as to why it was determined that an unknown scribe inserted "ἐν" before the word "Jerusalem": "the insertion of ἐν relieves the grammatical ambiguity."[958]

Comparative English Translations of the Last Phrase in Luke 2:38

English Geneva (1560)	KJV (1611/1769)	English Revised (1885)	Douais-Rheims* (1899)	RSV (1952)	NAS (1977)	NKJ (1982)	ESV (2004)
& spake of him to all that loked for redemption in Ierusalem	and spake of him to all them that looked for redemption in Jerusalem	and spake of him to all them that were looking for the redemption of Jerusalem	and spoke of him to all that looked for the redemption of Israel	and spoke of him to all who were looking for the redemption of Jerusalem	and continued to speak of Him to all those who were looking for the redemption of Jerusalem	and spoke of Him to all those who looked for redemption in Jerusalem	and to speak of him to all who were waiting for the redemption of Jerusalem

Others who "looked for" or "awaited" redemption [a word study of προσδεχόμενος]:

> Luke 2:25 NKJ), "And behold, there was a man in Jerusalem whose name *was* Simeon, and this man *was* just and devout, waiting for the Consolation of Israel, and the Holy Spirit was upon him"
>
> Luke 23:51 (NKJ), "He had not consented to their decision and deed. He *was* from Arimathea, a city of the Jews, who himself was also waiting for the kingdom of God."
>
> Acts 24:15 (NKJ), "I have hope in God, which they themselves also accept [or "expect"; προσδέχομαι], that there will be a resurrection of *the* dead, both of *the* just and *the* unjust"

2   God opens the heart of the person so that he may come to Him, Acts 16:14 (cf. I Sam 10:9, John 6:65):

    a.   God reveals the identity of Jesus, Matt 16:16-17

    b.   God removes the veil over the heart in Jesus Christ, Isa 25:7; 2 Cor 3:16; cf. 2 Cor 4:3-4

    c.   Therefore salvation is all God's doing, 1 Cor 1:30 (notice the importance and varieties of the translations of the prepositions ἐξ αὐτοῦ and ἀπὸ θεου)

---

[958]BibleWorks 8.0.

Translations of 1 Cor 1:30

Byzantine Textform	French Geneva (1669)	French Geneva (my trans)	English Geneva (1560)	English Standard Version	Revised Standard Version	King James Version	New American Standard	Le Semeur (1999)*	ABS's CEV[⊕] (2005)**
Ἐξ αὐτοῦ δὲ ὑμεῖς ἐστε ἐν χριστῷ Ἰησοῦ, ὃς ἐγενήθη ἡμῖν σοφία ἀπὸ θεοῦ, δικαιοσύνη τε καὶ ἁγιασμός, καὶ ἀπολύτρωσις·	Or c'est de lui que vous estes en Jesus Christ, qui vous a esté fait de par Dieu sapience, et justice, et sanctification, et redemption	Thus it is from him that you are in Jesus Christ, you who were made by God wisdom, righteous-ness, sanctifica-tion, and redemption	But ye are of him in Christ Iesus, who of God is made vnto vs wisedome and righteous-nesse, and sanctifica-tion, and redempcion	He is the source of your life in Christ Jesus, whom God made our wisdom and our righteous-ness and sanctifica-tion and redemption	He is the source of your life in Christ Jesus, whom God made our wisdom, our righteous-ness and sanctifica-tion and redemption	But of him are ye in Christ Jesus, who of God is made unto us wisdom, and righteous-ness, and sanctifica-tion, and redemption	But by His doing you are in Christ Jesus, who became to us wisdom from God, and righteous-ness and sanctifica-tion, and redemption	By him, you are united to the Christ, who has become for us this wisdom that comes from God: in Christ, in fact, is found for us, acquital, purification, and liberation from sin	You are God's children. He sent Christ Jesus to save us and to make us wise, acceptable, and holy.

*Note the subtle changes added to the text to allow for priests giving absolution, while removing the fully divine element of salvation. French text (translation mine): "Par lui, vous êtes unis au Christ, qui est devenu pour nous cette sagesse qui vient de Dieu: en Christ, en effet, se trouvent pour nous l'acquitte-ment, la purification et la libération du péché."
**Note the removal of both "by/of Him" and "from God" from the text, as well a the "in Christ Jesus"!

d.   Therefore all our boasting should be in the Lord, 1 Cor 1:31

3.   God grants repentance, 2 Tim 2:25

4.   He brings belief to the heart, John 6:29

5.   The person who receives the salvation available through Christ becomes born-again, born of the Spirit, and born from above, John 3:3-8, Eph 4:24, 1 Pet 1:3, 22-23 (cf. Psa 104:30)

6.   God's Spirit confirms to the spirit of the believer that he is a child of God, Rom 8:16.

7.   In Jesus Christ, God the Holy Spirit immediately seals the new believer, 2 Cor 1:22, Eph 1:13, 4:30 (cf. Acts 2:38-39; Gal 4:6)

G. God Bestows the Blessings of Salvation:

Introduction: A warning from the Lord, Jer 18:7-11 (cf. Jer 1:9-10)

1.   Salvation and Eternal Life:
   a.   Pardon for sin, Psa 32:1-2, Isa 55:6-7, John 1:29, 17:2, 1 John 1:9
   b.   Deliverance from Hell, John 5:24
   c.   Reconciliation with God, 2 Cor 5:18-19
   d.   Eternal life, John 1:12, 3:16, 6:40, 47, 14:6, Rom 6:23, Titus 3:7, 1 John 5:13
   e.   A crown of righteousness in glory, 2 Tim 4:8
   f.   Heaven awaits those who are being saved, Matt 25:46; John 14:1-3; Rev 21-22

2.   Transformation:
   a.   "In Him you have been made complete," Col 2:10.
   b.   God transforms the Christian "from glory to glory," 2 Cor 3:18
   c.   God (through Christ) grants a spiritual gift(s) to his children, 1 Cor 12:7, Eph 4:7
   d.   The Holy Spirit instructs in God's ways, Neh 9:30, John 14:26, 16:13
   e.   God sustains the Christian, Psa 18:35, 55:22, 63:8, 119:116, Isa 50:4, Heb 1:3
   f.   God makes the fruit of the Spirit are available to the Christian (love, joy, peace, patience, kindness, goodness, faithfulness, gentleness, self-control) Gal 5:22-23
   g.   God fills with all goodness, knowledge, and ability to admonish, Rom 15:14
   h.   Reason for living, Matt 6:33, 22:37, Rom 12:1-2, Eph 1:5, 2:10, Heb 12:28

       i. God gives the Christian hope through His word, Psa 119:49

3. Entrance into His family:
  a. Adoption as His child, John 1:12, Gal 3:2, 4:7, Eph 1:5
  b. Inheritance with Christ, Rom 8:17, Eph 3:6

4. Blessing and Grace:
  a. An advocate before the Father, 1 John 2:1
  b. Every spiritual blessing in Christ Jesus, Rom 8:32, Eph 1:3, Phil 4:19, 2 Pet 1:3 (cf. Psa 34:9-10)
  c. "For of His fulness we have all received, and grace upon grace," John 1:16

5. Free access to His throne, Eph 2:18, Heb 4:16

BIG IDEA #2: MAN'S PLACE IS EVANGELISM IS ABSOLUTELY NECESSARY, BUT REALLY MINIMAL

A. Some verses put man in his place:

1. Luke 17:10, note the various translations of this verse…

Some Translations of ἀχρεῖος in Luke 17:10

Nestle-Aland	English Geneva [and KJV]	New American Standard	Revised Standard [and NIV]	French Francais Courant	French *Le Semeur*	ABS's CEV[E]
δοῦλοι ἀχρεῖοί ἐσμεν	We are vnprofitable seruants	We are unworthy slaves	We are unworthy servants	We are simple servants	We are only servants without particular merit	We are merely servants
οὕτως καὶ ὑμεῖς, ὅταν ποιήσητε πάντα τὰ διαταχθέντα ὑμῖν, λέγετε ὅτι δοῦλοι ἀχρεῖοί ἐσμεν, ὃ ὠφείλομεν ποιῆσαι πεποιήκαμεν	So likewise yee, when yee haue done all those things, which are commanded you, say, We are vnprofitable seruants: wee haue done that which was our duetie to doe	"So you too, when you do all the things which are commanded you, say, 'We are unworthy slaves; we have done *only* that which we ought to have done.'"	So you also, when you have done all that is commanded you, say, 'We are unworthy servants; we have only done what was our duty	«Il en va de même pour vous: quand vous aurez fait tout ce qui vous est ordonné, dites: ‹Nous sommes de simples serviteurs; nous n'avons fait que notre devoir.› »	Il en est de même pour vous. Quand vous aurez fait tout ce qui vous est commandé, dites: «Nous ne sommes que des serviteurs sans mérite particulier; nous n'avons fait que notre devoir.»	And that's how it should be with you. When you've done all you should, then say, "We are merely servants, and we have simply done our duty."

Note these NT parallels:
  Matt 25:30, "And cast out the worthless slave [τὸν ἀχρεῖον δοῦλον] into the outer darkness; in that place there shall be weeping and gnashing of teeth
  Philemon 1:10-11, "I appeal to you for my child Onesimus, whom I have begotten in my imprisonment, who formerly was useless [ἄχρηστος] to you, but now is useful both to you and to me."
  ἄχρηστος in the same Louw-Nida word group as ἀχρεῖος (65.30-65.39)

2.   1 Cor 3:7, note some diverse translations of this powerful text:

Some Translations of 1 Corinthians 3:7

Neste-Aland 27th ed.	Latin Vulgate	French Jacques Lefevre (1530)	French Geneva	King James Version (1611/1769)	New American Standard	French Segond (1910)	New Living Translation	New Jerusalem Bible*	French Le Semeur	Cont English Version*
ἐστίν τι οὔτε	neque ... est aliquid neque	not ... is anything	not ... is anything	neither is ... any thing	neither ...is anything	ce n'est pas ... qui est quelque chose	aren't important	neither ... count for anything	Little matters who ... What counts is	What matters isn't those who ..., but
ὥστε οὔτε ὁ φυτεύων ἐστίν τι οὔτε ὁ ποτίζων ἀλλ' ὁ αὐξάνων θεός.	itaque neque qui plantat est aliquid neque qui rigat sed qui incrementum dat Deus	Parquoy ne celui qui plante n'est rien / ne celuy quy arouse: mais Dieu qui donne accroissement	C'est pourquoy, ni celui qui plante n'est rien, ni celui qui arrose: mais Dieu qui donne l'accroissement	So then neither is he that planteth any thing, neither he that watereth; but God that giveth the increase	So then neither the one who plants nor the one who waters is anything, but God who causes the growth	en sorte que ce n'est pas celui qui plante qui est quelque chose, ni celui qui arrose, mais Dieu qui fait croître.	The ones who do the planting or watering aren't important, but God is important because he is the one who makes the seed grow	In this, neither the planter nor the waterer counts for anything; only God, who gives growth	Peu importe, en fait, qui plante et qui arrose. Ce qui compte, c'est Dieu qui fait croître.	What matters isn't those who planted or watered, but God who made the plants grow.

B. Yet God Chooses to Use Man to "Save" Others:

1.   "That I might save some":
     1 Cor 9:22, "To the weak I became weak, that I might win the weak; I have become all things to all men, so that by all means [or: effort] **I may save** some"

2.   "Save others":
     Jude 22-23, "And have mercy on some, who are doubting; **save** others, snatching them out of the fire; and on some have mercy with fear, hating even the garment polluted by the flesh."

3.   "Whether you will save your husband? … whether you will save your wife?"
     1 Cor 7:16, "For how do you know, O wife, whether **you will save** your husband? Or how do you know, O husband, whether **you will save** your wife?"

4.   "Deliver"
     Prov 24:11-12, "**Deliver** those who are being taken away to death, And those who are staggering to slaughter, O hold *them* back. If you say, 'See, we did not know this,' Does He not consider *it* who weighs the hearts? And does He not know *it* who keeps your soul? And will He not render to man according to his work?"

C. Similarly God Chooses to Use Man that Others Might "Believe":

1.   "Servants through whom you believed":
     1 Cor 3:5, "What then is Apollos? And what is Paul? Servants **through whom you believed**, even as the Lord gave *opportunity* to each one."

2.   "Because of what you said that we believe":
     John 4:42, "And they were saying to the woman, 'It is no longer because of what you said that **we believe**, for we have heard for ourselves and know that this One is indeed the Savior of the world.'"

3.   For example, the jailer "believed" and was "saved"!
     Acts 16:28-34, "But Paul cried out with a loud voice, saying, "Do not harm yourself, for we are all here!' And he called for lights and rushed in, and trembling with fear he fell down before Paul and Silas, and after he brought them out, he said, 'Sirs, what must I do **to be saved**?' They said, '**Believe** in the Lord Jesus, and you will be saved, you and your household.' And they spoke the word of the Lord to him together with all who were in his house. And he took them that *very* hour of the night and washed their wounds, and

immediately he was baptized, he and all his *household*. And he brought them into his house and set food before them, and rejoiced greatly, **having believed** in God with his whole household."

4. Peter's invitation in Acts 2 included for listeners to "save themselves" from a crooked generation:
    Acts 2:40. "And with many other words he solemnly testified and kept on exhorting them, saying, '**Be saved** [imperative aorist passive 2nd person pl] from this perverse generation!'"

5. In fact, God used Paul to literally "save some" (as it were from this discussion):
    1 Cor 9:22b, "I have become all things to all men, that **I may** by all means **save some**"

FURTHER THOUGHT ON THE HOLY SPIRIT IN EVANGELISM:

1. The Holy Spirit provides the aid to bring souls to Christ and grow His Church:
    Acts 9:31 (Darby), "The assemblies then throughout the whole of Judaea and Galilee and Samaria had peace, being edified and walking in the fear of the Lord, and were increased through the comfort [or: help] of the Holy Spirit [καὶ τῇ παρακλήσει τοῦ ἁγίου πνεύματος ἐπληθύνοντο]."

Prayer in Evangelism

Introduction:

a. The quandary of prayer: when is prayer truly effective in the throne room of God?

When the idea of a prayer need comes to our minds?
> Who gives us the idea to pray? God or man or the Bible?

When the idea of the prayer is formulated into words in our minds?
> When our mind speaks those words as a prayer to God, as in silent prayer?

When our minds send the impulses to our vocal chords, these latter beginning to shape the sounds as they are sent by the brain?
> When the air begins to rush through our vocal chords, developing the words in prayer, as our mind sent it, those being in our own individual language, dialect, and idiomatic forms?
> When the sound of our prayer is available to be heard externally by another person who may be praying with us or who is within earshot?

How, then, does the laying on of hands seem to accentuate the power of a prayer?

It can be seen from these questions, to which many others may be added, that prayer is a mystery
> And yet it is requested of us by God
> And it is part of His plan for our salvation and spiritual growth!

b. Paul on prayer for evangelism:
> Eph 6:18-20 (NKJ), "praying always with all prayer and supplication in the Spirit, being watchful to this end with all perseverance and supplication for all the saints—and for me, that utterance may be given to me, that I may open my mouth boldly to make known the mystery of the gospel, for which I am an ambassador in chains; that in it I may speak boldly, as I ought to speak."
> Col 4:2-4, "Continue earnestly in prayer, being vigilant in it with thanksgiving; meanwhile praying also for us, that God would open to us a door for the word, to speak the mystery of Christ, for which I am also in chains, that I may make it manifest, as I ought to speak."
> 2 Thess 3:1-2, "Finally, brethren, pray for us, that the word of the Lord may run *swiftly* and be glorified, just as *it is* with you, and that we may be delivered from unreasonable and wicked men; for not all have faith."
> Rom 10:1, "Brethren, my heart's desire and prayer to God for Israel is that they may be saved."

c. The help of the Holy Spirit in prayer, Rom 8:26-27

d. A knowledge of the spiritual battle being waged, 2 Cor 10:3-5.

e. Food for Thought:

1) We live in a renewed time of emphasis on prayer, when some even speak of "prayer evangelism"—as if praying for someone is equivalent to or more spiritually effective than sharing the gospel with them.[959] A position hard to justify theologically or practically in the accounts of the Book of Acts

2) While praying "on site with insight" seems to be a good lead into evangelism…

3) We must be reminded of Samuel Zwemer's emphatic words that "prayer is not evangelism" (*No Salvation without Substitution* [1944]), as this must have been a problem in his day (as can be exemplified by Chafer's antecedent book [1911])

4) Gregory Frizzell's book, *Iceberg Dead Ahead*, explained and exemplified the tension involved:

> When it comes to prayer, repentance, and evangelism, it should never be *either/or*—it must always be *both/and*! There should never be any tension between "evangelism" and "prayer" people. In Scripture and

---

[959]"Fundamentally, then, the personal element in true soul-winning work is more a service of pleading *for* souls than a service of pleading *with* souls. It is talking with God about men from a clean heart and in the power of the Spirit, rather than talking to men about God. But let no one conclude that such intercessory prayer is not a service demanding time and vitality. If faithfully entered into this ministry, as has been pointed out, will result in an opportunity to direct Spirit-moved men to the faithful provisions and promises of God" (Lewis Sperry Chafer, *True Evangelism or Winning Souls by Prayer* [1st ed. Philadelphia: Sunday School Times, 1911; 2nd ed., Philadelphia: Sunday School Times, 1919; Wheaton, IL: Van Kampen; Grand Rapids: Zondervan, 1967; Grand Rapids: Kregel, 1993], 69).

in revival history, true evangelism and prayer are inseparately united. Make no mistake, to pray without doing evangelism is false piety. Yet to evangelize without fervent prayer and repentance ignores an absolutely essential principle of spiritual power. It may also reflect a subtle (but dangerous) attitude of self-reliance.[960]

5) While prayer is important and essential, the Great Commission never stated, "Go into all the world and pray for all people." In fact, the ministry of Paul in the book of Acts has very little on prayer, especially when discussing Paul's custom of evangelism (Acts 17:2-3).

Frizzell exemplifies one thing, prayer, among quite a number, that can keep soul winners from focusing on proclamation of the Gospel to win souls:

a) Have they prayed enough? (Chafer)
b) Have they built enough of a relationship to show the love of God? (Pippert, Aldrich)
c) Have they met any of the person's so-called needs? (Bosch, Sjogren)
d) Are they doing it for their glory or the glory of God?
e) Have they built a worldview bridge? (Mittleberg)
f) Have they taken enough time? (Mittleberg)

Any and all of these elements can co-opt biblical evangelism and leave the soul winner frozen with trying to accomplish a multitude of preparations for or additions to the Gospel, prior to attempting to share the Gospel. And as these notes will show, I believe in prayer, but I equally believe in the need for obedience in NT evangelism.

1. Effective Prayer Starts with the Righteousness that God Gives:

a. When God does not hear prayer:
Psa 66:18-19, "If I regard wickedness in my heart, The Lord will not hear; But certainly God has heard; He has given heed to the voice of my prayer"
Prov 28:9, "He who turns away his ear from listening to the law, Even his prayer is an abomination"
Isa 1:15, "So when you spread out your hands *in prayer*, I will hide My eyes from you; Yes, even though you multiply prayers, I will not listen. Your hands are covered with blood"

b. When God hears prayer:
Prov 15:8, "The sacrifice of the wicked is an abomination to the LORD, But the prayer of the upright is His delight"
Prov 15:29, "The LORD is far from the wicked, But He hears the prayer of the righteous"
James 5:16, "The effective prayer of a righteous man can accomplish much"

2. Teaching Concerning Prayer in Evangelism:

a. Prayer for evangelism in general:
1) Prayer can allow the political freedom to proclaim the Gospel, 1 Tim 2:1-4 (cf. Prov 21:1; Jer 29:7; Acts 9:31).
2) Prayer for doors to be opened for the Gospel, Col 4:3 (cf. 1 Cor 16:9)
3) Prayer that the Word of God may spread rapidly, 2 Thess 3:1 (cf. Psa 147:15)
4) Prayer as long as there are some who are unsaved, 1 Tim 2:4; 2 Thess 3:2

b. Prayer and workers:
1) Prayer is the impetus for workers in evangelism, Matt 9:36-38; Luke 10:2 (e.g. Acts 13:2)
2) Prayer is important for those involved in evangelism, Eph 6:19-20; 2 Thess 3:1-2
3) Your prayer life will make you become available, Matt 9:36-38; Luke 10:2

c. Prayer for and in specific evangelistic situations (cf. Prov 3:5-6, Isa 30:21):

1) Prayer as preceding bold evangelism, Acts 1:14ff, 4:23-31; 13:2

2) Prayer as the catalyst for boldness in evangelism:
Acts 4:31, "And when they had prayed, the place where they had gathered together was shaken, and they were all filled with the Holy Spirit, and *began* to speak the word of God with boldness."
Eph 6:18-20, "With all prayer and petition pray at all times in the Spirit, and with this in view, be on the alert with all perseverance and petition for all the saints, and *pray* on my behalf, that utterance may be

---

[960]Gregory Frizzell, *Iceberg Dead Ahead! An Urgent Call to "God-Seeking Repentance"* (Oklahoma City: Baptist General Convention of Oklahoma, 2007), 60.

given to me in the opening of my mouth, to make known with boldness the mystery of the gospel, for which I am an ambassador in chains; that in *proclaiming* it I may speak boldly, as I ought to speak."

Col 4:2-4, "Devote yourselves to prayer, keeping alert in it with *an attitude of* thanksgiving; praying at the same time for us as well, that God may open up to us a door for the word, so that we may speak forth the mystery of Christ, for which I have also been imprisoned; in order that I may make it clear in the way I ought to speak."

3) Prayer for the Word of God to be effective, Rom 1:16, Heb 4:12

d. Prayer can allow God to open a heart to salvation:
1) God desires the salvation of all men, 1 Tim 2:1-4, 2 Pet 3:9
2) The Holy Spirit must convict the heart of the individual to see his need for salvation, John 16:8-11.
3) God will answer the prayer in His will, John 14:13-14, 1 John 5:13-15 (not forgetting 1 Cor 7:16)

3. Persevering prayer for someone's salvation (cf. Luke 18:1-8):
a. God desires the salvation of all men, 1 Tim 2:4, 2 Pet 3:8-9
b. Jesus must reveal God to the person, Matt 11:27, Luke 10:22
c. The Spirit of God is needed to convict men of their need for Jesus, John 16:8 (cf. Zech 4:6; e.g. 1 Cor 2:1-5)
d. God will answer prayer in His will, John 4:13-14, 1 John 5:14-15
e. The individual needs to decide for themselves, 1 Cor 7:16
f. There is a time when God will no longer hear prayer for a person or group, Jer 7:16, 14:11

4. Biblical Examples of Prayer in Evangelism:
a. A prayer life while evangelizing, Luke 5:15-16
b. Prayer for the lost, Rom 9:1-5 (cf. Matt 9:35-37)

5. Practical Insights:

a. Pray daily for opportunities to share the Gospel.

b. Pray for the unsaved when the Lord places them on your heart.

c. Keep a list of names of people with whom you have shared the gospel or who God lays on your heart, and pray through this list daily, weekly, or periodically (depending upon how long it is)

d. Cover the sharing situation with prayer: before, during and after:
1) Pray as specifically as possible;
2) It is a spiritual battle and prayer is needed to have spiritual effectiveness;
3) Fervent prayer before, during, and after evangelism gives us an urgency that adorns the gospel presentation with its importance

e. If sharing is done two-by-two, one person can intercede while the other is talking.

f. Pray for the continued work of the Holy Spirit in the hearts of those with whom you have shared the Gospel.

Conclusion:

Here is the prayer of the soul winner:

Acts 4:29-30 (NKJ), "Now, Lord, look on their threats, and grant to Your servants that with all boldness they may speak Your word, by stretching out Your hand to heal, and that signs and wonders may be done through the name of Your holy Servant Jesus."

Will you pray that God will grant you to speak His word with all boldness today?

Fasting in Evangelism

Introduction: Although somewhat mysterious, much like prayer, and often indirectly cause and effect (hence not "name and claim"), fasting may in fact have a role in the spiritual battle being wages for the souls of men…

1. **Reasons for Fasting and Prayer:**
   a. To realign the priority of the spiritual, Matt 4:2-4
   b. To humble oneself before God and seek Him, 2 Kg 21:27-29, Ezra 8:21, Esther 4:16, Jonah 3:5-10
   c. Because the Bridegroom has been taken away, Matt 9:15 (pointing to the longing for His return, Rev 21:17)
   d. For spiritual power, Mark 9:29 (cf. Matt 17:21)
   e. For spiritual insight and understanding into some dimension of the Word of God, Dan 9:1-3
   f. For wisdom and direction:
       1) In decision making, Acts 14:23 (see also Acts 13:1-3)
       2) In one's actions, Neh 1:4
   g. In order to accomplish God's will: John 4:32-34, "And Jesus said to them, 'My will is to do the will of Him who sent Me, and to accomplish His work.'"

2. **Teaching about fasting:**
   a. There are biblical exhortations to fast, Esther 9:31, Joel 2:12
   b. Jesus taught that His followers **would** fast, Matt 9:14-15, Mark 2:18-19, Luke 5:33-35
   c. Fasting while not dealing with known wickedness is sinful, Isa 58:1-12
   d. Fasting weakens the body, Psa 109:24 (cf. 1 Sam 28:20)
   e. Interpersonal dimensions of fasting:
       1) One should not fast to be seen by men, Matt 6:16, i.e. proper motivation
       2) Effort should be made to keep a cheerful countenance while fasting, Matt 6:16 (cf. Neh 2:1)
       3) Care should be taken to avoid appearing unkempt while fasting, Matt 6:17-18 (e.g. not wearing ashes on one's forehead; cf. Neh 9:1, Dan 10:3)
   f. There is a place for abstinence in the marriage relationship for the purpose of prayer,[961] 1 Cor 7:5
   g. There are times when one should not fast, 1 Sam 14:24-30, Matt 9:15

3. **Practical considerations in fasting:**

   Introduction: Satan will try to sabotage a fast,[962] Matt 4:1-11, Luke 4:1-13

   a. Reasons for **beginning a fast**:
       1) Following an obvious act of God in life, Acts 9:8-9
       2) For a specific enquiry from the Lord:
           a) For protection, 2 Sam 12:16-17, Ezra 8:21, Esth 4:11
           b) For insight into God's Word, Dan 9:3
       3) When asking for the Lord's help, 2 Chron 20:3, Esth 4:3
       4) After a pronouncement of judgment from God, 1 Sam 28:20
       5) As a sign of repentance in confession, Neh 9:1-2
       6) When hearing of a great calamity, Neh 1:4
       7) When mourning the loss of a loved one, 1 Sam 31:13, 2 Sam 1:12
       8) As a practice of seeking the Lord, Dan 10:2-3, Acts 13:2

   b. Reasons for **ending a fast**:
       1) A concrete answer to prayer or enquiry, 2 Sam 12:19-20, Acts 9:19 (cf. Ezra 8:23), Dan 9:20-21, 10:2-4, 13.7
       2) When the event for which one has fasted has taken place, 2 Sam 12:19-23, Esth. 4:16, 5:1

---

[961]Dr. Robert E. Coleman included this consideration as one of seven spiritual disciplines for his Discipleship Evangelism class.

[962]From a sermon by Stephen Goold at Crystal Evangelical Free Church, New Hope, MN, delivered on January 19, 1992.

3) The ending of a specified period of time, Acts 12:3, 14:23 (cf. Dan 10:2-4, 13[963])

4) Ending a fast too soon (Saul), 1 Sam 28:23

  c. Practical considerations:

    1) How should young children eat when the mother and/or father are fasting?

    2) When hosting guests for a meal, how should one fast? Matt 9:15.

4. Types of fasting:

  a. The absolute fast:

    1) No bread or water, Ezra 10:6, Acts 9:9

    2) No food, just water (by deduction), Matt 4:1-4, Luke 4:1-4

  b. No tasty food, nor meat, nor wine, Dan 1:10, 10:3

  c. An abnormal diet, Matt 3:4

  d. Abstinence in marriage, 1 Cor 7:5

5. Some examples of fasting:

  a. In the Old Testament: 1 Sam 28:20, 31:13, 2 Sam 1:12, 2 Chron 20:3, Ezra 8:21, Neh 1:4, 9:1, Esther 4:3, 16, Dan 9:3, 10:3

  b. In the New Testament, Matt 3:4, 4:2, Acts 13:2-3, 14:23

6. Fasting and Prayer for Evangelism:

  a. To see the spiritual need of others, and the primacy of this need, Matt 4:2-4

  b. For deepened spiritual insight in the proclamation of God's Word, Dan 9:1-3

  c. For spiritual power to evangelize with boldness, Matt 17:21, Eph 6:19-20

  d. For humility and proper respect of the message in evangelism, 2 Kg 21:27-29, Ezra 8:21

  e. For wisdom in the use of time and funds to evangelize, Neh 1:4, Acts 14:23

---

[963]C. F. Keil & Franz Delitzsch, *Commentary on the Book of Daniel* (Grand Rapids: Eerdmans, 1986), 408: "So that the question as to the beginning and the end of the fast is not answered from the text, and, as being irrelevant to the matter, it can remain undecided."

Chapter 11 Appendixes

God the Evangelist:
An Analysis of Gen 4:6-7

Gen 4:6-7	Analysis
So the LORD said to Cain,	Speech: The Eternal One is speaking to Cain Notice also that the Eternal One comes at the proper time, between the temptation and the sin being committed Is this not quite similar to God's promised help in temptation? 1 Cor 10:13, "No temptation has overtaken you except such as is common to man; but God *is* faithful, who will not allow you to be tempted beyond what you are able, but with the temptation will also make the way of escape, that you may be able to bear *it*" Notice that this speech appears to be analogous to God speaking to the conscience of Cain, Rom 2:14-15 Although it is likely that this is an example of God addressing Cain directly According to the analysis of Keil and Delitzsch, God did not completely discontinue direct speech to men after the Garden of Eden Notice also the link between this kind of speech and Paul's evangelism, Rom 2:16 Likewise, evangelizing is a matter of direct speech: In fact, it is in actuality God speaking to others through us: Matt 10:20, "It is not you who speak, but the Spirit of your Father who speaks in you" Such that: Matt 10:40, "He who receives you receives Me, and he who receives Me receives Him who sent Me" Luke 10:16, "He who hears you hears Me, he who rejects you rejects Me, and he who rejects Me rejects Him who sent Me" John 13:20, "Most assuredly, I say to you, he who receives whomever I send receives Me; and he who receives Me receives Him who sent Me" We do not know God's perfect timing, but God does: Notice how He sent Philip to the Ethiopian Eunuch just at the time when he was questioning what Isa 53 meant (Acts 8) When we enter the ministry of evangelizing, we join God where He is, and He leads us supernaturally; and His timing is always perfect Could it be that we sometimes become God's "way out" of temptation for people as we approach them with the Gospel (1 Cor 10:13)? This is for sure the case as we seek to pull people away from their "pride of life" to humble themselves before the mighty hand of God! Could not the same be true of discipleship or true Christian fellowship? A word of godly counsel at the proper time to keep a brother or sister from sin?
"Why are you angry? And why has your countenance	God speaks directly to the problem, or the impending problem Notice: (1) The impact of temptation on the facial characteristics of Cain—the war being waged in the soul prior to his sin, and ultimately leading him into his sin (cf. Deut 15:9)

fallen?"	(2) God initiates the conversation; He does not wait for Cain to come to Him, but He seeks out Cain; is that not very gracious of God?

(2) God initiates the conversation; He does not wait for Cain to come to Him, but He seeks out
   Cain; is that not very gracious of God?
(3) God asks a question, thereby not judging Cain, but allowing Cain to evaluate the situation
   himself

God initiates the redemptive conversation with Cain, as we ought to be willing to initiate redemptive
conversations with people around us:
   We will see that ultimately, the conversation was to discuss the sin issue (from the chapter before,
      that is Gen 3)
   So here we have God's first conversation with man after sending Adam and Eve out of the
      Garden, and it is a redemptive conversation, whose warning is ultimately rejected by man
   By the way, the issue is sin—it is not facial expressions or even restoration of a relationship

Notice that God was speaking with "unsaved" Cain:
   Likewise, we have the impression that God truly does speak to unsaved people, even those that
      remain unsaved, e.g. Acts 24:24-26

Isn't that another gracious act?

   God is actually speaking to unsaved people all around us, and we do not realize it, unless we
      speak to them about spiritual things
      Although, we will find that some have a seared conscience, 1 Tim 4:3
      Others are blind, 2 Cor 4:3-4; etc.

   God speaks to all men through sickness, pain, and even dreams, Job 33

   He makes Himself clear in His speech to man (Rom 1), although that does not:
      Duplicate, replace, or conflict with our needing to fulfill the Great Commission
      Take the place of our needing to evangelize so that lost people can hear and be saved; thus
         excusing us from needing to evangelize

Notice that God used the same method as Satan, asking a question (Gen 3:1)

   Questions seem to be an effective rhetorical device to get individual man to consider his individual
      spiritual lot
      It is interesting that in both Gen 3 and Gen 4, Satan won out:
         In Gen 3, Eve falls for the temptation
         In Gen 4, Cain ignores the warning of God and continues on to kill his brother Abel

   In fact, numerous questions are found throughout the pages of the NT in relation to evangelism
      conversations, some of which are used to begin conversations:
      Jesus in John 5:6
      Philip in Acts 8:30

Notice that God first addressed the symptom on His way to addressing the core issue:
   Therefore, God uses a stair-step approach to the problem, coming at it indirectly, by dealing with
      the uncomfortable symptom
   Jesus uses a stair-step approach with His disciples when He asks them "Who do men say that I
      am?" and then "But who do you say that I am?" (Matt 16:13, 15)
   Jesus went from the general to the particular in speaking with Nicodemus, John 3:3, 7
   Similarly with asking for a drink of water, John 4:7, 11

Notice that this lesson could also be called, "God the Psychologist":
   God was psychoanalyzing Cain's symptoms:
      Angry heart
      Downcast face
   Notice how the sin that was taking root in Cain's heart was in the process of destroying his

	relationship with his brother, as well as his relationship with God, to whom he never responds—apparently ignoring God and His admonition! However, he is not leaving accountability to Himself, nor sin, nor Cain's individual responsibility for "doing well" out of the equation Notice that sometimes the spiritual state of another person is discernible to the evangelist, both in a positive sense and in a negative sense: Positively, Paul noted that the lame man from Lystra had faith in Jesus to be made well on his first hearing of the Gospel (Acts 14:8-9) Negatively, Paul noted that Elymas the sorcerer was filled with a spirit of deceit and fraud (Acts 13:9-10) If God reveals to us that spiritual state, following His leading, we ought to speak to it and/or use it in our witness
[7] "If you do well, will you not be accepted?"	God gave Cain a way out, an ultimatum as it were in verse 7 Yet, He began with the good side of the equation Is this not the prime example of "speech seasoned with salt to give grace to those who hear"? (Col 4) I am made to wonder, if Jesus coming to this earth to deal with mankind, did not ponder how His father dealt with mankind in his sin, as in this example (Gen 4) Remember the words of Jesus "O faithless and perverse generation, how long shall I be with you? How long shall I bear with you? Bring him here to Me'" (Mat 17:17; and parallels)? "If you do well" God was preaching good news to Cain It was good for him if he would only receive it or accept it (have a hearing of faith) It was clear that the psychological state in which Cain was living as he was contemplating and meditating on killing his brother, as jealousy and bitterness was consuming his soul, was not healthy nor helpful to him "Will you not be accepted" Here is a hint of accountability to God Our lifestyle being acceptable to God "Well done, thou good and faithful servant" Remember the unheeded words of warning of righteous Lot to the people of Sodom? Gen 19:7, "Please, my brethren, do not do so wickedly!" Which godly preaching they rejected: Gen 19:9, "This one came to stay *here*, and he keeps acting as a judge" Bringing destruction upon themselves: Gen 19:24, "Then the LORD rained brimstone and fire on Sodom and Gomorrah, from the LORD out of the heavens" Yet also remember that the people of Nineveh did receive the words of Jonah: Jonah 3:4, "Yet forty days, and Nineveh shall be overthrown!" Which advice they did receive: Jonah 3:5, "So the people of Nineveh believed God, proclaimed a fast, and put on sackcloth, from the greatest to the least of them" And God relented and accepted their repentance: Jonah 3:10, "Then God saw their works, that they turned from their evil way; and God relented from the disaster that He had said He would bring upon them, and He did not do it"
"And if you do not	"If you do not do well"

do well, sin lies at the door."	God gives the negative side of the ultimatum The result of falling prey to sin, actually resulting in death, Rom 6:23; James 1:15
	This is the warning, and this is the most difficult part of evangelism, warning Notice Paul speaks of "warning every man" as part of preaching Jesus, "Christ in you the hope of glory," Col 1:27-28
	So, the Gospel message of one of warning of impending doom: Mark 1:15, "The time is fulfilled, and the rulership of God is at hand, repent and believe the Good News"

	Remember that God was giving Cain a chance before He fell into sin
	  Was this not gracious of God?
	  And does this not make Can's sin even more heinous and worthy of judgment?

	Is this not the role of every man's conscience prior to their falling into sin? (Rom 2:14-15)
	  And does not the fact that man has a conscience condemn him before a holy God?
	  And show him his need for a Savior?

	Oh the riches of the grace of God poured out upon rebellious and sinful mankind!

	"Sin lies at the door"
	  Out of these words, we see sin personified as a roaring lion
	  This ravenous animal is crouching and waiting for an opportune time
	  It is waiting at the door, looking for an unguarded moment
	  There is a terrible urgency to see this animal called "sin"
	  And not to open that door to him

	The way to not open the door to him is given to Cain as "If you do well"
	  Not following through with the ruminations of his mind, with his deceitful scheming
	  Yet he went on and lied to Cain in the next verse

	It appears then that Cain could have obeyed the admonition of God
	  But here we have the weakness of the Law, although it offers regulations by which we should "do well," it only ends up condemning us, because we cannot "do well"
	  What then could Cain have done?
	  The same thing that Eve did not do!
	  Cry out to God for help and mercy

	Whenever our conscience condemns us, which, by the way, happens repeatedly every day, we ought to cry out to God for His strength and mercy toward us

	Yes, Cain needed Jesus
	  He needed Jesus before the murder
	  He needed Jesus after the murder
	  Yet his only concern was for himself, his reputation, his skin

	Notice, however, that God gives us a list of forgiven murderers in the Bible, notably:
	  Moses (Egyptian)
	  David (Uriah)
	  Saul of Tarsus, Paul (Stephen)

	The perceptive reader will notice that these are among the most important persons in the Bible Yes, there is hope, even for the murderer!
"And its desire *is* for you, but you	"And its desire *is* for you" God, the Evangelist, taught Cain about sin

should rule over it."	He gave him a lesson in harmatology

He did not speak about His transcendence, nor His glory, nor His worthiness to be praised:
  He did not come as the Shekinah glory to amaze Cain with His brilliance
  He did not come explaining his sovereignty and preeminence

God came as a teacher, teaching about what sin was seeking to do in Cain's heart:

  What sin wants to do
  And how he could overcome sin

  Notice, however, the weakness of the Old Covenant
  It is true that Cain needed to rule over sin
  But it is also true that he could not rule over it

  Again, this shows us our need for Jesus
  And we can say thank you to the Lord for placing us on this side of the cross of Christ
  We can conquer sin, not in our own strength, but by the Holy Spirit residing in our hearts!

  If God had left us with this "Rule" that He gave to Cain, "If you do well… if you do not do well" then
  we would all be doomed to eternal damnation
  By the way, there are many works salvation religions today
  Perhaps the Church of Rome being the chief among those that call themselves Christian

  But where the Old Covenant was weak, in the New Covenant herein is our strength

Notice also that God made a world where Cain could ignore His teaching, to his own peril
  Is this not what God saw when He looked down on the earth in Gen 6:5?
  Man doing "only evil continually"?

"but you should rule over it"

Thus, the words of God end with an ultimatum , "if, then; if not, then"
  And the response to this ultimatum is noted by the works of Cain in the next verse
  He spoke to his brother
    Likely some kind of lie
    John 8:44 ties together the murderer and the lie
  He killed his brother
    Hatred leading to violence, Matt 5:21-22

This evangelistic conversation ends with God the Evangelist leaving Cain with a warning!

  Sometimes or even oftentimes in our evangelism, especially when dealing with someone whom
    we can sense is hardened, should we not leave the contact with a some kind of warning?
    Heb 3;15; 4:7, "Today, if you will hear His voice, Do not harden your hearts"
    2 Cor 6:2, "Behold, now *is* the accepted time; behold, now *is* the day of salvation"

  Consider also the example of John the Baptist, Jesus, and the disciples:
    Matt 3:2, "Repent, for the kingdom of heaven is at hand!"
    Matt 4:17, "Repent, for the kingdom of heaven is at hand."
    Matt 10:7, "The kingdom of heaven is at hand."
    Mark 1:15, "The time is fulfilled, and the kingdom of God is at hand. Repent, and believe in the gospel."
    Mark 6:12, "So they went out and preached that *people* should repent"
    Mark 16:15-16, "Go into all the world and preach the gospel to every creature. He who believes and is baptized will
      be saved; but he who does not believe will be condemned"
    Luke 24:46-47, "Then He said to them, "Thus it is written, and thus it was necessary for the Christ to suffer and to
      rise from the dead the third day, and that repentance and remission of sins should be preached in His name to all
      nations, beginning at Jerusalem"
    Acts 2:38, "Repent, and let every one of you be baptized in the name of Jesus Christ for the remission of sins; and
      you shall receive the gift of the Holy Spirit"

	So the ball is in man's court to respond to the message that God has given:
	  The evangelist delivers God's message, and it is up to man to respond
	  And notice that even God was rejected when He warned Cain

Expectant Evangelism's Theological Foundations

God's Election
("which we know not but by the event,"
John Owens)

+

The Verbal Proclamation of the Gospel
(which is taught and exemplified in Scripture,
and unto which we are commanded)

+

The Dynamic Power of God's Word

+

The Work of the Holy Spirit

=

A Hearing of Faith
(at the designated time in their lives,
for those unto whom it is foreordained)

+

An Invitation to Salvation
(which is taught and exemplified in Scripture,
and unto which we are commanded)

=

An Opportunity for Instantaneous Conversion

(At This Point the Four Soils of the Parable of the Sower
Differentiate the Responses of Persons)

CHAPTER 12
Spiritual Elements to Evangelism

1. **Reasons why people have not yet come to Christ:**

    a. Sample reasons:
        1) **Ignorance**: they have never heard the Gospel, Rom 10:14-15.
        2) **Sin**: some root of sin has hardened their hearts to spiritual things, John 3:20.
        3) **Deceit**: they have been deceived by false teaching about salvation, 1 Tim 4:1.
            e.g. They may think that they are already saved, even though it is not by faith alone…
        4) **Pride** (rebelliousness): they do not want to humble themselves before the Lord, 1 Pet 5:6.

    b. Complimenting spiritual reasons:
        1) God may be hardening their hearts, Prov 1:28-29, Isa 6:10
        2) Satan may be blinding their eyes, 2 Cor 4:3-4

2. **God's Work of Conviction:**

    Introduction: The spiritual element of conviction is one that the evangelist does not control directly:
        1) We may use particular verses that should lead to conviction of sin
        2) We may be "prayed up" for sharing the gospel
        3) But only God and his Word can judge the secret intentions in the heart of man, Rom 2:16; Heb 4:12-13

    a. The Gospel convicts lost people:
        1) Of "sin, righteousness, and judgment," John 16:8
        2) Of "righteousness, self-control, and the judgment to come," Acts 24:25

    b. The Gospel reveals the hidden motives of men
        1) "When God will judge the secrets of the hearts of men," Rom 2:16
        2) "For the word of God… is a discerner of the thoughts and intentions of the heart," Heb 4:12

    Spiritual and expectant evangelism must be aware of God's hidden working in the heart:
        1) Discerning the receptivity of the person being engaged with the gospel
        2) Seeking to apply principles of God's Word with love and power to "cast down every argument … that exalts itself against the knowledge of God," 2 Cor 10:5

3. **Profile of the Open Heart**:[964]

    These are characteristics to look for while sharing the Gospel…

    a. He will "receive" the evangelist, Matt 10:40; John 13:20 (cf. John 1:12)

    b   He will listen, Acts 16:14; 1 John 4:6; cf. Luke 10:16.

    c. He will hear the Word:
        1) Hear and act upon the Word, Matt 7:24-25; Luke 6:47-48
        2) Having a hearing of faith, Gal 3:2, 5
        3) Hear and believe, John 5:24

    d. He will be a "man of peace," Luke 10:6

    e   He will display a contrite heart toward sin (versus arrogance or indifference):
        1) The afflicted soul, Isa 58:10, cf. Psa 22:24-26; 116:10
        2) The afflicted and needy, Ps 74:21
        3) The brokenhearted, Psa 34:18; 147:3; Isa 61:1
        4) The contrite and lowly of spirit, Isa 57:15
        5) The humble and contrite of spirit, Isa 66:2
        6) The broken and contrite heart, Psa 51:17

---

[964]See also Chapter 18, "Levels of Openness," "The Open Person," "Profile of an open heart."

   f.   Even lost persons may display a spiritual interest:
1) The devout or pious men in Jerusalem before Pentecost, Acts 2:5
2) The godfearers (τοῖς σεβομένοις) thoughout book of Acts, Acts 10:22; 13:43; 17:4, 17
3) Came to Jerusalem to worship, Acts 8:27

Discussion: Some high Calvinists take the previous characteristics as showing that God is working in persons prior to their hearing of the Gospel (hence undermining the *sola Scriptura* of salvation). If we accept that God must needs work in, with, and by His Word, then another explanation needs be sought. Two possibilities:

1) They are seeking the God revealed within them (Rom 1:19) and in their consciences (Rom 2:14-15)—if so, this needs to be reconciled with Rom 3:11
   Answer: Sure revelation does not constitute a redemptive seeking after, especially before the hearing of the gospel, which is the power of God.

2) God is at work outside of His word, which opens up a problem with Heb 4:12-13, the need for evangelism, God working through sacraments, etc.
   Comment: This option does not appear to correspond with the sensus plenior of Scripture.

It is clear that the devout, the pious, and the godfearers are not those who say, "Lord, Lord" (Matt 7:22-23). Thus we see levels of saved and lost people being described in the Bible via the Parable of the Sower and in other places (a lost godfearer and a saved carnal Christian). Very interesting! Also note that the Apostle Paul worked harder than the other apostles (1 Cor 15:10).

4. Spiritual Problems in Evangelism:

Introduction: There are spiritual problems with a lack of understanding or misplaced understanding that must be surmounted in evangelism.

   a.   A misunderstanding of spiritual things:
1) Misunderstanding the spiritual application of an example, John 3:4; 4:11, 15
2) In fact, this was why Jesus spoke in parables, using word pictures, so that those not meant to understand would not, while to others it would be revealed, Matt 13:10-17; Mark 4:10-13; Luke 8:9-10
3) By contrast the Centurion who understood the spiritual nature of things, and was commended for it. In Luke 7:6-9 Jesus said he had great faith, "I say to you, not even in Israel have I found such great faith."

   b.   Misplacing the power behind miracles:
1) As coming from Satan, Matt 12:24 (cf. Mark 3:22; Luke 11:15)
2) As coming from the men themselves, Acts 14:13

Only God through the gospel can overcome these spiritual blind spots, 2 Cor 4:2-3

5. Biblical Presuppositions—from General Revelation:

Introduction: Differentiation between General Revelation, Natural Revelation, and Special Revelation:

   a)   **General Revelation**—God's revelation to all men, at all times, in all places, which is non-salvific, e.g. Psa 19:1-6; it leads only to sure judgment (Rom 1:20) and further depravity (Rom 1:21; cf. Psa 36:1-4)

   b)   **Special Revelation**—God's revelation of Himself directly (as to Moses), through His Son (when He was on earth), and through His Word. *Sola Scriptura* limits salvific revelation in God's dealings with man to the Word of God, the Bible, Psa 19:7-13 (the theme of Psalm 119).

   c)   **Natural Revelation**—the belief that general revelation contains the possibility or opportunity for salvation outside of special revelation (i.e. the Gospel or the Word of God), often attributed to Thomistic theology (Thomas Aquinas).

One can assume certain innate truths to be in the hearts of those whom the Gospel is shared, even if they won't outwardly admit them. These are a part of general revelation (as it were, divine *preparatio evangelica*). It is not necessary to share these facts with the person. Rather, they can be a guide as you speak the Gospel with boldness.

a. Presuppositions concerning God:

1) All people have a knowledge of God, Rom 1:18-21 (cf. Isa 26:10)

   a) v 18, "men who suppress the truth"

   b) v 19, "that which is known about God is evident within them"

   c) v 19, "for God made it evident to them"

   d) v 20, "have been clearly seen"

   e) v 20, "being understood"

   f) v 20, "so that they are without excuse"

   g) v 21, "For even though they knew God"

2) Men stand in awe of God because of general revelation, Psa 65:8 (e.g. Jon 1:9-14)

3) All people have seen the glory of God, Psa 97:6 (cf. Psa 19:1-4; 50:6; 52:15)

4) "To Thee all men come," Psa 65:2

5) "He has set eternity in their hearts," Eccl. 3:11 (cf. Acts 17:26-28).

b. Presuppositions concerning sin:

1) Everyone has a conscience that accuses and defends, based on the Law of God written in their hearts, Rom 2:14-15

2) All people know of God's righteous commands, and of the death penalty for sin, Rom 1:32

Translations of δικαίωμα τοῦ θεοῦ in Rom 1:32

Wycliffe, Tyndale, Bishop's	Rotter-dam	Young's, Darby, NKJ	CSB	Noye's; ERV, ASV, NAS	KJV, Webster's	NIV (1984); NET; ESV	NJB⊞	NAB⊞ (1991)	RSV	BBE	DRA⊞	NIRV
Righteousness of God	Righteous sentence of God	Righteous judgment of God	God's just sentence	Ordinance of God	Judgment of God	God's righteous decree	God's ordinance	The just decree of God	God's decree	Law of God	Justice of God	That God's commands are right

Notice also, how the message taught in Rom 1:32 is reversed by the Latin Vulgate's addition of a negated verb form (non intellexerunt):

Consider the three Latin versions:[965]

    VUC Rom 1:32 Qui cum justitiam Dei cognovissent, non intellexerunt quoniam qui talia agunt, digni sunt morte: et non solum qui ea faciunt, sed etiam qui consentiunt facientibus.

    VULM Rom 1:32 qui cum iustitiam Dei cognovissent non intellexerunt quoniam qui talia agunt digni sunt morte non solum ea faciunt sed et consentiunt facientibus

    NOV Rom 1:32 Qui cum iudicium Dei cognovissent, quoniam qui talia agunt, digni sunt morte, non solum ea faciunt, sed et consentiunt facientibus.

These changes are noticeabled in the 1899 Douay-Rheims translation of this verse:

    DRA Rom 1:32 Who, having known the justice of God, did not understand that they who do such things, are worthy of death; and not only they that do them, but they also that consent to them that do them.

    NAS Rom 1:32 and, although they know the ordinance of God, that those who practice such things are worthy of death, they not only do the same, but also give hearty approval to those who practice them.

    NKJ Rom 1:32 who, knowing the righteous judgment of God, that those who practice such things are deserving of death, not only do the same but also approve of those who practice them.

---

[965]VUC=1598 Clementine Vulgate with 1880 glosses by Migne; VULM=1983 German Bible Society edition; NOV=1982 Nova Vulgata from Rome. This last version takes the prior version of the Vulgate and amends it to coincide with the Nestle-Aland 26th edition of the Greek New Testament, as part of John XXIII's (and hence Vatican II's) aggiornamento strategy in infiltrating and neutering the work of the Bible Societies (see my paper on "Worldwide Bible Translations and Original Language Texts"; available at: http://www.evangelismunlimited.com/ubs-spcu_text20090116b.pdf; and "Rome, Bible Translation, and the Oklahoma City Green Bible Collection"; available at: http://www.evangelismunlimited.com/rbt_paper20110611a.pdf).

The addition of the "did not understand," completely negates the teaching of this verse, and its universal applicability to man in his natural state. There are several issues at stake in the interpretation of this verse, but this is the most obvious. This change adversely affects a presuppositionalist viewpoint, as man is made to not understand God's law or His judgment of sin.

    3) God's judgment prepares people for the Gospel, Psa 58:11

c. Some appear to be waiting to hear of Christ:
    1) Isaiah 25:9, 42:4,[966] 45:24, 51:5, 60:9
    2) Note the parable of Christ which seems to parallel this teaching, Mark 4:26-29

d. However, some anthropological truths:
    1) All men are blinded to the light of the Gospel, 2 Cor. 4:4
    2) All men are spiritually dead and by nature children of wrath, Eph 2:1-3
    3) All men are under the empire of sin, etc., Rom 3:9-11

e. Conclusion:
    1) Although men have general revelation which points them to God, they need the special revelation of the Gospel in order to be saved:

> 2. This Promise of *Christ,* and Salvation by him, is revealed only by the Word of God; neither do the Works of Creation, or Providence, with the light of Nature, make discovery of *Christ,* or of *Grace* by him; so much as in a general, or obscure way; much less that men destitute of the Revelation of him by the Promise, or Gospel; should be enabled thereby, to attain saving Faith, or Repentance.[967]

Likewise:

> Only in Eden has general revelation been adequate to the needs of man. Not being a sinner, man in Eden had no need of the grace of God itself by which sinners are restored to communion with Him, or of special revelation of this grace of God to sinners to enable them to live with God.[968]

    2) It is obvious that Christian's do not need to assert the latest apologetic arguments to prove the existence of God, or to prove the validity of the Christian worldview. God has already done this prevenient work through nature and conscience. Ours is to be obedient to preach repentance for the forgiveness of sins to those that God supernaturally makes open to this message.

6. Times of openness:

Introduction:

While not wanting to be guided by the vain teachings of men, as God's ways are above man's ways, and his thoughts are above man's thoughts…

There are certain crisis times in life, allowed by God, which sometimes allow people to be more open to spiritual things. These crisis times have been put on a continuum (Holme's Stress Scale) by how much stress they put on a person. are also important times in which one may minister to others in tangible ways, as well as by sharing the Gospel of Jesus Christ.

The book of Job, Elihu's speech teaches us that God speaks to people in their consciences, through dreams and through difficult times (Job 33:14-28):

> "Indeed God speaks once, Or twice, yet no one notices it. In a dream, a vision of the night, When sound sleep falls on men, While they slumber in their beds, Then He opens the ears of men, And seals their instruction, That he may turn aside from his conduct, And keep man from pride; He keeps his soul from the pit, And his life from passing over into Sheol.
> "Man is also chastened with pain on his bed, And with unceasing complaint in his bones; So that his life loathes bread, And his soul favorite food. His flesh wastes away from sight, And all his bones stick out. Then his soul draws near to the pit, And his life to those who bring death.

---

[966]C.F. Keil and F. Delitzsch spoke of this verse as indicating a *"gracia preparatur."*

[967]*Second London [Baptist] Confession* (1677), Chapter 20, "Of the Gospel, and of the extent of the Grace thereof," from William L. Lumpkin, *Baptist Confessions of Faith,* rev. ed. (Valley Forge: Judson, 1959, 1969).

[968]Benjamin B. Warfield, *The Inspiration and Authority of the Bible* (Philippsburg, NJ: Presbyterean and Reformed, 1948), 75-76.

"If there is an angel as mediator for him, One out of a thousand, To remind a man what is right for him, Then let him be gracious to him and say, 'Deliver him from going down into the pit, I have found a ransom.' Let his flesh become fresher than in youth, Let him return to the days of his youth vigor; Then he will pray to God, and He will accept him, That he may see His face with joy, And that He may restore his righteousness to man. He will sing to men and say, 'I have sinned and perverted what is right, and it is not proper for me. He has redeemed my soul from going to the pit, And my life shall see the light.'"

Behold, God does all these oftentimes with men, To bring back his soul from the pit, That he may be enlightened with the light of life" The following indicates some of these times of stress. We should be aware of these as we minister the Gospel. Fred Jennings described these as "points of pain."[969]

In modern psychology certain "points of pain" are placed on "Holmes Stress Scale" (it must be noted that this stress scale betrays its North American context, as it does not contain bombing campaigns, war, famine, torture, being a prisoner of war, being in a refugee camp, having house and property confiscated, etc.). I have included the top twelve stresses on Holmes' scale:

Death in family	100
Divorce	73
Marital separation	65
Jail term	63
Death of a close family member	63
Personal injury or illness	53
Marriage	50
Fired at work	47
Marital reconciliation	45
Retirement	45
Change in health of family member	44
Pregnancy	40
etc.	

7. Be Aware of Possible Spiritual Steps:

Introduction, Isaiah 5:1-2:

There seems to be spiritual steps in the reception of the Gospel (especially when seen from a human point-of-view, as identified by sociological analysis or the psychology of conversion).[970]

It must be remember that conversion is a spiritual jump from blind to seeing. For example, some persons in the Bible jump from one extreme to the other:
  a) Demoniac from Gerasenes in Mark 5
  b) Woman at the well, John 4
  c) Saul of Tarsus, Acts 9
  d) Philippian jailer, Acts 16

Therefore the expansion of these steps:

---

[969]From his comments in the Biblical Evangelism class at Crown College on September 17, 1992.

[970]The Engel scale follows the conversion process in a more systematic cognitive approach. This scale was originally proposed by Dr. James Engel of the Wheaton Graduate School (source: Edward Dayton, "To Reach the Unreached," Ralph D. Winter and Steven C. Hawthrone, eds., *Perspectives on the World Christian Movement* (Pasadena, CA; William Carey, 1981), 591). Here are the eleven stages of awareness of the Gospel that make up the Engel Scale:

1)	No awareness of Christianity	-7
2)	Awareness of the Existence of Christianity	-6
3)	Some knowledge of the Gospel	-5
4)	Understanding the Fundamentals of the Gospel	-4
5)	Grasp of Personal Need	-3
6)	Challenge and Decision to receive Christ	-1
7)	CONVERSION	
8)	Evaluation of the Decision	+1
10)	Incorporation into a Fellowship of Christians	+2
11)	Active in Propogation of the Gospel	+3

a) Does not to diminish the need for instantaneity of witness nor the fact of its corollary, instantaneous conversion.

b) Nor do steps imply that human categories can and ought to be applied to evangelism, thereby easily trumping the divine work of the power of the gospel, Rom 1:16, by human types of persuasion, 1 Cor 1:17

The following steps are expansions of the teaching of two elderly missionary women (Jeanne & Mabel) who spent 40 years of their lives in door-to-door ministry in Quebec to begin three churches—in a very difficult area. The metaphor used in Isaiah 5 is one of the farmer seeking to raise up a crop—a parallel idea to the NT parable of the sower.

a. In sharing the Gospel, clear the ground of rocks: the hindrances of false ideas, Acts 14:14-18

b. In sharing the Gospel, work the soil:
1) The law is a tutor to grace, Rom 3:19-20; 7:5; Gal 3:24
2) Set a foundation of repentance, Mark 1:4 (cf. Luke 3:3), 15; Luke 5:32; 24:47; Acts 20:21
3) Warn the wicked to wake them up, Ezek 3:16-21, "You shall surely die!"
4) "Break up the fallow ground, and do not sow among thorns," Jer 4:3 (e.g. Isaiah 5:1-2)
5) Gene Edwards writes, "It is impossible to witness effectively unless you give the Holy Spirit opportunity to prepare the heart."[971] (i.e. the necessity of the Sword of the Spirit to be applied to the heart).

c. In sharing the Gospel, sow the seed of the Gospel, Luke 8:11

d. In sharing the Gospel, water the ground, 1 Cor 3:7.
Watering the ground is done through teaching of the Word.

e. In sharing the Gospel, God must cause the growth, 1 Cor 3:7.
God's working shows the need for prayer and continued nourishing from the Word.

f. In sharing the Gospel, harvest of the crop, John 4:35-36; 15:16.
True repentance and faith in Christ leading to eternal life shows the maturation to salvation of the Gospel in the life of the open heart.

---

[971]Gene Edwards, *How to Have a Soul Winning Church* (Springfield, MO; Gospel Publishing, 1962), 117.

Chapter 12 Appendix

Concerning Politically Correct Recipients of the Gospel

Introduction: Are there certain people, certain religions, or certain groups that are out-of-bounds for evangelism? In an age of ecumenism and tolerance and in a day when churches are signing non-proselytism agreements, how does the Bible speak to the issue of the recipients of the Gospel?

1. For the sake of understanding the boundaries of toleration, let us try to identify ways to determine a politically correct recipient of the Gospel

    a. Do they say that they are members of another church?
        For example: "I'm Catholic!"
        1) In which case, one has to determine whether salvation in that church is in accordance with the Gospel of Jesus Christ
        2) The mere fact of questioning the salvific teachings of another church, however, flies in the face of Christian toleration
        3) There is the added problem that the individual may not know, may not care about, or may not even accept the means of salvation as taught in their own church
        3) The Evangelical and Catholics Together Statement of 1994, for example, decried the idea of Evangelicals evangelizing among Catholics,[972] as did the 1994 Colson-Neuhaus Declaration.[973]

    b. Do they say that they are baptized?
        For example: "I was baptized when I was younger!"
        1) In some sacramental and some Evangelical churches, baptism is salvific or equivalent to being "born again"; hence, for those groups the baptism answer should end the Gospel conversation
        2) Again, from a biblical standpoint, baptism is a non-salvific ordinance, thus this question becomes a mute point

    c. Do they say that they believe in God?
        For example: "I'm Jewish!"
        1) If we were to broaden the parameters of faith and conversion, some would say that a mere belief in God is all that is needed to be saved
        2) Questioning a person who believes in God about their salvation is deemed not politically correct
        3) However, it is clear that belief in God is not enough, as "even the demons believe" in a monotheistic God and shutter, James 2:19

    d. Do they say that they are a Christian, and yet have no assurance of salvation?
        1) Is the biblical doctine of assurance of salvation a strong enough that it can be the foundation upon which personal evangelism can be built (i.e. the "Assurance Questions")?

---

[972]"Today, in this country and elsewhere, Evangelicals and Catholics **attempt to win 'converts'** from one another's folds. In some ways, this is perfectly understandable and perhaps inevitable. In many instances, however, such efforts at recruitment undermine the Christian mission by which we are bound by God's Word and to which we have recommitted ourselves in this statement. …At the same time, our commitment to full religious freedom compels us to defend the legal freedom to **proselytize** even as we call upon Christians to refrain from such activity" ("Evangelicals and Catholic Together: The Christian Mission in the Third Millennium," in Keith A. Fournier, with William D. Watkins, *A House United? Evangelicals and Catholics Together: A Winning Alliance for the 21st Century* [Colorado Springs: NavPress, 1994], 346).

[973]"There is a necessary distinction between evangelizing [non-Christians] and what is today commonly called proselytizing or 'sheep stealing.'" For "in view of the large number of non-Christians in the world and the enormous challenge of the common evangelistic task, it is neither theologically legitimate nor a prudent use of resources for one Christian community to proselytize among active adherents of another Christian community." Thus, "We condemn the practice of recruiting people from another community for the purposes of denominational or institutional aggrandizement" (Geisler and MacKenzie, *Roman Catholics and Evangelicals: Agreements and Differences* [Grand Rapids: Baker, 1995], 493).

2) Does therefore a Christian involved in personal evangelism have the right to "teach" or "edify" another Christian who does not believe in assurance of salvation?

3) In what way is assurance of salvation a salvific issue?

4) Note the issue of assurance of salvation in the Baptist Faith and Message.[974]

e. Conclusion: Any attempt to restrict the potential recipients of the Gospel to a certain underclass restricts both the universiality of the Great Commission and the universal need of salvation by grace through faith alone

2. The Bible is clearly universalistic as to the necessity for evangelism

a. The above Great Commission notes on the universality of recipients of the Gospel holds true, all need to hear

b. The above "Profile of the Open Heart" compels the Christian to share with anyone who will listen to the Gospel

c. The necessity for all Christians to regularly share the Gospel following the example fo the New Testament also bears out the universiality of the recipients

3. On the other hand, non-proselytism agreements are:

a. Reminiscent of the admonitions against the Lollards and the Methodists, "Stay out of my parish!"

b. Imply that the elements related to salvation and conversion in a statement of faith are not relevant in light of denominational cooperation

c. Imply that the Christian should not obey the Great Commission and share the Gospel "in the whole world ... to all creation" (Mark 16:15)

d. Imply a theological subjectivism, by which all roads lead to heaven, either within the scope of identified Christianity or even often outside of it!

---

[974]"All true believers endure to the end. Those whom God has accepted in Christ, and sanctified by His Spirit, will never fall away from the state of grace, but shall persevere to the end. Believers may fall into sin through neglect and temptation, whereby they grieve the Spirit, impair their graces and comforts, and bring reproach on the cause of Christ and temporal judgments on themselves; yet they shall be kept by the power of God through faith unto salvation" ("V. God's Purpose of Grace," par 2, Baptist Faith and Message 2000; available from http://www.sbc.net/bfm/default.asp; accessed 14 Aug 2002; Internet).

CHAPTER 13
Before Sharing the Gospel

Introduction:

1. What makes for Effective Evangelism?

    "If there were such a thing as a typical convert in Quebec it would be a person who is 30 years old who, seeking meaning in his/her life, had first seen the gospel lived out by a friend or family member of his/her own generation, then *heard it presented six to ten times*. Once these conditions are met, then this person would be apt to make his/her *final decision for Christ in a church meeting or crusade or camp* (48%), again accompanied by his believing friend or family member."[975]

2. The Heartbeat of Evangelism:

    There are differing styles of evangelism. There are differing types of evangelism. Christians have differing personalities and spiritual gifts and non-Christians have differing spiritual needs. In fact, the Bible does not zero in on one style of evangelism, but rather encourages many.[976] Yet with all these differences, *the heartbeat of evangelism remains the same.*

    Paul's heartbeat for evangelism is an encouragement. The Apostle Paul sought to reach people in any way he could. He wrote, "I have become all things to all men, that I may by all means save some" (1 Cor 9:22; cf. Col 1:28-29). Paul sought to be all things to all men. Everything he did had the goal of the salvation and growth of every person that he met. The Gospel was the central point of all his relationships. In fact, he saw himself as a fellow-worker with the Gospel (1 Cor 9:23).

    However, a question arises from the text: does "that I may by all means save some" imply a multiplicity of means of salvation? or a multiplicity of means of conversion? or a multiplicity of means of proclamation? or a multiplicity of effort in seeking to reach the lost? Let's look at the translation history of this text:

Translation of ἵνα πάντως τινὰς ("by all means"?) in 1 Corinthians 9:22b for a Multiplicity of Means

1990 Migne Clementine Vulgate	1530 Lefevre; [cf. 1550 Louvain*]	1899 Douay-Rheims*	1534 Olivetan; 1560 French Geneva	1973 French Jerusalem Bible*	1995 Contemp English Version*	1560 English Geneva	1611 King James Version [cf. ASV; RSV; NAS; NKJ; CSB; ESV]	1984 New International Version	1992/1999 French *Le Semeur*
facerem omnibus omnia factus sum ut omnes facerem salvos	Jay este faict toutes chose a tous / affin q' je les sauvasse tous	I became all things to all men, that I might save all	je me suis fait toutes choses à tous, afin qu'absolument j'en sauve quelques-uns.	Je me suis fait tout à tous, afin d'en sauver à tout prix quelques-uns	I do everything I can to win everyone I possibly can.	I am made all things to all men, that I might by all meanes saue some	I am made all things to all *men*, that I might by all means save some	I have become all things to all men so that by all possible means I might save some	C'est ainsi que je me fais tout à tous, afin d'en conduire au moins quelques-uns au salut par tous les moyens
"all" is translated to save "all"			"all" is translated or implied to mean "all effort"			"all" is translated to mean "by all means"			
Two implications: theological universalism, all people can be saved; ecclesial, a church for all the people of a territory			Implications: "all" refers to effort expended in evangelism; only a few will be reached			Implications: "all" refers to using all methods; only a few will be reached			

Greek τινὰς is masculine plural indefinite accusative of τὶς, meaning someone, something, a certain one, a certain thing, anyone, anything.

---

[975]Wesley Peach, "Evangelism—Distinctively Quebec," Arnell Motz, ed. *Reclaiming a Nation* (Richmond, B.C.; Church Leadership, 1990), 160. Italics mine.

[976]Merrill Tenney, *John, the Gospel of Belief* (Grand Rapids: Eerdmans, 1948). Tenney points out that Jesus employed a multiplicity of methods in the twenty-one personal interviews he engaged in, as recorded by John (cited in Bill Hull, *Jesus Christ Disciple Maker* [Minneapolis: Free Church, 1984], 23).

The Apostle Paul expanded on this idea in 1 Cor 10:33. "Just as I also please all men in all things, not seeking my own profit, but the profit of many, that they may be saved." Any of His personal goals, dreams, desires and tastes are subordinated to the greater purpose of the salvation of souls. The use of the inclusive "all" in the above verses is powerful and overwhelming.

It would seem from the context, and from Acts 15:11 (see Chapter 1), that Paul is refering to all effort in reaching the lost, as is emphasized in the French Geneva tradition.

Paul continues expounding on this thrust in his life as he writes in 2 Cor 12:15: "I will most gladly spend and be expended for your souls." Paul brings out the complete abandonment of himself in his ministry. No cost is too great—not even his own life!

One last quote from the Apostle Paul lets us understand his heartbeat:

> "And we proclaim Him, admonishing every man and teaching every man with all wisdom, that we may present every man complete in Christ. And to this purpose also I labor, striving according to His power, which mightily works within me," Col 1:28-29

The total commitment of the Apostle Paul is no secret. Why are these a model for the Christian? Paul, inspired by the Holy Spirit, wrote, "Be imitators of me, even as I am of Christ" (1 Cor 4:16, 11:1)

Paul has communicated his surrender to the Gospel. This surrender is a reminder of the complete surrender of Jesus Christ. "I am the good shepherd and I lay down My life for the sheep." (John 10:14-15) "For even the Son of Man did not come to be served, but to serve, and to give His life a ransom for many." (Mark 1045) In the apostle Paul, we find a beautiful example of a Christian becoming conformed to the image of Jesus Christ.

3. The Importance of (a) the one means of salvation, and (b) the biblical means of salvation:
   a. That **there is one means of salvation** (see chart on Acts 15:11 at the beginning of chapter 1) or of receiving grace!
      That Wayne Grudem in his theology muddied the waters with a multiplicity of means is disconcerting to say the least! Perhaps the confusing phrase is the "within the fellowship of the church." Here was what Grudem wrote:

   > "We may define means of grace as follows: *The means of grace are activities within the fellowship of the church that God uses to give more grace to Christians.*"[977]

   Grudem then listed 11 "means of grace," numbered in the following order:

   > "1. Teaching the Word of God
   > "2. Baptism
   > "3. The Lord's Supper
   > "4. Prayer for one another
   > "5. Worship
   > "6. Church discipline
   > "7. Giving
   > "8. Spiritual gifts
   > "9. Fellowship
   > "10. Evangelism
   > "11. Personal ministry to individuals"[978]

   He continued saying that the Roman Catholic Church has seven means of grace (listing them), which differ in meaning with the Protestants:

   > "Catholics view these as "means of salvation" that make people more fit to receive justification from God. But on a Protestant view, the means of grace are simply a means of additional blessing within the Christian life, and do not add to our fitness to receive justification from God."[979]

---

[977] Wayne Grudem, *Systematic Theology* (Grand Rapids: Zondervan, 1994), 950.

[978] Ibid., 951.

[979] Ibid., 951-52.

If this was truly the case, that he is speaking of "additional blessing" following justification, then why does Grudem include "evangelism" as number 10 of his 11 "means of grace"? Is it not through evangelism alone (or by the proclamation of the Word of God alone) that the "grace of salvation" is conferred on the lost? "Faith comes by hearing and hearing by the word of Christ" (Rom 10:17)? They are not "within the fellowship of the church" until they have become disciples (Matt 28:19), then they can be taught everything that God has commanded.

It would seem that Grudem is confused on the "Protestant" or Evangelical manner of grace at this point!

Note that the word "manner" is less slippery in English as is "means," which is written in the plural form, even if it has a singular meaning

For example, see in Chapter 1 the chart explaining the translation of the word τρόπος in Acts 15:11

A similar problem is found with use of the English word "orders" in Acts 1:2.

b. On the biblical means or method of salvation:
1) The manner in which you received it, 1 Cor 15:1-2
2) The impossibility of other manners of evangelizing, Gal 1:8-9
3) The drifting away from a New Testament manner, Gal 3:1-5

4. Evangelism Diagnostic:
Whatever the style or method: Is it biblical? Are you abandoned to the cause of evangelism? Will you give yourself completely for lost souls? Abandon yourself for the lost souls around you. This is the only worthwhile and lasting call. Give of yourself in any way you can. There is no limit to what can be done for the Lord through a life fully abandoned to His call.

A. The Principle of Availability:
1. John 4:35;
2. Col 4:6, cf. Eph 4:29;
3. 1 Pet 3:15.

Interesting Opposites Related to Availability

Passage	One Side	Other Side	Synopsis	Application
2 Tim 4:2	In [good] season	Out of season	There is no time when the Gospel ought not be ready on our lips	We ought always be available to share the Gospel
Rom 1:14	Greek	Barbarian	There are no cultural boundaries in evangelism	We ought not limit God's possibility of using us to reach people from any possible tribe or tongue
Rom 1:14	Wise	Foolish	There are no educational boundaries in evangelism	We ought not limit God's using us to reach all socio-economic levels of people
1 Cor 9:17	Of glad heart	Grudgingly	Emotions ought not guide our activity in evangelizing	Our changing emotions and desires should not limit our commitment to actively evangelize

B. Spiritual Preparation:
1. Reasons for spiritual preparation:
a. "Always being ready to make a defense to anyone who asks you," 1 Pet 3:15
b. "Let no unwholesome word proceed from your mouth, but only such a word as is good for edification according to the need of the moment, that it may give grace to those who hear." Eph 4:29
c. "Let your speech always be with grace, seasoned as it were, with salt, so that you may know how to respond to each person." Col 4:6

2. Aspects of spiritual preparation:
    a. Realize your complete dependency on God, Psa 144:1; Prov 21:31
    b. Consecrate yourself to God and to His will, Jos. 3:5; 1 Pet 3:15
    c. Don't compromise the holiness of God in your daily life, Jos. 7

3. Be wise as a serpent:
    a. Evangelizing is not for fools, but for the wise
    b. Wise as a serpent is listed first, therefore be on the alert, as you are on your way to share the Gospel
        1) Watch out for traps
        2) There is no glory in forcing yourself to be arrested to be seen by men
    c. Know the tricks of your enemy, the serpent of old, the Devil
        1) He will send distractions and temptations

4. Be gentle as a dove:
    a. While you are being wise as a serpent, take the opportunities God gives you to share the Gospel
    b. We must share the Gospel with patience and tenderness (2 Tim 2:2), and in love and humility (2 Tim 3:10)

C. Pray for an opportunity to share the Gospel:

1. Pray specifically for unsaved people whom God places on your heart, and be alert for opportunities to share with them, 1 Pet 3:15 (cf. Col 4:5-6).
2. Be open to God's answering a prayer that He wants to answer, John 14:13-14, 15:7-8, 1 John 5:13-15
3. Take the opportunity when He brings it your way (Eph 5:15-16; Col 4:6)!

D. Transparency in Testifying:

1. When not to speak, 1 Pet 3:1;
2. When to speak, Acts 4:19-20;
3. Why speak, Luke 12:4-5; Rom 10:14-15;
4. What to say, Eph 4:29 (cf. Col 4:5-6);

E. The Importance of Questions and Discussion:

1. The place of reasoning, Acts 17:17;[980]
2. Paul must have reasoned when he "confounded the Jews," Acts 9:22;
3. Stephen's adversaries "were unable to cope with his wisdom," Acts 6:10.

F. Dealing with Diversions:

1. The need for wisdom, Matt 10:16
2. Diversions may be honest openness on the part of the contact, be sensitive;
3. Jesus and the Woman at the Well, John 4;
4. Don't get into an argument, Prov 29:9 (win the battle, but lose the war);
5. Noting body language, e.g. Acts 24:25 (cf. John 16:8);
6. Redirecting the conversation to the Gospel, Rom 1:18-20

G. Be Positive!

1. Prov 15:2 (NKJV), "The tongue of the wise uses knowledge rightly."
2. Prov 10:32, "The lips of the wise bring forth what is acceptable."
3. Prov 15:4, "A soothing tongue is a tree of life."

H. Remember the Power of God's Word:

1. Eph 6:17
2. Heb 4:12
3. 1 Pet 1:23
4. Isaiah 55:11

---

[980]Note the Engel Scale.

Conclusion: Do not underestimate the power of God's Word. Use the Bible in your witness.

I. Go in the Joy of the Lord:

Often struggles and discouragements precede the sharing of the Gospel. This is because a spiritual battle is being waged. Usually rejoicing accompanies and almost always precedes the sharing of the Gospel. Isaiah 52:7-10 speaks of this joy.

Several chapters later, Isaiah 55:12 tells of the rejoicing that accompanies the preaching of the Gospel:

> For you will go out with joy, And be led forth with peace;
> The mountains and the hills will break forth into shouts of joy before you,
> And all the trees of the field will clap their hands.

Many Psalms echo the same truth (Psa 9:1, 26:7, 40:16, 70:4, 75:1, 79:13, 105:1, 107:22)

Joy in the Lord is an essential part of a powerful witness. Rejoice in the Lord (Phil 4:4) and be prepared for a joyous time of sharing.

J. Act as an ambassador for Jesus Christ:

Introduction:
   a. Be aware of how you come across, I Samuel 16:7
   b. Be aware of cultural norms:
      1) "Respect what is right in the sight of all men," Rom 12:17
      2) Ministry with the others in mind, 1 Cor 9:19-23, 10:32-33 ("give no offense," "seek to please all men in all things … so that they may be saved").

1. Personal Hygiene (cf. 1 Cor 9:19):
   a. Bad breath
   b. Body odor

2. Dress:
   It is good to dress appropriately to the people whom you are trying to reach. John the Baptist might be an example of one who dressed in a contrast to the society around him (Mark 1:6). However, his society had a prophetic office associated with his dress, and his ministry was effective (Mark 1:5). However, our societies often define role by dress. Some thought in this area might be good.

3. Actions:
   Your actions, the look in your eye, and where you look when you are talking with people are among the things that people see immediately when the meet someone else. Be considerate, look people in the eyes, and ask God for a genuine love for those you are going to—the same love that God had for man when He sent Jesus as a sacrifice for sins.

K. Go for it!

Introduction: Just do it!

1. "Finally, be strong in the Lord, and in the strength of His might," Eph 6:10

2. "Be on the alert, stand firm in the faith, act like men, be strong," 1 Cor 16:13

3. "No man will *be able to* stand before you all the days of your life. Just as I have been with Moses, I will be with you; I will not fail you or forsake you. Be strong and courageous, for you shall give this people possession of the land which I swore to their fathers to give them. Only be strong and very courageous; be careful to do according to all the law which Moses My servant commanded you; do not turn from it to the right or to the left, so that you may have success wherever you go. This book of the law shall not depart from your mouth, but you shall meditate on it day and night, so that you may be careful to do according to all that is written in it; for then you will make your way prosperous, and then you will have success. Have I not commanded you? Be strong and courageous! Do not tremble or be dismayed, for the LORD your God is with you wherever you go," Joshua 1:5-9

Chapter 13 Appendixes

Thoughts on Requiring Relationship as a Preparation for the Gospel

Introduction:

The topic of the order of salvation is fresh on the minds of theologians and church historians. Questions were asked in various scholastic periods in the history of the churches: What is the proper order of salvation? What is included in the order of salvation? Is it the physical sacrament? Is it faith alone? Does regeneration precede repentance? Etc.

There is also a parallel discussion. This discussion is not necessarily by theologians and historians, but rather by practicioners. The discussion centers around what human efforts validate the Gospel prior to its being presented. In many cased, these human efforts are unconsciously added to the order of salvation as preparatory graces to the Gospel, much like the preaching of John the Baptist was a divine preparation for Jesus. These human efforts include relationship, apologetics, service, lifestyle, etc. Evangelism without these prior human efforts is sometimes mocked. In this appendix the topic of necessitating a prior relationship is addressed. The reader is encouraged to soak in the words of the Bible, as well as to ponder the response and rejection of Jesus' hometown people, who saw the perfect Son of God grow up in their midst.

A. There are many examples of very significant conversations between strangers in the Bible, for example:
1. Abraham's servant asks a for the hand of a stranger to marry Isaac after prayer, Gen 24:10-27.
2. Elijah speaks to widow from Zarephath, because God said, "I have prepared a widow there to provide for you," 1 Kings 17:9-14
3. Two disciples were sent to get the colt for the triumphal entry from the city of Bethphage, and to answer anyone who asked them what they were doing, Luke 19:29-34
4. Peter and John are told to enter the city [of Jerusalem] and follow a man carrying a pitcher of water and to speak to the owner of the house he enters, Luke 22:8-13
Preliminary conclusion: It seems like God enjoys working in, with, and through conversations with strangers!

B. There are numerous examples in the Bible of the Gospel being discussed one-on-one between total strangers (with the understanding that no one was a stranger to Jesus):
1. Jesus and Nicodemus, John 3:1-21
2. Jesus and the Woman at the Well, John 4:7-26
3. Philip and the Ethiopian Eunuch, Acts 8:26-40
4. Paul and Lydia, Acts 16:14
5. Paul and Silas and the Philippian Jailer, Acts 16:28-32
6. Paul speaking to "those who happened to be present" at the market place in Athens, Acts 17:17
Furthermore: Many of the healings in the Book of Acts were also of complete strangers, e.g. lame man from Lystra, Acts 14:8-10; girl with a spirit of divination, Acts 16:16-18

C. There are also numerous examples of spiritual truth being proclaimed by a stranger to a group of people:
1. Jonah and the people of Nineveh, Jonah. 3
2. John the Baptist's preaching
3. Much of Jesus' public ministry:
    a. Note those with whom Jesus had a long relationship did not believe:
        1) Jesus' hometown:
        Matt 13:57, "Now He did not do many mighty works there because of their unbelief"
        Mark 6:6, "And He marveled because of their unbelief"
        2) Jesus' brothers, John 7:5, "For even His brothers did not believe in Him":
            a) Note their cynical comments to Him, vv 3-4

b) Note also the sharp response of Jesus (vv 6-8), which may have ultimately led to their salvation!

b. Note that those who had known Jesus the longest sought to kill Him after He preached to them:
   1) Other than his home town who tried to kill Jesus, Luke 4:28-20
   2) Compare with John 10:31-33

c. Note the often repeated comment of Jesus:
   Matt 13:57, "So they were offended at Him. But Jesus said to them, 'A prophet is not without honor except in his own country and in his own house'"
   Mark 6:4, "But Jesus said to them, "A prophet is not without honor except in his own country, among his own relatives, and in his own house'"
   Luke 4:24, "Then He said, "Assuredly, I say to you, no prophet is accepted in his own country"
   John 4:44, "For Jesus Himself testified that a prophet has no honor in his own country"

d. Consider that, against human common-sense, Jesus was passionate to move to the next town, Mark 1:36-39; Luke 4:42-44

4. Paul's sermons on his missionary journeys as recorded in the Acts are almost exclusively preached to complete strangers.
   E.g. "Brethren, if you have any word of exhortation for the people, say it," Acts 13:15

D. The most lasting and deep friendship is based not on longevity, but in the bond of the Holy Spirit.

E. Conclusion: Lukasse writes of the need for proclamation when building a friendship, "When we put it [proclamation] off too long, it may be difficult to broach the subject at all."[981]

---

[981]Lukasse, *Churches with Roots: Planting Churches in Post-Christian Europe* (Bromley: STL, 1990), 73-74.

INTRODUCING A BIBLICAL THEOLOGY FOR

PERSONAL EVANGELISM

Personal Evangelism Composite Chart
[a chronological graphic guide to the next section of notes]

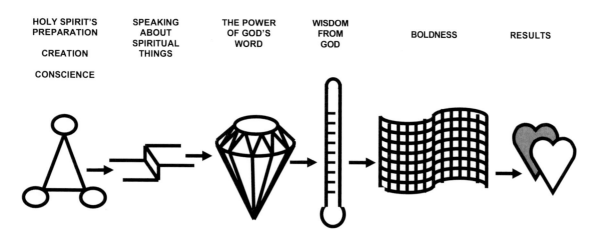

HOLY SPIRIT'S PREPARATION

CREATION

CONSCIENCE

SPEAKING ABOUT SPIRITUAL THINGS

THE POWER OF GOD'S WORD

WISDOM FROM GOD

BOLDNESS

RESULTS

CHAPTER 14
Beginning a Spiritual Conversation

Introductory Thoughts

Dealing with Strangers is Difficult in Most Cultures:

Luigi Barzini says of the French, "In France a man's privacy is sacred – even on the street."[982]

Taylor explains how to start conversations with strangers:[983]
1. Starting Reference Point: "To go into a café and start talking to another customer could easily be considered an invasion of his or her privacy, or even a proposition on you part."
2. Third Party Introduction: "Your best bet at a bar or café or shop is to wait until other customers have been presented to you through the waiter, bartender or clerk."
3. Starting Conversation: "In the beginning, the less said about your personal life or theirs, the better."

How does this impact the possibility of immediate conversations with strangers about the Gospel? E.g. I met a church planter who would not share the Gospel in a community until he befriended a "man of peace."

On the other hand, listen to some of the dating advice of Andrea McGinty, founder of the dating business called, "It's Just Lunch," and relate her advice to evangelism:
"1. Don't take dating too seriously…
"2. Improve your outlook and your luck will change…
"3. Take a proactive approach. Get off the couch and get out there! The weather's great. Dating is a numbers game. The more potential people you meet, the more likely you are to find "the one."
"4. Get the word out. Tell everyone you meet that you are available; casually mention that you're on the lookout for eligible dates.
"5. Be open. Be open to meeting someone new everywhere you go. There are lots of opportunities throughout your regular day to meet new people.
"6. Create a ripple effect. It's smart to talk to anyone, anywhere, even if the person doesn't seem to be your type. You never know who the person might introduce you to in the future."[984]

Let's apply some of Andrea's advice to evangelism by changing some words:
3. Take a proactive approach. Get off the couch and get out there! The weather's great. Evangelism is [seems to be] a numbers game. The more potential people you meet, the more likely you are to find "an interested person."
4. Get the word out. Tell everyone you meet that you are interested in their souls; casually mention that you're on the lookout for open people.
5. Be open. Be open to sharing the Gospel with someone new everywhere you go. There are lots of opportunities throughout your regular day to meet new people.
6. Create a ripple effect. It's smart to talk to anyone, anywhere, even if the person doesn't seem to be open. You never know if they might be interested in the Gospel, or if they might introduce you to someone who is in the future.

Notice Paul's words about evangelism:
"Or did I commit a sin in humbling myself that you might be exalted, because I preached [evangelized] the gospel of God to you without charge?" 2 Cor 11:7

---

[982]Sally Adamson Taylor, *Culture Shock: A Guide to Customs and Etiquette—France* (Portland: Graphic Arts Center, 1990, 1996), 134.

[983]*Ibid.*, 38-40.

[984]Andrea McGinty, "Dating Advice for Summer," *Southwest Airlines World Traveler* (June 2006), 42.

The Great Commission and Prior Relationship:

Introduction:

    Leighton Ford sought to built an argument for friendship/relational/servant/fellowship evangelism through use of the word "wait" in reference to "wait" for the reception of the Holy Spirit (Acts 1:4).

> "Not until they could show the fellowship of truth and demonstrate the deeds of truth, were they ready to speak the words of truth"[985]

However, using this text to show the need to "wait" to exemplify fellowship and deeds prior to sharing the Gospel is a *non sequetor*.

God at work in preparing total strangers—I Kings 17:8-16:

    Elijah speaking to the Sidonian Widow:
        Example of stranger-to-stranger spiritual communication
        God prepared her heart to receive Elijah, v. 9, "Arise, go to Zarephath, which belongs to Sidon, and stay there; behold, **I have commanded** a widow there to provide for you."
        Elijah saw a widow gathering sticks (she was busy), v. 10
        Asked her for bread, v. 11
        [note the parallel passages of Jesus and the Woman at the Well (John 4) and Abraham's servant and Rebekah (Gen 24)]

    Note the NT parallel of Philip and the Ethiopian Eunuch—Acts 8:26-29:
        The Eunuch was reading Scripture…
        "But an angel of the Lord spoke to Philip saying, 'Get up and go south to the road that descends from Jerusalem to Gaza.' (This is a desert *road*.) So he got up and went; and there was an Ethiopian eunuch, a court official of Candace, queen of the Ethiopians, who was in charge of all her treasure; and he had come to Jerusalem to worship, and he was returning and sitting in his chariot, and **was reading the prophet Isaiah**. Then the Spirit said to Philip, 'Go up and join this chariot.'"

    Note the NT parallel of Ananias and Saul—Acts 9:11-12:
        Saul was praying…
        "Get up and go to the street called Straight, and inquire at the house of Judas for a man from Tarsus named Saul, **for he is praying**, and he has seen in a vision a man named Ananias come in and lay his hands on him, so that he might regain his sight."

---

[985]Leighton Ford, *The Christian Persuader* (New York: Harper and Row, 1966), 68-78.

Issue: Is stranger-to-stranger evangelism valid? Where do the examples of the Bible fit?

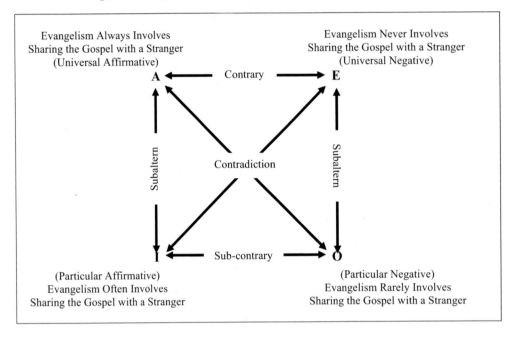

a. What does the Bible teach?

b. What are the biblical examples?

c. The interesting case of Paul evangelizing Aquila and Priscilla, Acts 18:2-3, 18, 26.

Beginning a Conversation

1. **Some biblical personal evangelism situations showing ways to enter into spiritual subjects:**

   a. Beginning with a common point of interest:
   1) Abraham's servant addresses Rebekah, a complete stranger, and offers Isaac in marriage to her after this conversation starter, Gen 24:17, "Please let me drink a little water from your jar."
   2) Elijah and the Widow from Zarephath, 1 Kings 17:10, "please give me a little water in a jar, that I may drink."
   3) Jesus and the Woman at the Well, John 4:7, "Give me a drink" (using the method of Abraham's servant).

   b. Questions about a current event:

   1) Jesus to two disciples on the road to Emmaus (not an evangelistic conversation, but a conversation started with strangers as they did not recognize Jesus, v. 16 and 31; they were also on-the-move walking, v. 13-15), Luke 24:13-25:
      Q1 "What are these words that you are exchanging with one another as you are walking?" Luke 24:17
         R_x1 "Are You the only one visiting Jerusalem and unaware of the things which have happened here in these days?"
      Q2 "What things?" Luke 24:19
         R_x2 "But also some women among us amazed us. When they were at the tomb early in the morning, and did not find His body, they came, saying that they had also seen a vision of angels, who said that He was alive. And some of those who were with us went to the tomb and found it just exactly as the women also had said; but Him they did not see."
      S "O foolish men and slow of heart to believe in all that the prophets have spoken! ..."

2) Seeking to stop false worship of themselves, Paul asked a rhetorical question: "Men, why are you doing these things?" Acts 14:15
  Whereas Simon the Sorcerer accepted the worship of men, Acts 8:9-10

c. Asking a question:[986]

1) Consider to the questioning sequence of Jacob in Gen 29:4-6:
  Q1 "My brothers, where are you from?"
    R_X1 "We are from Haran"
  Q2 "Do you know Laban the son of Nahor?"
    R_X2 "We know *him*."
  Q3 "Is it well with him?" (hashalim low?)
    R_X3 "It is well (shalom), and behold, Rachel his daughter is coming with the sheep."
  Remember that in this situation, it would seem that Jacob was speaking Hebrew, and the "sons of the east" (29:1) would have spoken Aramaic (cf. Gen 31:47)

2) Jesus to His disciples (again not a direct evangelism situation, but applicable none-the-less), Matt 16:13-20 (parallel in Luke 9:18-20):
  Q1 "Who do people say that I am?" v. 13
    R_X1 "Some *say* John the Baptist; and others, Elijah; but still others, Jeremiah, or one of the prophets"
  Q2 "Who do you say that I am?" v. 15
    R_X2 "Thou art the Christ, the Son of the living God."

3) Jesus asked the sick man at the pool of Bethseda, John 5:6-7:
  Q "Do you wish to be made well?"
    R_X "Sir, I have no man to put me into the pool when the water is stirred up, but while I am coming, another steps down before me."
  S "Arise, take up your pallet, and walk"

4) Jesus asked the man born blind, John 9:35-38:
  Q "Do you believe in the Son of Man?"
    R_X "And who is He, Lord, that I may believe in Him?"
  S "You have both seen Him, and He is the one who is talking with you"
    R_X "Lord, I believe."

5) Jesus asked two questions of those on the road to Emmaus (see point above)

6) Philip asked the Ethiopian Eunuch a question, Acts 8:30-38:
  Q1 "Do you understand what you are reading?"
    R_q1 "Well, how could I, unless someone guides me?"
  Scripture Reading (Isa 53:7-8):
    R_q2 "Please *tell me*, of whom does the prophet say this? Of himself or of someone else?" Acts 8:34
  Philip's explanation—evangelizes him about Jesus (Acts 8:35)
    R_q3 "Look! Water! What prevents me from being baptized?"
  R_a "*And Philip said, 'If you believe with all your heart, you may.' And he answered and said, 'I believe that Jesus Christ is the Son of God.' And he ordered the chariot to stop; and they both went down into the water, Philip as well as the eunuch; and he baptized him.*"

7) Sequence of theological questions, Acts 19:2-5:
  Q1 "Did you receive the Holy Spirit when you believed?" Acts 19:2
    R_X1 "No, we have not even heard whether there is a Holy Spirit."
  Q2 "Into what then were you baptized?"
    R_X2 "Into John's baptism."

---

[986]Randy Newman in *Questioning Evangelism* (Grand Rapids: Kregel, 2004) made the statement, "We can have better results from our evangelizing. Our efforts can produce more fruit advancing the kingdom further than has been recently achieved. … Perhaps the most important component to this kind of evangelism is answering questions with questions rather than giving answers" (26). Similarly, Sjogren, Ping's, and Pollock's chapter titled, "Active Wondering," includes hundreds of very helpful questions (Steve Sjogren, Dave Ping, and Doug Pollock, *Irresistible Evangelism* (Loveland, CO: Group, 2004)*, 127-45).

S   "John baptized with the baptism of repentance, telling the people to believe in Him who was coming after him, that is, in Jesus"

R$_a$ "And when they heard this, they were baptized in the name of the Lord Jesus"

d.   Initiating conversation with a statement:

1)   Jesus to His disciples, "Follow Me!" Matt 4:19; 9:9; Mark 1:17; 2:14; Luke 5:27; 9:59; John 1:43

2)   Peter and John to the Lame beggar, Acts 3:3-6:
a)   "Look at us!" v. 4
b)   "I do not possess silver and gold ..." v. 6
c)   God performs a miracle

3)   Paul cries out "Stand upright on your feet" to the lame man in Lystra, Acts 14:10

e.   Replying to a question: (e.g. Ezek 24:49, Jonah 1:8-9):

1)   In response to questions roused by the preaching of John the Baptist:
Q1 Luke 3:10, "And the crowds were questioning him, saying, 'Then what shall we do?'"
Q2 Luke 3:12, "And *some* tax collectors also came to be baptized, and they said to him, 'Teacher, what shall we do?'"
Q3 Luke 3:14, "*Some* soldiers were questioning him, saying, 'And *what about* us, what shall we do?'"

2)   Question of the self-justifying lawyer, Luke 10:25-29:
Q1 "Teacher, what shall I do to inherit eternal life?" Luke 10:25
R$_x$1 Jesus responds by quoting Deut 6:5 and Lev 19:18
Q2 "And who is my neighbor?" Luke 10:29

3)   "Good Teacher, what shall I do to inherit eternal life?" Mark 10:17 (cf. Luke 18:18); notice the difference in the Matthew 19:16 version: "Teacher, what good thing shall I do that I may obtain eternal life?"

4)   Samaritan Woman sequence, John 4:9, 11-12:
Q1 "How is it that You, being a Jew, ask me for a drink since I am a Samaritan woman?"
Q2 "Sir, You have nothing to draw with and the well is deep; where then do You get that living water?"
Q3 "You are not greater than our father Jacob, are You, who gave us the well, and drank of it himself and his sons and his cattle?"

5)   After the feeding of the 5,000 in John 6:
Q1 "Rabbi, when did You get here?" John 6:25 (they understood that some kind of miracle had occurred, cf. 6:2, 11-14)
R$_x$1 "You seek me not because you saw sings, but because you ate the loaves, and were filled..." John 6:26
Q2 "What shall we do, so that we may work the works of God?" John 6:28
Jesus: "This is the work of God, that you believe in Him whom He has sent," John 6:29
Q3 "What then do You do for a sign, so that we may see, and believe You? What work do You perform?" John 6:30

6)   Pilate and Jesus sequence in John 18:
Q1 "Are You the King of the Jews?" John 18:33
R$_q$1 "Are you saying this on your own initiative, or did others tell you about Me?" John 18:34
Q2 "I am not a Jew, am I?" (rhetorical question) John 18:35
Pilate about Jesus' Jewish ancestry: "Your own nation and the chief priests delivered You up to me," John 18:35
Q3 "What have You done?"
R$_x$3 My kingdom is not of this world. ..." John 18:36
Q4 "So You are a king?" John 18:37
R$_x$4 "You say *correctly* that I am a king. ...." John 18:37
Q5 "What is truth?" (last recorded words of conversation) John 18:38

7) Following the Pentecostal speaking in tongues:
   Q1 "What does this mean?" Acts 2:12
   Peter's sermon
   Q2 "What shall we do, brothers?" Acts 2:37

8) Classic salvation question:
   Q1 "What must I do to be saved?" Acts 16:31
   R_X1 "Believe in the Lord Jesus, and you shall be saved, you and your household," Act 16:31

9) Prior to Sotics and Epicureans forcefully bringing Paul to Areopagus, Acts 17:18-20
   Q1 "What would this idle babbler wish to say?
   R_X1 "He seems to be a proclaimer of strange deities"
   Narrator, "because he was evangelizing Jesus and the resurrection"
   Q2 "May we know what this new teaching is which you are proclaiming [speaking]?For you are bringing some strange things to our ears; so we want to know what these things mean"

10) Notice as well the tricky questions that the Pharisees asked Jesus in Matt 22:15-46; Mark 12:28-37; Luke 20:1-40, can we expect any different?
   Consider also in this light the many Inquisition questions gathered by Thomas Aquinas in his *Summa*

f. Replying to a statement:
    1) Jesus to several, Matt 8:19-22; Luke 9:57-58, 61-62
    2) Jesus to Nicodemus, John 3:3
    3) As to the Rich Young Ruler, Mark. 10:18.
    4) Jesus and the Thief on the Cross, Luke 23:42-43, "Jesus, remember me when You come in Your kingdom!" And He said to him, "Truly I say to you, today you shall be with Me in Paradise."

g. Reaching out to an inquisitive individual:
    1) Jesus and Zaccheus, Luke 19:5

h. Responding to an invitation:
    1) Jesus at Sychar, John 4:40-41
    2) Peter to men from Cornelius:
       Q1 "Behold, I am the one you are looking for; what is the reason for which you have come?" Acts 10:21
          R_X1 "Cornelius, a centurion, a righteous and God-fearing man well spoken of by the entire nation of the Jews, was *divinely* directed by a holy angel to send for you *to come* to his house and hear a message from you," Acts 10:22
       Q2 "I ask for what reason you have sent for me," Acts 10:29
          R_X2 "Four days ago to this hour, … And so I sent to you immediately, and you have been kind enough to come. Now then, we are all here present before God to hear all that you have been commanded by the Lord," Acts 10:30-33
       S3 "I most certainly understand *now* that God is not one to show partiality, … through His name everyone who believes in Him receives forgiveness of sins," Acts 10:34-43
       E4 "While Peter was still speaking these words, the Holy Spirit fell upon all those who were listening to the message," Acts 10:44
          R_X4 "Surely no one can refuse the water for these to be baptized who have received the Holy Spirit just as we *did*, can he?" Acts 10:41
    3) Paul to Felix and Drusilla, Acts 24:24-25

i. Speaking with aggressive individuals:
    1) In Athens the Stoics and Epicurians took the offensive on Paul—note the progressively more aggressive language:
       a) Marketplace conversations:
          (1) Paul was reasoning (διαλέγομαι) with whomever happened to be present, Acts 17:17
          (2) The Stoics and Epicurians were conversing/dialoguing (συμβάλλω) with Paul, Acts 17:18
          (3) Paul was evangelizing (εὐαγγελίζω) Jesus and the resurrection, Acts 17:18

(4) The Stoics and Epicurians felt that Paul was [ignorantly] throwing around words (Gk. σπερμολόγος; Lat. *seminiverbius*; Matthew Henry, "this scatterer of words")

    (a) It is highly likely that they meant to mock Paul and get some free laughs, much like when Paul was the *piece de resistance* [the main course] at the gathering in Caesarea (Acts 25:23ff.) when he was brought before King Agrippa with great pomp and likewise before all the important men of the city

    (b) It is also highly likely that this hapax legomena (σπερμολόγος) was meant as a derogatory term

  b) Terminology for taking Paul to "Mars Hill" was quite harsh:

    (1) They took him (ἐπιλαμβάνομαι), Acts 17:19, same word used in (these following include all the NT uses of that same form of the verb):

      (a) Crucifixion narrative, Luke 23:26)

      (b) When Paul was seized and dragged before the authorities, Acts 16:19

      (c) When Sosthenes was dragged and beaten, Acts 18:17

      (d) When they grabbed Paul in Jerusalem and threw him out of the city to kill him, Acts 21:30

    (2) And brought him (ἄγω), Acts 17:19

    (3) Both words are also used together in Acts 9:27 of Barnabas bringing Paul to the Apostles

j. Rebuking a disruptive individual:

  1) Jesus rebuking the demoniac from Gerasenes:

    Mark 5:7, "What business do we have with each other, Jesus, Son of the Most High God? I implore You by God, do not torment me!"

    Mark 5:8, "Come out of the man, you unclean spirit!"

  2) Slave girl with a spirit of divination, Acts 16:18

k. Mentioning Christ in conversation:

  1) John the Baptist to two disciples, John 1:35-36

l. Testifying about what Jesus had done (cf. Job 33:27-28):

  1) The Man from Gerasenes, Mark 5:20; Luke 8:39

  2) The Woman at the Well, John 4:39

m. Finding someone for the purpose of sharing Christ:

  Introduction: This fits with the purpose of Christ "to seek and to save those who are lost" (Luke 19:10). Thus Jesus sought out persons for conversation.

  Hence the complaint of the Pharisees and scribes: Luke 15:2 (NKJ), "And the Pharisees and scribes complained, saying, "This Man receives [literally: "looks for," from προσδέχομαι] sinners and eats with them."

  1) Andrew and Simon Peter, John 1:41

  2) Philip and Nathanael, John 1:45

  3) Jesus and the paralytic, John 5:14

  4) Jesus and the man born blind, John 9:35

  5) Paul and Lydia, Acts 16:14

  6) Paul in Athens, Acts 17:17

n. Starting a conversation by mistake:

  1) Eli began his conversation with Hannah because he falsely assumed that she was drunk, 1 Sam 1:12-14

    a) In the resulting conversation, he spoke a blessing into her life, 1 Sam 1:16!

2. Some General Principles:

Introduction: The way to begin a conversation is dependent on the specific situation, the style of evangelism and the personality of the one who is witnessing. However, several general principles can be applied.[987]

a. Flexibility, sensitivity and creativity is needed to start spiritual conversations with others.

b. Begin with a common point of interest:

1) Evaluate what the person would be interested in by his appearance.

2) Some ideas of possible areas of interest:
   a) What you or the other person is doing
   b) The weather
   c) Some known news item that might spark the interest of the individual.

c. Ask a question, make a comment or ask for help. These and other openers are all valid ways to start a conversation. Some possible questions:

1) On the church campus (as in Block Party or other special event):
   a) Hi, my name is _____, have we met before?
   b) Are you from _____? How long have you lived here?

2) Further questions, or off church site:
   a) Are you a praying man?
   b) Has the Lord given you a church that you attend?
   c) Are you a believing person?
   d) Do you consider yourself a spiritual person?

d. Be friendly and cheerful as it is appropriate to the context (culturally and socially).

e. Some Bible verses provide appropriate social guidelines for evangelizing: [988]
   1) Respect was is right in the sight of all men, Rom 12:17
   2) Honor all men, 1 Pet 2:17
   3) Give no offense, 1 Cor. 10:32-33; 2 Cor. 6:3
   4) To speak evil of no one, to be peaceable, gentle, showing all humility to all men, Titus 3:2
   5) Not returning evil for evil, or reviling for reviling, 1 Pet. 3:8-9

f. Remember the importance of a person's name, Luke 19:5, 3 John 14 (e.g. John 1:47-51).

3. Further Ideas for Starting Spiritual Conversations:

a. In street evangelism or door-to-door, I usually get right to the point (as will be noted in the next Chapter)

b. In stores, workers have name tags, or someone might tell you their name:

1) If you know the biblical meaning of a name, you can say something like:
   a) "Jonathan! That's a great name! Do you know that it's a biblical name?"
   b) "Do you know what it means?"
   c) "It means, the Lord is gracious!"
   d) "Has the Lord been gracious to you?"

---

[987]Edwards has a practical discussion of ways to begin a evangelistic conversation (Edwards, 116-30).

[988]Charles Grandison Finney, *Finney on Revival,* arranged by E. E. Shelhamer (Minneapolis: Bethany House, n.d.), 66-74 is a chapter entiltled, "To Win Souls Requires Wisdom." The need to be respectful is number 9 of his 22 practical and insightful points. R.A. Torrey in *How to Work for Christ* (Westwood, NJ; Revell, 1901), 174-75, wrote, "Be courteous," and "Avoid unwarranted familiarities with those with whom you deal."

2) If you know something about a biblical character by that name, you can something like:
   a) "Daniel! Now that's a great name! Did you know that your name comes from the Bible?"
   b) "Did you know that Daniel was a prophet of God?"
   c) "He was thrown into a lions den one time, because he would not stop praying to God"

3) There are many names with which these ideas can be used:
   a) Benjamin means "Son of my right hand"
   b) Joshua means "The Lord saves"—this is a particularly good name to use, as its NT Greek transliteration is "Jesus"
   c) Daniel means "Beloved of God"

c. Tattoos:
1) Often tattoos have meanings for people
2) A comment like, "That's a great looking tattoo! What does it mean to you?" can be a great conversation starter

d. Jewelry:
1) Sometimes jewelry can be a good conversation starter
2) For example, "That is a massive cross! Do you know what happened on the cross?"
3) Or again, "That's a great looking cross! Aren't you glad that we also celebrate Easter?"

e. More direct questions (as will also be elaborated further in the next chapter):
1) "How are you doing spiritually?"
2) "Do you have peace with God?"
3) "What is the condition of your soul?" (ascribed to Wesley)

f. Be ready for God to open your eyes, as you ask Him to open your mouth. There are many ways to enter into spiritual conversations with others!

4. Things to Look for:[989]

There are several things to look for when first addressing a person on a spiritual level:

a. Contrite heart:
1) A contrite heart evidences the preparatory work of the Holy Spirit

b. Points of Pain/Need:
1) Often God may bring points of pain in a person's life that make them open to the Gospel (as noted in the previous lesson).

c. Pattern of Prayer:
1) Give attention to the fact that someone may be praying for the individual you are contacting for Christ
2) You may want to ask the person if someone is praying for them.

d. Witness of the Word:
1) Sometimes the contact may have an unexplainable urge to read the Word of God, even prior to becoming a Christian, you may be an answer to the urgings of the Holy Spirit in their heart.

Conclusion: As you look for these items, you will likewise note if God is speaking through you to the person, John 6:45

5. Lifestyle Evangelism Situations:

a. **Definition**: People we see regularly in an everyday context will require a different conversational opening than in initiative evangelism situations. These lifestyle contacts are often found in the workplace and in living situations. Unsaved family members can also be put into the lifestyle category.

---

[989]Points b-d adapted from comments of Fred Jennings, Spiritual Emphasis Week, Crown College, 16-18 September 1992.

b. **Socratic Evangelism**:

1) Use points of conversation to bring in a biblical approach to the subject in an appropriate manner in order to spark interest in spiritual things. Strong intentionality is often needed to accomplish this. To this end, questions can be very helpful. There seems to be a renewed emphasis on the place of questions, as noted in a footnote above.

2) Steve Sjogren offers many helpful suggestions for asking questions, which he called "Active Wondering"; in this chapter he provided "99 Wondering Questions," such as:

   a) "Would you share the greatest piece of wisdom ever passed on to you?"
   b) "How did 9/11 affect your view God and the world?"
   c) "If you could ask God three questions, what would they be?"
   d) "How would you change the way you were raised?"[990]

   While Sjogren seemed to teach against an outright initiative approach to evangelism, communicated an anti-seminary mindset,[991] and taught a non-substitutionary approach to the Gosple,[992] his "Active Wondering" chapter fits perfectly with initiating Gospel conversations!

3) Likewise, Randy Newman wrote of another type of Socratic evangelism, which he calls "Solomonic Soulwinning" that is, answering questions with questions:

   "We can have better results from our evangelizing. Our efforts can produce more fruit advancing the kingdom further than has been recently achieved. ... Perhaps the most important component to this kind of evangelism is answering questions with questions rather than giving answers." [993]

   The heart of Newman's book is an apologetic response to seven questions frequently asked by non-Christians.

4) Follow up on the interest shown on a given subject can be done by guiding the conversation towards the Gospel. This is where knowledge of the entire breadth of various subjects in the Bible becomes helpful (e.g. see the Book of Psalms).

c. **Servant Evangelism**:

1) Actively look for ways to serve the people that the Lord has laid on your heart, asking God to provide openings to share the Gospel, following the pattern of Titus 3, "to be ready for every good work, to speak evil of no one, to be peaceable, gentle, showing all humility to all men," Titus 3:1-2

2) Service will provide proximity to the people, which can sometimes lead to open doors for sharing the Gospel

d. **The Use of Testimony**:

1) Be open to share your testimony in conjunction with the subject discussed, weaving in the main points of the Gospel, including the prayer to accept Christ.

---

[990]Steve Sjogren, Dave Ping, and Doug Pollock, *Irresistible Evangelism* (Loveland, CO: Group, 2004), 127-45.

[991]"He [Steve] was finally going to fulfill a lifelong dream. In September he would be attending seminary for the first time. He tells about his experience:

"...As the day wore on, my disappointment and cynicism increased, Maybe you've heard this uncharitable adage: Those who can, do. Those who can't, teach. Those who can do neither, lecture. Seminary was feeling more and more like a bad dream in which I had died and gone to church hell. My punishment was to be eternally lectured by folks who were totally out of touch with present-day life and ministry" (ibid., 41-42).

[992]"Many Christians talk about developing an intimate *personal relationship* with God, but the message they present to not-yet-Christians focuses almost exclusively on explaining how the atoning death of Jesus satisfies the requirements of God's justice. ...Talking about doctrines such as justification by faith and atonement by the substitutionary death of Jesus is usually unnecessarily confusing. These doctrines may accurately explain what happens (in a legal sense) when we pray to accept Jesus, but they don't paint a very relational picture.

"...Relationship is the heart of the matter" (ibid., 149).

[993]Randy Newman, *Questioning Evangelism* (Grand Rapids: Kregel, 2004), 26.

    2) The testimony often will not deal directly with salvation or conversion, but with some other aspect of life; this is where Scripture can gently be quoted on whatever the topic may be

    3) As interest persists, challenge the friend to accept Christ and ask if you can pray with/for him.

  e. **Follow-up**:

    1) As in any style of evangelism, when spiritual things are touched upon, the reproach of Christ is felt, which will divide the interested and the uninterested

    2) You have planed the seed for the uninterested, so then focus on the interested, while remaining as conversant as possible with the uninterested

    3) Share the Gospel, etc.

6. Contact Evangelism Situations:

  a. **Door-to-door evangelism**:

    1) Begin with your name, the name of the church or organization you are with, and the reason you are there—"to share the Gospel, of how Jesus died on the cross for your sins and rose again."

    2) In door-to-door it is often good to be straight forward and lead right into the Gospel. Some diversion onto another topic might be good to lighten up the conversation. But get to the Gospel quickly.

    3) Silence will work against you. Be ready to speak immediately when somebody gets to the door.

    4) Sometimes a questionnaire can be effective. A good concise questionnaire leading to the Gospel can flow naturally into an effective time of sharing the Gospel (sample questionnaires follow in this chapter).

    5) Be thoughtful and considerate of the person. Real Christian love shows through.

    6) An honest mention of how much time may be necessary.

  b. **Street evangelism** (one-on-one or several people):

    1) A friendly salutation is a good start.

    2) Entering right into the purpose of the encounter (to share the Gospel of Jesus Christ) with the individual is helpful right away.

    3) Be aware of how much time the person has and summarize the Gospel appropriately.

7. Example of Starting a Conversation:

In 1754, Baptist home missionary John Gano had this conversation with his landlord in North Carolina:

  "Landlord — "Are you a trader?"

  "Mr. Gano — "Yes."

  "L. — "Do you find trading to answer your purpose?"

  "G. — "Not so well as I could wish."

  "L. — "Probably the goods do not suit."

  "G. — "No one has complained of the goods."

  "L. — "You hold them too high."

  "G. — "Any one may have them below his own price."

  "L. — "I will trade with you on these terms."

  "G. — "I will cheerfully comply with them. Will not gold tried in the fire, yea, that which is better than the fine gold, wine and milk, durable riches and righteousness, without money and without price, suit you?"

  "L. — "Oh, I believe you are a minister."

  "G. — "I am, and I have a right to proclaim free grace wherever I go."

  "This," says Mr. Gano, "laid the foundation for the evening's conversation, and I must acknowledge his kindness, though he was not very desirous of *trading*, after he discovered who I was."[994]

Conclusion—Regarding the Need for Personal Work:

    As a rule, the intensity of the appeal is in inverse proportion to the area covered; in other words, the greater your audience, the smaller the probability of your appeal coming home to a single heart. I once heard Henry Ward Beecher say, "The longer I live, the more confidence I have in those sermons preached where one man is the minister and one man is the congregation; where there's no question as to who is meant when the preacher says, 'Thou art the man.'" Years after this, I heard the Rev. Dr. Nevius speak similarly as to the mission field in China.

---

[994]Excerpt from John Gano's Journal ("John Gano [1736-1804]"; available at: http://www.therestorationmovement.com/gano,john.htm; accessed: 20 Oct 2008).

He said he wanted no great preachers in his field. That was not the sort of missionary who were needed in China. If he could find a man who could talk familiarly, face to face, with another man, wherever he met him, he had missionary work for that kind of man in China. This is the way to do Christian work in China, or in America. …

It is not merely that individual work is a helpful addition to other work of the minister, but that it is the chief work, and that from it come strength and power for other work.[995]

---

[995]Charles G. Trumbull, *Taking Men Alive,* 33-34.

Chapter 14 Appendix

Admonitions to Guide Our Evangelism from 2 Timothy

1. Do not be ashamed of the Gospel, 2 Tim 1:8
    a. Do not be ashamed to the testimony of the Lord
    b. Do not be ashamed of me [Paul] His prisoner:
        1) Was this a hint that Timothy may have been ashamed of the evangelism methodology of Paul that landed him in prison?
    c. Paul himself was not ashamed of himself nor of his evangelizing, but rather he was fully assured that his being in prison was because he was a herald of the Gospel, and that he was in God's safekeeping, 2 Tim 1:12
    d. Then Paul gave examples of those who were and were not ashamed of him:
        2 Tim 1:15, "This you know, that all those in Asia have turned away from me, among whom are Phygellus and Hermogenes"
        2 Tim 1:16-17, "he Lord grant mercy to the household of Onesiphorus, for he often refreshed me, and was not ashamed of my chain; but when he arrived in Rome, he sought me out very zealously and found *me*"

2. Join me in suffering for the Gospel, 2 Tim 1:8
    a. Was it not true from the context that Timothy was so shameful of evangelizing, that he needed to be prodded by Paul to press on in the work of evangelizing?
    b. Timothy's timidity in evangelizing was a real problem, which Paul dealt with gently, but directly (reminiscent of Matt 10:33; Mark 8:38; Luke 9:26; 12:9):
        "*This is* a faithful saying: For if we died with *Him*, We shall also live with *Him*.
        "If we endure, We shall also reign with *Him*. If we deny *Him*, He also will deny us.
        "If we are faithless, He remains faithful; He cannot deny Himself" (2Tim 2:11-13)
    c. Finally, Paul commanded Timothy to "do the work of an evangelist":
        2 Tim 4:5, "But you be watchful in all things, endure afflictions, do the work of an evangelist, fulfill your ministry"

3. Various other admonitions:
    a. Retain the standard of sound teaching, 2 Tim 1:13
    b. Guard the treasure entrusted, 2 Tim 2:14
    c. Be strong in the grace that is in Christ Jesus, 2 Tim 2:1
    d. Suffer hardship with me as a soldier, 2 Tim 2:3
    e. Flee youthful lusts, 2 Tim 2:22

4. Be diligent as a workman, rightly "dividing" the word of truth, 2 Tim 2:15

5. The need to avoid quarrels:
    a. Not to wrangle about words, 2 Tim 2:14
    b. Avoid worldly and empty chatter, 2 Tim 2:16-17
    c. Refuse foolish and ignorant speculation, 2 Tim 2:23
    d. The Lord's bondservant must not be quarrelsome, 2 Tim 2:24

6. Proper characteristics:
    a. The need for gentleness, 2 Tim 2:24
    b. The need for love and patience, 2 Tim 3:10

7. What about avoiding "Striving" in 2 Tim 2:24 (KJV)?
    a. Does this admonition encourage us to avoid discussing spiritual things with others?
    b. Let's study what the verb means, looking at how it has been translated:
        Psalm 46:10 (NAS) "Cease *striving* and know that I am God; I will be exalted among the nations, I will be exalted in the earth."

An Analysis of the Translation of 2 Tim 2:24

Wycliffe, 2nd ed (1388)	Tyndale (1534)	KJV (1611/1769)	Webster's (1833)	Bible in Basic English (1949/1964)	RSV (1952)	NET (2005)
But it bihoueth the seruaunt of the Lord to chide not; but to be mylde to alle men, able to teche,	But the servaunt of the lorde must not stryve: but must be peasable vnto all men and apte to teache and one that can suffre: the evyll in meknes	And the servant of the Lord must not strive; but be gentle unto all *men*, apt to teach, patient,	And the servant of the Lord must not contend; but be gentle to all {men}, apt to teach, patient,	For it is not right for the Lord's servant to make trouble, but he is to be gentle to all, ready in teaching, putting up with wrong,	And the Lord's servant must not be quarrelsome but kindly to every one, an apt teacher, forbearing,	And the Lord's slave must not engage in heated disputes but be kind toward all, an apt teacher, patient,

    c.   It would seem that the verb does not mean that one ought not enter into discussion with others (even uncomfortable discussion), but rather avoid being quarrelsome.

    d.   Herein, the application of this admonition to evangelism should be tempered by two things:

        1)   The commands of the Great Commission

        2)   The examples of obedience of the Great Commission in the Book of Acts

Chronological Issues in Determining the Usefulness of Using or Purposes in Using Various Conversations in the Bible For Training in Personal Evangelism

In order to properly place each conversation in its proper place in the development of salvation history, let us begin by considering the distinctions between the Old and New Covenants. Then considering distinctions among and within New Testament books.

Consider the possibilities: when is the exact break between the Old Covenant and the New Covenant?
- The annunciation to Mary?
- The birth of John the Baptist?
- The birth of Jesus the Christ?
- The baptism of Jesus the Christ?
- The transfiguration event?
- The death of Christ?
- The resurrection of Christ?
- The giving of the Great Commission?
- The ascension of Christ?
- The coming of the Holy Spirit at Pentecost?

While all of these may or may not have a level of plausibility, depending largely on theological presuppositions of the subscriber, it appears that the death of Christ is the preferred possibility for several reasons:
- In Luke 23:45, at the end of the crucifixion, the curtain dividing the Holy of Holies from the Holy Place was torn, signifying by a miraculous act, that the old had gone, behold the new had come;
- Jesus, then sensing in His Spirit that all had been accomplished, in Luke 23:46, breathed His last breathe;
- In Matt 27:50-51, that reverses the order of the last breath and the tearing of the curtain, we also find mention of an earthquake and saints being raised to life for a brief time, prior to the resurrection of Christ (Matt 27:51-52)!
- Further, Jesus came to "fulfill" and He said the rulership (kingdom) of God was "at hand." Therefore, during His lifetime, He still gave an expectation of a future event that had not yet happened.

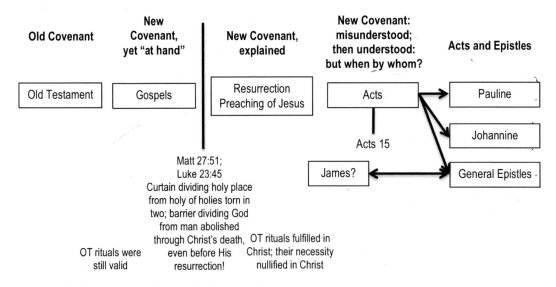

Whilde Jesus gradually revealed His death and resurrection throughout His life; even after the events, the disciples did not understand their meaning (cf. Luke 24). When came their breakthrough?

Or consider:
- In the apostles full understanding of the doctrine of salvation (as it relates to the OT law), where does the Jerusalem council fit in? Where they not to be the pillars of the church, and those who would remember the teachings of Jesus and pass them on?
- In the Pauline conception of justification by faith, where does that fit in with Acts 15?

- Therefore, do not (1) the Jerusalem Council and (2) the special revelation to Paul actually fill out the apostles' understanding and the NT's teaching of the concept of the doctrine of salvation (especially it appears as regards (a) the OT food laws, laws of association, and circumcision, and (b) justification by faith alone)? And if this is so, does this not provide another important doctrinal marker in the history of the preaching of salvation?
- If so, how does this relate to the developing sacramental or ritualistic doctrine of salvation in the "Early Church" and passed down to our time and further evolving in the traditions of the territorial churches?
- How do we interpret the teachings of Christ in the Gospels in light of the view after Acts 15? (esp. Sermon on the Mount; cf. Matt 22:34-40 and parallels)?
- How do we apply the examples of "evangelism" in the Gospels (Synoptic and Johannine), as well as those in Acts prior to Acts 15?
- Where does Book of James fit into this schema?
- Why did it appear that there were still some who (1) followed the prohibition laws of Acts 15 (e.g. 1 Cor 9-10) and (2) were believers and zealous for the law (Acts 21)?

Considering the full expression of the knowledge of the gospel chronologically in the New Testament:
- John the Baptist: His message, and the disciples of John the Baptist in Acts 19
- The Apostles in Matt 10; Mark 6; Luke 9 and 10
- Jesus gradually unfolding His death and resurrection to the Apostles (hence, the gospel)
- The Gospel in John, as considered in light of the Pauline Gospel and its pre-cross topic with a post-cross writing
- The disciples on the road to Emmaus and Jesus explaining the cross and resurrection, Luke 24
- The Great Commissions and their impact on the preaching of the gospel
- The Gospel proclamation in Acts
  - Pre-Jerusalem Council
  - Post-Jerusalem Council
  - Complexities of the Jerusalem Council on Acts 21 and "those of James" in Gal 2
- Paul's explanation of the gospel in Romans (et al.) as the final explanation of the gospel of justification by faith alone
- What of the offense of the cross, in light of observing the law?

CHAPTER 15
Getting into Spiritual Things

Introduction:

The Gospel is the most important subject of conversation. Yet, in friendship-type evangelism, as well as all other one-on-one types of evangelism, the hardest barrier to cross is the spiritual barrier. There are several truths concerning this stage in the sharing process, and there are also practical principles concerning this stage.

1.   The Goal of Sharing is a Conscience-to-Conscience Conversation about the Gospel!

Because it is so personal, conscience-to-conscience, this may very well be one of the reasons that evangelizing can be so threatening to Christians:

a.   Some NT verses describing this idea:

    1)   2 Cor 5:11 (ESV) "Therefore, knowing the fear of the Lord, we persuade others. But what we are is known to God, and I hope it is known also to your conscience."

    2)   Heb 4:12-13 (Gen), "For the worde of God is liuely, and mightie in operation, and sharper then any two edged sword, and entreth through, euen vnto the diuiding asunder of the soule and the spirit, and of the ioints, and the marow, and is a discerner of the thoughtes, and the intents of the heart. Neither is there any creature, which is not manifest in his sight: but all things are naked and open vnto his eyes, with whome we haue to doe."

    3)   Rom 2:14-16 (ESV), "For when Gentiles, who do not have the law, by nature do what the law requires, they are a law to themselves, even though they do not have the law. They show that the work of the law is written on their hearts, while their conscience also bears witness, and their conflicting thoughts accuse or even excuse them on that day when, according to my gospel, God judges the secrets of men by Christ Jesus."

        a)   The phrase "according to my gospel," uses the Greek preposition kata [], which often means "against" (with the genitive) or "through" (with the accusative)

        b)   Since "gospel" is in the accusative, another wording would be "through my gospel"

        c)   2:16 would therefore read thus: "on that day when, through my gospel, God judges the secrets of men by Jesus Christ"

        d)   If this is a correct reading, then there are several resulting considerations:

            (1)   The gospel becomes the instrument of judgment

            (2)   The gospel becomes the instrument of judgment on the day it is shared

            (3)   Jesus so embodies the power of the gospel, that it is actually Him judging the hearts of men through the instrument of the gospel!

    4)   1 Cor 2:12 (NAS), "For our proud confidence is this, the testimony of our conscience, that in holiness and godly sincerity, not in fleshly wisdom but in the grace of God, we have conducted ourselves in the world, and especially toward you"

    5)   2 Cor 4:2 (NKJ), "But we have renounced the hidden things of shame, not walking in craftiness nor handling the word of God deceitfully, but by manifestation of the truth commending ourselves to every man's conscience in the sight of God"

    6)   A result of this conscience-to-conscience communication: 2 Cor 4:1-4 (Wycliffe 2nd ed), "Therfor we that han this admynystracioun, aftir this that we han getun merci, faile we not, but do we awei the preue thingis of schame, not walkinge in sutil gile, nether doynge auoutrye bi the word of God, but in schewynge of the treuthe comendynge vs silf to ech conscience of men bifor God. For if also oure gospel is kyuerid, in these that perischen it is kyuerid; in which God hath blent the soulis of vnfeithful men of this world, that the liytnyng of the gospel of the glorie of Crist, which is the ymage of God, schyne not."

b.   Consider the example of Samson and Delilah:

    1)   After she pestered him for many days, and after he had told her half-truths and lies (Judges 17), then he shared with her all that was in his heart… and she knew it:

        Judges 16:16-18, "And it came about when she pressed him daily with her words and urged him, that his soul was annoyed to death. So he told her all *that was* in his heart and said to her, 'A razor has never come on my head, for I have been a Nazirite to God from my mother's womb. If I am shaved, then my strength will leave me and I shall become weak and be like any *other* man.' When Delilah saw that he had told her all *that was* in his heart, she sent and called the lords of the Philistines, saying, 'Come up once more, for he has told me all *that is* in his heart.' Then the lords of the Philistines came up to her, and brought the money in their hands."

2. Some thoughts:

    a) Evangelism is truly sharing all that is in one's heart (cf. John 4:25)

    b) Sharing all one's heart is threatening!

    c) Other people recognize when we are sharing all that is in our heart, perhaps because:

        1) This is the degree to which we should seek the Lord, Deut 4:29, "But from there you will seek the LORD your God, and you will find *Him* if you search for Him with all your heart and all your soul"

        2) This degree to which our love for the Lord should go, Deut 6:5, "And you shall love the LORD your God with all your heart and with all your soul and with all your might"

        3) This is the degree to which we should serve the Lord, Deut 11:13, "And it shall come about, if you listen obediently to my commandments which I am commanding you today, to love the LORD your God and to serve Him with all your heart and all your soul…"

        4) God will test if we love Him to this extent, Deut 13:3, "you shall not listen to the words of that prophet or that dreamer of dreams; for the LORD your God is testing you to find out if you love the LORD your God with all your heart and with all your soul" (cf. 2 Chr 32:31)
            (a) In this light, is our obedience in evangelizing a test of our love for God, and/or Jesus? I truly think that it is!

        5) Our obedience of God and His Word should be "with all of our heart," Deut 26:16, "This day the LORD your God commands you to do these statutes and ordinances. You shall therefore be careful to do them with all your heart and with all your soul"

        6) Ultimately, praise the Lord, our love for God is a work of God in our hearts, Deut 30:6, "Moreover the LORD your God will circumcise your heart and the heart of your descendants, to love the LORD your God with all your heart and with all your soul, in order that you may live"

        7) And yet, our responsibility to obey is not annexed away, Deut 30:10, "if you obey the LORD your God to keep His commandments and His statutes which are written in this book of the law, if you turn to the LORD your God with all your heart and soul"

        8) All that is in God's heart seems to be directly related to what is in His Word, 2 Kgs 10:30, "And the LORD said to Jehu, 'Because you have done well in executing what is right in My eyes, *and* have done to the house of Ahab according to all that *was* in My heart, your sons of the fourth generation shall sit on the throne of Israel'"
            (a) Is this not also true of our Lord's Great Commission?
            (b) Is not obedience to the Great Commission the way of blessing in our time?

        9) See also, 1 Sam 9:19; 12:20, 24; 14:7; 2 Sam 7:3; 1 Kgs 2:4; 2:44; 8:48; 11:37; 14:8; 15:14; 2 Kgs 23:3, 25; 1 Chr 17:2; 28:9; 2 Chr 6:38; 15:12, 15; 22:9; 31:21; 34:31; Psa 9:1; 86:12; Prov 3:5; Jer 29:13; 32:41; Joel 2:12; Zeph 3:4.

    d) Sharing all one's heart can be used against the person sharing it
        1) Hence all the warnings about persecution from the lips of Jesus (cf. Matt 10:16…)
        2) Hence all the examples of persecution in the Bible, including the crucifixion of Jesus!

    e) Interestingly, Philip's question to the Ethiopian Eunuch included the concept of "all your heart," perhaps as a caveat (with the baptism of Simon the Sorcerer happening not long before this event):
        1) Acts 8:37 (NKJ), "Then Philip said, 'If you believe with all your heart, you may.' And he answered and said, 'I believe that Jesus Christ is the Son of God.'"
        2) Please notice:
            (a) The concept of "all your heart" seems to be a caveat for true baptism;
            (b) By antithetic, there is the possibility of not believing "with all your heart":
                (1) As was the case of Simon the Sorcerer, as the thought of his heart was not right (Acts 8:21-23; cf. Deut 29:18-19)
                (2) As was also the case of some who believed in the Book of John (John 8:31ff; 12:42-43; cf. John 2:23-25)

(c) Again, the baptizer does not know the inner heart of the person being baptized, all he can see is the outer man:
(1) See his eyes (Matt 6:22-23) and
(2) Hear his words (Matt 12:34).
(d) In this case we have the verbal confession of the baptized before he is baptized, "I believe that Jesus Christ is the Son of God"
(e) Notice also that the Bible is clear, a verbal confession alone does not save, Matt 7:21!

e) It is very fascinating that, in the entire Bible, there are only several other examples of sharing all that is in one's heart:
1) The queen of Sheba shared all that is in her heart to Solomon, 1 Kgs 10:2; 2 Chr 9:1

2. The Truths in Opening the Conversation into the Gospel:

a. This is where one must be willing to carry the "shame of the cross."

b. Likewise, this is a most crucial barrier to cross for the eternal destiny of the person with whom you are talking:

Johan Lukasse wrote of crossing this barrier, "Some people are not open to the Gospel. They hide behind an armour of indifference as soon as spiritual things are touched upon."[996] Yet until we seek to cross this barrier we cannot ascertain a person's spiritual condition in order to guide them on to the Savior.

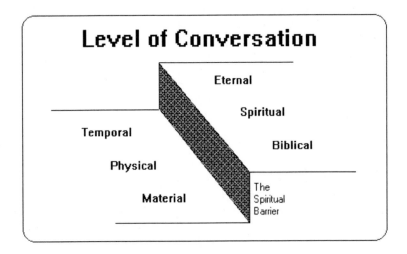

c. This is where the spiritual battle becomes evident:

"Never to the present day can I speak to a single soul for Christ without being reminded by Satan that I am in danger of harming the cause by introducing it just now. If there is one thing that Satan is sensitive about, it is the danger of a Christian's harming the cause he loves by speaking of Christ to a needy soul. He [Satan] has more than once, or twice, or thrice, kept me from speaking on the subject by his sensitive pious caution, and he has tried a thousand times to do so. Therefore my experience leads me to suppose that he is urging other persons to try any method for souls except the best one.

"Have we not the answer here to the question which was passed over a moment ago, as to why this work is the hardest work in the world? Just because it is the most effective work for Christ, the Devil opposes it most bitterly, and always will while he is permitted to oppose anything good. The Devil strikes hardest and most persistently at the forces which will, if effective, hurt his cause most. He devotes his chief energies to those from whom he has most to fear; their sides he never leaves. Therefore the worker who seeks to win individuals to Christ may rest assured that he has, by entering upon that work, served notice upon the Devil for a life-and-death conflict; and that notice will be accepted by the Devil as an obligation to swerve the worker from his

---

[996]Johan Lukasse, *Churches with Roots: Planting Churches in Post-Christian Europe* (Bromley: STL, 1990),
79.

purpose whenever, by any subtle means in the Devil's power, this can be done. Let us write down large in our mental or real note-books the Devil's favorite argument:

> *"His favorite argument with a believer is that just now is not a good time to speak on the subject. The lover of Christ and of souls is told that he will harm the cause he loves by introducing the theme of themes just now."*[997]

d. This is where the Holy Spirit can begin to work through the Word of God.
Gene Edwards wrote, "In order to be an effective soul winner, YOU MUST LEARN TO WORK TOGETHER WITH THE HOLY SPIRIT."[998]

3. Select Biblical Examples of Getting into Spiritual Things:

a. In response to "What shall we do?"—often in preaching context:
Introduction: A wrong "what shall we do?" question, John 6:28 (cf. Matt 19:16)
1) Luke 3:10, 12, 14
2) John 6:28
3) Acts 2:37
4) Acts 9:6 (Jesus dealing with Saul)
4) Acts 16:30

b. Direct:
1) John 3:3, "Truly, truly, I say to you, unless one is born again he cannot see the kingdom of God."
2) Acts 8:30, "Do you understand what you are reading?" Acts 8:30
3) Acts 22:1, "Brethren and fathers, hear my defense which I now offer to you"—his testimony!

c. From the general to the particular:
1) Jesus in Matthew 16:13, and 15 (cf. Luke 9:18, 20):
    a) "Who do people say the Son of Man is?"
    b) "But who do you say that I am?"
2) Jesus and Nicodemus, John 3:
    a) "Truly, truly, I say to you, unless one is born again he cannot see the kingdom of God," John 3:3
    b) "Do not be amazed that I said to you, 'You must be born again,'" John 3:7
3) Jesus with the Woman at the Well, John 4:
    a) "Give Me a drink," John 4:7
    b) "If you knew the gift of God and who it is who says to you, 'Give Me a drink,' you would have asked Him, and He would have given you living water," John 4:11
4) Zaccheus, Luke 19:
    a) "Zaccheus, hurry down, for today I must stay at your house," Luke 19:5
    b) "Today salvation has come to this house, because he, too, is a son of Abraham," Luke 19:9
5) Paul in Romans (using NKJ):
    a) Third person:
    "And even as they did not like to retain God in *their* knowledge, God gave them over to a debased mind, to do those things which are not fitting," Rom 1:28 (third person continues until verse 32)
    b) Transition:
    "who, knowing the righteous judgment of God, that those who practice such things are deserving of death, not only do the same but also approve of those who practice them," Rom 1:32
    c) Second person:
    "Therefore you are inexcusable, O man, whoever you are who judge, for in whatever you judge another you condemn yourself; for you who judge practice the same things," Rom 2:1
    d) Brought home forcefully:
    "But in accordance with your hardness and your impenitent heart you are treasuring up for yourself wrath in the day of wrath and revelation of the righteous judgment of God, who 'will render to each one according to his deeds,'" Rom 2:5-6

d. Of Jesus:
1) "Behold the Lamb of God," John 1:36
2) "We have found Him of whom Moses in the Law and also the Prophets wrote—Jesus of Nazareth, the son of Joseph," John 1:45

---

[997]Trumbull, *Taking Men Alive*, 44-45.
[998]Edwards, 116-17.

3)   "Are you saying this on your own initiative, or did others tell you about Me?" John 18:34

e.   Felt Need:
1)   Bethsaida sick man, John 5:
a)   "Do you wish to be made well?" John 5:6
b)   Jesus found him ... "Behold, you have become well; do not sin anymore, so that nothing worse happens to you." John 5:14
2)   Blind Bartimaeus, Matt 20:
a)   "What do you want Me to do for you?" Matt 20:32
b)   "Go; your faith has made you well," Mark 10:52 (cf. Luke 18:42).

f.   Transition from Healing:
1)   Man born blind, John 9:
a)   "Go wash in the pool of Siloam," John 9:7
b)   Jesus found him ... "Do you believe in the Son of Man?" John 9:35
c)   "You have both seen Him, and He is the one who is talking to you." John 9:37
2)   Ten lepers, Luke 17:
a)   "Jesus, Master, have mercy on us!" Luke 17:13
b)   "Go show yourselves to the priests," Luke 17:14
c)   "Where not ten cleansed? ..." Luke 17:17
d)   "Stand up and go; your faith has made you well," Luke 17:19

g.   Getting into Theological Issues in Conversation:
1)   "Did you receive the Holy Spirit when you believed?" Acts 19:2
2)   "Into what baptism were you baptized?" Acts 19:3

Some Critical Thinking:

A theology of salvation is vitally important! It was important enough to Paul and Barnabas that they "had great dissension and debate," Acts 15:2—note the salvation issues in Acts 15:1 and 5—the Judaizers were saying that Paul's evangelism was not appropriate, because he was not teaching properly. Again, a theology of salvation is important—it impacts both our evangelism message and method!

In other words, theological discussion and debate is not always inappropriate, even in evangelism contexts, as in Acts 19:2-3!

Some initial thoughts:

Notice the role of questions in the above biblical examples. As it turns out, there are at least 602 questions in the New Testament.[999] Not all of them are in narratives, but many of them are.

Jesus used questions to probe into the hearts of men. Paul used questions to essay the spiritual convictions of men.

It would seem that it is virtually impossible to share the Gospel with someone without some wise use of pertinent questions.

4.   **Practical Principles in Beginning to Share the Gospel:**

a.   Several Acrostics:

1)   Darrell Robinson suggests the helpful acronym FIRM as a guide to moving conversations into the Gospel (these are especially helpful in church visitation):
F—Family
I—Interests
R—Religion
M—Message

2)   I believe that it is CWT that proposed the following acrostic:
F—Family
I—Interests
R—Religious experience
E—Exploratory questions

---

[999]In the Byzantine Textform, there are 568 uses of τίς as an interrogative pronoun and 34 uses of the interrogative pronoun ποῖος.

   3) Bill Bright, in his Campus Crusade training used the acrostic LETUS:
      L—Love
      E—Establish rapport
      T—Talk about Jesus
      U—Use stories (if time allows)
      S—Sequence of questions[1000]

   Each fo these is helpful in beginning spiritual conversations whether casually or in an initiative setting (such as door-to-door).

   b. Initial questions to get *a pulse* of the person's spiritual state:

      1) **Some sample questions**:
         a) "On a scale of 1-100, what is your chance of going to heaven?"[1001]
         b) "Do you think that there is [only] one way to get to heaven? (from Matthew Inman)
         c) "How are you doing spiritually?"
         d) "Have I told you what Jesus did for me?"
         e) "Have you ever heard the Gospel?"
         f) "Do you get the chance to go to church?"
         g) "What do you think of Jesus?" (Matt 16:13, 15; Luke 9:18, 20)
         h) "Have you ever heard about Jesus?" If yes, "What do you think of Him?"
         i) "Are you a good person?" (beginning question for "Way of the Master" [see below])
         j) "At what point are you in your spiritual pilgrimage?"[1002]
         k) "Have you come to know Jesus in a personal way or would you say you are still in the process?"[1003]

      2) When a church, the Gospel, the name of Jesus or any other spiritual thing is mentioned, the person sharing can begin to get a pulse of where the other person is spiritually. You will know whether to back off, approach the subject in a different way or go right into the Gospel presentation.

   c. **More direct questions** can get right to the point:

      1) Some sample questions:

         a) "Way of the Master" (Ray Comfort)-type sequence:
            (1) "Do you consider yourself a good person?"[1004]
            (2) "Have you heard of the Ten Commandments?" "Do you think that you have obeyed those?"
               [look at the Ten Commandments; then…]
            (3) "Are you good enough to get to heaven?"

         b) The "Evangelism Explosion," Assurance Questions,[1005] Exploratory Questions, or Continuous Witness Training-type of questions are very direct and excellent for getting a good pulse of the person (EE's may have been adapted from Donald Grey Barnhouse):
            (1) "If you were to die tonight, where would you go?"
            (2) "If you were to die tonight and stand before God and He said, "Why should I let you into my heaven," how would you answer?"

[1000]Bill Bright, *Witnessing Without Fear: How To Share Your Faith with Confidence* (San Bernardino, CA: Here's Life, 1987), 101.

[1001]This question was developed by David Elliot, who used it effectively at bus stops in downtown Kansas City. Elliot was Associate Pastor of Evangelism at Roanoke Baptist church, Kansas City, MO.

[1002]Joseph Aldrich gave this as a sample "Interest Question" in *Lifestyle Evangelism* (Portland, OR: Multnomah, 1981), 223.

[1003]Darrell Robinson, *People Sharing Jesus* (Nashville: Nelson, 1995), 63.

[1004]Ray Comfort and Kirk Cameron. *Way of the Master* (Gainesville, FL: Bridge-Logos, 2006), 203.

[1005]Notice how important is the doctrine of assurance to the evangelist. Without it we have no basis for our evangelism!

    c) From Keith Fordham:
       (1) If you died tonight would you go to heaven or hell?
       (2) Would you like to know?

    d) Bill Fay's "Five Questions":[1006]
       (1) Do you have any kind of spiritual beliefs?
       (2) To you, who is Jesus Christ?
       (3) Do you think there is a heaven and hell?
       (4) If you died, where would you go? If heaven, why?
       (5) If what you are believing is not true, would you want to know?

    e) C. S. Lovett's "X-ray Approach Technique":[1007]
       (1) "Are you interested in spiritual things?"
       (2) "Have you ever thought of becoming a Christian?"
       (3) "Suppose someone where to ask you, 'What is a Christian,' what would you say?"

    f) FAITH question: "In your personal opinion, what do you understand it takes for a person to go to heaven?"

    g) Tom Johnston's thought-provoking questions:
       (1) "How are you doing spiritually?"
       (2) "Do you feel that you have peace with God?"
       (3) "Can I show you a verse that speaks of having peace with God?" [Rom 5:1]

    h) "Have you heard of the four spiritual laws?" (from *Four Spiritual Laws*)

    i) As a follow-up to "Do you ever get to go to church?" or "Is there a good church in your town?"—"Does your church ever talk about being born again?"

    j) "Are you a born-again Christian?" ... "Tell me about it." (Harry Saultnier of the Pacific Garden Mission)

       I used this question one time at a Kansas City Royals game, and here is a synopsis of the conversation, after I gave the man a Gospel tract:
         "Have you ever been born again?"
         "No, I don't think I need to be. I've been a Christian all my life!"
          [He had previously told me that he was from an infant baptizing denomination]
         "Then I guess Jesus was wrong when He said, 'You must be born again!'"
         The man gave me a puzzled look. He took the tract I handed to him, and later I saw him reading it!

    k) "What have you done with Jesus?" (cf. Matt 27:22, Mark 15:12)

    l) "What is the condition of your soul?" (John Wesley)

    m) "Are you saved?" (R.A. Torrey)

    n) "What are you depending on to get to heaven?" (Larry Moyer)

    o) "You know we will all stand before God and give an account. Are you ready to meet God?"

    p) "If you die and go to hell, who cares?" (as the introduction for a Gospel tract).

2) Some Comments:

    a) It is important not to answer the question for the person with which you are sharing, and not even to give choices if possible. This allows the person to think about spiritual things, and make up their mind on their own.

    b) From the answer or answers to the questions you ask, you can direct the Gospel presentation to the weakness in the answer. You can ask yourself:
       (1) How does this person view salvation?

[1006]William Fay, *Share Jesus Without Fear* (Nashville: Broadman, 1999), 33.
[1007]C. S. Lovett, *Soul-Winning Made Easy* (Baldwin Park, CA: Personal Christianity, 1959), 24-25.

          (2) Does this person understand that he/she is a sinner saved by grace?

          (3) Is the death of Jesus Christ important to this person—does he think he is saved without referring to the cross as his only hope?

          (4) Does this person have assurance of salvation?

      c) As the Gospel is shared, it is important to go over all the major areas. However, some people will already understand one aspect and need biblical clarification on another. Sensitivity, love, and boldness are needed.[1008]

    d. Don't feel like you need to apologize for having the Gospel of Jesus bubbling out of you, John 4:14 -> v. 39

[1008]Finney, 68, "Bring the great and fundamental truths to bear upon the person's mind."

Chapter 15 Appendix

Evangelism Methodology of Philbert Hamelin
(Martyred in 1557)

From Jean Crespin, *Histoire des vrays Tesmoins de la verite de l'evangile, qui de leur sang l'ont signée, depuis Jean Hus iusques autemps present* [*History of the True Witnesses to the Truth of the Gospel, Who with Their Blood Signed, from John Hus to the Present Time*] (Geneva, 1570; reproduction, Liège, 1964), 450. Translation mine:

"Philbert Hamelin, a former priest, converted at Saintes, France, was imprisoned in 1546 for the Gospel. For fear of his life, he faked a renunciation. He fled to Geneva where he established a printing press. After 12 years in Geneva, being married with children, he returned to share the Gospel in the place where he had renounced it. So, as a Bible colporteur, he planted churches [*petites communautés évangéliques*] in the area of his hometown. He was arrested in Saintes, and refused to escape jail, lest the jailor be put at risk, and because…

…Those who have the work of announcing the Gospel to others [should not] seek to escape and break out of prisons for fear of danger, instead of maintaining, even in flames, the doctrine that he had announced.[1009]

[The following paragraph described Hamelin's ministry of personal evangelism]

"Many faithful spoke of him, how when he went along in the country, often he would spy out and find field workers at the hour of their break, as they are accustomed to do, at the foot of a tree, or in the shade of a haystack. There he would feign like he was resting with them, taking the opportunity with little methods and by easy speech, to teach them to fear God, and to pray both before and after the break, inasmuch as it was him [the Lord] who gave them all things for the love of His Son Jesus Christ. And after that, he would ask the poor peasants if they would like it if he prayed to God on their behalf. Some took great pleasure in this and were edified, others were astonished, hearing things that they were not accustomed to hearing. Not a few would run after him with hostile intent [Fr. "aucuns luy couroyent-sus"], because he would show them that they were on the way to damnation, if they did not believe in the Gospel. After he received their curses and outrage, he often had this warning in his mouth, 'My friends, you do not now know what you are doing, but one day you will understand, and I pray God to do such a grace on your behalf.'"

[Hamelin was brought before the tribunal of Bordeaux, where he was degraded of his rank as priest and burned alive in 1557. For fear of his preaching, trumpets were sounding at his funeral [pyre], and he was strangled before his body was burned.]

[1009]Cited in Matthieu LeLièvre, *Portraits et récits Huguenots,* premiere série (Toulouse: Société des Livres Religieux, 1903), 125. Translation mine.

CHAPTER 16
The Personal Testimony and Power of Story

Introduction: One challenge to the Gospel is moving from objective propositional truth to subjective existentialism (story). One of the ways this change can be seen is with the current fascination with the Story of the Gospel over the Message of the Gospel. For this reason, I begin with a timeline on the contemporary use of story.

Brief Timeline of the Use of Story in Contemporary Evangelism

1973:

"The Decade [1970s] is full of new challenges. One of them is to learn a new love—to love to *do and tell* the story."[1010]

"If we do, it will be a great time to be alive and in mission. For it will mean that the church-centered and the world-centered will have moved beyond their present impasse to find each other at the rendezvous point out ahead—a place where they have learned together to *tell* and *celebrate* the Tale, and to *do* and *be* it."[1011]

Fackre then explains God's Story in a chapter entitled "Catechism for Skye [his teen-age daughter]: Telling the Tale."[1012]

1977:

In his chapter 11, "Tell Me the Old, New Story," Ford explained how to share the Gospel and how to share your own story.[1013]

Ford quoted David Hubbard (unpublished paper), "God knew what He was doing when He told the most significant things about Himself, not in proverbs, nor in sonnets, nor in chronological lists, nor in theological propositions, but in a story."[1014]

1994:

"Our goal is to uncover the crystalline simplicity of God's Story (with a capital *S*). Once we see how we have become a part of that Story, we can better understand how to tell and model our own story (with a small *s*) to others."[1015]

"We have our traditional ways of doing evangelism, but many of us are beginning to realize that the old paradigm of evangelism isn't working like it used to.... We must find a *new* paradigm."[1016]

"After considerable study, prayer, and contemplation, I have come to the conclusion that narrative evangelism is the new paradigm for evangelism in the postmodern age. It is simple. It is biblical. It is practical. And it is endlessly adaptable."[1017]

2000:

Jimmy Long, for example, proposes the following main points in his chapter on evangelizing Postmoderns, the following outline are headers in his text:[1018]
1. Trends in the Shift to Postmodernism
2. The Message of Hope
3. The Method: Loving Community
4. The Mode of Transmission: Story

[1010]Gabriel Fackre, *Do and Tell: Engagement Evangelism in the '70s* (Grand Rapids: Eerdmans, 1973), 15.

[1011]Ibid., 29.

[1012]Ibid., 30-45.

[1013]Leighton Ford, *Good News Is for Sharing: A Guide to Making Friends for God* (Elgin, IL: David C. Cook, 1977).

[1014]Ibid., 130.

[1015]Leighton Ford, *The Power of Story: Recovering the Oldest, Most Natural Way to Reach People for Christ* (Colorado Springs: NavPress, 1994), 14.

[1016]Ibid., 50.

[1017]Ibid., 52.

[1018]Jimmy Long, "Generating Hope: A Strategy for Reaching the Postmodern Generation" in *Telling the Truth: Evangelizing Postmoderns,* ed. D. A. Carson (Grand Rapids: Zondervan, 2000).

5. The Mandate: The Great Commandment, "I can assure you that for people who are postmodern, the Great Commandment can initially be a more compelling mandate than the Great Commission."[1019]

6. The Postmodern Conversion Process:[1020]

    a) "First of all people start out with a discontentment of life."

    b) "Next they have contact with Christians. We enter into their community, and they enter into our community."

    c) "Then they become converted to the community. They start coming … They may even start experiencing God in worship as part of a worshiping community."

    d) "However, we need to make sure that they are converted not only to the community but to the King of the community, Jesus Christ."

    e) Here is a chart of Long's *ordo salutis* as explained above:

Jimmy Long's *Ordo Salutis*

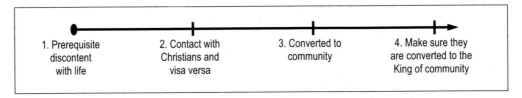

Food for Contemplation: Is something wrong with Jimmy Long's order of salvation/theology of conversion? Does this follow the teaching of the epistles or the examples in the book of Acts?

Some thoughts:[1021]

1) What if the person is satisfied with their life, not being convicted by God's Law [due to a seared conscience, 1 Tim 4:2?]

2) What if the unsaved person has had "negative experiences" in his interaction with Christians, as is noted to be the main theme of John Shore's book, *I'm O.K. and You're Not: The Message We're Sending to Unbelievers and Why We Should Stop*?[1022]
    [Perhaps, if anything, pitting Shore against Long shows the fallacies in both of their points.]
    [Noticing these approaches also shows the need to keep the Holy Spirit working through the Word of God as essential in the process of salvation]

Storying: Story from an Academic Approach—The following exemplifies the use of story in contemporary academia (as opposed to the objectivity of linear propositional truth, i.e. the Ten Commandments, the Gospel, etc.):

a. Samuel Byrskog, *Story as History – History as Story: The Gospel Tradition in the Context of Oral History* (Boston: Brille, 2002), 386 pp.

    "Samuel Byrskog employs models from the interdisciplinary field of oral history as presented by Paul Thompson, coupled with insights from cultural anthropology, in order to examine the interaction between the present and past as the gospel tradition evolved. The ancient Greek and Roman historians, with their use of eyewitness testimonies as sources to the past and as central elements in interpretive and narrativizing processes of the present, serve as the basis for unraveling culture-specific patterns of oral history, and thus for conceptualizing similar patterns during the development of the gospel tradition" (Brille Academic Publishers, unnamed catalogue, Autumn/Winter 2003, 11).

[1019]Ibid., 331.

[1020]Ibid., 334.

[1021]I am indebted to the comments of my student Benjamin Clay for the first two points listed here.

[1022]Shore, John. *I'm OK—You're Not: The Message We're Sending to Unbelievers and Why We Should Stop* (Colorado Springs: NavPress, 2007).

b. Kevin Vanhoozer, *The Drama of Doctrine* (Westminster John Knox, 2005); the author explained his book in an interview with *Trinity Magazine.* By the way, "Kevin Vanhoozer has been described by Oxford University's Alister McGrath as 'one of the most significant younger theological voices of our generation.'"[1023]

"TM [*Trinity Magazine*]: How does the church participate in the drama [referring to his book]?

"KV: The church is a company of players who have become, in the words of the apostle Paul, a 'spectacle to the world' (1 Cor 4:9). Christians are 'costumed interpreters,' clothed in the righteousness of Christ and charged with being the 'theater of the gospel.' To be precise, the church is to perform the Scriptures in the power of the Spirit. The most important form that our biblical interpretation takes is not the commentary but the community: the church is to show the world what the Gospel *means* through the way it shapes its life together. When the church performs the gospel, it becomes an enacted parable that exhibits the kingdom of God before the watching world.

"For example, the church performs the atonement by exercising its ministry of reconciliation (2 Cor 5:18). The church does not bring reconciliation about—only the cross can do that—but witnesses in word and deed to the reconciliation already achieved in Christ. The church participates in the cross, when it becomes a theater of reconciliation. Or, to put it somewhat differently, the church demonstrates her understanding of—performs—the doctrine of the atonement by living as though the dividing walls (Eph 2:14) of racial and ethnic hostility really were broken down."[1024]

Vanhoozer ended his interview with the following paragraph:

"The most important this the church should be doing is cultivating and embodying Christian wisdom in its corporate life and in the everyday lives of individual believers. Evangelicals neglect doctrine to their own peril and to the peril of their Christian witness. My prayer is that Christians today will rediscover the vitality of theology to the point where they are willing not only to die for the truth of Jesus Christ but to *live* for it."[1025]

The Limitation of Story (reconsidering: "Jesus, the best story teller there ever was!"):[1026]

1. Were not the parables of Jesus meant to hide the truth from the masses of people?

Matt 13:10-17, "And the disciples came and said to Him, 'Why do You speak to them in parables?' And He answered and said to them, 'To you it has been granted to know the mysteries of the kingdom of heaven, but to them it has not been granted. For whoever has, to him shall *more* be given, and he shall have an abundance; but whoever does not have, even what he has shall be taken away from him. Therefore I speak to them in parables; because while seeing they do not see, and while hearing they do not hear, nor do they understand. And in their case the prophecy of Isaiah is being fulfilled, which says, 'You will keep on hearing, but will not understand; And you will keep on seeing, but will not perceive; For the heart of this people has become dull, And with their ears they scarcely hear, And they have closed their eyes Lest they should see with their eyes, And hear with their ears, And understand with their heart and return, And I should heal them.' But blessed are your eyes, because they see; and your ears, because they hear. For truly I say to you, that many prophets and righteous men desired to see what you see, and did not see *it*; and to hear what you hear, and did not hear *it*."

Luke 8:9-10, "And His disciples *began* questioning Him as to what this parable might be. And He said, 'To you it has been granted to know the mysteries of the kingdom of God, but to the rest *it is* in parables, in order that seeing they may not see, and hearing they may not understand.'"

John 10:6, "This figure of speech Jesus spoke to them, but they did not understand what those things were which He had been saying to them."

[1023]*Trinity Magazine* (Spring 2006): 19.

[1024]*Ibid.,* 20-21.

[1025]*Ibid.,* 21.

[1026]"Jesus told stories that seemed very simple and clear, but his stories are rarely as simple or as straightforward as they seem. Some (though not all) of them work on four levels. First, they are marvelous stories that capture the imagination of the reader or hearer. Second, they teach moral behavior, what it is to be a truly good person, the way of life that is pleasing to the Lord. Third, they teach about the kingdom of God, how God's kingdom is different from earthly kingdoms. Fourth, they teach us about Jesus Himself" (Jerram Barrs, *The Heart of Evangelism* [Wheaton, IL: Crossway, 2001], 223). Notice that Barrs seems overlook Jesus' own explanation that He primarily spoke in parables to hide the truth from the masses of people.

John **14:21-22,** "and he who loves Me shall be loved by My Father, and I will love him, and will disclose Myself to him. Judas (not Iscariot) said to Him, 'Lord, what then has happened that You are going to disclose Yourself to us and not to the world?'"

2. Likewise, explanations of the parables were given only to His disciples and His followers (and even with these explanations they still did not understand, cf. Matt 15:16; 16:9; Luke 24:25-26):

Matt **13:34-35,** "All these things Jesus spoke to the multitude in parables; and without a parable He did not speak to them, that it might be fulfilled which was spoken by the prophet, saying: 'I will open My mouth in parables; I will utter things kept secret from the foundation of the world.'" (citing Psa 78:2)

Mark **4:10-12,** "And as soon as He was alone, His followers, along with the twelve, *began* asking Him *about* the parables. And He was saying to them, 'To you has been given the mystery of the kingdom of God; but those who are outside get everything in parables, in order that while seeing, they may see and not perceive; and while hearing, they may hear and not understand lest they return and be forgiven.'"

Mark **4:33-34,** "And with many such parables He was speaking the word to them as they were able to hear it; and He did not speak to them without a parable; but He was explaining everything privately to His own disciples."

Mark **7:17-18,** "When He had entered a house away from the crowd, His disciples asked Him concerning the parable. So He said to them, 'Are you thus without understanding also?'"

John **16:25, 29,** "'These things I have spoken to you in figurative language; an hour is coming when I will speak no more to you in figurative language, but will tell you plainly of the Father.' … His disciples said, 'Lo, now You are speaking plainly, and are not using a figure of speech.'"

Introducing Story—Four Approaches to "Storying the Gospel":

1. **Narrative Evangelism**:
   a. Parallel is the parables of Jesus
   b. Using real life situations to teach spiritual truths
   c. This is encouraged especially in the context of postmodern or relational evangelism:
      1) Which tends to be negative to propositional truth
      2)-Which tends to emphasize a long duration of relationship for effective witness
   d. Alvin Reid's caution: "Some have gone too far with narrative evangelism, elevating stories of people above *the* story of the gospel. We can, however, integrate the narrative to illustrate and explain the Gospel."[1027]

2. **Telling Our Story**—the Personal Testimony:
   a. Sharing a personal testimony as a witness to the life change that Jesus Christ can bring, Mark 5:19-20, and Luke 8:38-39
   b. Sharing what we have learned from Jesus, John 4:39
   c. Sharing about receiving eternal life, 1 Tim 6:12

   d. **STRENGTHS OF THE PERSONAL TESTIMONY**:
      1) A personal testimony is *experiential/existential*—it is real life, God at work in your life; God at work in the world!
      2) A personal testimony *adds credibility* to the sharing situation—showing the honesty and openness of the testifier.
      3) A personal testimony makes the Gospel presentation *interesting*.
      4) A personal testimony *cannot be refuted*—no one can rightfully say, 'This didn't happen to you!'
      5) A personal testimony *allows the Gospel to be shared* in a first-person way, minimizing the threat, while possibly maximizing the application (although the powerful weapon is the Word of God, not the story).
      6) A personal testimony may be more *non-threatening* for the listener (while perhaps being more threatening to the testifier).

[1027]Alvin Reid, *Radically Unchurched* (Grand Rapids: Kregel, 2002), 138.

    e. **POSSIBLE WEAKNESSES OF THE PERSONAL TESTIMONY**:

      1) May move away from the need for the presentation of the Gospel message

      2) May be a move away from the propositional truths of the Gospel

      3) May be a move away from the actual power in evangelizing being the Gospel (Rom 1:16) and the sword of the Spirit (Heb 4:12-13)

3. **Telling His Story—Parable Form or Directly**:

    a. Telling the Story of Jesus in Narrative Form:

      1) Directly, e.g. Jesus Video

      2) In parable form, e.g. C.S. Lewis, *The Chronicles of Narnia*:

> "The hidden presentation of the Gospel is on of the beauties of storytelling. It is possible to teach people about Jesus through stories, even when those people are not yet eager to know about Him. Again, C. S. Lewis is a wonderful example of this. His Narnia stories about the lion, Aslan, have introduced many people to Jesus, people who would normally not go to church or read the Bible or attend an evangelistic meeting. People are entranced with Aslan and through loving him come to worship the Lion of Judah, Christ Himself."[1028]

> Notice, however, that Barrs own experience with Lewis (and Tolkien) came not from a secular point-of-view, but from one of growing up in a Christian home. Barrs also confessed that even from a Christian point-of-view, he did not understand the Gospel story through those books:

> "My parents, along with so much else that was good, for which I owe them eternal thanks, introduced me to the writings of C. S. Lewis and J. R. R. Tolkien. My father read the Narnia stories by C. S. Lewis and Tolkien's *the Hobbit* and *Lord of the Rings* to us when we were children. Though I did not understand the Christian story that lies so closely beneath the surface of those books, they did create a longing for the world they represented."[1029]

    b. May or may not quote from Scripture

    c. May or may not deal directly with the Gospel or with "propositional truths" of the Gospel, e.g. 1 Cor 15:3-6

4. **Chronologically Storying the Gospel**:

    a. Sharing the message of the Gospel story beginning chronologically in one of several fashions (depending on one's view of the atonement):

      1) Beginning with the creation of man (Genesis 1 and 2), the fall (Genesis 3), the substitutionary lamb (Leviticus 4) and/or the Passover (Exodus 12, etc.), and other pertinent Old Testament portions before speaking about the life and ministry of Jesus Christ

      2) Beginning with God, His creation of man, and His rulership over creation, to the kingdom of God through the rulership of Christ (perhaps a *Christus Victor*—kingdom theology approach to evangelism)

    b. Method One was popularized by New Tribes Mission in their work with unreached tribal peoples; Method Two was popularized by Philip Jensen of Matthias Media (Australia) in Carson's book on Evangelizing Postmoderns

    c. Interesting approaches to the Gospel message

    d. May or may not fit into the normal understanding of the εὐαγγέλιον from a New Testament perspective:

      a. Compare Paul's Acts 17 sermon on Isaiah 42:5-8 with his description of the Gospel in 1 Corinthians 15:1-8

[1028]Jerram Barrs, *The Heart of Evangelism*, 227.

[1029]Ibid., 118.

b.   See my chart on the five audiences in the book of Acts and the respective approach to sharing the Gospel to each.[1030]

A Biblical Look at the Place of Personal Testimony:

A.   Some Testimonies in the Bible:
1.   Job 33:13-28, especially vv. 27-28
2.   Deut 6:20-25 (compare this passage with 1 Peter 3:15)
3.   Psa 66:16-20
4.   Mark 5:19-20; Luke 8:39:
a.   By the way, is not this command of Christ already found in Psa 73:28 or 118:17?
5.   John 4:39-42:
a.   John 4:39, "And from that city many of the Samaritans believed in Him because of the word of the woman who testified, 'He told me all the things that I *have* done'"
6.   Acts 19:18, "Many also of those who had believed kept coming, confessing [forth] and disclosing their practices" (ἐξομολογούμενοι καὶ ἀναγγέλλοντες τὰς πράξεις αὐτῶν)
7.   1 Tim 6:12, making a confession of eternal life in the presence of many witnesses.

B.   When to Give Testimony:
1.   When Jesus has saved you, John 4:39; Mark 5:19
2.   When on trial for your faith, Luke 21:13
3.   Always ready, 1 Pet 3:15
4.   At all times, Psa 34:1

C.   Types of Testimonies:
1.   In the recorded ministry of the Apostle Paul:
a.   Paul's conversion testimony:
1)   As recorded by Luke, Acts 9:1-19
2)   As recounted by Paul to the hostile crowd in Jerusalem, Acts 22:1-21
3)   As recounted by Paul as a defense of King Agrippa, Acts 26:1-23
b.   Paul recounts his conversion and theological development, Galatians 1:13-2:21
c.   Paul recounts his Jewish credentials, which he counts as rubbish, Philippians 3:1-7
d.   Paul explains his ministry as a church planting evangelist, 1 Thess 2:1-12
2.   Some classifications of testimonies:
a.   Testimony of conversion—Believing audience
b.   Testimony of Christ's work in a specific instance—Believing audience
1)   "This is my story"
c.   Testimony of conversion, background and ministry call—Believing audience
1)   For admission into seminary
2)   For a pastoral search committee or congregation
d.   Testimony (a) or (b) as an evangelistic tool—Unsaved audience

D.   The Three-Minute Testimony:
1.   The sharing of a testimony is an excellent way to bring the Gospel alive to people. It lets others know that Jesus is actually alive, and that He does work in our lives.
2.   The preparation and memorization of a short concise testimony is important. However, care should be taken to relating to the person when sharing the testimony. It is easy to sound like a tape-recorder if the testimony is a memorized to rigidly:
a.   Your testimony will be different to people of different ages and cultural or social groupings.
3.   What are some principles in preparing a three-minute testimony?

E.   The Ten-Second Testimony:
1.   For use in door-to-door, street evangelism, or spontaneous evangelism situations
2.   Basically a short version of the three minute testimony, à la Deut 6:20-25; Job 33:27-28

[1030]Johnston, *Charts for a Theology of Evangelism*, Chart 35, "Context of the Gospel in Acts," 63.

I. Preparing an Evangelistic Testimony:

Introduction: The reason for a three-minute testimony is to have a brief concise knowledge of how we came to Christ, and what He has done and is doing in our lives. In Acts 4:20, "Peter and John said, 'For we cannot stop speaking what we have seen and heard.'" The Apostle Paul shares his testimony on several occasions in the Acts (Acts 22:1-21, 26:1-23, cf. Job 33:26-28). These both give an idea of what should be a part of a brief testimony. This outline is based on the Navigator 2:7 training:[1031]

A. Lead-In, Acts 26:2-3
B. **Before**, Acts 26:4-11
C. **How**, Acts 26:12-20
D. **After**, Verses 21-23
E. Close, Acts 26:24-29

II. Method:

A. The salvation testimony may be divided into three segments:
1. **Before** I came to Christ
2. **How** and **why** I came to Christ
3. **Since** (**after**) I have come to Christ

B. If Christ was accepted as a youth, a significant adult experience showing you the need for spiritual growth may be highlighted.

C. Write your testimony on two sheets of paper (one side only); this limits the testimony to three minutes, preparing you to be succinct.

III. Requirements in Preparing a Testimony for This Class:

A. The expected audience should be:
1. Someone your age
2. Someone your gender
3. Someone unsaved

B. Other requirements:
1. Please emphasize conversion or spiritual recommitment, as appropriate to best communicate your commitment to Christ to someone your age and gender.
2. Please do not:
   a. Mention that you grew up in the church unless it directly relates to your conversion or spiritual recommitment
   b. Discuss meeting your spouse, unless it directly relates to your conversion or spiritual recommitment
   c. Mention your call to the ministry, unless it directly relates to your conversion or spiritual recommitment
   d. Turn your testimony into a "preachimony", telling about a Bible verse or concept rather than what God has done for you or how He reached you.
2. Please use one verse, or no more than two, without the reference
3. Length should be two pages, double-spaced (approximately 3 minutes when read aloud).

IV. Share Your Testimony:

Share your Testimony in a natural way as you share the Gospel. You can share your testimony in other situations also. Be open to appropriate times to tell others what Jesus has done for you!

[1031]*The 2:7 Series: Leader Training Clinic, Part I* (Colorado Springs: Navigators, 1988), 21.

CHAPTER 17
What Is the Gospel?

Introduction:

The German Pietist August Hermann Francke (1663-1727) once said:

> "As far as I am concerned, I must preach that should someone hear me only once before he dies, he will have heard not just a part, but the entire way of salvation and in the proper way for it to take root in his heart."[1032]

Likewise, a Century later the Anglican Robert Bickerseth, Bishop of Ripon (1857-1884) said:

> "No sermon was worthy of the name which did not contain the message of the Gospel, urging the sinner to be reconciled to God."[1033]

So what is this Gospel and how does it take root in a heart? What does it mean to urge sinners to be reconciled to God? As can be expected, there have been many deviations from the Gospel in the past, and it can only be anticipated that deviations will continue. So let's begin by giving an overview, and then examining recent terminology…

Chapter Summary: Approaches to Understanding the Content of the Personal Gospel….
- A. Preamble to Studying the Message of the Gospel:
    1. Historical Excursus on Terminology
    2. Several Preliminary Issues Related to the Gospel
- B. Some Shallow Wells for Summarizing the Gospel Message:
    1. Kerygma as Expressing the Gospel?
    2. Creeds as Expressing the Gospel?
- C. Analyzing Four Biblical Foci for Message:
    1. Deut 6:20-25
    2. Luke 24:46-47
    3. 1 Cor 15:1-8
    4. Gal 1:6-10
- D. Considering Biblical Terms for the Gospel
    1. Biblical Terms for the Gospel
    2. Biblical Concepts that Are Sometimes Made Equivocal
- E. Three Further Biblical Approaches to Discerning the Gospel Message:
    1. The 52 evangelistic conversations in the Gospels and the Book of Acts
    2. Five audiences in the Book of Acts
    3. The Book of Romans
- F. The Simple Gospel, with Several Historical Examples

[Addendum for teachers and students: Begin by looking at Point F, "The Simple Gospel, with Historic Examples." Then working back through points E and then D. Point D, "Considering Biblical Terms for the Gospel," was the original main point of this chapter. Point C should then bring further clarity to the essence of the Gospel message. Points A and B should confirm why the remainder of the chapter is necessary in the first place.]

[1032]Paulus Scharpff, *History of Evangelism: Three Hundred Years of Evangelism in Germany, Great Britain, and the Unites States of America.* Helga Bender Henry, trans. (Grand Rapids: Eerdmans, 1964, 1966), 46.

[1033]M. C. Bickerseth, *A Sketch of a Life and Episcopate of the Right Reverend Robert Biskerseth, D.D., Bishop of Ripon, 1857-1887* (London, 1887), 27f.; cited in David Bebbington, *Evangelicalism in Modern Britain: A History from the 1730s to the 1980s* (London: Unwin Hyman, 1989; Grand Rapids: Baker, 1992), 5.

A. Preamble to Understanding the Message of the Gospel:

1. Historical Excursus on Terminology:

a. Lately several terms have been added to the word "Gospel" to enhance or complete its meaning. Some of these are "Social Gospel" versus "Personal Gospel," "Full Gospel" and "Whole Gospel." A historical survey would be in order here:

1) **"Social Gospel"** was coined during the 1880s by Modernists to describe their type of ministry and missions which was interested in more than just the soul, but rather the whole man.[1034] In the case of Harnack and Hermann, the item added to the Gospel was a thorough (Christian and secular) education. Their view was that in the philosophical arena, Christianity stands head and shoulders above all other systems. Thus one ought not to fear to teach other systems. The philosophical emphasis of the day was exemplified by the Chair of Harvard University's Department of Philosophy (1849-1898), Josiah Royce, in his *The World and the Individual* (1899-1901) and *The Problem and Christianity* (1913).[1035] "You must be born again" was considered individualistic and unrelated to the socialist patterns of thought prevalent at that time.

2) **"Individual Gospel," "Personal Gospel," "Simple Gospel"** (2 Cor 11:3), and **"Pauline Gospel"** were terms used by Fundamentalists to counter the social practice of the Modernists. Fundamentalists also spoke of "soul-winning" during this era. While Modernists sought to find a social gospel in the life of Jesus, Fundamentalists affirmed that there was no distinction between Jesus and Paul. Therefore, the Book of Romans became the foundational theological book in the Bible School movement of the day.

3) **"Full Gospel 1"**: A. B. Simpson, founder of the Christian and Missionary Alliance church seems to have coined the term "full gospel." According to Simpson's usage, "full gospel" stood for the four roles of Jesus (related to the atonement): Jesus as Savior, Sanctifier, Healer, and Coming King. It would seem that R. A. Torrey, principal at Moody Bible Institute used the "Full Gospel" in a similar vein.[1036]

4) **"Full Gospel 2"**: The Assembly of God church (AG) broke from the Christian and Missionary Alliance over the issue of "sign gifts." The AG affirmed that speaking in tongues was the sign [gift] of the reception of the Holy Spirit.[1037] This teaching also became known as the "full gospel."

5) **"Whole Gospel 1"**: In 1922, J. E. Conant, a Fundamentalist [Presbyterian] in the aforementioned debate, formulated a watchword when he used the word "whole" three times in one sentence: "The main work of the whole Church in the whole world throughout the whole Age is witnessing to the salvation there is in Christ. Anything outside of this forfeits the promised presence and blessing of him who said, 'Lo, I am with you all the days, even unto the consummation of the Age'"[1038] Conant's emphasis was that there ought be nothing added to the Simple Gospel.

[1034]"Social Gospel" was a common term following Josiah Royce's ardent anti-individualism. "Social Gospel" was used from the mid-1890s to 1920 to refer to a societal, communal, or humanitarian approach to missions. Note for example: Adolf Harnack and Wilhelm Hermann, *Essays on the Social Gospel* (London: Williams & Norgate, 1907); Harry F. Ward, *Social Evangelism* (New York: Missionary Education Movement of the United States and Canada, 1915); and Walter Rauschenbusch, *A Theology for the Social Gospel* (New York: Macmillan, 1917; Nashville: Abingdon, 1978).

[1035]"Josiah Royce," Stanford Encyclopedia of Philosophy; available at http://plato.stanford.edu/ entries/royce/; accessed 8 Jan 2007; Internet.

[1036]Torrey, Reuben A. *The Missionary's Message—The Full Gospel.* Los Angeles: Biola, n.d.

[1037]"8. The Initial Physical Evidence of the Baptism in the Holy Spirit. The baptism of believers in the Holy Spirit is witnessed by the initial physical sign of speaking with other tongues as the Spirit of God gives them utterance. Acts 2:4 The speaking in tongues in this instance is the same in essence as the gift of tongues, but is different in purpose and use. 1 Corinthians 12:4-10; 1 Corinthians 12:28" (16 Fundamental Truths of the Assemblies of God (Full Text); available at http://ag.org/top/Beliefs/Statement_of_Fundamental_Truths/sft_full.cfm; accessed: 22 Feb 2007; Internet).

[1038]Conant, *Every-Member Evangelism*, 29.

6) **"Whole Gospel 2"**: Following the Lausanne 1974 Conference in worldwide Evangelicalism, the concept of "whole gospel" became used in relation to ministering to the needs of the whole man, body, mind, soul, and spirit, and not only to his spiritual needs (championed by John R. W. Stott). This terminology was used by Evangelical relief and development agencies to substantiate their existence alongside the traditional evangelistic ministries. This term also morphed into other terms, such as **"Holistic/Wholistic Evangelism/ Ministry,"** being meeting the needs of the whole man, and **"Servant/Servanthood/Ministry Evangelism,"** serving people to show the love of Jesus as a preferred or necessary human preparation to the Gospel.

7) **Prosperity Gospel**:[1039] So coined because it emphasizes the blessings of the Gospel, without much emphasis on the promised persecution and hardship of the true Gospel lifestyle (e.g. John 15:18-21; 16:33). Paul wrote to Timothy, "Remember my chains" (Col 4:18; 2 Tim 2:8-9). Furthermore, at times, passages appear to be twisted to focus uniquely on the financial blessings that are supposed to accompany a relationship with Christ. Clearly, the emphasis of the New Testament is quite the opposite. Jesus was born into a very poor family, never having a home of his own. Paul was in and out of prison, beaten times without number, often in hunger, thirst, exposure (2 Cor 11:27), and need (Phil 4:16).

8) **Health and Wealth Gospel**, as an offshoot of the **Prosperity Gospel**, which as the title suggests, posits that its adherents are promised a supernatural health and wealth. The emphasis of this Gospel is clearly in this life and not on the life to come (1 Cor 15:19), much as those whose "god is their belly" (Rom 16:18; Col 3:18-19). Furthermore, God never promised supernatural health to anyone, but merely protection for a time (Acts 18:9-10), and an additional number of years to Hezekiah (2 Kings 20:5-6)

Preliminary conclusion to historical interlude on emanations of the word "Gospel":

Evangelism morphing into Christian education. The Gospel morphing into a social teaching. Adding the necessity of speaking in tongues as a sign of receiving the Holy Spirit. Adding the need to meet the physical, economic, political, and/or emotional needs of people prior to sharing the Gospel. All of these and more have been debated in the history of the Church. Therefore, while a discussion of the "Gospel" seems elementary at first glance, it carries with it number of significant issues, proven divisive by past debates and the existence of multiple denominations which often differ on their understanding of the Gospel.

b. Other historical emanations:

1) Master of Sentences, Peter the Lombard (d. 1164) and his **"Signs and Symbols"** approach to the Gospel:
   a) "Signs" and "symbols" referred directly to the sacraments of the Roman Catholic church, through which Lombard taught that salvation was wrought by stages of grace or benefits of grace from the hand of the priest.
   b) The purpose of his writing being "a zeal for the house of God."[1040]
   c) Purposefully reframing the question in his attack against Manicheans (the Petrobusian or so-called "Albigenses" of his day [and Evangelicals today]), "Master Peter" gathered sentences from "the ancient fathers" as his authority, thereby further moving the

---

[1039]Both the Prosperity Gospel and the Health and Wealth Gospel were added to this list at the recommendation of Matt Queen, Professor of Evangelism at Southwestern Baptist Theological Seminary. Thanks, Matt!

[1040]"The truth of the One proffering delights us, but the immensity of the labor frightens: the desire of making progress exhorts, but the infirmity of failing discourages, which (infirmity) zeal for the house of God conquers. 'Catching fire from this (zeal), our faith against the errors of carnal and animal men' we have studied to wall with the round shields of the Tower of David and/or to show rather that (it is) walled and to open those things withdrawn from theological inquiries and also to put on display [traducere] the knowledge of ecclesiastical sacraments to the limited extent of our understanding" (Master Peter Lombard, "Prologue," *Four Books of Sentences*; accessed 16 May 2006; from http://www.franciscan-archive.org/lombardus/opera/ls-prolo.html; Internet).

substance of Roman Catholic studies away from the Word of God and into philosophical theology.[1041]

d) He wrote of the importance of making a good confession, therefore his purpose was salvific and ultimately evangelistic to his view of the Gospel.[1042]

e) Lombard reframed the question of salvation as being an issue of signs and symbols (i.e. Baptism, the Eucharist, Holy Unction, etc.)[1043]

f) Space not permitting, the reader is asked to further consider the impact of Master Peter's reframing the question away from hearing the Gospel and receiving its message by faith alone through grace alone.

g) Comparatively, see also in my *Book of Charts on a Theology of Evangelism* Erasmus' and Blaise Pascal's philosophical approach to the Gospel.[1044]

2) Aquinas' **Natural Theology** morphed into a centralized "**Christian Worldview**"

   a) Socinius' "**Moral Philosophy**" in which theology was boiled down to this lowest common denominator, to the exclusion of the authority of Scripture, the deity of Christ, the Trinity, the substitutionary atonement, etc.

   b) Finney's "**Moral Government**" became the Central Interpretive Motif by the time of his 1878 *Systematic Theology*. It would seem moral government became the apologetic and philosophical grid by which he communicated his Gospel. It was not too far a field of the Socinian "**Moral Philosophy**" prevalent in the earlier part of the century.

      (1) Does not Finney's emphasis on moral philosophy, or a Christian worldview, compromise the gospel and evangelism?

         (a) For example, most historic cooperating documents [statements of faith or confessions] emphasize the message of the Gospel, a few, the method of proclamation of the Gospel [e.g. Hubmaier's 26 conclusions])

[1041] "*They have a reason for (their) wisdom in superstition*: because mendacious hypocrisy follows defection from the faith, so that even in (their) words there is a piety, which has lost (its) conscience, and they render that simulated piety impious with every mendacity of words, contriving to corrupt the sanctity of the Faith with the instructions of false doctrine and forcing upon others an itching of the ears under the novel dogma of their own desire, who as students of contention war without the restraint of treaties [sine foedere] against the truth.' 'For between the assertion of truth and the defense of pleasure there is a persistent battle, so long as both the truth grasps itself and the will for error guards itself.' Therefore lest they be able to pour forth the venom of their iniquity upon others, to both turn the Church into (something) hateful to God and to stop up mouths of these (Her sons), we willing to exalt the light of the truth upon a candlestick, in much labor and sweat, with God as (our) surety, have compiled this volume in four distinct books, from the testimonies of the truth founded in eternity" (ibid.).

[1042] "In which you shall again find the examples and doctrine of (our) elders, (and) in which we have brought to light through a sincere profession of faith in the Lord [dominicae fidei] the fraudulence of the viper's doctrine, have embraced an approach for demonstrating the truth and have not inserted the danger of an impious profession, using a temperate means of guidance among both. But if our voice has sounded out at little anywhere, it has not departed from the limits of the Fathers" (ibid.).

[1043] "While considering the contents of the Old and New Law again and again by diligent chase [indagine], the prevenient grace of God has hinted to us, that a treatise on the Sacred Page is [versari] chiefly about things and/or signs. For as Augustine, the egregious Doctor, says in the book *on Christian Doctrine*: « Every doctrine is of things, and/or signs. But even things are learned through signs. But here (those) are properly named things, which are not employed to signify anything; but signs, those whose use is in signifying ». But of these there are some, whose every use is in signifying, not in justifying, that is, which we do not use except for the sake of signifying something, as (are) some Sacraments of the Law [legalia]; others, which not only signify, but confer that which helps inwardly, as the evangelical Sacraments (do). « From which it is openly understood, what are here named signs: those things namely, which are employed to signify something. Therefore every sign is also some thing. For because it is no thing, as Augustine said in the same (book), it is entirely nothing; but conversely not every thing is a sign », because it is not employed to signify anything. And since the studious and modest speculation of theologians is intent upon these, it turns toward the Sacred Page to hold the form prescribed in doctrine. Of these, therefore, there is to be an orderly discussion [disserendum est] by us who want, with God as (our) leader, to open an approach towards understanding to some extent the things divine; and first we would discuss in an orderly manner things, afterwards signs." (Peter the Lombard, *Sentences,* Book 1, Chapter 1, *Every doctrine concerns things and/or signs*; accessed 16 May 2006; from http://www.franciscan-archive.org/lombardus/opera/ls1-01.html; Internet).

[1044] Thomas P. Johnston, *Charts for a Theology of Evangelism* (Nashville: Broadman, 2007), 50-54.

(b) Might there be a comparison on some level between Finney's emphasis on "Moral Philosophy" and the 1907 assessment of the General Baptists in 1750?

> A new assembly was formed, and in 1750 the major part of the General Baptists [in England] had become Unitarian in their beliefs. This was followed by worldliness, lax discipline, the superficial preaching of mere morality, and the members fell away in large numbers.[1045]

c) A parallel concept to "**moral philosophy**" was the German "**Weltanschauung**," defined by question.com as:

> "**World view**; a conception of the course of events in, and of the purpose of, the world as a whole, forming a philosophical view or apprehension of the universe; the general idea embodied in a cosmology."

The notion of **Weltanschauung** gained popularity in Germany in the late 19th Century, being popularized in American academia in the early 20th Century.[1046] It was applied to philosophy, theology, and then psychoanalysis in the 1950s and 1960s. Today **Weltanschauung** has morphed into the concept of a "**Christian worldview**."

d) Today "**Christian Worldview**", a grandchild of Aquinas' **Natural Theology** and a cousin to Socinius' "**Moral Philosophy**" is gradually replacing the word "Gospel" for some in their efforts to "influence the world for Christ" (a codeword for evangelism) and as a basis for unity among all "Christians." Similarly with emphasis on a **Christian worldview** is the concept of "**Connecting with God**" alongside of or in the place of repenting of individual sin and believing in the substitutionary work of Christ.

Terms other than the word "gospel" bring further distinctions and debates when discussing the "gospel." These are translating the word εὐαγγέλιον, the meaning of the cross, as well as issues of salvation.

2. **Several Preliminary Issues Related to the Gospel:**

   a. **Some thoughts on the translation of εὐαγγέλιον (or "Gospel"):** Instead of being translated "Gospel," should not the Greek noun εὐαγγέλιον be translated "**Good News**" or "**Glad Tidings**"?

      1) Arguments to use words other than "Gospel" are made for several reasons:

         a) The term "Gospel" today has unique Christian implications which the term "εὐαγγέλιον" did not seem to have in the 1st Century, and it is therefore not properly understood by non-acculturated Christians in the context of its NT usage (this is largely a dynamic equivalent argument):
            (1) The term may derive from a combination of "God's-spelling," also forming the terms gospelling and gospel; hence gospelling the gospel
            (2) Others have posited that "spell" is derived from witchcraft in which spells are cast; these then consider that the term "spell" had something to do with the reception of the Holy Spirit
            (3) Non-use of the word "Gospel" may also be tainted by anti-Pauline Gospel tendencies, as well as non-conversionist sentiment.

[1045]Henry C. Vedder, *A Short History of Baptists* (Philadelphia: American Baptist, 1907, 1926, … 1945), 239.

[1046]For example: Horace B., Samuel, *Modernities* (New York: E. P. Dutton, 1914), Wincenty Lutoslawski, *The World of* Souls (London: Allen a& Unwin, 1924; New York: Dial, 1924; New York: MacVeagh, 1924); Albert Schweitzer and Charles E. B. Russell, *Indian Thought and Its Development* (Boston: Beacon, 1935; New York: H. Holt, 1936; London: Hodder & Stoughton, 1936); Herbert Reichert, *Studies in the Weltanschauung of Gottfried Keller* (Ph.D. Thesis, University of Illinois, 1942), published as *The Philosophy of Gottfried Keller* (Chapel Hill, 1949).

b) Likewise, the OT use of "Gospel" in 2 Sam 4:10, shows that there was a secular nature to the term, much like the OT use of the verb εὐαγγελίζω to announce the news of victory in battle (cf. 1 Sam 31:9; 2 Sam 1:20; 4:10…), thereby arguing against the use of a strictly spiritual term in translation

   (1) Similarly, in 1 Thess 3:6 Paul used the verb εὐαγγελίζω to describe when Timothy brought him relational good news of the Thessalonian church's view of him

2) However, there are some arguments to keep the use of the word "Gospel":

   a) 2 Samuel 4:10 is the only OT use of the noun εὐαγγέλιον, and it is the only plural use of the word in the entire Bible, therefore limiting its usefulness for strict comparison with the NT usage; a nuanced theological NT use of a word which already exists in the LXX is not unusual, but to be expected

   b) The contemporary English use of the word "Gospel" follows Paul's 1 Corinthians 15 use of the word

   c) One could consider the use of the word "**Bible**" similarly:
      (1) While there are many books (βιβλίον) in the world, there is only one **Bible**; hence the authority lies in the definite article
      (2) While there is a relative amount of good news in the world, there is only one "**Good News**"—"**the Good News**" (with definite article and capitalized as a proper noun), rather than merely another item of "**good news**"

   d) Because of the uniqueness and distinct nature of what the NT defines as the "**Gospel**" (as we shall see below), it seems appropriate that unique Christian terminology has developed to translate the term

3) Therefore, this author deems it advisable to use the term **Gospel** (with caps) in order to translate one word for one word; if one is convinced of the need to use **Good News** or **Glad Tidings** (for whatever reason), it would seem advisable to also capitalize these to show that they are referring to a proper noun.

b. **Thoughts on Individualism versus Socialism (or a Communal/Community Emphasis):**

Introduction: As noted in the above presentation, the concepts of individualism and socialism have been hotly debated in the history of the church in the United States (and in England).[1047] The impact of moving away from the New Testament's individual salvation has always led to a move away from the fundamentals of the faith. Therefore, as these notes affirm an individual Gospel <u>and</u> an individual work of the Gospel, several verses will have to suffice to show the individual emphasis of the Bible as regards salvation and accountability. Yes, there are verses on the corporate nature of the faith, but these refer to spiritual growth and the church. Again the problem is confusing the contexts and emphases.

1) Before attempting to address the topic of "individualism," let us consider the alternatives:
   a) Individual salvation as coming forward and making a decision for Christ at an evangelistic meeting?
   b) An individual being brought in when he/she is three weeks old to be baptized by the parish priest or pastor?
   c) If (a) is an example of individualism and (b) is not, then it is an issue of heredity and parentage, and has very little to do with "individualism" per se
   d) Or what of the opposite of individual salvation, communal salvation: what is communal salvation, and how does it look, and how does it operate spiritually?

[1047]"It is inaccurate to argue—as often happens—that individualism is simply an 'invention' of the West. Rather, the Christian gospel of necessity emphasizes personal responsibility and personal decision; therefore individualism in Western culture is primarily a fruit of Christian mission. …

"Principalities and powers, governments and nations cannot come to faith—only individuals can" (Bosch, *Transforming Mission*, 416).

e) Before answering what is almost an ad hominem argument, the framing of the question must be understood in all of its particularities.

2) Verses on individualism:

   a) In Old Testament:

   (1) A Level of Individualism:
   Lev 4:27, "Now if anyone of the common people sins unintentionally in doing any of the things which the LORD has commanded not to be done, and becomes guilty..."
   Deut 18:19, "And it shall come about that whoever will not listen to My words which he shall speak in My name, I Myself will require *it* of him"
   > The actual Hebrew is even more emphatic in its individualism: "It shall be a man who does not harken unto the words which he shall speak in my name I Myself will require of him."
   > The only plural in this verse is "the words"—everything else is singular, with an intensification of the subject for the verb "require"
   Prov 9:12, "If you are wise, you are wise for yourself, And if you scoff, you alone will bear it"
   Isaiah 28:16, "Therefore thus says the Lord God, 'Behold, I am laying in Zion a stone, a tested stone, A costly cornerstone *for* the foundation, firmly placed. He who believes *in it* will not be disturbed.'"
   > [This verse includes the term "he who believes" which is also used many times in the Gospel of John]
   Ezek 18:4, "Behold, all souls are Mine; the soul of the father as well as the soul of the son is Mine. The soul who sins will die"

   (2) There Is also a Level of Anti-individualism in the OT:
   Deut 12:8-9, "You shall not at all do as we are doing here today—every man doing whatever *is* right in his own eyes—for as yet you have not come to the rest and the inheritance which the LORD your God is giving you"
   Judges 21:25, "In those days *there was* no king in Israel; everyone did *what was* right in his own eyes" (cf. Judges 17:6)

   This predicament led to a centralized form of worship and religious control in the OT:
   Deut 12:10-11, "But *when* you cross over the Jordan and dwell in the land which the LORD your God is giving you to inherit, and He gives you rest from all your enemies round about, so that you dwell in safety, then there will be the place where the LORD your God chooses to make His name abide. There you shall bring all that I command you: your burnt offerings, your sacrifices, your tithes, the heave offerings of your hand, and all your choice offerings which you vow to the LORD"
   2 Chron 7:12, "Then the LORD appeared to Solomon by night, and said to him: 'I have heard your prayer, and have chosen this place for Myself as a house of sacrifice'"

   Not so in the NT:
   John 4:21-24, "Jesus said to her, 'Woman, believe Me, the hour is coming when you will neither on this mountain, nor in Jerusalem, worship the Father. You worship what you do not know; we know what we worship, for salvation is of the Jews. But the hour is coming, and now is, when the true worshipers will worship the Father in spirit and truth; for the Father is seeking such to worship Him. God *is* Spirit, and those who worship Him must worship in spirit and truth.'"
   1 Cor 6:19-20, "Or do you not know that your body is the temple of the Holy Spirit *who is* in you, whom you have from God, and you are not your own? For you were bought at a price; therefore glorify God in your body and in your spirit, which are God's"

   So also with individual accountability, which is to be guided by an individual sense of duty for one's neighbor (see also below Rom 14:4):
   1 Cor 9:23-24, "All things are lawful for me, but not all things are helpful; all things are lawful for me, but not all things edify. Let no one seek his own, but each one the other's *well-being*"

b) In New Testament:

(1) Necessity for an Individual Response to the Gospel:
>   Because "you" in English can be either singular or plural, I have shown when the words in Greek are singular or plural in the brackets
>
>   John 3:3, "Jesus answered and said to him, 'Truly, truly, I say to you [singular], unless one is born [singular] again, he cannot [singular] see the kingdom of God.'"
>
>   John 3:7, "Do not marvel that I said to you [singular], 'You [plural] must be born [infinitive] again.'" (last line literally, "it is necessary for you-all to be born again)
>
>   John 3:16, "For God so loved the world, that He gave His only begotten Son, that whoever believes [singular] in Him should not perish, but have eternal life"
>
>>   [In fact, the book of John is replete with the singular form of the verbal form πιστεύων in English "who/whoever believes," John 3:15, 16, 18 (twice), 36; 5:24; 6:35, 40, 47; 7:38; 11:25, 26; 12:44, 46; 14:12]
>>
>>   [The singular is also found in the phrase, "all who believe" (πᾶς ὁ πιστεύων) is found 6 times in the NT: John 3:15, 16; 12:46; Acts 13:39; Rom 10:11; 1 John 5:1]
>
>   John 3:18, "He who believes in Him is not judged; he who does not believe has been judged already, because he has not believed in the name of the only begotten Son of God"
>
>   Acts 16:30-31, "and after he brought them out, he said, 'Sirs, what must I do [singular] to be [infinitive] saved [singular]?' [31] And they said, 'Believe [singular] in the Lord Jesus, and you shall be saved [singular], you [singular] and your [singular] household [singular].'"
>
>   Rom 1:16, "For I am not ashamed of the gospel, for it is the power of God for salvation to everyone who believes [participle-present-active-dative-masculine-singular], to the Jew first and also to the Greek"
>
>   Rom 10:8-10, "But what does it say? 'The word is near you, in your mouth and in your heart'—that is, the word of faith which we are preaching, that if you confess [singular] with your mouth Jesus *as* Lord, and believe [singular] in your heart that God raised Him from the dead, you shall be saved [singular]; for with the heart man believes [singular], resulting in righteousness, and with the mouth he confesses [singular], resulting in salvation.
>
>   Rom 10:13, "for 'Whoever will call [singular] upon the name of the LORD will be saved.'"

(2) Judgment as Individuals:
>   1 Cor 3:12-15, "Now if any man builds on the foundation with gold, silver, precious stones, wood, hay, straw, each man's work will become evident; for the day will show it because it is *to be* revealed with fire, and the fire itself will test the quality of each man's work. If any man's work which he has built on it remains, he will receive a reward. If any man's work is burned up, he will suffer loss; but he himself will be saved, yet so as through fire"
>
>   2 Cor 5:10, "For we must all appear before the judgment seat of Christ, so that each one may be recompensed for his deeds in the body, according to what he has done, whether good or bad"
>
>   1 Pet 1:17, "If you address as Father the One who impartially judges according to each one's work, conduct yourselves in fear during the time of your stay *on earth*"
>
>   Rev 20:12-13, "And I saw the dead, the great and the small, standing before the throne, and books were opened; and another book was opened, which is *the book* of life; and the dead were judged from the things which were written in the books, according to their deeds. And the sea gave up the dead which were in it, and death and Hades gave up the dead which were in them; and they were judged, every one *of them* according to their deeds"

(3) Individual accountability:
>   Matt 25:14-15, 19, , "For *it is* just like a man *about* to go on a journey, who called his own slaves, and entrusted his possessions to them. [15] "And to one he gave five talents, to another, two, and to another, one, each according to his own ability; and he went on his journey. ... Now after a long time the master of those slaves came and settled accounts with them. [20] And the one who had received the five talents... [22] And the one who *had received* the two talents...[24] And the one also who had received the one talent..."
>
>   Mark 3:38, "For whoever is ashamed ['Ος γὰρ ἐὰν ἐπαισχυνθῇ (all singular)] of Me and My words in this adulterous and sinful generation, the Son of Man will also be ashamed of him when He comes in the glory of His Father with the holy angels."

Rom 14:4, "Who are you to judge the servant of another? To his own master he stands or falls; and stand he will, for the Lord is able to make him stand."

Rom 14:12, "So then each one of us will give an account of himself to God ["Αρα οὖν ἕκαστος ἡμῶν περὶ ἑαυτοῦ λόγον δώσει τῷ θεῷ]"

1 Cor 11:28, "But let a man examine himself [δοκιμαζέτω δὲ ἄνθρωπος ἑαυτὸν], and so let him eat of the bread and drink of the cup"

2 Cor 13:5, "Test yourselves *to see* if you are in the faith; examine yourselves! Or do you not recognize this about yourselves, that Jesus Christ is in you—unless indeed you fail the test?"

Gal 6:4-5, "But each one must examine his own work, and then he will have *reason for* boasting in regard to himself alone, and not in regard to another. For each one will bear his own load"

[Word studies on "one," "anyone," "each one," and "you" (sing) should suffice to show the plethora of instruction in the Bible on individual accountability]

(4) Individual giftedness:

1 Cor 12:7, "But to each one is given the manifestation of the Spirit for the common good"

1 Cor 12:11, "But one and the same Spirit works all these things, distributing to each one individually just as He wills"

1 Cor 12:18, "But now God has placed the members, each one of them, in the body, just as He desired"

Eph 4:7, "But to each one of us grace was given according to the measure of Christ's gift"

1 Pet 4:10, "As each one has received a *special* gift, employ it in serving one another as good stewards of the manifold grace of God"

(5) Individual Reward:

1 Cor 3:8, "Now he who plants and he who waters are one; but each will receive his own reward according to his own labor [ἕκαστος δὲ τὸν ἴδιον μισθὸν λήψεται κατὰ τὸν ἴδιον κόπον]"

2 Cor 5:10, "For we must all appear before the judgment seat of Christ, so that each one may be recompensed for his deeds in the body, according to what he has done, whether good or bad"

Eph 6:7, "With good will render service, as to the Lord, and not to men, knowing that whatever good thing each one does, this he will receive back from the Lord, whether slave or free"

(6) Individual Convictions:

Rom 14:5, "One person regards one day above another, another regards every day *alike*. Each person must be fully convinced in his own mind"

2 Cor 9:7, "Let each one *do* just as he has purposed in his heart; not grudgingly or under compulsion; for God loves a cheerful giver"

2 Tim 3:14-15, "You [singular], however, continue in the things you [singular] have learned and become convinced of, knowing from whom you [singular] have learned *them*; and that from childhood you [singular] have known the sacred writings which are able to give you [singular] the wisdom that leads to salvation through faith which is in Christ Jesus."

3) Verses on socialism or the social nature of Christianity:[1048]

a) The creation blessing (which some turn into the "Cultural Mandate"), Gen 1:28, "And God blessed them; and God said to them, 'Be fruitful and multiply, and fill the earth, and subdue it; and rule over the fish of the sea and over the birds of the sky, and over every living thing that moves on the earth.'"

b) Verses on the impact of the Christian on the world, e.g. "you are the salt of the earth" (Matt 5:13), in the context of social impact it is changed into a command, "you must be the salt of the earth" (see my chart on approaches to the meaning of salt)[1049]

[1048]The admission of Charles Colson regarding a lack of NT material on engagement in politics is applicable here, "When we turn to the New Testament, admittedly we do not find verses specifically commanding believers to be engaged in politics or the law or education or the arts. But we don't need to, because the cultural mandate given to Adam still applies" (Charles Colson and Nancy Pearcey, *How Now Shall We Live?* [Wheaton, IL: Tyndale House, 1999], 296).

c) The "Kingdom of God" in the Gospels, particularly in Matthew: the rulership of God exerted in a new way by the revelation of Jesus, is turned into the rulership of man over creation and the cosmos through the social teachings of Jesus

d) The 62 "one another" [ἀλλήλων] commands in the New Testament, e.g. "love one another," John 13:34-35

e) Other verses affirm the community of the saints, after conversion:
Rom 11:17-18, "But if some of the branches were broken off, and you, being a wild olive, were grafted in among them and became partaker with them of the rich root of the olive tree, [18] do not be arrogant toward the branches; but if you are arrogant, *remember that* it is not you who supports the root, but the root *supports* you"
1 Cor 12:12, "For even as the body is one and *yet* has many members, and all the members of the body, though they are many, are one body, so also is Christ"
1 Cor 12:27, "Now you are Christ's body, and individually members of it."
[Now here's an interesting verse combining individualism with community!]
Eph 2:19-22, "So then you are no longer strangers and aliens, but you are fellow citizens with the saints, and are of God's household, having been built upon the foundation of the apostles and prophets, Christ Jesus Himself being the corner *stone*, in whom the whole building, being fitted together is growing into a holy temple in the Lord; in whom you also are being built together into a dwelling of God in the Spirit"
1 Pet 2:4-5, "And coming to Him as to a living stone, rejected by men, but choice and precious in the sight of God, [5] you also, as living stones, are being built up as a spiritual house for a holy priesthood, to offer up spiritual sacrifices acceptable to God through Jesus Christ"
1 Pet 2:9-10, "But you are a chosen race, a royal priesthood, a holy nation, a people for *God's* own possession, that you may proclaim the excellencies of Him who has called you out of darkness into His marvelous light; for you once were not a people, but now you are the people of God; you had not received mercy, but now you have received mercy"

f) It would seem that these verses on the life of the church are wrongly used to affirm a social element to salvation, actually negating, altering, or ignoring all of the prior verses on an individual salvation!

Conclusion: It must be noted that none of the verses dealing with community overturn, diminish, or dismiss the examples of and teaching on an individualistic salvation and individual accountability in the New Testament.

4) The NT's alarming approach to family relationships, in light of the Gospel and evangelism!

Intro: Surprising and even alarming are the words of Jesus regarding family relationships in light of His Gospel! For Jesus, His Gospel and its proclamation superceded any and all social relationships, even those of the nuclear family, which is without a doubt the most basic social construct in humanity. These insights ought not be ignored as the social aspect of faith in Christ is discussed. In fact, perhaps it is for this very reason that Jesus is so direct and unabashed in this teaching!

a) Jesus' teaching before He sent His disciples "On Mission," and parallels:
Matt 10:21, "Now brother will deliver up brother to death, and a father *his* child; and children will rise up against parents and cause them to be put to death"
Matt 10:34-36, "Do not think that I came to bring peace on earth. I did not come to bring peace but a sword. For I have come to 'set a man against his father, a daughter against her mother, and a daughter-in-law against her mother-in-law'; and 'a man's enemies *will be* those of his *own* household.'"
Luke 12:51-53, "Do *you* suppose that I came to give peace on earth? I tell you, not at all, but rather division. For from now on five in one house will be divided: three against two, and two against three. Father will be divided against son and son against father, mother against daughter and daughter against mother, mother-in-law against her daughter-in-law and daughter-in-law against her mother-in-law."

[1049]Johnston, *Charts for a Theology of Evangelism*, Chart 60, "Five Interpretations of 'Salt' in Matthew 5:13,"

Matt 10:37, "He who loves father or mother more than Me is not worthy of Me. And he who loves son or daughter more than Me is not worthy of Me"

Luke 14:26, "If anyone comes to Me and does not hate his father and mother, wife and children, brothers and sisters, yes, and his own life also, he cannot be My disciple"

b) Following Jesus, family relationships, and the end times:

Mark 13:12, "Now brother will betray brother to death, and a father *his* child; and children will rise up against parents and cause them to be put to death"

Luke 21:16, "You will be betrayed even by parents and brothers, relatives and friends; and they will put *some* of you to death"

c) Further teaching in the Gospels regarding family relationships, hometown people, and following Jesus:

Matt 4:21-22, "Going on from there, He saw two other brothers, James *the son* of Zebedee, and John his brother, in the boat with Zebedee their father, mending their nets. He called them, and immediately they left the boat and their father, and followed Him" (Mark 1:20

Matt 12:46-50, "While He was still talking to the multitudes, behold, His mother and brothers stood outside, seeking to speak with Him. Then one said to Him, 'Look, Your mother and Your brothers are standing outside, seeking to speak with You.' But He answered and said to the one who told Him, 'Who is My mother and who are My brothers?' And He stretched out His hand toward His disciples and said, 'Here are My mother and My brothers! For whoever does the will of My Father in heaven is My brother and sister and mother'" (Mark 3:31-35; Luke 8:19-21)

Matt 13:54-57, "And when He had come to His own country, He taught them in their synagogue, so that they were astonished and said, 'Where did this *Man* get this wisdom and *these* mighty works? Is this not the carpenter's son? Is not His mother called Mary? And His brothers James, Joses, Simon, and Judas? And His sisters, are they not all with us? Where then did this *Man* get all these things?' So they were offended at Him. But Jesus said to them, 'A prophet is not without honor except in his own country and in his own house.' Now He did not do many mighty works there because of their unbelief"

Mark 10:29-30, "So Jesus answered and said, 'Assuredly, I say to you, there is no one who has left house or brothers or sisters or father or mother or wife or children or lands, for My sake and the gospel's, who shall not receive a hundredfold now in this time—houses and brothers and sisters and mothers and children and lands, with persecutions—and in the age to come, eternal life'" (Matt 19:25; Luke 18:29-30)

Luke 9:59-60, "Then He said to another, 'Follow Me.' But he said, 'Lord, let me first go and bury my father. Jesus said to him, 'Let the dead bury their own dead, but you go and preach the kingdom of God.'"

Luke 9:61-62, "And another also said, 'Lord, I will follow You, but let me first go *and* bid them farewell who are at my house.' But Jesus said to him, 'No one, having put his hand to the plow, and looking back, is fit for the kingdom of God.'"

John 7:3-5, "His brothers therefore said to Him, 'Depart from here and go into Judea, that Your disciples also may see the works that You are doing. For no one does anything in secret while he himself seeks to be known openly. If You do these things, show Yourself to the world.' For even His brothers did not believe in Him"

d) Paul on faith, family, and individual salvation (notice the underlying assumption that not all believers have children who walk with the Lord):

1 Cor 7:12-13, 15-16, "But to the rest I, not the Lord, say: If any brother has a wife who does not believe, and she is willing to live with him, let him not divorce her. And a woman who has a husband who does not believe, if he is willing to live with her, let her not divorce him. ... But if the unbeliever departs, let him depart; a brother or a sister is not under bondage in such *cases*. But God has called us to peace. For how do you know, O wife, whether you will save *your* husband? Or how do you know, O husband, whether you will save *your* wife?"

1 Tim 3:4-5, "one who rules his own house well, having *his* children in submission with all reverence (for if a man does not know how to rule his own house, how will he take care of the church of God?)"

1 Tim 3:12, "Let deacons be the husbands of one wife, ruling *their* children and their own houses well"

1 Tim 5:14-15, "Therefore I desire that *the* younger *widows* marry, bear children, manage the house, give no opportunity to the adversary to speak reproachfully. For some have already turned aside after Satan"

Titus 1:6, "if a man is blameless, the husband of one wife, having faithful children not accused of dissipation or insubordination"

e) On the behavior of "some" in the context of the social bonds of the church:

1 Tim 1:5-7, "Now the purpose of the commandment is love from a pure heart, *from* a good conscience, and *from* sincere faith, from which **some**, having strayed, have turned aside to idle talk, desiring to be teachers of the law, understanding neither what they say nor the things which they affirm"

1 Tim 5:13, "And besides they learn *to be* idle, wandering about from house to house, and not only idle but also gossips and busybodies, saying things which they ought not"

1 Tim 6:10, "For the love of money is a root of all *kinds of* evil, for which **some** have strayed from the faith in their greediness, and pierced themselves through with many sorrows"

1 Tim 6:20-21, "O Timothy! Guard what was committed to your trust, avoiding the profane *and* idle babblings and contradictions of what is falsely called knowledge—by professing it **some** have strayed concerning the faith. …"

Conclusion: A serious analysis of the social aspects of conversion must be done keeping in mind the promise fracture of family relationships prophesied by Jesus, as well as the weakness of the social construct of the church to assure the spiritual growth of those within it, from a biblical point-of-view. With these verses in mind, the individualistic aspects of conversion, though derided by some, appear far more biblical than any social construct that may be theorized.

c. **The Cross**. Some thoughts about what the Cross is not (also note my book of charts):[1050]

1) Not merely self-discipline (as Christianized Stoicism), 1 Cor 9:27

2) Not merely self-effacement (as Christianized Buddhism), Gal 2:20

3) Not merely an example of solidarity with the human predicament (as Christianized Socialism or Liberalized Christianity), Matt 25:35-36

4) Not merely an example to be worshipped and imitated (as Catholicized Christianity), Phil 2:12

5) Not merely God showing us how much He loves us and how much He wants to have a relationship with us (Liberalized Protestantism).

Rather the Cross refers to the instrument of death upon which Jesus Christ paid the sin debt of the world—to which we ought not add anything!

d. **"Lordship Salvation"** versus **"Free Grace."** In the 1980s, another battle began resurfacing in which some felt that repentance was necessary prior to believing. On the other hand, the free grace people felt that requiring outward signs of repentance was adding to the grace of God. The issue was as follows: must a person be broken by the law (unto repentance), before they can understand God's grace in Jesus Christ (unto faith), and if so, how does this repentance manifest itself? Consider the holiness movement (late 1800s) as a historical precedent to this issue, as well as the division between the General and Particular Baptists (late 1600s):

1) Consider that Luke's Great Commission only uses the word repentance as the focal point of the preaching of the Gospel:

Luke 24:47, "and that repentance for forgiveness of sins should be proclaimed in His name to all the nations, beginning from Jerusalem"

2) It appears, therefore, that it is not a matter of either/or, but a matter of both/and

---

[1050]Johnston, *Charts for a Theology of Evangelism*, Chart 26, "Views of Bearing One's Cross," 45.

e. **A Hermeneutical Comment:**

The words of Christ in John 16:12-13 bring up another point as to where and why the Gospel may be found:

> "I still have many things to say to you, but you cannot bear *them* now. However, when He, the Spirit of truth, has come, He will guide you into all truth; for He will not speak on His own *authority,* but whatever He hears He will speak; and He will tell you things to come" (John 16:12-13).

Several comments…

1) Even in the upper room discourse, with Judas absent (John 13:30), when Jesus was no longer using figurative speech (John 16:29-30), there were "many things" which Jesus still needed to say to His disciples.

  a) Similarly, the disciples on the road to Emmaus (from among the inner circle of disciples), although they knew the historical fact about the death and resurrection of Jesus, they did not understand it; Jesus had to interpret His own death and resurrection for them, which resulted in Luke's Great Commission (Luke 24:46-47).

2) Not only does this affirm the need for the epistles of the New Testament, but it also shows that the fullness of divine revelation (in a progressive sense) was not yet complete.

3) The words of Jesus, "it is finished" in Revelation 21:6, closes the addition of the "many things" expected due to John 16:12, 25

4) Between these two (John 16:12, 25 and Revelation 21:6), come the Book of Acts and the writings of Paul. In these writings the Gospel is more fully explained, as we shall see below. Based on John 16:12-13, 25 (which may refer to the resurrection narrative, especially that of Luke 24), one can therefore prioritize the more complete revelation of the Pauline Gospel (as it is called) over and above the varieties of interpretations from the "Gospels" which are made to emanate from the accounts of the life of Jesus (Golden Rule, virtues, living like Christ, servicing others as priority as prioritative over preaching the Gospel, etc.):

  a) Hence, consider Paul's audacity [in a positive sense] in making his preaching of the Gospel the measuring stick:

    (1) "According to my Gospel," Rom 2:16; 16:25; 1 Tim 1:11

    (2) A Gospel other/besides/otherwise/contrary than what "we" (Paul and "all the brethren that are with me" Gal 1:2) have preached: Gal 1:8-9, "But even though we, or an angel from heaven, should preach to you a gospel contrary to that which we have preached to you, let him be accursed. As we have said before, so I say again now, if any man is preaching to you a gospel contrary to that which you received, let him be accursed."

Comparative Translations of the preposition παρά in Gal 1:8-9

Byzantine	Vulgate	Wycliffe (1382)	Wycliffe (1388)	Tyndale (1534)	Geneva (1560)	Bishop's (1995); cf. KJV; Webster's; NKJ	James Murdock (1852); cf. Young's	Darby (1884, 1890)	English Revised (1885); cf. ASV; NIV**	RSV (1952); NAS	New Jerusalem (1985)
παρ'	Praeter-quam/ praeter id	bisydis that/ out .. that	bisidis that/ bisidis that	eny other ... then	otherwise, then	any other ... then	differently from	as ... besides	any ... other than	a ... otherwise	a ... other than the one
		As adverb to euangelisid and euangelise	As adverb to prechid and preche	As adjective to supplied nouns: gospell and thinge	As adverb to preach	As adjective to supplied noun: Gospel	As adverb of announce	As adverb of announce glad tidings	As adjective of gospel	As adjective of gospel	Unequi-vocally rerefing to the gospel message
Ἀλλὰ καὶ ἐὰν ἡμεῖς ἢ ἄγγελος ἐξ οὐρανοῦ εὐαγγελί-ζηται ὑμῖν παρ' ὃ εὐηγγελι-σάμεθα ὑμῖν, ἀνάθεμα ἔστω.	sed licet nos aut angelus de caelo evangelizet vobis praeter-quam quod evangeliz-avimus vobis anathema sit	But thouy we, or an aungel of heuene, euangelisid to you, bisydis that that we han euangelisid to you, cursid be he.	But thouy we, or an aungel of heuene, prechide to you, bisidis that that we han prechid to you, be he acursid.	Neverthe-lesse though we oure selves or an angell from heven preache eny other gospell vnto you the that which we have preached vnto you holde him as a cursed.	But thogh that we, or an Angel from heauen preache vnto you otherwise, then that which we haue preached vnto you, let him be accursed.	Neuerthe-lesse, though we, or an Angel from heauen, preache any other Gospel vnto you, then that which we haue preached vnto you, let hym be accursed.	But if we, or an angel from heaven, should announce to you differently from what we have announced to you, let him be accursed.	But if even *we* or an angel out of heaven announce as glad tidings to you anything besides what we have announced as glad tidings to you, let him be accursed.	But though we, or an angel from heaven, should preach unto you any gospel other than that which we preached unto you, let him be anathema.	But even if we, or an angel from heaven, should preach to you a gospel contrary to that which we preached to you, let him be accursed.	But even if we ourselves or an angel from heaven preaches to you a gospel other than the one we preached to you, let God's curse be on him.
⁹ Ὡς προειρήκα-μεν, καὶ ἄρτι πάλιν λέγω, εἴ τις ὑμᾶς εὐαγγελί-ζεται παρ' ὃ παρελάβετε, ἀνάθεμα ἔστω.	⁹ sicut praedix-imus et nunc iterum dico si quis vobis evangeliz-averit praeter id quod accepistis anathema sit	⁹ As I bifor seide, and now eftsoone I seye, if ony schal euangelise out taken that that ye han takun, cursid be he.	⁹ As Y haue seid bifore, and now eftsoones Y seie, if ony preche to you othere thinge vnto you then that ye han vndur-fongun, be he cursid.	⁹ As I sayde before so saye I now agayne yf eny man preache eny other thinge vnto you then that ye have receaved holde him accursed.	⁹ As we said before, so say I now againe, If anie man preache vnto you otherwise, then that ye haue receiued, let him be accursed.	⁹ As we sayde before, so say I nowe agayne, yf any man preache any other Gospell vnto you, then that ye haue receaued, let hym be accursed.	⁹ As I have just said, and now I again say it, that if any one announce to you differently from what ye received, let him be accursed.	⁹ As we have said before, now also again I say, If any one announce to you as glad tidings anything besides what ye have received, let him be accursed.	⁹ As we have said before, so say I now again, If any man preacheth unto you any gospel other than that which ye received, let him be anathema.	⁹ As we have said before, so now I say again, If any one is preaching to you a gospel contrary to that which you received, let him be accursed.	⁹ I repeat again what we declared before: anyone who preaches to you a gospel other than the one you were first given is to be under God's curse.

*The Bible in Basic English changed the verb evangelize into the phrase "be a preacher of good news"; hence, "But even if we, or an angel from heaven, were to be a preacher to you of good news other than that which we have given you, let there be a curse on him. ⁹ As we have said before, so say I now again, If any man is a preacher to you of any good news other than that which has been given to you, let there be a curse on him.

**Notice that the NIV, quite uniquely, supplies the term "message" at the end of Gal 2:6, thereby supplying the interpretation of Gal 1:8-9 as referring to the message and not the method.

(3) Making himself the model of imitating Christ: 1 Cor 11:1, "Be imitators of me, just as I also am of Christ" (given in the context of evangelism).

(4) Then, fortunately, the Book of Acts faithfully recorded the ministry of Paul for us to imitate![1051]

[1051]Martin Luther, *A Commentary on St. Paul's Epistle to the Galatians* (Westwood, NJ: Revell, n.d.), 201-05.

This very important distinction, regarding the centrality of a Pauline Gospel, was communicated in a sermon of R. A. Torrey, former President of Moody Bible Institute, who had studied at the Universities of Leipzig and Erlangen in the 1882-1883.[1052]

In fact, without making this distinction one's view of the Gospel is relegated to a nuance between or some dialectic of James, Jesus, and Paul, which is reminiscent of Paul's concern as noted in 1 Cor 1:12-13.

Notice that Vatican II's *Dei Verbum* clearly placed "the Gospels" as the preeminent texts of the NT, as they are considered to coincide with the Church of Rome's theology.[1053] The same teaching was reaffirmed in the *Catechism of the Catholic Church*, §125-127:

"§125 The *Gospels* [Matthew, Mark, Luke, (and John)] are at the heart of all Scriptures 'because they are our principal source for the life and teaching of the Incarnate Word, our Saviour.'
"§126 We can distinguish three stages in the formation of the Gospels:
"1. *The life and teaching of Jesus.* …
"2. *The oral tradition.* …
"3. *The written Gospels.* [notice how a "Pauline Gospel" is framed out of the question]
"§127 The fourfold Gospel [a reference to the four books] holds a unique place in the Church, as is evident both in the veneration which liturgy accords it and in the surpassing attraction it has exercised on the saints at all times."[1054]

Furthermore, notice what Pope Gregory VII wrote in his 1075 "Dictatus Papae":

"That no chapter or book may be recognized as canonical without his authority [for *Quod nullum capitulum nullus que liber canonicus habeatur absque illius auctoritate*]"[1055]

f. **Culture and Message:**

1) Some place a very high value on being culturally relevant

2) However, adding culture into the mix of the message can yield unexpected results:

   a) It can lead to picking and choosing what would or what would not be relevant to a given culture, as interpreted in the finite mind of the observer

   b) Then leading to picking and choosing as to what parts of the Bible to emphasize, and naturally then, what parts of it to deemphasize

---

[1052]"We are sometimes asked how we know that the apostles correctly reported what Jesus said—'they may have forgotten?' True, they might forget, but Christ Himself tells us that in the Gospels we have not only the apostles' recollection of what He said but the Holy Ghost's recollection, and the Spirit of God never forgets. In John 16:13,14, Christ said that the Holy Ghost should guide the apostles into "all truth"; therefore in the New Testament teaching we have the whole sphere of God's truth. The teaching of the apostles is more complete than that of Jesus Himself, for He says in John 16:12, 13, 'I have yet many things to say unto you, but ye cannot bear them now. Howbeit, when he, the Spirit of Truth, is come, he shall guide you into *all truth*.' While His own teaching had been partial, because of their weakness, the teaching of the apostles, under the promised Spirit, was able to take in the whole sphere of God's truth" (R. A. Torrey, "Ten Reasons Why I Believe the Bible to Be the Word of God," in Roger Martin, *R. A. Torrey: Apostles of Certainty* [Murfreesboro, TN: Sword of the Lord, 1976], 283).

[1053]"It is common knowledge that among all the Scriptures, even those of the New Testament, the Gospels have a special preeminence, and rightly so, for they are the principal witness for the life and teaching of the Incarnate Word, our Saviour" (Paul VI, Vatican II: Dogmatic Constitution on Divine Revelation: *Dei Verbum* [18 November 1965]; §18; available from http://listserv.american.edu/catholic/church/vaticanii/dei-verbum.html; accessed: 10 October 2005; Internet).

[1054]*Catechism of the Catholic Church* (Latin text © 1993, Libreria Editrice Vaticana; English translation for United Kingdom, © 1994, Geoffrey Chapman; Translation subject to revision in light of the *edition typical*; London: Geoffrey Chapman, 1994), §125-127.

[1055]Gregory VII, *Dictatus Papae*; from Brian Pullan, *Sources for the History of Medieval Europe from the Mid-Eighth to the Mid-Thirteenth Century* (Oxford: Basil Blackwell, 1971), document no. III 9, translated from Gregory VII's *Register*, no. II 55a.; available at: http://faculty.cua.edu/pennington/churchhistory220/topicfive/ DictatusPapaePullan.htm (online); accessed 4 July 2011; Internet.

    c)   It can lead to overriding the idea of preaching the "whole counsel of God" (Acts 20:27) for a higher motive, that of being culturally-sensitive:

        (1) It may inadvertently places the onus of responsibility on parsing culture, rather than properly illuminating the Word of God

        (2) The study of the Word of God may then take second place behind the *a priori* study of culture

        (3) According to Acts 20:27, placing culture above the Word of God in this way leads to bloodguilt

    d)   It can lead to disobeying the command, "Do not omit a word" (Jer 26:2):

        (1) Words and terms are regularly omitted by culturally relevant preachers who do not want to be rejected because of their culturally-insensitive message

        (2) Sometimes it would seem that culturally-relevant preachers would rather have the approval of men than that of God, John 12:42-43

        (3) As words and terms are changed, then theological systems are changed, often without knowing it, or without caring about it

3)   It may be that being culturally-relevant is not all that it is cracked up to be!

B. Some Shallow Wells for Summarizing the Gospel Message:

1. Kerygma (κήρυγμα) as Expressing the Gospel?[1056]

Introduction: Since 1936, much of the debate over the message of the Gospel has centered around the term *kerygma*. The issue in divergent definitions of the *kerygma* seems to be "what Gospel did the preachers in the book of Acts preach?" C. H. Dodd's *The Apostolic Preaching and its Development* masterfully reframed the question away from the Book of Romans, to the Book of Acts, and away from the Five Fundamentals of the Faith.[1057] This shift to a more nebulous definition of the Gospel was welcomed by younger more broad-minded Evangelicals of his time.

A focus on *kerygma*, therefore, moved the debate away from the clarity of the Book of Romans, a Pauline Gospel, or the "Roman Road" (e.g. total depravity, justification by faith alone, emphasis on eternal life) to a debate over the content of the various messages in the Book of Acts (with a special focus on Acts 17). The next logical step was to shift from the Book of Acts to develop a Gospel uniquely from the social teachings of Jesus, which is exactly what took place among mainstream Protestants of the middle 1900s (e.g. the *Christian Century* magazine with Reinhold Niebuhr as its editor).[1058] As for the social teachings of Jesus, this teaching and its practice had already been developed in the early 20th Century by Adolf Harnack[1059] and Walter Rauschenbusch.[1060] In that light, the proposal of Dodd was like a synthesis or mid-point between the Pauline Gospel and the social teachings of Jesus, corresponding to Gustav Aulen's *Christus Victor*.[1061]

A 20th Century Progression in Understanding the Message of the Gospel

Pauline Gospel (as in Romans)	→	The Kerygma (from Acts)	→	The Social Teachings Of Jesus (from the Synopics)*

*The Gospel of John is often deemed by social theologians to emphasize Manichean tendencies (light versus darkness; world as evil; and spiritual versus temporal, e.g. the new birth and eternal life).

    a. C.H. Dodd, 1936:[1062]
       (1) Prophecies are fulfilled, and the new age is inaugurated by the coming of Christ
       (2) He was born of the seed of David
       (3) He died according to the Scriptures to deliver us out of the present evil age
       (4) He was buried
       (5) He rose on the third day according to the Scriptures
       (6) He is exalted at the right hand of God
       (7) He will come again as judge and Savior.

[1056]Historical from Lewis Drummond, *The Word of the Cross: A Contemporary Theology of Evangelism* (Nashville: Broadman, 1992).

[1057]Cardinal Joseph Ratzinger (now Benedict XVI), Prefect of the Congregation for the Doctrine of the Faith, described the five fundamentals from the 1895 Niagara Bible Conference as "inerrancy of Scripture, the deity of Christ, the virginal birth, vicarious expiation, and the bodily resurrection" (Commission biblique pontificale, *L'interprétation de la Bible dans l'Église* [Montreal: Fides, 1994], 18).

[1058]See Reinhold Niebuhr, "Billy Graham's Christianity—and the World Crisis" (*Christian and Society* [Spring 1955], 3-4), "Literalism, Individualism, and Billy Graham" (*Christian Century,* 23 May 1956, 641-42), "Proposal to Billy Graham" (*Christian Century,* 8 August 1956, 921-22), and "After Comment, the Deluge" (*Christian Century,* 4 November 1957, 1034-35).

[1059]Adolf von Harnack and W. Herrmann, *Essays on the Social Gospel* (London: Williams and Norgate, 1907).

[1060]Walter Rauschenbusch, *Theology for the Social Gospel* (New York: Macmillan, 1917; Nashville: Abingdon, 1990).

[1061]Gustav Aulén, *Christus Victor: An Historical Study of the Three Main Types of the Idea of the Atonement*, trans. A. G. Hebert (1930; New York: Macmillan, 1969).

[1062]C.H. Dodd, *The Apostolic Preaching and its Development* (London: Hodder and Stoughton. 1936).

   b. James Stewart, 1953:[1063]
       (1) Incarnation
       (2) Forgiveness
       (3) Cross
       (4) Resurrection
       (5) Simply: Christ

   c. Roland Allen, 1962[1064]

   d. Douglas Webster, 1966:[1065]
       1) "The person and character of Jesus Christ. He really did live."
       2) "The teaching of Jesus Christ. He said certain things about God, about life, about the
           kingdom of God, and about human destiny ... [as] no one had [ever] spoken before."
       3) "The death of Jesus Christ. The death of our Lord was a turning point in history ... and God
           was active in it."
       4) "The resurrection of Jesus Christ.

   e. Hans Conzelmann, 1969:[1066]
       1) The promise of salvation
       2) The connection with Scripture
       3) The newness of Christian existence

   f. Michael Green, 1970:41[1067]

The following chart illustrates the reframing of the question which took place following C. H.
       Dodd's study on the "Apostolic preaching," as compared with the Lucan Great Commission and
       the "Roman Road."

Comparative of C. H. Dodd's *Kerygma*

C. H. Dodd's *Kerygma*	Luke 24:46-47	The Roman Road

a. Prophecies are fulfilled, and the new age is inaugurated by the coming of Christ
b. He was born of the seed of David
c. He died according to the Scriptures to deliver us out of the present evil age
d. He was buried
e. He rose on the third day according to the Scriptures
f. He is exalted at the right hand of God
g. He will come again as judge and Savior.
	a. "Thus it is written,
	
	b. that the Christ would suffer and
	
	c. rise again from the dead the third day,
	
	d. and that repentance for forgiveness of sins
	
	e. would be proclaimed in His name
	
	f. to all the nations, beginning from Jerusalem
		1. **Need** (Why?):
		  a. God says that all are sinners, Rom 3:10, 23
		  b. God tells us the reason all are sinners, Rom 5:12
		2. **Consequence** (What?) God tells us the result of sin, Rom 6:23
		3. **Remedy** (How?) God tells us of His concern for sinners, Rom 5:8-9
		4. **Condition** (Who?) God's way of salvation is made plain, Rom 10:9-10, 13
		5. **Results**: God tells us the results of salvation, Rom 5:1, 8:1
		6. **Assurance**: God gives the saved sinner assurance, Rom 8:16

Conclusion: A look at historical definitions of *kerygma* proves subjective and inconclusive. Many
       authors disagree on exactly what is the *kerygma*. Imagine a Gospel tract with C.H. Dodd's points
       as the message! Thus seeking a Gospel message in the various views of the *kerygma* proves
       disappointing; one must look elsewhere…

[1063]James Stewart, *A Faith to Proclaim* (New York: Scribner, 1953).

[1064]Roland Allen, *Missionary Method's: St. Paul's or Ours?* (Grand Rapids: Eerdmans, 1962).

[1065]Douglas Webster. *Yes to Missions* (London: SCM, 1966).

[1066]Hans Conzelmann, *An Outline of the Theology of the New Testament* (London: SCM, 1969).

[1067]Michael Green, *Evangelism in the Early Church* (London: Hodder and Stoughton. 1970).

2. Creeds as Expressing the Gospel?

a. Does the "Apostle's Creed" (or any similar creed) contain enough of the Gospel to bring a person to Christ?

1) In some liturgical churches, the entire congregation recites the Apostles Creed following a statement such as, "Let us now proclaim our faith!"

2) Let us similarly compare the Apostles Creed with some 1 Cor 15:1-8 and the Roman Road Gospel presentation…

Comparative of Apostles Creed

Apostles Creed	1 Corinthians 15:1-9	The Roman Road
I believe in God, the Father Almighty, the Creator of heaven and earth, and in Jesus Christ, His only Son, our Lord: Who was conceived of the Holy Spirit, born of the Virgin Mary, suffered under Pontius Pilate, was crucified, died, and was buried. He descended into hell. The third day He arose again from the dead. He ascended into heaven and sits at the right hand of God the Father Almighty, whence He shall come to judge the living and the dead. I believe in the Holy Spirit, the holy catholic church, the communion of saints, the **forgiveness of sins**, the resurrection of the body, and life everlasting. Amen.[1068]	1 Now I make known to you, brethren, the gospel which I preached to you, which also you received, in which also you stand, 2 by which also you are saved, if you hold fast the word which I preached to you, unless you believed in vain. 3 For I delivered to you as of first importance what I also received, that **Christ died for our sins** according to the Scriptures, 4 and that He was buried, and that He was raised on the third day according to the Scriptures, 5 and that He appeared to Cephas, then to the twelve. 6 After that He appeared to more than five hundred brethren at one time, most of whom remain until now, but some have fallen asleep; 7 then He appeared to James, then to all the apostles; 8 and last of all, as to one untimely born, He appeared to me also. 9 For I am the least of the apostles, and not fit to be called an apostle, because I persecuted the church of God.	1. **Need** (Why?): a. God says that all are sinners, Rom 3:10, 23 b. God tells us the reason all are sinners, Rom 5:12 2. **Consequence** (What?) God tells us the result of sin, Rom 6:23 3. **Remedy** (How?) God tells us of His concern for sinners, Rom 5:8-9 4. **Condition** (Who?) God's way of salvation is made plain, Rom 10:9-10, 13 5. **Results**: God tells us the results of salvation, Rom 5:1, 8:1 6. **Assurance**: God gives the saved sinner assurance, Rom 8:16

3) What is missing in the Apostles Creed?
   a) Notice it is "individualistic" using the word "I"
   b) Notice that it does mention the word "believe", whereas it nowhere mentions repentance
   c) While it does mention sin, it does so in a philosophical way, e.g. "I believe that there exists forgiveness of sins"
   d) Nor does it mention the need to be individually justified by faith (born again)
   e) Nor does it provide a method or manner of salvation, as expressed by Francke above, and as found in Acts 15:11
   f) The mention of the "believing in … the holy catholic church" is problematic, as regards the degradation and execution of John Hus[1069]

[1068]"The Apostles Creed," from: http://www.reformed.org/documents/apostles_creed.html; accessed 28 Nov 2005; Internet.

[1069]Remembering that John Hus was burned at the stake because he was said to have denied this line, "I believe in the Holy Spirit, the holy catholic church." Here is part of the sentence against John Hus: "This most holy synod of Constance, invoking Christ's name and having God alone before its eyes, therefore pronounces, decrees and defines by this definitive sentence, which is here written down, that the said John Hus was and is a true and manifest heretic and has taught and publicly preached, to the great offence of the divine Majesty, to the scandal of the universal church and to the detriment of the catholic faith, errors and heresies that have long ago been condemned by God's church and many things that are scandalous, offensive to the ears of the devout, rash and seditious, and that he has even despised *the keys* of the church and ecclesiastical censures. He has persisted in these things for many years with a

      g)   What this say about the validity of the Apostles Creed (or of any other creed for that matter) in matters of salvation?

   4) By the way, the "Nicene Creed" takes salvation a step farther by affirming baptismal regeneration: "I acknowledge one Baptism for the remission of sins"[1070]

b. Or (for comparisons sake) what if we turned the "Four Spiritual Laws" into a Creed (as the theological basis for a Campus Crusade Church)?

The Four Spiritual Laws as a Creed

We believe that God loves us and offers a wonderful plan for our lives
We believe that men are sinful and separated from God, therefore they cannot know and
    experience God's love and plan for their lives
We believe that Jesus Christ is God's only provision for sin, through Him we can know and
    experience God's love and plan for our lives
We believe that we must individually receive Jesus Christ as Savior and Lord, then we can know
    and experience God's love and plan for our lives

---

c. Conclusions:

   1) Creeds are also disappointing as a source of absolute truth for knowing the Gospel, for there is not enough of the simple Gospel contained in them to bring the sinner to salvation!

   2) Likewise, false teachers constantly look for nuances and loopholes in creeds upon which to capitalize

   3) From a biblical point of view, perhaps Luke 24:46-47, 1 Cor 15:1-8, or Gal 1:6-9 provide better starting points to understand the NT Gospel

   4) We begin with an OT comparative…

---

hardened heart. He has greatly scandalised Christ's faithful by his obstinacy since, bypassing the church's intermediaries, he has made appeal directly to our lord Jesus Christ, as to the supreme judge, in which he has introduced many false, harmful and scandalous things to the contempt of the apostolic see, ecclesiastical censures and the keys" ("Sentence of degradation against J. Hus" (online); "Council of Constance, Part Four"; From: http://www.dailycatholic.org/history/16ecume4.htm; accessed 23 Sept 2004; Internet).

    [1070]"The Nicene Creed" (online); from: http://www.ccel.org/ccel/schaff/creeds2.iv.i.i.i.html; accessed 13 Oct 2005; Internet.

C. Four Biblical Foci for Message:

1. Deuteronomy 6:20-25:

Deut 6:20-25, "When your son asks you in time to come, saying, 'What *do* the testimonies and the statutes and the judgments *mean* which the LORD our God commanded you?' [21] then you shall say to your son, 'We were slaves to Pharaoh in Egypt; and the LORD brought us from Egypt with a mighty hand. [22] 'Moreover, the LORD showed great and distressing signs and wonders before our eyes against Egypt, Pharaoh and all his household; [23] and He brought us out from there in order to bring us in, to give us the land which He had sworn to our fathers.' [24] "So the LORD commanded us to observe all these statutes, to fear the LORD our God for our good always and for our survival, as *it is* today. [25] "And it will be righteousness for us if we are careful to observe all this commandment before the LORD our God, just as He commanded us"

- a. That this passage exemplifies the Old Covenant message of salvation is found in its use of two words:
  - 1) εὖ—to be well, "that it might be well with you"
  - 2) ζάω—to find life, hence to live, "that you may live"
  - 3) ἐλεημοσύνη—to [receive] mercy [righteousness], "that we may receive mercy"
- b. Explanation of salvation:
  - 1) We were slaves—to Pharaoh in Egypt
  - 2) The Lord took us out:
    - a) With a mighty hand and an outstretched arm
    - b) With signs and wonders, great and terrible
  - 3) And He brought us:
    - a) To give us this land
    - b) Which He promised to our fathers
- c. Conditions to salvation:
  - 1) Observing all the statutes of the Lord
  - 2) Constantly fearing the Lord
  - 3) Keep doing all the commandments of the Lord, just as He commanded
- d. Hence, persons receiving salvation:
  - 1) The [physical and/or spiritual?] sons of those who are in the household of faith, and who teach their sons
  - 2) Those willing and able to keep and obey all the commandments of the Lord, just as He gave them to be observed!

2. Luke 24:46-47:

Introduction: A two-fold message: the Gospel and the preaching.
- 1) Note that the **divine preparation** to Christ was John the Baptist' preaching a baptism of repentance for the forgiveness of sins:
  - a) "It is he who will go *as a forerunner* before Him in the spirit and power of Elijah, TO TURN THE HEARTS OF THE FATHER'S BACK TO THE CHILDREN, and the disobedient to the attitude of the righteous, so as to make ready a people prepared for the Lord," Luke 1:17
  - b) "And you, child, will be called the prophet of the Most High; For you will go on BEFORE THE LORD TO PREPARE HIS WAYS; To give to His people *the* knowledge of salvation By the forgiveness of their sins, Because of the tender mercy of our God, With which the Sunrise from on high will visit us, TO SHINE UPON THOSE WHO SIT IN DARKNESS AND THE SHADOW OF DEATH, To guide our feet into the way of peace,"Luke 1:76-79
  - c) "And he came into all the district around the Jordan, preaching a baptism of repentance for the forgiveness of sins; as it is written in the book of the words of Isaiah the prophet, 'THE VOICE OF ONE CRYING IN THE WILDERNESS, "MAKE READY THE WAY OF THE LORD, MAKE HIS PATHS STRAIGHT. EVERY RAVINE WILL BE FILLED, AND EVERY MOUNTAIN AND HILL WILL BE BROUGHT LOW; THE CROOKED WILL BECOME STRAIGHT, AND THE ROUGH ROADS SMOOTH; AND ALL FLESH WILL SEE THE SALVATION OF GOD,"'" Luke 3:3-6
  - d) "When the messengers of John had left, He began to speak to the crowds about John, 'What did you go out into the wilderness to see? A reed shaken by the wind? But what did you go out to see? A man dressed in soft clothing? Those who are splendidly clothed and live in luxury are

found in royal palaces! But what did you go out to see? A prophet? Yes, I say to you, and one who is more than a prophet. "This is the one about whom it is written, "BEHOLD, I SEND MY MESSENGER AHEAD OF YOU, WHO WILL PREPARE YOUR WAY BEFORE YOU." I say to you, among those born of women there is no one greater than John; yet he who is least in the kingdom of God is greater than he.' When all the people and the tax collectors heard *this*, they acknowledged God's justice, having been baptized with the baptism of John. But the Pharisees and the lawyers rejected God's purpose for themselves, not having been baptized by John," Luke 7:24-30

    2) Hence John's baptism was a preparation for the Gospel:

        a) Similarly, Paul calls the Law a tutor to bring us to Christ, Gal 3:24-25

        b) Note the role of this tutor in the powerful preaching of Apollos, that prepared the way for Paul's effective ministry in Ephesus, Acts 18:24-19:20

    3) Therefore, a contemporary emphasis on using the Ten Commandments as a preparation for the Gospel is positive. However, perhaps an unclear emphasis is proponents to think that use of the Ten Commandments provides a spiritual panacea for "true" salvation, and therefore that no seed will fall on the shallow or weed-infested soils, as prophesied by Jesus.[1071]

  a. Luke 24:46, the Gospel (note parallel with 1 Cor 15 above):

    1) "Thus it is written,

    2) "That the Christ would suffer and

    3) "Rise again from the dead the third day,"

  b. Luke 24:47, the Preaching (includes desired response to, purpose for, and call to preaching):

    1) "And that repentance…

Some interesting translations of "Repent ye" in Matt 4:17

New American Standard (1976)	Tyndale (1534)	English Geneva (1560)	Latin Vulgate (435)	Wycliffe* (1388)	French Lefevre* (1530)	French Louvain* (1550)	Douay-Rheims* (1899)
Repent	Repet	Amend	[do penance]	Do ye penaunce	[do penance]	[do penance]	Do penance
From that time Jesus began to preach and say, "Repent, for the kingdom of heaven is at hand."	From that tyme Iesus begane to preache and to saye: repet for ye kigdome of heven is at honed.	From that time Iesus began to preache, and to say, Amende your liues: for ye kingdome of heauen is at hand	exinde coepit Iesus praedicare et dicere paenitentiam agite adpropinquavit enim regnum caelorum	Fro that tyme Jhesus bigan to preche, and seie, Do ye penaunce, for the kyngdom of heuenes schal come niy	Des lhors Jesus commencea a enseigner et dire: faictes penitence / car le royaume des cieul y est approche	Dés lors Jesus commenca a enseigner et dire. Faictes penitence car le royaume des cieux approchera	From that time Jesus began to preach, and to say: Do penance, for the kingdom of heaven is at hand

*Translated either directly from the Latin Vulgate or with a prioritative Latin Vulgate; the Late Middle French "faictes penitence" translates into the English "do penance."

When Jerome translated the Latin Vulgate, he used the term "do penance" at least 29 times. For example, the word "penance" is found 66 times in the Douay-Rheims Bible (a very literal translation of the Latin Vulgate into English in 1899), and the phrase "do penance" is found 29 times, "did penance" is found 5 times, and "done penance" is found 3 times; see the Douay-Rheims of Matt 3:2, "And saying: Do penance: for the kingdom of heaven is at hand"; Matt 3:8, "Bring forth therefore fruit worthy of penance"; Matt 3:11, "I indeed baptize you in the water unto penance, but he that shall come after me, is mightier than I, whose shoes I am not worthy to bear; he shall baptize you in the Holy Ghost and fire"; Matt 11:20, "Then began he to upbraid the cities wherein were done the most of his miracles, for that they had not done penance"; Matt 11:21, "Woe to thee, Corozain, woe to thee, Bethsaida: for if in Tyre and Sidon had been wrought the miracles that have been wrought in you, they had long ago done penance in sackcloth and ashes"; Matt 12:41, "The men of Ninive shall rise in judgment with this generation, and shall condemn it: because they did penance at the preaching of Jonas. And behold a greater than Jonas here"; Mark 6:12, "And going forth they preached that men should do penance"; Luke 3:3, "And he came into all the country about the Jordan, preaching the baptism of penance for the remission of sins"; … Acts 2:38, "But Peter said to them: Do penance, and be baptized every one of you in the name of Jesus Christ, for the remission of your sins: and you shall receive the gift of the Holy Ghost" …

[1071]"As I began to look at church growth records from around the country, I found to my horror that 80 to 90 percent of those making a decision for Christ were falling away from the faith. That is, modern evangelism was creating 80 to 90 of what we commonly call backsliders for every hundred decisions for Christ. … The tragedy of modern evangelism is that, around the turn of the twentieth century, the church forsook the Law in its capacity to convert the soul and drive sinners to Christ" (Kirk Cameron and Ray Comfort, *The School of Biblical Evangelism: 101 Lessons* [Gainesville: Bridge-Logos, 2004], 26).

2) "For forgiveness of sins"

    a) Notice that "repentance for the forgiveness of sins" was the preaching of John the Baptist, Luke 3:3

        (1) "As John Wesley advised a young evangelist, for effective evangelism, preach 90 percent Law and 10 percent grace"[1072]

        (2) Note that John the Baptist also included the need for baptism as the act affirming true repentance

    b) Note that the preparatory preaching of John the Baptist also became the application to or close of the Gospel as found in v. 46

    c) Repentance was a central theme in the preaching of Jesus:

        (1) In Luke, we do not find a summary statement of the early preaching of Jesus, such as we find in Matthew and Mark:

            (a) Matt 4:17, "From that time Jesus began to preach and say, 'Repent, for the kingdom of heaven is at hand.'"

            (b) Mark 1:14-15, "And after John had been taken into custody, Jesus came into Galilee, preaching the gospel of God, and saying, 'The time is fulfilled, and the kingdom of God is at hand; repent and believe in the gospel.'"

        (2) Rather in Luke we find that he preached (Luke 4:14, "And Jesus returned to Galilee in the power of the Spirit; and news about Him spread through all the surrounding district") followed by his first encounter in Nazareth

        (3) However, Luke brings in the concept of repentance in 5:32, "I have not come to call the righteous but sinners to repentance."

    d) Summary Thoughts about repentance and Luke 24:47:

        (1) We seem to have a sandwich (chiastic) pattern in Gospel proclamation:

            (a) Repentance as preparation (Law as tutor), Gal 3:24
Notice that the Gospel in Romans begins not with God's love, but with His wrath because of sin, Rom 1:18ff.

            (b) The Gospel (death of Christ for sins, His burial and resurrection)

            (c) Repentance for the forgiveness of sins

3) "Would be proclaimed

4) "In His name

5) "To all the nations,

6) "Beginning from Jerusalem."

Conclusion: This commission uniquely presents both Christ's work and man's responsibility both to respond to this message by repentance and then to proclaim this message. It also provides a divine interpretive grid for all the sermons of the Book of Acts, which are, as we have seen, seemingly contested as to what Gospel they actually proclaim—see kerygma notes above.

3. 1 Corinthians 15:1-8:

Introduction: A proper understanding of 1 Corinthians 15 was central to the Protestant Reformation's view of the Gospel as faith alone and grace alone.

    a. An Exegetical Look:

        1) Introduction: "First importance" (v. 3)

        2) The Gospel, vv. 1-2:
            a) I make known
            b) Which I preached
            c) Which you received

[1072]Cameron and Comfort, *The School of Biblical Evangelism,* 21.

       d) In which you stand

          (1) "Stand" is placed between the reception and the affirmation of salvation

          (2) note that there is a shift in Paul from "the word" in the OT, such as Psa 119, to "the Gospel" in the NT (although Luke in Acts retains use of "word" for the message)

          (3) Notice the parallel plea of Psa 119:28, "Strengthen me according to Your word":

              (a) Which is from the piel stem of the Hebrew verb *koom* (qal stem: raise up, get up; piel stem: "put in place, set up," establish, cause to stand)

              (b) The Greek LXX reads βεβαιόω, meaning confirm, establish, fulfill

              (c) The French and English Geneva both read, "raise mee vp" (Relève-moi selon ta parole);

              (d) Perhaps another translation in English may be, "Raise me up to stand"

       e) By which you are saved

    3) Christ, vv. 3-8:

       a) Died for our sins

          (1) according to the Scriptures, Exod 12; Lev 4; Psa 22; Isa 52-53, etc.

       b) Buried

          [i.e. He was really dead]

       c) Raise on the third day

          (1) According to the Scriptures:

              (a) Concerning the resurrection of Christ, Psa 16:8-10

              (b) Concerning resurrection in general, Isa 25:8; 26:19; 53:10-11; Ezek 37:9-10; Dan 12:2

              (c) Concerning resurrection on the third day, Hos 6:2

          (2) Further issues regarding the three days:

              (d) On **number of days included in three days**: "the same day … the next day … the third day," Lev 7:16-18; 19:6

              (e) On the guiltlessness of the murderer, "being that he hated him not before yesterday, nor before the thrice (three days)", Deut 19:4, 6

       d) Appeared to James, then to the apostles

          [i.e. He was really alive]

          (1) This verb for appeared, or was seen (ὁράω), is found 4 times in verses 5-8

    4) Other verses highlighting the importance of the death and resurrection of Christ (see lists below):

       a) The centrality of the cross, cf. 1 Cor 2:2

       b) The importance of the resurrection, 1 Cor 15:19

 b. A Thematic Look:

    Introduction: What is emphasized and what is not emphasized in the Gospel?

    1) What is emphasized?

       a) Use of the word "Gospel" is important here. It is not just "angelo" or "message".

       b) Notice the Geneva Bible's emphasis on the manner of the evangelizing in 15:2:

          "And whereby ye are saued, if ye keepe in memorie, after what maner I preached it vnto you, except ye haue beleeued in vaine"

          Which follows the French Geneva Bible translation:

          "Et par lequel vous estes aussi sauvez, si vous retenez en quelle maniere je vous l'ai annoncé: si ce n'est que vous ayez creu en vain"

       c) The Person of Christ

       d) The death of Christ **for sin**

          (1) Paul also accentuated sin in Rom 1-3; 6-7

       e) The burial of Christ

       f) The resurrection of Christ **in three days**

       g) The appearing of Christ

2) What is **not** emphasized?
   a) The incarnation (100% God-100% man versus a synthesized 50%-50%)
   b) The birth of Christ (interesting in light of the heavy emphasis placed on the celebration of Christmas)
   c) The Virgin Mary—her role as Mediatrix of all graces, Queen of heaven, etc…
   d) The example of Christ—His lifestyle (e.g. His incarnation into and participation in human existence)
   e) The miracles of Christ—His service to mankind
   f) Love (e.g. "It's all about love!"):[1073] the love of Christ, the love of God, or man's response of love
   g) The inauguration of the kingdom age, here and now
   h) The kingdom of God, i.e. His current reign on earth as King
   i) Christ's reign as king, following His resurrection from the dead
   j) Society's needs, and its maddening complexities (Pannenberg)
   k) Man's physical needs
   l) A Christian worldview (Colson), a moral philosophy (Socinius)
   m) A paradigm shift (Bloesch), the Gospel as a change of gears from the Old Testament (downgrading the newness of the New Covenant in Christ's blood)
   n) The glory of God—rather the message is the death, burial, and resurrection of Christ
   o) Man's ability: neither his ability to understand his problem, nor to save himself
   p) Man's response (other than verses 1-2)

3) Rather:
   a) The Gospel is the power of God unto salvation, Rom 1:16
   b) The Word of God is living and active, Heb 4:12

4. Galatians 1:6-9:

Introduction: Key verses for the Reformation, this passage discusses the Gospel specifically in relation to its propagation—evangelization. As such it includes certain special highlights related to the Gospel evangelized. The issue for Luther was to look at the Book of Acts and see if the Roman Catholic church was preaching in any way similarly to the apostles in the Book of Acts. He did not find that to be the case.

a. Notice Several Translations to Discern the Issues Involved:
   GEN (1560), 6 Je m'estonne qu'en delaissant Christ qui vous avoit appellez par grace, vous estes subitement transportez à un autre Evangile: Qui n'est pas un autre [Evangile:] mais il y en a qui vous troublent et qui veulent renverser l'Evangile de Christ. Or quand bien nous-mesmes, ou un Ange du ciel, vous evangelizeroit outre ce que nous vous avons evangelizé, qu'il soit execration. Ainsi que nous avons déja dit, maintenant aussi je [le] dis derechef, Si quelqu'un vous evangelize outre ce que vous avez receu, qu'il soit execration.
   GNV (1560), I marueile that ye are so sone remoued away vnto another Gospel, from him that had called you in the grace of Christ, [7] Which is not another *Gospel*, saue that there be some which trouble you, and intende to peruert the Gospel of Christ. [8] But thogh that we, or an Angel from heauen preache vnto you otherwise, then that which we haue preached vnto you, let him be accursed. [9] As we said before, so say I now againe, If anie man preache vnto you otherwise, then that ye haue receiued, let him be accursed.
   MRT (1699), Je m'étonne qu'abandonnant [Jésus-] Christ, qui vous avait appelés par sa grâce, vous ayez été si promptement transportés à un autre Evangile. Qui n'est pas un autre [Evangile], mais il y a des gens qui vous troublent, et qui veulent renverser l'Evangile de Christ. Mais quand nous-mêmes [vous évangéliserions], ou quand un Ange du Ciel vous évangéliserait outre ce que nous vous avons évangélisé, qu'il soit anathème. Comme nous l'avons déjà dit, je le dis encore maintenant : si quelqu'un vous évangélise outre ce que vous avez reçu, qu'il soit anathème.
   KJV (1611), I marvel that ye are so soon removed from him that called you into the grace of Christ unto another gospel: Which is not another; but there be some that trouble you, and would pervert the gospel of Christ. But though we, or an angel from heaven, preach any other gospel unto you than that

---

[1073]"The *model* He gave us is love . . . the *method* He gave us is love . . . the *motive* He gave us is love . . . the *message* He gave us is love" (Charles Arn, "Response to Thom Rainer, Recovering Our Purpose" *American Society for Church Growth* [1995]).

which we have preached unto you, let him be accursed. As we said before, so say I now again, If any *man* preach any other gospel unto you than that ye have received, let him be accursed.

ASV (1901), I marvel that ye are so quickly removing from him that called you in the grace of Christ unto a different gospel; which is not another *gospel* only there are some that trouble you, and would pervert the gospel of Christ. But though we, or an angel from heaven, should preach unto you any gospel other than that which we preached unto you, let him be anathema. As we have said before, so say I now again, if any man preacheth unto you any gospel other than that which ye received, let him be anathema.

NJB (1976), I am astonished that you are so promptly turning away from the one who called you in the grace of Christ and are going over to a different gospel—not that it is another gospel; except that there are trouble-makers among you who are seeking to pervert the gospel of Christ. But even if we ourselves or an angel from heaven preaches to you a gospel other than the one we preached to you, let God's curse be on him. I repeat again what we declared before: anyone who preaches to you a gospel other than the one you were first given is to be under God's curse.

FBJ, Je m'étonne que si vite vous abandonniez Celui qui vous a appelés par la grâce du Christ, pour passer à un second évangile—non qu'il y en ait deux ; il y a seulement des gens en train de jeter le trouble parmi vous et qui veulent bouleverser l'Évangile du Christ. Eh bien ! si nous-mêmes, si un ange venu du ciel vous annonçait un évangile différent de celui que nous vous avons prêché, qu'il soit anathème ! Nous l'avons déjà dit, et aujourd'hui je le répète : si quelqu'un vous annonce un évangile différent de celui que vous avez reçu, qu'il soit anathème !

SEM (1999), Je m'étonne de la rapidité avec laquelle vous abandonnez celui qui vous a appelés par la grâce du Christ, pour vous tourner vers un autre message. Comme s'il pouvait y avoir un autre message! Non, il n'en existe pas d'autre, mais il y a des gens qui sèment le trouble parmi vous et qui veulent renverser le message du Christ. Eh bien, si quelqu'un --- même nous, même un *ange du ciel --- vous annonçait un message différent de celui que nous vous avons annoncé, qu'il soit maudit. Je l'ai déjà dit et je le répète maintenant: si quelqu'un vous prêche un autre message que celui que vous avez reçu, qu'il soit maudit!

b.   Issues:

v. 6, Who or what is being turned from?

v. 6, The emphasis on the swift nature of the reversal?

v. 6, Does the turn involves a turning from grace or from Christ?

vv. 8-9, Is not the issue herein the method of evangelizing?

D. Considering Biblical Terms for the Gospel:

1. Biblical Terms for Gospel:[1074]

a. εὐαγγέλιον - εὐ, good; ἀγγέλιον, news, tidings; hence, good news, gald tidings, or Gospel (76 occurrences in New Testament):

Introduction:

    a) εὐαγγέλιον (gospel) is **not used** in John's Gospel or John's epistles, although it is used once in Revelation (14:6). However, λόγος (word) is used 36 times in the Gospel of John, 7 times in the epistles of John, and 18 times in Revelation.

    b) εὐαγγέλιον (gospel) is not found in the book of Luke and is found only twice in the Book of Acts (15:7 and 20:24). It is clear that there is a variance in terminology used for the Gospel. However, λόγος (word) is used 32 times in the Gospel of Luke and 65 times in the Book of Acts.

    c) εὐαγγέλιον is found 9 times in Romans. λόγος is used 7 times in Romans.

    d) Twenty-five uses of "gospel" in the NASB come from translating the word εὐαγγελίζω (evangelize) as "preach the gospel," rather than from the Greek word εὐαγγέλιον.

1) The use of εὐαγγέλιον (Gospel) without modifiers:
Matt 26:13; Mark 1:15; 13:10; 14:9; 16:15; Rom 1:16; 11:28; 1 Cor 4:15: 9:14 (twice); 9:18 (twice); 9:23; 15:1; 2 Cor 4:3; 8:18; Gal 1:11; 2:2, 5, 7; 4:3, 15; Eph 3:6; Phil 1:5, 7, 12, 16, 27 (twice); 2:12; 4:3, 15; 1 Thess 1:5; 2:4; 2 Thess 2:14; 2 Tim 1:8, 10; Phm 13

2) εὐαγγέλιον with different modifiers:

    a) Gospel of God: Mark 1:14; Rom 1:1; 15:16; 2 Cor 11:7; 1 Thess 2:2, 8, 9; 1 Pet 4:17
        (1) Gospel of the grace of God, Acts 20:24
        (2) Glorious gospel of our blessed God, 1 Tim 1:11

    b) Gospel of Christ: Rom 15:19; 1 Cor 9:12; 2 Cor 2:12; 9:13; 10:14; Gal 1:7; Phil 1:27; 1 Thess 3:2:
        (1) Gospel of His Son, Rom 1:9
        (2) Gospel of Jesus Christ, Mark 1:1
        (3) Gospel of our Lord Jesus Christ, 2 Thess 1:8
        (4) The light of the Gospel of the glory of Christ, 2 Cor 4:4

    c) Gospel of the kingdom: Matt 4:23; 9:35; 24:14
        (1) Gospel of the kingdom of God: [𝔐—Mark 1:14]

    d) Gospel with personal pronouns:
        (2) My Gospel, Rom 2:16; 16:25; 2 Tim 2:8
        (3) Our Gospel, 2 Cor 4:3; 1 Thess 1:5; 2 Thess 2:14

    e) Other modifying words:
        (1) "The defense and confirmation of the gospel," Phil 1:7
        (2) Word of the Gospel (τὸν λόγον τοῦ εὐαγγελίου), Acts 15:7
        (3) Truth of the gospel, Gal 2:5, 14; Col 1:5
        (4) Mystery of the gospel, Eph 6:19
        (5) Eternal Gospel, Rev 14:6
        (6) Faith of the Gospel, Phil 1:27
        (7) Hope of the Gospel, Col 1:23
        (8) Glorious Gospel, 1 Tim 1:11
        (9) Gospel of your salvation, Eph 1:13
        (10) Gospel of peace, Eph 6:15
        (11) Another gospel, 2 Cor 11:4
        (12) A different gospel, Gal 1:6

3) Places where the NASB inserts the word "gospel" as a partial translation of the verb εὐαγγελίζω (evangelize) or once for προευαγγελίζομαι (Gal 3:8): Matt 11:5; Luke 3:18; 4:18; 7:22; 9:6; 16:16; 20:1; Acts 8:25, 40; 14:7, 15, 21; 16:10; Rom 1:15; 15:20; 1 Cor 1:17; 9:16 (twice), 18; 2 Cor 10:16; Gal 1:8, 9; 4:13; 1 Pet 1:12; 4:6

[1074]Chapter 7, Defining Evangelizing, "Biblical Terms for Evangelism," is a parallel study to this one, focusing on the propagation of the message rather than on the message.

4) The use of εὐαγγέλιον in different contexts:
   a) The proclamation of the Gospel of salvation, Mark 1:14; 13:10; 16:15; 1 Cor 15:1-8
   b) The Gospel as a body of truth, Gal 1:6-12; 2 Thess 1:8; 1 Tim 1:10-11
   c) The Gospel as the four biographies of Jesus found in the four early books of the New Testament, Mark 1:1

b. Biblical terms for the Gospel dealing with Jesus Christ:
   Introduction:
   a) Preaching Christ and preaching the Gospel used synonymously, 2 Cor 4:3-6
   b) Christ as a body of truth, Eph 4:20
   1) "Christ," Acts 8:5; Phil 1:15, 17, 18
   2) "Christ crucified," 1 Cor 1:23
   3) "Faith in Jesus Christ," Acts 24:24
   4) "Jesus," Acts 8:35; 28:23; Rev 17:6
   5) "Jesus Christ," Rom 16:25
   6) "Jesus Christ, and Him crucified," 1 Cor 2:2
   7) "Jesus Christ as Lord," 2 Cor 4:5
   8) "Lord Jesus Christ," Acts 28:31
   9) "Mystery of Christ," Col 4:3
   10) "Testimony of Jesus," Rev 1:2
   11) "The resurrection of the Lord Jesus," Acts 4:33 (e.g. Luke 24:9-11, John 20:24-25)
   12) "This is the Christ," Acts 9:22; 17:3; 18:25 (cf. Acts 28:23)
   13) "This is the Son of God," John 1:34
   14) "Bear my name," Acts 9:15
   15) "Christ is proclaimed," Phil 1:18
   16) "Demonstrating by the Scriptures that Jesus was the Christ," Acts 18:28
   17) "Explaining and giving evidence that the Christ..." Acts 17:3
   18) "Preached Jesus," Acts 8:35
   19) "Preaching Jesus as the Christ," Acts 5:42
   20) "Preaching the good news of the kingdom of God and the name of Jesus Christ," Acts 8:12
   21) "Preaching the Lord Jesus," Acts 11:20
   22) "Proclaim Jesus," Acts 9:20 (cf. Acts 9:22)
   23) "Saying, 'This Jesus whom I am proclaiming to you is the Christ,'" Acts 17:3
   24) "Solemnly testifying ... that Jesus was the Christ," Acts 18:5
   25) "Solemnly testifying ... repentance toward God and faith in our Lord Jesus Christ," Acts 20:21
   26) "That I might preach Him [Jesus] among the Gentiles, Gal 1:16 (cf. Col 1:28)
   27) "To preach the unfathomable riches of Christ," Eph 3:8
   28) "Teaching of the Lord," Acts 13:12

c. Passages with the word *kerygma* (κήρυγμα):
   1) "The preaching of Jonah," Matt 12:41
   2) "The preaching of Jonah," Luke 11:32
   3) "My gospel and the preaching of Jesus Christ," Rom 16:25
   4) "The foolishness of the message preached," 1 Cor 1:21
   5) "My message and my preaching were not..." 1 Cor 2:4
   6) "Then our preaching is in vain," 1 Cor 15:14
   7) "In order that the proclamation might be accomplished," 2 Tim 4:17
   8) "The proclamation which was entrusted," Titus 1:3

d. Biblical Terms dealing with the Word:
   1) "Word" (τὸν λόγον), Acts 8:4; 14:25; 16:6; 18:5; 2 Tim 4:2
      a) Acts 8:4, lit "They therefore who had been scattered went about evangelizing the word" [Οἱ μὲν οὖν διασπαρέντες διῆλθον εὐαγγελιζόμενοι τὸν λόγον]
   2) "Word" (ῥῆμα), 1 Pet 1:25; 2:2
      a) I Pet 1:25, lit "And this is the word by which you were evangelized" [τοῦτο δέ ἐστιν τὸ ῥῆμα τὸ εὐαγγελισθὲν εἰς ὑμᾶς]
      b) It must be remembered that the word ῥῆμα was used quite extensively in the OT (467 times), e.g. Deut 6:6, "And these words [ῥῆμα], which I am commanding you today, shall be on your heart"
   3) "Word of Christ," Rom 10:17

4) "Word of God" (ὁ λόγος τοῦ θεοῦ), Acts 4:31; 6:7; 8:14; 11:1; 13:5, 7, 44, 46; 17:13; Col 1:25
    a) Notice that this word is used also of the message following the reception of the Gospel, Acts 6:2; 18:11
5) "Word of God's message," 1 Thess 2:13; Rev 1:2
6) "Word of His grace," Acts 14:3
7) "Word of life," Phil 2:16
8) "Word of reconciliation," 2 Cor 5:20
9) "Word of the cross," 1 Cor 1:18
10) "Word of the Gospel," Acts 15:7
11) "Word of the Lord" (ὁ λόγος τοῦ κυρίου), Acts 12:24; 13:44, 48, 49; 15:36; 16:32; 19:10, 20; 1 Thess 1:8; 2 Thess 3:1
    a) Notice that Paul used "Lord" synonymously for Jesus Christ, 1 Cor 6:14
    b) Notice that this term is used also of the message following the reception of the Gospel, Acts 8:25; 15:35
    c) Note the impact of changing from "word" to "message":

Comparative Translations of 2 Thess 3:1

Byzantine	Latin	Wycliffe 2nd (1388)	Tyndale (1534); cf. Coverdale; Geneva; Bishops	KJV (1611, 1769)	Etheridge (1849)	Young's (1862, 1887, 1898)	ESV (1885); cf. ASV	Bible in Basic English (1949)	RSV (1952)	NIV (1984)	New Jer Bible (1985); cf. NET; CSB	ABS' CEV (1991)
Τὸ λοιπὸν, προσεύχεσθε, ἀδελφοί, περὶ ἡμῶν, ἵνα ὁ λόγος τοῦ κυρίου τρέχῃ καὶ δοξάζηται, καθὼς καὶ πρὸς ὑμᾶς	de cetero fratres orate pro nobis ut sermo* Domini currat et clarificetur sicut et apud vos	Britheren, fro hennus forward preye ye for vs, that the word of God renne, and be clarified, as it is anentis you	Furthermore brethren praye for vs that the worde of god maye have fre passage and be gloryfied as it is with you	Finally, brethren, pray for us, that the word of the Lord may have free course, and be glorified, even as it is with you	Henceforth, my brethren, pray for us, that the word of our Lord may run and be glorified in every place, as among us	As to the rest, pray ye, brethren, concerning us, that the word of the Lord may run and may be glorified, as also with you	Finally, brethren, pray for us, that the word of the Lord may run and be glorified, even as it is with you	For the rest, my brothers, let there be prayer for us that the word of the Lord may go forward with increasing glory, even as it does with you	Finally, brethren, pray for us that the word of the Lord may speed on and triumph, as it did among you	Finally, brothers, pray for us that the message of the Lord may spread rapidly and be honoured, just as it was with you	Finally, brothers, pray for us that the Lord's message may spread quickly, and be received with honour as it was among you	Finally, our friends, please pray for us. This will help the message about the Lord to spread quickly, and others will respect it, just as you do.

*Not verbum.

Comparative Translations of 1 Pet 1:25b

Byzantine	Latin	Wycliffe, 1st ed. (1382)[1075]	Tyndale (1534)	KJV (1611, 1769)	Darby (1884, 1890)	ASV (1901)	RSV (1952)	NIV (1984)	New Jerusalem (1985)	ABS' CEV (1991)	Johnston's Evangelistic (2010)
Τοῦτο δέ ἐστιν τὸ ῥῆμα τὸ εὐαγγελισθὲν εἰς ὑμᾶς	hoc est autem verbum quod evangelizatum est in vos	sothely this is the worde[,] that is euangelizide to zou	And this is the worde which by the gospell was preached amonge you	And this is the word which by the gospel is preached unto you	And this is the word which by the gospel hath been preached unto you	And this is the word of good tidings which was preached unto you	That word is the good news which was preached to you	And this is the word that was preached to you	And this Word is the Good News that has been brought to you	Our good news to you is what the Lord has said	And this is the word by which you were evangelized

[1075]Josiah Forshall and Frederic Madden, *The Holy Bible, Containing the Old and New Testaments, with the Apocryphal Books, in the Earliest English Versions Made from the Latin Vulgate by John Wycliffe and His Followers* (Oxford: University Press, 1850).

12) "Word of truth." Col 1:5
13) "Words," 2 Tim 4:15

Comparative Translations of λόγοις in 2 Tim 4:15

Byzan-tine	Latin	Wycliffe, 2nd ed. (1388)	Tyndale (1534)	Geneva (1560)	KJV (1611, 1769)	ASV (1901)	Bible in Basic English (1949)	RSV (1952)	NAS (1977)	NKJ (1982)	NIV (1984)	ABS' CEV (1991)
λόγοις	verbis	Wordis	preach-ynge	preaching	words	→words	teaching	message	teaching	words	message	what we preach
ὃν καὶ σὺ φυλάσσου, λίαν γὰρ ἀνθέσ-τηκεν τοῖς ἡμετέροις λόγοις.	quem et tu devita valde enim restitit verbis nostris	Whom also thou eschewe; for he ayenstood ful greetli oure wordis.	of whom be thou ware also. For he withstode oure preach-ynge sore.	Of whome be thou ware also: for he withstode our preaching sore.	Of whom be thou ware also; for he hath greatly withstood our words	of whom do thou also beware; for he greatly withstood our words.	But be on the watch for him, for he was violent in his attacks on our teaching.	Beware of him yourself, for he strongly opposed our message.	Be on guard against him yourself, for he vigorously opposed our teaching.	You also must beware of him, for he has greatly resisted our words.	You too should be on your guard against him, because he strongly opposed our message.	Alexander opposes what we preach. You had better watch out for him.

14) "Scripture" (τῆς γραφῆς), Acts 8:35
15) "Scriptures" (τῶν γραφῶν), Acts 17:2, 11; 18:28; cf. Acts 18:24
16) "Sacred writings" (τὰ ἱερὰ γράμματα), 2 Tim 3:15

e. Terms dealing with God:
    1) "The Father has sent the Son to be the Savior of the world," 1 John 4:14
    2) "The kingdom of God," Mark 1:15; Luke 9:60; Acts 28:23, 31
    3) "The whole purpose of God," Acts 20: 27
    4) "Faith toward God," 1 Thess 1:8
    5) "Gospel of God," Mark 1:14; Rom 1:1; 15:16; 2 Cor 11:7; 1 Thess 2:2, 8, 9; 1 Tim 1:11; 1 Pet 4:17
    6) "Gospel of the grace of God," Acts 20:24
    7) "Gospel of the kingdom of God," Luke 16:16 (cf. Mark 1:15)
    8) "Grace of God in truth," Col 1:6
    9) "Hope in the living God," 1 Tim 4:10
    10) "Knowledge of God," 2 Cor 10:5
    11) "Repentance toward God and faith in our Lord Jesus Christ," Acts 20:21
    12) "Salvation of God," Acts 28:28
    13) "The testimony of God," 1 Cor 2:1
    14) "Word of God," Acts 4:31; 6:7; 8:14; 11:1; 13:5, 7, 44; 17:13; Col 1:25
    15) "Word of God's message," 1 Thess 2:13; Rev 1:2.

f. Terms dealing with aspects of salvation:
    1) Grace:
        a) "The grace of God," Acts 13:43
        b) "The grace that is spreading," 2 Cor 4:15
    2) Salvation:
        a) "Gospel of your salvation," Eph 1:13
        b) "Salvation of God," Acts 28:28
        c) "Way of salvation," Acts 16:17
    3) Repentance:
        a) "Repentance for forgiveness of sin," Luke 24:47
        b) "Repentance leading to a knowledge of the truth," 2 Tim 2:25
        c) "Repentance toward God and faith in our Lord Jesus Christ," Acts 20:21
        d) Notice that repentance was the summary of God's message to Israel through His prophets, Jer 35:14-17 (and a lack of repentance led to their demise!)

    4) Faith:
- a) "Faith toward God," 1 Thess 1:8
- b) "The faith," Acts 13:8; 1 Tim 4:1
- c) "Your faith," Phm 6 (NIV)

    5) Righteousness, self-control and the judgment to come, Acts 24:25

    6) Terms dealing with an invitation:
- a) "And let him who hears say, 'Come!'" Rev 22:17
- b) This example is clearly reminiscent of the two word message and invitation of Jesus, "follow Me," Luke 5:27; 9:59; John 1:43

g. Terms dealing with ἀλήθειαν - truth, John 8:32; 18:37; Rom 2:8; 2 Thess 2:12; 1 Tim 4:3 (cf. John 14:6):
1) "Knowledge of the truth," 1 Tim 2:4; 2 Tim 2:25; Titus 1:1; Heb 10:26
2) "Love of the truth," 2 Thess 2:10
3) "Message of truth," Eph 1:13
4) "Repentance leading to a knowledge of the truth," 2 Tim 2:25
5) "Way of God in truth," Matt 22:16 (cf. Mark 12:14)
6) "Way of truth," 2 Pet 2:2
7) "Word of truth," 2 Cor 6:7

h. Terms dealing with the message:
1) κήρυγμα - preaching, message: Matt 12:41; Luke 11:32; Rom 16:25; 1 Cor 1:21; 2:4; 15:14; 2 Tim 4:17; Titus 3
- a) "The preaching of Jesus Christ," Rom 16:25
2) διδαχῇ - teaching: "being amazed at the teaching of the Lord," Acts 13:12
- a) διδαχῇ τοῦ κυρίου, Acts 13:12
3) ῥήματα - message, "the whole message of this life," Acts 5:20
- a) πάντα τὰ ῥήματα τῆς ζωῆς ταύτης, Acts 5:20
4) λόγος - word, message:
- a) "Message of truth," Eph 1:13
- b) "Word [in you] of exhortation" (λόγος ἐν ὑμῖν παρακλήσεως), Acts 13:15
5) From the OT:
- a) πρόσταγμα τῆς ἀφέσεως (Deut 15:2), meaning "ordinance of release [or: remission, cancellation, pardon]"

i. Other terms speaking of the Gospel:
1) ὁδός - way, Acts 9:2; 19:9, 23; 24:24, 22:
- a) "I am the way," John 14:6
- b) "New and living way," Heb 10:26
- c) "Way of salvation," Acts 16:17
- d) "Way of truth," 2 Pet 2:2
2) οἰκονομία - stewardship, administration:
- a) "Administration of God," 1 Tim 1:4
- b) "Administration of the mystery," Eph 3:9
- c) "Stewardship," Eph 3:2 (cf. 1 Cor 9:17; Col 1:25)
3) ἀπολογία - a defense, an answer (8 NT uses, my translations below):
- a) "Brethren and fathers, hear **my plea** which I now *offer* to you," Acts 22:1
  Could ἀπολογία not also be translated "plea"?—since the Gospel needs no defense!

Translations of Acts 22:1

Byzantine	Latin Vulgate	Wycliffe 2nd ed (1388)	Tyndale (1534)	Geneva (1560)	KJV (1611, 1769)	Bible in Basic English (1949)
	Rationem [from *ratio*]	Resoun [reason]	Answere [answer]	Defence [defense]	Defence [defense]	Story of my life
Ἄνδρες ἀδελφοὶ καὶ πατέρες, ἀκούσατέ μου τῆς πρὸς ὑμᾶς νυνὶ ἀπολογίας.	viri fratres et patres audite quam ad vos nunc reddo rationem*	Britheren and fadris, here ye what resoun Y yelde now to you.	Ye men brethren and fathers heare myne answere which I make vnto you.	Ye men, brethren & fathers, heare my defence now towards you.	Men, brethren, and fathers, hear ye my defence *which I make* now unto you	My brothers and fathers, give ear to the story of my life which I now put before you.

*Jerome used the verb *reddo* and the noun *ratio* in pairs in numerous places, for different Greek verbs and nouns:

ἀποδίδωμι and λόγος: Dan 6:2; Matt 12:36; Luke 16:2; [Acts 19:40 (BGT)]; 1 Pet 4:5

ἀπολογέομαι: Acts 19:33; 25:8; 26:1, 24

δίδωμι and λόγος: Acts 19:40 (Byz)

ἐγω and ἀπολογία: Acts 22:1

λόγος and δίδωμι: Heb 13:17 (Vulgate splits the noun and verb as follows: *quasi rationem pro animabus vestris reddituri*)

λόγος and δίδωμι: Rom 14:12

b) "For it is only right for me to feel this way about you all, because I have you in my heart, since both in my imprisonment and in **the plea** and confirmation of the gospel, you all are partakers of grace with me," Phil 1:7

c) "At my first **plea** no one supported me, but all deserted me; may it not be counted against them," 2 Tim 4:16

d) "Eager to always **plead** with all that ask," 1 Pet 3:15

History of Translating πρὸς ἀπολογία in 1 Peter 3:15

Migne's Clementine Vulgate	Wycliffe 2nd ed (1388)	Tyndale (1534)	King James (1611/1769)	Murdock (1852)	Young's (1862)	Douay-Rheims (1899)	New American Bible (1970)	New American Standard (1977)	New Living Trans (2004)	Johnston Modified (2007)
ad satisfac-tionem*	redi to satisfac-cioun	To geve and answere	to *give* an answer	for a vindication	for defence	to satisfy	to give an explanation	to make a defense	to explain it	to plead
Dominum autem Christum sanctificate in cordibus vestris parati semper ad satisfac-tionem omni poscenti vos rationem de ea quae in vobis est spe	But halewe ye the Lord Crist in youre hertis, and euermore be ye redi to satisfac-cioun to ech man axynge you resoun of that feith and hope that is in you,	but sanctifie the Lorde God in youre hertes. Be redy all wayes to geve an answere to every man that axeth you a reason of the hope that is in you and that with meaknes and feare:	and *be* ready always to *give* an answer to every man that asketh you a reason of the hope that is in you with meekness and fear:	but sanctify the Lord the Messiah, in your hearts. And be ye ready for a vindication, before every one who demandeth of you an account of the hope of your faith,	and the Lord God sanctify in your hearts. And *be* ready always for defence to every one who is asking of you an account concerning the hope that *is* in you, with meekness and fear;	being ready always to satisfy every one that asketh you a reason of that hope which is in you	Always be ready to give an explanation to anyone who asks you for a reason for your hope	always *being* ready to make a defense to everyone who asks you to give an account for the hope that is in you	And if you are asked about your Christian hope, always be ready to explain it	always eager to plead with everyone who requests a word about the hope that is in you

*The 1979 Nova Vulgata changed the translation of this important word to "ad defensionem," clearly locking in an rational apologetic usage.

4) "The grace that is spreading," 2 Cor 4:15

5) "Eternal life," 1 John 1:2

6) "The kingdom," Acts 20:25

7) "Hope of Israel," Acts 28:20

Millard Erickson added a warning:

> Because the Gospel has been, is, and will always be the way of salvation, the only way, the church must preserve the Gospel at all costs.[1076]

Conclusion:

> The terms for the Gospel point to the roles of God and Jesus, the Gospel message, aspects of salvation and the blessings of salvation. These are all used to speak of the Gospel. This should free the herald of the Gospel to utilize the breadth of the Gospel message to meet the needs of the person with whom he is sharing, following the leading of the Holy Spirit.

> Consider the following chart to explain the full breadth of terminology to describe the Gospel message…

BIBLICAL TERMS FOR THE GOSPEL[1077]
(Also see Book of Charts)

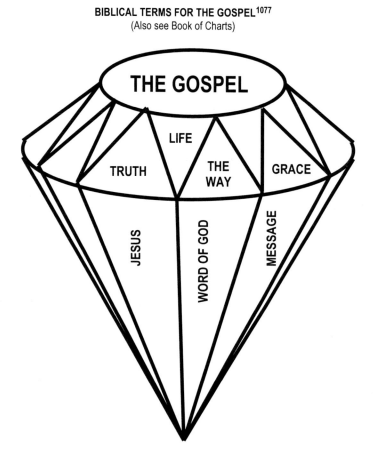

2. **Biblical Concepts that Are Sometimes Made Equivocal:**

a. **God's love, John 3:16**:

   1) With a complete emphasis on love to the exclusion of anything else, for example:

> "The *model* He gave us is love . . . the *method* He gave us is love . . . the *motive* He gave us is love . . . the *message* He gave us is love."[1078]

[1076]Erickson, *Christian Theology,* 1066.

[1077]Johnston, *Charts for a Theology of Evangelism,* Chart 34, "Terms for the Gospel in Acts," 62.

[1078]Charles Arn, "Response to Thom Rainer, Recovering Our Purpose" *American Society for Church Growth* (1995).

2) Note that Paul starts his Gospel to the Romans with the wrath of God for sin, love is not discussed until chapter 5, verse 5!

  a) Rom 1:18, "For the wrath of God is revealed from heaven against all ungodliness and unrighteousness of men"
  b) Rom 2:5, "But because of your stubbornness and unrepentant heart you are storing up wrath for yourself in the day of wrath and revelation of the righteous judgment of God"
  c) Rom 2:8, "but to those who are selfishly ambitious and do not obey the truth, but obey unrighteousness, wrath and indignation"
  d) Rom 3:5, "The God who inflicts wrath is not unrighteous, is He?"
  e) Rom 4:15, "for the Law brings about wrath"
  f) Rom 5:8-9, "But God demonstrates His own love toward us, in that while we were yet sinners, Christ died for us. Much more then, having now been justified by His blood, we shall be saved from the wrath *of God* through Him"

    (1) The love of God and the wrath of God meet in 5:8-9:
      (a) The grace of God is best understood in relationship to God's unfailing mercy in spite of man's reprehensible sinful nature and actions, cf. Eph 2:1-6
      (b) Any understanding of the love of God, without the complementary foundation of man's sinful nature, can easily become skewed and misunderstood, quickly leading to false teaching
    (2) Rom 5:8 is the second use of the word "love" ("love of God") in Romans; the first use is in Rom 5:5, "and hope does not disappoint, because the love of God has been poured out within our hearts through the Holy Spirit who was given to us"
      (a) Notice in this case, the issue is not our love for God, but rather it is God's love imputed to us (placed in us, because it was not there in the first place)
      (b) When is it placed in us? When we receive the Holy Spirit (when we are born again)
      (c) John highlighted the priority of God's love in 1 John 4:10, "In this is love, not that we loved God, but that He loved us and sent His Son *to be* the propitiation for our sins."

Conclusion:
  a) The lost must first be convinced that they are under the wrath of God for their sin, outside of the forgiveness available in Christ.
  b) Notice that when the Holy Spirit comes, He will convict the world of sin, righteousness, and judgment (John 16:8)
    (1) The Holy Spirit does not convince mankind of a lack of love
    (2) If we want to work together with the Holy Spirit, we must emphasize sin, righteousness, and judgment
  c) This is where the Law becomes a schoolmaster to bring us to Christ, Gal 3:24

b. Abundant life vs. eternal life:

1) While several NT verses seem to highlight the importance of this present life:
  a) John 10:10b, "I came that they may have life, and have *it* abundantly"
    Does the περισσός (found once in John; often translated "abundantly") contradict the Johanine emphasis on "eternal life" (15 times in the Gospel of John; 6 times in 1 John; "life eternal" found twice in the Gospel of John)?
    Should περισσός rather be translated "exceedingly": "I came that they may have life, and have *it* exceedingly"
    Paradoxically, the more our present lives focus on eternal life, the more abundant they are in this life!

Comparing a Temporal Versus an Eternal Emphasis

Emphasis	Temporal	Eternal
Difficulties in This Life	Sufferings due to the difficulties of life in this world, Job 5:7	Sufferings due to the proclamation of the Gospel, Matt 5:11-12
Passion of Christ	Emphasize Jesus' physical sufferings, in being beaten and scourged	Emphasize Jesus' spiritual suffering, in taking the the sins of the world, and the penalty for those sins, and being abandoned by His Father
	Emphasize Jesus' relational sufferings, in being denied and abandoned by His disciples	
Emphasis in the Gospel Presentation	The abundant life, here and now, John 10:10	Eternal life and a future in heaven, John 3:16
Corresponding Emphasis in the Great Commission	Making a difference in the world	Leading souls to salvation

b) Acts 3:19, "Therefore repent and return, so that your sins may be wiped away, in order that times of refreshing may come from the presence of the Lord"

c) James 4:14 "What is your life?" (KJV, RSV, NKJ, NIV)

d) And similarly, seeking to emphasize the "life" of Jesus (as opposed to His death):

  (1) Rom 5:10, "For if while we were enemies, we were reconciled to God through the death of His Son, much more, having been reconciled, we shall be saved by His life"

  (2) Notice that the "by His life" can be interpreted numerous ways:

    (a) Robertson relates it to Heb 7:25, "ever living to intercede for them"

    (b) Rom 4:25 speaks of Christ's resurrection unto life for our justification

    (c) Liberalizing theologians, however, find in this verse a salvific quality in the life of Christ, unrelated to His death[1079]

  (3) Similarly, perhaps Acts 10:38, "'*You know of* Jesus of Nazareth, how God anointed Him with the Holy Spirit and with power, and *how* He went about doing good, and healing all who were oppressed by the devil; for God was with Him'" (cf. Acts 1:1-2)

2) Many New Testament verses actually negate the *a priori* of making current life the priority of God's salvation:

a) "If we have hoped in Christ in this life only, we are of all men most to be pitied," 1 Cor 15:19—verses 12-19 speak of people who preach the resurrection of Christ *sans* emphasizing the resurrection of men (sound applicable). In there case, "your faith is worthless; you are still in your sins" (1 Cor 15:17)

b) Another example of a misplaced emphasis is Esau who traded one meal (in the present) for the blessing of the birthrite (in the future; cf. Gen 25:31-34; Heb 12:14-17). Hebrews actually calls him "an immoral and godless person like Esau."

c) Psa 17:13-14, "Deliver my soul from the wicked with Your sword, From men with Your hand, O LORD, From men of the world, whose portion is in *this* life, And whose belly You fill with Your treasure; They are satisfied with children, And leave their abundance to their babes."

d) Phil 3:18-19 (KJV), "For many walk, of whom I have told you often, and now tell you even weeping, *that they are* the enemies of the cross of Christ: Whose end *is* destruction, whose God *is their* belly, and *whose* glory *is* in their shame, who mind earthly things."

[1079]Note that this follows with Walter Rauschenbusch's dismissing an emphasis on the death of Christ as being non-apostolic and non-biblical: "These traditional theological explanations of the death of Christ have less authority that we are accustomed to suppose. The fundamental terms and ideas—"satisfaction," "substitution," "imputation," "merit"—are post-biblical ideas, and are alien from the spirit of the gospel" (Walter Rauschenbusch, *A Theology for the Social Gospel* (New York: Macmillan, 1917; Nashville: Abingdon, 1978], 242-43).

e) Mark 8:35, "For whoever wishes to save his life shall lose it; but whoever loses his life for My sake and the gospel's shall save it" (cf. Matt 10:39; 16:25-26; Luke 9:24-25; 17:33; John 12:25, "He who loves his life loses it; and he who hates his life in this world shall keep it to life eternal")

f) 1 Timothy 6:12, "Fight the good fight of faith; **take hold of the eternal life** to which you were called, and you made the good confession in the presence of many witnesses."

(1) An emphatic use of λαμβάνω, meaning "to take hold of, grasp"

(2) The word for "take hold" is ἐπιλαμβάνομαι; fortunately, it is not unique in the NT, but is found 38 times in the OT and 19 times in the NT! Therefore the translation should not be too much of a problem:

(a) When Jesus reached out his hand and "took hold" of Peter, when he was sinking in the water, Matt 14:31;

(b) When Jesus "took hold" of the blind man, led him out of town, and healed him, Mark 8:23

(c) Jesus "took hold" of a child, to teach His disciples, Mark 9:47

(d) Jesus "took hold" of the man with dropsy (condition of swollen tissues), Luke 14:4

(e) The scribes and pharisees sent spies to try to "catch," "seize," or "take hold" of Jesus in his words, Luke 20:20; which entrapment they were unable to do, Luke 20:26

(f) The guards "took hold" of Simon of Cyrene and forced him to carry the cross of Jesus, Luke 23:26

(g) Barnabas "took hold" of Paul and brought him to the apostles who were scarred of him, as he had persecuted the church, Acts 9:27

(h) The masters of the girl with the spirit of Python "took hold" of Paul and brought him to the authorities in the marketplace, Act 16:19

(i) The Epicurian and Stoic philosophers "took hold" of Paul and brought him to the Areopagus to explain himself, Acts 17:19

(j) Acts 18:17, "And they [the Jews] all **took hold** of Sosthenes, the leader of the synagogue, and *began* beating him in front of the judgment seat."

(k) At the false accusation of Paul, "And all the city was aroused, and the people rushed together; and **taking hold** of Paul, they dragged him out of the temple; and immediately the doors were shut. And while they were seeking to kill him, a report came up to the commander of the *Roman* cohort that all Jerusalem was in confusion. And at once he took along *some* soldiers and centurions, and ran down to them; and when they saw the commander and the soldiers, they stopped beating Paul. Then the commander came up and **took hold** of him, and ordered him to be bound with two chains; and he *began* asking who he was and what he had done" (Acts 21:30-33)

(l) Acts 23:18, "So he took him [Paul's young nephew] and led him to the commander and said, 'Paul the prisoner called me to him and asked me to lead this young man to you since he has something to tell you.'"

(m) 1 Tim 6:12, "Fight the good fight of faith; take hold of the eternal life to which you were called, and you made the good confession in the presence of many witnesses"

(n) 1 Tim 6:18-19, "*Instruct them* to do good, to be rich in good works, to be generous and ready to share, storing up for themselves the treasure of a good foundation for the future, so that they may **take hold** of that which is life indeed."

(o) Heb 2:16, "For he in no sort **tooke on** him the Angels nature, but hee **tooke on** him the seede of Abraham:"

(p) Heb 8:9, "Not like the covenant which I made with their fathers On the day when I **took** them by the hand To lead them out of the land of Egypt; For they did not continue in My covenant, And I did not care for them, says the Lord" (a quote of Jer 31:32).

(3) Yet note the varied translations of 1 Tim 6:12, likely due to varying views as to how to gain and if to emphasize eternal life!

Comparative Translations of ἐπιλαμβάνομαι in 1 Tim 6:12
[Issues here are eternal life received or achieved? And eternal life as the emphasis or not?]

Tyndale (1534); Bishop's	Geneva (1560); Murdock; Darby; NAB; NKJ	KJV (1611, 1769); Webster's; Young's; English Revised; Douay-Rheims; ASV	Young's (1862, 1898)	RSV (1962); NAS; NIV	Bible in Basic English (1949, 1962)	New Living Translation (2004)	ABS' Cont English Version (1991)	New Jerusalem (1985)	ABS' Good News Translation (1992)
Lay hand on	Laye hold of	Lay hold on	Be laying hold on	Take hold of	Take for yourself	Hold tightly	Claim	Win the	Win the … for yourself
Fyght the good fyght of fayth. **Laye honde on** eternall lyfe where vnto thou arte called and hast professed a good profession before many witnesses.	Fight the good fight of faith: **laye holde of** eternal life, whereunto thou art also called, & hast professed a good profession before many witnesses.	Fight the good fight of faith, **lay hold on** eternal life, whereunto thou art also called, and hast professed a good profession before many witnesses	be striving the good strife of the faith, **be laying hold on** the life age-during, to which also thou wast called, and didst profess the right profession before many witnesses.	Fight the good fight of the faith; **take hold of** the eternal life to which you were called when you made the good confession in the presence of many witnesses.	Be fighting the good fight of the faith; take for yourself the life eternal, for which you were marked out, and of which you gave witness in the eyes of all	Fight the good fight for the true faith. Hold tightly to the eternal life to which God has called you, which you have confessed so well before many witnesses	Fight the good fight for the faith and **claim** eternal life. God offered it to you when you clearly told about the faith, while so many people listened	Fight the good fight of faith and **win** the eternal life to which you were called and for which you made your noble profession of faith before many witnesses	Run your best in the race of faith, and **win** eternal life **for yourself**; for it was to this that god called you when you firmly professed your faith before many witnesses.

3) Simultaneously numerous NT verses do emphasize eternal life, John 3:16; 5:24; Rom 6:23; et al.

In the NKJ translation of the Synoptic Gospels, the phrase "eternal life" is found 8 times

In the NKJ translation of Johannine writings, the phrase "eternal life" is found 15 times and the phrase is found "everlasting life" 8 times, for a total of 23 times

In the NKJ translation of the Pauline epistles, the phrase "eternal life" is found 7 times and the phrase "everlasting life" is found 3 times, for a total of 10 times

Thus, the direct terms for eternal life are found 41 times in the NT, compared with the 3 verses used to emphasize abundant life here-and-now!

4) Paul even speaks of the promise of eternal life (as something found imbedded in the OT):
   a) Is it not found in the resurrection promises in the OT?
   b) Could it not also be found in Deut 5:29? "Oh that they had such a heart in them, that they would fear Me, and keep all My commandments always, that it may be well with them and with their sons **forever**!"
      (1) Notice the Segond Revise Geneve here: "Oh ! s'ils avaient toujours ce même coeur pour me craindre et pour observer tous mes commandements, **afin qu'ils soient heureux à jamais**, eux et leurs enfants"
   c) Notice also Jesus' words to the Jews in John 5:39, "You search the Scriptures, because you think that in them you have eternal life; and it is these that bear witness of Me":
      (2) Notice that Jesus accused the Jews of seeking "eternal life" in the Scriptures, and yet not being willing to go through him—they were half right (cf. John 20:31; 1 Tim 3:15)
      (3) Notice also, however, that they did consider eternal life something to be sought after, e.g. Deut 8:1, "that you might live"

c. Sin as mere privation (e.g. Augustine):

Introduction: Sin as privation implies that there is some goodness in man, but that man merely lacks some attributes of perfection, such as "falling short of the glory of God," falling short of righteousness, holiness, etc. In total depravity, there is no inherent goodness in man at all. Various, verses and terms become the battle ground on this issue. Some argue that…

1) Sin as mere privation:

    a) Based on the *a priori* reading of Eccl 3:11 to describe the state of fallen mankind as:
        (1) Having eternity in their hearts
        (2) Therefore, they all have a God-shaped void that only God can fill (enter Pascal's philosophical approach and his vacuum theory).
        (3) Therefore, the big issue of mankind is not sin, *per se* (as in Rom 6:23), but the privation of a relationship with God
        (4) Therefore, all that is needed is to show man that he will only be satisfied in a right relationship with God (note the relational view of evangelism, the Gospel, and the atonement)
        (5) This is sometimes used as a backdoor method to lead people to Christ without preaching "repentance for the forgiveness of sins," Luke 24:47
        (6) Notice that this very popular argument is based almost solely on a philosophical interpretation of Eccl 3:11; if it is such a good argument, why is it not clearly used by Jesus or in the Book of Acts?

    b) However:
        (1) If sin is mere privation of some divine virtue, how can the Apostle John speak of someone practicing sin (1 John 3:4), and likewise Paul mention the "deeds of the flesh which are evident" (Gal 5:19-21), concluding, "of which I forewarn you just as I have forewarned you that those who practice such things shall not inherit the kingdom of God."
        (2) Or how can Jesus say, "He who is without sin among you, let him *be the* first to throw a stone at her," if sin is a privation? That would mean that "he who is without without cast the first stone"!

    c) Rather:
        (1) Sin is more than mere privation, it is active indwelling corruption, Deut 32:5; Mark 7:20-23
        (2) This depraved nature necessarily leads to acts of rebellion against the law of God, Lev 4:27-28; 1 John 3:4
        (3) Notice the summary statement of King David in Psalm 14:1 (cf. Psa 53:1):
            (a) "The fool has said in his heart, 'There is no God.'
            (b) "They are corrupt
            (c) "They have committed abominable deeds" ("and have committed abominable iniquity" [Psa 53:1, KJV])
            (d) "There is no one who does good"

    d) Note my study on "Total Depravity According to Jesus" which includes: (1) his words to the Pharisees; (2) Mark 7:20-23; and (3) the sayings of Jesus regarding the corruption of "this generation"

2) Sin in the NT as primarily "missing the mark" (ἥμαρτον) of God's perfection, rather than the entire corruption of man.

3) Sin as "looking for love in the wrong places": Sometimes in the "it's all about love" theological approach, sin is seen as "looking for love in the wrong places":
    a) Perhaps some psychologists would want to put a positive spin on sin:
        (1) Through using situation ethics: yes, sin is wrong, but it was the best of two bad options (e.g. "she had to go into prostitution to support her children")
        (2) Through behavioral psychology: yes, sin is wrong, but it was a part of the environment of the sinner, or it was all that he/she knew to do or could do

b) However, much more than an naive or ignorant selfishness:
   (1) God has written his laws on the hearts of all men, Rom 2:14-15
   (2) Sin in its essence is intentional and unintentional acts of rebellion against the written law of God (Lev 4:27-28; 1 John 3:4); stemming from man's depraved nature (Gen 6:5; Eph 2:1-3)

4) Extent of sin (ὑστεροῦνται) = "falling short of the glory of God" rather than being "deprived of the glory of God"; notice the rainbow of translations on this commonly used gospel verse (also notice the rainbow of views of man's depravity or man's problem as a lack of relationship)…

Notice the Variety of Translations of Rom 3:[22]23 (arranged semi-thematically)

[Translation differences seem to focus on the theological weight of the term ὑστερέω; moving from a substitutionary model of the atonement to the reconciliation model (from total depravity to relational separation)]

Sample English Translations of Rom 3:23

	destitute	deprived	come short	lacke the prayse that is of valour	fallen short	*egent*	Do need	Lack	are far from	are far from being as good as	are not good enough to share in	is far from saving presence	are utterly incap-able of
Greek Byzan-tine*	**English Bishops' (1568, 1595)**	**English Geneva (1560)**	**KJV (1611)**	**Tyndale (1534)**	**Tischen-dorf's potential-ity (1869-1872)**	**Latin Vulgate (early 400s)**	**Douay-Rheims✠ (1899)**	**New Jeru-salem✠ (1985)**	**Bible in Basic English (1941/ 1949)**	**World-wide English NT (1969)**	**Easy-to-Read Version (2006)**	**Good News Trans✠ (1993)**	**The Message (1993)**
πάντες γὰρ ἥμαρτον καὶ ὑστεροῦν-ται τῆς δόξης τοῦ θεοῦ	"For all haue synned, and are destitute of the glorie of God"	"For there is no difference: for all haue sinned, and are depriued of the glorie of God"	"For all haue sinned, and come short of the glory of God"	"for all have synned and lacke the prayse that is of valoure before God"	"if all have sinned and fallen short of the glory of God"**	omnes enim peccave-runt et egent gloriam Dei	"For all have sinned and do need the glory of God"	"all have sinned and lack God's glory"	For all have done wrong and are far from the glory of God	"All have done wrong and all are far from being as good as God"	"All have sinned and are not good enough to share God's divine greatness"	"everyone has sinned and is far away from God's saving presence"	"we are utterly incapable of living the glorious lives God wills for us"
Greek verb ὑστερέω (20 LXX and 16 NT uses) make it a definable term; at issue seem to be theological presup-positions	"Deprived" implies a calculated privation from the outside; whereas "destitute" seems to imply a natural condition	A more mild transla-tion of the French Geneva, while implying a removal of ability from the outside	"Come short" implies that an individual lacks the ability to achieve the desired end of "the glory of God," cf. Gen 3:5	Tyndale appeared to bridge the Latin Vulgate's transla-tion of this text with the Greek	Tisch: παντες γαρ: Epiph οι γαρ παντες (ita enim legendum pro eo quod editum est ει γαρ παντες)	It appears that future Catholic transla-tions focused on the lexical definition of the word *egent*, from *egeo*, to want, be in need	Strict transla-tion of Vulgate; implies a neutral condition in which sin is a "lack of" rather than an evil condition or evil actions, cf. Psa 14:1	Another literal transla-tion of the Latin Vulgate	Notice the removal of the verb "to sin", and the emphasis on onto-logical or spiritual distance from God	Lacking in or falling short of the moral standard of God	Again, lacking in moral equality with God to share His greatness	Relational dimen-sion high-lighted, influen-cing a reading that sin is primarily relational, hence, the atone-ment is primarily restora-tion of relation-ship	Notice the emphasis on inability to live a certain way, rather than an actual state of being

*The Nestle-Aland 27th edition matches the Byzantine Textform in this verse.

**Surmised translation based on a question in Tischendorf's apparatus; for which he cited Epiphanius, Bishop of Salamis of Cypern of Constantine (A.D. 368-402). One wonders how long it took him to find this variant.

Sample French Translations of Rom 3:23*

Greek Byzantine	entirely destitute of	utterly deprived of	cannot attain to	are deprived of	are deprived of	are deprived of	egent	are in need of	do need	are deprived of … the presence	are deprived of … the … presence
Greek Byzantine	French Geneva (1560-1669)	French Martin (1699)	French Darby (1859)	French Ostervald (1744)	French Louis Segond (1910)	French Jerusalem Bible (1973); Segond 21 (2007)	Latin Vulgate (early 400s)	French Jacques leFevres d'Étaples* (1530)	French Louvain* (1899)	French Bible Francais Courant (1997)	French le Semeur (1992, 1999)[1080]
πάντες γὰρ ἥμαρτον καὶ ὑστεροῦνται τῆς δόξης τοῦ θεοῦ	"for there is [absolutely] no difference: seeing as all have sinned, and are entirely destitute of the glory of God"	"for there is absolutely no difference, seeing as all have sinned, and are utterly deprived of the glory of God"	"for all have sinned and cannot attain to the glory of God"	"For there is no difference, because all have sinned, and are deprived of the glory of God"	"For all have sinned and are deprived of the glory of God"	"All have sinned and are deprived of the glory of God"	omnes enim peccaverunt et egent gloriam Dei	"Certainly there is [absolutely] no difference: for all have sinned & are in need of the glory of God"	"For there is no difference: For all have sinned and have need the glory of God"	"all have sinned and are deprived of the presence of the glorious God"	"All have sinned, in fact, and are deprived of the glorious presence of God"
Greek verb ὑστερέω (20 LXX and 16 NT uses) make it a definable term; at issue seem to be theological presuppositions	From: "car il n'y a nulle difference: veu que tous ont peché, et sont entierement destituez de la gloire de Dieu"	From: "car il n'y a nulle différence, vu que tous ont péché, et qu'ils sont entièrement privés de la gloire de Dieu."	From: "car tous ont péché et n'atteignent pas à la gloire de Dieu:	From: "Car il n'y a point de distinction, puisque tous ont péché, et sont privés de la gloire de Dieu,"	From: "Car tous ont péché et sont privés de la gloire de Dieu"	From: "tous ont péché et sont privés de la gloire de Dieu,"	It appears that future Catholic translations focused on the lexical definition of the word *egent*, from *egeo*, to want, be in need	From: "Certes il ny a nulle difference: car tous on peche et ont besoing de la gloire de Dieu"	From: "Car il n'y a aucune difference: Car tous ont péché & ont besoing de la gloire de Dieu"	From: "tous ont péché et sont privés de la présence glorieuse de Dieu"	From: "Tous ont péché, en effet, et sont privés de la glorieuse présence de Dieu"

One cannot help but notice in these translations three different foci—is the main issue in describing sin:

> A problem of nature: entirely destitute or deprived of (as in completely lacking a limb or being deprived of electricity; i.e. not there; there is none)?
>
> A problem of achievement: cannot attain to a goal (unachievable)?
>
> A problem of privation: deprived of (as in deprived of joy) or in need of (lacking joy)?

Rule of thumb: "Scripture best interprets Scripture"; therefore, Rom 3:10-20 is quite clear on which of the above is being referenced by Paul; likewise, other verses, such as Gen 6:5 and Isa 59:3-8.

Further comments:

a) Of other uses of ὑστερέω, often translated "fall short" (16 uses in NT):

(1) In John 2:3 we have this verb used when the wine "gave out"; wherein Mary told Jesus, "They have no wine" [Οἶνον οὐκ ἔχουσιν]—clearly not a matter of lacking a mere percentage, but completely lacking—they were totally deprived or destitute of wine!

(2) In Phil 4:12, we have the word used as the opposite of abundance, in parallel to suffering hunger (cf. Luke 15:14)

(3) In Heb 4:1 and 12:15 it is used of falling short or being deprived of saving grace

(4) In 1 Cor 1:7; 8:8; and 12:24, of "lacking" or being deprived of any spiritual gifts, grace, or honor

(5) In 2 Cor 11:5, 9; 12:11, of Paul's ministry lacking with comparison to the effervescent ministry of the "super apostles"

[1080]By the way, publisher information on this version states, "This IBS translation of the Entire Bible is for the French language; an estimated 124,000,000 people speak this language as their mother tongue. This translation uses an informal language style and applies a meaning-based translation philosophy. It is translated from the Biblical languages and was completed in June 1999" ("La Bible du Semeur"; available from http://www.biblegateway.com/versions/index.php?action=getVersionInfo&vid=32; accessed: 24 Aug 2006; Internet).

(6) Notice in the OT, in the famous writing on the wall in Dan 5:25; the explanation for the second word "tekel," or, "You have been found deficient"; the Greek LXX used the term ὑστερέω.

b) Of other available Greek terms:

(1) The verb ἀπορφανίζω (1 NT use in 1 Thess 2:17) was available to Paul, which clearly communicates relational separation,[1081] would Paul have been interested in using a more relationally-oriented term that includes the communication of the concept of "for a time"

(2) The verb χρήζω was available to Paul, he used it twice (Rom 16:2; 2 Cor 3:1); further, he used the cognate noun χρεία, "in need," 18 times (incl. Heb) and once in Acts 20:34

(3) The verb ἔνδεια was also available to Paul, found 13 times in the OT LXX, and 7 times in the apocryphal books; according to Liddell-Scott, its meaning is "want, need, lack"; it is used physically, as in "lacking food" (Deut 28:20, 57), "lacking needs" (Prov 6:11; 14:23; 24:34), "lacking bread" (Amos 4:6; Ezek 4:16), "Lack of shelter" (Isa 25:4), "eat in want" (Ezek 12:19)and metaphorically, as in "lacking sense" (Prov 6:32), "lacking truth" (Prov 10:21)

(4) The term, σταθμός, meaning lack, as in needing to weigh in a balance to measure due to lack (Ezek 4:16); this term would appear to fit with the use of scales to consider that God provides what is lacking to us, because of "grace", after we do our best

c) The problem seems to be not with the Greek, but with the English use of "lacking", which has a more nuanced meaning than the Greek appears to have

d) Therefore we are left with several theological approaches to the sin nature of man, total depravity, moral privation, or relational privation; and thus to three potential theological categories, Substitutionary Atonement, Reconciliation Model, or some other lesser model. Which will the translator choose? It appears that a more conciliatory and nuanced rendering won the day in the 1611 King James Version, with the translation "fall short" (among Protestant translations).

(1) "Fall short" is used by the ASV, RSV, NAS, NIV, NKJ, ESV, CSB (hence all major 20th Century English translations)

(2) How the translation of this word has impacted doctrinal confessions through the years is difficult to say

(3) For example, whereas the 1833 [Baptist] New Hampshire Confession emphasized "utter depravity" (in the wake of the Unitarian Movement among U.S. Congregationalists), no 20th Century Baptist Confession appears to emphasize this same concept

f) Note also that almost all Evangelical Gospel presentations include Rom 3:23. Therefore, the proper translation of this verse is not without importance!

g) The International Bible Society's French *Le Semeur* (1999) and a new family of other translations (GNT) have gone over-and-above to reverse the Reformation translation of the French Geneva Bible, and to extract total depravity from Romans 3:23, while still using the verb "to deprive"

h) Notice that Catholic translations which utilize the Latin Vulgate as their authoritative version emphasize something like "do need", focusing on the lack of a percentage of grace, which being conferred through the Sacraments, affirms their Pelagianism

i) It appears that German translations also have a significant variety of translations of this same term.

[1081]"85.17 ἀπορφανίζω: (a figurative extension of meaning of ἀπορφανίζω 'to cause to be an orphan,' not occurring in the NT) to cause someone to be spacially separated, with the implication of additional emotional deprivation – 'to separate and to deprive.' ἀπορφανισθέντες ἀφ᾽ ὑμῶν πρὸς καιρὸν ὥρας 'separated from you for a time' or 'separated and deprived of your company for a time' 1 Th 2.17" (*Louw-Nida Lexicon*; Bibleworks 8.0).

4) The old "Remove-Key-Theological-Phrases-from-the-Bible-when-Translating" trick, while saying that removal is absolutely necessary because of supposedly "out-of-date words and phrases" (see for example the "out-of-date words and phrases" in the KJV):

Removing Key Total Depravity Phrases from the Text*
From Teaching Total Depravity to Communicating Social Misdeeds
(also see appendix to Chapter 8, Jesus on Total Depravity)

Text and Term	Byzantine Textform	King James Version (1611/1769)	New American Standard (1977)	New International Version (1984)	English New Jerusalem (1985)	God's Word to the Nations (1995)	IBS's French Le Semeur (1992/1999)**	Bible in Basic English (1941/1964)	ABS's Contemp English Version (1995)	ABS' Good News Trans (1992)
Rom 1:18 Against all ngodliness and Unrighteousness of men	Ἀποκαλύπτεται γὰρ ὀργὴ θεοῦ ἀπ' οὐρανοῦ ἐπὶ πᾶσαν ἀσέβειαν καὶ ἀδικίαν ἀνθρώπων τῶν τὴν ἀλήθειαν ἐν ἀδικίᾳ κατεχόντων·	For the wrath of God is revealed from heaven against all ungodliness and unrighteousness of men, who hold the truth in unrighteousness;	For the wrath of God is revealed from heaven against all ungodliness and unrighteousness of men, who suppress the truth in unrighteousness,	The wrath of God is being revealed from heaven against all the godlessness and wickedness of men who suppress the truth by their wickedness,	The retribution of God from heaven is being revealed against the ungodliness and injustice of human beings who in their injustice hold back the truth	God's anger is revealed from heaven against every ungodly and immoral thing people do as they try to suppress the truth by their immoral living	From the heights of heaven, God manifests against the men who do not honor him and do not respect his will. They also dishonest-ly smother the truth.	For there is a revelation of the wrath of God from heaven against all the wrong-doing and evil thoughts of men who keep down what is true by wrong-doing;	From heaven God shows how angry he is with all the wicked and evil things that sinful people do to crush the truth.	God's anger is revealed from heaven against all the sin and evil of the people whose evil ways prevent the truth from being known.
Eph 2:3 By nautre... Children of Wrath (or enfant de colère)	καὶ ἦμεν τέκνα φύσει ὀργῆς, ὡς καὶ οἱ λοιποί·	and were by nature the children of wrath, even as others	and were by nature children of wrath, even as the rest.	Like the rest, we were by nature objects of wrath.	our nature made us no less liable to God's retribution than the rest of the world.	So, because of our nature, we deserved God's anger just like everyone else	Also were we, by nature, destined to undergo the wrath of God as the rest of mankind.	and the punish-ment of God was waiting for us even as for the rest	and we were going to be punished like everyone else.	In our natural condition we, like everyone else, were destined to suffer God's anger
Eph 5:6 Sons of disobedience (or fils de rébellion)	Μηδεὶς ὑμᾶς ἀπατάτω κενοῖς λόγοις· διὰ ταῦτα γὰρ ἔρχεται ἡ ὀργὴ τοῦ θεοῦ ἐπὶ τοὺς υἱοὺς τῆς ἀπειθείας.	Let no man deceive you with vain words: for because of these things cometh the wrath of God upon the children of disobedience	Let no one deceive you with empty words, for because of these things the wrath of God comes upon the sons of disobedience.	Let no one deceive you with empty words, for because of such things God's wrath comes on those who are disobedient.	Do not let anyone deceive you with empty arguments: it is such behaviour that draws down God's retribution on those who rebel against him.	Don't let anyone deceive you with meaningless words. It is because of sins like these that God's anger comes to those who refuse to obey him	May no one trick you by arguments without value: it is these disorders that draw the wrath of God on those who refuse to obey him.	Do not be turned from the right way by foolish words; for because of these things the punish-ment of God comes on those who do not put them-selves under him.	Don't let anyone trick you with foolish talk. God punishes everyone who disobeys him and says foolish things.	Do not let anyone deceive you with foolish words; it is because of these very things that God's anger will come upon those who do not obey him.

*It almost seems like translators antagonistic to Evangelical theology go through Calvin's *Institutes* and Shedd's *Theology* to find the verses and terms that they use to describe doctrines like Total Depravity. Then to undermine these Gospel doctrines, they twist the words in any way they can so that these doctrines cannot be read from those verses.

**The French reads as follows: Rom 1:18, "Du haut du ciel, Dieu manifeste sa colère contre les hommes qui ne l'honorent pas et ne respectent pas sa volonté. Ils étouffent ainsi malhon-nêtement la vérité."; Eph 2:3, "Aussi étions-nous, par nature, destinés à subir la colère de Dieu comme le reste des hommes."; Eph 5:6, "Que personne ne vous trompe par des arguments sans valeur: ce sont ces désordres qui attirent la colère de Dieu sur ceux qui refusent de lui obéir."

d. Sin as a mere negation from 1 Cor 6:12:

1) The argument continues with "all things are permissible"

2) But sin is something that is "not useful," therefore supposedly undermining that [1] sinfulness is not a part of man's nature, nor that [2] sin is a willful or ignorant action

3) To use 1 Cor 6:12 to define sin is to take the verse out of context; many other verses show that sin is indeed a part of man's nature, as well as a definite thought or action whether willfully or from ignorance.

Questioning Sin as a Mere Negation and the Translation of Deuteronomy 32:4-5

French Revised Geneva* (1979)	Wycliffe (1388)	English Geneva (1560)	King James Bible (1611/1769)	New International Version (1984)	The NET Bible (2004, 2005)	New Jerusalem Bible (1985)	God's Word to the Nations (1995)	IBS' French Le Semeur* (1999)
[4] He is the Rock; his works are perfect, for all his ways are righteous;	[4] The werkis of God ben perfit, and alle hise weies ben domes;	[4] Perfect is ye worke of the mighty God: for all his wayes *are* iudgement.	[4] *He is* the Rock, his work *is* perfect: for all his ways *are* judgment:	[4] He is the Rock, his works are perfect, and all his ways are just.	[4] As for the Rock, his work is perfect, for all his ways are just.	[4] He is the Rock, his work is perfect, for all his ways are equitable.	[4] He is a rock. What he does is perfect. All his ways are fair.	[4] He is like a rock, His works are perfect. All that he does is righteous.
He is a faithful God and without iniquity,	God is feithful, and without ony wickidnesse;	God is true, and without wickednes:	a God of truth and without iniquity,	A faithful God who does no wrong,	He is a reliable God who is never unjust,	A trustworthy God who does no wrong,	He is a faithful God, who does no wrong.	He is a faithful God, who does not commit injustice,
He is righteous and upright.	God is iust and riytful.	iust, & righteous is he.	just and right *is* he.	upright and just is he.	he is fair and upright.	he is the Honest, the Upright One!	He is honorable and reliable.	He is a righteous God and straight.
[5] If they have corrupted themselves ,	[5] Thei synneden ayens hym,	[5] They haue corrupted them selues toward him	[5] They have corrupted themselves,	[5] They have acted corruptly toward him;	[5] His people have been unfaithful to him; they have not acted like his children– this is their sin.	[5] They have acted perversely,	[5] He recognizes that his people are corrupt.	[5] But you, toward him, have corrupted yourselves,
unto him is not the fault; the shame is to his children,	and not hise sones in filthis, `that is, of idolatrie;	by their vice, not being his children,	their spot *is* not *the spot* of his children:	to their shame they are no longer his children,		those he fathered without blemish,	To their shame they are no longer his children.	you are no longer his sons, because of your defect,
false and perverse race.	schrewid and waiward generacioun	*but* a frowarde and crooked generacion.	*they are* a perverse and crooked generation	but a warped and crooked generation	They are a perverse and deceitful generation.	a deceitful and underhand brood.	They are devious and scheming.	perverted people, depraved!

*Translation mine; The ABS' *Good News Translation* (revised, 1992) is just as equivocal: "The LORD is your mighty defender, perfect and just in all his ways; Your God is faithful and true; he does what is right and fair. But you are unfaithful, unworthy to be his people, a sinful and deceitful nation" (Deut 32:4-5).

Questioning Sin as a Mere Negation and the Translation of Genesis 6:5
[Note sin as an act (Natural Headship of Adam), rather than as a state of being (Federal Headship of Adam)]

French Revised Geneva* (1979)	Wycliffe (1388)	English Geneva (1560)	King James Bible (1611/1769)	New International Version (1984)	The NET Bible (2004, 2005)	New Jerusalem Bible (1985)	God's Word to the Nations (1995)	French Le Semeur* (1999)
5 The Eternal saw that the wickedness of men was great on the earth, and that all the thoughts of their heart carried itself every day uniquely toward evil.	5 Sotheli God seiy that myche malice of men was in erthe, and that al the thouyt of herte was ententif to yuel in al tyme,	5 When the Lord sawe that the wickedness of man was great in the earth, and all the imaginacions of the thoghts of his heart *were* onely euil continually,	5 And GOD saw that the wickedness of man *was* great in the earth, and *that* every imagination of the thoughts of his heart *was* only evil continually.	5 The LORD saw how great man's wickedness on the earth had become, and that every inclination of the thoughts of his heart was only evil all the time.	5 But the LORD saw that the wickedness of humankind had become great on the earth. Every inclination of the thoughts of their minds was only evil all the time.	5 Yahweh saw that human wickedness was great on earth and that human hearts contrived nothing but wicked schemes all day long.	5 The LORD saw how evil humans had become on the earth. All day long their deepest thoughts were nothing but evil.	5 The Eternal saw that men were doing more and more evil on the earth: unto the length of the day, their hearts conceived nothing but evil.

*Translation mine; Notice the ABS' *Good News Translation* (revised, 1992) on this verse: "When the LORD saw how wicked everyone on earth was and how evil their thoughts were all the time," [on to the next verse].

e. Sin as mere relational separation, Isa 59:2:

1) Seemingly ignoring that sin is the separating factor, "But your iniquities have made a separation between you and your God, And your sins have hidden *His* face from you so that He does not hear"

2) Or by redefining sin as a lack of something, e.g. love, righteousness, glory of God

3) Removing two aspects of the substitutionary atonement:
   a) Preeminent issue of man's sin
   b) Preeminent issue of remission of sins

f. The new birth as merely a new or renewed relationship, John 15:15:

1) Ignoring man's need for a complete change in nature ("You must be born-again"), Eph 2:3

2) Ignoring the fact of imputed righteousness, Isa 64:6, "For all of us have become like one who is unclean, And all our righteous deeds are like a filthy garment; And all of us wither like a leaf, And our iniquities, like the wind, take us away"

g. The Gospel as mere "truth", cf. Eph 1:13:

1) Once the Gospel is reduced to mere truth (often via worldview), then follows the mantra, "All truth is God's truth"; thereby downgrading the Gospel to empirically-derived (and ever-changing) truth found in sociology, anthropology, psychology, etc.

2) One result of the Gospel as mere truth, is man's mere acceptance of the truthfulness of the truth claims of Christianity:
   a) An example of this is C.S. Lewis' being surprised by theism; he *Surprised by Faith* explains his wrestling match with the concept of theism, to which he finally acquiesced
   b) Where is repentance for the forgiveness of sins (Luke 24:47; Acts 2:38) in this system of belief?

3) It must be remembered that the true Gospel is and will always be foolishness to those that are perishing (1 Cor 1:18), and to Gentiles (v. 23).

h. Some unequivocal emphases:
1) Man as totally depraved, Gen 6:5; Deut 32:4-5; Eph 2:1-3
2) Man as sinful from conception, Psa 51:5; 58:3

Translating Verses on Man as Sinful from Birth

Verse	LXX (200 BC)	Vulgate (435)	Wycliffe (1388)	Geneva (1560)	KJV (1611, 1769)	NAB (1901)	ASV (1901)	RSV (1952)	NIV (1984)	New Jerusalem (1985)	NET (2004)	French Le Semeur (1992, 1999)*
Psa 51:5 (a)	ἰδοὺ γὰρ ἐν ἀνομίαις συνελήμφθην	ecce in iniquitate conceptus sum	Y was conseyued in wicked-essis	Beholde, I was borne in iniquitie	Behold, I was shapen in iniquity	True, I was born guilty, a sinner	Behold, I was brought forth in iniquity	Behold, I was brought forth in iniquity	Surely I was sinful at birth	remember, I was born guilty	Look, I was guilty of sin from birth	I am, since my birth, / marked by sin
Psa 51:5 (b)	καὶ ἐν ἁμαρτίαις ἐκίσσησέν με ἡ μήτηρ μου	et in peccato peperit me mater mea	and my modir concey-uede me in synnes	and in sinne hathe my mother conceiued me	and in sin did my mother conceive me	even as my mother conceived me	And in sin did my mother conceive me	and in sin did my mother conceive me	sinful from the time my mother conceived me	a sinner from the moment of conception	a sinner the moment my mother conceived me	Since within my mother / I was conceived, sin attached itself to me
Psa 58:3 (a)	ἀπηλλοτρι ώθησαν οἱ ἁμαρτωλοὶ ἀπὸ μήτρας	alienati sunt peccatores a vulva	Synneris weren maad aliens fro the wombe	The wicked are strangers from ye wombe	The wicked are estranged from the womb	The wicked have been corrupt since birth	The wicked are estranged from the womb	The wicked go astray from the womb	Even from birth the wicked go astray	Since the womb they have gone astray, the wicked,	The wicked turn aside from birth	From the stomach of their mother, / the wicked wander
Psa 58:3 (b)	ἐπλανήθη σαν ἀπὸ γαστρός ἐλάλησαν ψεύδη	erraverunt ab utero loquentes mendacium	thei erriden fro the wombe, thei spaken false thingis	euen from the belly haue they erred, and speake lies	they go astray as soon as they be born, speaking lies	liars from the womb, they have gone astray	They go astray as soon as they are born, speaking lies	they err from their birth, speaking lies	from the womb they are wayward and speak lies	on the wrong path since their birth, with their unjust verdicts	liars go astray as soon as they are born	since their birth, / they spread lies

* Original French Le Semeur, Psa 51:[5]7, "Je suis, depuis ma naissance, / marqué du péché; depuis qu'en ma mère / j'ai été conçu, le péché est attaché à moi." Psa 58:4[3], "Dès le ventre de leur mère, / les méchants s'égarent, depuis leur naissance, / ils profèrent des mensonges."

3) Sin as active rebellion against the Law of God (e.g. Lev 4:27-28; 10 Commandments)
4) Christ as actually bearing our sin as a substitute, 2 Cor 5:21; 1 John 2:2; et al.
   Among other issues in the translation of 2 Cor 5:21 is the word which is modified by the negative term μὴ:
   The unsuspecting reader may think that it modifies the word "sin"; thus, "he knew no sin"
   The μὴ being placed before the verb "know", seems to imply the following as a better translation, "he knew not sin"; which translation is found in the 19th Century in Etheridge (1849), Young's (1862) ["did not know sin"], Darby (1884).

On Translating Substitutionary Atonement Verses
[Note the varying views of the atonement proffered in the contemporary Bible Society translations]

Verse	KJV (1611/1769)	NAS (1977)	ABS' Good News Trans (1993)	IBS' French Le Semeur (1992) Trans. mine*	ABS' Contemp English Version (1991)	Rome's New Jerusalem Bible (1985)
2 Cor 5:21	For he hath made him to be sin for us, who knew no sin; that we might be made the righteousness of God in him.	He made Him who knew no sin to be sin on our behalf, that we might become the righteousness of God in Him.	Christ was without sin, but for our sake God made him share our sin in order that in union with him we might share the righteousness of God.	He who was innocent of all sin, God condemned him as a sinner in our place so that, in union with the Christ, we might become just in the eyes of God.	Christ never sinned! God treated him as a sinner, so that Christ could make us acceptable to God.	For our sake he made the sinless one a victim for sin, so that in him we might become the uprightness of God

Verse	KJV (1611/1769)	NAS (1977)	Good News Trans (1993)	French *Le Semeur* (1992) Trans. mine*	Contemp English Version (1991)	New Jerusalem Bible (1985)
1 Pet 2:24	Who his own self bare our sins in his own body on the tree, that we, being dead to sins, should live unto righteousness: by whose stripes ye were healed	and He Himself bore our sins in His body on the cross, that we might die to sin and live to righteousness; for by His wounds you were healed	Christ himself carried our sins in his body on the cross, so that we might die to sin and live for righteousness. It is by his wounds that you have been healed.	He took our sins on himself and carried them in his body, on the cross, in order that dead to sin, we might live a just life. Yes, it is *by his wounds that you have been healed*.	Christ carried the burden of our sins. He was nailed to the cross, So that we could stop sinning and start living right. By his cuts and bruises you are healed.	He was bearing our sins in his own body on the cross, so that we might die to our sins and live for uprightness; through his bruises you have been healed
1 Pet 3:18	For Christ also hath once suffered for sins, the just for the unjust, that he might bring us to God, being put to death in the flesh, but quickened by the Spirit	For Christ also died for sins once for all, *the* just for *the* unjust, in order that He might bring us to God, having been put to death in the flesh, but made alive in the spirit;	For Christ died for sins once and for all, a good man on behalf of sinners, in order to lead you to God. He was put to death physically, but made alive spiritually.	The Christ himself suffered death for sins, once for all. He the innocent, he died for the guilty, in order to bring you to God. He was put to death in his body but was brought back to life by the Spirit.	For Christ died once for our sins. An innocent person died for those who are guilty. Christ did this to bring you to God, When his body was put to death And his spirit was made alive.	Christ himself died once and for all for sins, the upright for the sake of the guilty, to lead us to God. In the body he was put to death, in the spirit he was raised to life
1 John 2:2	And he is the propitiation for our sins: and not for ours only, but also for *the sins of* the whole world.	and He Himself is the propitiation for our sins; and not for ours only, but also for *those of* the whole world.	And Christ himself is the means by which our sins are forgiven, and not our sins only, but also the sins of everyone.	For he appeased the wrath of God against us in offering himself for our sins—and not only for ours, but also for those of the entire world.	Christ is the sacrifice that takes away our sins and the sins of all the world's people.	He is the sacrifice to expiate our sins, and not only ours, but also those of the whole world

*French originals of 2 Cor 5:21, "Celui qui était innocent de tout péché, Dieu l'a condamné comme un pécheur à notre place pour que, dans l'union avec le Christ, nous soyons justes aux yeux de Dieu." 1 Pet 2:24, "Il a pris nos péchés sur lui et les a portés dans son corps, sur la croix, afin qu'étant morts pour le péché, nous menions une vie juste. Oui, c'est *par ses blessures que vous avez été guéris*." 1 Pet 3:18, "Le Christ lui-même a souffert la mort pour les péchés, une fois pour toutes. Lui l'innocent, il est mort pour des coupables, afin de vous conduire à Dieu. Il a été mis à mort dans son corps mais il a été ramené à la vie par l'Esprit". 1 John 2:2, "Car il a apaisé la colère de Dieu contre nous en s'offrant pour nos péchés --- et pas seulement pour les nôtres, mais aussi pour ceux du monde entier."

5) God reckoning [λογίζομαι] as righteous, Rom 4:3-12
   By the way, the *Louw-Nida Lexicon* does not hide its disapproval of the concept of imputed righteousness.[1082]

[1082]"4.46 δικαιόω ; δικαίωσις, εως *f*; δικαιοσύνη, ης *f*: to cause someone to be in a proper or right relation with someone else - 'to put right with, to cause to be in a right relationship with.' Some scholars, however, interpret δικαιόω, δικαίωσις, and δικαιοσύνη in the following contexts as meaning 'forensic righteousness,' that it to say, the act of being declared righteous on the basis of Christ's atoning ministry, but it would seem more probable that Paul uses these expressions in the context of the covenant relation rather than in the context of legal procedures. δικαιόω: δικαιούμενοι δωρεὰν τῇ αὐτοῦ χάριτι διὰ τῆς ἀπολυτρώσεως τῆς ἐν Χριστῷ Ἰησοῦ 'by the free gift of his grace in delivering them through Christ Jesus, they are put right with him' Ro 3.24. δικαίωσις: ἠγέρθη διὰ τὴν δικαίωσιν ἡμῶν 'he was raised to life in order to put us right with (God)' Ro 4.25. δικαιοσύνη: δικαιοσύνη γὰρ θεοῦ ἐν αὐτῷ ἀποκαλύπτεται ἐκ πίστεως εἰς πίστιν 'how God puts people right with himself is revealed in it as a matter of faith from beginning to end' Ro 1.17. Some scholars, however, understand the phrase δικαιοσύνη θεοῦ in Ro 1.17 as referring to God's faithfulness to his promises made to Abraham. In other words, the focus would be upon God's moral integrity, but it is difficult to relate this interpretation to the statement about faith in Ro 1.17b.

"It may be difficult in some languages to find a succinct expression equivalent to 'to be put right with.' Sometimes the closest equivalent may be 'to be related to as one should be.' In some instances the implication of a right relationship may be expressed by phrases involving 'acceptance.' For example, Ro 3.24 may be expressed as 'by the free gift of God's grace they are accepted by him through Christ Jesus who sets them free.' Similarly, Ro 4.25 is sometimes expressed as 'he was raised to life in order to cause us to be accepted by God.' There are, however, certain dangers involved in terms indicating 'acceptance,' since this might imply God's reluctance to accept people apart from the atoning work of Jesus Christ, while in reality it was God who was in

Sample Translations of the Concept of Justification

Passage	Greek	KJV	NAS	ABS' CEV (1991)
Rom 3:24	δικαιούμενοι δωρεὰν τῇ αὐτοῦ χάριτι διὰ τῆς ἀπολυτρώσεως τῆς ἐν χριστῷ Ἰησοῦ·	Being justified freely by his grace through the redemption that is in Christ Jesus:	being justified as a gift by His grace through the redemption which is in Christ Jesus;	But God treats us much better than we deserve. And because of Jesus Christ, he freely accepts us and sets us free from our sins.
Rom 4:2	Εἰ γὰρ Ἀβραὰμ ἐξ ἔργων ἐδικαιώθη, ἔχει καύχημα, ἀλλ᾽ οὐ πρὸς τὸν θεόν.	For if Abraham were justified by works, he hath *whereof* to glory; but not before God.	For if Abraham was justified by works, he has something to boast about; but not before God.	If he became acceptable to God because of what he did, then he would have something to brag about. But he would never be able to brag about it to God.
Rom 4:5	Τῷ δὲ μὴ ἐργαζομένῳ, πιστεύοντι δὲ ἐπὶ τὸν δικαιοῦντα τὸν ἀσεβῆ, λογίζεται ἡ πίστις αὐτοῦ εἰς δικαιοσύνην.	But to him that worketh not, but believeth on him that justifieth the ungodly, his faith is counted for righteousness.	But to the one who does not work, but believes in Him who justifies the ungodly, his faith is reckoned as righteousness,	But you cannot make God accept you because of something you do. God accepts sinners only because they have faith in him.
Heb 11:4	δι᾽ ἧς ἐμαρτυρήθη εἶναι δίκαιος	by which he obtained witness that he was righteous	through which he obtained the testimony that he was righteous	God was pleased with him
Heb 11:7	καὶ τῆς κατὰ πίστιν δικαιοσύνης ἐγένετο κληρονόμος	and became heir of the righteousness which is by faith	and became an heir of the righteousness which is according to faith	And Noah was given the blessings that come to everyone who pleases God
Heb 11:33	οἳ διὰ πίστεως κατηγωνίσαντο βασιλείας, εἰργάσαντο δικαιοσύνην, ἐπέτυχον ἐπαγγελιῶν	Who through faith subdued kingdoms, wrought righteousness, , obtained promises	who by faith conquered kingdoms, performed *acts of* righteousness, obtained promises	Their faith helped them conquer kingdoms, and because they did right, God made promises to them

6) God appointing to eternal life, Acts 13:48; Romans 6:23

i. **Some sacramental considerations of salvation**:
   1) Conversion theology in Mary's "Magnificat" (Luke 1:46-55)
   2) Conversion theology in the Book of James
   3) The hyper-literalistic reading of John 6:53-56 (which flies in the face of the misunderstanding of the spiritual for the Woman at the Well and Nicodemus)

Christ reconciling the world to himself. Therefore, one should clearly avoid a rendering which would seem to suggest different types of motivation in the Godhead" (*Louw-Nida* in BibleWorks 8.0).

Comparing Translations: Eph 2:1-3

Byzantine Textform	New American Standard (1977)	IBS's French *Le Semeur* (my translation)	ABS's Contemp English Version (1991)
Καὶ ὑμᾶς ὄντας νεκροὺς τοῖς παραπτώμασιν καὶ ταῖς ἁμαρτίαις,	1 And you were dead in your trespasses and sins,	1 Hithertofore, you were dead because of your faults and you sins.	1 In the past you were dead because you sinned and fought against God.
ἐν αἷς ποτὲ περιεπατήσατε κατὰ τὸν αἰῶνα τοῦ κόσμου τούτου, κατὰ τὸν ἄρχοντα τῆς ἐξουσίας τοῦ ἀέρος, τοῦ πνεύματος τοῦ νῦν ἐνεργοῦντος ἐν τοῖς υἱοῖς τῆς ἀπειθείας·	2 in which you formerly walked according to the course of this world, according to the prince of the power of the air, of the spirit that is now working in the sons of disobedience.	2 By these actions, you conformed at that time your manner of life to that of this world and you had followed the chief of the bad spiritual powers, this spirit that works now in the men who are rebellious against God.	2 You followed the ways of this world and obeyed the devil. He rules the world, and his spirit has power over everyone who doesn't obey God.
ἐν οἷς καὶ ἡμεῖς πάντες ἀνεστράφημέν ποτε ἐν ταῖς ἐπιθυμίαις τῆς σαρκὸς ἡμῶν, ποιοῦντες τὰ θελήματα τῆς σαρκὸς καὶ τῶν διανοιῶν, καὶ ἤμεν τέκνα φύσει ὀργῆς, ὡς καὶ οἱ λοιποί·	3 Among them we too all formerly lived in the lusts of our flesh, indulging the desires of the flesh and of the mind, and were by nature children of wrath, even as the rest.	3 We also, we had hithertofore all been a part of these men. We had lived according to our desires [that being] of men delivered over to themselves and we had accomplished all that our body and our spirit could do to us. Also we had been, by nature, destined to suffer the wrath of God as the rest of men.	3 Once we were also ruled by the selfish desires of our bodies and minds. We had made God angry, and we were going to be punished like everyone else.

*My translation of "1 Autrefois, vous étiez morts à cause de vos fautes et de vos péchés. 2 Par ces actes, vous conformiez alors votre manière de vivre à celle de ce monde et vous suiviez le chef des puissances spirituelles mauvaises, cet esprit qui agit maintenant dans les hommes rebelles à Dieu. 3 Nous aussi, nous faisions autrefois tous partie de ces hommes. Nous vivions selon nos désirs d'hommes livrés à eux-mêmes et nous accomplissions tout ce que notre corps et notre esprit nous poussaient à faire. Aussi étions-nous, par nature, destinés à subir la colère de Dieu comme le reste des hommes."

The reader will consider all the theological variations injected into the *Le Semeur* translation. There is some incredible word crafting in this text to change its meaning. For example:

v 1 "Because of" changes the verse to teach the Natural Headship of Adam; hence removing Total Depravity from this text.

v 1 Downgrades trespasses to faults (following the French Jerusalem translation), whereas the French Protestant Segond reads "offenses" [meaning transgression] here, clearly indicating a transgression of the law of God

v 2 Addition of the word "actions", again to reemphasize the Natural Headship of Adam

v 2 Addition of the phrase "at that time" (along with the subjective tense throughout verses 2-3) to provide for the Roman teaching that baptism washes away the sinful nature inherited from Adam

v 2 "Manner of life" is amply used in *Le Semeur* almost in the sense of Behavioral Psychology

v 2 Addition of the verb "that you had followed" to again inject a Natural Headship dimension to Satan's dominion over the world

v 2 Insertion of "bad spiritual" to provide further unnecessary clouding of the meaning

v 2 Cannot allow "sons of disobedience" or the even stronger French Protestant reading "fils de rebellion" [sons of rebellion], as it implies Adam as Federal Head, and the sin nature as Total Depravity; thus they translate "men who are rebellious against God" focusing on the problem of sin being the act, and not the man's sinful nature; even the state of sinning is only a momentary problem "now"

v 3 Verse 3 is divided in an interesting way to categorize people, perhaps providing for the distinction between the baptized and non-baptized in Roman theology, as noted above in the additional phrase "at that time" in verse 2.

v 3 The possibility of man's lust being a part of his nature is removed from this text through the elaborate reinterpretation of "according to the lusts" into the phrase "according to our desires [that being] of men delivered over to themselves"

v 3 "We had accomplished all that our body and our spirit could do to us" provides in a strange way for the outside locus of sin v 3 "Destined to suffer" again removes the teaching that man's very nature is sinful (total depravity); allowing the text to teach that man's very nature is evil and depraved would be Manichean, something the Roman church has violently opposed since the 12th Century

Translating the preposition "in" in τί ἦν ἐν τῷ ἀνθρώπῳ **[What was in man], John 2:25**

Byzantine Textform	New American Standard, 1977	New Jerusalem Bible, 1985	IBS's *Le Semeur,** 1992, 1999	New American Bible, 1991	ABS's Contemp English Version, 1995
καὶ ὅτι οὐ χρείαν εἶχεν ἵνα τις μαρτυρήσῃ περὶ τοῦ ἀνθρώπου· αὐτὸς γὰρ ἐγίνωσκεν τί ἦν ἐν τῷ ἀνθρώπῳ	and because He did not need anyone to bear witness concerning man for He Himself knew what was in man	He never needed evidence about anyone; he could tell what someone had within.	In fact, he did not need to be informed about men for he knew what was in the depths of their heart	and did not need anyone to testify about human nature. He himself understood it well.	No one had to tell him what people were like. He already knew.

*My translation of "En effet, il n'avait pas besoin qu'on le renseigne sur les hommes car il connaissait le fond de leur cœur."

E. Three Further Approaches to Discerning the Gospel Message:

1. The Fifty-Two Evangelistic Conversations:[1083]

Introduction: In the 52 evangelistic conversations in the Gospels and the Book of Acts, based on my analysis, the following are aspects of the Gospel shared:

1. The Message:
    a. The person of Jesus, 47 times
    b. The Word of God, 2 times
    c. Serving God, Law and prophets, hope of the resurrection, 1 time
    d. Testimony, 1 time.

2. As far as methodology, Whitesell included excellent lists of Jesus' methodology from five authors:[1084]
    a. G. Campbell Morgan, *The Great Physician* (New York: Revell, 1937).
    b. Charles G. Trumbull, *Taking Men Alive* (New York: Association Press, 1907).
    c. F. V. McFatridge, *The Personal Evangelism of Jesus* (Grand Rapids: Zondervan, 1939).
    d. Robert H. Bothwell, "New Testament Principles of Personal Evangelism," B.D. Thesis, Northern Baptist Theological Seminary, 1941.
    e. Charles F. Kemp, *Physicians of Soul* (New York: Macmillan, 1947).
    f. It would be interesting to study the differences between these prior mentioned books and Robert Coleman's *The Master Plan of Evangelism* (Old Tappan, NJ: Revell, 1963), especially in light of the "Discipleship Movement" of the 1970s-1980s.

Conclusion: The message in the ministry of Jesus is unique because He was the incarnate Word of God, every word proceeding from His mouth was God's Word.

I. Five Audiences in the Book of Acts:

Introduction: There are five distinct audiences in the Book of Acts, clearly differentiated by the use of different words. These audiences are:

(1) Gentiles (both τὰ ἔθνη [13 uses in Acts], the Gentiles, and τοὺς Ἑλληνιστὰς [13 uses in Acts (various forms)] the Greeks)

(2) Jews

[1083]The idea for this study came from a chart titled "Interviews in the Gospel of John" in Merrill C. Tenney's *John: The Gospel of Belief, An Analytical Study of the Text* (Grand Rapids: Eerdmans, 1948), 316. In this chart, Tenney lists 27 interviews of Jesus in the Gospel of John, some of which were evangelistic. Faris D. Whitesell listed 50 personal evangelism conversations in his *Basic New Testament Evangelism* (Grand Rapids: Zondervan, 1949), 35 attributed to Jesus (ibid., 107-08) and 15 in the Book of Acts (ibid., 112).

[1084]Faris D. Whitesell, *Basic New Testament Evangelism* (Grand Rapids: Zondervan, 1949), 108-11.

(3) Godfearers (both σεβομένος, "one who worships God" [6 times], and φοβουμενος, "God-fearing" [3 times in Acts])

(4) Disciples of John the Baptist

(5) Believers.

Each group has sermons (or conversations for the Disciples of John the Baptist), directed to that group in particular, other sermons are for Jews and Godfearers. Some principles for developing an effective Gospel message can be derived from a study of these sermons. The following charts this idea.

The Content of the Gospel: the Five Named Audiences in the Book of Acts:[1085]

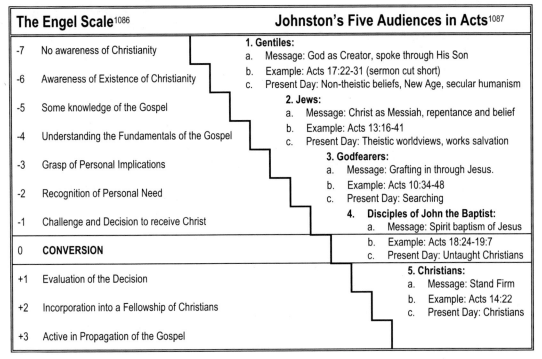

The Engel Scale[1086]	Johnston's Five Audiences in Acts[1087]
-7 No awareness of Christianity	**1. Gentiles:** a. Message: God as Creator, spoke through His Son
-6 Awareness of Existence of Christianity	b. Example: Acts 17:22-31 (sermon cut short) c. Present Day: Non-theistic beliefs, New Age, secular humanism
-5 Some knowledge of the Gospel	**2. Jews:** a. Message: Christ as Messiah, repentance and belief
-4 Understanding the Fundamentals of the Gospel	b. Example: Acts 13:16-41 c. Present Day: Theistic worldviews, works salvation
-3 Grasp of Personal Implications	**3. Godfearers:** a. Message: Grafting in through Jesus.
-2 Recognition of Personal Need	b. Example: Acts 10:34-48 c. Present Day: Searching
-1 Challenge and Decision to receive Christ	**4. Disciples of John the Baptist:** a. Message: Spirit baptism of Jesus
0 CONVERSION	b. Example: Acts 18:24-19:7 c. Present Day: Untaught Christians
+1 Evaluation of the Decision	**5. Christians:** a. Message: Stand Firm
+2 Incorporation into a Fellowship of Christians	b. Example: Acts 14:22 c. Present Day: Christians
+3 Active in Propagation of the Gospel	

Note 1: While the Gospel message never changes, the emphasis of the Gospel is different in different cases. It may be that Rom 15:8-9 explain this differentiation:

"For I say that Christ has become a servant to the circumcision on behalf of the truth of God to confirm the promises *given* to the fathers, and [whereas] for the Gentiles to glorify God for His mercy; as it is written, 'Therefore I will give praise to Thee among the Gentiles, And I will sing to Thy name.'"

Note 2: Some studies of the *kerygma* mentioned in the first point in this section, may deal exclusively with the message of the Apostles to the Jews, and may ignore or treat as one the other named audiences in Acts.

[1085]Johnston, *Charts for a Theology of Evangelism*, Chart 35, "Context of the Gospel in Acts," 63

[1086]"Engel Scale" (by James Engel, Wheaton Graduate School) taken from Edward R. Dayton, "To Reach the Unreached" in Ralph D. Winter and Steven C. Hawthorne, eds., *Perspectives on the World Christian Movement: A Reader* (Pasadena, CA: William Carey Library, 1981): 591.

[1087] Johnston's Five Audiences" from Thomas P. Johnston, *Evangelism and Discipleship: A Biblical Introduction* (Deerfield, IL: Evangelism Unlimited, Inc., 1997): 57. Revised by author for "A Theology of Mission – Through the Lens of the Book of Acts" (Seminar paper, Southern Baptist Theological Seminary, 1999).

J. The Book of Romans:

Introduction:

The Book of Romans has been and continues to be the most important theological book to NT Christians. It cannot be and must not be ignored nor reinterpreted by equivocating theologians.

Why is the Book of Romans so important? Because Paul stated that his purpose was "to evangelize" (Rom 1:15) among the Romans; which goal he accomplished through this book! More on that below...

Some theologians' antagonism to the Book of Romans and to its teaching are evidence of its importance message. For example, as one theologian described the Book of Romans as "Paul's ironic gospel":[1088]

> "As the eschatological community continues to live in the midst of an unchanged world, Paul **ironizes**. Thus the 'cursed' Jesus is the means of Christian blessing (Gal 3:10-14). His death is the fount of life (Rom 5:17-19). One must die in order to live (Gal 2:19-20; Rom 6:1-4).
> "Such ironic inversions are common the in the NT. Others, like **the inversion of righteousness in Romans**, are more distinctively Pauline."[1089]

In marked contrast, however, notice how the same author cannot help but express praise for the general epistles (Hebrews, James, 1-2 Peter, 1-3 John).[1090]

1. A Preliminary Look at the Organization of the Book of Romans:

Theme verses:

1) The theme verb of the Book of Romans is εὐαγγελίζω, "to evangelize"—notice the following:
   a) Based on his obligation or indebtedness, to make everyone hear the Gospel:

   Rom 1:14, "I am a debtor both to Greeks and to barbarians, both to wise and to unwise."

   b) Paul is eager to do evangelize in verse 15, using the verb εὐαγγελίζω in the infinitive-aorist-middle:

   Rom 1:15, "So, as much as is in me, *I am* ready to preach the gospel to you who are in Rome also" [οὕτως τὸ κατ' ἐμὲ πρόθυμον καὶ ὑμῖν τοῖς ἐν Ῥώμῃ εὐαγγελίσασθαι.]

   c) Which desire he fulfilled by writing the Book of Romans, evangelizing or sharing the Gospel with the Romans, maybe in a pattern similar to what he did in the synaguoge in Thessalonica, Acts 17:2-3, or in the marketplace at Athens, Acts 17:16-18!

[1088]Notice his other comments: "Like the Prophets, then, the primary mythic function of the Apostle is **succession**. Of course, the presence of Jesus diminishes the move away from the Gospel [read: Gospels]" (Richard G. Walsh, *Reading the Bible: An Introduction* [Notre Dame, IN: Cross Cultural, 1997], 445-46); "Put concisely, they [Paul's letters] call the churches to realize more fully or to return to the gospel. That is, Paul exhorts, advises, and counsels his churches **to act according to** his apostolic understanding of their **shared mythic identity** (hence, the frequent familial language)" (ibid., 452); "As attempts to exercise apostolic authority and mythic interpretation, the letters [of Paul] are **open-ended stories**. The communities may not heed Paul" (ibid., 452-53). Emphasis in original.

[1089]Ibid., 456. Emphasis from the original.

[1090]"The general epistles are remarkably free from the phatic language which structures letters. Thus, while Hebrews has a letter closing, it has no opening. Conversely, James has no closing. 1 john has neither opening nor closing....

"While James, Hebrews, and I john are more specific, their addresses mark them as **encyclicals**....

"Not surprisingly, the body of these letters is not a specific response to a specific occasion. Rather, the letters are **sermons, which reflect upon the foundational traditions** of the authors/communities.

"The traditions are applied generally. In essence, the audiences should hold onto their traditions, resist apostasy, and live in accord with tradition."

"The commitment to tradition creates a particular narrative voice. Whether apostle (1-2 Pet), servant (Jas; Jude; 2 Pet), or elder (2-3 Jn), that voice is **the authoritative guardian of tradition**.

"These **priestly custodians** exhort within and for an already established conventional wisdom (Jas) or apostolic tradition (2 Pet; 1-2 Jn; Jude). They do not substantively extend or create myth. They strive to maintain it in the face of apostasy" (ibid., 474-76; emphasis in original).

d) Paul then explained why he was eager to evangelize them immediately through the letter to the Romans; notice the series of prepositional phrases modifying the verb "evangelize":

(1) "For" Paul was not ashamed of the Gospel of Christ:

Rom 1:16, "For [Οὐ γὰρ] I am not ashamed of the gospel of Christ, for it is the power of God to salvation for everyone who believes, for the Jew first and also for the Greek."

(2) "For" in it the righteousness of God is revealed:

Rom 1:17, "For in it the righteousness of God is revealed [Δικαιοσύνη γὰρ θεοῦ ἐν αὐτῷ ἀποκαλύπτεται] from faith to faith; as it is written, 'The just shall live by faith.'"

(3) "For" the wrath of God is revealed (notice the repetition of the word "revealed"):

Rom 1:18-19, "For the wrath of God is revealed ['Αποκαλύπτεται γὰρ ὀργὴ θεοῦ] from heaven against all ungodliness and unrighteousness of men, who suppress the truth in unrighteousness, because what may be known of God is manifest in them, for God has shown *it* to them."

(4) "For" since the creation of the world:

Rom 1:20, "For since the creation of the world His invisible *attributes* are clearly seen, being understood by the things that are made, *even* His eternal power and Godhead, so that they are without excuse," …

2) If this logical string is correct, and it makes perfect sense, then this is why the Book of Romans is such a great sourcebook for the simple Gospel:

a) Paul was so eager to evangelize the Romans, that he actually did just that, through writing the Book of Romans!

b) Karl Barth even hinted at this purpose in his commentary on Romans (writing a ½ paragraph on Rom 1:14-15, and then 7½ pages on 1:16-17):

"Even the Christians in Rome are included in the forces of the gentiles, to whose service he has admittedly been consecrated. … Meanwhile, however, only the written word is available. He must therefore use it as best he can to promote a common knocking at the doors of the kingdom and united movement towards it."[1091]

3) Now, most scholars view Rom 1:16-17 or portions thereof to be the theme verses, seemingly ignoring that Paul actually evangelized them through his authorship of the Book of Romans:

a) While some Evangelical commentators virtually passed over Rom 1:15 focusing rather on Rom 1:14, e.g. H. C. G. Moule,[1092] Donald Grey Barnhouse,[1093] R. Kent Hughes[1094]

b) Douglas J. Moo seemed to summarize the thoughts of the majority of commentators in a section titled Rom 1:8-15, "Thanksgiving and Occasion" (followed by a section of commentary on Rom 1:16-17, "The Theme of the Letter"; Moo's treatment of "preaching the Gospel"):

"Paul now relates what he has generally said in v. 14 to the specific situation of his desire to come to Rome: 'and so my desire is to preach the gospel also to you in Rome.' That Paul includes the Roman Christians among those to whom he wants to preach the gospel is, at first sight, strange. Some commentators therefore think that Paul is talking here about what he planned to do in the past when he had hoped to come to Rome. But v. 15 is tied to v. 14, which uses the present tense. Others think that he is indicating his desire to preach the gospel to Spain, on behalf of the

---

[1091]Karl Barth, *The Epistle to the Romans,* translated by Edwyn C. Hoskyns (London: Oxford, 1933, 1950), 34.

[1092]Handley G. C. Moule, *The Epistle of Paul to the Romans* (London: Hodder and Stoughton, 1894), 31.

[1093]Chapter 14, "Debtors," Romans 1:14-15, in Donald Grey Barnhouse, *Romans* (Grand Rapids: Eerdmans, 1952, 1953), 1:146-56.

[1094]"Paul's Second Ministry Motivation: A Sense of Obligation (vv. 14, 15), almost a page in Chapter 2, "Paul's Motivation for Ministry, Romans 1:8-17," in R. Kent Hughes, *Romans: Righteousness from Heaven* (Wheaton, IL: Crossway, 1991), 26.

Roman Christians. But this requires us to import too much from the end of the letter. Another possibility is that 'you' refers generally to Romans and that Paul is speaking of his desire to evangelize in Rome. But it is more natural to take 'you' to refer to the Roman Christians; in this case, 'preach the gospel' will refer to the ongoing work of teaching that builds on initial evangelization. As P. Bowers has pointed out, 'the gospel' in Paul includes 'not simply an initial preaching mission but the full sequence of activities resulting in settled churches."[1095]

(1) Notice Moo's use of the word "strange" at the end of his second sentence to perhaps express his view of Paul's use of the word "evangelize"

(2) While coming close to stating that the main theme and purpose of the Book of Romans is found in the verb "evangelize," that idea does not appear to be on Moo's radar screen, nor anyone else's that he cites.

(3) Note for example Charles Hodge[1096]

(4) Or C. E. B. Cranfield:

(a) Of the theme verses:

"These one and a half verses [1:16b-17] are at the same time both an integral part of Paul's expression of his readiness to preach the gospel in Rome and also the statement of the theological theme which is going to be worked out in the main body of the epistle."[1097]

(b) Of the word "evangelize" in verse 15:

"…But Paul's preaching the gospel to them (εὐαγγελίσασθαι is here used of preaching the gospel to believers) [cites G. Friedrich, *TWNT* 2:717] is in no way incompatible with his receiving comfort and encouragement from them…"[1098]

(c) Of the dative ὑμῖν (you, plural) with no preposition, the word from which is derived the predicate "to you" in "evangelize to you", Cranfield has no discussion of the possible range of meanings, such as:
[1] To evangelize "with you"—there is a fellowship in the Gospel work that is sweet (Phil 1:5)
[2] To evangelize "to you" or "unto you"—the meaning he assumes
[3] To evangelize "among you" (indicating the wider group of Romans), notice, for example, how Paul spoke of the Cretans in Titus 1:12-13

4) However, as a presentation of the Gospel of Christ, notice how the book is organized…

2. **The Gospel plan in Romans?**

Introduction:
1) Note that Paul begins with the wrath of God against sin, Rom 1:18
2) He does not speak of love until Rom 5:5, 8

a. Sin, Rom 1:18-3:20

b. Righteousness by faith in Jesus Christ, not by works, Rom 3:21-5:21

c. More on sin, its wages and the battle for purity, Rom 6-7

[1095]Douglas J. Moo, *The Epistle to the Romans* (Grand Rapids: Eerdmans, 1996), 62-63.

[1096]"*To preach the gospel.* The verb εὐαγγελίσασθαι is commonly followed by some word or phrase expressing the subject of the message—kingdom of god, gospel, word of God, Christ. In writing to Christians, who knew what the glad tidings were, the apostles often, as in the present case use the word absolutely so that the word by itself means, to preach the gospel, &c. See chap. xv. 20; Acts xvi. 7; Gal iv. 13" (Charles Hodge, *Commentary on the Epistle to the Romans* [1886; Grand Rapids: Eerdmans, 1950], 28).

[1097]C. E. B. Cranfield, *A Critical and Exegetical Commentary on the Epistle to the Romans* (Edinburgh: T & T. Clark, 1975), 87.

[1098]Ibid., 86.

    d. Coming to Christ by merely saying, "Thank you!" Rom 7:25:

        Example: This was the salvation experience of missionary C. T. Studd:

> "I got down on my knees and I did say 'thank you' to God. And right then and there joy and peace came into my soul. I knew then what it was to be 'born again,' and the Bible which had been so dry to me before, became everything."[1099]

        1) The word for thank you in the Byzantine Greek of this verse is Εὐχαριστω (eucharisto). This word, and its use to describe the Lord's Supper in the Roman Catholic Church, might be indicative that it was first the Greek Orthodox church that replaced conversion through a sinner's prayer with taking the bread [and cup] of communion for salvation!

        2) Whatever the case, the simple action of receiving salvation by an attitude of thanksgiving in the heart has been repeatedly anathematized by Rome, as in the Council of Trent.[1100]

    e. Coming to God by faith alone, Rom 8:1-11:36:
        1) The link between believing and evangelizing is made in the rhetorical questions of Rom 10:14-15

    f. Implications of life of faith in Christ, Rom 12:1-15:13

    g. Return to his indebtedness to the Gentiles and his life as an evangelist, Rom 15:14-33
        1) Paul again brings up that his goal to evangelize where Christ has not been named, Rom 15:20

    h. Final greetings, Rom 16:1-27

  3. **Romans as an evangelistic conversation**—Paul's interesting uses of second person singular: Or: **How Paul evangelizes a.k.a. the Book of Romans**!

    Introduction:

      In the day that Paul shares the gospel:

> Rom 2:16 (CSB), "on the day when God judges what people have kept secret, according to my gospel through Christ Jesus"
>
> There were particular days when Paul shared the gospel
>
> It seems that it was on those days and at those times that God judged the secrets in the hearts of men
>
> According to Paul's gospel—"[on account of] Paul's gospel"
>
> > (Thayer on κατὰ): g. used of the cause; *through, on account of, from, owing to* (in accordance with i. e. *in consequence of, by virtue of*).
>
> Through Christ Jesus

      It is intuitive to the personal evangelist that, when and only when the gospel goes forth from his mouth, it is then that the Holy Spirit begins his work of conviction (cf. John 16:8; e.g. Acts 24:25)

      Romans 2:16 applies this concept to the gospel message in the Book of Romans

---

[1099]"Charles Studd"; available at: http://en.wikipedia.org/wiki/Charles_Studd (online); accessed: 11 Oct 2012; Internet.

[1100]"But though it is necessary to believe that sins neither are remitted nor ever have been remitted except gratuitously by divine mercy for Christ's sake, yet it must not be said that sins are forgiven or have been forgiven to anyone who boasts of his confidence and certainty of the remission of his sins, resting on that alone, though among heretics and schismatics this vain and ungodly confidence may be and in our troubled times indeed is found and preached with untiring fury against the Catholic Church" (Council of Trent, Decrees Concerning Justification, Chapter ix, Against the Vain Confidence of the Heretics"; available at: http://www.forerunner.com/chalcedon/ X0020_15._Council_of_Trent.html; accessed: 8 Jan 2005; Internet).

"Canon 12. If anyone says that justifying faith is nothing else than confidence in divine mercy,[117] which remits sins for Christ's sake, or that it is this confidence alone that justifies us, let him be anathema" (ibid., "Canons Concerning Justification").

Paul uses 71 verbs in the second person singular in the book of Romans (8.1%). In all the books that are not written to individuals, excepting Hebrews, Paul uses the second singular 124 times, the percentages work out to Galatians (5.4%), 1 Corinthians (2.5%), Colossians (2.5%), 2 Corinthians (2.0%), Ephesians (1.9%), Philippians (1.0%). In 1 and 2 Thessalonians, Paul did not use second person singular.

These uses need to be highlighted in our minds, as English translations use the same word "you" for both singular and plural, nor do our verb endings identify the difference between the second person singular and plural. This blending can cause significant confusion or misapplication for the English-only interpreter of the Bible, especially as it relates to an anti-individualism prevalent in English biblical scholarship

Five times he uses the vocative masculine singular (2:1, 3; 9:20; 10:16; 11:3). Again, only other times he uses vocative, other than in the Pastorals, Philemon, and Hebrews, is twice in First Corinthians (7:16; 15:55). Therefore, it is quite unusual in a book written to a city of churches.

The first seven uses of the word "Jew" in Romans, such as "to the Jew first," from 1:16 to 3:1, are all in the singular, as if Paul was speaking of the individual Jew with whom he is sharing the gospel, cf. 2:16, "in the day … according to my gospel":

Paul uses the plural of "Jew" twice (3:29; 9:24), then when speaking of the call to conversion he returns to the singular, 10:12:

Rom 10:12, "For there is no distinction between Jew and Greek, for the same Lord over all is rich to all who call upon Him"

a. Consider Paul's use of questions, as he guides the conversation about the Gospel—many of which are in the first person plural:

1) For example in chapter 3:
Rom 3:1, "Then what advantage has the Jew? Or what is the benefit of circumcision?"
Rom 3:3, "What then? If some did not believe, their unbelief will not nullify the faithfulness of God, will it?"
Rom 3:5, "But if our unrighteousness demonstrates the righteousness of God, what shall we say? The God who inflicts wrath is not unrighteous, is He?"
Rom 3:6, "For otherwise how will God judge the world?"
Rom 3:7, "But if through my lie the truth of God abounded to His glory, why am I also still being judged as a sinner?"
Rom 3:8, "And why not *say* (as we are slanderously reported and as some affirm that we say), "Let us do evil that good may come "?"
Rom 3:9, "What then? Are we better than they?"
[pause in questions for teaching from Scriptures]
Rom 3:27, "Where then is boasting? It is excluded. By what kind of law? Of works?"
Rom 3:29, "Or is God *the God* of Jews only? Is He not *the God* of Gentiles also?"
Rom 3:31, "Do we then nullify the Law through faith?"

b. Therefore it is clear that Paul is using one-to-one dialogue (singular) in his argumentation in the Book of Romans! Let's therefore consider how he uses it…

1) Of individual guilt before God, Rom 2:1-5:
Comprising 8 uses of second person singular, 2:1 (4 times), 3 (twice), 4, 5;
Comprising 2 uses of the vocative, 2:1, 3.
a) Of man who self-righteously judges others, while committing the same offenses himself, v 1
b) A convicting wake-up call expressing the sure judgment of God, v 3
Reminiscent of Nathan's words to King David, 2 Sam 12:7
c) Of God's longsuffering in delaying judgment, v 4
d) Of man's storing up judgment unto the day of wrath, v 5
Individual guilt in verse 5 is then reinforced by individual accountability in verse 6, with the use of a quote of the OT:
Rom 2:6, "who 'will render to each one according to his deeds'" (Psa 62:12; Prov 24:12)

2) [Rom 2:16, in the plural, Paul explains that it is after reinforcing sin and judgment for sin that God judges the secrets in the hearts of "men"—a plural term; confirming the universiality of this work of God through the powerful gospel]

3) Of individual guilt before God of the self-righteous and judgmental Jew, Rom 2:18-25:
    Comprising 15 uses of the second person singular, 2:18 (twice), 19, 21 (twice), 22 (twice), 23 (twice), 25 (twice).
    a) Of the advantages of the Jew due to knowledge of the Law of Moses, vv 17-20
    b) Of the hypocrisy of the Jew who does not perfectly follow the Law of Moses, vv 21-23
    c) Of the guilt of the Jews because of this hypocrisy, v 24
    d) Of the unprofitability of circumcision, if one does not perfectly obey the entire Law of Moses, v 25

4) Comments as in direct address:
    a) Rom 2:17 (NKJ), "Indeed [Behold], you (sg.) are called a Jew…" [Ἴδε σὺ Ἰουδαῖος ἐπονομάζῃ]
    b) Rom 7:1, "For I speak to them that know the Law"

5) In quotes of the OT, Rom 3:4; 7:7.

6) Of questioning guilt before God, Rom 9:19-33:
    Comprising 4 uses of second person singular, 9:19, 20 (twice), 33;
    Comprising one use of the vocative, 9:20.
    a) Of those who scorn God's choosing some unto salvation and not others; or, of Jews who scorn God's choosing Gentiles, while simultaneously not choosing all Israelites, vv 19-20

7) In call to profess and believe, Rom 10:6-9:
    Comprising of 4 uses of second person singular, 10:6, 9 (thrice).
    a) Of the individual's need to submit to the simple gospel of Jesus, v 6
    b) Of the individual's need to receive salvation by confessing and believing, v 9

8) In a lament for the disbelief of the majority, including the majority of Jews, Rom 10:16-11:3:
    Comprising 2 uses of the vocative, 10:16; 11:3.

9) Israel's role in light of God's NT plan of redemption, Rom 11:10-24:
    Comprising of 14 uses of second person singular, 11:10, 17 (twice), 18 (thrice), 19, 20 (thrice), 22 (twice), 24 (twice).
    Here, the reader of Romans can see and feel Paul debating with a rabbi who may disagree with the gospel in a certain synagogue (with an open scroll of Isaiah) or in the marketplace of a certain city

10) In admonitions to responding to persecution (Rom 12:20-21), dealing with secular governments (13:3-4), and the relationship between the law of love and the ten commandments (13:9):
    Comprising of 5 uses of the second person singular, 12:20 (thrice), 21 (twice); 13:3 (thrice), 4 (twice), 9 (5 times).

11) On convictions and judging others, Rom 14:4-22:
    Comprising of 8 uses of second person singular, 14:4, 10 (twice), 15 (twice), 20, 22 (twice).

c. Paul also uses expressive conjunctions as expected in a good discussion, for example:
    Rom 3:2, "Much in every way! For first of all…" [Πολὺ κατὰ πάντα τρόπον· πρῶτον μὲν γὰρ ὅτι]
    Rom 5:3, "And not only that, but also…" [Οὐ μόνον δέ, ἀλλὰ καὶ]
    Rom 5:5, "Now … because" [ἡ δὲ … ὅτι]
    Rom 5:6, "For when" [Ἔτι γὰρ]
    Rom 5:7, "For scarcely … yet perhaps" [Μόλις γὰρ … ὑπὲρ γὰρ]
    Rom 5:8, "But" [… δὲ …]
    Rom 5:9, "Much more then" [Πολλῷ οὖν μᾶλλον]
    Rom 5:10, "For if" [Εἰ γὰρ]
    Rom 5:10, "For if" [Εἰ γὰρ]; "much more" [πολλῷ μᾶλλον]
    Rom 5:11, "And not only that" [οὐ μόνον δε,]

Rom 5:17, "For if" [Εἰ γὰρ]; "much more" [πολλῷ μᾶλλον]

Rom 5:19, "For just as through" [ὥσπερ γὰρ διὰ]; "so also through" [οὕτω καὶ διὰ]

Conclusion: It is quite convicting when God's Word addresses us in direct address, through use of the vocative and the second person plural. Here we look over Paul's shoulder as he evangelizes lost people and exhorts new believers in the Christian faith. Not only does he ask many penetrating questions, but he also makes extensive use of lively conjunctions to make his points.

4. **The Roman Road**:

   a. **Need** (Why?)

     1) God says that all are sinners, Rom 3:9-10, 23

     2) God tells us the reason all are sinners, Rom 5:12

   b. **Consequence** (What?) God tells us the result of sin, Rom 6:23

   c. **Remedy** (How?) God tells us of His concern for sinners, Rom 5:8-9

   d. **Condition** (Who?) God's way of salvation is made plain, Rom 10:9-10, 13

   e. **Results**: God tells us the results of salvation, Rom 5:1, 8:1

   f. **Assurance**: God gives the saved sinner assurance, Rom 8:16

Question: Is this Pauline method as old or older than the Paulicians of the 8th and 9th Century? It is at least as old as the Apostle Paul who wrote it!

K. The Simple Gospel, with Historical Examples:

Introduction: The "Simple Gospel" has been derived from 1 Cor 15:1-8. It is generally similar to the kerygma as noted in Rom 16:25. In this kerygma of primary importance is Christ and his death and resurrection. From this flows the message of the Gospel as generally understood in most evangelical circles.

The Waldensian Bible, Luther, Hubmaier, and Spurgeon provide four historical precedents of gospel plans—including what some call "prooftexts" for the use of specific verses:

1. The second "Ritual" in the back of a Waldensian Bible dating from 1230-1330AD[1101]—Notice the Great Commission passages in this Medieval Gospel presentation, as well as the emphasis on Holy Spirit baptism.

[1101]"If he is to be consoled in a field, may he make amends [*melioramentum*], and may he take the book from the hand of the elder. The elder must admonish and preach with appropriate testimonies, and with such words that are convenient to a consolement [*consolamentum*]. And may he say as such:

"Peter, you want to receive the spiritual baptism, by which is given the Holy Spirit in the church of God, with the holy preaching, with the laying on of hands of 'good men.' Of this baptism our Lord Jesus-Christ says, in the gospel of Saint Matthew (xxviii, 19, 20), to his disciples: 'Go and instruct all the nations, and baptize them in the name of the father and of the son and of the Holy spirit. And teach them to keep all the things which I commanded you. And behold that I am with you for ever until the consummation of the age.' And in the gospel of Saint Mark (xvi, 15), he says: 'Go unto all the world, preach the gospel to every creature. And he that believes and is baptized will be saved, but he that does not believe will be condemned.' And in the gospel of Saint John (iii, 5) he says to Nicodemus: 'In truth, in truth I tell you that no man will enter the kingdom of God if he has not been regenerated by water and the Holy spirit.' And John the Baptist spoke of this baptism when he said (gospel of Saint John, i, 26-27, and gospel of Saint Matthew iii, 2): 'It is true that I baptize with water; but he who is to come after me is stronger than I: I am not worthy to tie the strap of his sandals. He will baptize you with the Holy spirit and with fire.' And Jesus-Christ says in the Acts of the Apostles (i, 5): 'For John baptized with water, but you will be baptized by the Holy Spirit.' This Holy baptism by the laying on of hands was instituted by Jesus-Christ, according to the report of Saint Luke, and he says that his friends would do it, as was reported by Saint Mark (xvi, 18): 'They will lay their hands on the sick, and the sick shall be healed.' And Ananias (Acts ix, 17 and 18) did this baptism to Saint Paul when he was converted. And later Paul and Barnabas did it in many places. And Saint Peter and Saint John did it upon the Samaritans. For Saint Luke says so much in the Acts of the Apostles (viii, 14-17): 'The apostles who were in Jerusalem having heard that those in Samaria had received the Word of God, sent unto them Peter and John. Whom having arrived prayed for them so that they received the Holy spirit, for he had not yet descended upon any of them. So they laid their hands upon them, and they receive the Holy spirit.' This Holy baptism by which the Holy spirit is given, the church of God has kept it up until now, and it has come from 'good

2.   Martin Luther's four fundamental points of Christianity (from his Wartburg Castle Address, 1522)[1102]

men' to 'good men' up until now, and it will be so until the end of the world. And you must hear that the power is given to the church of God to bind and unbind, and to forgive sins and hold them, as Jesus says in the gospel of Saint John (xx, 21-23): 'As the father has sent me, I send you also. When he had said these things, he blew and told them: Receive the Holy spirit; those unto whom you forgive the sins, they will be forgiven them, and those of whom you retain them, they will be retained.' And in the gospel of Saint Matthew, he saint to Simon Peter (xvi, 18, 19): 'I tell you that you are Peter, and on this rock I will build my church, and the doors of hell will have no strength against it. And I will give you the keys of the kingdom of heaven. And something that you bind on earth, it shall be bound in the heavens, and something that you unbind on earth, it shall be unbound in the heavens.' And in another place (Matthew xviii, 18-20) he says to his disciples: 'In truth I tell you that something that you bind on earth, it shall be bound in the heavens, and something that you unbind on earth, it shall be unbound in the heavens. And again in truth I tell you: if two or three persons gather on earth, all things, whatever they ask, will be accorded them by my father who is in heaven. For there where two or three persons are gathered in my name, I am there in their midst.' And in another place (Matthew x, 8), he says: 'Heal the sick, raise the dead, cleanse lepers, chase [out] demons.' And in the gospel of Saint John (xiv, 12), he says: 'He who believes in me will do the works that I do.' And in the gospel of Saint Mark (xvi, 17-18), he says: 'But those who believe, these signs will follow them: in my name they will chase [out] demons, and they will speak in new languages, they will remove serpents, and if they drink something deadly, it will do no ill to them. They will lay their hands on the sick and they will be healed.' And in the gospel of Saint Luke (x, 19), he says: 'Behold I have given you the power to walk on serpents and scorpions, and on all the forces of the enemy, and nothing will harm you.'

"If you want to receive this power and this strength, you must hold all the commandments of Christ in the new testament according to your power. And know that he has commanded that man does not commit adultery, neither homicide, neither lies, that he swear no oath, that he does not take nor steal, nor that he does to others that which he does not want done to himself, and that man forgives whoever has done him wrong, and that he loves his enemies, and that he prays for those who slander him and for his accusers and that he blesses them, and if he is struck on one cheek, that he extend [to him] the other one, and if someone takes his shirt [Occ. *la gonella*; Fr. *la 'gonelle'*], that he allow [him] his coat, and that he does not judge nor condemn, and many other commandments that are commanded by the lord to his church. For Saint John says in the epistle (first, ii, 15-17): 'O my very dear [ones], may you not love the world, nor the things that are in the world, the love of the father is not in it. For all that is in the world is the lust of the flesh, the lust of the eyes, and the pride of live, which is not from the father, but from the world; and the world will pass, likewise its lusts, but who does the will of God dwells eternally.' And Christ says to the nations (Saint John, vii, 7): 'The world cannot hate you, but it hates me, because I bear witness of it, that its works are bad.' And in the book of Solomon (Ecclesiastes i, 14), it is written: 'I saw the things that are done under the sun, and behold all are vanity and torment of spirit.' And Jude brother of James says for our instruction in the epistle (verse 23): 'Hate this soiled garment which is fleshly.' And by these testimonies and by many others, you must keep the commandments of God, and hate the world. And if you do well up until the end, we are assured that your soul will have eternal life."

And may he say, "I have this desire, pray God that he gives me the strength for it." And may one of the "good men" make amends, with the believer, to the elder, and may he say: "*Parcite nobis*. For all the sins that I may have done or said or thought or worked, I ask forgiveness of God, and of the church and to you all." And may the Christians say: "By God and by us and by the church may they be forgiven you, and we pray God that he may forgive you them." And then they must console him. And may the elder take the book and place it on his head, and the other "good men" each with his right hand, and may they say the "*parcias*" and three *adoremus*, and then:

"And then they must console him. And may the elder take the book and place it upon his head, and the other 'good men' each with his right hand, and may they say the *parcias* and three *adoremus*, and then: '[in Latin] *Pater Sanctu, suscipe servum tuum in tua justifia, et mitte gratiam tuum et spiritum sanctum tuum super eum.*' And may they pray with the preaching, and the one who guides the holy service must say in a quiet voice the '*sixaine*' [a prayer]; and when the '*sixaine*' is said, he should say three *Adoremus*, with the preaching out loud, and then 'the Gospel' [a Latin version of John 1:1-5, 10-17]. And when the Gospel is said, they must say three *Adoremus* and the '*gratia*' and the '*parcias*.'

"And then they must make peace between themselves (to hug) and with the book. And if there are believers, they must also make peace, and may the believers, if there are any, make peace with the book between them. And then may they pray God with 'Double' and with '*veniae*', and they will have delivered him [the preaching]" (L. Clédat, "Rituel Provençal," in L. Clédat, *Le Nouveau Testament traduit au XIIIe siècle en langue provençale suivi d'un rituel cathar [The New Testament translated in the 13th Century in the Provençal language followed by a Cathar ritual]* (Paris, 1887; Geneva: Slatkine, 1968), ix-xxvi. Translation mine).

[1102]"It is given to me to resound the Gospel in your ears.... How much is it not necessary for each of us to be undergirded with principles to sustain us at this important hour!... These principles, they are the great doctrines of Christianity.... I will be as brief as possible.

"And first, that we are in our nature children of wrath and that all our thoughts, our affections and our works serve us as nothing, now there is a fundamental truth. We must always have at our disposition several solid passages of

3. Balthasar Hubmaier's five points in his tract, "Summary of the Entire Christian Life" (1525)[1103]

Scripture to prove it. The Bible is full of declarations that contain the essence of this doctrine; but the third verse of the 2nd chapter of Ephesians goes more directly to the point. Write it in your spirit: *We are all,* says the Apostle, *children of wrath.*

"Secondly, the great an merciful Jehovah sent us his unique son, in order that we might believe in him, and that by faith in this Savior we would be freed from the law of sin and might become the children of God. *To all who believe in his name,* says Saint John, *he gave them the right to become children of God.* To defend this article, we must also arm ourselves of proofs taken from Scripture, and that, like Achilles shield, serve us to thwart the flaming darts of the evil one. Heretofore, to speak the truth, I have not found a fault in one or the other of the fundamental points of the Christian religion. I have often preached, before you, on these articles, and, I am not ashamed to note it, many of you have a much better state than me to defend the authority of the Scriptures.

"But there is a third point, my dear friends, that needs to captivate your attention,—that is that we ought to do good one to another, as the example of Jesus Christ, who showed us his love by his deeds. Without this love, the faith is a cold speculation and without any usefulness. Also saint Paul has said: [quote of 1 Cor 13:1]....

"Fourthly, continued Luther, we have need of patience. There must be persecutions. Satan never sleeps...

The Christian, enriched by his spiritual gifts, dreams not of his own advantage; full of goodwill for his brother, he renounces for love's sake those things which he is free to practice. *All is permitted,* says saint Paul, *but all is not convenient.* All have not made the same progress in the faith...." (Martin Luther, "Fragment of the Discourse that Luther Pronounced at Wittenberg upon Returning from the Castle of Wartburg [1522], in Franck Puaux, *Histoire de la Réformation Française* [Paris: Michel Lévy Frères, 1859], 408-9; translation mine).

[1103]"First, Christ, when he teaches a Christian life, says: amend your lives and believe in the gospel. Now to amendment of life belongs the taking heed to our way, and remembering our sins of commission and ommission. Then we will confess that we have disobeyed God, and will come to Him for help. We find that there is no health in us, but rather poison, wounds, and all impurities....

"Again: The Samaritan must come—that is to Christ—who brings medicine with him, wine and oil, and pours it upon the wounds of the sinner. Wine He gives to men in the repentance of their sins, and oil with which he annoints the sores and mollifies them, saying: believe in the gospel; this wine and this oil clearly show that I am the physician who has come into the world to make the sinner righteous and godly. The gospel teaches also that I am the only gracious, reconciling, interceding, peacemaker with God our Father. He who believeth on me, shall not be damned, but hath eternal life....

"Thirdly, after man, inwardly and by faith, has surrendered himself to a new life, he must testify to it, outwardly and openly in the churches of Christ, in whose fellowship he enrolls himself, according to the ordinance and institution of Christ....

"...He shall testify this publicly when he receives the water of baptism.

"Fourthly: because man recognizes that by nature he is an evil, worm-eaten poisonous tree, and can, of himself, bear no good fruit, therefore he makes this profession and open confession, not relying upon human strength or power, for that would be presumption and audacity, but on the name of God the Father, and the Son, and the Holy Ghost. In the name of our Lord Jesus Christ, that is, in the grace and strength of God, for these strengths are all one.

"From all this follows that this outward baptism unto Christ is nothing else than a public profession of the inward obligation. By it, man confesses publicly that he is a sinner, and admits his guilt. Yet he believes that Christ, through His death, has atoned for his sins, and that by the resurrection has made him righteous in the sight of God, our heavenly Father. Therefore he has determined to confess openly and publicly the faith and the name of Jesus Christ. Also he has promised to live henceforth according to the Word of Christ, but not in human strength, lest the same thing befall him as befell Peter. Without me ye can do nothing, says Christ, but in the power of God the Father, and the Son, and the Holy Ghost. Man must, by word and deed, confess and magnify the name and praise of Christ, so that others through us may become holy and blessed. Just as we, through others who have preached Christ to us, have come to faith, and that the kingdom of God may increase.

There follow persecution, crosses, and all sorts of tribulations for the sake of the gospel in this world. For this world hates life and light and loves darkness. The world does not want to be convicted of sin, but to be deemed pious and just in its own works, and to make its own rules of life. By that means it presumes that it will find salvation and it despised the unpretentious, plain and simple rules of Christ. Here the old Adam shows himself, that is the corrupt nature that we received from the womb of our mothers. He does not want to give up his old ways...

"The flesh should be mortified; yet it strives to live and act according to its lusts. But the spirit of Christ conquers, and brings a man to good fruitage, which bears witness to a good tree. A man must exercise himself day and night in all that concerns the praise of God and brotherly love.

"This is a summary and a proper ordering of an entire Christian life. It begins with the Word of God. The follow acknowledgement of one's sin, and the forgiveness of the sin, through faith. Faith is not idle, but industrious in all good Christian works. But those alone are good works which God himself has bade us to do, and for which we will give an account at the last day. (Matt. 26)

4.   Spurgeon's 1859 tract, titled "Ark of Safety"[1104]

"Fifthly: after we, in faith, out of the Word of God, have recognized clearly and plainly the inestimable and inexpressible goodness of God, we must be thankful therfor [sic] to God our Heavenly Father, who so ardently loved the world, that he did not spare his only begotten Son, who was given to death for our sakes…. [then discussed the Lord's Supper]" (Balthasar Hubmaier, "A Summary of the Entire Christian Life," W. O. Lewis, ed., trans. by G. D. Davidson [Liberty, MO: Archives, William Jewell College Library], 1:59-63).

[1104]"God's people are always safe. But God's people are only safe through *the blood*, because He sees the blood mark on their brow. They are bought with the precious blood of Christ. Nothing can hurt them, because 'the blood' is upon them.

"Christ Jesus, like the lamb, was not only a divinely–appointed victim, but He was *spotless*. Had there been *one* sin in Christ, He had not been capable of being our Saviour; but He was without sin. Turn, then, your eye to the cross, and see Jesus bleeding there and dying *for you*. Remember, **'For our sins not His own, He died to atone.'**

"The blood is *once shed* for the remission of sin. The paschal lamb was slain every year, but Christ, once for all, hath put away sin by the offering of Himself. He has said, 'It is finished.' Let that ring in thy ears.

"The blood of Christ, nothing but it, can ever save the soul. If some foolish Israelite had despised the command of God, and had said, 'I will sprinkle something else upon the doorposts,' or, 'I will adorn the lintel with jewels of gold and silver,' he must have perished; *nothing* could save his household but the sprinkled blood. My works, my prayers, my tears, can not save me; *the blood*, the blood has power to redeem. Nothing but the blood *alone,* of Jesus has the slightest saving power. Oh, you that are trusting in baptism, confirmation, or the Lord's supper, nothing but the blood of Jesus can save. If you make ordinances the basis of *your soul's salvation*, they are lighter than a shadow. There is not-I repeat it again-the slightest atom of saving power anywhere but in the blood of Jesus. THE BLOOD stands out in the *only* rock of our salvation.

"'Oh,' says one, 'I could not trust in Christ if I *felt* my sins more!' Sir, is thy repentance to be a part-saviour? *The blood* is to save thee, not thy tears; *Christ's death, not thy repentance.*

"'Nay,' says another, 'but I feel that I do not value the blood of Christ *as I ought*, and therefore I am afraid to believe.' My, friend, that is another insidious form of the same error. God does not say, 'When I see your estimate of the blood of Christ, I will pass over you; no, but when I see *the blood.*'

"'Nay,' says another, 'but if I had more faith, then I should have hope.' That, too, is a very deadly shape of the same evil. You are not to be saved by the efficacy of your faith, but by the efficacy of the blood of Christ.

"Faith comes from meditation upon Christ. Turn, then, your eye, not upon faith, but upon Jesus. It is not *'your hold of Christ'* that saves you, it is *'His hold of you.'*"

"'Oh,' says another, 'if I had such and such an experience, then I could trust!' Friend, it is not thine experience; it is the blood. God did not say, 'When I see your experience,' but, 'When I see *the blood of Christ.*'

"Yet again, we may say of the blood of Christ, it is *all-sufficient*. There is no case which the blood of Christ cannot meet; there is no sin which it can not wash away. There is no multiplicity of sin which it can not cleanse, no aggravation of guilt which it cannot remove. Ye may be double-dyed like scarlet, you may have lain in the lye of your sins these seventy years, but the blood of Christ can take out the stain. 'The blood of Christ cleanseth us from *all* sin.'

"But go further. The blood of Christ saves *surely*. Perhaps says one who is believing in Christ, 'Well, *I hope* it will save.'

"My friend that is a slur upon the honor of God. If any man gives you a promise and you say, 'Well, I *hope* he will fulfill it,' is it not implied that you have at least some doubt as to whether he will or not? Now, I do not hope that the blood of Christ will wash away my sin. I know it is washed away by His blood; and that is true faith, which does not hope about Christ's blood, but says: *I know it is so;* that blood *does* cleanse.

"The Israelite, if he was true to his faith, did not go inside, and say, 'I hope the destroying angel will pass by me;' but he said: '*I know* he will; I know God can not smite me. There is a blood-mark there; I am secure beyond doubt; there is not the shadow of a risk of my perishing.'

"O sinner, I have not the shadow of a doubt as to whether Christ will save you, *if* you trust in His blood! I know He will. I am certain His blood can save; and I beg you, in Christ's name, believe it; believe that the blood is *sure* to cleanse, not only that *it may* cleanse, but that *it must* cleanse. If we have that blood upon us we must be saved, or else we are to suppose a God unfaithful.

"And yet again, he that hath this blood sprinkled upon him is saved *completely*. Not a hair of the head of an Israelite was disturbed by the destroying angel. So that he believeth in the blood is saved from all things. There is a destroying angel *for Egypt*, but there is *none for Israel*. There is a hell for the wicked, but none for the righteous. Christ saves completely; every sin washed, every blessing insured.

"This brings us to the ONE CONDITION.

"'When I *see* the blood, I will pass over you.'

"Sinner, I have a word from the Lord for thee: if you feel your need of a Saviour, that blood is able to save you, and you are bidden simply to trust that blood, and you shall be saved. If you can rely simply on the blood of Christ, that blood is able to save. Leave off doing altogether; get Christ *first*, and then you may do as much as you like. See the Saviour hanging on the cross; turn your eye to Him, and say, 'Lord I trust Thee; I have nothing else to trust to; sink or

The three essential items to a Gospel presentation are (1) sin, (2) the work of Jesus, and (3) commitment. These are the core that should not be missed in a Gospel presentation, particularly in a Christianized area. In a pagan or non-evangelized area, one may begin with an explanation of God as creator. In a Christianized area, many often begin with the love of God or peace with God, bridging to anthropology and the sinfulness of man.

1. Sin:

    a. Several Principles:

        1) Without a knowledge of personal accountability for sin, there can be no true repentance, confession or forgiveness.

        2) Here is a need for understanding of the holiness, justice and judgment of God to understand the need for the death of Jesus Christ for sin.

        3) The Holy Spirit convicts of sin, righteousness, and judgment, but there are three biblical requirements for the Holy Spirit to work most powerfully:

            (a) That the person who is sharing the Gospel be a pure vessel.

            (b) That the Word of God be used in the testifying, Heb 4:12.

            (c) That the fact and accountability of sin be made clear in the witness.

        4) There is an innate knowledge of sin and of its consequences in man, Rom 1:32:

            (a) Some consciences may be seared by years of sin.

            (b) Sharing about sin and personal accountability for sin from the Bible will allow the Spirit to soften the heart, John 16:8

    b. Stages in an understanding of sin:[1105]

        1) The fact of personal sin, Eccl 7:20, Rom 3:9-12, 23

        2) Personal accountability for sin, Eccl 12:13-14, Rom 3:19-20, Heb 9:27, Rev 20:15

        3) Personal punishment for personal sin, Rom 6:23; 7:11; James 1:15; cf. Ezek 18:4; Gal 6:7-8

2. The Work of Jesus Christ (Luke 24:46):

The work of Jesus Christ speaks chiefly of the death and resurrection of .Jesus. In evangelism it is especially necessary for the person who is being shared with to understand that Jesus Christ died and rose again for them. ,although no one can understand the complete depth and significance of the death and resurrection of Jesus, there are some basic aspects which are important for a saving knowledge.

    a. The death of Jesus for sin, Isa 53:5-6, Rom 5:8,6: 10, 1 Pet 2:24.

    b. The resurrection of Jesus, Rom 4:25, 1 Cor 15:20

    c. The forgiveness due to the death of Jesus, Isa 53:5-6, 2 Cor 5:21, Col 2:13, 1 Pet 2:24.

3. Commitment (Luke 24:47):

It is important that the person who is being shared with understand that a commitment must be made. This is often where someone who has been open will begin to be ill at ease. However, this is the time for boldness and a sense of urgency.

Every person who hears the Gospel should be encouraged to make some type of commitment. This is where the different types of commitments are good to keep in mind. Refusing some type of

---

swim, my Saviour, I trust Thee.' And as surely, sinner, as thou canst put thy trust in Christ, thou art safe. He that believeth shall be saved, be his sins ever so many; he that believeth not shall be damned, be his sins ever so few, and his virtues ever so many. Trust in Jesus *now*, Jesus only" (C. H. Spurgeon, "Salvation and Safety" [a.k.a. "The Blood," 12 Dec 1859] *Royal Dainties*, no. 169 [Minneapolis: Asher Publishing Co., affiliated with The Union Gospel Mission, n.d.], 1, 2, 3, 4; found at http//www.wheaton.edu/bgc/ archives/docs/tract01.html; Internet, accessed 4 January 2001).

[1105]Note the content of the preaching of Devereux Jarrett, an Anglican revivalist clergymen who preached in State of Virginia beginning in 1773, "I endeavor to expose, in the most alarming colors, the guilt of sin, the entire depravity of human nature—the awful danger mankind are in by nature and practice—the tremendous curse to which they are obnoxious, and their utter inability to evade the sentence of the law and the strokes of divine justice by their own power, merit, or good works" (W. M. Geweher, *The Great Awakening in Virginia* [Durham, NC: Duke University, 1930], 139; quoted in W. L. Muncy, Jr., *Evangelism in the United States* [Kansas City, KS: Central Seminary, 1945], 53-54).

commitment is refusing the Gospel. However, a seed has been planted, and there might be openness in the future—if that is available.

a. The need for a commitment to Christ:
1) The command to call for commitment, Luke 24:27
2) The need for commitment, Matt 10:38-39, 2 Cor 5:15
3) The urgency of a commitment, Heb 3:7, 2 Cor 6:2

b. The aspects of commitment to Christ:
1) Repentance, Isa 55:6-7, Mark 1:15; Luke 24:47
2) Belief, Mark 1:15-16, John 5:24, Acts 16:30-31
3) Acceptance, John 1:12, Rev 3:20

c. The role of works:
1) God is the initiator and giver of salvation, John 3:16, Rom 5:8
2) Works show man his sinfulness, Rom 3:19-20
3) Salvation is not by works, Eph 2:8-9
4) Works necessarily follow true salvation, Eph 2:10, James 2:17, "Even so faith, if it has no works, is dead, being by itself."

CHAPTER 18
Levels of Openness

A. Formulating the Gospel to the Perceived Spiritual Needs:

1. Sensitivity and perception are needed to be open to the individual with whom the Gospel is being shared. This will allow the Gospel presentation to be tailored to the individual.

2. Knowing the person's spiritual background will help you to understand some presuppositions he may have. This includes religious upbringing, as well as any contact he may have had with the Gospel in the past.

3. The person may mention a death in the family or some other event which may open the door on the spiritual. Be sensitive, but you can use these things as illustrations or applications of biblical truth.

4. If you can see one or several ideas or presuppositions hindering the person from accepting Christ, formulate the Gospel to meet those presuppositions head on. It is wise not to start an intellectual or theological debate which often leads nowhere. The best approach is to show them what God's Word has to say on the given misunderstanding, and let them deal with God's Word.

5. In a predominantly Christian land, many will pretend to be Christian (Psa 81:15 KJV, NASB). These must hear the Gospel, in order that they might understand the commitment required.

6. It must always be kept in mind that the eternal destiny of the individual is at stake in their understanding the Gospel. Tact, love and boldness are needed to keep to the important issues.

B. Different Levels of Openness to the Gospel:[1106]

Introduction: Among the most disconcerting aspects of evangelism is the range of responses to the Gospel. This is especially true when a neighbor, friend, co-worker or family member do not respond to the Gospel as we would like. Sometimes there is a positive response which later turns into a sour relationship. What then?

This study seeks to look at the responses of various individuals. Jesus' Parable of the Sower gives a biblical buttress for such a study (Matt 13:3-9, 18-23; Mark 4:3-9, 13-20; Luke 8:5-8, 11-15). In this parable, Jesus spoke of four types of seed. Some seed fell on the road, some on rocky soil, some among thorns and some on good soil. Likewise as we sow the seed of the Gospel, we will elicit varying responses. There will be those who are closed to the Gospel. Others will be indifferent to the claims of Christ. Some will be spiritually stagnant, they will have heard the message without allowing it to impact their lives. And still others will be open to the claims of Christ.

One example of different responses to the Gospel was the ministry of Paul in Thessalonica and Berea. Luke gives us the differentiation in Acts 17:11, comparing these two towns with two phrases or words:
1) Berea was "more noble-minded" (οὗτοι δὲ ἦσαν εὐγενέστεροι τῶν ἐν Θεσσαλονίκῃ) than Thessalonica
2) Berea "received the word with great eagerness" (οἵτινες ἐδέξαντο τὸν λόγον μετὰ πάσης προθυμίας), as compared with Thessalonica
3) Berea was actually "examining the Scriptures daily *to see* whether these things were so" (αθ᾽ ἡμέραν ἀνακρίνοντες τὰς γραφὰς εἰ ἔχοι ταῦτα οὕτως), the comparative being that those in Thessalonica did not.

[1106]Many introductions to evangelism contain hints on how to reach various kinds of individuals. See R.A. Torrey, *How to Work for Christ* (New York; Fleming H. Revell, 1901), 33-170, for a biblical look at different levels of openness to the Gospel and how to deal with them. Also see G. Michael Cocoris, *Evangelism: A Biblical Approach* (Chicago; Moody, 1984), 149-65. Eugene M. Harrison spends a good portion of his *How to Win Souls* (Wheaton, IL; Scripture Press, 1952), 54-139, dealing with various types of people, as does William Evans in *Personal Soul-Winning* (Chicago; Moody, 1910).

It is important to note that we have the same evangelist, the same method, the same message in both Thessalonica and Berea. The difference was in the people, in other words, the soil of their hearts.

Listen to the words of the Apostle Paul in Rom 10:16, of those who did not listen:
KJV, "But they have not all obeyed the gospel"
ASV, "But they did not all hearken to the glad tidings"
NAS, "However, they did not all heed the glad tidings"
NIV, "But not all the Israelites accepted the good news"
GK, Ἀλλ' οὐ πάντες ὑπήκουσαν τῷ εὐαγγελίῳ.

Yet a similar word is used of Lydia of Thyatira, who did listen:
KJV, "heard *us*: whose heart the Lord opened, that she attended unto the things which were spoken of Paul"
ASV, "heard us: whose heart the Lord opened to give heed unto the things which were spoken by Paul"
NAS, "was listening; and the Lord opened her heart to respond to the things spoken by Paul"
NIV, "listening... . The Lord opened her heart to respond to Paul's message"
GK, ἤκουεν ἧς ὁ κύριος διήνοιξεν τὴν καρδίαν προσέχειν τοῖς λαλουμένοις ὑπὸ τοῦ Παύλου

Let us note these various responses and consider how we ought to deal with them in a biblical fashion.

1. **The Open Person**:

   a. Some biblical examples of individuals open to the Gospel:
      1) Andrew, Matt 4:18-20, Mark 1:16-18, John 1:36-40
      2) Peter, Matt 4:18-20, Mark 1:16-18, Luke 5:10-11, John 1:41-42
      3) James and John, Matt 4:21-22, Mark 1:19-20, Luke 5:10-11
      4) Philip, John 1:43-44
      5) Nathanael, John 1:45-51
      6) Paralytic, Matt 9:2-8, Mark 2:1-5, Luke 5:18-26
      7) Levi (or Matthew), Matt 9:9, Mark 2:14, Luke 5:27-28
      8) Man from Gerasenes, Matt 8:28-34, Mark 5:1-20, Luke 8:26-39
      9) Woman with Hemorrhage, Mark 5:25-34
      10) Syrophoenician Woman, Matt 15:21-28, Mark 7:24-30
      11) Zaccheus, Luke 19:5-10
      12) Nicodemus, John 3:1-21
      13) Woman at the Well, John 4:6-29
      14) Royal Officer, John 4:46-53
      15) Man Blind from Birth, John 9:35-39
      16) Sinful Woman, Matt 26:6-13, Mark 14:3-9, Luke 7:36-50, John 12:1-8
      17) Thief on the cross, Luke 23:42-43
      18) Soldier at crucifixion, Matt 27:54, Mark 15:39, Luke 23:47
      18) Lame beggar, Acts 3:3-6
      20) Ethiopian Eunuch, Acts 8:26-41
      21) Cornelius, Acts 10
      22) Proconsul, Acts 13:6-12
      23) Lydia, Acts 16:13-15, 40
      24) Jailer, Acts 16:23-24
      25) Titius Justus, Acts 18:7
      26) Crispus, Acts 18:8
      27) Apollos, Acts 18:24-28
      28) Dionyius the Aeropagite and Damaris, Acts 17:34

   b. Examples of groups or gatherings of people open to the Gospel:
      1) City of Sychar, John 4:39-42
      2) Three thousand souls, Acts 2:41
      3) Multitudes of both men and women, Acts 5:14
      4) The multitudes with one accord, Acts 8:6
      5) A great many people [in Antioch of Syria], Acts 11:26

6) Nearly the whole city [of Pisidian Antioch], Acts 13:44
7) A great multitude both of Jews and Greeks, Acts 14:1

c. Profile of an open heart:[1107]
   1) An open heart is often recognizable, Acts 14:9 (cf. Matt 6:22-23)

A Brief Look at the Greek Word ἀτενίζω

Usage: Used 14 times in New Testament
Passages: Luke 4:20; 22:56; Acts 1:10; 3:4, 12; 6:15; 7:55; 10:4; 11:6; 13:9; 14:9; 23:1; 2 Cor 3:7, 13
Lexical Meaning: Look intently, fix one's eyes, fix one's gaze
Explanation: This word is used in the sense of a critical evaluative stare (Luke 4:20; Acts 11:6; 23:1). It is used of a perplexed stare seeking to evaluate a vision (Acts 10:4) or an event (Acts 1:10), or a perplexed look of admiration (Acts 3:12). It results in a judgment about a person's character (Luke 22:56), their faith (Acts 3:4; 14:9), lack of faith (Acts 13:9), and their state of divine glory (Acts 6:15; 2 Cor 3:7, 13). It is also used of an assured gaze in faith into heaven (Acts 7:55).
Application for Evangelism: Often God will allow the openess or hardness of heart of a person to become evident to the evangelist as a response to the hearing of the Gospel. This special insight may then be used to guide the conversation toward calling for commitment, or to provide appropriate warnings to a hardened heart.

---

   2) Look for a contrite heart, Psa 51:19; Isa 57:15; Matt 5:3-4; Luke 6:21
   3) They will listen 1 John 4:6
   4) Look for a man of peace, Luke 10:6; Matt 5:5, 9

d. Do not delay (Prov 3:27-28), but take advantage of a heart opened by the Holy Spirit. We know that no one seeks God without God's prompting, John 15:16, Rom 3:11. However, they may close up in the future (John 3:8) or they may never get another opportunity to respond to the Gospel.

> Wherever you have reason to believe that a person within your reach is awakened, do not sleep till you have poured in the light upon his mind, and have tried to bring him to *immediate repentance.* Then is the time to press the subject with effect.[1108]

e. Share the Gospel:
   1) Make sure that the person is following and understanding the Gospel through occasional questions.
   2) Explain the need for a commitment.
   3) Ask the person to pray to make a commitment to Jesus.

f. You may sense that the person is open but not ready right away:
   1) Give appropriate warning verses (found below in section on "The Non- Committal Person)
   2) Pray with them for their heart and eyes to be open.
   3) Pray for them, for another opportunity to share the Gospel, and for their heart to remain open.
   4) Actively seek out opportunities to meet with the person.

g. Follow-up:
   1) Pray for the person while you are still with him/her.
   2) Share one of several assurance verses to encourage the young believer, John 5:24, Rom 10:9, 1 John 5:13. Ask him/her to memorize one of these.
   3) Leave a Bible or New Testament with the person if they do not have one readily available, if you have one for them.
   4) Try to get the person's name and address, and seek to set up an appointment within the next week.
   5) If the person is not the same sex, it is preferable to seek someone else of the same sex and age to follow the person up.

[1107]See also Chapter 12, "Spiritual Elements," 3. "Profile of an Open Heart."
[1108]Charles Finney, *Finney on Revival,* 68-69. Points 12 and 13 of his 22 points on evangelism.

2. **The Closed Person**:

Introduction: Sometimes it is a temptation to move into a "dialogue" type of interchange with closed persons (e.g. "Muhammad says this about Jesus." "The Bible says this about Jesus." "Your view is just as valid as my view, just so you have a view." ...). It is in these cases that the Bible takes a strong stand on absolute truth, and even provides harsh words for those who blaspheme...

a. Some biblical examples of closed persons: (some of these will also be dealt with under the heading "Messengers of Satan")
    1) Individuals:
        a) High priest, Matt 26:57, 62, 63, 65, Acts 5:17
        b) Captain of the Temple guard, Acts 4:1, 5:24
        c) Saul of Tarsus, Acts 7:58-8:3, 9:1
        d) Herod the king, Matt 2:1 (the Great) Acts 12:1-3, 19 (Agrippa I)
        e) Elymas the magician, Acts 13:6-11
        f) Demetrius the silversmith, Acts 19:24ff.
        g) The ethnarch of Damascus under Aretas, 2 Cor 11:32-33
        h) Alexander the coppersmith, 2 Tim 4:14-15
    2) Groups of people:
        a) Scribes, Matt 9:3; 12:38; 15:1, 26:57; 27:41-43
        b) Pharisees, Matt 9:11, 34; 12:2, 14, 24, 38; 15:1, 12-14; 19:3; 21:45-46; 22:34, 41; 27:62-66
        c) Jesus' hometown people, Matt 13:57; Mark 6:1-6; Luke 4:16-30
        d) Chief priests and elders of the people, Matt 21:23, 45-46; 26:3-5, 14 (chief priests), 47, 57 (elders), 59; 27:1, 6 (chief priests), 12, 20, 41-43, 62-66 (chief priests); 28:11-15; Acts 4:1 (priests), 23; 5:24 (chief priests)
        e) Sadducees, Matt 22:23, 34; Acts 4:1
        f) Council, Acts 4:15; 5:34; 6:15
        g) Synagogue of the freedmen, Acts 6:9
        h) The Jews, Acts 9:23, 29 (Hellenistic Jews), 12:3; 13:45, 50; 14:19 ...

b. A closed heart is often evident, Acts 13:9-11 (cf. Matt 6:22-23).

c. When sharing the Gospel:
    1) All the Christian is accountable for is to seek to sow the seed of the Gospel in love:
        a) Some people will be closed
        b) Be firm and clear, but do not push too hard. Let the Holy Spirit cut through
        c) Jesus showed righteous anger when dealing with certain closed people (Matt 23:13ff., John 2:13-22), as did the Apostle Paul (Acts 13:9-11)—however, make sure that there is no anger due to pride (Prov 29:8)
        d) "Like a trampled spring and a polluted well is a righteous man who gives way before the wicked," Prov 25:26
    2) It is often good to leave the closed person with something to make him think (Prov 26:5, 2 Cor 5:20):
        a) "Are you sure that you would go to heaven if you died tonight?"
        b) "Remember that you will stand before God and give an account some day! Are you ready for that?"
        c) "Make sure your ready in God's way, not in your own!"
        d) "What will you do with Jesus?" or "What have you done with Jesus?"
        e) "So then are you rejecting Jesus? Don't reject Jesus, I urge you!"

> f) Notice the closing words of Bible colporteur Philbert Hamelin (m. 1557) as recorded in Jean Crespin's martyrology:
>
> > "My friends, you do not know now what you are doing, but one day you will know, and I pray that God will give you that grace."[1109]
>
> 3) Jesus also said "Do not throw pearls before swine," Matt 7:6. This may be a reminder not to lose one's time with people who are closed, hardened and antagonistic to the Gospel.[1110]

d. After sharing the Gospel:
   1) Be sensitive to the continued spiritual needs of the closed person, 1 Pet 3:15
   2) Be transparent with this person, and open to their needs
   3) Do not seek to avoid the closed person, Prov 24:1
   4) Love your closed neighbor, Matt 22:39; cf. Prov 14:21; Matt 5:43-47
   5) Don't make yourself a nuisance to your closed neighbor, Prov 25:17
   6) **Pray** for this person and wait for the Holy Spirit to open up the door for the Gospel

3. **The Continuously Non-Committal Person**:

Introduction: No decision is the greatest sin one can commit, for it is sin against the Holy Spirit (Luke 12:10, Heb 10:26-27), and it is disobeying God's greatest command (Matt 22:36-38).

a. Some biblical examples of continuously non-committal people:
   1) Individuals:
      a) Rich Young Ruler, Matt 19:16-26, Mark 10:17-22, Luke 18:18-30
      b) Pilate, Matt 26:11-26, Mark 15:1-15, Luke 23:1-7, 13-25, John 18:33-19:16
      c) Herod, Luke 23:8-12
      d) Felix and Drussila, Acts 24:24-25
      e) Agrippa, Bernice and Festus, Acts 25:23-26:32
   2) Groups:
      a) Multitude, John 6:66; multitudes, Matt 20:9 > Matt 27:22-23
      b) Many, John 12:14, 24-26
      c) Rulers, John 12:42-43
      d) People at Areopagus to Paul, "We shall hear you again concerning this," Acts 17:32
      e) Jews, Acts 21:20, "You see, brother, how many thousands there are among the Jews of those who have believed, and they are all zealous for the Law"

b. Characteristics of non-committal people:
   1) They may have ulterior motives:
      a) Not wishing to lose great wealth, Rich Young Ruler, Matt 19:22; Mark 10:22; Luke 18:23, "for he was extremely rich"
      b) Hoping for a bribe, Felix, Acts 24:26
      c) Wanting to see a miracle, Herod, Luke 23:8
      d) Wanting to please the crowds, Pilate, Matt 27:19-24
      e) Wanting the ability to dispense the Holy Spirit, Simon the Sorcerer, Acts 8:18-19
   2) They may simply want to argue, 1 Tim 6:3-5 (and similar)

c. Reasons for the non-committal person:
   1) "Surely this great nation is a wise and understanding people," Deut 4:6
   2) "Thine enemies will give feigned obedience to Thee," Psa 66:3
   3) "Those who hate the Lord would pretend obedience to Him," Psa 81:15

d. No decision is a decision against Christ:
   1) Matt 12:30, "He who is not with Me is against Me; and he who does not gather with Me scatters." (cf. Luke 11:23)

[1109]Jean Crespin, *Histoire des vrays Tesmoins de la verite de l'evangile, qui de leur sang l'ont signée, depuis Jean Hus iusques autemps present* (Geneva, 1570; reproduction, Liège, 1964), 450; Matthieu LeLièvre, *Portraits et récits Huguenots,* premiere série (Toulouse, Société des Livres Religieux, 1903), 123.

[1110]*The Mindest of Eternity,* Chapter 6, Section I.F., "When Do You Shake the Dust Off Your Feet?" discusses the topic in detail.

        2)   Luke 16:13, "No servant can serve two masters."

   e.   A choice must be made:

        1)   Deut 30:15-19, v. 19, "So **choose life** in order that you may live, you and your descendants"

        2)   Ezek 18:32, "'For I have no pleasure in the death of anyone who dies,' declares the Lord God, 'Therefore, **repent and live**'"

        3)   Luke 9:59, "And He said to another, '**Follow Me**'"

        4)   John 14:11, "**Believe Me** that I am in the Father, and the Father in Me; otherwise believe on account of the works themselves" (cf. John 10:31f)

        5)   Heb 4:2, "For indeed we had good news preached to us, just as they also; but the word they heard did not profit them, because it was not **united by faith** in those who heard"

        6)   Heb 11:6, "Without **faith** it is impossible to please Him"

   f.   The urgency of making a decision for Jesus:

        1)   2 Cor 6:2, "behold, **now** is 'the acceptable time,' behold, **now** is 'the day of salvation."

        2)   Heb 3:7-8 (Psa 95:7-8), "**Today** if you hear His voice, do not harden your heart"

   g.   Something to keep him thinking: "I hope that you don't die tonight!"

4.   **The Messenger of Satan**:

Introduction: A group that I overlooked until I counseled a student recently, and considered my ministry and the Book of Acts anew!

   a.   Satan seems to send his mercenaries to attack at key junctures in the propagation of the Gospel:

        1)   Ananias and Sapphira, Acts 5:1-11

        2)   Simon the sorcerer, Acts 8:9-24

        3)   Bar-Jesus or Elymas the magician, Acts 13:6-12

        4)   The priest of Zeus, Acts 14:8-18

        5)   Slave-girl with a spirit of divination, Acts 16:16-24

        6)   Demetrius the silversmith, Acts 19:24-41

   b.   Their link with the proclamation of the Gospel:

        1)   Luke emphasizes the location of their meeting:

            a)   The priest of Zeus' temple was "outside the city gate" or "at the city gate," Acts 14:13

            b)   Slave-girl meets Paul as he goes to the "place of prayer," Acts 16:16, the same place where Paul spoke to Lydia, cf. Acts 16:13

        2)   Which came first, contact with Elymas or with Sergius Paulus?

            a)   Elymas is mentioned first in the text, perhaps because:

               (1)   He is the emphasis of this passage and the ensuing miracle, or

                  (a)   This is when Paul's name is changed from "Saul" to "Paul"

                  (b)   This is when the order of the names changes from "Barnabas and Paul" to "Paul and Barnabas"

                  (c)   This interpretation would make the salvation of Sergius Paulus secondary to the episode

               (2)   He led Paul and Barnabas to Sergius Paulus—doubtful as he opposed their teaching

            b)   It would seem that Sergius Paulus' interest in the Gospel preceded Elymas' opposition to the Gospel

        3)   Demetrius the silversmith spoke at a meeting of his trade guild following the revival that broke out, Acts 19:23

            a)   His words led to a riot, Acts 19:28-29

            b)   which led to Paul's leaving town, Acts 20:1

   b.   Their reception of the Gospel:

        1)   Ananias and Sapphira seemed to be members of the church in Jerusalem, and were giving to the work of the ministry, Acts 5:1-2

        2)   Simon the sorcerer seemed to believe, was baptized, and continued on with Philip, Acts 8:13, although (a) his "heart was not right before God," Acts 8:21, (b) his desire for the Holy Spirit showed that he was caught "in the gall of bitterness and in the bondage of iniquity," Acts 8:23, and (c) he despised the admonition of Peter by getting in the last word, Acts 8:24

(perhaps his problem was the priesthood of the believer, each person coming to God for themselves?)

3) Elymas the magician opposed Barnabas and Saul, and sought to turn the proconsul away from the faith, Acts 13:8

4) The priest of Zeus turned the healing into a reason to worship his god in his way, Acts 14:13

5) The slave-girl must have heard the message, for her statement concerning Paul and his ministry was correct: "These men are bond-servants of the Most High God, who are proclaiming to you the way of salvation," Acts 16:17

6) It seems that someone must have shared the Gospel with Demetrius, who was probably convicted but rejected the Gospel, and then considering the outcome of the Gospel for his profession, he spoke against it at a meeting of his guild, Acts 19:26

c. Their types:

1) **Theological false prophets**—try to turn persons away from the Gospel, e.g. Acts 15:1, 5

2) **Financial false prophets**—want to "make a buck" with their deceit, 2 Cor 2:17:
   a) There are some very deceptive liars on the street!
   b) Not only do these false prophets sell idols, prayer shawls, jewelry, statues, or other trinkets, but they also beg for money of Christians by their treachery, cf. Ezek 13:18-23
   c) They are trained in greed, 2 Pet 2:14 (cf. 1 Tim 6:5)

3) **Immoral false prophets**—deceive weak women, 2 Tim 3:6
   a) "Having eyes full of adultery that never cease from sin," 2 Pet 2:14

4) **Selfishly-Motivated prophets**—to draw away disciples after them, Acts 20:30

d. How they were dealt with:

1) Ananias and Sapphira were dealt with directly by Peter, and they died, Acts 5:3-10

2) Peter called Simon the sorcerer directly by confronting him, Acts 8:20-23

3) Paul spoke very forthrightly to Elymas the magician, even calling down blindness on him, Acts 13:9-11 (this could be said to be a good example of a "power encounter" in the ministry of Paul)

4) Paul was forced to disclaim the reverence of the crowd, and sought to turn the focus to God, Acts 14:14-18

5) Paul waited "many days" before confronting the spirit within the slave-girl, he became greatly annoyed and cast out the spirit, Acts 16:18

6) Paul was not allowed to oppose Demetrius at the riot and he left town, Acts 19:30; 20:1; cf. 2 Tim 4:14-15

e. Result on the ministry:

1) "A great fear came over the whole church, and over all who heard of these things," Acts 5:11

2) No result is recorded following the incident with Simon the Sorcerer, Acts 8:24

3) The proconsul believed and was "amazed at the teaching of the Lord," Acts 13:12

4) Several results in Acts 14:
   a) The Jews from Antioch and Iconium allied themselves with the priest of Zeus, the crowds "stoned Paul and dragged him out of the city, supposing him to be dead," Acts 14:19
   b) Paul returned to the city of Lystra immediately (i.e. he did not flee), Acts 14:20, and Paul returned following his time in Derbe, Acts 14:21
   c) There were disciples (presumably from that city) that gathered around Paul, Acts 14:20, as well as a church in Lystra, Acts 14:21-23
   d) Was this persecution in Lystra, or similar persecution elsewhere why John Mark "deserted them in Pamphylia," Acts 15:39, thus causing a rift between Paul and Barnabas, Acts 15:36-40, and then allowing the Holy Spirit though Luke to focus on the ministry of Paul, Acts 15:41ff?

5) A series of results ensued after Paul cast the spirit out of the slave-girl:
   a) Persecution of Paul and Silas: (1) Anger by the profiteers who owned the slave-girl, (2) a riot, (3) Paul and Silas beaten with rods, "when they had stuck them with many blows" and (4) imprisonment and bound in stocks.
   b) The salvation of the Philippian jailer and his family, Acts 16:27-34

   c) Apology from the chief magistrates, Acts 16:35-39

   d) Encouragement of the saints in Lydia's house, Acts 16:40

  6) Paul avoided going back to Ephesus when he spoke to the Elders, Acts 20:17

 f. Lessons:

  1) Messengers of Satan come in many types, and have varying responses to the Gospel:

   a) Within the church and outside the church, cf. 2 Cor 11:26

   b) Even the Apostle Peter was a messenger of Satan to Jesus in one instance, Matt 18:21-23

  2) The greatest challenges lead to greater usefulness for Christ:

   a) Paul's name was changed during his encounter with Elymas, Acts 13:9

   b) Paul likely had his "third heaven" experience when left for dead, Acts 14:19-20 (he was stoned only once, 2 Cor 11:25)

  3) Paul seemed to be harassed by specifically evil persons throughout his ministry.

  4) Adversaries do not rule out effective ministry, 1 Cor 16:8-9

  5) "So then, you will know them by their fruits," Matt 7:20

  6) "Be shrewd as serpents and innocent as doves," Matt 10:16

5. **The Spiritual Stagnant**:

 a. The reality of spiritual stagnancy:

  1) Jer 12:2, "Thou hast planted them, they have also taken root; they grow, they have even produced fruit. Thou art near their lips but far from their mind."

  2) 2 Tim 4:3, "For the time will come when they will not endure sound doctrine."

  3) Rev 2:4, "But I have this against you, that you have left your first love."

 b. Teaching about dealing with the spiritually stagnant:

  1) Ezek 3:20-21, "Again, when a righteous man turns away from his righteousness and commits iniquity, and I place an obstacle before him, he shall die; **since you have not warned him,** he shall die in his sin, and his righteous deeds which he has done shall not be remembered; but **his blood I will require at your hand**. However, **if you have warned** the righteous man that the righteous should not sin, he shall surely live because he took warning; and **you have delivered yourself**."

  2) 1 Thess 5:14, "And we urge you brethren, **admonish the unruly**, encourage the fainthearted, help the weak, be patient with all men."

  3) Jude 22-23, "And have mercy on some, who are doubting; save others, snatching them out of the fire; and on some have mercy with fear, hating even the garment polluted by the flesh."

 c. How to deal with the spiritually stagnant:

  1) Warn them.

  2) Admonish, encourage and help them, with great patience.

  3) Have mercy and seek to save them.

  4) We will be held guilty for ignoring the stagnant and not warning them!

6. Conclusion:

 a. "He who hears, let him hear; he who refuses, let him refuse," Ezek 3:27

  ἀκούων ἀκουέτω καὶ ὁ ἀπειθῶν ἀπειθείτω

 b. "Go to the exiles, to the sons of your people, and speak to them, **whether they listen or not**, *'Thus says the Lord God.'"* Ezek 3:11

  ἐὰν ἄρα ἀκούσωσιν ἐὰν ἄρα ἐνδῶσιν

 c. "And even if our gospel is veiled, it is veiled to those who are perishing, in whose case the god of this world has blinded the minds of the unbelieving, that they might not see the light of the gospel of the glory of Christ, who is the image of God, 2 Cor 4:3-4

 d. "Did you receive the Spirit by the works of the Law, or by hearing with faith?" Gal 3:2

  ἐξ ἔργων νόμου τὸ πνεῦμα ἐλάβετε ἢ ἐξ ἀκοῆς πίστεως

 e. "For indeed we have had good news preached to us, just as they also; but the word they heard did not profit them, because it was not united by faith in those who heard," Heb 4:2

  καὶ γάρ ἐσμεν εὐηγγελισμένοι καθάπερ κἀκεῖνοι· ἀλλ᾽ οὐκ ὠφέλησεν ὁ λόγος τῆς ἀκοῆς ἐκείνους μὴ συγκεκραμένους τῇ πίστει τοῖς ἀκούσασιν

 f. "Therefore, since it remains for some to enter it, and those who formerly had good news preached to them failed to enter because of disobedience," Heb 4:6

  ἐπεὶ οὖν ἀπολείπεται τινὰς εἰσελθεῖν εἰς αὐτήν καὶ οἱ πρότερον εὐαγγελισθέντες οὐκ εἰσῆλθον δι᾽ ἀπείθειαν

Chapter 18 Appendix

Illustrations

Introduction: Spiritual truths can often be difficult to grasp. This is especially the case if the person is hearing the Gospel concepts for the first time.

Jesus often used illustrations as he taught spiritual truths. This allowed those who heard him to understand the truths He was relating, realizing that at times the illustrations hid the meaning from the people (cf. Matt 13:10-17).

Here are some common illustrations which can be of help in different sharing situations. They are not meant to be exhaustive, but rather illustrative of what can be taught effectively with illustrations. The illustrations have been categorized by the spiritual truth which they are meant to illustrate.[1111]

1. **Sin**:
   a. The Definition of sin:
      1) Taking the wrong road to get to a vacation cabin. You can never get to the cabin on the wrong road.
   b. The Progression of sin:
      1) Sin is like an icicle which forms on a gutter. When it gradually gets too big, the gutter will come down.
      2) Sin is like worms attacking a tree. Things look fine from the outside until a strong wind comes and the tree falls. Then all the rot on the inside is made evident. The tree was weakened from within.
   c. The Cords of Sin:
      1) Sin is like a frog who jumps into a saucepan when it is cold. He feels comfortable and doesn't jump out even when the temperature of the water goes up. Eventually he boils to death, but he never knows it until it is too late. This is like the cords of sin. Proverbs 5:22-23.
      2) Sin is like a mouse that sees a beautiful cat. The mouse is attracted to the beautiful fur on the cat until the moment he comes too close. The cat pounces, and it is too late.
      3) Sin is like a deep chasm which gives off heat and warmth. The sinner keeps creeping closer, never getting enough heat. Then he gets too close and falls into the pit.

2. **The Justice of God**:
   a. A man kills ten people. He then flees to the mountain. Ten years later he comes back to civilization and gets caught. A good friend is his judge. Would it be right for the good friend to release the killer? He is sentenced to 1,000 strikes with a lash. … (continued under "The Sacrifice for Sin")
   b. In the banking industry, if a person was to withdraw more money than he had in his account he is penalized for his error (even if he believes that all things are subjective, the banker doesn't think so!). It is a cause and effect relationship. So also with the justice of God. God requires perfection. And because man has sinned against God, he does not arrive at the perfection that God requires. He is left owing to God. God must see that the debt is paid.

3. **Spiritual Need**:
   a. A man buys a '57 Corvette. But it has no battery. Let's say that he cannot buy a battery. Will that car run? No it needs a battery. Similarly, without God we are spiritually dead.

4. **Repentance**:
   a. The road to the vacation cabin illustration. If a left turn has been taken instead of a right turn along the road somewhere. The only way to get to the cabin is make a 180 degree turn and head

---

[1111]D. James Kennedy has good illustrative material for use in personal evangelism in *Evangelism Explosion* (Wheaton, IL: Tyndale House, 1977), 105-10. There are also many illustration books available. However, the best illustrations are those taken from the life of the illustrator.

back and find the right way. Even so, sin is going down the wrong path. The sinful lifestyle must be turned from to walk in righteousness.

5. **The Sacrifice for Sin**:
   a. The hand illustration: The Bible or another object is held in the right hand to show the weight of man's sin. Then the object is transferred to the other hand, showing that Jesus bore the weight of man's sin. This is good to illustrate Isaiah 53:5-6 and/or 2 Cor 5:21 (also Col 1:21-22).
   b. (continued from "Justice of God") A take-off on the killer of ten men illustration. The killer has another friend who decides to take the penalty of the 1,000 lashes for him. This other friend does so and dies in the process. Now when the killer stands before the judge, his record is clean, for the penalty has been paid.
   c. Father as judge illustration: A person who is guilty of a crime comes before the court. The penalty is declared by the judge. Then the judge takes off his robe, and the guilty person sees that it is his/her father. He comes around the bench and asks to take the penalty for the person. That's what Jesus did for us!

6. **Contra Self-justification**:
   a. Swimming to Hawaii illustration: No matter how good a swimmer is, no one can swim from California to Hawaii. I may get 500 feet. An ironman may swim 50 miles. But no one can make it all the way to Hawaii. God demands perfection. No one can claim a perfect life, other than Jesus. That's why we need His death to speak for us.

7. **Free Choice**:
   a. The robot does not have free choice. It must do what it is programmed to do. Man, however, can decide to do what he wants. Man has free choice.

8. **Faith**:
   a. The tightrope walker's challenge. A tightrope walker successfully crosses a tightrope across the Niagara Falls pushing a wheel barrel. Upon his return, he asks the crowd if they feel that he is able to cross with the wheel barrel full of rocks. The crowd agrees that he can do this, and he does. Then he asks if they feel he can take a person across in the wheel barrel. They wholeheartedly agree. No one is willing to accept the challenge. They don't have faith when their life is at stake.
   b. The chair illustration. A person may believe that a chair will hold him. But he doesn't put this belief into practice until he actually sits in the chair.

Conclusion: 1 Thessalonians 5:14

CHAPTER 19
Smokescreens and Objections
(Street Apologetics)

Introduction—Understanding the Balance:

Tearing down the [false] stronghold in which they trust:

Prov 21:22, "A wise man scales the city of the mighty, And brings down the stronghold in which they trust."

Yet not being involved in vain disputes:

1 Tim 6:20-21, "O Timothy, guard what has been entrusted to you, **avoiding worldly *and* empty chatter *and* the opposing arguments** of what is falsely called 'knowledge'—which some have professed and thus gone astray from the faith. Grace be with you."

Titus 3:9, "But **shun foolish controversies and genealogies and strife and disputes about the Law**; for they are unprofitable and worthless."

Silencing those that must be silenced:

Titus 1:10-11, "For there are many rebellious men, empty talkers and deceivers, especially those of the circumcision, who must be silenced because they are upsetting whole families, teaching things they should not *teach*, for the sake of sordid gain."

Knowing what issues are important:

Notice that Jesus avoided the obviously false statement of his followers, in order to teach them a deeper truth…

Preparatory statement:

John 8:30-32, "As He spoke these things, many came to believe in Him. Jesus therefore was saying to those Jews who had believed Him, 'If you abide in My word, *then* you are truly disciples of Mine; and you shall know the truth, and the truth shall make you free.'"

False statement of disciples:

John 8:33, "They answered Him, 'We are Abraham's offspring, and have never yet been enslaved to anyone; how is it that You say, "You shall become free"?'"

Sample verses reminding Jews that they were slaves in Egypt (not to mention Babylon or Rome):

Exod 13:3, 14; 20:2; Lev 26:13; Deut 5:6, 15; 6:12, 21; 7:8; 8:14; 13:5, 10; 15:15; 16:12; 24:18, 22; Judges 6:8; Neh 9:36; Micah 6:4:

Exodus 20:1-3, "Then God spoke all these words, saying, 'I am the LORD your God, who brought you out of the land of Egypt, out of the house of slavery. You shall have no other gods before Me.' [remainder of Ten Commandments]."

Deut 5:4, 6-7, "The LORD spoke to you face to face at the mountain from the midst of the fire, … He said, 'I am the LORD your God, who brought you out of the land of Egypt, out of the house of slavery. You shall have no other gods before Me' [remainder of Ten Commandments]."

Deut 6:12, "then watch yourself, lest you forget the LORD who brought you from the land of Egypt, out of the house of slavery."

Deuteronomy 8:14, "then your heart becomes proud, and you forget the LORD your God who brought you out from the land of Egypt, out of the house of slavery."

Jesus, overlooked this clear false statement, responding:

John 8:34-38, "Jesus answered them, 'Truly, truly, I say to you, everyone who commits sin is the slave of sin. And the slave does not remain in the house forever; the son does remain forever. If therefore the Son shall make you free, you shall be free indeed. I know that you are Abraham's offspring; yet you seek to kill Me, because My word has no place in you. I speak the things which I have seen with *My* Father; therefore you also do the things which you heard from *your* father.'"

Jesus exemplified that there are deeper issues that are more important than catching a person in a false statement. Ours is a wrestling match for their soul!

In John 8, the deeper issue was freedom from sin.

Reaching the Intelligent:

Acts 13: Sergius Paulus, "a man of intelligence"

Notice the false prophet, Bar-Jesus (son of Jesus), has gotten to him first

Notice that Sergius Paulus took the initiative to summoned Barnabas and Saul

Notice the opposition of Elymas

Notice that Sergius was not saved through apologetics or rational argument, but after a power encounter in which Elymas was cursed and blinded

The text reads, "Then the proconsul believed when he saw what had happened, being amazed at the teaching of the Lord" (Acts 13:12).

Acts 17: Paul "evangelizing" the "Epicureans and Stoics"

Paul was broadcasting the Gospel in the marketplace, v 17

The Epicureans and Stoics (opposing views) seemed to be aggressively volleying thoughts with Paul (συμβάλλω), v 18

Paul, however, was "evangelizing Jesus and the resurrection," v 18

The Epicureans and Stoics, became aggressive, and brought Paul to the Areopagus (perhaps hoping that he would not stand a chance in such a milieu, much like we will see in Acts 25-26)

The Holy Spirit, through Luke, takes a stab at those who are always looking for some new thought or idea, v 21

Acts 25-26: Paul showing his "great learning"

Festus arranges his first formal gathering in the auditorium—King Aggripa is in the audience, as well as all the prominent men of the capital city and commanders of the Army, 25:23

The stage is set and Paul is the main act, 25:23

They are looking forward to some laughs from this Jew who is so adamantly disliked by his own people, 25:24-27

Paul, however, brings a sobering message of salvation, three times sharing the Gospel with them, 26:2-23

Festus, not the one presiding, but the one who set up the whole affair, cuts in on Paul and calls him out of his mind because of his great learning, 26:24

Paul responds politely to Festus, 26:25

Then Paul addresses Agrippa, the one in charge, and brings him to the point of decision, 26:25-29

It is interesting to note that in his defense Paul did not mention that the only reason that he was still in prison was that the former governor, Felix, wanted a bribe from him, 24:26-27

In none of these cases can it be found that Paul appeals to Socrates, Plato, or Aristotle; Paul did not discuss worldview in any of these cases, rather he evangelized the foolishness of the cross (1 Cor 1:18)! Does not Paul's methodology correspond to Luke's Great Commission (Luke 24:46-47)?

Now some may be ignorant or have valid objections, much like Elymas was putting into the mind of Sergius Paulus. There is a need for gentleness with the broken (Isa 42) and firmness with the stubborn (Ezek 2-3).

Meeting Common Objections Biblically:

Introduction: The Queen of Screen—"The Woman at the Well" (John 4)

1. Shows how Jesus dealt with some common objections

2. Exemplifies common objections:
   - v. 9   Social objection—sexism, racism
   - v. 11   Misunderstanding spiritual I (similar to Nicodemus, John 3:4)
   - v. 12   Historic religious smokescreen I
   - v. 15   Misunderstanding spiritual II
   - v. 19-20   Historic religious smokescreen II
   - v. 25   Great religious expectation (as a last straw)

3. Jesus seems to be wrestling with her mind and soul to bring her to the point of submission to God, Prov 21:22

Though each person is an individual and thinks independently, there are common ways of thinking which people have to reject a Gospel presentation. The testifier must stand up to these lies by showing what God has to say in His Word.

There is a sense in which the wisdom of God manifested in the Gospel message is foolishness to unsaved man (1 Cor 1:20-21). Thus, without the Holy Spirit no one will be argued logically into the Kingdom of God. The Holy Spirit must convict of the heart of sin, righteousness and judgment (John 16:8-11). Yet, it is sometimes appropriate to be able to defend the faith when it is necessary (1 Pet 3:15). Argument should be avoided in making this defense (Prov 26:5, 29:9, Titus 3:9), and retreat may be necessary due to hardness of heart (Prov 26:4, Matt 7:6).

These objections can be understood in two ways: denying the authority of God and affirming the rights of self. Isaiah 47:10 speaks of these:

> "And you felt secure in your wickedness and said, 'No one sees me,' Your wisdom and your knowledge, they have deluded you; for you have said in your heart, 'I am, and there is no one besides me.'"

If a person rejects the Gospel they have a false sense of security, and are deluding themselves. Good reasoning from God's Word, the Bible, along with the power of the Holy Spirit may help loosen the veil over their eyes that they may "see the light of the Gospel of the glory of Christ" (2 Cor 4:4).

R. A. Torrey reminds his readers of two points pertinent here:

> "1. Never lose your temper when trying to lead a soul to Christ.
> "2. Never have a heated argument with one whom you would lead to Christ."[1112]

In his book, *Witnessing without Fear,* Bill Bright devoted a chapter to, "How to Handle Hostility, Questions and Resistance."[1113] He explained how to turn the questions that people have into opportunities to share the Gospel. Paul gave the following advice to Timothy:

> "To be ready for every good deed, to malign no one, to be uncontentious, gentle, showing every consideration for all men" (Titus 3:1-2)

The "all men" in the text above provides the clue that these admonitions ought to be applied to evangelism. Furthermore, Johan Lukasse offers some helpful advice when we encounter people who incessantly bring up smokescreens:

> "We might well meet people, for example, who enjoy a good discussion but are not really interested. We should not waste our time with them and fail to be available to those who are interested and are sincerely searching in some way."[1114]

Several common objections to the Gospel will be noted with some biblical passages to serve as answers. These are not intended to be exhaustive, but they may prove helpful when encountering individuals with objections.[1115]

[1112]R.A. Torrey, *How to Work for Christ* (Westwood, NJ; Revell, 1901), 174-75.

[1113]Bill Bright, *Witnessing Without Fear* (San Bernardino, CA: Here's Life, 1987), 139-55.

[1114]Johan Lukasse, *Churches with Roots: Planting Churches in Post-Christian Europe* (Bromley: STL, 1990), 36.

[1115]R.A. Torrey, *How to Work for Christ* (Westwood, NJ; Revell, 1901), 114-32, teaches how to deal with skeptics in a innovative and practical sense. Josh McDowell's books, *Evidence that Demands a Verdict* and *More Evidence* (San Bernardino, CA: Here's Life Publishers), give a thorough examination of the truth of the resurrection. This is especially relevant in evangelism amongst the educated who are skeptical to the Gospel.

1. Some **Objections** and **Smokescreens** in the Bible:

   Introduction: A compilation of some examples of what wicked men say in the Bible.[1116] These need to be applied to contemporary issues and thought. However, the essence of the objections and smokescreens don't change, as they are a part of fallen human nature.

   a. Indicating a rejection of God:
      1) "And they say to God, 'Depart from us! We do not even desire the knowledge of Thy ways. Who is the Almighty that we should serve Him, and what would we gain if we entreat Him?" Job 21:14-15

   b. Indicating that there is no God (thus no accountability):
      1) "There is no God!" Psa 14:1, 53:1
      2) "He does not punish! There is no God!" Psa 10:4

   c. Indicating that God does not see our evil (thus no accountability):
      1) "The Lord does not see, nor does the God of Jacob pay heed." Psa 94:7
      2) "No one sees me." Isa 47:10
      3) "Who will see them [traps]?" Psa 64:6
      4) "The Lord does not see us; the Lord has forsaken the land." Ezek 12:8
      5) "God has forgotten, He hides His face and never looks." Psa 10:11
      6) "He will not see our latter ending." Jer 12:4

   d. Indicating that God is ignorant of our ways (thus no accountability):
      1) "How will God know? Is there knowledge with the Most High?" Psa 73:11
      2) "Who hears?" Psa 59:8

   e. Indicating God's inability to achieve some end:
      1) "Can God prepare a table in the wilderness?" Psa 78:19-20

   f. Indicating a pride of life:
      1) "I am, and there is no one besides me." Isa 47:10
      2) "I shall not be shaken, from generation to generation I will be free from harm." Psa 10:6

   g. Plotting against the godly:
      1) "Let us completely subdue them." Psa 74:8
      2) "Let us possess for ourselves the pasture of God." Psa 83:13
      3) "Now we are ready, we have devised a perfect plan." Psa 64:7
      4) "God has forsaken him; pursue and seize him, for there is none to deliver." Psa 71:11

   h. Judging the godly:
      1) "Aha, Aha!" Psa 40:15
      2) "Aha, our desire!" "We have swallowed him up!" Psa 35:25
      3) "When will he die, and his name perish?" Psa 41:5
      4) "A wicked thing is poured down upon him, that when he lies down, he will not rise up again." Psa 41:8
      5) "Where is your God?" Psa 42:10

2. **Self-Justification**:

   a. There are several examples of self-justification in the responses of people:
      1) "Follow the Golden Rule and you'll be O.K."
      2) "You don't need to know the whole Bible, just follow the Golden Rule, God will accept you."
      3) "If I can forgive myself, then it's O.K." (cf. Luke 6:37)
      4) "I've never killed anybody. I think God will accept me."

[1116]The idea for this study came from Lloyd M. Perry in a class entitled, "Variety in Preaching," as a suggestion for an innovative sermon series.

b. Examples of this in the Bible:

1) Prov 30:12, "This is the way of the adulterous woman: She eats and wipes her mouth, And says, 'I have done no wrong.'"

2) Hosea 12:8, "And Ephraim said, 'Surely I have become rich, I have found wealth for myself; In all my labors they will find in me no iniquity, which would be sin."

3) The parable of the Pharisee and the Publican, Luke 18:9-14
   a) The problem was that the Pharisee was comparing himself to man and not to God, e.g. Matt 5:48
   b) Jesus made it clear that the self-righteous was **not** justified, Luke 18:14

c. Concerning self-justification:
1) Who has a clear conscience? No one, Prov 20:9 (cf. Eccl. 7:20)
2) A clear conscience does not justify, 1 Cor 4:4
3) Man's personal ideas about justification have little value, Prov 12:15, 14:12, 16:25, 28:26
4) Man may justify his actions, but it's God who justifies, Prov 16:2, 21:2
5) In fact God's common grace withholds mankind from living to the fullness of corruption according to his nature.

d. The Bible is clear that man is sinful and perverse, in great need of salvation. The Bible also clearly maintains that salvation is not by works, but that it is made evident through obedience to the Bible:
1) Sin:
   a) Man is utterly sinful, Gen 6:5, Rom 3:10-20, 23
   b) Men know that they are sinners, Rom 1:32
   c) Because of his sin, man cannot save himself, Job 14:4, Rom 3:19-20
2) Salvation:
   a) It is essential, John 3:3-7, 5:24, Acts 16:30-31, Rev 20:15
   b) It is not by works, Rom 3:20, 4:3-5, Gal 2:16, Eph 2:8-9, Titus 3:5 (cf. Psa 49:7-9)
   c) No one will be justified by the works of the law, Rom 3:20, Gal 2:16
   d) A clear conscience does not necessarily mean purity before God, Prov 30:12, 1 Cor 4:3-4
3) Obedience:
   a) Obedience to the Word, John 14:21, 1 John 2:3-6
   b) Not an anarchy, where everybody does what is right in there own eyes, Deut 12:8, Judges 21:25, Prov 16:2, 25, Rom 3:17-18.

e. Straightforward speech to the self-righteous:
1) Are they obedient to the Great Commandment (Matt 22:37)?
2) Are they perfect (Matt 5:48)?
3) Is there clear sin in their life? "The word of the Lord came to me saying, 'Son of man, make known to Jerusalem her abominations." Ezek 16:1-2 (cf. Ezek 22:2).

3. **Subjectivism**:

a. There are several examples of a subjective attitude which is found quite common:
1) "All religions are the same in their essence, they all lead to God and show us how to get there."
2) "It doesn't matter what you think just so you love your neighbor."
3) "How do you know that you have the truth?"
4) "You know the real problem in the world? People like you! It's people like you that start all the wars, because you think there's an absolute and there isn't. There is no absolute!"

b. Biblical examples of subjectivism:
Introduction: *The Spiritual Exercises of Ignatius Loyola* (1533):
   "Rules for Thinking in the Church," Number 13:
        If we wish to be sure that we are right in all things, we should always be ready to accept this principle: I will believe that the white that I see is black, if the hierarchical Church so defines it. For I believe that between the Bridegroom, Christ our Lord, and the Bride, His Church, there is

but one spirit, which governs and directs us for the salvation of our souls, for the same Spirit and Lord, who gave us the Ten Commandments, guides and governs our Holy Mother Church.[1117]

1) Isa 5:20, "Woe to those who call evil good, and good evil; Who substitute darkness for light and light for darkness; Who substitute bitter for sweet, and sweet for bitter!"
2) John 18:38, "And Pilate said to Him, 'What is truth?'"

c. The fallacy of subjectivism must be dealt with.
1) There is objective truth in nature: if I jump off a roof, I will fall. The law of gravity cannot be counteracted even with the best intentions. In fact, the same is true with all laws of nature. Nature is an objective reality.
2) If truth is subjective, then there is no right or wrong (see Rom 1:32):
   a) In such a case, Adolph Hitler was a good guy, because he was acting as he felt best. This is absurd, yet it shows that the subjectivity must be limited.
   b) If I say I am 27 years old, and if someone else says that I am 42 years old, then it is clear that one person has to be right and the other wrong. Yet in a subjective understanding of things, there is no absolute and both can be right. It is absurd to think that there is no absolute reality—that is the only way to understand things.
   c) If I overdraw my account, the objectivity of how much money is truly in the account is not in question to the banker. When I go to buy gas, the objectivity of the amount owed for the gasoline bought is not an issue. The issue is for me to pay it. If there is objectivity in such simple transactions in all of life, how can one deny the existence of objectivity in spiritual matters?
3) God has revealed Himself by objective truth:
   a) Jesus Christ perfectly revealed His Father, John 12:45, 14:9, 1 John 5:20
   b) Jesus Christ is Truth, John 14:6, 1 John 5:20
   c) God's Word is truth, Psa 119:142, 151, 160, Prov 30:2-6

4. **Universalism**:

a. Common statements:
1) "I think that God is a God of love. He's never going to condemn anybody!"
2) "We're all human, and we all make mistakes. I think that God's heart is big enough to forgive us. He's the One that wants us to forgive others, isn't He?"
3) "Everybody's going up there. God wouldn't send anybody to hell."
4) Theological: The Bible says that Christ died for sinners, bringing righteousness to all men (Rom 5:18). Not believing in universalism is saying that Christ's death is not enough or not efficacious.
5) Essentially universalism is the idea that everybody will be saved some day somehow.

b. The Bible's response to universalism:
1) Regarding a good God not condemning anybody:
   a) Yes, goodness and love are characteristics of God
   b) Yet, truth and justice are also characteristics of God
   c) The condemnation of the unrepentant sinner is inevitable (cf. Rom 1:32, and the innate knowledge of condemnation)
2) Regarding the blanket forgiveness of God:
   a) God loves the world and offers the world forgiveness (cf. 1 John 2:2)
   b) The forgiveness of God is conditional on seeking it His way
   c) God's way is through accepting the gift of forgiveness and righteousness through faith in Jesus Christ
3) Regarding the person of Christ and the resurrection:
   a) Regarding salvation only in Christ, John 14:6; Acts 4:12[1118]

[1117]*The Spiritual Exercises of St. Ignatius,* Translated by Anthony Mottola, Ph.D., with an Introduction by Robert W. Gleason, S.J. (Garden City, NY: Doubleday, 1964), 140-41; Imprimi Potest, John J. McGinty, S.J.; Nihil obstat, John P. Sullivan, M.A.; Imprimatur, Francis Cardinal Spellman.

         b) Regarding the importance of the resurrection, 1 Cor 15:19[1119]

    4) Regarding the ultimate salvation of all men:

         a) It is clear from Scripture that Christ died for all men (cf. 1 John 2:2)

         b) It is also clear from Scripture that most of mankind rejects Christ (cf. Matt 7:13-14, John 1:10-11)

         c) One must accept and follow Christ to be saved (cf. John 1:12-13)

5. **Questioning God's Fairness**:[1120]

    a. An example: "What about those who have never heard?"

    b. They are *without excuse*: "For since the creation of the world His invisible attributes, His eternal power and divine nature, have been clearly seen, being understood through what has been made, so that they are without excuse," Rom 1:20 (cf. Rom 2:1)

    c. God has given them a conscience that condemns, Rom 2:11-16

6. **Atheism, Evolution, and Reincarnation**:

Introduction: These ideas are combined because they essentially comprise similar fallacies and error. They may be held simultaneously or individually by any given person.

    a. The common statements are:

        1) "I don't believe in God."

        2) "I believe in evolution."

        3) "I believe we have several lives to live," or "I believe in reincarnation."

    b. The innate knowledge of God as creator:

        1) In Romans 1:21 Paul explains that all men have known God. However, he goes on to say that man has suppressed this knowledge of God to follow their sinful hearts. God can awaken the objectivity of His reality to the person being shared with. Continue sharing with the assumption that the individual you are speaking with knows God. One day he will stand before God and give an account. Warn him.

        2) Man's move has been to glorify the creation rather than the creator, Rom 1:22-25. Therefore, having their minds darkened (v. 21), becoming fools (v. 22), and choosing to believe a lie (v. 25).

    c. How does the Bible respond to these statements?

        1) Psa 14:1 and 53:1 say, "The fool has said in his heart, 'There is no God.'" Although this may not be a verse to use in all sharing circumstances. It lets the person know pretty clearly where he stands with respect to the Bible.

        2) Atheism is a subjective form of thought, which is proven by the "I" in "I don't believe in God." You can talk about subjectivity as above. These type of debates tend to be unproductive, bringing in Prov 16:25 et al.

        3) Evolution gives no reason for living, other than procreation and existence. There is no reason for existing because man is an animal. One the other hand, the Bible says that God made man for a reason, to know Him, to have fellowship with Him and to obey him. He gives man this abundant life in Jesus Christ (John 10:10):

            a) The Big Bang theory can sometimes make the evolutionary mind think about a beginning. Then it is important to ask what their was before the beginning. Modern scientific theories show that matter is not eternal, but that it is decomposing. The Bible says, "In the beginning," (Gen 1:1), clearly showing that matter is not eternal.

[1118]Numerous books on apologetics deal with the issue of Christ, for example: Lee Strobel, *The Case for Christ* (Grand Rapids: Zondervan, 1996); James W. Sire, *Why Good Arguments often Fail: Making a More Persuasive Case for Christ* (Downers Grove, IL: InterVarsity, 2006).

[1119]Some books on apologetics also deal with the resurrection, for example: Josh McDowell, *Evidence that Demands a Verdict* (San Bernardino, CA: Here's Life, 1979).

[1120]Dick Dowsett in *God That's Not Fair* (Bromley, Kent, UK; STL Books, 1982) covers the topic of God's justice in condemning to eternal judgment.

          b)   Einstein's second theory of relativity is also an interesting point to bring up. It states that "all things tend towards disorder." This conflicts fundamentally with the theory of evolution which asserts the opposite: that all living creatures grow more and more complex as they interact with one another.

    4)   Reincarnation as it is understood in the Western societies fits closely with the idea of evolution. It also affirms that a person comes back to life after death in some other life.

          a)   The Bible clearly affirms that there is one death (Heb 9:27) after which comes judgment for every person. One death, as death is understood in the Bible, affirms one earthly life.

          b)   Belief in reincarnation causes every doctrine of Scripture to be put in doubt. The Bible cannot tell the whole truth. Salvation from judgment and hell after death is not reasonable. The reason for the death and resurrection of Jesus become unclear. Some may say they are Christians and believe in reincarnation. However, the Bible and reincarnation are in no way compatible.

7.   **Historicity and Truth Claims of the Bible**:

    a.   These are called to doubt:

       1)   "The Bible is an old book from a society so different than ours, how can we understand it?"

       2)   "The Bible was written by men. And we know that men make mistakes."

       3)   "The Bible is full of errors anyways."

    b.   The Bible's response:

       1)   The hardened hearts of some will not allow them to understand the Bible, 2 Cor 4:3-4

       2)   The effectiveness of the Bible as God's Living Word must be assumed by faith (Isa 55:10-11, Rom 1:16, Eph 6:17, Heb 4:12), even if the person does not agree with it. One may say, "If you were to believe the Bible, then…"

       3)   Verses attesting the Bible's authority, consistency and truthfulness may be helpful if the person is not a staunch antagonist regarding God's Word. These may be: Psa 119:128, 160, 2 Tim 3:16-17, 2 Pet 1:20-21.

       4)   Some specific arguments concerning supposed falsehoods in the Bible may be considered. Yet, the Gospel must be the focus of the conversation.

    c.   Several situations dealing with God's Word:

       1)   For the person saying that there are many interpretations, 2 Pet 1:20-21 is a good verse to point out.

       2)   For the person saying they believe in God and yet not in the Bible, Psa 119:1-4 and John 14:21 can be good starting points to show them what God's Word says.

8.   **Conclusion**: In all these debating types of situations, the evangelist must not forget why he is speaking to the person—to bring them to a knowledge of Christ and the Gospel. This must not be forgotten and set aside for a heated intellectual discussion (Matt 7:6). Remember the power of God's Word and the Gospel—not that of our wisdom!

Chapter 19 Appendixes

Individual and Group Evangelizing

Introduction: How many people should go out in evangelism on a team? Should evangelism even be "done" or is it primarily an activity of the church in worship? This brief study shows the variety of examples in the Bible…

1. Individual (one person by himself): Jer 22:1; 26:1-2; Jonah 3:1-3; Mark 5:19-20; Luke 18:5-7; John 3:1-2; 4:6-8; 5:14; 9:35-38; Acts 17:16-17

   Individual by inference, Matt 10:1-10; Luke 9:1-6

2. Two-by-two: Mark 6:7-9; Luke 10:1; Acts 13:2-4; 15:39-40; 19:22

3. Group of men only: Acts 16:3, 11; 20:4

4. Group of men and women: Luke 8:1-3; Acts 18:18

Conclusion: This variety of approaches ought to encourage, rather than discourage individual evangelism, as some are apt to do,[1121] or even mixed gender evangelism, which is at times necessary (in public places with appropriate safeguards), but may it also show the preeminence of two-by-two evangelism.

By the way, the book of Acts has no examples of "community evangelism" nor of "worship evangelism." Some seek to equate Paul and Silas singing while in prison for evangelizing, after being beaten and with feet bound to stocks, with a worshiping church service with its architecture, safety, musical instruments, and worship leaders. However, this comparison is quite a stretch, and it's existence in no way contradicts or countermands the vaste evidence of individual evangelism in the New Testament. Proponents of community evangelism are likely ascribing to it based on something other than the authority of the New Testament. And if the use of an outside authority is the case, they cannot say that they stand on the inerrancy of Scriptures in matters of faith and practice.

One student recently wrote on a Contact Report form (related to street evangelism): Why is it that pastors and teachers are congregationally-oriented, but evangelists are not (cf. evangelists, pastors, and teachers in Eph 4:11)? His question concerns both the individual evangelism of the evangelist, as well as the location for evangelism.[1122]

[1121]Mark Mittelberg explained how he moved from "Lone Ranger Evangelism" to "Church-Based Evangelism" in his *Building a Contagious Church* (Grand Rapids: Zondervan, 2000), 23.

[1122]For a summary of some locations for evangelism in the New Testament, please see *UE*, Chap 7, I, 3, "Movement and Location of Evangelism Ministry"

Evangelizing and Territorial Issues

Introduction: Consider this verse from Deuteronomy:

> Deut 23:24, "When you enter your neighbor's vineyard, then you may eat grapes until you are fully satisfied, but you shall not put any in your basket."

1. If the concept of the "vineyard" is taken to mean a church territory or parish, or perhaps even the member of another church, then the figurative meaning of this verse may take on interesting meaning;

2. If the concept of "putting grapes into a basket" signifies spiritual harvesting, via evangelizing, along with the prior territorial interpretation, then here are three distinct historical approaches to this subject.

A. Council of Spier (1524), "Whose region, His religion!"

1. This statement expresses the territorial church view that made its way into the United States before the Revolution. Each colony in the colonial period had its own religion, for the most part, whose clergy were supported by taxes;

2. The territorial church model during the colonial period in the U.S. was modeled from the European State Churches: Roman Catholic (France, Spain, Italy, Austria, etc.); Anglican (England); Reformed (parts of Switzerland); etc.;

3. The exception to the State Church model was Pennsylvania; and its was from the free-market church model of Pennsylvania that came the First Amendment of the U.S. Constitution:

> "Congress shall make no law respecting an establishment of religion, or prohibiting the free exercise thereof; or abridging the freedom of speech, or of the press; or the right of the people peaceably to assemble, and to petition the Government for a redress of grievances."

B. John Wesley, "The world is my parish!" (~1740):

1. Interestingly, as to U.S. politics and the Constitution, about 30 years before the founding of the U.S. came the First Great Awakening (~1740);

2. One of the fiery preachers of the First Great Awakening was John Wesley, who was an Anglican minister. When he would travel (or itinerate) and preach in another Anglican parish, the minister there sometimes objected, saying, "Go elsewhere, this is my parish." Wesley's reply was, "The world is my parish. Consider:

   a. This idea was in keeping with Christ's Great Commission (aka. His resurrection preaching), which was not restrictive in any way, but universal to each and every Christian!

   > Matt 28:19, "Go therefore and make disciples of all the nations…"
   > Mark 16:15, "And He said to them, 'Go into all the world and preach the gospel to every creature."
   > Luke 24:47, "and that repentance and remission of sins should be proclaimed in His name to all nations…"
   > Acts 1:8, "…and you shall be witnesses to Me in Jerusalem, and in all Judea and Samaria, and to the end of the earth."

   b. Wesley's breaking down the parish mentality was necessary for freedom of worship;
   c. Note that the parish mentality was used against an OT prophet:

   > Amos 7:12-13, "Then Amaziah said to Amos, 'Go, you seer, flee away to the land of Judah, and there eat bread and there do your prophesying! But no longer prophesy at Bethel, for it is a sanctuary of the king and a royal residence."

3. Roger Finke and Rodney Stark, *The Churching of America: Winners and Losers in Our Religious Economy*, Rev Ed. (Rutgers University Press, 2005), communicate the phenomenon of the growth and decline of churches in a "free market economy" of churches.

C. Colson-Neuhaus on "Sheep-stealing":

1. Projecting a return to the territorial or parish mentality, the Colson-Neuhaus Statement decried when members of one Christian group have the temerity to evangelize among the (past or present) members of another religious group:

> "There is a necessary distinction between evangelizing [non-Christians] and what is today commonly called **proselytizing or 'sheep stealing.'**" For "in view of the large number of non-Christians in the world and the enormous challenge of the common evangelistic task, it is neither theologically legitimate nor a prudent use of resources for one Christian community to **proselytize** among active adherents of another Christian community." Thus, "**We condemn the practice of recruiting people** from another community for the purposes of denominational or institutional aggrandizement."[1123]

2. Notice the protectionism assumed by Colson-Neuhaus, calling down a condemnation;

3. Notice the antagonism projected to the evangelist who would dare to evangelize someone from another Christian group (e.g. a Baptist having the audacity to evangelize [a present or former] Roman Catholic or Greek Orthodox);

4. Notice the lack of concern for the souls of lost people, whoever's fold from which they may have come (which radiates a lack of belief in biblical conversion on their part);

5. Notice the assumption of false motives, "for the purposes of denominational or institutional aggrandizement," which seems to communicate a jealousy on the part of those who do not have growing churches and are not evangelizing!

Conclusion 1: So we have come full circle. Perhaps this study shows that there is nothing new under the sun, as well as the constant societal and religious pressures under which evangelists must fulfill their calling!

D. On the Use of an Implement—or Evangelism Methodology?

Deut 23:25, "When you enter your neighbor's standing grain, then you may pluck the heads with your hand, but you shall not wield a sickle in your neighbor's standing grain."

1. Continuing to use figurative interpretation, as with verse 24, that the neighbor is another Christian denomination, and that plucking heads refers to evangelizing, then to what may a "sickle" refer?
   a. Could not a sickle, as a manufactured implement, refer to an organized methodology?
   b. If this is the case, then, could this verse (on a stretch of allegorical interpretation) be prohibiting the forming of gospel presentations and gospel literature directed to bring people from another Christian group to Christ (for example Roman Catholics or Russian Orthodox)?

2. In this case, quite likely, we see an example of allegorical interpretation of the OT stretched beyond its limits:
   a. The reader may be interested to note how this form of interpretation can be used as it relates to not cutting down "trees for food" in Deut 20:19-20:

   > Deut 20:19-20, "When you besiege a city a long time, to make war against it in order to capture it, you shall not destroy its trees by swinging an axe against them; for you may eat from them, and you shall not cut them down. For is the tree of the field a man, that it should be besieged by you? Only the trees which you know are not fruit trees you shall destroy and cut down, that you may construct siegeworks against the city that is making war with you until it falls."

   b. Again, in this case, if waging war and the destruction of trees means destroying the writings of false teachers and leaders, then perhaps "trees for food" are the writings of the enemy suitable for consumption that ought not be destroyed, but used for food?
   c. On the other hand, elsewhere Deuteronomy teaches the complete destruction of idols and their trappings, Deut 7:25-26:

   > Deut 7:25-26, "The graven images of their gods you are to burn with fire; you shall not covet the silver or the gold that is on them, nor take it for yourselves, lest you be snared by it, for it is an abomination to

---

[1123]Geisler and MacKenzie, *Roman Catholics and Evangelicals: Agreements and Differences* (Grand Rapids: Baker, 1995), 493.

the LORD your God. And you shall not bring an abomination into your house, and like it come under the ban; you shall utterly detest it and you shall utterly abhor it, for it is something banned."

    d.   Thereby showing how the trickiness of allegorical interpretation can be used to negate the clear teaching of Scripture elsewhere!

Conclusion 2: As is taught in most classes on biblical interpretation, allegorical interpretation can be tricky, and should never contradict the clear teaching of the Scriptures. This rule is especially important, as the NT provides the Christian the proper interpretation and application of the OT.

Length of Time Evangelizing

Introduction: While the Bible teaches "now" evangelism, it may be necessary to spend some time reasoning, opening, setting forth, and confronting (cf. Acts 17:2-3). We should expect people to be touched by the Holy Spirit speaking through the Word of God immediately. Yet here are some passages that seem to indicate how much time was spent in evangelism (*before* being kicked out of or removing himself from the synagogue):

1. Apparent immediate conversion, Acts 8:26-39; 16:13-14, 25-34

2. After a full day of conversation, Acts 28:23-24

    Note the verbs used:
    >   Explained [ἐκτίθημι, main verb]
    >   Solemnly testified [διαμαρτύρομαι, participle]
    >   Persuading [πείθω, participle]

3. The next Sabbath, Acts 13:44

4. Three Sabbaths, Acts 17:2-3

    Note the verbs used:
    >   Reasoned [διαλέγομαι, main verb]
    >   Explaining – opening [διανοίγω, participle]
    >   Demonstrating – giving evidence [παρατίθημι, participle]
    >   Proclaim [καταγγέλλω, participle]

5. Three months, Acts 19:8

    Note what he did during this time:
    >   Spoke boldly [παρρησιάζομαι, main verb]
    >   Reasoning [διαλέγομαι, participle]
    >   Persuading [πείθω, participle])

Conclusion: In the chapter "Follow-up Is Important," I discuss the varied lengths of time spent on follow-up. It goes from no follow-up (Mark 1:38; Luke 4:42-44; Mark 5:18-20, Luke 8:38-39 [e.g. John 8:11]; Acts 8:39; 18:20), to no follow-up mentioned (Acts 13:12-13), to several days of follow-up (John 4:40-42; Acts 10:48; 20:6), to extended follow-up (Mark 3:13-14; Acts 11:26; 17:14; 18:11; 19:10; 20:31). Ascribing to a required length of time in follow-up is not a valid argument.

Similarly, in evangelism, there is a recent interest in taking extended time in evangelism, allowing the supposed "human aspects" of evangelism to take effect (friendship, lifestyle, service, or apologetics).[1124] Imposing a required length of time, and especially shunning or degrading "now" evangelism, though popular, is unhelpful and not consistent with Scripture.

[1124]"I've learned the hard way that pressing people to take steps for which they are not ready will backfire. In some cases it can even short-circuit the whole process" (Mark Mittelberg, *Building a Contagious Church* [Grand Rapids: Zondervan, 2000], 59). See also Steve Sjogren (*Conspiracy of Kindness* (Ann Arbor, MI: Servant, 1993), 22-24; and Robert Webber, *Ancient-Future Church: Making Your Church a Faith-Forming Community* (Grand Rapids: Baker, 2003), 67.

Concerning the Average Age of Converts

Introduction: A possible fallacy, common in established church areas (e.g. in the U.S.), is that *most* people come to Christ prior to 18 years of age. This figure is especially true when it involves second generation Christians.

However, when the Bible provides examples of named converts, they are *almost always* mature persons:

1. Woman at the well, married five times, John 4:17-18

2. Those in established careers:
    a. Zaccheus (tax collector), Luke 19:2
    b. Nicodemus (a ruler of the Jews), John 3:1
    c. Ethiopian eunuch (in charge of Candace's treasure), Acts 8:27
    d. Cornelius (Centurion), Acts 10:1-2
    e. Priscilla and Aquila (tentmakers), Acts 18 (circumstances of conversion unclear from text)

3. Those with families: Cornelius, Lydia the seller of purple fabrics, Philippian jailer

4. Of the man born blind, "Ask him; he is of age [an adult], he will speak for himself," John 9:21

5. Probably young adults: rich young ruler, Thief on the cross, and Saul (who became Paul) who was already well-educated prior to his salvation.

Conclusion: Although important, evangelization needs to be more than just reaching children. By the way, France recently (May 2000) passed a law against mental manipulation of children or the elderly.

When Do You Shake the Dust Off Your Feet?

Introduction: An African gentleman from Uganda recently told me that we should leave Muslim persons alone (cf. Matt 13:24-30) and not share the Gospel with them. God will decide those that are his at the end of time. What of this view? Is this a matter of shaking the dust off of one's feet, as far as a religious groups goes?

"Jesus presented another parable to them, saying, "The kingdom of heaven may be compared to a man who sowed good seed in his field. But while his men were sleeping, his enemy came and sowed tares among the wheat, and went away. But when the wheat sprouted and bore grain, then the tares became evident also. The slaves of the landowner came and said to him, 'Sir, did you not sow good seed in your field? How then does it have tares?' And he said to them, 'An enemy has done this!' The slaves said to him, 'Do you want us, then, to go and gather them up?' But he said, 'No; for while you are gathering up the tares, you may uproot the wheat with them. 'Allow both to grow together until the harvest; and in the time of the harvest I will say to the reapers, "First gather up the tares and bind them in bundles to burn them up; but gather the wheat into my barn"'" (Matt 13:24-30).

1. The teaching of Jesus, Matt 10:14-15, Mark 6:10-11, Luke 9:5; 10:10-11:

    a. Examples (in principle) in the life of Jesus:
        1) Teaching in parables so that they did not understand, Matt 13:10-17
        2) Jesus not able to do miracles in His hometown because of their unbelief, Matt 13:54-58

    b. Principles:
        1) Shaking the dust off our feet means we engage people in conversation until they have the opportunity to reject the Gospel
            a) We must make it personal
        2) Shaking the dust off our feet includes houses and cities, cf. Matt 10

    c. Points of application:

        1) Have you ever shaken the dust off your feet?
            a) It *is* commanded in God's Word in the context of the evangelism training of Jesus!

        2) If you are not sharing the Gospel there will be no opportunity to shake the dust off of your feet!
            a) Notice in Matthew it says "nor heed your words"
            b) In Mark it says, "does not listen to you"
            c) Both imply a verbal witness of the Gospel
            d) Is God using your vocal cords to share the Gospel message with the lost?

        3) Shaking the dust off your feet implies that this is far more than a marketing campaign, such as mass mailings and the distribution of invitations to church:
            a) Evangelizing—to the point of shaking the dust—implies an urgency
            b) Evangelizing—to the point of shaking the dust—implies the urgent need to make a decision

        4) You cannot get to the point of shaking the dust off of your feet until you are engaged in an evangelistic witness:
            a) You must bring the person to the point of decision in order to shake the dust off of your feet with integrity
            b) Smiling, handing a tract, praying a nice prayer, and going on to the next door is not enough
            c) In order to shake the dust off your feet, there needs to be an engaging spiritual conversation
            d) This goes against our nature as people—not wanting to be offensive:
                (1) By the way, Paul did say, "Give no offense either to Jews or to Greeks or to the church of God" (1 Cor 10:32)
                (2) Nevertheless, the Gospel is an offense to those who are perishing (e.g. 2 Cor 2:15-16; Gal 5:11)
            e) **"Shaking the dust off of your feet" seems to be Jesus saying that we ought to engage people to the point of decision**

5) If you have not shaken the dust off of your feet (hence no open rejection of the Gospel), then there is opportunity for continued witness
    a) It seems implied that if we have not shaken the dust off of our feet that we should go back to the same house or apartment
    b) Jesus made it clear in Matthew that He is including homes in the receiving or rejecting

6) Have you maximized those open doors that did not lead to shaking the dust off of your feet?
    a) This is perhaps a common area of weakness in evangelism:
        1) We don't engage people to the point of decision
        2) We don't capitalize on the opportunities and open doors that God provides
    b) We are scatter shooting the Gospel when God wants us to use a rifle and engage individuals!

2. Principles from the example of the apostles, Acts 13:49-52; 18:5-6:
    a. Notice that this shaking was symbolic and not ritualistic
    b. Shaking the dust off their feet was not a ritual to bring a voodoo-type of fear on the people
    c. The goal of the shaking was *not* to induce persons to the fear of God and repentance, rather it is a visible symbol of coming judgment
    d. Shaking the dust off their feet did *not* mean that the word was *not* having success, see Acts 13:48-49
    e. Shaking the dust off their feet did not imply that they felt their method of evangelism was wrong or needed to be adjusted
    f. Shaking the dust off their feet included when a political system did not provide them freedom to evangelize (i.e. freedom of speech)
    g. Shaking the dust off their feet did not discourage the believers

3. Parallel teaching:
    a. "He who corrects a scoffer gets dishonor for himself Do not reprove a scoffer, lest he hate you," Prov 9:7-8
    b. "Do not speak in the hearing of a fool," Prov 23:9
    c. "Do not answer a fool according to his folly. Answer a fool as his folly deserves," Prov 26:4-5
    d. "When a wise man has a controversy with a foolish man, the foolish man either rages or laughs, and there is no rest," Prov 29:9
    e. "Do not give what is holy to dogs, and do not throw pearls before swine, lest they trample them under their feet and turn and tear you to pieces," Matt 7:6

    "Verse 6 is not a directive against evangelizing the Gentiles, especially in a book full of various supports for this, not least 28:18-20 (10:5, properly understood, is no exception)."[1125]

4. Recognizing when to shake the dust off your feet:[1126]
    a. Occasions: in evangelistic situations when the Gospel is being communicated, Acts 13:16-41, "Shook the dust off their feet," 18:5, "Shook out garments."
    b. Responses to the Gospel necessitating this unfortunate retreat:
        1) Contradiction, Acts 13:45
        2) Resistance, Acts 18:6
        3) Blasphemy, Acts 13:45, 18:6
        4) Persecution, Acts 13:50
    c. These responses necessitate appropriate warning, Acts 13:46-47, 18:6
    d. A public shaking of the dust off one's feet or garments thereby signifies "disassociating himself from the pollution of those lands and the judgment in store for them."[1127]

[1125]Donald A. Carson, *The Expositor's Bible Commentary: Matthew* (Grand Rapids: Zondervan, 1984), 185.

[1126]"Levels of Openness: The Closed Person" (above) gives a practical look at this idea of shaking the dust off of one's feet.

[1127]Carson, *Matthew,* 246.

Evangelism, Spiritual Fatigue and Recuperation

Introduction: John 6:33, "These things I have spoken to you, so that in Me you may have peace. In the world you have tribulation, but take courage; I have overcome the world."

1. The Fact of Spiritual Drain in Ministry:
   a. Elijah, 1 Kgs 19
   b. Jonah, Jonah 4
   c. Jesus:
      1) During the temptation, Matt 4:11, Mark 1:13
      2) Jesus' exhausted sleep in the boat, Luke 8:22-25
      3) The woman with a hemorrhage, Mark 5:40
      4) During His prayer at Gethsemane, Luke 22:39-47
   d. Paul, 1 Cor 2:3-5, 2 Cor 7:5-6 (almost to the point of depression!)

2. Spiritual drain and a burden for people, Matt 9:35-38 (2 Cor 11:28-29):
   a. The strain of people seeking ministry
   b. A burden for people developing due to great spiritual needs

3. Spiritual drain and discouragement:
   a. Elijah, 1 Kgs 19:2-4
   b. The apostle Paul, Acts 18:9-10

4. The need for rest and recuperation:
   a. God giving restful sleep, Psa 4:8, 127:2, Prov 19:23 (e.g. 1 Kgs 19:5-6; Jer 31:26; Mark 4:37-38):
      1) The Apostle Paul writes of sleepnessless in the ministry, 2 Cor 6:5, 11:27 (cf. Psa 102:7)
      2) Remembering that too much sleep is laziness, Prov 6:10-11, 26:14
      3) Also remembering that meditation on God's Word is more important than sleep, Psa 119:147-148 (cf. Jos 1:8, Ps. 1:2)
      4) Also remembering that the disciples were sleeping when they should have been praying, Matt 26:40-46; Mark 14:37-41; Luke 22:45-46
   b. Extended private prayer and meditation as means of rest and recuperation:
      1) Jesus getting alone, Matt 14:13, 23, Mark 1:35, Luke 4:42, 5:15-16, 21:37-38, John 8:1-2 (with His disciples, Mark 14:13ff.)
      2) Meditation:
         a) "Cease striving and know that I am God," Psa 46:10
         b) Waiting on the Lord, Isa 40:30-31
   c. The need to get away:
      1) Mark 6:31, "And He said to them, 'Come away by yourselves to a lonely place and rest a while.'"
      2) Luke 9:10, "And when the apostles returned, they gave an account to Him of all that they had done. And taking them with Him, He withdrew privately to a city called Bethsaida."
   d. Rest through being a guest:
      1) Jesus was a guest on numerous occasions, Matt 9:10-13, Mark 14:3-11, Luke 7:36-50, 10:38-42, 14:1-24, 19:1-10, 24:28-31, John 2:1-11
      2) Jesus did not refrain from ministry in these circumstances. However, it must have afforded Him some rest.
   e. Prolonged recuperation after a missionary journey, Acts 14:28

5. Promises for rest, peace, and renewed strength, Prov 1:33, Isa 40:29-31, Jer 31:25, Heb 4:9-11

6. Spiritual fatigue and perseverance in doing good:
   a. Teaching: Gal 6:9, 2 Thess 3:13 (cf. Phil 3:12 and Heb 10:36)
   b. Ministering while under spiritual fatigue, Mark 6:33ff., John 4:6; 2 Cor 7:5

CHAPTER 20
Results, Reactions, and Responses

Introduction:

1.   Consider the relationship of the messenger with the Godhead:[1128]
     Link of the messenger and God, Acts 17:30
          Cf. Deut 18:18-19, "I will raise up a prophet from among their countrymen like you, and I will put My
              words in his mouth, and he shall speak to them all that I command him. And it shall come about that
              whoever will not listen to My words which he shall speak in My name, I Myself will require *it* of
              him."
     Link of the messenger with Christ, Acts 13:47
     The messenger assumed, so that they may hear, be taught of God, and come to Christ, John 6:45
     The world's reception of Christ, John 1:11-13; 15:18-21; 16:1-3
     Persecution because of world's hatred of God, Rom 8:36, "Just as it is written, 'For Thy sake we are
         being put to death all day long; We were considered as sheep to be slaughtered'" [quote of Psa
         44:22]
     There are numerous other verses on this issue; the following show the spiritual link of the messenger
         with the Godhead:

Relationship of the Messenger with the Godhead

Text	Messenger	Prophets	Christ	God
Exod 16:8		… And what are we? Your grumblings are not against us …		for the LORD hears your grumblings which you grumble against Him. … … but against the LORD.
1 Sam 8:7		And the LORD said to Samuel, "Listen to the voice of the people in regard to all that they say to you, for they have not rejected you,		but they have rejected Me from being king over them
Psa 69:9			For zeal for Thy house has consumed me, …have fallen on me	And the reproaches of those who reproach Thee…
Ezek 3:6		Who should be willing to listen to you		I have sent you to them
Ezek 3:7		Yet the house of Israel will not be willing to listen to you		Since they are not willing to listen to Me
Matt 5:11	Blessed are you when people insult you and persecute you and falsely say all kinds of evil against you		On account of me	
Matt 5:12	Rejoice and be glad, for your reward in heaven is great	For in the same way they persecuted the prophets who were before you		
Matt 10:40	He who receives you		Receives Me, and he who receives Me	Receives Him who sent Me

---

[1128]Please refer to the notes on "Hearing to Believe," as an Appendix of Chapter 2.

Text	Messenger	Prophets	Christ	God
Mark 9:37	[by analogy] Whoever receives one child like this in My name		receives Me and whoever receives Me does not receive Me	but Him who sent Me
Luke 6:22	Blessed are you when men hate you, and ostracize you, and insult you, and scorn your name as evil		For the sake of the Son of Man	
Luke 6:23	Be glad in that day and leap for joy, for behold your reward is great in heaven	For in the same way your fathers used to treat the prophets		
Luke 6:26	Woe to you when all men speak well of you	For their fathers used to treat the false prophets in the same way		
Luke 10:16	The one who listens to you And the one who rejects you		Listens to Me Rejects Me, and he who rejects Me	Rejects the One who sent Me
John 13:20	Receives whom I send		Receives Me	Receives Him who sent Me
John 15:20	Remember the word that I said to you, "A slave is not greater than his master." ... They will also persecute you They will keep yours also		If they persecuted Me ... If they kept My word ...	
John 15:21	But all these things they will do to you		For My name's sake	Because they do not know the One who sent Me
John 16:2-3	They will make you outcasts from the synagogue, but an hour is coming for everyone who kills you to think that he is offering a service to God		... Or Me	These things they will do because they have not known the Father ...
Heb 11:24-26		By faith Moses, when he had grown up, refused to be called the son of Pharaoh's daughter; choosing rather to endure ill-treatment with the people of God, than to enjoy the passing pleasures of sin; ...than the treasures of Egypt; for he was looking to the reward.	considering the reproach of Christ greater riches...	
Heb 12:3-4		...so that you may not grow weary and lose heart. You have not yet resisted to the point of shedding blood in your striving against sin	For consider Him who has endured such hostility by sinners against Himself,	
1 John 4:5-6	[context] They are from the world; therefore they speak *as* from the world, and the world listens to them		listens to us; does not listen to us. By this we know the spirit of truth and the spirit of error	We are from God; he who knows God... he who is not from God

Not everyone has warmly received this teaching. Notice for example the words of Lesslie Newbigin, at one time General Secretary of the International Missionary Council:

"I can never be so confident of the purity and authenticity of my witness that I can know that the person who rejects my witness has rejected Jesus. I am witness to him who is both utterly holy and utterly gracious. His holiness and his grace are far above my comprehension as they are above that of the hearer."[1129]

While we are not the final arbiters or the judges of man's conscience—God is!—our evangelizing or lack of it does bring about eternal consequences, both positive and negative (2 Cor 2:15-16).

2. A graphic portrayal of some of this relationship:

Charting the Relationship of the Evangelist with the Godhead

Part One: Reception and Rejection
(Matt 5:11;12; 10:40; Luke 10:16, et al.)

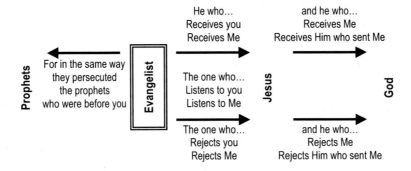

Part Two: Person, Proclamation, and Persuasion
(2 Cor 5:20-6:1)

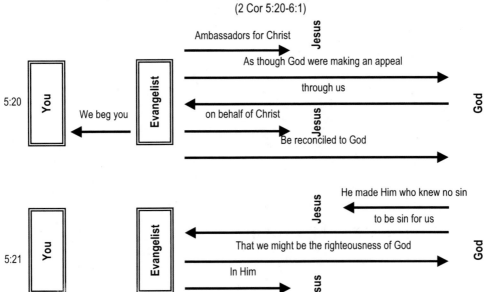

―――――――――――――――――

    [1129]Lesslie Newbigin, "Cross-currents in Ecumenical and Evangelical Understandings of Mission," *International Bulletin of Missionary Research*, vol 6 (1982), 146-51; cited in Bosch, *Transforming Mission*, 413.

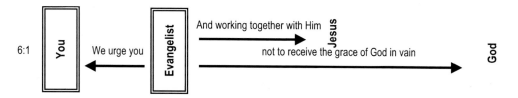

2 Cor 6:2 then provides God's invitation to the sinner; In this regard to our relationship with the Godhead in evangelism, also consider also 1 Cor 3:5-9, 10f.; 9:23

3. Consider the antitheses of the above chart:
   a. John 15:19, "If you were of the world, the world would love its own; but because you are not of the world, but I chose you out of the world, therefore the world hates you"
   b. 1 John 4:5, "They are from the world; therefore they speak *as* from the world, and the world listens to them"
   c. Gal 1:10, "For am I now seeking the favor of men, or of God? Or am I striving to please men? If I were still trying to please men, I would not be a bond-servant of Christ"

   Conclusion: Consider therefore how dangerous it is to seek to sugarcoat the Gospel so that the world accepts it.

The Difficulty of This Life and Translations of 1 Corinthians 7:26

Greek	Latin Vulgate	English Geneva	King James Version	American Standard Version	New American Standard	English Standard Version	French Segond [trans mine]
Νομίζω οὖν τοῦτο καλὸν ὑπάρχειν διὰ τὴν ἐνεστῶσαν ἀνάγκην	existimo ergo hoc bonum esse propter instantem necessitatem	I suppose then this to bee good for the present necessitie	I suppose therefore that this is good for the present distress	I think therefore that this is good by reason of the distress that is upon us	I think then that this is good in view of the present distress	I think that in view of the present distress	Behold therefore what I esteem good, because of the difficult times that are approaching

4. Willingness to bear the reproach of Christ:
   a. Moses bore the reproach of Christ, Heb 11:24-26
   b. Paul's willingness to bear the reproach of the cross, Gal 5:11; 1 Cor 4:10-13; etc.

5. Lack of willingness to bear the reproach of Christ:
   a. Peter's denial of Christ, John 18:15-18
   b. The believers among the rulers, John 12:42-43
   c. Seeking to be greater than the Master, John 15:18-20
   d. Baruch's possible seeking great things for himself, Jeremiah 45

The evangelist says: "Today if you hear His voice, do not harden your heart" (Heb 3:7-8): How do people respond?
Consider the varieties of responses in the Bible…

A. Reactions to the Gospel Message in the Bible:

1. Inward reactions of people:
   a. "Was listening; and the Lord opened her heart to respond," Acts 16:14
   b. "They received the word with great eagerness," Acts 17:11
   c. "Were being persuaded," Acts 28:24
   d. "Pierced to the heart," Acts 2:37
   e. "Turned to the Lord," 18:8
   f. "Believed," Acts 4:4; 11:21; 17:12
   g. "Some men joined him and believed," Acts 17:34
   h. "Hearing, believed and were baptized," Acts 18:8
   i. "Many also of those who had believed kept coming, confessing and disclosing their practices," Act 19:18

j.   "Were becoming obedient to the faith," Acts 6:7
k.   "But when the young man heard this statement, he went away grieved; for he was one who owned much property," Matt 19:22; cf. Mark 10:22; 18:33
l.   "Frightened," Acts 24:25
m.   "Cut to the quick," Acts 5:33 ("and were intending to slay them"), 7:54
n.   "Everyone marveled," Mark 5:20 (cf. John 7:15, Acts 2:7, 4:13)
o.   "Amazed," Matt 7:28, 12:23, Mark 1:22, Luke 4:32, Acts 2:7, 13:12
p.   συγχέω and συγχύννω:
     1)   "Bewildered," Acts 2:6
     2)   "Confounding" the Jews, Acts 9:22 (cf. Acts 6:10, 21:27)
q.   "Greatly disturbed," Acts 4:2
r.   "Did not believe," Mark 16:13
s.   "Would not believe," Luke 24:11, Acts 28:24
t.   "Refused to believe," Mark 16:11
u.   "Were becoming hardened and disobedient," Acts 19:9
v.   "Were filled with jealousy," Acts 5:17, 13:45 (cf. Acts 17:5)

2.   Positive outward reactions of people:
     a.   Repentance, Jonah 3:7-9, confirmed through baptism, Matt 3:2, 7, Luke 3:3, 7
     b.   Commitment confirmed through baptism, Acts 2:41, 8:36, 38, 16:15, 33, 18:8
     c.   "Joining" the believers, Acts 2:47, 5:14, 17:34
     d.   Invited the disciples to their house, Acts 16:15, 33
     e.   Washing of wounds, Acts 16:33

3.   Negative outward reactions of people:
     a.   "And they put him out," John 9:34
     b.   Cried out and covered their ears, Acts 7:57
     c.   Gnashed their teeth at him, Acts 7:54 (cf. Psa 37:12)
     d.   Began a riot and persecution, Acts 13:50, 14:5, 16:22, 17:13, 19:23-41, 21:27
     e.   Picked up stones to stone, John 8:59, 10:31 (cf. Num 14:10)
     f.   Stoned, Acts 7:58, 14:19
     g.   Flogged, Acts 5:40
     h.   Scourged, Matt 27:26, Mark 15:15
     i.   Beat with a reed, Mark 15:19, with rods, Acts 16:22-23
     j.   Beat Him with their fists and slapped Him, Mark 14:65
     k.   Slapped them, John 18:22-23, Acts 23:2
     l.   Put them in jail, Acts 4:3, 16:23
     m.   Put forward false witnesses, Acts 6:13
     n.   Followed for harmful reasons, Acts 16:33-34, 17:4, 34

B.   Examples of Verbal Responses to the Gospel in the Bible:

1.   Positive responses:
     a.   "And it will be said in that day, 'Behold this is our God for whom we have waited that He might save us. This is the Lord for whom we have waited; Let us rejoice and be glad in His salvation.'" Isa 25:9
     b.   "Who knows, God may turn and relent, and withdraw His burning anger so that we shall not perish?" Jonah 3:9
     c.   "Thou art the Christ, the Son of the living God." Matt 16:18
     d.   "This is the Savior of the world," John 4:42
     e.   "This is certainly the Prophet," John 7:40
     f.   "This is the Christ," John 7:41
     g.   "Truly this man was the Son of God!" Mark 15:39
     h.   "And who is He, Lord, that I may believe in Him?" John 9:36
     i.   "Yes, Lord; I have believed that You are the Christ, the Son of God, even He that comes into the world." John 11:27
     j.   "My Lord and my God!" John 20:28
     k.   "What shall we do brethren?" Acts 2:37
     l.   "Sirs, what must I do to be saved?" Acts 16:30

2.   Responses indicating possible continued interest:
     a.   Nicodemus questioned the idea of being "born-again," John 3:4 (cf. John 7:50, 19:39)
     b.   "What does this mean?" Acts 2:12

     c.   "Asked for another hearing," Acts 13:42

     d.   "What would this babbler wish to say?" Acts 17:18

     e.   "He seems to be proclaiming strange deities," Acts 17:18

     f.   "May we know what this new teaching is, we want to know therefore what these things mean." Acts 17:19-20

     g.   "Go away for the present, and when I find time, I will summon you," Acts 24:25

3. No response:

     a.   "But the people did not answer him a word," 1Kings 18:21

4. Negative responses:

     a.   "This is *one* of them!" Mark 14:69; "You are *one* of them too!" Luke 22:58; "Surely you too are *one* of them; for even the way you talk gives you away," Matt 26:73

     b.   "You also were with Jesus the Nazarene," Mark 14:67; "This man was with Him too," Luke 22:56

     c.   "Surely the Christ is not going to come from Galilee, is He?" John 4:40

     d.   Accusations, cf. Acts 6:11-14; 21:28, 24:2-8:

         1) "These men are throwing our city into confusion, being Jews, and are proclaiming customs which it is not lawful for us to accept or to observe, being Romans," Acts 16:20-21

         2) "These men who have upset the world have come here also; and Jason has welcomed them, and they all act contrary to the decrees of Caesar, saying that there is another king, Jesus," Acts 17:6-7

         3) "Men, you know that our prosperity depends upon this business. You see and hear that not only in Ephesus, but in almost all of Asia, this Paul has persuaded and turned away a considerable number of people, saying that gods made with hands are no gods *at all*. Not only is there danger that this trade of ours fall into disrepute, but also that the temple of the great goddess Artemis be regarded as worthless and that she whom all of Asia and the world worship will even be dethroned from her magnificence," Acts 19:25-27

     e.   Reviled:

         1) "They reviled him and said, 'You are His disciple, but we are disciples of Moses. We know that God has spoken to Moses, but as for this man, we do not know where He is from,'" John 9:28-29

     f.   Sneering, 2 Chr 30:10; Acts 17:32

     g.   Mocking, Matt 27:29, 31, 41; Mark 15:20, 31; Luke 22:63; 23:11, 36; Acts 2:13

     h.   Laughed them to scorn, 2 Chr 30:13; cf. Matt 9:24; Mark 5:40; Luke 8:53

     i.   Appeared to be jesting, Gen 19:14

     j.   "Speaking evil of the Way," Acts 19:9

     k.   Contradiction and blasphemy, Acts 13:45, 18:6 (e.g. John 8:33, 39, 41)

     l.   Threatened and ordered not to speak in the name of Jesus, Acts 4:21:

         1) "And when they had summoned them, they commanded them not to speak or teach at all in the name of Jesus," Acts 4:18

         2) "We gave you strict orders not to continue teaching in this name, and yet, you have filled Jerusalem with your teaching and intend to bring this man's blood upon us," Acts 5:28

         3) "They took his advice; and after calling the apostles in, they flogged them and ordered them not to speak in the name of Jesus, and *then* released them," Acts 5:40

     m.   "Go you seer, flee away to the land of Judah and there eat bread and there do your prophesying! But no longer prophesy at Bethel, for it is a sanctuary of the king and a royal residence," Amos 7:12-13

     n.   "Do not prophecy in the name of the Lord, that you might not die at our hand." Jer 11:21

     o.   "Away with him!" Acts 21:36

     p.   "Away with such a fellow from the earth, for he should not be allowed to live!" Acts 22:22

     q.   "He is deserving of death!" Matt 26:66

     r.   "You must die!" Jer 26:8

     s.   "A death sentence for this man!" Jer 26:11

     t.   "Let Him be crucified!" Matt 27:22-23; "Crucify Him!" Mark 15:13-14, Luke 24:21.

5. Derogatory names and terms:

     a.   "They are lazy," Exod 5:8; "You are lazy, very lazy," Exod 5:17

     b.   "Is it you, you troubler of Israel?" 1 Kg 18:17

     c.   "Is he not just speaking parables?" Ezek 20:49

     d.   "You are telling a lie! The Lord has not sent you to say…" Jer 43:2

     d.   "He is possessed by Beelzebub," Mark 3:22

     e.   "Do we not rightly say that you are a Samaritan and have a demon?" John 8:48

     f.   "Now we know you have a demon," John 8:52

     g.   "You were born entirely in sins, and you are teaching us?" John 9:34

h. "And said, 'Sir, we remember that when He was still alive <u>that deceiver</u> said, "After three days I *am to* rise again."'" Matt 27:63

i. "Paul, you are out of your mind! Your great learning is driving you mad," Acts 26:24

C. Present-Day Common Reactions and Responses to the Gospel:

Introduction: Some reactions and responses to the Gospel in the Bible have been sighted earlier.[1130] Following are examples of common reactions today. It is interesting to see how they parallel the reactions in God's Word.

John 13:20 clarifies what is implied by the reception of the witnessing Christian, "Truly, truly, I say to you, he who receives whomever I send receives Me; and he who receives Me receives Him who sent me." These words are good to ponder upon as we consider personal evangelism.

1. Some responses of people to a Gospel presentation:
   a. Showing openness:
      1) "I've never heard about this"

   b. Showing Some Knowledge:
      1) "I have a sister who's into this kind of stuff" [of handing out Gospel tracts on the street]
      2) "One time I used to be into this stuff, but I fell away."
      3) "I tried that. It didn't work for me!"

   c. Showing no apparent interest:
      1) "I feel comfortable with what I believe."
      2) "No time!" "Too busy!" Or "In a hurry!"
      3) "Not my cup of tea!"
      4) "Grow up!"
      5) "I already have my own religion!" [from an older French man on the boardwalk of a beach]
      6) "You mind your business, I'll mind mine!"
      7) "I have made a decision not to become a Christian!"
      8) "No!"

2. Some unusual responses for not making a commitment to Christ:
   a. From a Buddhist: "I can't do that because Jesus has too many enemies!"
   b. From a Muslim: "If you have a Muslim mom, you cannot go to a Christian mom!"
   c. From a Muslim: "If I pray this prayer will that make me a Christian?" "Yes." "Then I cannot do that!"
      1) This man was plagued by multiple demons, and often asked Christians to pray for him
      2) I had been trying to explain to him that he needed the Holy Spirit in his heart to protect him from the demons; hence, sharing the Gospel
   d. From a French woman: "There are some sins that I do not want to give up!"

3. Some non-verbal reactions to the Gospel or to a Gospel tract:
   a. Great interest
   b. Casual interest
   c. Looking the other way or ignoring the mention
   d. Looks of hatred
   e. Sometimes violence and cursing

4. Remember:
   Be aware that rejection in the vast majority of cases is not due to the evangelist, but it is due to Jesus Christ (cf. Luke 10:16). Samuel had a similar rejection from the Israelites, 1 Sam. 8:7-8.

[1130]As examples of reactions and responses to the Gospel in the Bible are noted, it is interesting to note that things have not changed too much through the years!

D. The Spiritual Results of a Verbal Witness:

1. General Results:
   a. God and His Salvation Are Made Known:
      1) Luke 10:9-11, The kingdom of God "comes near" to those who hear the Gospel, whether they accept it or reject it.
      2) 2 Cor 2:14, "and manifests through us the sweet aroma of the **knowledge of Him** in every place."
      3) 2 Cor 10:5, "We are destroying speculations and every lofty thing raised up **against a knowledge of God**, and we are taking every thought captive to the obedience of Christ."
   b. God is feared, Psa 76:8 (cf. Jos. 4:24, e.g. Acts 24:25, 26:24-32)
   c. God is glorified, John 15:8, 17:4 (cf. 2 Cor 4:15)
   d. God's blessing will be passed on, Jer 4:2 (cf. Psa 67)

2. Results to the hearers:
   a. God's Word will bear fruit in their heart, Isa 55:10-11
   b. They will have a knowledge of God and will gain a fear of God, Jos. 4:24, 1 Kings 8:43, 60, Psa 22:27, 67:2-3, 145:11-12 (cf. Psa 76:8, James 2:19)
   c. Feigned obedience among those who do not accept, Psa 66:3, 81:15

3. Decisions are made:

   Introduction: I have many corollary notes on this point elsewhere:
      1) *Evangelizology*, an Appendix following Chapter 2, "Hearing to Believe"
      2) *Evangelizology*, Chapter 7, G. Five Categories of New Testament Terms for Evangelism, 5. Result.
      3) In *Charts for a Theology of Evangelism*, "Hearing and Believing Selections in the New Testament."[1131]

   a. Decisions for salvation, John 5:24, Acts 4:4, Rom 10:14, 17 (cf. Acts 16:18):
      1) Psa 51:13, "*Then* I will teach transgressors Thy ways, And sinners will be converted to Thee."
      2) Psa 40:3, "And He put a new song in my mouth, a song of praise to our God; Many will see and fear, And will trust in the LORD"
      3) Luke 15:7, "I tell you that in the same way, there will be *more* joy in heaven over one sinner who repents, than over ninety-nine righteous persons who need no repentance"
      4) John 6:45, "It is written in the prophets, 'And they shall all be taught of God.' Everyone who has heard and learned from the Father, comes to Me."

   b. Hearts are hardened to the Word of God, Isa 6:9-10 (the most quoted OT passage in NT), Jer 6:10 (cf. Acts 17:32)

4. Results to the testifier:
   a. Joyful exuberance, Psa 9:14, 105:2-3, 126:5-6, Isa 55:12
   b. Giving of thanks, 2 Cor 4:15

5. THE RESULTS OF NO VERBAL WITNESS OF GOD'S WORD:
   A. DENIAL OF CHRIST BY BELIEVERS, LUKE 12:9 (CF. MATT 26:70, 72, 74)
   B. IGNORANCE OF GOD'S WAYS, ISAIAH 5:13-14
   C. NO CHANCE FOR SALVATION, ROM 10:14 (CF. ROM 10:17)

[1131]Johnston, *Charts for a Theology of Evangelism*, Chart 39, "Hearing and Believing Selections in the New Testament," 72-75.

Appendix

Lessons from Paul's Chains

"This salutation by my own hand—Paul. Remember my chains. Grace *be* with you. Amen."
Col 4:18 (NKJ)

Introduction:
  The reality of Paul's chains led to strained relationships, Phil 1:16
  Are there lessons in these strained relationships to be learned?
  Did this strain ever lead to friction as to methodology of evangelism?

1. The reality of Paul's afflictions and chains:
  Jesus prophesied that Paul would face many afflictions, Acts 9:15-16
  Paul's ministry included many afflictions, Acts 9:23-24; 13:45, 50-51; 14:5-6, 19-20; 15:2; 16:22-23;
  Paul spoke of his afflictions on numerous occasions, 1 Cor 4:9-13; 2 Cor 6:4
  Paul enumerated his afflictions to the Corinthian church, 2 Cor 11:22-33

2. Introducing the stressed relationships because of Paul's chains:
  Because of Paul's chains, some were ashamed of him, 2 Tim 1:8
  Because of Paul's chains, it appears that some turned away from the faith, 2 Tim 1:15
  Because of Paul's chains, some were commended, 2 Tim 1:16-18; Heb 10:34
  Because of Paul's chains, some preached Christ from envy and strife, Phil 1:15-16

3. In response, Paul explained the beneficial role of affliction or chains in the Christian life:
  God's teaching through affliction, 2 Cor 1:3-7; grace through affliction, 2 Cor 8:1-2; etc.]
  It must not be forgotten that the affliction mentioned by Paul always relates directly to that which came
      from persecution because of the verbal testimony of the Gospel! 2 Tim 1:8-11
      Rather than self-imposed afflictions of poverty, chastity, and abstinence
      Or rather than the trials of life that come to everyone
  Using the Pauline passages on affliction without acknowledging the evangelistic context is doing a
      massive discredit to the context, and leads to much false interpretation and distorted teaching!
      Further, this distortion goes down into the very heart of evangelism, the Great Commission, and
          salvation
      Further, this distortion contradicts the teaching of Jesus in Matt 10 as He sent out His disciples]

4. Did some Christian leaders, hetero-teachers, or false teachers in the Bible teach a chainless evangelism
    methodology, that being without affliction?
  Those who:
      Use carnal wisdom, 2 Cor 1:12
      Peddle the Word, 2 Cor 2:27
      Use weapons of the flesh, by inference from 2 Cor 10:3-5
  In actuality they are:
      Preaching another Gospel, 2 Cor 11:4
  Those who commend themselves (2 Cor 10:12), boasting of another man's work (2 Cor 10:13-16)
      In actuality these who preached such were:
          Some of the most imminent apostles? 2 Cor 11:4-6; cf. Gal 2:6-10
          Some were even false apostles, 2 Cor 11:13-15
      Where not these men boasting of their accomplishments?
      Where they not boasting about their superior methodologies, i.e. wisdom and tact in staying out of
          prison?
      Where these early super-apostles not focusing on their superior lifestyle?
  Segmented evangelism, much like segmented marketing, Gal 2:9
      Contra Great Commission, Matt 28:19-20; Mark 16:15

Contra Paul's going to the Jew first, Rom 1:16-17; Acts 17:2-3
Leading to hypocritical evangelizing, Gal 2:11-16
Servant evangelism, remembering the poor, Gal 2:10
Isn't it interesting that those who practice half-way evangelism accuse those who practice initiative or expectant evangelism of being prejudicial, when in fact they are the ones who are prejudicial?

5. Where these not examples of "false brethren" [ψευδαδέλφοις] as recounted as contributing to all the affliction of the Apostle Paul? See 2 Cor 11:26 (cf. Gal 2:4, secretly brought in).

Conclusion: The great danger of chainless evangelism!
Changes the method of the propagation of salvation
Changes the Great Commission, worldview, and orientation of the Church and the church
Changes the message of salvation, to the point of rendering salvation null and void

CHAPTER 21
Commitment and the Prayer of the Sinner

Introduction:

1. The two main sticky points in evangelism regard the initiating of conversations with strangers and calling for immediate repentance

2. As regards calling for commitment, these notes will seek to show that calling persons to immediate repentance is not only biblically valid, but also biblically necessary in the proclamation of the Gospel (lest we change the another Gospel)

3. Calling for commitment implies two points:
   a. It is evangelism by faith, a holy expectation that God's Word to be living and active (Heb 4:12) and open the hearts of hearers (Acts 16:14)
   b. It is evangelism in hope, hope for a harvest, as it is written, "The plowman ought to plow in hope," 1 Cor 9:10

4. Jesus gives the example of calling for commitment in John:

   John 4:9-10:

   > "Then the woman of Samaria said to Him, 'How is it that You, being a Jew, ask a drink from me, a Samaritan woman?' For Jews have no dealings with Samaritans"
   > "Jesus answered and said to her, 'If you knew the gift of God, and who it is who says to you, "Give Me a drink," **you would have asked Him**, and He would have given you living water'"

   Interestingly, early in His conversation with the woman, Jesus stated that the gift of eternal life by the Holy Spirit was just a request away!

   John 9:35-38, note the two different uses of the word "believe," both as a call to commitment and as an affirmation of commitment:

   > "Jesus heard that they had put him out, and finding him, He said,
   >   Q   'Do you **believe** in the Son of Man?'
   > "He answered,
   > R_X1 'Who is He, Lord, that I may **believe** in Him?'
   > "Jesus said to him,
   >   S   'You have both seen Him, and He is the one who is talking with you.'
   > "And he said,
   > R_X2 'Lord, I **believe**.'
   > "And he worshiped Him."

5. Furthermore, God affirms verbal affirmations of Him and to Him throughout His Word:
   Deut 6:21, "Then you shall say* to your son, 'We were slaves to Pharaoh in Egypt; and the LORD brought us from Egypt with a mighty hand...'"
       *2nd person, singular.
   Deut 26:13, "And you shall say* before the LORD your God, 'I have removed the sacred *portion* from *my* house, and also have given it to the Levite and the alien, the orphan and the widow, according to all Thy commandments which Thou hast commanded me; I have not transgressed or forgotten any of Thy commandments'"
       *2nd person, singular.
   2 Sam 22:4 "I call upon the LORD, who is worthy to be praised; And I am saved from my enemies"
   1 Chron 16:8, "Oh give thanks to the LORD, call upon His name; Make known His deeds among the peoples" (cf. Psa 18:3; 105:1)
   Psa 4:3, "But know that the LORD has set apart the godly man for Himself; The LORD hears when I call to Him"
   Psa 28:1, "To Thee, O LORD, I call; My rock, do not be deaf to me, Lest, if Thou be silent to me, I become like those who go down to the pit"
   Psa 55:16, "As for me, I shall call upon God, And the LORD will save me"
   Psa 116:13, "I shall lift up the cup of salvation, And call upon the name of the LORD"
   Psa 116:17, "To Thee I shall offer a sacrifice of thanksgiving, And call upon the name of the LORD"

Psa 145:18, "The LORD is near to all who call upon Him, To all who call upon Him in truth"

Prov 2:3 (ESV), "yes, if you call* out for insight and raise your voice for understanding"

*2nd person, singular.

Isa 12:4, "And in that day you will say, 'Give thanks to the LORD, call on His name. Make known His deeds among the peoples; Make *them* remember that His name is exalted'"

Isa 44:5, "This one will say, 'I am the LORD'S'; And that one will call on the name of Jacob; And another will write *on* his hand, 'Belonging to the LORD,' And will name Israel's name with honor"

Isa 55:6, "Seek the LORD while He may be found; Call upon Him while He is near"

Mal 1:9, "But now will you not entreat God's favor, that He may be gracious to us? With such an offering on your part, will He receive any of you kindly?" says the LORD of hosts"

Cf. Mal 1:9 (NEG), "Priez Dieu maintenant, pour qu'il ait pitié de nous! C'est de vous que cela vient: Vous recevra-t-il favorablement ? Dit l'Éternel des armées" (cf. Acts 8:22)

[See also the many commands in the OT and NT to speak and proclaim, as listed in *Evangelizology*, Chap 2 and Chap 10]

A. The Commitment to Christ Is at the Heart of Expectant Evangelism:

Introduction:

J. Hudson Taylor, famous missionary to China in the 19th century, expected that there would always be one or two commitments to Jesus Christ the first time a Chinese village had ever been exposed to the Gospel:

> "The gospel itself is the power of God unto salvation to everyone that believeth. Now, there are different ways of preaching the gospel. There is the plan of preaching the gospel and looking forward to the gradual enlightenment of the people, to their being saved as it were by a process of gradual instruction and preaching. And there is another method of preaching the gospel; *believing it to be the power of God unto salvation;* preaching it in the *expectation* that He who first brought light out of darkness can and will at once and instantaneously take the darkest heathen heart and create light within. That is the method that is successful. It has been my privilege to know many Christians – I am speaking within bounds when I say a hundred – who have accepted Jesus Christ as their Saviour the first time they ever heard of Him. The gospel itself is the power of God unto salvation" [1132]

This expectant evangelism led to the conversion of many Chinese to Christ, as well as encouraging a great thrust of missionaries into this land (cf. those who accepted Christ in Athens "joined him," Acts 17:34)

A concrete call for commitment is essential to the bold proclamation of the Gospel. "Simply informing our neighbor is not enough, *he has to make a choice.* The Bible spells this out for us very clearly."[1133] In fact, there is an urge for a pluralistic approach allowing for non-commitment. This merely leads to an uncommitted life. Without a call to commitment, the Gospel message is not complete.

Introductory Verses—as reference point (2 Cor. 5:20-6:2).

1. Preaching unto commitment was a part of Luke's Great Commission: "and that repentance for forgiveness of sins would be proclaimed in His name," Luke 24:47

2. Without commitment to Christ there is no salvation:
   a. It is necessary to "call upon the name of the Lord," Rom 10:13
      1) Is not this "calling" verbally "confessing" followed by or accompanied by "believing" (Rom 10:9)?
      2) Is not this "calling" also "believing" followed by or accompanied by verbally "confessing" (Rom 10:10)?
   b. The call to follow Christ necessarily includes a complete abandonment of oneself to Christ, Matt 10:38-39

[1132]J. Hudson Taylor, "The Source of Power," *Ecumenical Missionary Conference, New York, 1900* (New York, American Tract Society, 1900): 1:91. emphasis mine.

[1133]Johan Lukasse, *Churches with Roots: Planting Churches in Post-Christian Europe* (Bromley: STL, 1990), 75.

3.   There is a verbal element to a commitment to Christ:

a.   Notice the conditional related to a verbal commitment, "if you confess with your mouth," Rom 10:9; "with the mouth he confesses," Rom 10:10

1)   Consider also what type of confession is Paul alluding to in this text?

a)   Is the singular "if you confess" meant to have plural corporate-worship emphasis?
(1)   Is it therefore analogous to the recitation of a creed, which is summarized as "Jesus is Lord" (as exemplified in the NASB translation, as compared to the NKJ)?
(2)   Is it perhaps adhering to a type of proto-confession that "Jesus is Lord" (1 Cor 12:3)?

b)   Is it individually confessing a Person and His lordship over one's life?

In which case, is Paul's statement a return to the concept found at the end of Romans 7? Rom 7:24-25a, "Wretched man that I am! Who will set me free from the body of this death? Thanks be to God through Jesus Christ our Lord!"

Consider, unfortunately, that the simple action of receiving salvation by giving thanks as an expression of a heart attitude has been anathematized by Rome in the Council of Trent.[1134]

c)   Is this confession (1) to God in prayer; (2) to a pastor, priest, or church body; (3) is this confessing before an adulterous and sinful generation (Mark 8:38); (4) or all of the above?

d)   Notice how these various interpretations appear to be emphasized by different translations of the same Greek words!

Concerning the Translation of Rom 10:9

Byzantine Greek*	English Geneva (1560); cf. KJV, NKJ	Darby (1884); cf. ERV; ASV; NAS	RSV (1952); cf. NJB[*]; NAB[*]; NLT; NET; ESV	NIV (1984); cf. CSB
[Two nouns: no verb, conjunction, or preposition]	**Profession**	**Lordship**	**Confession**	**Creedal Confession**
κύριον Ἰησοῦν	the Lord Jesus	Jesus as Lord	that Jesus is Lord	"Jesus is Lord"
ὅτι ἐὰν ὁμολογήσῃς ἐν τῷ στόματί σου κύριον Ἰησοῦν, καὶ πιστεύσῃς ἐν τῇ καρδίᾳ σου ὅτι ὁ θεὸς αὐτὸν ἤγειρεν ἐκ νεκρῶν, σωθήσῃ·	For if thou shalt confesse with thy mouth the Lord Iesus, and shalt beleue in thine heart, that God raised him vp from the dead, thou shalt be saued	that if thou shalt confess with thy mouth Jesus as Lord, and shalt believe in thine heart that God has raised him from among the dead, thou shalt be saved	because, if you confess with your lips that Jesus is Lord and believe in your heart that God raised him from the dead, you will be saved	That if you confess with your mouth, "Jesus is Lord," and believe in your heart that God raised him from the dead, you will be saved

*There appears to be no variant between the Greek Orthodox Text, Byzantine Textform, and the Nestle-Aland 27th edition in this phrase.

b.   This confession parallels the teaching of Jesus, Matt 10:32; Luke 12:8
c.   This verbal confession follows the order of the verbs in Deut 30:14
d.   The primacy of the verbal also follows the order in sin, Psa 36:2; Rom 3:13-18
e.   The primacy of the verbal is typified in God who hears the cry of His people, Psa 106:44

[1134]"But though it is necessary to believe that sins neither are remitted nor ever have been remitted except gratuitously by divine mercy for Christ's sake, yet it must not be said that sins are forgiven or have been forgiven to anyone who boasts of his confidence and certainty of the remission of his sins, resting on that alone, though among heretics and schismatics this vain and ungodly confidence may be and in our troubled times indeed is found and preached with untiring fury against the Catholic Church" (Council of Trent, Decrees Concerning Justification, Chapter ix, Against the Vain Confidence of the Heretics"; available at: http://www.forerunner.com/chalcedon/ X0020_15._Council_of_Trent.html; accessed: 8 Jan 2005; Internet).

"Canon 12. If anyone says that justifying faith is nothing else than confidence in divine mercy, which remits sins for Christ's sake, or that it is this confidence alone that justifies us, let him be anathema" (ibid., "Canons Concerning Justification").

4. Some incomplete aspects of commitment:

    a. Commitment as mere cognitive knowledge of the Trinity and the role of God and that of the Son:
        1) John 17:3, "This is eternal life, that they may know You, the only true God, and Jesus Christ whom You have sent"
        2) John 17:30, "by this we believe that You came from God"
        3) John 5:24, "Truly, truly, I say to you, he who hears My word, and believes Him who sent Me, has eternal life, and does not come into judgment, but has passed out of death into life"

    b. Commitment as mere intellectual or verbal assent as regards the deity of Christ, 1 John 2:23, "the one who confesses the Son has the Father also"

    c. Commitment as mere verbal assent, 1 Cor 12:3, "Therefore I make known to you that no one speaking by the Spirit of God says, 'Jesus is accursed'; and no one can say, 'Jesus is Lord,' except by the Holy Spirit"

    d. Thoughts:
        1) Rather the above are examples of the **results of** saving faith, rather than the **means of** or **instruments of** saving faith
        2) True commitment, however, includes repentance for the forgiveness of sins (Luke 24:47; Acts 5:31, etc.), as well as faith in Jesus Christ (Acts 20:21).
        3) One must remember:
            a) Matt 7:21-23, 'Not everyone who says to Me, 'Lord, Lord,' shall enter the kingdom of heaven, but he who does the will of My Father in heaven. Many will say to Me in that day, 'Lord, Lord, have we not prophesied in Your name, cast out demons in Your name, and done many wonders in Your name?' And then I will declare to them, 'I never knew you; depart from Me, you who practice lawlessness!'"
            b) James 2:19, "You believe that God is one. You do well; the demons also believe, and shudder"

5. The urgent nature of a call to commitment:

    a. A call to commitment allows the testifier to share to the point of "shaking the dust off his feet" (i.e. acceptance or rejection), see Matt 10:14-15, Mark 6:10-11, Luke 9:5; 10:10-11; Acts 13:49-52; 18:5-6
        See the Appendix after Chapter 19, "When do you shake the dust off your feet?"

    b. A call to commitment to Christ gives the opportunity for acceptance or rejection of the Gospel

    c. A call to commitment parallels the biblical importance of "today", Heb 3:7-8, "Today if you hear His voice, harden not your heart" (cf. 2 Cor 6:2; Heb 3:13, 15; 4:7)

    d. "But God said to him, 'You fool! This *very* night your soul is required of you; and *now* who will own what you have prepared?'" Luke 12:20

    e. A call to commitment to Christ allows future follow-up in the Gospel

    f. A call to public commitment to Christ allows for public profession of Christ, Luke 12:8-9

6. Regarding the "Prayer of the Sinner" or the "Sinner's Prayer":

    a. Is there some kind of a trophy to be given to the evangelists who brings someone to the point of decision, without explaining to them how to receive Christ through prayer?

    b. Does not antagonism to the sinner's prayer come primarily from churches who practice infant baptism, and who do often disbelieve in individual conversion—of the necessity of each individual by his own volition to decide for [or against] Christ?

    c. Likewise, is it not true that the vast majority of those who are quite negative toward salvation being tendered through a "sinner's prayer" simultaneously and paradoxically affirm either that:

        (1) The verbal **prayer** over the baby at infant baptism somehow brings the unknowing child into the covenant family of God, brings the new birth, provides the washing of regeneration, cleanses them from original sin, etc. (depending on the specific church's doctrine): e.g. Anglican[1135] and Presbyterian[1136]; or

---

[1135]"Baptisme is not only a signe of profession, and marke of difference, whereby Christian men are discerned from other that be not christened: but is also a signe of regeneration or newe byrth, whereby as by an instrument, they that receaue baptisme rightly, are grafted into the Church: the promises of the forgeuenesse of sinne,

(2) The [physical] **water** poured over the baby's head as a sign and symbol given to the church has the spiritual power to accomplish these same ends

(3) That a simple **prayer** over the bread and the cup transform these simple elements:

    (a) Into the very body and blood of Christ (although it is admitted that the *accidens* never change), or

    (b) Into some consubstantial presence of Christ in the elements (consider the impact of the outside locus)

(4) Or that the verbal response of Mary to the angel Gabriel is an example to be followed?

        Luke 1:38, "And Mary said, 'Behold, the bondslave of the Lord; be it done to me according to your word.' And the angel departed from her"

    (a) Let's look at this response of Mary as a "sinner's prayer," that is, a verbal declaration in agreement to divinely revealed truth:

        [1] Mary was visited by an angel, definitely she was to receive truth from God

        [2] The text of Scripture uses the verb evangelize (εὐαγγελίζω) for Gabriel's announcement of the birth of John to Zacharias in Luke 1:19; therefore, Gabriel's announcement to Mary could also be considered true evangelizing by virtue of this earlier parallel text

        [3] In the case of Gabriel's announcement, Mary needed to do nothing, everything was acted upon her by the Holy Spirit; all that was needed from her was a repectful subservience

        [4] in fact, it may even be said that her verbal response was not prescriptive, but descriptive; so that future generations would know how she responded; therefore, no verbal response to the Gospel is necessary (as in a sinner's prayer), but merely the baby's passive reception of the waters of Holy Baptism

    (b) Some concerns about using Mary's response as the prototype for the reception of the Gospel:

        [1] in this narrative text, Luke 1:38 does not appear prescriptive, but rather descriptive of what actually happened

        [2] That Mary was a godly young lady and a devout follower of the Old Covenant, there is no doubt; nevertheless, "by the works of the [Old Testament] Law, no flesh will be justified in his sight" (Rom 3:20; Gal 2:16; cf. Rom 3:28; Gal 3:2, 5); Paul went so far as to say, "For as many as are of the works of the Law are under a curse" (Gal 3:10)

        [3] Based on the fact that Mary was favored among women (Luke 1:28), it appears that this event and its unfolding were unique in the history of mankind, and not meant to be repeated nor prescriptive

        [4] The angel Gabriel never spoke the Luke 24:46-47 or the 1 Cor 15:1-8 gospel to Mary, calling on her to repent of her sins and believe in Christ, which gospel is the commanded "proclamation" of the church; thus how can she be said to be responding of a gospel, if it was never proclaimed to her?

        [5] Likewise, in Luke 1:47, Mary acknowledged that God was indeed her Savior, proving that she, in fact, did need a Savior

---

and of our adoption to be the sonnes of God, by the holy ghost, are visibly signed and sealed: fayth is confyrmed: and grace increased by vertue of prayer vnto God.

    "The baptisme of young children, is in any wyse to be retayned in the Churche, as most agreable with the institution of Christe" (Article XXVII, "Thirty-Nine Articles of the Church of England" [Matthew Parker, 1572]; available at: http://www.episcopalian.org/efac/1553-1572.htm; accessed: 21 Oct 2004; Internet).

    [1136]"94. What is baptism? A. Baptism is a sacrament, wherein the washing with water in the name of the Father, and of the Son, and of the Holy Ghost, doth signify and seal our ingrafting into Christ, and partaking of the benefits of the covenant of grace, and our engagement to be the Lord's. 95. To whom is baptism to be administered? A. Baptism is not to be administered to any that are out of the visible church, till they profess their faith in Christ, and obedience to him; but the infants of such as are members of the visible church are to be baptized" ("Westminster Shorter Catechism; available at: http://www.shortercatechism.com/resources/wscformats/BPC_wsc.doc; accessed: 1 Dec 2005; Internet).

[6] This event, when viewed from the position of the *sensus plenior* of Scripture, does not match with any other examples of the positive reception of the gospel in Luke-Acts, nor elsewhere (e.g. Acts 9:3-6; 13:12; 16:14; 30-31; 17:2-4; 28:23-24).

(c) Considering the unfortunate results of isogesis on this text as prescriptive for all who are to come to the Gospel:

[1] This statement of Mary (Luke 1:38) becomes a type of a "sinner's prayer" for those of the Roman Catholic persuasion

[2] This statement of Mary becomes the source for her veneration and the reason for seeking to address prayers to her, in order to emulate the humble relinquishment of her will to that of the divine plan for her life; if taken too far, this example can be used to promote an absurd unthinking fatalism, in which one acts "just as an old man's stick which serves him who holds it in his hand"[1137]

[3] This statement of Mary, as an example of her humble subservience to the divine will, appears to affirm the Benedictine "Vow of Obedience"—which is one of the three Benedictine vows on which "Western" [Roman Catholic] monasticism was founded

[4] This statement of Mary has become foundational for an extreme obedience within Roman Catholicism, such as the Jesuits[1138] and Cardinal Lavigerie, who founded the White Fathers;[1139] this level of obedience is never disaffirmed by the popes, but rather, those who display and encourage such obedience are the founders of orders after they affirm such obedience.

[1137]"Let us with the utmost pains strain every nerve of our strength to exhibit this virtue of obedience, firstly to the Highest Pontiff, then to the Superiors of the Society; so that in all things, to which obedience can be extended with charity, we may be most ready to obey his voice, just as if it had been issued from Jesus Christ our Lord..., leaving nay work, even a letter, that we have begun and have not yet finished; by directing to this goal all our strength and intention in the Lord, that holy obedience may be made perfect in us in every respect, in performance, in will, in intellect; by submitting to whatever may be enjoined on us with readiness, with spiritual joy and perseverance; by persuading ourselves that all things [commanded] are just; by rejecting with a kind of blind obedience all opposing opinion or judgment of our own; and that in all things which are ordained by the Superior where it cannot be clearly held [*definiri*] that any kind of sin intervenes. And let each one persuade himself that they that live under obedience ought to allow themselves to be borne and ruled by divine providence working through their Superiors exactly as if they were a corpse which suffers itself to be borne and handled in any way whatsoever; or just as an old man's stick which serves him who holds it in his hand wherever and for whatever purpose he wish use it...." ("Obedience of the Jesuits," in Henry Bettenson, *Documents of the Christian Church* [London: Oxford University Press, 1963], 261).

[1138]"Thirteenth Rule. To be right in everything, we ought always to hold that the white which I see, is black, if the Hierarchical Church so decides it, believing that between Christ our Lord, the Bridegroom, and the Church, His Bride, there is the same Spirit which governs and directs us for the salvation of our souls. Because by the same Spirit and our Lord Who gave the ten Commandments, our holy Mother the Church is directed and governed" ("Rules for Thinking in the Church," from St. Ignatius Loyola, *The Spiritual Exercises of St. Ignatius,* translated by Anthony Mottola, S.J., imprimatur, Cardinal Spellman [Garden City, NY: Image Books, Doubleday, 1964], 140-41).

[1139]"This is my spiritual testament.

"I begin it by declaring, in the presence of eternity that will open itself before me, that I want to die with the same convictions in which I have always lived, that being obedience and devotion without limits to the Holy Apostolic Seat and to our Holy Father the Pope, Vicar of Jesus Christ on the earth. I have always believed, and I believe all that they teach and in the sense that they teach it. I have always believed, and I believe that outside of the Pope or against the Pope, there can be in the Church nothing but trouble, confusion, error, and eternal loss. He alone was created as the foundation of unity and as a consequence [of that] of life, and all that regards things of salvation.

"I have the signal honor of remaining very close to the Holy Apostloc Seat by my character of priest, bishop, and by my title of cardinal of the Holy Roman Church. Without a doubt these honors which are strongly above my misery and my weakness are done to confound me, in this moment that I ponder my presence before the tribunal of God, but I want to see in it even greater gratitude and faithfulness to the Seat of Peter and before our Holy Father the Pope, who has lavished me with the marks of his confidence and of his goodness.

"I have served him with my best, all that I was able. Not being able to do anything now, I pray that the Lord will accept the sacrifice that I have offered Him in my life and in my sufferings that will accompany my death, for the prolongation of the precious days of Leo XIII [his contemporary Pope] and in the triumph of his magnanimous designs" ("Spiritual Testament," in Cardinal Lavigerie [1825-1892], *Ecrits d'Afrique* [Paris: Bernard Grasset, 1966], 235-36; translation mine).

[5] Further, is not this example of humble subservience to the divine decree applied to all of Rome's faithful, as they must humbly accept the *ex cathedra* decrees of the sitting Pope as infallible?[1140]

And yet are not the prayer of the contrite heart in repentance and faith considered of no effect? What of the Pharisee and the publican?

> Luke 18:13-14, "And the tax collector, standing afar off, would not so much as raise *his* eyes to heaven, but beat his breast, saying, 'God, be merciful to me a sinner!' [14] "I tell you, this man went down to his house justified *rather* than the other; for everyone who exalts himself will be humbled, and he who humbles himself will be exalted."

d. Is not salvation through the prayer of faith or the "Prayer of the Sinner" the reason that those against whom was aimed the Second Council of Orange (A.D. 529) were said to be guilty of the error of Pelagius;[1141] which condemnation also Cramner[1142] repeated against the Anabaptists?

e. If the "prayer of a sinner" is not the response of the contrite heart to the Gospel message, than what is?

7. Examples of calling for commitment—note how many times questions are used:

a. Some examples from the Old Testament:
   1) "How long will you hesitate between two opinions?" 1 Kings 18:21
   2) "Trust in the Lord," is found in the imperative 5 times in the Book of Psalms, three of which are in Psalm 115:9-11:

      > "O Israel, trust in the LORD; He is their help and their shield.
      > "O house of Aaron, trust in the LORD; He is their help and their shield.
      > "You who fear the LORD, trust in the LORD; He is their help and their shield.

   3) "Behold, I set before you the way of life and the way of death." Jer 21:8
   4) "Therefore say to the house of Israel, 'Repent, turn away from your idols, and turn your faces away from your abominations'" Ezek 14:6
   5) "Therefore, repent and live." Ezek 18:32 (see context of vv. 30-32)
   6) "Turn back, turn back from your evil ways! Why then will you die , O house of Israel?" Ezek 33:11

b. New Testament examples:
   1) Matt 11:28-30, "Come to Me, all who are weary and heavy-laden, and I will give you rest. Take My yoke upon you, and learn from Me, for I am gentle and humble in heart; and you shall find rest for your souls. For My yoke is easy, and My load is light"
   2) "But who do you say that I am?" Matt 16:15
   3) "You do not want to go away also, do you?" John 6:67
   4) "Do you believe in the Son of Man?" John 9:35
   5) "Jesus said to her, 'I am the resurrection and the life; he who believes in Me shall live even if he dies, and everyone who lives and believes in Me shall never die. Do you believe this?'" John 11:25-26
   6) "Now why do you delay? Get up and be baptized, and wash away your sins, calling on His name," Acts 22:16

[1140]"This is why, binding ourselves faithfully to the traditions received since the origin of the Christian faith for the glory of God our Savior, for the exaltation of the Catholic religion and for the salvation of the Christian peoples, with the approbation of the Holy Council, we teach that it is a dogma revealed by God:

"when the Roman Pontiff speaks *ex cathedra*, meaning when, filling his calling as pastor and doctor of all Christians, he defines, in virtue of his supreme apostolic authority, that a doctrine in the matter of faith or morals must be held by the entire Church, he enjoys, by virtue of the divine assistance that has been promised to him in the person of Holy Peter, of this infallibility which the Redeemer desired be bestowed upon His Church when she defines doctrine on faith or morals; by consequence, these definitions of the Roman Pontiff are irreformable in themselves and not subject to the consensus of the Church.

"*[Canon]* If anyone, a thing which displeases God, had the presumption to contradict our definition: may he be anathema [accursed]" (*Symboles et Définitions de la Foi Catholique*, edited by Heinrich Denzinger, Peter Hünermann, and Joseph Hoffman [Paris: Cerf, 2005], §3074-3075; translation mine).

[1141]See the Appendix following Chapter 10.

[1142]"Originall sinne standeth not in the folowing of Adam, as the Pellagianes doe vainelie talke, whiche also the Anabaptistes doe now a daies renue, but it is the fault, and corruption of the nature of euery manne…" (Article VII, "Forty-Two Articles of the Church of England" [Thomas Cramner, 1553]; available at: http://www.episcopalian.org/efac/1553-1572.htm; accessed: 21 Oct 2004; Internet).

7) Paul using Habakkuk 1:5 in Acts 13:40-41, "Take heed therefore, so that the thing spoken of in the Prophets may not come upon *you*: 'Behold, you scoffers, and marvel, and perish; For I am accomplishing a work in your days, A work which you will never believe, though someone should describe it to you.'"

8) Paul using Isaiah 6:9-10 in Acts 28:25-28, "And when they did not agree with one another, they *began* leaving after Paul had spoken one *parting* word, 'The Holy Spirit rightly spoke through Isaiah the prophet to your fathers, saying,

> "Go to this people and say, 'You will keep on hearing, but will not understand; And you will keep on seeing, but will not perceive; For the heart of this people has become dull, And with their ears they scarcely hear, And they have closed their eyes; Lest they should see with their eyes, And hear with their ears, And understand with their heart and return, And I should heal them.'"

Let it be known to you therefore, that this salvation of God has been sent to the Gentiles; they will also listen.'"

9) "King Agrippa, do you believe the Prophets? I know that you do." Acts 26:27

8. Various calls to commitment (see the wide variety of biblical commitment terminology in Chapter 8, "Evangelism and Conversion"):

a. The commitment to accept Jesus for who He is, John 4:26, 29, 39-42, Acts 8:35-38
For example: "Would you like to accept Jesus Christ as your personal Savior?"

b. The commitment to repent, Luke 24:47; Acts 2:38; 3:19; 20:20-21

c. The commitment to believe, Acts 16:30-31

d. The commitment to accept the need for the new birth, John 3:3, 7

e. The commitment to call on the name of the Lord, Rom 10:13
For example: "Would you like to call on the name of the Lord to be saved right now?"
Or else: "Won't you call on the name of the Lord to be saved?"
Or even: "What's keeping you from calling on the name of the Lord to be saved?"

f. There is a level of intensity and urgency that grows as we consider the enormity of the weight of (1) man's sin; (2) that Christ is the only way; (3) the shortness of time; and (4) the absolute need to confess Christ verbally in space and time!

Types of Commitment

---

1) The commitment to seek God either:
   a) In general (the seeker's prayer)
   b) In the Bible
2) The commitment to agree with God that they are a sinner, which can lead to true repentance
3) The commitment to receive, accept, and believe in Christ
4) The commitment to follow Christ in New Testament baptism
5) A recommitment to God either:
   a) To get into the fellowship of the church
   b) To give one's life completely to God's will
   c) To read the Bible
   d) To turn from a specific sin

---

9. Principles in calling for commitment:

a. Follow the thrust of your Gospel presentation, focused to the spiritual need of the individual

b. Be aware of the different types of commitments possible:

1) The model invitation—2 Cor. 5:20-6:2
   a) 5:20 and 6:1, the plea for an invitation
   b) 6:2, use a Scripture, and from that Scripture
      (1) Making use of Scripture follows the example of Paul in Acts 13:40-41 and 28:25-28

        c) 6:2, build an invitation.

    2) The commitment to seek God either:
        a) In general (see the Seeker's Prayer below)
        b) In the Bible:
            (1) Through reading the Gospel of John every day for 30 days (Bill Bright's 30-day challenge to the honest atheist or agnostic)
            (2) Through reading the Bible in general:
                (a) Luther recommended reading the Gospel of John, the Book of Acts, and Romans, as well as all the epistles of Paul and those of Peter, in the 1522 preface to his New Testament
                (b) Hudson Taylor distributed Gospels of Luke

    3) The commitment to turn over one's life to Christ:
        a) The commitment to repent of sin
            (1) See possible Sinner's Prayers below
        b) Note the prayer of faith as found variously in many Gospel tracts

    4) A recommitment to God either:
        a) To get into the fellowship of the church
        b) To give one's life completely to God's will
        c) To read the Bible
        d) To turn from a specific sin

  c. John 9:35-39 and Stephen Olford on commitment:[1143]

    Invitation #1 [from general]: John 9:35, "Jesus heard that they had put him out, and finding him, He said, 'Do you believe in the Son of Man?'"

    Response #1a, John 9:36, "Who is He, Lord…?"
      Olford #1—Satisfy the mind: "I **must** be saved"
        a) Mental assent to the need for repentance for the forgiveness of sin
        b) Mental assent to the value of the blood of Jesus in cleansing from sin

    Response #1b, John 9:36, "…that I may believe in Him?"
      Olford #2—Stir the heart: "I **can** be saved" [John 9:36]
        a) Personal recognition to the need for repentance and confession

    Invitation #2 [to particular]: John 9:37, "Jesus said to him, 'You have both seen Him, and He is the one who is talking with you.'"

    Response #2, John 9:38, "Lord, I believe"
      Olford #3—Strengthen the will: "I **will** be saved" [John 9:38]
        a) Personal recognition that "now is the acceptable time."

  d. Restraint in calling for a commitment may lead to a hardness of heart, where "the last state of that man becomes worse than the first," Matt 12:45.

10. Results of a concrete commitment:
  a. Public commitment leads to public profession, Matt 3:6-8
  b. Public commitment leads to public confession, Luke 12:8-9 (cf. Mark 8:38)
  c. Public commitment brings public accountability, Mark 14:66-71

11. Conclusion: Charles Finney gave some good advice concerning commitment:

    "It is generally *best to be short,* and not to spin out what we have to say. Get the attention as soon as you can to the very point; say a few things and press them home, and bring the matter to an issue. If possible, get them to repent and give themselves to Christ at the time. This is the proper issue. Carefully avoid making an impression that you do not wish them to repent *now.*"

[1143]Stephen Olford, *The Secret of Soul-Winning* (Chicago: Moody Press, 1963), 65-66.

"Wherever you have reason to believe that a person within your reach is awakened, do not sleep till you have poured in the light upon his mind, and have tried to bring him to *immediate repentance.* Then is the time to press the subject with effect." [1144]

B. Prayer ending the Sharing Situation:

Introduction:

The commitment is made more concrete through prayer. If the person is not willing to pray, often the person who is sharing can pray for the person. Prayer can be a capstone to a good sharing opportunity, and it can also open the door to a future conversation. Many people appreciate an honest and transparent prayer for them and their salvation.

1. Principles in praying with someone:

    a. If they are open, ask him/her if he/she wants to pray to make a commitment to Jesus Christ.
       1) If yes:
          a) Sometimes a written prayer can be helpful, but if they can pray on their own that is also good. Have them read the written prayer aloud first, then if they agree with it, have them read it as a prayer to God. If there is no written prayer, they may repeat a prayer after the person sharing with them.
          b) Ask the person if you can pray for them. Then, pray to reaffirm the commitment made.
       2) If no, ask if you can pray for this person yourself. Then pray directly for this person and for their spiritual need.

    b. If there has been no openness to the Gospel, it may not be good to pray. Usually in this case there will be no interest in prayer.

    c. If a specific need has been mentioned, such as a sick person or a broken relationship, ask if it would be possible to pray for this need. In this situation wisdom is needed, and boldness is also needed to pray for the spiritual needs of the third party.

[1144]Finney, 68-69. Points 12 and 13 of his 22 points on evangelism.

Considering stages in the prayer of the sinner:
Old Testament and New Testament

Stages	Deut 21:1-6	Lev 4:27-31	Acts 16:11-15	Acts 16:25-31
Discovery	[1] If a slain person is found lying in the open country in the land which the LORD your God gives you to possess, *and* it is not known who has struck him	[27] 'Now if anyone of the common people sins unintentionally in doing any of the things which the Lord has commanded not to be done, and becomes guilty, [28] if his sin which he has committed is made known to him,	[11] So putting out to sea from Troas, we ran a straight course to Samothrace, and on the day following to Neapolis; [12] and from there to Philippi, which is a leading city of the district of Macedonia, a *Roman* colony; and we were staying in this city for some days. [13] And on the Sabbath day we went outside the gate to a riverside, where we were supposing that there would be a place of prayer; and we sat down and began speaking to the women who had assembled. [14] A woman named Lydia, from the city of Thyatira, a seller of purple fabrics, a worshiper of God, was listening; and the Lord opened her heart to respond to the things spoken by Paul.	[25] But about midnight Paul and Silas were praying and singing hymns of praise to God, and the prisoners were listening to them; [26] and suddenly there came a great earthquake, so that the foundations of the prison house were shaken; and immediately all the doors were opened and everyone's chains were unfastened. [27] When the jailer awoke and saw the prison doors opened, he drew his sword and was about to kill himself, supposing that the prisoners had escaped. [28] But Paul cried out with a loud voice, saying, "Do not harm yourself, for we are all here!" [29] And he called for lights and rushed in, and trembling with fear he fell down before Paul and Silas, [30] and after he brought them out, he said, "Sirs, what must I do to be saved?"
Preparation	[2] then your elders and your judges shall go out and measure *the distance* to the cities which are around the slain one. [3] It shall be that the city which is nearest to the slain man, that is, the elders of that city, shall take a heifer of the herd, which has not been worked and which has not pulled in a yoke; [4] and the elders of that city shall bring the heifer down to a valley with running water, which has not been plowed or sown, and shall break the heifer's neck there in the valley.	then he shall bring for his offering a goat, a female without defect, for his sin which he has committed.	[accomplished in the death of Christ on the cross, 1 Pet 3:18]	[accomplished in the death of Christ on the cross, 1 Pet 3:18]
Mediation	[5] Then the priests, the sons of Levi, shall come near, for the LORD your God has chosen them to serve Him and to bless in the name of the LORD; and every dispute and every assault shall be settled by them.	[29] He shall lay his hand on the head of the sin offering and slay the sin offering at the place of the burnt offering. [30] The priest shall take some of its blood with his finger and put it on the horns of the altar of burnt offering; and all *the rest of* its blood he shall pour out at the base of the altar. [31] Then he shall remove all its fat, just as the fat was removed from the sacrifice of peace offerings; and the priest shall offer it up in smoke on	[accomplished through Christ, 1 Pet 2:24]	[accomplished through Christ, 1 Pet 2:24]

		the altar for a soothing aroma to the Lord. Thus the priest shall make atonement for him,		
Prayer	6 All the elders of that city which is nearest to the slain man shall wash their hands over the heifer whose neck was broken in the valley; 7 and they shall answer and say, 'Our hands did not shed this blood, nor did our eyes see *it*. 8 Forgive Your people Israel whom You have redeemed, O LORD, and do not place the guilt of innocent blood in the midst of Your people Israel.'	n/a	n/a	31 They said, "Believe in the Lord Jesus, and you will be saved, you and your household."
Statement of Forgiveness	And the bloodguiltiness shall be forgiven them. 9 So you shall remove the guilt of innocent blood from your midst, when you do what is right in the eyes of the LORD.	and he will be forgiven.	["The Spirit Himself testifies with our spirit that we are children of God," Rom 8:16]	["The Spirit Himself testifies with our spirit that we are children of God," Rom 8:16]
Follow-Up	n/a	n/a	15 And when she and her household had been baptized, she urged us, saying, "If you have judged me to be faithful to the Lord, come into my house and stay." And she prevailed upon us.	32 And they spoke the word of the Lord to him together with all who were in his house. 33 And he took them that *very* hour of the night and washed their wounds, and immediately he was baptized, he and all his *household*. 34 And he brought them into his house and set food before them, and rejoiced greatly, having believed in God with his whole household.

2. Different examples of possible prayer:

   a. The Seeker's Prayer: "Lord, if You are really there, I want to know You."
     1) Admonition to seek the Lord, Isaiah 55:6-7
     2) "I do believe; help my unbelief," Mark 9:24

   b. OT Sample Prayers of Sinners:
     1) Josh 2:13, "and spare [take alive] my father and my mother and my brothers and my sisters, with all who belong to them, and deliver our lives [souls] from death" (cf. Psa 33:19)
     2) Num 21:7, "Therefore the people came to Moses, and said, 'We have sinned, for we have spoken against the LORD and against you; pray to the LORD that He take away the serpents from us.' So Moses prayed for the people"
       Cf. This example became the basis for Jesus sharing truths about salvation with Nicodemus in John 3:14-16
     3) 1 Kings 8:46-50, "When they sin against You (for there is no man who does not sin) and … if they take thought in the land where they have been taken captive, and repent and make supplication to You in the land of those who have taken them captive, saying, '**We have sinned** [*chata*, ἁμάρτάνω] **and have committed iniquity** [*avah*, ἀνομέω]**, we have acted wickedly** [*rasha*, ἀδικέω]'; if they return to You with all their heart and with all their soul … then hear their prayer and their supplication in heaven Your dwelling place, and maintain their cause, and forgive Your people who have sinned against You and all their transgressions which they have transgressed against You."
     4) Psa 6:4, "Return, O LORD, rescue my soul; Save me because of Your lovingkindness."[1145]

[1145]The phrase "save me" is found 20 times in the NASB translation of the Book of Psalms, and 29 times in the Bible. I have listed only four of these in this section.

5) Psa 13:5, "But I have trusted in Your lovingkindness; My heart shall rejoice in Your salvation."

6) Psa 26:11, "...Redeem me, and be gracious to me"[1146]

7) Psa 32:3-5, "When I kept silent *about my sin*, my body wasted away Through my groaning all day long. For day and night Thy hand was heavy upon me; My vitality was drained away *as* with the fever heat of summer. Selah. I acknowledged my sin to Thee, And my iniquity I did not hide; **I said, 'I will confess my transgressions to the LORD'**; And Thou didst forgive the guilt of my sin. Selah."

8) Psa 38:18, 21-22, "For I confess my iniquity; I am full of anxiety because of my sin. ... Do not forsake me, O LORD; O my God, do not be far from me! Make haste to help me, O Lord, my salvation!"

9) Psa 41:4, "O Lord, be gracious to me; Heal my soul, for I have sinned against Thee."

10) Psa 51:9-10, "Hide Thy face from my sins, And blot out all my iniquities. Create in me a clean heart, O God, And renew a steadfast spirit within me"

11) Psa 51:14, "Deliver me from bloodguiltiness, O God, the God of my salvation" (Psalm 51 is like a sinner's plea to God for forgiveness and mercy)

12) Psa 71:2, "In Your righteousness deliver me and rescue me; Incline Your ear to me and save me"

13) Psa 79:9, "Help us, O God of our salvation, for the glory of Your name; And deliver us and forgive our sins for Your name's sake"

14) Psa 119:17 (ESV), "Deal bountifully with your servant, that I may live and keep your word"

15) Psa 119:25 (ESV), "My soul clings to the dust; give me life according to your word!"

16) Psa 119:88 (ESV), "In your steadfast love give me life, that I may keep the testimonies of your mouth."

17) Psa 119:107 (ESV), "I am severely afflicted; give me life, O LORD, according to your word!"

18) Psa 119:146, "I cried to You; save me And I shall keep Your testimonies."

19) Psa 119:154 (ESV) "Plead my cause and redeem me; give me life according to your promise!"

20) Psa 119:170, "Let my supplication come before Thee; Deliver me according to Thy word"

21) Psa 119:175, "Let my soul live that it may praise Thee, And let Thine ordinances help me"

22) Isa 6:5, "Woe is me, for I am ruined! Because I am a man of unclean lips, And I live among a people of unclean lips; For my eyes have seen the King, the Lord of hosts"

23) Jer 17:14, Heal me, O LORD, and I will be healed; Save me and I will be saved, For You art my praise."

c. Sample NT Sinner's Prayers:

1) Matt 9:27-29, "Have mercy on us, Son of David!" ... "Do you believe that I am able to do this?" They said to Him, "Yes, Lord" ... "It shall be done to you according to your faith" (notice in this case that we have two persons responding simultaneously; cf. Mark 10:47)

2) Matt 15:22, "Have mercy on me, Lord, Son of David..."

3) Matt 20:30-31, "Lord, have mercy on us, Son of David!" (again two men, and they were both healed; cf. Luke 18:38-39)

4) Luke 5:8, "Go away from me Lord, for I am a sinful man, O Lord."

5) Luke 17:13, "Jesus, Master, have mercy on us!"
   a) Note that while all ten are crying out to Jesus for help, and all ten had their outward leprosy cured, only one had his soul saved, Luke 17:16, "Now one of them, when he saw that he had been healed, turned back, glorifying God with a loud voice, and he fell on his face at His feet, giving thanks to Him. And he was a Samaritan"
   b) Nine were not crying out for an eternal salvation; they were crying out to Jesus for temporal assistance only; the tenth was crying out for eternal salvation!
   c) The conversion ratio for this miracle was one out of ten

6) Luke 18:13, "God, be merciful to me the sinner!"
   a) Jesus explained that "I tell you, this man went down to his house justified rather than the other," Luke 18:14.
   b) The use of the verb "justify" exemplifies salvation language, does it not?

7) Luke 18:38, 39, "Jesus, Son of David, have mercy on me!" ... "Son of David, have mercy on me!"

8) John 9:38, "And he said, 'Lord, I believe.' And he worshiped Him."

9) Acts 8:37, *"And Philip said, 'If you believe with all your heart, you may.' And he answered and said, 'I believe that Jesus Christ is the Son of God.'"*

[1146]The phrase "redeem me" is found four times in the NASB translation of the Bible: once in Job 6:23, and three times in Psalms 26:11; 119:134, 154.

10) Rom 7:24-25, "Wretched man that I am! Who will set me free from the body of this death? Thanks be to God [χάρις δὲ τῷ θεῷ] through Jesus Christ our Lord! So then, on the one hand I myself with my mind am serving the law of God, but on the other, with my flesh the law of sin"

   a) In Rom 7 as in 1 Cor 15 we find the word charis, or "thanks", which combined with Christ giving thanks at the Lord's Supper (cf. Matt 26:26 [BYZ]; 26:27; Mark 14:23; Luke 22:17, 19; 1 Cor 11:24) seemed to evolve into the name for the Lord's Supper being called the Eucharist [from εὐχαριστέω, the giving of thanks]

   b) Then the Eucharist (taking of communion) eventually took the place of the sinner's prayer of thanks, which prayer is offered once for salvation, and later repeatedly in gratitude for salvation

11) 1 Cor 15:57, "but thanks be to God [τῷ δὲ θεῷ χάρις], who gives us the victory through our Lord Jesus Christ"

12) 1 Tim 1:15, "It is a trustworthy statement, deserving full acceptance, that Christ Jesus came into the world to save sinners, among whom I am foremost *of all*."

13) Rev 5:12, "saying with a loud voice, 'Worthy is the Lamb that was slain to receive power and riches and wisdom and might and honor and glory and blessing.'"

d. Content of prayers of commitment:

1) Minimal content of a prayer to commitment:

   a) Luke 18:13, "God, be merciful to me the sinner!"

   b) Rom 10:13, "for 'Whoever will call upon the name of the LORD will be saved'"

   c) 1 Cor 12:3, "Therefore I make known to you, that no one speaking by the Spirit of God says, 'Jesus is accursed'; and no one can say, 'Jesus is Lord,' except by the Holy Spirit"

   d) 1 John 4:2, "By this you know the Spirit of God: every spirit that confesses that Jesus Christ has come in the flesh is from God"

   e) While simplicity and brevity is sometimes helpful—this does not imply that theological minimalism is to be preferred (overlooking the fundamental teachings of the Bible)

2) Normally prayers of commitment include content from:

   a) 1 John 1:9:
      (1) Confession of sin

   b) Luke 24:47:
      (1) Repentance for the forgiveness of sins

   c) Mark 1:15:
      (1) Repentance and belief of the Gospel

   d) Rom 10:9-10:
      (1) Confessing Jesus as Lord
      (2) Believing the God raised Him from the dead

   e) John 1:12:
      (1) Receive Him
      (2) Believe in His name

   f) Other verses and concepts may also be added to these concepts:
      (1) The affirmation that Jesus is the Son of God, and/or fully God and fully man (especially important if this was denied in the prior discussion)

3) It must be noted that the words of a prayer are important, as "confess[ing] with your mouth"

   a) Just like it is important to have proper words in worship music, as it is "put it on their lips" (NAS) or "put it in their mouths" (NKJ) Deut 31:19

4) It must also be noted that God hears the words *and* sees the heart, Luke 18:14

e. Sample prayers of commitment:

1) Several Historic examples:

a) 1280 AD, from the end of a Waldensian Gospel presentation:[1147]

Please notice that this call to commitment appears ritualistic with the following repeated prayers repeated in a liturgical way (the exact phraseology of each prayer is uncertain, but :

Parcite Nobis—"spare us"; *Parcite Nobis* seems to refer to the following prayer:
> "*Benedicite parcite nobis, Amen.*
> "*Fiat nobis secundum verbum tuum.*
> "*Pater et Filius et Esperitus Sanctus parcat vobis omnia peccata vestra.*
> "*Adoremus Patrem et Filium et Esperitum sanctum [III vegadas].*"[1148]

Being translated as (from Latin and Provençale):
> "[Bless] O spare us, Amen.
> "Unto us according to your word [cf. Luke 1:38; 2:29].
> "The Father and Son and Holy Spirit forgive you all your sins.
> "Let us worship the Father and Son and Holy Spirit [three times]."

Parcias—"spared";

Adoremus—"we adore," appears to be an alternate spelling of adoramus.

These somewhat follow the liturgical approach to the sinners prayer of both Luther and Tyndale, as described below[1149]

b) 1519 AD Sinners Prayer of Martin Luther: Consisting of a the Ten Commandments, the Creed, and the Lord's Prayer

According to Yarnell, Tyndale's 1526 *Pater Noster*—"our Father"—closely follows Luther's 1519, "An Exposition of the Lord's Prayer for Simple Laymen." Not having access to Luther's prayer, my remarks will be based on Yarnell's 2004 publishing of Tyndale's "Sinner's Prayer" below.

c) 1526 AD Sinners Prayer of William Tyndale, from the end of his preface to the book of Romans, consisting of a revision of the 1519 Luther's Prayer:

[1147]"And Jude brother of James says for our instruction in the epistle (verse 23): 'Hate this soiled garment which is fleshly.' And by these testimonies and by many others, you must keep the commandments of God, and hate the world. And if you do well up until the end, we are assured that your soul will have eternal life."

And may he say, "I have this desire, pray God that he gives me the strength for it." And may one of the "good men" make amends, with the believer, to the elder, and may he say: "*Parcite nobis.* For all the sins that I may have done or said or thought or worked, I ask forgiveness of God, and of the church and to you all." And may the Christians say: "By God and by us and by the church may they be forgiven you, and we pray God that he may forgive you them." And then they must console him. And may the elder take the book and place it on his head, and the other "good men" each with his right hand, and may they say the "*parcias*" and three *adoremus*, and then:

"And then they must console him. And may the elder take the book and place it upon his head, and the other 'good men' each with his right hand, and may they say the *parcias* and three *adoremus*, and then: '[in Latin] *Pater Sanctu, suscipe servum tuum in tua justifia, et mitte gratiam tuum et spiritum sanctum tuum super eum.*' And may they pray with the preaching, and the one who guides the holy service must say in a quiet voice the '*sixaine*' [a prayer]; and when the '*sixaine*' is said, he should say three *Adoremus*, with the preaching out loud, and then 'the Gospel' [a Latin version of John 1:1-5, 10-17]. And when the Gospel is said, they must say three *Adoremus* and the '*gratia*' and the '*parcias*.'

"And then they must make peace between themselves (to hug) and with the book. And if there are believers, they must also make peace, and may the believers, if there are any, make peace with the book between them. And then may they pray God with 'Double' and with '*veniae*', and they will have delivered him [the preaching]" (L. Clédat, "Rituel Provençal," in L. Clédat, *Le Nouveau Testament traduit au XIIIe siècle en langue provençale suivi d'un ritual cathar [The New Testament translated in the 13ᵗʰ Century in the Provençal language followed by a Cathar ritual]* (Paris, 1887; Geneva: Slatkine, 1968), ix-xxvi. Translation mine).

[1148]Ibid., vi.

[1149]Malcolm Yarnell, "The First Evangelical Sinner's Prayer Published in English"; *Southwestern Journal of Theology* (Fall, 2004): Vol 47, Num 1, pp. 36-37. I am indebted to Jacob Willard for pointing out to me this excellent resource.

As exemplified on the right,[1150] Tyndale's Sinners prayer is organized antiphonally. There is lengthy introductory paragraph, which emphasizes sin, and the need for prayer based on the OT law and the hope of the Gospel promises:

> "**Here foloweth a treates (to fill upp** the leefe with all) of the pater noster / very necessary and profitable / wherein (yff thou marke) thou shalt perceive what prayar is and what belongeth to prayar. … Noote this also / that prayar is nothinge else save a morninge of the sprite / a desyre / a longyng for that which she lacketh / as the sick morneth and soroweth in his hert longynge after health. And un to prayar ys requered the lawe and also the gospell / that is to saye the promyses of God. … Prayar ys the effecte and worke off fayth / and the sprite thorowe fayth prayeth continually wyth mornynges passynge all utterance of speache / confessing: and knowleging hir grievous bondage / hir lacke and wekenes / and desyringe help and succre. …"[1151]

Following this introduction, the prayer breaks into antiphonally ordered quotes of Scriptures. Eight antiphonal sections begin with "The Sinner," followed by seven sections titled "God." The final sentence of the eighth sinner's section reads as follows (the passage being cited will be familiar to the reader, Mark 9:24, along with an explanation of its spiritual implications):

> "The father answered I belefe lorde / helpe myne unbelefe / that is to saye / heale myne unbelefe and geve me perfect belefe and strngthe the weaknes off my fayth and increase it."[1152]

[Please find a modern reading of Tyndale's entire prayer appended to this chapter.]

    d)   1689 AD Prayer on behalf of Penitents of Claude Brousson[1153]

The Synner

O oure father which art in hevē/ what a gret eate space ys betwen the god vs? Howe therefore shall we thy children here on erth/ banesshed and exiled from the in this vale of misery and wretchednes/ come home to the in to oure naturall countre?

God

The child honoureth hys hys father/ and the servaūt hys master. Yf I be youre father wher ys myne honoure. Yf I be youre lorde where ys my feare. Malachias.j. For my name thorowe you and by youre meanes ys blasphemen rayld apon and evyll spoken of Esaias. lij.

The Sinner.

Alas O father that ys trueth/ we knowledge oure synne and treaspace/ neverthelesse yet be thou a mercifull father/ and deale not wyth vs as cordig to oure deservynges/ nether iudge vs by the rigorousnes off thi lawe/ but geve vs grace that we maye so lyve/ that thy holy name maye be halowed and sanctified in vs. And kepe ous re bitter/ that we nether do ner speake/ no/ that we not once thynke or purpose any thinge/ but that which is to thyne honoure and prayse/ and as bove all thinges make thy name and honoure to be soughte of vs and not oure awne name god vayne glory. And off thi myghty power bringe to passe in vs/ that we maye love and feare the as a sonne hys father.

God

Howe can myne honoure and name be halowed amonge you/ when youre hertes and thoughtes are all wayes enclined to evyll/ and ye in

---

[1150]Yarnell explained how he found this remarkable Sinner's Prayer, a scan of which is found on the right side of the page: "It was only by accident—leaving aside the question of divine providence—that this unique prayer was discovered. While reading through the original documents collected *en masse* at the Bodleain Library at Oxford University, this author was concerned to discover Tyndale's doctrine of royal priesthood, especially as evidenced in his biblical commentaries. Having finished a thorough reading of Tyndale's preface to Paul's book of Romans, an unexpected document was found appended to that preface. This was a surprise because both of the authoritative editions of the collected works of Tyndale, which had been previously consulted, neglected to reprint the document" (ibid. 32; the scan on the left hand side of the page is from page 38).

[1151]Ibid., 39.

[1152]Ibid., 43.

[1153]"When the sermon was over, the preacher asked whether there was any among his hearers wishing to be reconciled to God and His Church, and to re-enter the communion of saints … Then, any who were so minded came forward and knelt before the preacher, who began to remonstrate with them and showed them how enormous was the sin they had committed in forsaking Christ. That being done, they were asked to say whether they did repent, and would henceforth live and die in *the Reformed faith*, in spite of the allurements and threats of the world; whether they heartily renounced the errors of the Church of Rome, the Mass and all thereto appertaining…. (This was done in much detail.)

e) Spurgeon's tract, "Ark of Safety":

"Sinner, I have a word from the Lord for thee: if you feel your need of a Saviour, that blood is able to save you, and you are bidden simply to trust that blood, and you shall be saved. If you can rely simply on the blood of Christ, that blood is able to save. Leave off doing altogether; get Christ *first*, and then you may do as much as you like. See the Saviour hanging on the cross; turn your eye to Him, and say, '**Lord I trust Thee; I have nothing else to trust to; sink or swim, my Saviour, I trust Thee.**' And as surely, sinner, as thou canst put thy trust in Christ, thou art safe. He that believeth shall be saved, be his sins ever so many; he that believeth not shall be damned, be his sins ever so few, and his virtues ever so many. Trust in Jesus *now*, Jesus only."[1154]

2) From *Steps to Peace with God*:

"Dear Lord Jesus, I know that I am a sinner and need Your forgiveness. I believe that You died for my sins. I want to turn from my sins. I now invite you to come into my heart and life. I want to trust and follow You as Lord and Savior. In Jesus' name. Amen."[1155]

3) From *The Four Spiritual Laws*:

"Lord Jesus, I need you. Thank You for dying on the cross for my sins. I open the door of my life and receive You as my Savior and Lord. Thank you for forgiving my sins and giving me eternal life. Take control of the throne of my life. Make me the kind of person You want me to be."[1156]

4) From *Bridge to Life*:

"Lord Jesus, please come into my life and be my Savior and Lord. Please forgive my sins, and give me eternal life."[1157]

5) From Jim Anderson's *Facts of Life*:

"Dear Lord Jesus, I know that I am a sinner, I believe the Bible is true when it says I can't save myself. But I also believe you died for me. I believe you rose up from the dead. I believe you paid for my sins. I accept you now as my personal Savior. I want to thank you for coming into my life now and making me your very own. Help me to do right, to live for you. Teach me what you want me to know about the Bible. Guide me to Christian friends and help me to be faithful in maintaining Christian fellowship. Thank you, Jesus, Amen."[1158]

6) From *There Is Hope*:

"O God, I know that I am a sinner and deserve hell. I know that Jesus died on the cross and rose again for me. I ask you to forgive me of my sin. I want you to come into my heart and take control of my live. In Jesus' name, Amen."[1159]

f. The prayer of recommitment: These are more specific to the need of the moment. Often the person will know how to pray, and will just need encouragement to pray aloud. Sometimes there

---

They had to answer Yes to all these questions, each individually. After this, they had to promise not to attend Mass any more, and to take great care not to pollute themselves with Babylon, either by marriage or in other ways; not to allow their children to be trained in it, but, on the contrary, to instruct them in the principles of our religion. Each having duly promised, the minister then proclaimed the remission of their sins, saying, 'In the name and authority of Jesus Christ, and as a faithful minister of His Word, I declare to you the remission of all your sins, and there is now no condemnation for you, since you are in Jesus Christ.' Then followed a prayer on their behalf.

"Forty-two of us were admitted in this manner, the rest of the flock having been received back at previous gatherings. The number of the communicants was about two hundred and fifty, men and women" (Matthieu Lelièvre, *Portraits et Récits Huguenots,* 274-82; translated and quoted by Rubens Saillens in his *The Soul of France* (London: Morgan and Scott, 1917), 86-87).

[1154]C. H. Spurgeon, "Salvation and Safety," *Royal Dainties*, no. 169 (Minneapolis: Asher Publishing Co., affiliated with The Union Gospel Mission, n.d.), 4; found at http//www.wheaton.edu/bgc/ archives/docs/tract01.html; Internet, accessed 4 January 2001.

[1155]From *Steps to Peace with God* (Minneapolis: World Wide Publications, n.d.).

[1156]From the *Four Spiritual Laws* (San Bernardino, CA: Campus Crusade for Christ, 1965).

[1157]From *Bridge to Life* (Colorado Springs, CO: NavPress, 1969).

[1158]From *Facts of Life* (Belton, MO: Jim Anderson Evangelistic Association, n.d.).

[1159]From *There Is Hope* (Deerfield, IL: Evangelism Unlimited Inc., 1986).

will be a period of silence, but don't rush them. Give them the time to get the courage to talk to God.

3. How to Lead Individuals in Prayer:

Introduction: There are different methods of leading a person in prayer. The setting and the conversation will guide the personal worker in choosing the best way to lead the contact in a prayer of commitment.

   a. **Verbal guidance methods**:

      1) **The repeat after me method**:
         a) The personal worker goes through the prayer phrase-by-phrase
         b) The contact is asked to repeat each phrase after the worker

      2) The same method is effective for large groups who have come forward for an altar call, especially with lack of counselors to deal individually with everyone.

      3) **The three prayer method** (adapted from CWT—Continuous Witness Training):
         a) **The prayer of understanding**: the evangelist leads the contact in a prayer of understanding, asking God to understand the Scriptures and to open the eyes of the contact to see Christ for who He is
         b) **The prayer of faith**: the evangelist leads the contact in a prayer to repent of his sin and place his faith in Jesus Christ
         c) **The prayer of confirmation**: the evangelist leads the contact to pray a prayer confirming his intent to be baptized, to join the fellowship of believers, and to continue on with the Lord.

   b. **Written guidance method**:
      1) Providing a written prayer of repentance, confession, and faith
      2) The read-the-prayer-aloud-first method:
         a) The worker asks the contact to read a prayer from a Gospel tract aloud
         b) After the contact has completed the prayer, the evangelist asks the person if the prayer expresses the desire of their heart.
         c) If the contact says that it does, the worker then asks the person to read it again as a prayer to God.
         d) The worker may then pray for the contact following his/her prayer.

   c. **The spontaneous prayer method**:
      1) The "pray whatever is on your heart to pray" method:
         a) Personal worker asks the interested contact to tell God in his own words how he would like to respond to the Gospel
         b) The evangelist may then pray for the new believer who has expressed what is in his heart to God!

4. **Concerning "Corporate" Commitment to Christ**:

   a. **Is reciting a Creed** (in liturgical churches) **a "corporate" parallel to the "individualistic" sinner's prayer** (in conversionistic churches)?

     Introduction: Some liturgical churches state prior to saying the Apostles Creed, "Let us now proclaim our faith." First of all, in what way is this a proclamation of one's faith? Does this fulfill the Great Commission's mandate to proclaim the Gospel?

      1) Is the entire congregation reciting a creed (Apostles Creed, the Nicene Creed, the Creed of Chalcedon, the Creed of Athanasius, also known as *Quicunque Vult*, "Whosoever will") similar to a communal/social saying of the sinner's prayer? Why or why not?

Note, for example, the first lines of the 8th Century "Creed of Athanasius":[1160]

1.	Whosoever will be saved, before all things it is necessary that he hold the Catholic faith,
2.	Which Faith except every one do keep whole and undefiled, without doubt he shall perish everlastingly.
3.	And the Catholic faith is this: "that we worship one God in Trinity, and Trinity in Unity;
4.	Neither confounding the Persons; nor dividing the Substance.
5.	For there is one Person of the Father, another of the Son, and another of the Holy Ghost.
6.	But the Godhead of the Father, of the Son, and of the Holy Ghost, is all one: the Glory Equal, the Majesty Coeternal.
7.	Such as the Father is, such is the Son: and such is the Holy Ghost.
8.	The Father uncreate, the Son uncreate: the Holy Ghost uncreate.
9.	The Father is incomprehensible, the Son incomprehensible and the Holy Ghost incomprehensible.
10.	The Father is eternal, the Son eternal: and the Holy Ghost eternal.
11.	And yet they are not three Eternals: but one Eternal.
12.	As there are not three uncreated, nor three incomprehensibles: but one uncreated and one incomprehensible....
	[this creed often recited on Pentecost Sunday is quite long, being 40 sentences long]

2) Or compare the Nicene Creed with 1 Corinthians 15:1-9 and the "Roman Road" Gospel presentation:

Nicene Creed (325)	1 Corinthians 15:1-9	The Roman Road

I believe in one GOD THE FATHER Almighty; Maker of heaven and earth, and of all things visible and invisible.
 	
And in one Lord JESUS CHRIST, the only-begotten Son of God, begotten of the Father before all worlds [God of God], Light of Light, very God of very God, begotten, not made, being of one substance [essence] with the Father; by whom all things were made; who, for us men and for our salvation, came down from heaven, and was incarnate by the Holy Ghost of the Virgin Mary, and was made man; and was crucified also **for us** under Pontius Pilate; he suffered and was buried; and the third day he rose again, according to the Scriptures; and ascended into heaven, and sitteth on the right hand of the Father; and he shall come again, with glory, to judge both the quick and the dead; whose kingdom shall have no end.
 	
And [I believe] in the Holy Ghost, the Lord and Giver of Life; who proceedeth from the Father [and the Son]; who with the Father and the Son together is worshiped and glorified; who spake by the Prophets. And [I believe] one Holy Catholic and Apostolic Church.[1161] **I acknowledge one Baptism for the remission of sins**; and I look for the resurrection of the dead, and the life of the world to come. Amen.[1162]
	1 Now I make known to you, brethren, the gospel which I preached to you, which also you received, in which also you stand, 2 by which also you are saved, if you hold fast the word which I preached to you, unless you believed in vain.
	
	3 For I delivered to you as of first importance what I also received, that **Christ died for our sins** according to the Scriptures, 4 and that He was buried, and that He was raised on the third day according to the Scriptures, 5 and that He appeared to Cephas, then to the twelve.
	
	6 After that He appeared to more than five hundred brethren at one time, most of whom remain until now, but some have fallen asleep; 7 then He appeared to James, then to all the apostles; 8 and last of all, as to one untimely born, He appeared to me also.
	
	9 For I am the least of the apostles, and not fit to be called an apostle, because I persecuted the church of God.
		1. **Need** (Why?):
		  a. God says that all are sinners, Rom 3:10, 23
		  b. God tells us the reason all are sinners, Rom 5:12
		
		2. **Consequence** (What?) God tells us the result of sin, Rom 6:23
		
		3. **Remedy** (How?) God tells us of His concern for sinners, Rom 5:8-9
		
		4. **Condition** (Who?) God's way of salvation is made plain, Rom 10:9-10, 13
		
		5. **Results**: God tells us the results of salvation, Rom 5:1, 8:1
		
		6. **Assurance**: God gives the saved sinner assurance, Rom 8:16

a) What are the similarities?

b) What are the differences?
    (1) Note the emphasis (or lack of it) on sin
    (2) Note the emphasis (or lack of it) on the atonement

[1160]"Creed of Athanasius"; accessed 24 Sept 2004; from http://www.rca.org/aboutus/beliefs/athanasian.php; Internet.

[1161]Consider the footnote above, as regards the martyrdom of John Hus for disavowing the Catholic church, as is stated in both the Apostles and Nicene creeds.

[1162]"The Nicene Creed" (online); from: http://www.ccel.org/ccel/schaff/creeds2.iv.i.i.i.html; accessed 13 Oct 2005; Internet.

(3) Note the voice of the text (I, you, he, we; individual or communal emphasis)

c) Are the salvific elements of the Gospel blunted in the Nicene Creed?

d) Is a congregation reading or reciting this creed similar to an individual reading a Sinner's Prayer? Why or why not?

e) Notice the power of a creed (or hymn, or chorus), as it is literally putting word in someone else's mouth—"put it on their lips":

Deut 31:19, ""Now therefore, write this song for yourselves, and teach it to the sons of Israel; **put it on their lips**, in order that this song may be a witness for Me against the sons of Israel"

b. Questions Relative to "Worship Evangelism":

Introduction:

Does Acts 16:25-26 provide an example of worship evangelism (cf. Psa 137:3)?
What about the teaching of 1 Cor 14:23-25?
The importance of the words in a song: "put it on their lips/in their mouths" (Deut 31:19)

Further questions:

What can be learned about the illegitimate worship of Nadab and Abihu (Lev 10:1-11)?
What does Saul's "worship" after he disobeyed say about worship (1 Sam 15:17-31)?
What can be learned about the illegitimate worship of Jeroboam (1 Kgs 12:25-33)?
What about the teaching of Isaiah 1:10-15?

1) Is the congregation singing a worship song, such as "Now Is the Time for Worship," an communal invitation or a communal call to commitment?

a) Is it similar to an group (community) saying a sinner's prayer together or an individual saying a sinner's prayer? Why or why not?

b) Is it evangelistic? If so, how?

c) Does it negate the need for a spoken invitation during preaching? And if it does, what elements need to be in the song to make it a biblical invitation song? If it does not, how can it be applied individually, rather than corporately?

d) What of the theology in "Now Is the Time to Worship" (as an example)? [1163]

Words	Comments
Come, now is the time to worship	Herein is the evangelistic invitation #1 Changes the "now" of 2 Cor 6:2 from a "now" of conversion to a "now" of worship!
Come, now is the time to give your heart	Herein is the evangelistic invitation #2
Come, just as you are to worship	Affirmation of "come as you are"
Come, just as you are before your God, Come	Herein is the evangelistic invitation #3 While lost sinners come unconditionally, they ought not remain in that state!
One day every tongue will confess You are God	Who is the "You" in this statement? Is Belief in the deity of Christ sufficient for salvation?
One day every knee will bow	Is this a universalistic statement (in a triumphalist sense) in this context?
Still, the greatest treasure remains for those	What treasure remains for unbelievers? Is it not hell that awaits those who don't "choose Jesus now"?
Who gladly choose You now	Herein is the evangelistic invitation #4 What of Jesus, His death for our sin, repentance for our sin and faith in Him? What are singers "gladly choosing"? A relationship with Jesus? Repentance for sin and faith unto death? Is it clear? If not, why not?

2) So what about worship evangelism?

a) In what way are people evangelized through worship?

b) In what way is worship evangelism existential (for the non-believer) through experiencing the true worship of a Christian?

[1163]Words by Brian Doerksen, from http://www.audiblefaith.com/pages/sg200065; accessed 7 Sept 2006.

    c)   In what way is the singing of choruses evangelistic?

    d)   How about if the words of the choruses speak only of the sovereignty, kingship, friendship, or love of Christ, and say nothing about our sin and the blood of Christ that cleanses from sin?

        (1) Herein we see the five views of the atonement portrayed in worship choruses and hymns

    e)   How about if the commitment called for in the chorus seems to avoid:

        (1) "Repentance for the forgiveness of sin" (cf. Luke 3:3; 5:32; 24:47; Acts 2:38; 5:31; 20:21)

        (2) Belief in "Christ", but rather only mentions belief in "God" (thereby affirming that the corporate congregation and individual singers are not atheistic)

        (3) Now let's compare the following songs related to their emphasis on the doctrine of the atonement…

Worship Songs Comparative[1164]

Take Me into the Holy of Holies[1165]	Above All[1166]	Here I Am to Worship[1167]	We Want to See Jesus Lifted High[1168]
Take me past the outer courts Into the secret place, Past the brazen altar, Lord, I want to see Your face. …. Take me in to the Holy of Holies, **Take me in by the blood of the Lamb;** … Take the coal, cleanse my lips, Here I am. © *Dave Browning 1986 Glory Alleluia Music, CCLI #19272*	Verse 1 Above all powers, above all kings Above all nature and all created things Above all wisdom and all the ways of man You were here before the world began … Chorus **Crucified laid behind a stone You lived to die rejected and alone Like a rose trampled on the ground You took the fall and thought of me above all** Rebecca St. James.	Light of the world, … And here I am to worship, here I am to bow down, **here I am to say that you're my God,** you're altogether lovely, altogether worthy, altogether wonderful to me. King of all days, … **All for love's sake became poor.** **I'll never know how much it cost to see my sin upon that cross.** I'll never know how much it cost to see my sin upon that cross.	We want to see Jesus lifted high A banner that flies across this land That all men might see the truth and know He is the way to heaven We want to see, we want to see We want to see Jesus lifted high … *Written by Doug Horley* © *1993 Kingsway's Thankyou Music, CCLI# 1596342*

*I have highlighted texts referring to the atonement.

        (4) What is taught in the above songs about the meaning of the atonement, and the required commitment resulting from that meaning?

        (5) Does it matter what is being sung or not?

        (6) Do not these songs put words "on our lips" (Deut 31:19), "in our mouths", and therefore "in our hearts" (Deut 30:14)?

        (7) Does it matter? Absolutely it matters!

[1164]Songs abbreviated for copyright reasons.

[1165]From http://www.growingchristians.org/mfgc/rock/TakeMeIn.html; accessed 28 Nov 2005.

[1166]From http://www.christianguitar.org/csong11678/Rebecca-St.-James-Above-All; accessed 28 Nov 2005.

[1167]From http://www.azlyrics.com/lyrics/plusone/hereiamtoworship.html; accessed 15 Feb 2006.

[1168]From http://www.justworship.com/worshipsongs/wewanttoseejesusliftedhigh.html; accessed 27 April 2007.

f) Further Food for Reflection: Do the following versions of "A Mighty Fortress Is Our God" express the theological agenda of the translators?

Five Versions of "A Mighty Fortress Is Our God"[1169]

Ein' Feste Burg [from: http://ingeb.org/Lieder /einfest9.html; Accessed: 8/12/04]	A Mighty Fortress Is Our God [*The Hymnal for Worship and Celebration* (Waco, TX: Word, 1986), 26]	A Mighty Fortress Is Our God [from: http://ingeb.org/spiritua/ amightyf.html; Accessed: 8/12/04]	A Mighty Fortress Is Our God [*Lutheran Book of Worship* (Minneapolis: Augsburg, 1978), 229]	A Mighty Fortress Is Our God [*Lutheran Book of Worship* (Minneapolis: Augsburg, 1978), 228]
Words and music: Martin Luther (1483-1546), 1529.	Words: tr. Frederick H. Hedge (1805-1890), 1853.	Words: tr. Catherine Winkworth (1829-1878).	Words: tr. Hymnal version, 1978.	Words: tr. Hymnal version, 1978.
1. Ein' feste Burg ist unser Gott, Ein gute Wehr und Waffen; Er hilft uns frei aus aller Not, Die uns jetzt hat betroffen. Der alt' böse Feind, Mit Ernst er's jetzt meint, Groß' Macht und viel List Sein' grausam' Rüstung ist, Auf Erd' ist nicht seinsgleichen.	1. A mighty fortress is our God, A bulwark never failing; Our helper He amid the flood Of mortal ills prevailing. For still our ancient foe Doth seek to work us woe— His craft and pow'r are great, And, armed with cruel hate On earth is not his equal.	1. A mighty Fortress is our God, A trusty Shield and Weapon; He helps us free from every need That hath us now o'ertaken. The old evil Foe Now means deadly woe; Deep guile and great might Are his dread arms in fight; On Earth is not his equal.	1. A mighty fortress is our God, A sword and shield victorious; He breaks the cruel oppressor's rod And wins salvation glorious. The old satanic foe, Has sworn to work us woe! With craft and dreadful might He arms himself to fight. On earth he has no equal.	1. A mighty fortress is our God, A sword and shield victorious; He breaks the cruel oppressor's rod And wins salvation glorious. The old evil foe, Sworn to work us woe, With dread craft and might He arms himself to fight. On earth he has no equal.
...	...	...	...	...
3. Und wenn die Welt voll Teufel wär Und wollt uns gar verschlingen, So fürchten wir uns nicht so sehr, Es soll uns doch gelingen. Der Fürst dieser Welt, Wie sau'r er sich stellt, Tut er uns doch nichts, Das macht, er ist gericht', Ein Wörtlein kann ihn fällen.	3. And tho this world with devils filled, Should threaten to undo us, We will not fear, for God hath willed, His truth to triumph thru us. The prince of darkness grim, We tremble not for him— His rage we can endure, For lo, his doom is sure: One little word shall fell him.	3. Though devils all the world should fill, All eager to devour us. We tremble not, we fear no ill, They shall not overpower us. This world's prince may still Scowl fierce as he will, He can harm us none, He's judged; the deed is done; One little word can fell him.	3. Though hordes of devils fill the land All threat'ning to devour us. We tremble not, unmoved we stand; They cannot overpow'r us. Let this world's tyrant rage; In battle we'll engage! His might is doomed to fail; God's judgment must prevail! One little word subdues him.	3. Though hordes of devils fill the land All threat'ning to devour us. We tremble not, unmoved we stand; They cannot overpow'r us. This world's prince may rage, In fierce war engage. He is doomed to fail; God's judgment must prevail! One little word subdues him.

d. Is there the need for an individual Gospel to be received individually? What of the corporate language in the Bible?

1) How do we change gears from (1) speaking to the group to (2) dealing with individual penitents (to use an old term)?
   a) Where acceptance or rejection can take place (i.e. "shaking the dust off our feet")?
   b) Where there's no question as to who is being addressed when the prophet says, "you are the man!" 2 Sam 12:7?

2) Herein we see that an individual Gospel demands an individual response. Thus individualistic churches (who believe in the substitutionary atonement and being born again) demand an individual response often denoted through a[n individualistic] public invitation.

e. Notice how theology and practice (including worship) meet at the point of evangelism and commitment to Christ!

[1169]Verses abbreviated for copyright reasons.

Chapter 21 Appendix

Luther's 1519 "Enflamed Dialogue," based on the Lord's Prayer, with Tyndale's 1526 translation as the "Prayer of the Sinner"

Luther's "Enflamed Dialogue" was apparently translated into French the same year of its appearance in Germany, and then put into poetry by the sister of the King of France, Marguerite de Valois.[1170] The following is Tyndale's Introduction to this unique prayer, as it appeared in his 1526 commentary on Romans (as did apparently the "enflamed dialogue" of Luther):

"Here follows a treatise (to fill up the leaf with all) of the Lord's Prayer, very necessary and profitable, wherein (if you mark [it]) you shall perceive what prayer is and all that belongs to prayer. The sinner prays the petitions of the Lord's Prayer, and God answers by the Law, as though he would put him from his desire. The sinner acknowledges that he is worthy to be put back, nevertheless faith holds fast to God's promises, and compels him, for truth's sake, to hear his petition. Mark this well and take it for a sure conclusion, when God commands us in the Law to do anything, he commands not therefore, that we are able to do it, but to bring us unto a knowledge of ourselves, that we might see what we are and in what miserable state we are in, and know our lack. That thereby we should turn to God and to acknowledge our wretchedness unto him, and to desire him that of his mercy he would make us that [which] he bids us to be, and give us the strength and power to do that which the Law requires of us. Note this also, that prayer is nothing else save a mourning of the spirit, as the sick [person] mourns and sorrows in his longing after health.

"And unto prayer is required the Law and the gospel, that is to say the promises of God. The office of the Law is only to utter sin and declare what miserable damnation and captivity we are in. Is it not a miserable, yea a fearful and horrible damnation and captivity we are in? Is it not a miserable, yea a fearful and horrible damnation we are in, when our very hearts are so fast bound and locked under the power of the devil, that we cannot once as much consent unto the will of almighty God, our Father, Creator, and Maker: yea and yet see not this so great, so sharp, so cruel, and terrible vengeance of God upon us, until the Law come.

"The Law brings a man unto the knowledge of himself, and compels him to mourn, to complain, to sorrow, to confess, and to acknowledge his sin and misery, and to seek help. The Gospel entices, draws, and shows from whence to fetch help, and binds us to God through faith. Faith is the anchor of all health and holds us fast to the promises of God which are the sure Law—neither works neither yet any other things can quiet a man's conscience, save only faith and trust in the promises of God. Faith suffers no wind, no storm, no tempest of adversity or temptation, no threatenings of the Law, no crafty subtlety of the devil to separate us from the love of God in Christ Jesus. That is to say, to make us believe that God loves us not in Christ and for Christ's sake. Prayer is the effect and work of faith, and the spirit through faith prays continually with mournings passing all utterance of speech, confessing and acknowledging here grievous bondage, here lack and weakness, and desiring help and succor. Now do you see that there is not so great a distance between heaven and earth, as between prayer and mumbling a pair of Matins or mumbling 'Our Father's' and honoring God with the lips.

"I pass over with silence, how without all fruit, yea how with terrible ignorance the lay and unlearned people say the 'Our Father' and also the '[Apostles] Creed' in the Latin tongue. Moreover, they never pray which feel not the working of the Law in their hearts, nor have their consciences shaken and bruised, and as it were beaten to powder with the thunderbolt thereof. Consider and behold yourself therefore diligently as in a mirror and then come and confess your sin, your lack and poverty unto God without all manner of feigning and hypocrisy, mourning and complaining over your horrible damnation, bondage, and captivity, and with strong faith pray God to have mercy on you for Christ's sake, to fulfill his promises, to give his Spirit, to release you, to strengthen you, to fulfill all his godly will in you, to pour the riches and treasure of his spiritual gifts on you, and to make you such a one as his heart has pleasure and delight in. And above all things desire him to increase your faith, and pray after the manner and example of this treatise here following."[1171]

[1170]"L'Oraison Dominicale: Dialogue entre Dieu et l'âme résumant l'explication du Pater de 1529," in Henri Strohl, *La Substance de l'Évangile de Luther: Témoignages choisis, traduits et annotés* (Carrières-sous-Poissy, France: "La Cause," 1934), 313-322. Stohl explained: "This 'enflamed dialogue' was put into verse by the sister of Francis 1st at the time that she was still the duchess of Angoulême. She, without doubt, worked from a version of French prose accomplished in Strasbourg. The translation [her rendition] is sometimes a superb commentary of the text of Luther, of which Marguerite grasped the full depth of meaning. Will Grayburn Moore, *La Réforme allemande et la littérature française, recherches sur la notoriété de Luther en France* (Strasbourg: La faculté des lettres à l'université, 1930), see p 186ff., for the complete text, p 431ff.

[1171]My modernization of the following: "**Here foloweth a treates (to fill upp** the leefe with all) of the pater noster / very necessary and profitable / wherein (yff thou marke) thou shalt perceave what prayer is and all that belongeth to prayar. The sinner prayeth the peticions off the pater noster / and God answereth by the lawe / as though he wolde putt hym from hys desyre. The sinner knowlegeth that he is worthy to be put backe / nevertheless fayth cleveth fast to gods promises / and compelleth hym / for his truethes sake / to heare her petición. Marke this well and take it for a sure conclusion / when god commaundeth us in the lawe to doo any thinge / he commaundeth not therefore / that we are able to do yt / but to bryng us un to the knowlege of oureselves / that we might se what we are and in what miserable state we are in / and knowe our lack / that thereby we shuld torne to god and to knowlege oure wretchednes un to hym / and to desyre him that of his mercy he wold make us that he biddeth us be / and to geve us strength and power to doo that which the lawe requireth of us. Noote this also / that prayar is nothinge else save a morninge of the sprite / a desyre / and a longyng for that which she lacketh / as the sick morneth and soroweth in his hert longynge after health. And un to prayar ys requered the lawe and also the gospell / that is to saye the promyses of God. The office off the lawe is only to utter sinne and declare what miserable damnación and captivité we are in. Is it not a miserable ye a fearefull and an horrible damnación and captivité we are in. Is it not a miserable / ye a fearefull and an horrible damnación and captivité that we are in / when oure very hertes are so fast bound and locked under the po-

« Oraison Dominicale » de Luther en 1519	Luther's 1519 Lord's Prayer (Johnston's translation)	Tyndale's 1526 Prayer of the Sinner[1172]	Tyndale's 1526 Prayer (Johnston's modernization)	Scriptural Allusions
L'âme. O notre Père qui es aux cieux, nous somme tes enfants, sur terre, séparés de toi, dans la misère. Quelle grande distance y a-t-il entre toi et nous ; comment pourrons-nous retourner à toi et dans notre patrie ?	*The Soul.* Oh our Father, who is in heaven, we are your children, on earth, separated from you, in great misery. What a great distance there is between you and us; how can we return to you and to our motherland?	**THE SYNNER** Oure father which arte in heven / what a greate space ys betwen the and us: How therefore shall we thy children here on erth / baneshed and exiled from the in this vale of misery and wretchednes / come home to the in to oure naturall countre?	**The Sinner** Our Father which are in heaven, what a great space is between you and us. How therefore shall we, your children, here on earth, banished and exiled in this vale of misery and wretchedness, come home to you in our natural country?	Isa 55:10-11 Luke 15:26
Dieu, *Malachie I. —* « Un enfant honore son père et un serviteur son maitre. » Si je suis votre père, où est l'honneur que vous me devez ? Si je suis votre Seigneur, me craignez-vous et me respectez-vous ? Car mon saint nom est blasphémé et déshonoré chez vous et par vous (*Esaïe*, LII).	*God,* *Malachi 1. —* "A child honors his father and a servant his master." If I am your father, where is the honor that you owe me? If I am your Lord, do you fear me and do you respect me? For my holy name is blasphemed and dishonored among you and by you (Isaiah 52).	**GOD** The child honoureth hys hys father / and the servaunt his master. Yf I be youre father wher ys myne honoure. Yf I be youre lorde where y s my feare. Malachias.i. For my name thorowe you and by youre meanes ys blasphemen rayld apon and evyll spoken of Esaias.lii.	**God** The child honors his own father, and the servant his master. If I be your father, where is my honor? If I be your Lord, where is my fear? (Malachi 1). For my name through you and by your means is blasphemed, railed upon, and evil spoken (Isaiah 52).	Mal 1:6 Isa 52:5
La première demande. *L'âme. —* O Père, ce n'est que trop vrai. Nous reconnaissons notre péché. Sois un père miséricordieux et ne nous tiens pas compte de nos offenses, mais donne-nous ta grâce afin que nous vivions ainsi que ton saint nom soit sanctifié en nous. Empêche-nous de penser, de dire, de faire, d'avoir ou de nous proposer ce qui ne pourrait pas contribuer à ta louange et à ta gloire, afin que nous recherchions avant toutes	*The First Request.* *The Soul. —* Oh Father, that is only all too true. We recognize our sin. Be a gracious father and do not take into account our sins, but give us your grace in order that we may live in such a way that your name would be sanctified in us. Hinder us from thinking, saying, doing, having or from proposing to ourselves that which would not contribute to your praise and to your glory, in order that we may diligently	**THE SINNER** Alas O father that ys trueth / we knowledge oure synne and treaspace / nevertelesse yet be thou a mercifull father / and deale not wyth us according to oure deservynges / nether iudge us by the rigorousnes off thi lawe / but geve us grace thatwe maye so lyve / that thy holy name maye be halowed and sanctified in us. And kepe oure hertes / that we nether do ner speake / no / that we not once thynke or purpose any thinge / but that which is to thyne honoure and prayse / and above all thinges make thy	**The Sinner** Alas, our Father that is truth. We acknowledge our sin and trespass. Nevertheless, please be a merciful Father, and do not deal with us according to what we deserve, neither judge us by the rigors of your Law, but give us grace that we may so live, that your name may be hallowed and sanctified in us. And keep our hearts that we neither do nor speak. No, that we not once think or purpose anything, but that which is to your honor and praise. And above all things, make your name and honor be sought of	Psa 32:5 1 Cor 10:31 Psa 115:1

(ciiʳ / ciiᵛ) wer of the devill / that we can not once as moch as consent un to the will of allmyghty God / oure father / creator / and maker: ye and yet se not this so greate / so sharpe / so cruel / and terrible vengeance of God apon us / untyll the lawe come. The law then bringeth aman un to the knowlege of him selfe / and compelleth him to morne / to complayne / to sorowe / to confesse and knowledge hys synne and miserie / and to seke help. The gospell entyseth draweth and sheweth from whence to fetche helpe / and coupleth us to God thorowe fayth. Fayth ys the ancre of all health and kepeth us fast un to the promyses of God which are the sure lawe nether workes nether yet any other thynge can quiette a mans conscience save only fayth and trust in the promyses of God. Fayth sofreth no wynde no storme no tempest of adversité or temptacion / no threat enynges of the lawe / no crafty sotylte off the devyll to seperatt us from the love of God in Christe Jesu / that ys to saye / to make us beleve that god loveth us not in Christe and for Christes sake. Prayar ys the effecte and worke off fayth / and the sprite thorowe fayth prayeth continually wyth mornynges passynge all utterance of speache / confessing: and knowleging hir grevous bondage / hir lacke and wekenes / and desyringe helpe and succre. Nowe seiste thou that there is not so greate distaunce betwene heven and erth / as betwene prayar and momblynge a payre of matenses or numbryng pater nosters and honourynnge God wyth the lyppes / I passe over wyth sylence / howe wyth oute all frute / ye with howe terrible ignouraunce the laye and unlerned people sa- (ciiᵛ /ciiʳ) ye the pater noster and also the crede in the latyne tonge. Moreover they never praye which fele not the workynge of the lawe in their hertes / and have their consciences shaken and broysed and as it were beaten to pouder wyth the thunderboltetheirof. Consyder and beholde thi sylfe theirfore in the lawe diligently as in a glass / and then come and confesse thi synne / thi lack and poverte un to god wyth out all maner faynynge and ypocrisy / morninge and complaynynge over thine horrible damnación / bondage and captivité and wyth a stronge fayth praye god to have mercy on the for Christs sake / to fulfyll hys promyses / to geve the hys sprite / to loose the / to strengthe the / to fullfyl all hys Godely wyll in the / to poure the ryches and treasure off hys spirituali gyftes in to the / and to make the soche a wone as hys herte hath pleasure and delectación in. And above all thynges desyre hym to encreace thy fayth / and praye after the maner and ensample of this treates here folowynge. (ciiiʳ / ciiiᵛ)" (Malcolm Yarnell, "The First Evangelical Sinner's Prayer Published in English"; *Southwestern Journal of Theology*, 47:1 [Fall, 2004], 39-40.)

[1172]Yarnell, "The First Evangelical Sinner's Prayer," 40-43.

choses la gloire de ton nom et non pas notre vaine gloire. Fais que nous t'aimions comme des enfants aiment, craignent et vénèrent leur père.	seek before all else the glory of your name and not at all our vain glory. Make us love you as children love, fear, and respect their father.	name and honoure to be soughte of us and not oure awne name and vayne glory. And off thi myghty power bringe to passein us / that we maye love and feare the as a sonne hys father.	us and not our name and vain glory. And by your mighty power bring to pass in us—that we may love and fear you as a son his Father.	
Dieu, *Esaïe II, Genèse VIII. —* Comment mon honneur et mon nom pourraient-ils être sanctifiés chez vous, quand vos pensées et votre cœur tout entier sont enclins au mal et dans les liens du péché ? Et pourtant personne ne peut chanter ma louange en pays étranger. (Psaume CXXXVII).	*God,* *Isaiah 2, Genesis 8. —* How can my honor and my name be sanctified among you, when your thoughts and hearts are so entirely inclined to evil and in the bonds of sin? And moreover no one can sing my praise in a strange land (Psalm 137).	**GOD** How can myne honoure and name be halowed amonge you / when youre hertes and thoughtes are all wayes enclined to evyll / and ye in *(ciiiᵛ/ciiiʳ)* bondage and captivité under synne / moare over seinge that noman can synge my laude and prayse in a straunge countre psal.cxxxvi.	**God** How can my honor and name be hallowed among you, when your hearts and thoughts are always inclined to evil? And you are in bondage and captivity under sin? Moreover, seeing that no man can sing my laud and praise in a strange country (Psa 136[137])	Gen 6:5 Psa 137:4
La deuxième demande. *L'âme. —* O Père, c'est vrai, nous reconnaissons que tous nos membres sont enclins au mal et que le monde, la chair et le diable veulent régner en nous et chasser ton honneur et ton nom. C'est pourquoi nous te supplions, délivre-nous de cette misère, établis ton règne, afin que le péché soit expulsé et que nous soyons rendus pieux, afin que toi seul règnes en nous et que nous devenions ton royaume en mettant à ton service toutes les forces de notre âme et de notre corps.	*The Second Request.* *The Soul. —* Oh Father, it is true, we recognize that all our members are inclined to evil and that the world, the flesh, and the devil want to reign in us and chase away your honor and your name. That is why we beseech you, deliver us from that misery, establish your reign, in order that sin would be expulsed and that we may be rendered holy, in order that you alone reign in us and that we become your kingdom by placing at your service all the strength of our souls and bodies.	**THE SINNER** O father that ys trueth / we fele our membres ye and also the very hertes of us prone and ready to sine and that the world / the flesshe / and the devyll rule in us / and expell the due honoure of thyne holy name. Wherefore we beseche the moost mercyfull father / for the love that thou hast un to thie sonne christe / helpe us out of this miserable bondage / and latt thi kingdome come / to dryve oute the synne / to loose the bondes off satan / to t ame the flesshe / to make us ryght eous and parfecte / and to cleve un to the / that thou only mayst raigne in us / and that we may be thi kingdome and possession / and the obey with all our power and strengthe / both with in and with oute.	**The Sinner** O Father, that is truth. We feel our members, yea and also our very hearts prone and ready to sin, and that the world, the flesh, and the devil rule in us, and expel the due honor of your holy name. Wherefore we beseech you most merciful Father, for the love that you have unto your Son, help us out of this miserable bondage, and thy kingdom come, to drive out the sin, to loose the bonds of Satan, to tame the flesh, to make us righteous and perfect, and to cleave unto you. That you alone may reign in us, and that we may be your kingdom and possession, and that we obey you with all our power and strength, both within and without.	Repentance Confession Faith Justification by faith; imputed righteousness
Dieu, *Deutér. XXXII. —* Je détruis celui auquel je veux aider et je tue, je rends pauvre et réduis à rien celui que je veux amener à la vie, au salut et que je veux rendre riche et pieux. Mais vous ne voulez accepter que je pense et que j'agisse ainsi (Psaume LXXVII). Comment dois-je donc vous aider ? Que puis-je faire de plus ? (Esaïe, V).	*God,* *Deuter. 32. —* I destroy he whom I want to help and I kill them, I render poor bring to naught him who I want to being to life, salvation, and whom I want to render rich and holy. But you do not accept that I think and act in this way (Psalm 77). How then can I help you? What more can I do for you? (Isaiah 5).	**GOD** Whom I helpe them I destroye. And whom I make lyvinge / safe / riche and good / them I fill condemne and cast them awaye / make them bedgers and bring them to noughte. But so to be cured off me ye wil not sofre psalme.lxxvii. Howe then shall I heale you / ye and what can I do moare? Iesaias.v.	**God** Whom I help, them I destroy. And whom I make living, safe, rich, and good, them I will condemn and cast them away, make them beggars and bring them to naught. But so to be cured by me will you not suffer? (Psa 77) How then shall I heal you, yea, and what shall I do more? (Isa 5)	Psa 78 Isa 5:4
La troisième demande. *L'âme. —* Nous regrettons de n'avoir ni compris, ni accepté ce que ta	*The Third Request.* *The Soul. —* We regret that we have not understood nor accepted that	**THE SINNER** That ys to us greate sorowe and greffe / that we can nether understonde nor sofre thi	**The Sinner** That is to us great sorrow and grief, that we can neither understand nor suffer your	Tyndale adds the concept of blindness and

main salutaire voulait faire pour nous. O Père, donne-nous ta grâce et ton aide afin que nous laissions agir ta volonté divine en nous.	which your salvific hand wanted to do for us. O Father, give us your grace and your help that we may allow you to work your divine will in us.	wholsome hande / Wherefore helpe deare father / open oure eyes / and worke pacience in us / that we maye understonde thi wholsome honde / and also paciently sofre thi Godly will to be fulfylled in us.	wholesome hand. Wherefore, help dear Father, open our eyes, and work patience in us, that we may understand your wholesome hand. And also patiently suffer your godly will to be fulfilled in us.	healing to this section: Psa 119:18; Isa 35:5; 42:7; Luke 24:31; Acts 9:8, 17-18
Et si cela nous fait mal, continue, corrige, tranche, frappe, brûle. Fait toujours ce que tu veux, afin que seule ta volonté se fasse et non pas la nôtre.	And if it hurts us, continue, correct, cut out, strike, burn. Always do what you want, in order that only your will be done and not ours.	Furthermore though thi moost wholsome cure (ciiiiʳ/ciiiiᵛ) be never so paynfull unto us / yet goo forewarde therewyth / punesh / bete / cutt / burn / destroye / brynge to noughte / damne / caste doune unto hell / and do whatsoever thou wylte / that thi wyll only maye be fulfylled and not oures.	Furthermore, though this most wholesome cure be ever so painful to us; yet go forward with it—punish, beat, cut, burn, destroy, bring to naught, damn, cast into hell, and do whatever you will—that your will may be fulfilled and not ours.	Notice also how Tyndale seems to add to Luther's list of verbs, expanding on Luther's ideas.
Ne souffre pas, cher Père, que nous entreprenions et accomplissions quelque chose selon notre idée, notre volonté. Car notre volonté et la tienne sont contraires ; la tienne seule est bonne, bien qu'elle ne nous semble pas toujours telle, la nôtre est mauvaise, bien qu'elle ait parfois belle apparence.	Do not suffer, dear Father, that we undertake or accomplish anything according to our ideas, our will. For our will and your will are contrary; yours is only good, even though it does not always seem to be so, and ours is bad, even though it sometimes has a beautiful appearance.	Forbydde deare father and in no wyse sofre us to folowe oure awne good thoughtes and ymaginacions / nether to prosecute our awne wyll / meanynge and purpose. For thi wyll and oures are clene contrary one to the other / thyne only good / though it other wyse appere un to our blynde reason / and oures evyll / though oure blindnes se it not	Forbid, dear Father, and in no wise suffer us to follow our own thoughts and imaginations, neither to execute our own will, meaning, and purpose. For your will and ours are clean contrary to one another. Yours is only good, though it appears otherwise to our blind reason; and ours evil, though [in] our blindness [we] see it not.	
Dieu, *Psaume LXXVII. —* Il est arrivé souvent que l'on m'aimait des lèvres et que le cœur était loin de moi. Et quand j'ai entrepris de les corriger, ils se sont enfuis et se sont soustraits à mon action, comme tu le lis au Psaume LXXVII : « Ils se sont convertis au jour de la bataille. »	**God,** *Psalm 77. —* It has happened quite often that they love me with their lips and that their heart is far from me. And when I make an effort to correct them, they flee and elude my action, as you read in Psalm 77, "They were converted in the day of battle."	**GOD** I am well served and dalte wyth all / that men love me wy th their lyppes and their hertes are farre from me / and when I take them in hande so make them better and to amende them / then runne they backeward / and in the mydds of there curynge / whyle their heal th ys a workinge / they wythdrawe themselves from me / as thoug readeste psalme.lxxvii.conversi sunt in die belli. They are tourned backe in the daye of batayle that ys to saye /	**God** I am well served and dealt with all, that men love me with their lips and their hearts are far from me. And when I take them in hand, so to make them better, and to help them, then they run backward, and in the midst of their curing, while their health is working, they withdraw from me, as you read in Psalm 77 (Lat. *conversi sunt in die belli*). They are turned back in the day of battle, that is to say.	Psa 78:36 Isa 29:13; Matt 15:8-9; etc.
Ils avaient bien commencé et m'avaient décidé à m'occuper d'eux, mais ils s'en sont retournés et sont retombés dans leur péché à mon déshonneur.	They started well so that I decided to take care of them, but then they turned back and relapsed into their sin to my dishonor.	they whych began well and committed them selves un to me / that I shulde take them in hande and cure them are gonne backe from me in tyme of temptacion and kylling of the flesshe / and are retourned to sinne and un to dishonouring of me agayne.	They which began well and committed themselves unto me, that I should take them in hand and cure them are gone back from me in time of temptation and killing of the flesh, and are returned to sin and unto [the] dishonoring of me again.	Psa 78:9; trans. "turned back in the day of battle"
La quatrième demande. *L'âme. —* Hélas, Père, c'est vrai. Nul homme n'est fort par lui-même (I Rois II). Qui pourra subsister devant toi, si tu ne nous fortifies	*The Fourth Request.* *The Soul. —* Alas, Father, that is true. No man is strong in-and-of himself (1 Kings 2). Who could subsist before you, if you do not	**THE SYNNER** O father it is true / no man can be strong in his awne stengthe / in the seconde chapter of the fyrst of the kinges. Ye and who is able to sofre and abyde	**The Sinner** O Father it is true. No man can be strong in his own strength. In the second chapter of the First of the Kings. Yea and who are able to suffer	1 Sam 2:4, 7-10 (?)

et ne nous réconfortes toi-même ? C'est pourquoi, cher Père, attaque-toi à nous, accomplis ta volonté afin que nous devenions ton royaume, à ta louange et à ta gloire.	strengthen us and you yourself do not console us? That is why, dear Father, spur us on, accomplish your will in order that we may become your kingdom, to your honor and your glory.	before thyne hande / yff thou the silfe strengthe and comforte us not. Wherefore moost mercifull father thake us un to thi cure / fulfyll *(ciiii^v/cv^r)* thi wyll in us / that we may be thi kyngdome and inheritaunce / un to thi laude and praysyng.	and abide before your hand, if you yourself do not strength and comfort us? Wherefore, most merciful Father, take us unto your cure, fulfill your will in us that we may be your kingdom and your inheritance, unto you laud and praise.	Like the Good Samaritan [Hubmaier's "Summary," Part 2]
Mais, cher Père, donne-nous ta force en cette affaire par ta parole sainte, donne nous notre pain quotidien. Imprime en nos cœurs l'image de ton cher fils Jésus-Christ qui est le vrai pain céleste, afin que, fortifiés par lui, nous acceptions et supportions joyeusement que notre volonté soit contrecarrée et détruite et que ta volonté s'accomplisse.	But, dear Father, give us your strength in this matter by your holy word, give us our daily bread. Print on our hearts the image of you dear son Jesus Christ who is the true bread from heaven, in order that, strengthened by him, we may accept and joyfully support that our will be thwarted and destroyed and that your will may be accomplished.	Also deare father strengthe and comforte us in soche busines with thi holy worde / geve us oure dayly breed / grave and printe this deare sonne Jesus in oure hertes / that we strengthed thorowe hym maye cherefully and gladly sofre and endure the destroyinge and killynge of oure will / and the fulfyllinge off thi will.	Also, dear Father, strengthen and comfort us in such business with your Holy Word. Give us our daily bread. Engrave and print your Son Jesus in our hearts, that we, strengthened through him may cheerfully and gladly suffer and endure the destroying and killing of our will, and the fulfilling of your will.	Deut 6:7
Accorde aussi ta grâce à toute chrétienté, envoie-nous des prêtres et des prédicateurs instruits qui ne nous enseignent pas de vaines fables, mais ton saint Evangile et Jésus-Christ.	Grant also your grace to all Christianity, send us instructed priests and preachers who will not teach vain fables, but your holy Gospel and Jesus Christ.	Ye and sheed oute thi grace a pon all christente and send learned prestes and preachers / to teache us thie sonne Jesus purely / and to feade us with the worde off thi holy Gospell / and not with the dreeggs and chaffe of fabelles and mens doctrine.	Yea, and shed out your grace upon all Christianity and send priests and preachers, to teach us your Son purely. And feed us with the word of your Holy Gospel, and not with the dregs and chaff of fables and men's doctrine.	Calling for Reformation Psa 1:4 2 Tim 4:4
Dieu, **Jérémie V et ailleurs. —** Il n'est pas bon de donner aux chiens les choses saintes et le pain des enfants.	**God,** **Jeremiah 5 and elsewhere.** **—** It is not good to give to dogs holy things and the bread of children.	**GOD** Yit is not good to caste pearles before syne / nether to geve holy things and the childrens bred unto the dogges and houndes.	**God** It is not good to cast pearls before swine, neither to give holy things and the children's bread to the dogs and hounds.	Matt 7:6 Matt 15:26
Vous péchez journellement, et quand je veux vous faire prêcher jour et nuit, vous n'écoutez pas et ma parole est méprisée.	You sin daily, and while I want you to preach day and night, you do not listen and my word is despised.	Ye synne continually with out ceasynge / and though I lett my word be preached a monge you never so moche / yet ye folowe not / nether obeye / but despice it.	You sin continuously without ceasing, and though I let my word be preached among you ever so much, yet you follow it not, neither obey, but despise it.	Gen 6:5 Psa 78:10 Isa 5:34
La cinquième demande. **L'âme. —** O Père, aie pitié et ne nous refuse pas le pain quotidien. Nous regrettons de n'avoir pas apprécié ta sainte parole et nous te prions d'avoir patience avec tes pauvres enfants. Remets-nous ce péché. Ne nous juge pas, car nul ne pourrait être considéré comme juste par toi.	**The Fifth Request.** **The Soul. —** Oh Father, have mercy and do not refuse us daily bread. We regret that we have not appreciated your holy word and we ask you to have patience with your poor children. Forgive us this sin. Do not judge us, for no one can be considered righteous by you.	**THE SYNNER** 0 father have mercy on us / and denye us not that breed of love / it greveth us sore / even at the very herte rotes of us / that we can not satisfye thi word and folowe it / we desyre the therefore to have pacience with us thie poure and wretched cheldren / and to forgeve us oure treaspace and gylt / and iudge us not after thi lawe / for no man is rightewes in thy presence.	**The Sinner** O Father, have mercy on us, and deny us not that bread of love. It grieves us much, even at the very root of our hearts, that we cannot satisfy your word and follow it. We desire you therefore to have patience with us, your poor and wretched children. And forgive us our trespass and guilt. And judge us not according to your Law. For no man is righteous in your presence.	Matt 18:26, 29 Luke 11:4 Eccl 7:20; Luke 17:10
Ne tiens compte que de ta promesse, afin que nous pardonnions à ceux qui nous	Take into account only your promise, in order that we may forgive those who have	Loke on thi promyses / we forgeve our treaspasers and that wyth all oure hertes / and	Look on your promises, we forgive our trespassers, and that with all of our hearts, and	

ont offensé, parce que tu nous as promis ton pardon. Non pas que nous ayons mérité ton pardon par notre pardon. Mais tu es véridique et tu as promis dans ta grâce de pardonner à tous ceux qui pardonnent à leur prochain. Nous mettons notre confiance en ta promesse.	trespassed against us, because you have promised your forgiveness. Not that we merit your forgiveness because of our forgiveness. But you are true and you have promised in your grace to forgive all those who forgive their neighbors. We place our confidence in your promise.	un to soche haste thou promysed forgevenes / not that we thorowe soch forgevenes are worthy of thy forgevenes / but th- *(cvʳ/cvᵛ)* at thou arte true / and of thi grace mercy haste promysed forgevenes un to all them that forgeve their neghbours / in this thi promyse therfore is all our hope and truste.	unto such hasten your promised forgiveness. Not that we through such forgiveness are worthy of forgiveness, but that you are true, and of your gracious mercy hasten promised forgiveness unto all them that forgive their neighbors. In this promise is all our hope and trust.	Exod 34:6-7 Matt 6:12; Luke 11:4
Dieu, *Psaume LXXVII. —* Bien souvent je pardonne et je délivre, et vous ne persévérez pas. Vous etes gens de peu de foi. Vous ne savez pas vieller et persévérer avec moi, vous retombez bien vite dans la tentation (Matthieu XXVI).	*God,* *Psalm 77. —* Very often I forgive and I deliver, and you do not persevere. You are people of little faith. You do not know how to watch and persevere with me, you very quickly relapse into temptation (Matthew 26).	**GOD** I forgeve you often and loose you ofte / and ye never abyde stedfaste. Children of lytle fayth are ye. Ye can not watche and endure with me a lityll while / but attonce faulle agayne in to temptacion / Matthew xxvi.	**God** I forgive you often, and you never abide steadfast. Children of little faith are you! You cannot watch and endure with me a little while. But once again fall into temptation, Matt 26	James 1:8 Matt 26:40-41; Mark 14:40
La sixième demande. *L'âme. —* Nous sommes faibles et malades, ô Père, et les assauts de la chair et du monde sont puissants et variés. O cher Père, soutiens-nous et ne nous laisse pas tomber en tentation et retomber dans le péché, mais donne-nous ta grâce afin que nous puissions persévérez et combattre vaillamment jusqu'à notre fin. Car sans ta grâce et ton aide nous ne pouvons rien.	*The Sixth Request.* *The Soul. —* We are weak and sickly, oh Father, and the assaults of the flesh and of the world are strong and varied. Oh dear Father, uphold us and do not allow us to fall into temptation and relapse into sin, but give us the grace in order that we may persevere and fight valiantly up until our end. For without your grace and your help we can do nothing.	**THE SYNNER** Weake are we o father and feble / and the temptacion greate and manyfold / in the flesshe and in the world. Kepe us father with thi myghty power / and lett us not faule in to temptacion and synne agayne / butt geve us grace thatt we maye abyde stondynge / and fighte manfully un to the ende / for with oute thi grace we can do nothynge.	**The Sinner** Weak are we, O Father, and feeble. And the temptation [is] great and manifold, in the flesh and in the world. Keep us, Father, with your mighty power, and let us not fall into temptation and sin again. But give us grace that we may abide standing, and fight manfully unto the end, for without your grace we can do nothing.	John 16:33 1 John 2:15-17 Eph 6:10-11, 13; 2 Tim 4:7 1 Cor 16:13 John 15:5
Dieu, *Psaume II. —* Je suis juste, et droit est mon jugement. C'est pourquoi le péché ne peut rester impuni. Et il faut que vous enduriez l'adversité. Que vous en souffriez est une conséquence de votre péché qui m'oblige à le punir et à l'entraver.	*God,* *Psalm 2. —* I am righteous, and upright is my judgment. That is why sin cannot remain unpunished. And it is necessary that you endure affliction. That you may suffer by it is a consequence of your sin that requires me to punish it and shackle it.	**GOD** I am ryghteous and ryghte ys my iudgment and therfore sinne maye not be unpunesshed / ye and ye muste sofre evyll and affliccion / and as twytchinge that ye have temptacion theirby / that is your sinnes faulte only / which compelleth me their un to / to kyll it and to heale you / For sinne can with no nother medicine be drawen out of you / but thorowe adversité and soferynge off evyll.	**God** I am righteous and my judgment is right. And therefore sin may not go unpunished. Yea, and you must suffer evil and affliction, and as doubtful that you have temptation thereby, that is only your sins fault, which compels me thereunto, to kill it and to heal you. For sin can with no other medicine be drawn out of you, but through adversity and suffering of evil.	Deut 32:4 2 Thess 1:4-6 Psa 66:10-11
La septième demande. *L'âme. —* Parce que le malheur est pour nous une tentation et menace de nous faire tomber dans le péché, délivre-nous-en, cher Père, afin que, libérés de tous péchés et de tous malheurs par ta volonté divine, nous devenions ton royaume et nous	*The Seventh Request.* *The Soul. —* Because hardship is for us a temptation and threatens to cause us to fall into sin, deliver us from it, dear Father, in order that, liberated from all sins and from all hardships by your divine will, we may become your kingdom and we may	**THE SYNNER** For as moche then as adversité tribulación affliccion and evyll which fyghte agaynste synne geve us temptacion / delyver us out of them / *(cvᵛ/cviʳ)* finishe thi cure and make us thorowe whole / that we loosed from synne and evyll maye be un to the a kyngdome / to laude	**The Sinner** For as much then as adversity, tribulation, affliction, and evil, which fight against sin give us temptation, deliver us out of them. Finish your cure and make us thoroughly whole. That we loosed from sin and evil may be unto you a kingdom, to laud,	2 Thess 1:4-6 2 Thess 1:10-11

te louions, te glorifions et te sanctifions éternellement. *Amen.* Comme tu nous as enseigné et ordonné et que tu as promis de nous exaucer, nous espérons et sommes assurés, Père très cher, que pour faire honneur à ta parole véridique, tu nous donneras tout cela dans ta grâce et ta miséricorde.	praise you, may glorify you, and may sanctify you eternally. *Amen.* As you taught and commanded us and you have promised to answer us, we hope and we are assured, very dear Father, that in order to do honor to your truthful word, you will give us all this by your grace and by your mercy.	/ to prays / and to sanctify the / amen. And seinge thou haste taughte us thus to praye / and has promysed also to heare us / we hope and are sure that thou wylte graciously and mercifully graunte us oure peticions / for thi veritees sake / and to the honouring off thy trueth / Amen.	to praise, and to sanctify you. Amen. And seeing that you have taught us to pray in this way, and have also promised to hear us, we hope and are sure that you will graciously and mercifully grant us our petitions, for your truth's sake, and to the honoring of your truth. Amen.	
Si quelqu'un demandait, enfin : « Que faire si je ne pouvais croire que je serai exaucé ? » Réponse : Fais comme le père de l'enfant possédé (Mark IX). Quand Christ lui dit : « Peux-tu croire ? Toutes choses sont possible pour celui qui a la foi », ce père s'écrie en larmes : Seigneur, je crois, viens au secours de ma foi si elle est trop faible. A Dieu soit honneur et gloire.	If someone would ask, lastly: "What can I do if I cannot believe that I will be answered?" Answer: Do as the father of the possessed (Mark 9). When Christ told him: "Are you able to believe? All things are possible for him who has faith," this father cried out with tears: Lord, I believe, come to the aid of my faith if it is too weak. To God be honor and glory.	Finally some man wyll say happly / what and yff I can not beleve that my prayer ys heard. I answere. Then do as the father of the possessed dyd in the .ix. of marke / when Christ sayd unto hym/ yff thou couldeste beleve / all thynges are possible un to hym that beleveth. The father answered I believe lorde / helpe myne unbelefe / that is to saye / heale myne unbelefe and geve me perfect belefe and strengthe the weaknes off my fayth and encrease it. *(cvi^r)*	Finally, some man will possibly say: "What if I cannot believe in my heart that my prayer is heard?" I answer: "Then do as the father of the possessed did in the 9th of Mark, when Christ said unto him, 'If you could believe, all things are possible unto him that believes.'" The father answered, "I believe, help mine unbelief." That is to say, heal mine unbelief and give me perfect belief and strengthen the weakness of my faith and increase it.	Mark 9:23 Mark 9:24 Rom 4:20

CHAPTER 22
Is an Invitation Necessary
for Effective Evangelistic Preaching?

Introduction:

a. The invitation is very controversial in some circles.[1173] How should a pastor or evangelist view the invitation with this kind of continual pressure? We begin with a definition

b. Definition: The invitation is a definite and clear, step-by-step explanation of what it takes for an individual to become a Christian according to the Bible:
    1) Regular use of a sinner's prayer is advisable.
    2) The invitation should use of some public sign made to the pastor or evangelist of the person's decision to give their heart to Christ, such as coming forward to the altar or front pew, standing up, or raising one's hand
        a) The more public the sign, the more public the commitment!
        b) An public invitation, although not uncommon in culture (e.g. political rallies), in a spiritual sense is counter-cultural, asking the person to step away from peers, in the midst of peers, to follow Christ, and Christ alone

c. Historically: The invitation is perfectly in line with Evangelical Christianity in the history of the church. For example, note the words of the German Lutheran Pietist August Hermann Francke (1663-1727) once said:

    "As far as I am concerned, I must preach that should someone hear me only once before he dies, he will have heard not just a part, but the entire way of salvation and in the proper way for it to take root in his heart."[1174]

d. Some introductory verses on the invitation:

    1) Old Testament theme verses for the invitation, Psa 95:6-11 (cf. Heb 3:7-4:13)

    2) New Testament theme verses for the invitation, 2 Cor. 5:20-6:2
        a) 5:20 and 6:1, the plea for an invitation
        b) 6:2, use a Scripture, and from that Scripture
        c) 6:2, build an invitation.

    3) A model invitation, Acts 13:38-41:
        a) Context of the invitation—forgiveness of sins, faith alone, vv 38-39:
            (1) Proclamation of forgiveness of sins [following Luke 24:27]
            (2) Emphasis on justification by faith
        b) Two part invitation:
            (1) Warning, v 40, "Therefore take heed"
            (2) Use of Scripture, v 41, [quote of Hab 1:5] "Behold, you scoffers, and marvel, and perish…"

    4) Furthermore:
        a) The summaries of preaching in the Book of Matthew are invitations:
            Of John the Baptist: "Now in those days John the Baptist came, preaching in the wilderness of Judea, saying, 'Repent, for the kingdom of heaven is at hand,'" Matt 3:1-2
            Of Jesus: "From that time Jesus began to preach and say, 'Repent, for the kingdom of heaven is at hand'" (Matt 4:17)
            Of the disciples: "And as you go, preach, saying, 'The kingdom of heaven is at hand.'" Matt 10:7

[1173]For example Erroll Hulse has written a biblical analysis against the invitation in *The Great Invitation* (Hertfordshire, England; Evangelical Press, 1986). Roger Carswell has heard the invitation called "Protestant Absolution" (Carswell, Roger. *And Some as Evangelists: Growing Your Church through Discovering and Developing Evangelists* [Fearn, Ross-shire, Great Britain: Christian Focus, 2002, 2005], 141).

[1174]Paulus Scharpff, *History of Evangelism: Three Hundred Years of Evangelism in Germany, Great Britain, and the Unites States of America.* Helga Bender Henry, trans. (Grand Rapids: Eerdmans, 1964, 1966), 46.

      b) The last words of the sermon of Paul in Acts is an invitation, Acts 28:25-28

      c) Toward the end of John's biography of Jesus:

         (1) John included Jesus' call for Thomas to believe, John 20:27-28

         (2) Then John included a call to the reader, John 20:30-31

5) Before one rejects the invitation, due to certain deductive arguments of systematic [or philosophical] theology, it would be good to consider:

    a) How this rejection necessitates the reinterpretation of the examples and preaching in the Bible, necessitating a "dispensational" distancing from New Testament preaching as not applying to the current age

    b) How this rejection impacts a plenary look at the New Testament in building a theology; the implication being that the rejection of an invitation implies or necessitates the ignoring of some clear aspects of New Testament theology and practice

1. Why Use an Invitation?

a. "Shaking the dust off your feet" demands that the Gospel be shared to the point of rejection!

1) Christ commands shaking the dust off of one's feet following a negative response,[1175] Matt 10:14-15, Mark 6:10-11, Luke 9:5; 10:10-11:

    a) This includes a negative response to:

       (1) Hearing the Gospel

       (2) The invitation to repent and believe in the Gospel

       (3) Even being received into someone's home!

    b) While numbers of women gathered in Philippi at the place of prayer, only Lydia was recorded as having listened, Acts 16:13-14; the demon-possessed slave girl, on the other hand, knew enough of the message of Paul and Silas to mock them, Acts 16:16-17

2) Rejection is thus confirmed or acknowledged through the shaking off the dust from one's feet

    a) Is this not synonymous to Isaiah's calling the heavens and the earth as a witness *against* Israel, Isa 1:2-3?

    b) Or asking Israel to sing a song as a witness against themselves, Deut 31:19

b. Sharing the Gospel to the point of warning someone:

1) Two verses:

    a) "When I say to the wicked, 'You shall surely die'; and you do not warn him or speak out to warn the wicked from his wicked way that he may live, that wicked man shall die in his iniquity, but his blood I will require at your hand," Ezek 3:18

    b) "Yet if you have warned the wicked, and he does not turn from his wickedness or from his wicked way, he shall die in his iniquity; but you have delivered yourself," Ezek 3:19

2) What does sharing the Gospel to the point of warning mean for an invitation?

    a) Sharing the Gospel is more than informing

    b) Sharing the Gospel also includes telling negatives

    c) Warning implies telling the person how to avoid the danger—this is where the invitation comes in

c. Similarly, the command to preach repentance implies an invitation!

1) "And that repentance for forgiveness of sins should be proclaimed," Luke 24:47

2) The preaching of repentance is found throughout the book of Acts, e.g. Acts 2:38; 3:19; 5:31; 8:22; 17:30; 20:21; 26:20 (cf. Acts 13:38-39)

3) Perhaps the preaching of repentance is what led antagonists of apostolic proclamation to use the verb καταγγέλλω [protesting or countermanding], Acts 4:2; 16:17, 21; cf. Acts 17:13

d. And as a parallel, preaching for someone to "turn from their wicked ways" implies decisional preaching:

1) Three examples of this should suffice, Isa 55:6-7; Jer 35:14-16; Eze 18:29-32; Acts 26:20

[1175]See more extensive treatment in the notes above titled, "When do you shake the dust off of your feet?" following Chapter 19.

2) However, interestingly enough, false teachers avoid preaching repentance and turning from sin, Jer 23:14, 17, are these not sometimes the same ones that are also against an invitation?

2. Historical (Part One):

Introduction: Often a historical view combined wth a theological understanding provides clarity for how or why methodologies develop

a. The Eucharist as Sacramental Invitation!?

1) In sacramental churches, parishioners are asked to come forward every week, row by row, family by family, to receive the Eucharist:
   a) In the Anglican church they receive both kinds (wafer and wine)
   b) In the Roman church they receive one kind (wafer), with a brass spatula held under the wafer to make sure that the "Body of Christ" does not fall to the ground

2) In the case of those not wanting to receive the eucharist (in the Episcopal/Anglican tradition):
   a) They move out of the row, into the aisle, and return to their seat after everyone else has left the aisle, or
   b) They go forward and cross their arms as a signal to the priest/pastor, so that he/she knows to bless them (pray for them) rather than to give them the wafer

3) This method of giving the elements is clearly public invitation with a very long history (the Gallican Missal was canonized by Gregory I [590-604] for the entire Western or Latin church):

   a) It is public; it is personal; it is individual; it is voluntary (while there is peer pressure to join in with everyone else)

   b) It is accompanied with a liturgical reinactment of the Gospel, through:
      (1) The liturgical prayer of confession of sin
          (a) While this prayer may warm the heart of a truly born again person, the unsaved repeat it as they would a Mother Goose rhyme (especially when it was in Latin)
      (2) The affirmation of the audience receiving absolution of sins
      (3) The reciting of the Apostles Creed
      (4) A "Gospel" reading from one of the Gospels

   c) It provides for a universalistic salvation to all who come forward for the element(s):
      (1) The 1 Cor 11:27-31 warning is often not given
      (2) Grace is deemed bestowed through receiving the elements *ex opere operato*, regardless of the spiritual condition or contrition of the person administering the sacrament or the spiritual condition of the person receiving the sacrament
      (3) Therefore, the mere coming forward along with the reception of the Eucharist is deemed to bestow grace

   d) It corresponds with a non-conversionistic sacramental theology of salvation as discussed in Chapter 8 and 17, whereby one is not saved by hearing and believing, but by submitting to a prescribed ritual of the church, be it Roman, Anglican, Lutheran, or Orthodox.

b. Medieval Preaching for Military Crusades:

1. Urban II (1088-1099) and Innocent III (1198-1216) or their legates preached in the open air to large crowds calling them to come forward for a public commitment to fight in the crusades, at which time they received a cloth cross which they were to sew to their garments until they had completed their crusade vow.[1176] This was [falsely] called, "the preaching of the Cross."

[1176]Jonathan Riley-Smith, *What Were the Crusades?* 3rd ed (San Francisco: Ignatius, 1977, 1992, 2002), 37-43.

2. Likewise, Bernard of Clairveaux (who took his monastic vows in 1113), was sent by Papal Legate and Cardinal, Bishop of Ostia Albéric to "preach the cross" (i.e. stamp out the "heretics") in Southern France, and particularly to preach against the "heresy" of the not-yet-titled "Albigenses."[1177] His [fanatical] anti-Albigensian and pro-Church-of-Rome views led him to ask a crowd to raise their hands as a sign to show that they would repress the "heresy" of the Albigenses.[1178]

Conclusion: Yes, there are documented improper uses of invitations in the history of the churches; this fact in itself, however, does not automatically negate the proper use of public invitations; Satan, the angel of Light, often seeks to take what is holy and discredit it through profane use!

3. **Biblical Overview**:[1179]

    a. Biblical Examples of Invitations—exemplary, not exhaustive:

        1) The invitation is the evangelist extending [voicing] God's call to sinners:

            a) Sample invitations in the Old Testament:

                (1) Torah and Historical Books:

Gen 3:9, "Where are you?"

Exod 19:12, "You shall set up bounds for the people all around, saying, 'Beware that you do not go up on the mountain or touch the border of it; whoever touches the mountain shall surely be put to death." [a geographic boundary]

Exod 32:26, "Whoever is for the Lord, come to me!"

Num 16:21, 24, "Separate yourselves from among this congregation, that I may consume them instantly." "Get back from around the dwellings of Korah, Dathan, and Abiram." [a necessary change in geography]

Num 21:8, "Then the Lord said to Moses, 'Make a fiery serpent, and set it on a standard; and it shall come about, that everyone who is bitten, when he looks at it, he will live."

Num 25:1-9, command to slay idolaters

Deut 11:26-28, "See, I am setting before you today a blessing and a curse: the blessing, if you listen to the commandments of the LORD your God, which I am commanding you today; and the curse, if you do not listen to the commandments of the LORD your God, but turn aside from the way which I am commanding you today, by following other gods which you have not known"

Jos 24:14-16, "'Now, therefore, fear the LORD and serve Him in sincerity and truth; and put away the gods which your fathers served beyond the River and in Egypt, and serve the LORD. And if it is disagreeable in your sight to serve the LORD, choose for yourselves today whom you will serve: whether the gods which your fathers served which were beyond the River, or the gods of the Amorites in whose land you are living; but as for me and my house, we will serve the LORD.' And the people answered and said, 'Far be it from us that we should forsake the LORD to serve other gods...'" (cf. Jos 24:24-27)

1 Kgs 18:21, "Elijah came near to all the people, 'How long will you hesitate between two opinions? If the Lord is God, follow Him; but if Baal, follow him.' But the people did not answer a word" (1 Kgs 18:37-38)

2 Kgs 23:1-3, called all the people to Jerusalem to hear the Word of the Lord.

                (2) Latter Prophets:

Isa 1:18, "'Come now, and let us reason together,' says the Lord. 'Though your sins are as scarlet, they will be white as snow; though they are red like crimson, they will be like wool.'"

Isa 55:1-6, "Ho! Every one who thirsts, come to the waters; and you who have no money come, buy and eat. Come, buy wine and milk without money and without cost." ... "Seek the Lord while He may be found; call upon Him while He is near. let the wicked forsake

---

[1177]Jean Duvernoy, *Le Catharisme: La Religion des Cathares* (Toulouse, France: Privat, 1976), 227-33.

[1178] Jean Duvernoy, *Le Catharisme: Histoire des Cathares* (Toulouse, France: Privat, 1979), 205.

[1179]This section amalgamates ideas from R. Alan Streett, *The Effective Invitation* (Old Tappan, NJ: Revell, 1980; Grand Rapids: Kregel, 1995), a message by Dr. Lane Adams, "Extending the Invitation" (preached at the Billy Graham School of Evangelism on June 20, 1990 at Wheaton College), as well as my own observations from Scriptures and practice.

his way, and the unrighteous man his thoughts; and let him return to the Lord, and He
will have compassion on him, and to our God, for He will abundantly pardon."

Jer 21:8, "Behold, I set before you the way of life and the way of death."

Jer 31:22, "How long will you go here and there, O faithless daughter?"

Jer 35:15, "Turn now every man from his evil way and amend your deeds, and do not go
after other gods to worship them. Then you will dwell in the land which I have given to
you and to your forefathers; but you have not inclined your ear or listened to Me"

Ezek 18:32, "Therefore, repent and live." Ezek 18:32

Ezek 33:11, "Turn back, turn back from your evil ways! Why then will you die, O house of
Israel?"

b) Select invitations in the Gospels:

Matt 4:17, "From that time Jesus began to preach and say, 'Repent, for the kingdom of heaven is
at hand'"

Matt 4:19, "And He said to them, 'Follow Me, and I will make you fishers of men'" (cf. Mark
1:17)

Matt 7:13, "Enter by the narrow gate"

Matt 8:22, "But Jesus said to him, 'Follow Me; and allow the dead to bury their own dead'"

Matt 9:9, "And as Jesus passed on from there, He saw a man, called Matthew, sitting in the tax
office; and He said to him, 'Follow Me!' And he rose, and followed Him" (cf. Mark 2:14;
Luke 5:27-28)

Matt 11:28, "Come to Me, all who are weary and heavy laden, and I will give you rest"

Matt 14:29, "Come!"

Matt 16:24, "Then Jesus said to His disciples, 'If anyone wishes to come after Me, let him deny
himself, and take up his cross, and follow Me'"

Matt 19:21, "Jesus said to him, "If you wish to be complete, go *and* sell your possessions and
give to *the* poor, and you shall have treasure in heaven; and come, follow Me" (cf. Mark
10:21; Luke 18:22)

Matt 22:4, "Come to the wedding feast" (cf. Luke 14:17)

Matt 25:6, "Behold, the bridegroom! Come out to meet *him*"

Matt 25:34, "Then the King will say to those on His right, 'Come, you who are blessed of My
Father, inherit the kingdom prepared for you from the foundation of the world'"

Matt 28:6, "Come, see the place where He was lying."

Mark 1:14-15, "And after John had been taken into custody, Jesus came into Galilee, preaching
the gospel of God, and saying, 'The time is fulfilled, and the kingdom of God is at hand;
repent and believe in the gospel'"

Mark 3:3, "And He said to the man with the withered hand, 'Rise and *come* forward!'" (cf. Luke
6:8)

Mark 5:30-34, "Who touched My garments?"

Mark 6:12, "And they went out and preached that *men* should repent"

Mark 6:31, "And He said to them, 'Come away by yourselves to a lonely place and rest a while.'"

Mark 10:14, "Permit the children to come to Me; do not hinder them; for the kingdom of God
belongs to such as these" (cf. Luke 18:16)

Luke 5:32, "I have not come to call the righteous but sinners to repentance"

[teaching] Luke 9:23, "If anyone wishes to come after Me, let him deny himself, and take up his
cross daily, and follow Me" (cf. Mark 8:34; Matt 10:38; 16:24)

Luke 9:59, "And He said to another, 'Follow Me!'"

Luke 13:3, "I tell you, no, but unless you repent, you will all likewise perish" (cf. Luke 13:5)

Luke 17:16-19, "Go and show yourselves to the priests!"

Luke 19:5-7, "Zaccheus, hurry and come down, for today I must stay at your house."

John 1:39, "Come, and you will see"

John 1:43, "Follow Me!" (cf. John 10:27)

John 1:46, "Come and see"

John 4:29, "Come, see a man who told me all the things that I *have* done; this is not the Christ, is
it?"

John 11:43, "Lazarus, come forth!"

John 21:12, "Come *and* have breakfast"

John 21:19, "Follow Me!"

John 21:22, "Jesus said to him, 'If I want him to remain until I come, what *is that* to you? You
follow Me!'"

c) Sample invitations in the Acts:

2:38-39, "Repent, and let each of you be baptized in the name of Jesus Christ for the forgiveness of your sins; and you shall receive the gift of the Holy Spirit. For the promise is for you and your children, and for all who are far off, as many as the Lord our God shall call to Himself."

3:19, "Repent therefore and return, that your sins may be wiped away, in order that times of refreshing may come from the presence of the Lord"

3:26, "For you first, God raised up His Servant, and sent Him to bless you by turning every one *of you* from your wicked ways."

8:22-23, "Therefore repent of this wickedness of yours, and pray the Lord that if possible, the intention of your heart may be forgiven you. For I see that you are in the gall of bitterness and in the bondage of iniquity."

13:38-39, "Therefore let it be known to you, brethren, that through Him forgiveness of sins is proclaimed to you, and through Him everyone who believes is freed from all things, from which you could not be freed through the Law of Moses"

16:31, "And they said, 'Believe in the Lord Jesus, and you shall be saved, you and your household.'"

17:30, "Therefore having overlooked the times of ignorance, God is now declaring to men that all everywhere should repent"

26:19-20, "Consequently, King Agrippa, I did not prove disobedient to the heavenly vision, but *kept* declaring both to those of Damascus first, and *also* at Jerusalem and *then* throughout all the region of Judea, and *even* to the Gentiles, that they should repent and turn to God, performing deeds appropriate to repentance"

26:24-28, "And while *Paul* was saying this in his defense, Festus said in a loud voice, 'Paul, you are out of your mind! *Your* great learning is driving you mad.' But Paul said, 'I am not out of my mind, most excellent Festus, but I utter words of sober truth. For the king knows about these matters, and I speak to him also with confidence, since I am persuaded that none of these things escape his notice; for this has not been done in a corner. King Agrippa, do you believe the Prophets? I know that you do.' And Agrippa *replied* to Paul, 'In a short time you will persuade me to become a Christian.'"

d) Sample invitations in the Pauline Letters:

Rom 12:1-2, "I urge you therefore, brethren, by the mercies of God ..."

Rom 15:30, "Now I urge you, brethren, by our Lord Jesus Christ ..."

Rom 16:17, "Now I urge you, brethren, keep your eye on those ..."

2 Cor. 5:20, "... we beg you on behalf of Christ, be reconciled to God."

2 Cor. 6:1-2, "We also urge you not to receive the grace of God in vain"

2 Cor. 10:1ff., "Now I, Paul, myself urge you by the meekness and gentleness of Christ..."

Phil 4:2, "I urge Euodia and I urge Syntyche to live in harmony in the Lord."

Col 4:17, "And say to Archippus, 'Take heed to the ministry which you have received in the Lord, that you may fulfill it.'"

1 Thess 4:10, "But we urge you, brethren, to excel still more."

1 Thess 5:14, "And we urge you, brethren, admonish the unruly, encourage the fainthearted, help the weak, be patient with all men."

1 Tim. 1:3-4, "As I urged you upon my departure for Macedonia, remain on at Ephesus, in order that you may instruct certain men not to teach strange doctrines ..."

1 Tim. 6:13-14, "... Therefore, I want younger *widows* to get married, bear children, keep house, *and* give the enemy no occasion for reproach."

2 Tim. 4:1-2, "I solemnly charge *you* in the presence of God and of Christ Jesus, who is to judge the living and the dead, and by His appearing and His kingdom: preach the word

Phm 10, "I appeal to you for my child ..."

e) Sample invitations in Hebrews:

Heb 4:1 (NKJ), "Therefore, since a promise remains of entering His rest, let us fear lest any of you seem to have come short of it"

Heb 4:14 (KJV), "Seeing then that we have a great high priest, that is passed into the heavens, Jesus the Son of God, let us hold fast *our* profession"

Heb 13:19, "And I urge *you* all the more to do this"

Heb 13:22, "But I urge you, brethren, bear with this word of exhortation"

f) In Peter:

1 Peter 2:11, "Beloved, I urge you as aliens and strangers to abstain from fleshly lusts, which wage war against the soul"

    2) Examples in the NT that necessitated some type of an invitation—a separation of respondents from the crowds of listeners:

        a) Verbal responses, Jos 24:16; John 9:38; Acts 2:37; 16:31; 26:28

        b) Baptism, Acts 2:41

        c) Counting the converts, Acts 2:41, 4:4, 6:7, 11:21

        d) Multitudes coming to Christ, Acts 5:14, 6:1, 7, 8:6, 12, 10:44, 48, 11:21, 24, 12:24, 14:1, 17:4

        e) Those who believed, Acts 16:33-34, 17:12, 19:18

        f) Those who became followers or joined the apostles, Acts 13:43, 16:14-15, 17:4, 34

    3) Other invitations:

        a) God's invitation for Moses to remove his sandals, Exod 3:5

        b) Jesus' invitation for a man to be healed, Matt 12:13

  b. Biblical Teaching on the Invitation:

    1) The Gift of Exhortation:

        a) For all Christians, 2 Cor 5:18-20

        b) As a particular gift, Rom 12:8

        c) A Requirement for pastors and elders, 2 Tim 4:2, 5, Titus 1:7-9

        d) Encouragement to exhort, Tit. 2:6

    2) The Abundant Use of the Word "Come" in the Bible, Isa 1:18; 55:1, 3, 6-7; Matt 11:28; 19:14; 22:2-5; Mark 10:21; John 5:40; 6:37; 7:37-39; Rev 22:17

    3) The Concept of Fishing for Souls, Matt 4:19; Mark 1:17; Luke 5:10

    4) Teaching Concerning Sowing and Reaping, John 4:35-38 (cf. Psa 126:5-6; Amos 9:13)

4. Reasons for an Invitation:

  a. The Gospel always demands a response, Luke 24:47

  b. Gives an opportunity for response:

    1) For people to get right with God

    2) For people to make a public Profession of faith in Christ, Luke 12:8

    3) For people to make a concrete commitment to Christ

  c. Allows for counseling with the penitent, e.g. Luke 3:10, 12, and 14; Acts 2:37

  d. Prepares for a verbal declaration of Christ, Rom 10:9-10

  e. Provides an example for the congregation:

    1) Of the need for salvation

    2) Of people coming to Christ

    3) Of the pastor's example in reaching out to the lost

    4) Of how to give an invitation

  f. An invitation keeps evangelism, the Gospel, and spiritual accountability before the people.

5. Lack of an Invitation:

  a. May involve scattering the sheep—a characteristics of false prophets, Jer 10:21; 23:1-2; Ezek 34:5-6, 20-24; Zech 11:14-17

    1) Matt 12:30, "He who is not with Me is against Me; and he who does not gather with Me scatters" (cf. Luke 11:23)

  b. May show a lack of emphasis on preaching the Gospel, contra 1 Cor 1:17; 2:2

  c. May show a lack of emphasis on conversion—"You must be born again," John 3:7

  d. May show a lack of commitment to decisional preaching

6. What an Invitation Does Not Mean:

    a. An invitation does not necessarily imply that the Gospel has been proclaimed

    b. An invitation does not necessarily imply that the Word of God has been proclaimed

    c. An invitation does not necessarily imply belief in the substitutionary atonement, the inerrancy of Scripture, etc.

    d. Nor does responding to an invitation does not necessarily imply genuine repentance and faith.

7. The Anatomy of an Individual Invitation:

    a. Sample (notice this was an individual invitation given before and in the midst of a large group of people, Acts 25:23):

        Acts 26:27, "King Agrippa, do you believe the Prophets? I know that you do."

    b. Here are some aspects of this invitation of the Apostle Paul:
        1) The individual invitation is respectful, "King Agrippa"
        2) The individual invitation is personal, "Agrippa" (by name)
        3) The invitation is in the form of a question, "do"
        4) The invitation focuses on the heart issues, "do you believe?"
        5) The invitation is related to faith in the testimony of the Scriptures, "the prophets"
        6) The invitation is calculated to move the person toward professing Christ, "do you believe the prophets?" He did not say, "Do you believe the Gospel?" or "Do you believe in Jesus?"
        7) The invitation comes from the heart of the person giving it, "I know"
        8) The invitation is based on perceived knowledge of the individual, "I know that you do"
        9) The invitation is expectant of a positive response, "I know that you do"

    c. Notice that King Agrippa understood exactly what Paul's invitation was seeking to accomplish:

        Acts 26:28, "And Agrippa *replied* to Paul, 'In a short time you will persuade me to become a Christian.'"

    d. Notice also that Paul was not ashamed of Agrippa receiving this implication from his question!

        Acts 26:29, "And Paul said, 'I would to God that not only you, but also all who hear me today, might become both almost and altogether such as I am, except for these chains.'"

8. The Invitation and Theology:

    a. Some oppose the invitation because of theological reasons,[1180] the words of John Owen (1616-1683), a Puritan theologian should be kept in mind:

        The mixed distribution of the elect and reprobates, believers and unbelievers, according to the purpose and mind of God, throughout the whole world, and in the several places thereof, in all or most of the single congregations, is another ground of holding out a tender of the blood of Jesus Christ to them for whom it was never shed, as is apparent in the event by the ineffectualness of its proposals. The ministers of the gospel, who are stewards of the mysteries of Christ, and to whom the word of reconciliation is committed, being acquainted only with revealed things (the Lord lodging his purposes and intentions towards particular persons in the secret ark of his own bosom, not to be pried into), *are bound to admonish all, and warn all men, to whom they are sent; giving the same commands, proposing the same promises, making tenders of Jesus Christ in the same manner, to all, that the elect, whom they know not but by the event, may obtain, whilst the rest are hardened.* Now, these things being thus ordered by Him who hath the supreme disposal of all, - namely, first, that there should be such a mixture of elect and reprobate, of tares and wheat, to the end of the world; and secondly, that Christ, and reconciliation through him, should be preached by men ignorant of his eternal discriminating purposes; there is an absolute necessity of two other things: First, that the promises must have a kind of unrestrained generality, to be suitable to this dispensation before recounted. Secondly, that they must be proposed to them towards whom the Lord never intended the good things of the promises, they having a share in this proposal by their mixture in this world with the elect of God. So that, from the general proposition of Christ in the promises, nothing can be concluded concerning his death for all to whom it is proposed, as having another rise and occasion. The sum is: The word of reconciliation being committed to men unacquainted with God's distinguishing

---

        [1180]For example, Iain Murray, *The Invitation System* (Edinburgh: Banner of Truth, 1967) and Erroll Hulse, *The Great Invitation: Examining the Use of the Invitation System in Evangelism* (Welwyn, Hertfordshire, England: Evangelical Press, 1986).

counsels, to be preached to men of a various, mixed condition in respect of his purpose, and the way whereby he hath determined to bring his own home to himself being by exhortations, entreaties, promises, and the like means, accommodated to the reasonable nature whereof all are partakers to whom the word is sent, which are suited also to the accomplishment of other ends towards the rest, as conviction, restraint, hardening inexcusableness, it cannot be but the proposal and offer must necessarily be made to some upon condition, who intentionally, and in respect of the purpose of God, have no right unto it in the just aim and intendment thereof. Only, for a close, observe these two things: - First, that the proffer itself neither is nor ever was absolutely universal to all, but only indefinite, without respect to outward differences. Secondly, that Christ being not to be received without faith, and God giving faith to whom he pleaseth, it is manifest that he never intendeth Christ to them on whom he will not bestow faith.[1181]

Not, then, any more to trouble the reader with a declaration of that in particulars which he cannot but be sufficiently convinced of by a bare overlooking of these reasons, - namely that this author is utterly ignorant of the way of reasoning, and knows not how tolerably to express his own conceptions, nor to infer one thing from another in any regular way, I answer, - First, that whatsoever the Scripture holds forth as a truth to be believed is certainly so, and to be embraced. Secondly, that the Scripture sets forth the death of Christ, to all whom the gospel is preached [unto], as an all sufficient means for the bringing of sinners unto God, so as that whosoever believe it and come in unto him shall certainly be saved. Thirdly, what can be concluded hence, but that the death of Christ is of such infinite value as that it is able to save to the utmost every one to whom it is made known, if by true faith they obtain an interest therein and a right thereunto, we cannot perceive. *This truth we have formerly confirmed by many testimonies of Scripture, and do conceive that this innate sufficiency of the death of Christ is the foundation of its promiscuous proposal to elect and reprobate.* Fourthly, that the conclusion, if he would have the reason to have any colour or show of an argument, should at least include and express the whole and entire assertion contained in the proposition, - namely, "That Christ is so set forth to be the Saviour of the world, that whosoever of the particulars believe," etc. And then it is by us fully granted, as making nothing at all for the universality of redemption, but only for the fullness and sufficiency of his satisfaction. Of the word *world* enough hath been said before.[1182]

9. Methods for the Invitation:[1183]

a. Looking up at preacher

b. The raising of hands
I was interested to have found an account of the raising of hands in 1145 AD:

"Saint Bernard [of Clairveaux] was better received [later in Albi, France]. He preached on the day of St Peter (June 29), before a crowd whom he brought to unanimously repress heresy by raised hands. But some letters having arrived from Cîteaux [of the Cistercians], led him to make haste in traveling to the north."[1184]

c. Standing up (as opposed to bowing down, cf. Dan 3:9-18)

d. Coming forward:
1) To meet the pastor or another person at the front (see example below of Claude Brousson's invitation in 1689)
2) To kneel for prayer
3) To go into an inquiry area (cf. Luke 3:10-14)
4) To sit on the "Anxious Bench" (i.e. front pew; often ascribed to Finney)

e. Filling out a commitment card on the table or in the pew

f. Talking to the pastor at the exit of the service, e.g. "please come talk to me before you leave today"

g. Evening home inquiry meetings, as in the time of Jonathan Edwards

---

[1181]John Owen, *Death of Death in the Death of Christ* (Edinburgh: Banner of Truth, 1959), 201-02. Emphasis mine.

[1182]Ibid., 264. Emphasis mine.

[1183]Faris D. Whitesell wrote *Sixty-Five Ways to Give Evangelistic Invitations* (Grand Rapids: Zondervan Publishing House, 1945). He gives a solid overview of methods for giving an invitation. Similarly, R. Alan Streett in *The Effective Invitation* speaks of historical and present methods of giving an invitation on pages 81-130.

[1184]Jean Duvernoy, *Le Catharisme: Histoire des Cathares* (Toulouse: Privat, 1979), 205. Translation mine.

h. Combinations of the above, for example, two classic "two step" invitations are:

1) Raised hands and come forward:
   a) Have persons raise their hands for prayer
   b) Pray for those who raised their hands
   c) Ask those who raised their hands to come forward as a public testimony to their commitment (whatever that is corresponding to the message)

2) Look up and come forward:
   a) Have the audience bow their heads in prayer
   b) Ask those who have been convicted by the message to look up
   c) Pray for those who looked up
   d) Ask those who looked up if they would like to make their commitment public through coming forward

h. Care ought to be taken that fleshly coercion be avoided for the sake of bragging about numbers; the invitation is a holy time with holy ends, and it ought to be kept holy!

10. Historical (Part Two):

Introduction: Much like Francke's quote above, many seem unaware of a public invitation prior to Charles Finney (circa 1820), or perhaps even prior to the First Great Awakening (circa 1740), for example:

"If one accepts that the altar call was not used prior to the eighteenth century, and, as has already been stated, it does not seem to have been, with the possible exceptions of isolated incidents, it becomes necessary to ask, did the great evangelists of the seventeen hundreds use it?"[1185]

a. The Invitation in the 1230-1330 Cathar Ritual:

Introduction: Bound at the end of a small handwritten New Testament, titled "Waldensian Bible," at the close of a second Gospel presentation on baptism in the Spirit and separation from the world, was the following call to decision:

[Last sentences of Gospel presentation, which began "If he must be consoled in the field"]: "And Jude brother of James says for our instruction in the epistle (verse 23): 'Hate this soiled garment which is fleshly.' And by these testimonies and by many others, you must keep the commandments of God, and hate the world. And if you do well up until the end, we are assured that your soul will have eternal life."

"And may he say, 'I have this desire, pray God that he gives me the strength for it.'"

"And may one of the 'good men' make amends [Occitan: *meloirer*; French: *melioramentum*], with the believer, to the elder, and may he say: '*Parcite nobis*' [a short prayer, titled 'spare us']"

"Good Christians, we pray you by the love of God that you accord this good that the God has given you to this friend present here" [speaking of the baptism of the Holy Spirit by the laying on of hands]

"And then may he make amends, and may he say: 'Spare us. For all the sins that I may have done or said or thought or accomplished, I ask forgiveness of God, and of the church, and of you all.'

"And may the Christians say: 'By God and by us and by the church may they be forgiven you, and we pray to God that he may forgive them of you.'

[1185]David Malcolm Bennett, *The Altar Call: Its Origins and Present Usage,* foreword by Mark Noll (Lanham, MD: University Press of America, 2000), 1. Bennett referred to his treatment of the topic as follow: "Though one cannot discount the possibility of isolated uses of the public invitation in the first sixteen hundred years of church history, there appears to be no justification for believing that the practice was common during those centuries, and may never have been used at all. Certainly, for most of that period the bulk of the church was either calvinistic or sacramentalist, and it would seem unlikely that this form of evangelism would have found favor with either party. Calvinists strongly emphasized the role of God, rather than the convert in Christian conversion, and one would not expect to find them using a form of evangelism which so strongly emphasized human response. In the case of sacramentalists, if grace conveyed through baptism marks the entry into the church, then there is little room left for a distinct conversion experience. Thus it would seem unlikely that this method of evangelism was used prior to the eighteenth century, at least not in a regular or systematic way. Some research was done on the practices of the Anabaptists (sixteenth century) and the early Baptists (seventeenth century), on the grounds that something akin to the altar call might have been used by them in their efforts to identify suitable candidates for baptism, but nothing was found to indicate such a practice. Neither has any other solid evidence of it being used by anybody else prior to the eighteenth century been discovered" (*ibid.,* xiv-xv).

"And then they must console him. And may the elder take the book and place it upon his head,[1186] and the other 'good men' each with his right hand, and may they say the *parcias* and three *adoremus*, and then: '[in Latin] *Pater Sanctu, suscipe servum tuum in tua justifia, et mitte gratiam tuum et spiritum sanctum tuum super eum.*' And may they pray with the preaching, and the one who guides the holy service must say in a quiet voice the '*sixaine*';[1187] and when the '*sixaine*' is said, he should say three *Adoremus*, with the preaching out loud, and then 'the Gospel' [a Latin version of John 1:1-5, 10-17]. And when the Gospel is said, they must say three *Adoremus* and the '*gratia*' and the '*parcias*.'

"And then they must make peace between themselves (to hug) and with the book. And if there are believers, they must also make peace, and may the believers, if there are any, make peace with the book between them. And then may they pray God with 'Double' and with '*veniae*', and they will have delivered him [the preaching].[1188]

b. Claude Brousson (1689):

The following is the translation of a 1689 invitation given by the French Huguenot Claude Brousson, a trained lawyer and a Reformed église du désert (underground church) preacher/revivalist/missionary (1689-1693, 1695-1696, 1697-1698). On his third mission trip from Switzerland into France, Brousson was betrayed, tried for preaching the Gospel (labeled as insurrection against the king, much like Jesus [Luke 23:14] and Paul [Acts 24:5]), and died by strangulation and then being stretched on a wheel in France:

"When Louis XIV revoked the Edict of Nantes on October 17, 1685, making it illegal to be Protestant in France, Brousson fled to Switzerland. Several years later, because of his concern for all the churches and believers in France, Brousson returned to revive the underground church. He went from city to city preaching in fields and forests, and reorganizing the Reformed [Huguenot] churches. He was hunted like a criminal on his three missionary journeys. Finally, on his third missionary tour, a traitor denounced him, and he was captured at his hiding place. He was sentenced to be broken alive on the wheel November 4, 1698, but the judge secretly ordered that he be strangled first. Here is a first-hand account of the public invitation he gave to his hearers during his first trip to France, restoring "apostates" who had recanted to Catholicism:

"'When the sermon was over, the preacher asked whether there was any among his hearers wishing to be reconciled to God and His Church, and to re-enter the communion of saints … Then, any who were so minded came forward and knelt before the preacher, who began to remonstrate with them and showed them how enormous was the sin they had committed in forsaking Christ. That being done, they were asked to say whether they did repent, and would henceforth live and die in *the Reformed faith*, in spite of the allurements and threats of the world; whether they heartily renounced the errors of the Church of Rome, the Mass and all thereto appertaining.… (This was done in much detail.) They had to answer Yes to all these questions, each individually. After this, they had to promise not to

---

[1186]It appears that the usage of the "book on the head" parallels Rome's ordination of a Bishop, going back to the end of the 5th Century (DS326). Some differences are: (1) in the case of Rome the book consists of the Gospels; in the case of the Cathars it consists of a New Testament; (2) in the case of Rome the ritual is to ordain a Bishop; in the case of the Cathars it is for the conversion of a layman.

[1187]"Sixaine" or "sizain" is likely a reference to a poem with six lines (*Dictionnaire Larousse*). This may, for example, refer to the six blessings of Number 6:24-26: "The LORD bless you, and keep you; The LORD make His face shine on you, And be gracious to you; The LORD lift up His countenance on you, And give you peace."

[1188]"Rituel Provençal," translated from Occitan into French by L. Clédat, in *Le Nouveau Testament traduit au XIIIe siècle en langue provençale suivi d'un ritual cathar* [*The New Testament translated in the 13th Century in the Provençal language followed by a Cathar ritual*], edited by L. Clédat (Paris, 1887; Geneva: Slatkine, 1968), ix-xxvi. Translation from French into English mine. Clédat in this text published Manuscript #36 [PA36] from the *Palais des Arts* of the Municipal Library of Lyons, France. Both Clédat and Duvernoy (http://jean.duvernoy.free.fr) provide a history of the provenance of this manuscript.

Several things must be noted in light of this manuscript. It is [to my research] the only know "Cathar Ritual" available contemporaneously. As such, the 200 year Cathar civilization (~1105-1305) has been extirpated from historical knowledge. Notice, for example, the sarcastic words of Sabatini: "A serious heretical outbreak had been occurring in Southern France. There, it would seem, all the schisms that had disturbed the Church since her foundation were gathered together Arians, Manichaeans, and Gnostics to which were added certain more recent sects, such as the Cathars, the Waldenses, and the Boni Homines, or Good People" (Rafael Sabatini, *Torquemada and the Spanish Inquisition: A History*, 2nd ed. [London: Stanley Paul, 1913], 32; available at: http://www.archive.org/stream/ torquemadaandthe00sabauoft/torquemadaandthe00sabauoft_djvu.txt; accessed 4 Jan 2010; Internet). Therefore, one must ask the question, why has this manuscript survived? Nevertheless, it provides valuable information on this civilization of Christians, some of whom appear to have been thoroughly biblical and Evangelical.

attend Mass any more, and to take great care not to pollute themselves with Babylon, either by marriage or in other ways; not to allow their children to be trained in it, but, on the contrary, to instruct them in the principles of our religion. Each having duly promised, the minister then proclaimed the remission of their sins, saying, 'In the name and authority of Jesus Christ, and as a faithful minister of His Word, I declare to you the remission of all your sins, and there is now no condemnation for you, since you are in Jesus Christ.' Then followed a prayer on their behalf. …

"'Forty-two of us were admitted in this manner, the rest of the flock having been received back at previous gatherings. The number of the communicants was about two hundred and fifty, men and women.

"'Tell our former pastor, M. Modens, that nearly half of his flock are now restored, and by God's grace the rest will soon follow. The churches at Uzès, Nîmes, Sommières, etc., have all received the same blessing and are now restored. Our foes may say and do what they will, the Holy Spirit has had mercy on us and has reconquered our souls.'"[1189]

   c. **Another Call to Commitment**: Listen to Spurgeon's appeal in the tract, "Ark of Safety":

"Sinner, I have a word from the Lord for thee: if you feel your need of a Saviour, that blood is able to save you, and you are bidden simply to trust that blood, and you shall be saved. If you can rely simply on the blood of Christ, that blood is able to save. Leave off doing altogether; get Christ *first*, and then you may do as much as you like. See the Saviour hanging on the cross; turn your eye to Him, and say, 'Lord I trust Thee; I have nothing else to trust to; sink or swim, my Saviour, I trust Thee.' And as surely, sinner, as thou canst put thy trust in Christ, thou art safe. He that believeth shall be saved, be his sins ever so many; he that believeth not shall be damned, be his sins ever so few, and his virtues ever so many. Trust in Jesus *now*, Jesus only."[1190]

11. Concerning Abuses:
   a. Regarding the belief that a geographic movement saves anybody—rather it is an opportunity to deal with hearts tenderized by the Word of God
   b. Extensive Emotionalism, especially non-biblical pressure (e.g. "Old Yellar")
   c. Prolongation, moving into human (psychological/emotional) pressure for a response
   d. Routine, always using the same invitation (rather than using an invitation from the text from which comes the message just preached)

12. Ideas for the Invitation:

Introduction:
   1) Prepare and memorize six different versions of the invitation[1191]
   2) Alternate use of these invitations along with the emphasis of the passage you are preaching
   3) Always use a sinner's prayer

   a. John 3:16

   b. The ABC's:
      1) Admit you are a sinner (Rom 3:23);
      2) Believe in Jesus only (Rom 6:23); and
      3) Confess Christ before men (Rom 10:9-10)

   c. Call on the name of the Lord to be saved, Rom 10:13

   d. The Roman Road:
      1) All Have sinned (Rom 3:23);
      2) the wages of sin is death (Rom 6:23);
      3) Christ has paid the price of sin (Rom 5:8);

[1189]From Matthieu Lelièvre, *Portraits et Récits Huguenots,* 274-82; translated and quoted by Rubens Saillens in his *The Soul of France* (London: Morgan and Scott, 1917), 85-87; emphasis mine. See also Léopold Nègre, *Vie et Ministère de Claude Brousson, 1647-1698* (Paris: Sandoz et Fischbacher, 1878), 71-73.

[1190]C. H. Spurgeon, "Salvation and Safety," *Royal Dainties,* no. 169 [Minneapolis: Asher Publishing Co., affiliated with The Union Gospel Mission, n.d.], 4; found at http//www.wheaton.edu/bgc/ archives/docs/tract01.html; Internet, accessed 4 January 2001.

[1191]The advice to memorize six different invitations and rotate them came to me from Bill Mackey, as he was training revival preachers for the simultaneous revival called "Celebrate Jesus 2000," at the Southern Baptist Theological Seminary in May 2000.

   4) We must be justified by faith in Jesus Christ (Rom 4:5);

   5) Confess and believe (Rom 10:9-10)

e. John 1:12

f. Col 2:13

g. Rev 3:20

h. 1 John 1:9-2:2

i. Please note Keith Fordham's advise to Sunday School teachers.[1192]

13. Closing advise on the Invitation:[1193]

a. Be honest in the invitation. Honest about the commitment.

b. Don't use an invitation in public unless you can give private invitations!

c. Your sermon should always have an invitation and pressure.

[1192]"When you come to the close of your lesson, please have all members of the class to bow their heads. Ask for those who have trusted Christ as their personal Savior to raise their hands. Comment on how wonderful it is to bear this testimony. This will make it easier for those who have not trusted the Lord to respond to the invitation, which follows:

"Then ask your class, as their heads are bowed, if there are those who feel themselves backslidden and feel the need of rededicating their lives to raise their hands for prayer. Then explain that being a member of the Sunday school is not being a member of the Church. If there are those who have not transferred their church membership, they need to do so this morning. Then ask those who would desire to take that step to indicate it by raising their hand. (Some have members of their families who are already members of the church and their families ought to be complete in the church.) Those who are Baptists elsewhere should keep the solemn agreement that they made when they joined the church where their membership now is (Ephesians 3:21, 5:24). Have prayer for these who have raised their hands, if any.

"Now make one final appeal to the unsaved of your class. Show the necessity of confessing Christ (Romans 10:9, Matthew 10:32-33). State the importance of doing it right now (James 4:14, 2 Cor.6:2). Ask if they will pray with you. Then pray aloud, asking God to give them the faith and repentance. Ask God to help them pray the prayer of Luke l8: 13 ["God, be merciful to me, the sinner!"]. Repeat the words, if necessary, so they will know what they need to pray. Then ask each one to pray what he feels in his heart he should pray. Pause a moment as they pray.

"Ask the class to continue with bowed heads and those who will this morning, right now, confess Jesus as Savior, stand to their feet. Have prayer of thanksgiving for God's love and willingness to take care of us and to answer our prayer for salvation, rededication and surrender. Note the ones who stand so you can deal with them individually. Give each one who makes a decision the assurance that the whole class is concerned and rejoices with them in their decision. Briefly fill out a decision card for each one. Get complete details later. Get name and decision made. Tell them if they have trusted the Lord that they should make it public and follow Him in baptism. Use Romans 10:9-10 and also verse 11. Explain the meaning of baptism if necessary. The baptismal service will be that night or at their earliest convenience, but they should make their public profession today. Ask them to sit with you in the closing assembly of the Sunday school in the auditorium and as the pastor gives the invitation to go forward with you, making their decision public. At the time for the morning service, go with your department to the auditorium. Ask those who have made decisions to sit next to you. Keep your class quiet in case there is a delay in moving to the auditorium. KEEP PRAYING!" (Keith Fordham, Email attachment, 5 Jan 2006).

[1193]Lane Adams, "Giving a Public Invitation," Billy Graham School of Evangelism, held in Wheaton, IL, June 1990.

CHAPTER 23
Immediate Follow-Up and Evaluation

A. Preparing for Follow-Up:

Introduction:
Every open contact should be followed up in some way. The primary aspect of follow up is prayer. No matter where the person is going, the Holy Spirit (Rom 8:26-27) can intercede for this person through the prayers of a believer. One should keep in mind that because of political or cultural tensions, follow up may not always be done in a systematic way. Following are some practical measures to keep in mind for follow-up.

1. General principles:
    a. Leave a verse for him to memorize, such as 1 John 5:13. Mark it in the Bible or on the tract, so that he will remember where to find it.
    b. "Here another warning is needed. Never tell one who has just professed faith in Christ that he is saved. Let the Holy Spirit tell him that, through the Word, and then let him tell you."[1194]
    c. Most people will not initiate continued contact—so the evangelist has to be aware to take the initiative in this area.
    d. Often it is easiest to meet the person in the same environment in which he was first met, to make better contact.

2. If the person lives in close proximity:
    a. General ideas:
        1) Ask the person for coffee, a meals or to church as the situation allows.
        2) Find out how things are going, and see how he has done on his memory verse.
        3) Decide on and begin going through a follow-up Bible study with the person.
    b. Immediate follow-up from R. A. Torrey:[1195]
        1) Confess Christ with the mouth before men every opportunity you get (Rom 10:9-10; Matt 10:32-33)
        2) Be baptized and partake regularly of the Lord's Supper (Acts 2:38-42; Luke 22:19; 1 Cor 11:24-26)
        3) Study the Word of God daily (1 Pet 2:2; Acts 20:32; 2 Tim 3:13-17; Acts 17:11)
        4) Pray daily, often and in every time of temptation (Luke 11:9-13; 22:40; 1 Thess 5:17)
        5) Put away out of your life every sin, even the smallest, and everything you have doubts about, and obey every word of Christ (1 John 1:6-7; Rom 14:23; John 14:23)
        6) Seek the society of Christians (Eph 4:12-16; Acts 2:42, 47; Heb 10:24-25)
        7) Go to work for Christ (Matt 25:14-29)
        8) When you fall into sin don't be discouraged, but confess it at once, believe it is forgiven because God says so and get up and go on (1 John 1:9; Phil 3:13-14)
    c. Immediate follow-up from Bill Fay:[1196]
        1) How many sins has Christ paid for? (1 John 2:2)
        2) How many of your sins does Christ remember? (Heb 10:17; 2 Cor. 5:17)
        3) Where does Christ live? (Gal 2:20)
        4) Let's pray
        5) Who has been praying for you?
        6) Do you know where your friend goes to church?
        7) Do you know your friend's phone number? Let's call him now!

[1194]Joseph C. MacAulay and Robert H. Belton, *Personal Evangelism* (Chicago; Moody, 1956), 130.
[1195]R. A. Torrey, *How to Work for Christ* (New York: Revell, 1910), 102.
[1196]From Bill Fay, *Share Jesus Without Fear* (Nashville: Broadman, 1999), 72-78.

8. May I take you to church?
9) Read the Gospel of John.
10) I will call you tomorrow to see if the Word became different.

   d. The first meeting:[1197]
      1) Questions the new believer may have
      2) The matter of faith and feelings
      3) Assurance of salvation
      4) Walk through the "Five Facts":
         (a) Christ has come into your heart, Rev 3:12
         (b) Your sins have been forgiven, Col 1:14
         (c) You have become a child of God, John 1:12
         (d) You have received eternal life, John 5:24
         (e) You have begun the great adventure for which God created you, John 10:10; 2 Cor. 5:17; 1 Thess 5:18.
      5) Give him a copy of the Transferable Concept *How to Be Sure that You Are a Christian.*
      6) Encourage him to read the Gospel of John
      7) Pray together.

3. If the person lives a distance away:
   a. Give your name, address and phone number to him, mentioning why you are giving it to him. The emphasis should be to stay in contact with him to encourage him in a relationship with Jesus.
   b. Ask him if he would like to give you his name, address and phone number. Mention that you want to write him or contact him to see how things are going, and encourage him spiritually. Say that he will not get on a mailing list sending regular literature or asking for money—and then make sure you don't do that. Write one or two letters to the person encouraging him towards a local church body or a contact person (if you yourself cannot contact him for some reason). Try to keep in contact by phone to offer encouragement, and keep the address in a file for continued reference.

3. If the person is closed to continued contact:
   a. Respect that wish. However, you can continue to pray for this person and ask the Lord that He would open his heart and lead others to speak to him.
   b. Remember that it often takes many contacts and much prayer for a person to come to Christ (John 4:38).
   c. The person closing up to further contact may be a sign that the Gospel has fallen on shallow soil, Matt 13:20-21
   d. For this reason we should never be proud about our achievement if we are privileged to pray with someone to receive Christ (Luke 17:10).

B. Linking the New Convert to the Local Church:

1. Ask if you can pick up the person to bring them to church (giving the day and time)

2. Ask them to make their decision for Christ public by going forward at the invitation—that next Sunday

3. Explain that their first step of Christian obedience is water baptism in the local church

---

[1197]Adapted from Bill Bright, *Witnessing without Fear* (San Bernardino, CA: Here's Life, 1987), 161-62.

Chapter 23 Appendix

Evaluation after Evangelistic Conversations

Introduction:

The mood of the evangelist after he has shared the Gospel will vary from that of tremendous joy to depression. It is important to evaluate the sharing situation in order to continue sharing the Gospel more appropriately. Often if one is discouraged, he may decide that he will never share the Gospel again. Evaluation may avoid this pitfall.

1. Questions to ask oneself:
   a. Was this individual truly lost? How do I know?
   b. Did I share the Gospel with the person(s) in question?
   c. Was I able to make use of Scripture in my witness?
   d. Could I have used a better way to reach the person's heart?
   e. Did I avail myself of the openness of the individual?

2. Common lessons learned in evangelism:
   a. "We have a great salvation in Jesus Christ!"
   b. "What a privilege to share the greatness of the glories of Jesus Christ!"
   c. "I need to know my Bible better"
   d. "There are **many** needy people"
   e. "I need to do this more often"

3. Comforting thoughts following evangelism situations:
   a. If the person was not a Christian, an unsaved person had the opportunity to hear of Christ through your witness.
   b. If they accepted Christ, all heaven is now rejoicing! Luke 15:10
   c. If God's Word was quoted or shared from, it will accomplish God's purpose, Isa 55:11
   d. God can use me in my weakness, 1 Cor 2:3, 2 Cor 12:10

CHAPTER 24
Baptism and Evangelism

A. Introduction:

1. Three commands:
   a. To evangelize—"Go into all the world and preach the gospel to all creation"
   b. To preach conversion—"You must be born again!"
   c. To baptize—"Let each of you be baptized in the name of Jesus Christ"

2. Three promises:
   a. "The harvest is plentiful, but the laborers are few"
   b. "Whosoever calls on the name of the Lord will be saved"
   c. "I will build My church!"

3. "One baptism," Eph 4:5:
   a. This one baptism was exemplified by John the Baptist, when he baptized Jesus, Matt 3:16; Luke 3:21
   b. This one baptism was practiced by the apostles and church leaders in the Book of Acts, e.g. John 4:1-2; Acts 8:38
   c. This one baptism was preceded by the repentance of the one requesting it, and took place in enough water for complete immersion (insofar as possible):

   > "First. Observe concerning Baptism: Baptism shall be given to all those who have learned repentance and amendment of life, and who believe truly that their sins are taken away by Christ, and to all those who walk in the resurrection of Jesus Christ, and wish to be buried with Him in death, so that they may be resurrected with Him, and to all those who with this significance request it [baptism] of us and demand it for themselves. This excludes all infant baptism, the highest and chief abominations of the pope. In this you have the foundation and testimony of the apostles. Mt. 28, Mk. 16, Acts 2, 8, 16, 19. This we wish to hold simply, yet firmly and with assurance."[1198]

   James Cuthbert spoke with unusual candor and eloquent clarity on the biblical conformity and historicity of baptism by immersion.[1199]

   d. Yet, there is biblically a differentiation between the baptism of the Holy Spirit, which takes place at salvation, and water baptism, which takes place after salvation as a witness to that salvation

B. Why believer's baptism?

1. Because it is commanded in the New Testament by Jesus Christ, as part of the Great Commission, Matt 28:20
2. Because it is exemplified by Jesus Christ—who Himself was baptized by John the Baptist, Matt 3:13-17; Mark 1:9-11; Luke 3:21-22
3. Because it is the only method of baptism exemplified throughout the book of Acts, Acts 2:41; 8:12, 36; 9:18; 10:48; 16:15; 16:33; 18:8; 19:5
   a. In which case, consistency in applying the "Regulative Principle" (must be taught and exemplified in Scripture), leaves no other choice but believers baptism
4. Because it is consistent with a conversionist theology, Rom 6:3-4
5. Because it allows for a professing membership:
   a. As opposed to that of the non-professing church of the multitudes [1 Cor 10:5] (which is a foregone conclusion in a State-Church-type system), or
   b. A verbal confession only membership, Gal 3:27; cf. 2 Cor 6:14-18

[1198]"Schleitheim Confession [1527]," in *Baptist Confessions of Faith*, ed. by William L. Lumpkin (Valley Forge: Judson, 1959, 1969), 25.

[1199]James H. Cuthbert, An Address on Baptism, Delivered in the Wentworth-Street Baptist church on Sunday Evening, June 11th, 1854 (Charleston, SC: James, Williams, and Gitsinger, 1854), 16-22.

C. What of believer's baptism?

1. The NT order is absolute: repentance and faith first, baptism second:

   a. The order in the command of Christ is clear, Matt 28:19-20:
      1) First a disciple is won as a disciple
      2) Next he is baptized, as the first step of obedience
      3) Finally, after he is baptized, he is taught to obey all that Christ has commanded in the fellowship of the church

   b. This same order is taught in Mark 16:16:
      1) He who has believed
      2) And has been baptized.

   c. This was also order of the baptism in the Book of Acts is clear in several places:
      1) Acts 2:38:
         a) Repent
         b) And each of you be baptized
      2) Acts 8:12:
         a) They believed
         b) And they were baptized, men and women alike
      3) Acts 8:35-39:
         a) Philip evangelized
         b) The Eunuch asked to be baptized
         c) Philip confirmed that he was baptized upon confession of his faith
         d) They both went in and out of the water (strongly implying baptism by immersion)

   d. In fact, the NT never departs from this order.
      1) Much to the chagrin of others who adhere to infant baptism, although they try to find it in the phrases "and her household" (Acts 16:15, "after she and her household had been baptized"), or again, "Cornelius was waiting for them and had called together his relatives and close friends. ... and he ordered them to be baptized," Acts 10:24, 48)
      2) Consider, for example, the rhetorical question of James H. Cuthbert:

         "In other words, what place can infant baptism find in a church where the ministers of Christ are authorized to administer the ordinance only on a personal and voluntary profession of faith?"[1200]

   e. Note also that adherance to believers baptism is often related to belief in the evangelism mandate.

   f. By the way, many have died as martyrs, because of their belief and observance that believer's baptism was the only God-ordained method of baptism![1201]

2. Baptism is a sign of true repentance:
   a. It is a sign of leaving the old life, Rom 6:3-4
      1) Which sometimes means clearly leaving an old religious system or church.
   b. People who believe and do not want to be baptized is a sign that they have not repented of their past life
   c. One must remember that Simon the Sorcerer believed and was baptized (Acts 8:12), yet after wanting to buy the power of the Holy Spirit, Peter said, "You have no part of portion in this matter" (Acts 8:21)—therefore confirming that he was not saved!

[1200]Ibid., 16.

[1201]See Thieleman J. van Bracht, *The Bloody Theater or Martyrs Mirror of the Defenseless Christians Who Baptized Only Upon Profession of Faith, and Who Suffered and Died for the Testimony of Jesus, Their Savior, From the Time of Christ to the Year A.D. 1660*, trans by Joseph F. Sohm (1660; 1748; 1837; 1853; Scottdale, PA: Herald Press, 2007).

D. Benefits of believers baptism?

1. Allows for obedience of the command of Christ, and follows the example of Christ and the Book of Acts

2. Provides a clear break for the baptismal candidate:
    a. From a life of sin
    b. From baptism in a past church that likely did not emphasize conversion

3. May differentiate between the seed sown in shallow soil and the other soils in follow-up, cf. Matt 13:20-21

4. Provides a NT method of counting professions of faith, Acts 2:41

5. Provides a visual examples of:
    a. The washing of regeneration, Titus 3:5
    b. Death to the life of sin, and being raised to newness of life, Rom 6:3-4

6. Provides a point of entry into the local church membership, 1 Cor 12:3

7. Provides a cooperative commonality between like-minded churches

E. Baptism and Salvation:

1. To equate salvation directly with baptism confuses the work of the Holy Spirit
    a. Does the Holy Spirit need a physical object (like water) in order to be sacramentally-present to bring salvation?
    b. Is the presence of the Holy Spirit, sacramentally enduing the water with His power, so effective as to bring salvation to an infant, even though he cannot respond to the Gospel by repentance an faith, as the Scriptures everywhere else show to be necessary?

2. In fact, baptism is not mentioned in key places, where if it were endelibly linked to salvation it should be mentioned:
    a. Baptism is not mentioned as a response in Luke's Great Commission, Luke 24
    b. Further, 1 Cor 15:1-8, the great passage where Paul explains the Gospel, does not mention Baptism

3. While Paul was sent to preach salvation (Acts 20:18-21 et al.), he specifically states that Christ did not send him to baptize, subordinating this ordinance below that of evangelizing, 1 Cor 1:17
    a. Where baptism crucial and pivotal to the work of the Holy Spirit in salvation, Paul could not have made this statement
    b. Rather, we find that Paul taught the need for a hearing of faith, Gal 3:1-5; Heb 4:2

F. Some Confusing Aspects of Infant Baptism:

1. Infant baptism removes many of the symbolic elements of baptism, as they relate to conversion (as noted above)

2. Infant baptism blurs the lines in salvation, particularly the need for instantaneous conversion, by inserting an intermediate state—baptized, but not yet saved?

    a. In the Presbyterian Church of America, infant baptism must be "confirmed" at a later date, which process is also made into a "cycle of life" event at a predetermined age:
        1) The words sometimes used in baptism: "He has commanded us to place the mark of the covenant upon our children"
            This author is unfamiliar with the location of this command in the New Testament.
        2) The caveat: "grace and salvation are not so inseparably annexed unto it as that no person can be regenerated or saved without it, or that all that are baptized are undoubtedly regenerated" (Westminster Confession, see below)
        3) Thus "Confirmation" becomes an act in which the faith of the infant baptism is "confirmed" by the party who received that infant baptism
            Perhaps the Bible accepts confirmation by "fruits of repentance"?

    4) In this "cycle of life" program, whence comes genuine individual repentance and faith? Here we find built in an anti-individualism toward those believing in "You must be born again!"

  b. This problem is also addressed by Jose Prado Flores (a.k.a. Pepe), in his book written to re-evangelize baptized Roman Catholics. He appears to sound somewhat Evangelical in his first lines:[1202]

> "One can synthesize Jesus' salvific work with only one word: He evangelized. To summarize the activity of the Church, one word is sufficient: to evangelize.
>
> "Evangelizing is announcing and initiating the Kingdom of God in this world with the power of the Holy Spirit. This was the motive for which the Son of God came to this earth. With this same motive he sent his apostles.
>
> In the beginning of the Primitive Church, only the converted were baptized. Today, it is the inverse, we have to convert those who are [already] baptized.
>
> "In the first years of the Christian era, the Church made itself the missionary and proclaimed the Good News of salvation in the whole world. Today it is the Church herself who must be evangelized from the interior. The Church is no longer the boat who fishes for men in the world, but it is rather the lake itself where Jesus throws out his nets to fish for those who no longer believe."[1203]

Several portions are of particular interest in this writing:

    1) His statement within the kerygma that he teaches, that "Jesus has already saved you."[1204]

    2) An interesting paragraph on Mary as part of the evangelizing process:

> "Evangelization has a model that we cannot forget: Mary. Jesus who is dying on the cross, who rose and intercedes for us is really and truly her son; she gave him to us by the action of the Holy Spirit. Jesus is the unique mediator that she gave us. She therefore collaborated in a certain way in the birth of all and of every believer."[1205]

    3) The citing of Paul VI's 1975 encyclical *Evangelii Nuntiandi* here and there (e.g. p. 138).

    4) In a section on the importance of the church, this book emphasizes community groups, as well as the whole Church, Dioceses, and individual parishes.[1206] This section appears to be a response to the so-called "Catholic Charismatic" movement initiated in the late 1960s,and to the 1975 Encyclical of Paul VI, which sternly warned small groups from straying from the oversight of their local priests.

3. Infant baptism tends to confuse the importance of conversion, as conversion loses its significance as resulting in a complete change of nature:

  a. For the strict Calvinist, it would seem that infant baptism confirms that the children of the saved enter a "Covenant of Grace", infant baptism being the symbolic act of their entering that covenant:

    1) Infant Baptism ties "Irresistible Grace" to a human act, rather than to divine election:

      a) It turns election and predestination into a work—a human work

      b) It makes salvation a man-oriented thing, and it introduces the Augustinian and Medieval doctrinal concept of signs and symbols into the mix—wherein God salvifically flows the powers of His grace through the physical specimens of the water (in this case)

[1202]"He spent a period of catechetical study at the pastoral Institute Lumen Vitae in Belgium, from which he returned in a completely special way to form leaders for Charismatic Renewal" (José Prado Flores, *Comment évangéliser les baptisés* [How to Evangelize the Baptized], translated from Spanish by Valérien Gaudet, preface by Émilien Tardif, M.S.C. [cf. *Missionarii Sacratissimi Cordis* or Missionaries of the Most Sacred Heart]; [Ste-Foy, Québec : Éditions Anne Sigier, 1989 ; Nouan-Le-Fuzelier, France : Éditions du Lion de Juda, 1989], 7; translation mine from the French).

[1203]Ibid., 15 ; translation mine.

[1204]He elaborated this heading for his point in outline form: "Jesus does not save you. He has already saved you" (*ibid.*, 85); translation mine.

[1205]Ibid., 133-134; translation mine.

[1206]Ibid., 144-147.

2) If such is the case, then the change of nature is not in space and time at the point of conversion, but rather it is removed to the foundations of the world in election and predestination, therefore blurring the importance of:
   a) The hearing of the Gospel for salvation,
   b) The need for a hearing of faith, and
   c) The act, time, and manner of conversion

3) Some high Calvinists therefore consider any discussion of a "manner of salvation" as man-made, while perhaps ignoring the "log in their own eye," that of infant baptism as administered by man

4) Two sources of truth to which Calvin found solace on infant baptism were:

   a) The ancient doctors:

   "For there are not a few in this sorry sequel, and principally those who want to contradict the Doctors: who being preoccupied with pride and presumption, see not a drop of all that we tell them: or more likely by obstinacy and malice deliberately close their eyes in order not to see clearly, when it is presented to them with clarity"[1207]

   "Therefore as it is, there is no doctor so ancient, that does not confess that always it [infant baptism] has been the usage since the time of the Apostles. I wanted to touch on this point in passing, not for any other reason, than to advise the simple, that it is an impudent accusation of these inventors to make us believe that ancient observance is [actually] a superstition newly forged, and to feign that it was sold by the Pope: as it is the case that the entire Church has hitherto maintained it that never has it been thought that it came from the papacy, nor that we heard not speak of it. As for the rest, [p. 17] I do not demand that ancient practice serve as proof of anything, unless it finds itself founded on the word of God. . I know that the custom of man does not give authority to the Sacraments: likewise that for proper use, one ought not regulate according to the same. Let us come then to the true rule of God, as we have said: being, unto the word, which here ought alone to have the place. Their intention is, that we cannot communicate baptism, unless unto him who requests it, making profession of [his] faith and repentance. And likewise that the Baptism of little children is the invention of men, against the word of God."[1208]

   If such is actually true, then Calvin fell prey to Medieval Scholasticism, the very thing that he said elsewhere that he was trying to avoid.

   b) The [Second] Council of Orange (529 A.D.)[1209]

   This so-called Augustinian council placed the reception of grace at [infant] baptism; and undermined the need for evangelism and evangelists among previously infant baptized people. In essense, it paved the way for the Medieval persecution of and inquisition of those who did not adhere to infant baptism as a proper, final, and unrepeatable means of salvation.

b. Some Lutherans place infant baptism as part of the "call" in Rom 10:13:
   1) Confirmation then allows the infant baptized to confirm the vow of the parents at baptism i.e. their calling on the Lord on behalf of the infant at baptism
   2) In this view, it becomes necessary in evangelism to find out if the contact has been baptized, since, if he/she has been baptized, they do not need to respond to the Gospel, since they already have responded positively to the Gospel vicariously through their parents
   3) Furthermore, the rite of infant baptism necessitated some type of confirmation of the baptism vows of the parents by the infant recipient of baptism; hence "Confirmation"

[1207]Jehan Calvin, "Brief Instruction … against the [combined] errors of the … the Anabaptists" (Geneva: Jehan Girard, 1544); from *Corpus Reformatorum*, vol 35; Ioannis Calvini, *Opera Quae Supersunt Omnia*, vol. 7 (Brunsvigae: Schwetschke, 1868), 45-142; from Google Books: Ioannis_Calvini_Opera_quae_supersunt_omn.pdf; accessed 4 Aug 2009; Internet; translation mine.

[1208]Ibid.

[1209]See Appendix following Chapter 10.

4. Infant baptism can also tend towards a universalistic approach to salvation:
    a. All those who have been baptized are saved, whether they are born again or not
    b. This complexity is why the Catholic church equates infant baptism with being "born again,"[1210] as do the Anglican and Methodist churches, and, in order to make baptism a symbol of something that happens in heaven,[1211] they teach that baptism washes away of original sin

5. Infant baptism renders some aspects of evangelism unclear, particularly that of the call to conversion for one who has already been baptized:
    a. Annulling the need for the New Testament practice of an invitation to salvation
    b. Making the prayer of the repentant sinner (a "Sinner's Prayer") null and void

6. Infant baptism blurs or mutes personal accountability in discipleship:
    a. As the first act of Christian discipleship, Christ places the burden of accountability on the person being baptized, just like the decision for Christ is the personal responsibility of the person who is making the profession of faith (Mark 16:16; Matt 28:19)
    b. Without the personal accountability of baptism, how can the person involved be held personally accountable for any other act of discipleship, such as "observing whatsoever the Lord has commanded," Matt 28:20
    c. Personal and individual accountability is one of the primary motivations of living a holy life:
        Gal 6:7-8, "Do not be deceived, God is not mocked; for whatever a man sows, this he will also reap. For the one who sows to his own flesh shall from the flesh reap corruption, but the one who sows to the Spirit shall from the Spirit reap eternal life."
        1 Thess 4:6, "For this is the will of God, your sanctification; *that is*, that you abstain from sexual immorality; … *and* that no man transgress and defraud his brother in the matter because the Lord is *the* avenger in all these things, just as we also told you before and solemnly warned *you*."

F. Moving a new believer from faith to baptism:

1. Affirm assurance of salvation:
    a. Allow for the new believer to share his commitment to Christ through testimony to others
    b. Go public with decision by going forward for salvation at the next Sunday service (as applicable and possible)

2. Teach baptism as the first step of obedience (beginning a life of confessing Christ before men):
    a. Note different approaches to baptism or lack of it in follow-up materials[1212]
    b. Go public with baptism the next Sunday:
        1) Some teach the need for a new believers class prior to baptism, this does not follow the Bible's pattern, and seems unnecessary
        2) What is important is that the baptismal candidate does not think that baptism saves him

G. Some complexities for further thought:

1. Following a single-church revival:
    a) Should baptisms be done immediately each night of the revival after people come forward to profess Christ?
    b) Should the baptismal service be held on the last night of the revival?
    c) Should the evangelist baptize the new converts, or should the pastor baptize them?

[1210]*Catechism of the Catholic Church*, §1213, 1215, 1238.

[1211]"For as Augustine, the egregious Doctor, says in the book *on Christian Doctrine*: 'Every doctrine is of things, and/or signs. But even things are learned through signs. But here (those) are properly named things, which are not employed to signify anything; but signs, those whose use is in signifying.' But of these there are some, whose every use is in signifying, not in justifying, that is, which we do not use except for the sake of signifying something, as (are) some Sacraments of the Law [legalia]; others, which not only signify, but confer that which helps inwardly, as the evangelical Sacraments (do)." (Peter the Lombard, *Book of Sentences,* Book 1, Distinction 1, Chapter 1; available from: http://www.franciscan-archive.org/lombardus/opera/ls1-01.html; Accessed: 16 May 2006; Internet).

[1212]Johnston, *Charts for a Theology of Evangelism*, Chart 31, "Comparing Follow-Up Tools," 56-57.

2. Of multi-church crusades:
   a) Should there be baptisms each night as part of the multi-church crusades, or should a baptismal service be organized on the last night, or should each individual church have one?
   b) Is it confusing to church members and new believers to organize crusades with other denominations who do not have the same views regarding believers baptism?

3. Should persons be baptized the same day as seems exemplified in the book of Acts, or should it be at an appropriate time as seems exemplified in Matt 3:13?

4. Can there be baptism prior to a local church being planted in a pioneer area (i.e. no local church is available, such as on the mission field)?
   a. Similarly, are new converts baptized into Christ, into a local church fellowship, or both?

5. Does the requirement of believer's baptism assure a redeemed membership?

6. Who is to initiate the request for baptism?
   a) The new believer (Acts 8:36)
   b) The preacher (Acts 2:38), or
   c) The parents of the child (by inference, Acts 16:15)

7. Is baptism merely symbolic, or is there some sacramental benefit?
   a. Or is some covenantal grace conferred through baptism
   b. Is a baptized believer somehow brought into the family of God in a way that he was not through verbal confession of Christ?

8. Can believer's baptism be held high without drifting into baptismal regeneration?

9. What is the theological weight of believer's baptism?
   a. Does not an emphasis on believer's baptism (after the fact) necessarily signify a corresponding belief in the substitutionary atonement—He did it all?
   b. Does not an emphasis on believer's baptism also necessarily signify belief in instantaneous conversion—"You must be born-again" (John 3:7)?
   c. What of believer's baptism and election and predestination? [see above]

10. What may baptism mean for those who hold to various views of the atonement?
   a. Example theory—following the example of Christ
   b. Kingdom theory—entering the kingdom or kingdom work inaugurated by Christ
   c. Reconciliation theory—connecting with Christ, beginning a relationship of service for Christ, and/or living for Christ
      1) The reconciliation approach seems to be where Martin Luther was on infant baptism (entering a covenant community) and the Lord's Supper (consubstantiation)
      2) The reconciliation approach seems to be the view toward which many seeker-friendly churches have evolved, as well as the child of the seeker-friendly movement, the emergent church movement.
   d. Substitutionary theory—a symbol of death to sin (repentance) and life in the resurrection power of Christ (faith), Rom 6:3-4

10. What of "Baptism in the Name of Jesus Only":
   a. This phrase is used by the United Pentecostal Church to describe their adherence to the pattern of Acts 19:5-6, after which baptism there was included "speaking with tongues and prophesying"
   b. While baptism is commanded and repeated in the Book of Acts, and while the Trinitarian formula is given in Matt 28, speaking in tongues is only mentioned in three places in the Book of Acts (Acts 2:3-4; 10:46; and 19:6), and it provided a theological purpose (affirming true conversion; showing that disciples of John the Baptist were not saved without hearing the post-resurrection Gospel of Christ) and ethnological purpose (advance of Gospel from Jews to Gentiles)

Several Historical Curiosities:

1. On the mode of baptism (pre-165 A.D.), Didache 7:1-4:

    [1] "And concerning baptism, thus baptize ye: Having first said all these things, baptize into the name of the Father, and of the Son, and of the Holy Spirit, in living water.

    [2] "But if thou have not living water, baptize into other water; and if thou canst not in cold, in warm.

    [3] "But if thou have not either, pour out water thrice upon the head into the name of Father and Son and Holy Spirit.

    [4] "But before the baptism let the baptizer fast, and the baptized, and whatever others can; but thou shalt order the baptized to fast one or two days before"

    a) On the mode of baptism:

        In living water, cold or warm

        Pouring is a last resort

        Pouring is to be done in three parts, in the name of the Father, in the name of the Son, and in the name of the Holy Spirit

        It can be conjectured, therefore, that baptism by immersion was also done thrice, which was also another method in the Early Church[1213]

    b) On preparation for baptism:

        It is clear that a time period of preparation was added between conversion and baptism, a move away from the examples of Acts 2, 8, 10, 16, and 18

        Further, was added the human element of fasting

        It must be understood that by the time of the Second Council of Orange (529 A.D.), the ritual of baptism itself was made into a reception of grace

        One cannot presume that infants are considered in this portion, as the baptismal candidate is required to prepare by fasting

2. On rebaptism:

    a) Rebaptism brought in the authenticity of infant baptism, which is strongly held by Rome since prior to:

        1) Augustine's *Contra Donatisten* (402-412)

            (a) It appears that this entire controversy was sparked by a Donatist who dared to rebaptize one previously baptized as a Roman Catholic

            (b) Furthermore, Augustine was so energetic against the Donatists that he called not only for political repression, but also for physical discipline.[1214]

[1213]"But with respect to trine immersion in baptism, no truer answer can be given than what you have yourself felt to be right; namely that, where there is one faith, a diversity of usage does no harm to holy Church. ... But, inasmuch as up to this time it has been the custom of heretics to immerse infants in baptism thrice, I am of opinion that this ought not to be done among you; lest, while they number the immersions, they should divide the Divinity, and while they continue to do as they have been used to do, they should boast of having got the better of our custom" (Gregory I, Epistle xliii, "To Leander Bishop of Hispalis" [A.D. 591]; available at: http://www.ccel.org/ccel/schaff/ npnf212.iii.v.i.xxx.html; accessed: 26 Aug 2008; Internet).

[1214]"For the Donatists met with the same fate as the accusers of the holy Daniel. For as the lions were turned against them, so the laws by which they had proposed to crush an innocent victim were turned against the Donatists; save that, through the mercy of Christ, the laws which seemed to be opposed to them are in reality their truest friends; for through their operation many of them have been, and are daily being reformed, and return God thanks that they are reformed, and delivered from their ruinous madness ...

"...If the true Church is the one which actually suffers persecution, not the one which inflicts it, let them ask the apostle of what Church Sarah was a type, when she inflicted persecution on her hand-maid. ... But if we investigate the story further, we shall find that the handmaid rather persecuted Sarah by her haughtiness, than Sarah the handmaid by her severity: for the handmaid was doing wrong to her mistress; the mistress only imposed on her a proper discipline in her haughtiness ...

"26. But God in His great mercy, knowing how necessary was the terror inspired by these laws, and a kind of medicinal inconvenience for the cold and wicked hearts of many men, and for that hardness of heart which cannot be softened by words, but yet admits of softening through the agency of some little severity of discipline, brought it about that our envoys could not obtain what they had undertaken to ask" (Augustine, "Epistle concerning the Correction of the

    2) Second Council of Orange (529):[1215]

        (a) This entire document is based on the effectualness of [infant] baptism, to wash away original sin and regenerate the sould of the recipient

        (b) This document makes the questioning of a[n infant] baptized individual's salvation heretical

        (c) Therefore, post-Orangian, it is against Rome's Tradition to share the Gospel with [infant] baptized Catholics, call them to commitment, and it is especially wrong to [re]baptize them!

    3) Hence succinctly states the 1994 *Catechism of the Catholic Church*:

        "Thus the two principal effects [of baptism] are purification from sins and new birth in the Holy Spirit."[1216]

  b) If the pre-conversion baptism is deemed invalid, as believed by this author, then it ought to be applied biblically after conversion

3. Notice that the 13th Century so-called Cathars, spent a significant time describing the need for the "Baptism of the Holy Spirit" in their Gospel presentation and/or manual of church order:[1217]

Donatists" [or epistle clxxxv], translated by J. R. King, in Philip Schaff, *Ante-Nicene Fathers* (online); available at: http://www.ccel.org/ccel/schaff/npnf104.doc; accessed 24 April 2007).

[1215]Please see the addendum at the end of Chapter 10.

[1216]*Catechism of the Catholic Church* (London: Geoffrey Chapman, 1994), §1262.

[1217]"Peter, you want to receive the spiritual baptism, by which is given the Holy Spirit in the church of God, with the holy preaching, with the laying on of hands of 'good men.' Of this baptism our Lord Jesus-Christ says, in the gospel of Saint Matthew (xxviii, 19, 20), to his disciples: 'Go and instruct all the nations, and baptize them in the name of the father and of the son and of the Holy spirit. And teach them to keep all the things which I commanded you. And behold that I am with you for ever until the consummation of the age.' And in the gospel of Saint Mark (xvi, 15), he says: 'Go unto all the world, preach the gospel to every creature. And he that believes and is baptized will be saved, but he that does not believe will be condemned.' And in the gospel of Saint John (iii, 5) he says to Nicodemus: 'In truth, in truth I tell you that no man will enter the kingdom of God if he has not been regenerated by water and the Holy spirit.' And John the Baptist spoke of this baptism when he said (gospel of Saint John, i, 26-27, and gospel of Saint Matthew iii, 2): 'It is true that I baptize with water; but he who is to come after me is stronger than I: I am not worthy to tie the strap of his sandals. He will baptize you with the Holy spirit and with fire.' And Jesus-Christ says in the Acts of the Apostles 9 i, 5): 'For John baptized with water, but you will be baptized by the Holy Spirit." This Holy baptism by the laying on of hands was instituted by Jesus-Christ, according to the report of Saint Luke, and he says that his friends would do it, as was reported by Saint Mark (xvi, 18): 'They will lay their hands on the sick, and the sick shall be healed.' And Ananias (Acts, ix, 17 and 18) did this baptism to Saint Paul when he was converted. And later Paul and Barnabas did it in many places. And Saint Peter and Saint John did it upon the Samaritans. For Saint Luke says so much in the Acts of the Apostles (viii, 14-17): "The apostles who were in Jerusalem having heard that those in Samaria had received the Word of God, sent unto them Peter and John. Whom having arrived prayed for them so that they received the Holy spirit, for he had not yet descended upon any of them. So they laid their hands upon them, and they receive the Holy spirit.' This Holy baptism by which the Holy spirit is given, the church of God has kept it up until now, and it has come from 'good men' to 'good men' up until now, and it will be so until the end of the world. And you must hear that the power is given to the church of God to bind and unbind, and to forgive sins and hold them, as Jesus says in the gospel of Saint John (xx, 21-23): 'As the father has sent me, I send you also. When he had said these things, he blew and told them: Receive the Holy spirit; those unto whom you forgive the sins, they will be forgiven them, and those of whom you retain them, they will be retained.' And in the gospel of Saint Matthew, he saint to Simon Peter (xvi, 18, 19): 'I tell you that you are Peter, and on this rock I will build my church, and the doors of hell will have no strength against it. And I will give you the keys of the kingdom of heaven. And something that you bind on earth, it shall be bound in the heavens, and something that you unbind on earth, it shall be unbound in the heavens.' And in another place (Matthew xviii, 18-20) he says to his disciples: 'In truth I tell you that something that you bind on earth, it shall be bound in the heavens, and something that you unbind on earth, it shall be unbound in the heavens. And again in truth I tell you: if two or three persons gather on earth, all things, whatever they ask, will be accorded them by my father who is in heaven. For there where two or three persons are gathered in my name, I am there in their midst.' And in another place (Matthew x, 8), he says: 'Heal the sick, raise the dead, cleanse lepers, chase [out] demons.' And in the gospel of Saint John (xiv, 12), he says: 'He who believes in me will do the works that I do.' And in the gospel of Saint Mark (xvi, 17-18), he says: 'But those who believe, these signs will follow them: in my name they will chase [out] demons, and they will speak in new languages, they will remove serpents, and if they drink something deadly, it will do no ill to them. They will lay their hands on the sick and they will be healed.' And in the gospel of Saint Luke (x, 19), he says: 'Behold I have given you the power to walk on serpents and scorpions, and on all the forces of the enemy, and nothing will harm you.'

a. This "dry baptism" used the symbol of the Bible held over the head of the candidate instead of the use of water

b. Quite a contrast to the "Holy Water" used for infant baptism by the Church of Rome, as described by the Medieval Martyr, Gerard de la Motte (d. 1227):

> 15. In baptism they leave out the most important part, namely the preaching of the Gospel; and add their own, conjure salt, grease, spittle, and tapers, and exorcise the devil from children which he never possessed."[1218]

c. This baptism is interesting in light of the Anabaptist Balthasar Hubmaier's view of Spirit Baptism (see below)

d. And it is also interesting as related to Spirit Baptism taught in contemporary Charismatic[1219] or Pentecostal churches[1220]

"If you want to receive this power and this strength, you must hold all the commandments of Christ in the new testament according to your power. And know that he has commanded that man does not commit adultery, neither homicide, neither lies, that he swear no oath, that he does not take nor steal, nor that he does to others that which he does not want done to himself, and that man forgives whoever has done him wrong, and that he loves his enemies, and that he prays for those who slander him and for his accusers and that he blesses them, and if he is struck on one cheek, that he extend [to him] the other one, and if someone takes his shirt [Occ. *la gonella*; Fr. *la 'gonelle'*], that he allow [him] his coat, and that he does not judge nor condemn, and many other commandments that are commanded by the lord to his church. For Saint John says in the epistle (first, ii, 15-17): 'O my very dear [ones], may you not love the world, nor the things that are in the world, the love of the father is not in it. For all that is in the world is the lust of the flesh, the lust of the eyes, and the pride of live, which is not from the father, but from the world; and the world will pass, likewise its lusts, but who does the will of God dwells eternally.' And Christ says to the nations (Saint John, vii, 7): 'The world cannot hate you, but it hates me, because I bear witness of it, that its works are bad.' And in the book of Solomon (Ecclesiastes I, 14), it is written: 'I saw the things that are done under the sun, and behold all are vanity and torment of spirit.' And Jude brother of James says for our instruction in the epistle (verse 23): 'Hate this soiled garment which is fleshly.' And by these testimonies and by many others, you must keep the commandments of God, and hate the world. And if you do well up until the end, we are assured that your soul will have eternal life" (L. Clédat, "Rituel Provençal," in L. Clédat, *Le Nouveau Testament traduit au XIIIe siècle en langue provençale suivi d'un ritual cathar [The New Testament translated in the 13th Century in the Provençal language followed by a Cathar ritual]* (Paris, 1887; Geneva: Slatkine, 1968), ix-xxvi. Translation mine).

[1218]Gerard de la Motte, "A Summary of the Doctrine of the Papists [1218]," from Thieleman J. van Bracht, *The Bloody Theater* ..., (1660; Scottdale, PA: Herald Press, 2007), 314.

[1219]For example, the Sixteen Fundamental Truths of the Assembly of God reads as follows on Baptism in the Holy Spirit: "7. The Baptism in the Holy Spirit:

"All believers are entitled to and should ardently expect and earnestly seek the promise of the Father, the baptism in the Holy Spirit and fire, according to the command of our Lord Jesus Christ. This was the normal experience of all in the early Christian Church. With it comes the enduement of power for life and service, the bestowment of the gifts and their uses in the work of the ministry. Luke 24:49; Acts 1:4; Acts 1:8; 1 Corinthians 12:1-31.

"This experience is distinct from and subsequent to the experience of the new birth. Acts 8:12-17; Acts 10:44-46; Acts 11:14-16; Acts 15:7-9.

"With the baptism in the Holy Spirit come such experiences as:
- an overflowing fullness of the Spirit, John 7:37-39, Acts 4:8
- a deepened reverence for God, Acts 2:43, Hebrews 12:28
- an intensified consecration to God and dedication to His work, Acts 2:42
- and a more active love for Christ, for His Word and for the lost, Mark 16:20

"8. The Initial Physical Evidence of the Baptism in the Holy Spirit:
"The baptism of believers in the Holy Spirit is witnessed by the initial physical sign of speaking with other tongues as the Spirit of God gives them utterance. Acts 2:4.

"The speaking in tongues in this instance is the same in essence as the gift of tongues, but is different in purpose and use. 1 Corinthians 12:4-10; 1 Corinthians 12:28" (Assembly of God, "Statement of Fundamental Truths" (online); available at: http://ag.org/top/Beliefs/Statement_of_ Fundamental _Truths/sft_full.cfm; accessed: 22 Feb 2007; Internet).

[1220]"THE BAPTISM OF THE HOLY SPIRIT

"John the Baptist, in Matthew 3:11, said, 'He shall baptize you with the Holy Ghost, and with fire.' Jesus, in Acts 1:5, said, 'Ye shall be baptized with the Holy Ghost not many days hence.'

"Luke tells us in Acts 2:4, 'They were all filled with the Holy Ghost, and began to speak with other tongues [languages], as the Spirit gave them utterance.'

4. Balthasar Hubmaier (m. 1528) spoke of three baptisms:
   a. The inward baptism of the Holy Spirit
   b. Water baptism, an outward expression of an inward change (believer's baptism)
   c. Baptism by blood, the "mortification of the flesh" in willingness to be martyred for Christ.[1221]

5. Notice Article 28 of the 42 Articles of the Church of England (authored in 1553 by Thomas Cranmer, Archbishop of Canterbury):

   > "Baptisme is not onelie a signe of profession, and marke of difference, wherby Christien menne are discerned from other that bee not Christened, but it is also a signe, and seale of our newe birth, whereby, as by an instrument thei that receiue Baptisme rightue, are grafted in the Churche, the promises of forgeuenesse of Sinne, and our Adoption to bee the sonnes of God, are visiblie signed and sealed, faith is confirmed, and grace increased by vertue of praier vnto God. The custome of the Churche to Christen yonge children, is to bee commended, and in any wise to bee reteined in the Churche."[1222]

   a. Note all the salvific graces associated with infant baptism:

   While apparently not questioning the use of the "Sign and Seal" language of Augustin and Peter the Lombard, Cranmer added the following graces associated with infant Baptism:

   1) "Our new birth";
   2) "Grafted into the Church";
   3) "The promises of forgivenss of sin";
   4) "Our adoption as sons of God"
   5) "Faith is confirmed"
   6) "Grace increased"

   Cranmer did, however, did remove the exorcism associated with Roman Catholic Infant Baptism, as well as its supposed removal of original sin (which did not help Adolf Hitler very much).

   b. Note also that the power of the baptism in this case is vested in the prayer over the water—quite amazing for some who are often so vehemently against a "Sinner's Prayer":
   1) "By vertue of praier vnto God"

   c. Note also that Cranmer included that the baptism of young children was to be retained in the Church, quite an insertion into the 42 Articles if it was not an issue in the church!

6. Of the mode of Baptism:

   a. The only examples of Baptism in the Bible are by [complete] immersion in the water (where that was available)

   b. Some advocate other means, such as sprinkling[1223] or pouring, which lack the Rom 6:3-4 analogy of burial with Christ

---

"The terms 'baptize with the Holy Ghost and fire,' 'filled with the Holy Spirit,' and the 'gift of the Holy Ghost' are synonymous terms used interchangeably in the Bible.

"It is scriptural to expect all who receive the gift, filling, or baptism of the Holy Spirit to receive the same physical, initial sign of speaking with other tongues.

"The speaking with other tongues, as recorded in Acts 2:4, 10:46, and 19:6, and the gift of tongues, as explained in I Corinthians, chapters 12 and 14, are the same in essence, but different in use and purpose.

"The Lord, through the Prophet Joel, said, 'I will pour out my spirit upon all flesh' (Joel 2:28).

"Peter, in explaining this phenomenal experience, said, 'Having received of the Father the promise of the Holy Ghost, he [Jesus] hath shed forth this, which ye now see and hear' (Acts 2:33).

"Further, 'the promise is unto you, and to your children, and to all that are afar off, even as many as the Lord our God shall call' (Acts 2:39) (United Pentecostal Church, "International Articles of Faith"; available at: http://www.upci.org/doctrine/articlesoffaith.asp; accessed: 27 Feb 2007; Internet).

[1221]"Balthasar Hubmaier: Truth Is Unkillable" (online); available at: http://cat.xula.edu/tpr/people/h%FCbmaier/; accessed 11 Aug 2006; Internet.

[1222]"XXVIII. Of Baptisme" (online); available at: http://www.episcopalian.org/efac/1553-1572.htm; accessed 21 Oct 2004; Internet.

[1223]Note the teaching of Methodist William Arthur: "One word as to the mode of this baptism. In this case we have one of the perfectly clear accounts contained in Scripture of the mode wherein the baptizing element was applied to the person of the baptized. The element here is fire, the mode is shedding down—'hath shed forth this.' 'It sat upon each of them.' Did baptism mean immersion, they would have been plunged into the fire, not the fire shed upon them.

7. Note that Billy Graham became a Southern Baptist when he was baptized with the people he led to Christ at a one of his early revivals at the Southern Baptist church in East Patalka, Florida (circa 1938):

> "When bother Underwood and the deacons learned that their young soul winner was a Presbyterian who had never been immersed according to the biblical pattern, they persuaded him to join a clutch of his converts in being baptized in the nearby Silver Lake."[1224]

It appears that this latter baptism was Graham's third baptism:[1225]

> "As a minister of the gospel, Graham felt called to be associated with the Southern Baptist Convention of churches. Graham was earlier baptized by sprinkling in 1919 at Chalmers Memorial Church.[1226] Later, being convinced of his need for baptism by immersion, he was baptized by Rev. John R. Minder, dean of Trinity Bible Institute.[1227] However, wanting to identify with a local church, he was baptized a third time under the auspices of a Southern Baptist church. Graham found among the Southern Baptists a group that believed in evangelism and the revival ministry to which he felt called.[1228]

By the way, Graham's third baptism followed the Landmark Baptist view that baptism is an ordinance meant to be performed in the context of the local church.[1229]

The only other case in which the mode of contact between the baptizing element and the baptized persons is indicated in this: 'And were all baptized to Moses in the cloud and in the sea.' They were not dipped in the cloud, but the cloud descended upon them; they were not plunged into the sea, but the sea sprinkled them as they passed. The Spirit signified by the water is *never once promised under the idea of dipping*. Such an expression as 'I will immerse you in my Spirit,' 'I will plunge you in my Spirit,' or 'I will dip you in clean water,' is unfamiliar to the Scripture. But 'I will pour out my Spirit upon you,' 'I will sprinkle clean water upon you,' is language and thought familiar to all readers of the Bible. The word 'dip,' or 'dipped,' does not often occur in the New Testament; but when it does, the original is *never* 'baptize,' or 'baptized'" (William Arthur, *The Tongue of Fire or, The True Power of Christianity* [New York: Abingdon-Cokesbury, 1856]), 25-26).

[1224]William Martin, *A Prophet with Honor: The Billy Graham Story* (New York: William Morrow, 1991), 76.

[1225]Thomas P. Johnston, *Examining Billy Graham's Theology of Evangelism* (Eugene, OR: Wipf & Stock, 2003), 10-11.

[1226]Chalmers Memorial was an Orthodox Presbyterian church.

[1227]Trinity Bible Institute was loosely affiliated with the Christian and Missionary Alliance and the Gospel Tabernacle movement.

[1228]Graham wrote, "Early in 1939, Woodrow came to me and said, 'I think you ought to be ordained. That would give you a standing in the Baptist Association and would be of great benefit to you in many ways'" (Billy Graham, *Just As I Am* [New York: Harper Collins, 1997], 56).

[1229]"All other baptism, even immersion of a believer, was considered 'alien' [non-Baptist], that is, coming from an organization other than the church" (H. Leon McBeth, *The Baptist Heritage: Four Centuries of Baptist Witness* [Nashville: Broadman, 1987], 452).

Chapter 24 Appendix

Eight Views of Baptism

Infant baptism represents the unconsciousness and insensibility of the person presumably receiving that baptismal grace through the proxy faith of a third party, parent, priest, or pastor; the effectiveness of the baptismal water is rendered valid by virtue of the prayer of this or another third party, presumably infusing the water with the Holy Spirit, whch provides sacramental power—not unlimited Holy Spirit power, but limited in what it represents:

1. A physical substance endued with the Holy Spirit power was argued to be a Christological mystery;
2. While saving faith has no limits, the spiritual efficacy of the sacrament is supposed to be limited by that which it represents.

In sharp contradistinction, **believers baptism** requires a prior profession of faith, based on the prayer of the person who is receives the grace of salvation thereby; baptism is only an outward symbol of the regeneration that has already taken place.

Roman Catholic Council of Trent (1546)	Martin Luther, "The Large Catechism" (1529)	Anglican Thirty-Nine Articles (1572) [Matthew Parker]	Methodist Book of Discipline (1784, 1808) [John Wesley]	John Calvin *Institutes*, Bk 4, Ch. 15, (~1546)	Westminster Confession (1646)	Alexander Campbell, *The Christian System* (1871)	Anabaptist Balthasar Hubmaier, "Summary of the Entire Christian Life" (1 July 1525)
Non-conversionistic			Conversionistic?		Conversionistic		
Infant Baptism						Believer's Baptism	
Sacramental Meaning[1230] [application of the physicial water of baptism as instrumentality]						Obedience	
Infant baptism as providing remission of sins	Infant baptism as efficient call [cf. Rom 10:13]	Infant baptism as "a sign of regeneration"	Infant baptism as a sign of regeneration	Infant baptism as seal of irresistible grace	Infant baptism as sign and seal of the covenant of grace	Beleivers baptism as "the means of receiving" the benefits of salvation	Believers baptism as a public testimonial·of a prior inward profession
3. ...if he denies that that [the] merit of Jesus Christ is applied both to adults and to infants by the sacrament of baptism rightly administered in the form of the Church, let him be anathema. ... 4. If anyone denies that	OF BAPTISM. "...But, in the first place, we take up Baptism, by which we are first received into the Christian Church. However, in order that it may be readily understood we will treat of it in an orderly manner, and keep only to that which it is necessary for us to know. For how it is to be maintained and defended against heretics and sects we	XXVII. *Of Baptisme.* Baptisme is not only a signe of profession, and marke of difference, whereby Christian men are discerned from other that be not christened: but is also a signe of regeneration	XVII—*Of Baptism* Baptism is not only a sign of profession and mark of difference whereby Christians are distinguished from others that are not baptized; but it is also a sign of regeneration or the new	1. BAPTISM is the initiatory sign by which we are admitted to the fellowship of the Church, that being ingrafted into Christ we may be accounted children of God. Moreover, the end for which God has given it (this I have	CHAPTER XXVIII. *Of Baptism.* I. Baptism is a sacrament of the New Testament, ordained by Jesus Christ, not only for the solemn admission of the party baptized into the visible Church, but also to be unto him a sign and seal of the covenant of	CHAPTER XVI. BAPTISM. OF THE ACTION. III. 1. ...All authorized Greek dictionaries, ancient and modern, with one consent, affirm that action to be immersion; and not sprinkling or pouring. THE SUBJECT OF BAPTISM. IV. Characters,	[THREE] Thirdly; after man, inwardly and by faith, has surrendered himself to a new life, he must testify to it, outwardly and openly in the churches of Christ, in whose fellowship he enrolls himself, according to the ordinance and institution of

[1230]Amazingly, this sacramental view, by its very nature, leads to a dualistic view of the material world: some physical objects are holy objects and others are not. Those who did not believe in this dualism of physical objects were themselves called "dualistic," in that they were framed to believe that physical objects could not be holy, only spiritual objects could be holy (thus the material world was evil by negation). In the first 1500 years of the church, the names Manichean and Docetic were applied to those people who felt that Holy Spirit power impacted the soul directly by the unseen filling from above (John 3:8). These latter folks were archheretics, as they did not believe in the sacraments as taught by both major territorial churches!

infants, newly born from their mothers' wombs, **are to be baptized**, … for this reason truly baptized for the remission of sins, in order that in them what they contracted by generation may be washed away by regeneration.

5. **If anyone denies** that by the grace of our Lord Jesus Christ which is conferred in baptism, the guilt of original sin is remitted, or says that the whole of that which belongs to the essence of sin is not taken away, but says that it is only canceled or not imputed, **let him be anathema**. … But this holy council perceives and confesses that in the one baptized there remains concupiscence or an inclination to sin, which, since it is left for us to wrestle with, cannot injure those who do not acquiesce but resist manfully by the grace of Jesus Christ; indeed, he who shall have striven lawfully shall

---

will commend to the learned.

"In the first place, we must above all things know well the words upon which Baptism is founded, … namely, where the Lord Christ speaks in the last chapter of Matthew, v. 19: 'Go ye therefore and teach all nations, baptizing them in the name of the Father, and of the Son, and of the Holy Ghost.'

"Likewise in St. Mark, the last chapter, v. 16: 'He that believeth and is baptized shall be saved; but he that believeth not shall be damned.' …

"Comprehend the difference, then, that Baptism is quite another thing than all other water; not on account of the natural quality, but because something more noble is here added; for God Himself stakes His honor His power and might on it. Therefore it is not only natural water, but a divine, heavenly, holy, and blessed water, and in whatever other terms we can praise it,—all on account of the Word, which is a heavenly, holy Word, that no one can sufficiently extol, for it has, and is able to do, all that God is and can do [since it has all the virtue and power of God comprised in it]. Hence also it derives its essence as a Sacrament, as St. Augustine also taught: *Accedat verbum ad elementum et fit sacramentum*. That

---

or newe byrth, whereby as by an instrument, they that receaue baptisme rightly, are grafted into the Church: the promises of the forgeuenesse of sinne, and of our adoption to be the sonnes of God, by the holy ghost, are visibly signed and sealed: fayth is confyrmed: and grace increased by vertue of prayer vnto God.

The baptisme of young children, is in any wyse to be retayned in the Churche, as most agreable with the institution of Christe.

---

birth.

The Baptism of young children is to be retained in the Church.

---

shown to be common to all mysteries) is, first, that it may be conducive to our faith in him; and, secondly, that it may serve the purpose of a confession among men. The nature of both institutions we shall explain in order. Baptism contributes to our faith three things, which require to be treated separately. The first object, therefore, for which it is appointed by the Lord, is to be a sign and evidence of our purification, or (better to explain my meaning) it is a kind of sealed instrument by which he assures us that all our sins are so deleted, covered, and effaced, that they will never come into his sight, never be mentioned, never imputed. For it is his will that all who have believed, be baptised for the remission of sins. Hence those who have thought that baptism is nothing else than the badge

---

grace, of his ingrafting into Christ, of regeneration, of remission of sins, and of his giving up unto God, through Jesus Christ, to walk in newness of life: which sacrament is, by Christ's own appointment, to be continued in his Church until the end of the world.

II. The outward element to be used in the sacrament is water, wherewith the party is to be baptized in the name of the Father, and of the Son, and of the Holy Ghost, by a minister of the gospel, lawfully called thereunto.

III. Dipping of the person into the water is not necessary; but baptism is rightly administered by pouring or sprinkling water upon the person.

IV. Not only those that do actually profess faith in and obedience unto Christ, but also the infants of one or both believing parents are to be baptized.

V. Although it be a great sin to contemn or neglect this ordinance, yet grace and salvation are not so inseparably annexed unto it as that no person

---

not persons, as such, are the subjects of baptism. Penitent believers—not infants nor adults, not males nor females, not Jews nor Greeks; but professors of repentance towards God, and faith in Christ—are the proper subjects of this ordinance.

THE MEANING OF BAPTISM.

VI. Baptism is, then, designed to introduce the subjects of it into the participation of the blessings of the death and resurrection of Christ; who "died for our sins," and "rose again for our justification." But it has no abstract efficacy. Without previous faith in the blood of Christ, and deep and unfeigned repentance before God, neither immersion in water, nor any other action, can secure to us the blessings of peace and pardon. It can merit nothing. Still to the believing penitent it is the *means* of receiving a formal, distinct, and specific absolution, or release from guilt. Therefore, none but those who have first believed the testimony of God and have

---

Christ. By that he informs the Christian churches, that is to say all brethren and sisters who live in the faith of Christ, that he has been instructed by the Word of Christ, and that he has already surrendered himself, in accordance with the will and law of Christ, to regulate his deeds, both positive and negative, by it. This he announces honestly and frankly. He promises that he will fight under Christ's battle, and strive even unto death. He asks to be baptized in water, by which means he may testify publicly his faith and intentions. … From all this it follows that the outward baptism unto Christ is nothing else than a public profession of the inward obligation. By it, man confesses publicly that he is a sinner, and admits his guilt. Yet he believes that Christ, through His death, has atoned for his sins, and by His resurrection has made him righteous in the sight of God, our heavenly Father. Therefore he has

be crowned. ... But if anyone is of the contrary opinion, let him be anathema.[1231]	is, when the Word is joined to the element or natural substance, it becomes a Sacrament, that is, a holy and divine matter and sign. ... "Here you see again how highly and precious we should esteem Baptism, because in it we obtain such an unspeakable treasure, which also indicates sufficiently that it cannot be ordinary mere water. For mere water could not do such a thing, but the Word does it, and (as said above) the fact that the name of God is comprehended therein. But where the name of God is, there must be also life and salvation, that it may indeed be called a divine, blessed, fruitful, and gracious water; for by the Word such power is imparted to Baptism that it is a laver of regeneration, as St. Paul also calls it, Titus 3:5."[1232]			and mark by which we profess our religion before men, in the same way as soldiers attest their profession by bearing the insignia of their commander, having not attended to what was the principal thing in baptism; and this is, that we are to receive it in connection with the promise, "He that believeth and is baptised shall be saved" (Mark 16:16)."	can be regenerated or saved without it, or that all that are baptized are undoubtedly regenerated. VI. The efficacy of baptism is not tied to that moment of time wherein it is administered; yet, notwithstanding, by the right use of this ordinance, the grace promised is not only offered, but really exhibited and conferred by the Holy Ghost, to such (whether of age or infants) as that grace belongeth unto, according to the counsel of God's own will, in his appointed time. VII. The sacrament of Baptism is but once to be administered to any person.	repented of their sins, and that have been intelligently immersed into his death, have the full and explicit testimony of God, assuring them of pardon. To such only as are truly penitent, dare we say, "Arise and be baptized, and wash away your sins, calling upon the name of the Lord," and to such only can we say with assurance, "You are washed, you are justified, you are sanctified in the name of the Lord Jesus, and by the Spirit of God." But let the reader examine with care our special essay on the Remission of Sins, in which this much-debated subject is discussed at considerable length.[1233]	determined to confess openly and publicly the faith and name of Jesus Christ. Also he has promised to live henceforth according to the Word of Christ, but that not in human strength, lest the same thing befall him that befell Peter. Without me ye can do nothing, says Christ, but in the power of God the Father, and the Son, and the Holy Ghost. Man must, by word and deed, confess and magnify the name and praise of Christ, so that others through us may become holy and blessed. Just as we, through others who have preached Christ to us, have come to faith, and that the kingdom of Christ may be increased.[1234]

[1231]Council of Trent (19th Ecumenical Council), Fifth Session, 17 June 1546; from http://www.forerunner.com/chalcedon/X0020_15._Council_of_Trent.html; accessed 1 Jan 2005; Internet.

[1232]Martin Luther, The Large Catechism, "Part Fourth: Of Baptism"; available at: http://www.gutenberg.org/cache/epub/1722/pg1722.txt (online) accessed 27 Sept 2012; Internet.

[1233]Alexander Campbell, *The Christian System, in Reference to the Union of Christians, and the Restoration of Primitive Christianity, as Plead in the Current Reformation* (Cincinnati: Bosworth, Chase and Hall, 1871), 55-57.

[1234]Balthasar Hubmaier, "Summary of the Entire Christian Life"; from "The Writings of Balthasar Hubmaier," collected and photographed by W. O. Lewis, translated by G. D. Davidson (Liberty, MO: Archives, William Jewell College Library), 1:57-66.

CHAPTER 25
The Parable of the Sower

The Parable of the Sower can be a tremendous encouragement to the evangelist. In this parable, Jesus spoke of some realities of evangelism and follow-up. These are timeless truths that transcend the limitations of worldview or culture. Whoever goes forth sowing the seed of the Gospel will encounter a number of reactions. They will also face some obstacles in the follow-up of new converts. Jesus shares this parable to prepare and encourage the evangelist for some of the realities of spiritual warfare.[1235]

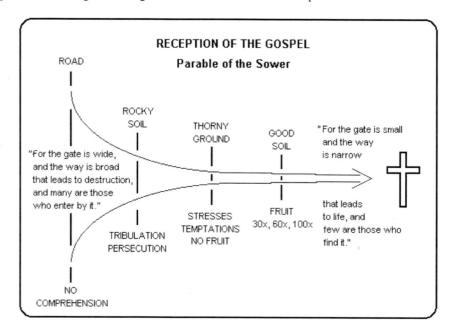

1. Introduction:

   a. Sample antecedent Scripture:
      1) Regarding the Word of God as rain, Deut 32:1-2
      2) Regarding vineyards and fruit, Isa 5:1-7
      3) Regarding seed and sowing, Psa 126:5-6; Isa 55:10-11 (cf. 2 Cor 9:10)

   b. There will be different kinds of people:
      1) The wide and narrow roads, Matt 7:13-14
      2) You will be the smell of death to those who are dying and the aroma of life to those who are being saved, 2 Cor 2:15-16

   c. The Bible gives us hints about the different kinds of people we will encounter:
      1) Some will listen, some will not, "And go to the exiles, to the sons of your people, and speak to them and tell them, whether they listen or not, 'Thus says the Lord God.'" Ezek 3:11 (cf. Ezek 2:5, 7)
      2) Likewise, the Bereans were more noble-minded (εὐγενής) and spiritually eager than the Thessalonians, which appears unrelated to the message or the messenger (same message, same messenger), Acts 17:10
      3) Similarly, the parable of the sower gives us four soils of the heart, Matt 13:4-9, 18-23; Mark 4:3-9, 14-20; Luke 8:5-8, 11-15

[1235]Also see a different rendition of this chart in my *Charts for a Theology of Evangelism,* Chart 8, "Lessons from the Parable of the Sower."

2. Understanding the differing soils:[1236]

   a. The characteristics of the seed sown on *the road:*

     1) No comprehension, Isa 1:2-3; 6:9-10; John 5:39-40; Acts 28:25-27; 2 Cor 3:15; 4:3

     2) Other characteristics of those not accepting Jesus Christ:

       a) Foolishness, Psa 53:1-3; Prov 1:28-31

       b) Wickedness, Prov 16:4; Rom 1:21-32; Eph 2:1-3

       c) Ignorance, Rom 10:14; Eph 2:12

     3) Some thoughts:

       a) Most seed inevitably will fall on the road, as most are headed for destruction (cf. Matt 7:13-14), the truth of the many and the few is taught multiple times in the New Testament, e.g. 1 Cor 9:22

       b) Therefore, seeking "whole nation evangelism" or "people movements" may not be in accord with this teaching in the Bible

       c) Likewise, seeking to evangelize, without the rejection of those on the road, may be like trying to be better than our Master (Luke 11:29; John 6:66-67; 15:20).

   b. The characteristics of the seed sown in *rocky soil:*

     1) Tribulation and persecution

     2) Other biblical characteristics of those "falling away" – using the terminology of Jesus:

       a) Unfaithfulness, Psa 73:27; John 15:6

       b) Falling away from the faith, Heb 6:4-6; 10:26-29

       c) Willful sin, Heb 10:26-31; 2 Pet 2:20-21

       d) Practicing evil, Matt 7:21; 13:30; 25:11-12

       e) Stumbling blocks, Matt 13:41-42; Luke 17:1-2

       f) Sin against the Spirit, Gen 6:3; Mark 3:28-29; Luke 12:10; cf. 1 John 5:16

     3) Some thoughts:

       a) We can expect that a certain number of "converts" are seed in shallow soil or rocky soil

       b) This seed that does not last is part of God's predisposed response some will have to the Gospel

       c) That some seed falls in the rocky soil is not the fault of the evangelist or the method (presupposing the good seed is sown), but rather rocky soil is part of God's sovereign predisposition in the harvest.

   c. The characteristics of the seed sown on *thorny ground:*

     1) Cares of the world:

       a) "Dissipation [overeating] and drunkenness and the worries of life," Luke 21:34

       b) "Wood, hay, and straw," 1 Cor 3:12-15

       c) "Entangles himself in the affairs of everyday life," 2 Tim 2:4

       d) "Turn away their ears from the truth and turn aside to myths," 2 Tim 4:4; "so that we may not drift," Heb 2:1

       e) "The sin which so easily entangles us," Heb 12:1

       f) "You therefore, beloved, knowing this beforehand, be on your guard so that you are not carried away by the error of unprincipled men and fall from your own steadfastness," 1 Pet 3:17

     2) Temptation, Matt 24:48-51; 1 Cor 3:16-17; 6:15-20; 10:1-6; Heb 6:4-6

     3) Fruitlessness, Matt 7:21-23; 25:24-30; John 15:2, 6; 2 Pet 1:8-9

     4) Some thoughts:

       a) That some will receive the Gospel, will pass the test of persecution because of the Word, and yet will not bear fruit (i.e. do not reproduce themselves Christians) is inevitable in the local church

       b) It is doubtful that these fruitless weed-entangled Christians merely need proper discipleship to be "made" fruitful

       c) Theologically speaking, are these carnal Christians or were they never saved in the first place? It is hard to discern biblically. However, the reality of their existence is evident.

[1236]Similarly, Jesus has three levels of persons mentioned in Luke 19:11-27—those who hated, those who used their talents, the one who buried his talent.

    d. The characteristics of the seed sown in *good soil:*

       1) Fruitful, Matt 25:46-47; Mark 1:17; John 4:36-38; 15:2, 4-5, 16; Eph 2:10; Phil 2:12-13; James 2:14-16

       2) Overcomer, Matt 24:13; 1 John 5:4-5; Rev 2:7, 11, 17, 26-28; 3:5, 12, 21; 21:7

       3) Awaiting Christ, Matt 24:46-48; 1 Thess 1:7-10

       4) Further characteristics of those living *fruitful lives:*

          a) Direction of their life is Christ, John 20:21; Rom 8:29; 1 Cor 11:1; Phil 3:12-14; Heb 12:1-4

          b) It calls for a complete commitment, Matt 10:39; Rom 6:11; 2 Cor 5:15; Gal 2:20; 5:16

          c) It calls for a heavenly perspective, Matt 4:4; 6:33; Col 3:1-3; Heb 11:6-16

       5) Some thoughts:

          a) Only a certain percentage of those who respond to the Gospel will ever bear fruit

          b) In the context it is most logical that the fruit in question is the Word of the Gospel sown in the lives of others, in other words, multiplying believers; to see fruit in this context as anything else, such as merely the fruit of the Spirit (Gal 5:22-23), the fruit of one's words (James 3:12), or the fruit of one's teaching (Matt 7:15-20), seems quite shallow and/or avoiding the obvious

  3. Applying the principles:[1237]

Question: Is it possible to avoid sowing in the "shallow soil"?

       1) T. J. Bach, former General Secretary of the Scandinavian Alliance Mission, said: "In all Christians Christ is present; in some Christians Christ is prominent; but in few Christians Christ is preeminent" (e.g. 1 Cor 10:5)

       2) Ray Comfort, however, seemed to struggle with the shallow soil, as expressed in this quote:

> "As I began to look at church growth records from around the country, I found to my horror that 80 to 90 percent of those making a decision for Christ were falling away from the faith. That is, modern evangelism was creating 80 to 90 of what we commonly call backsliders for every hundred decisions for Christ. ... The tragedy of modern evangelism is that, around the turn of the twentieth century, the church forsook the Law in its capacity to convert the soul and drive sinners to Christ."[1238]

Note that Comfort gave an arbitrary date when the Gospel no longer was preached with the Law as a precedent. He was perhaps unfamiliar with the preaching of the Southern Baptist Mordecai Ham, who preached sin for two weeks without an invitation in the 1930s before spending two weeks on the Gospel, and then two weeks of separation from the world.

It seems that Comfort's real problem was the fact that some seed will fall in shallow soil. No matter how good the Gospel is, this fact remains true—some seed will fall in shallow soil. There is no way around it.

However, Comfort's point was good, the Christian is under obligation to preach "the whole counsel of God" without omitting a word.

       3) Often "human elements" are promoted as providing the panacea for avoiding the "shallow soil"—when in actuality these human additions often produce even more shallow decisions!

          a) Depth of relationship

          b) Love of the service rendered

          c) Positive Christian lifestyle

          d) Cogent apologetic arguments

       4) Discipleship or multiplication can also be brought up as the answer to the problem of the "shallow soil."

[1237]Thomas P. Johnston, *Charts for a Theology of Evangelism*, Chart 8, "Lessons from the Parable of the Sower."

[1238]Kirk Cameron and Ray Comfort, *The School of Biblical Evangelism: 101 Lessons* (Gainesville: Bridge-Logos, 2004), 26.

    a.   Applications to theology:

        1) While coming from the framework of eternal security, this parable shows the reality of evangelism and follow-up as hard work.

        2) Real-life evangelism and follow-up cause one to wrestle with an experiential understanding of foundational principles. This parable matches with experience.

    b.   Applications to evangelism:

        1) There is no indication in the text that the sower:

            a) Was wrong to sow on the road or in the shallow soil; or

            b) Knew what kind of soil upon which he was sowing the seed.

        2) Someone falling by the spiritual wayside does not necessarily show that (1) the Gospel presentation, or (2) the style of evangelism was wrong. In the parable of Jesus the same seed was sown (the same way) in all four places; someone falling away likely points to the wrong type of soil.

        3) Often the method of proclamational evangelists is sullied because all of their converts do not continue on with the Lord:

            a) This same difficulty is true of all types of true evangelism (including relational)

            b) This difficulty comes because some seed will necessarily fall on shallow ground.

            c) Perhaps shallow soil (and counterfeits) should be understood as a sign of true evangelism (cf. Matt 13:24-30)

        4) Prayer for the Lord to direct to open hearts that the seed may fall on good ground should precede evangelism.

    c.   Applications to follow-up:

        1) As a priority, the Christian should seek to nurture those who are characterized as the good soil (cf. 2 Tim 2:2).

        2) The evangelist, however, should make a concerted effort to nurture all of those whom he has led to the Lord, as he cannot be sure of their true spiritual state (cf. 1 Sam 16:7).

4.   Further considerations:

    a.   From Deut 11:10-12:

    Just as there are physical differences between lands—Egypt needing to be irrigated, Israel receiving rain—so there are appears to be spiritual differences between places

    If the illustration is applied even farther, as in the case of irrigation, the difference is mostly in follow-up, the watering, cf. 1 Cor 3:6-8

    b.   From Isa 5:1-7:

    In the case of the vineyard of the people of Israel, fences were built around it, as well as a winepress

    But because of its bad fruit, God promised to destroy its fences and allow it to be trampled underfoot and filled with weeds, and that it would receive no more rain

CHAPTER 26
Follow-Up Is Important!

I. Preliminary Definitions:

Introduction:

Several points make follow-up a natural outflow of evangelism. The evangelist's new relationship with the newly saved contact "in Christ" should give the evangelist concern for his spiritual welfare (cf. Acts 15:36; 2 Cor 11:28). This concern led Paul to be curious of those he led to Christ and prompted his second missionary journey. Repeatedly the NT authors discuss their concern for those they led to Christ and their joy or regret in hearing news of them. This concern led to continual prayer on their behalf.

A. Some Thoughts on Nomenclature:

Evangelist Mordecai Ham (though whom Billy Graham was saved) typically preached six week revivals: two weeks on sin, two weeks on salvation, and two weeks on separation. In those days Fundamentalists (as they were called) did not speak of follow up or discipleship, rather they spoke of separation from sin. This fact should not be ignored in a day when discipleship has changed to become spiritual disciplines as Evangelical culture moves away from the Great Commission as proclamational evangelism.

The following Latin terms show the complexities involved in seeking to define distinctions between evangelism and discipleship, the imitation of Christ and/or the apostles, or seeking to provide a sequel to the life of Christ or the apostles. These terms (not exhaustive) are taken from the 1999 comments of French Medievalists Jean-Louis Biget and Jacques Dalarun in *Evangile et Evangelisme (XIIe-XIIIe siècle)*:

- *Sequela Christi* versus *imitatio Christ*;

- *Vita apostolica* or *imitatio apostolorum*;

- *Vita evangelica, regula evangelica,* and *vir evangelicus*;

- *Identificatio Christi*.[1239]

Jean Gonnet and Amedeo Molnar summarize the complexity of the Medieval conception of the imitation of the Apostles (*conversatio apostolic*).[1240] To these semantic debates may also be included a German term for the itinerant Medieval evangelists—*Wanderprediger*, as well as the itinerant preaching ministry of "hermits" [Fr. *Les ermites*].[1241]

[1239]Jean-Louis Biget, "Introduction," and Jacques Dalarun, "Conclusion," in *Évangile et évangélisme (XIIe-XIIIe siècle)*, Cahiers de Fanjeaux 34 (Toulouse, France: Éditions Privat, 1999), 7-9, 326-333.

[1240]"As to the precise modes of the application of the imitation of the apostles will birth an ensuing dispute between the monks, the clergy, and the canons, upon which will also grate, at a certain moment, the critical discussions of the Cathars [pure ones or Albigenses] and the Waldenses. What is exactly meant by *conversatio apostolic*? Life in common with its observances, or the ministry of souls? Or both at the same time? The monks, already lay people, became very often clergy, especially in the beginning of the 12th Century, and from the beginning they considered themselves similar to the canons, Thus, as they practiced the apostolic life in a manner more perfect than did the canons themselves, they esteemed that they were the true successors of the apostles. Meanwhile, being that an old tradition prohibited from exercising any kind of ministry by both monks and canons, in particular that of preaching, these retorted that it was not the fact of preaching, of baptizing or of exercising other ministries, but in the fact that they have the virtues of the apostles which consists of imitation [of their lifestyle] to which they conform. As for the canons, they replied that they participated much more than the monks in the ministry of the apostles, in the fact that they were clergy well before them. The Waldenses, as well as the Cathars, specified after this that those who live and preach like the apostles are their true imitators, and in this only consists the legitimacy of their mandate, received directly from God and not through the intermediary of the Church" (Jean Gonnet and Amedeo Molnar, *Les Vaudois au Moyen Age* [Torino, Italy: Claudiana, 1974], 23-24; translation mine.

[1241]Ibid., 24.

Concluding Points on Medieval Nomenclature:

- These distinctions were directly related to views of conversion and the work of conversion (evangelism)
- If they are related to a theology of conversion, then it follows that the 12th-13th Century debate was also directly related to views of systematic theology
- And because a plethora of theological views exist today, this 12th and 13th Century debate on defining the Great Commission continues today
- Arguing from views of the Great Commission without also considering the underlying views of conversion and the work of conversion is not only counterproductive, but dangerous, as it ignores the heart of the matter—the work of the cross and conversion
- Please also note my paper, "Dying for the Great Commission: A Thirteenth Century Struggle over Definition" found at www.evangelismunlimited.org, and the historical addendum at the end of this chapter

B. **Some Distinctions from Medieval Nomenclature**:
  1. "Now he who plants and he who waters are one" [or at least they ought to be one!], 1 Cor 3:8
  2. The same message applies to all, Col 1:28-29; cf. 1 Cor 2:2

Thirteen Views of Discipleship

Impacting Others (the outer life)							Personalistic/Individualistic (the inner life)					
Win disciples		Multiply disciples			Mentor leaders			Follow Christ			Follow the Apostles	
Do the work of an evangelist, 2 Tim 4:5; win disciples, Acts 14:21 (see NIV)	Teach others to win disciples	Teach others to win disciples and live the Christian life	Teach others to live the Christian life and win disciples	Teach others to live the Christian life	Teach others to teach and lead others	Teach others to lead others	The conse-crated life as a constant testing of one's faith, James 1:3	Identifica-tion with Christ	Imitate Christ	Live as a sequel to the life of Christ	Live as the apostles	Imitate the apostles
Opus evangelistae	Opus evangelii		Regula evangelii				Probatio fidei vestrae	Identifica-tio Christi	Imitatio Christi	Sequela Christi	Vita apostolica	Imitatio apostolorum

Questions follow:
What is being a man of the Gospel (*vir evangelicus*)?
What about the life of the Medieval wandering preacher (*Wanderprediger*)?

Four Views of Witnessing

Proactive Evangelism	Reactive Evangelism	Passive Evangelism, e.g. 1 Pet 3:15	Lifestyle Evangelism or Silent Evangelism
Initiating witnessing conversations	Proactively bearing witness when in conversation	Bearing witness when asked	Living as a witness

C. **The Relationship of the Beginning of Faith and the Continuation of Faith**:

  1. The message is the same:
     a. Christ, Col 1:24-29, esp vv 28-29
     b. Christ crucified, 1 Cor 2:2

  2. The response to the message is the same:
     a. The first reception of the Holy Spirit—the hearing of faith, Gal 3:2

Translations of ἐξ ἀκοῆς πίστεως in Galatians 3:2c

Vulgate	French Geneva, Louis Segond, NEG	English Geneva	KJV, DRA✝, ASV, NKJ	NAS, ESV, CSB	NAB✝	NIV, NET	NJB✝	CEV✝	French Le Semeur*
ex auditu fidei	Par la predication de la foi [by the preaching of the faith]	By the hearing the faith preached	By the hearing of faith	By hearing with faith	from faith in what you heard	by believing what you heard	by believing in the message you heard	by hearing about Christ and having faith in him	because you welcomed with faith the Good News that you heard
Jerome provided a word-for-word translation of the Greek: ἐξ ἀκοῆς πίστεως	The noun akoe is rendered "preaching"	The noun akoe is rendered the participle, "hearing" with the addition of verb "preached"	The verb "preached" is eliminated	Removal of the definite article "the"	The words "hear" and "faith" are reversed	"Faith" is turned into the verb "believing"	Emphasis on the "message", rather than on the reception of the verbal communication of the message (cf. Gal 1:8-9)	Cannot allow the particularity of a "hearing of faith" stand alone; must add concepts to cloud the potent term	"Hearing" and "faith" rearranged; add "welcomed" as main verb to "with faith" further downplaying that concept; addition of "the Good News" as the message

*My translation of "parce que vous avez accueilli avec foi la Bonne Nouvelle que vous avez entendue."

    b.   Method of He who works miracles in His church—the hearing of faith, Gal 3:5

  3.   Paul's question: do we begin by the hearing of faith, and then continue on in the faith by some kind of spiritual disciplines?

    a.   "Are you so foolish? Having begun by the Spirit, are you now being perfected by the flesh?" Gal 3:3

    b.   In fact, going back to the flesh (meaning the practices of the OT Law), is a weak and feeble substitute to the hearing of faith, Gal 4:9, "But now that you have come to know God, or rather to be known by God, how is it that you turn back again to the weak and worthless elemental things, to which you desire to be enslaved all over again?"

    c.   Several things seem to emanate from an emphasis on the spiritual disciplines:
      1)   There seems to be a subtle pride in the spiritual disciplines (Gal 5:26), which causes a rejection of or looking down on those who do not follow the same path (Gal 4:29)
      2)   The study of the Bible can become primarily for the sake of looking for more spiritual disciplines to follow, which can then become suffocating and legalistic, Gal 5:7-9
         a)   As Luther stated that Christ then becomes another Moses, another Law-giver[1242]
      3)   Personal spiritual disciplines can become selfish spiritual pursuits, wherein self becomes the focus, and others get in the way (therefore leading to cenobitic monasticism)
         a)   Rather, Paul admonishes the principle of love for one another, Gal 5:13-14

[1242]"Therefore, beware lest you make Christ into a Moses, and the gospel into a book of law or doctrine, as has been done before now, including some of Jerome's prefaces. In fact, however, the gospel demands no works to make us holy to redeem us. Indeed, it condemns such works, and demands only faith in Christ, because He has overcome sin, death and hell for us. Thus it is only by our own works, but by His work, His passion, and death, that He makes us righteous, and gives us life and salvation. This is in order that we might take to ourselves His death and victory as they were our own" (Martin Luther, "Preface [to the New Testament]" [1522]; from John Dillenberger, *Martin Luther: Selections...* [Garden City, NY: Doubleday, 1961], 14-19; from Bertram Lee Woolf, ed. and trans., *The Reformation Writings of Martin Luther*, vol 2, *The Spirit of the Protestant Reformation*, [London: Lutterworth Press, 1956], 278-79).

b)   And Jesus gave us the Great Commission, in which He focused on the preaching of the gospel to others

d.   Remember that the Benedictine vows and other monastic vows have been lauded as reforming principles within the church (particularly in the later medieval times). Unfortunately, the opposite was true. The affirmation of monastic vows was rather counter-reforming:
  a.   It led the church farther away from by the Scriptures alone, by faith alone, and by grace alone
  b.   It led the church into greater darkness and superstition.

e.   By the way, the law of liberty is tough to handle, this is why Paul clearly delineated the deeds of the flesh and the fruit of the Spirit, Gal 5:16-23

D.   Several Definitional Distinctions (cf. Acts 14:21-23):

1.   **Evangelism** is the proclamation of the Gospel resulting in the beginning of faith

2.   **Follow-up** is defined as establishing the young believer in the basics of a spiritual walk and growth to maturity.

3.   **Discipleship** (noun) or the corresponding **discipling** (verb) is defined as equipping the growing believer for service in ministry and daily life.

4.   **Mentoring** is a secular term, that can overlap in meaning with **discipling**, which generally refers to spiritual mentoring

5.   **Spiritual Disciplines** provides programmatic areas for growth in the Christian life, and are defined variously by various authors and practitioners

6.   Two related conceptions:

  a.   **Multiplication** is established as the ultimate goal of discipling:
    1)   Resulting in pouring one's life into another so that they can pour their lives into a third party
    2)   The end result of this one-on-one mentoring is presumed **exponential growth**, which is called "multiplication"
    3)   See the Appendix to this chapter, "An Assessment of Multiplication"

  b.   **Addition** is sometimes negatively defined in contrast to multiplication, as those who are only interested in evangelizing lost souls;
    1)   Such persons are sometimes caricatured as short-sighted and falsely single-minded
    2)   Such persons are often considered overly literalistic as to the methods of evangelism in the Gospels and the Book of Acts

  c.   One example of **multiplication** in the business world is the pyramid marketing scheme, by which a business is grown through mentoring others who as it were become financial sponsors of those who brought them into the business

  d.   The Navigators went through a slight crisis when the organization was 21 years old, as by that time the "2 times 2 to the 21st power factor" should have allowed them to reach 2.1 million people for Christ; other unforeseen issues were at stake, such as:
    1)   The fact that most who were saved and discipled through the Navigators would not join them once they graduated from college; in fact most would join local churches
    2)   The inevitable seed sown in shallow or weed infested soil
    3)   The disquieting issue of missional drift (Eph 4:14), promised by Paul (Acts 20:29-30)

  e.   See also in this regard the Appendix following this chapter, "Who Takes the Initiative in Follow-Up?"

7.   Corresponding definitions:

  a.   **Pre-evangelism** is founded upon a relational view of evangelism, pre-evangelism is considered anything that a person does to build a relationship with another person in order to share the Gospel with them after a certain [definite or indefinite] point in time

1) The danger is that it can be deemed his relationship, service, lifestyle, or apologetic arguments that will decide whether or not the person with whom he has decided to build a relationship will be elect unto salvation!

b. **Pre-discipleship** is also founded upon a relational view of evangelism, adding the pressure to the would-be evangelist/discipler, that how he builds the relationship will eventuate the ultimate salvation and spiritual nurture of the person whom he has chosen to be his future disciple.

E. A Working Definition:

Biblical follow-up is the nurture of a new or young Christian into the basics of a walk with the Lord, through teaching, modeling, guiding and encouraging the young Christian at several levels: Scripture meditation, prayer and obedience. These effect his life through developing his three major relationships: a passion for God, a passion for souls, and a passion for the brethren:

1. Biblical follow-up is:
    a. The nurture of a new or young Christian, 1 Thess 5:14
    b. Into the basics of a walk with the Lord, John 15:4; Col 2:6-7

2. Through the young Christian:
    a. Teaching, Matt 28:20
    b. Modeling, Mark 1:17; 3:14
    c. Guiding, Mark 10:42-45; John 15:15; 1 Pet 5:1-2
    d. Encouraging, 1 Thess 5:11; Heb 10:24

3. At several levels:
    a. Scripture meditation, Jos 1:8; Psa 1:1-3; 119:1-2
    b. Prayer, Luke 11:1
    c. Obedience, 1 John 2:3-4

4. Developing his three major relationships:
    a. A passion for God, Psa 63:1
    b. A passion for souls, Mark 1:17
    c. A passion for the brethren, Heb 10:24-25

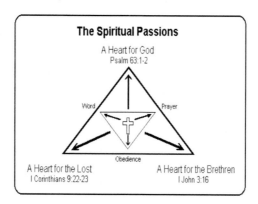

F. A Brief History of Some Translations (for historical context):

The following chart provides a historical overview of the translation of the word μαθητεύω in major English translations. It goes without saying that due to the worldwide influence of the British and Foreign Bible Society (est 1804) and English missions in the Great Century of Missions (1792-1910), English translations have had a major influence on most translations around the world.

Perhaps several observations are in order. It would seem that Young's Literal Translation of 1862 broke new ground with his use of the word "disciple" rather than "teach" or "instruct." Showing the possible power of the translation of one word, it is interesting to note that this version comes ten years prior to A. B. Bruce's *The Training of the Twelve,* 1st edition (1872), which highlighted the discipleship ministry of Jesus. Following this era, all English translations utilized the word "disciple" in Matt 28 and Acts 14. The RSV, NKJV, and NIV prefered using the word "trained" or "instructed" in Matt 13. The NIV also broke new ground in its translation of μαθητεύω in Acts 14 by using the verbal prefix "won" rather than "made." This new approach leads to my own preference of "win disciples" for the Great Commission of Matt 28!

A Historical Overview of the Translations of the Four NT Uses of μαθητεύω

Texts	Greek Nestle-Aland 27th Ed	Latin Vulgate	Wycliffe 2nd ed (1388)	Geneva (1560)	KJV (1611/ 1769)	Young's Literal (1862/ 1898)	Darby's English (1884/ 1890)	ASV (1901)	RSV (1952)	NAS (1977)	NKJ (1982)	NIV (1984)	Johnston's Evangelistic[1243]
Matt 13:52	μαθητευ-θεὶς	doctus	wise man in law	which is taught	*which is* instruct-ted	having been discipled	discipled	who hath been made a disciple	who has been trained	who has become a disciple	instructed	who has been instructed	who has been won over*
Matt 27:57**	ἐμαθητεύ-θη τῷ Ἰησοῦ	discipulus erat Iesu	was a disciple of Jhesu	who had also him self bene Iesus disciple	was Jesus' disciple	was discipled to Jesus	was a disciple to Jesus	was Jesus' disciple	was a disciple of Jesus	Had also become a disciple of Jesus	had also become a disciple of Jesus	had himself become a disciple of Jesus	had also become a disciple of Jesus
Matt 28:19	Πορευ-θέντες μαθητεύ-σατε πάντα τὰ ἔθνη	euntes ergo docete omnes gentes	Therfor go ye, and teche alle folkis	Go there-fore, and teache all nacions	Go ye there-fore, and teach all nations	having gone, then, disciple all the nations	Go *therefore* and make disciples of all the nations	Go ye therefore, and make disciples of all the nations	Go therefore and make disciples of all nations	Go therefore and make disciples of all the nations	Go therefore and make disciples of all the nations	Therefore go and make disciples of all nations	Go win disciples from all nations
Acts 14:[20]21	μαθητεύ-σαντες ἱκανούς	docuis-sent multos	tauyte manye	had taught manie	had taught many	having disciple many	having made many disciples	had made many disciples	had made many disciples	had made many disciples	made many disciples	won a large number of disciples	won many disciples

*Other translations may be "who has been [thoroughly] trained" or "who has been discipled in." All of these follow the meaning discussed in Friberg: "17286 μαθητής, οῦ, ὁ (1) as one who directs his mind to something *learner, disciple, pupil* (LU 6.40); (2) in a more technical sense *disciple, apprentice*; specifically in the NT as one who attached himself to a spiritual leader, such as Jesus (MT 12.1), John the Baptist (JN 3.25); (3) in a broader sense *disciple, follower*, one who adhered intellectually and spiritually to religious leaders, such as Jesus (AC 11.26), the Pharisees (MT 22.16), John the Baptist (AC 19.1), Moses (JN 9.28b)."

**Perhaps the Joseph of Arimathea verse (Matt 27:57) best provides the context to understand the Great Commission in Matthew 28. He "had become a disciple" (Geneva, NAS, NKJV, NIV). The aorist tense seems to refer to the beginning of faith, rather than to the continuation of faith. Likewise, Matt 28:19 is in the aorist, speaking of the beginning of faith, rather than its continuation.

[1243]I must give credit to Samuel Zwemer for preceding me in coining the term "win disciples" (Samuel Zwemer, *Evangelism Today: Message not Method,* 4th ed. [New York: Revell, 1944], 17).

Further English Translations of μαθητεύω in Matt 28:19

Version	Good News Translation* (1993)	The Message (1993)	God's Word to the Nations (1995)	Holman Christian Standard (2003)	New Living Translation (2004)
Matt 27:57	His name was Joseph, and he also was a disciple of Jesus	A disciple of Jesus, arrived. His name was Joseph	Joseph arrived. He … had become a disciple of Jesus	Joseph came, who himself had also become a disciple of Jesus	Joseph, … who had become a follower of Jesus
Matt 28:19	Go, then, to all peoples everywhere and make them my disciples	Go out and train everyone you meet, far and near, in this way of life	So wherever you go, make disciples of all nations	Go, therefore, and make disciples of all nations	Therefore, go and make disciples of all the nations

French translations of μαθητεύω in Matt 28:19

Version	Geneva (1560)	Martin (1707)	Ostervald (1744)	Darby NT (1859)	Segond (1910)
French	Allez donc, et endoctrinez toutes nations	Allez donc, et enseignez toutes les nations	Allez donc et instruisez toutes les nations	Allez donc, et faites disciples toutes les nations	Allez, faites de toutes les nations des disciples
English Equivalent	Go therefore, and indoctrinate all nations	Go therefore, and teach all the nations	Go therefore and instruct all the nations	Go therefore, and make all nations disciples	Go, make disciples from all nations

Interaction with this chart:

The Matthean Great Commission during the time of Calvin [in French] was literally "to indoctrinate" all nations. This fact brings to light his efforts in writing his *Institutes of the Christian Religion* to teach Francis I, the King of France, about the "Reformed" faith.

One must confess that without a definite article, the French Darby translation has the feel of a "disciple the nations" emphasis (similar to that being bantied about in Church Growth circles today), almost in a triumphalist sense, as if it were possible for everyone in a culture to be converted, which would contradict Matt 7:13-14 (among other things).

While the translation "make disciples" in English has a linear feel, the French it is more punctiliar. For example "Do what I told you!" in French would be "Fais ce que je t'ai dis!" using the same verb for make. In English we speak of "making one's bed," something that takes time. In the French Great Commission the verb "faites" (or make) is different than "fabriquer" (or make—e.g. "Made in France" is "Fabriquer en France"), or "developer" (to develop). It is more like "do". However, we cannot rightly say in English, "do disciples", that is why "win disciples" may be a more clear translation of "faites des disciples," if in fact this is what the text implies.

With the translation "make disciples" we are drawn into a discussion of who makes the disciple, how is a disciple made, and when is a disciple made? Obviously, for those who believe in infant baptism + baptismal regeneration, the disciple is made by pouring water on the head of an infant. For evangelicals, however, does this verse imply that it is the Christian's responsibility to share the Gospel (leaving the results to God), or does it teach that it is the Christian's responsibility to actually make [shape] the disciple? What is Christ responsible for, and for what is the Chrisitian responsible? It would seem that with an emphasis on evangelism, Christ is responsible for making making a new creation (2 Cor 5:17). Whereas with an emphasis on discipleship, it would seem that the Christian is responsible for making the new creation. It is amazing at the complexity of issues loaded into one verb.

The following chart shows the major English translations of Luke 6:40, another favorite verse of the discipleship movement. Perhaps some reasons for preferring this verse are:

- Its emphasis upon the "scribe" and his "master," or "pupil" and his "teacher," which can be used to emphasize human mentoring, rather than mentoring in Christ and His words (cf. Matt 23:8-10); by the way, there is a long history of writings on pedagogy, with a never ending variety of philosophies and methodologies into which the Christian can be drawn (and a strong draw is there), perhaps trying to find links between the Bible and human philosophy, rather than uniquely focusing on the revealed things in the Scriptures[1244]
- Its emphasis on "perfection," which plays into the hand of the monastic movement, with its heavy dependence upon Greek philosophy
- Its connotation of a long period of apprenticeship, again moving away from instantaneous justification by faith, 2 Cor 5:21 (sometimes also called washing, 1 Cor 6:11 [ἀπελούσασθε]; Tit 3:5 [λουτροῦ]; one may also see the applicability of the completed cleansing in John 15:3 [ἤδη ὑμεῖς καθαροί] and John 13:10-11 [καὶ ὑμεῖς καθαροί ἐστε])

A Historical Overview of the Translation of κατηρτισμένος δὲ πᾶς in Luke 6:40
"A pupil is not above his teacher; but everyone, after he has been fully trained, will be like his teacher"

Latin Vulgate (435)	Geneva (1560)	KJV (1611/ 1769)	Young's Literal (1862/ 1898)	Darby's English (1884/ 1890)	ASV (1901)	RSV (1952)	NAS (1977)	NKJ (1982)	NIV (1984)
perfectus autem omnis	but whosoeuer *will be* a perfite disciple	but every one that is perfect	but every one perfected	but every one that is perfected	but every one when he is perfected	But every one when he is fully taught	but everyone, after he has been fully trained	but everyone who is perfectly trained	But everyone who is fully trained

One can understand how translations shape theology and practice, particularly in the case of key verses. If one considers overemphasizes a prolonged period of discipleship, perhaps meditation on Luke 17:10 will provide a sober reminder of our complete dependency on God's grace, "So you too, when you do all the things which are commanded you, say, 'We are unworthy slaves; we have done *only* that which we ought to have done.'" The brief explanation of Francois Lambert d'Avignon as to why he left the Franciscan order to join Luther in 1523 may be in order here (See Historical Addendum below).

G. Finding the Balance between Evangelism and Discipleship:

1. Various approaches:
   a. No Follow-up: e.g. Ray Comfort, "I don't see follow-up anywhere in the New Testament."[1245]
   b. Discipleship Prior to Evangelism: e.g. Robert Coleman, "Remarkable as it may seem, Jesus started to gather these men before He ever organized an evangelistic campaign or even preached a sermon in public."[1246]

[1244]This author is reminded of the course he took in seminary titled, "The Psychological and Sociological Foundations of Christian Education." Primary works on this topic often begin with Sigmund Freud and work their way through modern psychology, moving to Piaget and educational theory, then focusing on moral development theories.

[1245]Ray Comfort, "Hell's Best Kept Secret," audio tape.

[1246]Robert E. Coleman, *The Master Plan of Evangelism* (Old Tappan, NJ: Revell, 1964), 21. Coleman's context is as follows, "His concern was not with programs to reach the multitudes, but with men who the multitudes would follow. Remarkable as it may seem, Jesus started to gather these men before he ever organized an evangelistic campaign or even preached a sermon in public" (Robert E. Coleman, *The Master Plan of Evangelism* [Old Tappan, NJ: Revell, 1983], 27). However, the preaching of Jesus in Matt 4:17, Mark 1:14-15, and Luke 4:44 preceded His calling of his disciples in Matthew 4:18-22, Mark 1:16-20, and Luke 5:10-11. His lack of considering these passages may render Coleman's *a priori* statement based on chronology in the discipleship training of Jesus void. A look at A. B. Bruce's *The Training of the Twelve,* 4th ed. (1894; Grand Rapids: Kregel, 1971), ix, shows that Bruce, upon whom Coleman relied, did not deal with any of the early preaching passages in his analysis. Coleman's *a priori* then led him to state of

    c. Discipleship as evangelism: e.g. Myron Augsburger.[1247]

2. The debate over the primacy of discipleship over evangelism or evangelism over discipleship is not a small issue. Notice how it impacts one's view of the mission of the church, and/or the Great Commission:

    a. While the watchword, "The evangelization of the world in this generation," was gaining currency, leading to the greatest zeal for world evangeliztion in the history of the church, according to David Barrett,[1248] The strongest antagonism to the Watchword, which ended up with John R. Mott changing from "mere evangelization" to a "larger evangelism," came from the German "father" of the "science of missions," Gustav Warneck:

> "From the beginning, the Watchword had been espoused and welcomed in North America, Britain, and Scandinavia, but had received a cool reception from the rest of Europe, Germany in particular. A fair number of German books had, it is true, been published in the 1890s, including O. Märker's *Die Evangelisation* (Stuttgart, 1896) and J. Schneider's *Evangelisation und Gemeinschaftspflegen* (Gutersloh, 1897). But the leading German theologian and founder of the science of missions, Gustav Warneck, was a severe critic and the major detractor from 1895-1910. In his classic work *Evangelische Missionslehre* (1902) he devoted most of Chapter 32 to combating what he considered to be the naivete and fallacy of the movement for world evangelization. He was first, but certainly not the last, to criticize proponents of world evangelization on the specious grounds that they were advocating 'blosse Kundmachung' (mere proclamation) rather than the building up of Christians and churches."[1249]

    b. Gustav Warneck took the air out of the Student Volunteer Movement watchword, "The Evangelization of the World in This Generation," by advocating for discipleship (Christian maturity) equal to or over evangelization.[1250]

---

mass evangelism, "Victory is never won by the multitudes" (Coleman, *The Master Plan*, 36). He also then shared his views about local church evangelism programs, "we have launched one crash program after another to reach the multitudes.... But we have failed..." (ibid., 38).

[1247]Myron Augsburger, *Evangelism as Discipling* (Scottsdale, PA: Herald, 1983).

[1248]"Mott's conclusions reiterated throughout the book [*The Evangelization of the World in This Generation* (New York, 1900)] and subsequently, can be given in the words of his address of 28 April 1900 to the Ecumenical Missionary Conference, New York:
"'There is a large and increasing number of Christians who believe that it is the duty of the Church to evangelize the world in this generation, but also that it is actually possible to accomplish the task.'
"1900-1914: The Highwater Mark of the Watchword
"This theme and its brilliant articulation by Mott set the scene for an unprecedented surge of enthusiasm for foreign missions from the USA and Europe. Together with it came a zeal for total evangelization of the world unmatched in Christian history" (David B. Barrett, *Evangelize! A Historical Survey of the Concept* [Birmingham, AL: New Hope, 1987], 28).

[1249]Ibid., 29.

[1250]"In view of the ambiguous definitions which have been and are still given of the watchword "evangelisation," [referring to John R. Mott's] it is difficult to say exactly what is to be understood by it. [John R.] Mott in his book, *The Evangelization of the World in this Generation* (London, 1900), written with a burning enthusiasm, explains that it means "that a sufficient opportunity shall be offered to all men to become acquainted with Jesus Christ as their Redeemer, and to become His disciples," but not "Christianisation in the sense of interpenetration of the world with Christian ideas," although educational, literary, and medical work are not excluded, and the proclamation of the Gospel is not to be of a superficial character. Dr. [A. T.] Pierson understands the word as only "preaching and testimony. These two words embrace all that is meant by evangelisation." What the definitions lack in clearness is supplied by the principles laid down as to methods of practical action. ...
"This last task is the task of missions [the solid founding of the Christian church]; the limitation of this task to mere evangelisation confounds means and goal. Mere preaching does not suffice; it is to be the means of laying the foundation of the Church. ...mere announcement of the Gospel is not sufficient for this" (Gustav Warneck, *Outline of the History of Protestant Missions*, 3rd English edition, translation of the 8th German edition of 1904 [New York: Revell, 1906], 406-07).

c.   The Watchword changed from "The Evangelization of the World," to the more socially-oriented "Christianization of the World in This Generation":

1)   The combined impact upon young student minds of Albrecht Ritschl's attack on the substitutionary atonement, Adolf Harnack's emphasis on the social Gospel, and Ernst Troelsch's social theology of the Church cannot be underestimated

d.   The issue of biblical emphasis is not a minor issue!

3.   Thus the debate between the "evangelism" or "soul-winning" camp and the "discipleship" or soul-building" camp has a long-standing history:

a.   Note the words of Scarborough acknowledging this debate:

"It is not wise to say that *soul winning* is the main thing or that *soul building* is the main thing. They are Siamese twins of God's gospel, going hand in hand, and they ought to keep up with each other.... And this leads me to say that the main thing in the Kingdom of God is the evangelistic spirit, the martial note and conquest tread."[1251]

b.   Where can we find the balance? An analysis at Ezek 3:17-21:

Ezekiel 3 on the Interrelationship of Evangelism and Discipleship

Concept	To the Wicked [evangelism]	To the Righteous [Discipleship]	Analysis
Command	Ezek 3:17, "whenever you hear a word from My mouth, warn them from Me"	Ezek 3:17, "whenever you hear a word from My mouth, warn them from Me"	Same Command
Verb used	"Warn" (Ezek 3:17) "Warn... speak out to warn" (Ezek 3:18) "If you have warned" (Ezek 3:19)	"Warn" (Ezek 3:17) "You have not warned him" (Ezek 3:20) "If you have warned" (Ezek 3:21)	Same verbal forms
Response to the warning	"He does not turn from his wickedness or from his wicked way (Ezek 3:19)	"He does not sin (Ezek 3:21) "Because he took warning (Ezek 3:21)	Opposite responses to the warning
Accountability for disobedience	Ezek 3:18, "but his blood I will require at your hand"	Ezek 3:20, "but his blood I will require at your hand"	Same accountabililty for disobedience
Result of obedience	Ezek 3:19, "but you have delivered yourself"	Ezek 3:21, "and you have delivered yourself"	Same result of obedience

c.   Some thoughts from Ezek 3:17-21:

1)   There is a distinction between ministry to the wicked and that to the righteous
a)   Quite similarly as there is a distinction between evangelizing the unsaved and encouraging the Christian

2)   While there is a distinction between the two, both are guided by the same command, have opposite responses to the same warning, and yet retain the same level of accountability:
a)   Therefore, it is not a question of "either-or" but of "both-and"
b)   Ignorance of one (such as evangelism), quite often leads to misemphasis in the other (discipleship)

3)   Which, then is the priority of the believer? Matt 28:19-20 shows that:
a)   When a person is lost, they need to be won as a disciple
b)   When a person is saved, and in the family of God through believer's baptism, they need to be taught to obey all the Christ commanded

4)   Further statements of Jesus also clarify:
a)   His main mission was to seek and to save that which was lost (Matt 18:11; Luke 19:10)

[1251]L. R. Scarborough, *Recruits for World Conquest* (New York: Revell, 1914), 58.

b) In view of the large percentage of lost people in the world (Matt 7:13-14), the reality is that evangelism is desperately needed to reach lost souls

I. A Final Introductory Theological Consideration:

1. How much emphasis can be placed on the Christian using culturally-based techniques of following up new believers, without displacing God's effective operation in salvation and spiritual growth, by faith alone?

    Eph 1:19-20 (NKJ), "and what *is* the exceeding greatness of His power toward us who believe, according to the working of His mighty power [κατὰ τὴν ἐνέργειαν τοῦ κράτους τῆς ἰσχύος αὐτοῦ] which He worked in Christ [ἣν ἐνήργησεν ἐν τῷ χριστῷ] when He raised Him from the dead and seated *Him* at His right hand in the heavenly *places*"

    Eph 3:6-7 (NKJ), "that the Gentiles should be fellow heirs, of the same body, and partakers of His promise in Christ through the gospel, of which I became a minister according to the gift of the grace of God given to me by the effective working of His power [κατὰ τὴν ἐνέργειαν τῆς δυνάμεως αὐτοῦ]."

    Phil 3:21 (NKJ), "who will transform our lowly body that it may be conformed to His glorious body, according to the working by which He is able even to subdue all things to Himself."

    Col 1:29 (NKJ), "To this *end* I also labor, striving according to His working which works in me mightily"

    Col 2:11-12, "In Him you were also circumcised with the circumcision made without hands, by putting off the body of the sins of the flesh, by the circumcision of Christ, buried with Him in baptism, in which you also were raised with *Him* through faith in the working of God [διὰ τῆς πίστεως τῆς ἐνεργείας τοῦ θεοῦ], who raised Him from the dead"

2. This begs the question: are there follow-up "techniques" that are not culturally-based human techniques?

    a. Yes, I believe that there are

3. What are these techniques?

    a. Let's first look at biblical terminology, particularly verbs describing the methodology of follow-up used primarily in (but not limited to) the Book of Acts...

    b. [by the way, is this not using the "Regulative Principle" for defining biblical follow-up?]

II. New Testament Verbs for Follow-Up/Discipleship/Fellowship:

Chart of Verbs and Verbal Nouns in Follow-Up, Discipleship, or Local Church Contexts by Category

Explanation: The first number in the chart represents the assigned number in the following notes; the second number corresponds to the number of evangelistic New Testament uses of the word in these notes (a zero indicates an Old Testament Septuagint use).

Comparative: This chart was developed to provide a comparison of verbs in evangelism contexts with verbs in follow-up and discipleship contexts

Disclaimer: This chart is not exhaustive and categories are general in nature; because cognate verbs and nouns are kept together and due to differing contexts, there may be some overlap or duplication in categories. There ought not be be repeated use of the same verb.

Follow-Up 1	Follow-Up 2	Life in the Church	Physical Presence or Action	Attitudes
Exhort/Encourage (1) παρακαλέω [18]; (n1) παράκλησις [1]; (2) συμπαρακαλέομαι [1]; (3) παραμυθέομαι [1]; (4) κατανοέω + παροξυσμός [1].	**Teach with Passion** (14) παραγγέλλω [1]; (15) ἐπαγωνίζομαι + πίστις [1]; (16) δέομαι [1]; (17) προβιβάζω [0].	**Role of Spiritual Leaders** (30) ποιμαίνω [3]; (31) ἀγρυπνέω [1]; (32) καταρτίζω [5].	**Gather** (44) συνάγω [3]; (n10) συναγωγή [1]; (n11) ἐπισυναγωγή [1]; (45) συνέρχομαι [3].	**Love** (57) ἀγαπάω [12]; (n11) ἀγάπη [1]; (n12) φιλαδελφία [2].
Establish/Build Up (5) στηρίζω [3]; (6) ἐπιστηρίζω [4]; (n2) στερέωμα [1]; (7) οἰκοδομέω [7]; (n3) οἰκοδομή [1].	**Preach/Proclaim** (18) κηρύσσω [1]; (19) καταγγέλλω [1]; (20) παρατείνω + λόγος [1]; (21) ἐπιτιμάω [2]; (22) ἐλέγχω [5]; (23) ὑποδείκνυμι [1]; (24) ὁμιλέω [1].	**Regarding Erring Members** (33) πορεύομαι [2]; (34) ζητέω [1].	**Greeting and Sending Off** (46) ἀσπάζομαι [3]; (47) ἀπασπάζομαι [1]; (48) ἐπιπίπτω + τράχηλος [1]; (49) καταφιλέω [1].	**Mutual Subjection** (58) ὑποτάσσω [2]; (59) ἡγέομαι [1].
Bear Witness (8) μαρτυρομαι [3]; (9) διαμαρτύρομαι [3]; (10) ἐπιμαρτυρέω [1].	**Entrust/Impart** (25) παρατίθημι [1]; (26) μεταδίδωμι + χάρισμα [1].	**Reports and Testimonies** (35) ἀναγγέλλω [5]; (36) ἀπαγγέλλω [1]; (37) ἐκδιηγέομαι [1]; (38) ἐξηγέομαι [1]; (39) ἐξομολογέω [4].	**Remain** (50) μένω [3]; (51) ἐπιμένω [1].	**Oneness of Mind** (60) φρονέω [1]; (61) ἀνέχω [2].
Teach/Instruct (11) διδάσκω [8]; (n4) διδασκαλία [4]; (12) νουθετέω [3]; (13) διαλέγομαι [2].	**Speak/Say** (27) λέγω [2]; (28) προλέγω [4]; (n5) ἐν λόγω [1]; (29) λαλέω [2].	**Receiving Instruction** (40) ἀναγνώσει [1]; (n6) διδαχη + ἀπόστολος [1]; (41) μανθάνω [6].	**Depart/Separate** (52) ἀφίσταμαι [1]; (53) ἀφορίζω [2]; (54) ἐξέρχομαι [3]; (55) στέλλω /στέλλομαι [1]; (56) ἀποτρέπω [1].	**Oneness of Care** (n13) φιλόστοργος [1]; (n14) προηγέομαι [1]; (62) προσλαμβάνω [1].
		Theological Debate and Decision Making (n7) στάσις [1]; (n8) ζήτησις [1]; (n9) συζήτησις [1]; (42) τάσσω [1]; (43) ὁράω + λόγος [1].		**Attitudes to Avoid** (63) κρίνω [1]; (n15) γίνομαι + κενόδοξος [1]; (64) προκαλέω [1]; (65) φθονέω [1].

Introduction to verbs below: Interestingly, two main verbal groups for follow-up in the Book of Acts seem to follow the precedent of Deut 3:28:

Deut 3:28, "But charge Joshua and **encourage** him and **strengthen** him; for he shall go across at the head of this people, and he shall give them as an inheritance the land which you will see"

Acts 14:22, "**strengthening** the souls of the disciples, **encouraging** them to continue in the faith, and *saying*, "Through many tribulations we must enter the kingdom of God"

Comparing "Encourage" and "Strengthen" in Deut 3:28 and Acts 14:22

Deut 3:28				Acts 14:22	
Hebrew	**Greek LXX (Rahlfs)**	**Vulgate (Migne)**	**NAS**	**Greek Byzantine Textform**	**NAS**
Chazaq	κατισχύω	corrobora	encourage	ἐπιστηρίζω	Strengthening
Amets	παρακαλέω	conforta	strengthen	παρακαλέω	Encouraging

A. Specific Verbs for Follow-Up in the Book of Acts (with a limited sampling of others):[1252]

    1. To exhort/encourage:

        a. παρακαλέω and cognate:

           1) παρακαλέω [18] – beg, urge, encourage, request, ask, appeal, exhort:
This verb is used 2 times in contexts that are unclear (as far as evangelizing or not evangelizing), 2 Cor 5:20; 2 Tim 4:2; however, it seems by far to be predominantly a verb directed to the exhortation of believers

Acts 2:40, "And with many other words he solemnly testified and kept on **exhorting** them, saying, 'Be saved from this perverse generation!'"

Acts 14:22, "strengthening the souls of the disciples, **encouraging** them to continue in the faith, and *saying*, 'Through many tribulations we must enter the kingdom of God.'"

Acts 15:32, "Judas and Silas, who themselves were prophets, said much **to encourage** and strengthen the brothers."

Acts 16:40, "And they went out of the prison and entered *the house of* Lydia, and when they saw the brethren, they **encouraged** them and departed."

Acts 20:1, "And after the uproar had ceased, Paul sent for the disciples and when he had **exhorted** them and taken his leave of them, he departed to go to Macedonia"

Acts 20:2, "And when he had gone through those districts and had given them **much exhortation** [exhorted them with many words], he came to Greece"

1 Cor 14:31, "For you can all prophesy one by one, so that all may learn and all **may be exhorted**"

2 Cor 5:20, "Therefore, we are ambassadors for Christ, as though God **were making an appeal** through us; we beg you on behalf of Christ, be reconciled to God"

2 Cor 6:1, "And working together *with Him*, we also **urge** you not to receive the grace of God in vain"

1 Thess 2:11, "just as you know how we *were* **exhorting** and encouraging and imploring each one of you as a father *would* his own children"

1 Thess 3:2, "and we sent Timothy, our brother and God's fellow worker in the gospel of Christ, to strengthen and **encourage** you as to your faith"

1 Thess 5:11, "Therefore **encourage** one another, and build up one another, just as you also are doing"

[1252]These terms are merely the beginning of a study, based primarily in the Book of Acts. They are meant to provide a comparative to the study of the terms for evangelizing in Chapter 7.

Translations of the edification verbs in 1 Thess 5:11

Greek	Latin (435)	Wycliffe 2nd ed (1388)	Eng Geneva (1560)	King James (1611, 1769)	Young's (1862)	Darby (1885)	American Standard (1901)	Revised Standard (1952)	New King James (1982)	New Jeru-salem* (1985)	IBS's French Le Semeur (1992, 1999)*	ABS's CEV* (1995)
παρακαλεῖτε ἀλλήλους	consolamini invicem	comforte ye togidere	exhorte one another	comfort yourselves together	comfort ye one another	encourage one another	exhort one another	encourage one another	comfort each other	give encourage-ment to each other	encourage ye one another	you must encourage
οἰκοδομεῖτε εἰς τὸν ἕνα	aedificate alterutrum	edefie ye ech other	edifie one another	edify one another	build ye up, one the one	build up each one the other	build each other up	build one another up	edify one another	keep strengthen-ing one another	mutually help ye to grow in the faith**	help each other

*My translation of, "encouragez-vous les uns les autres" and "aidez-vous mutuellement à grandir dans la foi."
**Another equivocal paraphrase, this time removed from the root meaning of the word, and emphasizing growing in "the faith."

1 Tim 6:2, "These things teach and **exhort**"

1 Tim 5:1-2, "Do not sharply rebuke an older man, but *rather* **appeal** to *him* as a father, *to the* younger men as brothers, the older women as mothers, *and* the younger women as sisters, in all purity."

2 Tim 4:2, "preach the word; be ready in season *and* out of season; reprove, rebuke, **exhort**, with great patience and instruction"

Titus 2:15, "These things speak and **exhort** and reprove with all authority"

Heb 3:13, "But **encourage** one another day after day, as long as it is *still* called 'Today,' lest any one of you be hardened by the deceitfulness of sin"

1 Pet 5:12, "Through Silvanus, our faithful brother (for so I regard *him*), I have written to you briefly, **exhorting** and testifying that this is the true grace of God. Stand firm in it!"

n1) παράκλησις [1] – exhortation, encouragement; appeal, request; comfort, consolation:

1 Tim 4:13 (NKJ), "Till I come, give attention to reading, to **exhortation**, to doctrine."

2) συμπαρακαλέομαι [1] – mutually encourage, Rom 1:12

Rom 1:12, "that is, that I may **be encouraged together** with you *while* among you, each of us by the other's faith, both yours and mine"

Does not this term express the complexity of follow-up and spiritual nurture? Here we have the Apostle Paul admitting that he is not coming as the "know it all," but rather that he is seeking mutual encouragement. Yes, at times, new believers have things that they can teach those who have been saved for quite some time—and that is because of "mutual faith" and the Holy Spirit residing in them. This should keep us all humble.

3) παραμυθέομαι [1] (4 NT uses) – encourage, cheer up; console, comfort

1 Thess 2:11, "just as you know how we *were* exhorting and **encouraging** and imploring each one of you as a father *would* his own children"

4) κατανοέω + παροξυσμός [1] – consider to encourage, Heb 10:24:

Heb 10:24, "and let us consider how to stimulate one another to love and good deeds"

1) κατανοέω (verb, 14 NT uses) – to perceive, consider, observe

2) παροξυσμός (noun, 2 OT uses, 2 NT uses) – stimulation, provocation, irritation; OT: sharp disagreement

2. To establish/build up:

a. στηρίζω and cognate:

5) στηρίζω [3] – establish (Friberg: literally setting up something so that it remains immovable *fix (firmly), establish, support* [16:26]); note the figurative use in Luke 9:51, "he fixed his face to go to Jerusalem":

Luke 22:32, "but I have prayed for you, that your faith may not fail; and you, when once you have turned again, **strengthen** your brothers"

Rom 1:11, "For I long to see you so that I may impart some spiritual gift to you, that you **may be established**"[1253]

> The Latin Vulgate translated στηρίζω in this verse with the verb *confirmo*, from which word is derived the term for the "Sacrament of Confirmation"

1 Thess 3:2 "and we sent Timothy, our brother and God's fellow worker in the gospel of Christ, to **strengthen** and encourage you as to your faith"

6) ἐπιστηρίζω [4] – strengthen, establish, cause to be firm:

In the Book of Acts, ἐπιστηρίζω is never used in an evangelistic context.

Acts 14:22, "**strengthening** the souls of the disciples, encouraging them to continue in the faith, and *saying*, 'Through many tribulations we must enter the kingdom of God.'"

Acts 15:32, "Judas and Silas, who themselves were prophets, said much to encourage and **strengthen** the brothers."

Acts 15:41, "And he was traveling through Syria and Cilicia, **strengthening** the churches"

Acts 18:23, "And having spent some time *there*, he departed and passed successively through the Galatian region and Phrygia, **strengthening** all the disciples"

n2) στερέωμα [1] (noun, used once in the NT [23 times in LXX]) – steadfastness, firmness:

Col 2:5, "For even though I am absent in body, nevertheless I am with you in spirit, rejoicing to see your good discipline and the **stability** of your faith in Christ"

b. οἰκοδομέω and cognates:

7) οἰκοδομέω [7] – build, edify, build up:

This verb is found 507 times in the OT LXX and 40 in the Nestle-Aland NT, primarily in its literal sense in the OT and the Gospels

Acts 9:31, "So the church throughout all Judea and Galilee and Samaria enjoyed peace, **being built up**; and, going on in the fear of the Lord and in the comfort of the Holy Spirit, it continued to increase."

Acts 20:32, "And now I commend you to God and to the word of His grace, which is able **to build *you* up** and to give *you* the inheritance among all those who are sanctified."

1 Cor 8:1, "Now concerning things sacrificed to idols, we know that we all have knowledge. Knowledge makes arrogant, but love **edifies**."

1 Cor 10:23, "All things are lawful, but not all things are profitable. All things are lawful, but not all things **edify**"

1 Cor 14:4, "One who speaks in a tongue **edifies** himself; but one who prophesies **edifies** the church."

1 Cor 14:17, "For you are giving thanks well enough, but the other man is not **edified**"

1 Thess 5:11, "Therefore encourage one another, and **build up** one another, just as you also are doing."

n3) οἰκοδομή [1] – building up:

Rom 14:19, "So then let us pursue the things which make for peace and the **building up of** one another"

3. To bear witness:

a. μαρτυρέω and μαρτυρομαι verbal group:

Introduction: The interesting 1669 French Geneva Bible's use of the word "protest" in the context of edification:

Gal 5:3, "Et derechef **je proteste** à tout homme qui se circoncit, qu'il est obligé d'accomplir toute la Loi." [As a translation of μαρτυρέω]

[1253]Roman 1:11 provides an interesting case study for spiritual growth. Depending on the translation and the interpretation of this verse, it could be understood as speaking of the "impartation of some grace" in the sacraments of the Roman Catholic Church, for example, the Sacrament of Confirmation, for which the Latin verb *confirmo* is used to translate στηρίζω in this verse. Elsewhere in the NT στηρίζω is also translated by Jerome into the Latin *confirmo* (Luke 22:32; Rom 14:24; 1 Thess 3:2, 13; 2 Thess 2:17; 3:3; James 5:8; 1 Pet 5:10; 2 Pet 1:12; Rev 3:2), or else merely as *firmo* (Luke 9:51; 16:26). Lewis defines *firmo* as, "to make firm, strengthen, fortify, sustain; fig. to fortify, strengthen, secure, confirm, assure, reinforce, make long lasting." *Confirmo* appears to have an almost identical meaning, along with its ritualistic religious connotations.

Rev 22:18, "Or **je proteste** à chacun qui oit les paroles de la prophetie de ce livre, que si quelqu'un ajouste à ces choses, Dieu ajoustera sur lui les playes escrites en ce livre." [As a translation of μαρτυρέω]

2 Tim 2:14, "Ramentoi ces choses, **protestant** devant le Seigneur qu'on ne debatte point de paroles: qui est une chose qui ne revient à aucun profit, [mais] à la ruïne des auditeurs." [As a translation of διαμαρτύρομαι]

8) μαρτυρομαι [3] – to testify, declare:

Acts 20:26, "Therefore **I testify** to you this day, that I am innocent of the blood of all men" (use of verb to a saved audience)

Eph 4:17, "This I say therefore, and **affirm together** with the Lord, that you walk no longer just as the Gentiles also walk, in the futility of their mind"

1 Thess 2:11, "just as you know how we *were* exhorting and encouraging and **imploring** each one of you as a father *would* his own children"

Variations in Translating of μαρτύρομαι

Passage	French Geneva Revised	New International	New American Standard	King James Version	New Living Translation	Douay-Rheims✠	New Jerusalem✠
Acts 20:26	Declare [déclare]	Declare	Testify	Take you to record	Say plainly	Witness	I swear
Eph 4:17	Declare [déclare]	Insist	Affirm [together with]	Testify	With [the Lord's] authority	Testify	Attest
1 Thess 2:11[12]	Plead [conjurant]	Urging	Imploring	Charged	Urged	Comforting	Appealing

9) διαμαρτύρομαι [3] – solemnly testifying, testify emphatically, **warn** (cf. Luke 16:28):

This verb is translated "warn" in Luke 16:28, and it also used 7 times in the Book of Acts for evangelizing, translated as solemnly testify in the NAS

Acts 2:40, "And with many other words he **solemnly testified** and kept on exhorting them, saying, 'Be saved from this perverse generation!'"

Acts 8:25, "And so, when they had **solemnly testified** and spoken the word of the Lord, they started back to Jerusalem, and were preaching the gospel to many villages of the Samaritans"

1 Thess 4:6, "*and* that no man transgress and defraud his brother in the matter because the Lord is *the* avenger in all these things, just as we also told you before and **solemnly warned** *you*"

10) ἐπιμαρτυρέω [1] – to bear witness (1 NT use):

1 Pet 5:12, "Through Silvanus, our faithful brother (for so I regard *him*), I have written to you briefly, exhorting and **testifying** that this is the true grace of God. Stand firm in it!"

4. Teach/instruct:

a. διδάσκω and cognate:

11) διδάσκω [8] – teach:

This verb is also used 17 times for evangelizing.

Matt 28:20, "**teaching** them to observe all that I commanded you; and lo, I am with you always, even to the end of the age"

Acts 15:35, "But Paul and Barnabas stayed in Antioch, **teaching** and preaching [evangelizing], with many others also, the word of the Lord"

Acts 18:11, "And he settled *there* a year and six months, **teaching** the word of God," (e.g. Acts 18:24-19:7)

Col 1:28, "We proclaim Him, admonishing every man and **teaching** every man with all wisdom, so that we may present every man complete in Christ"

Col 3:16, "Let the word of Christ richly dwell within you, with all wisdom **teaching** and admonishing one another with psalms *and* hymns *and* spiritual songs, singing with thankfulness in your hearts to God"

1 Tim 4:11, "Prescribe and **teach** these things"

1 Tim 6:2, "These things **teach** and exhort"

2 Tim 2:2, "And the things which you have heard from me in the presence of many witnesses, these entrust to faithful men, who will be able **to teach** others also"

n4) διδασκαλία [4]:

1 Tim 4:13 (NKJ), "Till I come, give attention to reading, to exhortation, to **doctrine**."

Chronological Comparative Translations of διδαχή and διδασκαλία in the NT

Texts	Greek	Latin	Wycliffe 2nd Edition (1388)	Tyndale (1534)	KJV (1611, 1769)	James Murdock (1852)	John Darby (1884, 1890)	Young's Literal (1862, 1898)	NAS (1977)	NKJ (1982)	NIV (1984)	NJB* (1985)
Matt 16:12			techyng	Doctrine	doctrine	Doctrine	doctrine	teaching	teaching	doctrine	teaching	teaching
	διδαχή	Doctrina	Thanne thei vndur-stooden, that he seide not to be war of sourdowy of looues, but of the techyng of Farisees and Saducees.	Then vnderstode they how that he bad not them beware of the leven of breed: but of the doctrine of the Pharises and of the Saduces.	Then understood they how that he bade *them* not beware of the leaven of bread, but of the doctrine of the Pharisees and of the Saddees.	Then understood they, that he did not bid them beware of the leaven of bread, but of the doctrine of the Pharisees and of the Saddees.	Then they compre-hended that he did not speak of being beware of the leaven of bread, but of the doctrine of the Pharisees and Sadducees.	Then they understood that he did not say to take heed of the leaven of the bread, but of the teaching, of the Pharisees and Sadducees.	Then they understood that He did not say to beware of the leaven of bread, but of the teaching of the Pharisees and Sadducees.	Then they understood that He did not tell *them* to beware of the leaven of bread, but of the doctrine of the Pharisees and Sadducees.	Then they understood that he was not telling them to guard against the yeast used in bread, but against the teaching of the Pharisees and Sadducees.	Then they understood that he was telling them to be on their guard, not against yeast for making bread, but against the teaching of the Pharisees and Sadducees.
2 Tim 4:2			doctryn	Doctryne	doctrine	instructive-ness	doctrine	teaching	instruction	teaching	careful instruction	with care to instruct
	διδαχή	Doctrina	preche the word, be thou bisi couenabli with outen rest, repreue thou, biseche thou, blame thou in al pacience and doctryn.	preache the worde be fervent be it in season or out of season. Improve rebuke exhorte with all longe sufferinge and doctryne.	Preach the word; be instant in season, out of season; reprove, rebuke, exhort with all long-suffering and doctrine.	Proclaim the word; and persist [in it] with diligence, in time and out of time; admonish, and rebuke, with all patience and instructive-ness.	Proclaim the word; be urgent in season *and* out of season, convict, rebuke, encourage, with all long-suffering and doctrine.	preach the word; be earnest in season, out of season, convict, rebuke, exhort, in all long-suffering and teaching,	preach the word; be ready in season *and* out of season; reprove, rebuke, exhort, with great patience and instruction.	Preach the word! Be ready in season *and* out of season. Convince, rebuke, exhort, with all longsuffering and teaching.	Preach the Word; be prepared in season and out of season; correct, rebuke and encourage-- with great patience and careful instruction	proclaim the message and, welcome or unwelcome, insist on it. Refute falsehood, correct error, give encourage-ment -- but do all with patience and with care to instruct.

Texts	Greek	Latin	Wycliffe 2nd Edition (1388)	Tyndale (1534)	KJV (1611, 1769)	James Murdock (1852)	John Darby (1884, 1890)	Young's Literal (1862, 1898)	NAS (1977)	NKJ (1982)	NIV (1984)	NJB* (1985)
1 Tim 4:6	τῆς καλῆς διδασκαλίας	bonae doctrinae	good doctrine	good doctryne	good doctrine	the good doctrine	the good teaching	the good teaching	the sound doctrine	the good doctrine	the good teaching	the good doctrine
			Thou puttynge forth these thingis to britheren, schalt be a good mynystre of Crist Jhesu; nurschid with wordis of feith and of good doctryne, which thou hast gete.	Yf thou shalt put the brethren in remem-braunce of these thynges thou shalt be a good minister of Iesu Christ which hast bene norisshed vp in the wordes of the fayth and good doctryne which doctryne thou hast continually followed.	If thou put the brethren in remem-brance of these things, thou shalt be a good minister of Jesus Christ, nourished up in the words of faith and of good doctrine, whereunto thou hast attained.	If thou shalt inculcate these things on thy brethren, thou wilt be a good minister of Jesus the Messiah, being educated in the language of the faith, and in the good doctrine which thou hast been taught.	Laying these things before the brethren, thou wilt be a good minister of Christ Jesus, nourished with the words of the faith and of the good teaching which thou hast fully followed up.	These things placing before the brethren, thou shalt be a good ministrant of Jesus Christ, being nourished by the words of the faith, and of the good teaching, which thou didst follow after,	In pointing out these things to the brethren, you will be a good servant of Christ Jesus, constantly nourished on the words of faith and of the sound doctrine which you have been following.	If you instruct the brethren in these things, you will be a good minister of Jesus Christ, nourished in the words of faith and of the good doctrine which you have carefully followed.	If you point these things out to the brothers, you will be a good minister of Christ Jesus, brought up in the truths of the faith and of the good teaching that you have followed.	If you put all this to the brothers, you will be a good servant of Christ Jesus and show that you have really digested the teaching of the faith and the good doctrine which you have always followed.
1 Tim 4:13	διδασκαλία	Doctrinae	Teching	doctryne	doctrine	teaching	Teaching	teaching	teaching	doctrine	Teaching	Teaching
			Tyl Y come, take tent to redyng, to exortacioun and teching.	Till I come geve attendaunce to redynge to exhortacion and to doctryne.	Till I come, give attendance to reading, to exhortation, to doctrine.	Until I come, be diligent in reading, and in prayer, and in teaching.	Till I come, give thyself to reading, to exhortation, to teaching.	till I come, give heed to the reading, to the exhortation, to the teaching;	Until I come, give attention to the public reading of Scripture, to exhortation and teaching.	Till I come, give attention to reading, to exhortation, to doctrine.	Until I come, devote yourself to the public reading of Scripture, to preaching and to teaching.	Until I arrive, devote yourself to reading to the people, encourag-ing and teaching.
1 Tim 5:17	λόγος and διδασκαλία	verbo et doctrina	in word and teching	in the worde and in teachinge	in the word and doctrine	in the word and in doctrine	in word and teaching	in word and teaching	at preaching and teaching	in the word and doctrine	preaching and teaching	at preaching and teaching
			The prestis that ben wel gouernoures, be thei had worthi to double onour; moost thei that trauelen in word and teching.	The elders that rule wel are worthy of double honoure most specially they which laboure in the worde and in teachinge.	Let the elders that rule well be counted worthy of double honour, especially they who labour in the word and doctrine.	Let the elders who conduct themselves well, be esteemed worthy of double honor; especially they who labor in the word and in doctrine.	Let the elders who take the lead among the saints well be esteemed worthy of double honour, specially those labouring in word and teaching;	The well-leading elders of double honour let them be counted worthy, especially those labouring in word and teaching,	Let the elders who rule well be considered worthy of double honor, especially those who work hard at preaching and teaching.	Let the elders who rule well be counted worthy of double honor, especially those who labor in the word and doctrine.	The elders who direct the affairs of the church well are worthy of double honor, especially those whose work is preaching and teaching.	Elders who do their work well while they are in charge earn double reward, especially those who work hard at preaching and teaching.

In comparing the two words used for translating διδαχή and διδασκαλία (not to mention, λόγος, ῥῆμα, or λογικός):

"Doctrine" is a noun, and corresponds to the Greek word that is a noun

It implies a certain body of truth

The same is true of the Greek noun διδαχή, which is also translated either doctrine or teaching

"Teaching" is a verb, used as a participle, and does not correspond in type with the Greek word (which would only be important for literal translations)

One problem with using the word "doctrine" to translate is that "doctrine" may be seen to imply only polemic theology or philosophy, and not issues of lifestyle and methodology

In this case the broad participle "teaching" would consider more than just polemic theology

"Teaching", however, seems more problematic, as it does not necessarily emphasize what is taught, but how it is taught, as there are textbooks and classes on "principles for teaching," "classical pedagogy," "psychology of educational," ect.:

Therefore, in our text above, in the move from "doctrine" to "teaching," the emphasis may easily shift from "teaching right doctrine" to "using proper teaching methods to communicate something"

Likewise, there can be a comparable shift in emphasis:

From the doctrinal portions of Paul,

To learning teaching principles from the parables of Jesus, who was "the best teacher that ever lived!"

This shift toward method of teaching may be best represented in the NIV and NJB translations of 2 Tim 4:2, where they have moved beyond use of the word "teaching", to say "careful instruction" and "with care to instruct"—again reminiscent of carefully crafted lesson plans and object lessons

Also, using the verb "teaching" in English blurs distinctions in English-only study of:

The 30 NT uses of the noun διδαχή (instruction)

The 21 NT uses of the noun διδασκαλία (doctrine)

The 91 NT uses of the verb διδάσκω (to teach)

The KJV has 50 NT uses of the word English word "doctrine[s]"

The NKJ has 38 NT uses of the word "doctrine[s]":

20 of these are translations of διδασκαλία

17 of these are translation of διδαχή

One of these is in the translation of the verb ἑτεροδιδασκαλέω

The RSV has 16 uses o the word "doctrine[s]"

The NAS has 14 NT uses of "doctrine[s]"

12 for διδασκαλία

2 in the translation of the verb ἑτεροδιδασκαλέω

The ESV has 13 uses of "doctrine[s]"

The Holman Christian Standard has 8 total NT uses of "doctrine[s]"

The NIV, however, has 7 NT uses of the word "doctrine[s]":

1 Tim 1:3, for ἑτεροδιδασκαλέω

1 Tim 1:10, for διδασκαλία

1 Tim 4:16, for διδασκαλία

1 Tim 6:3, for ἑτεροδιδασκαλέω

2 Tim 4:3 for διδασκαλία

Tit 1:9, for διδασκαλία

Tit 2:1, for διδασκαλία

The NET Bible has 2 uses of "doctrine[s]"

Matt 15:9 for διδασκαλία

Mark 7:7 for διδασκαλία

The New Living Translation has no uses of "doctrine[s]"

It must be noted that there are a total of 51 uses of both the nounts διδαχή and διδασκαλία in the NT, not including 2 uses of the verb ἑτεροδιδασκαλέω

> n4) διδασκαλία (continued):
>> 1 Tim 5:14, "Let the elders who rule well be considered worthy of double honor, especially those who work hard at preaching and **teaching**"
>> 2 Tim 3:16 (NKJ) All Scripture *is* given by inspiration of God, and *is* profitable for **doctrine**, for reproof, for correction, for instruction in righteousness,

Translations of the Role of Scripture as It Relates to "Doctrine" in 2 Tim 3:16-17

[again related to the translation of the Greek term: διδασκαλία]

Wycliffe 2nd Edit (1388)	Tyndale (1534)	Geneva (1560)	King James (1611, 1769)	James Murdock (1852)	Young's Literal (1862, 1898)	New Jerusalem Bible⚜ (1985)	Contemp English Version⚜ (1995)
to teche	to teache	to teache	for doctrine	for instruction	for teaching	… teaching them to be upright	for teaching
For al scripture inspirid of God is profitable to teche, to repreue, to chastice, to lerne in riytwisnes, [17] that the man of God be parfit, lerud to al good werk.	For all scripture geve by inspiracion of god is proffitable to teache to improve to amende and to instruct in rightewesnes [17] that the man of god maye be perfect and prepared vnto all good workes.	For the whole Scripture is giuen by inspiration of God, and is profitable to teache, to correct and to instructe in rightousnes, [17] That the man of God may be absolute, being made perfite vnto all good workes.	All scripture is given by inspiration of God, and is profitable for doctrine, for reproof, for correction, for instruction in righteousness: [17] That the man of God may be perfect, throughly furnished unto all good works.	All scripture that was written by the Spirit, is profitable for instruction, and for confutation, and for correction, and for erudition in righteousness; [17] that the man of God may become perfect, and complete for every good work.	every Writing is God-breathed, and profitable for teaching, for conviction, for setting aright, for instruction that is in righteousness, [17] that the man of God may be fitted -- for every good work having been completed.	All scripture is inspired by God and useful for refuting error, for guiding people's lives and teaching them to be upright. [17] This is how someone who is dedicated to God becomes fully equipped and ready for any good work.	Everything in the Scriptures is God's Word. All of it is useful for teaching and helping people and for correcting them and showing them how to live. [17] The Scriptures train God's servants to do all kinds of good deeds.

n4) διδασκαλία (continued):

Titus 2:7-8 (Young's) "concerning all things thyself showing a pattern of good works; in **the teaching [doctrine]** uncorruptedness [ἀδιαφθορία], gravity, incorruptibility [ἀφθαρσία], [8] discourse sound, irreprehensible [ἀκατάγνωστον], that he who is of the contrary part may be ashamed, having nothing evil to say concerning you"

b. (12) νουθετέω [3] – instruct, teach, warn:

Rom 15:14, "And concerning you, my brethren, I myself also am convinced that you yourselves are full of goodness, filled with all knowledge, and able also to **admonish** one another"

Col :28, "We proclaim Him, **admonishing** every man and teaching every man with all wisdom, so that we may present every man complete in Christ"

Col 3:16, "Let the word of Christ richly dwell within you, with all wisdom teaching and **admonishing** one another with psalms and hymns and spiritual songs, singing with thankfulness in your hearts to God"

c. (13) διαλέγομαι [2] – reason:

This verb is also used 4 times for evangelizing, cf. Acts 19:8-9

Acts 19:9, "But when some were becoming hardened and disobedient, speaking evil of the Way before the multitude, he withdrew from them and took away the disciples, **reasoning** daily in the school of Tyrannus"

Acts 20:9, "And there was a certain young man named Eutychus sitting on the window sill, sinking into a deep sleep; and as Paul **kept on talking**, he was overcome by sleep and fell down from the third floor, and was picked up dead"

5. To teach with passion:

a. (14) παραγγέλλω [1] – command, order; warn, prescribe (30 NT uses, one for evangelism [Acts 17:30], quite a number dealing with direct instruction):
1 Tim 4:11, "**Prescribe** and teach these things"

Comparing Translations of παραγγέλλω in Various Verses
(with English contexts)

Verses	Greek Form	Latin Vulgate	Geneva Bible (1560)	English Revised (1885)	NASB (1977)	Cont English Version* (1995)
Acts 10:42	παρήγγειλεν	Praecepit	And he commanded vs to preache vnto the people	And he charged us to preach unto the people	And He ordered us to preach to the people	God told us to announce clearly to the people
Acts 17:30	παραγγέλλει	Adnuntiat	but now he admonisheth all men euerie where to repent	but now he commandeth men that they should all everywhere repent	but now commands all men everywhere to repent	But now he says that everyone everywhere must turn to him
2 Thess 3:6	Παραγγέλλομεν	Denuntiamus	We commande you, brethren	Now we command you, brethren	Now we command you, brethren	My dear friends, ..., I beg you
1 Tim 1:3	παραγγείλης	Denuntiares	that thou maiest commande some, that thei teache none other doctrine	that thou mightest charge certain men not to teach a different doctrine	in order that you may instruct certain men not to teach strange doctrines	and warn certain people there to stop spreading their false teachings
1 Tim 4:11	Παράγγελλε	Praecipe	These things commande and teache	These things command and teach	Prescribe and teach these things	Teach these things and tell everyone to do what you say

b. (15) ἐπαγωνίζομαι + πίστις [1] – contending for the faith:

   Jude 3, "Beloved, while I was making every effort to write you about our common salvation, I felt the necessity to write to you appealing that you **contend earnestly for the faith** which was once for all delivered to the saints"

c. (16) δέομαι [1] – "beg," beseech:

   2 Cor 5:20, "Therefore, we are ambassadors for Christ, as though God were making an appeal through us; **we beg** you on behalf of Christ, be reconciled to God"

d. (17) προβιβάζω [0] – Koine meaning (Gingrich): "put forward, cause to come forward"; LXX meaning (Lust, Eynikel, and Hauspie): "to teach" [a translation of the Hebrew *shanan*: "to repeat", "say again"):

   Deut 6:6-7, "And these words, which I am commanding you today, shall be on your heart; and you shall **teach** them **diligently** to your sons and shall talk of them when you sit in your house and when you walk by the way and when you lie down and when you rise up."

6. To preach/proclaim:

a. (18) κηρύσσω [1] – preach:

   2 Tim 4:2, "**preach** the word; be ready in season *and* out of season; reprove, rebuke, exhort, with great patience and instruction"

   It would seem that the "in good season" (εὐκαίρως) for preaching is within the context of the local church, where preaching and teaching ought to be expected; likewise, it would seem that the "out of season" (ἀκαίρως) is outside of the context of the local church, such as in street evangelism, door-to-door, etc.

b. (19) καταγγέλλω [1] – proclaim, challenge, etc.:

   Col 1:28, "We **proclaim** Him, admonishing every man and teaching every man with all wisdom, so that we may present every man complete in Christ"

c. (20) παρατείνω + λόγος [1] – prolonged speech:

   Acts 20:7, "Paul *began* talking to them, intending to depart the next day, and he **prolonged his message** until midnight"

d. (21) ἐπιτιμάω [2] – to mete out due measure, hence to censure:

   Luke 17:3, "Be on your guard! If your brother sins, **rebuke** him; and if he repents, forgive him"

   2 Tim 4:2, "preach the word; be ready in season *and* out of season; reprove, **rebuke**, exhort, with great patience and instruction"

e.   (22) ἐλέγχω [5] – expose, convict, reprove:

1 Tim 5:20, "Those [elders] who continue in sin, **rebuke** in the presence of all, so that the rest also may be fearful *of sinning*"

2 Tim 4:2, "preach the word; be ready in season *and* out of season; **reprove**, rebuke, exhort, with great patience and instruction"

Titus 1:9, "holding fast the faithful word which is in accordance with the teaching, that he may be able both to exhort in sound doctrine and to **refute** those who contradict [ἀντιλέγω]"

Titus 1:13, "For this cause **reprove** them severely that they may be sound in the faith"

Titus 2:15, "These things speak and exhort and **reprove** with all authority"

f.   (23) ὑποδείκνυμι [1] – to show, warn:

Acts 20:35, "In everything I **showed** you that by working hard in this manner you must help the weak…"

g.   (24) ὁμιλέω [1] – talk, converse (5 OT uses; 4 NT uses, all in Luke-Acts: Luke 24:14, 15; Acts 20:11; 24:26):

[From which word is derived the English "homiletics"—being instruction on how to talk or converse in public]

Acts 20:11, "And when he had gone *back* up, and had broken the bread and eaten, he **talked with them** a long while, until daybreak, and so departed"

7.   To entrust/impart:

a.   (25) παρατίθημι [1] – entrust:

2 Tim 2:2, "And the things which you have heard from me in the presence of many witnesses, these **entrust** to faithful men, who will be able to teach others also"

b.   (26) μεταδίδωμι + χάρισμα [1] – impart a [spiritual] gift:

Rom 1:11, "For I long to see you so that I may **impart** some spiritual **gift** to you, that you may be established"

8.   To speak/say:

a.   λέγω and cognate:

27) λέγω [2] – say, speak:

Acts 2:40, "And with many other words he solemnly testified and kept on exhorting them, **saying**, 'Be saved from this perverse generation!'"

Eph 4:17, "This **I say** therefore, and affirm together with the Lord, that you walk no longer just as the Gentiles also walk, in the futility of their mind"

28) προλέγω [4] – forewarn, say, say in advance:

2 Cor 13:2, "I **have previously said** when present the second time, and though now absent I **say in advance** to those who have sinned in the past and to all the rest *as well*, that if I come again I will not spare *anyone*"

Gal 5:21, "envying, drunkenness, carousing, and things like these, of which I **forewarn** you, just as I have **forewarned** you, that those who practice such things will not inherit the kingdom of God"

1 Thess 3:4 [NKJ], "For, in fact, we **told** you **before** when we were with you that we would suffer tribulation, just as it happened, and you know"

1 Thess 4:6, "*and* that no man transgress and defraud his brother in the matter because the Lord is *the* avenger in all these things, just as we also **told you before** and solemnly warned *you*"

n5) ἐν λόγῳ [1] - translated "in preaching":

1 Tim 5:17, "Let the elders who rule well be considered worthy of double honor, especially those who work hard at **preaching** and teaching"

b.   (29) λαλέω [2] – saying:

Acts 8:25, "And so, when they had solemnly testified and **spoken** the word of the Lord, they started back to Jerusalem, and were preaching the gospel to many villages of the Samaritans"

Heb 13:7, "Remember those who led you, who **spoke** the word of God to you; and considering the result of their conduct, imitate their faith"

B. Other verbs regarding life in the church:

Introduction: 1 Cor 14:26-33

1. Concerning the role of spiritual leaders:

    a. (30) ποιμαίνω [3] – shepherd, tend [like a shepherd], feed; rule (cf. Matt 2:6; 1 Cor 9:7; Jude 12; Rev 2:27; 7:17; 12:5; 19:15):

        John 21:16, "He said to him again a second time, 'Simon, *son* of John, do you love Me?' He said to Him, 'Yes, Lord; You know that I love You.' He said to him, '**Shepherd** My sheep.'"

        Acts 20:28, "Be on guard for yourselves and for all the flock, among which the Holy Spirit has made you overseers, **to shepherd** the church of God which He purchased with His own blood"

        1 Pet 5:2, "**shepherd** [ποιμάνατε] the flock of God among you, exercising oversight not under compulsion, but voluntarily, according to *the will of* God; and not for sordid gain, but with eagerness"

    b. (31) ἀγρυπνέω [1] – keep watch (4 NT uses; Mark 13:33; Luke 21:36; Eph 6:18):

        Heb 13:17, "Obey your leaders, and submit *to them*; for they keep watch over your souls, as those who will give an account. Let them do this with joy and not with grief, for this would be unprofitable for you."

Translations of "for they keep watch over your souls" in Heb 13:17

Latin Vulgate	Wycliffe (1388)	DRA* (1899)	Greek Byzantine Textform	Tyndale (1534); Bishops; Geneva; KJV; Websters; Darby; NJB	Young's Literal (1862)	English Rev (1885); ASV	Bible in Basic English (1949); NAS; NKJ; NET; CSB	RSV (1952); ESV	Good News Trans* (1993)	New Living Trans (2004)	Complete Jewish Bible (1998)	NAB* (1970)	NIV (1984)	CEV* (1993)	God's Word to the Nations (1995)
Pervigilant quasi rationem pro animabus vestris	for thei perfitli waken, as to yeldinge resoun for youre soulis	For they watch as being to render an account of your souls	αὐτοὶ γὰρ ἀγρυπνοῦσιν ὑπὲρ τῶν ψυχῶν ὑμῶν	for they watch for youre soules	for these do watch for your souls	for they watch in behalf of your souls	for they keep watch over your souls	for they are keeping watch over your souls	They watch over your souls without resting	Their work is to watch over your souls	for they keep watch over your lives	for they keep watch over you	They keep watch over you	They are watching over you	They take care of you
Use word "souls"									**Uses word "lives"**		**Do not use "soul"***				

*One problem with removing the word "souls" (other than the fact that God placed the word there) is the application of this verse to secular rulers, as did one of my students recently.

    c. (32) καταρτίζω [5] (13 NT uses) – to restore, mend, complete:

        Introduction: This word has quite an interesting semantic range: from fully training a disciple to restoring a sinful brother. A very rich verb indeed!

        Luke 6:40 "A pupil is not above his teacher; but everyone, after he has been **fully trained**, will be like his teacher"

        1 Cor 1:10, " Now I exhort you, brethren, by the name of our Lord Jesus Christ, that you all agree, and there be no divisions among you, but you **be made complete** in the same mind and in the same judgment"

        2 Cor 13:11, " Finally, brethren, rejoice, **be made complete**, be comforted, be like-minded, live in peace; and the God of love and peace shall be with you"

        Gal 6:1, "Brethren, even if a man is caught in any trespass, you who are spiritual, **restore** such a one in a spirit of gentleness; *each one* looking to yourself, lest you too be tempted"

        1 Thess 3:10, "As we night and day keep praying most earnestly that we may see your face, and **may complete** what is lacking in your faith?"

This amazing verb is also found in two doxologies (thus another indication of God and the Christian cooperating to accomplish the same work in people's lives):

Heb 13:20-21, "Now the God of peace, who brought up from the dead the great Shepherd of the sheep through the blood of the eternal covenant, *even* Jesus our Lord, **equip** you in every good thing to do His will, working in us that which is pleasing in His sight, through Jesus Christ, to whom *be* the glory forever and ever. Amen"

1 Pet 5:10, "And after you have suffered for a little while, the God of all grace, who called you to His eternal glory in Christ, will Himself **perfect**, confirm, strengthen *and* establish you"

2. Regarding Erring Members:

a. (33) πορεύομαι [2] (154 NT uses) – to go, proceed, walk:

Matt 18:12, "What do you think? If any man has a hundred sheep, and one of them has gone astray, does he not leave the ninety-nine on the mountains and **go** and search for the one that is straying?"

Luke 15:4, "What man among you, if he has a hundred sheep and has lost one of them, does not leave the ninety-nine in the open pasture, and **go** after the one which is lost, until he finds it?"

Metaphorical use:

Acts 9:31 So the church throughout all Judea and Galilee and Samaria enjoyed peace, being built up; and, **going on** in the fear of the Lord and in the comfort of the Holy Spirit, it continued to increase"

b. (34) ζητέω [1] – to seek:

Matt 18:12, "What do you think? If any man has a hundred sheep, and one of them has gone astray, does he not leave the ninety-nine on the mountains and go and **search** for the one that is straying?"

3. Reports and Testimonies:

a. Cognates of ἀγγέλλω:

35) ἀναγγέλλω [5] (18 NT uses) – report, rehearse, recite, disclose:

Acts 14:27, "When they had arrived and gathered the church together, they *began* **to report** all things that God had done with them and how He had opened a door of faith to the Gentiles"

Acts 15:4, "And when they arrived at Jerusalem, they were received by the church and the apostles and the elders, and they **reported** all that God had done with them"

Acts 19:18, "Many also of those who had believed kept coming, confessing and **disclosing** their practices"

Acts 20:20, "how I did not shrink from **declaring** to you anything that was profitable, and teaching you publicly and from house to house"

Acts 20:27, "For I did not shrink from **declaring** to you the whole purpose of God"

36) ἀπαγγέλλω [1] – announce, tell:

Acts 15:27, "Therefore we have sent Judas and Silas, who themselves will also report the same things by word *of mouth*."

b. (37) ἐκδιηγέομαι [1] – "tell, relate" (2 NT uses; in LXX from Hebrew saphar, "count, recount, relate"), Psa 118:17; Ezek 12:6;

Acts 15:3, "Therefore, being sent on their way by the church, they were passing through both Phoenicia and Samaria, describing in detail the conversion of the Gentiles, and were bringing great joy to all the brethren"

c. (38) ἐξηγέομαι [1] – tell, relate, explain, report; make known:

Acts 21:19, "And after he had greeted them, he *began* to relate one by one the things which God had done among the Gentiles through his ministry"

d. Of testimonies during services:

39) ἐξομολογέω [4] (10 total NT uses), to confess, pray:

Matthew 3:6 and they were being baptized by him in the Jordan River, as they **confessed** their sins

Mark 1:5 And all the country of Judea was going out to him, and all the people of Jerusalem; and they were being baptized by him in the Jordan River, **confessing** their sins

Acts 19:18, "Many also of those who had believed kept coming, **confessing** and disclosing their practices"

> James 5:16 Therefore, **confess** your sins to one another, and pray for one another, so that you may be healed. The effective prayer of a righteous man can accomplish much

4. On receiving instruction:

   a. (40) ἀναγνώσει [1] – for the public reading of Scripture:
   1 Tim 4:13 (NKJ), "Till I come, give attention to **reading**, to exhortation, to doctrine."

   b. (n6) διδαχή + ἀπόστολος [1] – the apostles teaching:
   Acts 2:42 (NKJ), "And they continued steadfastly **in the apostles' doctrine** and fellowship, in the breaking of bread, and in prayers."

   c. (41) μανθάνω [6] – learn:
   1 Cor 4:6, "that in us **you might learn** not to exceed what is written"
   1 Cor 14:31, "For you can all prophesy one by one, so that all **may learn** and all may be exhorted"
   Eph 4:20, "But you did not **learn** Christ in this way"
   Phil 4:9, "The things you have learned and received and heard and seen in me, practice these things; and the God of peace shall be with you"
   2 Tim 3:14, "You, however, continue in the things **you have learned** and become convinced of, knowing from whom **you have learned** *them*"
   Titus 3:14, "And let our *people* also **learn** to engage in good deeds to meet pressing needs, that they may not be unfruitful"

5. Theological debate and decision making:

   a. Theological debate:

      n7) στάσις [1] (9 NT uses), meaning dissension, rebellion, standing:
      Acts 15:2, "And when Paul and Barnabas had great **dissension** and debate with them, *the brethren* determined that Paul and Barnabas and some others of them should go up to Jerusalem to the apostles and elders concerning this issue"

      n8) ζήτησις [1] (7 NT uses), meaning debate, controversy, discussion:
      Acts 15:2, "And when Paul and Barnabas had great dissension and **debate** with them, *the brethren* determined that Paul and Barnabas and some others of them should go up to Jerusalem to the apostles and elders concerning this issue"

      n9) συζήτησις [1] (2 NT uses; this use is ζήτησις in NA27), meaning dispute, discussion:
      Acts 15:7, "After there had been much **debate**, Peter stood up and said to them, 'Brethren, you know that in the early days God made a choice among you, that by my mouth the Gentiles would hear the word of the gospel and believe'"

   b. Decision-making:

      42) τάσσω [1] (9 NT uses), meaning to arrange, appoint, order:
      Acts 15:2, "And when Paul and Barnabas had great dissension and debate with them, *the brethren* **determined** [to set up] that Paul and Barnabas and some others of them should go up to Jerusalem to the apostles and elders concerning this issue"
      1 Cor 16:15, "Now I urge you, brethren (you know the household of Stephanas, that they were the first fruits of Achaia, and that they have **devoted** themselves for ministry to the saints)"

      43) ὁράω (695 NT uses) + λόγος (331 NT uses) [1] (2 total uses of these verbs in a compound clause, the other is Luke 1:29):
      Acts 15:6, "The apostles and the elders came together **to look** into this **matter**"
      Συνήχθησάν τε οἱ ἀπόστολοι καὶ οἱ πρεσβύτεροι ἰδεῖν περὶ τοῦ λόγου τούτου

C. Verbs indicating physical presence or physical action:

   1. Gather:

      a. συνάγω and cognate nouns:

         44) συνάγω [3] – to assemble:
         Acts 4:31, "And when they had prayed, the place where they had gathered together was shaken, and they were all filled with the Holy Spirit, and *began* to speak the word of God with boldness"
         Acts 15:6, "And the apostles and the elders came together to look into this matter"

1 Cor 5:4, "In the name of our Lord Jesus, when you are assembled, and I with you in spirit, with the power of our Lord Jesus"

n10) συναγωγή [1] – assembly:

James 2:2, "For if a man comes into your assembly with a gold ring and dressed in fine clothes, and there also comes in a poor man in dirty clothes"

n11) ἐπισυναγωγή [1] – assembling together:

Heb 10:25, "not forsaking our own assembling together, as is the habit of some, but encouraging *one another*; and all the more, as you see the day drawing near"

b. (45) συνέρχομαι [3] – to come together, assemble:

1 Cor 11:18, "For first of all, when you come together as a church, I hear that there are divisions among you, and in part I believe it" [verb also found in 11:17, 20, 33, 34]

Comparing Translations: 1 Cor 11:18-20

Byzantine Textform	New American Standard (1977)	IBS's French *Le Semeur* (my translation)	ABS's Contemp English Version* (1995)
[18] Πρῶτον μὲν γὰρ συνερχομένων ὑμῶν ἐν ἐκκλησίᾳ, ἀκούω σχίσματα ἐν ὑμῖν ὑπάρχειν, καὶ μέρος τι πιστεύω.	[18] For, in the first place, when you come together as a church, I hear that divisions exist among you; and in part, I believe it.	[18] To begin with I hear it said that when you hold a gathering, there are among you divisions. --- I am inclined to believe that there is a portion of truth in what is recounted.	[18] I am told that you can't get along with each other when you worship, and I am sure that some of what I have heard is true.
[19] Δεῖ γὰρ καὶ αἱρέσεις ἐν ὑμῖν εἶναι, ἵνα οἱ δόκιμοι φανεροὶ γένωνται ἐν ὑμῖν.	[19] For there must also be factions among you, in order that those who are approved may have become evident among you.	[19] No doubt must it be that there be divisions within you, so that the Christians who have proven themselves be clearly recognized in your midst!	[19] You are bound to argue with each other, but it is easy to see which of you have God's approval.
[20] Συνερχομένων οὖν ὑμῶν ἐπὶ τὸ αὐτό, οὐκ ἔστιν κυριακὸν δεῖπνον φαγεῖν.	[20] Therefore when you meet together, it is not to eat the Lord's Supper,	[20] Thus, when you gather yourselves together, one cannot truly call that "taking the supper of the Lord,"	[20] When you meet together, you don't really celebrate the Lord's Supper.

*My translation of: "[18] Tout d'abord j'entends dire que lorsque vous tenez une réunion, il y a parmi vous des divisions. --- J'incline à croire qu'il y a une part de vérité dans ce qu'on raconte. [19] Sans doute faut-il qu'il y ait chez vous des divisions, pour que les chrétiens qui ont fait leurs preuves soient clairement reconnus au milieu de vous! [20] Ainsi, lorsque vous vous réunissez, on ne peut vraiment plus appeler cela «prendre le repas du Seigneur»,"

1 Cor 14:23, "If therefore the whole church should assemble together and all speak in tongues, and ungifted men or unbelievers enter, will they not say that you are mad?"

1 Cor 14:26, "What is *the outcome* then, brethren? When you assemble, each one has a psalm, has a teaching, has a revelation, has a tongue, has an interpretation. Let all things be done for edification."

2. Greeting and sending off:

a. ἀσπάζομαι and cognate:

46) ἀσπάζομαι [3] – greet, welcome, visit:

Acts 21:7, "and after greeting the brethren, we stayed with them for a day"
Acts 21:19, "And after he had greeted them"
2 Cor 13:12-13, "Greet one another with a holy kiss. All the saints greet you"

47) ἀπασπάζομαι [1] – say good-bye, take leave, embrace:

Acts 21:6 (Geneva), "Then when we had embraced one another"

b. (48) ἐπιπίπτω + τράχηλος [1] – fell on his neck, embrace (also used in Luke 15:20):

Acts 20:37, "And they *began* to weep aloud and embraced Paul, and repeatedly kissed him"

c. (49) καταφιλέω [1] – kiss, repeatedly kiss:

Acts 20:37, "And they *began* to weep aloud and embraced Paul, and repeatedly kissed him"

3. Remain:

    a. μένω and cognate:

        50) μένω [3] – remain, dwell, abide:

            Acts 21:7, "and **abode** with them one day"

            Acts 21:8, "and entering into the house of Philip the evangelist, who was one of the seven, **we abode** with him"

            1 John 2:19, "They went out from us, but they were not *really* of us; for if they had been of us, **they would have remained** with us; but *they went out*, in order that it might be shown that they all are not of us"

        51) ἐπιμένω [1] – remain, stay, continue, keep on, persist

            Acts 21:10, "And as **we were staying** there for some days"

4. Depart/Separate:

    52) ἀφίσταμαι [1] – leave, go away, desert, commit apostasy; keep away; incite [a revolt]

        Acts 19:9, ἀποστὰς ἀπ' αὐτῶν ἀφώρισεν τοὺς μαθητὰς - **he departed** from them, and separated the disciples

    53) ἀφορίζω [2] – separate, take away, exclude; set apart, appoint:

        Acts 19:9, ἀποστὰς ἀπ' αὐτῶν ἀφώρισεν τοὺς μαθητὰς - he departed from them, and **separated** the disciples

        2 Cor 6:17, "'Therefore, come out from their midst and **be separate**,' says the Lord. 'And do not touch what is unclean; And I will welcome you.'" [quoting Isa 52:11]

    54) ἐξέρχομαι [3] (222 NT uses), go out, come out, get out, come away:

        Positively stated:

            2 Cor 6:17, "'Therefore, **come out** from their midst and be separate,' says the Lord. 'And do not touch what is unclean; And I will welcome you.'" [quoting Isa 52:11]

            Heb 13:13, "Hence, let us **go out** to Him outside the camp, bearing His reproach."

        Negatively stated:

            1 John 2:19, "They **went out** from us, but they were not *really* of us; for if they had been of us, they would have remained with us; but *they went out*, in order that it might be shown that they all are not of us."

    55) στέλλω / στέλλομαι [1] – withdraw, keep away, stand aloof (2 NT uses):

        2 Thess 3:6 (NAS), "Now we command you, brethren, in the name of our Lord Jesus Christ, that you **keep aloof** from every brother who leads an unruly life and not according to the tradition which you received from us."

Translations of στέλλω / στέλλομαι in 2 Thess 3:6b

Byzantine	Vulgate	Wycliffe 2nd ed. (1388); cf. Tyndale; Bishops; Geneva; KJV; Young's; Darby; English Revised (1885); ASV (1901); NKJ (1982)	Bible in Basic English (1949, 1964); cf. RSV; NIV; New Jerusalem*; ESV (2001); CSB (2003); NET (2004)	NASB (1977);	God's Word for the Nations (1995)	New Living (2004)
	Subtraho*	Withdraw	Keep away	Keep aloof	Not to associate	Stay away
	Active emphasis		Passive emphasis			
στέλλεσθαι ὑμᾶς ἀπὸ παντὸς ἀδελφοῦ ἀτάκτως περιπατοῦντος, καὶ μὴ κατὰ τὴν παράδοσιν ἣν παρέλαβον παρ' ἡμῶν	ut subtrahatis vos ab omni fratre ambulante inordinate et non secundum traditionem quam acceperunt a nobis	that ye withdrawe you from ech brother that wandrith out of ordre, and not aftir the techyng, that thei resseyueden of vs	to keep away from all those whose behaviour is not well ordered and in harmony with the teaching which they had from us	that you keep aloof from every brother who leads an unruly life and not according to the tradition which you received from us	not to associate with any believer who doesn't live a disciplined life and doesn't follow the tradition you received from us	Stay away from all believers who live idle lives and don't follow the tradition they received from us

*Subtraho (Charlton T. Lewis, *An Elementary Latin Dictionary* [1890]): **sub-trahō** trīxī, trīctus, ere, to draw from below, drag out, draw off, carry off, withdraw, take away, remove.

56) ἀποτρέπω [1] – to turn away from, avoid (1 NT use; no use in LXX):

2 Tim 3:4-5, "treacherous, reckless, conceited, lovers of pleasure rather than lovers of God; holding to a form of godliness, although they have denied its power; and **avoid** such men as these"

Translating ἀποτρέπω in 2 Tim 3:5

Greek Byzantine	Latin Vulgate*	Wycliffe (1388)	Tyndale (1534)	Eng. Geneva (1560)	Bishops (1595)	KJV (1611, 1769); Webster's	Young's (1862)	Darby (1884)	English Revised (1885); ASV	Bible in Basic English (1949)
καὶ τούτους ἀποτρέπου	et hos devita	And eschewe thou these men	and soche abhorre	turne away therefore from suche	turne away from these	from such turn away	and from these be turning away	and from these turn away	from these also turn away	Go not with these
RSV (1952)	NAB* (1971)	NASB (1977)	NKJ (1982)	NIV (1984)	NJB* (1985)	ABS' CEV* (1992)	ABS' GNT* (1993)	ESV (2001); CSB	NLT (2004)	NET (2004)
Avoid such people	Reject them	and avoid such men as these	And from such people turn away!	Have nothing to do with them	Keep away from people like that	Don't have anything to do with such people	Keep away from such people	Avoid such people[!]	Stay away from people like that!	So avoid people like these

D. Verbs about attitude:

1. Love:

a. (57) ἀγαπάω [12] – love (142 NT uses):

John 13:34, "A new commandment I give to you, that you **love** one another, even as I have loved you, that you also **love** one another"

John 13:35, "By this all men will know that you are My disciples, if you have **love** for one another"

John 15:12, "This is My commandment, that you **love** one another, just as I have loved you"

John 15:17, "This I command you, that you love one another"

Rom 13:8, "Owe nothing to anyone except to love one another; for he who loves his neighbor has fulfilled *the* law"

1 Pet 1:22, "Since you have in obedience to the truth purified your souls for a sincere love of the brethren, fervently **love** one another from the heart"

1 John 3:11, "For this is the message which you have heard from the beginning, that **we should love** one another"

1 John 3:23, "And this is His commandment, that we believe in the name of His Son Jesus Christ, and **love** one another, just as He commanded us"

1 John 4:7, "Beloved, **let us love** one another, for love is from God; and everyone who loves is born of God and knows God"

1 John 4:11, "Beloved, if God so loved us, **we also ought to love** one another"

1 John 4:12, "No one has beheld God at any time; if **we love** one another, God abides in us, and His love is perfected in us"

2 John 5, "And now I ask you, lady, not as writing to you a new commandment, but the one which we have had from the beginning, that **we love** one another"

    b. (n11) ἀγάπη [1] – love (131 NT uses):

        1 Pet 4:8, "Above all, keep fervent in your **love** for one another, because love covers a multitude of sins"

    c. (n12) φιλαδελφία [2] – brotherly love (6 NT uses):

        Rom 12:10, "Be devoted to one another in **brotherly love**; give preference to one another in honor"

        Heb 13:1, "**Let love of the brethren** continue" (Ἡ φιλαδελφία μενέτω).

2. Mutual subjection:

    a. (58) ὑποτάσσω [2] – subject, subordinate:

        Eph 5:21, "and **be subject** to one another in the fear of Christ"

        1 Pet 5:5, "You younger men, likewise, **be subject** to your elders; and all of you, clothe yourselves with humility toward one another, for God is opposed to the proud, but gives grace to the humble"

    b. (59) ἡγέομαι [1] – lead, guide; think, consider, regard:

        Phil 2:3, "Do nothing from selfishness or empty conceit, but with humility of mind **let each of you regard** one another as more important than himself"

3. Oneness of mind:

    b. (60) φρονέω [1] – think, form or hold an opinion, judge; set one's mind on, be intent on; have thoughts or attitudes, be minded or disposed:

        Rom 12:16, "**Be of the same mind** toward one another; do not be haughty in mind, but associate with the lowly. Do not be wise in your own estimation"

    d. (61) ἀνέχω [2] – endure (patiently), put up with, bear with:

        Eph 4:2, "with all humility and gentleness, with patience, **showing forbearance** to one another in love"

        Col 3:13, "**bearing with** one another, and forgiving each other, whoever has a complaint against anyone; just as the Lord forgave you, so also should you"

4. Oneness of care:

    a. Three terms in Rom 12:10, Τῇ φιλαδελφίᾳ εἰς ἀλλήλους φιλόστοργοι· τῇ τιμῇ ἀλλήλους προηγούμενοι·:

        1) φιλαδελφία (n12 above)

        n13) φιλόστοργος [1] – loving, dearly devoted:

            Rom 12:10, "**Be devoted** to one another in brotherly love; give preference to one another in honor"

        n14) προηγέομαι [1] – go before, outdo, consider better, esteem more highly:

            Rom 12:10, "Be devoted to one another in brotherly love; **give preference** to one another in honor"

    b. (62) προσλαμβάνω [1] – receive, accept: Rom 15:7, "Wherefore, **accept** one another, just as Christ also accepted us to the glory of God"

5. Attitudes to avoid:

    a. (63) κρίνω [1] – judge, think, consider; decide, propose, intend; pass judgment on:

        Rom 14:13, "Therefore **let us not judge** one another anymore, but rather determine this—not to put an obstacle or a stumbling block in a brother's way"

    d.   Three negatives in Gal 5:26:
        Μὴ γινώμεθα κενόδοξοι, ἀλλήλους προκαλούμενοι, ἀλλήλοις φθονοῦντες.

        n15) γίνομαι + κενόδοξος [1] – conceited, boastful:
            Gal 5:26, "Let us not **become boastful**, challenging one another, envying one another"

        64) προκαλέω [1] – provoking:
            Gal 5:26, "Let us not become boastful, **challenging** one another, envying one another"

        65) φθονέω [1] – envy, jealous:
            Gal 5:26, "Let us not become boastful, challenging one another, **envying** one another"

E. Content and Themes for Proper Follow-up:

    1. Content: the Word of God:
        Heb 13:7, "Remember those who led you, who **spoke** the word of God to you; and considering the result of their conduct, imitate their faith"
        1 Pet 2:2, "like newborn babes, long for the pure milk of the word, that by it you may grow in respect to salvation"

    2. Theme: Evangelism Training:

        a.   Fishing for men:
            Matt 4:19, "And He said to them, 'Follow Me, and **I will make you** fishers of men.'"
            Mark 1:17, "And Jesus said to them, 'Follow Me, and **I will make you become** fishers of men.'"

        b.   Taking men alive:
            Luke 5:10, "and so also James and John, sons of Zebedee, who were partners with Simon. And Jesus said to Simon, 'Do not fear, **from now on** you will be **catching men.**'"

        c.   Eagerness to share the Gospel:
            1 Peter 3:15, "but sanctify Christ as Lord in your hearts, always *being* ready to make a defense to everyone who asks you to give an account for the hope that is in you, yet with gentleness and reverence"

    3. Theme: Teaching to observe:
        Matt 28:19-20, "Go therefore and make disciples of all the nations, baptizing them in the name of the Father and the Son and the Holy Spirit, **teaching them to observe** all that I commanded you; and lo, I am with you always, even to the end of the age."

    4. Theme: Admonitions to go and grow:
        1 Cor 15:58, "Therefore, my beloved brethren, be steadfast, immovable, always abounding in the work of the Lord, knowing that your toil is not *in* vain in the Lord"
        Phil 2:12-13, "So then, my beloved, just as you have always obeyed, not as in my presence only, but now much more in my absence, work out your salvation with fear and trembling; for it is God who is at work in you, both to will and to work for *His* good pleasure"
        Col 2:6-7, "As you therefore have received Christ Jesus the Lord, *so* walk in Him, having been firmly rooted *and now* being built up in Him and established in your faith, just as you were instructed, *and* overflowing with gratitude"

    5. Theme: Walk in holiness:
        1 Thess 4:3, "For this is the will of God, your sanctification"[1254]

[1254]1 Thess 4:3a became a favorite verse for the Holiness Movement in the U.S. (coming out of the "National Holiness Camp Meeting" in Vineland, NJ, in 1867), and of those churches which proceeded out of this movement, e.g. 1880, The Holiness Church; Church of God (Anderson); 1881, Christian and Missionary Alliance; 1886, The (original) Church of God, The Church of God (Cleveland, TN), The Peniel Mission, Mennonite Brethren in Christ; 1894, The Church of the Nazarene; 1897, Pilgrim Holiness Church, African-American Church of God in Christ; 1898, Pentecostal Holiness Church; 1900, The Apostolic Faith Mission; 1907, Assemblies of God; 1914, Assemblies of God (General Council).

Translations of 1 Thess 4:3

Byzantine	Latin	Wycliffe (1388); cf. Bishop's	Tyndale (1534)	Geneva (1560); cf. KJV; Darby; ERV; ASV	NAB* (1901, 1991)	BBE (1949, 1962)	RSV (1952)	NAS (1977); cf. NKJ; ESV; JCSB	NIV (1984)	NET (2005)	NJB* (1985)	NLT (2004)	French Le Semeur (1992, 1999)*	ABS's CEV* (1995)
Τοῦτο γάρ ἐστιν θέλημα τοῦ θεοῦ, ὁ ἁγιασμὸς ὑμῶν, ἀπέχεσθαι ὑμᾶς ἀπὸ τῆς πορνείας·	haec est enim voluntas Dei sanctificatio vestra [4:4] ut abstineatis vos a fornicatione	For this is the wille of God, youre holynesse, that ye absteyne you fro fornycacioun.	For this is the wil of god even that ye shuld be holy 4 and that ye shuld abstayne from fornicacion	For this is of God euen your sanctifi-cation, & that ye shulde abisteine from fornica-tion	his is the will of God, your holiness: that you refrain from immoral-ity	For the purpose of God for you is this: that you may be holy, and may keep your-selves from the desires of the flesh	or this is the will of God, your sanctifi-cation: that you abstain from unchas-tity	For this is the will of God, your sanctifi-cation; that is, that you abstain from sexual immoral-ity	It is God's will that you should be sanctified: that you should avoid sexual immoral-ity	For this is God's will: that you become holy, that you keep away from sexual immoral-ity	God wills you all to be holy. He wants you to keep away from sexual immoral-ity	God's will is for you to be holy, so stay away from all sexual sin	What God wants is that you maintain a holy life: that you abstain from all immoral-ity	God wants you to be holy, so don't be immoral in matters of sex.

*Original French "Ce que Dieu veut, c'est que vous meniez une vie sainte: que vous vous absteniez de toute immoralité"

1 Peter 1:14-16, "As obedient children, do not be conformed to the former lusts *which were yours* in your ignorance, but like the Holy One who called you, be holy yourselves also in all *your* behavior; because it is written, 'You shall be holy, for I am holy'"

6. Theme: Warning:

   a. προσέχω – pay attention; beware, be on guard:
Matt 7:15, "**Beware** of the false prophets, who come to you in sheep's clothing, but inwardly are ravenous wolves."

   b. σαλεύω – totter, shake, disturb (what false prophets will seek to do):
2 Thess 2:2, "that you may not be quickly **shaken** from your composure or be disturbed either by a spirit or a message or a letter as if from us, to the effect that the day of the Lord has come."

   c. ἐξαπατάω – deceive, cheat, seduce (what false prophets seek to do):
2 Thess 2:3, "Let no one in any way deceive you, for *it will not come* unless the apostasy comes first, and the man of lawlessness is revealed, the son of destruction"

Question: Is there ever a time we ought to be "leaving the elementary teaching about the Christ" (Heb 6:1)? What about Paul's thoughts as expressed in 1 Cor 2:2 and Col 1:28-29? Notice that after writing this, the author of Hebrews spent significant time on Jesus as the new Mediator (Heb 7-8), the atonement (Heb 9-10), faith (Heb 11), and perseverance (Heb 12).

F. Verb indicating the opposite of proper follow-up:

  1. Verbs indicating the improper action:

    a. πλανάω and cognate:

      1) πλανάω – deceive, lead astray, mislead:
Matt 24:11, "And many false prophets will arise, and will **mislead** many."
Matt 24:24, "For false Christs and false prophets will arise and will show great signs and wonders, so as to **mislead**, if possible, even the elect."
Luke 21:8, "And He said, 'See to it that you be not misled; for many will come in My name, saying, "I am *He*," and, "The time is at hand"; do not go after them."

      2) ἀποπλανάω – mislead:
Mark 13:22, "for false Christs and false prophets will arise, and will show signs and wonders, in order, if possible, **to lead** the elect **astray**."

    b. ἀποσπάω – draw away, lead away, draw:
Acts 20:30, τοῦ ἀποσπᾶν τοὺς μαθητὰς ὀπίσω αὐτῶν – **draw away** disciples after themselves

c. ἀπόλλυμι – ruin, destroy:

1 Cor 8:11, "For through your knowledge he who is weak **is ruined**, the brother for whose sake Christ died"

d. σκανδαλίζω – scandalize, cause to stumble or fall, offend:

1 Cor 8:13, "Therefore, if food **causes** my brother **to stumble**, I will never eat meat again, that I might not cause my brother to stumble"

2. Results of the false teaching:

a. ἀφίστημι – fall away, become apostate:

1 Tim 4:1, "But the Spirit explicitly says that in later times some **will fall away** from the faith, paying attention to deceitful spirits and doctrines of demons"

b. ἀποστρέφω – turn from, turn away, reject:

2 Tim 4:4, "and **will turn away** their ears from the truth, and will turn aside to myths."

c. ἐκτρέπω – turn, turn away:

2 Tim 4:4, "and will turn away their ears from the truth, and **will turn aside** to myths."

d. παραρρέω – flow by, slip away, fig. drift away [be carried away]:

Heb 2:1, "For this reason we must pay much closer attention to what we have heard, lest we drift away *from it*."

Translations of παραρρέω in Heb 2:1

Vulgate	Wycliffe 2nd ed (1388)	Tyndale (1534)	Geneva (1560)	Bishops (1595); KJV	Murdock (1852)	Young's (1862, etc.)	Darby (1884)	ERV (1885); ASV	DRA✠ (1899)	BBE (1949)	RSV (1952); NAS; ESV	NKJ (1982)	NIV (1984); NJB✠; NET	NAB✠ (1985)	CSB (2003)
peref-fluamus	we fleten awei*	we perysshe	we shulde let them slippe	we should let them slippe	lest we fall away	we may glide aside	we should slip away	we drift away *from them*	we should let them slip	we might be slipping away	we drift away from it	we drift away	we do not drift away	we may not be carried away	we will not drift away

*we floaten away.

Two French versions may bring further insight into the history of interpretation:

Heb 2:1 (FGB 1669), "Pour cette cause il nous faut prendre de plus prés garde aux choses que nous avons ouies, afin que nous ne venions point à nous écouler"

[My translation] "For this reason we must take much closer attention to the things which we have heard, in order that we not-at-all come to drift"

Heb 2:1 (NEG 1975), "C'est pourquoi nous devons d'autant plus nous attacher aux choses que nous avons entendues, de peur que nous ne soyons emportés loin d'elles"

[My translation] "Because of this we must far more cling to those things which we have heard, for fear that we be driven far from them"

e. παραφέρω – carry away, remove:

Heb 13:9, "Do not be carried away by varied and strange teachings; for it is good for the heart to be strengthened by grace, not by foods, through which those who were thus occupied were not benefited"

G. Differentiating Emphases Between Verbs for Evangelism and Verbs for Follow-Up:

1. Perhaps Acts 8:25 provides the best example of the change in terminology, as verbs for both evangelism and follow-up are found in the same verse

2. Differentiation: Some verbs are used for both evangelism and follow-up (διαλέγομαι[reason], διαμαρτύρομαι[solemnly testify], διδάσκω [teach]), while other verbs are used exclusively for follow-up (παρακαλέω [encourage], ἐπιστηρίζω [establish], οἰκοδομέω [edify]):

a. There is a sense in which the message for the saved and the lost is Christ, Col 1:28

b. Note the verbs that are uniquely used for Christian to Christian interaction, there is a clear distinction between telling lost souls about salvation and the encouragement and edification of those who are already saved

3. Some verses groups verbs directed to both saved and lost, however, according to the usage in the Book of Acts and elsewhere, these verb strings are normally directed to the saved:
    Col 1:28: καταγγέλλω (proclaim), νουθετέω (admonishing), and διδάσκω (teaching)
    1 Thess 2:11[12]: παρακαλέω (exhort), παραμυθέομαι (encourage), and μαρτύρομαι (testify)
    2 Tim 4:2: κηρύσσω (preach), ἐλέγχω (reprove), ἐπιτιμάω (rebuke), and παρακαλέω (exhort)

4. What can we learn?
    a. There seems to be a marked shift in terminology from Gospel proclamation (evangelism) to exhortation and encouragement once a person is saved
    b. Evangelism of the lost has a very different feel than exhorting the saved—a primary tendency is to confuse the two:
        1) Does not the seeker church model of preaching confuse this differentiation in terminology?
        2) Can this difference not also explain the shallow teaching in some churches where believers are not exhorted and strengthened in the Word?
    c. The greater majority of communicatory verbs in the book of Acts are evangelistic verbs, directed to the lost
    d. The English-language's lack of clarity in translating some proclamational verbs (e.g. εὐαγγελίζω) may hide some of this differentiation from English-only readers, as well as color the research of those who do know the original languages

H. What can we learn about biblical follow-up (based on the concept of the sufficiency of Scriptures)?

1. The apostles never trained in new believers for cultural accommodation, neither do we find any concrete evangelism training programs

2. We have no concrete examples of a follow-up methodology or program, even when it would be obvious to the context:
    a. Such as Paul training in Priscilla and Aquila before they joined him on a mission trip in Acts 18, in fact, we hear nothing of their conversion through their employment of Paul!

3. Amazingly, there is even little emphasis on church planting or leadership development methodologies, other than brief descriptions of what happened and perhaps what was said
    a. In fact the closest thing we have to a methodology is the giving of regulations by James in Acts 15 and repeated Acts 21, which ended up bringing further confusion that Paul dealt with in 1 Corinthians and Galatians, not to speak of all the ecclesiastical regulations of Rome wherein they affirm the precedent of James!

4. Then, what do we have? Patterns of Christians beginning life together in fellowship, while fulfilling the Great Commission among those who are not a part of the church.

III. Biblical Aspects of Follow-up:

A. Follow-Up Is Important!

1. God desires the Christian to continue to minister after the conversion of the contact!

However, this should in no way negate the validity of itinerant evangelism, itinerating mission teams, street preaching, and street evangelism which are exemplified and taught throughout the NT!

a. In the first Great Commission passage (Matt 28:19-20), Jesus commands His disciples to "win disciples":

1) This includes "baptizing", the identification with the body of Christ, as well as with a local church body.

2) This includes the "teaching" all of the commands of Christ (quite a task in itself).

b. Christians are to bear fruit that remains:

1) That remains eternally, John 4:36; 15:16; Gal 6:8

2) In general, Matt 28:19-20; John 15:16; Col 1:28-29.

c. The one who brings a person to Christ has a special place as "a father" to the new believer, 1 Cor 4:14-15, e.g. 2 Cor 12:14 (cf. 1 Cor 9:1-2; Phil 2:22; 2 Tim 1:2; Philm 10, 12):[1255]

1) Are you regularly leading others to Christ? Have you ever led anyone to Christ?

2) Dawson Trotman's follow-up question: "Are they living for Christ now?" Please note the context of this question:

"You are going out to the foreign field. You hope to be used by the Lord in winning men and women to Christ. Is that right?"

"Yes."

"You want them to go on and live the victorious life, don't you? You don't want them just to make a decision and then go back into the world, do you?"

"No."

"Then may I ask you something more? How many persons do you know by name today who were won to Christ by you and are living for Him?"

The majority had to admit that they were ready to cross an ocean and learn a foreign language, but had not won their first soul who was going on with Jesus Christ. A number of them said that they got many people to go to church; others said they had persuaded some to go forward when the invitation was given.

I asked, "Are they living for Christ now?" Their eyes dropped. I then continued, "How do you expect that by crossing an ocean and speaking a foreign language with people who are suspicious of you, whose way of life is unfamiliar, you will be able to do there what you have not yet done here?"

These questions do not apply to missionaries and prospective missionaries only. They apply to all of God's people. Every one of His children ought to be a reproducer.[1256]

Several comments of interest to these statements of Trotman:

(1) Notice his communicated antagonism to just making a decision: "just to make a decision"—by the way, this antagonism is the pivotal key which drives the discipleship movement!

(2) Notice his reference to the "old-fashioned" methodology of "persuaders", who would personally invite others to come forward during the invitation

(3) Trotman also missed the "gift of the missionary," which may allow someone from a second culture to have a larger impact than even someone from their own culture, even with linguistic and other cultural barriers:

[1255]In this case follow-up is understood as a type of spiritual parenting, cf. Psa 127:3-5. This spiritual parenting can lead to a fulfillment of Isa 54:1, "'For the sons of the desolate one will be more numerous than the sons of the married woman,' says the Lord."

[1256]Dawson Trotman, *Born to Reproduce* (Colorado Springs: NavPress, 1984), 18-19.

> (a) This second culture ministry is a given in the Great Commissions of
> Matthew, Mark, Luke, and Acts
>
> (b) Short term ministry in other cultures is clearly exemplified in Scripture, as
> Paul ministered where they spoke Lyconian (Acts 14) and in Europe (Acts
> 16)
>
> (4) Giving the Christian the title of "reproducer" is not as biblical as some other
> titles, such as "fishers of men" or "evangelist"—again we find the same move
> that was noted above (Chapter 10) as exemplified in Howard Hendricks.[1257]

d. Paul describes those who came to faith in Christ under his ministry as "children of promise,"
Gal 4:28.

e. Paul had a passionate concern for the churches he founded:

> 2 Cor 11:2 (my trans), "For I am zealous for you with a godly zeal [Ζηλῶ γὰρ ὑμᾶς θεοῦ ζήλῳ]; for I
> betrothed you to one husband, that to Christ I might present you *as a pure virgin*" (cf. John 2:17)
>
> 2 Cor 11:28-29, "Apart from *such* external things, there is the daily pressure upon me *of* concern for
> all the churches. Who is weak without my being weak? Who is led into sin without my intense
> concern?"

f. The lasting spiritual fruit of an evangelist is a testimony to his ministry, 2 Cor 3:1-3

g. Evangelism without proper follow-up can be work "in vain", Gal 4:11; Phil 2:16;
1 Thess 3:2-5; 2 John 8 (cf. 1 Cor 15:58):

REASONS FOR VAIN LABOR IN THE NEW TESTAMENT		
Passage	Problem	Application
Gal 4:11	Theological drift: soteriology	Teach sound doctrine
Phil 2:16	Practical drift	Train in righteousness
1 Thess 3:5	Drift due to persecution	Prepare for persecution
2 John 8	Theological drift: Christology	Teach sound doctrine

One possible example of vain labor, as far as theological drift is concerned, is
involvement in evangelism with non-evangelical churches, in which case the follow-up
would be done with some theological lack of clarity on issues like total depravity and
justification by faith alone. Yes, God can truly save someone, and yes, God can do the
follow-up. However, it puts the new believer into a situation whereby he woud not be
properly fed the pure milk of the word.

h. Samuel D. Faircloth's comments conclude this point:

> "It is unscriptural as well as deplorably neglectful to leave new converts without adequate
> spiritual nurture and care."[1258]

[1257]"'Make disciples' is the mandate of the Master (Matthew 28:19-20). We may ignore it, but we cannot
evade it. Our risen Christ left this legacy—the magna charta of the church. He provided both the model and the method.
His life—and death—recast the lives of men. He demonstrated that you have not done anything until you have changed
the lives of men. 'Follow Me,' He urged His men. And then that staggering assurance: 'Lo, I am with you *always*...'
Somehow we have forgotten that this promise is linked to a process. We cannot embrace the *promise* and ignore the
process" (Howard Hendricks, "Foreword," in Walter A. Hendrichsen, *Disciples Are Made—Not Born: Making
Disciples Out of Christians* [Wheaton, IL: Victor, 1974; 23rd printing, 1985], 5; Italics from original).

[1258]Samuel D. Faircloth, *Church Planting for Reproduction* (Grand Rapids; Baker, 1991), 175.

2. **The Apostle Paul as** *the Example* **for Biblical Spiritual Growth and Follow-up**, Acts 9:17-30 (compare this list with the chart "Comparing Follow-Up Tools"):[1259]

   a. Immediate occurrences, v. 18-19:
      1) Blindness removed
      2) Regained his sight
      3) Was baptized
      4) Was strengthened, broke his fast

   b. After several days, vv. 19-22:
      1) With the disciples (changed his companions)
      2) Began to evangelize (test of true faith)
      3) His reputation changed
      4) His early spiritual growth

   c. After many days, vv. 23-30:
      1) Organized persecution
      2) Protection of the believers

   d. **NOT an example** of follow-up nor of initiation into the clergy, Acts 21:21-27:

      Introduction: Unfortunately seeking to:
         a) Appease those who were "zealous for the Law," v. 21
         b) Show that Paul also was not telling Jews to abandon the law, v. 21
         c) Appease heresay, v. 21-22
      1) Four men appointed by the church, v. 23
      2) They "made a vow," v. 23
      3) They had to go through a ritual of purification, v. 24
      4) The purification rite cost them money, v. 24
      5) They needed to receive a special haircut to show their vow (compare Medieval "tonsure"), v. 24
      Conclusion: Notice how some churches have used this text as a precedent for entering the Holy Orders!

3. **Some Follow-up precedents in the Old Testament**:

   a. Follow-Up Advice:
      1) "Cast away, each of you, the detestable things of the eyes, and do not defile yourselves with the idols of Egypt; I am the Lord your God." Ezek 20:7
      2) "And I said to their children in the wilderness, 'Do not walk in the statutes of your fathers, or keep their ordinances, or defile yourselves with their idols. I am the LORD your God; walk in My statutes, and keep My ordinances, and observe them. And sanctify My Sabbaths; and they shall be a sign between Me and you, that you may know that I am the LORD your God.'" Ezek 20:18

4. **Concerning Length of Follow-Up:**

   a. In the Gospels:

      1) No apparent follow-up:
         a) Jesus did not stay with the crowds, but went on to the next city, Mark 1:37-38; Luke 4:42-44 (cf. John 2:23-25).
         b) Jesus did not allow the [former] demoniac from Gerasenes to stay with him, Mark 5:18-20, Luke 8:38-39; e.g. John 8:11, Acts 8:39-40
            1) Note that the town's people wanted Christ to depart, Mark 5:17; cf. Matt 8:34

      b) Shorter Follow-up:
         a) Jesus stayed two days in Sychar, Samaria, John 4:40-42.
         b) Jesus stayed in the house of Zaccheus, Luke 19:5

      3) Disciples were with Jesus approximately three years, Mark 3:13-14.

[1259]Johnston, *Charts for a Theology of Evangelism*, Chart 31, "Comparing Follow-Up Tools" 56-57.

    b. In the Acts:

        1) No follow-up, Acts 8:39, "And when they came out of the water, the Spirit of the Lord snatched Philip away; and the eunuch saw him no more, but went on his way rejoicing."

        2) No mention of follow-up of the first recorded convert from Paul's first missionary journey: "Then the proconsul believed when he saw what had happened, being amazed at the teaching of the Lord. Now Paul and his companions put out to sea from Paphos and came to Perga in Pamphylia; but John left them and returned to Jerusalem," Acts 13:12-13

           a) Later Barnabas went to Cyprus with John Mark, Acts 15:39

        3) Did not stay: "When they asked him to stay a little longer [in Ephesus], he did not consent," Acts 18:20

        4) Contact took the initiative: First European convert pleaded that Paul and Silas stay with her: "A woman named Lydia, from the city of Thyatira, a seller of purple fabrics, a worshiper of God, was listening; and the Lord opened her heart to respond to the things spoken by Paul. And when she and her household had been baptized, she urged us, saying, 'If you have judged me to be faithful to the Lord, come into my house and stay.' And she prevailed upon us," Acts 16:14-15 (it is likely that a church ended up being founded in her home, 16:40)

        5) Several days, Acts 10:48, "Then they asked him to stay on for a few days"

        6) Seven days in Troas, Acts 20:6

        7) Some follow-up, Acts 17:14, "and Silas and Timothy stayed there [in Berea]."

        8) One year of teaching in Antioch, Acts 11:26

        9) One and a half years in Corinth, Acts 18:11, "And he settled there a year and six months, teaching the word of God among them."

        10) Extended follow-up in Ephesus (after not consenting in Acts 18:20-21):

           a) Three months in synagogue (Acts 19:8) + Two years at school of Tyrannus (Acts 19:10)

           b) Three years, Acts 20:31

5. Follow-up Encouragement (Acts 16:40):

    a. In the Gospels:

        1) Jesus to demoniac from Gerasenes, "Go home to your people and report to them what great things the Lord has done for you, and *how* He had mercy on you," Mark 5:19

    b. In the Book of Acts:

        1) The Jerusalem Council (Acts 15:19-21, parallel in Acts 15:29):

            "Therefore it is my judgment that we do not trouble those who are turning to God from among the Gentiles [with forced circumcision (Acts 15:1, 5) or following the whole law (Acts 15:5)], but that we write to them that they abstain:

           a) from things contaminated by idols and
           b) from fornication and
           c) from what is strangled and
           d) from blood.

            "For Moses from ancient generations has in every city those who preach him, since he is read in the synagogues every Sabbath."

          Conclusion: However, the authority of these admonitions may be blurred a bit by:
            (1) The Jerusalem church, being zealous for the law, rather than for Jesus Christ or their salvation, were rather acting like a hierarchical church (Acts 21:20-25)

(2) The book of Romans on food (Rom 14)
(3) The book of 1 Corinthians on eating meat (1 Cor 8-11)
(4) The book of Galatians on the role of the Law
(5) Also note the way that some hierachical churches have interpreted this passage
     as being a precedent for all of their non-biblical regulations!

On the Translation of Acts 15:20

Byzantine Textform	Tyndale (1534)	Geneva (1560)	KJV (1611)	Webster's (1833)	Young's (1862, 1887, 1898)	ERV (1885); Douay-Rheims*; ASV	Bible in Basic English (1949)	RSV (1952)
ἀλλὰ Ἐπιστεῖλαι αὐτοῖς τοῦ ἀπέχεσθαι ἀπὸ Τῶν ἀλισγημάτων τῶν εἰδώλων	but that we write vnto them that they abstayne them selves from filthynes of ymages	But that we send vnto them, that they abstaine themselues from filthinesse of idoles,	But that we write unto them, that they abstain from pollutions of idols,	But that we write to them that they abstain from pollutions of idols,	but to write to them to abstain from the pollutions of the idols,	but that we write unto them, that they abstain from the pollutions of idols,	But that we give them orders to keep themselves from things offered to false gods,	but should write to them to abstain from the pollutions of idols
καὶ τῆς πορνείας	from fornicacion	and fornication,	and *from fornication,*	and {from} lewdness,	and the whoredom,	and from fornication,	and from the evil desires of the body,	and from unchastity
καὶ τοῦ πνικτοῦ	from straglyd	and that that is strangled,	and *from* things strangled,	and {from} things strangled,	and the strangled thing;	and from what is strangled,	and from the flesh of animals put to death in ways against the law,	and from what is strangled
καὶ τοῦ αἵματος	and from bloude	and from blood	and *from* blood	and {from} blood	and the blood	and from blood	and from blood	and from blood

Byzantine Textform	NAS (1977)	NKJ (1982)	NIV (1984)	NJB* (1985)	NLT (2004)	NET (2005)	ABS' GNT* (1993)	ABS' CEV* (1991)
ἀλλὰ Ἐπιστεῖλαι αὐτοῖς τοῦ ἀπέχεσθαι ἀπὸ Τῶν ἀλισγημάτων τῶν εἰδώλων	but that we write to them that they abstain from things contaminated by idols	"but that we write to them to abstain from things polluted by idols,	Instead we should write to them, telling them to abstain from food polluted by idols,	we should send them a letter telling them merely to abstain from anything polluted by idols,	Instead, we should write and tell them to abstain from eating food offered to idols,	but that we should write them a letter telling them to abstain from things defiled by idols	Instead, we should write a letter telling them not to eat any food that is ritually unclean because it has been offered to idols;	We should simply write and tell them not to eat anything that has been offered to idols.
καὶ τῆς πορνείας	and from fornication	*from* sexual immorality,	from sexual immorality,	from illicit marriages,	from sexual immorality,	and from sexual immorality	to keep themselves from sexual immorality;	They should be told not to eat the meat of any animal that has been
καὶ τοῦ πνικτοῦ	and from what is strangled	*from* things strangled,	from the meat of strangled animals	from the meat of strangled animals	from eating the meat of strangled animals,	and from what has been strangled	and not to eat any animal that has been strangled,	strangled or that still has blood in it. They must also
καὶ τοῦ αἵματος	and from blood	and *from* blood.	and from blood	and from blood	and from consuming blood	and from blood	or any blood	not commit terrible sexual sins

2) Direct quotes:
   a) Acts 2:40-41, "Be saved from this perverse generation!" (cf. Deut 32:5)—this was
      the follow-up of past generations, who emphasized "Separation" (cf. Acts 19:9; e.g.
      Mordecai Ham)
   b) Acts 14:22, "Through many tribulations we must enter the kingdom of God"
      (cf. John 16:33)—of all the follow-up programs listed in my book of charts, none of

them highlight the promise of persecution! Is this omission because they are developed in the United States?[1260]

    3) Further follow-up explanations:
      a) Acts 11:23, "began to encourage them all with resolute heart to remain true to the Lord"
      b) Acts 13:43, "urging them to continue in the grace of God" (cf. 2 Cor 5:20-6:2)
      c) Acts 18:23, "strengthening all the disciples"

6. Other Aspects of Follow-Up:

  a. Salvation issues:
    1) Emphasis on faith as the active agent, Mark 5:34, John 1:50-51, cf. Eph 2:8-9
    2) Assurance of salvation:
      a) Forgiveness of sin, John 8:11, cf. Rom 8:1
      b) Eternal life, Luke 23:42, cf. John 5:24

  b. Change of relationship:
    1) Emphasis on following Christ, John 1:38-39, 43
    2) Emphasis on being "with" Jesus, Acts 4:13
    3) Joining with the apostles, Acts 13:43, 17:4, 34

  c. Baptism as part of follow-up, Acts 2:41; 8:12-16, 36-38, 9:18; 10:47-48; 16:15, 33; 18:8; 19:5 (cf. Matt 28:19-20)

  d Encouragement to share what Christ had done immediately, Mark 5:18-20, Luke 8:39; e.g. John 1:41, 44-45; 4:28-29

  e. A focus on God's Word:
    1) In the Gospels, John 4:40-42, 50
    2) In the Book of Acts, Acts 8:25, 13:44, 18:11, 20:32
    3) In the epistles, 1 Thess 2:13

  f. Healing after salvation, Mark 5:34, John 5:14, cf. John 14:26

  g. Call to holy living, John 5:14, 8:11, cf. 1 Pet 1:14-16

  h. Emphasis on the great things God will do, John 1:50-51

7. The apostle Paul was involved in follow-up:

  a. His concern for those he led to the Lord (and those he didn't lead to the Lord, Col 2:1-3):

    1) Individuals, Col 1:28-29 (e.g. 2 Cor 2:12-13)

    2) Churches he founded, Acts 13:47, 20:18-21, 25-27, 2 Cor 11:2, 28, 12:21, 1 Thess 2:17-3:10:
      a) The Thessalonian church, as many of the churches founded by the apostle Paul (Pisidian Antioch, Iconium, Lystra, Philippi, Berea and Athens), had sporadic follow-up by the Apostle. He seems to have sent co-workers to work in follow-up and nurture. Paul sent Timothy to Thessalonica for a season—to give a foundation to the brethren (1 Thess 3:2). During this same time it seems that Silas was left in Berea (Acts 17:15-16).
      b) It is interesting to note the relatively small amount of follow-up done in some of the churches founded. Yet nurture of churches seems to be a major thrust of the second and third missionary journeys of Paul, Acts 15:36 (cf. 2 Cor 11:28). There are two extended ministries of the Apostle Paul as recorded in the Bible:
        (1) Ephesus: two years, Acts 19:10; three years, Acts 20:31
        (2) Corinth, one year and 6 months, Acts 18:11
      c) Paul's foundational desire was to plant new churches where Christ was not named, as is evident in Rom 15:20-21

[1260]Ibid.

    b.   Aspects of the apostle Paul's follow-up:

        1) He prayed for those he led to the Lord, 1 Cor 1:4-9; Eph 1:15-23; 3:14-19; Phil 1:9-11; Col 1:3, 9-12; 1 Thess 1:2-5; 2 Thess 1:3-4.

        2) He visited the churches he had founded to encourage them, Acts 14:21-23; 15:36; 20:17; 1 Cor 16:5-7

        3) He wrote letters to individuals and churches encouraging them in the faith:
            a) Individuals, 1 Tim 1:1-2; 2 Tim 1:1-2; Tit 1:1, 4; Philm 1
            b) Churches, Rom 1:1, 7; 1 Cor 1:1-2; 2 Cor 1:1; Gal 1:1-2; Eph 1:1; Phil 1:1; Col 1:1-2; 1 Thess 1:1; 2 Thess 1:1

        4) He loved, exhorted and disciplined wayward members from afar:
            a) Love, his intense concern when believers were led into sin, 2 Cor 11:29 (e.g. 2 Cor 12:19-21)
            b) Disciplined, 1 Cor 5:3; 1 Tim 1:20
            c) Exhorted, Phil 4:2-3, Col 4:17

        5) He had a ministry while he was at the Churches:
            a) He preached, Acts 14:22; 20:7-11, 18-35
            b) He exhorted, 2 Cor 5:20 (cf. 2 Cor 11:2)
            c) He disciplined where it was needed, Gal 2:11-13

        6) Follow-up was one of his passions, 2 Cor 11:2, "For I am zealous for you with a godly zeal [Ζηλῶ γὰρ ὑμᾶς θεοῦ ζήλῳ]"

        7) Follow-up was one of his reasons for living:
            a) Phil 1:24, "yet to remain on in the flesh is more necessary for your sake"
            b) 1 Thess 3:8 [NKJ], "For now we live, if you stand fast in the Lord"

        8) No follow-through by the Christians he led to Christ would have been ministry "in vain," Gal 4:11; Phil 2:16; 1 Thess 3:5 (cf. Gal 2:2)—see chart above

8. Special teaching in the epistles:

    a.   Distinctions of spiritual maturity or spiritual giftedness:

        1) Weak:
            a) The weaker brother, Rom 15:1-3; 1 Cor 8:9-13
            b) The weak, 1 Cor 12:22; 1 Thess 5:14
            c) The one who is weak in the faith, Rom 14:1ff

        2) Distinctions in honor:
            a) Less honorable, 1 Cor 12:23
            b) Unseemly and seemly, 1 Cor 12:23-24

        3) Other spiritual distinctions:
            a) The disorderly, 1 Thess 5:14
            b) The fainthearted, 1 Thess 5:14
            c) Those who are doubting, Jude 22-23

    b.   Specific advice related to distinction:
        1) Not eating meat to avoid scandalizing a brother, 1 Cor 8:9-13
        2) Give greater honor to the less honorable and unseemly, 1 Cor 12:23-24

9. **The importance of emphasizing ministry to fellow-believers**, e.g. follow-up, Gal 6:10, "So then, while we have the opportunity, let us do good to all men, and especially to those in the household of the faith."

10. In conclusion we quote from the Amsterdam Affirmations read by Billy Graham and affirmed by 4,000 evangelists at the close of the International Conference for Itinerant Evangelists in 1983:

"We are responsible to arrange for the spiritual care of those who come to faith under our ministry, to encourage them to identify with the local body of believers, and seek to provide for the instruction of believers in witnessing to the Gospel."[1261]

IV. Further Issues Concerning the New Convert:

A. The temptation will be to give the new Christian a leadership position too quickly:

1 Tim 3:6, "*and* not a new convert, lest he become conceited and fall into the condemnation incurred by the devil."

B. Do not embroil the new Christian in theological debates and controversies:

1. Scripture:

Rom 14:1 (Greek), Τὸν δὲ ἀσθενοῦντα τῇ πίστει προσλαμβάνεσθε μὴ εἰς διακρίσεις διαλογισμῶν

Rom 14:1 (French Geneva Revised), "Accueillez celui qui est faible dans la foi, et ne discutez pas les opinions"

Rom 14:1 (My translation), "Welcome he who is weak in the faith, and do not discuss opinions [points-of-view]"

Rom 14:1 (Geneva), "Him that is weake in the faith, receiue vnto you, but not for controuersies of disputations"

Rom 14:1 (NIV), "Accept him whose faith is weak, without passing judgment on disputable matters"

Rom 14:1 (ESV), "As for the one who is weak in faith, welcome him, but not to quarrel over opinions"

2. False teachers, however, do embroil new followers into their particularities:

Matt 23:15, "Woe to you, scribes and Pharisees, hypocrites, because you travel about on sea and land to make one proselyte; and when he becomes one, you make him twice as much a son of hell as yourselves"

Acts 13:10 [Elymas the Magician was making crooked the straight ways of the Lord]

3. False teachers also teach the need for special acts of obedience to accompany salvation; acts which are not taught in the NT (baptism, however, is commanded in the NT, Matt 28:19-20):

The OT is one place where false teachers can find a number of biblical commands to add to faith alone; circumcision was the struggle of the NT church

Gal 5:2-3, "Behold I, Paul, say to you that if you receive circumcision, Christ will be of no benefit to you. And I testify again to every man who receives circumcision, that he is under obligation to keep the whole Law."

V. Comparing Follow-Up Tools (see my chart on this in Book of Charts):[1262]

A. Disclaimer: Some models on the Chart are specifically for follow-up of new believers (*Survival Kit* and *Beginning Steps*), while others seem helpful for the nourishment of believers (*MasterLife* and *A Call to Joy*).

B. The chart begins with Acts 9 as the model for early spiritual growth.

C. It must be noted that:

1. Few models deal with baptism and the importance of the church—a particular weakness of parachurch materials!

2. None of the models deal with persecution, this omission is peculiar (perhaps due to their North American provenance):

a) Especially because dealing with persecution was one of the first follow-up comments in the Book of Acts (e.g. Acts 14:22)

b) Especially in light of the fact that those who fall away in the Parable of the Sower do so because of persecution!

[1261]Billy Graham, *A Biblical Standard for Evangelists* (Minneapolis; World Wide, 1984), 109.

[1262]Johnston, *Charts for a Theology of Evangelism*, Chart 31, "Comparing Follow-Up Tools" 56-57.

Chapter 26 Appendixes

Who Takes the Initiative in Follow-Up?

Introduction: Since the onset of the discipleship movement, the onus of responsibility for follow-up has been placed on the shoulders of the evangelist. This set of notes seeks to investigate the verbs used to describe the follow-up in the Book of Acts to determine (1) the subjects and objects of those verbs, and (2) the voices of the verbs. In this way, God will speak for Himself by the verbs that He has placed in His Word.

A. An overview of who took the initiative in the New Testament:[1263]

1. The recipient of the evangelism took the initiative:
   a. John 4:40, the Samaritans asked Jesus to stay, so He stayed two days
   b. Acts 5:14, "and all the more believers [participle present active nominative masculine plural] in the Lord, multitudes of men and women, were constantly added [indicative imperfect passive 3rd person plural] to *their number*"
   c. Acts 8:36, The eunuch said to Philip, "Look, some water, what prevents me from being baptized"
   d. Acts 13:42-44, the hearers begged that they speak again on the next Sabbath, they obliged; many followed Paul and Barnabas after the first hearing, they spoke to them urging them to continue in the grace of God
   e. Acts 16:15, Lydia "was baptized" (aorist passive) and urged them to stay with her
   f. Acts 16:30-34, Philippian jailer took the initiative by asking "What must I do to be saved?"; Paul and Silas then spoke the word of the Lord to him and his household; the jailer released them and washed their wounds; he was baptized (aorist passive); he fed them; he rejoiced because he and his household had believed
   g. Acts 17:18-19, "they took hold of him and brought him to the Areopagus;" sounds quite forceful, similar words used of arresting someone!
   h. Acts 17:34a, "But some men joined him [participle aorist passive nominative masculine plural] and believed [indicative aorist active 3rd person plural]"
   i. Acts 18:8b, "and many of the Corinthians when they heard [participle, present, active, nominative, plural] were believing [imperfect, active, 3rd person, plural] and being baptized [imperfect, passive, 3rd person, plural]"

2. There was a mixed initiative (through the evangelist preaching for commitment, and through listener verbally responding):
   a. Matt 3:2-7, Luke 3:3-14, John the Baptist took the initiative by going out and preaching repentance; the listeners took the initiative going out to him, by coming for baptism, and by asking what they should do
   b. Matt 16:15-28, Jesus asked a question, and Peter answered
   c. Acts 2:36-37, Peter took the initiative by telling the crowd at Pentecost that they were responsible for the death of Christ; the listeners took the initiative by asking, "Brethren, what shall we do"

3. The Lord (or His Word, or His Spirit) taking the initiave, along with the recipients:
   a. Acts 2:47b, "And the Lord was adding [indicative, perfect, 1st person, singular] to their number day by day those who were being saved [participle, present, passive, accusative, masculine, plural]"
   b. Acts 6:7, "And the word of God kept on spreading [from αὐξάνω, to grow; indicative imperfect active 3rd person singular]; and the number of the disciples continued to increase [indicative imperfect passive 3rd person singular] greatly in Jerusalem, and a great many of the priests were becoming obedient [indicative imperfect active 3rd person plural] to the faith"

[1263]Verses included were gleaned from Chapter 20, positive reactions or responses.

    c. Acts 13:50-52, Paul and Barnabas were driven out of the district; somehow they shook the dust off their feet (although there were some believers), and yet the disciples were filled with joy and the Holy Spirit

4. No follow-up recorded:
    a. John 7:40-41
    b. Mark 15:39
    c. John 3:4, both the conversion of and follow-up of Nicodemus are unclear from the text, although we have him speaking in John 7:50-51 and bringing spices in John 19:39

5. No continued follow-up at all:
    a. Even though it was requested: Mark 5:18-19, "And as He was getting into the boat, the man who had been demon-possessed was entreating Him that he might accompany Him. And He did not let him, but He said to him, 'Go home to your people and report to them what great things the Lord has done for you, and *how* He had mercy on you.'"
    b. Jesus did not stay even though it was requested: Mark 1:38; Luke 4:42-44
    c. He saw him no more: Acts 8:39, "And when they came up out of the water, the Spirit of the Lord snatched Philip away; and the eunuch saw him no more, but went on his way rejoicing"
    d. Even though it was requested, Acts 18:19-20

6. The evangelist took the initiative by himself:
    a. John 5:14, Jesus went to find the man that he had healed; the man seems to have turned on Jesus in vv. 15-16
    b. John 9:35-38, follow-up of prior contact for the purpose of evangelism, follow-up after conversion unclear
    c. Jesus followed-up with miracle, John 11:27ff.
    d. Follow-up for Thomas seemed to be the presence of Jesus in, with, and by the Word of God, John 20:28-31
    e. Paul returned to Lystra after he had been stoned and left for dead, then he left the next day, Act 14:20
    f. Follow-up to establish churches where they had been, Acts 14:21-23
    g. The second missionary journey was initiated for follow-up, Acts 15:36

B. Some principles to be gleaned from this study:

1. The evangelist is responsible to preach with conviction and for commitment

2. The recipient of the message is primarily responsible for the follow-up!

3. Once the recipient shows interest in follow-up, it is then the responsibility of the evangelist to follow-up in so far as possible, although particulars of what follow-up actually means is unclear from the text, other than the knowledge that later churches were founded in many of the cities where there was a positive reception

4. The Bible is strangely silent on the nuts-and-bolts of a programatic follow-up mechanism (the church has been good at creating very intricate follow-up programs anyway, from the founding of monasteries and orders with their multiple vows and rules, to present day year long programs of follow-up)

Assessing Evangelizing in the Pastoral Epistles

Introduction: What is the relationship of evangelism to the functioning of the church as portrayed in the Pastoral Epistles. Is there a difference between the evangelistic priority as found in the Book of Acts and the teaching on ecclesiology as found in the Pastoral epistles? What are the issues? How is this to be understood?

1. **The relationship of the Pastorals to Eph 4:11 and the work of the evangelist:**

   Introduction: It was brought to my attention that the word "evangelist" is used only once in the pastorals, and that only speaking of Timothy.

   Question: Do evangelists have a rightful place in the leadership of the church (cf. Eph 4:11) if they are not specifically mentioned in the Pastorals (1 Timothy [2 Timothy] and Titus)?

   Response 1.1: As far as descriptive nouns, the word "pastor" is not found in the Pastorals, and the word prophet is found only once, and that of a certain Cretan prophets (Tit 1:12)

   Response 1.2: As far as descriptive nouns that are found in the Pastorals, Paul twice refers to himself with the string: preacher [or herald for κῆρυξ], apostle, and teacher (1 Tim 2:7; 2 Tim 1:11); evangelist is found once (2 Tim 4:5)

   Response 1.3: As far as the message of which the apostle Paul was a herald, in 1 Tim 1:7 Paul was referring to the truth that Christ gave "gave Himself as a ransom for all" (v. 6)—thus clearly referring to the Gospel. In 2 Tim 1:11, Paul was also referring to this Gospel message, "the appearing of our Savior Christ Jesus, who abolished death, and brought life and immortality to light through the gospel" (v. 10). This Gospel is specifically that message which is directed to the unsaved that they may come to Christ by faith—therefore referring to his role as an evangelist (cf. 1 Cor 9:16).

   Response 2.1: As far as verbs, "prophesy" is not used in the Pastoral, whereas "preach" is found several times [in the NAS], in 1 Tim 5:17, it is a translation of [those laboring] "in the word," and in 1 Tim 6:2, as a translation of "exhort," other than that, "preach" [κηρύσσω] is found only once in the pastorals! It is interesting that while the Pauline epistles use the verb evangelize [εὐαγγελίζω] 21 times, that word is not used in the Pastorals either.

   Response 2.2: We have to watch out for an argument from silence.

   Response 2.3: We have to maintain "plenary inspiration", as far as the example of the Book of Acts for ecclesiology. After all it is the Book of Acts that exemplifies congregational rule and provides insight as to the sending off and receiving missionaries.

2. **The relationship of the Pastorals to the Book of Acts:**

   Introduction: Someone once told me that while evangelism is found in the Gospels and the Book of Acts, it is not found in the epistles.

   Question: Is the ecclesiology of the Book of Acts different than, unrelated to, or from an era of the church that is not meant to be repeated or mimicked, and therefore is authoritatively secondary to the Epistles, and especially the Pastorals as regards ecclesiology?

   Response 1.1: "Plenary inspiration" seems to indicate that both the Pastorals and the Book of Acts are equally inspired. The only way to discount this is to make an artificial differentiation between the teaching and practice of the Apostolic Age and that of the Church Age. By the way, the entire New Testament was written in the Apostolic Age, thus making a stark difference between the two ages may lead to a dispensational problem, and perhaps a Process Theology problem.

   Response 1.2: Both the Book of Acts and the Epistles relate to the Church Age.

   Response 1.3: The Commission given by Christ to the Apostles at the end of each Gospel and at the beginning of the Book of Acts applies both to the Apostolic Church and to the post-Apostolic Church.

   Response 2.1: The lack of translation of the word εὐαγγελίζω as evangelize has led some English-only or English-primary readers of the Bible to think that mandate for or task of evangelism is not found in the Epistles. As mentioned above, the word is found in Paul 21 times (not counting 2 uses in Hebrews), and in Luke-Acts 25 times.

Response 2.2: The predominant number of denominations, theologians, and church historians that provide the majority of texts that we read do not believe in the substitutionary atonement, nor in instantaneous conversion ("You must be born again"), nor in New Testament evangelism. Therefore it is not surprising that their textbooks expunge evangelism from the theology of and history of the churches.

Response 2.3: Because of the helping verb "make" in "make disciples" in Matthew 28:19, non-instantaneous conversion people have interpreted "make" as providing for a lifetime of conversion, corresponding to a blending of passages on justification and sanctification, have ignored the proclamationally-oriented Great Commission passages, and have determined that the New Testament should be interpreted predominantly or uniquely as a manual for discipleship. In this context, it is no wonder that the verbal proclamation of evangelism is completely ignored.

Response 3.1: One must remember that when Luther read his Vulgate, he found the verb *evangelizare* perhaps 43 times as a direct translation of the 54 NT uses of the Greek εὐαγγελίζω, including three times in Gal 1:8-9. The evangelism of Johannes Tetzel, the seller of indulgences, was completely against the method of the Book of Acts. Therefore, the evangelism methodology of the Book of Acts was foundational in moving Luther to see the need for the Reformation.

3. **The relationship of the Pastorals and the Great Commissions:**

    Introduction: The concepts communicated here are twofold: (1) Matthean primacy as regards the Great Commission passages; and/or (2) ascribing to the principle of multiplication in 2 Timothy 2:2 as a Great Commission (see the chart on this verse in the next portion).

    Question 1: Does the Matthean Great Commission usurp or envelope all the other Great Commission passages, to the point that they are not even discussed as Great Commission passages?

    Response 1.1: There seems to be no reason that the Matthean Great Commission has risen to primacy, other than its emphasis on the linear element of training and teaching, which is picked up in the current translations of μαθητεύω as "make disciples," with an emphasis on the word "make."

    Response 1.2: The punctiliar elements of preaching in Mark and Luke, and testifying in Acts, are buttressed by Pauline theology, whereby faith comes by hearing, and hearing by the word of Christ, as well as by numerous analogies of Scripture, such as fishing for men, catching men alive, etc.

    Response 1.3: Those not adhering to the substitutionary atonement, but rather adhering to a reconciliation model of the atonement (relational), *Christus Victor,* liberation theology model, or the moral influence model *must necessarily* (especially the last three) oppose preaching as the only or primary emphasis of the Great Commission. For if they upheld preaching as the primary emphasis of the Great Commission they would be inconsistent with theology. And in actuality, the first thing to go when theological drift occurs is urgent evangelism.

    Question 2: Does 2 Timothy 2:2 constitute a Great Commission or does it contain all the characteristics of a Great Commission?

    Response 2.1: The main verb in this verb is the verb "commit" [παράθου]. This verb is considered to be an indicative aorist middle by some and an imperative aorist middle by others. In other words, it is not necessarily a command. Likewise, Luke's Great Commission contains an infinitive aorist passive (Luke 24:47), and in Luke 24:50 we find the only imperative, which is "wait." The issue is similar with John [πέμπω, present active indicative] and Acts [ἔσεσθέ, indicative future no voice or middle].

    Response 2.2: The verb παράθου [from παρατίθημι] in the middle voice means "commit, entrust, point out, prove." The secondary verb is the infinitive form of διδάσκω, meaning "to teach." These verbs are generally directed to those who are already Christians, and not to the lost as in the case of the other Great Commissions. Thus 2 Tim 2:2 has an interior focus rather than an exterior focus— develop leaders first, then evangelize second. Otherwise, if it is taken with an outward focus, it may be taken as meaning that we ought to seek to reach "leaders" with the Gospel first (like the athletes on a college campus), which does not seem to fit with 1 Cor 1:26, "For consider your calling, brethren, that there were not many wise according to the flesh, not many mighty, not many noble."

    Response 2.3: The verse is *not* given by Jesus Christ in a post-resurrection appearance (cf. Acts 10:42).

Response 2.4: The verse lacks the universality of the other Great Commission passages, (all nations, all the earth, all creation, unto the uttermost parts of the earth, etc.), but rather limits the emphasis only to "faithful men who will be able to teach others also."

Response 2.5: The verse lacks clarity as to the message, in two cases only using demonstrative pronouns, "What" [ἅ] and "these things" [ταῦτα]. There is a sense in which the message is not clear, as in Matthew—"all that I have commanded you," Mark—the Gospel, Luke—the death and resurrection and repentance for the forgiveness of sins, and Acts—"my witnesses." Granted, John 20:21 does not contain a specific message.

Response 2.6: It must be noted, however, that "teaching to obey" is part of Matthew's Great Commission, which is directly related to 2 Tim 2:2.

4. **The relationship of the Pastorals to evangelizing:**

   Introduction: The issue here relates to the presumed lack of the outward emphasis on evangelizing in the Pastorals, which therefore casts doubt on the necessity of emphasizing evangelizing in the local church, as some are fond to do (e.g. this author).

   Questions 1: Is there a lack of emphasis on evangelizing in the Pastorals, especially as regards ecclesiology?

   Response 1.1: Paul refers to his own ministry using the proclamational term "herald" [κῆρυξ] often used with an evangelistic emphasis (1 Tim 2:7; 2 Tim 1:11)

   Response 1.2: The fact that Paul was a prisoner for the Gospel, at least at the time of the writing of 2 Timothy [1:8], makes persecution for the "testimony of the Lord" (evangelizing) an obvious contextual issue in the proper interpretation of the Pastorals.

   Response 1.3: If the string of nouns used by Paul refers to a chronological order in ministry, Paul is first a herald [κῆρυξ], then he becomes an apostle to those who believe [ἀπόστολος], and finally he becomes their teacher [διδάσκαλος], 1 Tim 2:7; 2 Tim 1:11

   Response 1.4: In 2 Tim 1:11 Paul refers to his teaching role as being for the Gentiles [διδάσκαλος ἐθνῶν], a term most often used not for believers, but for non-believers

   Response 1.5: The admonition for Timothy to "Do the work of an evangelist" [ἔργον ποίησον εὐαγγελιστοῦ] is found in 2 Tim 4:5

   Response 1.6: The additional admonition in 2 Tim 4:5 "fulfill your ministry" [τὴν διακονίαν σου πληροφόρησον] seems to indicate that Timothy was not accomplishing the work of an evangelist as he should have been. πληροφορέω meaning to accomplish or carry out fully.

   Response 1.7: It may be ascertained that Timothy was ashamed of two things in 2 Tim 1:8: (1) the testimony of the Lord (clearly in the context, the Gospel message), and (2) that Paul was a prisoner because of the testimony of the Lord. Again, Paul is addressing Timothy's timidity as regards evangelizing.

   Response 1.8: In 2 Tim 4:17, Paul additionally used the word πληροφορέω to emphasize his evangelistic mission, "that by me the preaching **might be fully known**, and *that* all the Gentiles might hear" [ἵνα δι' ἐμοῦ τὸ κήρυγμα πληροφορηθῇ καὶ ἀκούσωσιν πάντα τὰ ἔθνη]. This includes the words preaching and hearing with the object being "the Gentiles," clearly referring to an evangelistic mission

   Response 1.9: Paul also portrays his mission in terms of the salvation of the chosen in 2 Tim 2:10, "For this reason I endure all things for the sake of those who are chosen, so that they also may obtain the salvation [ἵνα καὶ αὐτοὶ σωτηρίας τύχωσιν] which is in Christ Jesus *and* with *it* eternal glory," which verses, by the way sound like a restatement of 1 Cor 9:22-23

   Response 1.10: Paul explained that the result of Timothy "paying close attention" to himself and to his teaching would result in the salvation of those who heard him (1 Tim 4:16), clearly an evangelistic purpose, again a parallel to that found in 1 Cor 9:18-23; 10:32-11:1 and Col 1:28-29.

   Response 1.11: The "teaching[s]" or more accurately "words" [λόγοις] opposed by Alexander the Coppersmith, 2 Tim 4:14-15, was likely not some teaching within the church, as there is no evidence that Alexander was saved; rather it was likely referring to the evangelism of Paul in the marketplace (cf. Acts 17:16-17), similar to that referred to by Demetrius the Silversmith, Acts 19:26, "And you see and hear that not only in Ephesus, but in almost all of Asia, this Paul has persuaded and turned away a considerable number of people, saying that gods made **with** hands are no gods *at all*" (cf. 1 Thess 1:9-10)—this teaching, then, refers to evangelism outside the church!

Question 2: If there is this presumed lack of emphasis on evangelism in the pastorals, then should our churches be bound to the Great Commission given to the twelve apostles?

Response 2.1: If not, then a bifurcation is made between the teachings of Christ, hence the five Great Commission passages, and the teachings of the Apostle Paul, or more specifically Paul as expressed in the Pastorals. This dismemberment of the NT is indeed a pseudo-Dispensationalism—one in which the command of Christ (cf. 1 Cor 9:21) is deemed different than the example of Paul (cf. 1 Cor 11:1).

Response 2.2: If not, the law of Christ is nullified, the command of Christ is made void, and the new command of Christ to "love one another" (John 13:34-35) may as well be nullified as well.

Response 2.3: If not, then the commissioning (ἐντειλάμενος) given by Christ in Acts 1:2 and also mentioned in Acts 10:42, "He ordered us to preach to the people, and solemnly to testify" (παρήγγειλεν ἡμῖν κηρύξαι τῷ λαῷ καὶ διαμαρτύρασθαι), does not apply to the post-apostolic church, therefore adding third dispensation: (1) Christ and his teachings; (2) Paul and the apostolic times; (3) the post-apostolic church with the Pastorals as their only guide, which would lead us to another question, "Why chose the Pastorals and not, for example, the Johanine epistles or the Book of James?"

Summary: It would seem that the Great Commission passages *do* apply to the church, and has been shown, *there is no lack of emphasis on evangelizing* in the Pastorals. Similarly, it would seem that the reader has to purposefully ignore the context of the Book of Acts and the very message of the Pastorals in order to whitewash evangelization from their pages!

An Assessment of Multiplication

Introduction: The principle of multiplication—that proclamational evangelism brings only addition, whereas discipleship evangelism leads to geometric progression—has been taught to prioritize discipleship over evangelism.[1264] How does the concept of multiplication impact the Great Commission as studied in Chapter 7, "Defining Evangelizing," and Chapter 10, "The Great Commission"?**1.   Some proponents of multiplication develop their thoughts roughly as follows:**

a.   Presuppositions:

#1   A Christian (or believer) is different than a [true] disciple:
   a)   Using the "He who follows after Me" passages in Matthew and Luke
   b)   Contra Acts 11:26, "and the disciples were first called Christians in Antioch"

#2   Mentoring/training/discipleship takes a born-again Christian and produces a [true] disciple out of him/her

#3   That, based on 2 Tim 2:2, the Christian is to focus his attention primarily on those new believers who show potential to be leadership candidates:
   a)   Therefore, seemingly countering the words of Paul in 1 Cor 12:22-29, which encourages the church to bestow more abundant honor on the weak
   b)   However, seemingly affirmed by Jesus' Parable of the Sower, which teaches that some who seem to repent and believe actually either, are not saved (seed sown in the rocky soil) or are embrloied with life's issues (seed sown among the thorns)

On the Translations of 2 Timothy 2:2
[On whether the final clause is a result clause of teaching others, or another descriptor of the "faithful ones," e.g. "apt to teach"?]

Greek Byzantine Text	KJV; ERV; ASV; RSV; NAS; NKJ; CSB; ESV	Young's (1862)	Darby (1884)	Douais-Rheims✣ (1899)	Bible in Basic English (1949)	New Jerusalem✣ (1985)	NAB✣ (1970)	NIV (1984)	NET (2005)
οἵτινες ἱκανοὶ ἔσονται καὶ ἑτέρους διδάξαι	who shall be able to teach others also	who shall be sufficient also others to teach	such as shall be competent to instruct others also	who shall be fit to teach others also	so that they may be teachers of others	so that they in turn will be able to teach others	who will have the ability to teach others as well	who will also be qualified to teach others	who will be competent to teach others as well
Καὶ ἃ ἤκουσας παρ' ἐμοῦ διὰ πολλῶν μαρτύρων, ταῦτα παράθου πιστοῖς ἀνθρώποις, οἵτινες ἱκανοὶ ἔσονται καὶ ἑτέρους διδάξαι	And the things that thou hast heard of me among many witnesses, the same commit thou to faithful men, who shall be able to teach others also.	and the things that thou didst hear from me through many witnesses, these things be committing to stedfast men, who shall be sufficient also others to teach	And the things thou hast heard of me in the presence of many witnesses, these entrust to faithful men, such as shall be competent to instruct others also	And the things which thou hast heard of me by many witnesses, the same commend to faithful men, who shall be fit to teach others also	And the things which I have said to you before a number of witnesses, give to those of the faith, so that they may be teachers of others	Pass on to reliable people what you have heard from me through many witnesses entrust to faithful people who will have the ability to teach others	And what you heard from me through many witnesses entrust to faithful people who will have the ability to teach others as well	And the things you have heard me say in the presence of many witnesses entrust to reliable men who will also be qualified to teach others	And entrust what you heard me say in the presence of many others as witnesses to faithful people who will be competent to teach others as well

---

[1264]Walter A. Hendrichsen in *DisciplesAre Made--Not Born* (Wheaton, IL: Victor Books, 1974) has entitled chapter 11, "Multipying Your Efforts." This chapter is an excellent summary of the topic, and has been reprinted as chapter 6 in *Discipleship: The Best Writings From the Most Experienced Disciple Makers* edited by Billie Hanks, Jr. and William A. Shell (Grand Rapids, MI: Zondervan Publishing House, 1981).

    c) Preliminary thoughts on the interpretation of 2 Tim 2:2:

       (1) Please note that the word faithful ones (πιστοῖς is from the adjective πιστός found 63 times in the NT), and is used in the exact same form to describe all believers in Eph 1:1, Col 1:2, and 1 Tim 4:3

       (2) The restriction to men (πιστοῖς ἀνθρώποις), is related to men being considered the leaders of the church, 1 Tim 3:2, etc.

    d) Delving into 2 Tim 2:2:

       (1) Does Paul encourage Timothy to focus his teaching ministry solely or primarily on those "who have leadership potential?"

          (a) This leading to a hierarchy of men who have leadership potential, crack troups if you will, necessitating an artificial distinction between a mere Christian and a "disciple":

            [1] Faithful men would be considered people such as those on Paul's missionary team, i.e. those able to journey with Paul on a missionary trip

          (b) Which by necessity requires a [human] distinction among the parts of the body, that being locating and working only with those with a chosen aptitude, which problem Paul wanted to avoid in 1 Cor 12:22-29

            [1] Here is where the problem lies, making a human set of guidelines for who is or who is not the recipient of the teaching described

            [2] Once a human set of guidelines comes into place, then all the human sciences enter the picture to assist the pastor in determining who is or who is not worthy of his time; enter competition, pride, and favoritism

          (c) What chosen aptitude would be most apt to be considered, when seeking a set of criteria to determine who are the "faithful" to be trained?

            [1] "Ability to teach" follows from a predisposed reading that "faithful" is a special aptitude that is not a characteristic of all Christians

            [2] From which follows then, ability to lead

            [3] From which sometimes follows, ability to make money and give

       (2) Or does Paul call Timothy to teach all faithful men (all Christians without distinction), with the result that they will then be able to teach other Christians also?

          (a) Although this is not the usual reading of this text, it may be preferred

          (b) It does not appear that Paul is calling Timothy to focus on several apprentices in the ministry, but rather to pass on all that he taught Timothy to "many witnesses," just as he himself had done.

  b. Necessary definitions:

    #1 Itinerant evangelizing (preaching the Gospel) = addition, and produces…

      a) Mere decisions

      b) Merely born again Christians

      c) Not necessarily [true] disciples

    #2 Intentional discipleship = multiplication (2^{32} = 4.3 billion), and does produce both born-again Christians and [true] disciples, who:

      a) Produce fruit in keeping with their repentance

      b) Reproduce themselves

  c. Hermeneutical progression:

    #1 While Paul exemplified itinerant evangelizing, itinerant evangelizing was not the example of Jesus (*contra* Mark 1:38; Luke 4:42-44; 8:1-3; 9:1-2, 6; 10:1), nor is it taught or exemplified in the Epistles

    #2 The Book of Acts must be understood in its place and time as a part of the Apostolic Church, but is less relevant [especially methodologically] to a post-apostolic church:

      a) This division leads to a "dispensationalism" of evangelism methodology

      b) There is nowhere in the Bible wherein this claim can be verified

      c) This bifurcation is made between Pauline methodology and that of Jesus—only to lead to a bifurcation in conversion, and finally to soteriology

  #3 Jesus' only, primary, chronologically prior, or most important ministry example was that of long-term [one-on-one or small group] discipleship:

      a) Itinerant evangelism was not the primary public thrust of the ministry of Jesus (contra Mark 1:38; Luke 4:42-44, etc.)

      b) The public or itinerant evangelism ministry of Jesus was merely a "fishing pond" for the more important discipleship ministry

  #4 Matthew's Great Commission is therefore prior to, superior to, or more complete than the other Great Commission passages (e.g. in Mark 16; Luke 24; or Acts 1):

      a) Thus they can be ignored as relating to the Great Commission

      b) Often no attempt at correlating all the Great Commission passages is attempted

  #5 The aorist tense [a punctiliar emphasis] of μαθητεύω in Matthew 28:19 should therefore be translated:

      a) With the helping verb "make"—whereby "make" implies linear action, or an extended period of time, then, "make" almost becomes the most important verbal element of "make disciples"

      b) Rather than use the helping verb "win" (as in Acts 14:21, NIV), which implies instantaneity in becoming a disciple, or the beginning of faith, rather than its continuation in a prolonged period of initiation, growth, and development:

          (1) Several scholars consider Paul's second missionary journey to be two years in length, not allowing for a two or three year discipleship program (Nav 2:7-type program) to be implemented in every town, much less in the city of Derbe (Acts 14:20-21, after he had evangelized that city and won many disciples):

             (a) F. F. Bruce places the journey in A.D. 47-48[1265]

             (b) Frank Goodwin places Paul's First Missionary Journey as follows in his chronology: "First Missionary Journey, 45-47 A.D., 2 years."[1266] Allowing for a stay of a "long time" in Antioch of 2 years (Acts 14:28), hence 48-49 A.D.

      c) "Win" actually fits more clearly with a theology of instantaneous conversion ("You must be born again!"), as well as the New Testament examples of evangelism.

  d. Ensuing methodological results:

  #1 Itinerant evangelizing (addition) is understood as being only a part of the discipleship process, and therefore as only a [small and shrinking] part of the Great Commission

  #2 Intentional discipleship, however, is often considered more holistic and more inclusive of Christ's purposes for individual believers and His church on earth.

  #3 The building of a friendship with a lost person as being called "pre-discipleship"; thus combining the necessary preparatory grace of friendship in evangelism with the linear process of long-term discipleship to posit the starting of a friendship as "pre-discipleship"

2. Some considerations in light of the above:

  a. Jesus' ministry did include itinerant evangelism as the Central Interpretive Motif of the Gospels (Mark 1:38; Luke 4:42-43), as well as particular instances wherein Jesus did not allow someone to stay with him (Mark 5:18-20), thereby calling into question the *a priori* place of long-term discipleship as the only model of Jesus

---

[1265]"Chronological Table" in F. F. Bruce, *The Acts of the Apostles*, 2nd ed. (Grand Rapids: Eerdmans, 1952), 55.

[1266]"Outline Life of Paul" in Frank J. Goodwin, *A Harmony of the Life of St. Paul According to the Acts of the Apostles and the Pauline Epistles* (Grand Rapids: Baker, 1951), 7. Goodwin cited that he based his chronology on Hackett's commentary on Acts (Hovey ed.), which itself took into account information derived from the dates found in Josephus for the rulership of Aretas and Herod Agrippa I.

b. Joseph of Arimathea was deemed to have been a "disciple of Jesus" (μαθητεύω [Byz: indicative, aorist, active, 3rd person, singular], Matt 27:57), even though he did not walk with Jesus in prolongued training or equipping (John 19:38).

c. Paul's ministry in Acts was provided as a faithful representation of the ministry of Christ (1 Cor 11:1), and therefore provides Christians a divinely inspired example as to how to follow Christ.

d. Multiplication is difficult to prove from the Book of Acts (much as McGavran's finding "People Movements" throughout the Book of Acts was a stretch in his 1955 *Bridges of God*).

e. Acts 11:21 and 26 show the interchangeable use of the words "believer," "disciple," and "Christian"

f. The decentralization of, denigration of, antagonism to, and ultimate elimination of evangelism [note the progression in these four terms] due to an overemphasis on discipleship or multiplication proves difficult to reconcile with the Great Commissions in Mark, Luke, and Acts, unless Christ [and the authorship of the Holy Spirit] is divided (1 Cor 1:13)

g. Discipleship becomes for some the [ultimate] panacea that assures that the seed of the Gospel is sown in receptive soil, and it will not fall on shallow or weed-infested soil (cf. Matt 13; Mark 4; Luke 8); and therefore, that seed sown in shallow soil needed only discipleship to bring it to become seed sown in good soil; an interpretation which is tangential to the teaching of this parable

h. Discipleship (and its cousin the spiritual disciplines) can regenerate into a works methodology, then a works ministry, culminating in a works salvation:
   1) Is this not what happened in the Roman Catholic church with its sacramental system and its monastic leadership over the years?

3. **That being said, however:**
   a. The idea to focus on a few *seems* biblical, 2 Tim 2:2 (depending on how this verse is translated, interpreted, and applied)
   b. The Matthean Great Commission *does* include "teaching to obey," Matt 28:20 for all believers
   c. A proper follow-up *is* biblical and necessary when at all possible
   d. The planting and multiplication of churches *is* important and necessary.

Evaluation of the Impact of Sunday School on the Church

Introduction: We live about 150 years after the advent on the Sunday School movement within the local church in the United States. While there has been much good come from the Sunday School movement, there have also been ancillary results from the movement. The following charts seeks to look at the impact of the Sunday School upon local church ministry.

ISSUE	POSSIBLE NEGATIVE ANGLE	RESULTS	BIBLICAL INPUT	POSITIVE SIDE
Time	Shortens available time for worship service, to accommodate time for Sunday School	Adds time constraints to the worship service	Evangelizing-preaching-teaching is emphasized in the NT	Divides time in church between teaching/fellowship and worship/preaching
Definitional	Can make an unhelpful dichotomy between teaching and preaching	Can lead to fighting between soul-winning (evangelism) and soul-building (discipleship)	NT uses preaching (evangelizing) and teaching together	Keeps balance between wining disciples and teaching to obey all that Christ has commanded
Sunday School as Follow-up	Some may differentiate between the role of Sunday School and the follow-up of new converts	Lack of a "follow-up program" may be used to discourage evangelism, even when a complete program of Sunday School is in place	Differentiation between follow-up of new believers and establishing mature believers is difficult to prove from the NT	The Sunday School program can and should be used for the follow-up of new believers
Punctiliar versus Linear Emphasis	Can lead to a scenario wherein "You must be born again" is considered archaic, while a gradual catechetic or progressive enlightenment is deemed more relevant, based on secular psychological and educational theories	Can lead to a de-emphasis on evangelistic preaching, and an mis-emphasis on transformational studies, such as discipleship and the spiritual disciplines	The Bible places conversion (justification) before and prior to sanctification (spiritual growth and maturity)	Can and should provide an environment wherein teaching emphasizes "all that I have commanded you"
Age-Appropriate Learning	Can champion ministry in smaller, age-delineated groups, while denigrating preaching to non-discriminate large groups	Can lead to disagreement in defining age-appropriate issues of topical relevance, wherein man becomes the judge of what is relevant and what is not both practically and theologically	NT does not seem to divide the church by age groups; however, secular educational theory does	Takes into account issues through which different ages go, and their need for age-oriented fellowship, teaching, and ministry
Learning Environments	Can make a dichotomy between small group teaching and large group preaching	Can lead to arguments between the ineffectiveness of large groups (mass evangelism, mass meetings, or congregational settings) versus small groups (in smaller classrooms or home settings)	NT does not seem to emphasize differences in learning environments in the church	Takes into account different learning environments
Learning Styles	Can make a dichotomy between interaction-dialogue and preaching-monologue	Can lead to discussion of the benfits of the Socratic method, and varieties in styles of learning and teaching, while denigrating some of the very methods used by Jesus and the apostles	NT never mentions personality types as found in Greek philosophy, even though the "Four Personality Types" were available in the 2nd Century B.C.	Takes into account different learning styles

ISSUE	POSSIBLE NEGATIVE ANGLE	RESULTS	BIBLICAL INPUT	POSITIVE SIDE
Place for Bible Teaching	May tend toward less biblically-based preaching, as Sunday School is considered the place for "hard core" Bible teaching	Since Sunday School emphasizes Bible teaching, then in reaction (some may claim) that relevancy and motivational speech should guide homiletics	Moving from revealed truth to cultural relevance is an early indication of doctrinal downgrade	Expository preaching and expositional teaching should be the focus of everything in the church
Expectations*	Smaller churches (and church plants) may feel forced to emulate the age-group differentiation of much larger churches and their CE materials	Smaller churches and church plants often focus on the goal and expectation of staffing a "full range" of ages in their educational program	The nature of the church described in Acts and the Pastoral Epistles does not match the complexity of some educational expectations	Gives churches something on which to focus for growth, and provides places for new people to be plugged in to help in the ministry of the church
False Expectations**	A developed CE program seems to be the expectation in the U.S. for all "normal" churches	As 85% of U.S. churches are below 100 people, they cannot staff educational programs to the level for which books and CE materials are published	Again, the NT does not emphasize these educational complexities; wherein the NT may emphasize cell or house churches	Cell and house churches provide a NT alternative to these expectations; How can publishers accommodate smaller churches without a complete paradigm shift?
Personnel Needs	Can lead to the largest administrative arm of any church, with all of its programmatic complexities	Christian education often entails the largest administrative program in the church, as well as its most expensive branch	A NT church should focus on the winning souls and growing disciples, rather than developing extravagant educational hierarchies	Allows multiple people to be involved in ministry, albeit Program-Based Design ministry**
Space Needs	May lead to the need for numerous classrooms for Sunday School classes, apart from a large group worship service	Christian education entails the most expensive architectural element in the construction of a typical U.S. church, following the architectural norms and codes of public schools	NT churches were located in houses or rented quarters; in early U.S. history, the only space designed in churches was for congregational gathering; between 1900-1940, progressive U.S. churches added significant CE space	Need for more classroom space is a healthy sign of church growth
Inter-generational Nature of Church	Elaborate Sunday School programs may segment age groups, further augmenting the generation gap, and disallowing the younger to learn from older	Attendees may not learn from the whole range of God's people in the church	NT places importance on the older teaching (and modeling for) the younger	Allows for qualified (hopefully) older persons to teach classes of younger people
Need for Reliance on the Holy Spirit	As a whole age appropriate range of lessons are developed, repackaged lessons may not encourage the Sunday School teacher to grapple with the text of Scripture himself or herself	Sunday School teachers teach that which they have not received or inferred from the text, leaving the Holy Spirit out of the process of lesson preparation; the application points of some lessons may even be tangential to the text, further confusing the teacher and his class	The Bible places the onus of responsibility for teaching on the shoulders of the teacher as he individually grapples with the text; removing this responsibility is removing the inspiration of the Holy Spirit from the process	Sunday School materials can allow the teacher to provide a quality lesson without a lengthy time commitment, while controlling lesson plans allows the publisher to control the theology (for better or worse) and corresponding lessons learned from a given text of Scripture

*It would seem that once a Sunday School program is established, then the expectation is for the church to develop a complete music program.

**These Christian education [and other programmatic] expectations can lead to what Ralph Neighbour, Jr. calls Program-Based Design or PBD churches, in his *Where Do We Go From Here? A Guide for the Cell Group Church* (Houston: Touch, 1990). For example, see Thom Rainer's *Simple Church* (Nashville: Broadman, 2007). Rainer guides churches to rethink core values, so that they can actually minister effectively, while reshaping the expectations of how a true church should look.

Considering Differences Between Roman Catholic and Evangelical Spiritual Disciplines

Introduction: Contemporary books on the spiritual disciplines, a fairly new emphasis among Evangelicals, have often drawn from Medieval Roman Catholic sources, perhaps not realizing the significant gulf that divides the two both practically and doctrinally.

		Catholic Holy Orders	Catholic Non-Holy Orders	Evangelical
Participants in Spiritual Disciplines		Persons who have taken the Benedictine Vows of Poverty, Celibacy, and Obedience	Not expected to participate in spiritual disciplines, other than saying the regular saying of the Rosary, attendance at Mass, the buying and lighting of candles for prayer, etc.	All believers, ordained or non-ordained, are considered equal
Reasons for Spiritual Disciplines	**As Related to Salvation**	To add to the merits of Christ, Mary, and the Saints	To add to the merits of Christ, Mary, and the Saints	In gratitude for salvation, full and free
	As Related to Sanctification	To put to death the vices and increase the virtues	To put to death the vices and increase the virtues	In obedience to the commands of Christ, as well as the teaching and examples in the Bible
	As Related to Human Relationships	To obey the rule of the particular order, and the desires of the order's superior	To obey the local priest and ultimately the Pope	To live in relationship with others as Christ would desire
Content of Spiritual Disciplines	**Content Allowed**	The Sentences of Peter the Lombard	The Rosary and the Mass	The Bible
	Content Disallowed	Study of the Bible, until the theology of Lombard and Aquinas has been completely absorbed	Study of the Bible until very recently, and that only when read in submission to the hierarchy	Sinful, idolatrous, and wordly things
Practice of Spiritual Disciplines	**Secular Employment**	Because of a Vow of Poverty, secular work cannot and must not be done	Although work is encouraged, social welfare from the state is also encouraged	Evangelicals assume that all believers are to work, based on Acts 20:34; Eph 4:28; 1 Thess 4:11-12; 2 Thess 3:12
	Family	Because of the Vow of Celibacy, one does not have the demands (or joys) of family constraints	Marriage and the raising of a family is required for those who have not taken the vow of Holy Orders	Evangelicals assume that one ought to honor father and mother, and that marriage is a good thing, Heb 13:4; Prov 18:22
	Use of Time	One's time is completely devoted to a life of obedience to the rule of discipline of the particular order	While daily mass and the multiple times of saying the Rosary are expected of Roman Catholic lay persons, most knowing that it is very difficult to maintain this degree of "devotion" are just nominal catholics	Practical demands on time spent in pursuing "spiritual disciplines" are tempered by work and family

Historical Addendum

Francois Lambert d'Avignon on the Subtle Trap of Monasticism

François Lambert d'Avignon, "Histoire du moine racontée par lui-même, traduite du latin" [story of a monk told by he himself, translated from Latin], in Franck Puaux, *Histoire de la Réformation Française* (1523; Paris: Michel Lévy Frères, 1859), 1:412-17; taken from Gerdesius, *Historia christianismi renovati,* vol IV; translation mine.

"François Lambert, d'Avignon, useless servant of Jesus Christ, to the pious reader, may grace and peace be given to you in Jesus Christ.

"Received hithertofore into the minor orders [Observant Franciscans, a.k.a. O.F.M., *Ordo Fratrum Minorum*][1267] who take the title of observing, I during several years, wearing the costume of their order, announced the Word of God in a number of counties. Lately I was forced to remove their habit and their society. It is therefore necessary that I make known the causes and that I give my reasons for my way of acting. If I would not do this, the simple would be scandalized, not understanding that I was able to do so in a Christian fashion. To this end I composed two tracts: in the first, it is this: I expose several of the reasons for my leaving the minor orders; in the second, I make know what are the rules of this order of monks, and how one ought to think of such.

"When you will have read them, not only will you not be, dear reader, scandalized by my actions, but you will be convinced that I acted well. Goodbye, and may the grace of God be with you!

"In the town of Avignon, celebrated city of the Gaul's [Medieval French people-group], having lost my father when I was very young, I felt myself drawn to God by His Spirit. What struck me in particular about this city, was the exterior beauty of the minor orders called observants, and their appearance of great holiness. In the simplicity of my childhood, I thought that with these monks their interior responded to their exterior. With them I admired the decency of their clothing, the humility of their appearance, their lowered eyes, the softness of the voice, the crossing of their arms, the grace of their gestures. I admired their bare feet, their shaved and covered head, and other similar things. But what I did not recognize among them, was the spirit of a fox and the heart of a wolf hidden under their lambs wool.

"When I heard them in their public assemblies, I felt myself drawn to them and I thought that what they did was pleasing to God. When with lies they told me of life in the convent, the rest of the cloister, and the advantage of education and other similar things, they motivated me. But what they should have revealed to me, this they carefully hid from me.

"Feeling myself drawn to them more and more, I was fifteen years old when I was received into their order at Avignon. I was immensely deceived! But God permitted that I be in order that I might later understand His own wisdom. I do not doubt that it was all by the effect of His providence that I found myself in the midst of them, in order that after having been deceived by their exterior appearance, I exit their convent with a knowledge of the truth, to reveal to others all that there is of rottenness in these whitewashed sepulchers.

"During the year of my initiation, they carefully hid from me all the bad there was among them, in the fear that I would leave them. This is what they always do with their initiates, because they are assured that if they were to make known what they were, no one would want to be received among them; the initiation completed, they feared nothing, hardly assuring me that it was an unforgivable sin to leave their home.

"My initiation completed, just fifteen years and several days old, I made my vows, barely knowing what I was doing. It did not take long for me to get to know the convent, and how the interior [image] corresponded very little to the exterior [image]. Finding myself deceived during my abeyance [period of waiting], I was sad, afflicted, and languishing; my spirit did not have peace, and my heart was missing the repose that it had so desired. I moaned to live in the midst of all these godless.

"Called later to the ministry of the Word, I was tormented by those of the minor orders, because I did not preach for their cloister. And while the people eagerly listened to my sermons, these sorry people, deaf as vipers closed their ears and scorned the Word of the Most High; they said that I was a flatterer and corruptor of the Word of God. I was therefore always with them in dissension.

"After several years, I was named an apostolic missionary. In this new job description, besides the difficulties associated with my ministry, the monks were a continual cross for me. The function of apostolic missionary consists of

---

[1267]The reference to the *minorites* is made throughout this essay. It is a plural noun that signifies those of the minor orders, in particular Franciscans (founded in Southern France approximately 1208-1209), who were also known in French as *cordelier,* because of a rope that they tied around them. The Dominicans were also founded (also in Southern France approximately 1225) and were known in French as *capucins,* probably due to the skullcap that they wore. These orders were a Catholic response to the *hereticos* (Latin) *parfaits* (French for perfect ones), the name given by the Dominican inquisitors to the Albigenses of that time (also used of the Waldenses). The derogatory name Albigenses was first used by crusade preacher Jacques de Vitry in 1209, 80 years after Southern France was evangelized by Henry of Lausanne.

going out, as the apostles, to preach the Gospel to all the world, wherever the opportunity presents itself. While I with infinite difficulty fulfilled my duties, the minor brothers made efforts to destroy with their slander what God was doing through me. While I saw them furious and filled with hatred, I did not want to take all the means that I had in the exercise of my duties; this did not effect them, and they did not cease from persecuting the poor servant of Jesus Christ.

"Often, when tired from my many sermons, I entered into their convent, these wicked men, who should have given me rewards, sold me off to wickedness; their gossip, their mockery was the bread at each of my meals. Because of the weakness of my body I was not able to travel on foot, they hoped in this way to hinder me from attending to my ministry. They permitted nevertheless that my friends gave me donkeys to assist me; but in their cupidity they sold them several days later, or else gave them away according to their own desire.

"Four years ago, I was preaching the Gospel in a town in France; my audience, touched by my sermons and returning to their better sentiments, brought me masques, dice, [playing] cards, and other similar things to burn them; but several of these miserable monks, enemies of the truth, lifted numerous of these objects and notably a mask resembling a lascivious young girl. I therefore accused them of theft. From that time on they conspired against me in order to remove me from the ministry of the Word; they did not neglect anything to this end: they invented lies and false testimonies, but they did not tell them to me. God confounded the designs of these Ahitophels,[1268] to the end that I did not lose one opportunity to preach.

"One day, a miserable partisan of the antichristian [papal] bulls stood up against me. Sustained by the Spirit of God, I resisted him so well, that he was condemned by the judges of the town. My colleagues blamed me for having acted as I did.

"Bringing myself another day to one of the homes that gives hospitality to brothers of the minor orders, I learned that they were public libertines, usurers [one loaning at exorbitant interest] and players; I warned them in secret of what people were saying and thinking of them; they did not want to listen to me. Irritated, they condemned my advice, as they had not asked for it.

"A certain Cardinal of those we call *à latere* [cf. *légat*; papal legate] wanted one day that I preach before him. All of this excited the jealousy of my brothers, and especially of two elderly men whose behavior was very poor: one of them was the guardian [must be a title in the monastery]. The day of the preaching having arrived, furious, they went to the palace of the Cardinal and told him that I was sick; it was a lie. The fear of these two Babylonian elderly men was that I would not flatter them enough before the Cardinal and his following; when I found out the facts, I reprimanded the guardian who threatened me with imprisonment and torture.

"Becoming the provincial of his order [regional superintendent], this guardian remembered his old wickedness and wrote against my faithful and truthful speeches; fearing because of this to fall into their hands and to see my life broken, I resolved to leave the order and become *chartreux*.[1269] I had a great fear of returning into the society of men, for fear of becoming an object of scandal in all the places that I had preached the Gospel of Christ.—I told myself equally, if I can announce in peace the Word of God, I would then be able to show him what I could through writing. That was again an illusion, for they would not have permitted me to do so.

"Persecuted by the *minorites* [brothers of the minor orders], I was not received among the *chartreux,* although they admitted me with a greeting of peace. Removed from the latter by the intrigues of my older brothers, who saw me with spite, I returned to them and continued my circuit of preaching. It was not long before I was again persecuted.

"I had in my cell [small room] some very-evangelical books of the very illustrious doctor Martin Luther; they took these and placed them under lock and key. Then, without having examined them, the chapter condemned them and threw them in the fire. They should have at least read them before they cried out: they are heretical! They are heretical! This is how they act, condemning that which they do not know. I would say confidently, God knows that I am not lying, that there was in these books the truest theology of all the books of the monks of all time.

"Pardon me, good reader, to have taken so much time on the folly of these Pharisees.—Again however a few words to speak of the evil that these wicked men have done to me and to those like me who love the truth; wickedness so great that several volumes would not suffice to tell them all.

"Such are the men who proudly call themselves observant, when Jesus Christ, in the seventeenth chapter of Saint Luke [v 10], says: "When you have done all the things that are commanded you say, 'We are your useless servants!'" But these men, dear reader, in order that you might know it, despise the Holy Word even in the name that they carry [obervants]. They have placed in their rules, all the statutes of the other monks, in order to be able to, better than their brothers, call themselves observants,—but none do better than they wrong to the Church.—But how can men, who do not know their own rules nor do not want to understand them, how can they sincerely follow them?

"The glorious tomb of Jesus Christ was not yet open to me, and the rock of eternal wisdom under which was kept the loving truth of God, had not yet been rolled… How much I was mistaken!—Whom have they not seduced, these persistent enemies of the observance of the commands of God!—They persecute the one who announces to them the Holy Word and those among their brotherhood who push themselves to rigorously keep the rule. What would I have become among these godless men?

[1268]David's counselor who gave advice to the treasonous Absalom (cf. 2 Sam 15-17).

[1269]*Chartreux* [English, Cartusians], a Catholic religious order founded in 1084 by [St] Bruno.

"Having received letters of commissioning from the general or vice-general of the order (I do not remember which), I went from France to Germany.—I seized the first favorable opportunity to remove my pharisaical costume, persuaded that the form and color of the habit are of little importance. I protested to God that I would never have left my order, if, by staying in my convent, I would have been able to freely announce the Gospel; but as that was impossible for me, I had to do what I did. If I had done otherwise, I would have sinned against the precept of the Apostle Paul, "You were purchased with a great price—do not become the slaves of men" [1 Cor 7:23]. Thus, those that attached themselves to the foolish constitutions of men, do they not make themselves slaves? Me therefore who, seduced, made myself the slave of men, how could I do anything else but to observe this other precept of Saint Paul, "If you can become free, do it." Separated from the assembly of the wicked, I arrived at the academy of Wittenberg, the first of the universe, and that leaves nothing to be desired as regards evangelical studies. I regret if I may say so of being mute and of not being able to announce with my own voice to the people the Word of God.—But I will wait the command of the Lord: I will place myself under His hand, and I will attempt with all that I can, by my writings, to exhort the world to receive the Gospel.

"I tell you only, dear reader, a few of the reasons that constrained me to leave the *minorites*... but it must suffice that I told you only summarily. In a few days, you will receive a commentary concerning the rule of their order, that will help you understand the totality. In the meantime, in order that all the world may know what to wait for as far as my resolutions and convictions, I will say these three things:

"1st Hitherto seduced and ignorant of what I was doing, I pronounced vows contrary to the Christian profession of faith. Oh well! I renounce to all these inventions of the *minorites* and recognize that the holy Gospel is my rule and should be that of all Christians;

"2nd I retract what I have preached that does not conform to Christian truth. I pray all those who have heard me preach or who read my writings to reject all that is contrary to the Holy Books. I have confidence in Him who removed me from a captivity more difficult than that of Egypt, that I will repair with His divine help by my words and by my books my numerous errors;

"3rd As no one can come to the knowledge of the truth without being in disagreement with the Pope, I renounce him and all his decrees, and I no longer want to be a part of his reign of apostasy. I desire rather to be excommunicated by him, knowing that his reign is excommunicated and accursed of God...

"In another book, we will speak of these things in greater detail; we will do so for the name of Jesus Christ to whom be honor and glory."

[Puaux then narrated the following epilogue]

"Henceforth speaks Francois Lambert: his simple words, but full of conviction, reveals in him one of those righteous souls thirsting to drink from the pure source of Christian truth. Such are almost all of the Fathers of Protestantism: theirs was a desire to know God and to be faithful to Him, we recognize all of them.

"The monk Lambert dated his letter from Wittenberg, where he arrived in 1523. That same year he was married. He was the first French monk who broke the vow of celibacy, and found in a virtuous and pious woman the help that God in his kindness has given to man.

"Lambert tried to come back to France to preach here the truths of salvation, but he could not. He established himself in Marburg [Germany], where he became a professor of theology and died there at the age of 43. Let us now return to the thread of our narrative interrupted for but a moment."

Another 19th Century Protestant View of Monasticism and Monastic Vows

Note the parallel concerns from "Translators Note," in Jean Charles Léonard Simonde de Sismondi, *History of the Crusades against the Albigenses, in the Thirteenth Century* (London: Wightman and Cramp, 1826; New York: AMS, 1973), xxviii; quoting Venema's *Historia Ecclesiastica*, 5:115-26:

"7. They [the Waldenses] held only three ecclesiastical orders, bishops, priests, and deacons, and that the remainder were human figments; and that monasticism was a putrid carcase, and [monastic] vows the inventions of men; and that marriage of the clergy was lawful and necessary."

Teaching on the Benedictine Vows

The monastic vows began with the so-called "Benedictine Vows," derived from [St] Ambrose (340-397), being named for [St] Benedict (480-550), who was made famous by a writing of Gregory I [the Great], *Life of St. Benedict*, being vows of poverty, chastity, and obedience:

1. [Voluntary] poverty [aka. the abolition of private property or communism]:

   a. Thereafter living from begging or from alms given to the church

   b. With no income from secular employment [however encouraged manual labor for the monastery]

2. Chastity [with communal living, in one room if possible]:

   a. An irreversible vow of perpetual celebacy, henceforth being considered married to the church as:
      1) The Bride of Christ, for monks
      2) Christ as a husband, for nuns.

   b. The celibacy of the clergy being established as Canonical Law by the Second Council of Lyons (1274):

      "16. On bigamists [i.e. priests married to church and to a woman]
      "16 [or 22] Putting an end to an old debate by the present declaration, we declare that bigamists are deprived of any clerical privilege and are to be handed over to the control of the secular law, any contrary custom notwithstanding. We also forbid bigamists under pain of anathema to wear the tonsure or clerical dress."[1270]

3. Obedience:

   a. From *Rule of Benedict*:

      "They no longer live by their own judgement, giving in to their whims and appetites; rather, they walk according to another's decisions and directions, choosing to live in monasteries and to have an abbot over them."[1271]
      Of an abbott: "He is believed to hold the place of Christ in the monastery, since he is addressed by a title of Christ."[1272]

   b. The following are examples of the vows of obedience taken by Jesuits (an order founded by Ignatius Loyola [1491/1495-1556] as the Society of Jesus [S.J.], organized in Paris as part of the Roman counter-Reformation):
      1) From *The Spiritual Exercises of St. Ignatius*:

         "13. If we wish to be sure that we are right in all things, we should always be ready to accept this principle: I will believe that the white that I see is black if the hierarchical Church so defines it. For, I believe that between the Bridegroom, Christ our Lord, and the Bride, His Church, there is but one spirit, which governs and directs us for the salvation of our souls, for the same Spirit and Lord, who gave us the Ten Commandments, guides and governs our Holy Mother Church.".[1273]
         [Note how Psalm 139:12 can be read in light of this statement; note also the woe of Isaiah 5:20]

      2) From "The Obedience of the Jesuits":

         "Let us with the utmost pains strain every nerve of our strength to exhbit this virtue of obedience, firstly to the Highest Pontiff, then to the Superiors of the Society; so that in all things, to which obedience can be extended with charity, we may be most ready to obey his voice, just as if it had been issued from Jesus Christ our Lord..., leaving nay work, even a letter, that we have begun and have not

---

[1270]"The Second Council of Lyons—1274"; available from: http://www.geocities.com/Heartland/Valley/8920/churchcouncils/Ecum13.htm#On%20excommunication%201; accessed: 1 Sept 2005; Internet.

[1271]Robert C. Jones, "A Brief History of Monasticism"; available at: http://www.sundayschoolcourses.com/monastic/monastic.htm#_Toc476569431; accessed: 5 Oct 2005; Internet; quoted from *The Rule of Saint Benedict in English* (The Liturgical Press, 1982), Chap 5.

[1272]Ibid., quoted from *The Rule of Saint Benedict in English*, Chap 2.

[1273]St. Ignatius Loyola, *The Spiritual Exercises of St. Ignatius*, translated by Anthony Mottola, S.J., imprimatur, Cardinal Spellman (Garden City, NY: Image Books, Doubleday and Company, 1964), 140-41.

yet finished; by directing to this goal all our strength and intention in the Lord, that holy obedience may be made perfect in us in every respect, in performance, in will, in intellect; by submitting to whatever may be enjoined on us with reaness, with spiritual joy and perseverance; by persuading ourselves that all things [commanded] are just; by rejecting with a kind of blind obedience all opposing opinion or judgement of our own; and that in all things which are ordained by the Superior where it cannot be clearly held [*definiri*] that any kind of sin intervenes. And let each one persuade himself that they that live under obedience ought to allow themselves to be borne and ruled by divine providence working through their Superiors exactly as if they were a corpse which suffers itself to be borne and handled in any way whatsoever; or just as an old man's stick which serves him who holds it in his hand wherever and for whatever purpose he wish use it...."[1274]

3) Cardinal Lavigerie's *Spiritual Testament* (Lavigerie [1825-1892] was the Roman Catholic Bishop of Algiers, Bishop of Carthage, and founder of the White Fathers order [organized to reevangelize Equitorial Africa]; this testament was originally written in 1884):

> "Spiritual Testament
> "*In the name of the Father, of the Son and of the Holy Spirit. So may it be.*
> "This is my spiritual testament.
> "I begin it by declaring, in the presence of eternity that will open itself before me, that I want to die with the same convictions in which I have always lived, that being obedience and devotion without limits to the Holy Apostolic Seat and to our Holy Father the Pope, Vicar of Jesus Christ on the earth. I have always believed, and I believe all that they teach and in the sense that they teach it. I have always believed, and I believe that outside of the Pope or against the Pope, there can be in the Church nothing but trouble, confusion, error, and eternal loss. He alone was created as the foundation of unity and as a consequence [of that] of life, and all that regards things of salvation.
> "I have the signal honor of remaining very close to the Holy Apostloc Seat by my character of priest, bishop, and by my title of cardinal of the Holy Roman Church. Without a doubt these honors which are strongly above my misery and my weakness are done to confound me, in this moment that I ponder my presence before the tribunal of God, but I want to see in it even greater gratitude and faithfulness to the Seat of Peter and before our Holy Father the Pope, who has lavished me with the marks of his confidence and of his goodness.
> "I have served him with my best, all that I was able. Not being able to do anything now, I pray that the Lord will accept the sacrifice that I have offered Him in my life and in my sufferings that will accompany my death, for the prolongation of the precious days of Leo XIII [his contemporary Pope] and in the triumph of his magnanimous designs."[1275]

4. Numerous other "vows" or "rules" were added to the Benedictine vows as monastic orders multiplied and differentiated themselves from one another.

Conclusion: It must be noted that the Reformers took exception to all of these vows as derived from man and unbiblical (1 Tim 4:1-5). When the Reformers married (Lambert d'Avignon, 1523; Zwingli, 1524; Luther and Hubmaier, 1525; John Rogers, 1533; Calvin, 1540), they visibly turned from the human yoke of these vows that they had made (in the case of Lambert, Zwingli, Luther, and Hubmaier), rejecting the necessity of obeying the ecclesiastical laws of the Roman Catholic church.

However, for the Church of Rome, its laws are equally [or more] important than biblical commands, as can be seen by the prices attributed to the indulgences. For sins such as murder and rape had a same or lower "price" than ecclesiastical "sins":

> "Absolution for the one who reveals the confession of any penitent is taxed at seven *carlins*.
> "Absolution for the one who abuses a young girl is taxed at six *carlins*.
> "Absolution for the one who has killed his father, his mother, his brother, his sister, his wife, or any other relative or associate, being a lay person, is taxed at five *carlins*.
> "If there is adultery and incest one the part of lay people, they will need to pay for each head six *tournois*.
> "Permission to eat milk products when it is forbidden [prohibited] costs, for only one person, six *tournois*."[1276]

[1274]"Obedience of the Jesuits," in Henry Bettenson, *Documents of the Christian Church* (London: Oxford University Press, 1963), 261.

[1275]Cardinal Lavigerie (1825-1892), *Ecrits d'Afrique* (Paris: Bernard Grasset, 1966), 235-36. Translation mine.

[1276]"Old tariffs of indulgences and absolutions of the Roman Church," Franck Puaux, *Histoire de la Réformation Française* (Paris: Michel Lévy Frères, 1859), 1:406-07; translation mine.

The gravity of the "pretended" Reformation of the Church [as the Reformed Church was called by King Louis XIV of France, "RPR—Religion Prétendue Réformée"] was that it did not follow all the ecclesiastical laws and canon laws of the Church of Rome.

Hence the battle lines are drawn up at the canon laws of the Church of Rome, which Protestants and Anabaptists viewed as unwarranted additions to Scripture, that actually removed the power of salvation from the Gospel message.

A Biblical Critique of the Benedictine Vows

Of human vows based on the philosophy of men, does not Paul call them the commandments and ordinances of men, the basic principles of men, which have no value against fleshly indulgence?

- Col 2:18-23, "Let no one cheat you of your reward, taking delight in *false* humility and worship of angels, intruding into those things which he has not seen, vainly puffed up by his fleshly mind, and not holding fast to the Head, from whom all the body, nourished and knit together by joints and ligaments, grows with the increase *that is* from God. Therefore, if you died with Christ from the basic principles of the world, why, as *though* living in the world, do you subject yourselves to regulations—'Do not touch, do not taste, do not handle,' which all concern things which perish with the using-- according to the commandments and doctrines of men? These things indeed have an appearance of wisdom in self-imposed religion, *false* humility, and neglect of the body, *but are* of no value against the indulgence of the flesh"

1. Of the vow of poverty:

- Two New Testament passages seem to contradict the vow of poverty:
  - 2 Thess 3:10-12, "For even when we were with you, we commanded you this: If anyone will not work, neither shall he eat. For we hear that there are some who walk among you in a disorderly manner, not working at all, but are busybodies. Now those who are such we command and exhort through our Lord Jesus Christ that they work in quietness and eat their own bread"
  - Eph 4:28, "Let him who stole steal no longer, but rather let him labor, working with *his* hands what is good, that he may have something to give him who has need"
- In the Old Testament, the Levitical priest, when he leaves his hometown to go to Jerusalem, appears to keep the earnings of his inheritance, according to Deut 18:8, rather than to give up his right to possessions. The discerning reader will notice how this verse has led to variety in interpretation likely because of this very issue:
  - Deut 18:8 (NKJ), "They shall have equal portions to eat, besides what comes from the sale of his inheritance"
  - Deut 18:8 (NJB), "eating equal shares with them—what he has from the sale of his patrimony notwithstanding"
- Furthermore, "Voluntary Poverty" may feed an egotistical side, "I could be rich, but I have chosen to be poor as an example and for your benefit"
- Likewise "Voluntary Poverty" may appear to be pleasing men, and saying, "Look at me!" rather than saying "I am nothing, look at Him!" John 1:26-27; 3:30; 15:5
- Notice that Paul did not tell the rich to sell all that they had and give it to the poor (as was singularly the case for the Rich Young Ruler, Matt 19:21; Mark 10:21; Luke 12:33); Paul rather instructed them as follows:
  - 1 Tim 6:17-19, "Command those who are rich in this present age not to be haughty, nor to trust in uncertain riches but in the living God, who gives us richly all things to enjoy. *Let them* do good, that they be rich in good works, ready to give, willing to share, storing up for themselves a good foundation for the time to come, that they may lay hold on eternal life"
- Notice also that the poverty at the birth of Jesus was not voluntary on the part of Joseph and Mary, and the "no gold nor silver nor copper, nor bag, etc." (Matt 10:9-10; Luke 10:4) when Jesus sent His disciples was commanded (not voluntary), and both pragmatic and circumstantial, as was that of Paul, 1 Cor 6; 2 Cor 11; Phil 4
  - The disciples were commanded not to bring anything, which assumes that they had something to bring in the first place
  - This command allowed the disciples to respond immediately (e.g. Matt 4:20, "The immediately left their nets and followed Him"; Mark 1:18); they didn't go to the bank, go back home to get another pair of shoes, or grab a sack lunch.
- Likewise, when [St.] Dominic sent his followers to "beg food," this violated 2 Thess 3:12
- Rather, the so-called "Vow of Poverty" appears to be a self-determined choice to live the superior "contemplative life"[1277] (rejecting the need for work to earn a living), while necessitating that the rest of human society pay for the choice of a contemplative lifestyle (either through the church receiving money from the state from taxes or through the gifts of people):
  - This urge for the contemplative life appears to be based at least in part on the teaching of Aristotle[1278]
  - This almost forces *ipso facto*, that the person taking the vow becomes greedy for gain, as he has no other choice for income (Prov 1:19)

[1277]As to "Whether the active life is more excellent than the contemplative?", Aquinas taught: "On the contrary, Our Lord said (Lk. 10:42): 'Mary hath chosen the best part, which shall not be taken away from her.' Now Mary figures the contemplative life. Therefore the contemplative life is more excellent than the active" (Thomas Aquinas, *Summa Theologica*, SS, Q[182], A[1], "Whether the active life is more excellent than the contemplative?").

[1278]In his proof for dividing all of life into active and contemplative (Thomas Aquinas, *Summa Theologica*, SS, [Q]179, A[1], "Whether life is fittingly divided into active and contemplative?"), Aquinas quotes Aristotle five times (De Anima, ii. 4; iii. 10; ii. 4; Ethic, ix. 12; De Anima, iii. 7), Dionysius twice (both Div. Nom. iv), a homily by Gregory 1 once (Homily xiv, super Ezech.), and the Wisdom of Solomon 8:16.

- o True, when combined with the vow of celibacy, the complexity of supporting a wife and children is eliminated, but how about support of one's aging parents, as in the case of widows in 1 Tim 5:8?
  - 1 Tim 5:8, "But if anyone does not provide for his own, and especially for those of his household, he has denied the faith and is worse than an unbeliever"
- o Further, it appears that this contemplative lifestyle is not earned through the rigors of teaching and publishing, but rather assumed by the individual and his ecclesiastical society at a very young age (15-16 years old), before the individual has shown intellectual propensity for such an honor

- Therefore, it appears that when Gregory I promoted Benedict and his lifestyle (690-604 A.D.), including his "vow of poverty," it came to be used as a Public Relations technique:
  - o Luther explained the lavish lifestyle and meals of the monks when he traveled to Rome (who made come of their income by selling indulgences), comparing that to the languor of those outside the monasteries
  - o Likewise, the people of Geneva chronicled the lavish lifestyle and meals of the monks in their city when the monasteries were opened to the outside
  - o While this is not to say that there are not some monks, nuns, and priests, who suffer great privation both voluntarily and involuntarily, the so-called "vow of voluntary poverty" taken by some leaders in the Catholic Church, combined with the secrecy of Rome and its properties, appears to have been used as an effective public relations technique
  - o Could it be that the wealth gained by Protestants through capitalism has become a subject of envy? This author recommends to the reader a study of the history of capitalism in relationship to Reformation Geneva and the early Puritan United States of America.
- When the Catholic "vow of poverty" is compared to the Protestant or Evangelical scenario where marriage is involved, then further issues emerge:
  - o What of the 60-75% who go to seminary and never "make it" in the seminary? How are these individuals figured into the lifelong "vow of poverty" scenario? Surely there are a percentage in the Catholic model that take the vows and then "do not work out"; what happens to them?
  - o Whereas in the Protestant and Evangelical model, the normal pattern, which is not imposed, is that marriage occurs prior to, during, or after seminary, often children ensue, and thereupon a necessary period of 20-25 years occurs where the life of "contemplation" is impossible, due to raising children:
    - However, is that 20-25 year period in vain?
    - Are there not lessons in life, ministry, and theology gained in those years?
    - Furthermore, there is a built-in time of testing built-in prior to the minister entering into a period of the contemplative life

2. Of the vow of abstinence:

- Consider the following biblical passages:
  - o Contra 1 Tim 4:1-4, [against those] "who forbid marriage"
  - o Gen 2:18, "It is not good for the man to be alone; I will make him a helper suitable for him."
  - o Prov 18:22, "He who finds a wife finds a good thing, And obtains favor from the LORD"
  - o Matt 19:12, "He who is able to accept *this*, let him accept *it*."
- Paul specifically stated that he was not commanding some or any Christians to be single:
  - o 1 Cor 7:5-7, "Do not deprive one another except with consent for a time, that you may give yourselves to fasting and prayer; and come together again so that Satan does not tempt you because of your lack of self-control. But I say this as a concession, not as a commandment. For I wish that all men were even as I myself. But each one has his own gift from God, one in this manner and another in that."
- So also, consider the example of the godly Enoch, who begot sons and daughters while he walked with God:
  - o Gen 5:21-24, "Enoch lived sixty-five years, and begot Methuselah. After he begot Methuselah, Enoch walked with God three hundred years, and had sons and daughters. So all the days of Enoch were three hundred and sixty-five years. And Enoch walked with God; and he *was* not, for God took him."
- Consider also King David, a "man of God" (Neh 12:24, 26), who was also the father of many children. Consider also Zacharias, the father of John the Baptist, etc. Therefore, it is clear that the Bible does not teach or exemplify the need for celibacy to be a man of God.
- From whence then did this teaching the need for celibacy come, in order to achieve some type of higher holiness? Was it not based on Stoicism, sex being part of the base human nature, and abstinence being a higher self-control? Is this self-imposed piety not vanity, vainglory, and grossly distorted?
  - o Is this not strange in light of Rome's accusation that Evangelical leaders are Manichean (flesh is evil, spirit good), and yet Evangelicals allow sex within marriage? It appears that in this case it is Rome that is acting Manichean!

- o Note also teachings, such as Wisdom 4:1 (NJB), "Better to have no children yet to have virtue, since immortality perpetuates its memory; for God and human beings both recognise it"
- Furthermore, this particular vow seems to have led to systemic sexual problems within Catholicism:
- o Note, for example, the problems of homosexuality as described in a letter of Pope Leo IX, *Ad splendidum nitentis* (DS 687-688), in which he responded to Pierre Damien's *Liber Gomorrhianus,* which called for greater severity in dealing with homosexual clerics (see A.D. 1054 below)
- Does there not seem to be a problem of conflict of interests in those who have made a vow of abstinence seeking to convince others that such a vow is not only acceptable, but commendable?
- For the papal decree that all Roman clergy be celibate, and for comments on the backlash against those who are married, see A.D. 1079.

3. Of the vow of obedience:

- Contra Rom 14:12; Col 2:16; see also Gal 4:21ff.
- The vow of absolute obedience is to be given to God alone (Deut 26:14)—see below in 1534 and 1884 to understand how far the vow of obedience was taken;
- Contra personal accountability:
- o To study, 2 Tim 2:15;
- o To diligently search the Scriptures, Acts 17:11;
- o To be on the alert, Acts 20:31; 1 Cor 16:13; etc.

Furthermore, the monastic vows in general:

- Seem to contradict: Isa 2:22; Jer 17:5-8; 1 Cor 3:21
- Cause the monk to be unable to obey the Great Commission of preaching the Gospel to all creation (as they live in solitude or in communal life sometimes or often completely isolated from the outside world)
- o It was not until the 13th Century that Rome produced the "preaching orders" (so-called) where monks had the vocation to preach outside the monasteries (Franciscans and Dominicans)
- o The purpose for these "preaching orders" was to counter the Matthew 10-type of evangelistic ministry of the so-called heretical Cathar denominations (16 of them) and the Waldenses (aka. Poor Men of Lyons)
- o As for the Dominicans, when they were founded by Bishop Diego, they were told to utilize the methods of "the enemy" of Rome to spread Rome's message
- Remember also that the reading and studying of Scripture in the vernacular tongue was forbidden even to clerics (by the 11th-12th Centuries), which means:
- o The monks had to both learn and rely on their Latin readings in Peter the Lombard for their spiritual development and discipleship
- o They likely did not have access to the Scriptures (even in Latin) that disallowed the particular vows they had made, until long into their "Holy Orders," at which time they were called upon to debate with so-called "Heretics" on these very issues
- In their striving for self-imposed Stoic self-perfectionism, Cenobitic monks (those living completely alone, like [St.] Benedict of Nursia) could not obey, and thus had to disobey, the 62 "one another" commandments in the NT given to guide the interrelationships of Christians within the local church
- As regards the interpretation of Scripture:
- o While living in disobedience to the commands of Christ to "evangelize the lost" and to "love the brethren," these monks still presumably memorized and chanted the Psalms and still handwrote portions of Scripture (for the communal monks), until the reading of Scripture was forbidden to them
- o The result of the disconnect of lifestyle from the clear teaching of Scripture was the reinterpretation of evangelistic passages and themes in the Bible, as is now codified in Lombard and Aquinas

The monastic movement, with its emphasis on "personal spiritual disciplines," its reinterpretation of the Great Commission as evangelizing, and its role in the [Holy] Inquisition, has resulted in a strongly negative influence on the ministry of the Gospel in the history of the churches

It is interesting to note that while the living "above reproach" of the 1 Timothy 3 and Titus 1 regulations for church leadership were dropped as part of Augustine's quarrel against the Donatists, eventually they were replaced by the three Benedictine Vows, thereby usurping those standards of the Bible for church leadership ("Nature abhors a vacuum").

CHAPTER 27
God and the Bible in Follow-Up

Introduction: Who does the follow-Up?

1 Corinthians 3:5-8

Verse	Paul	Apollos	God
5	...and what is Paul? Servants through whom you believed,	What then is Apollos? ... Servants through whom you believed,	even as the Lord gave *opportunity* to each one
6	I planted,	Apollos watered,	but God was causing the growth. (ἀλλ ὁ θεὸς ηὔξανεν)
7	So then neither the one who plants ... is anything,	nor the one who waters is anything,	but God who causes the growth. (ἀλλ ὁ αὐξάνων θεός)
8	Now he who plants and he who waters are one;		
8	but each will receive his own reward according to his own labor*	but each will receive his own reward according to his own labor*	

[Gk. Verse 7, ὥστε οὔτε ὁ φυτεύων ἐστίν τι οὔτε ὁ ποτίζων ἀλλ ὁ αὐξάνων θεός]
*Emphasizing grace to labor, see 1 Cor 15:10

Main Theme: God is intimately involved in every aspect of follow-up (and discipleship)!

A. A Preliminary Theology of Follow-Up:

Introduction: **Who is ultimately responsible for the spiritual growth of the new believer?** Several choices emerge:

1. The one who led him to faith in Jesus Christ
2. The new believer himself
3. The local church
4. God

Much like the hypostatic union considered in evangelism, it is not surprising that the same pattern emerges as it comes to follow-up.

Often the contemporary Evangelist [or Christian] may be made to "take the blame" if a convert falls by the wayside. While there is a biblical responsibility to do what we can, there are clear biblical examples of no follow-up (Mark 5:17-20; Acts 8:38-40) and we have the repeated Parable of the Sower which explains that not all apparent receptions of the Word will persevere (Matt 13:20-21; et al.)

The Bible seems to place the following order of responsibility on the follow-up of the new believer (chronological and prioritative):

1. In the first place:
   a. God (1 Cor 3:6-7; Phil 1:6)

2. In second place:
   a. The one who led him to faith in Christ (Matt 28:19-20)
   b. The new believer himself (Col 2:6-7; 1 Pet 2:2)

3. In the third place:
   c. The local church (Eph 4:11-15)

There can be a huge amount of guilt placed on the Evangelist who led someone to Christ, if that person does not persevere in the faith. It is extremely important that the entire teaching of Scripture be considered on this suject.

Whereas Paul gave thanks to God for His ministry in follow-up…

On the translation of ὀφείλω [to owe, be indebted to] in 2 Thess 1:3
[On Paul's debt to God for His follow-up of the Thessalonians]

Byzantine	Latin Vulgate (435)	Wycliffe (1388)	My translation (2008)	Tyndale (1534); cf KJV; Webster's; RSV; NKJV	Geneva (1560); cf. Young's; Darby; ASV; NAS; NIV; ESV; NET	New Jerusalem Bible*; cf. NRSV; CSB	God's Word for the Nations (1995)	Bible in Basic English (1949, 1964)	New Living Translation (2004)
	Debemus	We owen	We are indebted to	We are bound	We oght	We must	We …have to	It is right	We can't help
Εὐχαριστεῖν ὀφείλομεν τῷ θεῷ πάντοτε περὶ ὑμῶν, ἀδελφοί, καθὼς ἄξιόν ἐστιν, ὅτι ὑπεραυξάνει ἡ πίστις ὑμῶν, καὶ πλεονάζει ἡ ἀγάπη ἑνὸς ἑκάστου πάντων ὑμῶν εἰς ἀλλήλους·	Gratias agere debemus Deo semper pro vobis fratres ita ut dignum est quoniam supercrescit fides vestra et abundat caritas uniuscuiusque omnium vestrum in invicem	We owen to do thankyngis eueremore to God for you, britheren, so as it is worthi, for youre feith ouer wexith, and the charite of ech of you to othere aboundith.	We are indebted to thank God always for you, brethren, as it is proper, that your faith grows exceedingly, and the love of every one of you toward one another abounds.	We are bounde to thanke God all wayes for you brethren as it is mete because that youre fayth groweth excedyngly and every one of you swymmeth in love towarde another betwene youre selves	We oght to thanke God alwayes for you, brethren, as it is mete, because that your faith groweth excedingly, and the loue of euerie one of you towarde another, abundeth,	We must always thank God for you, brothers; quite rightly, because your faith is growing so wonderfully and the mutual love that each one of you has for all never stops increasing.	We always have to thank God for you, brothers and sisters. It's right to do this because your faith is showing remarkable growth and your love for each other is increasing	It is right for us to give praise to God at all times for you, brothers, because of the great increase of your faith, and the wealth of your love for one another;	Dear brothers and sisters, we can't help but thank God for you, because your faith is flourishing and your love for one another is growing.

B. The Role of the Godhead in Follow-up:[1279]

1. God the Father and God the Holy Spirit seal the young Christian, 2 Cor 1:22, Eph 1:13, 4:30

2. God the Father perfects the work He has begun, Phil 1:6

On the Translation of πείθω [to persuade] in Philippians 1:6
[Persuaded in God's ability to secure the new believer]

Byzantine	Latin Vulgate (435)	Wycliffe (1388)	Tyndale (1534)	Geneva (1560)	KJV (1611, 1769), cf. Webster's; ERS; ASV; NKJV; NIV	NAS (1977)	Young's (1862, 1888, 1898)	Darby (1884, 1890)	New American Bible* (1901); cf. NRSV	New Jeru-salem* (1985)	God's Word for the Nations (1995)	Bible in Basic English (1949, 1964); cf. NLT	RSV (1952); cf. ESV; NET; CSB
	Confidens	Tristenynge	[I] am suerly certified	I am persuaded	Being confident	Confident	Having been confident	Having confidence	I am confident	I am quite confident	I'm convinced	I am certain	I am sure
πεποιθὼς αὐτὸ τοῦτο, ὅτι ὁ ἐναρξά-μενος ἐν ὑμῖν ἔργον ἀγαθὸν ἐπιτελέ-σει ἄχρι ἡμέρας χριστοῦ Ἰησοῦ·	confidens hoc ipsum quia qui coepit in vobis bonum opus perficiet usque in diem Christi Iesu	Tristen-ynge this ilke thing, that he that bigan in you a good werk, schal perfourme it til in to the dai of Jhesu Crist.	and am suerly certified of this that he which beganne a good worke in you shall go forthe with it vntyll the daye of Iesus Christ	And I am persuad-ed of this same thing, that he that hathe begne *this* good worke in you, wil performe it vntil the day of Iesus Christ,	Being confident of this very thing, that he which hath begun a good work in you will perform *it* until the day of Jesus Christ:	For I am confident of this very thing, that He who began a good work in you will perfect it until the day of Christ Jesus.	having been confident of this very thing, that He who did begin in you a good work, will perform *it* till a day of Jesus Christ,	having confidenc e of this very thing, that he who has begun in you a good work will complete it unto the day of Jesus Christ's day:	I am confident of this, that the one who began a good work in you will continue to complete it until the day of Jesus Christ.	I am quite confident that the One who began a good work in you will go on comple-ting it until the Day of Jesus Christ comes.	I'm convin-ced that God, who began this good work in you, will carry it through to comple-tion on the day of Christ Jesus.	For I am certain of this very thing, that he by whom the good work was started in you will make it complete till the day of Jesus Christ:	And I am sure that he who began a good work in you will bring it to comple-tion at the day of Jesus Christ.

3. God the Father causes the spiritual growth of the young Christian, 1 Cor 3:6-7

4. God seeks out the believer who is seeking Him, Psa 119:176; James 4:8

5. The Holy Spirit indwells and directs the young Christian, John 14:16-17, 26; 16:13.

6. The Holy Spirit gives the young Christian the desire to obey Him, Ezek 36:27

7. The Holy Spirit working through the Word of God (1 Thess 2:13) transforms the young Christian "from glory to glory," 2 Cor 3:17-18

8. Jesus Christ is the example for the young Christian, Rom 8:29 (cf. 1 Cor 11:1)

9. Jesus Christ and the Holy Spirit intercede for the young Christian, Rom 8:26-27, 34; Heb 7:25

[1279]For more information on this subject see also T. Johnston, *Mindset*, Chap 5, II.A., "The Christian and Leading for Evangelism."

C. The Role of the Bible in Spiritual Growth:[1280]

Introduction: The sure way to make sure that God is doing the follow up is through encouraging the new believer to feed on the pure milk of the Word of God, 1 Pet 2:2

Translations of λογικός in 1 Peter 2:2

Greek Byzantine*	Latin Vulgate (435)	Tyndale (1534)	English Geneva (1560)	Etheridge** (1841)	Darby (1884)	Douais-Rheims✠ (1899)	American Standard Version (1901)	New American Standard (1977)	New Jerusalem✠ (1985)	Good News Trans✠ (1993)
λογικός	rationale	reasonable	of the woorde	of the word	mental ... of the word	rational	spiritual	of the word	spiritual	spiritual
τὸ λογικὸν ἄδολον γάλα ἐπιποθή-σατε	rationale sine dolo lac concupis-cite	desyre that reasonable mylke which is with out corruptcion	desire the syncere milke of the worde	and be desirous of the word as of milk pure and spiritual	desire earnestly the pure mental milk of the word,	desire the rational milk without guile,	long for the spiritual milk which is without guile,	long for the pure milk of the word,	all your longing should be for milk—the unadul-terated spiritual milk—	who are thirsty for pure spiritual milk,
ἵνα ἐν αὐτῷ αὐξηθῆτε	ut in eo crescatis in salutem	that ye maye growe therin	that ye maye growe thereby	that by it you may increase unto life	that by it ye may grow up to salvation	that thereby you may grow unto salvation	that ye may grow thereby unto salvation	that by it you may grow in respect to salvation	which will help you to grow up to salvation	so that by drinking it you may grow up and be saved

*The Nestle Aland "critical" text adds to the last phrase the words "εἰς σωτηρίαν" [unto salvation], which is an example of a return to the priority of the Vulgate in some decisions of the Editorial Committee of the United Bible Society.

**The Etheridge is a literal translation of the New Testament Peshitta (a 2ⁿᵈ Century Syriac translation of the Bible)

1. The Bible is the acting agent for spiritual growth in the life of the Christian, Psa 119:38; 1 Thess 2:13 (cf. 2 Cor 3:17-18)

2. The Bible is the central reference point for follow-up, Acts 8:25; 13:44; 18:11; 20:32

3. The Bible is the standard for spiritual growth:

    a. Through its many admonitions to stand firm in its teaching:
       1) Encouraging a reverence for God's Word, Prov 13:13; Acts 17:11
       2) Do not go "to the right or to the left" of biblical teaching, Deut 5:32; 17:20; 28:14; Jos. 1:7.
       3) Inclining one's ear or heart towards the Word, Prov 2:2; 4:20; 5:1
       4) Treasuring the Word, Prov 7:1
       5) Not forgetting God's Word, Prov 3:1
       6) Not abandoning God's Word, Prov 4:2

    b. Because of the results of heeding its teaching:
       1) Brings spiritual growth, 1 Pet 2:2
       2) Brings blessing, Prov 8:32-34; Rev 1:3
       3) Renders the Christian adequate and equipped for every good work, 2 Tim 3:16-17 (cf. 1 Tim 4:6)

    c. Through its many examples of spiritual success and failure:
       1) Several examples of spiritual failure:
          a) David's adultery with Bathsheba, 2 Sam 11
          b) Abijam, "who's heart was not fully devoted to the Lord His God," 1 Kgs 15:3
          c) Peter's denial of Jesus, Mark 14:29-31, 66-72 (cf. Luke 12:8-9)
          d) Ananias and Saphira, Acts 5:1-11

[1280]T. Johnston, *Mindset*, "God's Word in the Nurture of the Christian," Chap 1, IV.E., also speaks on this point.

    2) Several examples of spiritual success (cf. Jos. 1:8; Psa 1:3):
      a) Jesus, the Example, Rom 8:29
      b) The exemplary life of Joseph, Gen 37-50
      c) The hall of faith, Heb 11

4. God encourages a regular diet of His Word:

   a. God's Word is an important part of a regular diet, Deut 8:3, Matt 4:4, Luke 4:4, 1 Pet 2:2 (cf. 1 Tim 4:6)

   b. Through personally handwriting God's Word, Deut 17:18:
    1) Recommended starting point for handwriting Scripture: 1 John, Romans, 2 Timothy, Gospel of John
    2) Recommended methodology and pace for writing of Scripture: daily writing from 3-7 verses on loose leaf paper, one book at a time; a more literal translation is highly recommended: e.g. KJV, NAS, NKJ, ESV
    3) Advanced students may also alternate in OT books, such as: Deuteronomy, Psalms, Isaiah, and Jeremiah, perhaps alternating days, weeks, or months, from NT writing to NT writing

   c. Through daily reading of His Word, Deut 17:19-20, Prov 8:34 (cf. Isa 50:4)

   d. Through memorization of the Word, Psa 119:11, Prov 22:18

   e. Through constant meditation and application of its teaching, Jos. 1:8, Psa 1:1-3 (e.g. Psa 77:11-12)

5. Results of meditation on the Word:
   a. God's Word keeps from sin, Psa 17:4; 119:9 (cf. 2 Cor 10:4-5)
   b. God's Word cleanses the heart, John 15:3; 17:17
   c. God's Word sustains the Christian, Psa 119:116

6. God the Holy Spirit gives the Christian the desire to obey His Word, Ezek 36:27

D. God's Word in the Nurture of the Christian:

Introduction: Remembering that God deals with us according to His Word, Psa 119:65

1. Commands concerning God's Word in the Christian life:
   a. Study, Psa 111:2; 2 Tim 2:15
   b. Meditation and memorization, Jos 1:8; Psa 1:1-3; 119:11, 147-148; Prov 7:3 (e.g. Psa 37:31)
   c. Obedience, Deut 5:1; 6:1-2; John 14:21; 1 John 2:3-6; Rev 1:3 (e.g. Jer 42:5-6)

2. God's Word and the Christian life:
   a. Life in the Word:
    1) God's Word "produces reverence for God," Psa 119:38
    2) God's Word builds up (οἰκοδομέω) the Christian, Acts 20:32
    3) God's Word transforms the Christian, 1 Thess 2:13
    4) God's Word cleanses the Christian's soul, John 15:3; 17:17; Eph 5:26 (cf. Tit. 3:5)
    5) God's Word becomes the lifeblood of the Christian, Deut 32:47 (cf. Deut 8:3; Matt 4:4)
    6) God's Word is a source of strength to the Christian, Psa 119:28 (e.g. Psa 130:5)
    7) God's Word nourishes the Christian, 1 Tim 4:6
    8) God's Word sustains the believer, Psa 119:116
    9) God's Word comforts the Christian, Psa 119:52
    10) God's Word revives the afflicted soul, Psa 107:20; 119:50, 93 (cf. Psa 119:37, 107, 156)
    11) God's Word heals those who cry out to Him, Psa 107:19-20
    12) God's Word chastens the Christian, Psa 94:12 (cf. Heb 4:12; 2 Tim 3:16)
    13) God's Word keeps the believer from sin, Psa 17:4; 119:11 (cf. Psa 119:133)
    14) God's Word formulates the Christian's songs, Psa 119:54, 172 (cf. Col 3:16)

   b. Maintaining life in the Word:
    1) The Christian should put his faith in a God who is true to His Word, Rom 10:17 (see Psa 105:19)

    2) The Christian should give attention to the Word, Prov 2:1; 16:20:

    3) The Christian should listen to the Word, Ezek 3:10

    4) The Christian should observe God's Word, Psa 119:56

    5) The Christian should take God's Word into his heart, Ezek 3:10

    6) The Christian should abide in the Word, John 8:31 (cf. John 15:7)

    7) The Christian should remember God's Word, Psa 119:52

    8) The Christian should let his mind dwell on the Word, Col 3:16 (cf. Col 3:1-2, e.g. Phil 4:8)

    9) "My words shall not depart from your mouth," Isa 59:21 (cf. Jos. 1:8)

    10) "Holding fast to the word of life," Phil 2:16

  c. Living out of fellowship with the Word (note the progression):

    1) Forgetting, Deut 4:9, 23; 8:11, 14, 19; 2 Kings 17:38; Psa 119:139; Prov 3:1

    2) Wandering, Psa 119:10, 21, 118

    3) Disbelieving the Word, Psa 106:24

    4) Not listening to God's voice, Psa 106:25 (cf. Jer 17:23; 36:31; 37:2; 44:5, 16, "we are not going to listen to you!")

    5) Refusing to listen, Jer 13:10 (cf. Jer 12:17)

    6) Turning from the Law, Prov 28:9

    7) Forsaking, Deut 31:16-17, Psa 89:30-34; 119:53, 87 (e.g. I Sam. 15:19-24; Jer 9:12-14)

    8) "Rebelled against the words of God, and spurned the counsel of the Most High." Psa 107:11

    9) Despising the Word, Prov 13:13

    10) Hating the Word of God, Psa 50:17

    11) To Jeremiah the prophet, "You are telling a lie!" Jer 43:2

3. Examples of the Role of God's Word in Christian Nurture:

  a God's Word in follow-up, Acts 8:25; 13:44; 18:11; 20:32

  b. Scripture meditation in the Bible:

    1) The example of the Apostles, Acts 6:2-4

    2) The example of a receptive group, Acts 17:11

    3) The example of right fellowship, Col 3:16

    4) The example and encouragement of Timothy, 2 Tim 3:14-15

Chapter 27 Appendixes

Growth and Development in the Christian Life

1. A Study of the word "grow," αὐξάνω, in the New Testament:

    a. Growth is achieved through God's Word, 1 Pet 2:2, "Like newborn babes, long for the pure milk of the word, that by it you may **grow** with respect to salvation" (αὐξηθῆτε)

    b. Growth is possible in a local church where members are using their gifts, and under sound teaching, Eph 4:11-15 (v 15), "But speaking the truth in love, we are to **grow up** in all aspects into Him, who is the head, even Christ" (αὐξήσωμεν)
        1) Growth is directly related to use of our spiritual gifts, 1 Tim 4:14

    c. Growth is achieved through a decision of the will, 2 Pet 3:17-18 (v 18), "But **grow** in grace and knowledge of our Lord and Savior Jesus Christ. To Him be the glory, both now and to the day of eternity. Amen" (αὐξάνετε):
        1) Growth is achieved through spiritual discipline, 1 Tim 4:7-8
        2) Growth is achieved through being driven to progress spiritually, 1 Tim 4:15
        3) Growth is achieved through perseverance, 1 Tim 4:16

    d. Growth should be the natural by product of the Christian life, both growth in righteousness and in effectiveness, Prov 4:18; 1 Tim 4:12

2. Levels of Nurture for Christian Growth:

    a. God's Word is the foundational catalyst for spiritual growth, 1 Pet 2:2; 2 Tim 3:14-17; cf. Deut 32:45-47.

    b. The Holy Spirit, Rom 8:16; cf. Gal 5:25

    c. Other Christians:
        1) The evangelist, John 15:16
        2) Another Christian, 1 Cor 3:6
        3) The local church, 1 Thess 5:11

Metaphors for the Christian Life

Introduction: Watchman Nee wrote *Sit, Walk, Stand*,[1281] which consists of a commentary on Ephesians in which he sets "forth the believers position in Christ, his life in the world, and his attitude to the enemy." (p. viii) His title provided the seed thought for this study.

1. **WALK**:

    a. Walking and the Godhead:
        1) Walking with God, Gen 5:24
        2) Walk in Christ, Col 2:6-7
        3) Walking in the Spirit, 2 Cor. 10:3; Gal 5:16, 25
        4) Walking to please God, 1 Thess 4:1

    b. Walk in a manner worthy:
        1) Of God, 1 Thess 2:12
        2) Of the Lord, Col 1:10
        3) Of the calling, Eph 4:1-3

    c. Walking and light:
        1) Walking with Christ is walking in the light, John 8:12
        2) Walking in the light of God's countenance, Psa 89:15
        3) Walk as children of light, Eph 5:8
        4) Walk in the light, 1 Jn 1:7

    d. Aspects of the walk:
        1) Walking in love, Eph 5:2, 2 Jn 6
        2) Walking by faith, 2 Cor 5:7
        3) Walking in newness of life, Rom 6:4
        4) Walk uprightly, Psa 84:11
        5) Walk wisely, Eph 5:15
        6) Walking with perseverance, Isa 40:31

    e. Walking and the Bible:
        1) Walk as Christ walked, 1 Jn 2:6
        2) Walk in God's ways, Deut 8:6; 10:12; 11:22; 19:9; 26:17; 28:19; 30:16; Psa 119:3; 128:1
        3) Walk in God's truth, Psa 86:11
        4) Walk according to the commandments, 2 Jn 6; "Make me walk in the path of Thy commandments," Psa 119:35
        5) Walk in the Law of the Lord, Psa 119:1; cf. Psa 78:10
        6) Walk in God's judgments, Psa 89:30
        7) Walk according to the pattern of good men, Phil 3:17

    f. Walking and sin:
        1) Not to walk acording to the flesh, Rom 8:4
        2) Not walking in the counsel of the ungodly, Psa 1:1
        3) Walking in white, Rev 3:6

2. **RUN** (cf. Hab 2:2, Gal 5:7):
    a. Running in God's ways, Psa 119:32
    b. Running with perseverance, Isa 40:31
    c. Running with endurance, Heb 12:1
    d. Running to win, 1 Cor 9:26-27
    e. Running victoriously, 2 Sam 22:30 (cf. Psa 18:29)
    f. Running in vain, Gal 2:2; Phil 2:16

[1281]Watchman Nee *Sit, Walk, Stand* (Fort Washington, PA; Christian Literature Crusade, 1957).

3. **WAIT**:

    a.   The Command to Wait on the Lord, Psa 27:14; 37:34; 46:10; Hos 12:6:
        1) The practice of waiting, Psa 37:3-6
        2) The attitudes of waiting, Psa 84:1-4; Isa 26:8

    b.   Affirmations of waiting on the Lord, Psa 25:5; 130:5-6

    c.   Waiting on God's Word, Psa 119:147 (cf. Psa 130:5, Isa 26:8)

    d.   Results of waiting on the Lord:
        1) Renewed strength, Isa 40:30-31
        2) Keep from shame, Psa 25:3

4. **STAND**:

    a.   Aspects of standing firm:
        1) The admonition to stand firm, Gal 5:1, Eph 6:11, 13, 14; 2 Thess 2:15
        2) The condition of standing firm, 1 Thess 3:8
        3) God's assistance in standing firm, Jude 24-25 (cf. Rom 14:4)

    b.   That in which we should stand firm:
        1) The Lord, Phil 4:1
        2) The faith, Rom 11:20; 1 Cor 16:13; 2 Cor 1:24
        3) The grace of God, Rom 5:2; 1 Pet 5:12
        4) The Gospel, 1 Cor 15:1-2
        5) The traditions which were taught, 2 Thess 2:15

    c.   Standing and unity: Phil 1:27

    d.   Standing and sin: Not "standing in the way of sinners," Psa 1:1

The "One Another" Commands in the New Testament

Introduction In Galatians 6:10 Paul states, "So then, while we have the opportunity, let us do good to all men, and especially to those who are of the household of faith."
  a.   A priority is established for relationships within the body of Christ.
  b.   An enlargement of Psa 37:27, "Depart from evil *and do good,* so you will abide forever."
  c.   Paul in 1 Timothy 3:15 states, "...I write so that you may know how one ought to conduct himself in the household of God, which is the church of the living God, the support and pillar of truth." The following from God's Word is how one ought to conduct himself in the household of God.
  d.   The following study highlights specific commands in the New Testament that include the reflexive term ἀλλήλων or in English "one another."

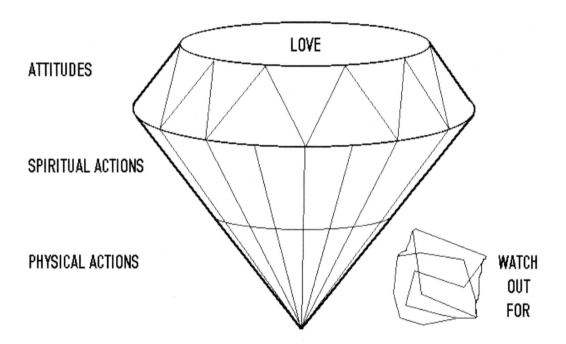

1.   Developing a Loving Attitude:
  a.   Attitudes we need to cultivate as Christians:
    1)   Clothe yourselves with humility toward one another, 1 Pet 5:5
    2)   Have the same mind towards one another, Rom 12:16
    3)   Accept one another, Rom 15:7
    4)   Be devoted to one another, Rom 12:10
    5)   Be subject to one another, Eph 5:21
    6)   Regard the another as more important than yourself, Phil 2:3
    7)   Bear with one another, Eph 4:2, Col 3:13
    8)   Show forbearance for one another, Eph 4:1-2
    9)   Live at peace with one another, 1 Thess 5:13
  b.   Attitudes to watch out for:
    1)   Watch out for a critical spirit, Rom 14:13 (cf. Heb 12:14-15; Rom 2:1-3)
    2)   Watch out for envy, Gal 5:26
  c.   The all encompassing attitude of love (cf. Matt 22:36-40):
    1)   Love one another, John 13:34-35; 15:12, 17; Rom 13:8; 1 Pet 1:22; 4:8; 1 John 3:11, 23; 4:7, 11, 12; 2 John 5; cf. Heb 13:1:
      a)   Love defined, "As I have loved you," John 13:34-35; 15:12

   b) Extent of love explained, "Fervently love one another," 1 Pet 1:22; 4:8
   2) Love is an obligation:
      a) Rom 13:8, it is something we owe our brother
      b) 1 John 3:11; 4:11, "we should love one another."

2. Living Out a Loving Attitude:
   a. General spiritual actions towards one another in the body of Christ (cf. 1 Thess 5:14):
      1) Build up one another, Rom 14:19; 1 Thess 5:11
      2) Admonish one another, Rom 15:14; Col 3:16 (teaching and admonishing)
      3) Encourage one another, 1 Thess 5:11; Heb 3:13
   b. Specific spiritual actions towards one another in the body of Christ:
      1) Speaking to one another with psalms, Eph 5:19
      2) Comfort one another, 1 Thess 4:18
      3) Bear one another's burdens, Gal 6:2
      4) Confess your sins to one another, James 5:16
      5) Consider how to stimulate one another to love and good deeds, Heb 10:24
      6) Pray for one another, James 5:16
   c. Physical actions towards one another in the body of Christ:
      1) Greet one another with a holy kiss, Rom 16:16; 1 Cor 16:20; 2 Cor 13:12; 1 Pet 5:14 ("kiss of
          love")
      2) Care for one another 1 Cor 12:25
      3) Serve one another, Gal 5:13; 1 Pet 4:10
      4) Give preference to one another, Rom 12:10
      5) Be hospitable to one another, 1 Pet 4:9; cf. Heb 13:2
      6) Have fellowship with one another, 1 John 1:7
      7) Be kind to one another, Eph 4:32
   d. Some things to watch for:
      1) Watch your words:
         a) Do not speak against one another, James 4:11 (cf. Prov 26:18-26)
         b) Do not complain against one another, James 5:9
         c) Do not lie to one another, Col 3:9 (cf. John 8:44)
         d) Do not provoke one another, Gal 5:26
         e) Do not bite and devour one another, Gal 5:15 (cf. Prov 11:10; 18:21)
         f) Do not consume one another, Gal 5:15
      2) Watch your actions: Do not repay evil for evil, 1 Thess 5:15
   e. The results of living out a loving attitude:
      1) 1 John 4:12, love for one another proves that God abides in us and is perfecting His love in us.
      2) 2 Thess 1:3, growth in faith is made evident through growth in love, which can be observed.
      3) 1 Thess 4:9-10, the practice of love is clearly visible.
      4) John 13:35, visible love is a witness to the world of an authentic disciple of Christ.

3. Material Dimensions to Christian Relationships, Matt 25:31-46; 1 Cor 16:1-3; 2 Cor 12:15; 1 John 3:17:
   a. Who these commands refer to: "brothers of Mine," "for the saints," "You [those in the Corinthian
       church]," "his brother."
   b. Helping financially, 1 John 3:17
   c. The cost of closing one's eyes:
      1) Judgment, Prov 21:13; 28:27; Matt 25: 25:31-46
      2) No manifestation of God's love, 1 John 3:17

CHAPTER 28
A Graphic Look at Biblical Follow-Up

Introduction:

The Bible is rich in metaphors and terminology for spiritual growth. Some of these concepts have been illustrated in this section to give graphic representation of the walk with God.

The general instruction is as follows:

"So walk ye in Him"

Col 2:6, "As you therefore have received Christ Jesus the Lord, *so* walk in Him, having been firmly rooted *and now* being built up in Him and established in your faith, just as you were instructed, *and* overflowing with gratitude"

"Abound more and more"

1 Thess 4:1 [KJV], "Furthermore then we beseech you, brethren, and exhort *you* by the Lord Jesus, that as ye have received of us how ye ought to walk and to please God, *so* ye would abound more and more"

Translations of ἵνα περισσεύητε μᾶλλον in 1 Thess 4:1

Wycliffe (1388) Young's (1862...)	English Revised (1885) American Standard (1901)	Tyndale (1534) Geneva (1560) Bishops (1595)	New King James (1982)	Darby (1885...)	King James (1611/ 1769) Webster's (1833)	Murdock (1852)	NAS (1977)	NJB* (1985)	DRA* (1899)	New American (1901/ 1991) Revised Standard (1952) Holman Christian Standard (2000) English Standard (2001) New Living Trans (2004) NET (2004)	New Interna-tional (1984)	New Revised Version (1989)	God's Word for the Nations (1995)	Bible in Basic English (1949...)
Abounde /abound the more	Abound more and more	Ye increace/ increase/ encrease more and more	Should abound more and more	Would abound still more	Would abound more and more	Would make progress more and more	May excel still more	Make more progress still	May abound the more	Do so even more	Do this more and more	Should do so more and more	Even more than you already do	More and more
that ye abounde the more	that ye abound more and more	that ye increace more and more	that you should abound more and more	that ye would abound still more	*so* ye would abound more and more	so ye would make progress more and more	that you may excel still more	but make more progress still	that you may abound the more	you do so even more	to do this more and more	you should do so more and more	even more than you already do	but more and more

A. **Stages in Spiritual Growth (2 Peter 1:4-11):**[1282]

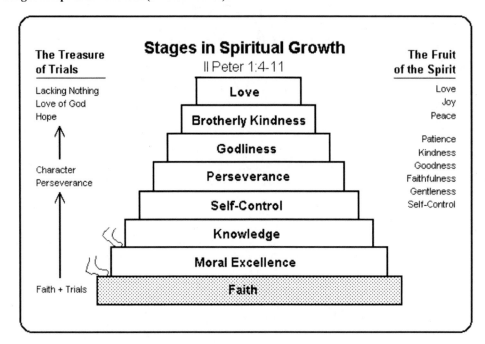

Introduction:
   a. The punctilear: justification, Rom 3:30; 2 Cor 5:21; Col 1:22
   b. The linear: sanctification, Rom 8:29; 1 Thess 4:3; Heb 12:14

1. The biblical context:
   a. The trials of life, Rom 5:3-5; James 1:2-4 (e.g. Jer 20:7-18; Heb 5:8; cf. Jer 6:21; Heb 12:11;
       1 Pet 4:19)
   b. The beatitudes, Matt 5:3-10
   c. Result: the fruit of the Spirit, Gal 5:22-23 (cf. 1 Cor 13:13)

2. Looking at 2 Pet 1:4-11:

   a. The Preceding Context, 2 Pet 1:2-4

   b. The Command, "Applying all diligence supply," 2 Pet 1:5

   c. The Stages and Their Emphases, 2 Pet 1:5-7
       1) Spiritual Qualities:
           a) Faith, Heb 11:6 (πίστις)
           b) Moral Excellence (ἀρετή)
           c) Knowledge (γνῶσις), 1 Cor 8:1

       2) Character qualities:
           a) Self-Control (ἐγκράτεια), Phil. 4:5 (ἐπιεικής)
           b) Perseverance (ὑπομονή), Jms 1:3; Rom 5:3-5 (-> love, cf. 1 John 4:11)

       3) Motivational qualities:
           a) Godliness (εὐσέβεια), 2 Cor 5:11
           b) Brotherly Kindness (φιλαδελφία)
           c) Love (ἀγάπη), 1 Cor 13:13

   [1282]This study was an expansion from a verbal illustration of Eileen Starr, a student at Trinity Evangelical
Divinity School in 1986, as she described her study of spiritual growth in relation to 2 Peter 1:4-11. The Treasure
of Trials is expanded in the following section.

    d.   The results, 2 Pet 1:8-9:
       1) Obedience: growth and fruitfulness, 2 Pet 1:8
       2) Laziness: stagnancy and fruitlessness, 2 Pet 1:9:
          a) Characteristics: blindness or shortsightedness
          b) Reason: Forgetting the greatness of the cross of Christ

    e.   The closing challenge, 2 Pet 1:10-11

B. The Mastery of the Body (1 Cor 9:27):

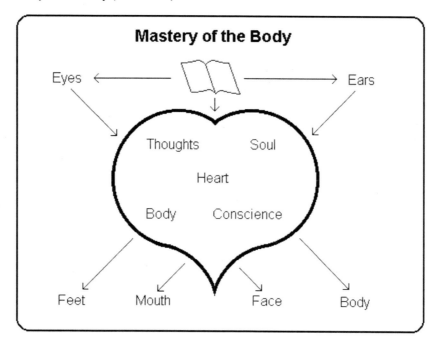

1.   Introduction—the importance of the mastery of the body:
    a.   Principle of Mastering the Body, 1 Cor 6:12; 9:27; 1 Thess 4:4
    b.   The Goal of Mastering the Body:
       1) Living a holy life, Mark 7:14-23; 1 Thess 4:3
       2) Approval from God, 1 Cor 9:27; 1 Thess 4:1
       3) Keeping a pure heart, Psa 78:8; Prov 4:23 (cf. Prov 27:19; e.g. Deut 4:9)
    c.   Mastering the Body, Spiritual Health and Physical Vitality, Prov 3:1-10; 4:20-27
    d.   Mastering the Body and Freedom from Sexual Sin:
       1) 1 Cor 6:12-20
       2) 1 Thess 4:1-8

2.   The Web Relationships:

    a.   The Input:
       1) The centrality of God's Word, Deut 30:14; Jos. 1:8; Psa 1:1-3; 19:7-8; 40:8; 119:11;
          Prov 2:1-5; 3:1; 4:1-2, 21; 5:1-5; 6:20-21; Isa 59:21; Jer 15:16; John 15:3; 17:17; 2 Tim
          3:14-17; Heb 4:12.
       2) Input through the eyes, Psa 19:8; 101:3; 119:15, 18, 30, 37, 82, 123, 148; Prov 4:21-22,
          25; 15:30; 16:2; 23:26; Psa 101:3; Matt 6:22-23; 1 John 2:11, 16
       3) Input through the ears, Prov 2:2; 4:20; 5:1; 15:30-31; 16:24; 17:4; 18:15; 22:17; 23:19;
          26:22.

    b.   The Inner Life (Prov 4:23):
       1) Inner life of the heart, Deut 30:14; Psa 19:7-8; 40:8; 119:11; Prov 2:2; 4:21-23; 15:13,
          30; 16:9, 23; 17:22; 19:3; 26:26; 27:19; Jer 15:16; 31:33; Matt 15:18-19

      2) Inner life of the thoughts, Gen. 4:5-8; Jos. 1:8; Psa 1:1-3; 19:7; 38:18; 119:33-40, 59, 72, 97, 127; Prov 2:11; 4:26-27; 5:2; 12:5; 15:31; 17:28; Rom 12:2; Phil. 4:8; 1 John 2:11

      3) Inner life and the body, Prov 15:30; 16:24; Matt 6:22-23; Rom 12:1; 1 Cor 3:16; 6:19; 9:27; 1 Thess 4:3-5

      4) Inner life of the soul, Prov 16:24

      5) Inner life of the conscience, Job 33:14-30; Prov 6:22 (cf. Rom 2:14-15)

  c. The Output:

      1) The inner life's effect on the path of the feet, Jos. 1:7; Psa 17:5; 119:59, 101, 105, 133; Prov 1:15-16; 2:4; 4:14-15, 26-27; 7:25; 16:2, 9, 17; 19:3; Rom 12:2.

      2) The inner life's effect on what comes out of the mouth, Deut 30:14; Jos. 1:8; Psa 17:3; 33:1; Prov 2:3; 4:24; 10:32; 16:23; 17:27-28; Isa 59:21; Matt 12:36-37; 15:11, 18; James 3:2-12 (esp. v. 6).

      3) The inner life's effect on the face, Gen. 4:5-8; Psa 33:1; 147:1; Prov 15:13, 15; 21:29; 25:23; 26:26; Isa 3:9; Acts 6:15 (cf. Prov 27:19)

         a) Link of the mouth to the countenance, Psa 43:5; Prov 25:23

      4) The inner life's effect on the body, Psa 38:3, 5-8; Prov 3:2, 8; 4:21-22; 16:24; 17:22; Rom 12:1.

3. Mastering the Body:

  a. Sin's Effect (Heb 3:13):

      1) On the body, Psa 32:3-4; Prov 5:11

      2) On the conscience, 1 Tim 4:2

      3) "For their heart continually went after their idols," Ez. 20:16

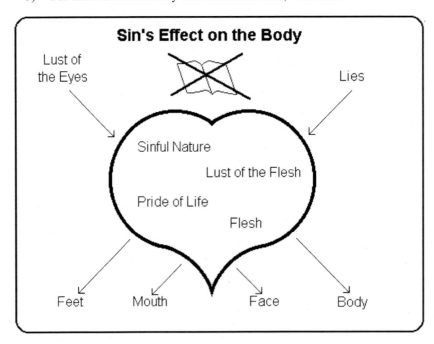

  b. Controlling the Input:

      1) Recognizing attacks on the input:

         a) The lust of the eye: greed, sexual lust, Matt 6:22-23

         b) Attacks on the ear: gossip, Prov 26:22; immoral stories or jokes, Eph 5:3; listening to lies, John 8:44 (cf. Psa 120:2)

      2) Discipline of input through the eyes, Job 31:1; Psa 119:82, 123

      3) The discipline of input through the ears:

         a) Focusing on the good, Prov 2:2; 4:20; 5:1; Isa 55:3; Phil. 4:8; Col 3:1-2

         b) Avoiding and ignoring the bad, Prov 17:4 (cf. Eph 5:3-4)

c.   Mastering the Inner Life:
    1)   Overcoming the fleshly nature:
        a)   The lust of the flesh, 1 Cor 6:10-11; 1 John 2:1-2
        b)   The boastful pride of life, Gen. 4:7; 1 Pet 5:5-7
    2)   Cleansing of the inner life:
        a)   Through the blood of Jesus, 1 John 1:7; Tit. 3:5 (cf. Heb 10:22)
        b)   Through the cleansing of God's Word, John 15:3; 17:17
        c)   Through wisdom and knowledge from God's word, Prov 2:10-22 (cf. Psa 17:4)
        d)   Through controling one's thought life, Prov 12:5; Phil. 4:8

d.   Considering the Output:
    1)   In general:
        a)   The "fruits" of one's life, Psa 1:3-4; Matt. 7:15-20; John 15:1-6
        b)   The role of reflection, Prov 2:11; 4:23; 21:12
    2)   Specifically:
        a)   Keeping the feet from evil, Psa 1:1; 17:5; Prov 4:27; 16:17; Jer 14:10
        b)   Setting a guard over our mouth, Psa 17:3; 120:2; 141:3; Prov 10:19; 30:8; Isa 59:21; Eph 4:29; 5:3-4
        c)   Offering our bodies as slaves to righteousness, Rom 6:11-14.

C. Developing the Spiritual Passions:

Introduction:
    a.   Jesus said that "we cannot serve two masters," Matt 6:24
    b.   Alexander I. Solzhenitsyn wrote, "There is no room in us for two passions."[1283]

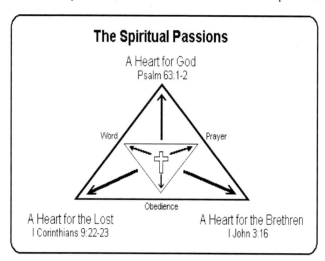

1.   Christ is the center
    a.   A passion to know Christ, Phil 3:8-10
    b.   He is the focus, Rom 8:29; Heb 12:1-2
    c.   We must abide in Him, John 15:1-8; 1 John 2:27-28

2.   Three central passions to Christian growth:

    a.   A passion for the Word, 1 Pet 2:2
        1)   An intense searching in the Word, Prov 2:1-9 (Psa 119:82)
        2)   Developing a heart for the Word, Psa 119:71-72
        3)   The goal: a passion for the Word, Psa 119:40, 97, 105, 131, 147-148

[1283]Alexander I. Solzhenitsyn, *The First Circle* (San Francisco, CA: Harper, 1966), 236.

      b.   A passion for Prayer, John 15:7

          1)   Seeking the Lord in Prayer, Deut 4:29; Jer 29:12-13

      c.   A Passion for Obedience, 1 John 2:3

          1)   The importance of obedience in the Old Testament, Deut 4:1-2, 5, 14, 40; Jos. 1:8; Psa 103:18; 119:57, 60 (see Jos 8:35; 11:15 for examples of obedience)

          2)   The importance of obedience in the New Testament, John 3:36; 14:21; 1 John 2:3-6; 5:2; 2 John 6; Rev 2:5, 26; 3:10 (Christ as an example of obedience, Luke 2:51; Heb 5:7-10)

      d.   Complimentary passions:

          1)   A passion for salvation, Psa 119:81

          2)   A passion for righteousness, Matt 5:6

3.   Growing in these spiritual passions:

      a.   A heart for God, Psa 63:1-2

          1)   Drawing near to God, Jms 4:8

          2)   Seeking God, 1 Chr 16:10-11; 2 Chr 7:14; Isa 55:6-7; Jer 29:12

          3)   A thirsting for God, Psa 42:1-2; 63:1-2; 143:6; Isa 55:1-2; John 4:13-14

          4)   Desiring nothing but God, Psa 73:25

          5)   An intense love for God, Deut 6:5; Matt 22:36-37

          6)   A fear of God, 2 Cor 5:11; 7:1; 1 Pet 2:17 (cf. Jer 2:19)

      b.   A heart for the lost, 1 Cor 9:19-23 (cf. Phil 3:18-19):[1284]

          1)   Following God's example, John 3:16; Rom 5:8

          2)   Obeying God, Mark 1:17; 16:15

          3)   Following Paul's example (e.g. 1 Cor 11:1), 1 Cor 9:19-23; Col 1:28-29

      c.   A heart for the brethren, 1 John 3:16[1285]

          1)   Learning to care for the brethren, 1 Thess 5:11

          2)   "Through love serve one another," Gal 5:13

          3)   Giving one's life for the brethren, John 15:12-13; 1 John 3:16

          4)   Applying all one's efforts, Col 1:28-29

[1284]This attitude is often exemplified in vibrant growth periods in the history of the churches. John Knox said, "Give me Scottland or I die!" John Wesley said, "The world is my parish." William Booth said, "My ambition is the souls of men!" Jim Elliot wrote, "I want to be a fork in the road of every man for or against Christ."

[1285]For greater depth in the Christian's attitudes toward his brothers, please see in T. Johnston, *Mindset,* Chap 11, II.D., "The Special Dimension of Christian Relationships."

D. The Navigator Wheel:[1286]

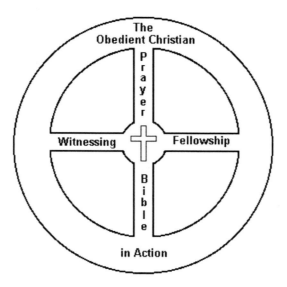

1. Christ the Center: 2 Cor 5:17; Gal 2:20

2. The Obedient Christian in Action: Rom 12:1; John 14:21

3. The Bible: 2 Tim 3:16; Joshua 1:8

4. Prayer: John 15:7; Phil 4:6-7

5. Fellowship (or discipleship): Matt 28:20; He. 10:24-25

6. Witnessing (or evangelism): Matt 4:19; Rom 1:16

E. The Battle Against Sin:

Introduction:

> Transgression speaks to the ungodly within his heart;
> There is no fear of God before his eyes.
> For it flatters him in his own eyes,
> Concerning the discovery of his iniquity and the hatred of it.
> Psa 36:1-2

Surely these verses allude to the unctuous coaxing of temptation in the human heart. Man's mind may wander as these alluring invocations draw him into the Temptor's trap. Even so, James reminds us "and sin when it is accomplished brings forth death." (James 1:15) Sin is never worth its pining pleasure. It always destroys.

Billy Graham associate, Cliff Barrows, speaking at a Billy Graham School of Evangelism (Wheaton College, June 1990) cited five words describing the downward progression of sin. The following are his words with my addition of verses:

a. Casualness, Jms 1:14

b. Carelessness, Prov 14:16

c. Callousness, Eph 4:18-19; Heb 3:13

d. Compromise, 2 Pet 2:15

e. Catastrophe, Prov 29:1

[1286]Used by permission. For an expansion of "The Navigator Wheel" please contact NavPress, Colorado Springs, CO or call 1-800-366-7788.

Likewise:

> "One evening, an old Cherokee told his grandson about a battle that goes on inside people. He said, 'My son, the battle inside all people is between two wolves. One is bad. It is anger, envy, sorrow, regret, arrogance, self-pity, guilt, resentment, inferiority, lies, false pride, superiority and ego. The other is good. It is joy, peace, love, hope, serenity, humility, kindness, benevolence, empathy, generosity, truth, compassion and faith.' The grandson thought about it for a while and asked, 'Which one wins?' The old Cherokee answered, 'The one you feed'"[1287]

1. The Battle:

   a. Iniquity can have dominion over us:
      1) "Do not let any iniquity have dominion over us," Psa 119:133
      2) "Slaves of sin," John 8:34; Rom 6:6, 12, 20
      3) Rom 7:13-23, v. 19, "For the good that I wish, I do not do; but I practice the very evil that I do not wish." (e.g. Psa 65:3)

   b. Sin is in direct opposition to God's working:
      1) "For the flesh sets its desire against the Spirit, and the Spirit against the flesh; for these are in opposition to one another, so that you may not do the things that you please." Gal 5:17
      2) "abstain from fleshly lusts, which wage war against your soul." 1 Pet 2:10
      3) "If anyone loves the world, the love of the Father is not in Him." 1 John 2:15

   c. Examples of the battle's outworking:
      1) Fruit, Matt 7:16-17
      2) Words, Gal 5:15; James 3:9-12; 4:1-3

   d. The Christian and freedom from the dominion of sin:
      1) Called to freedom, Gal 5:13
      2) The Spirit giving freedom, 2 Cor 3:17

   e) Working out that freedom:
      1) Through abiding in the words of Christ, John 8:31-32
      2) Through obeying the teaching of Christ, Rom 6:17-18
      3) Through offering our members as instruments of righteousness, Rom 6:13, 18
      4) Through becoming enslaved to God, Rom 6:22

2. The carnal nature:

   a. The mindset:
      Introduction: Psalm 106 exemplifies the pattern of disobedience found in man's devotion to God.
      1) Synonyms for the carnal mindset:
         a) Unbelieving, Psa 78:22
         b) Rebellious, Psa 78:17, 40, 56; Ezek 2:3-8
         c) Obstinate, Ezek 3:7-8
      2) Results of the carnal mindset:
         a) Forgetting God's deeds, Deut 4:23; 6:12; Psa 78:11, 42
         b) Wandering from the way, Prov 21:16
         c) Speaking against God, Psa 78:19
         d) Deceiving God with one's lips, Psa 78:36
         e) Spiritual defection, Isa 31:6
      3) The carnal mindset and the battle against sin:
         a) "The mind set on the flesh is hostile towards God," Rom 8:7 (cf. 1 John 3:6)
         b) "Those who are in the flesh cannot please God," Rom 8:8
         c) "For the mind set on the flesh is death," Rom 8:6

[1287](From an anomymous email).

    b. The deeds:
        1) "Now the deeds of the flesh are evident":
            a) **Spiritual**: lawlessness, Matt 7:23; unrighteousness, wickedness, Rom 1:29; idolatry, Col 3:5
            b) **Mental**: jealousy, envy, envyings, anger, wrath, malice, evil desire, desires, passion, greed, Rom 1:29; Gal 5:20, 24; Eph 4:19; Col 3:5, 8
            c) **Verbal**: boastful, challenging (one another), murder (cf. Prov 18:21), strife, deceit, enmities, strife, outbursts of anger, disputes, dissensions, factions, slander, abusive speech, bite & devour, Exod 20:16; Gal 5:15, 20, 26, Col 3:8; 2 Tim 3:2
            d) **Physical**: immorality, impurity, adultery, sensuality, murder, idolatry, drunkenness, carousings, every kind of impurity, Exod 20:13-15; Gal 5:19, 21; Eph 4:19; Col 3:5
            e) **Other**: Disobedient to parents, without understanding, untrustworthy, unloving, unmerciful, Rom 1:30-31; 2 Tim 3:2
        2) Terms for those who do the above deeds:
            a) **Spiritual**: Idolaters, Rom 6:9, haters of God, Rom 1:30, unbelieving, sorcerers, idolaters, Rev 21:8
            b) **Mental**: insolent, arrogant, boastful, inventors of evil, lovers of self, lovers of money, haters of good, conceited, lovers of pleasure, cowardly, Rom 1:30; 2 Tim 3:2-4; Rev 21:8
            c) **Verbal**: Gossips, slanderers, malicious gossips, treacherous, liars, Rom 1:29-30; 2 Tim 3:3-4; Rev 21:8
            d) **Physical**: Fornicators, adulterers, effeminate, homosexuals, murderers, immoral persons, Rom 6:9; Rev 21:8

    c. The result of living according to the carnal nature (Prov 11:31; Gal 6:7-8; Heb 2:2):[1288]
        Introduction: Remembering that... Sin is like a cancer that eats away at the soul.
        1) No peace, Isa 48:22
        2) A hard life, Prov 13:15
        3) A troubled life, Prov 12:21; 15:6
        4) Strife, Prov 17:19
        5) Sorrows, Psa 32:10 (e.g. Ps 107:18; Prov 5:11)
        6) Adversity, Prov 15:21
        8) Brings the curse of God, Prov 3:33
        9) Become like chaff which the wind drives away, Psa 1:4
      10) Resting in the assembly of the dead, Prov 21:16

    d. The result of a "Christian" living in sin:
        1) Living in sin for a time with repentance:
            a) The word becomes unfruitful, Matt 13:22
            b) No fruits of repentance, Matt 3:8; not doing the will of the Father, Matt 7:21
            c) Stern discipline (from God), Prov 3:10-11; 15:10; Heb 12:5-8; Rev 3:19
            d) "Repent and do the deeds you did at first; or else I am coming to you, and will remove your lampstand out of its place," Rev 2:5
            e) God giving His people over to their sin, Psa 81:12 (cf. 1 Tim 1:20)
            f) "If any man's work is burned up, he shall suffer loss; but he himself shall be saved, yet so as through fire." 1 Cor 3:15

        2) Continuing in sin without repentance:
            a) Deceitfulness of sin, Heb 3:13
            b) "For the time will come when they will not endure sound doctrine; but *wanting* to have their ears tickled, they will accumulate for themselves teachers in accordance to their own desires; and will turn away their ears from the truth, and will turn aside to myths," 2 Timothy 4:3-4
            c) Falling away from the Lord due to an unbelieving heart, Heb 3:12
            d) Falling away from the faith, 1 Tim 4:1; e.g. Matt 13:21

[1288]Please note the information in T. Johnston, *Mindset,* Chap 3, III.A.-C., which take a look at the fallen nature of man.

e) "You who have forsaken Me," declares the Lord, "You keep going backward. So I will stretch out My hand against you and destroy you; I am tired of relenting!" Jer 15:6

f) "Impossible to renew them again to repentance," Heb 6:4-6

g) Takes branch away, John 15:2, "if anyone does not abide in Me, he is thrown away as a branch, and dries up, and they gather them, and cast them into the fire, and they are burned." John 15:6

h) "I never knew you," Matt 7:23

i) "I will spit you out of My mouth." Rev 3:16

j) "It would be better for them not to have known the way of righteousness, than having known it, to turn away from the holy commandment delivered to them." 2 Pet 2:21 (cf. v. 20)

k) "When God heard, He was filled with wrath, and greatly abhorred Israel." Psa 78:59

l) "How much severer punishment do you think he will deserve who has trampled under foot the Son of God?" Heb 10:29

3. The spiritual nature:

  a. The mindset:
     1) "The mind set on the Spirit is life," Rom 8:6
     2) Abiding in Christ, John 15:1-6
     3) Walking in the Spirit, Rom 8:14

  b. The fruit of the Spirit, Gal 5:22-23; Col 3:12-14

4. Fighting the Battle:

  a. The work of Christ:
     1) The flesh has been crucified with Christ, Rom 6:6; Gal 2:20; 5:24
     2) "Consider yourself to be dead to sin," Rom 6:10-11 (cf. Col 3:5; 1 John 2:29)

  b. Putting to death the flesh:
     1) Lay aside the old self, Eph 4:22; Col .3:9
     2) Making no provision for the flesh, Rom 13:14
     3) "Putting to death the deeds of the body," Rom 8:13
     4) Abstain from fleshly lusts, 1 Pet 2:11
     5) "Depart from evil," Prov 16:17

  c. Living in the Spirit:
     1) "be transformed by the renewing of your mind," Rom 12:2
     2) " be renewed in the spirit of your mind," Eph 4:23
     3) "Set your mind on things above," Col 3:2
     4) "If we live by the Spirit, let us walk by the Spirit," Gal 5:25
     5) "For all who are being led by the Spirit of God, these are the sons of God," Rom 8:14
     6) "Put on the new self," Eph 4:24; Col 3:10, 12-14 (cf. 2 Cor 5:4)
     7) "Though the body is dead because of sin, yet the spirit is alive because of righteousness," Rom 8:10
     8) Pursuing righteousness, Prov 15:9
     9) Hungering and thirsting for righteousness, Matt 5:6
     10) "Slaves to righteousness," Rom 6:18-19

  d. Recommended prayer whenever temptation knocks at the door:

     "Father, I pray in the name of Your Son, the Lord Jesus Christ, that you will rebuke the evil one, help me to resist the Devil and to say 'no' to my sinful nature..."[1289]

[1289]This prayer was a suggestion of Pastor Lester Nelson of the Crystal Evangelical Free Church, given in December, 1991. The verses listed following the prayer were also the suggestion of Pastor Nelson. This list can be expanded to meet any of a number of needs. He suggested that a list of these verses may be kept in one's Bible for personal use, as well as for reference in "care giving" situations when encouraging other believers.

At this point a pertinent verse should be added, dealing with temptation in general or perhaps focusing on the particular temptation being faced.

1. Envy, 1 Cor 13:4; James 3:16
2. Love, John 15:9
3. Forgiveness, 1 Cor 10:13; Psa 25:11
4. Self-worth, Eph 2:10; Luke 4:13
5. Anxiety, Phil 4:6

5. Aspects of freedom from sin

   a. Renewed Desire:
      1) "Freedom from sin" the continual cry of the godly man, Psa 119:133 (cf. Psa 119:8, 176; 139:23-24)
      2) The place of the contrite heart, Psa 51:17; Matt 5:3-6
      3) God giving the desires of the heart, Psa 37:4

   b. God's Word:
      1) Freedom in the truth through abiding in the Word, Psa 17:4; 119:9; John 8:31-34 (cf. Prov 16:17)
      2) Freedom from the bondage of sin, through commitment to the truth, Rom 6:17-18

   c. Ministry: Freedom from selfishness for the sake of ministry, 1 Cor 9:19-23; 10:31-33 (cf. 2 Cor 12:15)

F. The Way of Obedience:

1. The Way of Obedience:
   a. A walk of faith, Heb 11:6
   b. A walk of grace, Eph 2:8-10
   c. A walk of obedience, Psa 119:1-3, 33-35, 44-48; James 1:22
   d. The reward of obedience, Psa 18:20-24

2. The Way of Disobedience:[1290]
   a. Forgetting God's Word: Deut 8:11, 14, 19; Psa 119:139 (e.g. Jer 18:15)
   b. Wandering from God's Word, Psa 119:118
   c. Disobeying God's Word, 1 Sam 15:19; 1 Chr 10:13-14
   d. The Word of God becomes a reproach, Jer 6:10
   e. Forsaking God's Word, Psa 119:53
   f. Rejecting God's Word, Jer 6:19
   g. Despising God's Word, 2 Sam 12:9

3. The Path of repentance:
   Introduction: Psa 119:58-60:
      1) The humble cry of the heart, Psa 119:58
      2) The turn of repentance, Psa 119:59
      3) The decision of the will, Psa 119:60
   a. The discipline of God, Psa 107:17-18; 119:67, 75, 176; Prov 3:11-12; 15:10; Heb 12:5-7 (e.g. Exod 20:26, "that I might make them desolate")
   b. Discipline leading to the fear of the Lord, Psa 119:120, 161; Heb 12:9-11; cf. Psa 118:18, e.g. Psa 107:10-16
   c. Plea of the heart to obey, Psa 119:8-10, 17, 33-34, 88,107:
      1) Repentance, Acts 2:38
      2) Forgiveness, 1 John 1:9
   d. Decision of the will to obey, Psa 119:30, 44, 106, 112 (cf. 2 Pet 2:22)
   e. The result: a deepened knowledge of God's Word (Psa 119:72) allowing continued growth and obedience, Psa 119:67.

[1290]T. Johnston, *Mindset*, Chap 1, IV.E.2.c., "Living out of fellowship with the Word," portrays the decline in the believer's relationship to the Word of God.

CHAPTER 29
Visitation Initiative—
Toward a Local Church Evangelism Strategy

Introduction:

Diagnostic Questions for Local Church Analysis:
- a. When do the unsaved hear the Gospel in our local church ministry?
  - 1) How do you know that those who are reached are unsaved?
  - 2) Is there a concerted effort to reach the unsaved through this ministry?
- b. When are the lost given an opportunity to commit their lives to Jesus Christ?
  - 1) Do they have the opportunity to receive salvation in Christ?
  - 2) How is their commitment confirmed?
  - 3) Are there solid avenues for the follow-up (and discipleship) of new converts?
- c. Are Christians being trained in personal evangelism through our church ministry?
  - 1) Does the church have a systematic training program for those interested?
  - 2) Are they given opportunities to share their faith and apply what they learn?
- d. Does our church have any type of accountability structure to encourage believers to continue in evangelism?
  - 1) How are they held accountable?
  - 2) Are there support groups in place to encourage the weary?

Are the above questions valid?
- a) If so, is the church accomplishing its first priority?
  - 1) If it is not accomplishing its first priority, why not?
- b) What needs to be done to help it accomplish its first priority?
  - 1) The following are some general points of encouragement

The next section seeks to answer two questions:

Why do we emphasize evangelism?

How do we emphasize evangelism?

I. Some Emphasis in Ministry Verses:

1. Emphasis Outward:
   a. At least three of the five Great Commission emphasize proclamational evangelism, pointing the church outward to a lost world
   b. Ephesians 4:11 includes three current ministers (if apostles and prophets are considered ceased gifts):
      1) Evangelists—outward focus
      2) Pastors—inward shepherding focus
      3) Teachers—inward teaching focus
   c. The Great Commission forces us to look out. Of the three leaders provided to the church, the evangelist is the leader with an outward focus.
   d. Like the evangelist Paul was encouraged by God to look outwardly:

   Acts 18:9-10, "And the Lord said to Paul in the night by a vision, 'Do not be afraid *any longer*, but go on speaking and do not be silent; for I am with you, and no man will attack you in order to harm you, for I have many people in this city.'"

2. Emphasis Inward:
   a. "Make disciples" in the Matthew 28 Great Commission passage can be made to have an almost exclusive inward emphasis, whereas, "teaching them to obey" in Matt 28:20 certainly does focus inwardly
   b. Two of the three leaders in Ephesians 4:11 have an inward focus: pastors and teachers

    c. Pastors are called to "shepherd the flock of God," Acts 20:28, 1 Peter 5:1-4

    d. Other verses point to the importance of relationships within the local church:

       1) The priority of relationship among believers, Galatians 6:10

       2) The 62 "one another" commands focus on relationships within the fellowship of the local church

3. Inward emphasis or outward emphasis? How can this apparent conflict be solved in the ministry of the local church? Can they both be in operation simultaneously?

    a. A look at the evangelistic strategy of the apostle Paul:

       1) Acts 17:16-17—in the synagogue (1) Jews, (2) Gentiles, and in the marketplace (3) whoever happened to be present

       2) Rom 1:14-17—to the Jew first, and also to the Greek

       3) But then, you say, that was the evangelistic strategy, not the church ministry strategy ...

    b. When churches were founded in cities, Paul visited the churches and ministered:

    Acts 11:20-26, "But there were some of them, men of Cyprus and Cyrene, who came to Antioch and *began* speaking to the Greeks also, preaching the Lord Jesus. And the hand of the Lord was with them, and a large number who believed turned to the Lord. And the news about them reached the ears of the church at Jerusalem, and they sent Barnabas off to Antioch. Then when he had come and witnessed the grace of God, he rejoiced and *began* to encourage them all with resolute heart to remain *true* to the Lord; for he was a good man, and full of the Holy Spirit and of faith. And considerable numbers were brought to the Lord. And he left for Tarsus to look for Saul; and when he had found him, he brought him to Antioch. And it came about that for an entire year they met with the church, and taught considerable numbers; and the disciples were first called Christians in Antioch"

    Acts 14:21-23, "...They returned to Lystra and to Iconium and to Antioch, strengthening the souls of the disciples, encouraging them to continue in the faith, and *saying*, 'Through many tribulations we must enter the kingdom of God.' And when they had appointed elders for them in every church, having prayed with fasting, they commended them to the Lord in whom they had believed"

    Acts 15:41; 16:5, "And he was traveling through Syria and Cilicia, strengthening the churches ... So the churches were being strengthened in the faith, and were increasing in number daily"

    Acts 16:40,"And they went out of the prison and entered *the house of* Lydia, and when they saw the brethren, they encouraged them and departed"

    Acts 19:1, "He found some disciples [in Ephesus]"

    Acts 20:7, "On the first day of the week, we assembled to break bread"

    Acts 20:17-38 [Address to Ephesian elders]

    Acts 21:4, "So we found some disciples, and stayed there [Tyre] seven days"

    Acts 21:7, "We reached Ptolemais where we greeted the brothers and stayed with them one day"

    Acts 28:14, "There we found believers and were invited to stay with them for seven days"

    c. Did the apostle continue evangelizing cities after churches were already founded there?

       1) While this leads to a certain argument from silence, certain hints are found toward the end of the Book of Acts (including Acts 18:9-10), along with material on Paul's ministry in the epistles (e.g. 1 Corinthians 9; 2 Corinthians 5-6; Colossians 1, etc.)

       2) e.g. Appolos evangelized the Jews in Ephesus, though it seemed that a church was already founded there—although the church may not yet have separated from the synagogue in that town, Acts 18:28 (cf. Acts 19:8-9).

       3) Paul evangelized in Rome (Acts 28:30-31), although a church was already founded in that town, as the believers from that church (or the churches) met Paul at the Appii Forum and the Three Taverns (Acts 28:14-15).

       4) Rom 1:15, "Thus, for my part, I am eager to preach the gospel to you [or "evangelize with you"] also who are in Rome"

To whom is any congregation ministering?

The Following are ideas based on knowledge of six distinct groups of people that a congregation should minister to (placed in order of importance, as long as all are being ministered to):

    1. Absentees, Luke 15

    2. Shut-ins, 1 Thessalonians 5:14

    3. Members, Acts 20:28

    4. Regulars, Acts 20:28

5. Visitors, 1 Corinthians 14:22 (could this not describe visitors?)
6. Community outreach, Acts 17:16-17
   Including groups, such as schoolteachers, the police, firemen, and other public authorities

The following notes have combined these six groups into four:

Absentee and visitor names can be tabulated from a Friendship Register or from a form that every attendee fills out every Sunday morning. Those that are ushering, on nursery duty, in choir, or on the platform may be left out, depending on when and how the form is filled in and collected.

It is recommended that Absentee names (kept by family last name) be collected in groups, such as A-1 (absent one Sunday), A-2 (absent two Sundays in a row), A-3 (absent three Sundays in a row), and A-4+ (absent four or more Sundays in a row). A similar procedure may be used for Visitors: V-1 (first time guest), V-2 (second time guest), V-3 (third time guest), and V-4 (fourth time guest). There are computer software packages available to assist churches in keeping these type of records. The following is based on a church having these names available for ministry.

I. Absentee Care-Giving, Luke 15:4-7; I Thessalonians 5:14:

A. Goal: To nurture those who have been absent from our fellowship and minister to the needs of those who may be drifting

B. Who?   The Church Secretary, the Shepherding Team (Pastors & Deacons) & the Care Giving Team

C. What?—Some ideas—these need to be decided upon by church leaders:
   1. Following the First Absence (A-1): Information Ministry (send them a bulletin with a handwritten note from someone), Telephone Contact (to see if there is a health or some other need)
   2. Following the *Second Absence* (A-2): Information Ministry Care-Giving Ministry (a team of trained Care-Givers visit all A-2s)
   3. Following the *Third Absence* (A-3): Information Ministry.

II. Member and Regular Care-Giving, Acts 20:28:

A. Goal: To visit in the homes of members and regulars every year

B. Who? The Church Secretary and the Shepherding Team (Pastor and trained deacons)

C. What? Someone from Shepherding Team visits the homes of all members and regulars once every 6 months.

III. Guest Evangelism and Enfolding, John 13:34-35:

A. Goal: To lovingly reach out with the Gospel to those who have come to us and enfold them into our fellowship.

B. Who? The Church Secretary, the Senior Pastor, the Intercessory Team, the Cookie Coordinator, the Care-Giving Team, the Hospitality Team and the Prayer Chain Ministry Leader.

C. What? (again, these need to be decided upon and tweaked by church leaders)
   1. Following 1st Sunday morning visit (V-1):
      a. Personal Handwritten Note from Pastor, Deacon, or Sunday School teacher;
      b. Intercessory Prayer Team: Designated intercessors begin to pray for names;
      c. Cookie/Muffin/Coffee Mug Ministry brings something to the home;
      d. Care-Giving Ministry: Trained care-givers visit the home and meet spiritual need encountered (if a decision is made for Christ in any of the Care-Giving visits, this moves them into another category not dealt with in this material).
   2. Following 2nd Sunday morning visit (V-2):
      a. Small Group [or Sunday School] Ministry. They are contacted and invited by an age-appropriate Sunday School class
      b. Hospitality Ministry: Someone is prepared to invite 2nd time visitors to lunch—the Sunday School is a good mechanism for this ministry

3. Following 3rd Sunday morning visit (V-3):

   a. Engraved New Testament: They are given an engraved New Testament with their initials and receive a second Care-Giving Visit

4. Following 4th Sunday Morning Visit (V-4):

   a. Prayer Chain Ministry: If they are saved, they are invited to consider being placed on a prayer chain (preferably with their Sunday School class or Small Group)

   b. Directory Ministry: A church directory is brought to their house, and their names are recorded for future editions of the Directory if they are interested.

IV. Community Outreach, Matthew 22:9; Acts 1:8; 17:17:[1291]

A. Goal: To have a **weekly** program geared to reaching the lost in our community with the Gospel, through any and every method available—care giving visitation and/or door-to-door visitation are encouraged here.

1. This weekly program is not meant to replace or supersede annual special events (Halloween, Thanksgiving, Christmas, or Easter), revivals, Vacation Bible School, or other such events.

2. This weekly program is designed to assist Block Parties, Servant Evangelism projects, etc.

3. Community outreach is designed to assure that a weekly evangelism thrust is taking place into the community.

B. Who? The Care Giving Team—they are dividing their time with the Guest Evangelism and Enfolding—or another team can be set up.

C. What? Three sample approaches:

1. Door-to-door with a needs-type questionnaire, getting into the Gospel

2. "Welcome Wagon" type of ministry—to new water hook-ups in the area (these names are available from the Water Company, but do not give information on apartment dwellers)

3. Street evangelism

4. Jail ministry

5. Brainstorms by Care-Giving Team à la *Conspiracy of Kindness* by Steve Sjogren.

V. Discussion Items for Evangelism:

A. Should not the pastors and deacons work together in care-giving as a *Shepherding Team*?

B. Should the regular care-giving responsibilities of the congregation be equally divided between pastors and deacons?

C. Given that one person can have vital contact within a group of no more than 80 people, if the church is larger, how should the congregation be divided?

1. Along relational lines

2. By geographical situation

3. By ministry or age (e.g. Sunday School classes)

4. In some other way?

D. The bigger question is: As a church grows, how is it best divided – by ministry ages (Sunday School), by cell-group or in geographical format?

E. Should non-members be allowed to be a part of our church's visitation teams?

VI. Making It Happen in the Local Church:

Introduction: The three "Es" mentioned by Darrell Robinson need to be kept in mind:[1292]

Exaltation

Edification

Evangelism

[1291]Mark Mittelberg's *Building a Contagious Church* (2000) not only contains numerous ideas for community outreach, it also provides the organizational structure to do it in the local church.

[1292]See Darrell Robinson, *Total Church Life* (Nashville: Broadman, 1997).

Implimentation: "Flake's Formula" for local church implimentation should be remembered here:
1. Discover the prospects
2. Expand the organization
3. Train the workers
4. Provide the space
5. Go get the people.[1293]

VI. Resources:

Robert Coleman, *The Master Plan of Evangelism* (Old Tappan, NJ: Fleming H. Revell Publishing, 1963)

Larry Gilbert, *Team Evangelism: How to Influence Your Loved Ones for Christ When You Don't Have the Gift of Evangelism* (Church Growth Institute; Lynchburg, VA, 1991)

Bill Hull, *Jesus Christ Disciple Maker, The Disciple Making Church,* and *The Disciple Making Pastor* (Old Tappan, NJ; Fleming H. Revell Company, 1984, 1990, 1988 respectively)

Lessons in Assurance, NavPress.

Ralph Neighbour, Jr. *The Shepherd's Guidebook* (Houston, TX; Touch Publications, Inc., 1988)

_____. *Where Do We Go from Here? A Guidebook for the Cell Group Church*, (Houston, TX; Touch Publications, Inc., 1990)

Darrell Robinson, *Total Church Life* (Nashville: Broadman, 1997)

Steve Sjogren, *Conspiracy of Kindness* (Ann Arbor, MI; Servant Publications, 1993)

SonLife Ministries, *Foundations for Youth Ministry* seminar (Wheaton, IL; SonLife Ministries, 1989)

R. Alan Streett, *The Effective Invitation* (Old Tappan, NJ: Revell, 1984).

[1293]See Charles Kelley, *How Did They Do It? The Story of Southern Baptist Evangelism* (New Orleans: Insight, 1993), 93.

Chapter 29 Appendixes

Church Evangelism: Schedules and Timing

There are times and seasons in the life of a church. The wise pastor will know how to lead his congregation into maximum effectiveness without burning them out. The following are ideas for the timing of various outreach programs in the local church, allowing perennial programs of evangelism with different levels of commitment and involvement. They are ideas that have been used in churches and do work.

Local Church

Weekly Outreach Schedule Ideas:

1. Weekly Visitation: Many churches find that a weekly visitation program is very effective in allowing for perennial evangelism. The implication is that the same thing is done every week. These are usually divided into two types of evangelism:

   a. Visiting visitors;

   b. Door-to-door visitation.

   This type of visitation normally involves the pastor, deacons, and/or other church leaders, as well as other interested people.

2. Varied Weekly Visitation: I have found that many urban churches will have different visitation programs on different Saturdays of the month, for example:

   a. First Saturday of the month: visit the local prison or jail;

   b. Second Saturday of the month: door-to-door visitation in the neighborhood of the church;

   c. Third Saturday of the month: visit the local nursing home;

   d. Fourth Saturday of the month: visit and assist at the homeless shelter;

   e. Fifth Saturday of the month: gather for training and prayer.

   Often, one person from each adult Sunday School class is designated as the evangelist to represent the class in these varied activities.

Monthly, Quarterly, or Seasonal Evangelism Events:[1294]

Quarterly one-day evangelism event:

One-day block parties;

Wild Game Night;

Women's Night Out.

Seasonal evangelistic events:

Super Bowl Party;

Easter Egg Hunt;

Fall festival;

Christmas pageant.

Depending on the size, interest, and location of the church, these events can be run on a quarterly or monthly basis.

[1294]For a number of examples see: *High Impact Events* (Alpharetta, GA: North American Mission Board, 2008).

Planning a High Impact Revival (once a year or twice a year):

In order to prepare for a host a High Impact Revival, preparation is of ultimate importance. Properly publicizing within the congregation and within the community can make a big difference. Inviting a God-called evangelist is also very important.[1295]

1. Plan for the revival at least one year in advance (if possible). This way you can often find an evangelist before he is booked up:

   It may be helpful to change around the revivals year-by-year or twice-a-year by using different venues and emphases:

   Tent revival;

   Youth revival;

   One-day revival;

   Sunday-to-Sunday revival;

   Association-wide revival.

   Remember to check the various civic calendars when planning a revival. If there is a major school event (school graduation or senior prom), or something like the Super Bowl or County Fair, these may negatively impact attendance. Your people should now about the important events in their town.

2. Six months before the revival, call together a special committee to head up the revival. Follow the Revival Preparation Manual provided by the evangelist, and make use of his publicity at the appropriate time;

3. Three months before the revival:

   Prepare the congregation by helping them focus on prayer for lost souls and prayer for the evangelist;

   Committees should be active in preparing various aspects of the revival: venue details, publicity details, working committees planning their role.

4. Host the evangelist, giving him time to prepare his heart for preaching.

5. Expect great things:

   Plan for a baptismal service on the closing night, while the evangelist is there. It will really encourage him!

   A follow-up committee should be in place to follow-up all contacts within 2 or 3 days of the end of the revival services.

A Month-by-Month Outreach Schedule:

June-July-August: designating summer months of the year for certain types of evangelism:

   a. The summer months (June, July, August) for door-to-door visitation (outdoors): e.g. one Saturday a month in June and July, every Saturday in August;

   b. The fall, winter, and spring months for member and regular visitation (indoors).

This idea:

   Takes the weather into consideration, allowing for ongoing evangelism when the weather is usually best for being outside;

   It also allows the church to meet new people who moved into the community during the summer months;

   Further, it feeds a new members initiative in the fall of the year.

[1295]See Keith Fordham and Tom Johnston, *The Worth and Work of the Evangelist* (Liberty, MO: Evangelism Unlimited, 2013).

September through November: designating the fall months for new member assimilation:

    a.   September for new member recruitment (resulting from Summer outreaches):

    b.   October and November for new member classes.

November and December: Christmas activities and events

January: January Bible Conference

February through May: revival or special evangelism event preparation:

    February: prayer emphasis;

    March: training in personal evangelism;

    April: canvas neighborhoods and publicize the revival or special event;

    May: host the revival and/or implement the special event

Associational Evangelism Ideas

Originally designed not just for fellowship between like-minded churches, the main purpose of church associations is the furthering of the Great Commission in and through the church association. There are three elements to the fulfilling of the Great Commission through associational missionaries and their associations:

1. Fostering, developing, and facilitating evangelism through the ministry of the association;

2. The multiplication of churches in the association; and

3. The revitalization of churches that already exist.

Association-wide evangelism efforts can be conducted in a number of ways. Two of them are simultaneous revivals and area crusades.

Simultaneous revivals:

Working with willing churches to plan and time a simultaneous revival two years into the future. The most important thing is to get buy in from the pastors of several churches, and to set a date that fits with the schedule of the churches and communities in question.

In a simultaneous revival, all the participating churches will have their revival at exactly the same time. Publicity will be coordinated centrally, publicizing all the participating churches, their pastors, and their evangelists.[1296] Often, the closing session of the simultaneous meeting can be in a larger civic auditorium and bring together people from all the participating churches.

Area crusades:

Area crusades are also organized to reach whole communities for Christ. Perhaps more difficult than the simultaneous revivals to get buy-in, these area-wide crusades take several years of planning in order to be effective.

Decisions must be made such as:

    a.   Who should be invited as a musician or evangelist to draw a crowd?

    b.   What churches will we invite to participate, and what churches will we not invite?

[1296]An excellent example and introduction to the simultaneous revival can be found in C. E. Matthews' two books: *The Department of Evangelism and the Simultaneous Revival Program* (Dallas: Baptist General Convention of Texas, 1946) and *The Southern Baptist Program of Evangelism* (Atlanta: Home Mission Board, SBC, 1949). It must be kept in mind that the simultaneous tent meetings was first used by Evangelist J. Wilbur Chapman in Pittsburg, Pennsylvania, in 1904. In 1908 the "Chapman-Alexander Simultaneous Campaign" launched its first simultaneous campaign in Philadelphia with great success. He divided the city of Philadelphia into 42 zones, worked with 21 evangelists, holding the simultaneous revival in half the city one week, had one week break in between, and held a simultaneous revival in the other half of the city in week three. The simultaneous revival method was also used by Billy Graham throughout the 1950s an into 1960s.

    c. What venue will we use, and how much will it cost? Can we handle the cost?

Church planting:

Associational missionaries can be targeting needy areas in his association for church planting. He can then direct local churches in his association to concentrate their home evangelism strategies in seeding these areas with the gospel in order to prepare for a church plant. A revival can be planned in the designated area to kick-off the church plant, and begin to develop the synergy of people needed to start an evangelistic church.

Six-month associational proposed church planting strategy:

    a. First month: designate location for church plant, with the help of the Evangelism Committee of the association;

    b. Second month:

        1) With the help of the Evangelism Committee, select a church planting pastor to head up the operation;

        2) Choose a name for the church plant; and

        3) Divide up evangelism initiatives in Months 3-5 between local associational churches, having them take one-week time slots for a select evangelism effort.

    c. Third through fifth months:

        1) Saturate the designated area with: prayer walking, door-to-door evangelism, and special events, all in the name of the new church plant; and

        2) The task of the church planter during this time will be to direct and oversee the evangelism efforts and the immediate follow-up of converts and contacts.

    d. During month six, the focus will change to the revival meetings:

        1) Evangelism efforts will include the revival meeting evangelist, dates, and venue; and

        2) The church planting pastor will focus his energies on assuring that the revival is a success, and the all contacts up to date attend the revival.

    e. Host a week-long, Sunday to Sunday revival meeting in the name of the local church within the designated area, using a God-called evangelist:

        1) The evangelist will introduce the pastor in the final Sunday morning service;

        2) The new pastor will baptize converts from the revival service on Sunday evening; and

        3) A new church will be well into its early stages of development.

Church revitalization:

Sponsoring, organizing, and implementing revivals in declining churches;

Hosting training clinics in declining churches, using books such as:

Chuck Lawless, *Discipled Warriors*; or

Arnold C. Cook, *Must My Church Die?*

Training and sending traveling praise teams and preachers from other associational churches.

Denominational Evangelism Ideas

Communication in the technological age:

Communication is changing very quickly. These ongoing changes impact how we publicize and how we make information and materials available to churches, pastors, and leaders.

It also changes the timelines for evangelism planning efforts. Some timelines can be reduced by more than half because of the ease of instant communications, Internet video conferencing, and the speed of transportation—if necessary.

Planning a five-year denominational evangelism effort:

Year One—Developing the Plan:

Planning and denominational leadership buy-in; and

Cooperation from every denominational agency, including the distribution of tasks and efforts.

Year Two—Formalizing the Plan:

Leadership recruitment for denominational effort;

Promotion to state leadership; and

Literature preparation.

Year Three—Communication and Leadership Recruitment:

Further promotion of effort to state leaders;

Promotion to associational leaders, and pastors;

Promotion to pastors and church leaders;

Sign-up and recruitment of grassroots leaders.

Year Four—Sunday School Recruitment:

Grassroots recruitment of whole churches, whole associations, whole state conventions

Inviting people to Sunday School and/or church[1297]

E.g. "A Million More in '54.

Year Five—Harvest:

Harvest revivals

E.g. simultaneous revivals in 1955.

[1297]Most will come if merely invited!

George Vasser's Church Planting (1537)

From: Thieleman J. van Braght, *The Bloody Theater or Martyrs Mirror of the Defenseless Christians Who Baptized Only Upon the Confession of Faith, and Who Suffered and Died for the Testimony of Jesus, Their Savior, From the Time of Christ to the Year A.D. 1660*, trans from the Dutch by Joseph Sohm, 2nd English edition (1660; 1837; 1886; Scottdale, PA: Herald Press, 2007), 446.

"George Vasser, and Leonhard Sailer, A.D. 1536

"In this year, Goerge Vasser, a minister of the Lord and His church, and Brother Leonard Sailer, his companion, were apprehended in Neudorf, in Austria, where they were passing through, and put in the stocks there. The next day, the Judge of Metling, and the whole council, as also other people with them, came and asked them on what account they were imprisoned there. They replied: 'For the faith of Christ, and the divine truth.'

"They then took them, and brought them into the market town of Metling, a distance of several furlongs from Neudorf, and two leagues from Vienna. On the whole way they testified with great boldness to the truth, and with many words declared to them the judgment of God, so that the Judge and all the others were amazed and dared not say a single word against it. Thereupon they put them into the common prison, in which they met all manner of ungodly and shameful impropriety on the part of their fellow prisoners, which daily caused them great sorrow of heart, so that they would rather have been cast into an offensive dungeon where they would not have been obliged to listen to this impiety.

"During their imprisonment they were much questioned with regard to infant baptism, the sacrament, and that we call them all ungodly and unbelieving; but they told them, that, as regards infant baptism, they were entirely welcome to it, and also said: "Because they call themselves Christians, but falsely bore the name of Christ, and did not move with a finger the least in Christ's commandments; therefore they should know that they were of the devil (John 8:44); and if they would not repent of their sins, God would destroy their false boast, so that they, along with the whole world, and the rich man would be cast into the abyss of hell, which would certainly come to pass, though they now did not believe it. Having been in prison nearly a whole year, and being fully prepared for death; yea, of good courage and cheer, and joyful in the Lord, they prayed that the Lord, the gracious God, would deliver them from this mortal tabernacle, and this wicked blind world; for they had a good hope and a great joy and a sincere desire to depart, and expected every hour, to die manfully and boldly, through the help and power of God, for the divine truth, and for the name of our Lord Jesus Christ, notwithstanding the pain and suffering, which might be inflicted upon them.

"However, through a special providence of God, they were wonderfully liberated, unharmed in their consciences, and came in peace to the church at Trasenhofen, and were joyfully received in the spirit, as good, worthy and beloved brethren.

"Further account of George Vaser, A.D. 1537

"In the following year, at the request of some of the zealous, the above mentioned George Vaser, was sent to Pechstall, in Austria, where he gladly began to teach the Word of God, notwithstanding he had just come out of prison in Metling. He gathered a group of believers, and established a church, according to the command of God. But he could not escape a certain deceiver, a genuine tool of all treachery, who, under a false appearance, pretended to learn the grounds of the truth of him as a minister, but, in the meantime appointed many servants, commanding them at a suitable time to apprehend George Vaser, which they faithfully did.

"He was then subjected to much cruel torturing, and while in prison was tempted in manifold ways; but he remained steadfast and faithfully followed unto death Him whom he had proclaimed in the faith; thus testifying with his blood (being executed with the sword), to the faith and the truth of God."

Recommendation from the Past:
Gilbert Tennent's 1740,
"The Danger of an Unconverted Ministry"

Source: Rev. Gilbert Tennent (1703-1764), "The Danger of an Unconverted Ministry" (from the Soli Deo Gloria title *Sermons of the Log College,* now out of print) (online); available at: http://www.sounddoctrine.net/Classic_Sermons/Gilbert%20Tennent/danger_of_unconverted.htm; accessed 20 Oct 2008; Internet.

"And Jesus, when He came out, saw much people and was moved with compassion towards them, because they were as sheep not having a shepherd." Mark 6:34

As a faithful ministry is a great ornament, blessing, and comfort, to the church of God (even the feet of such messengers are beautiful), so, on the contrary, an ungodly ministry is a great curse and judgment. These caterpillars labor to devour every green thing.

There is nothing that may more justly call forth our saddest sorrows, and make all our powers and passions mourn in the most doleful accents, the most incessant, insatiable, and deploring agonies, than the melancholy case of such who have no faithful ministry! This truth is set before our minds in a strong light in the words that I have chosen now to insist upon, in which we have an account of our Lord's grief with the causes of it.

We are informed that our dear Redeemer was moved with compassion towards them. The original word signifies the strongest and most vehement pity, issuing from the innermost bowels. But what was the cause of this great and compassionate commotion in the heart of Christ? It was because He saw much people as sheep having no shepherd. Why, had the people then no teachers? O yes! They had heaps of Pharisee-teachers that came out, no doubt, after they had been at the feet of Gamaliel the usual time, and according to the acts, cannons, and traditions of the Jewish church. But, notwithstanding the great crowds of these orthodox, letter-learned, and regular Pharisees, our Lord laments the unhappy case of that great number of people who, in the days of His flesh, had no letter guides, because those were as good as none (in many respects), in our Savior's judgment. For all them, the people were as sheep without a Shepherd.

From the words of our text, the following proposition offers itself to our consideration: that the case of such is much to be pitied who have no other but Pharisee-shepherds, or unconverted teachers.

[and so began this powerful First Great Awakening sermon that called believers to leave churches with unconverted preachers, to join under the ministry of a converted preacher, preached by the son of William Tennent, founder of the Log Cabin School, which became Princeton College, and later Princeton University. Here are some further excerpts:]

They often strengthen the hands of the wicked by promising him life. They comfort people before they convince them, sow before they plow, and are busy in raising a fabric before they lay a foundation. These foolish builders do but strengthen men's carnal security by their soft, selfish, cowardly discourses. They do not have the courage or honesty to thrust the nail of terror into sleeping souls.

Nay, sometimes they strive with all their might to fasten terror into the hearts of the righteous, and so to make those sad whom God would not have made sad! And this happens when pious people begin to suspect their hypocrisy, for which they have good reason, I may add that, inasmuch as Pharisee-teachers seek after righteousness, as it were, by the works of the law themselves, they therefore do not distinguish as they ought between Law and Gospel in their discourses to others. ...

And isn't this the reason why a work of conviction and conversion has been so rarely heard of for a long time in the churches till of late, that the bulk of her spiritual guides were stone-blind and stone-dead?

4. The ministry of natural men is dangerous, both in respect of the doctrines and practice of piety. The doctrines of original sin, justification by faith alone, and the other points of Calvinism, are very cross to the grain of unrenewed nature. And though men, by the influence of a good education and hopes of preferment, may have the edge of their natural enmity against them blunted, yet it's far from being broken or removed. It's only the saving grace of God that can give us a true relish for those nature-humbling doctrines; and so effectually secure us from being infected by the contrary. Is not the carnality of the ministry one great cause of the general spread of Arminianism, Socinianism, Arianism, and Deism, at this day through the world?

And alas! What poor guides are natural ministers to those who are under spiritual trouble? They either slight such distress altogether and call it "melancholy," or "madness," or daub those that are under it with untempered mortar. Our Lord assures us that the salt which has lost its savor is good for nothing. Some say, "It genders worms and vermin." Now, what savor have Pharisee-ministers? In truth, a very stinking one, both in the nostrils of God and good men. "Be these moral Negroes never so white in the mouth (as one expresses it), yet will they hinder instead of helping others in at the strait gate." Hence is that threatening of our Lord against them in Matthew 23:13: "Woe unto you, Scribes and

Pharisees, hypocrites; for ye shut up the Kingdom of Heaven against men; for ye neither go in yourselves, nor suffer those that are entering to go in."…

And indeed, my brethren, we should join our endeavors to our prayers. The most likely method to stock the church with a faithful ministry, in the present situation of things, the public academies being so much corrupted and abused generally, is to encourage private schools, or seminaries of learning, which are under the care of skilful and experienced Christians; in which those only should be admitted who, upon strict examination have, in the judgment of a reasonable charity, the plain evidences of experimental religion. Pious and experienced youths, who have a good natural capacity, and great desires after the ministerial work, from good motives, might be sought for, and found up and down in the country, and put to private schools of the Prophets, especially in such places where the public ones are not. …

4. If the ministry of natural men is as it has been represented, then it is both lawful and expedient to go from them to hear godly persons; yea, it's so far from being sinful to do this that one who lives under a pious minister of lesser gifts, after having honestly endeavored to get benefit by his ministry, and yet gets little or none, but finds real benefit elsewhere, I say, he may lawfully go, and that frequently, where he gets most good to his precious soul. He may do this after regular application to the pastor where he lives for his consent, proposing the reasons thereof when this is done in the spirit of love and meekness, without contempt of any, and also without rash anger or vain curiosity. …

Must we leave off every duty that is the occasion of contention or division? Then we must quit powerful religion altogether, for he who will live godly in Christ Jesus, shall suffer persecution. And particularly, we must carefully avoid faithful preaching, for that is wont to occasion disturbances and divisions, especially when accompanied with divine power. 1 Thessalonians 1:5–6: "Our gospel came not unto you in Word only, but in power," and then it is added that they "received the Word in much affliction." And, the Apostle Paul informs us in 1 Corinthians 16:9 that a great door, and an effectual one, was opened unto him, and that there were many adversaries. Blessed Paul was accounted a common disturber of the peace as well as Elijah long before him, and yet he left not off preaching for all that. Yea, our blessed Lord informs us that He came not to send peace on earth, but rather a sword, variance, fire, and division, and that even among relations (Matthew 10:34–36; Luke 12:49, 51–53). And also, while the strong man armed keeps the house, all the goods are in peace.

It is true, the power of the gospel is not the proper cause of those divisions, but the innocent occasion only. No, the proper and selfish lusts are the proper cause of those divisions. And very often natural men, who are the proper causes of the divisions aforesaid, are wont to deal with God's servants as Potiphar's wife did by Joseph; they lay all the blame of their own wickedness at their doors, and make a loud cry! …

Again, it may be objected that the aforesaid practice tends to grieve our parish-minister, and to break congregations in pieces.

I answer, if our parish-minister is grieved at our greater good, or prefers his credit before it, then he has good cause to grieve over his own rottenness and hypocrisy. And as for breaking congregations to pieces upon the account of people's going from place to place to hear the Word with a view to getting greater good, that spiritual blindness and death that so generally prevails will put this out of danger. It is but a very few that have gotten any spiritual relish. The most will venture their souls with any formalist, and be will satisfied with the sapless discourses of such dead drones. …

I beseech you, my dear brethren, to consider that there is no probability of your getting good by the ministry of Pharisees, for they are no shepherds (no faithful ones) in Christ's account. They are as good as none, nay, worse than none upon some account. For take them first and last, and they generally do more hurt than good. They strive to keep better out of the places where they live; nay, when the life of piety comes near their quarters, they rise up in arms against it, consult, contrive, and combine in their conclaves against it as a common enemy that reveals and condemns their craft and hypocrisy. And with what art, rhetoric, and appearances of piety, will they varnish their opposition of Christ's kingdom? As the magicians imitated the works of Moses, so do false apostles, and deceitful workers imitate the apostles of Christ.

I shall conclude the discourse with the words of the Apostle Paul from 2 Corinthians 11:14–15: "And no marvel; for Satan himself is transformed into an angel of light: Therefore it is no great thing if his ministers also be transformed as the ministers of righteousness; whose end shall be according to their works."

Spurgeon's 1856 Sermon, "Gospel Missions"

"Gospel Missions, by C. H. Spurgeon" (online); available at: http://www.wholesomewords.org/etexts/ spurgeon/chsmiss.html; accessed: 5 Nov 2008; Internet. [preached when Spurgeon was 22 years old]

"And the word of the Lord was published throughout all the region." Acts 13:49

I SHALL not confine myself to the text. It being an old custom to take texts when we preach, I have taken one, but I shall address you, at large, upon a subject which I am sure will occupy your attention, and has done for many days and years past — the subject of gospel missions. We feel persuaded that all of you are of one mind in this matter, that it is the absolute duty as well as the eminent privilege of the Church to proclaim the gospel to the world. We do not conceive that God will do his own work without instruments, but that, as he has always employed means in the work of the regeneration of this world, he will still continue to do the same, and that it becomes the Church to do its utmost to spread the truth wherever it can reach the ear of man. We have not two opinions on that point. Some churches may have, but we have not. Our doctrines, although they are supposed to lead to apathy and sloth, have always proved themselves to be eminently practical; the fathers of the mission were all zealous lovers of the doctrines of the grace of God; and we believe, the great supporters of missionary enterprise, if it is to be successful, must always come from those who hold God's truth firmly and boldly, and yet have fire and zeal with it, and desire to spread it everywhere. But there is a point on which we have great division of opinion, and that is as to the reason why we have had so little success in our missionary labours. There may be some who say the success has been proportionate to the agency, and that we could not have been more successful. I am far from being of their opinion, and I do not think they themselves would express it on their knees before Almighty God. We have not been successful to the extent we might have expected, certainly not to an apostolic extent, certainly with nothing like the success of Paul or Peter, or even of those imminent men who have preceded us in modern times, and who were able to evangelize whole countries, turning thousands to God. Now, what is the reason of this? Perhaps we may turn our eyes on high, and think we find that reason in the sovereignty of God, which hath withholden his Spirit, and hath not poured out his grace as aforetime. I shall be prepared to grant all men may say on that point, for I believe in the ordination of everything by Almighty God. I believe in a present God in our defeats as well as in our successes; a God as well in the motionless air as in the careering tempest; a God of ebbs as well as a God of floods. But still we must look at home for the cause. When Zion travails, she brings forth children; when Zion is in earnest, God is in earnest about his work; when Zion is prayerful, God blesses her. We must not, therefore, arbitrarily look for the cause of our failure in the will of God, but we must also see what is the difference between ourselves and the men of Apostolic times, and what it is that renders our success so trifling in comparison with the tremendous results of Apostolic preaching. I think I shall be able to show one or two reasons why our holy faith is not so prosperous as it was then. In the first place, *we have not Apostolic men;* in the second place, they *do not set about their work in an Apostolic style;* in the third place, we have *not Apostolic churches* to back them up; and in the fourth place, we have not *the Apostolic influence of the Holy Ghost* in the measure which they had it in ancient times.

I. First, WE HAVE FEW APOSTOLIC MEN IN THESE TIMES.

II. In the second place, WE DO NOT GO ABOUT OUR WORK IN AN APOSTOLIC STYLE.

… I have one more remark to make here with regard to the style in which we go to work. I fear that we have not enough of the divine method of *itinerancy.* Paul was a great itinerant: he preached in one place, and there were twelve converted there; he made a church at once; he did not stop till he had five hundred; but when he had twelve, he went off to another place. A holy woman takes him in; she has a son and daughter; they are saved and baptized — there is another church. Then he goes on; wherever he goes the people believe and are baptized, wherever he meets a family who believe, he or his companion baptizes all the house, and goes about his way still forming churches and appointing elders over them. We, now-a-days, go and settle in a place, make a station of it, and work around it by little and little, and think that is the way to succeed. No, no! ravage a continent; attempt great things and great things shall be done. But they say if you just pass over a place it will be forgotten like the summer shower, which moistens all, but satisfies none. Yes, but you do not know how many of God's elect may be there; you have no business to stop in one place; go straight on; God's elect are everywhere. I protest if I could not itinerate this country of England, I could not bear to preach. If I preached *here* always, many of you would become gospel hardened. I love to go ranging here, there, and everywhere. *My* highest ambition is this, that I may be found going through the entire land, as well as holding my head quarters in one position. I do hold that itinerancy is God's great plan. There should be fixed ministers and pastors, but those who are like apostles should itinerate far more than they do.

III. But I have a third thing to say which will strike home to some of us: that is, that WE HAVE NOT APOSTOLIC CHURCHES.

IV. But lastly, as the result of the other things which have gone before, and perhaps partly as the cause of them too, WE HAVE NOT THE HOLY SPIRIT IN THAT MEASURE WHICH ATTENDED THE APOSTLES.

Recommendation from the Past:
Charles Thwing's 1888 *The Working Church*

Charles F. Thwing [D.D.], *The Working Church* (New York: Baker and Taylor, 1888, 1889), 125-26.

Note. – In answer to the question "What can the ordinary church do to reach the masses?" the Rev. Dr. D. A. Reed (Proceedings of the Second Convention of Christian Workers in the United States and Canada, Sept. 21-28, 1887, p.32) has suggested these methods: - "In concluding, let me summarize: 'What can the ordinary church do to reach the masses?'

"(1) Let the services of the church be simple, pleasing, and attractive.

"(2) Have special evangelistic services in the evening, with good music.

"(3) Have a well-manned Sunday-school, with building suitable for class-rooms for a large number of adult classes; also where classes can meet during the week for literary and social purposes.

"(4) Have educational classes, and lectures on certain evenings, on the great burning questions of the day, by live, earnest men.

"(5) Where a church numbers over three hundred, have two pastors, or a pastor and a trained assistant, devoting his whole time to the work, under the direction of the pastor or supplementing him.

"(6) Make much of personal work, the efforts of individuals whose hearts are full of love for souls. Have a band of men and women trained in the Bible, who shall know how to use it and love to use it, ready to work in all meetings of an evangelistic character in the inquiry-room, ready to go and see individuals and converse with them about their spiritual needs, wise to win souls.

"(7) Have the parish districted, and find out where the people attend church, if possible; and if they do not attend, go for them and invite them, not once but many times.

"(8) Have branch chapels or cottage prayer-meetings, or both, in the districts where fewest people attend church. They will often go into these places when they will not go into the church.

"(9) Have a sufficient number of visitors for each district, so that too many families will not be given to any one.

"(10) Have classes into which those who are converted can enter and be instructed in the great doctrines of Christianity, and taught how to study the Bible with profit and pleasure, and how to engage in some form of Christian work.

"(11) Set the converts to work, watching, directing, encouraging them until they get to love it and consecrate themselves to it. Show them, by the teaching and example of pastor and older Christians, that the great aim of the church is to bear true witness to the gospel of Jesus Christ and save men. Show each Christian that he or she has a personal work to do with persons; that money and prayers are not sufficient; that sympathy and love and personal solicitude for the comfort and salvation of men are what the masses need.

"(12) Money, brains, consecration, and the aid of the Holy Spirit will enable any ordinary church to win the masses."

Toward Becoming an Evangelistic Pastor

Introduction:

Not having arrived myself, but in constant need of rejuvenating an evangelistic spirit, I write these notes as a pastor to pastors.

The following notes are suggestions for the pastor to develop and/or maintain an evangelistic heart. It is very likely that pastors can and will become embroiled in the cares of the world, the deceitfulness of riches, and the desire for greater things, just as any other Christian. Therefore, comes the question, are there tangible ways to develop or maintain an evangelistic spirit? Please consider the following suggestions based on John 4:35.

> *John 4:35, "Do you not say, 'There are yet four months, and then comes the harvest'? Behold, I say to you, lift up your eyes, and look on the fields, that they are already white for harvest."*

The question becomes, how do we lift up our eyes and look on the fields to see that they are white for harvest?

1. **"Behold, I say to you":**
   a. Begin by asking God for a heart for the lost
   b. Memorize and meditate on key verses on evangelism, such as John 4:35-38, 1 Cor 9:16-23, and 2 Cor 5:20-6:2, to put them on your tongue and in your heart that you may do them (cf. Deut 30:14)
   c. Notice the example of the Apostle Paul in Athens, who shared the Gospel daily:

   > *Acts 17:16, "Now while Paul was waiting for them at Athens, his spirit was being provoked within him as he was beholding the city full of idols. [17] So he was reasoning in the synagogue with the Jews and the God-fearing Gentiles, and in the market place every day with those who happened to be present.*

   Is this an example that you should follow? Ask God to give you the will and the opportunity.
   d. Also memorize 1 Cor 15:10 and Eph 5:15-16, as well as the Great Commission passages: Matt 28:18-20; Mark 16:15; Luke 24:44-49; John 20:21; and Acts 1:8

2. **"Lift up your eyes, and look on the fields":**

   a. Begin a program of door-to-door visitation to meet people in your church field who have nothing to do with your church, but are still your responsibility to reach:
      1) Starting from the neighborhood of the church, begin a systematic plan of door-to-door visitation of every home [saturation evangelism]
      2) Be sure to seek to share the Gospel in every home, to gauge people's responsiveness to the Gospel, which is the whole purpose of the exercise
      3) Be sure to pray with the people for their needs, even if they are not responsive to the Gospel
      4) Even one hour of door-to-door visitation can be a life-changing experience!

   b. Begin a prayer list of lost people you encounter in your church field—its length over time will break your heart, and show you the white harvest in a very short time!

   c. If you say, "door-to-door will not work in my area," then you have already negated a wonderful methodology through which you can actually meet and reach some of the people in your church field. Just because you are going door-to-door does not mean that you have to be nasty about it. Be loving, gracious, respectful, and bold.

3. **"That they are already white for harvest":**

   a. By faith expect people to be receptive to the Gospel the first time you speak with them; God has prepared them for you to "go and tell"

   b. By faith, always include a presentation of the simple Gospel in every sermon, along with an invitation to receive Christ

   c. Use stories of your actual evangelism opportunities in your sermons to encourage the saints in fulfilling the Great Commission

    d.   Begin organizing interested church members to join you in door-to-door visitation, they will provide you with fellowship and accountability in the work of the evangelist

    e.   Invite an evangelist to your church:
        1)   To help make evangelism the main focus of the church
        2)   To lead lost people to Christ and encourage the saints
        3)   To jump start a ministry of evangelism
        4)   To learn about the harvest from this gifted man.

    f.   Invite an evangelist on your staff or begin supporting an evangelist, and let your people hear how God is using this man in evangelism.

Conclusion: If you do these things, you will be well on your way to developing and maintaining a heart for the lost, which, by the way, needs to be continually nurtured throughout your ministry! You will quickly become obedient to God's command for all pastors: "Do the work of an evangelist!" (2 Tim 4:5).

Evangelism and the Lord's Supper

Introduction: Communion provides an interesting touch-stone to a theology of conversion and evangelism. A progression is delineated in the Chart below that exemplifies a slide that can take place in a theology of the Lord's Supper as it is related to evangelism. In this regard, one may recall the struggles related to Solomon Stoddard's "Half-way Covenant."

1	2	3	4	5	6	7	8	9	10	11	12
Communion only for those properly baptized				Communion only for those who are born again				Communion as an evangelistic tool		Communion as a sanctifying tool	
Baptized within a particular church	Baptized within a particular church association	Baptized as a believer (by immersion only)	Water baptized (may include infant baptism)			Open to all believers, regardless of baptism		Communion open to all regardless of conversion		Communion is an act leading to conversion	
Always giving a warning	Always giving a warning	Always giving a warning	Always giving a warning	Always giving a warning	Sometimes giving a warning	Framing the warning in a positive sense	Never giving a warning	Participation in Communion as a type of proclamation of the Gospel to the lost	Participation in Communion as a way to connect with God	Participation in Communion as a way to receive grace from God	Participation in Communion as a way to cooperate with the grace of God
Close-Close	Close*	Close/Open	Open**	Open	Open	Open	Open	Open	Open	Open	Open
Conversionistic					Non-Conversionistic					Salvific	
Particular Atonement				General Atonement							
Memorial						Presence				Con-sub-stantia-tion	Tran-sub-stantia-tion

*Close refers to "Close Communion," meaning that the Lord's Supper is limited to Christians, Baptized as indicated.
**Open refers to "Open Communion," meaning that the Lord's Supper is given more openly or generally, within the specified limitations.

Some further questions on the Lord's Supper:

Does it matter when the warning of 1 Cor 11:27-32 is not spoken at the celebration of the Lord's Supper?
Can the warning of 1 Cor 11:27-32 be restated in a positive way only, and yet still remain a warning?

Does it matter when the distinction between the saved and the lost is no longer made when giving/taking the Lord's Supper?
Is conversion really that important in taking the Lord's Supper?

Can the Lord's Supper rightly be given to lost people as a "proclamation of the Gospel" (cf. 1 Cor 11:26)?
Can the words of Paul in 1 Cor 11:27-32 be overruled by a higher purpose, that being:
  (1) Taking the opportunity to proclaim the Gospel, or
  (2) Providing the opportunity to infuse some level of grace [or the Holy Spirit, or Christ Himself] into the [dead?] soul of the lost person?
What is the implication to a theology of conversion if the Gospel can be savingly communicated to lost souls through giving them a piece of bread [and some juice]?
Or, is it the words of the Gospel proclaimed prior to giving lost people the bread and the cup that communicates the Gospel?

Is the warning of 1 Cor 11:27-32 always to be stated when giving the Lord's Supper?
Is the Lord's Supper for believer's only?
Is the Lord's Supper for baptized believer's only?

Where have our Baptist forefathers stood on this issue?
Where they right to take this stand?
Was this stand cultural or biblical-derived?

CHAPTER 30
Four Categories of Evangelism Programs

Introduction:

Notice the background of the struggle described in 1 Thess 3:6:

"That you always have good remembrance of us, greatly desiring to see us, as we also *to see* you"

What was the churches last memory of Paul?

Was it not Jason being brought before the authorities by the Jews, and being forced to give "a pledge" [ἱκανός] (Acts 17:8) due to the aggressive evangelism methodology of Paul?

[Geneva] "Notwithstanding when they had receiued sufficient assurance of Iason and of the other, they let them goe"

Was there a struggle over the evangelism methodology of Paul? It seems likely from that context

Yet in the case of Thessalonica, God overruled, and they remained open to fellowship with Paul

Which joy provides the only context for a non-evangelistic use of the verb "evangelize" [εὐαγγελίζω] in the New Testament (1 Thess 3:6)

That being coupled with the fact that they were walking in the faith (see 1 Thess 2:17-3:9)

By the way, struggles over methodology are not uncommon:

See also in Galatians:

How to preach? Pauline or not, Gal 1:8-9

Who to please? God or men, Gal 1:10

What to require? Circumcision or not, Gal 2:3

Whom to reach? Jews or Gentiles, Gal 2:7

How to reach? Not to forget the poor, Gal 2:10

Also note:

The hypocrisy in this area of:

False brethren, Gal 2:4

[Consider what he called them because of their divergent views on evangelism (preaching and conversion)]

Peter himself: "But when Cephas came to Antioch, I opposed him to his face, because he stood condemned," Gal 2:11

Certain men from James [τινας ἀπὸ Ἰακώβου], Gal 2:12

The party of the circumcision, Gal 2:12

Barnabas, Gal 2:13

Paul's unbending zeal in this area:

"For I would have you know, brethren, that the gospel evangelized by me is not according to man. For I neither received it from man, nor was I taught it, but *I received it* through a revelation of Jesus Christ," Gal 1:11-12

"But we did not yield in subjection to them for even an hour, so that the truth of the gospel might remain with you," Gal 2:5

"Those who were of reputation contributed nothing to me," Gal 2:6

Those of reputation are listed: "James and Cephas and John, who were reputed to be pillars, … and Barnabas," Gal 2:9

"I opposed him [Cephas/Peter] to his face," Gal 2:11

The relationship of method and message:

"But even though we, or an angel from heaven, should evangelize you contrary to that how we evangelized you, let him be accursed. As we have said before, so I say again now, if any man is evangelizing you contrary to that which you received, let him be accursed," Gal 1:8-9

"But we did not yield in subjection to them for even an hour, so that the truth of the gospel might remain with you," Gal 2:5

Notice the insertion of the word "message" in Galatians 2:6 in the NIV, NJB, GWN, and NET Bible:

Thereby forcing the application of the discussion as being "message" not "method"

[It seems that out of the thousands of manuscripts available to the Geman Bible Society, the word "message" appears in none in this part of Gal 2:6, so it has to be added to the NIV translation, rather than to the next so-called "critical edition" Greek text (perhaps there is still a chance for them to find it in some manuscript)]

Note the chart on Galatians 2:6 at the end of Chapter 10

While there are dozens and dozens of evangelism methods (see my *Charts for a Theology of Evangelism*), these notes will consider four major methods with local church evangelism programs available in our day:

1.   Initiative Evangelism Programs

2.   Lifestyle and Relational Programs

3.   Servant Evangelism Programs

4.   Special Event Evangelism

5.   Other

I. Initiative Evangelism Programs:[1298]

General Definition: Initiative Evangelism Programs—Programs that organize members to take the initiative in sharing their faith with visitors to church, strangers, friends, family, and neighbors.

Key Verse: Luke 14:23, "And the master said to the slave, 'Go out into the highways and along the hedges, and compel *them* to come in, so that my house may be filled.'"

General Strengths and Weaknesses (from student interaction):

Weaknesses:
Gospel sharing can become mechanical
"Cheese-factor"—can make the Gospel presentation sound cheesy
Getting people to do it
Does it address the questions that people are asking (e.g. heaven?)
Weekly visitation: can it burn out people? Is this rather a sign of laziness or fruitlessness?
Time commitment (FAITH requires 3.5 to 4 hours in one night; many split it into two nights)
Difficult to keep motivated for 13 weeks
Sometimes seen as program rather than tool

Strengths:
Gives a venue for the church to fulfill the Great Commission
Tied to the command "Go!"
Continually places the priority of evangelism before the people
Helps give people confidence
Equips the saints
Gain confidence in sharing the Gospel
Experienced people can then learn to share naturally in lifestyle situations
A memorized Gospel plan:
Keeps conversation on track
Ties Scripture to each point
Brings visit to [spiritual] conclusion

Other negative comments against initiative evangelism:
"You should not have to initiate conversations about Jesus, people will come to you"
"Most people truly want to hear the Gospel, it's the methods that we use that they do not like"

[1298]The order of these programs is chronological, as is possible to discern.

"If you serve people, they will see Jesus in you, which will then open up natural opportunities to share Christ"

"Preach the Gospel as often as you can, and if necessary use words" (ascribed to [St] Francis of Assisi)

Fill in the following blanks with one of the following types of evangelism: initiative evangelism, street preaching, street evangelism, door-to-door evangelism, tract evangelism, confrontational evangelism, aggressive evangelism, cold-turkey evangelism, etc.

"_____ is wrong!"

"_____ is unbiblical!"

"_____ is not my gift!"

"I have had bad experiences with _____!"

May the reader have his own convictions (Rom 14:4-5). And may the readers convictions fall into line with the biblical material on evangelism (2 Tim 3:17).

A. *Evangelism Explosion* (D. James Kennedy)—Initiative Evangelism[1299]
   History of Evangelism Explosion:[1300]

   1962, After he started ministering at a church plant which became Coral Ridge Presbyterian church, D. James Kennedy was invited to preach a revival in Decatur, GA, by a pastor he had known from seminary, Kennedy Smart

   Kennedy went out during the day in door-to-door evangelism, and D. James Kennedy preached in the evenings.

   Pastor Smart brought D. James Kennedy with him, and D. James Kennedy was sold on the necessity for this kind of evangelism

   1962-1967, D. James Kennedy led this kind of evangelism in his church, experimenting with various training delivery styles

   1967, D. James Kennedy held his first training clinic for pastors

   1970, D. James Kennedy published his first edition of *Evangelism Explosion* (Wheaton, IL: Tyndale House, 1970, 1977, 4th ed., 1994, 1996)

   1995, Evangelism Explosion was in every sovereign nation in the world

   2000, Evangelism Explosion was in every nation and territory of the world

   Methodology:
   Getting Contacts—oriented to (1) church visitors, (2) prospects, (3) new persons in town, and (4) strangers [my addition of categories 2-4]
   Gospel Plan Introduction:
   Their Secular Life
   Their Church
   Our Church
   Testimony
   Two Questions

[1299]"Many Christians can take comfort in the fact that the founder of Evangelism Explosion has not always been a soul winner. By his own admission, Dr. James Kennedy said he did not attempt to reach people for Christ because of a serious "back problem." He said the ailment involved a "wide yellow stripe that ran up his spine and connected to his jawbone." He was a shy minister who had trouble turning any conversation toward Christ. Ironically, a friend invited Kennedy to be the guest "evangelist" in a revival meeting. The majority of their time was spent visiting those who were known to be lost. During these personal visits, it became very apparent that the young Kennedy did not possess evangelistic skills. The hosting pastor assumed the evangelist's role and led over fifty people to Christ that week. Kennedy returned home both humiliated and challenged. He prayed for God to help him overcome his fears and reach out to the lost around him. The new dynamic of intentionally sharing the gospel transformed his church of seventeen people. As the senior pastor of Coral Ridge Presbyterian Church in Fort Lauderdale, Florida, his weekly messages are televised throughout America and in over fifty other international regions. He founded Evangelism Explosion and the principles of this approach to witnessing has been taught in over one hundred countries. Fear is not a legitimate reason to remain quiet about the gospel. It is something God can use to make us dependent and obedient servants of his. God used an evangelistic coward to launch a worldwide emphasis on evangelism. He could do the same through you or me" (from Bill Bright, *The Greatest Lesson I've Ever Learned*, [1991], 122–29).

[1300]From Leon Pannkuk, EE Regional Coordinator, special lecture, Midwestern Baptist Theological Seminary, 2 March 2006.

Gospel:
 Grace
 God
 Man
 Christ
 Faith

B. *Continuing Witness Training* or *CWT* (HMB/NAMB)—Initiative Evangelism

History:[1301]
 1969-1972, under Director of Evangelism, Kenneth Chafin, personal evangelism became the new method of Southern Baptist evangelism; expanding from C. E. Autrey's Cultivative Commitment Witnessing program, Chafin introduced the WIN—Witness Involvement Now program and the LES—Lay Evangelism School.
 1973-1982, C. B. Hogue developed three programs for personal evangelism: WOW—Win Our World, TELL—Training for Lifestyle and Leadership, and CWT—Continuous Witness Training. The Latter, CWT, won the field and became the backbone of Southern Baptist personal evangelism until 1997.
 1989-1997, Darrell Robinson also championed CWT during his tenure at the HMB. However, it was discontinued in 1997.
 The CWT approach was quite similar in many respects to Evangelism Explosion. The message portion of CWT was changed to become less like EE and more like the Roman Road approach to the Gospel.

Methodology:[1302]
 F.I.R.E.
 Family
 Interests
 Religion
 Exploratory Questions
 Gospel:
 God's Purpose
 Our Need
 God's Provision
 Our Response.

C. *Share Jesus Without Fear* (William Fay)

The Five Questions:
 1. Do you have any kind of spiritual beliefs?
 2. To you, who is Jesus Christ?
 3. Do you think there is a heaven and hell?
 4. If you died, where would you go? If heaven, why?
 5. If what you are believing is not true, would you want to know?

Share Scriptures:
 1. Rom 3:23
 2. Rom 6:23
 3. John 3:3
 4. John 14:6
 5. Rom 10:9-10
 6. 2 Cor 5:15
 7. Rev 3:20

[1301]Information from Charles Kelley, Jr., *How Did They Do It? The Story of Southern Baptist Evangelism* (New Orleans: Insight, 1993).

[1302]For more detail, see Alvin Reid, *Introduction to Evangelism* (Nashville: Broadman, 1998).

Bring to Decision:
1. Are you a sinner?
2. Do you want forgiveness of sins?
3. Do you believe Jesus died on the cross and rose again?
4. Are you willing to surrender your life to Jesus Christ?
5. Are you ready to invite Jesus into your life and into your heart?

What to Ask When Someone Receives Christ:
1) How many sins has Christ paid for? (1 John 2:2)
2) How many of your sins does Christ remember? (Heb 10:17; 2 Cor. 5:17)
3) Where does Christ live? (Gal 2:20)
4) Let's pray
5) Who has been praying for you?
6) Do you know where your friend goes to church?
7) Do you know your friend's phone number? Let's call him now!
8. May I take you to church?
9) Read the Gospel of John.
10) I will call you tomorrow to see if the Word became different.

D. *People Sharing Jesus* (Darrell Robinson)

Distinctives

1. Four stages of Preparation:
   a. The Soil Preparation Stage
      "When God's revived people respond to Him in surrender and obedience, they permeate their community with the presence of the living Lord.
      "... The change that God has wrought in your life affirms the Gospel and prepares the soil of a community to receive the seed of the Gospel."[1303]
   b. The Sowing Stage
   c. The Cultivation Stage
   d. The Harvest Stage

2. Seven steps in leading a person to Christ:
   a. Begin the conversation (using FIRM: Family, Interests, Religion, Message)
   b. Present the plan of salvation
   c. Ask the person to receive Christ
   d. Lead the person to pray
   e. Guide into assurance
   f. Instruct the new believer
   g. Follow-up.

E. F.A.I.T.H. (Lifeway)

Outline (copyrighted):
Faith
Available
Impossible
Turn
Heaven

Basically runs along the lines of EE or CWT, with one primary exception:
1. It is Sunday School based, so that each Sunday School class has a participating member (helps in three weaknesses in initiative programs, helpful in: [1] recruiting regular personnel for outreach, [2] providing accountability in evangelism, and [3] assisting in follow-up). In so doing, FAITH makes a philosophical link between CWT and Arthur Flake's *Building a Standard Sunday School* (1934).

[1303]Darrell Robinson, *People Sharing Jesus* (Nashville: Thomas Nelson, 1995), 135.

F. A historical biographical look:

Thwing, Charles Franklin. *The Working Church,* New York: Baker and Taylor, 1888; rev. ed. 1889; New York: Revell, 1913.

Wood, Verda. *Ringing Door Bells : the Art of Visiting.* Nashville: Baptist Sunday School Board, 1946.

Neighbour, Ralph W. Jr. *Knocking on Doors—Opening Hearts.* Houston: Touch, 1990.

II. Lifestyle and Relational Programs:

Some preliminary food for thought on relational approaches:

How are good works perceived by lost people?

As a reproach?

2 Cor 2:15-16, "For we are a fragrance of Christ to God among those who are being saved and among those who are perishing; to the one an aroma from death to death, to the other an aroma from life to life. And who is adequate for these things?"

1 Pet 2:11-12, "Beloved, I urge you as aliens and strangers to abstain from fleshly lusts which wage war against the soul. Keep your behavior excellent among the Gentiles, so that in the thing in which they slander you as evildoers…

Are we actually commanded to practice our righteousness before men?

Not really!

Matt 6:1, "Beware of practicing your righteousness before men to be noticed by them; otherwise you have no reward with your Father who is in heaven."

Is not practicing our righteousness before men (servant evangelism) hypocrisy like the Pharisees?

Matt 6:5, "And when you pray, you are not to be as the hypocrites; for they love to stand and pray in the synagogues and on the street corners, in order to be seen by men. Truly I say to you, they have their reward in full."

Matt 6:16, "And whenever you fast, do not put on a gloomy face as the hypocrites *do*, for they neglect their appearance in order to be seen fasting by men. Truly I say to you, they have their reward in full."

Matt 23:5-7, "But they do all their deeds to be noticed by men; for they broaden their phylacteries, and lengthen the tassels *of their garments*. And they love the place of honor at banquets, and the chief seats in the synagogues, and respectful greetings in the market places, and being called by men, Rabbi."

What of "letting our light shine" before men?

They do not glorify us, due to our good behavior, but God, due to His work in our lives!

Matt 5:16 "Let your light so shine before men, that they may see your good works and glorify your Father in heaven."

1 Pet 2:11-12, "Beloved, I urge you as aliens and strangers to abstain from fleshly lusts which wage war against the soul. Keep your behavior excellent among the Gentiles, so that in the thing in which they slander you as evildoers, they may because of your good deeds, as they observe *them*, glorify God in the day of visitation."

What of befriending lost people, to be like them as much as possible?

1 Cor 15:33, "Do not be deceived: 'Bad company corrupts good morals.'"

Eph 5:3-7 (NKJ), "But fornication and all uncleanness or covetousness, let it not even be named among you, as is fitting for saints; neither filthiness, nor foolish talking, nor coarse jesting, which are not fitting, but rather giving of thanks. For this you know with certainty, that no immoral or impure person or covetous man, who is an idolater, has an inheritance in the kingdom of Christ and God. Let no one deceive you with empty words, for because of these things the wrath of God comes upon the sons of disobedience. Therefore do not be partakers with them."

1 Thess 4:3-8, "For this is the will of God, your sanctification; *that is*, that you abstain from sexual immorality; that each of you know how to possess his own vessel in sanctification and honor, not in lustful passion, like the Gentiles who do not know God; *and* that no man transgress and defraud his brother in the matter because the Lord is *the* avenger in all these things, just as we also told you before and solemnly warned *you*. For God has not called us for the purpose of impurity, but in sanctification. So, he who rejects *this* is not rejecting man but the God who gives His Holy Spirit to you."

James 4:4, "You adulteresses, do you not know that friendship with the world is hostility toward God? Therefore whoever wishes to be a friend of the world makes himself an enemy of God."

1 John 2:15-17, "Do not love the world, nor the things in the world. If anyone loves the world, the love of the Father is not in him. [16] For all that is in the world, the lust of the flesh and the lust of the eyes and

the boastful pride of life, is not from the Father, but is from the world. [17] And the world is passing away, and *also* its lusts; but the one who does the will of God abides forever."

What of our relationship to our neighbor?

Matt 22:39, "You shall love your neighbor as yourself" (cf. Lev 19:18)

Prov 25:17, "Let your foot rarely be in your neighbor's house, Or he will become weary of you and hate you."

Historical Introduction:

1. Often Lifestyle Evangelism is confused with Relational Evangelism, however they are quite different from a theoretical point of view...

Preliminary definitions:

1) Lifestyle Evangelism is the notion that we can be true a witness for Christ by our lifestyle. The thought is that this lifestyle witness satisfies the demands of the Great Commission

2) Relational Evangelism requires the initiating of a friendship with someone prior to sharing the Gospel with them. It's presuppositions are:

a) The Gospel crosses more effectively over established relationships

b) Engaging strangers for Christ is against the spirit of the Gospel.

Lifestyle—from encyclical by Paul VI, *Evangelii Nuntiandi* (8 December 1975)

"21. Above all the Gospel must be proclaimed by witness. Take a Christian or a handful of Christians who, in the midst of their own community, show their capacity for understanding and acceptance, their sharing of life and destiny with other people, their solidarity with the efforts of all for whatever is noble and good. Let us suppose that, in addition, they radiate in an altogether simple and unaffected way their faith in values that go beyond current values, and their hope in something that is not seen and that one would not dare to imagine. Through this wordless witness these Christians stir up irresistible questions in the hearts of those who see how they live: Why are they like this? Why do they live in this way? What or who is it that inspires them? Why are they in our midst? Such a witness is already a silent proclamation of the Good News and a very powerful and effective one. Here we have an initial act of evangelization. The above questions will ask, whether they are people to whom Christ has never been proclaimed, or baptized people who do not practice, or people who live as nominal Christians but according to principles that are in no way Christian, or people who are seeking, and not without suffering, something or someone whom they sense but cannot name. Other questions will arise, deeper and more demanding ones, questions evoked by this witness which involves presence, sharing, solidarity, and which is an essential element, and generally the first one, in evangelization."[51]

"All Christians are called to this witness, and in this way they can be real evangelizers. We are thinking especially of the responsibility incumbent on immigrants in the country that receives them.

"41. Without repeating everything that we have already mentioned, it is appropriate first of all to emphasize the following point: for the Church, the first means of evangelization is the witness of an authentically Christian life, given over to God in a communion that nothing should destroy and at the same time given to one's neighbor with limitless zeal.

"69. Religious, for their part, find in their consecrated life a privileged means of effective evangelization. At the deepest level of their being they are caught up in the dynamism of the Church's life, which is thirsty for the divine Absolute and called to holiness. It is to this holiness that they bear witness. They embody the Church in her desire to give herself completely to the radical demands of the beatitudes. By their lives they are a sign of total availability to God, the Church and the brethren.

"As such they have a special importance in the context of the witness which, as we have said, is of prime importance in evangelization. At the same time as being a challenge to the world and to the Church herself, this silent witness of poverty and abnegation, of purity and sincerity, of self-sacrifice in obedience, can become an eloquent witness capable of touching also non-Christians who have good will and are sensitive to certain values.

"In this perspective one perceives the role played in evangelization by religious men and women consecrated to prayer, silence, penance and sacrifice."

2. Contemporary Relational Evangelism:

    Definition: Relational evangelism requires the *Preparatio Evangelica* of a relationship prior to
    sharing the Gospel.

    Numerous books teach a relational-type evangelism (organized chronologically):
    1976
    Gerald Borchert, *Dynamics of Evangelism* (Waco: Word, 1976).
    C. B. Hogue, *Love Leaves No Choice: Life-style Evangelism* (Waco, TX: Word, 1976).
    1977
    Leighton Ford, *Good News Is for Sharing: A Guide to Making Friends for Christ* (Elgin, IL:
        David C. Cook, 1977)
    1978
    James H. Jauncey, *One-on-One Evangelism* (Chicago: Moody, 1978).
    1979
    Richard S. Armstrong, *Service Evangelism* (Philadelphia: Westminster, 1979).
    Paul E. Little, ed., *His Guide to Evangelism* (Downers Grove, IL: InterVarsity, 1979).
    Wayne McDill, *Making Friends for Christ—A Practical Approach to Relational Evangelism*
        (Nashville: Broadman, 1979).
    Arthur McPhee, *Friendship Evangelism: the Caring Way to Share Christ* (Grand Rapids:
        Zondervan, 1979)
    Rebecca Manly Pippert, *Out of the Saltshaker and into the World: Evangelism as a Way of Life*
        (Downers Grove, IL: InterVarsity, 1979).
    1980
    Jim Petersen, *Evangelism as a Lifestyle* (Colorado Springs, CO: NavPress, 1980)
    Richard G. Korthals, *Agape Evangelism: Roots that Reach Out* (Wheaton, IL: Tyndale House,
        1980).
    1981
    Joseph Aldrich, *Lifestyle Evangelism* (Portland, OR: Multnomah Press, 1981).
    Joyce Neville, *How to Share Your Faith without Being Offensive* (New York: Seabury, 1981).
    Matthew Prince, *Winning through Caring: Handbook on Friendship Evangelism* (Grand Rapids:
        Baker, 1981).
    1984
    Neighbour, Ralph Jr. *The Journey into Discipleship: The Journey into Lifestyle Evangelism and
        Ministry* (Memphis: Brotherhood Commission of the SBC, 1984, 1987).
    1985
    Jim Petersen, *Evangelism for Our Generation* (Colorado Springs, CO: NavPress, 1985).
    1989
    Jim Petersen, *Living Proof* (Colorado Springs, CO: NavPress, 1989).
    1997
    Nick Pollard, *Evangelism Made Slightly Less Difficult: How to Interest Those Who Aren't
        Interested* (Downers Grove: InterVarsity, 1997).

3. An evaluation of Joseph Aldrich's *Life-Style Evangelism*/relational approach to evangelism:

    Introduction:
    Could not this approach not be considered a "moral-influence theory" of evangelism (i.e.
        "my lifestyle will draw people to Christ")?
    Furthermore, in Evangelical circles, God's General Revelation is considered insufficient to
        teach man His way of salvation, thereby necessitating Special Revelation.[1304]
    If God's "lifestyle" approach is/was not sufficient, why how can a person's lifestyle be
        considered sufficient?
    Could this not be a link between non-Evangelical practice leading to non-Evangelical
        theology?

[1304]"Only in Eden has general revelation been adequate to the needs of man. Not being a sinner, man in Eden
had no need of the grace of God itself by which sinners are restored to communion with Him, or of special revelation of
this grace of God to sinners to enable them to live with God" (Benjamin B. Warfield, *The Inspiration and Authority of
the Bible* [Philippsburg, NJ: Presbyterean and Reformed, 1948], 75-76).

    a.   Of "Proclamational Evangelism" Aldrich wrote:

> Although the proclamational approach to evangelism will have validity until Jesus comes, it is not a means by which the majority of Christians will reach their own private world.[1305]

    b.   He drew the following conclusion regarding confrontational/intrusional evangelism:[1306]

> The vast majority do *not* become Christians by confrontational, stranger-to-stranger evangelism. Furthermore, many are being kept from making an effective decision because of bad experiences with a zealous but insensitive witness.[1307]

    c.   While on one hand saying that expectant evangelism was legitimate, on the other hand Aldrich proclaimed that it was counter-productive, actually hindering "effective decision." In two pages of his *Lifestyle Evangelism* Aldrich came full circle:

        1)   Expectant evangelism is valid and legitimate.

        2)   Expectant evangelism is not practical.

        3)   Expectant evangelism hinders effective decisions.[1308]

    d.   Following his attack of expectant evangelism, Aldrich explained the benefits of his Relational/Incarnational Model using Maslow's "Hierarchy of Needs" to make his point[1309] (based on the use of George Hunter III).[1310]

        1)   Basis was Maslow's hierarchy of needs: "physiological needs" first , and work up to the safety/security needs, the love/affection needs, the self-esteem needs, and finally the self-actualization needs:

[1305]Joseph Aldrich, *Life-Style Evangelism,* 78. Aldrich defined "proclamational evangelism" by using the example of the early church: "The early church was planted because of the strong proclamational ministries of the apostles. They preached on street corners, in synagogues, and in marketplaces" (ibid.).

[1306]Aldrich defined "confrontational/intrusional evangelism" in this way: "The *confrontational/intrusional* model is probably the most common one. Generally the 'target audience' is a stranger" (ibid.). Thus any non-relationally-based one-on-one evangelism can fall into the category of "confrontational/intrusional." However, of the fifty-two personal evangelism conversations in the New Testament, thirty-seven were with complete strangers (understanding that no one was a stranger to Jesus), five were with previous acquaintances, and the prior relationship of ten is unclear from the text (see Thomas P. Johnston, "An Analytical Study of Personal Evangelism Conversations in the Gospels and the Book of Acts," Classroom lecture notes, *BIB/CHM 230X—Biblical Evangelism,* Spring 1995, photocopy], 7). Whitesell cited 35 examples of personal evangelism in the ministry of Jesus, another 15 examples of personal evangelism in the Book of Acts, for a total of 50 examples (Faris D. Whitesell, *Basic New Testament Evangelism* [Grand Rapids: Zondervan, 1949], 107-08, 112).

[1307]Aldrich, *Life-Style Evangelism,* 79; emphasis mine.

[1308]To back up this point, Aldrich quoted James Jauncey, *Psychology for Successful Evangelism* (Chicago: Moody, 1972), 123: "Just buttonholing a stranger, witnessing to him and pressing for a decision will likely do more harm than good. Most responsible people react negatively and often quite violently to this kind of assault. *It shows a fundamental lack of respect for human dignity and personality*" (Aldrich, *Life-Style Evangelism*, 80).

[1309]"I have used Maslow's Hierarchy of needs for years as a teaching tool. I find it helpful in determining what level of need a person is struggling to satisfy. Motivation to act appears to be directly related to need. If I can link a solution (the Gospel) to a felt need, I have created a favorable climate to meet that need. ... Maslow's model also lets us see how important genuine Christian fellowship can be as it is specifically targeted to meet these needs" (ibid., 90, 94).

[1310]"George Hunter suggests two further refinements which are full of insight. Relatively speaking, those near the top of the hierarchy of needs are stronger, more adequate people. Those at the bottom are weaker, more vulnerable ones" (ibid., 95; notes George Hunter, *The Contagious Congregation* [Nashville: Abingdon, 1979], 45-47).

ALDRICH'S USE OF MASLOW'S HIERARCHY OF NEEDS[1311]

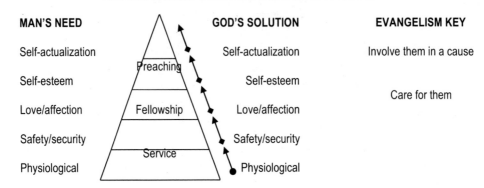

MAN'S NEED		GOD'S SOLUTION	EVANGELISM KEY
Self-actualization		Self-actualization	Involve them in a cause
Self-esteem	Preaching	Self-esteem	
Love/affection	Fellowship	Love/affection	Care for them
Safety/security	Service	Safety/security	
Physiological		Physiological	

The thief on the cross (Luke 23), the demoniac from Gerasenes (Mark 5), and the Woman at the Well (John 4) all show that the spiritual need was met first, and not visa versa. In John 6, the 5000 who were fed left Jesus by the end of the chapter.

2) Note that Sjogren's diagram was virtually identical in its approach: (1) Active kindness; (2) Active listening; (3) Active wondering; and (4) Active sharing.

SJOGREN'S USE OF MASLOW[1312]

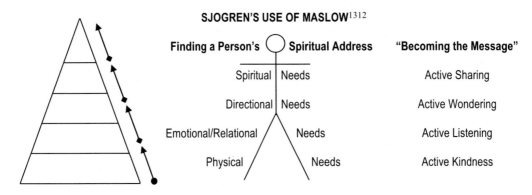

Finding a Person's ◯ Spiritual Address		"Becoming the Message"
Spiritual	Needs	Active Sharing
Directional	Needs	Active Wondering
Emotional/Relational	Needs	Active Listening
Physical	Needs	Active Kindness

While Sjogren [et al.] used different categories and solutions, while their premise was the same. They used Maslow's approach without stating it in the text, as did Aldrich above. One must begin with physical needs first, and then move up to spiritual needs.

Now listen to how far these presuppositions have taken Sjogren:

"Many Christians talk about developing an intimate *personal relationship* with God, but the message they present to not-yet-Christians focuses almost exclusively on explaining how the atoning death of Jesus satisfies the requirements of God's justice. ... Talking about doctrines such as justification by faith and atonement by the substitutionary death of Jesus is usually unnecessarily confusing.

"...Relationship is the true heart of the matter. ... Following Jesus is more than just a handy way to gain admittance into heaven or to avoid hell. It's more than a magic formula for salvation. It is *at least* as real and dynamic a relationship as marriage is."[1313]

Speaking about the subsitutionary atonement is "unnecessarilty confusing"? What else is Luke 24:46-47 or 1 Cor 15:1-8? His *a priori* has taken him far. By the way, notice the use of the word "natural" in the title. The word "natural" is often used in

---

[1311]Adapted from from *Life-Style Evangelism* © 1981, 1993 (pp. 94-95) by Dr. Joseph Aldrich. Used by permission of Multnomah Publishers, Inc.

[1312]Steve Sjogren, Dave Ping, and Doug Pollock, *Irresistible Evangelism: Natural Ways to Open Others to Jesus* (Loveland, CO: Group, 2004), 69.

[1313]Sjogren, Ping, and Pollock, *Irresistible Evangelism*, 149.

contradistinction to "supernatural", as in Christian Schwarz' *Natural Church Development* which we will discuss below.[1314]

b. Likewise, as Aldrich used Maslow as a basis, he also went around the Square of Opposition on Proclamational Evangelism, starting at the particular affirmative:[1315]

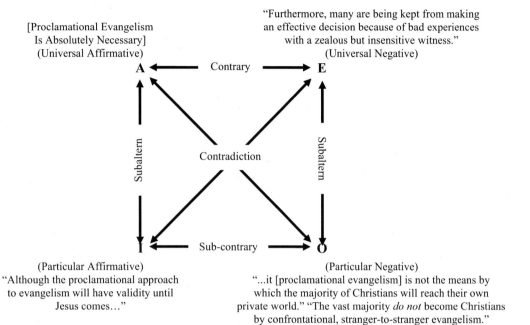

[Proclamational Evangelism Is Absolutely Necessary] (Universal Affirmative)

"Furthermore, many are being kept from making an effective decision because of bad experiences with a zealous but insensitive witness." (Universal Negative)

(Particular Affirmative) "Although the proclamational approach to evangelism will have validity until Jesus comes…"

(Particular Negative) "...it [proclamational evangelism] is not the means by which the majority of Christians will reach their own private world." "The vast majority *do not* become Christians by confrontational, stranger-to-stranger evangelism."

Strengths and Weaknesses:

Strengths:

1. Seeks to combine the Great Commission and the many admonitions to godly living in the Bible
2. Provides a practice-what-you-preach emphasis in evangelism ("Walk your talk and talk your walk")

Weaknesses:

1. Confuses the missionary nature of the Great Commission with personal spiritual disciplines

2. Changes evangelism from instantaneous preaching to long-term living; thereby changing conversion from instantaneous ("You must be born again") to gradual enlightenment ("renewing of the mind").

3. Undermines the "Separation" verses that tell us directly not to befriend the world (Eph 5:7; 1 Thess 4:3, 7):

   a. This lack of separation from the world seems to be a result of:
      1) The normal spiritual drift of churches, and
      2) A seeker-church mentality, in which there is a blending of the saved and the lost, with little or no distinction between the two, either in church organization nor in preaching

   b. Unfortunate unforeseen results of friendship evangelism:
      1) Saved persons are sometimes or often placed in compromising situations while seeking to "build friendships" with lost people (outside of the special events planned by the

---

[1314]Christian Schwarz, *Natural Church Development,* 3rd ed. (Wheaton, IL: ChurchSmart, 1998).

[1315]Aldrich, *Life-Style Evangelism,* 78-79.

church for the purpose of helping parishioners to build friendships with the unchurched); for example:

    a) One young woman called a Christian youth Saturday evening radio show, saying that she had been raped while trying to build a friendship with a lost young man so that she could share the Gospel with him; to say the least, she was devasted by the unbiblical methodological advice that she had received; the radio talk show host, who was promoting friendship evangelism on his show, had no response when she questioned the validity of friendship evangelism, nor to her tears!

    b) A collegiate sought to befriend a Muslim who he already knew to be very closed to the Gospel; assuming that if he befriended him he would open up, he asked this Muslim collegiate to be his roommate, resulting in a terribly difficult year with no change in the Muslim roommate's negative attitude toward the Gospel; friendship did not predispose his roommate to the Gospel, nor did it prove to be an efficacious preparation for the Gospel

2) Due to the lack of distinction between the saved and the lost (Lev 10:10), dating relationships can easily turn into marriages between saved and lost, thus leading to Christians to being unequally yoked with unbelievers (2 Cor 6:14)

3) Some unforeseen consequences of "friendship evangelism" are very tragic indeed!

4. The unforeseen results of Friendship Evangelism may actually be the result of building on an unsure foundation:

    a. Building on a foundation other than Christ and His Words is always a recipe for disaster, Matt 7:24-27

    b. "There is a way *which seems* right to a man, But its end is the way of death," Prov 14:12; 16:25

5. Lifestyle-relational evangelism exemplifies a methodological paradigm shift that simultaneously necessitates a theological paradigm shift…

THEOLOGICAL COMPARISION OF EXPECTANT AND LIFESTYLE EVANGELISM[1316]

	Expectant Evangelism	Theological Implications of Lifestyle Evangelism
1	Instantaneous conversion ("You must be born again!"), John 3:7; Acts 16:14; Rom 10:13 ("now is the acceptable time…")	Progressive conversion/gradual enlightenment (now evangelism is wrong-spirited)
2	Faith comes by hearing, Rom 10:17	Faith comes by seeing and hearing
3	Christ earned the right for the message to be shared, Rom 5:8; 1 Tim 1:15	Christians must earn the right to share the gospel with others
4	The word of God is the instrument of salvation, Rom 1:17; 1 Pet. 1:23	Sharing the gospel must be preempted by relationship, or some other human preparation
5	The lifestyle and miracles of Christ did not lead to faith in all those who observed them, John 12:37	The lifestyle of the Christian will lead the lost to become open to the message of the gospel
6	God must open the hearts of the lost by His Spirit operating through His word, Acts 16:14; Gal 3:1-5; 1 Thess 2:13	Our service, friendship, relationship, or apologetics will open the hearts of the lost prior to their considering the Gospel
7	Substitutionary atonement (judicial/objective), 2 Cor 5:21	Reconciliation model of the atonement (relational/toward subjective)
8	Preaching Christ, 2 Cor 4:5	Preaching ourselves and Christ
9	Christ alone saves, Acts 4:12; Rom 5:8-10, et al.	Christ's work needs human merits to be effective
10	Harvest is ripe, Amos 9:13; Luke 10:2; John 4:35	Harvest is not ripe; it needs additional cultivation and time
11	Must evangelize by faith, John 4:35	Must use natural relational rules

---

[1316]It is important to understand that, as within any movement, there are degrees of adherance to lifestyle evangelism. Various Scriptures are also cited by those adhering to lifestyle evangelism to affirm their position (e.g., see Aldrich, Joseph C. *Gentle Persuasion* [Portland, OR: Multnomah Press, 1988]).

	Expectant Evangelism	Theological Implications of Lifestyle Evangelism
12	Christians' lives should be consistent with the gospel; Christians should live holy lives, 1 Pet 1:14-16	Christians must practice "radical identification" and "eat meat" (à la 1 Cor 10:23 ff.) to relate to the lost.
13	Christians will be hated "without cause" (Psa 69:4) by a jealous, mocking, and reviling world due to their association with Christ, John 15:18-21	Christians are hated only because they are not relevant nor culturally sensitive nor are they open to the physical and emotional needs of the unsaved
14	The gospel is a reproach, Heb 11:26, e.g. 1 Cor 1:23; it will be avoided by evildoers, lest their deeds be exposed, John 3:20-21	The gospel need not be a reproach (i.e. a moral philosophy); natural man can and will accept Christianity's rational superiority with proper apologetics
15	Satan has blinded the minds of unbelievers so that they cannot see Christ, John 3:20-21, 2 Cor 2:17, 4:3-4	Man's sin has not fully blinded his mind; he can discern certain spiritual truths if properly communicated
16	Rejection of gospel is due to lack of comprehension and spiritual blindness, Matt 13:19, 2 Cor 4:3-4 – Christian only responsible to share, Ezek 3:18-19, with patience, 2 Tim 4:2, and gentleness, 1 Pet 3:15	Rejection of gospel is due to a lack of relational cultivation; guilt is placed on the rejected Christian for his lack of proper cultivation, leading to a further fear of sharing the gospel to the unsaved
17	Only "some" will be saved, although we must preach to "all" (1 Cor 9:22; the road to salvation is narrow (Matt 7:13-14)	"All" can be saved, if the Christian given enough time, enough prayer, enough relationship, enough service; on the other hand, rejection of the Gospel is primarily due to the lack of effort on the part of the Christian to properly cultivate the friendship[1317]
18	Persecution is promised, 2 Tim 3:12, and is a blessing, Matt 5:10-11, 1 Pet 4:12-14	Persecution is a sign that the method of evangelism is faulty, needing modification
19	Evangelism weapons are spiritual, 2 Cor 10:3-5	Must use both spiritual and carnal weapons (e.g., marketing techniques)
20	Evangelism is both urgent and the preeminent priority for the Christian: (1) Return of Christ, Matt 24:14 (2) Mankind is totally depraved, Rom 3:9-20 (3) Reality of hell, Matt 25:46 (4) Christians are accountable, Ezek 3:16-21, Acts 20:26	Evangelism is one of many important aspects of the Christian life (including the Great Commandment, the Creation Mandate, etc.): (1) Emphasis on here and now (2) Total depravity may be an overstatement (3) Some question the reality of a literal hell (4) Mentioning accountability is putting guilt trips on Christians
21	The Bible is authoritative in both doctrine and practice (i.e., the work of evangelism), 2 Tim 3:16-17; 1 Cor 11:1	The Bible is authoritative primarily for doctrine—the practice of evangelism must glean truth from culture
22	Expectant evangelism is absolutely necessary in the ministry of the local church: (1) Expectant evangelism is commanded, Mark 16:15, et al. (2) Expectant evangelism is exemplified, Acts 4:19-20; 5:29; cf. 2 Tim 4:1-5	Expectant evangelism is counter-productive, negative to the world's view of the church, cf. 1 Cor 4:10: (1) Reinterpret Great Commission as a gradual process, e.g., make disciples in Matt 28:19 (2) Adapt evangelism methodology to truths in anthropology, sociology, and psychology

Lessons from Lot on Lifestyle Evangelism:

Lot moved to and lived in Sodom as a righteous man:

> Gen 13:12-13, "Abram settled in the land of Canaan, while Lot settled in the cities of the valley, and moved his tents as far as Sodom. Now the men of Sodom were wicked exceedingly and sinners against the LORD."

Living among them, Lot's soul was tormented by the evil that he saw:

> 2 Pet 2:7-9, "and *if* He rescued righteous Lot, oppressed by the sensual conduct of unprincipled men (for by what he saw and heard *that* righteous man, while living among them, felt *his* righteous soul tormented day after day with *their* lawless deeds), *then* the Lord knows how to rescue the godly from temptation, and to keep the unrighteous under punishment for the day of judgment"

The men of Sodom distained Lot for his righteous verbalized stance, in protecting the men [angels] who came to visit the city:

> Gen 19:4-9, "Before they lay down, the men of the city, the men of Sodom, surrounded the house, both young and old, all the people from every quarter; and they called to Lot and said to him, 'Where are the men who came to you tonight? Bring them out to us that we may have relations with them.' But Lot went out to them at the doorway, and shut the door behind him, and said, 'Please, my brothers, do not act wickedly [Heb *ra'a'*]. Now behold, I have two daughters who have not had relations with man; please let me bring them out to you, and do to them whatever you like; only do nothing to these men, inasmuch as they have

---

[1317]Is this not the primary message of John Shore in *I'm OK—You're Not: The Message We're Sending to Unbelievers and Why We Should Stop* (Colorado Springs: NavPress, 2007)?

come under the shelter of my roof.' But they said, 'Stand aside.' Furthermore, they said, 'This one came in as an alien, and already he is acting like a judge; now we will treat you worse than them.' So they pressed hard against Lot and came near to break the door.

Lot's godly lifestyle (as stated by Peter and exemplified by the fact that his daughters were pure) did not lead the men of Sodom to seek Lot's God for salvation, Rather:
They distained him even more for seeking to hinder their wickedness,
They were ready to treat him worse than the men they planned to assault, and
Therefore God destroyed these cities in a notorious act of judgment!

Nowhere in the Bible is it found that the lifestyle of a follower of God is the power of God unto salvation of anyone.

A look at several lifestyle-oriented evangelism programs for the local church:

A. *Living Proof* (NavPress, CBMC)—Lifestyle Evangelism

History:

Two Books:
Jim Petersen, *Evangelism as a Lifestyle* (Colorado Springs: NavPress, 1980)
Jim Petersen, *Evangelism for Our Generation* (Colorado Springs: NavPress, 1985).
Combined:
Jim Petersen, *Living Proof* (Colorado Springs: NavPress, 1989).
Video Series

Some Reminders

Strengths and Weaknesses

B. Contagious Christian (Willowcreek Resource):
History
Some Reminders
Strengths and Weaknesses

C. Examples of Other Lifestyle-Oriented Evangelism Methodologies:
Prayer Evangelism?
Worship Evangelism?

D. Examples of Other Relational-Oriented Evangelism Methodologies:
Block Parties?

III. Servant Evangelism Programs:

Key Verses:

Matt 5:16, "Let your light shine before men in such a way that they may see your good works, and glorify your Father who is in heaven"

1 Pet 2:12, "Keep your behavior excellent among the Gentiles, so that in the thing in which they slander you as evildoers, they may because of your good deeds, as they observe *them*, glorify God in the day of visitation"

Likewise, Darrell Robinson found in Dorcas an example of Servant Evangelism, as she made tunics and garments for widows:

Acts 9:36-42 (NKJ), "At Joppa there was a certain disciple named Tabitha, which is translated Dorcas. This woman was full of good works and charitable deeds which she did. [37] But it happened in those days that she became sick and died. When they had washed her, they laid *her* in an upper room. [38] And since Lydda was near Joppa, and the disciples had heard that Peter was there, they sent two men to him, imploring *him* not to delay in coming to them. [39] Then Peter arose and went with them. When he had come, they brought *him* to the upper room. And all the widows stood by him weeping, showing the tunics and garments which Dorcas had made while she was with them. [40] But Peter put them all out, and knelt down and prayed. And turning to the body he said, 'Tabitha, arise.' And she opened her eyes, and when she saw Peter she sat up. [41] Then he gave her *his* hand and lifted her up;

and when he had called the saints and widows, he presented her alive. [42] And it became known throughout all Joppa, and many believed on the Lord."

This same emphasis is also discussed in relation to a widow who is a widow indeed:

> 1 Tim 5:9-10 (NKJ), "Do not let a widow under sixty years old be taken into the number, *and not unless* she has been the wife of one man, [10] well reported for good works: if she has brought up children, if she has lodged strangers, if she has washed the saints' feet, if she has relieved the afflicted, if she has diligently followed every good work."

Notice especially the people to whom she ministers, and the order in which they are listed:
Her children
Strangers, a parallel to traveling evangelists (Tit 3:13-14) or angels in disguise (Heb 13:1)?
Saints, clearly of those in the household of the faith
Afflicted (or oppressed, cf. Heb 10:32-34), as in remembering those in prison (Heb 13:3)

There also seems to be a clear parallel with the ministry of the excellent wife in Prov 31:

> Prov 31:20 (NKJ), "She extends her hand to the poor, Yes, she reaches out her hands to the needy"

In this light, how are we to understand the words of Jesus in Matt 6:1?

> Matt 6:1, "Beware of practicing your righteousness before men to be noticed by them; otherwise you have no reward with your Father who is in heaven"

Introduction: Considering the concept of service being a *Preparatio Evangelica* to the Gospel:

Four main approaches to "service":
1. Service allowing proximity to the contact for evangelism
2. Service as a necessary work which must precede the Gospel[1318]
3. Service as a replacement for communicating the Gospel
4. Service as part of "working out" one's salvation (e.g. in Roman Catholicism)

Notice some contemporary examples:

1. New Jerusalem Bible (Roman Catholic) translation of Rom 1:[1] 2, "set apart for the service of the gospel"; the NASB reads for this phrase, "set apart for the gospel of God"; the French 1910 Segond adds the word "announce," reading, "is à part pour annoncer l'Évangile de Dieu"; the Greek reads, ἀφωρισμένος εἰς εὐαγγέλιον θεοῦ. The argument is: what is meant by "unto the Gospel"?

2. Franklin Graham, "Jesus ministered to the physical needs of people before preaching the Good News to them" (BGEA monthly letter, September 2003, 2):
   a. This approach is very common and not-a-most-biblical concept
   b. The canonical order of verbs is almost always as such: preaching, proclaiming, then healing (Matt 9:35)

[1318]See my Chart 65, "Guide to Evangelical Drift Portrayed in Charts 66-75," in *Charts for a Theology of Evangelism* (Nashville: Broadman, 2007), 104-05. In this chart I have delineated the following 12 approaches to proclamation and service (please consider the progression):
(1) Service is a supernatural outflow of proclamation (the result of changed lives)
(2) Service is an opening for proclamation (to evangelize in closed countries)
(3) Service is a bridge to proclamation (allowing proximity for evangelism)
(4) Service is a preparatory grace for proclamation (providing relevance to the Gospel)
(5) Service is a preferred preparatory grace for proclamation (adding credibility to the Gospel)
(6) Service is a necessary preparatory grace for proclamation (adding power to the Gospel)
(7) Service is an equal partner to proclamation (the two mandates, spiritual and social; both are necessary together)
(8) Service is an end in itself, apart from proclamation (need not be to together; both are legitimate ends in themselves [often tied somehow to the Great Commission)
(9) Service is primary over proclamation (conversion agenda is secondary to social agenda)
(10) Service is proclamational evangelism (conversion agenda hinders social ends and means; proclamation is unnecessary [e.g. Francis of Assisi, "Preach the Gospel at all times, and if necessary use words"])
(11) Service is proclamational evangelism (proclamational evangelism is actually counterproductive)
(12) Service is proclamational evangelism (conversion agenda hinders church ends; proclamational evangelism is unbiblical and the method of heretics or the unlearned and ignorant).

    c.   In this case, healing is an affirmation of Christ's deity and a confirmation of the Gospel (Mark 16:20), rather than a preparation for the Gospel

Strengths (from student interaction):
1. Gets the church to minister outside of its four walls
2. Helps meet needs in the community
3. Allows for a "Go" emphasis in evangelism
4. Helps move Christians out of their comfort zone
5. Helps soften the hearts of individuals to the Gospel
6. Helps build trust relationships (e.g. overseas in closed countries)
7. Helps soften the hearts of Christians toward needy persons
8. Allows for those not gifted in evangelism to be involved in evangelism
9. Allows for the organization of a programmatic, non-proclamational approach to evangelism
10. Allows close contact with non-church-related and needy individuals
11. Allows for a level of non-negative attention from the world
12. Provides for world-friendly public relations—presence evangelism

Weaknesses (from student interaction):
1. Must work hard to remain evangelistic
2. "Love" can become the unique focus
3. Focus can move to the activities
4. Works primarily with those who have a discernible physical need of some type—can this lead to a Christian sense of superiority (cf. 1 Cor 15:19)?
5. May confuses the spiritual nature of the Great Commission with the addition of doing good deeds
6. May incline toward disbelief in the sufficiency of God's Word to convict and convert
7. Can be made to replace any other initiative form of evangelism, as it is marketed as a preferable evangelism method

Further weaknesses:
1. Servant evangelism may be seen as a "Bait and Switch" tactic for the Gospel
2. Servant evangelism can lead to a condescending (or patronizing) attitude toward others (as hinted above):
    a.   Likewise, servant evangelism may lead the church to focus their evangelism efforts only on those who are socially disadvantaged
    b.   James and John did encourage Paul to reach out to the poor in Gal 2:10
3. The mixed signals behind Servant Evangelism may lead to a lack of clarity as regards a commitment to Jesus unto death
4. Often over time, the "servant" part of the ministry remains, while the "evangelism" part moves to the sidelines; examples of this change over time are:
    a.   The Salvation Army, was at one time actually about preaching the Gospel and "salvation" when it was founded by William Booth
    b.   The International Missionary Conference movement morphed into the World Council of Churches, although it had included powerful 19th Century missionary conferences (with Hudson Taylor, Robert Speer, A. T. Pierson, etc.)
5. Does not using the financial assistance from church funds for evangelistic purposes…
    a.   Hinder the church's abiblity to assist those who are "widows indeed" (1 Tim 5:3-16)?

        1 Tim 5:16, "Do not let the church be burdened"

    b.   Give funds to those whom Paul said should be denied because of wanton or rebellious living (1 Tim 5:6)?

        1 Tim 5:6, "But she who lives in pleasure is dead while she lives"

    c.   Miss the point of Paul that financial assistance should only be given to those widows who have lived an exemplary Christian lifestyle (1 Tim 5:9-10)?

        1 Tim 5:9-10, "Do not let a widow under sixty years old be taken into the number, *and not unless she has been the wife of one man,* [10] well reported for good works: if she has brought up

children, if she has lodged strangers, if she has washed the saints' feet, if she has relieved the afflicted, if she has diligently followed every good work"

d. Further miss the point, that even for needy widows within the fellowship of the church, other avenues were to be sought out for those who did not meet the stringent qualifications (e.g. that their children take care of them or that they get married)?

e. How then could church funds be used to evangelize unsaved people, in a "Christian Social Welfare" sense, without contradicting Paul's teaching in 1 Timothy 5?

Consider also "**Reverse-Servant-Evangelism**" in the New Testament:

1. Why did not Jesus buy a bucket and bring water to the Woman at the Well? Rather he asked her for water, John 4:
   a. Was Jesus being chauvinistic? Was He too good to get His own water? I think not!
   b. Could not Jesus had made water gush out of a nearby rock, like Moses did when he struck the rock (Exod 17:6; Num 20:11)? That would really have gotten this unsavory woman's attention!
   c. Or how about creating a pulley system to help her get the water? Surely that was in His ability to do:
      1) Yet, Jesus did say in John that He did only the works that His Father wanted Him to do: "for the works which the Father has given Me to accomplish, the very works that I do" (John 5:36; cf. John 5:17; 8:28; 10:32, 37-38; 17:4)
      2) Therefore, Jesus was limited in what He could do by the will of His Father
      3) Also, Jesus could do no miracle because of their unbelief, Mark 6:5
      4) Notice how the miraculous did not lead the Jews in John 6 to faith in Christ, John 6:26-31
      5) John clearly wrote:
         John 12:37-38, "But although He had done so many signs before them, they did not believe in Him, [38] that the word of Isaiah the prophet might be fulfilled, which he spoke: 'Lord, who has believed our report? And to whom has the arm of the LORD been revealed?'"
      6) Likewise, an adulterous generation graved for a sign, but none would be given to it, Matt 12:39; 16:4
   d. Without wanting to be sarcastic or sacrilegious, Jesus specifically asked her [the Woman at the Well] to serve Him to begin the conversation with her
   e. And to think that the account of the Woman at the Well in John 4 is the primary account used for relational evangelism…

2. Likewise, when Jesus sent out His apostles on evangelistic mission trips, He specifically commanded them not to bring money, a change of clothing, or even a staff for the evangelistic mission trip, "for the workman is worthy of his wages," Matt 10:9-10; cf. Mark 6:8; Luke 9:3; 10:4:

   a. The apostles did not have the funds to buy anything (batteries, light bulbs, cookies, water, kool aid, hot chocolate, Christmas wrapping paper, etc.), nor even to make anything (quilts, etc.), for those with whom they shared the Gospel
      1) Perhaps there were no poor or needy people in the time of Jesus? Yes, Jesus said to Judas Iscariot, who seemed to be interested in serving the poor, "The poor you will have with you always," John 12:8
      2) Why did Jesus not train the apostles in felt-need evangelism in Matthew 10? Perhaps at issue is not meeting physical felt needs, but finding those whom God has given an ear to hear
   b. The apostles were left completely at the mercy of those to whom they first ministered the Gospel, remembering that they were going "to every city and place where He Himself [Jesus] was going to come," Luke 10:1
      1) Jesus sent them on Reverse-Servant-Evangelism: they needed to be served by those to whom they shared the Gospel

2) And in Luke 22:35, once Judas Iscariot had left, the apostles shared that they lacked nothing when they were sent out:

> "And He said to them, 'When I sent you out without purse and bag and sandals, you did not lack anything, did you?' And they said, '*No*, nothing'" (Luke 22:35)

3) Now what would these traveling preachers [cf. Medieval *Wanderprediger*, Poor Men of Lyons, etc.] have needed? (1) food, (2) a place to sleep, (3) his clothing washed, and (4) a place to clean up:

    a) Without these necessities what would life be like?
        (1) "To this present hour we are both hungry, thirsty, and are poorly clothed, and are roughly treated, and are homeless," 1 Cor 4:11
        (2) "In sleeplessness, in hunger," 2 Cor 6:5
        (3) "Through many sleepless nights, in hunger and thirst, often without food, in cold and exposure," 2 Cor 11:27

    b) Without these necessities, they would receive the curse of Deut 28:48 (as Paul did, Acts 9:16) for those who disobey the commands of God:

> "Because you did not serve the LORD your God with joy and a glad heart, for the abundance of all things; therefore you shall serve your enemies whom the LORD shall send against you, in hunger, in thirst, in nakedness, and in the lack of all things; and He will put an iron yoke on your neck until He has destroyed you" (Deut 28:47-48)

    c) Therefore:
        (1) "Bless those who curse you," Luke 6:28
        (2) "For, I think, God has exhibited us apostles last of all, as men condemned to death; because we have become a spectacle to the world, both to angels and to men," 1 Cor 4:9

c. Now, as mentioned above, Jesus specifically addressed and changed this command in Luke 22:35-36, when Judas Iscariot was not among them:

> "And He said to them, 'When I sent you out without purse and bag and sandals, you did not lack anything, did you?' And they said, '*No*, nothing.' And He said to them, 'But now, let him who has a purse take it along, likewise also a bag, and let him who has no sword sell his robe and buy one'" (Luke 22:35-36)

1) It seems like they can have a little more for their journey:
    a) A purse—for some money, which Judas was want to have, John 12:6
    b) A bag—for some extra clothing
    c) A sword—for protection—was urged upon them as more important than a robe!

2) They were still sent out, meaning:
    a) They had no long term reputation in the village, town, or city—there goes the basis for Lifestyle Evangelism!
    b) They were strangers, unacquainted with local lore and customs, and possibly even language (see Acts 14:11-12)

d. Why did Jesus send out His disciples as paupers?

1) Did not God say of the poor man: "All the brothers of a poor man hate him; How much more do his friends go far from him! He pursues *them with* words, *but* they are gone" (Prov 19:7)?

2) Why would Christ set up His disciples for such a fate?
    a) Was this because they are men of whom the world is not worthy, Heb 11:38?
    b) Was this so that the power was in the message and in nothing else, 1 Cor 1:17-21?

3. Paul, in the context of evangelism, even spoke of the right of the evangelist to earn his living from the Gospel, 1 Cor 9:11-14:

   a. While this principle is often applied to pastoral ministry (and not without other Scripture, 1 Tim 5:17-18), in 1 Corinthians 9 it is directed to the person who was privileged to lead the person to Christ

   b. There are examples of people who extended the ministry of hospitality to Paul in Acts:
      1) Lydia from Thyatira took in Paul and his team, Acts 16:15
      2) The Philippian jailer took in Paul and Silas into his house after his conversion, and fed them, Acts 16:34
      3) Jason took in Paul and Silas during their evangelistic ministry in Thessalonica, Acts 17:6-7

4. **Reverse Servant Evangelism** in the History of the Churches:

   a. The Waldenses or "Poor Men of Lyons" specifically followed the admonitions in the sending passages of Matthew, Mark, and Luke:

   b. As noted in Chapter 7, the Dominicans were specifically commanded to adopt the lifestyle of their "enemy" [the Albigenses and Waldenses]:
      1) Their method of following Matthew 10 was so effective that when the Roman Catholic Dominican order was founded, Dominic and his companions were given the mandate by Bishop Diego to "imitate" the Waldenses, by living a lifestyle of "voluntary poverty," begging for their food—which, by the way, the Waldenses did not do!
      2) Herein, by the way, we have an example of imitating a method without the message

Some Servant Resources:

A. *Servant Evangelism* (Sjogren, 1993)

   History:
   Steve Sjogren, *Conspiracy of Kindness* (Ann Harbor, MI: Servant, 1993)
   Steve Sjogren, Dave Ping, and Doug Pollock, *Irresistible Evangelism* (Group, 2003)

   Theology: The difference between Sjogren and Atkinson/Roesel

   Methodology—individual service

B. *Ministry Evangelism* (Atkinson and Roesel, 1995)

   History: Donald A. Atkinson and Charles L. Roesel, *Meeting Needs—Sharing Christ* (Nashville: Lifeway, 1995).

   Theology: The difference between Sjogren and Atkinson/Roesel

   Methodology—social service

C. *Servanthood Evangelism* (Reid and Wheeler, 1997):

   Definition: Alvin Reid and David Wheeler, "Intentionally Sharing Christ by Modeling Biblical Servanthood"

   Methodology—individual service

D. Operation Angel Food (2005):

   Definition: Low cost food is provided to needy families once-a-month. The families must come to church to receive the food, and initial contacts are made through church members.

   Involved churches can share the Gospel either in the church or at the homes of those who receive the food.

E. AERDO—or the Association of Evangelical Relief and Development Organizations all promote and raise funds among Evangelicals assuming the premises of Servant Evangelism, which were earlier defined by amalgamating Christianity with the psychology of Maslow's Hierarchy of needs, as noted above in Aldrich and Sjogren.

Historical perspective:
> The Salvation Army, founded by William Booth, later developed a similar strategy of serving people's needs as a bridge into their lives
>
> World Vision, founded by Bob Pierce in 1950, is the contemporary grandfather of most of the AERDO organizations.[1319]

IV. Special Event Evangelism:

Introduction: Special event evangelism, very common in our day, may include on campus events related to the Christian calendar: Christmas and Easter Pageants; or on-campus events not related to the Christian calendar: Super Bowl parties, fishing conventions, hot rod car expeditions, etc.; sometimes off-campus events may be included: going to a movie, a ball game, the amusement park, etc.

a.   Evaluation:

1)   Strengths:

a)   Special event evangelism generally focuses on culturally-compatible and culturally-acceptable types of events, often focusing on significant seasons (such as Christmas and Easter, but also New Year, Valentine's Day, etc.)

b)   Provides the church with a cataclysmic event, which assists the week-in and week-out of all of the other church's activities

c)   Generally provides for a "come and see", non-confrontational type of evangelism

2)   Weaknesses:

a)   Can become a competition between churches:
(1) Who can have a bigger stage production
(2) Who can have better music
(3) Who can have more animals involved

b)   Can provide smaller churches:
(1) A feeling of inferiority, because they are not able to produce Broadway-style musicals like First Church
(2) A false view of what it means to achieve success as a church

c)   Evangelism may be downgraded to:
(1) A "come and see" method only
(2) Use of special events as a non-confrontational strategy
(3) "Look at us" evangelism, rather than "Look at Him" evangelism

d)   May confuse:
(1) Entertainment with evangelism
(2) Church swapping with evangelism
(3) Church growth with evangelism

e)   May create a talent-based ecclesiology:
(1) Wherein a person's talent leads them to be of assistance to the church
(2) 1 Corinthians 12 addressed the need to honor the less presentable (12:20-26)

f)   May use worldly-methods to achieve spiritual ends.

g)   It must be considered whether unsaved people can truly experience the love of God in Christian fellowship, or whether their eyes are blinded to it.

[1319]Franklin Graham and Jeannette Lockerbie, *Bob Pierce: This One Thing I Do* (Dallas: Word, 1983).

V. Other Evangelism Programs:

   A. NET (NAMB)

     Introduction: *The NET* may possibly be considered a "postmodern" approach to evangelism, as it seeks to emphasize "storying the Gospel"

     History—use of story seeks to impact a non-propositional generation:
       One must consider, on the other hand, that Jesus used parables to hide the truth, not to make it plain, Matt 13:10-17, 34-35

     The following provides Alvin Reid's assessment of the NET:

       "Some have gone too far with narrative evangelism, elevating stories of people above *the* story of the gospel. We can, however, integrate the narrative to illustrate and explain the Gospel.
       "How, though, do we achieve this integration? The *Net* approach teaches believers how to share Christ by merging one's testimony with the Gospel.
       "The Net's approach takes into consideration the changes brought on by postmodernism. It trains the witness to weave his or her testimony into the clear, biblical presentation of the gospel."[1320]

   B. Block Parties

   C. Athletic Programs, e.g. Upward Basketball

[1320]Alvin Reid, *Radically Unchurched* (Grand Rapids: Kregel, 2002), 138.

Chapter 30 Appendixes

Some Possible Fallacies of Lifestyle Evangelism, Friendship Evangelism, or Relational Evangelism

Definitions:

Lifestyle Evangelism relates to (1) the belief that living a good life in front of lost people is true proclamation of the Gospel; or (2) the belief that living a good life in front of lost people is a necessary preparation prior to the proclamation of the Gospel

Friendship Evangelism is defined as recommending or requiring the building of a friendship with a lost person prior to gain the right to share the Gospel with this person

Much like **Friendship Evangelism**, **Relationship Evangelism** teaches that the Gospel message best crosses the lines of existing relationships; it therefore encourages and/or necessitates the building of relationships with lost people prior to or as a prerequisite to sharing the Gospel

Some Fallacies of Lifestyle Evangelism:

Fallacy #1: My transformed life in Christ will not be a reproach to lost people, cf. Lot in Sodom, Gen 19:6-10

Fallacy #2: Jesus was wrong when He said that the sinful men actually love deeds of darkness, hate the light, and will not come to the light lest their deeds be exposed, John 3:19-20

Fallacy #3: Experience proves that Jesus spoke in significant hyperbole when He said that the world would hate His disciples, John 15:18-20

Fallacy #4: Jesus made an overstatement when He told His disciples that telling others of faith in Him would divide friendships and bring enmity within families, Matt 10:21-22, 34-36

Fallacy #5: The example of Jesus with the unbelief of His family and hometown do not relate to Christians today, Matt 13:54-58; Mark 6:1-6; Luke 4:16, 28-30, even though Jesus made that comparison, John 15:18, promising persecution for His name, Matt 5:11-12; Luke 6:22-23; cf. 1 Pet 4:14

Fallacy #6: Any Christian who does not agree with lifestyle evangelism, likewise does not live a holy or godly life, and consequently lives an inconsistent life before lost people, and is therefore a reproach to the name of Christ

Fallacy #7: Christians must join sinners in their sinful lifestyles in order to earn the right to share the Gospel with them

Fallacy #8: Christians must live in a state of sinless perfection before they have earned the right to share the Gospel with anyone

Further Questions for Thought:

1. Is belief in lifestyle evangelism not symptomatic of seeking to apply a Christian Moral Philosophy to evangelism?

2. Does not belief in lifestyle evangelism necessitate the ignoring of certain portions of Scripture, therefore undermining plenary inspiration?

3. What happens to the urgency of evangelism when evangelism is reduced to a lifestyle-only evangelism?

Some fallacies of **Friendship Evangelism** and/or **Relationship Evangelism**:

Fallacy #1: James made an overstatement when He said that friendship with the world is enmity toward God, James 4:4; furthermore, He was not speaking of people in the world, He was speaking only of materialism and capitalism.

Fallacy #2: Paul was overly pious or pietistic when he discouraged being in fellowship with those who walk in darkness, 2 Cor 6:14-18

Fallacy #3: There will be no pressure to participate in deeds of darkness when one seeks to establish a friendship with lost people

Fallacy #4: Friendship with lost people will never result in mocking or persecution for not participating in their deeds of darkness, cf. Lot in Sodom, Gen 19:6-10

Further Question for Thought

1. How can non-judgmental separation from the world be followed, while keeping doors open for evangelistic relationships, à la 1 Cor 5:9-13 or 1 Cor 9:19-23?

2. Is there a difference between being friendly and friendship?

3. In what way is friendship developed through mutual interests and activities? And when does non-participation in mutual activities prohibit friendship?

4. In what way are the subtle issues involved in **Friendship Evangelism** or **Relational Evangelism** being discussed in Leviticus 10:10-11, the making of a distinction between the holy and unholy, between the clean and the unclean?

Great Commission, Activity, and Leadership

| **Great Commission Evangelism** | Necessarily ⟶ Leads to | **Evangelism Activity** | Necessarily ⟶ Leads to | **Need for Leadership** | Necessarily ⟶ Leads to | **Administrative Principles** |

Comments:
1. Leading people in evangelism always necessitates to some level of leadership and administration
2. There are two dangers here:
   a) Downgrading the leading of evangelism to a series of administrative principles (e.g. relying on the example of "Madison Avenue" techniques or the teachings of the *Harvard Business Review*)
   b) Placing the leading of evangelism into the hands of capable administrators, who are not time tested evangelists, and therefore do not have enough of a heart for evangelization for that to be a mark of their administrative talents

| **While all Evangelism Activity** | Necessarily ⟶ Leads to | **Increased Church Activity** | ⟶ | **Not All Church Activity** | Necessarily ⟶ Leads to | **Increased Evangelism Activity** |

Comments:
1. Whereas evangelization always leads to administration of some type, all church activity is not evangelism
2. The challenge comes from old administration resulting from old evangelization; following changes in church leadership, old administration can lead to continued complexity of administration without the corresponding evangelization which led to its necessity
3. Perhaps this is the greatest challenge of what Ralph Neighbour, Jr. called "Program Based Design" churches, which have old leadership structures without the older Great Commission emphasis
4. The result is a church with a lot of complex structure, but without the corresponding evangelistic zeal.

Evangelism, Activity, and Social Activity

| **Begin with an Evangelistic Church*** | Wooed into ⟶ Including | **Combined Evangelism with Social Activity** | plus approximately ⟶ 4 years of Social Activity | **Social Activity without Evangelization** |

*The soil wherein this process most effectively takes place is one in which church members are truly born again, having the love of Jesus shed abroad in their hearts. These members are sensitive to the needs of others, malleable to learn and grow, and open to the leadership of a pastor and others. They are sometimes described by God as bread that is eaten (Psa 14:4; 53:4)!

Consider by way of example:
1. A tree trimming crew is great, needful, and helpful in disaster relief and other situations, both for the help of needy church members, as well as for the help of society at large
2. The sale for participating on the tree trimming crew is evangelistic, "We are going to help meet needs and share the love of Jesus; come join our crew!"
3. Those with a heart for the lost will be the first to sign up for the tree trimming crew, even if they know nothing about trimming trees
4. How long does it take for the tree trimming crew to become another social arm of the church wherein no evangelism is taking place (when dealing with lost people), and/or wherein its services are not made available to needy people within the church—such as the elderly (Eph 6:10)?
5. Meanwhile the time and talents of those with a heart for evangelism are drained by putting them in charge of a social program, where there may be less and less opportunities to share the Gospel

6. At issue is not ceasing to provide help, but just being biblical and maintaining the original vision; when the love of Jesus is shed abroad in anyone's heart, they begin to see needs and consider how they can help out; it's a very good thing!

Comments:

1. Whereas the length of time for an evangelistic church to maintain social activity and drop their evangelistic thrust is primarily dependent upon the preaching and practice of the pastor

2. Often, truly evangelistic churches have enough social needs within their own membership (which is growing from their evangelization), that they will have less time and/or money to effectively meet the needs of their own people (e.g. helping widows that are widows indeed, 1 Tim 5), if social activity becomes their major evangelism strategy

3. A shift takes place in the mentality of a church, wherein the phrase in Ephesians 6:10, "especially to the household of the saints," is forgotten, as a church changes to emphasize social ministry as the major part of their evangelistic ministry

4. It does not take long for a church emphasizing social evangelism to begin to ignore or forget the needs of their own hurting brethren (e.g. helping widows that are widows indeed, 1 Tim 5), as they are swamped with the unending needs of the entire society (John 12:8); perhaps this shift takes 5 to 10 years, again depending on the pastor or the changes in pastoral staffing

5. Likewise, the Great Commission's emphasis on spiritual lostness changes to an emphasis on the social needs of men (in particular), and then those of the entire society (as a whole), and soon political decisions (as these impact society as a whole); showing comes a change in the church's view of the Great Commission toward the pressing socio-political and economic issues of the day (which are unending)

6. Meanwhile, membership can become more a matter of social health and social standing, than a matter of conversion or being "born again"

Begin with an Evangelistic Church → Add in Social Activity in Their Evangelization → Emphasize Social Needs for Outreach → Emphasize Good Social Standing for Membership → Downgrade Conversion in Preaching → Downgrade Conversion for Membership → Downgrade Conversion in Theology

Further Comments:

1. The above changes are readily observable in individual churches over time:
   a. It takes a very strong and faithful preacher of the Word to keep this inevitable drift from taking place

2. One of the great dangers of emphasizing social needs for outreach is seeking to please men in our evangelization:
   a. Pleasing men, rather than God, is never a good motive, John 12:42-43; Gal 1:10
   b. Please men is pleasing those who do not know that death is the end of their ways, Prov 14:12; 16:25
   c. Pleasing men will lead to seeking to avoid the offense of the cross and the offense of the Gospel preached, 1 Cor 1:18ff.; Gal 5:11
   d. Meanwhile, the true Gospel and the godly lifestyle of believers will always be the smell of death to those who are dying (the lost), 2 Cor 2:15-16

3. Sometimes emphasizing social needs leads churches to seek publicity from the world:
   a. However, often if the world (e.g. secular news outlets) will publicize the event, they will not allow a spiritual emphasis to be included in their coverage
   b. Some churches will (it seems) do almost anything to attract the world's attention
   c. Sometimes churches will hide their evangelistic or missional emphasis in order to get secular coverage, thereby hiding their Great Commission emphasis
   d. This slow (or not-so-slow) change leads to masking their conversionistic and Great Commission emphasis, even to those within their own church (this often begins by removing the denominational label in the church name, so as to remove potential stumbling blocks for lost people coming to the church).
   e. What does this do to their membership's view of the priority of the spiritual in the Great Commission?

4. The downgrade displayed in the above chart portrays the drift from being an evangelistic church to downgrading conversion in theology:
   a. This exemplifies a downgrade that has occurred generation after generation in the history of virtually all U.S. Protestant or Evangelical churches, as can be readily studied in U.S. denominational histories

b. It is up to the reader to determine where on the above chart:
    1) Comes the drift away from a New Testament practice
    2) Comes the drift away from a New Testament theology

Postmodern Evangelism Methodologies

The following have been posited as "postmodern" evangelism methodologies in contradistinction to "modern" methods.

	"Postmodern"	Vs.	"Modern"
Preparation	Worldview[1321]	Vs.	General revelation
	Service[1322]	Vs.	Irrelevant/Inauthentic
	Relationship[1323]	Vs.	Stranger-to-stranger
	Culturally Relevant[1324]	Vs.	Eternal orientation
	Prolonged time[1325]	Vs.	Instantaneous
Method	Incarnational[1326]	Vs.	Proclamational
	Dialogue[1327]	Vs.	Us/them mentality
	Narrative[1328]	Vs.	Outline
	Community[1329]	Vs.	Individual
	Worship[1330]	Vs.	Abstract cognitive
Message	Storying[1331]	Vs.	Biblical propositional statements
	Here and Now[1332]	Vs.	Eternal Life
	Relational[1333]	Vs.	Judicial
	Love (emotional)[1334]	Vs.	Gospel principles
Decision	Converted to community[1335]	Vs.	Converted to Christ
	Converted to the Christ of community[1336]	Vs.	Converted to the Christ of the cross
Duration	Process[1337]	Vs.	Punctiliar or instantaneous

[1321]Mark Mittelberg, *Building a Contagious Church* (Grand Rapids: Zondervan, 2000), 43.

[1322]Ardith Fernando, "The Uniqueness of Jesus Christ," in D. A. Carson, ed., *Telling the Truth: Evangelizing Postmoderns* (Grand Rapids: Zondervan, 2000), 125-26; Steve Sjogren, et al., *Irresistible Evangelism Natural Ways to Open Others to Jesus* (Loveland, CO: Group, 2004), 90.

[1323]Ardith Fernando, "The Uniqueness of Jesus Christ," in *Telling the Truth*, 124; Tony Jones, *Postmodern Youth Ministry: Exploring Cultural Shift, Cultivating Authentic Community, Creating Holistic Connections* (Grand Rapids: Zondervan and Youth Specialties, 2001), 122; and Brian McLaren, *More Ready Than you Realize: Evangelism as Dance in the Postmodern Matrix* (Grand Rapids: Zondervan, 2002), 55, 58, 61, 67, 135-137.

[1324]"Where does one go to find common ground? I refer to the moral argument, which argues for God from morality" (Ravi Zacharias, "The Touch of Truth," in *Telling the Truth*, 33, 34).

[1325]Mittelberg, 59. Robert Webber, *Ancient-Future Church: Making Your Church a Faith-Forming Community* (Grand Rapids: Baker, 2003), 67.

[1326]"We need to incarnate the truth" (Millard Erickson, *Truth or Consequences: The Promise or Perils of Postmodernism* [Downers Grove, IL: InterVarsity, 2001], 315).

[1327]Richard Bauckham, *Bible and Mission* (Grand Rapids: Baker, 2003), 99; Graham Johnston, *Preaching to a Postmodern World* (Grand Rapids: Baker, 2001), 78; Robert N. Nash, *An 8-Track Church in a CD World: The Church in a Postmodern World* (Macon, GA: Smyth and Helwys, 2001), 68-69; Sjogren, *Irresistible Evangelism*, 139.

[1328]Kevin Graham Ford, *Jesus for a New Generation* (Downer's Grove: InterVarsity, 1995), 218-39; and McLaren, *More Ready than You Realize*, 135.

[1329]Erickson, 289-305; Jones, 103-09; Jimmy Long, "Generating Hope: A Strategy for Reaching the Postmodern Generation" in *Telling the Truth*, 334; Leonard Sweet, *Postmodern Pilgrims* (Nashville: Broadman, 2000), 112-18; Webber, 61-63.

[1330]Fernando, 136; Long, "Generating Hope," 334; Nash, 69-72; Sweet, 43-45, 72-73.

[1331]Bauckham, 90-98; Erickson, 317-19; Leighton Ford, *The Power of Story: Recovering the Oldest, Most Natural Way to Reach People for Christ* (Colorado Springs: NavPress, 1994), 14, 50, 52; Jones, 27; McLaren, 135; Alvin Reid, *Radically Unchurched* (Grand Rapids: Kregel, 2002), 128-41; Sweet, 123-25.

[1332]Grenz, Stanley J., *What Christians Really Believe and Why* (Louisville, KY: Westminster John Knox, 1998), 163-65; Nash, 58-63.

[1333]Sjogren, 149.

[1334]Nash, 72, 119; Sweet, 31.

[1335]Long, 334; Webber, 55-69.

[1336]Long, 334.

[1337]McLaren, 137-40; Webber, 13.

Thoughts on the Emergent Church Movement

Understanding the Term "Emergent":
     One of the focal definitions for the term "emergent" is described by Joseph R. Myers in *The Search to Belong: Rethinking Intimacy, Community, Small Groups* (2003):

The Secret of Slime Mold
(Emergence Theory)

"The slime mold spends much of its life as thousands of distinct single-celled units, each moving separately from its other comrades. Under the right conditions, those myriad cells will coalesce again into a single, larger organism, which then begins its leisurely crawl across the garden floor, consuming rotting leaves and wood as it moves about. When the environment is less hospitable, the slime mold acts as a single organism; when the weather turns cooler and the mold enjoys a large food supply, 'it' becomes a 'they.' The slime mold oscillates between being a single creature and a swarm."[1338]
     The intriguing secret of slime mold is that there is no 'master planner' calling the cells to unite. The coming together is spontaneous. There is no apparent leader. There is no call to action. No vision statements, value statements, or mission statements. There is no "queen bee" or charismatic leader. The cells collect spontaneously when the environment triggers the response.
     When slime mold encounters a favorable environment, the mold emits a substance called acrasin or cyclic AMP. When this occurs, the slime mold cells unite with others in the area. When people encounter someone to whom they are attracted, there is a similar occurrence. The triggering mechanism? For people, there are several. Human beings communicate their desire to connect through eye dilation, facial expression (sometimes voluntary, sometimes involuntary), posture, body temperature, and, yes, we too emit chemicals called pheromones, which are decoded by those around us.
     When there is a favorable environment we make spontaneous choices regarding to whom we want to belong. This is the type of connection that people are looking for in their lives.
     Slime mold offers us an interesting insight: We humans could help by creating the healthy environments in which people naturally connect. If we would concentrate upon facilitating the environment instead of the result (people experiencing community), we might see healthy, spontaneous community emerge.[1339]

Several Considerations about Emergent:

     First of all, there are a number of emanations of the Emergent Church Movement (aka. "Postmodern Churches" or "Transformational Churches" [e.g. Mosaic Church]). Ed Stetzer delineated three eminations:
     (1) The Relevants (applying Gospel to culture),
     (2) The Reconstructionists (changing the form of the church to apply the Gospel to culture), and
     (3) The Revisionists ("questioning and revising the Gospel and the church").[1340]
Each of these would need to be interpreted and considered separately.

     Second, while the overall Emergent Church's emphasis on community is important, it seems to me that when the church consists of believers-only, community comes as a supernatural gift of the Holy Spirit, "Fellowship of the Spirit" (2 Cor 13:14). However, in the Seeker Church context, community must be [humanly] fostered as there is no given "fellowship of the Spirit" between believers and unbelievers. Likewise for the emergent, community provides a preparatory tool to open the door for discussing the Gospel in a non-threatening way. Note that Jesus in John 13:35 clearly stated "one another" to described the relationship among believers. While the believer is still to love his neighbor as himself, the latter context is not missional, but related to God-given obedience.

     [1338]Quoted from Steve Johnson, *Emergence: The Connected Lives of Ants, Brains, Cities, and Software* [New York: Scribner, 2001], 13; the paragraph is also quoted by Brian McLaren, *A Generous Orthodoxy: Why I Am Missional + Evangelical + Post/Protestant + Liberal/Conservative + Mystical/Poetic + Biblical + Charismatic/Contemplative + Fundamentalist/Calvinist + Anabaptist/Anglican + Methodist + Catholic + Green + Incarnational + Depressed-yet-Hopeful + Emergent + Unfinished Christian* (El Cajon, CA: EmergentYS, 2004; Grand Rapids: Zondervan, 2004), 276.
     [1339]Joseph R. Myers in *The Search to Belong: Rethinking Intimacy, Community, Small Groups* (El Cajon, CA: EmergentYS, 2003; Grand Rapids: Zondervan, 2003), 72-73.
     [1340]Ed Stetzer, "Understanding the Emerging Church (6 Jan 2006)"; available from: http://www.sbcbaptistpress.org/bpnews.asp?ID=22406; Internet.

Third, the renewed emphasis on the use of questions in evangelism is refreshing. Similarly, there are several questions used in the New Testament as regards evangelism, e.g. "Who do people say that I am? ... Who do you say that I am?" (Matt 16:13, 15), "Do you believe in the Son of Man?" (John 9:35), and "Do you understand what you are reading?" (Acts 8:30).

Fourth, however, disconcerting are:

1. The Emergent church's movement away from punctiliar salvation ("You must be born again")
2. The addition of community to the order of salvation ("Whosoever calls upon the name of the Lord will be saved")
3. The assumption of a wide road if the Gospel is properly communicated ("For the gate is small and the way is narrow that leads to life, and there are few who find it")
4. The antagonism to an emphasis on eternal life ("Those appointed for eternal life believed," "But the gift of God is eternal life," etc.)
5. The movement away from verbal and plenary inspiration ("Every word of God is tested").

Sample Books on, by, or related to the "Emergent" Church

2007

Kester Brewin, *Signs of Emergence* (Emersion, 2007).

Tim Keel, *Intuitive Leadership* (Emersion, 2007).

Joseph Myers, *Organic Community* (Emersion, 2007).

Doug Pagitt and Tony Jones, eds., *An Emergent Manifesto of Hope* (Grand Rapids: Baker, 2007).

Will and Lisa Samson, *Justice in the Burbs* (Emersion, 2007).

Robert Webber†, ed. *Listening to the Beliefs of Emerging Churches: Five Viewpoints* (Grand Rapids: Zondervan, 2007).

2006

Ray S. Anderson, *An Emerging Theology for Emerging Churches* (Downers Grove, IL: InterVarsity, 2006).

Scott A. Bessenecker, *The New Friars: The Emerging Movement Serving the World's Poor* (Downers Grove, IL: InterVarsity, 2006.

Tim Conder, *Church in Transition: The Journey of Existing Churches into the Emerging Culture* (El Cajon, CA: EmergentYS, 2006; Grand Rapids: Zondervan, 2006).

2005

George Barna, *Revolution* (Wheaton, IL: Tyndale, 2005).

Jonathan Campbell and Ryan K. Bolger, *The Way of Jesus: A Journey of Freedom for Pilgrims and Wanderers* (San Francisco: Jossey-Bass, 2005).

D. A. Carson, *Becoming Conversant with the Emergent Church: Understanding a Movement and Its Implications* (Grand Rapids: Zondervan, 2005).

Neil Cole, *Organic Church: Growing Faith Where Life Happens* (San Francisco: Jossey-Bass, 2005).

Eddie Gibbs and Ryan K. Bolger, *Emerging Churches: Creating Christian Community in Postmodern Cultures* (Grand Rapids: Baker, 2005).

Brian McLaren, *The Last Word and the Word After That* (San Francisco: Jossey-Bass, 2005).

Michael Moynagh, *emergingchurch.intro* (Grand Rapids: Monarch Books, 2005).

Greg Russinger and Alex Field, eds., *Practitioners: Voices Within the Emerging Church* (Ventura: Regal, 2005).

Steve Taylor, *The Out of Bounds Church? Learning to Create a Community of Faith in a Culture of Change* (Grand Rapids: Zondervan, 2005).

2004

Dan Kimball, *Emerging Worship: Creating Worship Gatherings for New Generations* (El Cajon, CA: EmergentYS, 2004; Grand Rapids: Zondervan, 2004).

Brian McLaren, *A Generous Orthodoxy: Why I Am Missional + Evangelical + Post/Protestant + Liberal/Conservative + Mystical/Poetic + Biblical + Charismatic/Contemplative + Fundamentalist/Calvinist + Anabaptist/Anglican + Methodist + Catholic + Green + Incarnational + Depressed-yet-Hopeful + Emergent + Unfinished Christian* (El Cajon, CA: EmergentYS, 2004; Grand Rapids: Zondervan, 2004).

Elmer Towns and Ed Stetzer, *Perimeters of Light: Biblical Boundaries for the Emergent Church* (Chicago: Moody, 2004).

2003—This year seemed to be "The Wave"!

Rob Bell, *Velvet Elvis* (Grand Rapids: Zondervan, 2003).

Michael Frost and Alan Hirsch, *The Shaping of Things to Come: Innovation and Mission for the 21st Century Church* (Peabody, MA: Hendrickson, 2003).

Dan Kimball, *The Emerging Church: Vintage Christianity for a New Generation* (El Cajon, CA: EmergentYS, 2003; Grand Rapids: Zondervan, 2003)

Brian McLaren, *The Story We Find Ourselves In: Further Adventures of a New Kind of Christian* (San Francisco: Jossey-Bass, 2003)

Brian D. McLaren and Tony Campolo, *Adventures in Missing the Point: How the Culture Controlled Church Neutered the Gospel* (El Cajon, CA: EmergentYS, 2003; Grand Rapids: Zondervan, 2003).

Joseph R. Myers, *The Search to Belong: Rethinking Intimacy, Community, Small Groups.* Forewords by John Wooden and Leonard Sweet (El Cajon, CA: EmergentYS, 2003; Grand Rapids: Zondervan, 2003).

Leonard Sweet, Brian McLaren, and Jerry Haselmayer, eds., *A Is for Abductive: The Language of the Emerging Church* (Grand Rapids: Zondervan, 2003).

Leonard Sweet, ed. *The Church in Emerging Culture: Five Perspectives* (El Cajon, CA: EmergentYS, 2003; Grand Rapids: Zondervan, 2003).

Dave Tomlinson, *The Post Evangelical* (London: SPCK, 1995; El Cajon, CA: EmergentYS/Grand Rapids: Zondervan, 2003).

Mike Yaconnelli, ed., *Stories of Emergence: Moving from Absolute to Authentic* (El Cajon, CA: EmergentYS, 2003; Grand Rapids: Zondervan, 2003).

2002

Brian McLaren, *More Ready than You Realize: Evangelism as Dance in the Postmodern Matrix* (Zondervan, 2002).

Leonard Sweet, *SoulSalsa: Survival Tips for Godly Living in the 21st Century* (Grand Rapids: Zondervan, 2002).

Robert E. Webber, *The Younger Evangelicals: Facing the Challenges of the New World* (Grand Rapids: Baker, 2002)

2001

Robert Lewis, *The Church of Irresistible Influence* (Grand Rapids: Zondervan, 2001).

Michael Moynagh, *Changing World, Changing Church* (Grand Rapids: Monarch, 2001).

Brian McLaren, *A New Kind of Christian: A Tale of Two Friends on a Spiritual Journey* (San Francisco: Jossey-Bass/Leadership Network, 2001).

Leonard Sweet, *SoulTsunami: 10 Life Rings for You and Your Church* (Grand Rapids: Zondervan, 2001).

2000

Brian McLaren, *The Church on the Other Side: Doing Ministry in the Postmodern Matrix,* revised and expanded version of *Reinventing Your Church* (Grand Rapids: Zondervan, 1998, 2000).

Leonard Sweet, *Postmodern Pilgrims: First Century Passion for the 21st Century Church* (Nashville: Broadman, 2000).

1998

Darrell L. Guder and Lois Barrett, *Missional Church: A Vision for the Sending of the Church in North America* (Grand Rapids: Eerdmans, 1998).

Some [older] Emergent Websites

www.anewkindofchristian.com
www.crcc.org
www.emergentvillage.com
www.emersionbooks.com
emergent-us.typepad.com
www.off-the-map.org
www.preachingplus.com
smartchristian.com
tallskinnykiwi.typepad.com
www.theooze.com
www.vintagefaith.com

Cooperation and Separation Issues?

Introduction: The conservatively-oriented New Testament Chrisatian may have issues with other Christians at various points. It is helpful to know which are the most important, which are secondary, and which are tertiary, as these issues are often sometimes muddled together in an ecumenical goulash ("It's just a matter of biblical interpretation"). The following issues and their assignment are meant to introduce the concepts and to show various hues of interpretation and application.

Level of Issue	Level Three (of less importance)	Level Two (important)	Level One (of highest importance)
Atonement issues			Substitutionary atonement versus any other model
Baptismal issues	Running water or use of a pool	Mode of believer's baptism by immersion	Believer's baptism versus infant baptism
			Belief in believer's baptism versus belief in the salvific validity of baptism as a sacrament [Augustine's "signs and symbols"]
Biblical Issues		e.g. Belief in multiple fulfillment of OT prophecy	Absolute authority of the Word of God
Calvinism issues		The exact order of the pre-creation decrees in the mind of God	Belief in predestination
		Limited atonement versus universal atonement	Total depravity of man
Charismatic issues		Speaking in tongues	Not adhering to a "health and wealth" or prosperity gospel
Conversion issues			Conversion versus non-conversionistic
			Belief in being born again versus indifference toward this doctrine
Creation Issues		Theistic evolution	God did created the heavens and the earth
Dispensational issues		Belief in the seven dispensations	
Ecclesial issues	Architecture (not too expensive please)		Priesthood of the believer and local congregational rule versus bishop rule or papal authority
End time issues	Pre-tribulation rapture	Premillennial return of Christ	Imminent return of Christ
Ethical issues*	Attendance at movies		Acceptance of homosexuality as an alternate lifestyle
Evangelism issues			The church's primary mission is to fulfill the Great Commission
	Exact Gospel presentation used, as there are many good ones	Sinners prayer	Initiative or expectant evangelism
		Altar call	Lost people must hear the Gospel to be saved
Gender issues		Ordination of deaconesses	Women preachers
Lord's Supper	Vessel in which the cup is passed or whether one partakes as a family, in small groups, or as a church		Belief in the non-salvific quality of the Lord's Supper versus assigning a sacramental grace to partaking of the symbols

*Many more issues may be added to the Ethical issues list. These examples may spark some interest in the mind of the reader.

Also see my charts on the atonement (*Charts for a Theology of Evangelism*, Charts 65-75)
    With whom will you cooperate?
    With whom will you separate?
    What are the boundaries for your theology and why?

Understanding Theological Change
Or: Interesting Differentiations among Conservative Evangelicals
Or: Battlegrounds in Church History

The following chart considers and interesting distinctions that I have noticed in my studies. As in any chart, it may be viewed as simplistic, dogmatic, or generalistic, and yet the distinctions hold some interesting parallels. Because this chart unites historical views and views of biblical authority with evangelism, it is included in this chapter for cautious consideration.

Considerations		Conservative Evangelical	Possibly "Moderating" Evangelical
Historical Theology	**General approach to the study of history**	Tend to be more watchful, skeptical, and even perhaps pessimistic in their analysis of the history of the churches	Tend to be more open, positive, broad-minded, and even ready to rethink past mores, considering their immediate predecessors to be too perhaps narrow-minded—the moderate may say that they were perhaps a bit naïve
	Patristics	Tend to be cautious to find value in [what remains of] Patristic writings or information on the growth and expansion of the "Church" in its early centuries	Tend to find normative value in the "Early Church's" evangelistic practices and in Patristic theology
	Monastic movement	Tend to be cautious in finding value in monasticism, with its Stoic roots, sacramental salvation, and biblically-tangential spiritual disciplines	Tend to find great value in the spiritual disciplines of the Roman monks, morphing into a positive view of their Medieval methods [minus Inquisition and crusades], and Ecclesial and sacramental message
	Medieval theology	Tend to recognize the sacramental nature of Medieval theology, and understand its antagonism to Evangelical soteriology	Tend to emphasize the devotional nature of Rome's Medieval theology, while depreciating both Rome's antagonism to and reframing the question in opposition to Evangelical soteriology
	Medieval history	Tend to recognize the central role of inquisition, martyrdom, and crusades in Rome's crushing of schimatic and "heretical" movements in Medieval history	Tend to ignore the compromising nature of inquisition, martyrdom, and crusades in Rome's approach to missions and practice in Medieval history
	Reformation	Tend to recognize, value, and include the importance of evangelism, martyrdom, and crusades, as well as the commonality of Evangelical doctrinal beliefs when interpreting the religious climate of the Reformation era	Tend to ignore evangelism, martyrdom, and crusades during the Reformation era, focusing only on the variations between theology and practice between various cultural-linguistic Protestant churches (à la Bossuet's *Variations*)
	Eighteenth and nineteenth Centuries	Tend to emphasize evangelism and [what became known as] Fundamental theology in the Nineteenth Century, considering with skepticism the development of "higher criticism" and with caution "textual criticism"	Tend to emphasize the social results of the Pietists in Germany and in the evangelism of Evangelicals in England during the Eighteenth and Nineteenth Centuries (e.g. Wilberforce)
	Roman Catholicism	Tend to distance themselves from Rome, vocally separating from its theology and practice	Tend to find value in Rome's social dogmas, while downplaying its soteriological and ecclesial differences, and encouraging cooperation with Rome whenever deemed pragmatic
Bible and Authority	**Translations of the Bible**	Tend to appreciate more literal translations of Scripture (including the use of "back translation"), in conjunction with belief in verbal inerrancy of the original autographs	Tend to appreciate dynamic translations of Scripture (accepting the translators' norms of cultural equivalency), in conjunction with a belief in the inerrancy of the ideas of the text (thought for thought) , not necessarily the words or scientific data
	Original texts of the New Testament	Tend to appreciate the plurality of texts, in other words the Majority Text, Byzantine Textform, or to use the more pejorative term "Textus Receptus"	Tend to appreciate the critical edition history of the German Bible Society's text of the New Testament Greek, in other words the Westcott-Hort-Tischendorff-Nestle-Aland-Metzger-Martini-Karavidopoulos text
	Of the Old Testament Septuagint	Tend to be more appreciative of the study of the OT Septuagint, because of the common Greek language with the NT, while not denying the uniqueness, necessity, and authority of the Hebrew original or the Masoretic Text	Tend to emphasize the linguistic differences between OT Septuagint Greek (2nd Century B.C. = 101-200 B.C.) and NT Koine Greek (1st Century A.D. = 52-98 A.D.), a temporal range of 151-298 years [e.g. Is there today a Greek NT available bound with an OT LXX without the apocryphal books from any Bible Society?]

Considerations		Conservative Evangelical	Possibly "Moderating" Evangelical
Bible	**Biblical authority**	Tend to emphasize the absolute authority and inerrancy of each word in the Bible in theology, practice, and church life	Tend to emphasize inerrancy in thoughts and ideas, while accepting a type of hypostatic union of the Bible with science and culture in theology, practice, and church life
Soteriology	**Atonement**	Tend to emphasize almost uniquely the Substitutionary Atonement (aka. judicial or forensic atonement)	Tend to emphasize a Reconciliation or Relational model of the atonement, with a life here-and-now emphasis in a theology of salvation (a type of middle view between the objective and subjective atonement)
	Conversion	Tend to emphasize the new birth as a complete change in nature, including making less of a distinction between a convert, a Christian, and a disciple of Christ	Tend to emphasize pre-evangelism, pre-discipleship, the discipleship process, spiritual disciplines, and sometimes a gradual enlightenment approach to salvation, including sometimes making a big distinction between a mere convert and a true disciple
	Evangelism	Tend to emphasize New Testament evangelism (initiative and expectant)	Tend to emphasize culturally "relevant" methods of evangelism, including but not limited to friendship, lifestyle, service, and apologetic evangelism (all of which have wide ranges of definition and application)

Could it be that actual doctrinal changes in actuality start at the bottom of the chart and move their way up to the top?

It is very unlikely that one would move from a "Moderating" position to the "Conservative" view, outside of revival. Water tends to flow downstream. Changes in the other direction, from "Conservative" to "Moderating," are so commonplace that they tend to be seen as the norm by those who accept the premise of change.

Further difficulty comes from several additional factors: (1) Those who have so changed seek to guise their change, at least for a while, so as not to lose their positions of leadership or their prominence. Similarly, they know how to speak to keep their "Conservative" constituencies at ease. Therefore they can often lead seminaries, denominations, and movements to change with them. (2) The changes themselves are incremental, taking place over a period of time, and are often very difficult to judge. (3) Those who go through these changes are usually good people with a good history and a good track record.

Inspiration or Some Other Divine Action:
Wherein Lays the Miracle?

Object of Divine Action	Bible	Evangelism	Christian Lives	Christian Community	"Holy Objects"
Divine Action	God's inspiration of the words of the Bible, 2 Tim 3:16-17	God accompanying His Word in witness	God transforming Christians to reveal His presence	God revealing His love through Christian fellowship	Christ's real body in the Host; God's grace bestowed through the instrument of holy physical objects
Result of Divine Action	Inerrancy, John 17:17	God's Word is living and active, Heb 4:12-13	Let your light shine before men in such a way that they may see your good works, Matt 5:16	By this will all men know that you are My disciples, if you have love for one another, John 13:34-35; cf. John 17:21, 23	Impartation of grace through the Eucharist
		The Holy Spirit convicting of sin, righteousness and judgment through the Word, John 16:8			Repetition of the sacrifice of the death of Christ
			Keep your behavior excellent among the Gentiles, 1 Pet 2:12		Other objects deemed holy as well, e.g. relics, holy water, statues, etc.
Considerations	The Bible affirms its truthfulness, eternality, and righteousness over and over	Numerous Scriptures affirm that it was the message of the Word of God that led to the salvation of the hearers, 1 Thess 2:13	Jesus was rejected in His hometown, where He lived the perfect sinless life	Salvation through this subjective witness was neither the example of the early church, nor was it the teaching of the early church	Virtually the entire message of life and salvation is lost through idolatry
Wherein Faith Is Placed?	In God who has faithfully spoken through His Word	In Jesus Christ as proclaimed by the Bible and the faithful evangelist	In the promise of [and possibility of] God's transforming power	In the fellowship of the Spirit, as only displayed through God's redeemed people	In the misplaced message that the physical realm can communicate or involve some type of saving grace
Evaluation	**Most unhindered divine revelation**	**Hindrance comes through the messenger omitting or changing the Word, Jer 26:2**	**Hindrance comes through the imperfect lives of believers**	**Hindrance comes through the inevitable animosity and strife in local churches**	**A salvific divine revelation is almost impossible with this type of idolatry**

Consider the lesson of Num 20:6-12 and Acts 15:7-11.

CHAPTER 31
Evangelism and Systematic Theology

Introduction:

➢ Introductory Thoughts

✓ Theology and practice are inseparably linked

The main point of this chapter is to show that message of the Gospel, the reception of that message, and the method of proclamation are inseparably linked and interrelated.

The Interrelationship of Message, Reception, and Propagation

Fragmented Approach
Assuming no interrelationship

Non-fragmented Approach
Acknowledging interrelationship

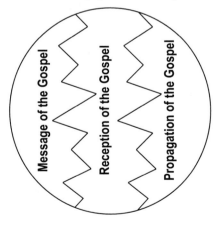

✓ Good theology leads to good practice
   Bad theology leads to bad practice, or…
   Bad practice may in fact point to bad theology!

✓ E.g. Note the theological foundation of Christian Schwartz' evangelism as communicated in his *Natural Church Development* material:

   ✓ *The ABC's of Natural Church Development*
      "There are some people who feel evangelism works best when you push people to commit their life to Christ. They do not even shy away from manipulative methods to reach this goal. No wonder many of us feel a strange sensation in our stomach when we hear the word 'evangelism.'
      "But it can be shown that 'pushy' manipulative methods represent the exact opposite of the practice we learn from growing churches."[1341]

   ✓ *Natural Church Development*
      On the last two pages of his *Natural Church Development,* Schwarz titles his topic "Church growth in the power of the Holy Spirit." In this very interesting portion, he reveals the relationship of his sociological work and the Holy Spirit inspired Word of God:
      "Natural church development is made up of principles God has created and revealed to us. This theme is woven through this whole book. It does not mean, however, that this book claims 'divine authorship.' That claim would be absurd. No, the *terminology* we have chosen to describe these principles is less than perfect. The *research techniques* we used to empirically identify the principles are flawed—like any scientific method. And the *materials* we have developed can be improved. But all of this does not change one basic fact: the *principles* that we have gropingly tried to search out and blunderingly tried to communicate find their source in God."[1342]
      What does Schwarz mean by "find their source in God"? His theological book may provide an answer …

   ✓ *Paradigm Shift in the Church*
      In a chapter titled "Functionality as a Theological Criterion?" Schwarz again reveals his theological emphases:
      The problem is that the term 'theological' is often identified with a static, ideological concept of truth…. But in fact (as this chapter will argue), to ask about the (practically demonstrable) functionality of church structures is an eminently theological concern. I would even say that a *functional* understanding of the church as an organization is the only legitimate way to justify the institutional side of the church theologically. …
      In this chapter I propose to demonstrate that the concepts of *truth* and *functionality* (understood as usefulness for church development) are theologically closer together than appears in conventional discussion…. What is a false church? My thesis is that it is a church whose structures have not been justified in terms of how useful they are for effective church development.[1343]

➢ If God predestines the Christian to salvation:
   ✓ Does that mean no evangelism is needed?
      ☞ To believe so would be disregarding the Great Commission
   ✓ Does that mean we need to share the truth but no persuasion or invitation is needed?
      ☞ To believe this would be disregarding the examples and teaching of the Bible
   ✓ We are to share the Gospel and call for commitment, even though we believe in predestination

➢ If God predestines the Christian to salvation, does He also predestine their spiritual growth?
   ✓ Does this not imply the sinless perfection of all who believe (e.g. Matt 5:48)?
   ✓ Otherwise there must be the possibility of the "carnal Christian" (e.g. 1 Cor 3:10-15)?
   ✓ And how about those who drift into theological error (e.g. Gal 1:6; 5:10)?
   ✓ Yet all our good works are "wrought in God" (John 3:21; Eph 2:10)?
   ✓ There are two warring natures in the believer (e.g. Gal 5:16-18).

[1341]Christian A. Schwarz, *ABC's of Natural Church Development* (Carol Stream, IL: ChurchSmart, n.d.), 16.

[1342]Christian Schwarz, *Natural Church Development,* 3rd ed. (Wheaton, IL: ChurchSmart, 1998), 126-27.

[1343]Christian Schwarz, *Paradigm Shift in the Church: How Natural Church Development Can Transform Theological Thinking* (Wheaton, IL: ChurchSmart, 1999), 65-66.

➢ There are actually a number of issues addressed in evangelism and systematic theology:
  ✓ The message of salvation
  ✓ The role of the preacher in salvation (his lifestyle or deeds, as well as his preaching)
  ✓ The role of the Word of God
  ✓ The role of the Holy Spirit
  ✓ The lostness of man
  ✓ Man's ability to understand the message and respond
  ✓ The order of conversion/salvation
  ✓ The role of Baptism in salvation
  ✓ The role of the church in salvation, etc.

Evangelism and Systematic Theology:

➢ Two Approaches to evangelism:
  ✓ Man-centered
  ✓ Christ-centered

EMPHASES IN EVANGELISM

Christ-Centered	Man-Centered
Supernaturally-oriented	Naturally-oriented
Instantaneous Conversion (e.g. "you must be born again")	Gradual Conversion (e.g. Schleiermacher's "quiescent self-consciousness")
Instantaneous Witnessing	Gradual Witnessing

➢ Christ-centered...
  ✓ Follows the teaching of the Bible
  ✓ Follows the examples of the Bible

➢ Man-centered...
  ✓ Seeks to please man, John 12:42-43; Gal 1:10?
  ✓ Focuses on man's ability, contra Phil 3:7-8?
  ✓ Focuses on man's righteousness, Phil 3:9?

FOCUS OF EVANGELISM I

"Look-at-Him Evangelism" [Substitutionary]	"Look-at-Me Evangelism" [Moral-influence theory; "people will be drawn to Christ by my life"]		
Christ's Righteousness, Christ's Life, Christ's Works, and Christ's Death	My Righteousness	My Life	My Works
2 Cor 4:5, "For we do not preach ourselves, but Jesus Christ as Lord" 1 Cor 2:2, "For I resolved to know nothing while I was with you except Jesus Christ and Him crucified" Phil 3:3, "for we are the *true* circumcision, who worship in the Spirit of God and glory in Christ Jesus and put no confidence in the flesh"	Matt 6:1ff (2-18), "Beware of practicing your righteousness to be seen by men" Rom 10:2-4, "For I testify about them that they have a zeal for God, but not in accordance with knowledge. For not knowing about God's righteousness and seeking to establish their own, they did not subject themselves to the righteousness of God. For Christ is the end of the law for righteousness to everyone who believes."	Matt 13:57, "And they took offense at Him. But Jesus said to them, 'A prophet is not without honor except in his hometown and in his *own* household.' And He did not do many miracles there because of their unbelief." Mark 6:4-6, "Jesus said to them, 'A prophet is not without honor except in his hometown and among his *own* relatives and in his *own* household.' And He could do no miracle there except that He laid His hands on a few sick people and healed them. And He wondered at their unbelief. And He was going around the villages teaching." Luke 4:23-24, "And He said to them, 'No doubt you will quote this proverb to Me, "Physician, heal yourself! Whatever we heard was done at Capernaum, do here in your hometown as well."' And He said, 'Truly I say to you, no prophet is welcome in his hometown." Luke 4:28-30, "And all *the people* in the synagogue were filled with rage as they heard these things; and they got up and drove Him out of the city, and led Him to the brow of the hill on which their city had been built, in order to throw Him down the cliff. But passing through their midst, He went His way."	John 10:32-33, "Jesus answered them, 'I showed you many good works from the Father; for which of them are you stoning Me?' The Jews answered Him, 'For a good work we do not stone You, but for blasphemy; and because You, being a man, make Yourself out *to be* God'" [therefore, even the good works of Jesus were not infallible preparations for His words, the Jews still wanted to kill Him!] John 6, Jesus performs signs (John 6:2); He feeds 5,000 men (v. 10-13); they believe that He is a prophet (v. 14); they want to crown Him king (v. 15); Jesus tells them that their motives are wrong (v. 26-27); He teaches them of the need for faith in Him (v. 35-40); they begin to grumble (v. 41-43; 60-61); all but the twelve leave Him (v. 66-67); Peter gets it right (v. 68-69). The signs and feeding of Jesus did not suffice for preparing the hardened hearts of the 5,000 men! (cf. Luke 11:14-16; John 12:37-41; Acts 14:8-20)

➢ Some thoughts on Matthew 25 and Social Responsibility:

✓ Consider the comments of Delos Miles in this regard:

> "Evangelist Billy graham defined evangelism in 1983 as 'the offering of the whole Christ by the whole Church, to the whole man, to the whole world.' If the world-renowned evangelist was right, and I believe he was, then evangelism and social involvement are two wings of the same gospel bird.
> "Evangelism and Christian social concern are two sides of the same coin. If one side of the coin is missing, that coin has lost its value. The lack of social conscience impugns the reputation of the holy God and leads to societal failure. Evangelism is surely a blood brother to social involvement."[1344]

✓ The litany of good works performed as discussed in Matt 25:34-39 are often used to promote a "two wings of a bird" approach to evangelism, hence evangelism plus social responsibility, or more likely, social responsibility plus evangelism:
- ☞ Hungry, you gave me something to eat
- ☞ Thirsty, you gave me something to drink
- ☞ A stranger, you invited me in
- ☞ Naked, you clothed me
- ☞ Sick, you visited me
- ☞ In prison, you came to me

✓ However, in Matt 25:40, it is very difficult to overlook to whom the ministry was performed, "one of these <u>brothers</u> of mine", and the parallel in 25:45, "one of the least of these"

✓ Is not the context of these terms found in Matt 10:42, "one of these little ones", in which case, it is referring to the traveling evangelists who have no money or food (Matt 10:9-10)?

[1344]Delos Miles, *Evangelism and Social Involvement* (Nashville: Broadman, 1986), 7.

✓ Using "these little ones" (Matt 25:45) and "these brothers of mine" (Matt 24:40) for evangelism results in the liberal "Fatherhood of God" and "brotherhood of man" concept, outside of a saving relationship with Jesus Christ

✓ Furthermore, churches that focus on social responsibility:

☞ Lose the radical distinction between the saved and the lost

☞ Begin to treat the saved and lost with the same care (thus their love grows cold for the brethren, in the name of their loving all men)

☞ Lack the funds to provide for the needy in their own churches, according to the command of the Scriptures, Gal 6:10, "So then, while we have opportunity, let us do good to all men, and especially to those who are of the household of the faith" (cf. Col 1:4), since the social needs of a lost world are overwhelming, and can easily and quickly sap the funds of any government, much less a local church or denominational entity

✓ Note how this whole discussion in Evangelicalism was preceded by and encouraged John R. W. Stott though his chairmanship of the 1974 Lausanne Conference on World Evangelism:

> "Stott's call to social responsibility used emotionally-charged language, including terms such as 'we are appalled' and 'radical compassion.'[1345] The commitment then reaffirmed the definition of the Lausanne Covenant. In a next section, the commission examined the issue of the relationship between evangelism and social responsibility. Three relationships were proposed: 'social activity is a *consequence* of evangelism,' 'social activity can be a bridge to evangelism,' and 'social activity not only follows evangelism as its consequence and aim, and precedes it as its bridge, but it also accompanies it as its partner.'[1346] Stott, however, was not satisfied to allow proposition one to stand on its own. He stated as part of proposition one, 'Social responsibility is more than just a consequence of evangelism; it is also one of its principal aims.... Social responsibility, like evangelism, should therefore be included in the teaching ministry of the church.'[1347] Thus, Stott could not allow proposition one to stand on its own under its own definition without having to insert his rhetoric relating to position three, and then restating it in proposition three—begging the question."[1348]

✓ This same discussion was telegraphed into the future by South African missiologist David J. Bosch as he sought to define "evangelism" in his 1991 *Transforming Mission*:

> "10. *Because of this, evangelism cannot be divorced from the preaching and practicing of justice.* This is a flaw in the view according to which evangelism is given absolute priority over social involvement, or where evangelism is separated from justice, even if it is maintained that, together with social justice, it constitutes 'mission.' ...
>
> "... At its heart, Jesus' invitation to people to follow him and become his disciples, is asking people whom they want to serve. Evangelism is, therefore, a call to service. ...
>
> "... God wills ... that within us—and through our ministry also in society around us—the 'fullness of Christ' be re-created, the image of God be restored in our lives and relationships."[1349]

➢ The Atonement—Two main views of the atonement—discounting Socinianism:

✓ Substitutionary atonement

✓ Example Theory

✓ With attempts at Mediation

[1345]John R. W. Stott, "Grand Rapids Report on Evangelism and Social Responsibility: An Evangelical Commitment," in *Making Christ Known: Historic Mission Documents from the Lausanne Movement, 1974-1989*, ed. John R. W. Stott (Grand Rapids: Eerdmans, 1996), 177.

[1346]Ibid., 181-82.

[1347]Ibid., 181.

[1348]Johnston, *Understanding Billy Graham's Theology of Evangelism* (Eugene, OR: Wipf & Stock, 2003), 132.

[1349]Bosch, *Transforming Mission*, 418.

FOCUS OF EVANGELISM II

View of Atonement	Substitutionary Atonement	Attempts at Mediation	Moral-Influence Theory
Emphasis of Atonement	Christ did it all; "It is finished!"— our salvation is paid full and free!		Christ was an example
Effect of Atonement	Faith alone is necessary		Works are necessary
Effect on Response to Gospel	Belief in Gospel uniquely		Faith and works
Effect of Method of Sharing the Gospel	Proclamational or Expectant Evangelism		Lifestyle or Service Evangelism

➢ Atonement and focus of Evangelism
  ✓ Is the focus Christ, or is the focus the Christian (Church, Christian society)?
  ✓ Disclaimer one: the Christian is to live a lifestyle in accordance with the Gospel
  ✓ Disclaimer two: the life of the Christian is important, as it should reflect the message of the Gospel
    ✓ Impact of soteriology on evangelism in general
    ✓ Impact of soteriology on particular aspects of evangelism.
➢ Note the two evangelism approaches listed by Delos Miles, and the "inductive" approaches to intentionality and their seeming negativity to expectant evangelism (compare with "Postmodern Evangelism Methodologies" above)… [next page]

Two Kinds of Contemporary Evangelism (1983)

Personal Evangelism[1350]

(Intentionality)

Deductive	Vs	*Inductive*
Receptivity (high)	Vs.	Receptivity (low)
Monological (telling)	Vs.	Dialogical (listening)
Short-term Gains	Vs.	Long Term Gains
Canned	Vs.	Spontaneous
Instant	Vs.	Incarnational
Religious Persons	Vs.	Secular Persons
Proclamational	Vs.	Affirmation (Petersen)[1351]
Propositional	Vs.	Point-of-Need (Hunter)[1352]
Stereotyped	Vs.	Service (Armstrong)[1353]
Contact	Vs.	Conversational (Pippert)[1354]
Functional	Vs.	Friendship (McPhee)[1355]
Rational	Vs.	Relational (McDill)[1356]
Traditional	Vs.	Target-Group (Neighbour)[1357]
Individual	Vs.	Household (Green, *et al*)[1358]
Lips	Vs.	Life-style (Aldrich)[1359]

[1350]From Delos Miles, *Introduction to Evangelism* (Nashville: Broadman, 1983), 254. The following footnotes found in Miles' chart, are taken directly from Miles' book.

[1351]Jim Petersen, *Evangelism as a Lifestyle* (Colorado Springs, NavPress, 1980). [Five years later Petersen wrote *Evangelism for Our Generation* (Colorado Springs: NavPress, 1985); the two books were combined to form *Living Proof* (Colorado Springs: NavPress, 1989).]

[1352]George G. Hunter, III, *The Contagious Congregation* (Nashville: Abingdon, 1979), 35-39. These are not Hunter's actual terms. He prefers the terms *deductive* and *inductive*, but his new inductive-grace model and inductive-mission model boils down to a point-of-need approach.

[1353]Richard Stoll Armstrong, *Service Evangelism* (Philadelphia: Westminster, 1979), especially Chapter 4. Armstrong bases his service evangelism on the model of Jesus Christ, the Suffering Servant. His is also very much a point-of-need approach.

[1354]Rebecca Manley Pippert, *Out of the Saltashaker and Into the World* (Downers Grove, IL: InterVarsity, 1979), 127-151, 173f.

[1355]Arthur G. McPhee, *Friendship Evangelism* (Grand Rapids: Zondervan, 1978).

[1356]Wayne McDill, *Making Friends for Christ* (Nashville: Broadman, 1979). McDill prefers the term *relational evangelism.*

[1357]Ralph W. Neighbour, Jr., and Cal Thomas, *Target-Group Evangelism* (Nashville: Broadman, 1975).

[1358]Michael Green, *Evangelism in the Early Church* (Grand Rapids: Eerdmans, 1970), 207-229. Green uses the term *household evangelism.* See also: Thomas O. Wolf, "Oikos Evangelism: Key to the Future," Ralph W. Neighbour, Jr., compiler, *Future Church* (Nashville: Broadman, 1980), 153-176; Ron Johnson, Joseph W. Hinkle, and Charles M. Lowry, *Oikos: A Practical Approach to Family Evangelism* (Nashville: Broadman, 1982).

[1359]Joseph C. Aldrich, *Life-Style Evangelism* (Portland: Multnomah, 1981); See also W. Oscar Thompson, Jr., *Concentric Circles of Concern* (Nashville: Broadman, 1981); C. B. Hogue, *Love Leaves No Choice* (Waco, TX: Word, 1976).

➢ The following logic chart may explain some of the theological considerations in evangelism:

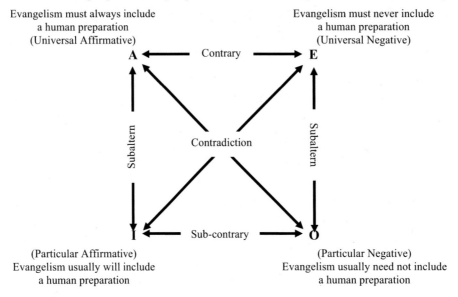

Evangelism must always include
a human preparation
(Universal Affirmative)

Evangelism must never include
a human preparation
(Universal Negative)

(Particular Affirmative)
Evangelism usually will include
a human preparation

(Particular Negative)
Evangelism usually need not include
a human preparation

➢ Or consider the following:

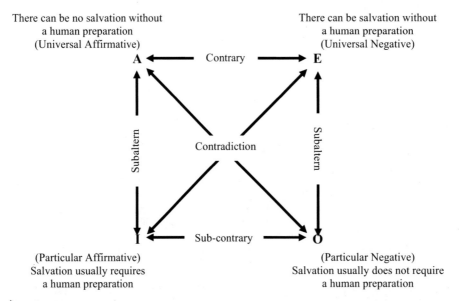

There can be no salvation without
a human preparation
(Universal Affirmative)

There can be salvation without
a human preparation
(Universal Negative)

(Particular Affirmative)
Salvation usually requires
a human preparation

(Particular Negative)
Salvation usually does not require
a human preparation

➢ Conclusion: The link between theology and practice is strong and important. Let us find at the cross the perfect balance of grace and truth, as well as be wise as serpents and gentle as doves!

Conclusions for Personal Evangelism

1. Several Dangers to Avoid in Personal Evangelism:

a. Becoming **routine** or **nonchalant** in the proclamation of the Gospel:
   1) Perhaps this is because of a loss of one's first love
   2) Some danger signs:
      a) Evangelism without fervent prayer in advance
      b) Sharing the Gospel without eye contact with the lost, including...
      c) No concern for the responses or thoughts of the prospect
      d) Lack of concern in beginning the conversation or in the end of the conversation
      e) Lack of urgency in calling for decision, or if the right words are used, they may seem fake

b. **Self-righteousness** regarding the proclamation of the Gospel:
   1) The Elijah attitude, "I alone am left," 1 Kings 19:10
      a) "I am the only one sharing the Gospel around here"
      b) "No one else cares for souls like I do"
   2) A pride resulting from obedience in this vital area can cause the evangelist to act without love, 1 Cor 13:2-4, leading to a critical spirit, and leading to a lack of the Holy Spirit's presence and power in witness

c. **Narrow-mindedness** and/or **rigidity**:
   1) Focusing on a method, rather than the Gospel:
      a) "My Gospel tract is the best" [implied, "and the only good one that we should use"]
      b) "My Gospel plan is the most effective" [or the only effective plan]
      c) "My evangelism methodology is the best or most effective methodology" [I have been using it to save souls for years]
   2) Looking to the temporal rather than the eternal, 2 Cor 4:18; and also...

d. **A critical spirit**, leading to a **root of bitterness**:
   1) Becoming judgmental of other people's methods of evangelism and/or of their lifestyles
   2) Jesus gave a poignant warning against this danger in Matt 7:1-2:

   > "Do not judge lest you be judged. For in the way you judge, you will be judged; and by your standard of measure, it will be measured to you" (Matt 7:1-2)

   3) Likewise, Paul reminded the Corinthians in 1 Cor 8:1, "Knowledge makes arrogant, but love edifies."
   4) Eph 4:31, "Let all bitterness and wrath and anger and clamor and slander be put away from you, along with all malice."

2. Some Closing Thoughts:

A. Are You Teachable?
There is much to learn in the area of evangelism. Unfortunately mistakes are made on real people. But this should not hinder anyone from sharing Christ. Doing it is the most important thing. A humble openness to continue to learn is also needed.

B. Are You Available?
No one will ever master evangelism completely except for Jesus Christ Himself. Likewise, no one will be able to master what is in these notes—I certainly have not! However, learning these principles and applications can allow the Holy Spirit to bring them to mind in the midst of a sharing situation. Intellectual preparation for maximum usefulness to the Holy Spirit is the goal in studying evangelism.

C. Are You Faithful?
See what works for you. Continue on with it. There is no boxed method for perfect evangelism—other than the clear teachings of and examples from the Word of God. Evangelism needs to come from the depths of your

soul. "Let the word of Christ dwell richly within you" (Col 3:16), then go forward for Him. The last thing these notes are ever meant to do is discouragement anybody from evangelism. Be encouraged and go for it!

R. G. Lee once said:

"Fishing for men is the greatest business in the entire universe. ... We must believe that it is the most important work that ever moved God's arm in power or sent a man's feet on Christian visitation—as well as the greatest work that ever laid claim upon the talents, education and abilities of Christians everywhere.

"... A winner of souls has the biggest job in the world."[1360]

Do you believe it?

[1360]"Interview with the Prince of Preachers, Dr. Robert G. Lee" (Studio Hall, CA: World Literature Crusade, n.d.), 7. "Interviewed by its founder and president, Dr. Jack McAlister."

Alphabetical Bibliography

The following books are arranged alphabetically. A chronological listing of the same books is found at the end of Chapter One. Books on church evangelism, personal follow-up, discipleship, church planting, church growth, the history of evangelism, or a theology of evangelism are generally not included in this bibliography. Inclusion does not constitute an endorsement, rather, this bibliography is an attempt to show the breadth of books on evangelism, especially in the 19th Century. An effort has been made to include books of all stripes, everywhere from the 1975 Papal encyclical of Paul VI, *Evangelii Nuntiandi—On Evangelization in the Modern World*, to L. R. Scarborough's 1919 *With Christ after the Lost*, C. G. Trumbull's 1907 *Taking Men Alive*, and W. B. Riley's 1904 *The Perennial Revival*. This bibliography does not include all works cited in the footnotes.

9Marks, *Reaching the Lost: Evangelism*, from "Healthy Church Study Guides." Wheaton, IL: Crossway, 2012.

Abraham, William J. *Logic of Evangelism*. Grand Rapids: Eerdmans, 1989.

Achtemeier, Mark and Andrew Purves, eds., *A Passion for the Gospel: Confessing Jesus Christ for the 21st Century*. Louisville: Geneva, 2000.

Adeney, David H. *The Unchanging Commission*. Chicago: Moody, 1955.

Adeney, Frances S. *Graceful Evangelism: Christian Witness in a Complex World*. Grand Rapids: Baker, 2010.

Alabama Baptist State Convention, Department of Evangelism. *Evangelize or Die!* Montgomery: The Convention, 1961.

Aldrich, Joseph C. *Gentle Persuasion*. Portland, OR: Multnomah, 1988.

Aldrich, Joseph C. *Life-Style Evangelism: Crossing Traditional Boundaries to Reach the Unbelieving World*. Portland, OR: Multnomah, 1981.

Allison, Lon and Mark Anderson. *Going Public with the Gospel: Reviving Evangelistic Proclamation*. Downers Grove, IL: InterVarsity, 2004.

Alphonson V. Washburn, *Reach Out to People: A People-to-People Emphasis*. Nashville: Convention, 1974.

Amberson, Talmadge R. *Reaching Out to People*. Nashville: Broadman, 1980.

Anderson, Ken. *A Coward's Guide to Witnessing*. Carol Stream, IL: Creation House, 1972.

Appelman, Hyman. *The Call to Conversion: Have You Been Born Again?* Philadelphia: Blakiston; New York: Revell, 1942.

Archibald, Arthur C. *New Testament Evangelism: How It Works*. Philadelphia: Judson, 1946, 1947.

Armstrong, Richard Stoll. *The Pastor as Evangelist*. Philadelphia: Westminster, 1984.

Armstrong, Richard S. *Service Evangelism*. Philadelphia: Westminster, 1979.

Armstrong, D. Wade. *Evangelistic Growth in Acts 1 & 2*. Nashville: Broadman, 1983.

Atkinson, Donald A. and Charles L. Roesel, *Meeting Needs/Sharing Christ: Ministry Evangelism in Today's New Testament Church*. Nashville: Lifeway, 1995.

Augsburger, Myron. *Evangelism as Discipling*. Scottsdale, PA: Herald, 1983.

Augsburger, Myron. *Invitation to Discipleship: The Message of Evangelism*. Scottsdale, PN: Herald, 1964.

Autrey, C. E. *Basic Evangelism*. Grand Rapids: Zondervan, 1959; Memphis: Brotherhood Commission, SBC, 1960.

Autrey, C. E. *You Can Win Souls*. Nashville: Broadman, 1961.

Azurdia, Arturo, *Connected Christianity: Engaging Culture Without Compromise*. Fearn, Ross-shire, Great Britain: Christian Focus, 2009.

Bader, Jesse M., ed. *The Message and Method of New Testament Evangelism: A Joint Statement of the Evangelistic Mission of the Christian Church*. New York: Round Table, 1937.

Bailey, Ambrose M. *Evangelism in a Changing World*. New York: Round Table Press, 1936.

Banks, Louis Albert. *The Revival Quiver*. Boston: Lee and Shepard, 1892.

Banks, Louis Albert. *Soul Winning Stories*. New York: American Tract, 1902; New York: George H. Doran, 1902.

Banks, William L. *In Search of the Great Commission: What Did Jesus Really Say?* Chicago: Moody, 1991.

Barna, George. *Evangelism that Works: How to Reach Changing Generations with the Unchanging Gospel*. Ventura: Regal, 1995.

Barnett, Minyard Merrill. *The Greatest of All Journeys: Soul Winner's Chart*. Fresno: CBF Press, 1950.

Barrett, David B. *Evangelize! A Survey of the Concept*. Birmingham, AL: New Hope, 1987.

Barrs, Jerram. *The Heart of Evangelism*. Wheaton, IL: Crossway, 2001, 2005.

Barrs, Jerram. *Learning Evangelism from Jesus*. Wheaton, IL: Crossway, 2009.

Bartlett, David L. and Ruth Fowler. *Moments of Commitment: Years of Growth: Evangelism and Christian Education*. St. Louis, MO: Christian Board of Publications, 1987.

Barton, Levi Elder. *Helps for Soul Winners*. Montgomery: Paragon, 1945.

Bassett, Paul, *God's Way*. Ambassador, 1981.

Baugh, Ken. *Getting Real: An Interactive Guide to Relational Ministry*. Colorado Springs, CO: NavPress, 2000.

Bayly, Joseph. *The Gospel Blimp*. Grand Rapids: Zondervan, 1960.

Beardsley, Frank G. *Religious Progress Through Revivals*. New York: American Tract Society, 1943.

Beasley, Gary M. and Francis Anfuso. *Complete Evangelism: Fitting the Pieces Together*. South Lake Tahoe, CA: Christian Equippers, 1991.

Bechtle, Mike. *Evangelism for the Rest of Us: Sharing Christ within Your Personality Style*. Grand Rapids: Baker, 2006.

Beginning Steps: A Growth Guide for New Believers [NIV]. Atlanta: North American Mission Board, 1993.

Benavides, Victor. *The Prepared Witness: A 30 Day Devotional*. Acworth, GA: M28 Evangelism, 2013.

Benavides, Victor. *Breaking the Evangelism Code: Evangelism Today*. Bloomington, IN: CrossBooks, 2011.

Bender, Urie A. *The Witness*. Scottdale, PA: Herald Press, 1965.

Benson, Clarence H. *Techniques of a Working Church*. Chicago: Moody, 1946.

Beougher, Timothy. *Overcoming Walls to Witnessing*. Minneapolis: Billy Graham Evangelistic Association, 1993.

Beougher, Timothy and Alvin Reid, eds., *Evangelism for a Changing World: Essays in Honor of Roy Fish*. Wheaton, IL: Harold Shaw, 1995.

Berge, Selmer Alonzo. *Evangelism in the Congregation*. Minneapolis: Faith Action Movement, 1944.

Best, W. E. *Life Brought to Light*. Houston: South Belt Assembly of Christ, 1992.

Biederwolf, William E. *Evangelism: Its Justification, Its Operation and Its Value.* New York: Revell, 1921.

Bierle, Donald A. *Surprised by Faith.* Excelsior, MN: H.I.S. Ministries, 1992.

Bisagno, John R. *How to Have an Evangelistic Church.* Nashville: Broadman, 1971.

Blackwood, Andrew Watterson. *Evangelism in the Home Church.* New York: Abingdon-Cokesbury, 1942.

Bock, Darrell L. and Mitch Glaser, *To the Jew First: The Case for Jewish Evangelism in Scripture and History.* Grand Rapids: Kregel, 2008.

Boer, Harry R. *Pentecost and Missions.* Lutterworth, 1961; Grand Rapids: Eerdmans, 1961, 1964.

Bolt, Peter. *Mission Minded.* London: St. Matthias Press, 1992.

Borchert, Gerald L. *Dynamics of Evangelism.* Waco, TX: Word, 1976.

Bothwell, Robert H. "New Testament Principles of Personal Evangelism." B.D. Thesis, Northern Baptist Theological Seminary, 1941.

Brealey, W. J. H. *Always Abounding: or, Recollections of the Life and Labours of the Late George Brealey, the Evangelist of the Blackdown Hills.* Kilmarnock, Scotland: John Ritchie, 1897; London: W. G. Wheeler, 1897; London: John F. Shaw, 1897; Glasgow: Pickering & Inglis, 1897; London: S. Bagster & Sons, 1897; New York: Gospel Pub. House, 1897.

Brennan, Patrick. *Re-Imagining Evangelization: Vision, Conversion, and Contagion.* Crossroad, 1994.

Bretscher, Paul G. *The Holy Infection: The Mission of the Church in Parish and Community.* In "The Witnessing Church Series." Saint Louis: Concordia, 1969.

Bright, Bill. *Witnessing Without Fear.* San Bernardino, CA: Here's Life, 1987.

Briner, Bob. *Roaring Lambs.* Grand Rapids: Zondervan, 1993.

Brock, Charles. *Let This Mind Be in You.* Kansas City, MO: Church Growth, 1990.

Brooks, W. Hal. *Follow Up Evangelism.* Nashville: Broadman, 1972.

Brown, Fred. *Secular Evangelism.* London: SCM, 1970.

Brown, Stanley C. *Evangelism in the Early Church: A Study in the Book of the Acts of the Apostles.* Grand Rapids: Eerdmans, 1963.

Brueggemann. *Biblical Perspectives on Evangelism: Living in a Three-Storied Universe.* Nashville: Abingdon, 1993.

Bryan, Dawson Charles. *Building Church Membership through Evangelism.* New York: Abingdon-Cokesbury, 1952.

Bryan, Dawson Charles. *Handbook on Evangelism for Laymen.* New York: Abingdon-Cokesbury, 1948.

Bryan, O. E. *The Ethics of Evangelism.* Louisville: The Southern Baptist Theological Seminary, 1920.

Burroughs, Prince Emanuel. *How to Win to Christ.* Nashville: Sunday School Board of the SBC, 1934; Nashville: Convention, 1934.

Burroughs, Prince Emanuel. *Winning to Christ.* Nashville: Tennessee Sunday School Board, 1914, 1923.

Cahill, Mark, *One Thing You Can't Do in Heaven.* Genesis Publishing; Rockwall, TX: Biblical Discipleship, 2002, 2003, 2004, 2005.

Cairns, Earle Edwin. *An Endless Line of Splendor: Revivals and Their Leaders from the Great Awakening to the Present.* Wheaton, IL: Tyndale House, 1986.

Caldwell, Max L., ed., *Witness to Win: Positive Evangelism through the Sunday School.* Nashville: Convention, 1978.

Callahan, Kennon L. *Visiting in an Age of Mission: A Handbook for Person-to-Person Ministry.* San Francisco: HarperSanFrancisco, 1994.

Callender, Willard D. *How to Make a Friendly Call.* Valley Forge, PA: Judson, 1982.

Calver, Clive. *Sold Out: Taking the Lid Off Evangelism.* London: Lakeland, Marshall, Morgan and Scott, 1980.

Calvin, John. *Come Out From Among Them: 'Anti-Nicodemite' Writings of John Calvin.* Trans. by Seth Solnitsky. Dallas: Protestant Heritage, 2001.

Cameron, Julia E. M. *Christ Our Reconciler: Presentations from the Third Lausanne Congress in Capetown, South Africa.* Downer's Grove: InterVarsity, 2012.

Cameron, Kirk and Ray Comfort. *The School of Biblical Evangelism: 101 Lessons.* Gainesville: Bridge-Logos, 2004.

Campbell, Robert C. *The Coming Revival.* Nashville: Broadman, 1939.

Careaga, Andrew. *E-vangelism: Sharing the Gospel in Cyberspace.* Lafayette, LA: Vital Issues, 1999.

Carey, William. "An Enquiry whether the Commission given by our Lord to His Disciples be not still Binding on Us," in *An Enquiry into the Obligations of Christians to use Means for the Conversion of the Heathen.* 1792.

Carson, Donald A., ed. *Telling the Truth: Evangelizing Postmoderns.* Grand Rapids: Zondervan, 2000.

Carswell, Roger. *And Some as Evangelists: Growing Your Church through Discovering and Developing Evangelists.* Fearn, Ross-shire, Great Britain: Christian Focus, 2002, 2005.

Cartwright, Lin D. *Evangelism for Today.* St. Louis: Bethany, 1934, 1943.

Cassidy, Michael. *A Passion for Preaching.* Pietermaritzburg, South Africa: African Enterprise, 1986, 2006.

Catholic Church. *Ministry through the Lens of Evangelisation.* Washington: USCCB (United States Conference of Catholic Bishops), 2003.

Chafer, Lewis Sperry. *True Evangelism or Winning Souls by Prayer.* 1st ed. Philadelphia: Sunday School Times, 1911; 2nd ed., Philadelphia: Sunday School Times, 1919; Wheaton, IL: Van Kampen; Grand Rapids: Zondervan, 1967; Grand Rapids: Kregel, 1993.

Chafin, Kenneth L. *The Reluctant Witness.* Nashville: Broadman, 1974.

Chambers, Oswald. *Workmen of God.* New York: Grosset and Dunlap, 1938.

Chan, Francis and Mark Beuving, *Multiply.* Colorado Springs: David C. Cook, 2012.

Chandler, Matt, Eric Geiger, and Josh Patterson, *Creature of the Word: The Jesus Centered Church.* Broadman-Holman, 2012.

Chang, Curtis. *Engaging Unbelief: A Captivating Strategy from Augustine and Aquinas.* Downers Grove, IL: InterVarsity, 2000.

Chapman, John C. *Setting Hearts on Fire: A Guide to Giving Evangelistic Talks.* Australia: Kingsford, NSW, Matthias, 1999.

Chapman, John C. *Know & Tell the Gospel: The Why and How of Evangelism.* London: Hodder & Stoughton, 1981 and Colorado Springs, CO: NavPress, 1985.

Chapman, J. Wilbur. *Present Day Evangelism.* New York: Revell, 1903, 1913.

Chappell, E. B. *Evangelism in the Sunday School.* Nashville: Methodist Episcopal Church, South, 1925.

Child, Kenneth. *In His Own Parish: Pastoral Care through Parochial Visiting.* London: SPCK, 1970.

Chirgwin, Arthur Mitchell. *A Book in his Hand: A Manual of Colportage.* London: United Bible Societies, 1954.

Clapp, Steve. *Christian Education as Evangelism.* Champaign, IL: Crouse Printing, 1982.

Clark, Elmer T., ed., *Methodism Vitalized,* Studies in Evangelism by Bishops John M. Moore, A. Frank Smith, W. N. Ainsworth, and Paul B. Kern. Nashville: Board of Missions, Methodist Episcopal Church, South, 1936.

Clark, Glenn, *Fishers of Men.* Boston: Little, Brown, 1928.

Claydon, David, ed. *A New Vision, A New Heart, A Renewed Call. Volumes One, Two, Three. Lausanne Occasional Papers from the 2004 Forum for World Evangelization* Pasadena, CA: William Carey Library, 2005.

Cocoris, Michael G. *Evangelism: A Biblical Approach.* Chicago: Moody, 1984.

Coggin, James E. *You Can Reach People Now.* Nashville: Broadman, 1971.

Coleman, Robert E. *Evangelism on the Cutting Edge.* Old Tappan, NJ: Revell, 1986.

Coleman, Robert E. *The Heart of the Gospel: The Theology Behind the Master Plan of Evangelism.* Grand Rapids: Baker, 2011.

Coleman, Robert E. *The Master Plan of Evangelism.* Old Tappan, NJ: Revell, 1963.

Coleman, Robert E. *The Master's Way of Personal Evangelism.* Wheaton: Crossway, 1997.

Coleman, Robert E. *"Nothing To Do But To Save Souls."* Wilmore, KY: Wesley Heritage, 1990.

Coleman, Robert E. *They Meet the Master: A Study Manual on the Personal Evangelism of Jesus.* Old Tappan, NJ: Revell, 1973.

Colle, Beau. *CB for Christians.* Nashville: Broadman, 1976.

Colquhoun, Frank. *The Fellowship of the Gospel: A New Testament Study in the Principles of Christian Cooperation.* Grand Rapids: Zondervan, 1957.

Comfort, Ray. *Hell's Best Kept Secret.* Bellflower, CA: self-published, 1989; Springdale, PA: Whitaker House, 1989; New Kensington, PA: Whitaker House, 2002; revised with study guide, Kensington, PA: Whitaker House, 2004.

Comfort, Ray and Kirk Cameron. *Way of the Master.* Gainesville: Bridge-Logos, 2006.

Conant, J. E. *Every Member Evangelism.* New York: Harper and Brothers, 1922; revised by Roy Fish, 1976.

Conant, J. E. *No Salvation without Substitution.* Grand Rapids: Eerdmans, 1941.

Conant, J. E. *Soul-Winning Evangelism: The Good News in Action.* Grand Rapids, 1963.

Conard, William W., ed. *Amsterdam 2000: The Mission of an Evangelist.* Minneapolis: World Wide Publications, 2001.

Condé, Bertha. *The Human Element in the Making of a Christian: Studies in Personal Evangelism.* New York: Scribners, 1917.

Conn, Harvey. *Evangelism: Doing Justice and Preaching Grace.* Grand Rapids: Zondervan, 1982.

Cook, Henry. *The Theology of Evangelism: The Gospel in the World of To-Day.* London: Carey Kingsgate, 1951.

Cooper, Raymond W. *Modern Evangelism: A Practical Course in Effective Evangelistic Methods.* New York: Revell, 1929.

Corbitt, J. Nathan and Vivian Nix-Early. *Taking It to the Streets: Using the Arts to Transform Your Community.* Grand Rapids: Baker, 2003.

Cowan, John F. *New Youth Evangelism: for Workers Among Young People of To-day.* New York: Revell, 1928.

Cox, Harvey. *Manual for Church in World Witness: with Procedures for Church in World Conferences and Study Groups.* New York : Division of Evangelism, American Baptist Home Mission Societies, 1960.

Crawford, Percy B. *The Art of Fishing for Men.* Philadelphia: The Mutual, 1935.

Crossley, G. *Everyday Evangelism.* Evangelical Press, 1987.

Crespin, Jean. *Histoire des vrays Tesmoins de la verite de l'evangile, qui de leur sang l'ont signée, depuis Jean Hus iusques autemps present* [*History of the True Witnesses to the Truth of the Gospel, Who with Their Blood Signed, from John Hus to the Present*]. Geneva, 1554, 1555, 1556, 1561, 1564, 1570; reproduction, Liège, 1964.

Crume, Thomas Clinton. *Evangelism in Action.* Louisville: Pentecostal, 1925.

Cullom, Peter E. *Visitation Evangelism Everywhere, as Did the Lord Jesus and Early Christians.* Washington, D.C.: Fishers of Men, 1965.

Cushman, Ralph Spalding. *The Essentials of Evangelism.* Nashville: Tidings, General Board of Evangelism, The Methodist Church, 1946.

Dalaba, Oliver V. *That None Be Lost.* Springfield, MO: Gospel Publishing, 1977.

Dale, Robert D. *Evangelizing the Hard-to-Reach.* Nashville: Broadman, 1986.

Daniels, Elam Jackson. *Techniques of Torchbearing.* Grand Rapids: Zondervan, 1957.

Davenport, Frederick Morgan, *Primitive Traits in Religious Revivals: A Study in Mental and Social Evolution.* New York: Macmillan, 1905.

Davenport, Ray W. *A Syllabus for Classes in Personal Evangelism,* 6th Ed. Whittier, CA: Ray W. Davenport, 1962.

Davis, D. Mark. *Talking about Evangelism: A Congregational Resource.* Cleveland: Pilgrim, 2007.

Davis, Freddy, *Worldview Witnessing: How to Confidently Share Christ with Anyone.* Otsego, MI: PageFree Publishing, 2007.

Dawson, Scott and Scott Lenning, *Effectively Sharing the Gospel in a Rapidly Changing World.* Grand Rapids: Baker, 2009.

Dawson, Scott, ed. *The Complete Evangelism Handbook: Expert Advice on Reaching Others for Christ.* Grand Rapids: Baker, 2006.

Dayton, Edward R. *That Everyone May Hear: Reaching the Unreached,* 3rd ed. MARC—Mission Advanced Research and Communication Center, 1983.

De Blois, Austen Kennedy. *Evangelism in the New Age.* Philadelphia: Judson, 1933.

de Jong, Pieter. *Evangelism and Contemporary Theology: A Study of the Implications for Evangelism in the Thoughts of Six Modern Theologians.* Nashville: Tidings, 1962.

Dean, Horace F. *Operation Evangelism: The Bob Jones University Lectures on Evangelism for 1957.* Grand Rapids: Zondervan, 1957.

Dean, Horace F. *Visitation Evangelism Made Practical: Reaching Your Community for Christ and the Church.* Grand Rapids: Zondervan, 1957.

Dean, John Marvin. *Evangelism and Social Service.* Philadelphia: Griffith & Rowland, 1913.

Dever, Mark and C. J. Mahaney. *The Gospel and Personal Evangelism.* Wheaton, IL: Crossway, 2007.

Deville, Jard. *The Psychology of Witnessing.* Waco: Word, 1980.

Dhavamony, Mariasusia, S.J. *Evangelisation.* Rome: Università Gregoriana, 1975.

Dobbins, Gaines S. *Evangelism According to Christ.* Nashville: Broadman, 1949.

Dobbins, Gaines S. *Good News to Change Lives: Evangelism for an Age of Uncertainty.* Nashville: Broadman, 1976.

Dodd, M. E. *Missions Our Mission.* Nashville: Sunday School Board of the SBC, 1930.

Douglas, J. D., ed. *The Calling of an Evangelist: The Second International Congress for Itinerant Evangelists, Amsterdam, The Netherlands.* Minneapolis: World Wide, 1987.

Douglas, J. D., ed. *The Work of an Evangelist: International Congress for Itinerant Evangelists, Amsterdam, The Netherlands, 1983.* Minneapolis: World Wide Publishing, 1984.

Douglas, Mack R. *How to Build an Evangelistic Church.* Grand Rapids: Zondervan, 1963.

Downey, Murray. *The Art of Soul-Winning.* Grand Rapids: Baker, 1957, 1983.

Drane, John. *Evangelism for a New Age.* Hammersmith, London: Marshall Pickering, 1994.

Drummond, Lewis A. *Evangelism—The Counter Revolution.* London: Marshall, Morgan and Scott, 1972.

Drummond, Lewis A. *Leading Your Church in Evangelism.* Nashville: Broadman, 1975.

Drummond, Lewis A. *The Word of the Cross: A Contemporary Theology of Evangelism.* Nashville: Broadman, 1992.

Duckworth, Jessicah Krey. *Wide Welcome: How the Unsettling Presence of Newcomers Ca Save the Church.* Minneapolis: Fortress, 2013.

Eakin, Mary Mulford. *Scuffy Sandals: A Guide for Church Visitation in the Community.* New York: Pilgrim, 1982.

Earle, Absalom B. [and J. C. Buttre]. *Bringing in the Sheaves.* Boston: James H. Earle, 1868, 1869, 1872.

Edwards, Gene. *How to Have a Soul Winning Church.* Springfield, MO: Gospel Publishing, 1962.

Edwards, Jonathan. *Jonathan Edwards on Revival: A Narrative of Surprising Conversions* [1736]*, The Distinguishing Marks of a Work of the Holy Spirit* [1941]*; An Account of the Revival of Religion in Northampton* [1740-1742]. Edinburgh: Banner of Truth, 1965.

Eims, Leroy. *Winning Ways: The Adventure of Sharing Christ.* Wheaton, IL: Victor, 1975.

Elliff, Tom. *What Should I Say to My Friend?* Richmond, VA: International Mission Board, 2009.

Ellis, Howard W. *Evangelism for Teen-Agers.* New York: Abingdon, 1958.

Ellis, Howard W. *Fishing for Men: Including a Suggested Scheme of Organization for Bands of "Fishermen" Together with a Plan and Program for Winning Those Who Are Lost and for Enlisting the Unenlisted Saved in the Service of Christ.* Grand Rapids: Zondervan, 1941.

Engel, James F. *Contemporary Christian Communications: Its Theory and Practice.* Nashville: Nelson, 1978, 1979.

Engel James F. and Wilbert Norton, *What's Gone Wrong with the Harvest? A Communication Strategy for the Church and World Evangelism.* Grand Rapids: Zondervan, 1975.

Evangelism in Action through Christ-Centered Messages: Twelve Evangelistic Sermons. Wheaton, IL: Van Kampen, 1951.

Evangelism in Depth: Experimenting with a New Type of Evangelism, as Told By Team Members of the Latin America Mission. Chicago: Moody, 1961.

Évangile et Évangélisme: XIIe-XIIIe Siècle. Cahiers de Fanjeaux 34. Toulouse, France: Éditions Privat, 1999.

Evans, William. *Personal Soul-Winning.* Chicago: Moody, 1910.

Everist, Norma Cook, ed. *Christian Education as Evangelism.* Minneapolis: Fortress, 2007.

Exum, Jack. *How to Win Souls Today.* Shreveport, LA: Lambert, 1970.

Fackre, Gabriel. *Do and Tell: Engagement Evangelism in the '70s.* Grand Rapids: Eerdmans, 1973.

Fackre, Gabriel. *Word in Deed: Theological Themes in Evangelism.* Grand Rapids: Eerdmans, 1975.

Faircloth, Samuel. *Church Planting for Reproduction.* Grand Rapids: Baker, 1992.

Faris, John T. *The Book of Personal Work.* New York: Doran, 1916.

Fay, William. *Share Jesus Without Fear.* Nashville: Broadman, 1999.

Feather, R. Othal. *A Manual for Promoting Personal Evangelism through the Sunday School.* Nashville: Convention Press, 1959.

Feather, R. Othal. *Outreach Evangelism through the Sunday School.* Nashville: Convention, 1972.

Finney, Charles G. *Lectures on the Revival of Religion: From Notes by the Editor of "New York Evangelist," Revised by the Author [1825].* From 6th American Edition, 2nd British Edition [hence 8th Edition]. London: Milner [Paternoster Row], 1838; 396 pages.

Finney, Charles G. *Lectures on Revival,* Kevin Walter Johnson, ed., a modified edition of *Lectures on Revivals of Religion,* 1835; Minneapolis: Bethany House, 1988; 288 pages.

Finney, Charles G. *Lectures on the Revival of Religion.* 9th Edition. London: Thomas Tegg, 1839; 396 pages.

Finney, Charles G. *Lectures on the Revival of Religion: A New Edition.* Revised and enlarged. Oberlin, OH: E. J. Goodrich, 1868; 445 pages.

Finney, Charles G. *Finney on Revival,* arranged by E. E. Shelhamer. 1834, 1839, 1850, 1868; Minneapolis: Bethany House, 1988; 120 pages.

Finney, Charles G. *True and False Repentance: Evangelistic Sermons.* Grand Rapids: Kregel, 1966.

Fish, Henry Clay. *Handbook of Revivals: For the Use of Winners of Souls.* Boston: J. H. Earle, 1874.

Fish, Roy. *Giving a Good Invitation.* Nashville: Broadman, 1974.

Flake, Arthur. *Building a Standard Sunday School.* Nashville: Sunday School Board of the Southern Baptist Convention, 1934.

Fletcher, Joseph. *Mission to Main Street: Five Study Units on the Work of the Church, the Function of the Lay Members, and the Place Where Witness Is Made.* Greenwich, CT : Seabury, 1962.

Fletcher, Lionel B. *The Effective Evangelist.* New York: George H. Doran, 1923; London: Hodder and Stoughton, 1923.

Ford, Kevin. *Jesus for a New Generation.* Downers Grove: InterVarsity, 1995.

Ford, Leighton. *The Christian Persuader: A New Look at Evangelism Today.* New York: Harper and Row, 1966.

Ford, Leighton. *Good News Is for Sharing: A Guide to Making Friends for Christ.* Elgin, IL: David C. Cook, 1977.

Ford, Leighton. *The Power of Story: Recovering the Oldest, Most Natural Way to Reach People for Christ.* Colorado Springs: NavPress, 1994.

Fordham, Keith. *"The Evangelist"—The Heart of God.* Del City, OK: Spirit, 1988, 1991, 2002.

Fordham, Keith and Tom Johnston. *The Worth and Work of the Evangelist—for Christ's Great Commission Church.* Liberty, MO: Evangelism Unlimited, 2013.

Foust, Paul J. *Reborn to Multiply: Tested Techniques for Personal Evangelism.* St. Louis: Concordia, 1973.

Freeman, Clifford Wade, ed. *The Doctrine of Evangelism.* Nashville: Baptist General Conference of Texas, 1957.

Frost, Toby, Bill Sims, and Monty McWhorter. *The Evangelistic Block Party Manual.* Atlanta: NAMB, 2003.

Fuller, Andrew. *The Gospel Worthy of All Acceptation.* 1784.

Gage, Albert H. *Evangelism of Youth.* Philadelphia: Judson, 1922.

Gager, Leroy. *Handbook for Soul Winners.* Grand Rapids: Zondervan, 1956.

Gall, James. *The Evangelistic Baptism Indespensable to the Church for the Conversion of the World.* Edinburgh: Gall and Inglis, 1888.

Geisler, Norman and David. *Conversational Evangelism.* Harvest House, 2009.

Geisler, Norman and Patrick Zukeran. *The Apologetics of Jesus: A Caring Approach to Dealing with Doubters.* Grand Rapids: Baker, 2010.

Gentry, Gardiner. *Bus Them in.* Grand Rapids: Baker, 1976.

George, Timothy and John Woodbridge. *The Mark of Jesus: Loving in a Way the World Can See.* Chicago: Moody, 2005.

Gesswein, Armin Richard. *Is Revival the Normal?* Intro. by Billy Graham. Elizabethtown, PA: McBeth, 1956.

Gilbert, Larry. *Team Evangelism—Giving New Meaning to Lay Evangelism.* Lynchburg: Church Growth, 1991.

Gill, John. *Body of Divinity.* London: George Keith, 1769; Tegg, 1839; Grand Rapids: Baker, 1978.

Gill, John. *The Cause of God and Truth.* London: Aaron Ward, 1735.

Gladden, Washington. *The Christian Pastor and the Working Church.* New York: Scribner's, 1898.

Godfrey, George. *How to Win Souls and Influence People for Heaven.* Grand Rapids: Baker, 1973.

Goodell, Charles L. *Motives and Methods in Modern Evangelism.* New York: Revell, 1926.

Goodell, Charles L. *Pastoral and Personal Evangelism.* New York: Revell, 1907.

Graf, Arthur E. *The Church in a Community: An Effective Evangelism Program for the Christian Congregation.* Grand Rapids: Eerdmans, 1965.

Graham, Billy. *A Biblical Standard for Evangelists.* Minneapolis: World Wide, 1984.

Graham, Franklin with Jeanette Lockerbie. *Bob Pierce: This One Thing I Do.* Waco: Word, 1983.

Green, Bryan S. W. *The Practice of Evangelism.* London: Hodder and Stoughton, 1951, 1952; New York: Scribner, 1951.

Green, Hollis L. *Why Churches Die: A Guide to Basic Evangelism and Church Growth.* Minneapolis: Bethany Fellowship, 1972.

Green, Hollis L. *Why Wait Till Sunday? An Action approach to Local Evangelism.* Minneapolis: Bethany Fellowship, 1975.

Green, Michael. *Evangelism in the Early Church.* Grand Rapids: Eerdmans, 1970.

Green, Michael. *Evangelism Now and Then: How Can What Happened in the Early Church Happen Now?* Downer's Grove, IL: InterVarsity, 1979; Rev. Ed. Grand Rapids: Eerdmans, 2004.

Green, Michael. *One to One: How to Share Your Faith with a Friend.* Nashville: Moorings, 1995.

Green, Oscar Olin. *Normal Evangelism.* New York: Revell, 1910.

Grindstaff, Wilmer E. *Ways to Win: Methods of Evangelism for the Local Church.* Nashville: Broadman, 1957.

Grubb, Norman P. *Continuous Revival.* Fort Washington, PA : Christian Literature Crusade, 1971.

Gumbel, Nicky. *Telling Others: The Alpha Initiative.* Eastbourne, Great Britain: Kingsway, 1994.

Ham, Edward E. *Fifty Years on the Battle Front with Christ: A Biography of Mordecai F. Ham.* Shelbyville, TN: Bible and Literature Missionary Foundation, 1950.

Hamilton, William Wistar. *The Fine Art of Soul-Winning.* Nashville: Sunday School Board of the SBC, 1935.

Hamilton, William Wistar. *Highways and edges.* Nashville: Broadman, 1938.

Hamilton, William Wistar. *Sane Evangelism.* Philadelphia: American Baptist, 1909.

Hamilton, William Wistar. *Wisdom in soul winning.* Nashville: Sunday School Board of the SBC, 1929.

Haney, David P. *The Ministry Evangelism Weekend: Preparation Manual.* Atlanta: Renewal Evangelism, 1976.

Hanks, Billie, Jr. *Everyday Evangelism: Evangelism as a Way of Life.* Nashville: Word, 1986.

Hanks, Billie, Jr. *Everyday Evangelism: How to Do It and How to Teach It.* Grand Rapids: Zondervan, 1983

Hannan, F. Watson. *Evangelism.* New York: Methodist Book Concern, 1921.

Harnack, Adolf and Wilhelm Hermann. *Essays on the Social Gospel.* London: Williams and Norgate, 1907.

Harney, Kevin G. *Organic Outreach for Ordinary People: Sharing Good News Naturally.* Grand Rapids: Zondervan, 2009.

Harrison, Eugene Myers. *How to Win Souls: A Manual of Personal Evangelism.* Wheaton, IL: Van Kampen, 1952; Wheaton, IL: Scripture Press, 1952.

Hartt, Julian N. *Toward a Theology of Evangelism.* New York: Abingdon, 1955

Havlik, John F. *The Evangelistic Church.* Nashville: Convention, 1976.

Havlik, John F. *People-Centered Evangelism.* Nashville: Broadman, 1970, 1971.

Hawthorne, Steve and Graham Kendrick, *Prayer Walking: Praying On Site with Insight.* Charisma House, 1996.

Haynes, Carlyle B. *Living Evangelism.* Takoma Park, WA: Review and Herald, 1937.

Head, Eldred Douglas. *Evangelism in Acts.* Fort Worth, TX: Southwestern Baptist Theological Seminary, 1950.

Heath, Elaine A. *The Mystic Way of Evangelism: A Contemplative Vision for Christian Outreach.* Grand Rapids: Baker, 2008.

Heck, Joel D. *The Art of Sharing Your faith.* Old Tappan, NJ: Revell, 1991.

Hedstrom, C. B. *"Pay Day—Some day": with Other Sketches from Life and Messages from the Word.* Grand Rapids: Zondervan, 1938.

Henderson, Jim. *a.k.a. Lost: Discovering Ways to Connect with the People Jesus Misses Most.* WaterBrook, 2005.

Henderson, Jim. *Evangelism Without Additives: What If Sharing Your Faith Meant Just Being Yourself?* WaterBrook, 2007.

Henderson, Robert T. *Joy to the World: An Introduction to Kingdom Evangelism.* Atlanta: John Knox, 1980.

Hendrick, John R. *Opening the Door of Faith: The Why, When, and Where of Evangelism.* Atlanta: John Knox, 1977.

Hendricks, Howard G. *Say It with Love: The Art and Joy of Telling the Good News.* Foreword by Billy Graham. Wheaton, IL: Victor, 1972, 1973.

Henrichsen, Walter A. *Disciples Are Made-not Born.* Wheaton, IL: Victor, 1974.

Henry, Carl F. H. *The Uneasy Conscience of Modern Fundamentalism.* Grand Rapids: Eerdmans, 1947.

Henry, Carl F. H. and W. Stanley Mooneyham, eds. *One Race, One Gospel, One Task: World Congress on Evangelism, Berlin, 1966.* 2 vols. Minneapolis: World Wide Publications, 1967.

Herrick, Carl E. *Modern Evangelism: A Practical Course in Effective Evangelistic Methods.* New York: Revell, 1929.

Hervey, George Winfred. *Manual of Revivals: Practical Hints and Suggestions from Histories of Revivals and Biographies of Revivalists, with Themes for the Use of Pastors and Missionaries Before, During, and After Special Services, Including the Texts, Subjects, and Outlines of the Sermons of Many Distinguished Evangelists.* New York: Funk and Wagnalls, 1884.

Hicks, Joseph P. *Ten Lessons in Personal Evangelism.* New York: Doran, 1922.

High School Evangelism. San Bernardino, CA: Campus Crusade for Christ, 1976.

Hinkle, J. Herbert. *Soul Winning in Black Churches.* Grand Rapids: Baker, 1973.

Hinson, William H. *A Place to Dig in: Doing Evangelism in the Local Church.* Nashville: Abingdon, 1987.

[Hocking Report]. *Rethinking Missions: A Laymen's Inquiry after One Hundred Years.* New York: Harper and Brothers, 1932.

Hirsch, Alan and Leonard Sweet. *The Forgotten Ways: Reactivating the Missional Church.* Grand Rapids: Brazos, 2009.

Hogue, C. B. *I Want My Church to Grow.* Nashville: Broadman, 1977.

Hogue, C.B. *Lifestyle Evangelism.* Atlanta, GA: Home Mission Board of the SBC, 1973.

Hogue, C. B. *Love Leaves No Choice: Life-style Evangelism.* Waco: Word, 1976.

Hollenweger, Walter. *Evangelism Today: Good News or Bone of Contention?* Belfast: Christian Journals, 1976.

Homrighausen, Elmer G. *Choose Ye This Day: A Study of Decision and Commitment in Christian Personality.* Philadelphia: Westminster, 1943.

Horton, Michael. *The Gospel Commission: Recovering God's Strategy for Making Disciples.* Grand Rapids: Baker, 2011.

Hough, Lynn Harold. *The Great Evangel.* Nashville: Cokesbury, 1936.

Houghton, Will H. *Lessons in Soul-Winning.* Chicago: Moody Bible Institute of Chicago, 1936.

Howard, David M. *The Great Commission Today.* Downers Grove, IL: InterVarsity, 1976.

Hulse, Erroll. *The Great Invitation.* Welwyn: Evangelical, 1986.

Humphrey, Heman. *Revival Sketches and Manual: in Two Parts.* New York: American Tract Society, 1859.

Hunt, Lionel A. *Handbook on Children's Evangelism.* Chicago, Moody, 1960.

Hunt, Stephen. *The Alpha Enterprise: Evangelism in a Post-Christian Era.* Aldershot, Hants, England: Ashgate, 2004.

Hussey, Joseph. *The Glory of Christ Vindicated, ...* London: William and Joseph Marshall, 1707; Philadelphia: printed by Joseph Crukshank for John M'Gibbons, 1771.

Hybels, Bill. *Just a Walk Across the Room: Simple Steps Pointing People to Faith.* Grand Rapids: Zondervan, 2006.

Hybels, Bill and Mark Mittelberg. *Becoming a Contagious Christian.* Grand Rapids: Zondervan, 1994.

Hyles, Jack. *Let's Go Soul Winning: A Step by Step Guide in How to Lead a Soul to Christ.* Murfreesboro, TN: Sword of the Lord, 1962.

Innes, Dick. *I Hate Witnessing! A Handbook for Effective Christian Communication.* Ventura, CA: Vision House, 1983.

Jacks, Bob and Betty. *Your Home a Lighthouse.* Colorado Springs: NavPress, 1986, 1987.

Jauncey, James H. *One-on-One Evangelism.* Chicago: Moody, 1978.

Jauncey, James H. *Psychology for Successful Evangelism.* Foreword by Leighton Ford. Chicago: Moody, 1972.

Jensen, Phillip and Phil Campbell. *Two Ways to Live: A Bible Study Explaining Christianity.* Kinsford, NSW, Australia: Matthias Media, 1998.

John, J. *God's Top Ten: Rediscovering the Basic Building Blocks for Life.* Eastbourne, Great Britain: Kingsway, 1995.

Johnson, Ben. *An Evangelism Primer: Practical Principles for Congregations.* Atlanta: John Knox, 1983.

Johnson Ben Campbell. *Speaking of God: Evangelism as Initial Spiritual Guidance.* Atlanta: Westminster John Knox, 1991.

Johnson, Daniel E. *Building with Buses.* Grand Rapids: Baker, 1974.

Johnston, E. A. *Asahel Nettleton: Revival Preacher.* Asheville, NC: Revival Literature, 2012.

Johnston, Howard A. *Enlisting for Christ and the Church.* New York: Association, 1919.

Johnston, James, ed. *Ecumenical Missionary Conference, New York, 1900: Report of the Ecumenical Conference on Foreign Missions, Held in Carnegie Hall and Neighboring Churches, April 21 to May 1.* New York: American Tract Society, 1900.

Johnston, James, ed. *Report of the Centenary Conference on the Protestant Missions of the World Held in Exeter Hall (June 9th-19th), London, 1888.* New York: Revell, 1888.

Johnston, Thomas P. *Charts for a Theology of Evangelism.* Nashville: Broadman, 2007.

Johnston, Thomas P. *Toward a Biblical-Historical Theology of Evangelism.* Liberty, MO: Evangelism Unlimited, 2006.

Johnston, Thomas P. *Examining Billy Graham's Theology of Evangelism.* Eugene, OR: Wipf and Stock, 2003.

Johnston, Thomas P. *Inquisition and Martyrdom (1002-1572): Being a Historical Study of Evangelism and Its Repression.* Liberty, MO: Evangelism Unlimited, 2008.

Johnston, Thomas P. *The Mindset of Eternity.* Deerfield, IL: Evangelism Unlimited, 1994.

Johnston, Thomas P., ed. *Mobilizing a Great Commission Church for Outreach.* Eugene, OR: Wipf and Stock, 2011.

Johnston, Thomas P., *Understanding Evangelizology.* Liberty, MO: Evangelism Unlimited, 2009.

Jones, Bob, Sr., *Evangelism Today: Where Is It Headed?* Greenville, SC: Bob Jones University, 1955.

Kallenberg, Brad. *Live to Tell: Evangelism in a Postmodern World.* Grand Rapids: Baker, 2002.

Kantonen, Talto A. *The Theology of Evangelism.* Philadelphia: Muhlenberg, 1954.

Kelley, Charles. *How Did They Do It? The Story of Southern Baptist Evangelism.* New Orleans: Insight, 1993.

Kemp, Charles F. *Physicians of the Soul.* New York: Macmillan, 1947).

Kennedy, D. James. *Evangelism Explosion.* Wheaton, IL: Tyndale House, 1970; rev ed, 1977; 4th ed, 1994, 1996.

Kernahan, A. Earl. *Christian Citizenship and Visitation Evangelism.* New York: Revell, 1929.

Kernahan, A. Earl. *Visitation Evangelism: Its Methods and Results.* New York: Revell, 1925, 1935.

Kilpatrick, Thomas B. *New Testament Evangelism.* 1911.

Knapp, Martin Wells. *Revival Kindlings.* Cincinnati: God's Revivalist Office, 1890.

Koo, Hongnak. *The Impact of Luis Palau on Global Evangelism.* Grand Rapids: Credo, 2010.

Koyama, Kosuke. *Waterbuffalo Theology.* Maryknoll, NY: Orbis, 1974.

Korthals, Richard G. *Agape Evangelism: Roots that Reach Out.* Wheaton, IL: Tyndale House, 1980.

Koukl, Gregory. *Tactics: A Game Plan for Discussing Your Christian Convictions.* Grand Rapids: Zondervan, 2009.

Kraft, Charles H. *Communicating the Gospel God's Way.* Pasadena: William Carey, 1979.

Kraft, Charles H. *Communication Theory for Christian Witness.* Nashville: Abingdon, 1983.

Kramp, John. *Out of Their Faces and Into Their Shoes: How to Understand Spiritually Lost People and Give Them Directions to Find God.* Nashville: Broadman and Holman, 1995.

Krass, Alfred C. *Evangelizing Neopagan North America.* Scottsdale, PA: Herald, 1982.

Krupp, Nate. *A World to Win: Secrets of New Testament Evangelism.* Minneapolis: Bethany Fellowship, 1966.

Kuhne, Gary. *The Dynamics of Personal Follow-Up.* Grand Rapids: Zondervan, 1976.

Kuiper, R. B. *God Centered Evangelism.* Grand Rapids: Baker, 1961, 1975; Carlisle, PA: Banner of Truth, 1966.

Laney, James T. *Evangelism: Mandates for Action.* New York: Hawthorn, 1975.

Larsen, David L. *The Evangelism Mandate: Recovering the Centrality of Gospel Preaching.* Wheaton: Crossway, 1992.

Laurie, Greg. *How To Share Your Faith.* Wheaton, IL: Tyndale House, 1999.

Lavin, Ronald J., ed., *The Human Chain for Divine Grace: Lutheran Sermons for Evangelical Outreach.* Philadelphia: Fortress, 1978.

Lawless, Chuck and Thom S. Rainer, eds. *The Challenge of the Great Commission: Essays on God's Mandate for the Local Church.* Louisville: Pinnacle, 2005.

Lawrence, J. B. *The Holy Spirit in Evangelism.* Grand Rapids: Zondervan, 1954.

Leavell, Frank H. *Christian Witnessing.* Nashville: Broadman Press, 1942.

Leavell, Roland Q. *The Christian's Business: Being a Witness.* Nashville: Broadman, 1964.

Leavell, Roland Q. *Evangelism: Christ's Imperative Command.* Nashville: Broadman, 1951.

Leavell, Roland Q. *Helping Others to Become Christians.* Atlanta: Home Mission Board, SBC, 1939.

Leavell, Roland Q. *The Romance of Evangelism.* New York: Revell, 1942.

Leavell, Roland Q. *Winning Others to Christ.* Nashville: Sunday School Board of the SBC, 1936; Nashville: Convention, 1936.

Lee, Robert G. *How to Lead a Soul to Christ.* Grand Rapids: Zondervan, 1955.

LeFlore, David. *Fast Food Evangelism: A Drive-Through Approach to Sharing the Gospel.* Orlando, FL: Bridge-Logos, 2007.

Legg. Steve. *A-Z of Evangelism: The Ultimate Guide to Evangelism.* London: Hodder and Stoughton, 2002.

Leith, John H. *Reformed Theology and the Style of Evangelism.* Edited by James C. Goodloe IV. Lousville, KY: Geneva Press, 1973; Eugene, OR: Wipf & Stock, 2010.

Lessons in Assurance. Colorado Springs: NavPress, 1980.

Levicoff, Steve. *Street Smarts: A Survival Guide to Personal Evangelism and the Law.* Grand Rapids: Baker, 1994.

Lewis, Edwin. *Theology and Evangelism.* Nashville: Tidings, 1952.

Lewis, Sinclair. *Elmer Gantry.* Berlin: E. Rowolht, 1928; New York: Harcourt, Brace, 1929.

Little, Paul E., ed. *His Guide to Evangelism.* Downers Grove, IL: InterVarsity, 1977, 1979.

Little, Paul E. *How to Give Away Your Faith.* Downers Grove, IL: InterVarsity, 1966.

Long, Jimmy. *Emerging Hope* (revision and expansion of *Generating Hope* [1997]). Downers Grove, IL: InterVarsity, 2004.

Long, Jimmy. *Generating Hope: A Strategy for Reaching the Postmodern Generation.* Downers Grove, IL: InterVarsity, 1997.

Lovett, Cummings Samuel. *Soul-Winning Made Easy.* Baldwin Park, CA: Personal Christianity, 1959, 1978.

Lovett, Cummings Samuel. *Visitation Made Easy.* Baldwin Park, CA: Personal Christianity, 1959.

Lovett, Cummings Samuel. *Witnessing Made Easy: the Ladder-Method.* Baldwin Park, CA: Personal Christianity, 1964, 1971.

Loud, Grover Cleveland. *Evangelized America.* New York, L. MacVeagh, the Dial Press, 1928; Toronto, Longmans, Green, 1928; Freeport, N.Y. : Books for Libraries Press, 1971.

Lowry, Oscar. *Scripture Memory for Successful Soul-Winning.* New York: Revell, 1934.

Lukasse, Johan. *Churches with Roots: Planting Churches in Post-Christian Europe.* Bromley: STL, 1990.

Lum, Ada. *How to Begin an Evangelistic Bible Study.* Downers Grove, IL: InterVarsity, 1971.

Mabie, Henry C. *Method in Soul-Winning: on Home and Foreign Fields.* New York: Revell, 1906.

MacAulay, J. C. and Robert H. Belton. *Personal Evangelism.* Chicago: Moody, 1956.

MacArthur, John, ed. *Evangelism: How to Share the Gospel Faithfully.* Nashville: Nelson, 2011.

MacArthur, John. *Nothing But the Truth: Upholding the Gospel in a Doubting Age.* Wheaton, IL: Crossway, 1999; Amazon: Kindle, n.d.

MacDonald, William C. *Modern Evangelism.* London: James Clarke, 1936, 1937.

Maclean, John Kennedy. *Triumphant Evangelism: The Three Years Mission of Dr. Torrey and Mr. Alexander in Great Britain and Ireland.* London: Marshall, 1907.

Mallalieu, W. F. *The Why, When and How of Revivals.* New York: Eaton and Mains; Cincinatti: Jennings and Pye, 1901.

Mallough, Don. *Grassroots Evangelism.* Grand Rapids: Baker, 1971.

Malone, Tom. *Essentials of Evangelism: Bob Jones University Lectures on Evangelism for 1958.* Murfreesboro, TN: Sword of the Lord, 1958.

Martin, Gerald E. *The Future of Evangelism.* Grand Rapids: Zondervan, 1969.

Martin, O. Dean. *Invite: What Do You Do after the Sermon?* Nashville: Tidings, 1973.

Martin, Ralph and Peter Williamson, eds. *John Paul II and the New Evangelization: How You Can Bring the Good News to Others.* Ann Arbor: Servant, 2006.

Martin, Roger. *R. A. Torrey: Apostle of Certainty.* Murfreesboro, TN: Sword of the Lord, 1976.

Marty, Martin E. *The Improper Opinion: Mass Media and the Christian Faith.* Philadelphia: Westminster, 1961.

Massee, Jasper C. *The Pentecostal Fire: Rekindling the Flame.* Philadelphia: Judson, 1930.

Massee, Jasper C. *Rekindling the Pentecostal Fire.* Butler, IN: Higley, 1930.

Matthews, C. E. *The Department of Evangelism and the Simultaneous Revival Program.* Dallas: Baptist General Convention of Texas, 1946.

Matthews, C. E. *The Southern Baptist Program of Evangelism.* Atlanta: Home Mission Board, SBC, 1949.

Mayfield, William H. *Restoring First Century Evangelism: for an Effective Program in Soul-Winning through the Rediscovery of the Witnessing Power of the Early Church: Evangelism Text Book and Training Manual.* Cincinnati: New Life, 1974.

McCloskey, Mark. *Tell It Often—Tell It Well.* San Bernardino, CA: Here's Life, 1986.

McCullough, William James. *Home Visitation Evangelism for Laymen: A Manual.* New York: American Baptist Home Mission Society, 1946.

McDill, Wayne *Evangelism in a Tangled World.* Nashville: Broadman, 1976.

McDill, Wayne. *Making Friends for Christ—A Practical Approach to Relational Evangelism.* Nashville: Broadman, 1979.

McDormand, Thomas Bruce. *Evangelism and a Saving Faith for Modern Man.* 1958.

McDowell, Sean. *Apologetics for a New Generation: A Biblical and Culturally Relevant Approach to Talking about God.* Harvest House, 2009.

McDowell, William Fraser. *That I May Save Some.* New York: Abingdon, 1928.

McFatridge, F. V. *The Personal Evangelism of Jesus* (Grand Rapids: Zondervan, 1939).

McKay, Charles L. *The Call of the Harvest.* Nashville: Convention Press, 1956, 1976.

McLaren, Brian D. *More Ready Than you Realize: Evangelism as Dance in the Postmodern Matrix.* Grand Rapids: Zondervan, 2002.

McLarry, Newman R., ed., *Handbook on Evangelism: A Program of Evangelism for Southern Baptists.* Nashville: Convention, 1965.

McPhee, Arthur. *Friendship Evangelism: The Caring Way to Share Your Faith.* Grand Rapids: Zondervan, 1979.

McRainey, Will. *The Art of Personal Evangelism.* Nashville: Broadman, 2003.

Menninger, Karl. *Whatever Became of Sin?* New York: Bantam, 1978.

Messages on Evangelism: Delivered at Florida Baptist Evangelistic Conference, 1961. Orlando: Golden Rule, 1961.

Metcalf, Harold E. *The Magic of Telephone Evangelism.* Atlanta: Southern Union Conference [of Seventh-Day Adventists], 1967.

Metzger, Will. *Tell the Truth: The Whole Message to the Whole Person by the Whole People.* Downers Grove, IL: InterVarsity, 1981, 1984

Miles, Delos. *Introduction to Evangelism.* Nashville: Broadman, 1983.

Miles, Delos. *Master Principles of Evangelism: Examples from Jesus' Personal Witnessing.* Nashville: Broadman, 1982.

Miller, Calvin. *A View from the Fields.* Nashville: Broadman, 1978.

Miller, Herb. *Evangelism's Open Secrets.* St. Louis: Bethany, 1977.

Miller, Herb. *Fishing on the Asphalt: Effective Evangelism in Mainline Denominations.* St. Louis: Bethany, 1983.

Miller, John C. *Evangelism and Your Church.* Phillipsburg, NJ: Presbyterian and Reformed, 1980.

Mims, Gene. *Kingdom Principles for Church Growth.* Nashville: Broadman, 1994, 2001.

Misselbrook, Lawrence Richard. *Winning the People for Christ: An Experiment in Evangelism.* London: Carey Kingsgate, 1957.

Misselbrook, Lewis. *Sharing the Faith with Others: A Program for Training in Evangelism.* Valley Forge, PA: American Baptist, 1979.

Mittelberg, Mark with Bill Hybels, *Building a Contagious Church: Revolutionizing the Way We View and Do Evangelism.* Grand Rapids: Zondervan, 2000.

Morgan, G. Campbell, *Evangelism.* Grand Rapids: Baker, 1976.

Morgan, G. Campbell, *The Great Physician.* New York: Revell, 1937.

Morgenthaler, Susan. *Worship Evangelism.* Grand Rapids: Zondervan, 1999.

Moseley, J. Edward, ed., *Evangelism—Commitment and Involvement.* St. Louis: Bethany, 1965.

Mott, John R. *Cooperation and the World Mission.* New York: International Missionary Council, 1935.

Moyer, R. Larry. *21 Things God Never Said: Correcting Our Misconceptions about Evangelism.* Grand Rapids: Kregel, 2004.

Moyer, R. Larry. *Free and Clear: Understanding and Communicating God's Offer of Eternal Life.* Grand Rapids: Kregel, 1997.

Moyer, R. Larry. *Larry Moyer's how-To Book on Personal Evangelism.* Grand Rapids: Kregel, 1998.

Mueller, Charles S. *The Strategy of Evangelism: A Primer for Congregational Evangelism Committees.* Saint Louis: Concordia, 1965.

Mumma, Howard. E. *Take It to the People: New Ways in Soul Winning—Unconventional Evangelism* New York: World, 1969.

Muncy, William L. *A History of Evangelism in the United States.* Kansas City, KS: Central Seminary, 1945.

Muncy, William L. *New Testament Evangelism.* Kansas City: Central Seminary Press, 1937.

Munro, Harry C. *Fellowship Evangelism through Church Groups.* St. Louis: Cooperative Association, Bethany, 1951.

Murphee, Jon Tal. *Responsible Evangelism: Relating Theory to Practice.* Toccoa Falls, GA: Toccoa Falls College, 1994.

Murphey, Buddy. *Drawing the Net: The Soul Winners Workbook.* Corpus Christi, TX: Buddy Murphey, 1969.

Murray, Arthur L. *Reaching the Unchurched.* New York: Round Table, 1940.

Myers, Joseph R. *The Search to Belong: Rethinking Intimacy, Community, and Small Groups.* Grand Rapids: Zondervan, 2003.

Neighbour, Ralph Jr. *The Journey into Discipleship: The Journey into Lifestyle Evangelism and Ministry.* Memphis: Brotherhood Commission of the SBC, 1984, 1987.

Neighbour, Ralph W. Jr. *Knocking on Doors—Opening Hearts.* Houston: Touch, 1990.

Neighbour, Ralph W. Jr., *Target-Group Evangelism.* Nashville: Broadman, 1975.

Neighbour, Ralph W., Jr., *The Touch of the Spirit.* Nashville: Broadman, 1972.

Neighbour, Ralph W. Jr. *Where Do We Go from Here? A Guidebook for the Cell Group Church.* Houston: Touch, 1990.

Neil, Samuel Graham. *A Great Evangelism.* Philadelphia: Judson, 1929.

Neville, Joyce. *How to Share Your Faith Without Being Offensive.* New York: Seabury, 1981.

New Testament Evangelism: The Eternal Purpose. Nashville, Convention, 1960.

Newman, Randy, *Questioning Evangelism: Engaging People's Hearts the Way Jesus Did.* Grand Rapids: Kregel, 2004.

Northey, James. *Outreach: Toward Effective Open-Air Evangelism.* London: Salvationist, 1976.

O'Brien, John A. *Bringing Souls to Christ: Methods of Sharing the Faith with Others.* Introduction by Francis Cardinal Spellman. Garden City, NY: Hanover House, 1955.

O'Brien, John A. *Winning Converts: A Symposium on Methods of Convert Making for Priests and Lay People.* New York: P. J. Kennedy, 1948.

Olford, Stephen F. *The Secret of Soul-Winning.* Chicago: Moody, 1963, 1981.

Orr, J. Edwin. *God Can——? "10,000 Miles of Miracles in Britain."* London: Marshall, Morgan and Scott, 1934; Grand Rapids: Zondervan, 1934.

Orr, J. Edwin. *The Promise Is to You: 10,000 Miles of Miracle—to Palestine.* London: Marshall, Morgan and Scott, 1935.

Orr, J. Edwin. *This Is the Victory: 10,000 Miles of Miracle in America.* London: Marshall, Morgan and Scott, 1936; Grand Rapids: Zondervan, 1936.

Overholtzer, J. Irvin. *Handbook on Child Evangelism.* Grand Rapids: Child Evangelism Fellowship, 1955.

Ownbey, Richard L. *Evangelism in Christian Education.* Nashville: Abingdon, 1941.

Packer, J. I. *Evangelism and the Sovereignty of God.* Downers Grove, IL: InterVarsity, 1961.

Packer, J. I. and Mark Dever, *Evangelism and the Sovereignty of God.* Downers Grove, IL: InterVarsity Press, 2012.

Palau, Luis and Timothy Robnett, *Telling the Story: Evangelism for the Next Generation.* Ventura, CA: Gospel Light, 2006.

Pannell, William. *Evangelism from the Bottom Up.* Grand Rapids: Zondervan, 1992.

Parr, Steve R. and Thomas Crites. *Evangelistic Effectiveness: Difference Makers in Mindsets and Methods.* Duluth, GA: Georgia Baptist Convention, 2012.

Paul VI. *Evangelii Nuntiandi—On Evangelization in the Modern World.* Rome: Vatican, 8 Dec 1975.

Payne, J. D. *Evangelism: A Biblical Response to Today's Questions.* Colorado Springs: Biblica, 2011.

Payne, J. D. *Missional House Churches: Reaching Our Communities with the Gospel.* Paternoster, 2008.

Payne, Tony. *Six Steps to Talking about Jesus: Practical Training for Small Groups.* Kingsford, NSW, Australia: Matthias Media, 2009.

Peace, Richard, *Holy Conversation: Talking About God in Everyday Life.* Downer's Grove, IL: InterVarsity, 2006.

Peale, Norman Vincent. *The Positive Power of Jesus Christ: Life-Changing Adventures in Faith.* Wheaton, IL: Tyndale House, 1980.

Peck, Jonas O. *The Revival and the Pastor.* New York: Eaton and Mains; Cincinatti: Curts and Jennings, 1894.

Peile, James H. F. *The Reproach of the Gospel: An Inquiry into the Apparent Failure of Christianity as a General Rule of Life and Conduct, with a Special Reference to the Present Time.* London: Longmans, Green, 1907.

Pell, Edward Leigh. *How Can I Lead my Pupils to Christ?* New York: Revell, 1919.

Penn-Lewis, Jessie. *Prayer and Evangelism*. Fort Washington, PA: Christian Literature Crusade, 1995.

Peters, George W. *Saturation Evangelism*. Grand Rapids: Zondervan, 1970.

Petersen, Jim. *Evangelism as a Lifestyle*. Colorado Springs, CO: NavPress, 1980.

Petersen, Jim. *Evangelism for Our Generation*. Colorado Springs, CO: NavPress, 1985.

Petersen, Jim. *Living Proof*. Colorado Springs: NavPress, 1989.

Phillips, Richard D. *Jesus the Evangelist: Learning to Share the Gospel from the Book of John*. Reformation Trust, 2007.

Phillips, William A. *The Follow-Up in Evangelism*. Philadelphia: The John Mason Jackson Fund of the American Baptist Publication Society, 1937.

Pickering, Ernest D. *The Theology of Evangelism*. Clarks Summit, PA: Baptist Bible College, 1974.

Pierson, A. T. *Evangelistic Work in Principles and Practice*. New York: Baker and Taylor, 1887; London: Dickinson, 1888; rev. ed., London: Passmore and Alabaster, 1892.

Pierson, A. T. *From the Pulpit to the Palm-Branch: A Tribute to Charles Haddon Spurgeon*. New York, A.C. Armstrong, 1892.

Pilavachi, Mike and Liza Hoeksma. *When Necessary Use Words: Changing Lives Through Worship, Justice and Evangelism*. Ventura: Regal, 2007.

Piper, John. *Don't Waste Your Life*. Crossway, 2004.

Piper, John. *Let the Nations Be Glad: The Supremacy of God in Missions*. Grand Rapids: Baker, 1993.

Piper, John, ed. *Finish the Mission: Bringing the Gospel to the Unreached and Unengaged*. Crossway, 2012.

Pippert, Rebecca Manley. *Out of the Saltshaker and into the World: Evangelism as a Way of Life*. Downers Grove, IL: InterVarsity, 1979.

Pippert, Rebecca Manley and Ruth Siemens, *Evangelism: A Way of Life*, A Lifeguide Bible Study. Downers Grove, IL: InterVarsity, 2000.

Platt, David. *Radical: Taking Back Your Faith from the American Dream*. Multnomah, 2010.

Plummer Robert L. and John Mark Terry, eds. *Paul's Missionary Method: His Time and Ours*. Downers Grove, IL: IVP Academic, 2012.

Pollard, Nicky. *Evangelism Made Slightly Less Difficult: How to Interest People Who Aren't Interested*. Downers Grove, IL: InterVarsity, 1997.

Porter, Douglas. *How to Develop and Use the Gift of Evangelism*. Lynchburg, VA: Church Growth, 1992.

Potter, Burtt. *The Church Reaching Out*. Durham, NC: Moore, 1976.

Poulton, John. *A Today Sort of Evangelism*. London: Lutterworth, 1972.

Powell, Sidney Waterbury. *Toward the Great Awakening*. New York: Abingdon-Cokesbury, 1949.

Powell, Sidney Waterbury. *Where Are the Converts?* Nashville: Broadman, 1958.

Prince, Matthew. *Winning Through Caring: Handbook on Friendship Evangelism*. Grand Rapids: Baker, 1981.

Prior, Kenneth Francis William. *The Gospel in a Pagan Society: A Book for Modern Evangelists*. Downers Grove, IL: InterVarsity, 1975.

Quere, Ralph W. *Evangelical Witness: The Message, Medium, Mission, and Method of Evangelism*. Minneapolis: Augsburg, 1975.

Rader, Lyell. *Re-discovering the Open Air Meeting; A Manual for Salvationist Soul-Winning*. Wilmore, KY: Asbury Theological Seminary, Evangelism Dept., 1966.

Rahn, David and Youth for Christ. *3Story: Preparing for a Lifestyle of Evangelism: Participant's Guide*. Grand Rapids: Zondervan-Youth Specialties, 2006.

Rainer, Thom. *Effective Evangelistic Churches: Successful Churches Reveal What Works and What Doesn't*. Nashville: Broadman, 1996.

Rainer, Thom. *Simple Church*. Nashville: Broadman, 2007.

Rainer, Thom. *Surprising Insights from the Unchurches and Proven Ways to Reach Them*. Grand Rapids: Zondervan, 2001.

Rainer, Thom. *The Unchurched Next Door: Understanding Faith Stages as Keys to Sharing Your Faith.* Grand Rapids: Zondervan, 2003.

Rand, Ronald R. *The Evangelism Helper*. Cincinnati, OH: The Vine, 1974.

Rand, Ronald R. *Won By One*. Ventura: Regal, 1988.

Randall, Rob, *Witnessing: A Way Of Life*. Criterion Publications, 1987.

Ratz, Calvin, Frank Tillapaugh, and Myron Augsburger. *Mastering Outreach And Evangelism*. Portland, OR: Multnomah (with Christianity Today), 1990.

Rausch, Thomas P., S.J., ed. *Evangelizing America*. Mahwah, NJ: Paulist, 2004.

Rauschenbusch, Walter. *A Theology for the Social Gospel*. New York: Macmillan, 1917; Nashville: Abingdon, 1978.

Ray, Michael D. *Soul Winning—The Heart Of God*. Hopewell Ministries, 1994.

Read, David Haxton Carswell. *Go and Make Disciples*. Nashville: Abingdon, 1978.

Reese, Martha Grace, *Unbinding the Gospel: Real Life Evangelism*. Afterword by Brian McLaren. St. Louis: Chalice, 2006.

Reid, Alvin. *Evangelism Handbook: Biblical, Spiritual, Intentional, Missional*. Nashville: Broadman, 2009.

Reid, Alvin. *Introduction to Evangelism*. Nashville: Broadman, 1998.

Reid, Alvin. *Radically Unchurched: Who They Are and How to Reach Them*. Grand Rapids: Kregel, 2002.

Reid, Alvin and David Wheeler, "Servanthood Evangelism." 1997.

Reid, Gavin. *To Reach a Nation: The Challenge of Evangelism in a Mass-Media Age*. London: Hodder and Stoughton, 1987.

Reisner, Christian F. *Disciple Winners*. New York: Abingdon, 1930.

Rice, John R. *The Evangelist and His Work*. Murfreesboro, TN: Sword of the Lord, 1968.

Rice, John R. *The Golden Path to Successful Soul Winning*. Wheaton, IL: Sword of the Lord, 1961.

Rice, John R. *We Can Have Revival Now*. Wheaton, IL: Sword of the Lord, 1950.

Richardson, Rick. *Evangelism Outside the Box: New Ways to Help People Experience the Good News*. Downers Grove, IL: InterVarsity, 2000.

Richardson, Rick. *Reimagining Evangelism: Inviting Friends on a Spiritual Journey*. Downers Grove, IL: InterVarsity, 2006.

Richardson, Rick, Terry Erickson, and Judy Johnson. *Reimaging Evangelism: Inviting Friends on a Spiritual Journey*, Participant's Guide. Downers Grove, IL: IVP Connect, 2008.

Riggs, Ralph, et al. *So Send I You—A Study In Personal Soul Winning*. Gospel Publishing, 1965.

Riley, W. B. *The Crisis of the Church*. New York: Cook, 1914.

Riley, W. B. *The Perennial Revival: A Plea for Evangelism*. Chicago: Winona Publishing, 1904; Philadelphia: American Baptist, 1916.

Rinker, Rosalind. *You Can Witness with Confidence*. Grand Rapids: Zondervan, 1962.

Roberts, Richard Owen. *Revival: What Is Revival? When Is Revival Needed? When Can Revival Be Expected? When Is Revival Dangerous? Will the Revival Last?* Wheaton, IL: Tyndale House, 1982.

Robinson, Darrell. *Incredibly Gifted*. Hannibal Press: Garland, TX, 2002.

Robinson, Darrell. *People Sharing Jesus.* Nashville: Nelson, 1995.

Robinson, Darrell. *Synergistic Evangelism.* Nashville: CrossBooks, 2009.

Robinson, Darrell. *Total Church Life.* Nashville: Broadman, 1997.

Robinson, Godfrey C. and Stephen Winward. *The King's Business—Handbook for Christian Workers.* Children's Special Service, 1957.

Rockey, Carroll J. *Fishing for Fishers of Men.* Philadelphia: United Lutheran, 1924.

Rockwell, Margaret. *Stepping Out: Sharing Christ in Everyday Circumstances.* Arrowhead Springs, CA: Here's Life, 1984.

Root, Jerry and Stan Guthrie, *The Sacrament of Evangelism.* Chicago: Moody, 2011.

Routh, Porter. *Witness To The World.* Convention Press, 1979.

Rueter, Alvin C. *Organizing for Evangelism: Planning an Effective Program for Witnessing.* Minneapolis: Augsburg, 1983.

Samuel, Leith. *Share Your Faith.* Grand Rapids: Baker, 1981.

Sanders, J. Oswald. *Effective Evangelism.* Kent, England: STL Books, 1982.

Sanderson, Leonard. *The Association in Evangelism.* Atlanta: Home Mission Board, SBC, 1958.

Sanderson, Leonard. *Personal Soul-Winning.* Nashville: Convention, 1958.

Sanderson, Leonard, ed. *Revival Plan Book.* Dallas: Division of Evangelism, Home Mission Board, Southern Baptist Convention, 1959-1960.

Sanderson, Leonard. *Using the Sunday School in Evangelism* Nashville: Convention, 1958.

Sanny, Lorne. *The Art of Personal Witnessing.* Chicago: Moody, 1957.

Savelle, Jerry. *Sharing Jesus Effectively: A Handbook on Successful Soul-Winning.* Tulsa, OK: Harrison House, 1982.

Scarborough, L. R. *Endued to Win.* Nashville: Sunday School Board of the SBC, 1922.

Scarborough, L. R. *Gay Lectures on Evangelism 1939.* 1939.

Scarborough, L. R. *How Jesus Won Men.* Nashville: Tennessee Sunday School Board, 1926.

Scarborough, L. R. *Recruits for World Conquest.* New York: Revell, 1914.

Scarborough, L. R. *A Search for Souls: A Study in the Finest of the Arts—Winning the Lost to Christ.* Nashville: Tennessee Sunday School Board, 1925.

Scarborough, L. R. *With Christ After the Lost.* Nashville: Tennessee Sunday School Board, 1919; New York: George H. Doran, 1919; Nashville: Broadman, 1919, 1952, 1953.

Scharpff, Paulus. *History of Evangelism: Three Hundred Years of Evangelism in Germany, Great Britain, and the United States of America,* trans. Helga Bender Henry. Grand Rapids: Eerdmans, 1966; trans *Geschichte der Evangelisation: Dreihundert Jahre Evangelisation in Deutschland, Großbritannien und USA.* Giessen, West Germany: Brunnen Verlag, 1964.

Scott, Bruce. *Gleanings for the Remnant.* Lynwood, IL: American Messianic Fellowship, 1988.

Sellers, Ernest O. *Personal Evangelism: Studies in Individual Efforts to Lead Souls into Right Relations to Christ.* Nashville: Sunday School Board of the SBC, 1923; New York: Doran, 1923.

Sellers, James Earl. *The Outsider and the Word of God: A Study in Christian Communication.* New York: Abingdon, 1961.

Setzler, Monitia, Barbara Oden, Gary Bulley, and David Strawn. *TouchPOINTS—Sowing Seeds, Volume One.* Nashville: On Target, 1996.

Shadrach, Steve, *The Fuel and the Flame: 10 Keys to Ignite Your College Campus for Jesus Christ.* Conway, AR: The Bodybuilders, 2003.

Sharing the Abundant Life on Campus. San Bernardino: Campus Crusade for Christ, 1972.

Shepherd, Norman. *The Call of Grace: How the Covenant Illuminates Salvation and Evangelism.* Phillipsburg, NJ: P&R, 2000.

Sheridan, Wilbur Fletcher. *The Sunday-Night Service: A Study in Continuous Evangelism.* Cincinnati: Jennings and Graham; New York: Eaton and Mains, 1908.

Sherrod, Paul. *Successful Soul Winning: Proven Ideas to Challenge Every Christian to Be a Personal Worker.* Lubbock, TX: P. Sherrod, 1974.

Shindler, Robert Doy. *From the Usher's Desk to the Tabernacle Pulpit: The Life and Labors of Charles Haddon Spurgeon.* New York: American Tract Society, 1892; New York: A. C. Armstrong, 1892; London: Passmore and Alabaster, 1892.

Shivers, Frank. *Christian Basics 101: A Handbook on Christian Growth.* Xulon Press, 2009.

Shivers, Frank. *The Evangelistic Invitation 101: 150 Helps in Giving the Evangelistic Invitation.* Sumter, SC: Hill Publishing, 2004.

Shivers, Frank. *Evangelistic Preaching 101: Voices from the Past and Present on Effective Preaching.* La Vergne, TN: Lightning Source, 2010.

Shivers, Frank. *How to Preach without Evangelistic Results.* Columbia, SC: Frank Shivers Evangelistic Association, 2012.

Shivers, Frank. *Revivals 101: A Concise 'How To" Manual on Revivals.* Sumter, SC: Victory Hill Publishing, 2008.

Shivers, Frank. *Soul Winning [101] with Illustrations and Sermons: 275 Helps for Winning the Lost.* Sumter, SC: Hill Publishing, 2006.

Shivers, Frank. *Spurs to Soul Winning: 531 Motivations for Winning Souls.* La Vergne, TN: Lightning Source, 2012.

Shoemaker, Samuel M. *The Experiment of Faith: A Handbook for Beginners.* New York: Harper, 1957.

Shoemaker, Samuel M. *The Conversion of the Church.* New York: Revell, 1932.

Shoemaker, Samuel M. *With the Holy Spirit and with Fire.* New York: Harper and Brothers, 1960.

Shore, John. *I'm OK—You're Not: The Message We're Sending to Unbelievers and Why We Should Stop.* Colorado Springs: NavPress, 2007.

Short, Roy Hunter. *Evangelism through the Local Church.* New York: Abingdon, 1956

Silvoso, Ed. *Prayer Evangelism.* Ventura: Regal, 2000.

Simpson, Michael L. *Permission Evangelism—When to Talk, When to Walk.* Colorado Springs: NexGen, Cook, 2004.

Singlehurst, Laurence. *Sowing, Reaping, Keeping: People-Sensitive Evangelism.* Nottingham: InterVarsity Press, 2006.

Sisson, Richard. *Training for Evangelism.* Chicago: Moody, 1979.

Sjogren, Steve. *101 Ways to Reach Your Community.* Colorado Springs: NavPress, 2001.

Sjogren, Steve. *Conspiracy of Kindness.* Ann Arbor: Servant, 1993.

Sjogren, Steve. *Servant Warfare: How Kindness Conquers Spiritual Darkness.* Ann Arbor: Servant, 1996.

Sjogren, Steve, Dave Ping, and Doug Pollock. *Irresistible Evangelism: Natural Ways to Open Others to Jesus.* Loveland, CO: Group, 2004.

Smith, Bailey E. *Real Evangelism: Exposing the Subtle Substitutes for That Evangelism.* Nashville: Broadman, 1978; Nashville: World, 1999.

Smith, Glenn C., ed. *Evangelizing Adults.* Washington, DC: Paulist National Catholic Evangelization Association; Wheaton, IL: Tyndale House, 1985.

Smith, Gordon T. *Transforming Conversion: Rethinking the Language and Contours of Christian Initiation.* Grand Rapids: Baker, 2010.

Smith, Oswald J. *The Consuming Fire: the Bob Jones University Lectures on Evangelism.* London: Marshall, Morgan, and Scott, 1954, 1957.

Smith, Oswald J. *The Passion for Souls.* London: Marshall, Morgan and Scott, 1950, 1965.

Smith, Oswald J. *The Revival We Need.* Foreword by Jonathan Goforth. London: Marshall, Morgan and Scott, 1933; 1940.

Smith, Sean. *Prophetic Evangelism: Empowering a Generation to Seize Their Day.* Shippensburg, PA: Destiny Image, 2005

Smith, Warren Cole. *A Lover's Quarrel with the Evangelical Church.* Authentic, 2009.

Southard, Samuel. *Pastoral Evangelism.* Nashville, Broadman, 1962; Atlanta: John Knox, 1981.

Speer, Robert E. *The Church and Missions.* London: James Clarke, n.d.; New York, George H. Doran, 1926.

Spencer, Ichabod. *Conversations with Anxious Souls Concerning the Way of Salvation.* New York: M. W. Dodd, 1853; Solid Ground, 2006.

Sprague, William B. *Lectures on the Revival of Religion.* 1832; London: Banner of Truth Trust, 1959.

Sprenger, Mike. *Blowing Your Cover: Workbook.* London: Monarch, 2006.

Spurgeon, Charles H. *The Soul Winner.* New York: Revell, 1895; Grand Rapids: Zondervan, 1947; Grand Rapids: Eerdmans, 1963, 1964, 1995.

Spurr, Frederic C. *The Evangelism for OUR Time.* London: Epworth, 1937: including "The Message of the Evangel—…for the purposes of living… about the whole of human life" (46). "Method of Evangelism: conventional methods [crusades] … have lost their appeal (52-53); (a) The pulpit dialogue (59); (b) "Every Christian an evangelist" (66).

Starkes, M. Thomas. *Interfaith Witness.* Memphis: Brotherhood Commission, SBC, 1971.

Stebbins, Tom. *Evangelism by the Book.* Camp Hill, PA: Christian, 1991.

Stewart, George. *The Practice of Friendship: Studies in Personal Evangelism with Men of the United States Army and Navy in American Training Camps.* New York: Association, 1918.

Stewart, George, Jr. and Henry B. Wright, *Personal Evangelism among Students: Studies in the Practice of Friendship in School and College.* New York: Association, 1920.

Stewart, James A. *Evangelism Without Apology: the Bob Jones University Lectures on Evangelism for 1959.* Grand Rapids: Kregel, 1960.

Stier, Greg. *Outbreak! Creating a Contagious Youth Ministry through Viral Evangelism.* Chicago: Moody, 2002.

Stilwell, H. F. *The Stewardship of Evangelism.* New York: Board of Missionary Cooperation of the NBC, 1925.

Stone, Bryan P. *Evangelism after Christendom: The Theology and Practice of Christian Witness.* Grand Rapids: Brazos, 2007.

Stone, John Timothy. *Winning Men; Studies in Soul-Winning.* New York: Revell, 1946.

Stott, John, ed. *Making Christ Known: Historic Mission Documents from the Lausanne Movement 1974-1989.* Great Britain: Paternoster, 1996.

Stott, John R. W. *Our Guilty Silence: The Church, The Gospel, The World.* Grand Rapids: Eerdmans, 1967, 1976.

Streett, R. Alan, *The Effective Invitation.* Old Tappan, NJ: Revell, 1984.

Stone, John Timothy. *Recruiting for Christ: Hand to Hand Methods with Men.* New York: Revell, 1910.

Strobel, Lee. *The Case for Faith.* Grand Rapids: Zondervan, 2000.

Strobel, Lee and Mark Mittelberg, *The Unexpected Adventure: Taking Everyday Risks to Talk with People about Jesus.* Grand Rapids: Zondervan, 2009.

Sunday School Board, *Ringing Door Bells: the Art of Visiting.* Nashville: Department of Young People's and Adult Sunday School Work, Sunday School Board, Southern Baptist Convention, 1936.

Swearingen, Thomas E. and Mary G. *Heeding the Spirit in Evangelism.* Birmingham: Keystone, 1965.

Sweazey, George E. *The Church as Evangelist.* San Francisco: Harper and Row, 1978.

Sweazey, George E. *Effective Evangelism: The Greatest Work in the World.* New York: Harper and Row, 1953, 1976.

Sweeting, George. *The Evangelistic Campaign: A Book of Helps for Passtor and Evangelist.* Chicago: Moody, 1955.

Tabb, Mark. *Mission to Oz: Reaching Postmoderns without Losing Your Way.* Chicago: Moody, 2004.

Target, George W. *Tell It the Way It Is: A Primer for Christian Communicators.* London : Lutterworth, 1970.

Taylor, Frederick Eugene. *The Evangelistic Church.* Philadelphia: Judson, 1927.

Taylor, William. *Seven Years Street Preaching in San Francisco: Embracing Incidents, Triumphant Death Scenes, Etc.* New York: Cartlon and Porter, 1856, 1857, 1858.

Templeton, Charles B. *Evangelism for Tomorrow.* New York: Harper, 1957.

Terry, John Mark. *Evangelism: A Concise History.* Nashville: Broadman and Holman, 1994.

Thompson, John L. *Urban Impact: Reaching the World through Effective Urban Ministry.* Eugene, OR: Wipf and Stock, 2011.

Thompson, W. Oscar, Jr. *Concentric Circles of Concern.* Nashville: Broadman, 1981.

Thwing, Charles Franklin. *The Working Church,* New York: Baker and Taylor, 1888; rev. ed. 1889; New York: Revell, 1913.

Torrey, Reuben A. *How to Work for Christ: A Compendium of Effective Methods.* New York: Revell, 1901; Los Angeles: Revell, 1920 [includes Book One, "Personal Work;" Book Two, "Methods of Christian Work;" and Book Three, "Preaching and Teaching the Word of God"]. 518 pages.

Torrey, Reuben A. *How to Bring Men to Christ.* New York: Revell, 1893; Chicago: Moody, 1910; Minneapolis: Bethany, 1977.

Torrey, Reuben A., ed. *How to Promote and Conduct a Successful Revival.* Chicago: Revell, 1901.

Torrey, Reuben A. *Individual Soulwinning.* Los Angeles: Biola, 1917.

Torrey, Reuben A. *Personal Work* [part one of *How to Work for Christ*]. New York: Revell, 1901.

Torrey, Reuben A. *The Missionary's Message—The Full Gospel.* Los Angeles: Biola, n.d.

Torrey, Reuben A. *The Wondrous Joy of Soul Winning.* London: The "One by One" Working Band; Los Angeles: Biola, n.d.

Tovey, Phillip. *Inculturation: The Eucharist in Africa.* Kiraz Liturgical Series 11. Piscataway Township, NJ: Gorgias, 2010.

Towns, Elmer L. *Evangelize Thru Christian Education.* Wheaton, IL: Evangelical Teacher Training Association, 1976.

Trimble, Henry Burton. *To Every Creature.* Nashville: Cokesbury, 1939.

Trotman, Dawson. *Born to Reproduce.* Colorado Springs: NavPress, 1984.

Truett, George W. *A Quest for Souls.* New York: Doran, 1917; Nashville: Broadman, 1917.

Trumbull, Charles G. *Taking Men Alive: Studies in the Principles and Practise of Individual Soul-Winning.* New York: The International Committee of the YMCA, 1907; 1915; New York: Revell, 1938.

Trumbull, Charles G. *What Is the Gospel? Straightforward Talks on Evangelism*. Philadelphia: Sunday School Times, 1918; New York: Harper and Brothers, 1918; Minneapolis: The Harrison Service, 1944.

Trumbull, Henry Clay. *Individual Work for Individuals: A Record of Personal Experiences and Convictions*. New York: The International Committee of the Young Men's Christian Associations, 1901.

Tull, Nelson F. *Effective Christian Witnessing*. Memphis: Brotherhood Commission, SBC, 1960, 1971.

Turnbull, Michael. *Parish Evangelism: A Practical Resource Book for the Local Church*. London: Mowbrays, 1980.

Turnbull, Ralph G., ed. *Evangelism Now*. Grand Rapids: Baker, 1972.

Tuttle, Robert, Jr. *Someone Out There Needs Me: A Practical Guide to Relational Evangelism*. Grand Rapids: Zondervan, 1983.

Van de Pijpekamp, Bob. *God Registers Them: Praying for Unknown People Groups*. Maarn, Holland: Euromission, 1992.

Visser 't Hooft, W. A. *The Background of the Social Gospel in America*. Haarlem: H. D. Tjeenk Willink and Zoon, 1928; St. Louis, MO: Bethany Press, 1963, 1968.

Voelkel, Jack. *Student Evangelism in a World of Revolution*. Grand Rapids: Zondervan, 1974.

Waggoner, Brad J. *The Shape of Faith to Come: Spiritual Formation and the Future of Discipleship*. Nashville: Broadman, 2008.

Walker, Alan. *The New Evangelism*. Nashville: Abingdon, 1975.

Walker, Jeremy. *The Brokenhearted Evangelist*. Grand Rapids: Reformation Heritage, 2012.

Walker, Louise Jeter . *Evangelism Today: An Independent Study Textbook*, 2nd ed. International Correspondence Institute, 1989.

Walker, Mickey. *Doulos: Personal Evangelism Notebook*. Bilbao, Spain: Operation Mobilization, 1983.

Walsh, John. *Evangelization and Justice: New Insight for Christian Ministry*. Maryknoll, NY: Orbis, 1982.

Ward, Harry Frederick. *Social Evangelism*. New York: Missionary Education Movement of the U.S. and Canada, 1915.

Ward, Mark Sr., *The Word Works: 151 Amazing Stories of Men and Women Saved through Gospel Literature*. Greenville, SC: Ambassador Emerald Int'l, 2002.

Warren, Max. *I Believe in the Great Commission*. Grand Rapids: Eerdmans, 1976.

Warren, Max. *Interpreters: A Study in Contemporary Evangelism*. London: Highway Press, 1936.

Washburn, Alphonso V. *Outreach for the Unreached*. Nashville: Convention, 1960.

Washburn, Alphonso V. *Reach Out to People: A People-to-People Emphasis*. Nashville: Convention, 1974.

Water, Mark. *Sharing Your Faith Made Easy: An Easy-to-Understand Pocket Reference Guide*. Hendricksen, 1999.

Watson, David. *I Believe in Evangelism*. Grand Rapids: Eerdmans, 1976; London: Hodder and Stoughton, 1976.

Weatherford, W. D. *Introducing Men to Christ: Fundamental Studies*. New York: Association Press, 1915.

Webber, Robert. *Ancient Future Evangelism: Making Your Church a Faith Forming Community*. Grand Rapids: Baker, 2003.

Weber, Jaroy. *Winning America to Christ*. Nashville: Broadman, 1975.

Webster, Douglas. *What Is Evangelism?* London: Highway Press, 1961.

Wee, Yan T. *The Soul-Winner's Handy Guide*, 3rd ed. Singapore: Y. T. Wee, 2011.

Welch, Bobby. *Evangelism Through Sunday School: A Journey of Faith*. Nashville: Lifeway, 1997.

Welch, Bobby and Doug Williams with David Apple, *Faith Evangelism: Discipling for Evangelism and Ministry*, Journal 1. Nashville: Lifeway, 2007.

Wells, David F. *God the Evangelist: How the Holy Spirit Works to Bring Men to Christ*. Grand Rapids: Eerdmans, 1987; Exeter, United Kingdom: Paternoster Press, 1987.

Wells, Robert J. and John R. Rice, eds. *How to Have a Revival*. Wheaton, IL: Sword of the Lord, 1949.

Wheeler, David. *Servanthood Evangelism*. Alpheretta, GA: North American Mission Board of the SBC, 2009.

White, F. C. *Evangelism Today*. London: Marshall, Morgan, and Scott, 1939.

White, Robert A. *How to Win a Soul*. Nashville: Southern Publication Association, 1971.

Whitesell, Faris D. *Basic New Testament Evangelism*. Grand Rapids: Zondervan, 1949.

Whitesell, Faris D. *Great Personal Workers*. Chicago: Moody, 1956.

Whitesell, Faris D. *Sixty-Five Ways to Give Evangelistic Invitations*. Grand Rapids: Zondervan, 1945.

Whitney, Donald S. *Spiritual Disciplines for the Christian Life*. Colorado Springs: NavPress, 1991.

Wiggins, Kembleton S. *Soul Winning Made Easier: The Psychology of Getting More Decisions*. Mountain View, CA: Pacific, 1975.

Wilder, Jack B. *Biblical Blueprints for Building Witnessing Churches*. Tigerville, SC: Jewel, 1969.

Wiles, Jerry. *How to Win Others to Christ: Your Personal, Practical Guide to Evangelism*. Nashville: Nelson, 1992.

Wilkins, Scott G. *REACH: A Team Approach to Evangelism and Assimilation*. Grand Rapids: Baker, 2005.

Williams, Derek. *One in a Million*. Berkhamsted. UK: Word Books, 1984.

Williams, Doug and Bobby H. Welch. *A Journey in Faith: Facilitator Guide*. Sunday School Board of the SBC, 1998.

Wilson, Walter Lewis. *Let's Go Fishing with the Doctor*. Findlay, OH: Fundamental Truth, 1936; Grand Rapids: Dunham, 1964.

Wilson, Jim. *Principles of War: A Handbook on Strategic Evangelism*. Moscow, ID: Community Christian Ministries, 1964, 1983, 1991; under the tilte *Against the Powers*, 1980.

Wimber, John. *Power Evangelism*. San Francisco: Harper and Row, 1986; North Pomfret, VT: Trafalgar Square, 2000.

Wood, Eernest J. *A Church Fulfilling Its Mission through Proclamation and Witness*. Nashville: SBC, 1964.

Wood, Frederick P. *Studies in Soul-Winning*. London: Marshall Brothers, National Young Life Campaign, 1934; Rev. Ed. London: Marshall, Morgan and Scott, 1934.

Wood, Verda. *Ringing Door Bells : the Art of Visiting*. Nashville: Baptist Sunday School Board, 1946.

Wright, Linda Raney. *Christianity's Crisis in Evangelism: Going Where the People Are*. Portland: Multnomah, 2000.

Yamamori, Tetsuanao. *God's New Envoys: A Bold Strategy for Penetrating "Closed Countries."* Portland, OR: Multnomah, 1987.

Zahniser, Charles Reed. *Case Work Evangelism: Studies in the Art of Christian Personal Work*. New York: Revell, 1927.

Studies of Hebrew Terms

Studies of Greek Terms

Scripture Studies

General Index